▶
▶
▶
▶
▶
▶
▶

UNDERSTANDING CHILD DEVELOPMENT

Spencer A. Rathus

Marist College

Peter Favaro, *Consulting Author*
Hofstra University

HOLT, RINEHART and WINSTON, Inc.
New York   Chicago   San Francisco   Philadelphia
Montreal   Toronto   London   Sydney   Tokyo

Publisher   Susan Meyers
Acquisitions Editor   Susan Arellano
Senior Project Manager   Françoise Bartlett
Art Director   Robert Kopelman
Production Manager   Stefania Taflinska
Photo Researcher   Nicki Harlan
Cover Photo   Jim Hendricks

Library of Congress Cataloging-in-Publication Data

Rathus, Spencer A.
    Understanding child development / Spencer A. Rathus.
        p. cm.
    Includes bibliographies and index.
    1. Child development.   I. Title.
    [DNLM: 1. Child Development.   WS 105 R235u]
RJ131.R36 1988
155.4—dc19
87-28710

ISBN 0-03-001837-4

Printed in the United States of America

8 9 0 1   039   9 8 7 6 5 4 3 2 1

Holt, Rinehart and Winston, Inc.
The Dryden Press
Saunders College Publishing

Photo credits are on page 653.

▶
▶
▶
▶
▶
▶
▶

This book is for
Allyn and Jordan
to share,
or else neither one of
them may have it.

Jordan at 2 years, 9 months

Allyn at 4 years, 8 months

►
►
►
►
►
►
►

► P R E F A C E ►

Writing a child development textbook—what a source of satisfaction! The story of child development is at once personal and universal. Writing this book afforded me not only the satisfactions of the proud father who, given the slightest opening, shows off photos of his children. It also afforded me the satisfactions of the scientist/author who can commit to pen and paper the methods and principles of a rigorous and fascinating discipline.

Another motive for writing *Understanding Child Development* was my dissatisfaction with the other books available for teaching the course. It seemed to me that they can be broadly broken down into (1) a group of straightforward, dry textbooks that present the field with accuracy and rigor, and (2) a group of "student-oriented" books that are entertaining but superficial. It was my goal to write a textbook that would also present the field as it is—with accuracy and rigor—but motivate the student by capturing the entertaining things that children do and allowing my own enthusiasm (and my own family experiences) to shine through. In that sense, *Understanding Child Development* is a personal as well as a scientific document. Writing this textbook allowed me to record some of the more meaningful and charming aspects of my own children's growth and development, and, at the same time, to outline the principles of development as they affect all of us.

Comprehensive and Balanced Coverage

The aim of *Understanding Child Development* is to communicate in content and form the excitement, relevance, and true scientific nature of the discipline of child development. Chapter 1 is a formal presentation of the history of ways of viewing child development and of contemporary research methods. Chapter 2 is an in-depth discussion of the major theories of child development that influence the field today. Chapters 3–5 cover the more biologically oriented areas of development: heredity, prenatal and neonatal development, and physical and motor development. Chapters 6–9 cover perceptual and cognitive de-

► ► ► ►

velopment. Chapters 10–13 cover social and emotional development, and Chapter 14 covers development of behavior disorders. The general thrust in Chapters 3–13 is from the biological to the cognitive to the social and emotional aspects of development. Although these topics and areas are presented consecutively as a way of organizing the textbook, the book also endeavors to show how they overlap and how understanding of one area enhances understanding of the others. In each area, great emphasis is placed on research methodology, up-to-date research findings, and theoretical integration of findings.

The Writing Style

Although *Understanding Child Development* provides an accurate picture of the scientific nature of child development, it was also written with the needs of students in mind. Feedback from dozens of professors has enabled me to craft the language and the vocabulary so that scientific concepts are made accessible to students. It is my belief that even the most abstract concepts can be presented in energetic prose when one writes and rewrites according to the suggestions of reviewers.

Understanding Child Development was also written for the instructor—the instructor who wants to teach from a textbook that is:

> comprehensive in its breadth
>
> rigorous in its depth
>
> accurate and up-to-date
>
> applied as well as theoretical
>
> clearly written
>
> interest-arousing
>
> easily understood
>
> well illustrated

Learning Aids and Features

The central task of a textbook is to provide students with clear information in a format that promotes learning. *Understanding Child Development* contains a number of learning aids and features designed to meet this goal.

Chapter Outlines

Each chapter begins with an outline that helps organize the subject matter for the student.

"Truth or Fiction?" Sections

These sections follow the chapter outlines. "Truth or Fiction?" items stimulate student interest by challenging common knowledge and folklore and by highlighting research findings that are presented in each chapter.

► ► ► ►

Many students consider themselves experts in child development. After all, they observed their own development and that of friends and siblings for many years. Also, some of them are parents. The "Truth or Fiction?" items prod them to reflect upon the accuracy of their observations and to reconsider from a scientific perspective some of the conclusions they might have drawn about children.

Glossaries

Understanding Child Development includes two glossaries: a marginal, running glossary and a traditional end-of-book glossary.

Running Glossary   The running glossary defines technical terms as they are used in the text. Technical terms are boldfaced in the text column the first time they appear. Then they are defined in the margins of the same pages. Ready access to glossary items permits students to maintain concentration on the chapter. Students need not flip back and forth between the chapter and a section at the end of the book in order to understand new terms as they are introduced.

When needed, technical terms are written phonetically to help students pronounce them. Students will not have to "unlearn" mispronunciations by making embarrassing errors in the classroom. In some cases, word origins are also provided—with emphasis on Greek and Latin roots of terms. Word origins always fascinated me in their own right. Also, they helped me in the development of my own general and technical vocabularies, and I wanted to share some of this information with students. Students will see that terms do not simply pop into the language out of nowhere, and that with a little bit of persistence and general knowledge of their own, they might be able to decode more new terms than they had imagined.

End-of-Book Glossary   Instructors have also indicated that they want a traditional, alphabetical glossary at the back of a textbook. *Understanding Child Development* meets this request.

Illustrations

A generous supply of photographs, figures, and drawings—many of them in full color—illustrates the basic concepts, themes, and research findings of the text. They have been carefully chosen and constructed in order to enhance understanding and stimulate interest.

"Focus on Research" Inserts

A number of "Focus on Research" inserts have been placed throughout the text in order to elaborate the scientific methods developmentalists use to expand knowledge. Examples of these inserts include amplified explanations of research methods and reports of a number of classical and contemporary studies:

How Do You Ease Your Child into Nursery School?—A Field Study (by Tiffany Field)

► ► ► ►

Cross-Species Research in Child Development

Operant Conditioning of Vocalizations in Infants

Breast-Feeding vs. Bottle-Feeding: Does It Make a Difference?

Studying Visual Acuity in Newborn Infants: How Do You Get Babies to Tell You How Well They Can See?

Strategies for Studying the Development of Shape Constancy

Strategies for Studying the Development of Object Identity and Object Permanence in Infants

Studying Egocentrism among Preoperational Children

A Potpourri of Experiments in Conservation

The Puzzle and the Pendulum (Piaget's pendulum problem)

Eidetic Imagery: How Do Researchers Determine Whether Children Have "Photographic Memories"?

What Happens to Brilliant Children? Some Notes on the Terman Studies of Genius

Strategies for Studying Genetic and Environmental Influences in IQ

The Strange Situation Method

Cross-Cultural Studies of the Development of Independence

Effects of Father-Absence on Girls: The Hetherington Study

Sugar and Spice and . . . Just What Are Little Girls (and Boys) Made Of?

What's Sweet for Jack Is Often Sour for Jill (on parental selective reinforcement of stereotypical masuline and feminine behavior patterns in infants)

The Stories of the Cups (Piaget's method for studying moral development)

Maternal Influences on Helping Behavior

"Close-Up" Inserts

"Close-Up" inserts highlight some of the issues in child development by using humor or a "personal touch." These inserts include:

How Much Do You Know about Child Development? (an enlightening pretest)

Does Ontogeny Recapitulate Phylogeny? *Or*, How One Dinosaur (Nearly) Became Extinct (a mini-horror story from the author's home)

The Odd Couple (how the film and TV series illustrate psychoanalytic concepts of oral-retentive and oral-expressive personality traits)

I Have My Nose Too Hard Scratched. How She Hurts. (An illustration of the immensity of the child's task of acquiring language)

On Yum-Yum, Da-Da, Wa-Wa, and Poo-Poo: Some Thoughts on "Motherese"

▶ ▶ ▶ ▶

"If It's Dark Outside, I Must Be Sleeping": Some Notes on Transductive Reasoning

Children's Concepts about Sex and Elimination

Smile, 'Cause When You're Smiling, Your Caregivers Smile with You

Chocolate Chip Cookie Therapy? (A children's fear-reduction method)

Working Mothers and Their Children: Must Women Who Want What's Best for Their Children Remain in the Home?

Do Girls Suffer from Penis Envy?

Noneducational Television Can Be Educational, Indeed, *Or*, "I'm Popeye, the Sailor Woman?"

The Girl in the Gilded Cage (on anorexia nervosa)

"Developing Today" Inserts

"Developing Today" inserts highlight some of the contemporary issues and scientific advances in child development. They include:

Genetic Engineering

Prenatal Surgery

A Family-Centered Approach to Childbirth

Are We Still Growing Taller Than Our Parents?

The Three R's in 70 Tongues: Debating the Uses of Bilingual Instruction

Selecting a Day-Care Center

Does TV Violence Contribute to Aggressive Behavior in Children?

A Weight-Loss Manual for Children (and Their Parents)

Can You Make Your Children "Immune" to Alcohol Abuse?

In-Text Applications

In addition to the material contained in the inserts, many in-text applications highlight the relevance of theory and research in child development to everyday life. In-text applications include:

Using avoidance learning to save a baby's life

The bell-and-pad method for bedwetting

Behavior modification in the classroom

Deciding whether or not to have children

Alternative methods of conception

Sex preselection

Teratogens

Children with AIDS

Methods of childbirth

▶ ▶ ▶ ▶

PREFACE

Development of reading skills

Black English

Language learning by deaf children

What to do about child abuse

Helping children cope with fears

Children in single-parent families

Mainstreaming of exceptional children

Treatment of behavior disorders of childhood

Chapter Summaries

Numbered chapter summaries review the material in a logical step-by-step manner. Care was taken to include many technical terms in the summaries.

"Truth or Fiction Revisited" Sections

"Truth or Fiction Revisited" sections complete each chapter. And so, each chapter is brought full circle: a sense of closure is provided by returning to issues raised in the chapter-opening "Truth or Fiction?" sections. By now the material has been discussed in the chapter and reviewed in the summary. The "Truth or Fiction Revisited" sections provide students feedback as to whether the objectives of the chapter have been met and erroneous views have been dispelled.

Summit, N.J.
December 1987

S.A.R.

► ► ► ►

►
►
►
►
►
►
►

► THE ANCILLARIES ►

The text is accompanied by a *Study Guide* written by Larry Fenson, developmental psychologist at California State University, San Diego. The *Study Guide* is designed to encourage reflection, not just rote memorization. Students are asked not just to define key terms and concepts but to review research cited in the text by analyzing specific research methods and findings. To hone their critical skills, students are asked to critique the research and to discuss the implications of selected procedures, theories, and findings.

Also included in the ancillary package is an *Instructor's Manual*, with lecture outlines and teaching suggestions, along with a *Test Bank* and a *Computerized Test Bank* for IBM and Apple PCs. Interactive software (IBM and Apple versions) and four video segments are also provided.

CHILD'S PLAY, provided by Peter Favaro, is an interactive guided-learning exercise that uses vignettes (about 150 in all) to emphasize important facts and ways of thinking about textbook material.

The vignettes are written in a style that helps students imagine what they might do or how they might think in certain situations. After presenting in a brief paragraph a given situation, the student is asked to make a choice. When the choice is made, the computer provides feedback and guides the student back through the thinking process to more accurate or efficient ways of understanding the material. The following is a sample vignette:

A 4-year-old child whom you are observing sits in a corner and begins growling at a plastic figure. He has transformed himself into a powerful monster about to bite the head off the figure. In his fantasy, he talks about ripping the arms off his victim and tearing off his legs. This child isn't experiencing any great stress or family problems and has never been a behavior problem before. What do you make of this behavior?

Sometimes a cluster of facts about an area are emphasized in a vignette, allowing several choices or levels of choice. Sometimes a single important fact is emphasized. Some vignettes discuss research; others direct students to the four or five major theoretical positions within the field of psychology by asking

► ► ► ►

THE ANCILLARIES

students to "interview" the proponents of these theories. We often want students to imagine what Freud would say or what Skinner would say about something. This is one of the hardest skills to teach most beginning psychology students. CHILD'S PLAY gives ample practice in these areas.

Many of the vignettes have "recap loops." A recap loop asks the student who has just gone through the experience of moving through a vignette if he or she would like a recap of the important facts discussed in the event.

Students who use CHILD'S PLAY will have the basic foundations reinforced, as well as gain a new perspective on child development. One reviewer notes that CHILD'S PLAY will "provide a means for students to start making the transition from pure theory and factual information to transference of the concepts to the real world."

A very special thanks to CHILD'S PLAY reviewers Richard Dean of Anne Arundel Community College and Richard L. Beattie of Mississippi State University.

Also included in the ancillary package are four video segments developed by Dr. Patricia Greenfield, who is a professor of developmental psychology at UCLA and a recent winner of the APA Division Two Teaching Award. She developed these videos in conjunction with her students at UCLA and uses them in her child development class. The four segments are examples of experiments in development and are entitled: "Babies Respond to a Visual Cliff: Baby X"; "The Effect of Gender Labels on Adult Response to Babies"; "Children Drawing: From Intellectual to Visual Realism"; and "Developing Social Skills through Play."

▶ ▶ ▶ ▶

►
►
►
►
►
►
►

► ACKNOWLEDGMENTS ►

The discipline of child development owes its progress and its scientific standing to experts who construct theory and conduct research in many different areas. Similarly, *Understanding Child Development* and its ancillaries owe a great deal of their substance and form to my colleagues, who provided expert suggestions and insights at various stages in their development. My sincere thanks to the following:

Nancy Hamblen Acuff, East Tennessee State University

Richard Beattie, Mississippi State University

Tom Berndt, Purdue University

Roberta Berns, Saddleback College

Dana Birnbaum, University of Maine, Orono

Donald Bowers, Community College of Philadelphia

Joseph Canale, Marist College

Glendon Casto, Utah State University

Nancy Denney, University of Wisconsin

Donna Duffy, Middlesex Community College

Linda Dunlap, Marist College

Mary Ellen Edwards, Edison Community College

Richard Fabes, Arizona State University, Tempe

Johanna Flynn, Emory University

Larry Goff, Dallas Community College

Bernard Gorman, Nassau Community College

Romayne Hertweck, Mira Costa College

Charles Hill, Whittier College

► ► ► ►

George Holden, Teachers College, University of Texas, Austin

Rosemary Hornak, Meredith College

Rick Ida, Diablo Valley College

Robert Kavanaugh, Williams College

Daniel Kee, California State College, Fullerton

Derl Keen, Fresno City College

Jan Kenney, Towson State College

Dene Klinzing, University of Delaware

Mary Levitt, Florida International University

Earldene McNeill, Eastfield College

Patricia Miller, University of Florida, Gainesville

Susan Nakayama-Siaw, California State Polytechnic, Pomona

Roger Page, Ohio State University

Jay Posner, Jackson Community College

Joseph Reish, Tidewater Community College

Cynthia Rohrbeck, George Washington University

Jo Rosauer, Iowa State University

Gerald Rubin, Virginia Community College

Toni Santimire, University of Nebraska, Lincoln

Midge Schratz, Marist College

Daniel Smothergill, Syracuse University

James Starzec, SUNY, Cortland

Sandra Stein, Ryder College

Jan Stivers, Marist College

Billie Underwood, Pima Community College

Amye Warren Leubecker, University of Tennessee, Chattanooga

I wish to pay special thanks to two colleagues whose help has been extraordinary. First is Peter Favaro of Hofstra University. His sensitive reading of the manuscript helped me correct many errors and include many omissions. He also supplied the CHILD'S PLAY software. Second is William R. Eidle, head of the Division of Social and Behavioral Sciences at Marist College, who made every effort to provide me with the time necessary to complete this book during 1987.

As always, I am indebted to the publishing professionals at Holt, Rinehart and Winston. It is a continuing privilege to work with them. Susan Meyers, Publisher of the Behavioral and Social Sciences, is to be credited for making the decision to publish the text at a crucial stage in its development. Susan Arellano, Psychology Editor, was broadsided with this project as she moved into her position, and it truly served as her baptism under fire. Her support, her organizational skills, and her practical suggestions all made major contributions to the text. I am grateful to Hilary Jackson for devising the mar-

► ► ► ►

keting campaign for the book. Françoise Bartlett, Senior Project Manager, is to be credited for overseeing the editing and coordinating all the activities necessary for turning a manuscript into a bound book. Fran has worked with me on a number of books at this point and has always made the editorial production process run smoothly. Frankly, I don't know what I'd do without her. Robert Kopelman directed the art program and is responsible for giving the text much of its visual impact. Stefania Taflinska ably managed the production of the book. I also want to thank Adina Genn, editorial assistant, for finding excellent reviewers and for her creative help with photo research. A special thanks goes to Steven Collins, Robin Finney, and the teachers at Kennedy-King Child Development Center for helping to make our cover a very special one.

Summit, N.J.
December 1987

S.A.R.

▶
▶
▶
▶
▶
▶
▶

▶ C O N T E N T S ▶ I N ▶ B R I E F ▶

▶ ▶ ▶ ▶

▶
▶
▶
▶
▶
▶
▶

CONTENTS

▶ ▶ ▶ ▶

► ► ► ►

► ► ► ►

▶ ▶ ▶ ▶

CHAPTER 7
LANGUAGE DEVELOPMENT   254

► ► ► ►

▶ ▶ ▶ ▶

► ► ► ►

► ► ► ►

CONTENTS

▶ ▶ ▶ ▶

UNDERSTANDING CHILD DEVELOPMENT

1

What Is Child Development?

▶
▶
▶
▶
▶
▶
▶

▶
▶
▶
▶
▶
▶
▶

T R U T H ▶ O R ▶ F I C T I O N ?

- Development and growth are synonymous terms.
- Children were once treated as the property of their parents.
- In medieval Paris, children were handed over to lower-class women for rearing shortly after birth and were not returned to their parents for several years.
- During the Middle Ages, girls were not educated, because it was thought that they lacked reason and were too emotional.
- Louis XIV took the throne of France at the age of 5.
- Children come into the world as "blank tablets"—without preferences or inborn differences in intelligence and specific talents.
- The development of the child parallels the evolution of our species.
- Although we have become more affluent, twentieth-century life has prolonged children's dependence on parents.
- Giving children early training in sitting up and walking significantly accelerates the development of these skills.
- Children's levels of intelligence are influenced by early learning experiences.
- Some theorists contend that children actively strive to understand and take charge of their worlds, whereas other theorists argue that children respond passively to environmental stimulation.
- Children who are dropped off at nursery school by their mothers are more likely to cry than children who are dropped off by their fathers.
- Boys who spend the first years of life in father-absent homes are more likely to be dependent than boys who do not.
- Teenaged girls who live with their divorced mothers are more likely to become involved in heterosexual activity than girls who live in intact homes.
- There are physical similarities between children with fetal alcohol syndrome (FAS) and the offspring of rats who were given alcohol during pregnancy.
- Researchers have followed some subjects in developmental research for more than 50 years.

1

My heart leaps up when I behold
  A rainbow in the sky:
So it was when my life began;
So it is now I am a man;
So be it when I shall grow old,
  Or let me die!
The Child is father of the Man. . . .
  ——*William Wordsworth*

Some things in life are obvious. One is that men and women are the parents of children. How, then, could the poet William Wordsworth create such problems for me in high school English by writing the line *The Child is father of the man?*

It took me a while to understand that Wordsworth was suggesting that the experiences of the child can shape the adult, or that the naive wonderment of the child can lay the groundwork for the intellectual development of the adult. But since we are accustomed to thinking of adults as shaping their children, it seems strange to view the process as also proceeding in the opposite direction. But it does. Our childhoods do help to form our adult traits, preferences, and patterns of thought, just as we foster their development in our children.

The development of children is what this book is about, but in our children we also see the mirrors of ourselves. We shall come to see that in a very real sense we cannot hope to understand ourselves as adults—we cannot catch a glimpse of the remarkable journeys we have taken—without understanding children.

Let us embark on our search for ourselves by answering a basic question: What *is* child development? Then we shall explore some of the reasons for studying child development. One of them, as suggested, is to gain insight into our own behavior as adults. But there are others, such as looking into the causes of developmental abnormalities and finding ways of preventing or treating them. Then we go on a brief tour of the history of child development. It may surprise you to learn that people were not particularly sensitive to the many ways in which children differ from adults until relatively recent times. Next we examine some controversies in child development, such as whether or not there are distinct stages of development. Then we consider scientific methods for the study of child development, and, finally, we examine some of the issues concerning ethics in developmental research. We shall see that many sophisticated methods for studying children have been devised, and that ethics helps determine the types of research that are deemed proper and improper.

What Is Child Development?

In order to define child development, let us have a look at two words whose meanings may seem self-evident, but may not be: *child* and *development.*

Child You have heard the word *child* all your life, so why bother to define it? We define it, because words in common usage are frequently used in inexact ways.

◀ ◀ ◀ ◀

1 WHAT IS CHILD DEVELOPMENT?

Child *A person undergoing the period of development from infancy through puberty.*

Infancy *Babyhood. The period of very early childhood, characterized by lack of speech; the first two years after birth.*

Puberty *(PEW-burr-tee). The stage of development characterized by changes that lead to reproductive capacity.*

Germ cells *The cells from which new organisms are developed. (See* ova *and* sperm cells.)

Conception *The process of becoming pregnant; the process by which a sperm cell joins with an ovum to begin a new life.*

Development *The processes by which organisms unfold features and traits, grow, and become more complex and specialized in structure and function.*

Motor development *The development of the capacity for movement, particularly as made possible by changes in the nervous system and the muscles.*

Growth *The processes by which organisms increase (and eventually decrease) in size, weight, power, and other traits as they develop.*

A **child** is a person undergoing the period of development from infancy to puberty—two more familiar words that are frequently used inexactly. The term **infancy** derives from Latin roots meaning "not speaking," and infancy is usually defined as the first two years of life, or the period of life prior to the development of complex speech. I stress the word *complex,* because many children have large numbers of words and use simple sentences well before their second birthday. **Puberty** refers to the period of development during which people gain reproductive capacity. However, child development textbooks usually include discussions of infancy and adolescence, and so shall we. In fact, we shall begin even before infancy. We shall describe the origin of **germ cells** and the process of **conception,** which is more complicated than most people think.

Development   **Development** is the orderly appearance, over time, of physical structures, psychological traits, behaviors, and ways of adapting to the demands of life. The changes brought on by development are both qualitative and quantitative. Consider **motor development.** As we develop, we gain the capacities to lift our heads, sit up, creep, stand, and walk. These changes are qualitative. However, within each of these qualititative changes, there are also developments that are quantitative. After babies begin to lift their heads, they lift them higher and higher. Soon after children walk, they also begin to run. And, as their running advances, they gain the capacity to go faster and faster.

Development also occurs across many dimensions simultaneously—physiological, cognitive, personality, social, emotional, and behavioral. Development is spurred on by internal factors, such as the genetic code, and external factors, such as learning and nutrition.

Growth and Development   Are **growth** and development synonymous? Not quite, although many people do use them interchangeably. Growth is usually used to refer to changes in size or quantity, whereas development also refers to changes in quality.

During the early days following fertilization, a newly conceived child *develops* rapidly as cells divide and begin to take on specialized forms. However, there is no gain, or *growth,* in mass, because the unborn child has not yet become "hooked into" external sources of nourishment. Language *development* refers to the processes by which the child's use of language becomes progressively more sophisticated and complex during the first few years of life. Vocabulary *growth,* by contrast, refers to the simple accumulation of knowledge of the meanings of new words.

Child Development: A Definition   Child development, then, is a field of inquiry that attempts to gain knowledge of the processes that govern the appearance and growth of children's physical structures, psychological traits, behavior patterns, and ways of adapting to the demands of life. Professionals from many fields are interested in child development. They include psychologists, educators, anthropologists, sociologists, nurses, medical researchers, and many others. Each brings his or her own brand of expertise to the quest for knowledge. Intellectual cross-fertilization enhances the skills of developmentalists and enriches the lives of children.

Let us now consider the many reasons that these professionals study child development.

▶ ▶ ▶ ▶

How Much Do You Know about Child Development?

▷
▷
▷
▷
▷ So, you think, what is there to learn about child development? After all, you were once a child. Having "gone through it," you should have emerged as something of an expert, right?

Perhaps you did. Perhaps you didn't. If you did, I must admit that you are far ahead of where I was as a student.

To test your knowledge of child development, indicate whether you think each of the following items is true or false by circling the T or F. Then compare your answers with the key at the end of the chapter.

1. **T—F** Conception takes place in the uterus.

2. **T—F** Pregnant women can have just one or two drinks a day without being concerned about their effects on the unborn child.

3. **T—F** Parents must spend the first few hours after birth with their newborn babies if adequate bonding is to take place.

4. **T—F** Newborn babies sleep about 16 hours a day.

5. **T—F** Children are born with all the bones they will ever have. The bones just grow larger as times goes on.

6. **T—F** Male and female human embryos appear identical until six or seven weeks after conception.

7. **T—F** Newborn babies usually cannot see for several hours.

8. **T—F** Babies a few months old prefer red and blue objects to yellow and green objects.

9. **T—F** Nine-month-old babies will usually crawl off the edges of beds, couches, and tables if they are not prevented from doing so.

10. **T—F** Children learn to fear stimuli that are associated with painful experiences.

11. **T—F** When objects are taken out of the sight of 2-month-old babies, they no longer exist so far as the baby is concerned.

12. **T—F** Although it may be difficult to measure intelligence in newborn babies, a child's IQ remains fixed from birth.

13. **T—F** Babies learn to smile from observing other people smile.

14. **T—F** Nine-month-old babies who fear strangers are likely to become anxious adults.

15. **T—F** Babies placed in day care grow less attached to their mothers than babies reared by their mothers in the home.

16. **T—F** Parents who demand more mature behavior from their children are more likely to get it.

17. **T—F** First-born children are usually more responsible than later-born children.

18. **T—F** It is better for parents in conflict to stay together "for the sake of the children" than to get a divorce.

19. **T—F** More attractive children are usually more popular with their peers.

20. **T—F** Boys are usually more aggressive than girls.

21. **T—F** Boys usually have greater verbal skills than girls.

22. **T—F** Children are basically selfish.

23. **T—F** Television violence contributes to aggressive behavior in child viewers.

24. **T—F** Most children who wet their beds simply outgrow the problem.

25. **T—F** Marijuana is the drug most frequently abused by adolescents.

► ► ► ►

Why Do We Study Child Development?

One motive for studying child development also applies to other areas of investigation: curiosity—the desire to learn about things that are little understood. Scientists still find curiosity a valid reason for studying child development. Despite the wealth of research that has been conducted, many important questions about development remain unresolved or only partly resolved.

Other motives have theoretical and practical aspects. We also study child development:

To Try to Gain Insight into Our Basic Nature

For centuries, philosophers, theologians, natural scientists, psychologists, and educators have held different perspectives on development and argued about the "basic" nature of children. They have argued over whether children are basically antisocial and aggressive, or prosocial and loving. They have argued over whether children are conscious and self-aware. They have disputed whether children have a natural curiosity that demands to unravel the mysteries of the universe, or whether children are merely mechanical reactors to environmental stimulation.

If their arguments had remained theoretical—subjects limited only to discussion in the seminar—they might have gained little notice. But their perspectives on child development have led to very different suggestions for child rearing and education. Thus, they have an important impact on the daily lives of children, parents, educators, and others who interact with children.

One motive for studying child development, then, is to determine which theoretical perspectives are supported by the evidence. The major theoretical perspectives on child development today are the maturational, psychoanalytic, learning-theory, cognitive-developmental, and ecological perspectives. We shall refer to each of them later on.

To Try to Gain Insight into the Origins of Adult Behavior

How do we explain the origins of **empathy** in adults? Of antisocial behavior? How do we explain the assumption of "masculine" and "feminine" behavior patterns? The origins of special abilities in language (reading, writing, spelling, articulation) and in mathematics?

There are various ways of explaining the origins of adult behavior. Some investigators look to situational influences—that is, the stimuli that impinge on the adult in the "here and now." Others look to adult decision making—to a mature weighing of the pluses and minuses in a situation. Still others tend to search for their answers in the processes of development.

Consider the example of sex roles. There is no question that society remains biased toward rewarding men for "masculine" behavior and rewarding women for "feminine" behavior. It also seems reasonable that men and women take society's system of rewards and punishments into account, if and when they weigh their satisfaction with their sex-role behavior. But the literature on child development shows that most boys and girls take on what is considered

Empathy *The ability to share another person's feelings or emotions. (From the Greek* en, *meaning "in," and* pathos, *meaning "feeling.")*

▶ ▶ ▶ ▶

"appropriate" sex-role behaviors during early childhood, largely through processes of **identification** and **socialization,** as we shall see in Chapter 12. There remains a good deal of controversy about the relative role of biology in the assumption of sex roles, but no discussion of the origins of sex-role behavior could be meaningful without reference to child development.

To Try to Gain Insight into the Causes, Prevention, and Treatment of Developmental Abnormalities and Problems

Fetal alcohol syndrome, PKU, SIDS, Down syndrome, autism, hyperactivity, dyslexia, child abuse—these are just a handful of the buzz words that stir fear in parents and parents-to-be. A major focus in child development research is the search for the causes of such problems, so that they can be prevented and, when possible, treated.

Let us mention just a few examples that will be discussed more thoroughly in later chapters. Research has made it possible to identify children with **PKU** at birth through analysis of samples of blood or urine. PKU may then be treated through reasonably effective dietary restrictions. In the future it may be possible for parents to preselect boys or girls with certainty. In that case, parents whose male children would be susceptible to sex-linked diseases such as muscular dystrophy and hemophilia could avert these tragedies by conceiving girls.

To Try to Optimize the Conditions of Development for All Children

Most children, fortunately, do not encounter developmental abnormalities. However, we remain concerned about optimizing the conditions of their development in order to foster positive traits. Most parents, for example, want their infants to feel secure with them. They want to provide the best in nutrition, so that their children will develop strong bones and muscles. They want to assure that major transitions, such as the transition from the home to the school, will be as stress-free as possible.

Note just a few of the issues that have been studied in recent years in an effort to optimize the conditions of development:

The effects of various foods and agents on the development of unborn children

The effects of intense parent–infant interaction immediately following birth on bonds of attachment

The effects of bottle-feeding versus breast-feeding on mother–infant attachment and on babies' health

The effects of nursery-school and day-care programs on parent–child bonds of attachment and on children's social and intellectual development

The effects of different patterns of child rearing on the fostering of independence and competence

How to raise children who share and empathize with others

The effects of **open education,** as compared to traditional education, on the academic achievement and personalities of children

▶ ▶ ▶ ▶

Optimizing Conditions of Development
Most parents and day-care facilities try to provide the best in nutrition to optimize the development of their children.

Of course, there is another reason that scientists study child development: They enjoy it. Much of the research in child development—as in the area of developmental abnormalities—takes on an appropriately serious, almost solemn tone. However, much of the research in other areas is great fun, just as children are fun.

And so there are many reasons for studying child development. In the next section we discuss the history of the field of child development. In contrast to today's preoccupation with children and their welfare, we shall see that throughout most of human history people did not believe that childhood offered very much to think about at all.

The Development of Child Development: A Brief History

Child development as a field of scientific inquiry has existed for little more than a century. Throughout the remainder of the course of human history attitudes toward children were quite varied. There were times when childhood was barely recognized as a special time of life. There were times when children toiled beside adults in the fields and in the factories. There were times when children were farmed out to **wet nurses,** and there were times when children were sold into slavery. Fortunately, there have also been times of enlightenment. In recent years, children have been granted civil rights and protection from abuse.

Ancient Times: Of "The Glory That Was Greece and the Grandeur That Was Rome"

Wet nurse *A milk-producing woman hired to suckle and, usually, to rear another woman's child.*

Commentaries on children are found in the writings of the Greek philosophers Plato and Aristotle. Plato characterized boys as sly, mischievous, and

▶ ▶ ▶ ▶

unruly. In *Laws* he advocated that children should be separated from parents and reared by the state, because parents reared children to behave in selfish ways. When children as adults served as public officials, Plato believed, such selfishness led to corruption (Borstelmann, 1983).

Although Plato perceived children as deceitful and difficult, he also believed that children have inborn knowledge of the world and of what is right. He saw the purpose of education as bringing out this knowledge. In fact, the word *education* is derived from Latin roots meaning "to lead out."

Aristotle shared Plato's concerns about parents rearing children to be selfish, but he believed that children should be reared within the family. The family unit, he wrote, provided social stability.

Infant mortality was high in ancient Greece and Rome, because of birth problems, illness, and, to a lesser degree, the practice of **infanticide.** Infanticide was usually limited to children with birth defects and to "excess" progeny, particularly girls.

Discipline was harsh, as if following the Old Testament advice that sparing the rod would spoil the child. Handcuffs, gags, foot shackles, and flagellation were not unknown as methods of disciplining children.

Children in these civilizations were the property of their parents. In the Roman **patriarchy,** the powerful father could arrange marriages and sell his children into slavery.

The Middle Ages

The Middle Ages in Europe produced magnificent cathedrals and the beginnings of city centers. However, they were also a time of ignorance and pestilence. Infant mortality remained high, and smallpox, infuenza, and plague assaulted children during the early years.

We hear little of parents deriving pleasure from their children during the Middle Ages. In centers such as Paris the majority of babies were separated from their mothers and consigned to wet nurses. Wet nurses nourished and reared them throughout infancy, sometimes through the age of 5. Children were **swaddled** to prevent their limbs from bending and to protect them from draughts. In Western Europe swaddling persisted into the eighteenth century; in Eastern Europe, into the twentieth century.

Legally, medieval children were treated as property and servants. They enjoyed no civil rights. They could be sent to the monastery or married without consultation.

The medieval concept of childhood, in short, was limited. Children were nurtured until 7, the "age of reason." Then they were expected to fend for themselves (Aries, 1962). They worked alongside adults in the home and in the field. They dressed as miniature adults. They ate and drank as adults. They even ruled nations. "Child's play" was adult play: When Louis XIV took the French throne at the age of 5, he dabbled in sexual games with his nursemaids. Well into the eighteenth century in England 7-year-olds could be convicted of capital crimes and hanged.

For much of the Middle Ages, artists depicted children as small adults. In paintings and sculptures of that era, shrunken men populate the laps of Madonnas. No attempt was made to naturally portray the proportions of the body of the child.

▶ ▶ ▶ ▶

Education was minimal. Wealthy boys were tutored at home. Some lower-class boys learned to write and to read Latin in the choir school. But girls were not educated, because it was thought that they lacked reason and were too emotional.

The Transition to Modern Times

The transition to modern times is marked by the Protestant Reformation and by the thinking of philosophers such as John Locke and Jean Jacques Rousseau.

The Reformation   The Protestant Reformation stirred various attitudes toward children. For one thing, it highlighted the importance of taking responsibility for the way in which one's children turned out. It also underscored the values of independence, self-reliance, and education. A Protestant view of interest to Americans is the Puritan approach to children, as seen in the early days of the settlement of New England.

The common belief is that the Puritans came to America from England in search of religious freedom. But a number of historians argue that they sought instead the freedom to establish their own religious tyranny—and such a tyranny they established over their own children. The Puritans viewed children as innately sinful. They believed that children would commit evil acts unless they were carefully guided by their parents and the community. As we shall see, once infants become self-aware at about 18 months, it is normal for them to begin to defy their parents more frequently. The Puritans intepreted their children's defiance as evidence of evil, and they tried to break their children's will by means of religious instruction and discipline.

On the other hand, the Puritans viewed their children as precious. For one thing, children helped them clear the fields and tend the crops. For another, few people populated the new land, and children were a major source of increase.

The Puritans also strongly believed in education, although education was slanted toward their own religious perspective. The value they placed on education is shown by the fact that they directed some of their scant resources toward the founding of Harvard College in 1637, when they had barely gained a foothold in the new land.

John Locke   The Englishman John Locke (1632–1704) was one of a number of seventeenth-century philosophers who formulated theories about childhood and offered advice to parents. Locke organized his thoughts during the Enlightenment, a period that saw great change in politics, science, and religion, and also the establishment of grammar schools for the education of the common boy. Girls were still second-class citizens. Girls, it was thought, would profit more from training in domestic skills than formal education.

Tabula rasa (TAB-you-luh RAH-suh). *A Latin phrase meaning "blank slate"—referring to the view that children are born without ethical, cultural, or vocational preferences, and that such preferences are shaped by the environment.*

Locke believed that the child came into the world as a **tabula rasa,** a "blank tablet" or clean slate that was written upon by experience. Despite the philosophical and religious legacy of the centuries, Locke did not believe that inborn predispositions (as toward good or evil) played an important role in the conduct of the child. Instead he focused on the role of the environment, or of experience.

▶ ▶ ▶ ▶

In his 1693 essay, *Some Thoughts Concerning Education,* Locke proposed that a system of rewards and punishments be used with children, if they were to become productive adults. He argued that children must be taught to seek social approval ("esteem" and "credit") and to avoid social disapproval ("shame" and "disgrace"). Parents could accomplish these aims by caressing and complimenting children when they behaved properly, and by showing a "cold and neglectful" response to them when they misbehaved. Locke believed that this approach, applied consistently, would work more powerfully than threats or spankings—and in doing so, he countermanded the folklore of the centuries. Praise and disapproval would teach children right from wrong and motivate them to do what was right.

Jean Jacques Rousseau   Rousseau (1712–1778), a Swiss–French philosopher, reversed the stance of the Middle Ages (and of the Puritans). Rousseau argued that children were inherently good and that, left to their own devices, children would develop into generous and moral individuals. In his *Émile, or On Education,* first published in 1762, Rousseau tried to convince parents that they could allow children to express their natural impulses without fear of corruption.

Rousseau believed that most children's problems stemmed from a society that sought to usher them into adulthood before their time. Rousseau saw many of the educational practices of his era as manipulative and doctrinaire. He argued that schools should be flexible, accommodating to the needs of the children, each one of whom Rousseau saw as unique in talents and temperament:

> Leave childhood to ripen in your children. . . . It is the child's individual bent that must be thoroughly known before we can choose the fittest moral training. Every mind has its own form, in accordance with which it must be controlled. . . . Oh, wise man, take time to observe nature; watch your scholar well before you say a word to him; first leave the germ of his character free to show itself. Do not constrain him in anything, the better to see him as he really is (*Émile*).

On the other hand, when it came to girls Rousseau was no more enlightened than other members of the "Enlightenment." Rousseau, too, thought that girls lacked reason. In the "natural" order of things, to him, girls were intended to provide love and comfort—not wisdom or industry.

Up to the Present Day

The modern age began with the Industrial Revolution, which brought the site of production from the home into the factory and moved vast numbers of people from the country to the city.

With the movement into the cities, family life became defined in terms of the nuclear unit of mother, father, and children, rather than the extended family. Within the smaller family group, children became more visible, fostering awareness of childhood as a special time of life. More families entered the middle class, and financial betterment made it possible for many children to actually have a childhood, rather than slave away in the fields or the factories.

The rise of mercantile capitalism also required workers who could read and write—who could keep records and send letters. Capitalism, the emergence of the nuclear family, the recognition of childhood, and the migration to the

► ► ► ►

1   WHAT IS CHILD DEVELOPMENT?

cities all contributed to the development of formal education through public schools. In many Western countries it became increasingly possible for the sons of lower- and middle-class families to achieve recognition and upward mobility through education. Still, despite increasing recognition of childhood as a special time of life, it was not unusual for boys and girls to labor in factories from dawn to dusk up through the early years of the twentieth century.

Only in the twentieth century were laws passed to protect children from severe labor. Only in the twentieth century were compulsory education laws passed that require that children—girls as well as boys—attend school until a certain age. In this century, too, laws have been passed preventing children from getting married or being sexually exploited. Whereas children were once considered the property of parents to do with as they wished, in this century strict laws have been passed protecting children from the abuse and neglect of parents and other caretakers. Juvenile courts have been introduced that grant special status to child offenders under the law, although adolescents who commit serious crimes can be treated as adults. No longer are 7-year-old children hanged.

In the nineteenth and twentieth centuries, there have also been many individuals who have contributed to the advancement of child development as a scientific field of study. They include Charles Darwin, G. Stanley Hall, Alfred Binet, Arnold Gesell, and many others.

Charles Darwin The Englishman Charles Darwin (1809–1882) is known as the originator of evolutionary theory. In his *On the Origin of Species,* published in 1859, Darwin suggested that child development paralleled the evolution of the human species. The idea that **ontogeny recapitulates phylogeny,** coined by a nineteenth-century German zoologist, expresses this view. The phrase means that the life cycle of a single organism retraces the evolution of its species.

The notion that ontogeny recapitulates phylogeny does not fully stand up. During the early days of development, human embryos do bear resemblances to the embryos of ancestral species, such as fish. However, as embryonic development proceeds, the embryos of different species become more and more dissimilar. Nevertheless, these nineteenth-century views can be credited with stimulating scientists to focus intensely on the sequences and timing of the developmental patterns of children.

Darwin himself was so fascinated by children that he was one of the first observers to keep a **baby biography.** Note this excerpt from his biography of his first-born son:

> During the first seven days various **reflex** actions, namely sneezing, hiccoughing, yawning, stretching, and of course sucking and screaming, were well-performed by my infant. On the seventh day I touched the naked sole of his foot with a bit of paper, and he jerked it away, curling at the same time his toes, like a much older child when tickled. The perfection of these reflex movements shows that the extreme imperfection of the voluntary ones is not due to the state of the muscles or of the coordinating centres, but to that of the seat of the will (Kessen, 1965, p. 118).

G. Stanley Hall G. Stanley Hall (1844–1924) received the first American doctorate at Harvard University (in psychology in 1878), and he was the first president of the American Psychological Association (1892). Hall is credited with founding child development as an academic discipline.

Ontogeny recapitulates phylogeny (on-TODGE-en-nee, fye-LODGE-en-nee). The nineteenth-century view that the development of the individual retraces the evolution of the species. (From the Greek ontos, meaning organism; phylon, meaning "tribe"; and genes, meaning "born.")

Baby biography A meticulous account of the development of a baby, attending to the sequences and timing of changes.

Reflex An inborn, stereotyped response to an environmental stimulus.

▶ ▶ ▶ ▶

Does Ontogeny Recapitulate Phylogeny? *Or*, How One Dinosaur (Nearly) Became Extinct

▷
▷
▷
▷

▷　At one point we had an epidemic of dinosaur bites at my house. Let me tell you about one of them.

My daughter Allyn is usually sensitive and empathic enough, but occasionally she has done or said things that show me one reason why Darwin and Hall believed that children go through a stage of "savagery." Occasionally I also glimpse notions of why philosophers over the centuries have written that children are unruly, mischievous, and—at an extreme—innately evil.

When Allyn was 5, she and her then 3-year-old sister Jordan were playing with Jordan's yellow stuffed triceratops. This is a two-feet-long dinosaur with three felt horns protruding from its head. On this occasion, as on others, Jordan pretended that the dinosaur bit her. The poor triceratops immediately went on the endangered list. Allyn's punishment was swift and certain:

"Oh, Jordan," she exclaimed, "let's smash its nose into the ground, pull its eyes out with a tweezers, and yank its stupid horns out until they're nice and bloody." Jordan was caught up in Allyn's enthusiasm, and the two of them proceeded to begin smashing the dinosaur against the floor.

I intervened to prevent the triceratops from getting scuffed up and to save 45 dollars (good dinosaurs don't come cheap).

In Chapter 10 we shall explore possible ways in which children's "pretend play" may foster their social and emotional development. Here let us note that "child's play," even at "tender ages," can be less than generous toward fantasized villains.

Children, of course, are not savages. Nor are they innately evil. But it is understandable why some people might have observed their behavior from time to time and considered them so.

Hall believed in Darwin's view that ontogeny recapitulates phylogeny. Hall suggested that children would be more susceptible to social control if parents allowed the "fundamental traits of savagery their fling." In this way children would recapitulate the social evolution of their species and more naturally arrive at "civilized" behavior.

Hall founded an institute for child study at Clark University in 1891. He adapted the new questionnaire method for use with large groups of children so that he could study the "contents of children's minds." In one study Hall asked children about their interests and activities in an effort to describe the sequence and timing of their developmental processes. Noting the differences in maturity among 400 Massachusetts first graders so tested, he suggested that teachers tailor their teaching methods to the needs of the individual child.

Not until Hall published his major two-volume work, *Adolescence*, in 1904, did **adolescence** become widely perceived as a separate stage of life. In preindustrial societies, children had generally taken on adult responsibilities

Adolescence The stage bounded by the advent of puberty at the lower end and the capacity to take on adult responsibilities at the upper end. Puberty is a biological concept, while adolescence is a psychobiological concept.

► ► ► ►

and worked side by side with parents at much earlier ages. In some societies, puberty had been taken as the sign of entry into adulthood. But the affluence and quality of industrial life in the twentieth century have contributed to a prolonged period during which postpubertal children often continue to acquire academic and vocational skills. Only gradually do they attain independence from parents.

Alfred Binet and Lewis Terman The Frenchman Alfred Binet (1857–1911), along with Theophile Simon, developed the first standardized intelligence test at around the turn of the century. Binet's purpose was twofold: to assess individual differences in intellectual functioning, and to identify public school-children who might profit from special education. Binet (1909) attempted to protect children by pointing out that a poor performance in school could reflect factors other than disobedience and laziness.

Lewis Terman (1877–1956), one of G. Stanley Hall's students, pioneered the mental-testing movement in the United States. Terman adapted Binet's scale to American needs at Stanford University in California, at which time it became known as the Stanford Binet Intelligence Scale. Terman administered the scale to a thousand children aged 3 to 18 and developed **norms** for each age group.

Arnold Gesell Arnold Gesell (1880–1961), another student of Hall's, was a major proponent of the maturational theory of child development, which focuses largely on the unfolding of genetically determined developmental sequences. Gesell argued that development is self-regulated by the unfolding of natural plans and processes.

Maturational processes tend to follow invariant sequences. In their motor development, for example, children sit up before they stand, and they crawl before they walk. Gesell's legacy is the chronicling of patterns of development. The Gesell Institute of Child Development has studied the patterns of behavior that tend to occur at various ages. Gesell Scales have been developed to assess social development, motor development, and so on.

Maturational theory remains a powerful influence in a number of areas of child development, including physical development (changes in size and weight, sexual maturation, and so on), motor development, language development, and cognitive development.

Sigmund Freud The Viennese physician Sigmund Freud (1856–1939) is the originator of **psychoanalytic theory.** Freud's views have been very influential in twentieth-century thought, and they reflect various historical trends. First, we could say that they represent a return to the view that children are innately selfish. Freud believed that primitive impulses, urges, and **instincts**—especially sexual and aggressive urges and instincts—reside deep within children. Children are driven to gratify these impulses, even at the expense of the needs and wishes of parents and others.

Freud arrived at this view from scientific, not religious, teachings. Influenced by Darwin, he believed that evolution had favored the "survival of the fittest"—as generally defined in terms of inborn sexual and aggressive prowess. But Freud also, in a sense, held children blameless for their "instincts" and encouraged parents to allow at them at least partial outlets.

Freud's major areas of focus were on the development of personality traits and psychological problems. His thinking about ways in which early ex-

Norms Standards that indicate how groups of children behave at certain ages.

Psychoanalysis The school of psychology, founded by Sigmund Freud, that emphasizes the importance of unconscious, primitive motives and conflicts as determinants of behavior and personality development.

Instinct An inborn tendency to behave in a way that is characteristic of one's species.

▶ ▶ ▶ ▶

Stage A period of development that differs markedly in quality from other periods. The development of stages is discontinuous.

Stage A period of development that differs markedly in quality from other periods. The development of stages is discontinuous.

Behaviorism The school of psychology that focuses on observable behavior only, and investigates relationships between stimuli and responses.

Passive In this sense, influenced or acted upon by environmental stimuli instead of acting upon the world.

Conditioning A simple form of learning in which stimuli are associated with responses. (See classical conditioning *and* operant conditioning *in* Chapter 2.)

Cognitive Concerning mental activities and functions, such as thought, language, intelligence, dreams, fantasies, and so on. (From the Latin cognoscere, meaning "to know.")

Active Influencing or acting upon the environment.

Peers Children of the same age. (More generally, people of similar background and social standing.)

Social-learning theory A school of psychology that studies the roles of conditioning and observational learning (see Chapter 2) in development and behavior.

perience may shape adult traits and interpersonal behavior have permeated our culture.

In Chapter 2 we shall see that Freud argued that there were specific **stages** of early childhood development. Freud's stages were marked by biological changes that made children particularly sensitive to certain types of interactions with parents and others who played central roles in their lives.

John B. Watson   Early in the twentieth century, John Locke's ideas found new expression in the **behaviorism** of the psychologist John B. Watson (1878–1958). Watson, like Locke, argued that children could be viewed as blank slates. Watson saw children as **passive,** as *reactors* to environmental stimulation, not as *actors.* In essence, children could be **conditioned** into doing—and choosing—almost anything. Watson eliminated any significant role for natural abilities, talents, or predispositions in children's development:

> The behaviorists believe that there is nothing from within to develop. If you start with a healthy body, the right number of fingers and toes, eyes, and a few elementary movements that are present at birth, you do not need anything else in the way of raw materials to make a man, be that a genius, a cultured gentleman, a rowdy, or a thug (Watson, 1928, p. 41).

Today, few scholars of child development would take this extreme environmental view. But it is interesting to note that Watson's ideas were very democratic. They suggested that any child might become a great scientist, writer, or president—given the proper learning opportunities.

Jean Piaget   The Swiss psychologist Jean Piaget (1896–1980) became known in the United States in the early 1960s. Piaget's focus had been on children's **cognitive** processes—their concepts, thought processes, mental imagery, and ways of solving problems. Piaget believed that children underwent distinct stages of cognitive development, during which their views of the world and their ways of approaching problems changed dramatically.

Piaget viewed children as **active** beings who are intrinsically motivated to try to make sense of the world. His view has a strong biological/maturational flavor. It is assumed that children's increasingly sophisticated patterns of thought are made possible largely by the development of the brain. But there is also a role for experience. Piaget believed that children's ideas about moral behavior—about what is right and just—are also influenced by their interactions with adults and, particularly, with **peers.**

While Watson and Freud minimized the role of conscious thought in child development, thought processes are the central focus of Piaget. To Piaget, child development *is* the dramatic change that occurs in the way that children of different ages conceptualize their worlds.

Recent Trends   A number of important events in the study of child development have taken place since the early 1960s. One has been the emergence of **social-learning theory,** which focuses largely on learning by observation, and on the environmental or situational influences on development, particularly in the areas of skill acquisition and social behavior. Social-learning theorists follow in the theoretical footsteps of Locke and Watson. However, they do not insist that children enter this world as "blank tablets," because research today suggests that many traits, including basic temperament, have an inherited com-

▶ ▶ ▶ ▶

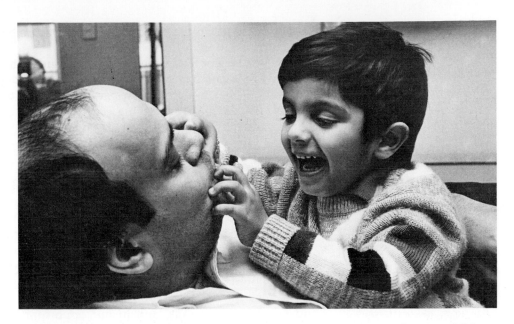

Attachment Much recent research in child development has focused on processes by which parents and children become attached.

Attachment The emotional bond between children and parents, as usually characterized by attempting to remain in contact and the showimg of distress upon separation.

Rooming-in The practice of having a newborn baby remain in the hospital room with the mother, as opposed to residing in the nursery.

Ecological Of the scientific approach that deals with the relations between living organisms and their environment. (See ecological theory in Chapter 2.)

Reciprocal Done, felt, or given in return. Referring to a mutual exchange in which each side influences the other.

ponent. Many social-learning theorists, in contrast to Watson, also see children as active, rather than passive—as attempting to gain knowledge about the environment and skills through purposefully observing the behavior of others in books, on television, and in everyday life.

Recent research by Mary Ainsworth and her colleagues has focused on the processes of **attachment** that characterize the formation of emotional bonds between children and parents. Other researchers have examined the effects of early mother–infant contact in the attachment process, including practices such as **rooming-in** at the hospital.

Many researchers such as University of Virginia psychologist Sandra Scarr and University of Colorado psychologists Robert Plomin and J. C. DeFries continue to attempt to ferret out the environmental and genetic determinants of various personality traits and of intelligence. Cornell University psychologist Urie Bronfenbrenner has advised us not to focus exclusively on children or on their environments as we seek the causes of behavior. From his **ecological** perspective, children and their settings have **reciprocal** influences upon one another.

Other issues have a particularly contemporary flavor. For example, Michael Lamb of the University of Utah has been exploring the role of the father in children's social and emotional development—a long-neglected issue. Researchers have been exploring the biological and experiential factors that contribute to the assumption of sex roles. Still other researchers have been examining the effects of day care on children's intellectual and social development and on bonds of attachment to their parents. Child abuse, the mainstreaming of exceptional children in the schools, the effects of environmental hazards on unborn children, the effects of televised violence, the effects of divorce, and single-parent families—these are just a handful of the other issues that have come under recent scrutiny.

As we have seen, philosophers, psychologists, and educators have held very different opinions as to the nature of children. Let us now turn our attention to some of the controversies that continue to color the field of child development.

▶ ▶ ▶ ▶

Controversies in Child Development

Nature *A term for all the processes within an organism that guide that organism to develop according to its genetic code.*

Nurture *A term for all the processes external to an organism that nourish it as it develops according to its genetic code or cause it to swerve or deviate from its genetically programmed course. Environmental factors that influence development.*

Genes *The basic building blocks of heredity.*

Maturation *The unfolding of genetically determined traits, structures, and functions.*

Primates *An order of mammals including humans, apes, and monkeys.*

Fetal *Of the fetus—the unborn child from about the ninth week of pregnancy until childbirth.*

Sex roles *Complex clusters of behavior that are considered stereotypical of men and women.*

Altruism *Unselfish concern for the welfare of others. Selflessness.*

We have already noted that developmentalists see things in very different ways. Let us consider some of the current controversies in the field.

Which Exerts the Greater Influence on Children: Nature or Nurture?

There is continuing interest in sorting out what human behavior is the result of **nature** (biology) and of **nurture** (environmental influences). What aspects of behavior originate in our **genes** and are biologically "programmed" to unfold in the child as time goes on, so long as minimal nutrition and social experience are provided? What aspects of behavior can be traced largely to such environmental influences as nutrition and learning?

Scientists seek the natural causes of behavior in our genetic heritage, the functioning of the nervous system, and in the process of **maturation.** Scientists seek the environmental causes of behavior in our nutrition, our cultural and family backgrounds, and in our opportunities to learn about the world, including our cognitive stimulation during early childhood and our formal education.

Arnold Gesell and Jean Piaget leaned heavily toward natural explanations of development. John Watson and other behaviorists leaned heavily toward environmental explanations. But today nearly all researchers would agree that, broadly speaking, nature and nurture each play important roles in child development. Consider the development of language. Language develops only in advanced **primates*** and appears to be based in structures found in certain areas of the brain. Thus, biology (nature) plays an indispensable role in language development. But children also come to speak the languages spoken by their caretakers. Parent–child similarities in accent and vocabulary provide additional evidence for an indispensable role for learning (nurture) in language development.

The nature–nurture question pervades practically every area of concern in child development—from **fetal** development to motor development, from intelligence to the acquisition of **sex roles** and **altruism.**

Is Development Continuous or Discontinuous?

Are developmental changes continuous or discontinuous? That is, do they occur gradually, or in major qualitative leaps that dramatically alter the ways in which children are structured and behave?

John Watson and other behaviorists assumed that behavior changes in minor increments. They tended to view even major behavioral changes as the summation of many individually learned response patterns. Maturational theorists, on the other hand, assume that there are periods of life during which behavior changes so dramatically and so rapidly that we can speak of there being discrete stages. Stage theorists such as Sigmund Freud and Jean Piaget

---

*I say "primates" rather than people, because there is currently a controversy as to whether or not apes can also acquire language, as we shall see in Chapter 7.

▶ ▶ ▶ ▶

saw development as discontinuous. Stage theorists see the sequences of development as invariant, although they allow for individual differences in the timing of the sequences and in how far children travel through the sequences.

Certainly it is useful to characterize physical development as consisting of stages. For the several years of middle childhood, children grow gradually larger. But then they undergo adolescent "growth spurts" during which gains become highly dramatic. In boys the muscle mass mushrooms and bodily hair develops. In girls fatty tissue forms breasts and hips.

Earlier it was noted that 7 was once considered the "age of reason." It is not coincidental that Jean Piaget hypothesized that at about the ages of 6 or 7 children tend to enter a new stage of cognitive development—the stage of concrete operations. At this time thought becomes dramatically more flexible, and children are able to focus on several elements of a problem at once as they seek a solution. The stage of concrete operations seems qualitatively different from the one that preceded it. Piaget argues that we cannot explain the difference in terms of children gathering just a bit more experience.

Many theorists look upon some developmental changes as continuous and others as discontinuous. Gains in height throughout middle childhood are largely continuous. Once babies begin to crawl, they show gradual or continuous improvements in muscle coordination. However, as noted, the relatively sudden physical changes of the onset of adolescence seem discontinuous. So does the sequence of events that lead from the infant's crawling to walking.

Scientists are still attempting to identify the areas of development that are continuous and discontinuous.

Are Children Active or Passive?

In the broad sense, all living organisms are active. However, in the field of child development, the question has a more specific meaning. Are children innately "programmed" to try to act upon and take charge of the world (are they active)? Or are children basically shaped by experience, so that they will fit within almost any behavioral or social mold (are they passive)?

The historical view of children as willful and unruly suggests that people have generally seen children as active—even if mischievous (at best) or evil (at worst). However, with John Locke there emerged a countervailing view. Locke and his intellectual descendants view children as passive beings (blank tablets) upon whom external experience writes features of personality and moral virtue. The passive view is seen in Watson's suggestion that children are born with physical features, but not internal predispositions toward preferences or adult vocations. B. F. Skinner, the Harvard University behaviorist, elaborated on Watson's views. Skinner asserted that children's preferences were shaped by experience. In his 1948 novel *Walden Two*, Skinner suggested that the continuous use of **reinforcement** shaped children to *want* to help their fellows and act virtuously.

Jean Piaget saw children as experimenting with and trying to take intellectual charge of their worlds from very tender ages. Even reflexes, wrote Piaget, soon lose their stereotypical quality as children intentionally adapt them to their needs.

At one extreme, educators who view children as passive may assume that they must be motivated to learn by their instructors. Such educators are likely to provide a traditional curriculum with rigorous exercises in spelling,

Reinforcement Any stimulus or change in the environment that follows behavior and increases the frequency of that behavior.

▶ ▶ ▶ ▶

music, and math to promote absorption of the subject matter. They are also likely to apply a powerful system of rewards and punishments to keep children on the straight and narrow.

At the other extreme, educators who view children as active may assume that they have a natural love of learning. Such educators are likely to espouse open education and encourage children to explore an environment rich with learning materials. Rather than attempting to coerce children into specific academic activities, such educators are likely to "listen to the children" to learn about their unique likes and talents, and then to support children as they pursue their inclinations.

These are extremes. Most educators would probably agree that children show major individual differences, and that some children require more guidance and external motivation than others. In other words, children can be "active" in some subjects and "passive" in others. Whether children who do not actively seek to master certain subjects are coerced tends to depend on how important the subject is to functioning in today's society, the age of the child, the attitudes of the parents, and many other factors.

Urie Bronfenbrenner (1977) argues that we miss the point when we assume that children are either entirely active or passive. Children are influenced by the environment, but children also influence the environment. The challenge is to observe the many ways in which children interact with their settings.

These controversies are theoretical. Scientists value theory for its ability to tie together observations and suggest new areas of investigation, but they also follow an **empirical** approach. That is, they engage in research methods, such as those described in the following section, in order to find evidence for or against various theoretical positions.

How Do We Study Child Development?

How many words does the average 2-year-old know? The average 3-year-old? What is the relationship between intelligence and achievement? What are the effects of aspirin and alcohol on the fetus? How can you rear children to become competent and independent? What are the effects of divorce on children?

These are just a few of the questions that are asked about child development. We may all have opinions as to the answers, but scientists insist that such questions be answered by research. Persuasive arguments, reference to authority figures, even tightly knit theories do not suffice. Scientific evidence is obtained by the *scientific method.*

The Scientific Method

There are four basic steps to the scientific method:

Step 1: Formulating a Research Question First is *formulation of a research question.* Our daily experiences, developmental theory, even folklore may all help generate questions for research. Daily experience with dropping off our children at day-care centers may stir us to undertake research to find out whether day

▶ ▶ ▶ ▶

Hypothesis (high-POTH-uh-sis). *A specific statement about behavior that is tested by research. (A Greek word meaning "groundwork" or "foundation.")*

Field study *A method of scientific observation in which children (and others) are observed in their natural environments.*

care influences children's intellectual or social development or the bonds of attachment between children and their mothers. Social-learning theory may prompt research into the effects of televised violence.

Step 2: Developing a Hypothesis   The second step is the *development of a hypothesis*. A **hypothesis** is a specific statement about behavior that is tested through research.

One hypothesis about day care might be that preschool children placed in day care will acquire greater social skills in relating to peers than will preschool children who are cared for in the home. A hypothesis about televised violence might be that elementary school boys who watch more violent television shows tend to behave more aggressively toward their peers.

Step 3: Testing the Hypothesis   The third step is *testing the hypothesis*. Scientists test the hypothesis through carefully controlled methods of observation, such as the field study, the correlational method, the experiment, and the case study.

For example, we could introduce day-care and nonday-care children to a new child in a college child-research center and observe how each group fares with the new acquaintance. Concerning the effects of televised violence, we could have parents help us tally which television shows their children watch and rate the shows for violent content. Each boy could receive a total "exposure to TV violence score." We could then gather teacher reports as to how aggressively the boys act toward their peers, and we could determine whether more aggressive boys also watch more violence on television. We shall describe research methods such as these in the following section.

Step 4: Drawing Conclusions about the Hypothesis   The fourth step is *drawing conclusions*. Finally, scientists draw conclusions about the accuracy of their hypotheses on the basis of the results of their research. When research does not bear out their hypotheses, they may modify the theories from which the hypotheses were derived. The results of scientific research frequently suggest new hypotheses and new studies based on these hypotheses.

In our research on the effects of day care, we would probably find that day-care children have somewhat greater social skills than children cared for in the home, as we shall see in Chapter 10. We would probably also find that more aggressive children spend more time watching televised violence, as we shall see in Chapter 13. But we shall also see in the following section (and in Chapter 13) that it might be wrong to conclude *from the evidence described* that TV violence *causes* aggressive behavior.

Now let us consider each of the research methods used by developmentalists. Then we shall discuss ethical issues concerning research with children.

The Field Study

Field studies of children are conducted in natural or "real-life" settings such as homes, playgrounds, and classrooms. In the field study, investigators observe the natural behavior of children, trying their best not to interfere with it. Interference could influence the results, so that investigators would be observing child–investigator interactions, and not genuine behavior "where it hap-

▶ ▶ ▶ ▶

How Do You Ease Your Child into Nursery School? —A Field Study (by Tiffany Field)

▷
▷
▷
▷
▷ All right, this is it. You're at the crunch. It's the day you've fantasized about and dreaded—Alison's first day at nursery school. And although you've done everything to "prepare" her—lengthy explanations and gradually longer stays in the care of babysitters—she's clutching and crying and begging you not to go. So now what?

Now, of course, many parents must insist that their children stay in nursery school and adjust. The alternative is to quit work, surrender the house, the car, and their "luxurious" life style—that is, eating and having a place to sleep. How do parents take leave of their children in such situations? How do the children adjust? A field study by *Tiffany Field*, Jacob Gewirtz, and their colleagues (1984) at the University of Miami Medical School provides some clues.

The Sample

One of the problems with the field study is that it may be difficult to find or recruit an adequate number of participants, or subjects. However, Tiffany Field and her colleagues had the advantage of being able to gather subjects from children at a full-day university nursery school that was designed to second as an observational research laboratory. Fifty-six children were included—infants (ages 3 to 17 months), toddlers (ages 18 to 29 months), and preschoolers (ages 30 to 69 months). The parents were predominantly middle class and well educated, of various ethnic backgrounds.

Another problem with the field study is that observations of subjects can be haphazard or inconsistent. However, Tiffany Field and her colleagues surmounted this problem by observing 15 randomly selected leave-takings over a six-week period for each child. Observations were made at the beginning of the fall semester by research assistants who were blind to the purposes of the study. An additional ten observations of leave-takings were made six months later.

Age and Sex Differences

Various correlations were observed between children's ages, sex, and behavior. For example, when they were being dropped off by their parents during the first semester, infants and toddlers were more likely than preschoolers to look at their parents, and preschoolers were more likely to look at and talk to their teachers, or to talk to other children.

Girls were more likely than boys to approach their teachers, and boys were more likely to immediately get involved in play activities. Preschoolers were most likely to kiss and hug their parents, and toddlers— the middle age group—were most likely to hover around, cry, complain, and try to cling to their parents. The parents of the toddlers—the group of children for whom adjustment was most difficult—were most likely to try to distract their children by getting them involved in activities in the schoolroom and then to "sneak out."

Being Dropped Off by Fathers versus Mothers

Children showed more crying and attention-getting behavior when they were dropped off by their mothers than when they were dropped off by their fathers. Mothers tended to take more time to leave and to make more of an effort to distract their children as they took their leave. It

▶ ▶ ▶ ▶

Tiffany M. Field in the "field"

could be that the children were aware that fathers, as a group, were less likely to tolerate attention-getting behavior when they were being dropped off. It could also be that the more distress the parent expects at leave-taking, the more distress the child is likely to show.

And Six Months Later

The observations made six months later showed that children of all age groups spent less time relating to their departing parents. There was less crying, less protesting. The children had generally adjusted to spending their days at nursery school.

Now, which children do you think showed the greatest distress when their parents left? Children whose parents left abruptly, or children whose parents stayed for several minutes, attempting to distract them and sneak out of the room? It turns out that the children of the lingering, distracting parents showed more distress.

Field Studies and Causality

But remember: This is a correlational field study, and it can be misleading to try to ferret out cause and effect from correlational studies. Do not conclude that parental lingering and distraction *caused* child distress. It could be that child distress caused the parents to linger and try to sneak out. Or it could be that causal effects were *bidirectional*—that is, that the children and parents influenced each other's behavior in a fluid, continuous fashion.

Also consider the question of why adjustment was most difficult for the toddlers. A correlational study can draw the connections between age and behavior, but it is useless to conclude that distress is *caused* by age. We need to undertake additional research to determine what is happening during toddlerhood that augments distress at leave-taking. It may be that toddlers are old enough to understand what is happening when their parents leave, but young enough to doubt their ability to while away the time apart—a hypothesis that cannot be borne out through the field study.

In any event, a comforting thought may be drawn from this study. Most children do adjust (and reasonably quickly) to nursery school, regardless of the amount of distress they show during the early days. So when the tears are streaming down your child's cheek and you wish you could disappear into a hole in the ground, tell yourself that in a few days, or within a couple of weeks, things will probably get better. Your child may even begin to look forward to nursery school—at least sometimes.

▶ ▶ ▶ ▶

pens." Thus researchers may try to "blend in with the woodwork" by sitting quietly in the back of a classroom, or by observing the class through a one-way mirror.

Figure 1.1 A Native-American Navajo Infant Strapped to a Cradleboard. *Many important field studies have been cross-cultural. For example, researchers have studied Navajo children who are strapped to cradleboards during the first year to see if their motor development is delayed significantly. Once released from their boards, Navajo children make rapid advances in motor development, suggestive of the role of maturation in motor development.*

Cross-Cultural Research   Many important field studies have been **cross-cultural.** Researchers have observed the motor behavior of Native American Navajo children who are strapped to cradle boards during the first year (see Figure 1.1). They have observed the social and intellectual development of children raised in Iranian orphanages. They have observed language development in the United States, Mexico, Turkey, Kenya, and China—seeking "universals" that might suggest a major role for maturation in the acquisition of language skills. They have also observed the ways in which children are socialized in the Soviet Union, in Israel, and in other nations in an effort to determine what patterns of child rearing lead to the development of personality traits such as independence and cooperation.

The field study is also an appropriate method for studying aspects of language development and the nature of **hyperactivity.** In order to determine the rate of growth of children's vocabularies, researchers can observe children of different ages and record the words they use. In the case of hyperactivity, researchers can observe children in classrooms and check off such target behaviors as calling out or getting out of one's seat each time they occur.

The field study is frequently the first type of study carried out in new areas of investigation. Through careful observation, scientists gather an initial impression of what happens in certain situations. In their interpretation of the data, they may use the mathematical **correlational** method, described below and in Chapter 9, to refine their observations of how strongly different **variables** are related. For example, they may explore whether the rate of vocabulary growth is related to sex or to cultural background. Afterwards, they may attempt to investigate cause and effect through experimental research.

The Correlational Method

In the correlational method, researchers determine whether one behavior or trait being studied is related to, or correlated with, another. Consider the variables of intelligence and achievement. Numerous investigations have found *positive* correlations between intelligence and achievement. This means that children who score high on intelligence tests are also likely to score relatively high on achievement tests and to attain high grades in academic subjects. In these studies, both variables, intelligence and achievement, are assigned numbers, such as **IQ** scores and numerical grades. Then these numbers are mathematically related and expressed as a *correlation coefficient.**

Some correlational studies investigate the behaviors and personality traits of children who are influenced by different cultural or family backgrounds. Numerous studies have been carried out, for example, to determine the relationships between divorce and children's behavior and adjustment. Most children of divorce live with their mothers. Many of these studies, therefore, address the effects of father-absence on children. One finding is that boys who

Cross-cultural   *With or of another culture.*

Hyperactivity   *A behavior disorder of childhood characterized by excessive restlessness, low tolerance for frustration, and short attention span.*

Correlated   *Associated, linked.*

Variables   *Quantities that can vary from child to child, or from occasion to occasion, such as height, weight, intelligence, attention span, etc.*

IQ   *Abbreviation for* intelligence quotient, *a score on an intelligence test.*

▶ ▶ ▶ ▶

*The mathematics of the correlation coefficient and some of the details of these studies are discussed in Chapter 9.

are reared in father-absent homes for the first five years or so tend to show fewer sex-typed "masculine" interests, greater dependence, and a "feminine" pattern of intellectual skills (that is, greater verbal skills than math ability).

Field studies may also use the correlational method. Consider the "field study" by Tiffany Field and her colleagues (1984) described in the nearby box. In this study there were numerous correlations—for example, correlations between children's ages and their behavior at leave-taking; correlations between sex of child and leave-taking behavior; correlations between sex of parent dropping off the child and leave-taking behavior; and parental behavior at leave-taking and level of child distress, to name but a few.

Correlational Research on the Daughters of Divorced Mothers   In the correlational research on intelligence and achievement, each variable is usually expressed as a numerical value. Intelligence test scores in a study may vary from 70 to 130, and academic achievment could vary from, say, 1 for F to 13 for A+. But correlational studies may also involve broad group assignments or conditions, as in a study on the effects of divorce by child psychologist E. Mavis Hetherington.

In this fascinating study, Hetherington (1972) correlated the home situations of 13- to 17-year-old girls with their levels of heterosexual interest and activity. Three groups of girls were studied: girls from intact homes, girls who lived with mothers who had been divorced, and girls who lived with mothers who had been widowed. Measures of heterosexual interest and activity were compared for the three groups.

Hetherington found that girls whose mothers were divorced showed the highest levels of heterosexual activity and interest. The daughters of widowed mothers, on the other hand, showed high levels of heterosexual *anxiety* and tended to distance themselves from males. For reasons that we consider in Chapter 12, father-absence due to divorce was linked to different behavior patterns than father-absence due to death.

Types of Measures   The Hetherington study also suggests the various types of observations and measures used in research on child development. The girls in this study were given interviews and personality tests. Their mothers were also interviewed. Moreover, the girls' **overt** behavior was observed and recorded in two situations—in a recreation center where they could choose to mingle either with males or females, and in the office with the interviewer. In the office, it was noted how closely they chose to sit to the (male) interviewer, and whether their general postures or "body language" were standoffish or "sexually inviting."

In other studies, peers have also been used as sources of information. In studies of childhood popularity and childhood depression, for example, children may be asked to answer questions such as the following about their friends or classmates: "Who is liked by almost everybody?" "Who smiles a lot?" "Who has a sad face lots of the time?" "Who stays by himself or herself?"

Patterns of Child Rearing   Much research has also been conducted to learn what patterns of child rearing are associated with positive traits, such as independence and competence with friends and in school. As we shall see in Chapter 11, Diana Baumrind (1973) found that these qualities are most likely to be found in children whose parents are strict, demand mature behavior, commu-

Overt   *Observable.*

▶ ▶ ▶ ▶

nicate effectively with their children, and show their children warmth and support.

Twin Studies   Correlational studies involving identical twins are used whenever possible in the effort to sort out the influences of nature and nurture. As identical twins possess the same genetic endowment (nature), it can be assumed that differences in behavior stem from environmental influences (nurture).

Most pairs of identical twins are reared in highly similar environments, usually in the same household. If their abilities and traits correlate strongly—which they do—it remains difficult to sort out the influences of nature and nurture. But now and then identical twins are separated shortly after birth because of family financial problems or other circumstances. If correlations for intelligence and personality traits between pairs of separated twins continue to be high, these correlations provide strong evidence for the importance of nature. In later chapters we shall report the findings of studies that have correlated the traits of identical twins reared together and apart.

Limitations of Correlational Research   Correlational studies can reveal relationships between variables, but they do not show cause and effect. It may seem logical that intelligence causes academic achievement, but studies on intelligence that measure the two variables and mathematically relate them do not show that one causes, or leads to, the other. Put it another way: We can construct two tests and label one an intelligence test and the other an achievement test. But if we find a positive correlation between test scores, it does not mean that the traits measured by one test were responsible for the traits measured by the other. This is because high scores on both tests could also be accounted for by other factors, such as test-wiseness and motivation to do well.

Similarly, studies that relate divorce to behavior and adjustment report different behavior patterns among children in intact homes and children of divorced parents. However, they do not show that divorce *causes* these adjustment problems. It could be that the factors that led to divorce (such as parental change, lack of commitment, or conflict) also led to adjustment problems among the children.

In the studies on patterns of child rearing, we must also ask *why* parents choose to raise their children in certain ways. It is possible that the same factors that lead them to make these choices also influence the behavior of their children.

In order to investigate cause and effect, researchers turn to the experimental method.

Experiment A method of scientific investigation that seeks to discover cause-and-effect relationships by introducing independent variables and observing their effects on dependent variables.

Treatment In an experiment, a condition received by participants so that its effects may be observed.

The Experiment

Most scientists would agree that the preferred method for investigating questions of cause and effect, such as whether pregnant women who drink alcohol are damaging their unborn children, is the **experiment**. In an experiment, a randomly selected group of subjects receives a **treatment**, such as a dosage of alcohol. The subjects are then observed carefully to determine whether the treatment makes a difference in their physiological features or their behavior.

▶ ▶ ▶ ▶

Independent variable *A condition in a scientifc study that is manipulated (changed) so that its effects may be observed.*

Dependent variable *A measure of an assumed effect of an independent variable.*

Experimental subjects (1) *Subjects receiving a treatment in an experiment.* (2) *More generally, participants in an experiment.*

Control subjects *Participants in an experiment who do not receive the treatment, but for whom all other conditions are held comparable to those of experimental subjects.*

Ethical *Moral, of a system of morals.*

Fetal alcohol syndrome *A cluster of symptoms, including mental retardation and characteristic facial features, found among the babies of women who drink alcohol during pregnancy.*

Cross-species *With or of another species.*

Experiments are used whenever possible, because they allow researchers to directly control the experiences of children and other subjects in order to determine the outcomes of a treatment. Experiments, like other research methods, are usually undertaken to test a hypothesis. For example, a social-learning theorist might hypothesize that television violence will cause aggressive behavior in children because of principles of observational learning. He or she might then devise an experiment in which children are purposefully exposed to televised violence in order to test this hypothesis. It is not enough to show that children who watch more violence on television behave more aggressively; such evidence is correlational. It may simply be that more aggressive children *prefer* violent television shows. We shall review this research—correlational and experimental—in Chapter 13.

Independent and Dependent Variables   In an experiment to determine whether alcohol damages the fetus, experimental subjects would be given a quantity of alcohol and its effects would be measured. Alcohol in this experiment would be an **independent variable,** a variable whose presence is manipulated by the experimenters so that its effects may be determined. The measured results or outcomes of an experiment are called **dependent variables.** Their presence or level presumably depends on the independent variables.

Experimental and Control Groups   Ideal experiments use experimental and control subjects, or experimental and control groups. **Experimental subjects** receive the treatment while **control subjects** do not. Every effort is made to ensure that all other conditions are held constant for both groups of subjects. By doing so we can have confidence that experimental outcomes reflect the treatments, and not chance factors or variation. In a study on the effects of alcohol on the fetus, pregnant females in the experimental group would be given alcohol (there could be several experimental groups, with each group receiving a different dose of alcohol), and pregnant females in the control group would not be given alcohol.

I would not be surprised if you are thinking, "Wait a minute! What researcher would take the chance of harming a fetus by purposefully asking pregnant women to drink alcohol?" Your objection would be right on the mark. **Ethical** considerations do prevent researchers from taking actions that might be harmful. However, correlational evidence does show a link between maternal drinking and so-called **fetal alcohol syndrome** (FAS). This link has prompted **cross-species** experiments with laboratory animals, as discussed in the nearby box.

Random Selection   It is also essential that subjects be assigned to experimental or control groups on a chance or random basis. We could not conclude much from an experiment on the effects of bottle-feeding versus breast-feeding, if the mothers were allowed to choose how to feed their babies. This is because, as a group, women who choose to breast-feed are seeking relatively closer relationships with their babies. And so, if women who breast-feed wind up with closer relationships to their children, we cannot attribute this difference to feeding practice itself. It may, instead, reflect the desire to establish close ties.

In an experiment on the effects of breast-feeding versus bottle-feeding, we would therefore have to assign women randomly either to breast- or bottle-

▶ ▶ ▶ ▶

Cross-Species Research in Child Development

▷
▷
▷
▷
▷   Ethical considerations prevent researchers from using exerimental methods that may be harmful to humans. For example, no researcher would administer alcohol to pregnant women in order to assess the consequences to their fetuses. Similarly, no researcher would wish to separate human children from other people in order to study the effects of isolation on personality development and behavior. However, only experimentation allows scientists to draw conclusions about cause and effect, and important questions concerning the effects of alcohol and other agents and the effects of social isolation need to be answered. For these reasons, researchers often turn to cross-species research and attempt to extend their findings to people.

Rats and Fetal Alcohol Syndrome

Pregnant rats have been exposed to potentially harmful substances, such as alcohol. Rats are frequently used in cross-species research because their body chemistry is similar to ours. Rats are also readily available, and their generations may be counted in weeks rather than years. Thus, it is possible to explore the effects of a treatment on future generations. In one experiment with rats, it was found that the fetuses of pregnant rats who were fed alcohol showed facial features similar to those of children with FAS, including a long upper lip, a small nose, and a narrow forehead (Sulik et al., 1981). This study supports the view that alcohol *causes*, and is not merely associated with, FAS.

Macaque Monkeys

Macaque monkeys have also been used extensively in biological and behavioral research projects that could not be carried out with humans. In one study by Virginia Gunderson and her colleagues (1986), the monkeys were prenatally exposed to mercury. As a result, they developed deficits in visual perception, which confirms correlational studies with human children.

Rhesus Monkeys and Social Isolation

Harry F. Harlow and his colleagues have conducted research on the effects of social isolation with one kind of frequently used macaque, the rhesus monkey. This research would be considered unethical with children. Rhesus infants were separated from their mothers shortly after birth and reared in isolation in order to study the effects of early social deprivation. (See Chapter 10.)

Generalizing to Humans

One of the problems with experimental research is that the experimental situation may be far removed from the everyday situation to which we would like to apply it. This shortcoming is highlighted in the case of cross-species research, in which we must always question whether we can generalize the findings to humans.

On the other hand, years of experience in medical research have suggested that rats and monkeys are similar to people in many aspects of their physiology, and so it may be that we can generalize from these animals to humans regarding certain aspects of physical development. But people are unique in their social development and in their language and cognitive abilities. It may be stretching the point to generalize to people in these areas of development. Nevertheless, rhesus monkeys show patterns of social behavior and attachment that are reminiscent of our own, and this similarity provides the rationale for the Harlow studies.

▶ ▶ ▶ ▶

Role models Persons who act out social roles that are observed and imitated by others.

Case study A carefully drawn biography of the life of an individual, or of the lives of a small group.

feeding, regardless of their personal preferences. As you can imagine, it is not a simple matter to enlist mothers to volunteer to participate in such a study. In one study, discussed in Chapter 4, a compromise was worked out in which women alternated between breast- and bottle-feeding.

Ethical and practical considerations also prevent researchers from doing experiments on the effects of divorce or of different patterns of child rearing. We cannot randomly assign some families to divorce, or to conflict, and other families to perpetual harmony. Nor can we randomly assign parents with an authoritarian bent to raising their children in a permissive manner, or vice versa. In some areas of investigation, we must be relatively satisfied with correlational evidence.

However, the experimental method has been admirably suited to aiding researchers in the gathering of many types of data in all areas of development. As noted earlier in the chapter, investigators in the area of motor development have subjected infants to early training or to lack of practice (independent variables) in motor skills in order to assess their effects on the development of these skills (the dependent variables). In the area of perceptual development (see Chapter 6), infants have been exposed to various visual and auditory stimuli (such as red or green circles, or loud or soft music), and their reactions—paying attention, showing distress, and so on—have been interpreted as suggestive of their perceptual abilities and their preferences. In the area of moral development (Chapter 13), children have been exposed to generous and aggressive **role models** (independent variables), and their resultant behavior (dependent variables) has been observed.

The Case Study

The **case study** is a carefully drawn account or biography of the behavior of an individual child. Parents who keep diaries of their children's activities are involved in informal case studies. In addition to direct observation, case studies include questionnaires and tests, and interviews with children's parents, teachers, and caretakers. Information gleaned from school and other records may be included. Scientists who use the case study method take great pains to record all the relevant factors in a child's behavior, and they are very cautious in drawing conclusions about what leads to what.

Sigmund Freud developed his own clinical case study method for use with his patients. He encouraged them to lie back and relax, and to recall events from their early childhoods. Of course, there are many problems with this method. People are bound to have gaps in memory, and they may purposefully distort their pasts because they are ashamed of some things they did. They may try to earn their interviewers' approval by telling them what they think their interviewers want to hear. The interviewer is also not immune to bias. Freud may have subtly distorted his subjects' life histories to fit his theoretical formulations. Other interviewers may similarly fall prey to bias.

Jean Piaget used the case study method in carefully observing and recording the behavior of his own children, as we shall see in Chapter 8. But Piaget also did small-scale experiments with his own children and those of others. For example, he would show an infant a toy. Then, when the infant began to reach for it, he would cover it with a piece of cloth to determine whether the infant would try to remove the cloth to reach the toy. If the infant did respond to the piece of cloth as a barrier, and attempt to remove it, Piaget

▶ ▶ ▶ ▶

Longitudinal research
The study of developmental processes by taking repeated measures of the same group of children at various stages of development.

Cross-sectional research
The study of developmental processes by taking measures of children of different age groups at the same time.

would conclude that the child's cognitive development had advanced to the point where the toy was *mentally represented*—that is, to the point where the infant had formed an image of the toy in his or her mind, and would continue to perceive this mental image in the absence of the toy.

The Baby Biography   Some of the most fascinating case studies of children are found in baby biographies. Baby biographies are careful observations of children that frequently begin just after birth. As was the case with Piaget's accounts of his own children, baby biographies often include accounts of "mini-experiments" in which a parent or the observer touches the child, or serves as a model for the child, and the child's responses are recorded. Child development students are frequently assigned baby biographies as course requirements.

In many instances, case studies, like field studies, form the basis for sophisticated correlational and experimental studies that follow. The early case studies of Freud and Piaget have led to countless experiments that have attempted to find evidence to support or to disconfirm their theories.

Longitudinal versus Cross-Sectional Research

The processes of development occur over time, and researchers have evolved two different strategies for comparing children of one age to children (or adults) of other ages. In **longitudinal research,** the same children are observed repeatedly over time, and changes in development, such as gains in height or changes in approach to problem solving, are recorded. In **cross-sectional research,** children of different ages are observed and compared. It is assumed that, when large numbers of children are chosen at random, the differences found in the older age groups are a reflection of how the younger children will develop, given time.

Longitudinal Studies   Some ambitious longitudinal studies have followed the development of children and adults for more than half a century. One, the Fels Longitudinal Study, began in 1929. Children were observed twice a year in their homes and twice a year in the Fels Institute nursery school. In this way, records could be amassed that followed their interactions with family and peers. From time to time, various investigators have dipped into the Fels pool of subjects, further testing, interviewing, and observing these individuals as they have grown into adults. In this way they have been able to observe, for example, the development of patterns of independence and dependence. In Chapter 11 we shall see that by the ages of 6 to 10, the behavior patterns shown by the children became predictive of their behavior as adults.

The Terman Studies of Genius also began in the 1920s to follow children who attained high IQ scores. As we shall see in Chapter 9, the men in this study, but not the women, went on to high achievements in the professional world. But it would be wrong to conclude that high intelligence is wasted in women. Contemporary studies of women show that those with high intelligence generally match the achievements of men and suggest that the women of the earlier era were held back by traditional sex-role expectations.

Most longitudinal studies span months or a few years, not decades. In Chapter 11, for example, we shall see that briefer longitudinal studies have found that the children of divorced parents undergo the most severe adjustment

Cohort effect *Similarities in behavior among a group of peers that stem from the fact that the group are approximately of the same age. (A possible source of misleading information in cross-sectional research.)*

Cross-sequential research *An approach that combines the longitudinal and cross-sectional methods by following individuals of different ages for abbreviated periods of time.*

problems within a few months following the divorce. But by two years afterward, most children tend to have regained their equilibrium, as indicated by improved academic performance, socially appropriate behavior, and other measures.

Longitudinal studies have a number of drawbacks. On a practical level, it can be difficult to enlist volunteers to participate in a study that will last a lifetime, and it can be more difficult to have the subjects provide updated addresses. Many subjects fall out of touch as the years pass; others die. The researchers, of course, must be very patient. In order to compare 3-year-olds with 6-year-olds, they must wait at least three years. And, in the early stages of such a study, the concept of comparing 3-year-olds with 21-year-olds remains a distant dream. When the researchers themselves are middle-aged or elderly, they must hope that the candle of yearning for knowledge will be kept lit by a new generation of researchers.

Cross-Sectional Studies Because of the drawbacks of longitudinal studies, most research that compares children of different ages is cross-sectional. Most investigators, in other words, gather data on what the "typical" 6-month-old is doing by finding children who are 6 months old *today*. When they expand their research to the behavior of typical 12-month-olds, they seek another group of children, and so on.

A major drawback to cross-sectional research is the so-called **cohort effect.** A cohort is a group of people born at about the same time. As a result, they experience cultural and other events unique to their age group. In other words, children and adults of different ages are not likely to have shared similar cultural backgrounds. People who are 60 years old today, for example, grew up without television. People who are 40 years old today grew up before the era of space travel. When they were children, no explorers had yet left the Earth. Today's 20-year-olds did not spend their earliest years with *Sesame Street*, a television program that has greatly influenced millions of a somewhat younger cohort of children. And today's children are growing up taking microcomputers and videogames for granted.

Children of past generations also grew up with very different expectations about sex roles and appropriate social behavior. Remember that women in the Terman study generally chose motherhood over careers. Today's girls are growing up with women role models as astronauts, candidates for national office, and even powerful athletes. Moreover, today more than 50 percent of mothers are in the work force, and their attitudes have changed.

In sum, today's 25-year-olds are *not* today's 5-year-olds as seen 20 years later. And today's 10-year-olds may not even be today's 5-year-olds as seen five years later. The times change, and their influence on children changes also. In longitudinal studies, we know that we have the same subjects as they have developed over five, ten, and twenty years. In cross-sectional research we hope that they will be comparable.

Cross-Sequential Research **Cross-sequential research** combines the longitudinal and cross-sectional methods in such a way that many of their drawbacks are overcome.

In the cross-sequential study, the full span of the ideal longitudinal study is first broken up into convenient segments. For example, let us assume

▶ ▶ ▶ ▶

that we wished to follow the sex-role attitudes of children from the age of 4 through the age of 12. The typical longitudinal study would take eight years. However, we can divide this eight-year span in half by attaining two samples of children (a cross section) instead of one: 4-year-olds and 8-year-olds. We would then interview, test, and observe each group at the beginning of the study and four years afterward. By the time of the second observation period, the 4-year-olds would have become 8 years old, and the 8-year-olds would have become 12.

An obvious advantage to this collapsed method is that the study is completed in four rather than eight years. Still, the testing and retesting of samples provides some of the continuity of the longitudinal study. By observing both samples at the age of 8 we can also determine whether they are, in fact, comparable, or whether the four years' difference in their birthdates is associated with cultural and other environmental changes that lead to different attitudes. The fact that both groups of children overlap in age at one point (8 years old), when the younger group is tested for the second time and the older group for the first time, may also provide insight as to whether the process of testing itself makes a difference in future performance. That is, differences between samples tested at the same age may reflect the experience of having been tested before, as well as other environmental differences.

This combined method may include more than two samples and briefer time spans. For example, it is possible to recruit five groups of subjects, not two. If these subjects are 2, 4, 6, 8, and 10 years old at the outset of the study, they can be followed for two years, until their ages overlap, and then be retested. In this way, ten years of "longitudinal" data can be acquired in two. Eight years are saved and some of the objections to longitudinal research are overcome. Quite a bargain.

Ethical Considerations in Studying Children

As noted, many types of research are carried out with lower animals that would be considered unethical with children. Because of the importance of the knowledge to be gained, many researchers consider it ethical to feed alcohol to pregnant rats and to deprive rhesus monkeys of early social experience. But these courses of treatment could not be carried out with pregnant women or with children.

Various professional groups, such as the American Psychological Association, the Society for Research in Child Development, and government review boards have proposed guidelines for research with children. The overriding purpose of these guidelines is to protect children from harm. These guidelines include the following:

- Researchers are not to use treatments or methods of measurement that may do physical or psychological harm to children.
- Children and their parents must be fully informed of the purposes of the research and about the research methods.
- Children and their parents must provide voluntary consent to participate in the study.
- Children and their parents may withdraw from the study at any time, for any reason.

▶ ▶ ▶ ▶

Debriefing *Receiving information about a just-completed procedure.*

- Children and their parents should be offered information about the results of the study.
- The identities of the children participating in a study are to remain confidential.
- Researchers should present their plans for research to a committee of their peers and gain the committee's approval before proceeding.

These guidelines present researchers with a number of hurdles to overcome before proceeding with and while conducting research. But since they protect the welfare of children, the guidelines are valuable.

However, one major dilemma is posed by one of these guidelines, and exceptions are sometimes sought. This is the guideline that suggests that children are to be informed of the purposes of the research. The problem is not that many children are too young to comprehend the research; in such cases, disclosure can be made to their parents.

But what of those cases in which disclosure of the study's purposes would render the study useless? Consider the Hetherington study on the daughters of divorced women. In one part of the study, the girls were given the opportunity to choose their seat for an interview. If the girls had first been told that the researchers wanted to find out how close they would sit to the interviewer, their choices would have been influenced by this information. Instead of acting spontaneously, the girls might have based their seating choice on the impression they wished to make.

Or consider a study in which children are exposed to films of adults who are acting aggressively and are then given the opportunity to act aggressively themselves. What would be the effect of informing children of the purposes of the study? And what if—in order to be perfectly aboveboard—the children were also informed that they would be observed through one-way mirrors? Such research could not be accomplished if full disclosure were insisted upon.

Because of this dilemma, researchers are sometimes given the go-ahead by committees of peers to make exceptions to the principle of full disclosure, so long as other safeguards are taken. Such safeguards might include disclosure of the study's purposes and methods to parents, if not the children themselves; reasonable assurance that the procedures will not be harmful; and **debriefing** of subjects after the study has been carried out.

Nothing in life is perfect. The ethical guidelines used today protect children reasonably well from being abused in research undertakings. When researchers make every reasonable effort to safeguard children from harm, and graciously allow them to withdraw from a study at any time, they are attempting to act ethically.

Summary

1. Childhood spans the years from infancy to puberty. Child development refers to the unfolding and growth of structures, traits, and behavior patterns throughout childhood.

2. Researchers study child development for many reasons: to try to gain insight into human nature (that is, to support or disconfirm theories of child development); to learn about the origins of adult behavior; to investigate

▶ ▶ ▶ ▶

the causes, prevention, and treatment of developmental abnormalities; and to optimize conditions of development for all children.

3. In recent years, for example, researchers have learned about the causes of PKU, hemophilia, Down syndrome, and many other genetic abnormalities. Researchers have also learned about substances that may harm the fetus when ingested by pregnant women, and they are investigating the effects of day care and various educational programs.

4. During ancient times, children were often considered the property of their parents. Plato believed that children were born with knowledge that could be brought out through education, and that children should be reared by the state to lessen their selfishness.

5. During the Middle Ages many babies were consigned to wet nurses for the first few years of life. Swaddling was common. Children frequently began to labor alongside their parents once they reached the age of 7. Education was minimal, and girls were considered too irrational to be educated at all.

6. The Protestant Reformation underscored the values of independence, self-reliance, and education. The Puritans saw children as innately sinful, but believed that guidance by the family and the community could foster socially productive behavior.

7. The seventeenth-century English philosopher John Locke argued that children entered the world as blank tablets, and that rewards (social approval) and punishments (parental disapproval) would foster proper behavior. The eighteenth-century Swiss–French philosopher Jean Jacques Rousseau argued that children were innately good and that improper behavior stemmed from a corrupt society. Rousseau saw the educational practices of his era as manipulative and doctrinaire. He believed that schools should be flexible, adapting to the individual needs of each child.

8. The Industrial Revolution and mercantile capitalism contributed to the advancement of public education. During the twentieth century, compulsory education laws were passed, along with laws that protect children from parental abuse and neglect and from adverse labor conditions.

9. Nineteenth-century scientist Charles Darwin, the originator of evolutionary theory, suggested that child development paralleled the evolution of the species—a view that is incorrect. The American psychologist G. Stanley Hall, who founded the field of child development a century ago, adopted Darwin's view. Hall suggested that it was natural for children to be allowed to give "savagery its fling." Hall also adapted the questionnaire method for use with children and is credited with heightening awareness of adolescence as a stage.

10. The mental-testing movement was pioneered by the Frenchman Alfred Binet and by Lewis Terman of Stanford University. Arnold Gesell was a major proponent of maturational theory, and work at the Gesell Institute focused on developing norms for behavior patterns at various ages.

11. Viennese physician Sigmund Freud's psychoanalytic theory presented children as innately selfish and largely at the mercy of primitive impulses and instincts. John Watson founded American behaviorism, which echoed the views of John Locke and focused on principles of learning in the shaping of behavior. Swiss psychologist Jean Piaget espoused a cognitive view. Pi-

▶ ▶ ▶ ▶

1   WHAT IS CHILD DEVELOPMENT?

aget viewed children as active beings who are intrinsically motivated to understand their worlds and solve problems.

12. There are three major contemporary controversies in child development: Does nature (heredity) or nurture (environmental influences) exert the greater impact upon children? Is development continuous (does it occur gradually) or discontinuous (does it occur in stages)? Are children basically active or passive?

13. Maturational theorists and cognitive theorists such as Piaget see children as active, with nature exerting the greater influence. Behaviorists view children as passive, with nurture—especially learning—as more important. Maturational theorists, psychoanalysts, and cognitive theorists generally see development as occurring in stages, while behaviorists see change as more continuous.

14. Developmentalists use the scientific method to gather evidence. The four steps of this method are: formulating a research question, developing a hypothesis, testing the hypothesis, and drawing conclusions about the hypothesis.

15. Developmentalists use various research methods to test hypotheses. The field study observes children's behavior "where it happens," in the natural setting. The baby biography is one example of an observational study.

16. The correlational method discovers relationships between variables, such as intelligence and achievement, or aspects of family life (such as patterns of child rearing and divorce) and children's adjustment to the demands of life. But the correlational method does not show cause and effect.

17. Experiments seek to show cause and effect by giving experimental subjects a treatment that is not received by control subjects. The effects of different levels of the treatment are then measured carefully. Experiments have shown, for example, that televised violence contributes to aggressive behavior in children.

18. The case study is a carefully drawn description of the behavior of an individual. Freud and cognitive-developmental theorist Jean Piaget both relied heavily on the case-study method.

19. In longitudinal research the same group of subjects is observed repeatedly at several points in time. In cross-sectional research, subjects of different ages are compared. Both types of research suggest developmental conclusions. Longitudinal research has the drawbacks of taking a long time and of loss of subjects over time. Cross-sectional research is troubled by the fact that older subjects may not be representative of younger subjects at advanced ages.

20. The cross-sequential method combines longitudinal and cross-sectional approaches. It saves researchers time and also answers some of the drawbacks of both types of research.

21. Ethics in child development research focus on protecting children from harm. In order to protect them, children or their parents are informed of research methods and purposes, they are given the opportunity to withdraw from research at any time, and their records are kept confidential. Animal studies may use methods that would not be acceptable with humans.

▶ ▶ ▶ ▶

Development and growth are synonymous terms. *False.* Growth refers to changes in size or quantity. Development is a more comprehensive term. Development refers both to changes in quality, as in the qualitative distinctions between thought processes in the 2-year-old and in the 5-year-old, and to growth.

Children were once treated as the property of their parents. *True,* especially in ancient Rome.

In medieval Paris, children were handed over to lower-class women for rearing shortly after birth and were not returned to their parents for several years. *True.* The women who reared them were called wet nurses, and children were frequently not returned to their natural parents until the age of 5.

During the Middle Ages, girls were not educated because it was thought that they lacked reason and were too emotional. *True.* Prejudice against girls and women has been with us throughout history.

Louis XIV took the throne of France at the age of 5. *True.*

Children come into the world as "blank tablets"—without preferences or inborn differences in intelligence and specific talents. *False.* Although the view of children as blank tablets or clean slates has been advanced by John Locke and behaviorists, evidence suggests that there are inherited components of children's psychological traits and basic temperaments.

The development of the child parallels the evolution of our species. *False.* There are similarities between the embryos of children and the embryos of ancestral species—but these similarities are limited to the first days of embryonic development.

Although we have become more affluent, twentieth-century life has prolonged children's dependence on parents. *True.* Today's children and adolescents remain in school to further their academic and vocational skills at ages when in centuries past they would have been working in the fields or in factories.

Giving children early training in sitting up and walking significantly accelerates the development of these skills. *False.* Training may lead to slight acceleration of motor development, but motor skills are by and large not acquired until children are "ready"—that is, until they have matured sufficiently.

Children's levels of intelligence are influenced by early learning experiences. *True.* Programs such as Head Start have improved children's performances on intelligence tests.

Some theorists contend that children actively strive to understand and take charge of their worlds, while other theorists argue that children respond passively to environmental stimulation. *True.* Theorists such as Piaget have viewed children as active, while Watson and other behaviorists have viewed children as passive.

Children who are dropped off at nursery school by their mothers are more likely to cry than children who are dropped off by their fathers. *True.*

▶ ▶ ▶ ▶

Mothers and fathers may communicate very different expectations to their children, even to toddlers.

Boys who spend the first years of life in father-absent homes are more likely to be dependent than boys who do not. True.

Teenaged girls who live with their divorced mothers are more likely to become involved in heterosexual activity than girls who live in intact homes. True.

There are physical similarities between children with fetal alcohol syndrome and the offspring of rats who were given alcohol during pregnancy. True. These include a longer upper lip, a smaller nose, and a narrower forehead.

Researchers have followed some subjects in developmental research for more than 50 years. True. Subjects have been followed for this length of time in a number of longitudinal research projects.

Answer Key to Questionnaire on Knowledge of Child Development, page 4

1. F	6. T	11. T	16. T	21. F
2. F	7. F	12. F	17. T	22. F
3. F	8. T	13. F	18. F	23. T
4. T	9. F	14. F	19. T	24. T
5. F	10. T	15. F	20. T	25. F

► ► ► ►

2

Theories of Development

▸
▸
▸
▸
▸
▸
▸

T R U T H ► O R ► F I C T I O N ?

- Children must crawl before they can walk.
- Giving infants early training in sitting up and walking accelerates the development of these skills.
- Conflict between children and their parents is inescapable.
- Children can be taught to wake up in the middle of the night if they are about to wet their beds.
- Punishment doesn't work.
- Psychologists successfully used painful electric shock to teach a nine-month-old infant not to vomit.
- Classroom behavior-modification procedures rely largely on old standbys such as ignoring children when they misbehave and praising them for desired behavior.
- Children can learn only by making mistakes.
- Children are budding scientists who actively intend to learn about and take intellectual charge of their worlds.
- Infants do not simply accept their parents' child-rearing approaches; even newborns influence their parents to treat them in certain ways.
- Children are influenced not only by their parents, schools, and other local agencies, but also by the ideals and values of the cultures in which they are reared.

"Give me a dozen healthy infants, well-formed," challenged John B. Watson in 1924, "and my own specified world to bring them up in, and I'll guarantee to take any one at random and train him to become any type of specialist I might suggest—doctor, lawyer, merchant-chief, and, yes, even beggar-man and thief, regardless of his talents, penchants, tendencies, abilities, vocations, and the race of his ancestors" (p. 82).

Watson, often referred to as the father of American **behaviorism,** was expressing a learning-theory view of children, in keeping with the ideas of the British philosopher John Locke, that children come into the world as a *tabula rasa* or "blank slate," and that their ideas, preferences, tendencies, and skills are shaped by their experiences. In Chapter 1 it was noted that there has long been a nature–nurture controversy in the study of children. In his theoretical approach to understanding children, Watson emphasized the role of *nurture,* or of the physical and social environments, for example, of parental training and approval.

Watson's view was a minority one in the long history of approaches to understanding children. *Nature,* or the inherited, genetic characteristics of the child, had long been the more popular explanation of how children get to be what they are. Just four years after Watson sounded his clarion call for the behavioral view, Arnold Gesell expressed the idea that biological **maturation** was the main principle of development in *Infancy and Human Growth:* "All things considered, the inevitableness and surety of maturation are the most impressive characteristics of early development. It is the hereditary ballast which conserves and stabilizes growth of each individual infant" (1928, p. 378).

Watson was talking largely about the behavior patterns children develop, while Gesell was perhaps focusing mainly on physical aspects of growth and development. Still, the behavioral and maturational perspectives remain at opposite ends of the continuum of theories of development. As noted by psychologist Sandra Scarr (1985), many scientists fall into the trap of overemphasizing the importance of either nature or nurture at the risk of overlooking the ways in which nature and nurture interact. Just as a child's environments and experiences influence the development of his or her biological endowment, children often place themselves in environments that are harmonious with their personal characteristics. Children, for example, are influenced by teachers and by other students; however, because of the psychological traits they bring into school with them, some children may choose to socialize as much as possible with other children, while other children may prefer the company of teachers, and still other children may prefer to remain by themselves as much as they can.

In this chapter we first define what is meant by theories of development. We show why it is important to try to construct theories and to show which theories are most helpful in understanding children. Then we examine five contemporary theoretical approaches to understanding children: the maturational, psychoanalytic, learning-theory, cognitive-developmental, and ecological approaches. We may as well confess at once that we shall conclude that each theoretical approach has contributed to our overall understanding of children.

Behaviorism *Watson's view that a science or a theory of development must study observable behavior only, and investigate relationships between stimuli and responses.*

Maturation *The unfolding of genetically determined traits, structures, and functions.*

▶ ▶ ▶ ▶

THEORIES OF DEVELOPMENT

Why Do We Have Theories of Child Development?

Child development is a scientific enterprise. As in other scientific enterprises, developmentalists seek to describe, explain, predict, and control the events they study.

Developmentalists attempt to describe and explain behavior in terms of concepts such as heredity, perception, language, learning, cognition, emotion, socialization, and sex roles. For example, we may describe learning as a process in which behavior changes as a result of experience. We can be more specific and also describe instances of learning in which children memorize the alphabet through repetition, or acquire gymnastic skills through practice in which their performance gradually approximates desired behavior. We may explain how learning occurs in terms of rules or principles that govern learning. Thus we might explain the trainer's use of words such as "fine" and "good" as "reinforcers" that provide the gymnast with "feedback."

When possible, descriptive terms and concepts are interwoven into **theories.** Theories are related sets of statements about events. Theories are based on certain assumptions about behavior, such as Watson's assumption that training outweighs talents and abilities, or Gesell's assumption that the unfolding of maturational tendencies is inevitable. Theories also allow us to derive explanations and predictions. Many developmental theories combine statements about psychological concepts (such as learning and motivation), behavior (such as reading or problem solving), and anatomical structures or biological processes (such as maturation of the nervous system). For instance, a child's ability to learn to read is influenced by his or her motivation, attention span, and level of perceptual development.

A satisfactory theory of development must allow us to predict behavior. For instance, a satisfactory theory concerning the development of sex roles will allow us to predict the circumstances under which children will acquire stereotypical masculine or feminine sex-typed behavior patterns, or a combination of these patterns. A broadly satisfying, comprehensive theory should have a wide range of applicability. A broad theory of the development of sex roles might apply to children from different cultural and racial backgrounds and, perhaps, to homosexuals as well as heterosexuals. If our observations cannot be adequately explained by or predicted from a given theory, we should consider revising or replacing that theory.

Many theories have been found incapable of explaining or predicting new observations. As a result they have been revised extensively. For example, Sigmund Freud's psychoanalytic view that assertive career women are suffering from unconscious **penis-envy** has met with criticism from his followers (such as Karen Horney) and his antagonists alike. So it is that most modern-day, or "neo," Freudians have developed different views concerning assertive behavior in girls.

The notion of controlling behavior is controversial. However, the goal of "control" does not mean that developmentalists seek to make children do their bidding—as if they were puppets dangling on strings. Instead, it means that professionals consult with parents, teachers, nurses, and children them-

Theory *A formulation of relationships underlying observed events. A theory involves assumptions and logically derived explanations and predictions.*

Penis-envy *In psychoanalytic theory, jealousy of the male sex organ attributed to girls in the phallic stage.*

▶ ▶ ▶ ▶

Stage theory *A theory of development characterized by hypothesizing the existence of stages.*

Stage *A distinct period of life that is qualitatively different from other stages. Stages follow one another in an orderly sequence.*

Discrete *Separate and distinct; made up of distinct parts.*

Maturational theory *Arnold Gesell's view that development is self-regulated by the unfolding of natural plans (that is, heredity) and processes.*

selves in order to promote the welfare of children. Psychologists, for example, may summarize and interpret theory and research on the effects of day care to help day-care workers provide an optimal child-care environment. Teachers may use learning theory to help children learn to read and write. In each case the professional is "controlling" the experiences that children will encounter, but it is clearly with the benefits of the children in mind, and also, ultimately, with the understanding and approval of parents.

Stage Theories versus Development as Continuous

The psychoanalytic theories of Sigmund Freud and Erik Erikson and the cognitive-developmental theory of Jean Piaget are **stage theories. Stages** are relatively **discrete** periods of development that differ in quality from other periods. Stages follow one another in a certain sequence. According to Freud, each stage of development—oral, anal, and so on—is ushered in by biological changes. Each stage is characterized by particular behaviors and holds a distinct potential for the development of various traits and conflicts.

Not all developmental theories are stage theories. Social-learning theorists, for example, view development as a continuous process in which the effects of learning mount gradually, with no major, sudden qualitative leaps.

Let us now consider what each of the major theoretical approaches has to say about the nature and development of the child.

Maturational Theory

Maturational theory focuses largely on the unfolding of genetically determined developmental sequences. Whereas the theory of Sigmund Freud assumes that biological maturation provides the foundation for changes in personality and emotional development, maturational theory, as propounded by Arnold Gesell (1880–1961), argues that all areas of development are self-regulated by the unfolding of natural plans and processes. Few contemporary students of child development would agree that maturation is the central factor in *all* areas of development. However, very few would dispute that maturation plays the major role in areas such as motor development.

Maturational processes tend to follow invariant sequences. In the case of motor development, children sit up before they stand, and they stand before they walk. It appears that these motor skills are made possible by the progressive maturation of certain parts of the nervous system. Numerous investigators have also wondered whether learning experiences have an important influence on motor development—whether, for example, training can accelerate children's progress through this sequence. In Chapter 5 we shall see that early training only slightly accelerates motor development. No amount of training, moreover, can teach these skills to children whose levels of maturation are not advanced enough to allow them. In maturational terms, children must be "ready" to acquire new behavior patterns. The unfolding of natural processes creates the foundation on which experiences can build.

A few studies have focused on the effects of purposefully *preventing* infants from practicing certain motor skills during the early months. When

▶ ▶ ▶ ▶

Arnold Gesell

children who are deprived of experience in this way are again permitted to move about freely at more advanced ages, they tend to acquire these motor skills almost literally overnight. When we are ready to learn, we tend to learn quickly. When we are not ready, learning proceeds tediously, if it occurs at all. Educators are understandably concerned with knowing when children are *ready* to acquire academic skills.

Maturational Theory and Psychological Traits

Most developmentalists freely admit to the prominent role of maturation in physical and motor development, but there is controversy concerning the prominence of maturation in the development of **psychological traits.** Psychological traits "steer" children to behave in similar ways across different situations. For example, the trait of sociability may steer a child to invite friends along when going to a museum, to share confidences with friends, and to befriend teachers.

According to psychologist Gordon Allport (1937, 1961), psychological traits are rooted in the nervous system, for which reason Allport referred to them as "neuropsychic structures." Critics have argued that Allport did not specify how traits were imbedded in the nervous system—an omission that needs to be addressed. But if we temporarily put aside the question of the exact biological nature of traits, there is evidence that predispositions toward a number of psychological traits are inherited. Much of this evidence is found in adoption studies and in comparisons of identical and fraternal twins.

It may be that genetic influences are strongest in traits that describe the child's general temperament, that is, the child's placement along dimensions of personality such as activity–lethargy, emotionality–impassivity, sociability–

Psychological trait *An aspect of personality that is inferred from behavior and assumed to give rise to behavioral consistency.*

▶ ▶ ▶ ▶

social detachment, and impulsivity–reflectiveness. Alexander Thomas and Stella Chess (1977) argue that children's temperaments reflect their basic activity levels, adaptability to new experiences, abilities to establish regular cycles of eating and sleeping, emotional reactivity, moods, and persistence. These factors combine in different ways, so that some children are "easy-going," but others are "difficult" or "slow to warm up."

A number of investigators, such as Daniels and Plomin (1985) and Kagan (1984), argue that children can inherit tendencies toward fearfulness, shyness, and timidity on the one hand, or toward uninhibited sociability on the other. Most children tend to inherit a balance of traits among these extremes.

Research suggests that identical twins resemble one another more strongly than fraternal twins on numerous traits. These traits include general irritability and sociability; persistence in performing cognitive tasks; and ability in cognitive tasks that assess verbal and spatial skills and perceptual speed (DeFries et al., 1987; Floderus-Myrhed et al., 1980; Matheny, 1983; Scarr & Kidd, 1983). Identical twins also show more similarity than fraternal twins in their early signs of attachment, such as smiling, cuddling, and expressing fear of strangers (Freedman, 1965; Scarr & Kidd, 1983).

Evaluation   And so, it may be that a number of tendencies toward temperament, attachment behaviors, and the development of cognitive skills are "built in." It may also be that their maturation—that is, the unfolding of the child's genetic code—plays a prominent role in their development. But there are differences of opinion. Consider temperament. Some researchers (e.g., Goldsmith & Campos, 1986) argue that if children do have "basic" temperaments, these temperaments ought to show stability over time. However, temperament does show some instability over time, as in one recent study which tracked the temperaments of 2-year-olds over 100 days (Hooker et al., 1987). Temperament is also generally measured by means of mothers' reports, and the accuracy of maternal reporting has been brought into question (Bates & Bayles, 1984; Matheny et al., 1987). At this time it may be safest to conclude that maturation appears to play a role in temperament, but that the impact of this role remains unclear.

There is also dispute about the role of maturation in intelligence. In Chapter 7 we shall see that nearly half of psychologists and educational specialists attribute differences in intelligence to the interaction of maturational and environmental influences. Moreover, in arriving at their conclusions, psychologists and educators were most impressed by research that compared the intelligence of adopted children with that of their natural and adoptive mothers (Snyderman & Rothman, 1987).

Let us heed Sandra Scarr's warning and note how children's environments interact with inherited tendencies in directing their development. Experience may foster major changes in the ways in which children adapt to the demands of everyday life. Society usually demands that impulsive children behave more reflectively. Parents may urge passive children to try to take more active charge of their lives. Shy and retiring children may be taught social skills and guided into more outgoing behavior. But it may also be that the child with average athletic potential will never become an Olympic gymnast, even with the best of training.

► ► ► ►

Repress *In psychoanalytic theory, to protect the individual from anxiety by ejecting anxiety-evoking ideas and impulses from awareness.*

Now let us consider another theory of development that relies upon the relationship between the biological maturation of the child and stages of development: psychoanalytic theory. Unlike Gesell's approach, the psychoanalytic approach focuses on what is presumed to be children's conflicts with their parents and society at large.

Psychoanalytic Theories

He was born with a shock of dark hair—in Jewish tradition, the sign of a prophet. In 1856, in a Czechoslovakian village, an old woman told his mother that she had given birth to an important man. The child was raised with great expectations. In manhood, Freud himself would be cynical about this notion. Old women, after all, earn more favors through good tidings than through forecasts of doom. But, in a sense, the prophecy about Freud may have been realized. Few have shaped our thinking about human nature as deeply as the compassionate physician from Vienna.

Sigmund Freud (1856–1939) is the father of psychoanalytic theories of development and of the form of psychotherapy called psychoanalysis. Freud focused on the emotional and social development of children, and on the origins of psychological traits such as dependence, obsessive neatness, and vanity.

The troubled adult undergoing psychoanalysis settles down on a couch and utters whatever thoughts pop into awareness. Patients are gently guided into reminiscences of childhood, because the psychoanalyst believes that adult problems originate in childhood conflicts that have been long **repressed.**

Sigmund Freud

► ► ► ►

Psychodynamic *Descriptive of Freud's view that various forces move through the personality and determine behavior.*

Conscious *Self-aware.*

Preconscious *In psychoanalytic theory, not in awareness but capable of being brought into awareness by focusing of attention.*

Unconscious *In psychoanalytic theory, not available to awareness by simple focusing of attention.*

Id *The psychic structure, present at birth, that represents physiological drives and is fully unconscious. (A Latin word meaning "it.")*

Ego *(EE-go). The second psychic structure to develop, characterized by self-awareness, planning, and the delay of gratification. (A Latin word meaning "I.")*

Superego *The third psychic structure, which functions as a moral guardian and sets forth high standards for behavior.*

Psychic structure *(SIGH-kick). In psychoanalytic theory, a hypothesized mental structure that helps explain different aspects of behavior.*

Defense mechanism *In psychoanalytic theory, an unconscious function of the ego that protects it from anxiety-evoking material by preventing accurate recognition of this material.*

A basic concept of psychoanalytic theories is that conflict between the child and society is inevitable. Children are viewed as possessing biological instincts that demand gratification. The social processes that limit the child's avenues for seeking this gratification—that guide the child into following parental wishes and social codes—also shape the child's personality.

In this section we explore Freud's theory of psychosexual development and Erik Erikson's theory of psychosocial development. Each is a stage theory. Each suggests that the child's experiences during early stages have implications for the child's eventual emotional balance and social adjustment.

Sigmund Freud's Theory of Psychosexual Development

Freud's view of personality is **psychodynamic.** Freud taught that personality in even young children is characterized by a dynamic struggle. Basic drives such as hunger, sex, and aggression inevitably come into conflict with social pressures to behave according to laws, rules, and moral codes. The laws and social rules become internalized. Children make them parts of themselves. After doing so, the dynamic struggle becomes a clashing of opposing *inner* forces. The major struggles lie *within.*

The Geography of the Mind: Warming Up to the Human Iceberg Freud believed that the human mind was like an iceberg. Only the tip of an iceberg rises above the surface of the water, while the great mass of it darkens the deep. Freud came to believe that people, because of their childhood experiences, are aware only of a small number of the ideas and the impulses that dwell within their minds. Our deepest images, thoughts, fears, and urges remain beneath the surface of conscious awareness, where little light illuminates them. He labeled the region that pokes through into the light of awareness the **conscious** part of the mind. He called the regions that lie below the surface the preconscious and the unconscious.

The **preconscious** mind contains elements of experience that are presently out of awareness, but can be made conscious simply by focusing on them, such as your phone number or what you ate for dinner yesterday. The **unconscious** mind contains genetic instincts and urges that we only partially perceive as hunger, thirst, sexuality, and aggression. Some unconscious urges cannot be experienced consciously, because mental images and words could not portray them in all their color and fury. Other unconscious urges, which are largely sexual and aggressive in nature, may be kept below the surface by repression.

Repression, or motivated forgetting, is the ejecting of unacceptable ideas from awareness. Repression protects children and adults from recognizing impulses they would consider inappropriate in light of their moral values.

The Structure of Personality: Id, Ego, and Superego Sigmund Freud labeled the clashing forces of personality the **id, ego,** and **superego.** These three **psychic structures** could not be observed directly, but their influence could be inferred from our behavior.

The id is present at birth. The id represents biological drives and is unconscious. It demands instant gratification of instincts without consideration of law, social custom, or the needs of others.

▶ ▶ ▶ ▶

Regression *A defense mechanism in which the individual, under stress, returns to behavior patterns that are characteristic of earlier stages of development. (From the Latin* re-, *meaning "back," and* gradi, *meaning "to go.")*

Rationalization *A defense mechanism in which the individual engages in self-deception by finding justifications for unacceptable ideas or behavior.*

Displacement *A defense mechanism in which ideas or impulses are transferred from threatening or unsuitable objects onto less threatening objects.*

Identification *In psychoanalytic theory, the unconscious assumption of the behavior of another person, usually the parent of the same sex.*

Eros *In psychoanalytic theory, the basic instinct to preserve and perpetuate life.*

Libido *(lib-BEE-doe). In psychoanalytic theory, the energy of Eros; the sexual instinct.*

Erogenous zone *An area of the body that is sensitive to sexual sensations.*

Psychosexual development *In psychoanalytic theory, the process by which libidinal energy is expressed through different erogenous zones during different stages of development.*

Oral stage *The first stage of psychosexual development, during which gratification is hypothesized to be attained primarily through oral activities, like sucking and biting.*

The ego begins to develop during the first year of life, when an infant experiences delays prior to receiving gratification. It blossoms as children learn to obtain gratification for themselves, without screaming or crying. The ego "stands for reason and good sense" (Freud, 1964, p. 76), for rational ways of coping with frustration. The ego curbs the appetites of the id and makes plans that are in keeping with social convention, so that a person can find gratification yet avoid the disapproval of others. The id lets children know that they are hungry. The ego creates the idea of walking to the refrigerator, microwaving some leftovers, and pouring a glass of milk. In Freudian theory, the ego also provides the conscious sense of self.

Defense Mechanisms   Although most of the ego is conscious, some of its business is carried out unconsciously. For instance, the ego also acts as a watchdog or censor that screens the impulses of the id. When the ego senses that socially unacceptable impulses are rising into awareness, it may use psychological defenses to prevent them from surfacing. Repression is one such psychological defense, or **defense mechanism.** Other important defense mechanisms include *regression, rationalization,* and *displacement.* In **regression,** the individual when under stress returns to a form of behavior characteristic of an earlier stage of development. For example, an adolescent may cry when he is not allowed to use the family car. **Rationalization** is the use of self-deceiving justifications for unacceptable behavior. For example, a fifth grader may blame her cheating on the teacher for leaving the room. **Displacement** is the transfer of ideas and impulses from threatening or unsuitable objects to less threatening objects. We shall see that Freud believed that children displace their sexual urges toward their own parents onto people outside the family, in part because of the incest taboo.

The superego develops throughout middle childhood, incorporating the moral standards and values of parents and significant members of the community through **identification.** Throughout life the superego monitors the intentions of the ego and hands out judgments of right and wrong.

The Stages of Psychosexual Development   Freud stirred controversy within the medical establishment of his day by arguing that sexual impulses, and their gratification, are central factors in children's development. He believed that children's most basic ways of relating to the world, such as sucking their mothers' breasts and moving their bowels, involve intense sexual feelings.

He also believed that one of the major instincts of the id is **eros,** the instinct to preserve and perpetuate life. Eros contains a certain amount of energy, which Freud labeled **libido.** This energy is psychological in nature and involves sexual impulses, so Freud considered it *psychosexual.* Libidinal energy is expressed through sexual feelings in different parts of the body, or **erogenous zones,** as the child develops. Freud hypothesized five stages of **psychosexual development:** oral, anal, phallic, latency, and genital.

The Oral Stage   During the first year of life, a child experiences much of the world through the mouth. If it fits, into the mouth it goes. This is the **oral stage** of psychosexual development. Freud argued that oral activities like sucking and biting bring the child sexual gratification as well as nourishment.

▶ ▶ ▶ ▶

Freud believed that children encounter conflicts during each stage of psychosexual development. During the oral stage conflict centers around the nature and extent of oral gratification. Early weaning can lead to frustration. Excessive gratification, on the other hand, can lead an infant to expect it will automatically be handed everything in life. Inadequate or excessive gratification in any stage can lead to **fixation** in that stage, according to Freud, and to the development of traits characteristic of that stage. Oral traits include dependency, gullibility, and optimism and pessimism.

Freud theorized that adults with an oral fixation can experience exaggerated desires for such "oral activities" as smoking, overeating, alcohol abuse, and nail biting. Like the infant whose very survival depends on the mercy of an adult, adults with oral fixations may have clinging, dependent interpersonal relationships.

The Anal Stage　During the **anal stage,** sexual gratification is attained through contraction and relaxation of the muscles that control elimination of waste products. The process of elimination, which was controlled reflexively during most of the first year of life, comes under voluntary muscular control, even if such control at first is not reliable. The anal stage is said to begin in the second year of life.

According to Freud, it is during the anal stage that children learn to delay the gratification of eliminating as soon as they feel the urge. The general issue of self-control may become a source of conflict between parent and child, and the issue of self-control frequently finds expression in toilet training. Anal fixations may stem from this conflict and lead to two sets of anal traits. **Anal-retentive** traits involve excessive use of self-control: perfectionism, a strong need for order, and exaggerated neatness and cleanliness. **Anal-expulsive** traits, on the other hand, "let it all hang out." They include carelessness, messiness, even sadism.

The Phallic Stage　Children are said to enter the **phallic stage** during the third year of life. At this time the major erogenous zone becomes the phallic region (the clitoris in girls). Parent–child conflict is likely to develop over masturbation, which parents may treat with punishment and threats. During the phallic stage children are theorized to develop strong sexual attachments to the parent of the opposite sex and begin to view the same-sex parent as a rival for the other parent's affections. Boys may want to marry Mommy, and girls may want to marry Daddy.

Feelings of lust and jealousy are difficult for little children to handle. They make home life tense indeed. So these feelings are largely repressed, although their influence is felt through fantasies about marriage and through vague hostilities toward the same-sex parent. Freud labeled this conflict in boys the **Oedipus complex,** after the legendary Greek king who unwittingly killed his father and married his mother. Similar feelings in girls give rise to the **Electra complex.** According to Greek legend, Electra was the daughter of the king Agamemnon. She longed for him after his death and sought revenge against his slayers—her mother and her mother's lover.

According to Freud, the intense conflicts of the phallic stage are normal developmental events. Normal development demands that they be experienced, and that they be resolved properly. The Oedipus and Electra complexes normally become resolved by about the age of 5 or 6, as children repress their

▶ ▶ ▶ ▶

THEORIES OF DEVELOPMENT

The Odd Couple

▷
▷
▷
▷

▷ In the film and television series *The Odd Couple*, Oscar Madison and Felix Ungar share an apartment after their wives have thrown them out. Oscar is messy. He drops everything everywhere, like a truck of junk on a bumpy road. Felix is excessively neat, the type of individual who will follow a smoker around the room with an ashtray.

According to psychoanalytic theory, both Felix and Oscar are fixated in the anal stage of psychosexual development. Their behavior patterns reflect the opposing ways in which they learned to adjust to a strict toilet-training process.

Felix became very well housebroken. His personality type is anal-retentive. He has a place for everything and everything is in its place. Neatness and spelling both count. But Oscar rebelled. According to psychoanalytic theory, his slovenliness may symbolize his resentment at being forced to use the potty when it was still difficult for him to exercise self-control. His personality is anal-expulsive. He is unkempt, disorganized, and careless.

hostilities toward the same-sex parent and identify with that parent. Identification leads to playing the social and sexual roles of the same-sex parent and internalizing that parent's values. Sexual feelings toward the opposite-sex parent are repressed for a number of years. When they re-emerge during adolescence, they are displaced onto socially appropriate members of the opposite sex.

The Latency Stage By the age of 5 or 6, Freud believed, the pressures of the Oedipus and Electra complexes motivate children to repress all sexual urges. Repression then leads them into the **latency stage,** a period of life during which sexual feelings remain unconscious. Children use this period to focus on schoolwork and to consolidate earlier learning, most notably, of appropriate sex-role behaviors. During the latency stage it is not uncommon for children to prefer playmates of their own sex.

The Genital Stage Freud wrote that we enter the final stage of psychosexual development, or **genital stage,** at puberty. Adolescent males again experience sexual urges toward their mothers and adolescent females toward their fathers. But the incest taboo provides ample motivation for keeping the true objects of these feelings repressed and displacing the feelings onto other adults or adolescents of the opposite sex. Even so, boys might still seek girls "just like the girl that married dear old Dad." Girls might still be attracted to men who resemble their fathers.

Freud believed that the thrust of Eros was aimed at the perpetuation of the species. He therefore assumed that people in the genital stage would prefer

Latency stage *The fourth stage of psychosexual development, characterized by repression of sexual impulses.*

Genital stage *The mature stage of psychosexual development, characterized by preferred expression of libido through intercourse with an adult of the opposite sex.*

► ► ► ►

to find sexual gratification through intercourse with a member of the opposite sex. In Freud's view, oral or anal stimulation, masturbation, and homosexual activity all represented pregenital fixations and immature forms of sexual conduct. They were not in keeping with the life instinct, Eros.

Evaluation of Freud's Theory of Psychosexual Development   Freudian theory has had tremendous appeal and has been a major contribution to twentieth-century thought. It is one of the richest theories of development, explaining the childhood origins of many varieties of behavior and traits. Freud's theory has also stimulated research on attachment, sex typing, moral development, and identification. But despite its richness, Freud's work has been criticized on many grounds.

For one thing, Freud developed his theory on the basis of contacts with patients who were experiencing emotional problems. He also concluded that most of his patients' problems originated in childhood conflicts. It is possible that he might have found less evidence of childhood conflict if his sample had consisted of less troubled individuals. He was also dealing with recollections of his patients' pasts rather than observing children directly. Such recollections are subject to errors in memory, and it may also be that Freud, as detective, subtly guided his patients into expressing ideas that were consistent with his own evolving theoretical views.

A number of followers of Freud, such as Erik Erikson and Karen Horney, have argued that Freud placed too much emphasis on human sexuality and neglected the relative importance of social relationships. Others have argued that Freud placed too much emphasis on unconscious motives—that people are motivated by conscious desires to achieve, to have aesthetic experiences, and to help others, as well as by the primitive, nameless urgings of the id.

Karen Horney

Erik Erikson

A number of critics note that "psychic structures" like the id, ego, and superego have no substance. They are little more than useful fictions, poetic ways to express inner conflict. It is debatable whether Freud himself ever attributed substance to the psychic structures.

Nor has Freud's theory of psychosexual development escaped criticism. People may begin to masturbate as early as the first year of life, rather than in the "phallic stage." As parents can testify from observing their children play "doctor," sexuality in the "latency" stage is not so latent as Freud believed. Much of Freud's thinking concerning the Oedipus and Electra complexes remains simple speculation. His views of female sexuality and sex-role behavior reflect the ignorance and prejudice of his times.

Once we have catalogued our criticisms of Freud's views, what of merit is left? A number of things. Freud pointed out that behavior is determined and not arbitrary. He pointed out that childhood experiences can have far-reaching effects on personality. He noted that we have defensive ways of looking at the world, that our cognitive processes can be distorted by our efforts to defend ourselves against anxiety and guilt. If these ideas no longer impress us as unique or innovative, it is largely because they have been so widely accepted since Freud first enuciated them.

Erik Erikson's Theory of Psychosocial Development

Throughout his early childhood in Germany, Erik Erikson did not know that his natural father had deserted his mother just before his birth in 1902 (Erikson, 1975). Young Erikson was raised by his mother and his stepfather, Theodor Homburger, a pediatrician. Though his mother and stepfather were Jewish, Erikson's blond hair and blue eyes resembled those of his natural father, a Dane. In his stepfather's synagogue he was considered a Gentile. To his classmates he was a Jew. He felt different from other children and alienated from his family. Like many children, he fantasized that he was adopted—the offspring of special parents who had abandoned him. "Who am I?" was a question that permeated his early years.

As he developed, Erikson faced another issue of self-identity: "What am I to do in life?" His stepfather encouraged him to follow in his footsteps and pursue medicine. But Erikson sought his own path. As a youth he studied art and traveled through Europe, leading the bohemian life of an artist. This was a period of serious questioning and soul-searching that Erikson would later label an **identity crisis.**

The turmoil of his personal quest for identity oriented Erikson toward his life's work: psychotherapy. He met Sigmund Freud and other psychoanalysts in Vienna, left his wanderings, and plunged into psychoanalytic training under the tutelage of Sigmund Freud's daughter, Anna Freud (Hall, 1983). After his graduation from the Vienna Psychoanalytic Institute in 1933, he came to the United States.

Erikson's psychoanalytic theory, like that of Freud's, focuses on the development of the emotional life and psychological traits—on social adjustment. But Erikson also focused on the development of self-identity. Out of the chaos of his own identity problems, Erikson had forged a personally meaningful life pattern. And his theory of development differed dramatically from that of his intellectual forebear, Sigmund Freud. To Erikson, development was not the outcome of environmental forces and intrapsychic conflict. Erikson's social re-

Identity crisis *According to Erikson, a period of inner conflict during which one examines one's values and makes decisions about life roles.*

▶ ▶ ▶ ▶

lationships had been more crucial than sexual or aggressive instincts as determinants of his development. It seemed to Erikson that he had developed his own personality through a series of conscious and purposeful acts.

Stages of Psychosocial Development Erikson (1963) extended Freud's five developmental stages to eight in order to include the developing concerns of the various seasons of adulthood. Rather than label his stages after erogenous zones, Erikson labeled stages after the traits and **life crises** that the child (and later, the adult) might develop and experience during that stage. The first stage of **psychosocial development,** for example, is labeled the stage of trust versus mistrust because of two possible major outcomes: (1) A warm, loving relationship with the mother during infancy may lead to a basic sense of trust in people and the world. (2) A cold, nongratifying relationship with **significant others** may lead to a pervasive sense of mistrust. Erikson's eight stages are outlined in Table 2.1.

Erikson proposed that our relationships with significant others as well as our levels of physical maturation give each stage its character. For example, the parent–child relationship and the infant's utter dependence and helplessness are responsible for the nature of the earliest stages of development. The 6-year-old's capacity to profit from the school setting reflects the cognitive capacities to learn to read and to understand the rudiments of mathematics, and the physical/perceptual capacities to sit relatively still and focus on schoolwork.

According to Erikson, early experiences exert a continued influence on future development. With proper parental support during the early years, most

Table 2.1 Erik Erikson's Stages of Development

TIME PERIOD	LIFE CRISIS	THE DEVELOPMENTAL TASK
Infancy (0–1)	Trust vs. mistrust	Coming to trust the mother and the environment—to associate surroundings with feelings of inner goodness
Early childhood (2–3)	Autonomy vs. shame and doubt	Developing the wish to make choices and the self-contol to exercise choice
Preschol years (4–5)	Initiative vs. guilt	Adding planning and "attacking" to choice, becoming active and on the move
Grammar school years (6–12)	Industry vs. inferiority	Becoming eagerly absorbed in skills, tasks, and productivity; mastering the fundamentals of technology
Adolescence	Identity vs. role diffusion	Connecting skills and social roles to formation of career objectives
Young adulthood	Intimacy vs. isolation	Committing the self to another; engaging in sexual love
Middle adulthood	Generativity vs. stagnation	Needing to be needed; guiding and encouraging the younger generation; being creative
Late adulthood	Integrity vs. despair	Accepting the timing and placing of one's own life cycle; achieving wisdom and dignity

Source: Erikson, 1963, pp. 247–269.

▶ ▶ ▶ ▶

children resolve early life crises productively. Successful resolution of each crisis bolsters their senses of identity—of who they are and what they stand for—and their expectations of future success.

Stages of Psychosocial Development   Let us now consider each of Erikson's stages of psychosocial development. Each stages carries a specific developmental task. Successful completion of this task depends heavily on the nature of the child's social relationships at each stage.

The developmental task of the first stage is to develop a sense of trust in the mother which will foster feelings of **attachment** and pave the way for the development of future intimate relationships.

During the second and third years, the central tasks are to develop and to exercise self-control. However, it is essential that the child take pride in the ability to choose to exercise self-control, rather than be compelled to show it out of feelings of shame and self-doubt.

Toilet training is one of the challenges faced during the second year. During this year, children are mobile and inquisitive. Warmly encouraging parents can provide guidance yet teach their children to be proud of their newly developing **autonomy.** But parents who demand too much too soon at this stage, or who are arbitrarily restrictive, can lead a child to perceive self-control as an unattainable goal. A lifelong pattern of self-doubt can follow.

During the fourth and fifth years, the central developmental task is to begin to organize activities in order to achieve goals—to become more assertive in attempting to attain goals.

During the grammar school years of about 6 to 12, the major developmental task is to acquire the basic academic and cultural skills that will enable one to achieve. A sense of industry will contribute to achievement motivation. A sense of inferiority may turn the child away from attempts to acquire skills and compete with peers.

During the grammar school years children learn to evaluate their competence by comparing their performance to that of peers. If grammar school children do well in their studies, in sports, and in their social activities, they are likely to develop a sense of industry and to become productive. Fine performance in, say, math may compensate for poor or average athletic performance, and vice versa. But if children fail consistently in most areas, they are likely to develop feelings of inferiority and to withdraw from the arenas of competition.

During the teenage years, the central developmental task is for adolescents to develop **ego identity**—that is, a sense of who they are and what they stand for. Adolescents may simply adopt the expectations others have for them, or they may examine expectations in the light of their own understanding of the world around them. One aspect of attaining ego identity is learning "how to connect the roles and skills cultivated earlier with the occupational prototypes of the day" (Erikson, 1963, p. 261)—that is, with jobs. But ego identity extends to sexual, political, and religious beliefs and commitments.

Erikson characterizes the life crisis of adolescence as that of ego identity versus **role diffusion.** If this crisis is resolved properly, adolescents develop a firm sense of who they are and what they stand for. Ego identity can then carry them through difficult times and color their achievements with meaning. But if they do not resolve this life crisis properly, they may experience role diffusion. In this case they spread themselves thin, running down one blind alley after

Attachment *Affectionate regard or devotion, as characterized by seeking closeness or contact with the object of attachment and showing distress upon separation.*

Autonomy *Self-direction; independence. (From the Greek autos, meaning "self," and nomos, meaning "law.")*

Ego identity *According to Erikson, one's sense of who one is and what one stands for.*

Role diffusion *According to Erikson, inconsistency in behavior that stems from lack of ego identity.*

▶ ▶ ▶ ▶

another and placing themselves at the mercy of leaders who promise to give them the sense of identity they cannot mold for themselves.

We shall briefly discuss Erikson's final three stages of development in order to provide a sense of continuity, but they concern adult development rather than child development.

The establishment of intimate relationships is a central task of young adulthood. Young adults who have evolved a firm sense of identity during adolescence are now ready, Erikson believes, to fuse their identities with significant others through relationships such as marriage and the formation of abiding friendships.

Erikson labels the life crisis of middle adulthood generativity versus stagnation. He describes generativity as including procreativity (having children), productivity (as in work), and creativity (Erikson, 1983). Generativity assumes that in middle life people are concerned about the welfare of the next generation, and work to make the world a better place in which to live.

The central task of late adulthood is to maintain our senses of who we are and what we stand for (ego integrity) in the face of deterioration of physical function and the specter of death. In order to maintain the integrity or wholeness of our egos, we must develop the wisdom to accept the limits of our own life spans within the ebb and flow of history; we must develop the capacity to begin to let go while we are still alive. Wisdom, according to theory, is more likely to come to those who have developed healthy personalities—reached the Eriksonian ideals—through the first seven stages of life.

Evaluation of Erikson's Theory of Psychosocial Development   Erikson's views have received much admiration and much criticism. They are appealing in that they emphasize the importance of human consciousness and choice and minimize the role—and the threat—of dark, poorly perceived urges. They are also appealing in that they paint us as prosocial and giving, whereas Freud portrayed us as selfish and needing to be forced into adherence to social norms.

There is also some empirical support for the Eriksonian view that positive resolutions of early life crises lead to more positive behavior later on. For example, Donald Pastor (1981) found that children who are securely attached to their mothers at the end of the first year—children who appear to have a sense of basic trust in their mothers—are more sociable with their peers than are insecure children several months later. Trust in the mother seems to develop into willingness to relate to others. There is also evidence that young adults who have not begun to establish themselves in a career (that is, to develop occupational identity) are less likely to form lasting marriages.

On the other hand, it has been argued that the positive resolutions Erikson proposes for several stages sound more like propaganda than science. For example, a person whose life crises have been positively resolved is expected to be generous and giving throughout middle adulthood, and to be capable of letting go during the later years. But many adults in their 40s are self-centered. Does this mean that they have not adequately resolved life's crises? And many in late adulthood look upon old age as a dirty trick without saving graces. Are their outlooks suggestive of faulty personality development? Does this mean that they failed to develop basic trust during their first year, or had similar difficulty at a later stage?

Still, Erikson has drawn a coherent pattern of development over the life span, and his views are fostering a good deal of research. As noted earlier in

▶ ▶ ▶ ▶

this section, the quest for identity has been supported by research as a major focus of adolescent development, and it does appear that early childhood social influences can have far-reaching effects.

Learning Theories

During the 1930s, psychologists derived from learning theory an ingenious method for helping 5- and 6-year-old children overcome bed-wetting. Most children at this age wake up and go to the bathroom when their bladders are full. But bed-wetters sleep through bladder tension and reflexively urinate in bed. The psychologists' objective was to teach *sleeping* children with full bladders to wake up rather than wet their beds.

They placed a special pad beneath the sleeping child. When the pad was wet, an electrical circuit was closed, causing a bell to ring and the sleeping child to waken. After several repetitions, most children learned to wake up *before* they wet the pad. How? Through a technique called classical conditioning, which we explain in this section.

The so-called bell-and-pad method for bed-wetting is an exotic example of the application of learning theory in child development. However, the great majority of applications of learning theory to development are found in everyday events. For example, children are not born knowing what the letters "A" and "B" sound like or how to scratch their ears. They learn these things. They are not born knowing how to do gymnastics. Nor are they born understanding the meanings of abstract concepts such as big, blue, decency, and justice. All these skills and knowledge are learned.

Learning theorists argue that **conditioning** and social learning make major contributions to the development of children's behavior patterns, even those that are initially reflexive. The newborn child's **rooting** and sucking are examples of **reflexes.** However, as we shall see in Chapter 4, many reflexes, such as the sucking reflex, no longer occur automatically after a month or so. If the child maintains such behaviors, it is because of learning.

In this section we discuss the theories of behaviorism and social learning and see how they are involved in child development. We shall see that children are capable of mechanical learning by association (as in the bell-and-pad method), but we shall also see that children are capable of intentional learning. Children purposefully engage in rote learning and trial-and-error learning. Children purposefully observe and imitate the behavior of other people. We shall also see how the principles of learning have been used in **behavior modification** to help children overcome behavior disorders or cope with adjustment problems.

Behaviorism

Behaviorism in the United States, as noted at the outset of the chapter, was founded by John B. Watson. Watson became convinced of the need for a behavioral approach when he was working on his doctoral dissertation at the University of Chicago in 1903. His research involved teaching rats to run routes through mazes by means of rewarding them with food. His professors, however, required that Watson speculate on what his rats were *thinking* at various

Conditioning *A simple form of learning in which associations between stimuli and responses are learned.*

Rooting *A reflex in which infants turn their mouths and heads in the direction of a stroking of the cheek or the corner of the mouth.*

Reflex *An unlearned, stereotypical response to a stimulus.*

Behavior modification *The systematic application of principles of learning to the reversal or amelioration of behavior problems.*

▶ ▶ ▶ ▶

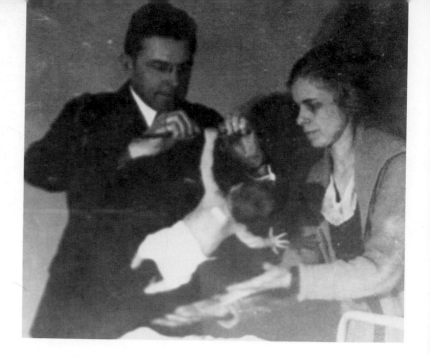

John B. Watson testing the grasping reflex of an infant

points in the maze. As a result of experiences such as these, Watson came to argue that scientists must address observable behavior only. Therefore, a scientific approach to development must focus on the observable behavior of humans. Thoughts, plans, fantasies, and other mental images were all private events—not subject to direct measurement—and must be omitted from theory.

Watson pointed to the research being conducted in Russia by Ivan Pavlov as a prime example of a scientific approach to behavior. Pavlov's research was in conditioning, in specifying the conditions that led to changes in behavior. Let us see how two types of conditioning—classical and operant—have contributed to behaviorism and to the understanding of development. Then we shall consider a more recently developed theory of learning that deals with children's cognitive processes as well as their overt behavior—social-learning theory.

Classical Conditioning **Classical conditioning** is a simple form of learning in which an originally neutral stimulus comes to bring forth, or **elicit,** the response usually brought forth by a second stimulus as a result of being paired repeatedly with the second stimulus. In the bell-and-pad method for bed-wetting, psychologists repeatedly paired *tension in the children's bladders* with a stimulus that woke them up (the bell). The children learned to respond to the bladder tension as if it were a bell—that is, they woke up.

Like many other important scientific discoveries, classical conditioning was discovered by accident. Russian physiologist Ivan Pavlov (1849–1936) was attempting to identify the nerve cells in the mouths of laboratory dogs that triggered a response from the salivary glands (see Figure 2.1). But his research efforts were hampered by the fact that the dogs often salivated at undesired times, such as when a laboratory assistant accidentally clinked a food tray.

Because of its biological makeup, a dog will salivate if a meat **stimulus** is placed on its tongue. Salivation in response to meat is unlearned, a reflex. Pavlov discovered that reflexes can be learned, or conditioned, through asso-

Conditioned response *A learned response to a previously neutral stimulus. Abbreviated* CR.

Unconditioned stimulus *A stimulus that elicits a response from an organism without learning. Abbreviated* US.

THEORIES OF DEVELOPMENT

Figure 2.1 Ivan Pavlov
Pavlov, his assistants, and an expert salivator at the Soviet Military Medicine Academy early in the century.

ciation. His dogs began salivating in response to clinking food trays, because clinking had been paired repeatedly with the arrival of food. The dogs would also salivate when an assistant entered the laboratory. Why? In the past the assistant had brought food.

As noted, Pavlov at first saw this uncalled-for canine salivation as an annoyance, an impediment to his work. But in 1901 he decided that his "problem" was worth looking into. And so he set about to show that he could train, or condition, his dogs to salivate in response to any stimulus he chose.

Trained salivary responses are called **conditioned responses** (CRs). They are responses to previously neutral stimuli that are learned, or conditioned.

Pavlov demonstrated conditioned reflexes by strapping a dog into a harness (see Figure 2.2). When meat was placed on the dog's tongue, the dog salivated. Pavlov repeated the process several times, each time preceding the meat by half a second or so with the ringing of a bell. After several pairings of meat and bell, Pavlov rang the bell but did *not* follow the bell with the meat. Still the dog salivated. It had learned to salivate in response to the bell.

Why? *Explanations for acquiring conditioned responses are made in terms of the conditions of learning:* The dog learned to salivate in response to the bell, *because* the ringing of the bell had been paired with meat. It is not scientific to say that the dog "knew" that food was on the way.

Why do I emphasize this distinction? To make a point about children. Babies are capable of learning even at birth, but it is also unscientific to talk about what babies "know." Instead, we can say that babies have *learned* to respond in certain ways, because of the conditions of learning. Also, the children trained to wake up by means of the bell-and-pad method essentially learned in their sleep. We cannot say that they "knew" that bladder tension and the bell had come to serve the same function. We can only say that the children, by repeated pairing of bladder tension and the bell, came to wake up in response to bladder tension alone.

In Pavlov's demonstration, the meat is an unlearned or **unconditioned**

Classical conditioning A simple form of learning in which one stimulus comes to bring forth the response usually brought forth by a second stimulus by being paired repeatedly with the second stimulus.

Elicit (ee-LISS-it). To bring forth; evoke.

Stimulus A change in the environment that leads to a change in behavior.

▶ ▶ ▶ ▶

LEARNING THEORIES

Figure 2.2 Pavlov's Demonstration of Conditioned Reflexes in Laboratory Dogs
From behind the two-way mirror to the left, a laboratory assistant rings a bell and then places
meat on the dog's tongue. After several pairings, the animal salivates in response to the bell
alone.

stimulus (US). Salivation in response to the meat is an unlearned or **unconditioned response** (UR). The bell was at first a meaningless or neutral stimulus (see Figure 2.3). It might have produced an **orienting reflex** in the dog because of its distinctness. But it was not yet associated with food. Then, through repeated association with the meat, the bell became a learned or **conditioned stimulus** (CS) for the salivation response. But salivation in response to the *bell (or CS)* is a learned or conditioned response (CR). A CR is a response similar to a UR, but the response elicited by the CS is by definition a CR, not a UR.

Emotional Learning Behaviorists argue that a good deal of emotional learning is acquired through classical conditioning. For example, we may learn to fear (CR) stimuli that cause pain (UR). Touching a hot stove is painful, and one or two incidents may elicit a fear response when a child looks at a stove or considers touching it again. Parents may yell at or smack a child who is about to touch a stove or run out into the street in hope that the child will learn to fear the dangerous activity. They associate the stove (CS) with smacking or yelling (painful USs), expecting that future perception of the stove will elicit fear (CR). The UR is the pain of the smack or loud, sharp sound.

Through classical conditioning, children learn to associate stimuli so that a simple, usually passive response made to one is then made in response to the other. Let us now turn our attention to operant conditioning, in which children learn to engage in certain behaviors because of their effects.

Operant Conditioning In **operant conditioning**, children learn to operate on the environment, or to engage in certain behavior, because of the *effects* of that behavior.

Unconditioned response An unlearned response. A response to an unconditioned stimulus. Abbreviated UR.

Orienting reflex An unlearned response in which an organism attends to a stimulus.

Conditioned stimulus A previously neutral stimulus that elicits a response, because it has been paired repeatedly with a stimulus that already elicited that response. Abbreviated CS.

Operant conditioning A simple form of learning in which an organism learns to engage in behavior that is reinforced.

▶ ▶ ▶ ▶

THEORIES OF DEVELOPMENT

Reinforcement *The process of providing stimuli following a response that have the effect of increasing the frequency of the response.*

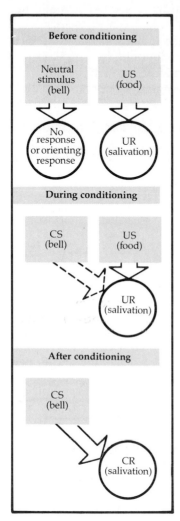

Figure 2.3 A Schematic Representation of Classical Conditioning
Prior to conditioning, food elicits salivation. The bell, a neutral stimulus, elicits no response or an orienting response. During conditioning, the bell is rung just before meat is placed on the dog's tongue. After conditioning the bell has become a CS that elicits salivation (the CR).

Harvard University psychologist B. F. Skinner introduced one of the central concepts of operant conditioning—the concept of **reinforcement.** Reinforcers are stimuli that increase the frequency of the behavior that they follow. Most children will increase the frquency of behavior patterns that earn them consequences such as a hug, an A on a test, attention, or social approval. And so, these consequences serve as reinforcers. Some children learn to conform their behavior to social codes and rules to earn the attention and approval of their parents and teachers. Other children, ironically, may learn to "misbehave," since misbehavior also draws attention. Children may especially learn to be "bad" when their "good" behavior is routinely ignored or is not "good enough" to earn approval. The poor student is more likely to be drawn into a delinquent subculture than the excellent student, since reinforcement is not likely to be provided by the mainstream culture—for example, teachers.

In operant conditioning, it matters little how the first desired response is made. The child can happen upon it by chance, as in random trial-and-error learning, or the child can be physically guided. A 2-year-old child may be shown how to turn the crank on a music box to play a tune by an adult placing his or her hand over the child's and doing the turning. The child is reinforced by the sound of music, and after training he or she will be able to turn the crank alone.

Children, of course, can frequently be verbally guided into desired responses when they are learning skills such as adding numbers, getting dressed, or sharpening pencils. But they then need to be informed when they have made

B. F. Skinner

▶ ▶ ▶ ▶

LEARNING THEORIES

the correct response. Knowledge of results is often all the reinforcement that motivated children need to learn new skills.

Operant conditioning is helpful in the explanation of the development of motor skills. Through trial and error, the infant learns that certain sensations within the muscles and joints of the arm are associated with bringing her arm and hand into her field of vision. By learning to produce these sensations in the arm, the child attains the reinforcement of seeing the arm in front of her. Soon she repeatedly produces these sensations in order to see her arm and her hand.

Various behaviors such as crying, smiling, and looking at specific objects have been conditioned in very young infants (Lancioni, 1980). For example, 4-month-old infants were conditioned to suck a pacifier vigorously, when sucking brought into focus a blurred checkerboard pattern that was being displayed on a television monitor (Siqueland & Delucia, 1969).

Let us pay a bit more attention to the important concept of reinforcement.

Types of Reinforcers Reinforcers increase the probability that operant behavior will be repeated. How do we know whether a stimulus is a reinforcer? Any stimulus that increases the frequency of the responses preceding it serves as a reinforcer. Most of the time food, social approval, and attention serve as reinforcers.

Skinner distinguished between positive and negative reinforcers. **Positive reinforcers** increase the frequency of operants when they are *applied*. Food and approval usually serve as positive reinforcers. **Negative reinforcers** increase the frequency of operants when they are *removed*. Children often learn to plan ahead, so that they need not fear that things will go wrong. Fear acts as a negative reinforcer in that its *removal* increases the frequency of the behaviors preceding it (such as studying for a quiz).

We can also distinguish between primary and secondary or conditioned reinforcers. **Primary reinforcers** are effective because of the biological makeup of the child. Food, water, adequate warmth (positive reinforcers), and pain (an example of a *primary negative* reinforcer) all serve as primary reinforcers. **Secondary reinforcers** acquire their value through being associated with established reinforcers. For this reason they are also termed *conditioned reinforcers*. We may seek money, because we have learned that it can be exchanged for primary reinforcers. Money, attention, social approval—all are conditioned reinforcers in our culture. For some children, teacher approval is a conditioned positive reinforcer. For other children, it is not, but peer approval is. Teachers must know what is reinforcing to particular children, if they are to be capable of modifying their behavior in the classroom.

Knowledge of results is often an effective reinforcer with children. Many children will work hard to improve skills in spelling, math, and myriad other areas simply for the sake of improvement. White (1959) has advanced the view that we have an **intrinsic** motive to master skills and will frequently learn how to solve problems and manipulate objects for the pleasure of doing so. Children, in other words, frequently find reinforcers for behaviors within rather than outside of themselves. The latter are called **extrinsic** reinforcers. Later in the chapter we shall see that developmentalist Jean Piaget believed that children are intrinsically motivated to understand their worlds.

In a study of the motive for mastery, Mark Lepper and his colleagues

Positive reinforcer A reinforcer that, when applied, increases the frequency of a response.

Negative reinforcer A reinforcer that, when removed, increases the frequency of a response.

Primary reinforcer An unlearned reinforcer, such as food, warmth, or pain.

Secondary reinforcer A reinforcer that gains its effectiveness through association with established reinforcers. Social approval and gold stars in school are secondary reinforcers.

Intrinsic Internal.

Extrinsic External.

THEORIES OF DEVELOPMENT

Operant Conditioning of Vocalizations in Infants

▷
▷
▷
▷

▷ A classical study by psychologist Harriet Rheingold and her colleagues (1959) demonstrates how reinforcement and extinction can influence the behavior of infants—in this case, of vocalization. A female researcher first observed the subjects, 3-month-old infants, for about half an hour to record "baseline" (preexperimental) measures of the frequency of their vocalizing. Infants averaged about 13–15 vocalizations each. During the conditioning phase of the study, the woman reinforced the vocalizations with social stimuli, such as encouraging sounds, smiles, and gentle touches. There was a significant increase in the frequency of vocalizing throughout this phase. By the end of an hour of conditioning spread over a two-day period, the average incidence of vocalizations had nearly doubled, to about 24–25 within a half hour. During the extinction phase, as during the baseline, the woman passively observed each infant, no longer reinforcing vocalization. After two half-hour extinction periods, average vocalizing had returned to near baseline, about 13–16 per half hour.

(1973) presented groups of preschool children with challenging puzzles. One group was promised a reward for doing the activity. A second group was reinforced for assembling the puzzle pieces by being allowed to play with appealing toys. A third group received no external reinforcement. Afterwards, all children were allowed to manipulate the puzzle pieces once more. Children who had not been promised a reward worked on the puzzles nearly twice as long as the children who had. Apparently the expectation of external reinforcement had compromised the intrinsic value of working on the puzzles for its own sake.

There is a message in this. We need not always be concerned about "payoffs" for learning for children. Once children become involved in an area of subject matter, and acquire the capacity to manipulate concepts in that area, they may enjoy working for hours simply for its own sake. External reinforcers for these children may change the nature of the learning task so that it becomes less enjoyable. Other children, however, may not find the development of even basic academic skills reinforcing. They may require regular external reinforcement for manipulating concepts and objects—if we are to involve them successfully.

Extinction **Extinction** results from repeated performance of operant behavior without reinforcement. After a number of trials, the operant behavior becomes inhibited; it is no longer shown.

There are many cases in which children's temper tantrums and crying at bedtime have been extinguished within a few days by simply having parents remain out of the bedroom after the children have been put to bed. Previously, the tantrums and crying had been reinforced by parental attention and com-

Extinction *In operant conditioning, the discontinuation of a response as a result of repeated performance of that response in the absence of reinforcement.*

▶ ▶ ▶ ▶

pany. By changing the reinforcement contingencies of the problem behavior, it was eliminated.*

Punishments **Punishments** are aversive events that suppress or decrease the frequency of the behavior they follow. Punishments, like rewards, can influence the probability that behavior will be shown. Punishments can rapidly suppress undesirable behavior and may be warranted in "emergencies," such as when a child tries to run out into the street. But many learning theorists agree that punishment is usually undesirable, especially in rearing children, for reasons such as the following:

1. *Punishment in and of itself does not suggest an alternate, acceptable form of behavior.*

2. *Punishment tends to suppress undesirable behavior only under circumstances in which its delivery is guaranteed.* It does not take children long to learn that they can "get away with murder" with one parent, or one teacher, but not with another.

3. *Punished children may withdraw from the situation.* A child who is severely punished at home may run away. A child who is repeatedly punished in school may cut class, become "sick," or drop out of school altogether.

4. *Punishment can create anger and hostility.* A child may express accumulated feelings of hostility against other children. After being spanked by their parents, children may hit smaller siblings or destroy objects in the home. Children now and then also try to hit their parents back, and, when they do, parents may increase the intensity of the punishment. A vicious cycle of increasing brutality can follow (Mulhern & Passman, 1981; Passman & Blackwelder, 1981).

5. *Punishment may generalize too far.* For example, the child who is punished severely for bad table manners may stop eating altogether. Overgeneralization is more likely to occur when the child does not know exactly why he or she is being punished.

6. *Punishment may be modeled as a way of solving problems or coping with stress.* Children learn by observing others. Even though children may not immediately perform the behavior they observe, they may perform it later on, even as adults, when their circumstances are similar to those of the **model.** Children, moreover, usually suggest that others use the disipline methods used by their parents (Wolfe et al., 1982), and many child abusers had been beaten by their own parents (Parke & Collmer, 1975).

7. *Children learn responses that are punished.* Whether or not children choose to *perform* punished responses, punishment focuses their attention on them. Allyn at the age of 2 somehow picked up the word

---

*I am not suggesting that children's bedtime crying or tantrums should always be ignored. True—much of the time children can be taught not to have tantrums or to cry in certain situations by ignoring them. However, as mentioned later in the chapter, ignoring them also gives them certain information about the nature of their worlds, and parents may wish to consider *everything* that their children are likely to learn when they respond to them in certain ways.

▶ ▶ ▶ ▶

THEORIES OF DEVELOPMENT

bitch and applied it to my wife. My wife was taken aback and used a harsh, punitive tone of voice in insisting that Allyn not repeat the word. I think you can guess the rest.

It is usually preferable to focus on rewarding children for desirable behavior than to punish them for unwanted behavior. By ignoring their misbehavior, or by using **time out** from positive reinforcement, we can consistently avoid reinforcing children for misbehavior.

To reward or positively reinforce children for desired behavior takes time and care. It requires that we pay attention to them when they are behaving well. If we take their desirable behavior for granted, and act as if we are aware of them only when they misbehave, we may be encouraging misbehavior. We must also physically or verbally guide them into making the desired responses.

Making Punishment Effective But if punishment is to be used with children, it is useful to keep the following in mind:

1. Immediate punishment is more effective than delayed punishment (Aronfreed, 1968). If the child cannot be punished immediately, it is useful to remind the child of the misbehavior before administering the punishment (Verne, 1977).

2. It has also been found helpful to explain why the misbehavior is worthy of punishment (LaVoie, 1973; Parke, 1977; Sears et al., 1957). Punishment, then, is less likely to seem arbitrary and to elicit hostility.

3. Consistent punishment is more effective than irregular punishment in gaining control.

4. Although intense punishment supresses behavior more rapidly than mild punishment, parents and teachers must be careful not to abuse children. Children who receive mild punishments are also more likely to come to believe in the rule that they broke (Lepper, 1981). Consistent mild or moderate punishment, along with an explanation and the encouragement of alternative behavior, is effective with most children.

Continuous versus Intermittent Reinforcement Some responses are maintained by **continuous reinforcement.** You become warmer every time you put on heavy clothing. You become less thirsty every time you drink water. But if you have ever watched people throwing money down the maws of slot machines, or "one-armed bandits," you know that behavior can also be maintained by **intermittent reinforcement.**

During the early stages of learning, it is useful to reinforce every correct response. In this way, the child quickly learns what is expected. In the classroom, the teacher may at first praise children each time they write or draw numbers and letters correctly. But once children have acquired basic skills in writing letters, teachers can turn to intermittent praise or reinforcement.

Learning theorists note that many parents unintentionally teach their children to cry or whine persistently by intermittently reinforcing these behavior patterns. Consider a child who cries when a parent refuses a request for potato

Time out *A behavior-modification technique in which a child who misbehaves is temporarily placed in a drab, restrictive environment in which reinforcement is unavailable.*

Continuous reinforcement *Reinforcement of every correct response.*

Intermittent reinforcement *Reinforcement of some, but not all, correct responses.*

► ► ► ►

Shaping *A procedure for teaching complex behaviors in which components of the behavior are reinforced separately, before they are combined into a complete performance.*

Successive approximations *A series of behaviors that become progressively more like the target behavior.*

chips before dinner, or a request to be picked up when the parent is busy at the stove. If the parent were consistent in ignoring the child's crying, learning theorists predict that it would eventually stop. Why? Because it is not being reinforced. But what happens when a parent ignores the crying on, say, nine occasions, but simply "hasn't the heart" to ignore the child on the tenth? The child's crying when denied potato chips or being picked up might then become increasingly persistent, because of intermittent reinforcement.*

Shaping   We can teach children complex behaviors by **shaping,** or at first reinforcing small steps toward the behavioral goals. At first it may be wise to smile and say "Good" when a reluctant child gathers the courage to get out on the dance floor, even if his partner's feet get flattened by his initial clumsiness. If a child is being taught to use the potty, the parent may first generously reinforce the learner simply for sitting on the potty for a while, even if he or she insists on wearing a diaper at the time. And pajamas or overalls over the diaper.

But as training proceeds, the parent can demand more before dispensing reinforcement. We can reinforce **successive approximations** to the goal. In teaching a 2-year-old child to put on her own coat, it helps first to praise her for trying to stick her arm into a sleeve on a couple of occasions. Then praise her for actually getting her arm into the sleeve. And so on. You will find that most children are actually highly motivated to put on their own coats, as they observe Mommy and Daddy doing. Rather than having to use copious amounts of praise to encourage them at the age of 2, you may have to use all your cleverness now and then to convince them *not* to wear a coat in a warm house.

We also shape complex athletic skills, such as gymnastics. Consider a 12-year-old girl who runs across the mat and then dives into a series of flips. Her coaches did not initially wait for her to complete the entire sequence before saying "Great!" At first, she was physically guided into single somersaults, and reinforced for each one. Then she repeatedly practiced single flips. Only after many months, perhaps years, of training did she undertake the competitive sequence.

The case of the young gymnast points up some of the theoretical issues surrounding reinforcement. For example, is the coach's "Great!" or the coach's smile reinforcing because it provides pleasure or motivation, or because it provides the girl with knowledge of results (information as to the correctness of her response)? In this example, reinforcement probably serves all these functions—motivation, provision of pleasure, provision of knowledge. Still, it is useful to keep in mind that in many cases children go on to fine-tune skills simply on the basis of knowledge of results at each step along the way. But the younger children are, the more important a smile and a pleasantly excited tone of voice of their teacher seem to be.

Applications of Operant Conditioning   Operant conditioning has numerous applications for child development. Here we shall focus on just a few.

---

*This is not the whole story. The parent will presumably also explain to the child *why* the request for potato chips or some other demand is being denied, so that the child has an opportunity to gain cognitive understanding of the situation. Also, the parent who repeatedly refuses the child may be imparting the *idea* that the world is a place of absolute rules where pleas and extenuating circumstances are of no avail. Radical behaviorists focus only on the behavioral effects of rearing children in certain ways, but most parents are also concerned about the ways in which their children are learning to think and feel. Thus they tolerate inconsistency in their own behavior.

▶ ▶ ▶ ▶

Socialization *A process in which children are encouraged to adopt socially desirable behavior patterns through a system of guidance, rewards, and punishments.*

Avoidance learning *A form of learning in which organisms learn to engage in responses that avert aversive (painful) stimulation.*

Ruminative *Repeatedly rejecting the contents of the stomach through the mouth; vomiting.*

Autistic *Socially withdrawn; self-absorbed.*

Socialization   Operant conditioning is used every day in the **socialization** of young children. For example, as we shall see in Chapters 11–13, parents and peers influence children to acquire gender-appropriate behaviors and appropriate social skills through the elaborate use of rewards and punishments. Thus boys may ignore other boys when they play with dolls and housekeeping toys, but play with boys when they use transportation toys.

Avoidance Learning   Techniques of **avoidance learning** have found applications with a number of children who are too young or distressed to respond to verbal forms of therapy. In one example, reported by Lang and Melamed (1969), a 9-month-old **ruminative** infant vomited regularly within 10–15 minutes after eating. Repeated diagnostic workups had found no medical basis for the problem, and medical treatments were to no avail. When the case was brought to the attention of Lang and Melamed, the infant weighed only nine pounds and was in critical condition, being fed by a pump.

The psychologists monitored the infant for the first physical indications (local muscle tension) that vomiting was to occur. When the child tensed prior to vomiting, a tone was sounded and followed by painful but (presumably) harmless electric shock. After two one-hour treatment sessions, the infant's muscle tensions ceased in response to the tone alone, and vomiting soon ceased altogether. At a one-year follow-up, the infant was still not vomiting and had caught up in weight.

This remarkable procedure included both classical and operant conditioning. Through repeated pairings, the tone (CS) came to elicit expectation of electric shock (US), so that the psychologists could use the painful shock only sparingly. The electric shock and, after classical conditioning, the tone served as punishments. The infant soon learned to suppress the behaviors (muscle tensions) that were reliably followed by the punishment. In so doing, he avoided the punishment.

This learning occurred at an age long before any sort of verbal intervention could have been understood, and it apparently saved the infant's life. Similar procedures have been used to teach very young, **autistic** children to avoid mutilating and otherwise injuring themselves, as we shall see in Chapter 14.

Behavior Modification in the Classroom   As noted earlier, adults may unwittingly reinforce undesirable behavior in children by attending to them when they misbehave, but ignoring them when they behave properly. The use of behavior modification in the classroom reverses this pattern: Teachers attend to children when they are behaving appropriately and, when possible, ignore (avoid reinforcing) misbehavior (Lahey & Drabman, 1981). The younger the child, the more powerful teacher attention and approval seem to be.

In one study, Madsen and his colleagues (1968) modified the behavior of three elementary school children who touched others, took others' property, turned around, made noise, and mouthed objects during lessons. First the teacher wrote out classroom rules on the blackboard. The children repeated them out loud. The teacher left the rules visible while inappropriate behavior was ignored and appropriate behavior was praised. Targeted behavior rapidly decreased, and the blackboard could be erased.

Similar approaches have reduced aggressive behavior and increased studying in schoolchildren. Descriptive praise seems more effective than a sim-

▶ ▶ ▶ ▶

ple "Good." Saying "It was very good the way you raised your hand and waited for me to call on you before talking out" reminds the child of the behavior that results in praise and prompts him or her to repeat it.

Among older children and adolescents, peer approval is frequently a more powerful reinforcer than teacher approval. Peer approval may maintain misbehavior, and teacher's ignoring it may allow peers only to become more disruptive. In such cases it may be necessary to separate troublesome children.

Teachers also frequently use time out from positive reinforcement to discourage misbehavior. In this method, disruptive children are placed in drab, restrictive environments for a specified time period, usually about ten minutes. When isolated, they cannot earn the attention of peers or teachers, and no reinforcing activities are present.

It may strike you that these techniques are not new. Perhaps we all know parents who have ignored their children's misbehavior and have heard of teachers making children "sit facing the corner." Perhaps what is novel is the focus on (1) avoiding punishment, and (2) being consistent so that undesirable behavior is not intermittently reinforced. But it should be noted that punishment can also decrease undesirable behavior in the classroom. For example, after-school detention has been found to reduce disruptive classroom behavior (Brigham et al., 1985).

Programmed Learning   B. F. Skinner developed an educational practice called **programmed learning.** Programmed learning is based on the assumption that any complex task, involving conceptual learning as well as motor skills, can be broken down into a number of small steps. These steps can be shaped individually and combined in sequence to form the correct behavioral chain.

Programmed learning does not punish errors. Instead, correct responses are reinforced. All children earn "100," but at their own pace. Programmed learning also assumes that it is the task of the teacher (or program) to structure the learning experience so that errors will not be made. So-called computer-assisted learning frequently relies on programs that reinforce correct responses and permit children to learn at their own pace.

Social-Learning Theory

Behaviorists tend to limit their discussions of human learning to the classical and operant conditioning of observable behaviors. They theorize that learning in children can be fully explained as the summation of numerous instances of the association of stimuli (classical conditioning) or the reinforcement of operant behavior (operant conditioning).

Social-learning theorists, such as Stanford University psychologist Albert Bandura, have run numerous experiments that show that much of children's learning also occurs by observing parents, other children, characters on television, teachers, and other people. In other words, children can also acquire operants—and expectations of reinforcement—by observing others. Children may need some practice to refine their skills, but they acquire much of the basic "know-how" through observation. Children may also choose to allow these skills to lie **latent.** For example, children (and adults) are not likely to imitate aggressive behavior unless they are provoked and believe that they are more likely to be rewarded than punished for aggressive behavior.

Programmed learning A learning method in which complex tasks are broken down into simple steps. The proper performance of each step is reinforced, while incorrect responses are not reinforced.

Social-learning theory A theory in the learning-theory tradition that includes cognitive factors and observational learning in the explanation and prediction of behavior.

Latent Hidden.

▶ ▶ ▶ ▶

THEORIES OF DEVELOPMENT

Albert Bandura

As viewed by the behaviorists, learning occurs by means of mechanical conditioning. There is no reference to thought processes that may occur as a result of conditioning and prior to the performance of responses. There is no role for *cognition*. Social-learning theorists, in contrast, suggest that learning alters the children's mental representations of the environment and influences their belief in their ability to act effectively upon the environment. However, children are theorized to choose whether or not to show the new behaviors they have learned. In social-learning theory children acquire operants without necessarily being directly reinforced. Children's values and expectations of reinforcement also influence the probability that they will attempt to imitate the behavior they observe. In social-learning theory there is a central role for cognition. Children are seen as active. They intentionally seek out or create environments in which reinforcers are available.

Observational Learning **Observational learning,** the type of learning of most interest to social-learning theorists, may account for most of human learning. It occurs when children observe parents cook, clean, or repair a broken appliance. There is evidence that children learn simple, "single actions" (such as separating halves of a toy barrel to find a smaller barrel within) by observation at as early as 12 months (Abravanel & Gingold, 1985). By the age of 24 months, children attempt to imitate most of the motor and social behaviors they observe in adults (McCall et al., 1977).

Observational learning takes place when children watch teachers solve problems on the blackboard or hear them speak in a foreign language. It takes place when children read books about the experiences of others. Observational learning does not occur because of direct reinforcement. Children can learn without engaging in overt responses at all. Learning will occur so long as children pay attention to the behavior of others.

Imitation and Identification *Identification* is a term derived from Freud's psychoanalytic theory, and it refers to children's attempts to internalize the traits of other people. However, from a social-learning theory perspective, identification may be viewed as a broad process of imitation through which children acquire behavior patterns that are similar to those of other people. Once children are a few years old, observational learning becomes intentional, and children appear to select models for imitation who show certain positive characteristics.

Models The people after whom children pattern their own behavior are termed *models* in social-learning theory. The traits that encourage children to attempt

Observational learning The acquiring of expectations and skills by means of observing others. In observational learning, skills can be acquired without their being emitted and reinforced.

► ► ► ►

to identify with models include warmth, competence, social dominance, and social status (Bandura, 1977). Traits such as these appear to give models access to the tangible rewards and social success to which children themselves aspire. Children are also likely to imitate the more powerful parent, whether the parent is the mother or the father, and daughters of powerful mothers are more likely to aspire to nontraditional, competitive career choices than are girls of mothers who take a back seat to their husbands (Lavine, 1982).

The Modeling of Sex Roles   In Chapter 12 we shall see that children appear to acquire their concepts of stereotypical masculine and feminine behavior through observational learning. Children also learn rules and principles from observing others as well as specific behavior patterns. Consider the area of moral development, which will be discussed at length in Chapter 13. Children old enough to make mature or immature moral judgments have been exposed to adult models who have made one type of judgment or the other. In these experiments, the children tended to show the types of moral reasoning displayed by the model when they faced new moral problems, regardless of the type of reasoning the children showed prior to the study (Bandura & McDonald, 1963; Cowan et al., 1969).

In later chapters we shall also see how helping behavior and aggression in children are fostered by observational learning.

Evaluation of Learning Theories   There is no question that learning theories have done an excellent job of allowing us to describe, explain, predict, and control many aspects of children's behavior. There have been thousands of innovative applications of conditioning and social-learning theory. For example, the use of the bell-and-pad method for bed-wetting is an example of behavior modification that probably would not have been derived from any other theoretical approach. The use of electric shock to save the life of the ruminative infant is another. Behavior modification has also been used in innovative ways to deal with autistic children, self-injurious children, and children showing temper tantrums and conduct disorders. Many of the teaching approaches found in educational television shows are also based on learning theory.

Despite the demonstrated effectiveness of behavior-modification procedures, there are a number of ways in which learning-theory approaches to child development have been criticized. First there is the theoretical question as to whether the conditioning process in children is truly mechanical. For example, a good deal of research with humans and with lower animals suggests that reinforcers may not condition responses in a mechanical sense, but rather provide the children with information as to when they have made desired responses (Rathus, 1987, pp. 234–236). There is reason to believe that conditioning may often change the way in which the child interprets the world, rather than simply changing responses to stimuli—especially in older children.

Second, it may be that learning theorists have exaggerated the role of learning in development. There is no question that learning is of major importance in the acquisition of motor skills, language, and academic skills. However, behaviorists such as Watson may have erroneously underestimated the prominence of biological-maturational factors in the appearance of temperament and basic psychological traits. That is, many learning theorists have not paid sufficient attention to the genetically based individual differences that may place limits on learning.

▶ ▶ ▶ ▶

Jean Piaget

However, many contemporary learning theorists take issue with Watson's (and Locke's) view that children are born as "blank slates." They allow for genetically determined individual differences. Social-learning theorists also focus on children's expectations, values, and abilities to make choices in their description, explanation, prediction, and control of behavior. They find a role for cognition.

Let us now consider a theory of development that places cognitive processes at the heart of development.

Cognitive-Developmental Theory

Cognitive-developmental theory focuses on the development of children's ways of perceiving and mentally representing the world, on the development of thought and logic, and on the development of the ability to solve problems. Cognitive-developmental theory has a strong biological bent in that it is assumed that the maturation of biological structures provides for an invariant sequence of stages of cognitive development. That is, maturation of the brain permits increasingly sophisticated patterns of thought. However, interaction with the world is also indispensable to cognitive development, since the world outside provides so many of the objects that are represented and manipulated in the mind. Moreover, children—as scientists—experiment upon the world in order to refine their ideas.

The leading proponent of cognitive-developmental theory in the twentieth century was Jean Piaget (1896–1980). Piaget was born in Neuchatel, Switzerland, and spent his childhood in this French-speaking "college town." His first intellectual love was biology, and he published his first scientific article at the age of 10. He then became a laboratory assistant to the director of a museum of natural history and engaged in research on mollusks (oysters, clams, snails, octopuses, squids, and—as my children have scientifically classified them— some other "squishy" things). The director soon died, and Piaget published their findings himself. On the basis of these papers, he was offered the curatorship of a museum in Geneva, but had to turn it down. After all, he was only 11.

During adolescence Piaget became immersed in a search for knowledge about knowledge itself. He studied philosophy, logic, and mathematics, but

Cognitive-developmental theory The stage theory that holds that the child's abilities to mentally represent the world and solve problems unfold as a result of the interaction between the maturation of neurological structures and experience.

▶ ▶ ▶ ▶

took his Ph.D. in biology. For the next three years he job-hopped, seeking a satisfying line of work. He dabbled in experimental psychology in 1918 but found the discipline too dull. He dabbled, too, in psychoanalysis, but found the views of Freud and his followers too speculative, too unscientific. In 1919 he studied psychopathology at the Sorbonne in Paris and learned how to conduct clinical interviews with patients in mental hospitals.

In 1920 Piaget suddenly, unexpectedly, found his vocation. He obtained a job at the Binet Institute in Paris, where work on intelligence tests was being conducted, and his initial task was to adapt a number of verbal reasoning items that had originated in England for use with French children. In order to do so, Piaget had to try them out on children of various age groups and see whether they could arrive at correct answers. The task was winding down to boredom until Piaget became intrigued by the children's *incorrect* answers. Another investigator might have shrugged them off and forgotten them. Young Piaget realized that there were methods to his children's madness. The wrong answers seemed to reflect consistent, if illogical, cognitive processes.

Piaget investigated these "wrong" answers by straying from the standard questioning format. He used the clinical method he had learned at the Sorbonne to probe the children's responses, to seek out the underlying patterns of thought that led to them. He continued in his work at the Binet Institute and began to publish a series of articles on children's thought processes. The head of the Institute Jean Jacques Rousseau in Geneva was so impressed by the writings of young Piaget that he offered him the directorship of child development research in 1921. At the age of 25, Piaget began his life's work in earnest.

Piaget wrote and published dozens of books and scores of articles, but his work was almost unknown in the English-speaking countries until the mid-1950s. For one thing, Piaget's writing is difficult to understand, even to native speakers of French. Piaget once remarked, in fact, that he was able to write so much because he was free of the task of having to *read* his own work (Cowan, 1978, p. 5). For another, it took him a number of years to formulate his full set of theoretical ideas. For a third, once formed, Piaget's views were very different from those of other developmentalists. Psychology in England and the United States was dominated by behaviorism and psychoanalysis, and Piaget's writings had a biological-cognitive flavor. They did not fit in.

Today the world of child development has been turned topsy-turvy. Many English-speaking developmentalists are trying to fit their views to those of Piaget. Volumes of research have been conducted just by scientists who have set out to dispute a point of Piaget's (Bryant, 1982).

Jean Piaget's View of the Nature of Children

Different theorists of child development have attempted to explain different types of events and have had very different views of the basic nature of children. Behaviorists such as John B. Watson have focused on the acquisition of overt behavior. They see children as blank slates which are written upon by experience—as reactors to environmental stimulation, not actors.

Freud's psychoanalytic theory focuses on personality and emotional development. It portrays children as largely irrational and at the mercy of instinctive impulses—as driven creatures caught between powerful sexual and aggressive urges and the stifling codes of parents and society.

▶ ▶ ▶ ▶

THEORIES OF DEVELOPMENT

Piaget was concerned with the ways in which children form concepts or mental representations of the world, and how they manipulate their concepts in order to plan changes in the external world. Freud believed that conscious thought represents only a small portion of what occurs in the mind, and an illusory portion at that. Piaget, by contrast, believed that thought processes are at the heart of what it is to be human. But Piaget, like the behaviorists, recognized that thoughts cannot be measured directly, and so he always tried to link his views on children's mental processes to observable behavior.

Piaget regarded maturing children as natural physicists who actively intend to learn about and take intellectual charge of their worlds. In the Piagetian view, children who squish their food and laugh enthusiastically are often acting as budding scientists. In addition to enjoying earning a response from parents, they are studying the texture and consistency of their food. (Parents, of course, often prefer that their children would practice these experiments in the laboratory, not the dining room.)

Piaget's Basic Concepts

Researchers from different perspectives tie together different concepts in theoretical packages. Psychoanalysts integrate concepts such as repression and anal traits into principles that govern personality development. Behaviorists tie together concepts such as stimulus and reinforcement into principles that govern processes of learning. Piaget used concepts such as *schemes, assimilation, accommodation,* and *equilibration,* and he tied them together to describe and explain cognitive development.

Schemes   Piaget defines the **scheme** as a pattern of action or a mental structure that is involved in acquiring or organizing knowledge. According to Piaget, *acting on the environment and acquiring knowledge occur simultaneously, or are equivalent forms of behavior.* As action patterns, schemes tend to be repeated and to occur in certain types of situations.

Among older children and adults, a scheme may be the inclusion of an object in a class. For example, the *mammal* class or concept includes a group of animals that are warm-blooded and nurse their young. The inclusion of cats, apes, buffalo, whales, and people in the mammal class involves a series of mental operations, or schemes, that expand the child's knowledge of the natural world.

But schemes need not involve words. Babies, for example, are said to have sucking schemes, grasping schemes, and looking schemes. As we shall see in Chapter 4, newborn babies tend to suck things that are placed in their mouths, to grasp objects placed in their hands, and to visually track moving objects. Piaget would say that infants' schemes give *meaning* to the objects around them. For instance, even in the first months of life infants are responding to objects around them as things-I-can-suck or things-I-can't-suck, things-I-can-grasp or things-I-can't-grasp.

Sucking and grasping are reflexes, but Piaget referred to them as schemes, because the concept of the reflex implies that children behave mechanically—that they do not act until they are stimulated. While neonates do respond mechanically to certain stimuli, they also show some flexibility in their behavior, and Piaget described their behavior as becoming active, intentional, and purposeful even within the first few weeks.

Scheme According to Piaget, an action pattern or mental structure that is involved in the acquisition and organization of knowledge.

▶ ▶ ▶ ▶

Piaget drew a connection between the wordless schemes of infants and the complex mental structures of older children and adults, because both involve the transformation of experience into knowing. Both reflect an active and organized quest for knowledge.

Assimilation: Food for Thought   The concept of **assimilation** reflects Piaget's early interest in biology. In biology, assimilation is the process by which food is digested and converted into the tissues that compose an animal. In the social sciences, "cultural assimilation" refers to the process by which people from foreign lands learn U.S. English and become integrated into U.S. culture.

The *cognitive* process of assimilation is akin to both biological and cultural assimilation. Cognitive assimilation is the process by which new events are responded to according to existing schemes or ways of organizing knowledge. Novel objects or events are never taken quite as they are. Instead, they are checked for fit against the child's mental structures or cognitive organizations. These organizations transform them into meaningful events. New events *mean* something, because they can (or cannot) be assimilated by existing schemes.

Children's cognitive organizations change dramatically as they mature and gain experience. Thus assimilation takes dramatically different forms at different ages. Infants, for example, usually try to place new objects in their mouths to suck, feel, or explore them. Piaget would say that the child is assimilating (fitting) a new toy or object into the sucking-an-object activity or scheme. At about the age of 6 or 7 months, infants can reach their toes and tend also to assimilate them to the sucking-an-object scheme.

Similarly, 2-year-olds who refer to sheep and cows as "doggies" or "bow-wows" can be said to be assimilating these new animals to the *doggy* scheme. As they develop, they will adapt by acquiring proper schemes for interpreting these animals. Their cognitive organization will blossom into a hierarchical structure in which dogs and sheep are assimilated as mammals, and mammals are further assimilated as animals.

According to Piaget, much children's play involves exercises in assimilation. Children often pretend that objects are what they want them to be. A piece of clay may become a mountain or an animal. A pile of blocks may be a castle or a spaceship, depending on what game the child is playing. Cognitive psychologists have suggested that playing with concepts can be intrinsically reinforcing. Children may tirelessly repeat games in which they assimilate objects to newly constructed schemes, because these games provide intellectual pleasure.

Assimmilation and accommodation, which is discussed in the next section, occur throughout life.

Accommodation   **Accommodation** is also a biological term, meaning a change in structure that permits an organism to adjust or adapt to a novel object or event, to a new source of stimulation.

As the term applies to cognitive development, *accommodation* is the transformation of existing ways of organizing knowledge, or schemes, so that new information can be incorporated. At first infants may be able to engage in reflexive rooting and sucking only when held in certain positions. But even within a few days, they accommodate to the demands imposed by new positions by twisting and turning their bodies to reach the nipple and other objects. They

► ► ► ►

Equilibration *The creation of an equilibrium or balance between assimilation and accommodation as a way of incorporating new events or knowledge.*

accommodate further by rejecting objects that are too large, that taste bad, or that are of the wrong texture or temperature. They gain knowledge that certain things are not to be sucked and may experiment with new ways to relate to them.

Two-year-olds may at first assimilate dogs, cats, and other animals to the doggy scheme. However, children accommodate to parental correction and the desire to be understood by creating new mental structures, such as classes or categories for cats, cows, sheep, and still other animals.

Equilibration Piaget theorizes that, when children can assimilate new events to existing schemes, they are in a state of cognitive harmony, or equilibrium. When something that does not fit happens along, their state of equilibrium is disturbed and they may try to accommodate to it. The process of restoring equilibrium is termed **equilibration.** Piaget believed that the attempt to restore equilibrium is the source of intellectual motivation and lies at the heart of the natural curiosity of the child.

Equilibration is most efficient when the processes of assimilation and accommodation work together. Then, when children encounter something new, they can try to fit it into existing concepts and also to generate new ideas. According to Piaget, the processes of assimilation and accommodation tend to come into balance by about the second birthday. As a result, the capacity for equilibration increases dramatically. Children become more efficient problem solvers, and their intellectual functioning blossoms.

Piaget's Stages of Cognitive Development

Piaget (1963) hypothesized that children's cognitive processes develop in an orderly sequence or series of stages. As is the case with motor development and language development, some children may be more advanced than others at particular ages, but the developmental sequence does not normally vary. Piaget identified four major stages of cognitive development: *sensorimotor, preoperational, concrete operational,* and *formal operational.* These stages will be discussed in Chapter 8.

Piaget believed that the cognitive developments of each stage, and of substages within, tend to be universal. One reason for this is that cognitive development largely depends on the maturation of the brain, and, assuming minimal nourishment, the course of maturation will be reasonably similar from child to child. Second, cognitive developments are also based on children's interactions with their environments. While it is true that no two children share precisely the same environment, the broad realities are compelling enough so that practically all children must learn to cope with them. For example, gravity affects us all. So all children have the opportunity to learn that dropped objects move downward. Children from different cultures may reach for very different objects, but all normally learn that reaching for things enables us to touch or grasp them.

Piaget also believed that the cognitive developments of one stage, or one substage, are made possible by the cognitive achievements of the preceding stage. In Chapter 8 we shall see how stage develops from stage, and how substage grows out of substage. We shall also find that many researchers, using a variety of methods, have found that Piaget may have been in error concerning

▶ ▶ ▶ ▶

his views on just when children are capable of doing certain things. However, here let it suffice to note that Piaget presents us with a view of children very different from the psychoanalytic and behaviorist views, and that Piaget has provided a strong theoretical foundation for researchers who are concerned with the sequences in children's cognitive development.

Ecological Theory

Ecology is the branch of biology that deals with the relationships between living organisms and their environment. The **ecological theory** of child development addresses aspects of psychological, social, and emotional development as well as biological development. Ecological theorists explain child development in terms of the interaction between children and their environment.

Consider the example of the ways in which parents interact with infants. Some parents may choose to feed newborns on demand, while others may decide to adhere to a schedule in which feedings are presented four hours apart. Certainly parental feeding plans will affect the child. But the basic (apparently inborn) temperaments of children differ, as noted by Thomas and Chess (1980), and some children are more likely to accept their parents' feeding patterns than others. Some children, that is, are basically "easy-going." Easy-going children are open to novel events and readily develop regular cycles of eating and sleeping. Easy-going children are likely to conform to a rigid feeding schedule. Other children are basically "difficult." Difficult children are less open to manipulation by others. They are more irritable, more likely to cry, and slow to develop regular cycles of eating and sleeping. Difficult children may not readily adapt to a rigid feeding schedule, and the parents' wishes may have to be modified if the peace is to be kept.

The point is this: Parents are part of the child's environment, and parents do have a major influence upon the child, but the influence is not a one-way street.

Focus on Reciprocal Processes

According to psychologist Urie Bronfenbrenner of Cornell University, the first proposition of ecological theory is that the traditional, unidirectional approach to understanding child-environment relationships is insufficient. The ecological approach allows for reciprocal processes—"not only the effect of A on B, but also the effect of B on A" (1977, p. 519). Children reciprocally act to influence the parents, and the developmental process cannot be completely understood unless we focus on the interactions between the child and the parents—not just maturational forces (nature) or parental child-rearing approaches (nurture).

As defined by Bronfenbrenner, the ecology of human development involves the "scientific study of the progressive mutual accommodation between an active growing human being and . . . the settings in which the developing person lives. . . ." "Difficult" children will foster very different kinds of "mutual accommodations" with their parents than "easy-going" children will.

Ecology The branch of biology that deals with the relationships between living organisms and their environment.

Ecological theory The view that explains child development in terms of the reciprocal influences between children and the settings that comprise their environment.

▶ ▶ ▶ ▶

THEORIES OF DEVELOPMENT

Microsystem *The immediate settings with which the child interacts, such as the home, the school, and the maternity ward. (From the Greek* mikros, *meaning "small.")*

Mesosystem *The interlocking settings that influence the child, such as the interaction of the school and the larger community when children are taken on field trips. (From the Greek* mesos, *meaning "middle.")*

Urie Bronfenbrenner

Sandra Scarr

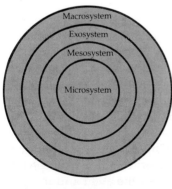

Figure 2.4 The Contexts of Human Development According to ecological theory, the systems within which children develop are embedded within larger systems. Children and these systems reciprocally influence one another.

Focus on the Larger Context: Systems within Systems

The development of the child is also influenced "by the relations between these settings [in which the developing person lives] and by larger contexts in which the settings are embedded" (Bronfenbrenner, 1979, p. 21). According to psychologist Sandra Scarr of the University of Virginia, we must expand our view "of the context in which development occurs. Children have not only an immediate family but contexts of neighborhood, community, and society in which they do or do not get medical care, day care, and school lunches. Parents have work lives and friendship groups that affect how much time of what quality they spend with the children" (1985, p. 501). She adds that we cannot understand children unless we examine the social and cultural aspects of behavior as well as the biological and psychological aspects.

Bronfenbrenner (1979, 1986; Bronfenbrenner & Crouter, 1983) suggests that we can view the setting or contexts of human development as consisting of four systems. Each of these systems is embedded within the next larger context. From narrowest to widest, these systems consist of the microsystem, the mesosystem, the exosystem, and the macrosystem (see Figure 2.4).

The Microsystem The **microsystem** involves the interactions between the child and other people in the immediate setting, such as the home, the school, or the maternity ward. For example, the presence of both parents in the maternity ward apparently encourages each parent to smile more frequently at the newborn child. Conversely, marital tension appears to contribute to maternal ineptness in feeding the child.

The Mesosystem The **mesosystem** involves the interactions among the various settings in which the child participates. For instance, the home and the school

▶ ▶ ▶ ▶

ECOLOGICAL THEORY

73

Exosystem Community institutions and settings that indirectly influence the child, such as the school board and the parents' workplaces. (From the Greek exo-, meaning "outside.")

Macrosystem The basic institutions and ideologies that influence the child, such as the American ideals of freedom of expression and equality under the law. (From the Greek makros, meaning "long" or "enlarged.")

interact during parent–teacher conferences. The school and the larger community interact when children are taken on field trips. The ecological approach addresses the joint impact of two or more settings on the child.

The Exosystem The **exosystem** involves the institutions in which the child does not directly participate, but which exert an indirect influence upon the child. For example, the school board is part of the child's exosystem in that board members construct curricula for the child's education, determine what books will be in the school library, and so forth. In similar fashion, the parents' workplaces determine the hours during which they will be available to the child, help determine what mood they will be in when they interact with the child, and so on. Studies that address the effects of adequate or inadequate housing, or television programs, church attendance, government agencies, or even the presence or absence of a telephone on children are all examining the interactions of the exosystem with the child.

The Macrosystem The **macrosystem** involves the interaction of children with the basic institutional and ideological patterns of their cultural settings. Cross-cultural studies examine children's interactions with their macrosystems. For example, American studies that investigate the ways in which children interact with cultural ideals such as freedom of expression and equality under the law involve the macrosystem.

Evaluation of Ecological Theory Perhaps the most valuable aspect of ecological theory is that it has helped make researchers aware of the systems with which children interact. This awareness has fostered research down relatively new avenues. For example, focus on interactions within the microsystem have led to the innovative research by Michael Lamb (see Chapter 11) on the important but previously ignored role of the father in child development. Other researchers have extended research within the immediate family to include the influences of peers.

Much research at the level of the mesosystem focuses on the shifts in setting that children encounter as they develop. For example, the health of the child requires interlocking relationships between parents and the health system, just as the education of the child requires interaction between parents and school personnel. At the level of the exosystem, researchers look into the effects of parents' work lives, welfare agencies, transportation systems, shopping facilities, and so on. At the level of the macrosystem, we may compare child-rearing practices in the United States to those of the Soviet Union and various third-world cultures.

In short, the powerful legacies of the ecological approach are that our perspectives on development are broadened and our research endeavors may be better organized. The ecological approach compels us at once to pay attention to the power of nature and also to regard the several systems of nurture with greater sophistication.

As Bronfenbrenner points out, a major test of the ecological approach is whether it fosters innovative research concerning the interactions between children and the multiple systems that influence them. It has already been shown that the ecological ("multisystemic") approach broadens the strategies for intervention in problems such as juvenile offending and child abuse (e.g., Belsky, 1980; Brunk et al., 1987; Henggeler et al., 1986; Rosenberg, 1987).

▶ ▶ ▶ ▶

THEORIES OF DEVELOPMENT

Bronfenbrenner (1977) suggests projects such as:

- Introducing a "curriculum for caring" in which students help care for children of working mothers, help families during crises, and visit the sick and the elderly
- Facilitating the entry of children into the educational system by acquainting families with school personnel and encouraging joint activities when children are still preschoolers
- Inducing businesses to create more flexible work schedules for parents

On Theories of Development: Some Integrating Thoughts

Now that we have explored the major theories of development, what can we conclude? After all, the theories do not all address the same aspects of development. One may focus on motor development, another on learning, another on emotional development, and still another on cognitive development. One theory may view development as involving a discrete sequence of stages, while another may view development as continuous.

We must also deal with the fact that many theoretical notions have been discarded, or at least revised and updated. For example, Erikson's views revise those of Freud, and social-learning theorists have updated the propositions of the behaviorists.

Nonetheless, despite the differences in the theories, and despite the need for revision, there may be emerging a central core of knowledge about children. For example, it would be erroneous to ignore the powerful role of maturation in the child's biological development and the appearance of the child's basic temperament, although the extent of the role of maturation is somewhat more open to dispute in the development of intelligence and academic skills.

Let us try to develop an integrating list of propositions on development—a theory-derived list that appears to have been generally supported by research as of today. Such a list might look like this:

1. The heredity of the child does provide for a measure of stability in development. For example, as we shall see in Chapter 5, children whose physical development is delayed by malnourishment tend to "catch up" when nourishment becomes more adequate. (Maturational theory.)

2. Children may not only inherit physical traits such as hair and eye color, but also predispositions toward basic temperament and factors such as basic ways of approaching cognitive tasks. (Maturational theory.)

3. Early childhood experiences can have far-reaching effects on adult personality and emotional life. (Freud's psychoanalytic theory.)

4. Our early social relationships influence our tendencies to view the world as generally benevolent or malevolent, and color our future relationships. (Freud's and Erikson's psychoanalytic theories.)

▶ ▶ ▶ ▶

5. To some degree we are the conscious architects of our own person- alities. (Erikson's psychoanalytic theory; social-learning theory; cog- nitive-developmental theory.)

6. Children are capable of learning to associate stimuli very early in life, long before they can verbalize the associations. (Learning the- ory.)

7. Rewards and, in many cases, punishments work. Pleasant stimuli tend to encourage children to repeat the rewarded behavior, while aversive stimuli tend to suppress the punished behavior. (Learning theory.)

8. Children also learn from observing the behavior of others—parents, siblings and peers, teachers, television characters, even characters in books. (Social-learning theory.)

9. Children do not only react mechanically to external stimulation. They also try to understand the world about them—to form accurate mental representations of external objects and to discover what leads to what. (Cognitive-developmental theory.)

10. We as children (and adults) tend to interpret new events according to existing ways of perceiving the world, but we can also accom- modate by changing the ways we perceive the world when new events do not "fit." (Cognitive-developmental theory.)

11. Children are not only influenced by their environments; children also influence their environments, so that the influences are recip- rocal. (Ecological theory; maturational theory.)

12. In order to develop a comprehensive understanding of the forces that act upon children, we must consider many interacting systems, ranging from systems as concrete as the immediate family to sys- tems as abstract as the ideals of the cultures in which children are reared. (Ecological theory.)

If it strikes you that there is some truth to each of these statements, then perhaps each theory of development has something of value to tell us. Each theory sheds light on meaningful aspects of development. In later chapters we shall return to these theories to see how they further enhance our understanding of child development.

▶ ▶ ▶ ▶

THEORIES OF DEVELOPMENT

Summary

1. Scientists who study child development seek to describe, explain, predict, and control various aspects of development. When possible, descriptive terms and concepts are interwoven into theories. Theories are based on assumptions about behavior, and theories allow us to derive explanations and predictions.

2. Stage theorists view development as consisting of discrete periods that differ from other periods in quality. Stages follow one another according to invariant sequences.

3. Maturational theory focuses on the unfolding of genetically determined developmental sequences. Maturational theorist Arnold Gesell argued that all areas of development are self-regulated by the unfolding of natural plans and processes. The sequences of motor development provide a powerful illustration of the role of maturation. According to maturational theory, training (e.g., in motor skills) accomplishes very little until we are ready to learn.

4. Maturational theory appears to apply to the unfolding of many psychological traits as well as to areas of physical development. Genetic influences appear strongest in traits that describe the child's general temperament, such as activity level, emotionality, and sociability. There is also evidence that heredity influences whether children are basically "easy-going" or "difficult" and factors that are related to attachment and to performance on cognitive tasks.

5. Sigmund Freud's psychoanalytic theory focuses on personality and emotional development and assumes that children are driven by instincts and inevitably encounter conflict with parents. Freud hypothesized the existence of three psychic structures: the id, which provides instinctive motives; the ego, which represents reason and makes plans; and the superego, which functions as the conscience. Defense mechanisms protect the ego from anxiety by repressing unacceptable ideas or distorting reality.

6. According to Freud, children undergo five stages of psychosexual development as psychosexual energy is transferred from one erogenous zone to another: the oral, anal, phallic, latency, and genital stages. Inadequate or excessive gratification in any stage can lead to fixation and the development of characteristic personality traits. Children are theorized eventually to identify with the same-sex parents by resolving the Oedipus and Electra complexes of the phallic stage.

7. Erik Erikson's psychoanalytic theory extends Freud's five stages of development to eight, including three that occur during adulthood. Erikson's theory concerns stages of psychosocial development rather than psychosexual development, since Erikson focuses on social relationships during each stage rather than the expression of sexual energy. Erikson also argues that personality development is largely conscious and based on making choices.

8. Learning theorists view development in terms of changes in behavior that result from experience. For example, in classical conditioning an originally neutral stimulus (the conditioned stimulus) comes to elicit the response usually brought forth by a second stimulus (the unconditioned stimulus) by being paired repeatedly with the second stimulus. ▶ ▶ ▶ ▶

9. In operant conditioning, children increase the frequency of behaviors that are reinforced. Children may acquire complex motor skills through shaping, in which successive approximations to the target behavior pattern are reinforced.

10. Positive reinforcers (such as food and approval) increase the frequency of behaviors when they are applied. Negative reinforcers (such as pain and fear) increase the frequency of the behaviors they follow when that behavior pattern results in their removal. Primary reinforcers (food, pain) are effective because of children's biological makeup. Secondary reinforcers (approval, money, fear) acquire their effectiveness through association with established reinforcers.

11. Social-learning theorists such as Albert Bandura have shown that children also learn by observing others. That is, children can also learn how to do things without emitting responses that are reinforced. Children appear to learn behavior patterns considered appropriate for their genders by means of observation.

12. Cognitive-developmental theory is a stage theory that focuses on the ways in which children mentally represent the world and solve problems. Jean Piaget viewed cognitive development as the child's way of adapting to the environment. Piaget saw children as budding scientists who purposefully seek to understand and influence the environment.

13. Piaget theorized that children respond to stimulation with organized actions or mental operations termed *schemes*. Children assimilate new events to existing schemes when possible, and, when they cannot, they accommodate by modifying their schemes. When children cannot respond effectively to new events, they experience cognitive disharmony and attempt to restore harmony. The restoration of harmony may demand both assimilation and accommodation—a back and forth process that is termed *equilibration*.

14. Ecological theorists focus on children's interactions with environmental systems. According to psychologist Urie Bronfenbrenner, the first proposition of ecological theory is that children and their environments exert reciprocal influences upon one another.

15. Ecological theory hypothesizes the existence of four systems that influence children: the microsystem, or immediate setting, such as the home or school; the mesosystem, which involves interactions among various settings (e.g., home and school interact in parent–teacher conferences); the exosystem, or influential institutions in which the child does not directly participate (e.g., the school board or the parents' workplaces); and the macrosystem, or cultural values, ideals, and institutions.

▶ ▶ ▶ ▶

Children must crawl before they can walk. True. As noted by maturational theorists, the stages of motor development follow a largely invariant sequence.

Giving infants early training in sitting up and walking accelerates the development of these skills. False. Training may slightly speed up the processes of motor development, but motor skills, by and large, are not acquired until children have matured to the point where they are ready to acquire them.

Conflict between children and their parents is inescapable. True, according to Freud's psychoanalytic theory, in which children's basic instincts are viewed as selfish and antisocial. However, other theorists might not agree.

Children can be taught to wake up in the middle of the night, if they are about to wet their beds. True. In the bell-and-pad method, bladder tension becomes a conditioned stimulus (CS) that elicits the response of waking up.

Punishment doesn't work. False. Punishment can suppress undesired behavior. However, most developmentalists prefer not to use punishment, because punishment can have undesirable "side effects," such as creating hostility or causing the child to withdraw.

Psychologists successfully used painful electric shock to teach a 9-month-old infant not to vomit. True. The dangerously malnourished infant in the case learned not to vomit and made dramatic gains in weight.

Classroom behavior-modification procedures rely largely on old standbys such as ignoring children when they misbehave and praising them for desired behavior. True. Behavior-modification procedures apply these methods and others as consistently as possible.

Children can learn only by making mistakes. False. In programmed learning, for example, children can acquire academic knowledge without making any errors.

Children are budding scientists who actively intend to learn about and take intellectual charge of their worlds. True, according to cognitive-developmental theory. Behaviorists, however, might not agree. In Chapter 8 we shall see how children appear to "take charge" during the several stages of cognitive development.

Infants do not simply accept their parents' child-rearing approaches; even newborns influence their parents to treat them in certain ways. True. Children differ in their basic temperaments. As pointed out by ecological theorists, influences between children and their environments are reciprocal.

Children are influenced not only by their parents, schools, and other local agencies, but also by the ideals and values of the cultures in which they are reared. True. Ecological theorists encourage us to focus on the various systems—immediate and extended—that interact with children as they develop.

▸ ▸ ▸ ▸

3

Heredity and Prenatal Development

▶
▶
▶
▶
▶
▶
▶

T R U T H ▸ O R ▸ F I C T I O N ?

- Fertilization takes place in the uterus.
- Identical twins are more likely than fraternal twins to share problems such as nail-biting and carsickness.
- Brown eyes are dominant over blue eyes.
- Sickle-cell anemia is most prevalent among blacks.
- It is not possible to learn the sex of one's child prior to birth.
- We can use sound waves to take "pictures" of unborn children.
- Equal numbers of boys and girls are conceived.
- "Yuppies" are more likely than nonprofessionals to develop fertility problems.
- Developing embryos have been successfully transferred from the womb of one woman to the womb of another.
- You can predetermine the sex of your child.
- Newly fertilized egg cells survive without any nourishment from the mother for more than a week.
- Your heart started beating when you were only one-fifth of an inch long and weighed a fraction of an ounce.
- If it were not for the secretion of male sex hormones a few weeks after conception, we would all develop as females.
- Embryos and fetuses "take what they need" from their mothers. Therefore, pregnant women need not be too concerned about their diets.
- Newborn babies whose mothers read *The Cat in the Hat* aloud during the last weeks of pregnancy prefer *The Cat in the Hat* to other stories.
- Fetuses suck their thumbs and hiccough, sometimes for hours on end.
- Surgery has been carried out on fetuses.
- Babies can be born addicted to narcotics and other drugs.
- Pregnant women who smoke risk having children who are low in birth weight.

On a summerlike day in October, Elaine and her husband Dennis rush out to their jobs as usual. While Elaine, a buyer for a New York department store, is arranging for dresses from the Chicago manufacturer to arrive in time for the spring line, a very different drama is unfolding in her body. Hormones are causing a follicle (egg container) in one of her **ovaries** to rupture and release an egg cell, or **ovum.** Elaine, like other women, possessed from birth all the egg cells she would ever have. How this ovum was selected for development and release this month is unknown. But for a day or so following **ovulation,** Elaine will be capable of becoming pregnant.

When it is released, the ovum begins a slow journey down a four-inch-long **fallopian tube** to the **uterus.** It is within this tube that one of Dennis's sperm cells will unite with it.

Like many other couples, Elaine and Dennis engaged in sexual intercourse the previous night. But unlike most other couples, their timing and methodology were preplanned. Elaine had used a nonprescription kit bought in a drug store to predict when she would ovulate. She had been chemically analyzing her urine for the presence of **luteinizing hormone.** Luteinizing hormone surges about one to two days prior to ovulation, and the results placed this day at the center of the period of time when Elaine was likely to conceive.

When Elaine and Dennis made love, he ejaculated hundreds of millions of sperm, with about equal numbers of Y and X sex **chromosomes.** By the time of conception only a few thousand had survived the journey to the fallopian tubes. Several bombarded the ovum, attempting to penetrate. Only one succeeded. It carried a Y sex chromosome. When a Y-bearing sperm unites with an ovum, all of which contain X sex chromosomes, the couple will conceive a boy. When an X-bearing sperm fertilizes the ovum, a girl is conceived. The fertilized ovum, or **zygote,** is 1/175th of an inch long—a tiny stage for the drama yet to unfold.

The genetic material from Dennis's sperm cell combines with that in Elaine's egg cell. Elaine is 37 years old, and in four months she will have an **amniocentesis** to check for the presence of **Down syndrome,** a chromosomal disorder that occurs more frequently among the children of couples in their 30s and 40s. Amniocentesis also provides information about the sex of the unborn child. And so, months before their son is born, Elaine and Dennis will start thinking about boys' names and prepare their nursery for a boy.

In this chapter we explore heredity and **prenatal** development. In a sense, development begins before the moment of conception. Development also involves the origins of the genetic structures that determine that the being conceived by Dennis and Elaine will grow arms rather than wings, a mouth rather than gills, and hair rather than scales. And so our discussion begins with an examination of the building blocks of heredity: genes and chromosomes. We describe the process of conception itself and find that the odds against any one sperm's uniting with an ovum are astronomical. We then trace human growth and development through the nine months of **gestation.** Although many parents feel that their pregnancies tend to drag on, especially toward the end, we see that the major organ systems and all the structures that make us human actually take form with great rapidity.

But first let us turn our attention to a very important issue that preceded the conception of Elaine and Dennis's new child: the decision to bear a child.

Ovary *A female reproductive organ located in the abdomen that produces female reproductive cells, or ova.*

Ovum *A female reproductive cell.*

Ovulation *The releasing of an ovum from an ovary.*

Fallopian tube *A tube that conducts ova from an ovary to the uterus.*

Uterus *The hollow organ within females in which the embryo and fetus develop.*

Luteinizing hormone *(LEW-ten-eyes-ing). A hormone produced by the pituitary gland that causes ovulation.*

Chromosomes *Rod-shaped structures composed of genes that are found within the nuclei of cells.*

Zygote *A fertilized ovum.*

Amniocentesis *(AM-nee-oh-sen-TEE-sis). A procedure for drawing and examining fetal cells sloughed off into amniotic fluid in order to determine the presence of various disorders.*

Down syndrome *A chromosomal abnormality characterized by mental retardation and caused by an extra chromosome in the twenty-first pair.*

Prenatal *Before birth.*

Gestation *The period of carrying young from conception until birth.*

▶ ▶ ▶ ▶

Children: To Have or to Have Not

Once upon a time marriage was equated with children. It was traditional for people to get married and, in what Hare-Mustin and Broderick (1979) refer to as the "motherhood mandate," it was traditional for women to bear at least two children and to rear them properly. In short, married women who could bear children usually did (Faux, 1984).

Today, this tradition—the motherhood mandate—as so many others, has to some degree broken down. More than ever, people see themselves as having the right to *choose* whether or not they will have children. Today from 10 to 25 percent of U.S. women do not want children (Cook et al., 1982; Gerson et al., 1984; Notman & Nadelson, 1982). U.S. couples are now also having fewer children than in the past—only 1.8 per couple (McFalls, 1983).

Women's own experiences as children influence their own desire for children. Women who report their own childhoods to have been filled with happiness and maternal love are more likely to want children of their own than are women whose memories are not so pleasant (Gerson, 1980, 1984).

Level of education and sex-role attitudes also play important roles. Women who do not have children are more likely to be white, urban, and highly educated than those who do (Faux, 1984). In a recent survey at a major university, 55 percent of the married faculty women under the age of 40 were child-free (Yogev & Vierra, 1983). Child-free women, black and white, are more likely to hold nontraditional, feminist beliefs than women with children. The latter group are more likely to endorse the stereotypical feminine sex role for women (Bram, 1984; Gerson, 1984; Scott & Morgan, 1983).

Fortunately for those women who choose not to have children, the tenor of the times seems reasonably supportive. It was once thought that women must have children in order to be fulfilled, but only 9 percent of the respondents in one recent survey endorsed this view (Knaub et al., 1983). In a survey by Hare-Mustin and Broderick (1979), only 22 percent of college students endorsed the view that having a baby is totally fulfilling. Only 12 percent considered the decision against having children unnatural or selfish.

Research on child-free women supports the view that children are not mandatory for women's fulfillment. Young married women without children report greater marital and general life satisfaction than do their counterparts with children (Doherty & Jackson, 1982; Gerson et al., 1984). The same finding holds for middle-aged women. Only among widows does it appear that children are a source of comfort. Widows with grown children appear to be more satisfied with their lives and to feel less isolated than their child-free counterparts (Beckman & Houser, 1982; Houser et al., 1984). The corollary here may be that it is erroneous for women to assume that having children will solve their problems or ensure their happiness (Baruch et al., 1983).

Keep in mind that the above findings on life satisfaction generally apply to couples who have *chosen* not to have children. For couples who want children but cannot have them, few situations are more frustrating.

What are some of the considerations involved in choosing to have, or not to have, children? Researchers have found several for each choice. Note that there are a number of pros and cons that will not impress you as good or valid reasons. They are included because other people have offered them. Ultimately you must be the judge. It's your life, and your choice.

▶ ▶ ▶ ▶

Reasons for Having Children   Researchers (Berelson, 1979; Campbell et al., 1982; Daniels & Weingarten, 1982; Hoffman & Manis, 1978) have compiled the following reasons for having children:

1. *Personal Experience.* Having children is a unique experience. To many people, no other experience compares with having the opportunity to love them, to experience their love, to help shape their lives, and to watch them develop.

2. *Personal Pleasure.* There is fun and pleasure in playing with children, taking them to the zoo and the circus, and viewing the world through their fresh, innocent eyes.

3. *Personal Extension.* Children carry on our genetic heritage, and some of our own wishes and dreams, beyond the confines of our own mortality. We name them after ourselves or our families, and see them as extensions of ourselves. We identify with their successes.

4. *Relationship.* Parents have the opportunity to establish extremely close bonds with their children.

5. *Personal Status.* Within our culture, parents are afforded respect *just because* they are parents. Consider the commandment: "Honor thy Father and thy Mother."

6. *Personal Competence.* Parenthood is a challenge. Competence in the social roles of mother and father is a potential source of gratification to people who cannot match this competence in their vocational or other social roles.

Reasons for Having Children
Parents report many reasons for having children, including personal experience, personal pleasure, and the opportunity to establish close bonds with them.

▶ ▶ ▶ ▶

3 HEREDITY AND PRENATAL DEVELOPMENT

7. *Personal Responsibility*. Parents have the opportunity to be responsible for the welfare and education of their children.

8. *Personal Power*. The power that parents hold over their children is gratifying to some people.

9. *Moral Worth*. Some people feel that having children provides the opportunity for a moral, selfless act in which they place the needs of others—their children—ahead of their own.

Reasons for Not Having Children   Researchers (Benedek & Vaughn, 1982; Bernard, 1975; Campbell et al., 1982; McFalls, 1983; Sunday & Lewin, 1985) have compiled the following reasons why couples may choose not to have children:

1. *Strain on Resources*. The world is overpopulated and it is wrong to place additional strain on limited resources.

2. *Increase in Overpopulation*. More children will only geometrically increase the problem of overpopulation.

3. *Choice, Not Mandate*. Motherhood should be a choice, not a mandate.

4. *Time Together*. Child-free couples can spend more time together and develop a more intimate relationship.

5. *Freedom*. Children can interfere with plans for leisure time, education, and vocational advancement. Child-free couples are more able to live spontaneously, to go where they please and do as they please.

6. *Other Children*. People can enjoy other than their own children. Adoption is a possibility.

7. *Dual Careers*. Members of child-free couples may both pursue meaningful careers without distraction.

8. *Financial Security*. Children are a financial burden, especially considering the cost of a college education.

9. *Community Welfare*. Child-free couples have a greater opportunity to become involved in civic concerns and community organizations.

10. *Difficulty*. Parenthood is demanding. It requires sacrifice of time, money, and energy, and not everyone makes a good parent.

11. *Irrevocable Decision*. Once you have children, the decision cannot be changed.

12. *Failure*. Some people fear that they will not be good parents.

13. *Danger*. The world is a dangerous place, with the threats, for example, of crime and nuclear war. It is better not to bring children into such a world.

The decision to have or not to have children is a personal one—one of the most important decisions we make. Let us now follow what happens during the earliest days of child development.

▶ ▶ ▶ ▶

Genetic Influences on Development

Spend a moment or two reflecting on some facts of life:

- People cannot breathe underwater (without special equipment).
- People cannot fly (again, without special equipment).
- Fish cannot learn to speak French or do an Irish jig, even if you raise them in enriched environments and send them to finishing school (which is why we look for tuna that taste good, not for tuna with good taste).
- Chimpanzees and gorillas can learn to use sign language.

We cannot breathe underwater or fly (without artificial devices), because we have not inherited gills or wings. Fish are similarly limited by their **heredity** and cannot speak French or do a jig. Chimpanzees and gorillas can express simple concepts through sign language (see Chapter 7), but they show no ability to speak. Although chimps and gorillas can make sounds, they have apparently not inherited humanlike speech areas of the brain.

Genetic influences, or the biological transmission of traits from one generation to another, play a significant role in the determination of human traits. Our inherited structures at once make our behaviors possible and place limits on them. The sets of traits that we inherit from our parents are referred to as our **genotypes.** But none of us, as we appear, is the result of heredity, or genotype, alone.

It turns out that heredity provides the biological basis for a **reaction range** in the expression of traits. Our inherited traits can vary in expression, depending upon environmental conditions. In addition to inheritance, the expression of our traits is also influenced by nutrition, learning, exercise, and—unfortunately—accident and illness. Our actual sets of characteristics at any point in time are referred to as our **phenotypes,** the product of genetic and environmental influences.

Developmentalists attempt to sort out the roles of heredity ("nature") and environmental influences ("nurture") in the development of various structures and behavior patterns. They are interested in the roles of nature and nurture in both physical development and in psychological factors such as intelligence, abnormal behaviors like anxiety and mood disorders, and social problems such as sociopathy.

Research suggests that genetic influences are not only a factor in physical traits such as height, race, and the color of the eyes, but also in personality traits such as **extraversion** (Loehlin et al., 1982), **neuroticism** (Scarr et al., 1981), shyness (Kagan, 1984; Plomin, 1982), dominance and aggressiveness (Goldsmith, 1983), and criminal behavior (Mednick, 1985). There is even a genetic influence on infants' communicative development, as measured by their production of words, level of communicative gesturing, and vocal imitation within a week of their first birthdays (Hardy-Brown & Plomin, 1985).

In a general sense it can be argued that all behavior reflects the interaction of nature and nurture. All organisms inherit a range of structures that set the stage for certain behaviors. Yet environmental influences such as nutrition and learning also figure in as to whether potential behaviors will be displayed. A potential Shakespeare who is reared in an impoverished neighborhood and never taught to read or write is unlikely to create a *Hamlet.*

Let us now turn our attention to the building blocks of heredity: *genes* and *chromosomes.*

▶ ▶ ▶ ▶

Genes and Chromosomes

The building blocks of heredity are called **genes.** Genes are the biochemical materials that regulate the development of traits. Some traits, such as blood type, appear to be transmitted by a single pair of genes—one of which is derived from each parent. Other traits, referred to as **polygenic,** are determined by combinations of pairs of genes.

Chromosomes, the rod-shaped genetic structures found in the nuclei of the body's cells, each consist of more than 1,000 genes. A normal human cell contains 46 chromosomes, which are organized into 23 pairs.

We may have about 100,000 genes in every cell within our bodies. Chromosomes consist of large, complex molecules of **deoxyribonucleic acid** (DNA). Genes occupy various segments along the length of chromosomes. The form of DNA was first demonstrated in the 1950s by the team of James Watson and Francis Crick (1958). As you can see in Figure 3.1, DNA takes the form of a double spiral, or helix, similar in appearance to a twisting ladder. In all living things, from one-celled animals to fish to people, the sides of the "ladder" consist of alternating segments of phosphate (P) and a simple sugar (S). The "rungs" of the ladder are always attached to the sugars and consist of one of two pairs of bases, either *adenine* with *thymine* (A with T), or *cytosine* with *guanine* (C with G). The sequence of the "rungs" is the genetic code that will unfold to cause the organism to grow arms or wings, skin or scales.

Mitosis and Meiosis

We all begin life as a single cell or zygote which divides again and again. There are two types of cell division: *mitosis* and *meiosis*. **Mitosis** is the cell-division process by which growth occurs and tissues are replaced. Through mitosis, the identical genetic code is carried into each new cell in the body. In order to accomplish this, the chromosomal strands of DNA break apart, or "unzip" (see Figure 3.2). One side of the "ladder" and one of the two elements of each "rung" remain in the nucleus of each new cell after division takes place. The double helix is then rebuilt in each cell: Each incomplete rung combines with the appropriate base from the material within the cell (that is, G with C, A with T, and so on) to form a complete ladder. As a consequence, the genetic code is identical in every cell of the body, unless **mutations** occur through radiation or other environmental influences. Mutations are also believed, on rare occasions, to occur by chance.

Sperm and ova are produced through **meiosis,** or reduction division. In meiosis, the 46 chromosomes within the cell nucleus first divide into 23 pairs. When the cell divides, one member of each pair goes to each newly formed cell. As a consequence, each new cell nucleus contains only 23 chromosomes, not 46. And so, a cell that results from meiosis has half the genetic material of one that results from mitosis.

Through reduction division, or meiosis, we receive 23 chromosomes from our fathers' sperm cells and 23 from our mothers' ova. When a sperm cell fertilizes an ovum the chromosomes form 23 pairs (Figure 3.3). Twenty-two of the pairs contain **autosomes,** which are chromosomes that look alike and possess genetic information concerning the same set of traits. The twenty-third pair consists of **sex chromosomes** that look different and determine our sex. We all receive an X sex chromosome (so called because of the "X" shape) from our mothers. If we also receive an X sex chromosome from our fathers, we develop

▶ ▶ ▶ ▶

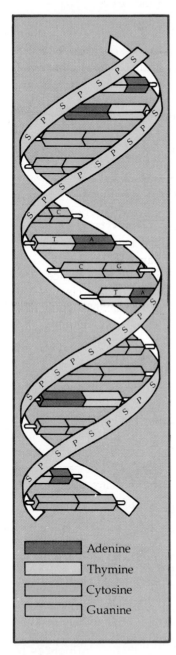

Figure 3.1 The Double Helix of DNA
DNA consists of phosphate, sugar, and a number of bases. It takes the form of a double spiral, or helix.

Adenine
Thymine
Cytosine
Guanine

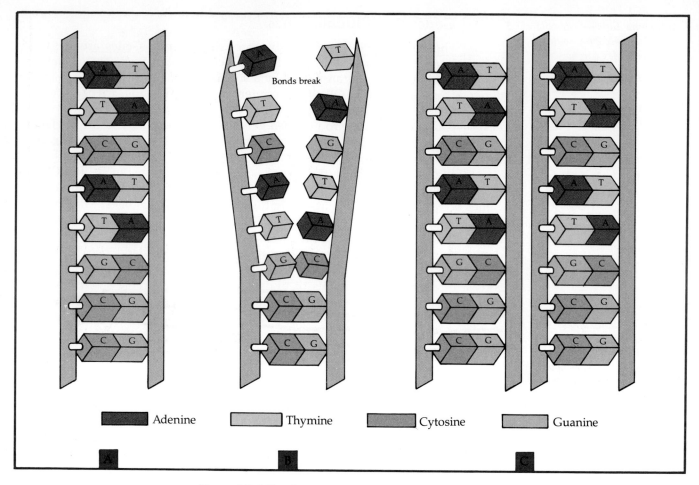

| Adenine | Thymine | Cytosine | Guanine |

Figure 3.2 Mitosis
Part A shows a segment of a strand of DNA prior to mitosis. During mitosis, chromosomal strands of DNA "unzip," as in Part B. One side of the "ladder" and one base of each "rung" remain in each new cell after division. As shown in Part C, the double helix is rebuilt in each new cell, as each incomplete "rung" combines with appropriate molecules within the cell.

into females. If we receive a Y sex chromosome (named after the "Y" shape) from our fathers, we develop into males.

Identical and Fraternal Twins

Now and then a zygote divides into two cells that separate so that each subsequently develops into an individual with the same genetic makeup. These individuals are known as identical or **monozygotic (MZ) twins.** The possible combinations of traits that can result from the combinations of so many thousands of genes is, for all practical purposes, unlimited. The chances that any two people will show completely identical traits, with the exception of MZ twins, are, for all practical purposes, nil.

If, on the other hand, the woman produces two ova in the same month, and they are both fertilized, they develop into fraternal or **dizygotic (DZ) twins.** Identical or MZ twins are important in the study of the relative influences of heredity and environment, because differences between MZ twins are the result of environmental influences (of nurture, not nature).

Monozygotic (MZ) twins
Twins that derive from a single zygote that has split into two; identical twins. MZ twins. Each MZ twin carries the same genetic code.

Dizygotic (DZ) twins Twins that derive from two zygotes; fraternal twins. DZ twins.

▶ ▶ ▶ ▶

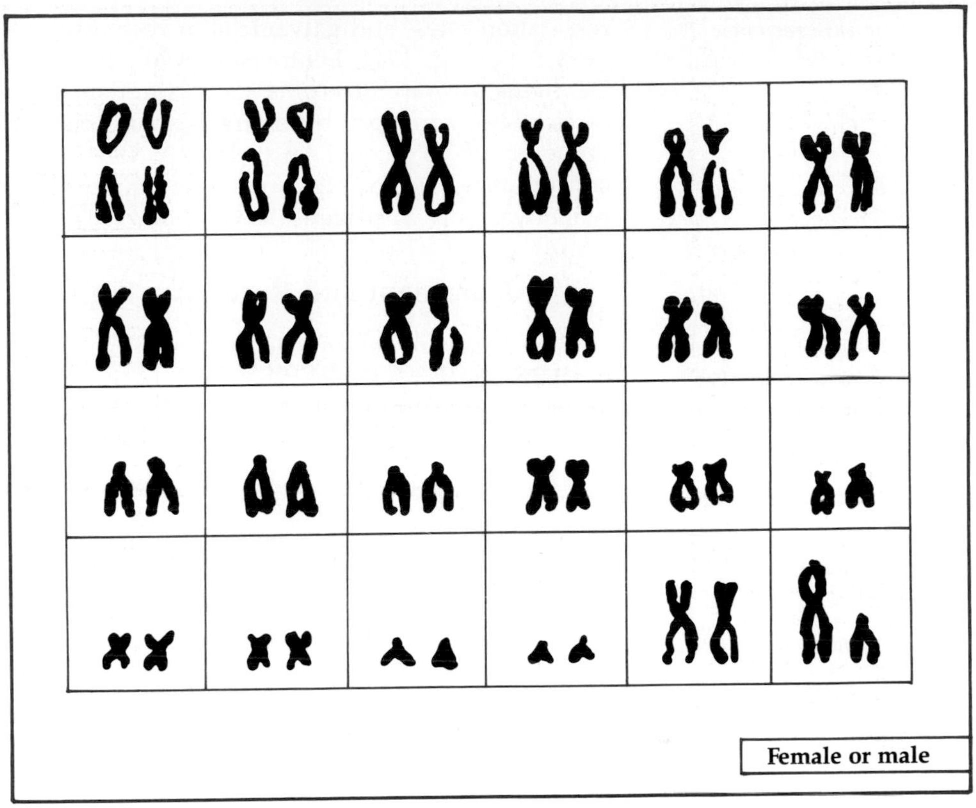

Figure 3.3 The 23 Pairs of Human Chromosomes
Sex is determined by the twenty-third pair of chromosomes. Females have two X sex chromosomes. Males have one X and one Y sex chromosome.

Female or male

Incidence of Twins MZ twins are rarer than DZ twins, occurring once in about every 270 pregnancies (Cassill, 1982; Scheinfeld, 1973). **Demographic** and environmental factors do not appear to have much impact on the incidence of MZ twins, but there is quite a bit of variation in the incidence of DZ twins. Consider ethnicity. Whites in the United States have about one chance in 93 of having DZ twins. Blacks have one chance in 95, whereas Asian-Americans have only about one chance in 150.

DZ twins run in families. If a woman's mother was a twin, chances are one in eight that she will bear twins. If a woman has previously borne twins, the chances similarly rise to one in eight that she will bear twins in subsequent pregnancies. Similarly, women who have borne several children stand increased likelihood of twins in subsequent pregnancies.

As women reach their 40s, ovulation becomes less regular, resulting in a number of months when more than one ovum is released. Thus the chances of twins increase with the woman's age. Fertility drugs also enhance the chances of multiple births.

Resemblances among Twins It is common knowledge that MZ twins look alike. MZ twins are also closer in height than DZ twins. This finding holds even when the identical twins are reared apart and the fraternal twins are reared together (Mittler, 1971; Newman et al., 1937). Other physical similarities between pairs of MZ twins may be more subtle, but they are also strong. For example, classic research shows that MZ twin sisters begin to menstruate about one to two months apart, whereas DZ twins begin to menstruate about a year apart (Petri, 1934). MZ twins are more alike than DZ twins in their pulse rates,

Demographic Having to do with vital statistics.

► ► ► ►

GENETIC INFLUENCES ON DEVELOPMENT

Galvanic skin response The amount of electricity conducted by the sweat in the palm of the hand; a measure of anxiety.

Autism A childhood disorder marked by problems such as failure to relate to others, lack of speech, and intolerance of change.

Enuresis (en-you-REE-sis). Lack of bladder control at an age by which control is normally attained.

Concordance Agreement.

Allele Each member of a pair of genes.

Homozygous Having two identical alleles.

Heterozygous Having two different alleles.

Dominant trait A trait that is expressed.

Recessive trait A trait that is not expressed when the gene or genes involved have been paired with dominant genes. But recessive traits are transmitted to future generations and expressed if they are paired with other recessive genes.

Modifier genes Genes that alter the action of the phenotypical expression of other genes.

Carrier A person who carries and transmits abnormalities, but does not show them.

respiration rates, and **galvanic skin response,** which is a measure of sweating (Jost & Sontag, 1944; Lehtovaara et al., 1965). MZ twins are more likely than DZ twins to share problems such as **autism** (Ritvo et al., 1985), sleepwalking, carsickness, constipation, **enuresis,** nail-biting (Bakwin, 1970, 1971a–d), even vulnerability to alcoholism (Schuckit, 1986, 1987). In the case of autism, the **concordance** rate for MZ twins was 96 percent. The concordance rate for DZ twins was only 24 percent (Ritvo et al., 1985).

Dominant and Recessive Traits

Traits are determined by pairs of genes. Each member of a pair of genes is referred to as an **allele.** When both of the alleles for a trait, such as hair color, are the same, the person is said to be **homozygous** for that trait. When the alleles for a trait differ, the person is **heterozygous** for that trait (Arms & Camp, 1987).

Gregor Mendel (1822–1884), the Austrian monk, established a number of laws of heredity through his work with plants. However, the progress of science did not permit him to discover in his lifetime the true biochemical nature of the gene. Still, Mendel realized that some traits may result from an "averaging" of the genetic instructions carried by the parents. When the effects of both alleles are shown, there is said to be incomplete dominance or codominance.

Mendel also discovered the "law of dominance." For example, the offspring from the crossing of purebred tall peas and purebred dwarf peas were tall, suggesting that tallness is dominant over dwarfism. We now know that many genes carry **dominant traits** or **recessive traits.** When a dominant allele is paired with a recessive allele, the dominant allele appears in the individual.

Brown hair, for instance, is dominant over blond hair. If one parent carries genes for only brown hair, and the other for only blond hair, the children will invariably have brown hair. But brown-haired parents may also carry recessive genes for blond hair, as shown in Figure 3.4. Similarly, the offspring of Mendel's crossing of purebred tall and purebred dwarf peas were not pure. They carried recessive genes for dwarfism.

If the recessive gene from one parent should combine with the recessive gene from the other, the recessive trait will be shown. Brown eyes are similarly dominant over blue eyes, and brown-eyed persons may carry recessive genes for blue eyes. As suggested by Figure 3.4, approximately 25 percent of the offspring of parents who carry recessive blue eye color will have blue eyes. Mendel had found that 25 percent of the offspring of parent peas that carried recessive dwarfism would be dwarfs.

Of course, there are more variations in eye color than brown and blue. We now know that in eye color and other traits, so-called **modifier genes** can alter the expression of traits. Some genes, in fact, "switch" other genes on or off at certain times of development. Sexual maturation and male-patterned baldness are examples of traits "switched on" in adolescence and adulthood.

Carriers People who bear one dominant gene and one recessive gene for a trait are said to be **carriers** of the recessive gene. In the cases of recessive genes that give rise to serious illnesses, carriers of those genes are fortunate indeed to have dominant genes that cancel their effects. Unfortunately, carriers can still transmit their recessive genes to their children.

▶ ▶ ▶ ▶

3 HEREDITY AND PRENATAL DEVELOPMENT

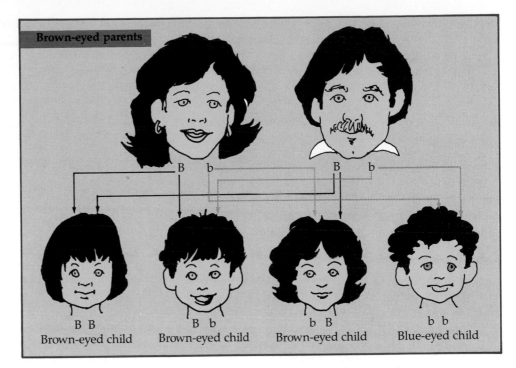

Brown-eyed parents

| B | b | | B | b |

| B B | B b | b B | b b |
| Brown-eyed child | Brown-eyed child | Brown-eyed child | Blue-eyed child |

Figure 3.4 The Transmission of Dominant and Recessive Genes from Generation to Generation
Brown eyes are dominant over blue eyes. Whenever a child carries one gene for brown eyes and one gene for blue eyes he or she will have brown eyes. In this example, two brown-eyed parents each carry a recessive gene for blue eyes. Children have an equal opportunity of receiving genes for brown eyes and blue eyes. The laws of probability are such that 25 percent of the children will show the recessive trait—blue eyes. The other 75 percent will show the dominant trait—brown eyes. But two of three children who show brown eyes carry the recessive trait for transmission to future generations. If a blue-eyed person has a child with someone who has brown eyes but carries a recessive gene for blue eyes, what is the probability that the child will have blue eyes?

Chromosomal and Genetic Abnormalities

A number of diseases reflect chromosomal or genetic abnormalities. Some chromosomal disorders reflect abnormalities in the autosomes (such as Down syndrome), while others reflect abnormalities in the sex chromosomes (as in XYY syndrome). Some genetic abnormalities, such as phenylketonuria, are caused by a single pair of genes, while others are caused by complex combinations of genes. **Multifactoral problems** reflect a genetic predisposition and environmental contributors. Diabetes mellitus, epilepsy, and peptic ulcers are but a few examples of the many multifactoral problems we encounter. A number of chromosomal and genetic abnormalities are discussed below and summarized in Table 3.1.

Multifactoral problems
Problems that stem from the interaction of heredity and environmental factors.

Chromosomal Abnormalities Occasionally children do not have the normal complement of 46 chromosomes. Behavioral as well as physical abnormalities may then result. The risk of chromosomal abnormalities rises with the age of the parents (Hook, 1981).

▶ ▶ ▶ ▶

Table 3.1 Some Chromosomal and Genetic Abnormalities

Cystic fibrosis	A genetic disease in which the pancreas and lungs become clogged with mucus, impairing the processes of respiration and digestion.
Down syndrome	A condition characterized by a third chromosome on the twenty-first pair in which the child shows a characteristic fold of skin over the eye and mental retardation. Risk increases as parents increase in age.
Hemophilia	A sex-linked disorder in which the blood fails to clot properly.
Huntington's chorea	A fatal neurological disorder with onset in middle adulthood.
Neural tube defects	Disorders of the brain or spine, such as *anencephaly*, in which part of the brain is missing, and *spina bifida*, in which part of the spine is exposed or missing. Anencephaly is fatal shortly after birth, but some spina bifida victims survive for a number of years, albeit with severe handicaps.
Phenylketonuria	A disorder in which children cannot metabolize phenylalanine, which builds up in the form of phenylpyruvic acid and causes mental retardation. Diagnosed at birth and controlled by diet.
Retina blastoma	A form of blindness caused by a dominant gene.
Sickle-cell anemia	A blood disorder that mostly afflicts blacks and obstructs small blood vessels, decreasing their capacity to carry oxygen, and heightening the risk of occasionally fatal infections.
Tay-Sachs disease	A fatal neurological disorder that afflicts Jews of European origin.

Down Syndrome In Down syndrome (formerly referred to as Down's syndrome), the twenty-first pair of chromosomes has an extra, or third, chromosome. Down syndrome is thought to be caused by faulty division of the twenty-first pair of chromosomes during meiosis. This abnormality becomes increasingly likely among older parents. With young mothers, Down syndrome occurs in about one birth in 1,500. By age 35 the figure rises to one birth in 300, and by age 45 to one birth in every 30 to 50 (Masters et al., 1985). Down syndrome is usually attributed to the mother, but it should be noted that fathers are responsible for Down syndrome in about 25 percent of cases.

The eyes of children with Down syndrome show a downward-sloping fold of skin at the inner corners, creating a superficial resemblance to Asians. For this reason, the disorder was once termed *mongolism*. However, this term is now recognized as racist and is no longer used.

Down-syndrome children also show a characteristic round face, protruding tongue, and a broad, flat nose. Their motor development lags behind that of normal children, and they are moderately to severely mentally retarded. About half of the girls born with Down syndrome die during the first year, but boys are relatively hardier. Because of their physical problems, most persons afflicted with Down syndrome die by middle age. At middle age they are also prone to memory loss and childish emotions that stem from a form of senility (Kolata, 1985).

The development and adjustment of children with Down syndrome are related to their acceptance by their families. Down-syndrome children reared in the home develop more rapidly and achieve higher levels of functioning than those reared in institutions. Although the birth of a child with Down syndrome is usually traumatic for a family, in most cases they gain acceptance and come to provide the family with a source of pleasure (Gath, 1985).

Sex-Linked Chromosomal Abnormalities A number of disorders stem from abnormal numbers of sex chromosomes and are therefore said to be sex-linked.

▶ ▶ ▶ ▶

Klinefelter's syndrome A chromosomal disorder found among males that is caused by an extra X sex chromosome and characterized by infertility and mild mental retardation.

Turner's syndrome A chromosomal disorder found among females that is caused by having a single X sex chromosome and characterized by infertility.

Phenylketonuria (fee-nill-key-tone-NEW-ree-uh). A genetic abnormality in which phenylpyruvic acid builds up and causes mental retardation.

Huntington's chorea A fatal genetic neurological disorder whose onset is in middle age.

An extra Y sex chromosome is associated with heightening of male secondary sex characteristics in men labeled "supermales." XYY males are somewhat taller than average and develop heavier beards. They are often mildly retarded, particularly in language development. In Chapter 13 we shall see that it was once speculated that XYY syndrome is linked to aggressive criminal behavior. However, most individuals with XYY syndrome do not show records of aggressive criminal behavior. Moreover, the XYY syndrome affects only one male in 1,000, and therefore it could not account for a significant number of aggressive crimes (Witkin et al., 1976).

Other sex-chromosomal abnormalities include Klinefelter's syndrome, Turner's syndrome, and the XXX "superfemale" syndrome. About one male in 500 has **Klinefelter's syndrome,** which is caused by an extra X sex chromosome (XXY). XXY males produce less testosterone than normal males, and the secondary sex characteristics, such as deepening of the voice and a male pattern of bodily hair, do not develop. XXY males are also infertile. XXY males usually have enlarged breasts and poor muscle development. In terms of cognitive functioning and personality, they are usually mildly mentally retarded, particularly in language skills.

About one girl in 10,000 has a single X sex chromosome and as a result develops **Turner's syndrome.** The external genitals of girls with this disorder are normal, but their ovaries are poorly developed, and they produce reduced amounts of estrogen. Because of low estrogen production, they do not develop breasts or menstruate. Girls with this problem are shorter than average and infertile. Psychologically, they are mildly retarded, especially in math and science-related skills.

About one girl in 1,000 has XXX sex chromosomal structure, giving rise to superfemale syndrome. "Superfemales" are normal in appearance. However, they tend to show lower-than-average language skills and poorer memory for recent events, suggestive of mild mental retardation (Rovet & Netley, 1983).

Genetic Abnormalities   A number of disorders have been attributed to defective genes.

PKU   The enzyme disorder **phenylketonuria** (PKU) is transmitted by a recessive gene and affects about one child in 14,000. Therefore, if both parents are carriers, PKU will be transmitted to one child in four (as in Figure 3.4). One child in four will *not* carry the recessive gene. The other two children in four will, like their parents, be carriers.

Children with PKU cannot metabolize *phenylalanine.* As a consequence, this protein builds up in their bodies as phenylpyruvic acid, and damages the central nervous system. The results are mental retardation and emotional disturbance. We have no cure for PKU, but PKU can be detected in newborn children through blood or urine analysis. Children with PKU who are placed on diets low in phenylalanine within three to six weeks after birth develop normally. These children also receive protein supplements (Lofenelac is one) that compensate for the nutritional loss.

Huntington's Chorea   **Huntington's chorea,** the disease that afflicted folk singer Woodie Guthrie, is a progressive degenerative disorder and is a dominant trait. Because its onset is delayed until middle adulthood, many individuals with the defect have borne children only to discover years later that they, and their

▶ ▶ ▶ ▶

Sickle-cell anemia *A genetic disorder that decreases the blood's capacity to carry oxygen.*

Tay-Sachs disease *A fatal genetic neurological disorder.*

Hemophilia *A genetic disorder in which blood does not clot properly.*

Sex-linked genetic abnormalities *Abnormalities due to genes that are found on the X sex chromosome, and thus more likely to be shown by male (who do not have an opposing gene) than female offspring.*

Muscular dystrophy *(DISS-tro-fee). A chronic disease characterized by progressive wasting away of the muscles.*

Genetic counseling *Advice concerning the probabilities that a couple's children will show genetic abnormalities.*

offspring, will inevitably develop the physical (uncontrollable muscle movements) and psychological (loss of intellectual functioning and personality change) symptoms.

Sickle-Cell Anemia **Sickle-cell anemia** and Tay-Sachs disease are both caused by recessive genes. Sickle-cell anemia is found in many groups, but has been particularly worrisome to blacks. It is carried by about two million black Americans (nearly one black in ten). One Hispanic American in 20 is also a carrier.

In sickle-cell anemia, red blood cells take on a sickle shape and clump together, obstructing small blood vessels and decreasing the oxygen supply. The result is increased likelihood of such possibly fatal conditions as pneumonia and heart and kidney failure and lesser problems such as painful and swollen joints and jaundice.

Tay-Sachs Disease **Tay-Sachs disease** is a fatal degenerative disease of the central nervous system that is most prevalent among Jews of East European origin. About one in 25 U.S. Jews carries the recessive gene for the defect, and so the chance that a Jewish couple will both carry the gene is about one in 625. Victims of Tay-Sachs disease gradually lose muscle control. They become blind and deaf, retarded and paralyzed, and die by the age of 5.

If both parents carry recessive genes for Tay-Sachs disease, the fetus stands a one in four chance of showing the disorder. Because of heightened awareness and careful screening, only 13 children with Tay-Sachs disease were born in 1980, as compared with about 100 in 1970.

Sex-Linked Genetic Abnormalities Some genetic defects, such as **hemophilia,** are carried on only the X sex chromosome. For this reason they are referred to as **sex-linked genetic abnormalities.** They also involve recessive genes. Females, who contain two X sex chromosomes, are less likely than males to show sex-linked disorders, since the potential for the disorder would have to be present in both of a female's sex chromosomes to be expressed. But such sex-linked diseases *are* shown by the sons of female carriers, since the genetic instructions carried in their X sex chromosomes are not canceled by genetic instructions on their Y sex chromosomes. Queen Victoria was a carrier of hemophilia and transmitted the blood disorder to many of her children, who, in turn, carried it into a number of the ruling houses of Europe. For this reason, hemophilia has been referred to as the "royal disease."

One form of **muscular dystrophy,** Duchenne's muscular dystrophy, is sex-linked. Muscular dystrophy is characterized by weakening of the muscles that can lead to wasting away, inability to walk, and sometimes death. Other sex-linked abnormalities include diabetes, color blindness, and some types of night blindness.

Genetic Counseling and Prenatal Testing

In an effort to help parents avert predictable tragedies, **genetic counseling** is becoming widely used. In this procedure, information about a couple's genetic backgrounds is compiled to determine the possibility that their union may result in genetically defective children. Some couples whose natural children would be at high risk for genetic diseases elect to adopt.

▶ ▶ ▶ ▶

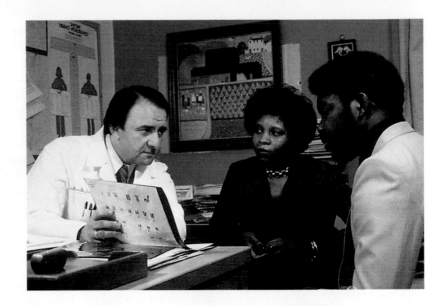

Genetic Counseling In genetic counseling, information about a couple's genetic backgrounds is assembled so that they can make judgments concerning the advisability of bearing children. They are also informed of methods such as amniocentesis, which allow them to learn whether their children will bear certain genetic defects in utero.

Amniocentesis Pregnant women may also confirm the presence of certain genetic and chromosomal abnormalities in their children through amniocentesis, a procedure carried out about 15 weeks after conception (Figure 3.5). Fluid is withdrawn from the amniotic sac (also called the "bag of waters") containing the fetus. Sloughed-off fetal cells are then separated from amniotic fluid, grown in a culture, and examined microscopically for genetic abnormalities.

Amniocentesis is commonly carried out with women who become pregnant past the age of 35, because the chances of Down syndrome increase dramatically as women approach or pass the age of 40 (Abrams & Bennet, 1981). But women carrying the children of aging fathers may also wish to have amniocentesis. About one in four cases of Down syndrome have been linked to abnormal cell division in sperm, and the sperm of aging men is at greater risk for faulty division (Holmes, 1978). Amniocentesis can detect the presence of sickle-cell anemia, Tay-Sachs disease, spina bifida, muscular dystrophy, and Rh incompatibility in the fetus. For these reasons, it is recommended for women who (or whose partners) carry sickle-cell anemia and Tay-Sachs disease. It is also recommended for those with family histories of the other three disorders.

The results of amniocentesis are not available until the pregnancy is well into the fifth month (Golbus et al., 1979). The amniotic fluid is drawn at 14–15 weeks after conception, and the growth and examination of the culture take another two to three weeks. Some women do not realize how long it takes to obtain the results of an amniocentesis and therefore begin their pregnancies with the idea that they can have an abortion if "things" are not progressing properly. However, they then find themselves in serious conflict over aborting an abnormal fetus whose major organ systems are almost fully formed and who is making dramatic gains in weight.

Amniocentesis also permits parents to learn the sex of their unborn child through examination of the twenty-third pair of chromosomes. But amniocentesis carries some risk of miscarriage and of complications such as cramping or bleeding, and it is unwise to have the procedure done solely for this purpose. If you were having an amniocentesis, would you want to know the sex of your unborn child, or would you prefer to wait?

▶ ▶ ▶ ▶

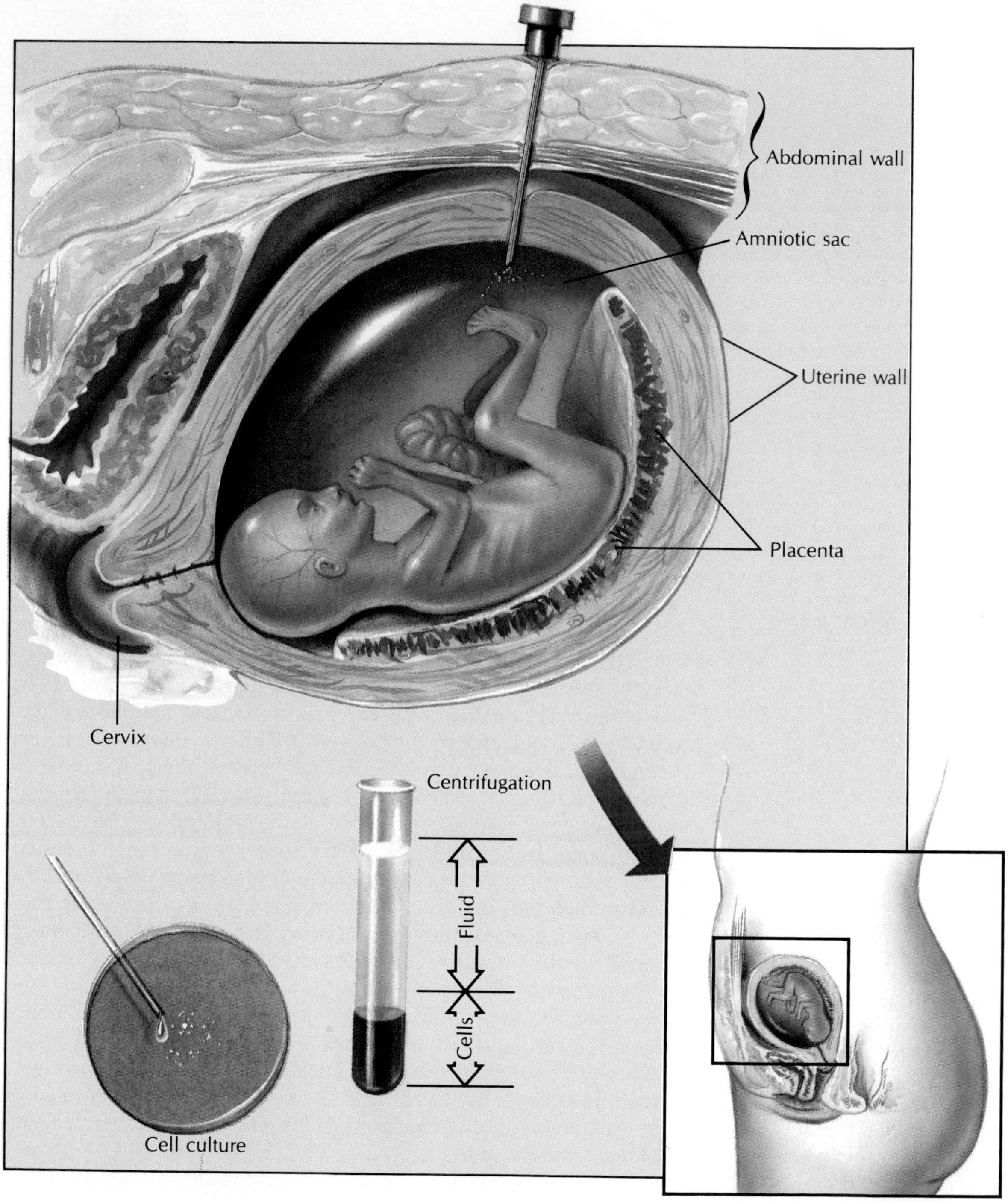
Abdominal wall
Amniotic sac
Uterine wall
Placenta
Cervix
Centrifugation
Fluid
Cells
Cell culture

Figure 3.5 Amniocentesis
This modern method for examining the genetic material sloughed off by a fetus into amniotic fluid allows the prenatal identification of certain genetic and chromosomal abnormalities. Amniocentesis also allows parents to learn the sex of their unborn child. Would you want to know?

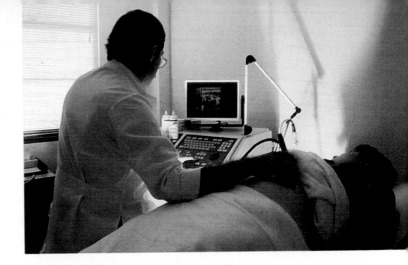

Ultrasound In the ultrasound technique, soundwaves are bounced off the fetus in utero and provide a "picture" that enables professionals to detect various abnormalities.

Ultrasound *Sound waves too high in pitch to be sensed by the human ear.*

Sonogram *A procedure for using ultrasonic sound waves to create a "picture" of an embryo or fetus.*

Chorionic villi sampling *(CORE-ee-ON-ick Vill-eye). A method for detecting genetic abnormalities that samples the membrane enveloping the amniotic sac and fetus.*

Ultrasound Another common method of prenatal testing is the use of **ultrasound** to form a picture of the fetus. The picture is referred to as a **sonogram.** "Ultrasound" is so high in pitch that it cannot be detected by the human ear. However, it can be "bounced off" the unborn child in the same way that radar is bounced off objects in order to form a "picture" of the object.

Ultrasound is used as an adjunct with amniocentesis in order to better determine the position of the fetus. In this way the physician can make sure that the needle enters the sac surrounding the fetus, and not the fetus itself. Ultrasound is also used to locate fetal structures when intrauterine transfusions are necessary for the survival of the unborn child in Rh disease.

Ultrasound has been used for about 20 years to track the growth of the fetus and detect certain gross abnormalities. Ultrasound can detect the baby's heartbeat within a month following conception. However, a panel assembled by the National Institutes of Health in 1984 warned that ultrasound, like amniocentesis, should not be used routinely. While listing 27 legitimate uses for ultrasound, the panel also noted that the long-term effects of ultrasound on mothers and children have been virtually unexplored. Moreover, experiments on cell cultures and laboratory animals with higher-than-normal levels of ultrasound have resulted in chromosomal damage, impaired immune systems, and retarded fetal growth. We do not know whether we should have concern about "normal" levels of ultrasound, but it certainly makes sense to be cautious when we are uncertain.

Chorionic Villi Sampling **Chorionic villi sampling** (CVS) is similar to amniocentesis. CVS is carried out during the seventh or eighth week of pregnancy. A small tube is inserted through the vagina into the uterus, and pieces of material from the outer membrane that contains the amniotic sac are snipped off. Results are available within days of the procedure. CVS is used in the place of amniocentesis. However, CVS is riskier to the fetus and, for this reason, is not so widely used.

Blood Tests The presence of a variety of disorders can be detected by testing the blood of the parents. For instance, the presence of the recessive genes for sickle-cell anemia and Tay-Sachs disease can be detected from analysis of blood

▶ ▶ ▶ ▶

GENETIC INFLUENCES ON DEVELOPMENT

Genetic Engineering

▷
▷
▷
▷
▷   In the recently developed technology of genetic engineering, the genetic structures of organisms are changed by direct manipulation of their reproductive cells. Even as you read these words, patents are pending on new life forms—mostly microscopic—that biologists and corporations hope will be marketable in some fashion or another.

Current research suggests that genetic engineering may lead to some other exciting results (McAuliffe & McAuliffe, 1983) in the not-too-distant future. They include:

- New vaccines for diseases like hepatitis and herpes
- Ways of detecting predispositions for disorders like cancer, heart disease, and emphysema by studying a newborn's (or fetus's) genetic code
- Prenatal screening for fatal hereditary diseases like Huntington's chorea and cystic fibrosis*
- Learning how "spelling errors" in the genetic code (for example, ATTC rather than ATGC in a given segment of DNA) may cause inherited diseases
- Modifying the genetic code of fetuses or children to prevent disease
- Creating new wonder drugs from the materials that compose DNA

The purposeful manipulation of genetic material also has its frightening aspects. Some fear that genetic manipulation can lead to future scenarios like that portrayed by Aldous Huxley in his still powerful 1932 novel *Brave New World.* Through a fictitious method called "Bokanovsky's Process," egg cells from parents who are identically suited for certain types of labor are made to "bud." From these buds up to

*In amniocentesis the general chromosomal structure, rather than the intricate and elusive genetic code, is examined.

96 people with identical genetic makeups can be developed—filling whatever labor niches are required by society.

In the novel the director of a "hatchery" is leading a group of students on a tour. One student is foolish enough to question the advantage of Bokanovsky's Process:

"My good boy!" The Director wheeled sharply round on him. "Can't you see? Can't you see?" He raised a hand; his expression was solemn. "Bokanovsky's Process is one of the major instruments of social stability!"

Major instruments of social stability (wrote the student).

Standard men and women; in uniform batches. The whole of a small factory staffed with the products of a single bokanovskied egg.

"Ninety-six identical twins working 96 identical machines!" The voice was almost tremulous with enthusiasm. "You really know where you are. For the first time in history." He quoted the planetary motto. "Community, Identity, Stability." Grand words. "If we could bokanovskify indefinitely the whole problem would be solved."

Through Bokanovsky's Process we might be able to eliminate certain genetic disorders. We might even be able to lower the incidence of crime, aggression, and abnormal behaviors. But I ask those of you who think that all this might be a good idea to consider that unless the parent was a genius, from none of these "bokanovskified" eggs would there emerge a Shakespeare, a Beethoven, or a Madame Curie. We might avoid tyrants, but we would also be bereft of individuals who might shape the world in ways we cannot foresee.

▶ ▶ ▶ ▶

samples. As noted, when both parents carry genes for these disorders, the disorders can be detected in the fetus by means of amniocentesis or CVS.

Another kind of blood test, the **alphafetoprotein assay,** is used to detect neural-tube defects. As a result of neural-tube defects, the alphafetoprotein (AFP) level in the mother's blood is elevated. However, the mother's AFP level also varies with other factors. For this reason, the diagnosis of neural-tube defect is confirmed by other methods of observation, such as fetoscopy.

Fetoscopy   In **fetoscopy** a narrow tube is surgically inserted through the abdomen into the uterus to allow examination of the fetus. A small lens can be attached to the fetoscope, permitting visual examination. A small needle may also be attached, which enables the direct withdrawal of a blood sample from the fetus. Unfortunately fetoscopy, like CVS, is riskier than amniocentesis and its use is quite limited.

Conception: Against All Odds

Conception is the union of a sperm cell and an ovum. Conception, from one perspective, is the beginning of a new human life. But conception is also the culmination of a fantastic voyage in which one of several hundred thousand ova produced by the woman unites with one of several hundred *billion* sperm produced by the man. As noted earlier, women are born with all the ova they will ever produce, but men produce sperm cells continuously and ejaculate hundreds of millions at a time.

Sperm cells develop through several stages. In one early stage, they are **spermatocytes,** each of which contains 46 chromosomes, including one X and one Y sex chromosome. Each spermatocyte engages in meiosis, meaning that it divides into two **spermatids,** each of which has 23 chromosomes. Half the spermatids have X sex chromosomes, and the other half have Y sex chromosomes, which is one reason that the numbers of men and women are rather balanced. It's not just good luck. But sperm with Y sex chromosomes appear to swim faster than sperm with X sex chromosomes. For this and other reasons, about 120–150 boys may be conceived for every 100 girls. However, male fetuses suffer a higher rate of **spontaneous abortion** than females, frequently during the first month of pregnancy. For this reason, some women who were carrying boys may menstruate almost on time and never realize that they had been pregnant. At birth boys outnumber girls by a ratio of only 106 to 100 (Purtillo & Sullivan, 1979). But since there is also a higher rate of infant mortality among boys, the numbers of males and females becomes even more equalized by the time they show an interest in pairing off.

Spermatids, in any event, mature into sperm cells with heads, cone-shaped midpieces, and tails. The head contains the cell nucleus that houses the 23 chromosomes. The midpiece contains structures that provide energy that permits the tail to lash back and forth in a swimming motion. Each sperm cell is about 1/500th of an inch long, one of the smallest types of cells in the body.

Four hundred million or so sperm are present in a typical ejaculation. This may seem a wasteful number, since only one can fertilize an ovum. But only one in 1,000 will ever arrive in the vicinity of an ovum. Millions deposited in the vagina simply flow out of the woman's body because of gravity, unless

▶ ▶ ▶ ▶

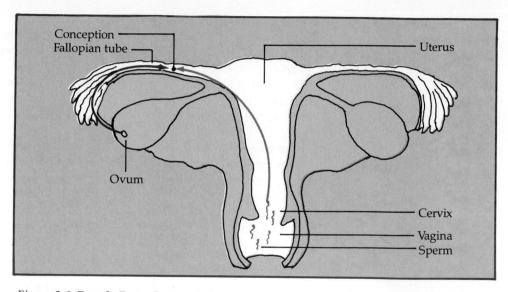

Figure 3.6 Female Reproductive Organs
Conception is something of an obstacle course. Sperm must survive the pull of gravity, vaginal acidity, risk winding up in the wrong fallopian tube, and surmount other hurdles before they reach the ovum.

she remains prone for quite some time. Normal vaginal acidity kills many more. Many remaining sperm swim through the cervix into the uterus (Figure 3.6), against the current of fluids that are continuously discharged from the woman's body. Some surviving sperm reach the fallopian tubes, where conception normally takes place, 60–90 minutes after ejaculation. Half of these, of course, enter the "wrong" tube—that is, the one without the egg. Perhaps 2,000 of those that enter the tube containing the egg manage to swim the final two inches against the currents generated by the cilia that line the tube.

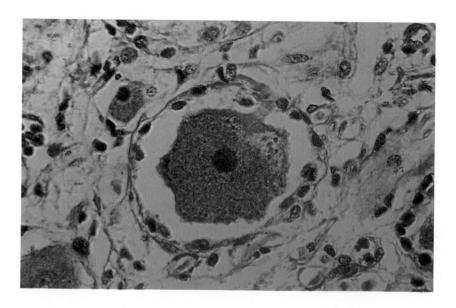

A Ripening Ovum in an Ovarian Follicle

▶ ▶ ▶ ▶

3 HEREDITY AND PRENATAL DEVELOPMENT

Although women at birth already contain their 400,000 ova, they are immature in form. Each ovum is contained in its own follicle, or capsule, within an ovary. The ovaries also produce the female hormones estrogen and progesterone.

At puberty, in response to hormonal command, some ova begin to mature. Each month one egg (occasionally more than one) is released from its ovarian follicle about midway during the menstrual cycle and enters a nearby fallopian tube. Contrary to popular belief, ova are released into the abdominal cavity and not directly into a fallopian tube. How they find their ways into these narrow tubes is one of the mysteries of biology. It might take three to four days for an egg to be propelled by cilia and, perhaps, contractions in the wall of the tube, the few inches to the uterus. Unlike sperm, eggs do not propel themselves.

If the egg is not fertilized, it is discharged through the uterus and the vagina—sloughed off, along with the **endometrium** that had formed to support an embryo—in the menstrual flow. During a woman's reproductive years, only about 400 ova (that is, one in 1,000) will ripen and be relased. How these ova are selected is also a mystery.

In an early stage of development, egg cells, like spermatocytes, contain 46 chromosomes. But each developing egg cell contains two X sex chromosomes, not a Y and an X sex chromosome. After meiosis, each ovum contains 23 chromosomes, one of which is an X sex chromosome.

Ova are much larger than sperm. (The chicken egg and the six-inch ostrich egg are each just *one cell.*) Human ova are barely visible to the eye, but their bulk is still thousands of times larger than that of sperm cells. Figure 3.7 shows sperm swarming around an egg.

The sperm that approach the egg secrete the enzyme **hyaluronidase,** which briefly thins the gelatinous layer called the **zona pellucida** that surrounds the egg. Only one sperm enters. Its "selection" is another biological mystery.

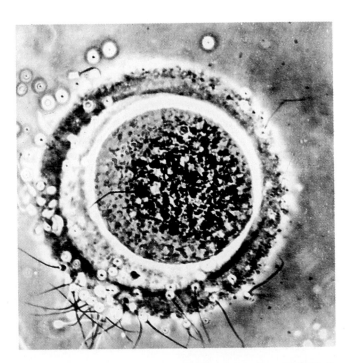

Figure 3.7 The Moment of Conception
This dramatic photograph shows the fertilization of an ovum by a sperm. Fertilization occurs in the fallopian tubes. Thousands of sperm may wind up in the vicinity of an ovum, but only one fertilizes it. How this sperm cell is "selected" remains one of the mysteries of nature.

▶ ▶ ▶ ▶

Then the zona pellucida thickens, locking other sperm out. The chromosomes from the sperm cell line up across from the corresponding chromosomes in the egg cell. Conception finally occurs as the chromosomes combine to form 23 new pairs with a unique set of genetic instructions.

Alternate Ways of Becoming Parents

As noted, for couples who want children, few problems are more frustrating than inability to conceive. Physicians are usually not concerned until couples who are trying to conceive have not done so for six months. The term *infertility* is usually not applied until the couple has not conceived for a year.

At least 10 to 15 percent of U.S. couples are infertile (Francoeur, 1985). In about four of ten cases, the problem lies with the man. In the other six, it lies with the woman.

Male Fertility Problems   Fertility problems in the male include (1) a low sperm count, (2) low sperm **motility,** (3) infectious diseases, and (4) direct trauma to the testes (Rathus, 1983). Low (or zero) sperm count is the most common problem with men.

Artificial Insemination   In some cases, multiple ejaculations of men with low sperm counts have been collected and quick-frozen. The sperm have then been injected into the woman's uterus at time of ovulation. This is one **artificial insemination** procedure. Sperm may also be collected from men with low sperm motility and injected into their partners' uteruses.

Artificial insemination is more likely to be used when the man is completely infertile. In such cases the woman can be artificially inseminated with the sperm of a donor who resembles the man in physical traits and ethnic background. The child then bears the genes of at least one of the parents.

Female Fertility Problems   Women may encounter infertility because of (1) lack of ovulation, (2) infections, (3) endometriosis, and (4) obstructions or malfunctions of the reproductive tract (Rathus, 1983).

The most frequent problem, failure to ovulate, may stem from causes such as hormonal irregularities, malnutrition, and stress. "Fertility" drugs such as clomiphene and pergonal contain hormones that help regulate ovulation. They have also been linked to multiple births. Most of the time when we hear of quadruplets and quintuplets being born, it is to women who have used such drugs (Austin & Short, 1972).

Local infections may impede passage of sperm or ova through the fallopian tubes and elsewhere. Infections include **pelvic inflammatory disease** (PID)—which actually refers to several diseases caused by bacteria, viruses, and the sexually transmitted disease, gonorrhea. Antibiotics are sometimes helpful.

Endometriosis   **Endometriosis** can block the fallopian tubes and also worsens the "climate" for conception for reasons that are not well understood. Endometriosis has been labeled the "yuppies' disease" because its effects are cumulative and experienced most strongly by women who have postponed bearing children. Hormone treatments and surgery are sometimes successful in reducing endometriosis to the point where women can conceive.

Motility Self-propulsion.

Artificial insemination Injection of sperm into the uterus in order to fertilize an ovum.

Pelvic inflammatory disease Any of a number of diseases that infect the abdominal region, impairing fertility. Abbreviated PID.

Endometriosis Inflammation of endometrial tissue sloughed off into the abdominal cavity rather than out of the body during menstruation. A disease characterized by abdominal pain and impairment of fertility.

▶ ▶ ▶ ▶

In vitro fertilization (VEE-tro). *Fertilization of an ovum in a laboratory dish.*

Embryonic transfer The *transfer of a 5-day-old embryo from the uterus of one woman to that of another.*

Surrogate mother A woman *who is artificially inseminated and carries to term a child who is then given to another woman.*

A number of recent methods have been developed to help women with blocked fallopian tubes and related problems bear children.

In Vitro Fertilization   Louise Brown, the world's first "test-tube baby," was born in England in 1978 after having been conceived by means of **in vitro fertilization** (IVF). In this method, ova are surgically removed from the mother's ovary and allowed to ripen in a laboratory dish. Then they are fertilized by the father's sperm. The fertilized egg is injected into the mother's uterus and becomes implanted in the uterine wall.

Donor IVF   A variation known as *donor* IVF can be used when the mother-to-be does not produce ova. In donor IVF, an ovum from another women is fertilized and injected into the uterus of the mother-to-be (Lutjen et al., 1984).

Embyonic Transfer   A related method under study for women who do not produce ova is termed **embryonic transfer.** A volunteer is artificially inseminated by the infertile woman's partner. After five days the embryo is removed from the volunteer and placed within the uterus of the mother-to-be, where it becomes implanted in the uterine wall and is carried to term (Bustillo et al., 1984). At this time, the in-vitro and transfer methods remain costly and are considered experimental.

Surrogate Mothers   **Surrogate mothers** have become increasingly used in recent years for women who are infertile. For a fee in the range of $10,000 to $20,000 plus medical expenses, the surrogate mother is artifically inseminated by the husband of the infertile woman and carries the baby to term. The surrogate signs a contract to turn the baby over to the wife of the father. As with artificial insemination by a donor, the baby carries the genes of one of the parents.

Superficially, surrogate motherhood might seem the mirror image of the technique in which a fertile woman is artificially inseminated with the sperm of a donor. But many important psychological and social issues are raised. For one thing, sperm donors usually do not know the identity of the women who have received their sperm. Nor do they observe their children developing within the mothers-to-be. However, surrogate mothers are involved in the entire process of prenatal development. They can become attached to their unborn children, and turning them over to other women once they are born can instill a devastating sense of loss. For this reason, some surrogate mothers have refused to part with their babies. Court cases have resulted, but the legal issues surrounding surrogate motherhood are not yet resolved.

Another objection to surrogate motherhood is voiced by social critics who view it as just one more example of exploitation of the poor. It is normally the wealthy who seek to use surrogate mothers, and it is normally the woman in need of extra income who consents to act as a surrogate. From this perspective, the surrogate mother then allows her body to be used (as a prostitute might allow her body to be used), and ultimately she must surrender the child that she might wish to retain.

We also have very few answers about the long-term effects of alternate ways of becoming parents on children (Elias & Annas, 1986). We are familiar with some of the questions that adopted children raise about their own value and about their natural parents. But what of the child conceived in a laboratory dish? What of the child turned over by a surrogate mother?

▶ ▶ ▶ ▶

Just as new technologies are enhancing the chances for infertile couples to become parents, new methods seem to be leading to the day when we can preselect the sex of our children. In sex preselection, too, there are major social and ethical issues.

Selecting the Sex of Your Child: Fantasy or Reality?

What would happen if we could select the sex of our children? Would we predominantly select boys or girls? Would it all balance out in the end?

According to a survey of 5,981 women, most women who would make a choice would select boys for their first children, but then balance the family with girls (Westoff & Rindfuss, 1974). Assuming that each woman in the study had two or more children, boys would still outnumber girls by a large margin. But only 39 percent of the women surveyed would select the sex of their child. Forty-seven percent would not, and 14 percent were not sure.

The proportion of male births would mushroom around the world. Shulan Jiao and his colleagues at the Chinese Academy of Sciences note that preference for boys is placing China's family-planning goal of one child per family in jeopardy. The problem stems from the "feudal idea that men are superior to women; thus, for a family to be without a male child is considered a misfortune" (Jiao et al., 1986, p. 357). Given the prejudice against girls, what would happen if the Chinese could select the sex of their children but remained pressured to have just one child per family? China's population problems would be eliminated in a generation.

A Potpourri of Folklore on Preselection of Sex In any event, folklore is filled with bizarre notions as to how to predetermine the sex of one's offspring. Some cultures have advised intercourse under the full moon to beget boys. Aristotle suggested making love during a North wind for sons, but a South wind if one favored daughters. Sour food was once advised to increase the chances of having a boy. Consumption of sweets, by contrast, would yield a girl. A husband yearning for a son could also try wearing his boots to bed. And on the thesis that boys were seeded by the right testicle, eighteenth-century French nobles were advised to have the left one removed. Needless to say, none of these measures work. More recent methods sound more reasonable, if less colorful. Still, not all scholars are convinced that they are much more reliable.

Shettles' Approach Landrum Shettles (Rorvik & Shettles, 1970; Shettles, 1972) reports that sperm bearing the Y sex chromosome are smaller than those bearing the X sex chromosome, and that they are faster swimmers. But sperm with the X sex chromosome are more durable. From these assumptions, Shettles and other researchers (Cherry, 1973; Kogan, 1973) derive a number of strategies for selecting the sex of one's children:

In order to optimize the chances of having a boy, (1) the man should abstain from ejaculating for several days prior to his partner's time of ovulation; (2) the couple should engage in sexual intercourse on the day of ovulation; (3) the man should be penetrating deeply at time of ejaculation; and (4) the woman can make the vagina more hospitable to Y-bearing sperm by douching beforehand with two tablespoons of baking soda per quart of warm water. This will lower vaginal acidity.

▶ ▶ ▶ ▶

In order to optimize the chances of having a girl, (1) the couple should engage in sexual intercourse about two days (or slightly more) before ovulation; (2) the woman can make the vagina *less* hospitable to Y-bearing sperm by douching with two tablespoons of vinegar per quart of warm water to raise vaginal acidity before intercourse; (3) the woman should avoid orgasm on the (debatable) assumption that orgasm facilitates the journey of sperm; and (4) the man should ejaculate with shallow penetration.

A combination of these methods has been asserted to result in the conception of a child of the desired sex in about 80 percent of cases (Kogan, 1973), but many professionals consider these figures to be exaggerated (Harlap, 1979; Karp, 1980; Simcock, 1985). The suggestions that rely on the relatively faster swimming of Y-bearing sperm are probably more useful than those that involve douching with vinegar or baking soda (Wallis, 1984).

In any event, over-the-counter kits for sex preselection are coming on the market. One of them, Gender Choice, contains ovulation-predicting equipment and chemicals that alter the acidity of the vagina. The manufacturer of the kit claims "up to 85 percent reliability" in preselecting a boy, and "up to 80 percent reliability" in preselecting a girl. Notice the *up to* preceding the percentages. There is no guarantee.

Sperm-Separation Procedures   California researcher Ronald Ericsson has devised a sperm-separation procedure based on the swimming rates of Y- and X-bearing sperm. Albumin, a thick liquid protein similar to egg white, impedes the progress of X-bearing sperm more so than that of the faster-swimming Y-bearing sperm. Ericsson places semen on top of a test tube containing albumin. The Y-bearing sperm migrate to the bottom more rapidly than the X-bearing sperm. They are collected and used in artificial insemination. Ericsson's method reportedly leads or has led to conception of boys 75 percent of the time, as compared with the usual 53 percent (Glass & Ericsson, 1982).

A method pioneered in Japan separates Y- from X-bearing sperm on the basis of the different electrical charges carried by the two types (Clark & Doi, 1983). An updated version of the dietary approach suggests that women who want to conceive a girl should eat foods rich in magnesium and calcium, whereas women who want a boy should choose foods rich in sodium and potassium (Stolkowski & Choukroun, 1981). Each of these approaches supposedly results in a success rate of about 80 percent.

Social critics brand sex-preselection technology as "stupendously sexist" (Powledge, 1981), even though many couples would use these methods to try to conceive daughters. However, there can be little doubt that the methods, if widely enough used, would see a dramatic increase in the proportion of boys in the United States and around the world.

Stages of Prenatal Development

The Chinese are nine months older than we are when they are the same age. Why? The Chinese date a person's age from the assumed time of conception rather than birth. The months following conception are eventful, indeed.

Pregnancy can be dated from the onset of the last menstrual period, in

▶ ▶ ▶ ▶

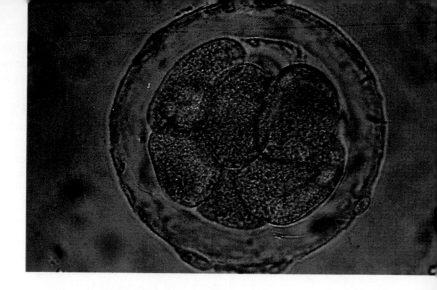

Early in the germinal stage of development, the dividing ball of cells as it has reached eight cells

which case the normal gestation period is 280 days. Pregnancy can also be dated from the assumed date of fertilization, which normally occurs two weeks after the beginning of the menstrual cycle. With this type of accounting, the gestation period is 266 days.

During the months following conception, the single cell formed by the union of sperm and egg will multiply—becoming two, then four, then eight, and so on. Tissues, organs, and structures will form that gradually take the unmistakable shape of a human being. By the time a fetus is ready to be born, it will contain hundreds of billions of cells—more cells than there are stars in the Milky Way galaxy. Prenatal development is divided into three periods: the germinal stage (approximately the first two weeks), the embryonic stage (the first two months), and the fetal stage. It is also common to speak of prenatal development as lasting for three trimesters of three months each.

The Germinal Stage

Germinal stage *The period of development between conception and the implantation of the embryo in the uterine wall.*

Period of the ovum *Another term for* germinal stage.

Blastocyst *A stage of development in which the zygote has the form of a sphere of cells surrounding a cavity of fluid.*

Embryonic disk *The platelike inner part of the blastocyst that differentiates into the* ecto-derm, mesoderm, *and* en-doderm *of the embryo.*

Trophoblast *The outer part of the blastocyst, from which the amniotic sac, placenta, and umbilical cord develop.*

▶ ▶ ▶ ▶

Within 36 hours after conception, the zygote suddenly divides into two cells. It then divides repeatedly, as it proceeds on its journey to the uterus. Within another 36 hours, it has become 32 cells. Three to four days are required to reach the uterus. The mass of dividing cells wanders about the uterus for another three to four days before beginning to become implanted in the uterine wall. Implantation requires another week or so. The period from conception to implantation is called the **germinal stage** or the **period of the ovum.** See Figure 3.8.

A few days into the germinal stage, the dividing cell mass has taken the form of a fluid-filled ball of cells called a **blastocyst.** A blastocyst already shows differentiation. Cells are separating into groups according to what they will become. Two distinct inner layers of cells are forming within a thickened mass of cells called the **embryonic disk.** They will become the baby.

The outer part of the blastocyst, or **trophoblast,** at first contains a single layer of cells. But the trophoblast rapidly differentiates into four membranes that will protect and nourish the embryo. One membrane produces blood cells until the embryo's liver can develop and take over this function. Then it dis-

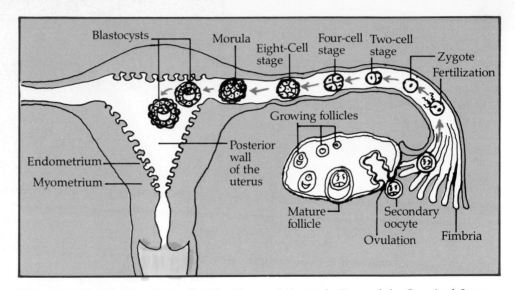

Figure 3.8 The Ovarian Cycle, Fertilization, and the Early Days of the Germinal Stage
The zygote first divides at about 36 hours after conception. Continuing division creates the hollow sphere of cells referred to as the blastocyst. The blastocyst usually becomes implanted in the posterior (back) wall of the uterus.

appears. Another membrane develops into the umbilical cord and the blood vessels of the placenta. A third develops into the amniotic sac, and the fourth becomes the chorion, which will line the placenta.

Prior to implantation, the dividing cluster of cells is nourished solely by the yolk of the original egg cell, and it does not gain in mass. The blastocyst can gain in mass only from outside nourishment, which it will gain once implanted in the uterine wall. Implantation is sometimes accompanied by perfectly normal bleeding as threadlike structures from the trophoblast rupture the small blood vessels that line the uterus at this time of the menstrual cycle. But bleeding can also be a sign of miscarriage, and so it concerns many women who want to become pregnant. Many women do in fact miscarry at this time, but their menstrual flows appear about on schedule, so that they may not even realize they had conceived. More boys than girls appear to be lost in this way, and miscarriage usually stems from abnormalities in the developmental process. Women who experience some nausea, bloating, changes in appetite, and tenderness in the breasts prior to their periods may have miscarried. However, most women who do not miscarry at time of implantation go on to have normal pregnancies and normal babies, despite earlier implantation bleeding.

The Embryonic Stage

Embryonic stage The stage of prenatal development that lasts from implantation through the eighth week, characterized by the development of the major organ systems.

Cephalocaudal From head to tail.

Proximodistal From the inner part (or axis) of the body outward.

The **embryonic stage** lasts from implantation until about the eighth week of development. During this stage, the major body organ systems differentiate. Development follows two general trends—**cephalocaudal** (Latin for from "head to tail"), and **proximodistal** (Latin for "near to far"). As you can note from the apparently oversized heads of embryos and fetuses at various stages of prenatal development (Figure 3.9), growth of the head takes precedence over the growth of the lower parts of the body. If you also think of the body as containing a central axis that coincides with the spinal cord, the growth

▶ ▶ ▶ ▶

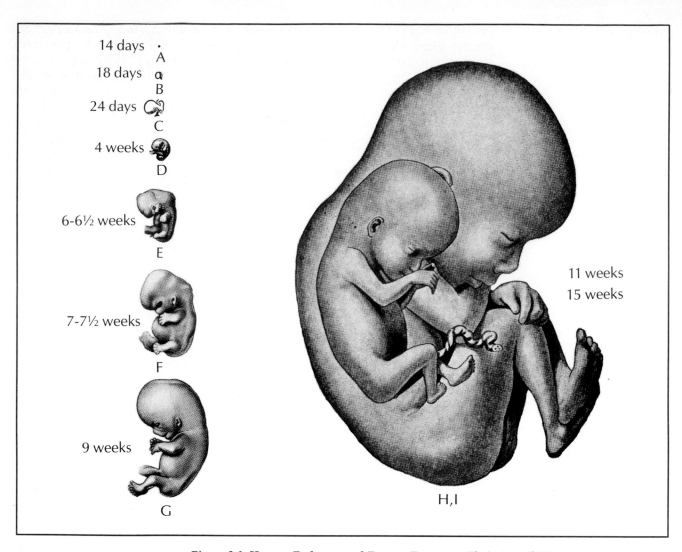

14 days · A
18 days B
24 days C
4 weeks D
6-6½ weeks E
7-7½ weeks F
9 weeks G
11 weeks
15 weeks
H,I

Figure 3.9 Human Embryos and Fetuses Drawn at Their Actual Sizes

Ectoderm *The outermost cell layer of the newly formed embryo, from which the skin and nervous system develop.*

Neural tube *A hollowed-out area in the blastocyst from which the nervous system develops.*

Endoderm *The inner layer of the embryo, from which the lungs and digestive system develop.*

Mesoderm *The central layer of the embryo, from which the bones and muscles develop.*

▶ ▶ ▶ ▶

of the organ systems close to this axis (that is, *proximal)* takes precedence over the growth of the extremities *(distal* areas). We do not know exactly why growth follows the cephalocaudal and proximodistal patterns, but we can note that the relatively early maturation of the brain and the major organ systems allows them to participate in the nourishment and further development of the unborn child.

During the embryonic stage, the outer layer of cells of the embryonic disk, or **ectoderm,** develops into the nervous system, sensory organs, nails, hair, teeth, and the outer layer of skin. At about 21 days, two ridges appear in the embryo and fold to compose the **neural tube,** from which the nervous system will develop. The inner layer, or **endoderm,** forms the digestive and respiratory systems, the liver, and the pancreas. A bit later during the embryonic stage the **mesoderm,** a middle layer of cells, becomes differentiated. The mesoderm develops into the excretory, reproductive, and circulatory systems, the muscles, the skeleton, and the inner layer of the skin.

During the third week after conception, the head and the blood vessels

Androgens Male sex hormones.

Amniotic sac The sac containing the fetus.

begin to form. During the fourth week, a primitive heart begins to beat and pump blood—in an organism that is only one-fifth of an inch in length. It will continue to beat without rest every minute of every day for perhaps 80 or 90 years. "Arm buds" and "leg buds" begin to appear toward the end of the first month. Eyes, ears, nose, and mouth begin to take shape. By this time, the nervous system, including the brain, has also begun to develop.

In accord with the principle of proximodistal development, the upper arms and legs develop first, followed by the forearms and lower legs. Next come hands and feet, followed at 6 to 8 weeks by webbed fingers and toes. By the end of the second month the limbs are elongating and separated; the webbing is gone. The head has become rounded and the facial features have become distinct—all in an embryo about one inch long and weighing *one-thirtieth* of an ounce. During the second month the nervous system begins to transmit messages. By the end of the embryonic period, teeth buds have also been formed. The embryo's own kidneys are filtering acid from the blood, and its own liver is producing red blood cells.

Hormones and Prenatal Sexual Differentiation   At about 5 to 6 weeks, when the embryo is only a quarter to a half an inch long, nondescript sex organs have been formed. By about the seventh week following conception, the genetic code (XY or XX) begins to assert itself, leading to changes in the internal and external sex organs. If a Y sex chromosome is present, testes will form and begin to produce **androgens** that prompt further masculinization of the sexual organs.

In the absence of male sex hormones, the embryo will develop female sex organs. Female sex hormones are not needed to induce these changes. If an embryo with an XY sex chromosomal structure were prevented from producing androgens, it would develop female sex organs—despite the genetic code.

The Amniotic Sac   The unborn child—embryo and fetus—develops within an **amniotic sac,** a protective environment in the mother's uterus. The sac is sur-

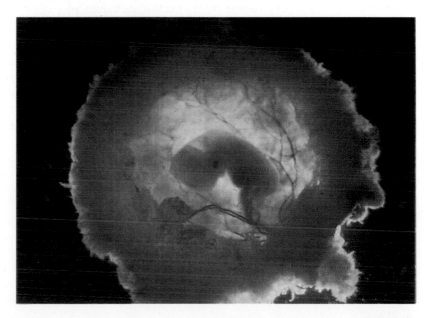

A Human Embryo at Seven Weeks
At this late part of the embryonic stage, the major organ systems have already become well differentiated.

▶ ▶ ▶ ▶

Amniotic fluid Fluid within the amniotic sac that suspends and protects the fetus.

Placenta (pluh-SENT-uh). An organ connected to the fetus by the umbilical cord. The placenta serves as a relay station between mother and fetus for exchange of nutrients and wastes.

Umbilical cord A tube that connects the fetus to the placenta.

rounded by a clear membrane and contains **amniotic fluid,** in which the developing child is suspended. Amniotic fluid serves as a "shock absorber," preventing the child from being damaged by the mother's movements. It also helps maintain an even temperature.

The Placenta   The **placenta** is a mass of tissue that permits the embryo (and, later on, the fetus) to exchange nutrients and wastes with the mother. The placenta is unique in origin; it grows from material supplied both by mother and embryo. Toward the end of the first trimester it will have become a flattish, round organ about seven inches in diameter and one inch thick—larger than the fetus itself. The fetus is connected to the placenta by the **umbilical cord.** The mother is connected to the placenta by the system of blood vessels in the uterine wall. The umbilical cord develops about five weeks after conception and reaches 20 inches in length. It contains two arteries through which maternal nutrients reach the fetus. A vein carries waste products back to the mother.

The circulatory systems of mother and unborn child do not mix. A membrane in the placenta permits only certain substances to pass through. Oxygen and nutrients are passed from the mother to the embryo. Carbon dioxide and other wastes are passed from the child to the mother, where they are removed by the mother's lungs and kidneys. Unfortunately, a number of other substances can pass through the placenta. They include some microscopic disease organisms—such as those that cause syphilis and German measles—and some drugs, including aspirin, narcotics, alcohol, and tranquilizers.

The placenta also secretes hormones that preserve the pregnancy, prepare the breasts for nursing, and stimulate the uterine contractions that prompt childbirth. Ultimately, the placenta passes from the woman's body after the child is delivered. For this reason it is also called the "afterbirth."

The Fetal Stage

The fetus begins to turn and respond to external stimulation at about the ninth or tenth week. By the end of the first trimester, all the major organ systems have been formed (Arms & Camp, 1987). The fingers and toes appear fully formed. The eyes can be clearly distinguished, and the sex of the fetus can be determined visually.

The second trimester is characterized by further maturation of fetal organ systems and dramatic gains in size. The brain continues to mature, contributing to the fetus's ability to regulate its own basic body functions. During the second trimester, the fetus advances from one *ounce* to two *pounds* in weight and grows three to four times in length, from about four to 14 inches.

During the second trimester, soft, downy hair grows above the eyes and on the scalp. The skin turns ruddy because of blood vessels that show through the surface. (During the third trimester, fatty layers will give the red a pinkish hue.)

Fetal Perception: Bach at Breakfast and Beethoven at Brunch?   When I was a beginning graduate student and knew everything, I was astounded by the naiveté of pregnant women who listened to Bach or Beethoven or who read Shakespeare in order to promote the cultural development of their fetuses. But in more recent years, I must confess that my wife and I have made more of an effort to "expose" our unborn children to good music as well.

► ► ► ►

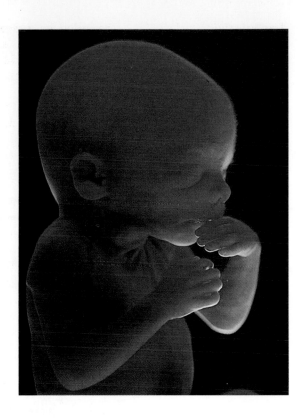

A Human Fetus at Twelve Weeks

Research shows that by the thirteenth week of pregnancy, the fetus does respond to sound waves. In a classic experiment, Sontag and Richards (1938) rang a bell near the mother and the fetus responded with muscle movements similar to those of the startle reflex shown after birth. During the third trimester, fetuses respond to sounds of different frequencies through a variety of movements and changes in heart rate, suggesting that by this time they can discriminate pitch (Bernard & Sontag, 1947).

A recent experiment by DeCasper and Fifer (1980) is even more intriguing. In this study, 16 women read the Dr. Seuss book *The Cat in the Hat* out loud twice daily during the final month and a half of pregnancy. After birth their babies were given pacifiers that could switch on one of two recordings, depending on how they were sucked. Sucking on them in one way would activate recordings of their mothers reading *The Cat in the Hat*. Sucking on them in another way would activate their mothers' readings of another book, *The King, the Mice, and the Cheese*, which was written in very different cadences. The babies "chose" to hear only *The Cat in the Hat*.

During the latter days of pregnancy, Bach at breakfast and Beethoven at brunch may not be a bad idea. It just may do more than help the food go down.

Fetal Movements In the middle of the fourth month, the mother usually detects the first fetal movements and may suddenly feel that the baby is "alive," although, of course, it has been alive from the moment of conception—and the germ cells from which it was formed were also of living material.

By the end of the second trimester, the fetus moves its limbs so vigorously that the mother may complain of being kicked—often at 4 A.M. It opens

▶ ▶ ▶ ▶

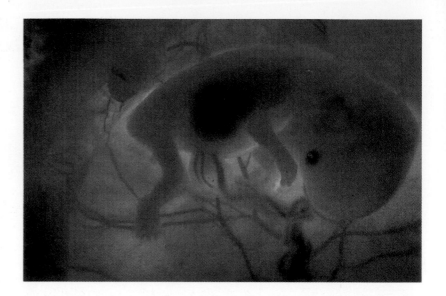

A Human Fetus at Four and One-Half Months

and shuts its eyes, sucks its thumb, alternates between periods of wakefulness and sleep, and perceives lights and sounds. It also turns somersaults, which can be clearly perceived by the mother. The umbilical cord is designed so that it will not break or become dangerously wrapped around the fetus, no matter how many acrobatic feats it performs.

Fetuses show different patterns of prenatal activity (Sontag, 1966). Slow squirming movements begin at about 5 or 6 months. Sharp jabbing or kicking movements begin at about the same time and increase in intensity until shortly prior to birth. There are also sharp spasms of the diaphragm, or fetal hiccoughs. Some fetuses have been known to hiccough for days on end, which can, understandably, be both distressing and alarming to the mother. However, hiccoughing fetuses do not seem to be at greater risk for developing serious problems after birth. Different fetuses show different levels of activity and different combinations of kinds of activities. Interestingly, prenatal activity predicts ac-

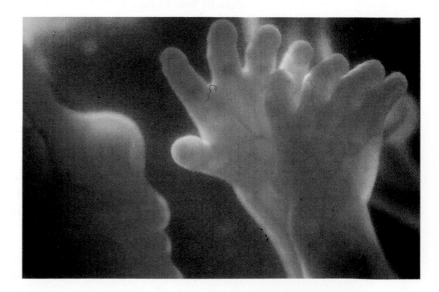

The Hands of a Human Fetus at Five Months

▶ ▶ ▶ ▶

Prenatal Surgery

▷
▷
▷
▷

▷ Six months into her pregnancy, Loretta Lyons' obstetrician told her that an ultrasound scan of her uterus had found a potentially fatal problem in her unborn child. A urinary tract blockage was threatening to destroy its kidneys. Until recently, Lyons could have done nothing but await the birth of a child doomed by irreversible damage to the kidneys and lungs. But in September 1983, surgeons at a university hospital inserted a tube through the mother and into the fetus to drain the obstructive fluids. After delivery in December, both mother and baby were doing quite well.

Prenatal surgery remains experimental. Only a few dozen women have received operations for urinary-tract obstructions in the fetus. Perhaps two dozen fetuses have been operated on to drain accumulations of cerebrospinal fluid in the brain, the cause of hydrocephalus.

The successes of prenatal surgery for urinary-tract blockages may be largely attributed to ultrasound scanning, which provides physicians with an accurate picture of a swollen bladder and enlarged kidneys. In one experimental procedure used at the University of California at San Francisco, ultrasound guides physicians as they force a hollow metal tube through the wall of the uterus into the swollen bladder of the fetus. A plastic shunt is then pushed through the tube into the bladder. Once in the bladder, it is positioned to provide a passageway from the bladder to the amniotic sac surrounding the fetus. Amniotic fluid is largely formed from fetal urine, and the shunt permits this process to continue despite blockage in the urinary tract. Additional surgery is undertaken after delivery in order to remove the shunt and permanently unblock the urinary tract itself.

tivity levels after birth. For instance, highly active fetuses show more advanced motor development six months after birth than do their more lethargic counterparts (Richards & Nelson, 1938). Moreover, fetuses who show wide variations in heart rate during the eighth month of prenatal development also show wide variations at the age of 20 years (Lacey & Lacey, 1958). That is, activity levels and predispositions toward emotional responsiveness—at least as measured by heart rate—tend to show developmental stability.

Toward the end of the second trimester, fetuses are nearing the **age of viability.** Still, only about one baby in ten born at the end of the second trimester who weighs less than two pounds will survive, even with expert medical care (Behrman & Rosen, 1976; Katchadourian, 1985).

During the third trimester, the organ systems of the fetus continue to mature. The heart and lungs become increasingly capable of sustaining independent life. The fetus gains about five and one-half pounds and doubles in length. Newborn boys average about seven and one-half pounds and newborn girls about seven pounds.

During the seventh month, the fetus normally turns upside down in the uterus so that delivery will be head-first. By the end of the seventh month,

Age of viability The age at which a fetus can sustain independent life.

▶ ▶ ▶ ▶

the fetus will have almost doubled in weight, gaining another one pound twelve ounces, and increasing another two inches in length. If born now, chances of survival are about 50 percent. If born at the end of the eighth month, the odds are overwhelmingly in favor of survival.

As the fetus grows it becomes cramped in the uterus, and movement is constricted. Many women become concerned that their fetuses are markedly less active during the ninth month than previously, but most of the time this change is normal.

Environmental Influences on Prenatal Development

Scientific advances have not only helped us chronicle the details of prenatal development. They have also made us keenly aware of the types of things that can go wrong and, in many cases, what we can do to prevent these problems. In this section we consider some of the environmental factors that have an impact on our prenatal development. These include the mother's diet, diseases and disorders of the mother, Rh incompatibility, drugs, smoking, maternal stress, and the mother's age.

The Mother's Diet

It is widely believed that fetuses "take what they need" from their mothers, even at the expense of their mothers' own nutritional needs. If this were true, pregnant women would not have to be highly concerned about their diets. However, malnutrition in the mother, especially during the last trimester when the fetus should be making rapid gains in weight, has been linked to low birth weights and heightened infant mortality during the first year (Newton, 1972; Stein et al., 1975). There is conflicting evidence as to whether maternal malnutrition leads to long-term effects among children who survive the first year. But at least one study (Richardson, 1972) reported that children whose mothers were malnourished during their pregnancies attained lower scores on intelligence tests and showed poorer school achievement than the children of well-nourished mothers.

Pregnant women who follow adequate diets do tend to experience fewer problems during pregnancy and to spend somewhat less time in labor. Their babies are more likely to be average or above average in size (Winick & Noble, 1966; Salkind & Haskins, 1982). Their babies are also less likely to contract colds and serious respiratory disorders.

Evidence on supplementing the diets of women who might otherwise be deficient in their intake of calories and protein shows modest positive effects on the motor development of their infants. As compared to a control group, the 12-month-old children of lower-class New York women who received dietary supplements showed motor gains, as measured by length of play (Rush et al., 1980). Women in a Taiwan study normally ate low-calorie diets high in rice, sweet potatoes and other vegetables, but low in animal protein. At 8 months of age, children of women who received calorie and protein supplements, like those in the New York study, showed significantly greater motor development

▶ ▶ ▶ ▶

than controls, as measured by crawling and sitting, pulling themselves to a standing position, and taking stepping movements (Joos et al., 1983).

Pregnant women require the following food elements in order to maintain themselves and to give birth to healthy babies: protein, most heavily concentrated in meat, fish, poultry, eggs, beans, milk, and cheese; vitamin A, found in milk and vegetables; vitamin B, found in wheat germ, whole grain breads, and liver; vitamin C, found in citrus fruits; vitamin D, derived from sunshine, fish-liver oil, and vitamin-D-fortified milk; vitamin E, found in whole grains, some vegetables, eggs, and peanuts; folic acid, found in leafy green vegetables; iron, concentrated heavily in meat—especially liver—egg yolks, fish, and raisins; the trace minerals zinc and cobalt, found in seafood; calcium, found in milk and stone-ground grains; and, yes, calories. It should be noted that women who are allergic to some of these foods, or who find them distasteful, can usually find substitutes. While women who eat a well-rounded diet do not require food supplements, most doctors recommend vitamin and mineral supplements to be on the safe side. However, women should not assume that "more is better," especially with vitamins and calories, as we shall see below.

Women can expect to gain quite a bit of weight during pregnancy because of the growth of the placenta, amniotic fluid, and the fetus itself. Most women will gain 20 to 25 pounds. Overweight women may gain less, and slender women may gain 30 pounds or so (Winick, 1981). Regular weight gains are most desirable, about one-half pound per week during the first half of the pregnancy, and one pound per week during the second half. Sudden large gains or losses in weight should be discussed with the doctor.

Over the years, the pendulum has swung back and forth on concepts of ideal weight gains during pregnancy. Early in the century it was believed that greater weight gains would assure proper nutrition for mother and fetus. During the 1960s and part of the 1970s, the watchword was quality, not quantity. Pregnant women were advised to watch their weight. It was felt that excess weight posed risks for the mother and might be hard to take off following pregnancy—both of which fears bear some truth. But now the pendulum has swung slightly again, so that women who put on more than two pounds per month are not necessarily seen as creating problems for themselves. It should also be noted that a woman in the seventh or eighth month who finds herself overshooting a weight-gain target of, say, 25–30 pounds, should avoid a crash diet—especially during the period when the fetus is making its most dramatic gains in weight.

Diseases and Disorders of the Mother

Many environmental influences or agents can harm the developing embryo and fetus. They are referred to as **teratogens,** from the Greek *teras,* meaning "monster." They include drugs such as thalidomide and alcohol, Rh-positive antibodies, metals such as lead and mercury, radiation, excessive hormones, and disease organisms such as bacteria and viruses. Many disease organisms cannot pass through the placenta and infect the embryo or fetus, but extremely small organisms, such as those responsible for syphilis, mumps, chicken pox, and measles, can. Pregnant women may also incur disorders such as toxemia that are not passed on to the child, but that affect the child by altering the environment within which the child is developing.

Teratogen An agent that gives rise to abnormalities in the embryo or fetus.

Syphilis A sexually transmitted disease which, in advanced stages, can attack major organ systems.

▶ ▶ ▶ ▶

Critical Periods of Vulnerability For the unborn child, there is a **critical period** or timespan when exposure to a particular teratogen is most harmful. This is because of the timing of the development of certain structures. For example, the heart develops rapidly during the third to fifth weeks after conception. As you can see in Figure 3.10, the heart is most vulnerable to teratogens at that time. The arms and legs, which develop somewhat later, are most vulnerable during the fourth through eighth weeks. Since the major organ systems differentiate during the embryonic stage, the unborn child is generally most vulnerable to teratogens during this six-week period of prenatal development.

Let us now consider the effects of specific teratogens.

Rubella (German Measles) **Rubella** is a viral infection. The embryos of women who contract rubella during the first month or two of pregnancy, when the major organ systems are undergoing rapid differentiation, run close to a 50 percent chance of incurring problems such as deafness, mental retardation, heart disease, or cataracts. The risk of major disorders declines as the pregnancy progresses and the embryo matures into a fetus. The fetal risk for such disorders

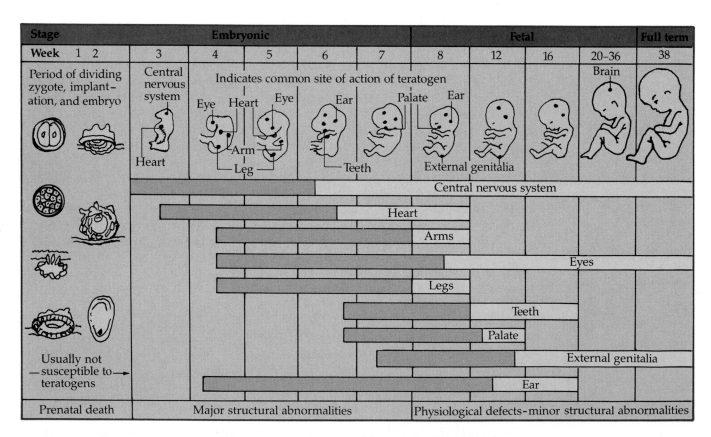

Figure 3.10 Critical Periods in Prenatal Development
The developing child is most vulnerable to teratogens during the embryonic period, when the organ systems are forming. The periods of greatest vulnerability for organ systems are shown in blue. Periods of lesser vulnerability are shown in yellow.

▶ ▶ ▶ ▶

drops to one in ten for women who contract rubella during the third month of pregnancy.

Nearly 85 percent of adult women have had rubella as children and acquired immunity in this way. Women who are uncertain as to whether they have had rubella may be tested and, if they are not immune, they can be vaccinated *prior to pregnancy.* Inoculation during pregnancy is risky because the vaccine gives the mother a mild case of the disease, thereby affecting the unborn child.

Because of increased awareness of rubella and inoculation, the incidence of rubella-related disorders in children has declined dramatically in the United States. The number of children born with defects caused by rubella dropped from about 20,000 in 1964–1965 to fewer than 100 in 1983 (Franklin, 1984).

Syphilis **Syphilis** is a sexually transmitted disease that is caused by the spiral-shaped bacterium *treponema pallidum.* Miscarriage, **stillbirth,** or **congenital** syphilis may result. Congenital syphilis can impair the vision and hearing, damage the liver, or deform the bones and teeth.

Blood tests are run routinely early in pregnancy to diagnose syphilis and other problems. Because treponema pallidum bacteria do not readily cross the placental membrane during the first months of pregnancy, the fetus will probably not contract syphilis if an infected mother is treated successfully with antibiotics before the fourth month of pregnancy.

Other sexually transmitted diseases in the mother which also affect the unborn child are chlamydia, genital herpes, and AIDS.

AIDS **AIDS** (acquired immune deficiency syndrome) cripples the body's immune system, leaving victims prey to a wide variety of fatal illnesses, including respiratory disorders and certain types of cancer. Fifty percent or more of the individuals who are infected by the AIDS virus are likely to develop full-blown cases of the disease. So far as we know, just about everyone who develops a full-blown case dies.

Information about AIDS is being gathered rapidly, and the picture it presents is changing just as rapidly. Early in the 1980s it was assumed that the virus that causes AIDS was transmitted primarily by means of homosexual contacts and blood transfusions. Individuals who shared hypodermic needles while "shooting up" drugs were also at risk. But it was assumed that most heterosexuals were safe from the disease, although women might receive the AIDS virus from bisexual partners. Now it is known that AIDS can be transmitted by heterosexual contact as well. Transmission of AIDS is bidirectional— the virus can be transmitted from women to men, as well as from men to women.

Evidence reported by Surgeon General C. Everett Koop (1987) indicates that the AIDS virus can be passed to children in utero. Research at Albert Einstein Medical Center in New York and elsewhere suggests that babies with congenital AIDS have characteristic facial features which may soon become known as a part of "fetal AIDS syndrome," according to pediatrician Stephen Levine (1987). The virus might also be transmitted to children by breastfeeding (Rogers, 1985). Children have also received AIDS through blood transfusions and during childbirth. In the African country of Rwanda, where children receive blood transfusions to treat malarial anemia, 22 percent of the AIDS sufferers are children (Serrill, 1987). During childbirth it is normal for blood vessels in

▶ ▶ ▶ ▶

the mother and the baby to rupture, providing another opportunity for an exchange of blood and transmission of the virus.

Bloodtests   Koop (1987) recommends that women considering pregnancy should have bloodtests to determine whether they have been exposed to the virus that causes AIDS. He adds, "I would think anybody who is getting married today would want to be tested and would want to know" whether his or her intended spouse had been infected as well. He noted that women who are discovered to have been infected and who are less than 13 weeks pregnant are being advised to have abortions. Apparently about 50 percent of those advised are doing so.

Controversy is rife about whether children with AIDS should be permitted to attend public schools. The medical wisdom of the moment is that the AIDS virus cannot be transmitted by the sort of "casual contact" that characterizes interactions among children. Even a bite from an AIDS victim is thought to be unlikely to transmit the virus, since relatively little of the virus is found in saliva. Nevertheless, children with AIDS are frequently ostracized in the schools, and many parents of healthy children boycott schools attended by victims. In some municipalities, the identities of children with AIDS are kept confidential to avoid ostracism, but some parents of healthy children contend that the anonymity of potential transmitters endangers their own children.

Pregnant women who have or who fear they have AIDS or other sexually-transmitted disorders should discuss them frankly with their physicians. In some cases, measures can be taken which will help protect their children.

Toxemia   **Toxemia** is a life-threatening disease, characterized by high blood pressure, that may afflict women late in the second or early in the third trimester. The first stage of toxemia, *preeclampsia,* is diagnosed by protein in the urine, swelling from fluid retention, and high blood pressure, and may be relatively mild. As preeclampsia worsens, the mother may have headaches and visual problems that reflect the heightened blood pressure, and there may be abdominal pain. *Eclampsia,* the final stage, may bring convulsions, coma, and, in some cases, death. Women with toxemia often have **premature** or undersized babies.

Toxemia appears to be linked to malnutrition, but the causes are unclear. Ironically, undernourished women may gain weight rapidly through fluid retention, but their swollen appearance may then discourage eating. Pregnant women who gain weight rapidly but have not increased their food intake should consult their obstetricians.

Toxemia A life-threatening disease that can afflict pregnant women and is characterized by high blood pressure.

Premature Born before the full term of gestation.

Rh incompatibility A condition in which antibodies produced by the mother are transmitted to the child and may cause brain damage or death.

▶ ▶ ▶ ▶

Rh Incompatibility

In **Rh incompatibility,** antibodies produced by the mother may be transmitted to a fetus or newborn infant and cause brain damage or death. *Rh* is a simple blood protein which is found in the red blood cells of some individuals and causes them to produce antibodies. Rh incompatibility occurs when a woman who does not have this factor, and is thus *Rh negative,* is carrying an *Rh-positive* fetus, which may happen if the father is Rh positive. This negative-positive combination occurs in about 10 percent of marriages in the United States, and resultant Rh incompatibility becomes a problem in a minority of the resultant pregnancies.

Rh incompatibility does not usually adversely affect a first child. Since mother and fetus have separate circulatory systems, it is unlikely that Rh-positive fetal red blood cells will enter the mother's body and cause her to produce antibodies. But the chances of an exchange of blood increase during childbirth, especially when the placenta detaches from the uterine wall. The mother then produces Rh-positive antibodies which may enter the fetal bloodstream during later pregnancies or deliveries and cause a condition known as *fetal erythroblastosis,* which may result in anemia, mental deficiency, or death to the fetus.

Fortunately, the blood-typing of pregnant women significantly decreases the threat of erythroblastosis. If an Rh-negative mother is injected with the vaccine Rhogan within 72 hours after delivery of an Rh-positive baby, she will not develop the dangerous antibodies. A fetus or newborn child at risk for erythroblastosis may also receive a preventive blood transfusion, which removes the mother's antibodies from its blood.

Drugs Taken by the Mother (and Father)

Many of us are familiar with the fetal problems caused by drugs such as **thalidomide,** a sedative used widely in the 1960s, that has been linked to birth defects such as missing or foreshortened limbs when taken during the embryonic stage. But we are not so likely to be aware that more common drugs, such as aspirin, have also been associated with problems in children born to users (Scher & Dix, 1983). Moreover, there is a good deal of controversy about the effects on the fetus of illegal recreational drugs such as cocaine and marijuana.

A special problem with cocaine and marijuana is the widespread perception that many of the "horror stories" associated with their use have been exaggerated in moralistic efforts to curb usage. However, research suggests that using these drugs during pregnancy may pose certain risks for the fetus, as shown in Table 3.2 (Chasnoff et al., 1985; Fried et al., 1984). In 1982, the National Academy of Sciences reported, for example, that high doses of marijuana during pregnancy cause birth defects in laboratory animals. However, the Academy also pointed out that no adequate studies have yet been carried out to determine whether marijuana harms the human fetus.

Another question is whether it is harmful to the fetus if its father uses such substances. Do drugs alter the genetic material in the father's sperm and consequently harm the child? Little is known about this. Another question is whether the father's use of certain substances during pregnancy will harm the fetus. Here we know a bit more. We shall see, for example, that cigarette smoke produced by the father or other people may indeed be detrimental to the fetus. Marijuana smoke may also be harmful.

In this section we discuss the effects of various drugs on the unborn child—prescription drugs, over-the-counter drugs, and illegal drugs. Pregnant women may, with their physicians' consultation, be able to find acceptable substitutes for widely used but potentially harmful drugs, such as aspirin. But one rule of thumb for a healthy pregnancy is to avoid nearly all drugs, and to use even apparently harmless drugs only with the obstetrician's consent.

Thalidomide A sedative used in the 1960s that has been linked to birth defects.

Thalidomide   Thalidomide was marketed in the early 1960s as a safe, mild sedative that would help pregnant women cope with insomnia and nausea. It

▶ ▶ ▶ ▶

Table 3.2 Possible Effects on the Fetus of Certain Agents during Pregnancy

AGENT	POSSIBLE EFFECT
Accutane	Malformation, stillbirth
Alcohol	Mental retardation, addiction, hyperactivity, undersize
Aspirin (large doses)	Respiratory problems, bleeding
Bendectin	Cleft palate? Heart deformities?
Caffeine (coffee, many soft drinks, chocolate, etc.)	Stimulates fetus; other effects uncertain
Cigarettes	Undersize, premature delivery, fetal death
Cocaine	Spontaneous abortion, neurological problems
Diethylstilbestrol (DES)	Cancer of the cervix or testes
Heavy metals (lead, mercury)	Hyperactivity, mental retardation, stillbirth
Heavy sedation during labor	Brain damage, asphyxiation
Heroin, Morphine, other narcotics	Addiction, undersize
Marijuana	Early delivery? Neurological problems? Birth defects?
Paint fumes (substantial exposure)	Mental retardation
PCB, dioxin, other insecticides and herbicides	Under study (possible stillbirth)
Progestin	Masculinization of female embryos, heightened aggressiveness?
Rubella (German measles)	Mental retardation, nerve damage impairing vision and hearing
Streptomycin	Deafness
Tetracycline	Yellow teeth, deformed bones
Thalidomide	Deformed or missing limbs
Vitamin A (large doses)	Cleft palate, eye damage
Vitamin D (large doses)	Mental retardation
X rays	Malformation of organs

A variety of chemical and other agents have been found harmful to the fetus, or are strongly implicated in fetal damage. Pregnant women should consult their physicians about their diets, vitamin supplements, and use of any drugs—including drugs available without a prescription.

was available in Germany and England without prescription. Within a couple of years, nearly 8,000 deformed babies had been born in these countries and elsewhere as a result of their mothers having taken thalidomide during pregnancy.

The experience of thalidomide provides a dramatic example of the critical periods for various teratogens. For example, the extremities undergo rapid development during the last four weeks of the embryonic stage (see Figure 3.10). Women using thalidomide between the fifth and seventh weeks following conception almost invariably gave birth to babies with deformed or absent limbs.

Antibiotics Several antibiotics may be harmful to the fetus. Tetracycline, which is frequently prescribed for flu symptoms and colds, may lead to yellowed teeth and deformed bones. Other antibiotics have been implicated in deafness and jaundice.

Hormones Women at risk for miscarriages have been prescribed hormones such as progestin and DES in order to help maintain their pregnancies.

▶ ▶ ▶ ▶

3 HEREDITY AND PRENATAL DEVELOPMENT

Progestin *A hormone used to maintain pregnancy that can cause masculinization of the fetus.*

DES *Abbreviation for* diethylstilbestrol, *a powerful estrogen that has been linked to cancer in the reproductive organs of children of women who used the hormone when pregnant.*

Progestin **Progestin** is similar in chemical composition to male sex hormones. When taken at about the time that male sex organs begin to differentiate in the embryo, it can promote the masculinization of the external sex organs in individuals with a female (XX sex chromosome) genotype. In Chapter 12 we shall see that children with XX genotypes and masculinized sex organs have been encouraged in some cases to develop as females, and, in others, as males. Progestin taken during the first trimester has also been linked to increased levels of aggressive behavior during childhood (Reinisch, 1981).

DES **DES** (short for *diethylstilbestrol*) is a powerful estrogen that was used commonly between the 1940s and the 1960s. DES appears to have caused cervical and testicular cancer in many of the children of women who used it to maintain their pregnancies. It appears that among DES users about one daughter in 7,000 will develop cancer in the reproductive tract (Orenberg, 1981).

There are other problems: Daughters of DES takers are more likely to miscarry their own children or to have premature deliveries (Barnes et al., 1980). Sons of DES users have higher-than-average rates of infertility (Stenchever et al., 1981). The women who used DES now also appear to be at greater risk for certain medical problems themselves. For example, former DES patients appear to have a higher-than-average risk for breast cancer (Greenberg et al., 1984).

Vitamins While pregnant women are usually prescribed daily multivitamins to maintain their own health and to promote the development of their unborn children, too much of a good thing can apparently be dangerous. The use of high doses of vitamins such as A, B_6, D, and K has been associated with birth defects. Vitamin A has been linked with cleft palate and eye damage, and vitamin D with mental retardation.

Narcotics Narcotics such as heroin and methadone readily cross the placental membrane. Narcotics are addictive, and the fetuses of women who use them regularly during pregnancy apparently can become addicted to them. There are reports of violent kicking of the fetus when their mothers suspend usage for a while (Desmond & Wilson, 1975). Then, when the mothers take the drug, the kicking subsides. It may well be that these fetuses are irritable because of periodic withdrawal symptoms.

Pregnant women who use narcotics regularly may also deliver addicted children. If they confide in their obstetricians, their newborn infants are usually given the narcotic shortly after birth so that they will not suffer withdrawal symptoms such as muscle tremors, fever, intestinal problems, difficulty in breathing, and, in severe cases, convulsions and death. The neonates are then usually withdrawn gradually from the drug. Still, infant mortality, usually from respiratory problems, is more likely to occur among the children of mothers addicted to narcotics.

It has not yet been shown whether the use of narcotics during pregnancy influences the long-term development of children who come through delivery and the first weeks of postnatal life without major problems. However, a number of researchers fear that repeated periods of withdrawal from narcotics are linked to oxygen deprivation in the brains of the fetuses, creating a risk of brain damage or neurological impairment (Householder et al., 1982).

Tranquilizers Tranquilizers such as Librium and Valium also cross the placental membrane. These drugs, which are frequently prescribed for everyday

▶ ▶ ▶ ▶

anxiety and tension, are suspected of causing birth defects such as harelip. Barbiturates—phenobarbital is one—are suspected of decreasing testosterone levels in boys and of creating reproductive problems (Gupta et al., 1982). Barbiturates are no longer widely prescribed, because in addition to their other drawbacks they are highly addictive.

Alcohol It has been known at least since the Golden Age of Greece that heavy drinking is a major cause for concern. Maternal use of alcohol has been associated with death of the fetus and neonate, malformations, and a variety of growth deficiencies (Streissguth et al., 1980). Alcohol can affect the formation of DNA (Brown et al., 1979), and strands of DNA are constantly being "unzipped" and reformed as the unborn child grows through the process of mitosis. Maternal drinking in the fifth month of pregnancy has been linked to lower **habituation** in the neonate, a suggestion of central-nervous-system dysfunction (Streissguth et al., 1983). That is, these children show lower adaptivity to repetitive stimuli and thus are more likely to be disturbed by repetitive noises while sleeping. Evidence also suggests that children of mothers who drank during pregnancy may encounter academic problems in school, even when they are average in intelligence (Shaywitz et al., 1980).

Fetal Alcohol Syndrome It may be that upwards of 40 percent of the children of severe alcoholics have **fetal alcohol syndrome** (Jones, 1975). Boston University psychiatrist Henry Rosett (Rosett & Sander, 1979) found that mothers who drink heavily (at least five drinks on one occasion and 45 drinks a month) were significantly more likely to deliver children with FAS than were moderate drinkers or nondrinkers. Infants with FAS are frequently undersized and have smaller-than-average brains. There are distinct facial features, including widely spaced eyes, a flattened nose, and an underdeveloped upper jaw. There may be mental retardation, lack of coordination, limb deformities, and heart problems (Adickes & Shuman, 1981). They suck less well than normal babies, are short for their weight, and tend not to catch up (Hollestedt et al., 1983).

At least one study has found evidence of FAS among 16 percent of the offspring of women who imbibed only one to two ounces of alcohol a day during the early days of the embryonic stage (Hanson et al., 1978). The critical period for the development of the facial features associated with FAS seems to be the third and fourth weeks of prenatal development, when the head is starting to take shape. At this stage of pregnancy, the mother may not realize that she is pregnant. She may simply think that she is "late," and many factors, including stress, can delay menstruation. Remember, too, that many women have light bleeding at time of implantation, and it is possible to confuse this "spotting" with menstruation. The message is this: Social drinkers who wait until pregnancy is confirmed before they abstain from alcohol may be waiting too long.

Not all physicians agree on the effects of light drinking. Many physicians allow their pregnant patients a glass of wine with dinner. Wayne State University obstetrician Robert J. Sokol (1984) argues that "It's questionable whether there has ever been a case of an FAS child born to less than a chronically addicted woman." George Washington University physician John Larken (1984) argues that there is no evidence that "one glass of wine has any damaging effect."

On the other hand, a recent study of 32,000 women reported that pregnant women who have as few as one or two drinks a day were more likely to

Anoxia *Deprivation of oxygen.*

miscarry than women who did not drink at all (Harlap & Shiono, 1980). Moreover, women who are "social drinkers," who have a couple of glasses of wine with dinner or an occasional cocktail, are more likely to give birth to babies who are of low birth weight and difficult to arouse (Barr et al., 1984; Streissguth et al., 1977, 1978). By the age of 4 children whose mothers had had only three to five drinks a week during midpregnancy show deficits that may predict academic difficulties. They show longer reaction times and attention deficits, as compared to 4-year-olds whose mothers had not drunk at all (Streissguth et al., 1984).

It seems that the safest course for a pregnant woman is to abstain from alcohol. If she does drink, drinking small amounts of alcohol may be less risky than drinking larger amounts, *but there is no guaranteed safe minimum.* It also makes sense for women who are trying to become pregnant—or who are not taking precautions against becoming pregnant—to assume that they may be conceiving a child any month, and to modify their drinking habits accordingly.

Smoking Cigarettes Cigarette smoke contains many ingredients, among them the stimulant nicotine and the gas carbon monoxide, both of which are transmitted to the fetus. The effects of nicotine are uncertain, but carbon monoxide decreases the amount of oxygen available to the unborn child. Insufficient oxygen, or **anoxia,** has been linked to mental retardation, learning disorders, and a host of behavioral problems. Lack of oxygen also retards the general growth rate.

Figure 3.11 Why Start a New Life under a Cloud?
This American Cancer Society poster dramatizes the risks
posed by maternal smoking during pregnancy.

▶ ▶ ▶ ▶

Women who smoke during pregnancy are likely to deliver babies who weigh less than women who do not smoke (Butler & Goldstein, 1973; Linn et al., 1982; Meredith, 1975; Nieberg et al., 1985). Birth weight is related to infant mortality, and women who smoke during pregnancy are also more likely to have stillbirths (Naeye, 1978), or to deliver babies who die soon after birth (see Figure 3.11). In 1980, the Surgeon General reported that women who smoke also run higher risks of spontaneous abortion and premature rupture of the amniotic sac. The combination of drinking and smoking during pregnancy places the child at yet greater risk for low birth weight than does either of these practices alone (Wright et al., 1983).

Maternal smoking may also have long-term effects. Four-year-olds whose mothers smoked at least 15 cigarettes a day during the second trimester showed lower attention span than the children of nonsmoking mothers (Streissguth et al., 1984). Children whose mothers smoked during pregnancy are more likely to demonstrate a poor attention span, hyperactivity, and other behavior disorders in school (Dunn et al., 1977; Naeye & Peters, 1984; Nichols, 1977). Schoolchildren whose mothers had smoked during pregnancy attain lower IQ scores, are more likely to be diagnosed as having minimal brain dysfunction, and show poorer social adjustment (Landesman-Dwyer & Emanuel, 1979). Their academic achievement throughout middle childhood may also suffer, as found in a comparison of math, spelling, and reading scores among children of smoking and nonsmoking mothers (Fogelman, 1980; Naeye & Peters, 1984).

The likelihood of birth problems is related to the amount of smoking by the mother. In one study, women who suspended smoking for just 48 hours in the third trimester showed an 8 percent increase in the amount of oxygen available to their festuses (Davies et al., 1979). I have found that some women are better able to quit smoking or to cut down during pregnancy when they conceptualize their sacrifice as temporary—as a burden they must bear for only a few months. The bonus is that, after making this "temporary sacrifice" and managing to get through the withdrawal symptoms, some choose not to return to smoking.

A father's smoking may also hold dangers. Men who smoke are more likely than nonsmokers to produce abnormal sperm. Evans (1981) found that men who smoke have children with higher rates of birth defects and infant mortality.

Maternal Stress

While pregnancy can be a time of immense gratification for women, it can also be a time of stress. The baby might be unplanned and unwanted. Parents might not have the financial resources or the room for the child. The mother might have to give up her job. Perhaps there is another infant in the home who requires attention. Then, too, the mother might be experiencing physical discomforts, such as nausea or high blood pressure, because of the pregnancy. She might also fear the birth process itself or be concerned as to whether the baby will be normal.

So there are many reasons why a pregnant woman might experience stress. But how does a mother's emotional state influence her unborn child? After all, there are no known mechanisms for transmitting psychological events such as worries, concerns, or radiant happiness through the placenta. The fact is that, although emotions are psychological feeling states, they also have phys-

▶ ▶ ▶ ▶

iological components. For example, they are linked to the secretion of hormones such as **adrenalin.** Adrenalin stimulates the mother's heart rate, respiration rate, and many other bodily functions. Hormones pass through the placenta and also influence—at least physiologically—the unborn child.

It has been known for half a century that fetal movements increase when the mother is experiencing stress (Sontag, 1944). However, there does not seem to be persuasive evidence that short-term stress harms the fetus, no matter how upsetting it is for the mother (Spezzano, 1981).

The effects of long-term maternal stress on the fetus are more open to question. There are some reports that anxious, stressed mothers are more likely to bear **colicky** children—children who show digestive problems, including frequent spitting up; irritability; and greater-than-average crying (Lakin, 1957). It has even been speculated that extreme stress during the third month of pregnancy, when the bones in the fetal jaw are developing, is a factor in causing cleft lip and cleft palate.

Of course it would be unethical to expose randomly selected pregnant women to persistent stress in order to observe the outcomes on their children. However, such experiments have been run with rats, and it appears that prenatal stress reactions can be reversed by providing a more congenial environment after birth (Spezzano, 1981).

There are also confounding factors in the research on the effects of maternal stress. For one thing, pregnant women who encounter stress from, say, financial or marital problems do not usually find life completely serene after delivery. And so, the apparent effects of prenatal stress may actually be due to stress encountered during infancy. It can also be difficult to sort out genetic and environmental influences on fetal emotional reactivity. MZ twins, for example, are more likely than DZ twins to be overanxious (Slater & Shields, 1969), suggesting that predispositions toward anxiety may be genetically transmitted.

In sum, while some reports on the effects of maternal stress have been alarming, evidence on the issue is less convincing. It makes sense for pregnant women to regulate the stress impacting upon them, just as it makes sense for most of us to be aware of and regulate the stress to which we are exposed. But it may be that the effects of maternal stress upon the fetus are mostly temporary.

The Mother's Age

From a biological vantage point, there is little doubt that the 20s are the ideal time for women to bear children (Kessner, 1973). Women in their middle teens and younger and women in their late 30s and beyond show dramatically greater incidences of miscarriage, birth defects, prematurity, and infant mortality.

Teenage women who become pregnant place a burden on bodies that may not have adequately matured to facilitate pregnancy and childbirth. Women beyond their middle 30s may have passed the point at which their reproductive systems function most efficiently. As noted, women possess all their ova in immature form at birth. Over 30 years, these cells are exposed to the slings and arrows of an outrageous environment of toxic wastes, chemical pollutants, and radiation, thus increasing the risk of chromosomal abnormalities.

▶ ▶ ▶ ▶

There is also evidence that women's fertility declines after age 30 (Schwartz & Mayaux, 1982). All these negatives are dismaying for the career woman who wants to delay marriage and bearing children until her 30s. Psychologically, many women, like many men, feel that they are only "coming into their own" as individuals in their 30s, after they have had an opportunity to assess their effectiveness in and feelings about the world of business. It seems cruel that the biological clock can be running out when the outlook remains youthful. On the other hand, many women do bear children successfully in their 30s and beyond. We cannot ignore statistics if we are to make realistic decisions, but it is comforting to know that we are people and not probabilities.

Summary

1. People have children for many reasons, including the pleasure of having children, the opportunity to extend themselves in others, and the belief that it is right to have children. People choose not to have children for many reasons, including lack of financial resources, desire to maintain personal freedom, and belief that it is morally wrong to bring children into a troubled world.

2. Prenatal development, like all development, reflects the interaction of genetic and environmental influences. Our genotypes are the composites of our traits, as carried in our genetic instructions. Our phenotypes, or actual shown traits, are influenced both by genetics (nature) and environmental factors (nurture).

3. With the exception of sperm and ova, human cells carry 46 rod-shaped chromosomes (23 pairs of chromosomes) in their nuclei. Chromosomes are composed of deoxyribonucleic acid (DNA), which takes the form of a double helix.

4. Genes are the units of heredity, and genes consist of segments of DNA. Some traits are transmitted by single pairs of genes, whereas others are polygenic—transmitted by more than one pair of genes. Genes provide a reaction range for the expression of inherited traits.

5. There are two types of cell division: mitosis and meiosis. Aging cells are replaced, and the body grows by means of mitosis, in which each of the 46 chromosomes in a "parent" cell "unzips." One side of each double helix is transmitted to each new cell. There they rebuild into the original 46 chromosomes.

6. Sperm cells and ova (egg cells) are formed by meiosis, or reduction division. Each pair of chromosomes splits, and 23 migrate into each sperm and ovum. At conception, the 23 chromosomes in the sperm cell align with the 23 in the ovum. Thus a zygote with 46 chromosomes (arranged in 23 pairs) is formed. The zygote develops by means of mitosis.

7. Girls carry two X sex chromosomes. Boys carry one X and one Y sex chromosome. Identical (monozygotic) twins are formed when one zygote divides into two organisms, each of which carries the identical genetic code. Fraternal (dizygotic) twins are conceived when two sperm fertilize two ova. MZ twins are important in the study of child development, because differences between pairs may be assumed to be due to environmental factors.

▶ ▶ ▶ ▶

8. Dominant genetic traits are expressed when they pair up with recessive genes. Recessive traits are not expressed unless they pair up with other recessive genes, or are unopposed by another gene (as in a sex-linked trait such as hemophilia or male patterned baldness).

9. There are a number of chromosomal abnormalities. In Down syndrome, which results in characteristic facial features and retardation, the twenty-first pair of chromosomes contains a third. The probability of Down syndrome increases with the age of the mother (or father!). Other chromosomal abnormalities, such as Klinefelter's syndrome and Turner's syndrome, stem from abnormal numbers of sex chromosomes.

10. There are also many genetic abnormalities. Phenylketonuria (PKU), sickle-cell anemia, and Tay-Sachs disease are caused by recessive genes, so it is possible to carry one of these disorders without developing it. In PKU there is a build-up of phenylpyrivic acid, causing mental retardation. PKU can be controlled by diet. Sickle-cell anemia afflicts mainly blacks and Hispanic Americans. Tay-Sachs disease afflicts mainly Jews of European origin. Hemophilia is a sex-linked genetic disorder.

11. Genetic counseling helps potential parents weigh the probabilities that their children will be afflicted by such disorders. These abnormalities can frequently be detected by amniocentesis or chorionic villi sampling, ultrasound, blood test, or fetoscopy.

12. Women possess all the ova they will ever produce at birth, while men produce sperm continuously. Diseases and malformations of the reproductive tract make 10 to 15 percent of couples infertile. New reproductive technologies have been brought to bear when fertility problems cannot be corrected: artificial insemination, in vitro fertilization (IVF), donor IVF, embryonic transfer, and surrogate motherhood.

13. Conception normally occurs in a fallopian tube. Methods have been devised for sex preselection that claim up to an 80 percent success rate. Some methods rely on the the facts that X-bearing sperm swim more slowly than Y-bearing sperm and that X- and Y-bearing sperm survive longer at certain vaginal pH levels. Social critics consider sex preselection to be "stupendously sexist."

14. During the germinal stage of prenatal development, the zygote divides repeatedly and develops into a fluid-filled ball of cells called a blastocyst. The baby will develop from the part of the blastocyst called the embryonic disk. Supportive tissues, such as the amniotic sac, the placenta, and the umbilical cord, develop from the trophoblast. The blastocyst becomes implanted in the uterine wall about ten to 14 days after conception.

15. The major organ systems are formed during the embryonic stage, which lasts from the second through the eighth weeks following conception. During this stage the amniotic sac, placenta, and umbilical cord are formed also. The placenta is formed by both mother and child and serves as the way station that transports nutrients from mother to unborn child, and wastes from child to mother.

16. The fetal stage lasts from the ninth week through birth, which takes place about 266 days (nine months) after conception. The fetal stage is marked by further gains in length and weight and maturation of organ systems.

► ► ► ►

17. Inadequate maternal diet has been linked to low birth weight and infant mortality. Various maternal disorders lead to birth defects or other problems in the child. There are critical periods during prenatal development when the embryo and fetus are most vulnerable to certain substances (called teratogens), because of the structures and systems that are differentiating at the time.

18. Maternal rubella (German measles) may cause deafness, heart disease, or retardation in the child. Congenital syphilis can cause loss of vision or hearing, and damage to bones and teeth. The fatal AIDS virus can also pass through the placenta and infect the child. Toxemia can kill mother and child, or cause premature birth or undersize. In Rh incompatibility, an Rh-negative mother produces Rh-positive antibodies in response to her blood's mixing with that of an Rh-positive fetus during delivery. *Subsequent* Rh-positive children are at risk.

19. Drugs taken by the mother pass through the placenta and can harm the child. Hormones used to maintain the pregnancy have caused cancer in children (DES) or masculinized the sex organs of female children (progestin). Children can be born addicted to narcotics. Alcohol can lead to fetal alcohol syndrome (FAS), characterized by certain facial features and the possibilities of retardation and heart problems. Smoking has been linked to undersized children, stillbirths, and academic problems during later years.

20. Periodic maternal stress probably has only temporary effects.

21. Women in their late 30s and older are more likely to have complications during pregnancy and to bear children with birth defects than women in their 20s. However, amniocentesis and other diagnostic procedures have made pregnancy beyond age 35 somewhat less stressful than it was in earlier years.

T R U T H ▸ O R ▸ F I C T I O N ▸ R E V I S I T E D

Fertilization takes place in the uterus. False. Conception usually occurs in the fallopian tubes.

Identical twins are more likely than fraternal twins to share problems such as nail-biting and carsickness. True. Identical twins are very much alike in certain behavior patterns as well as in their physical traits.

Brown eyes are dominant over blue eyes. True. Blue eye color is carried by a recessive gene.

Sickle-cell anemia is most prevalent among blacks. True. There is also a relatively high incidence among Hispanic Americans.

It is not possible to learn the sex of one's child prior to birth. False. Amniocentesis and ultrasound are two of the methods that can provide this information.

▶ ▶ ▶ ▶

We can use sound waves to take "pictures" of unborn children. *True.* Ultrasound waves provide a "sonogram" of the child.

Equal numbers of boys and girls are conceived. *False.* Greater numbers of boys are conceived.

"Yuppies" are more likely than nonprofessionals to develop fertility problems. *True.* Yuppies tend to delay childbearing, and fertility declines with age.

Developing embryos have been successfully transferred from the womb of one woman to the womb of another. *True.* Embryonic transfer is just one of several recent advances in reproductive technology.

You can predetermine the sex of your child. *Not with certainty.* However, a number of methods promise up to 80 percent success rates.

Newly fertilized egg cells survive without any nourishment from the mother for more than a week. *True.* They do so before they become implanted in the uterus.

Your heart started beating when you were only one-fifth of an inch long and weighed a fraction of an ounce. *True.* You reached this size about one month after conception.

If it were not for the secretion of male sex hormones a few weeks after conception, we would all develop as females. *True.* Male sex hormones spur the development of male sex organs.

Embryos and fetuses "take what they need" from their mothers. Therefore, pregnant women need not be too concerned about their diets. *False.* Women must attain adequate nutrition in order to give birth to healthy babies.

Newborn babies whose mothers read **The Cat in the Hat** *aloud during the last weeks of pregnancy prefer* **The Cat in the Hat** *to other stories.* *True.* The newborns had apparently perceived the rhythms of the story before they were born.

Fetuses suck their thumbs and hiccough, sometimes for hours on end. *True.* They also do somersaults and alternate periods of wakefulness and sleep.

Surgery has been carried out on fetuses. *True.* However, it is risky.

Babies can be born addicted to narcotics and other drugs. *True.* A variety of drugs crosses the placental membrance and influences the fetus.

Pregnant women who smoke risk having children who are low in birth weight. *True.* These children are at generally greater risk for physical problems and, later on, for academic problems.

▶ ▶ ▶ ▶

4

Birth and the Neonate: In the New World

C H A P T E R ▸ O U T L I N E

▸
▸
▸
▸
▸
▸
▸

▶
▶
▶
▶
▶
▶
▶

T R U T H ▸ O R ▸ F I C T I O N ?

- The fetus signals the mother when it is ready to be born.
- Soon after birth, babies are slapped on the buttocks to clear passageways for air and stimulate independent breathing.
- The way in which the umbilical cord is cut determines whether the child will have an "inny" or an "outy" as a "belly button."
- Local or regional anesthetics used by mothers during childbirth have no effect on the child.
- Women who give birth according to the Lamaze method experience no pain during labor.
- Most hospitals exclude fathers from participating in the birth process.
- Home births are as safe as hospital births for women who have given birth before and who are in good health.
- Once their physical needs have been taken care of, preterm infants should be left undisturbed as much as possible until they achieve normal birth weights.
- It is essential for parents to have extended early contact with their newborn children if adequate bonding is to take place.
- Breast-feeding and bottle-feeding are equally healthful for infants.
- Women cannot become pregnant while they are breast-feeding their babies.
- Newborn babies who are placed face down in comfortably warm water will attempt to swim.
- Newborn babies are capable of learning.
- Newborn babies require about twice the amount of sleep that adults do.
- Babies who are picked up as soon as they start to cry become spoiled and cry more often than babies whose mothers wait a while to pick them up.

During the last few weeks of her pregnancy, Elaine continued to, as she put it, "drag myself into work. I wasn't just going to sit home all day watching *As the World Turns* like a dunce." I have (secretly) watched *As the World Turns* since Dr. Bob Hughes was a little boy, and so I ignored part of what she said. Elaine added, "But since I was so exhausted by the time I got to the office, I sat behind my desk like—well—half a dunce. I also couldn't get my mind off the pregnancy—what it was going to be like when I finally delivered Jason, or, I should say, when he finally delivered me. I'd had the amniocentesis, but I was still hoping and praying everything would be normal with him. And it was just so darned* hard to get around."

During the last weeks of pregnancy it is normal, especially for first-time mothers, to worry about the mechanics of delivery and whether the child will be normal. As they near full **term,** women become increasingly heavy and, literally, "bent out of shape." It may require a feat of balance and ingenuity to get up from a chair or out of bed. Sitting behind a steering wheel—and still reaching the wheel—may become a challenge. Muscle tension from supporting the fetus and other intrauterine material may cause backaches. At this time many women have the feeling that their pregnancies will never come to an end.

They do, of course. Or else this book would not have been written.

Early in the last month of pregnancy, as noted in Chapter 3, the head of the fetus settles in the pelvis. This is called "dropping" or "lightening." Since lightening decreases pressure in the diaphragm, the mother may, in fact, feel lighter.

The first uterine contractions are called **Braxton-Hicks contractions** or false labor contractions. They are relatively painless and may be experienced as early as the sixth month of pregnancy. They tend to increase in frequency as the pregnancy progresses. Although they may be confused with actual labor contractions, real labor contractions are more painful and regular. In contrast to Braxton-Hicks contractions, real labor contractions are also usually intensified by walking. Braxton-Hicks contractions may serve to tone the muscles that will be used in delivery.

A day or so before labor begins, increased pelvic pressure from the fetus may rupture superficial blood vessels in the birth canal so that blood appears in vaginal secretions. The mucus tissue that had plugged the cervix and protected the uterus from infection becomes dislodged. At about this time one woman in ten also has a rush of warm "water" from the vagina. This "water" is actually amniotic fluid, and it means that the amniotic sac (or "bag of waters") has burst. The amniotic sac usually does not burst until the end of the first stage of childbirth, as described below. Indigestion, diarrhea, an ache in the small of the back, and abdominal cramps are also common signs that labor may be beginning.

The mechanisms that initiate and maintain labor are not fully understood, but the first step might be secretion of hormones by the adrenal and pituitary glands of the fetus. This would be logical, suggesting that the fetus has a way of signaling the mother when it is mature enough to sustain life outside the uterus. The fetal hormones would act by stimulating the placenta and the uterus to secrete **prostaglandins.** Prostaglandins, in turn, cause labor

Term *A set period of time.*

Braxton-Hicks contractions *The first, usually painless, contractions of childbirth.*

Prostaglandins *(pross-tuh-GLAND-ins). Hormones that stimulate uterine contractions.*

▶ ▶ ▶ ▶

*This word has been modified in order to maintain the decorum of a college textbook.

contractions by exciting the muscles of the uterus. It may be that throughout a good part of the pregnancy, other hormones produced by the placenta *inhibited* the action of prostaglandins. However, the production of these inhibitor hormones appears to weaken near full term. Later during labor the pituitary gland releases **oxytocin,** a hormone that stimulates contractions strong enough to expel the baby.

In this chapter we discuss the events of childbirth and the characteristics of the **neonate.** Arriving in the new world may be a bit more complex than you had thought, and it may also be that newborn babies can do a bit more than you had imagined.

The Stages of Childbirth

Childbirth begins with the onset of regular uterine contractions and is described in three stages.

The First Stage

In the first stage of childbirth, uterine contractions cause the cervix to become **effaced** and **dilated** to about 4 inches (10 cm) in diameter, so that the baby may pass. Most of the pain of childbirth is caused by the stretching of the cervix. When the cervix dilates easily and quickly, there may be little or no pain at all.

The first stage may last from a few minutes to a couple of days. Twelve to 24 hours is about average for a first pregnancy. Later pregnancies require about half this time. The initial contractions are not usually very painful. They may be spaced 15 to 20 minutes apart and last from 45 seconds to a minute.

As time elapses, contractions become more frequent, regular, and strong. A woman is usually informed to go the hospital when they are four to five minutes apart. She will usually be admitted to a labor room until the end of the first stage, where her husband typically remains with her.

"Prepping" If the woman is to be "prepped"—that is, if her pubic hair is to be shaved—it takes place now. The prep is intended to lower the chances of infection during delivery and to facilitate the performance of an **episiotomy** (described below). A woman may now also be given an enema in order to prevent an involuntary bowel movement during contractions of labor. However, many women find prepping and enemas degrading and seek obstetricians who do not perform them routinely. The medical necessity of these procedures has been questioned (Hahn & Paige, 1980).

Fetal Monitoring During the first stage of childbirth, **fetal monitoring** may be applied to monitor the mother's contractions and the response of the baby. In one kind of monitor, an electronic sensing device is strapped around the woman's abdomen. It can measure the fetal heart rate as well as the frequency, strength, and duration of the mother's contractions. Another type of fetal monitor is attached directly to the scalp of the baby. It measures the oxygen in the baby's bloodstream. An irregular heart rate, or a rapid falloff in heart rate, can be a sign of fetal distress. Abnormal heart rate or lower-than-normal levels of

▶ ▶ ▶ ▶

Forceps *A curved instrument that fits around the head of the baby and permits it to be pulled through the birth canal.*

Vacuum extraction tube *An instrument that uses suction to pull the baby through the birth canal.*

Transition *The initial movement of the head of the fetus into the birth canal.*

Perineum *The area between the female's genital region and the anus.*

oxygen alert the medical staff to possible birth problems, so that appropriate steps can be taken, such as speeding up the delivery by means such as **forceps** or the **vacuum extraction tube.** The forceps is a curved instrument that fits around the baby's head and allows the baby to be pulled out of the mother's body. The vacuum extraction tube relies on suction to pull the baby through the birth canal.

Transition When the cervix is nearly fully dilated, the head of the fetus begins to move into the vagina, or birth canal. This process is called **transition.** During transition contractions tend to come rapidly. The woman may encounter pain, nausea, or chills. Transition is usually over within a few minutes.

The Second Stage

The woman may be taken to a delivery room for the second stage of childbirth. The second stage follows transition. It begins when the baby first appears at the opening of the birth canal (Figure 4.1). The second stage is shorter than the first stage. It lasts from a few minutes to a few hours, and ends with the birth of the baby.

Only a couple of decades ago the husband was systematically excluded from the delivery room, and he was pictured, stereotypically, as pacing up and down awaiting news of the birth of his child. Today, however, the husband is more likely than not to participate in the birth process (May & Perrin, 1985). He is prepared for the childbirth along with his wife. He has learned how to support her during delivery—often by means of the Lamaze method, described later.

With each contraction in the second stage, the skin surrounding the birth canal stretches farther and the baby is propelled farther along. When the baby's head starts to emerge from the birth canal, it is said to have *crowned.* Typically, the baby then fully emerges within a few minutes.

The Episiotomy When the baby's head has crowned, the obstetrician, nurse, or midwife may perform an *episiotomy.* Most women do not feel the incision because pressure from the baby's emerging head tends to numb the area. The episiotomy, like prepping and the enema, is controversial and is not practiced in Europe. The incision may cause itching and, in some cases, stabbing pain as it heals. Discomfort may interfere with sexual relations for several months following delivery. Today an increasing number of U.S. obstetricians no longer perform the episiotomy routinely, although most physicians argue that an episiotomy is preferable to random tearing when they see that the tissue of the **perineum** is becoming severely effaced.

Whether or not an episiotomy is performed, the baby's passageway to the outside world is at best a tight fit. For this reason, the shape of the baby's head and facial features may be distended. The head may be molded (elongated), the nose may be flattened—as though our new arrival had been involved in a vicious prize fight—and the ears may be bent. Parents are frequently concerned about whether everything will return to its proper shape. First-time parents are often skeptical of assurances that cartilage and the bones of the neonate's skull are soft and that, in the great majority of cases, heads, noses, and ears return to their genetically preset courses. But they are, and they do.

▶ ▶ ▶ ▶

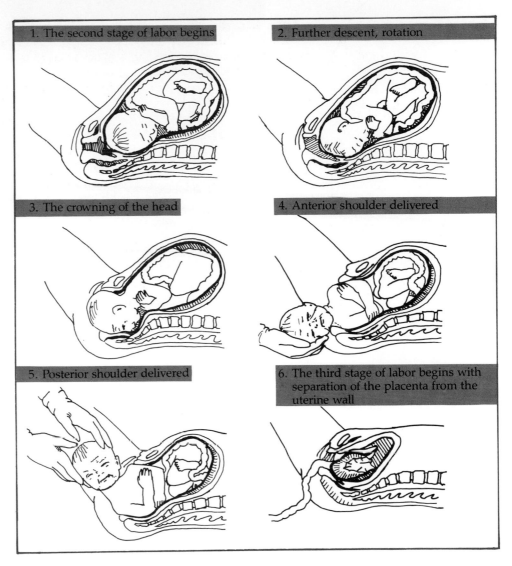

1. The second stage of labor begins
2. Further descent, rotation
3. The crowning of the head
4. Anterior shoulder delivered
5. Posterior shoulder delivered
6. The third stage of labor begins with separation of the placenta from the uterine wall

Figure 4.1 The Stages of Childbirth
In the first stage of childbirth, uterine contractions cause the cervix to become effaced and dilated to about four inches (10 cm) so that the baby may pass. The second stage begins when the baby begins to move into the birth canal (vagina) and ends with the birth of the baby. During the third stage of childbirth, the placenta separates from the uterine wall and, along with other fetal-support tissues, is expelled through the birth canal.

In the New World   Once the baby's head emerges from the mother's body, mucus is usually aspirated from its mouth by suction, so that the passageway for breathing will not be obstructed. Aspiration is frequently repeated when the baby is fully delivered. Because of the use of suction, the baby is no longer routinely held upside down to help expel mucus. There is also no need for the baby to be slapped on the buttocks to stimulate independent breathing, as we see in so many old films.

► ► ► ►

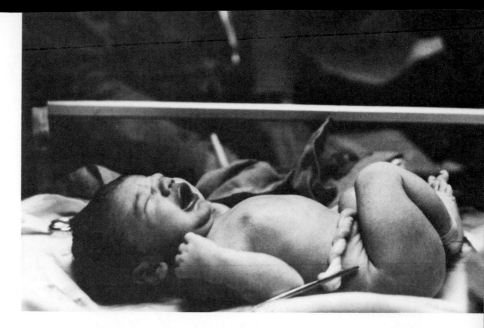

A Clamped and Severed Umbilical Cord *The stump of the cord dries and falls off in its own time. Whether the child will have an "inny" or an "outy" has nothing to do with the preferences of the obstetrician.*

Once the baby is breathing adequately on its own, the umbilical cord, through which it had received oxygen from the mother, is clamped and severed about 3 inches from the baby's body. At about 266 days after conception, mother and infant have finally become separate beings. The stump of the umbilical cord will dry and fall off in its own time. Whether the child will have an "inny" or an "outy" has nothing to do with the expertise or cosmetic preferences of the obstetrician.

The baby may then be taken by a nurse, so that various procedures can be performed while the mother is in the third stage of labor. Now the baby is usually given a plastic identification bracelet and footprinted. In most states it is required that drops of silver nitrate or an antibiotic ointment (erythromycin) be put into the baby's eyes to prevent gonorrheal infection. The newborn may also receive an injection of vitamin K, since neonates do not manufacture this vitamin. Vitamin K helps ensure that the baby's blood will clot normally in case of bleeding.

The Apgar Scale The baby's overall level of health is usually evaluated at birth according to the Apgar scoring system, developed by Virginia Apgar in 1953. Apgar scores are based on five signs of health, as shown in Table 4.1. The neonate can receive a score of 0, 1, or 2 on each sign. The total Apgar score can therefore vary from 0 to 10. A score of 7 or above usually indicates that the baby is not in danger. A score below 4 suggests that the baby is in critical condition and requires medical attention. By one minute after birth, most normal babies attain scores of 8 to 10 (Self & Horowitz, 1980).

An acronym using the name *APGAR* is commonly used to aid in remembering the five criteria:

A: the general *Appearance* or color of the newborn infant

P: the *Pulse* or heart rate

G: Grimace (the one-point sign of reflex irritability)

A: general *Activity* level or muscle tone, and

R: Respiratory effort, or rate of breathing.

► ► ► ►

Table 4.1 The Apgar Scale

SIGN	POINTS		
	0	1	2
APPEARANCE Color	Blue, pale	Body pink, extremities blue	Entirely pink
PULSE Heart rate	Absent (not detectable)	Slow—below 100 beats/minute	Rapid—100–140 beats/minute
GRIMACE Reflex irritability	No response	Grimace	Crying, coughing, sneezing
ACTIVITY LEVEL Muscle tone	Completely flaccid, limp	Weak, inactive	Flexed arms and legs; resists extension
RESPIRATORY EFFORT Breathing	Absent (infant is "apneic")	Shallow breathing; irregular, slow	Regular breathing; lusty crying

Source: Adapted from Virginia Apgar, "A Proposal for a New Method of Evaluation of the Newborn Infant." *Current Research in Anesthesia and Analgesia*, 32 (1953), 260–267.

The Third Stage

During the third or *placental* stage of childbirth, which may last from a few minutes to an hour or more, the placenta separates from the uterine wall and is expelled along with fetal membranes. There may be some bleeding, and the uterus begins the process of contracting to a smaller size. The attending physician sews the episiotomy and any tears in the perineum.

Some authorities include the initial period of recovery as a fourth stage of childbirth (Auvenshire & Enriquez, 1985; Jensen & Bobak, 1985). Later we shall discuss some of the psychological events of the postpartum period.

Methods of Childbirth

Until this century, childbirth typically was an intimate home procedure involving the mother, a **midwife,** family, and friends. In our culture today it is most often a hospital procedure performed by a physician who uses surgical instruments and anesthetics to help protect mother and child from infection, complications, and pain. While the use of modern medicine has saved lives, it has also made childbearing more impersonal. Social critics argue that it has, to a large degree, wrested from women control over their own bodies and, through drugs, denied many women the experience of giving birth.

In this section we consider a number of contemporary methods for facilitating childbirth.

Midwife *A woman who helps other women in childbirth. (From Old English roots meaning "with woman.")*

▶ ▶ ▶ ▶

Medicated Childbirth

In sorrow thou shalt bring forth children.
——Genesis 3:16

The Bible suggests that the ancients saw suffering during childbirth as a woman's lot. But during the past two centuries, the ascendance of modern medicine, along with the development of effective **anesthetics,** has led many people to believe that women need not experience discomfort during childbirth. Many women, in fact, deliver children while unconscious. Unconscious childbirth was popularized in England when Queen Victoria delivered her eighth child under chloroform anesthesia in 1853. Today some anesthesia is used in more than 90 percent of U.S. deliveries.

General anesthesia affects the entire body by putting the woman to sleep. Today sodium pentothal, a barbiturate, is injected into the vein of the arm, and, like the chloroform of old, achieves its anesthetic effect by putting the woman to sleep. **Tranquilizers** such as Valium and Librium, and orally-taken barbiturates such as sodium seconal, are not anesthetics, but they reduce anxiety which can compound the stress produced by pain. Narcotics such as Demerol also blunt perception of pain.

General anesthetics, tranquilizers, and narcotics decrease the strength of uterine contractions during delivery and, by crossing the placental membrane, lower the overall responsiveness of the neonate (Bonica, 1972; Brazelton, 1973; Scanlon et al., 1974). There is no doubt that they have immediate effects on the child, and the higher the dosage, the greater their impact.

The major question is whether these anesthetics have long-term effects on the child. Evidence is mixed. Some studies show no long-term effects. Others suggest that children whose mothers received heavy doses of anesthetics during delivery lag in their motor development and cognitive functioning at the ages of 1 year and beyond (Brackbill, 1976, 1979; Goldstein et al., 1976). But there is little suggestion that these effects are severe.

Regional or **local anesthetics** attempt to deaden the pain in certain areas of the body without generally depressing the mother or putting her to sleep. For these reasons it has also been hoped that they would also have less impact on the neonate. In the *pudendal block,* the mother's external genitals are numbed by local injection. In an *epidural block,* anesthesia is injected into the spinal canal, temporarily numbing and paralyzing the body below the waist. Anesthesia is injected directly into the spinal cord in the *spinal block,* which also numbs the body from the waist down.

However, it now appears that local anesthesia does decrease the strength and lower the activity levels of neonates, at least during the first eight hours following birth (Murray et al., 1981; Scanlon et al., 1974). Even low doses of local anesthesia make the baby less alert (Lester et al., 1982). Ann Murray and her colleagues (1981) compared babies of women who had received the anesthetic Bupivacaine by spinal block with babies of mothers who had received little or no medication during childbirth. Differences in physiological and motor responses were strongest on the first day, with the babies in the medicated group performing less well. Group differences in responsiveness decreased dramatically within five days. However, one month later, when the babies were apparently responding equally well, the spinal-block mothers reported that their babies were less sociable and harder to care for. Other researchers (e.g., Hollenbeck et al., 1984) have also found that medicated childbirth negatively influ-

Anesthetics *Agents that produce partial or total loss of the sense of pain. (From Greek roots meaning "without feeling.")*

General anesthesia *The process of eliminating pain by putting the person to sleep.*

Tranquilizer *A drug that reduces feelings of anxiety and tension.*

Local anesthetic *A method that reduces pain in an area of the body.*

ences parent–baby interactions during the month after birth. Why should this be so?

Medicated babies are less responsive after birth, and it is possible that their relationships with their mothers get off on the wrong foot. Perhaps the mothers' first impressions of less responsiveness persist, even when their babies have caught up. Perhaps subtle problems that we have not yet been able to detect persist and color the mothers' perceptions. We must also note that the Murray study and most others of the kind are "natural experiments." Mothers are not randomly assigned to medication or no-medication groups. Some mothers ask for medication, others do not. Thus, it might be that the same factors that influence some mothers to refuse medication also influence them to appreciate their children more. Given that questions remain about the effects of medicated delivery on the child, one such factor could be greater concern about the welfare of their babies. It could also be that the mothers who do not ask for medication are better prepared for childbirth—and child rearing.

It should also be noted that women who have general anesthesia and are unconscious throughout childbirth have more negative feelings about childbirth and the baby than women using any other method. Women who receive spinal or other "blocks" have relatively more positive feelings about childbirth and their babies, but they feel detached from the childbirth process (Leifer, 1980).

In any event, there is little convincing evidence that medicated childbirth leads to severe, long-term consequences for children. It is also clear that medication is now and then required to assure the physical well-being of both mother and baby. However, critics argue that anesthetics are used indiscriminately and that we have not heard the last word on their long-term effects. Critics also contend that medication has contributed to the institutionalization of child-bearing—putting the doctor in charge of what ought to be a family-centered event.

Natural Childbirth

Partly as a reaction against the use of anesthetics, English obstetrician Grantly Dick-Read endorsed **natural childbirth** in his 1932 book, *Childbirth Without Fear*. Dick-Read argued that women's labor pains were heightened by their fear of the unknown and resultant muscle tensions. Dick-Read presaged modern practices by educating women about the biological aspects of reproduction and delivery, by encouraging physical fitness, and by teaching them breathing exercises and relaxation.

Prepared Childbirth: The Lamaze Method

Most women who are pregnant for the first time expect pain and discomfort during childbirth (Leifer, 1980). Certainly the popular media image of childbirth is one in which the woman sweats profusely and screams and thrashes in pain.

The French obstetrician Fernand Lamaze (1981) shared this impression, until he visited the Soviet Union in 1951. He found that many Russian women appeared to bear babies without anesthetics or pain. Lamaze took back to Western Europe with him the techniques of the Russian women, which he referred

Natural childbirth Dick-Read's method of childbirth in which women use no anesthesia and are educated about childbirth and strategies for coping with discomfort.

▶ ▶ ▶ ▶

An Exercise Class for Pregnant Women
Years ago, the rule of thumb was that pregnant women were not to exert themselves. Today, it is recognized that exercise is healthful for pregnant women, because it promotes cardiovascular fitness and enhances muscle strength. Fitness and strength are assets during childbirth—and at other times.

to as the "psychoprophylactic" method. This term is a mouthful, but it simply means using psychological techniques to prevent pain in childbirth.

During the 1950s the techniques were brought to the United States as the **Lamaze method** or *prepared childbirth,* although Lamaze has always acknowledged his debt to the conditioning concepts of Ivan Pavlov (see Chapter 2). In essence, Lamaze argues that women can learn to *dissociate* uterine contractions from pain and fear by associating *other* responses with contractions. Women can be taught to think of pleasant images such as beach scenes while they are involved in delivery. They can also learn to lessen pain somewhat by means of breathing and relaxation exercises.

A woman attends Lamaze classes accompanied by a "coach." The coach is the person—usually the father—who will aid her in the delivery room by timing contractions, offering moral support, and coaching her in patterns of breathing and relaxation. During each contraction, the woman breathes in a specific, rehearsed manner. She is taught how to relax muscle groups throughout her body, then how to contract a single muscle while others remain at ease. The rationale is that during labor she will be able, upon cue, to keep other muscles relaxed while the uterus contracts (Ewy & Ewy, 1976). In this way she will conserve energy, minimize bodily tension and pain, and experience less anxiety. In an additional regimen, muscles that will be used during delivery, such as leg muscles, are strengthened through exercise.

The woman is also educated about childbirth and given an agenda of things to do during delivery. The father is integrated into the process, and it has been reported that the marital relationship is strengthened and the woman feels less alone during delivery as a result (Dooker, 1980; Wideman & Singer, 1984). The father as well as the mother takes pride in "their" accomplishment of childbirth (Bing, 1983). It also seems that women report less pain and request less medication when their husbands are present (Henneborn & Cogan, 1975).

The Lamaze method appears to have considerably decreased the stress of childbirth for many women. Women using the method have generally positive feelings about childbirth and about their babies (Leifer, 1980). Still, they usually report some pain during delivery and frequently use anesthetics. How, then, is the Lamaze method helpful? Perhaps it is in part because women en-

Lamaze method *A childbirth method in which women are educated about childbirth, learn to relax and breathe in patterns that conservve energy and lessen pain, and have a coach (usually the father) present during childbirth. Also termed* prepared childbirth.

▶ ▶ ▶ ▶

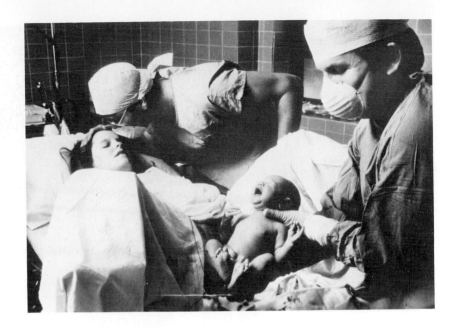

Today the father is usually integrated into the process of childbirth and takes pride in "his" accomplishment as well as that of his wife.

hance their self-esteem by regaining control over their own delivery (Dooker, 1980; May & Perrin, 1985). They become knowledgeable about childbirth and perceive themselves as the central actors in the process, not as passive victims who need the guidance of the doctor. The breathing and relaxation exercises do not fully eliminate pain, but they provide the woman with coping strategies and something to focus on besides fear and pain.

"Birth without Violence": The Leboyer Method

Natural and prepared methods of childbirth address the comfort of the mother. In *Birth without Violence,* French physician Frederick Leboyer (1975) advocates another form of reaction against the institutionalization of child-bearing by focusing on gently easing the infant into the world.

In the **Leboyer method** or *gentle birth,* the physician or midwife eases the baby along the birth canal, with fingers under its armpits. Hospital delivery rooms tend to be noisy, harshly lit places where babies are separated from their mothers after birth, so that the various procedures described earlier can be carried out and the mother can rest. Leboyer tames the hospital setting by lowering the lighting and instructing attendants to keep their voices hushed.

After birth, the baby is placed on its mother's warm abdomen and is held by her until it begins breathing strongly on its own. Only then is the umbilical cord cut. In other methods of childbirth, the umbilical cord is cut upon delivery. Leboyer has noted that his method permits the baby to escape the violence of being slapped on the buttocks, but as noted earlier, today babies are (gently) suctioned rather than slapped.

Next, the baby is given a warm bath—frequently by the father (Berezin, 1980). When it opens its eyes and flexes its limbs, it is returned to the mother for cuddling and suckling.

There is little research on the Leboyer method. One study compared babies delivered by the Leboyer method to babies delivered by other means an

Leboyer method A childbirth method that focuses on gently easing the neonate into the world. Also termed gentle childbirth.

▶ ▶ ▶ ▶

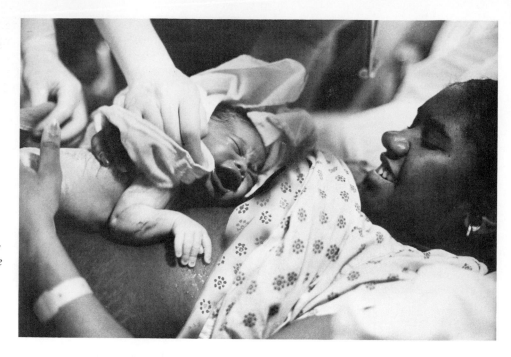

One of the practices of the Leboyer method is placing the neonate on the mother's abdomen after birth. This practice is widely adopted today even by mothers who do not use other aspects of the Leboyer method, and many parents and professionals believe that it is one element in the bonding process.

hour after birth, and at follow-ups of 24 hours, 72 hours, and 8 months (Nelson et al., 1980). No differences were found in the responsiveness of the babies nor in the health of the babies or their mothers. At 8 months the mothers reported that they *thought* that the Leboyer method had helped their children, even though their views were not supported by objective evidence. It seems that we generally expect more from "special" treatments and are disposed toward rating them positively.

Caesarean Section

In a **Caesarean section,** the baby is delivered by surgery rather than through the vagina. In this procedure, by which Julius Caesar is said to have been delivered (hence the name), incisions are made in the abdomen and the uterus, and the baby is removed. The incisions are then sewn up, and, in most cases, the mother is capable of walking about on the same day, although there is discomfort. In previous years, the incisions left visible scars, but today "C-sections" tend to be performed near the top line of the mother's pubic hair. This so-called "bikini cut" is all but invisible.

The C-section is becoming more common in the United States. It is used in about 20 percent of childbirths today, as compared with 10.4 percent in 1975 and 17 percent in 1980 (Clark & Witherspoon, 1984; Gleicher, 1984). The C-section is most likely to be used when normal delivery is expected to be difficult or threatening to the mother or the child. Difficult deliveries can occur when the mother is weak or fatigued, the baby is very large, or the mother's pelvis is small or misshapen. C-sections may also be performed when the baby is in the **breech position** (feet downward), in the **transverse position** (lying crosswise), or in distress.

The C-section has its advantages and disadvantages. For the mother it can be life-saving when the delivery is difficult or she is fatigued. Anesthetics

Caesarean section A method of childbirth in which the neonate is delivered through a surgical incision in the abdomen.

Breech position A feet-downward position in which the fetus's backside first enters the birth canal.

Transverse position A position in which the fetus lies crosswise across the opening to the birth canal.

▶ ▶ ▶ ▶

make the process pain-free. However, women receiving C-sections have a higher risk of infection than women who deliver vaginally, and their physical recoveries from childbirth are prolonged. Psychologically, C-sections frequently have depressing effects on women. Although women may anticipate childbirth with some trepidation, they may also view childbirth with pride, as one of the things that only they can do. Especially with the contemporary emphasis on women as the primary actors in childbirth, the C-section can cause women to see themselves as failures.

It is clearly safer for babies in the breech position to be born by C-section (Sachs et al., 1983). Babies born this way are also spared the process of squeezing through the birth canal. For this reason, they look better upon delivery. As of today, however, research has not uncovered any notable long-term differences between children who are born vaginally or by C-section.

Alternatives to the Hospital: Where Should a Child Be Born?

Most babies in the United States are born in hospitals. The advantage of hospital delivery is the availability of medical equipment and personnel in case of complications. But hospitals can be expensive and impersonal. Their use may reinforce the perception that pregnancy is an illness that requires medical treatment rather than a natural process. The hospital environment encourages "patients" to surrender responsibility to the physician and to take a passive role in their own well-being. For these reasons, in recent years many pregnant women, and fathers, have sought alternative birthplaces.

Alternate Birth Centers Alternate Birth Centers (ABCs) attempt to provide the back-up facilities found in hospitals and the atmosphere of a home delivery. Unheard of 20 years ago, there are now at least 1,000 of them in the United States. ABCs are frequently located within or adjacent to medical centers, so that medical equipment is typically outside the door in case of emergency.

The birthing room itself is usually decorated and furnished like a bedroom—cheerfully. Family, friends, and siblings of the baby may all be present. Women in labor move about, eat, drink, rest, or joke as they wish. After the birth, the family usually remains together. As in the Leboyer method, the neonate is placed on the mother's abdomen, where it has the opportunity to be cuddled and to experience eye contact. Later in the chapter we shall see that some researchers believe that this early eye contact is an important aspect of the mother–infant **bonding** process. Women generally report that the ABC experience permits them to exercise control and gain greater satisfaction from the process of childbirth (Montrose, 1978).

Before moving on to the next section, I must note another compelling reason for families to consider avoiding hospitals for purposes of childbirth. My wife and I were discussing a friend's pregnancy and my daughter Allyn, at 5 years 3 months, came up with one of her more diabolical schemes: "Let's go to the hospital and tell all the women they don't have babies in their stomachs, [but that] they have chickens in their stomachs. Then we'll spill marbles on the floor and they'll. . . ." (The rest is silence.)*

Bonding *The process of creating attachment (bonds of affection) between parent and child.*

*Serious students of child development are invited to get in touch with the author to learn the ugly details.

► ► ► ►

A Family-Centered Approach to Childbirth

▷
▷
▷
▷
▷ In recent years, childbirth has been becoming more family-centered, as opposed to hospital- or doctor-centered. In her book *The Psychology of Women,* Margaret Matlin (1987) of the State University of New York at Geneseo summarizes some of the trends toward family-centered childbirth:

1. Labor is not artificially induced simply because it is more convenient for the physician.
2. The motive for doing a Caesarean section in a given case is seriously considered.
3. Women are allowed to take an upright (sitting) position during delivery, rather than the flat-on-the-table, feet-in-the-stirrups approach.
4. Birth practices that have little or no health benefits—such as *routine* enema, shaving of the genital area, forbidding the consumption of food, and episiotomy—are reconsidered.
5. Routine use of anesthetics is reconsidered.
6. A supportive family member or friend is present.
7. Alternative physical locations for childbirth are explored.
8. Siblings are permitted to share in the birth of the new baby, and they are carefully prepared for the event (p. 369).

Home Births Home birth has also increased in popularity in recent years. Home delivery naturally provides familiar surroundings and also enhances the perception that the woman and her family are in control.

Some advocates of home delivery argue that when a pregnant woman is screened carefully for potential complications, and when she has a history of normal births, home delivery may be quite safe. Opponents assert that women cannot be screened for *every* possible complication and that home delivery poses unnecessary risks to mother and child. Many physicians, in fact, refuse to deliver babies in the home. Even midwives may prefer the birthing clinic, because of concern about lack of access to medical equipment and personnel in the case of the unexpected.

Birth Problems

Although the great majority of deliveries are "unremarkable" from a medical standpoint, perhaps every delivery is most remarkable from the parents' point of view. Still, there are a number of problems that can occur. In this section we discuss anoxia and preterm and low-birth-weight neonates.

▶ ▶ ▶ ▶

Anoxia

Prenatal **anoxia** can cause brain damage and associated problems such as intellectual deficiency and neurological impairment. Prolonged cut-off of the baby's oxygen supply during delivery is linked with these problems and can also cause cerebral palsy and, in extreme cases, death.

The fetus and emerging baby receive oxygen through the umbilical cord. Passage through the birth canal is tight, and the umbilical cord is usually squeezed during the process. If the squeezing is temporary, the effect is like holding one's breath for a moment, and no problems are likely to ensue. But if the squeezing is prolonged, anoxia can result. Prolonged squeezing is more likely during a breech presentation, when the baby's head presses the umbilical cord against the birth canal. C-sections are common when it is evident that the baby will be delivered feet first. Fetal monitoring helps detect anoxia before it becomes prolonged.

The transition from receiving oxygen through the umbilical cord to breathing is not always perfectly coordinated. This is another reason that slight oxygen deprivation at birth is not all that unusual. Again, brief periods of deprivation need not have long-term effects (Broman et al., 1975; Sameroff & Chandler, 1975).

Preterm and Low-Birth-Weight Children

Since the fetus makes dramatic gains in weight during the last weeks of pregnancy, prematurity and low birth weight usually go hand in hand. A baby is considered premature or **preterm** when birth occurs at or before 37 weeks of gestation, as compared with the normal 40 weeks. A baby is considered to have a low birth weight when it weighs less than 5½ pounds (about 2,500 grams). When a baby is low in birth weight, even though it is born at full term, it is referred to as **small-for-dates.** Small-for-dates babies, as a group, tend to remain shorter and lighter than their agemates (Cruise, 1973), while preterm babies who survive are more likely to achieve normal heights and weights.

About 7 percent of children are born preterm or low in birth weight (Miller, 1985). Infant mortality is the most immediate risk for low-birth-weight children. Three and one-quarter pounds (1,500 grams) seems to be something of a cut-off point. In a study of births in New York City over a period of one year, about 60 percent of infants below this birth weight died, as compared with a mortality rate of only 5.5 percent for babies born at between about 3¼ to 5½ pounds (1,500–2,500 grams) (Kessner, 1973).

Signs of Prematurity Preterm babies show characteristic signs of immaturity. They are relatively thin, because they have not yet formed the layer of fat that gives so many full-term children their round, robust appearance. They often have fine, downy hair referred to as **lanugo,** and an oily, white substance on the skin known as **vernix.** Lanugo and vernix disappear within a few days or weeks. If they are born six weeks or more prior to full term, their nipples will not yet have emerged. The testicles of boys born this early will not yet have descended into the scrotum. However, the nipples develop further and the testes descend after birth.

The muscles of preterm babies are immature. As a result, they show weakness in the vital sucking and breathing reflexes. They may lack the strength

Anoxia A condition characterized by lack of oxygen.

Preterm Born prior to completion of 37 weeks of gestation.

Small-for-dates Descriptive of neonates who are unusually small for their age.

Lanugo (lan-OO-go). Fine, downy hair that covers much of the body of the neonate, especially preterm babies.

Vernix An oily, white substance that coats the skin of the neonate, especially preterm babies.

▶ ▶ ▶ ▶

to suck and to expand their lungs in breathing. Babies born more than a month prior to full term may breathe irregularly, or suddenly stop breathing, showing a cluster of problems known as **respiratory distress syndrome.** About 20 percent of babies born one month early show the syndrome, and it is found more frequently among infants born still earlier (Behrman & Vaughan, 1983). Respiratory distress syndrome causes a large percentage of U.S. neonatal deaths. The immune systems of preterm babies may also be underdeveloped, making them vulnerable to infections.

Major strides have been made in helping low-birth-weight children survive. Still, low-birth-weight children who do survive often have problems, including lower-than-average verbal ability and academic achievement and various physical, motor, perceptual, and neurological impairments (Colletti, 1979; Holmes et al., 1982; Rose, 1983; Ross, 1985; Ungerer & Sigman, 1983). They also engage in less imaginative play. Preterm infants with very low birth weights are likely to show the greatest cognitive deficits (Caputo & Mandell, 1970; Field et al., 1981). Relatively heavier "preemies" achieve closer-to-average intelligence test scores and are more likely to be placed at age-appropriate grade levels.

Treatment of Preterm Babies Because of their physical frailty, preterm infants usually remain in the hospital and are placed in **incubators** that maintain a temperature-controlled environment and afford some protection from disease. They may be given oxygen, although excessive oxygen can cause permanent eye injury or a form of blindness referred to as **retrolintal fibroplasia.**

A generation ago, preterm babies were left as undisturbed as possible. For one thing, concern was aroused by the prospect of handling such a tiny, frail creature. For another, preterm babies would not normally experience interpersonal contact or other sources of external stimulation until full term.

Despite these rationales, experiments carried out over the past two decades have suggested that preterm infants profit from early stimulation just as do full-term babies. One type of approach "compensates" for early removal from the uterus by exposing preterm infants to treatments that provide features of the intrauterine environment. These treatments include recordings of mater-

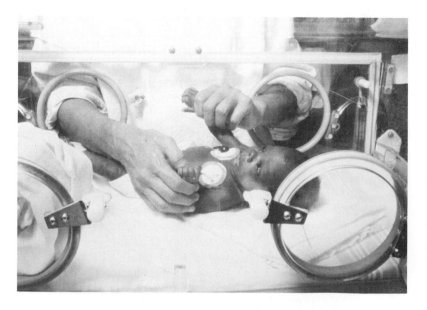

Stimulating a Preterm Infant It was once believed that preterm infants should be left as undisturbed as possible. Today, however, it is recognized that preterm infants usually profit from various kinds of stimulation.

▶ ▶ ▶ ▶

nal heartbeats as they might be heard from within the uterus and placement in incubator "waterbeds" and **womb simulators** whose movements presumably capture some of the sensations of floating within the amniotic sac (Korner et al., 1975).

A second approach has been to provide preterm infants with the types of experiences that full-term babies receive. And so preterm babies have been cuddled, rocked, talked and sung to, exposed to recordings of their mothers' voices, and had mobiles placed within view (Scarr-Salapatek & Williams, 1972). Kathryn Barnard and Helen Bee (1983) combined mechanical rocking with a recorded heartbeat for several 15-minute periods on a daily basis. Immediately following the treatment, the infants showed increased activity levels. At a two-year follow-up, they were significantly ahead in intellectual functioning. By and large, preterm infants exposed to stimulation tend to gain weight more rapidly, show fewer respiratory problems, and make generally greater advances in motor, intellectual, and neurological development than controls (Shaefer et al., 1980).

Parents and Preterm Neonates Parents, unfortunately, often do not treat preterm newborns as well as they treat full-term newborns. For one thing, preterm neonates are less attractive than full-term babies. Preterm infants usually do not have the robust, appealing appearance of many full-term babies, and their frailty may make their heads appear too large. Fear of making a mistake can further discourage parents from handling them, even when the hospital encourages it. Preterm children are also more likely to be abused by their parents in later years (Frodi, 1981).

Mothers of preterm babies frequently report that they feel alienated from them and harbor feelings of failure, guilt, and low self-esteem. Mothers of preterm infants also hold them differently; they cuddle them less and tend to keep them literally at arm's length (Leifer et al., 1972).

Once they come home from the hospital, preterm infants remain more passive than full-term infants (Field, 1980; Crnic et al., 1983), so they demand less interaction with parents. However, when their parents do interact with them during the first year, they are more likely to poke at them and prod them, rub them, and talk to them, apparently in an effort to prod them out of their passivity. Yet this high level of parental activity is not necessarily all positive in nature. Parents and preterm babies smile at one another less frequently during the first year than do parents and full-term babies (Field, 1980). Preterm babies also show less positive emotional tone in their vocalizations (Crnic et al., 1983).

People tend to encourage behavior they like and to discourage behavior that troubles them. As the first year progresses, mothers tend to respond with greater interest when their infants express positive feelings, and increasingly to ignore their infants' expressions of pain, sadness, and anger. Perhaps as a result of this "training," preterm infants express negative emotions decreasingly as they develop from 2½ to 7½ months of age (Malatesta et al., 1986).

Stereotyping of Preterm Babies An ingenious experiment by Marilyn Stern and Katherine Hildebrandt (1986) showed how devastating the stereotype of the preterm infant can be. Stern and Hildebrandt observed the reactions of 27 mothers to unfamiliar infants. All the infants were full term; however, half of them were assigned at random the label "premature." The infants labeled pre-

▶ ▶ ▶ ▶

mature were rated as significantly smaller and less cute (although they were not). The mothers liked them less and gave them less mature toys. The mothers also touched the "premature" infants less often. As a result of this stereotyping, the infants labeled premature were actually *less active* during the interaction than infants labeled full-term. Clearly, our expectations can create self-fulfilling prophecies. In the case of true preterm infants who *are* less active, perhaps an even more vicious cycle of expectation and response takes place.

Preterm babies are not only at risk for various physical defects and impairments. Parents' coping problems and hospital procedures pose psychological risks as well (Hack, 1983). Finally, let us note that preterm infants from middle- and upper-level income families fare better than preterm infants from lower-income families (Sigman et al., 1981). It appears that families who possess adequate resources can better promote the welfare of their preterm children. And longitudinal research does show that preterm children who are reared in consistently attentive, responsive environments attain higher intelligence test scores between the ages of 24 months and 8 years than those who are not (Beckwith & Parmelee, 1986).

This is both sad and promising. It is sad, because it means that the families who suffer in so many other ways also apparently create less adequate environments for the rearing of prematurely born children. But it is also promising, because it suggests that premature infants whose families are given the educational and financial resources to cope with their needs may be able to lower the risks they face (Field et al., 1980; Sameroff & Seifer, 1983).

The Postpartum Period

The weeks following delivery are called the **postpartum period.** The first few days postpartum are frequently happy ones. The long wait is over. The discomforts (and fear) of labor are done with. In the great majority of cases the baby is normal, and the mother may be pleased that she is getting her "figure back." However, a number of women experience significant feelings of depression at this time. In this section we discuss two issues concerning the postpartum period: maternal depression and bonding.

Maternal Depression

Women frequently encounter one of two types of depression during the postpartum period.

Postpartum period The period that immediately follows childbirth.

Maternity blues Crying and feelings of sadness, anxiety and tension, irritability, and anger that half or more of women experience for a couple of days or so after childbirth.

Maternity Blues The first type of depression is less severe. It is called **maternity blues,** and it is experienced by 50 to 80 percent of new mothers (Hopkins et al., 1984; Stein, 1982). The maternity blues are characterized by sadness, crying, anxiety and tension, irritability, and anger. Fortunately, they only last for about two days.

Great hormonal changes occur after delivery and may play a role. Estrogen and progesterone levels drop off, while prolactin and oxytocin are secreted to facilitate breast-feeding. Oxytocin also stimulates uterine contractions and reduces bleeding. Such hormonal changes can apparently trigger unpredictable episodes of crying and depressive feelings which, fortunately, do not

► ► ► ►

last. Maternity blues are also more common following a first pregnancy, and they may reflect adjustment problems. After all, new mothers are frequently overwhelmed by their new responsibilities and the changes that are about to take place in their daily lives. New fathers might experience "paternity blues" but for the fact that the child-rearing chores usually fall squarely on the shoulders of the mother.

Postpartum Depression   About 10 to 15 percent of women have severe feelings of depression that last for several weeks following delivery (Cutrona & Troutman, 1986; Hopkins et al., 1984; O'Hara et al., 1984). These feelings are termed **postpartum depression,** and they are characterized by extreme sadness, apathy, despair, feelings of worthlessness, difficulty concentrating, and physical symptoms such as headaches and digestive problems.

Postpartum depression may reflect physiological and psychological factors. The hormonal changes that may be involved in maternity blues may also be linked to postpartum depression. Moreover, women who encounter postpartum depression—as opposed to maternity blues—are more likely to have had depressive episodes prior to and during pregnancy (O'Hara et al., 1984). Depressive episodes have been linked to imbalances in **neurotransmitters** (Rathus, 1987). It may be that the aftermath of pregnancy creates problematic interactions between hormones and neurotransmitters in a number of women.

But it has also been found that women who encounter postpartum depression are under greater stress than women who do not. Postpartum depression, like maternity blues, may be heightened by concerns about maternal adequacy and the changes that will occur in personal and family life (Gansberg & Mostel, 1984; Hoffnung, 1984). Years of new responsibility lie ahead. For better or worse, life will never be the same, and change itself is usually stressful (Rathus & Nevid, 1986). Some women, of course, may feel depressed because they did not want or plan for the baby. It appears that women who feel helpless and guilty are more likely than others to encounter prolonged depressive episodes related to such issues (Cutrona, 1983).

Infants with difficult temperaments may also contribute to postpartum depression. Their intense emotional reactions, prolonged and vigorous crying episodes, and irregular sleeping and eating patterns are stressful in and of themselves. They also place a severe strain on the mother's sense of competence (Cutrona & Troutman, 1986). A network of social support is helpful to the mother at this time. Unfortunately, if she is isolated in the home, and if relatives live far away, such support may be hard to come by, and depression may persist.

Bonding

In Chapter 10 we shall fully explore the nature of parent–child attachment. Here let us consider the view that the first hours postpartum provide a special opportunity for bonding between parents and newborns.

The Kennell and Klaus Study   One study that more than any other has stirred controversy on this issue was carried out by physicians John Kennell and Marshall Klaus and their colleagues (Kennell et al., 1974). Kennell and Klaus held the belief that the first few hours after birth present a "maternal-sensitive" period during which the mother is particularly disposed, largely because of

▶ ▶ ▶ ▶

Breast-feeding versus Bottle-Feeding: Does It Make a Difference?

▷
▷
▷
▷

▷ The decision as to whether or not to breast-feed is not taken lightly by most parents. There are a number of concerns about the relative physical and psychological merits of breast- and bottle-feeding for infants. There are also political issues in that breast-feeding is associated with the stereotypical feminine role, and many mothers therefore ask themselves what breast- or bottle-feeding will "mean" for them as women.

Why do women formula- or bottle-feed their children? Financial pressures require many women to return to the work force. Some parents prefer to share child-feeding responsibilities, and the father, of course, is well equipped to hold a bottle. Other women find bottle-feeding more convenient and trouble-free (Manstead et al., 1983).

Today slightly over half of U.S. women breast-feed their children (Martinez & Krieger, 1985). White women are significantly more likely than black or Hispanic-American women to breast-feed (Fetterly & Graubard, 1984; Rassin et al., 1984). The percentage of breast-feeding mothers was higher early in the century, when formulas were less well-perfected and more difficult to prepare. The percentage was somewhat lower a couple of decades ago, when formula-feeding became more convenient, and it was generally believed that bottle-fed babies thrived just as well as breast-fed babies.

Mother's Milk: The Ultimate Fast Food?

Mother's milk has been referred to as the ultimate fast food or the perfect health food (Eiger & Olds, 1986). Mother's milk is superior to cow's milk or formula in its balance of nutrients (Alemi et al., 1981; Sadowitz & Oski, 1983). It contains more vitamins A and C and more iron than cow's milk. Breast milk is also served at the right temperature. Breast milk contains antibodies that help infants fend off diseases which the mother has had, or against which the mother has been inoculated, such as tetanus, chicken pox, typhoid, and small pox (Ogra & Greene, 1982). It helps prevent respiratory infections, helps prevent allergies, and is (almost always) free from infectious agents (Forman et al., 1984; Jelliffe & Jelliffe, 1983). Breast-feeding even seems to help the muscle tissue of the uterus to tighten up following delivery (Matlin, 1987). By and large, women who choose to breast-feed frequently offer the reason that breast-feeding will be better for their babies (Newton, 1971). Is it?

In attempting to answer this extremely important question, we must first note that long-term comparisons of breast-fed and bottle-fed U.S. children show few, if any, significant differences in the ultimate welfare of the children (Schmitt, 1970). However, breast-fed babies do seem to have somewhat fewer allergies, fewer digestive upsets (Larsen & Homer, 1978), and fewer infections of the respiratory system and gastrointestinal tract (Marano, 1979). On the other hand, alcohol, many drugs taken by the mother, and environmental hazards such as PCB are passed along to their babies through breast milk, and so breast milk may not always be so pure as it would seem.

The Selection Factor

Most studies concerning differences in feeding practices include children whose parents have *chosen* to breast- or bottle-feed. It may be that mothers who choose to breast-feed differ from mothers who elect to bottle-feed, and that these differences rather than the breast- or bottle-feed-

Bottle-Feeding versus Breast-Feeding *Bottle-feeding has been viewed as a way of liberating third world women to join the work force. Unfortunately, formulas have been watered down in many underdeveloped nations, so that bottle-fed children have been malnourished.*

ing per se account for differences in the mother–child relationship or in the welfare of the children. For example, one study found that mothers who breast-fed their babies spent more time holding and rocking them (Newton, 1979). Another reported that babies who are breast-fed on demand seem more secure (Newton, 1972). It is unlikely that these findings can be attributed to breast-feeding in and of itself. It could also be that mothers who choose to breast-feed, and to breast-feed on demand, are seeking closer relationships with their infants (Manstead et al., 1983).

In one of the few experiments on breast-feeding, mothers alternately breast- and bottle-fed their children. It was found that bottle-feeding was somewhat more stressful and anxiety-evoking because of its relative inconvenience, suggesting that bottle-feeding may introduce an element of stress into the mother–child relationship (Modahl & Newton, 1979). But it must be emphasized that the women in the experiment were alternating breast- and bottle-feeding, a practice that is rare in everyday life and carries stresses of its own.

Problems in the "Third World"

Some people have viewed bottle-feeding as more "modern" than breast-feeding, since it helps free women from a traditional task that hampers their availability to the work force. For this reason, bottle-feeding has found its way into a number of prein-dustrialized "third-world" nations as a method of hastening industrialization. Unfortunately, in many cases it has backfired. Many poverty-stricken mothers water down the formula, thus providing their babies with inadequate nutrition. In other cases the formula has been prepared under unsanitary conditions or placed in unsanitized bottles, causing infant deaths. For reasons such as these, in 1981 the World Health Organization voted to encourage a ban on the use of infant formulas in third-world nations.

In sum, breast-feeding appears to have some health benefits for children in terms of antibodies and decreased likelihood of allergic reactions. However, these differences are minor and the great majority of bottle-fed (U.S.) children have thrived. The current state of the evidence suggests that most U.S. women are probably well-advised to choose whether to breast- or bottle-feed on the basis of financial considerations or personal preferences, and not to be overly concerned about the long-term effects of their decisions on the physical or psychological development of their infants.

One more thing: Breast-feeding delays resumption of normal menstrual cycles, thus decreasing the likelihood that a nursing mother will become pregnant during the first few months after delivery (Short, 1984), but in no way assuring it. Nursing is unreliable as a birth-control method, and nursing mothers who wish to avoid pregnancy should not assume that they are "safe."

▶ ▶ ▶ ▶

hormone levels, to form a bond with the neonate. The researchers recruited 28 mothers and their full-term neonates for the study. Most of the women were unwed, impoverished, and poorly educated.

Half the women were randomly assigned to standard hospital procedure, in which their babies were whisked away to the nursery shortly after birth. Throughout the remainder of the hospital stay, the babies visited with their mothers for half-hour periods at feeding time. The other group of mothers spent a half-hour with their neonates within three hours after birth. They spent five hours a day with their infants for the remainder of the stay. The hospital staff encouraged and reassured the group of mothers who had extended contact.

Follow-ups over a two-year period suggested that extended contact had enormous benefits for the mothers and children (Klaus & Kennell, 1976). Extended-contact mothers were more likely than controls to cuddle their babies, pick them up and soothe them when they cried, enjoy their presence, and worry about them in their absence. At 1 year of age, the extended-contact infants outscored controls in physical and intellectual development. These advantages extended into the second year. Extended-contact mothers had more interaction with their infants. They were warmer, more encouraging, and less likely to give commands.

Since this landmark study, similar research has been carried out with subjects drawn from different social classes in various countries around the world. Most studies confirm the finding that extended early contact leads to better parent–child relationships and superior development, at least on a short-term basis (Goldberg, 1983; Thomson & Kramer, 1984). Studies on the effects of early extended *father* contact with newborns have shown comparable results. Extended-contact fathers engage in more face-to-face interaction with their infants several months afterward (Keller et al., 1981; Rodhölm, 1981).

A Critique   Critics note that these studies are fraught with methodological problems (Chess & Thomas, 1982; Goldberg, 1983; Lamb, 1982; Myers, 1984; Svejda et al., 1980; Thomson & Kramer, 1984). For one thing, sample size was generally limited. For another, the definition of "extended early contact" varied considerably from study to study. In the Rodhölm (1981) study, for example, fathers in the extended-contact group held their newborns for *ten minutes* after birth, whereas controls caught only a glimpse of their children. Compare this to the five hours a day in the Kennell and Klaus (1974) study.

To me, the most telling criticism is that we cannot sort out the effects of extended contact from those that stem from parents' knowledge that they were in a "special" group. Not only did mothers in the Kennell and Klaus study receive extra time with their babies, but the hospital staff showed active interest in them and gave them encouragement and support. Did their infants fare better because of superior "bonding," or because the hospital staff taught them that their relationships with their children were special and instructed them as to how to hold their babies, play with them, and care for them? Because of such criticisms as these, even Kennell and Klaus (1984) have toned down their views in their more recent writings. They now view the hours after birth as just one element in a complex and prolonged bonding process.

Regardless of the validity of these studies, awareness of the possible importance of early parent–child contact has revolutionized U.S. hospital policies. In 1983, when my youngest daughter Jordan was born in Princeton, New Jersey, her 2-year-old sister Allyn and I were encouraged to be with her at

► ► ► ►

certain hours of the day for "bonding time." What a difference from Margaret Matlin's experience:

> When my oldest daughter was born in 1970, a nurse yelled at me for un-wrapping her from her blanket-cocoon, and I contemplated hiding her under my bedsheets to prolong our visit beyond the specified 30 minutes. **Rooming-in** reminds everyone that the baby belongs to the mother, and not to the hospital (Matlin, 1987, p. 377).

Of course the first hours are "special." There has been a major life change for parents and siblings, and a new person has (literally) emerged upon the scene, with all the potential physical and emotional strengths and weaknesses to which we all fall heir. But research is not compelling that these hours are critical, or that failure to "form bonds" during this time will result in a second-rate parent–child relationship (Korsch, 1983). There are countless millions of fine parent–child relationships in which the parents were denied these early hours with their children (Rutter, 1981).

The message for parents may well be to relax and not worry about how well their "bonding" with their neonate is going. Still, like chicken soup, a little extra contact probably won't hurt.

Characteristics of Newborn Children

What is there to know about newborn babies? One pediatrician apparently believed he had summed up the wisdom of the centuries by instructing the mother of a newborn girl to "Feed her, change her, love her." This advice did recognize that neonates need to eat, that they eliminate waste products, and that they profit from social interaction, but it also suggests that newborn babies are simple creatures with only a few needs. In fact, neonates are quite complex, and they undergo rapid developmental changes right from their beginnings in the new world.

Many neonates come into the world looking a bit fuzzy, because the lanugo has not yet disappeared, although full-term babies show less of this downy substance than preterm babies do. Full-term babies also show something of the protective oily coating or vernix shown by preterm babies. It dries up within a few days.

Newborns tend to be pale, regardless of race. Their skin is thin, and the blood flowing through surface capillaries creates a pinkish cast. Tiny amounts of "witch's milk" sometimes issue from the nipples, in response to estrogen secreted by the placenta prior to birth. Estrogen may also cause baby girls to have bloody vaginal discharges, which are usually no cause for concern—though there is no harm in checking with the pediatrician.

In this section we discuss several aspects of the behavior of newborn children. Newborns may be utterly dependent on others, but they are probably more aware of their surroundings than you had imagined, and they make rapid adaptations to the world around them.

Reflexes

If soon after birth you had been held gently for a few moments with your face down in comfortably warm water, you would not have drowned.

▶ ▶ ▶ ▶

Reflex *An unlearned, stereotypical response to a stimulus.*

Voluntarily *Intentionally.*

Rooting reflex *A reflex in which infants turn their mouths and heads in the direction of a stroking of the cheek or the corner of the mouth.*

Instead of breathing the water in, you would have exhaled slowly through the mouth and engaged in swimming motions.* This swimming response is innate, or inborn, and it is just one of the many **reflexes** shown by neonates. Reflexes are simple, unlearned, stereotypical responses that are elicited by certain types of stimulation. They do not require higher brain functions; they occur automatically, without thinking.

Reflexes are the most complicated motor activities displayed by newborns. Neonates cannot roll over, sit up, reach for an object that they see, or raise their heads. In contrast to specific reflex actions, other motor behaviors seem diffuse and directionless indeed.

But let us return to our early venture into the water. If you had been placed into the water not a few moments but several months after birth, the results might have been very different, and disastrous. After a few months the swimming reflex, like many others, ceases to exist. However, at 6 to 12 months of age infants can learn how to swim **voluntarily.** In fact, the transition from reflexive swimming to learned swimming can be reasonably smooth with careful guided practice.

Many reflexes have survival value. Adults and neonates, for example, will reflexively close their eyes when assaulted with a puff of air or sudden bright light. Others seem to reflect interesting facets of the evolution of the nervous system. The swimming reflex seems to suggest that there was a time when our ancestors profited from being born able to swim. A number of reflexes are discussed below.

The Breathing Reflex The most basic reflex for survival is breathing. The breathing rate is regulated by the oxygen and carbon dioxide content of the blood and other bodily fluids. We take in oxygen and give off carbon dioxide. Higher percentages of carbon dioxide in the body cause us to inhale by contracting muscles that lift the ribs and lower the diaphragm; as a consequence, the chest cavity expands and air rushes into the lungs. We exhale by relaxing these muscles.

Newborns normally take their first breath before the umbilical cord is cut. The muscles of preterm babies may not be mature enough to sustain independent breathing. Also, the walls of the tiny air sacs within their lungs may tend to stick together "like the sides of a wet plastic bag" when they do not yet secrete a substance that lubricates the walls of the sacs (Arms & Camp, 1987, p. 666).

The breathing reflex continues to work for a lifetime, although we can take conscious control of breathing when we choose to. Don't worry if your children decide to hold their breaths now and then. Increasing discomfort will usually discourage them, and at worst they will lose consciousness because of buildup of carbon dioxide. Assuming that their regulation of breathing is working properly, reflexive breathing will take over and they will receive the oxygen they need (Arms & Camp, 1987, p. 675).

The Rooting Reflex In the **rooting reflex,** the baby turns the head and mouth toward a stimulus that prods or strokes the cheek, chin, or corner of the mouth. After a couple of months or so, the response becomes more finely tuned. The baby responds only to stimulation at the corner of the mouth and tends to move

*I urge readers not to test babies for this reflex. The hazards are obvious.

▶ ▶ ▶ ▶

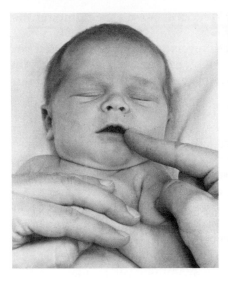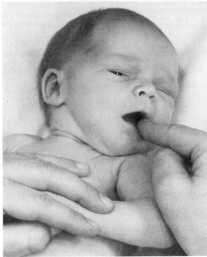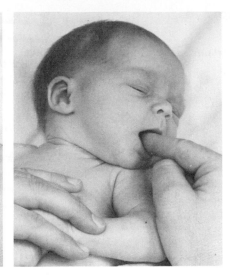

The Rooting Reflex *Tactile stimulation of the corner of the mouth elicits turning of the head toward the stimulus.*

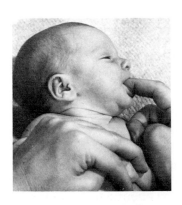

Testing the Sucking Reflex

Neural *Of the nervous system.*

Stupor *A state of slowed down or dulled responsiveness.*

Moro reflex *A reflex in which infants arch their backs and draw up their legs in response to a sudden change in position.*

the lips rather than turn the entire head. The rooting reflex facilitates finding of the mother's nipple, in preparation for sucking. New mothers might attempt to orient the baby's head toward the breast by gently pushing the *opposite* side of the face, but because babies tend to turn toward tactile stimulation on the face, this maternal tactic makes it more difficult for the baby to "find" the nipple.

The Sucking Reflex Babies suck by squeezing objects between the tongue and palate, and by contracting the cheek muscles, which creates suction. They will suck almost any object that touches the lips. For obvious reasons, the sucking reflex, like the breathing reflex, is basic to survival. The sucking reflex is accompanied by breathing through the nose and by the swallowing reflex, in which muscles in the throat cause food (or other material) to pass from the mouth into the stomach. The sucking reflex grows stronger during the first days after birth and can be lost if not stimulated. As the months go on, reflexive sucking becomes replaced by voluntary sucking.

Pediatricians learn a good deal about the adequacy of newborn babies' **neural** functioning by testing their reflexes. Shortly after birth, a finger or other object is placed about three to four centimeters into the baby's mouth to determine whether he or she has an adequately "strong suck." Absence or weakness of the sucking reflex may indicate immaturity (as in prematurity), **stupor** which can result from anesthetics used during childbirth, brain injury, or retardation.

Infants begin to chew their food at about 5 to 8 months, but components of the muscular activities involved in chewing begin to appear as early as the first week after birth (Sheppard & Mysak, 1984).

The Moro Reflex In the startle or **Moro reflex** (named after Ernst Moro, who first described the reflex in 1918), the back arches, the legs draw up, and the arms are brought forward in a hugging or embracing motion. The Moro reflex occurs when a baby's position is suddenly changed or support for the head and

▶ ▶ ▶ ▶

Palmar reflex *A reflex in which infants grasp objects that cause pressure against the palms.*

Stepping reflex *A reflex in which infants take steps when held under the arms and leaned forward so that their feet press against the ground.*

Placing reflex *A reflex in which infants lift their legs when pressure is placed against the top of the foot.*

Babinski reflex *A reflex in which infants fan their toes when the undersides of their feet are stroked.*

Plantar reflex *A reflex in which infants curl their toes downward in response to pressure against the balls of the feet.*

neck is suddenly lost. It can also be elicited by loud noises, by bumping the baby's crib, or by jerking the baby's blanket.

The Moro reflex is usually lost by six to seven months after birth (Kessen et al., 1970), although similar movements can be found in adults who suddenly lose support. Absence of the Moro reflex can indicate immaturity or **edema** of the brain, or other brain damage.

The Palmar Reflex During the first few weeks following birth, babies show an increasing tendency to reflexively grasp fingers or other objects pressed against the palms of their hands. In this grasping or **palmar reflex,** they use four fingers only (the thumbs are not included). The palmar reflex is stronger when babies are simultaneously startled. Most babies can support their own weight in this way. They can be literally lifted into the air as they reflexively cling with two hands. Some babies can actually support their weight with just one hand. The grasping reflex is usually lost by 3 to 4 months of age, and babies generally show voluntary grasping by 5 to 6 months.

The Moro and palmar reflexes, like the swimming reflex, may suggest something about our evolutionary history. Baby monkeys cling to their mothers' backs or abdomens, from which they can be dislodged by sudden jarring (Prechtl, 1965). Such jarring is likely to occur when the mother spies a predator and seeks to flee. The startle and grasping reflexes then work together to prevent the infant from falling off and possibly being left behind.

Absence of the grasping reflex may indicate depressed activity of the nervous system, which can stem from use of anesthetics during childbirth.

Stepping and Placing Reflexes One or two days after birth, babies show reflexes that mimic walking. When held under the arms and tilted forward such that the feet press against a solid surface, a baby will show a **stepping reflex** in which the feet are advanced alternately. A full-term baby "walks" heel-to-toe, whereas a preterm infant is more likely to remain on tiptoe.

The **placing reflex** is demonstrated by holding the baby upright and pressing the top part of the feet against a surface, such as the rung of a ladder. The baby will usually lift a foot and place it on top of the rung, as if climbing. The stepping and placing reflexes usually disappear by about 3 to 4 months of age.

Eliminatory Reflexes Babies urinate and have bowel movements by reflex activity. Urination occurs in response to the pressure of a full (or filling) bladder and bowel movements in response to pressure within the lower part of the large intestine. During the toilet-training process, infants learn to inhibit these reflexes, which otherwise would control elimination for a lifetime.

Other Reflexes Other reflexes that merit mentioning are the Babinski, plantar, withdrawal, and Babkin reflexes.

In the **Babinski reflex,** the neonate fans or spreads the toes in response to stroking of the foot from heel to toes. The Babinski reflex normally disappears toward the end of the first year, to be replaced by curling downward of the toes. Persistence of the Babinski reflex may suggest defects of the lower spinal cord, lagging development of nerve cells, or other disorders.

In the toe grasp or **Plantar reflex,** the baby curls the toes downward in response to pressure against the balls of the feet. The Plantar reflex usually

Withdrawal reflex *Reflexive recoiling from a painful stimulus.*

Babkin reflex *A reflex in which infants open their mouths and attempt to lift their heads in response to pressure against the palms when they are lying on their backs.*

Sensation *The stimulation of sensory receptors and the transmission of sensory information to the spinal cord and brain.*

disappears by 8 to 12 months, and its absence suggests defects in the lower part of the spinal cord.

In the **withdrawal reflex,** the baby recoils from an aversive stimulus, such as a pinprick or the touch of a heated bottle, by flexing the legs and crying. Depending on the site of painful stimulation, neonates may also flex their arms or twist their bodies. These responses have clear survival value. They frequently permit neonates to terminate contact with harmful objects, and they draw the attention of adults. The withdrawal reflex is strongest during the first two weeks after birth.

The **Babkin reflex** is elicited by pressing the palms of the neonate's hands while he or she is lying on the back. When so stimulated, the baby opens the mouth, closes the eyes, turns the head straight ahead, and may attempt to lift the head. The Babkin reflex is more complex than the rooting reflex, but it may be functionally similar. Like the rooting reflex, it appears to set the stage for sucking. The Babkin reflex usually disappears in three to four months, and its absence may indicate depressed activity of the brain or spinal cord.

Some reflexes, such as breathing and blinking the eye in response to a puff of air, remain with us for life. When reflexes disappear, they may do so because of maturation of the nervous system, or because they become integrated into learned behavior patterns. For example, loss of the Moro and Babinski reflexes indicates that the nervous system is maturing on schedule. The sucking reflex is gradually replaced by voluntary sucking after a number of months, and the reflexive elimination of waste products may not become inhibited for two to four years.

The Brazelton Neonatal Behavioral Assessment Scale   Boston pediatrician T. Berry Brazelton created a scale, the Brazelton Neonatal Behavioral Assessment Scale, that measures neonates' reflexes and other behavior patterns. The test screens neonates for behavioral and neurological problems by assessing four areas of behavior—motor behavior, including muscle tone and most reflexes; response to stress, as shown, for example, by the startle reflex; adaptive behavior, such as orientation to the examiner and responsiveness to cuddling; and control over physiological state, as shown by quieting oneself after being disturbed.

And so, neonates respond to their new environment. In order to respond, they must first *sense* and *perceive.* Let us now consider some of the sensory capabilties of the neonate.

Sensation and Perception

Earlier we asked what there is to know about newborn babies. Perhaps we could begin this section by asking what newborn babies are capable of knowing—or of perceiving about the new world. The answer is "quite a lot." In this section let us briefly differentiate between sensation and perception and summarize some information about the capabilities of neonates. In Chapter 6 we shall explore the development of perceptual processes in detail.

Some Definitions   **Sensation** is the stimulation of sensory receptors and the transmission of sensory information to the central nervous system (spinal cord or brain). Sensory receptors are located in sensory organs such as the eyes and ears, in the skin, and elsewhere in the body. The stimulation of these receptors

▶ ▶ ▶ ▶

is mechanical, resulting from the presence of physical sources of energy such as light, sound, touch, and so on.

Perception is not mechanical. Perception is the process by which sensations are organized into an inner representation of the world, providing the child with his or her own internal picture or map of reality. It seems that we are "prewired" to perceive certain types of sensory information in certain ways and to prefer some types of stimulation to others, but perception is also influenced by the child's expectations and learning experiences.

The infant's sensory (and motor) capabilities are closely related to the maturation of neurons and of certain areas of the brain. One of the issues concerning childhood sensation and perception is the degree to which nature and nurture influence various processes. Unborn children are capable of some sensory activity and may thus be said to be capable of "experiences" in utero. However, given adequate nutrition in utero, it is likely that the sensory capabilities of newborn children largely reflect the unfolding of their genetic potential, or nature.

Some Characteristics of the Neonate At birth the irises of the eyes widen reflexively to admit more light when it is dark, and they narrow to admit less light when the light is bright. Neonates can see, but are nearsighted by the standards of older children and adults. They can most clearly see objects seven to nine inches from their eyes. Newborns are also capable of tracking (following) moving visual stimuli, as long as the movement is slow and near the center of the visual field.

Fetuses respond to sounds in utero, and neonates can hear unless their ears are clogged with amniotic fluid. Newborns respond differently to sounds of different pitches and amplitude, and they appear to be prewired to respond to speech.

Neonates discriminate distinct odors and turn away from unpleasant ones. They are also sensitive to the smell of mothers' milk. Neonates can discriminate among tastes as they can among odors, preferring sweet tastes.

Learning

The perceptual limits of neonates suggest that they may not learn so rapidly as older children do. After all, we must sense and perceive clearly those things that we are to learn about. However, most if not all neonates seem capable of at least two basic forms of learning: classical and operant conditioning.

Classical Conditioning of Neonates In classical conditioning of neonates, involuntary responses are conditioned to new stimuli (Clifton, 1974; Stamps & Porges, 1975). In a typical study, this one by Czechoslovakian researcher Hanuš Papoušek (1967), newborn, 3-month-old, and 5-month-old infants were taught to show the rooting reflex in response to a bell.

The rooting reflex (UR) can be elicited by stroking the corner of the infant's mouth (US). Papoušek paired stroking of the infants' mouths with a bell (CS). After repeated pairings, the bell (CS) gained the capacity to elicit turning of the head (CR). In this case, the conditioned response was also a conditioned reflex.

▶ ▶ ▶ ▶

Papoušek, like other researchers (e.g., Lewis, 1969), found that a great many repetitions are required for young infants. Newborn infants required an average of 177 trials to reach the criterion of five successive responses to the bell. Three-month-old infants required an average of 42 trials, and 5-month-olds needed only 28. But research such as this shows that even newborns are equipped to learn that events peculiar to their own environments (bells or other conditioned stimuli) may mean that a meal is at hand—or, more accurately, at mouth. One neonate may learn that a light going on overhead precedes a meal. Another may learn that feeding is preceded by the rustling of a carpet of thatched leaves. The conditioned stimuli are culture-specific; the capacity to learn is universal.

Operant Conditioning of Neonates   Operant conditioning, like classical conditioning, can take place with neonates. Sameroff (1968, 1971), for example, modified the sucking reflexes of neonates through reinforcement with milk. Earlier in the chapter, we saw that the sucking reflex involves (a) pressing the nipple against the palate with the tongue, and (b) creating suction with the cheek muscles. Sameroff was able to increase the strength of either sucking component with neonates, *a* or *b,* by selectively reinforcing it with milk.

In the Papoušek (1967) study discussed above there was also an operant conditioning component. Through repeated pairing with stroking the corner of the mouth, a bell came to elicit the rooting reflex. However, rooting in response to the bell was also reinforced with milk.

The younger the child, the more important it is that reinforcers be administered rapidly. Among newborns it seems that reinforcers must be administered within a second after the desired behavior is performed if learning is to occur (Millar, 1972).

There are major individual differences in conditionability among newborn children. Some can be conditioned with relatively few trials, while others apparently cannot learn some conditioning tasks at all (Fitzgerald & Brackbill, 1976). However, it would be premature to attribute differences in conditionability to differences in "intelligence." Although intelligence is often loosely thought of as learning ability, conditionability is not comparable with the complex cognitive tasks that define intellectual performance in older children. And, as we shall see in Chapter 9, measures of intelligence in infants do not correlate very well with measures of intelligence that are taken at later ages.

Social Learning and Neonates   The results of research as to whether neonates can engage in social learning are not so clear.

In one experiment, for example, neonates only 0.7–71 hours old were found to "imitate" adults who opened their mouths and protruded their tongues (Meltzoff & Moore, 1983). In this study, the neonates were supported in a semiupright position in a padded infant seat. As they lay in the seat, an adult woman in their field of vision opened her mouth and protruded her tongue for 20 seconds. She then held her tongue in for 20 seconds, followed by another 20 seconds of protrusion. During periods when the woman protruded her tongue, the neonates did likewise at greater-than-chance frequencies.

But before you marvel too closely at this early "social learning," recognize that most scholars consider this early imitation reflexive (e.g., Abravanel & Sigafoos, 1984). In a relevant study, Sandra Jacobson (1979) found that 6-week-old babies stuck out their tongues when nonhuman stimuli, such as small

▶ ▶ ▶ ▶

balls or felt-tipped pens, were moved toward their mouths. In order for behavior to be considered imitative, it must occur in response to another person's engaging in the same (or highly similar) behavior. So this sort of neonatal behavior cannot properly be labeled imitative.

Most developmentalists agree that *voluntary* (as opposed to reflexive) imitation of other people's gestures and sounds generally appears at some time between 2 and 4 months of age.

Patterns of Sleeping

Sleep has always been a fascinating subject. After all, we spend about one-third of our adult lives sleeping. Newborn infants greatly outdo us, spending two-thirds of their time, or about 16 hours per day, in sleep. And in one of life's basic challenges to parents, neonates do not sleep their 16 hours in a row.

Individual infants require different amounts of sleep and follow different patterns of sleep, but virtually all infants distribute their sleeping throughout the day and night through a series of naps. The typical infant has about six cycles of waking and sleeping throughout a 24-hour period. The longest nap typically approaches four and one-half hours, and the neonate is usually awake for a little more than one hour during each cycle.

This pattern of waking and sleeping changes rapidly and dramatically over the course of the years. Even after a month or so, the infant has fewer but longer sleep periods, and will usually take longer naps during the night. Parents whose babies "do not know the difference between night and day" usually teach them the difference by playing with them during daytime hours, once feeding and caretaking chores have been carried out, and by putting them back to sleep as soon as possible when they awaken hungry during the night. Most parents do not require professional instruction in this "method." At 3:00 and 4:00 A.M. parents are not likely to feel playful—at least toward their children.

By the ages of about 6 months to a year, many infants begin to sleep through the night. Many infants start sleeping through the night earlier, and some people rarely sleep through the night at any age. A number of infants begin to sleep through the night for a week or so and then revert to their wakeful ways again for a while.

REM and NREM Sleep   Sleep itself is not a consistent state. Figure 4.2 shows that sleep can be divided into **rapid-eye-movement** (REM) sleep and **non-rapid-eye-movement** (NREM) sleep. Studies with the **electroencephalograph** (EEG) show that we can subdivide NREM sleep into four additional stages of sleep, each with its characteristic brain waves, but our discussion will be limited to REM and NREM sleep. REM sleep is characterized by rapid eye movements that can be observed beneath closed lids. The EEG patterns produced during REM sleep resemble those of the waking state, for which reason REM sleep is also called paradoxical sleep. However, we are hard to awaken during REM sleep. Adults who are roused during REM sleep report that they have been dreaming about 80 percent of the time. Adults report dreaming only about 20 percent of the time when they are awakened during NREM sleep. The reasons for dreaming remain a mystery, although the content of dreams most often parallels the experiences of the waking day.

Note from Figure 4.2 that neonates spend about half their time sleeping in REM sleep. By 6 months or so, REM sleep accounts for only about 30 percent

Rapid-eye-movement *A period of sleep during which we are likely to dream, as indicated by rapid eye movements. Abbreviated REM sleep.*

Non-rapid-eye-movement *Periods of sleep during which we are unlikely to dream. Abbreviated NREM sleep.*

Electroencephalograph *An instrument that measures electrical activity of the brain. Abbreviated EEG.*

▶ ▶ ▶ ▶

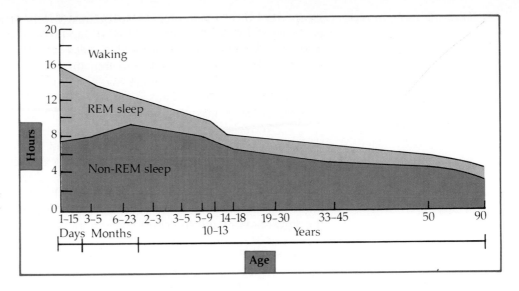

Figure 4.2 REM Sleep and NREM Sleep
Neonates spend nearly 50 percent of their time sleeping in rapid-eye movement (REM) sleep.
The percentage of time spent sleeping in REM sleep drops off to 20–25 percent for 2- to 3-year-
olds. As we mature, we sleep fewer hours, and most of the dropoff can be attributed to decline
in REM sleep.

of the baby's sleep, and by 2 to 3 years, the percentage of REM sleep drops off to about 20–25 (Coons & Guilleminault, 1982). There is a dramatic falling off in the total number of hours spent in sleep as we develop. Figure 4.2 shows that the major portion of the dropoff can be attributed to lessened REM sleep. The amount of NREM sleep actually increases slightly during the first couple of years, although the overall amount of sleep shows a steep decline. Why?

Autostimulation Theory There is no evidence for assuming that neonates dream in the way that older children and adults do. Roffwarg, Muzio, and Dement (1966) propose an **autostimulation theory** explanation of REM sleep in infants. According to this view, the brain requires a certain amount of neural activity in order to develop properly. This activity can be stimulated from internal or external sources. In older children and adults, external sources of stimulation are provided by activity, a vast and shifting array of sensory impressions, and, perhaps, thought processes during the waking state. The newborn, however, spends its brief waking periods largely isolated from the kaleidoscope of events of the world outside and is not likely to be lost in deep thought. Thus, in the waking state, he or she may not provide the brain with the needed stimulation. As a compensatory measure, the neonate spends relatively more time in REM sleep, which most closely parallels the waking state in terms of brain waves. While infants are in REM sleep, internal physiological stimulation spurs the brain on to appropriate development. Preterm babies spend even greater proportions of their time in REM sleep than full-term babies, perhaps— goes the argument—because they might require relatively greater stimulation of the brain.

A couple of studies provide some support for the autostimulation theory. In one, it was found that circumcised neonates spent less time in REM

Autostimulation theory The view that REM sleep in infants fosters the development of the brain by stimulating neural activity.

▶ ▶ ▶ ▶

Hindbrain *The back part of the brain.*

Cerebral cortex *The wrinkled surface area of the brain that makes possible the functions of thought and language.*

sleep than did noncircumcised neonates (Emde et al., 1971). The process of circumcision is highly stimulating to neonates, and perhaps this external experience decreases the amount of internal stimulation or autostimulation they require. In another, it was found that infants who spent a good deal of time fixating on visual stimuli while awake showed temporary decreases in REM sleep (Boismier, 1977). Again, external stimulation might have reduced the need for internal stimulation.

In this context, it is worth noting that one theory of dreams holds that they are caused by physiological activation of the **hindbrain** and integration of this activity by the **cerebral cortex** (Hobson & McCarley, 1977). The dream's content reflects the neural activity of parts of the cortex involved in vision, hearing, and memory. It could also be that in neonates the hind part of the brain also stimulates cerebral activity and development during REM sleep, although it is not until the child has experiences to draw upon that dreaming as we know it occurs.

Crying and Soothing

No discussion of the behavior of the neonate would be complete without mentioning crying—a comment that parents will view as an understatement. I have known a number of first-time parents who have attempted to follow an imaginary eleventh Commandment, "The baby shall not cry." Some parents have entered into conflict with hospital nurses who tell them not to worry when their babies are crying on the other side of the nursery's glass partition. Nurses frequently tell parents that their babies *must* cry, that crying helps clear their respiratory systems of any fluids that linger from the amniotic sac, and that it stimulates the circulatory system.

Whether crying is healthful and necessary remains an open question, but at least some crying among babies seems universal. Some scholars have thought of crying as a sort of "primitive language," but it is not. Languages, even "primitive," contain units and groupings of sounds that symbolize objects and events. Crying does not. Still, crying appears to be both expressive and functional. Crying, that is, serves as an infant's expressive response to aversive stimulation and also stimulates caretakers to do something to help. Crying thus "communicates" something, even though it is not a form of language.

Types of Crying   There are a number of different types of cries. Schaffer (1971) suggests the existence of three distinct patterns: crying that stems from (1) hunger, (2) anger, and (3) pain. Let us amplify this list and suggest additional patterns:

- A cry of hunger frequently begins in a halting, whining manner and gradually builds to a rhythmic, loud cry.
- A whining, fretful cry that starts and stops, growing gradually lower and slower, may indicate that the baby is irritable and fatigued and is about to fall asleep.
- A sudden loud, insistent cry associated with flexing and kicking of the legs may indicate colic (pain due to gas or other sources of distress in the digestive

tract). The baby may seem to hold his or her breath for a few moments, then gasp and begin to cry again.*

- A fretful cry associated with passing of air and green stool may indicate indigestion.
- A whining cry associated with listlessness and little movement may suggest illness and weakness.
- A shrill, sharp cry associated with a great deal of movement (or hardly any movement) may indicate injury.

Prior to parenthood, many people wonder whether they will be able to recognize the "meaning" of their babies' cries, but it usually does not take them long. Cries may also have special meaning for health professionals, to whom certain cries serve as a sign of abnormal development. For example, the cries of chronically distressed infants differ from those of normal infants in both rhythm and pitch. Patterns of crying may be indicative of problems ranging from chromosomal abnormalities to infections to fetal malnutrition (Porter et al., 1986; Zeskind, 1983).

Soothing Sucking is not only a means for ingesting food in the infant; it also seems to function as a built-in tranquilizer. Sucking on a **pacifier** decreases crying and agitated movement in neonates who have not yet had the opportunity to feed (Kessen et al., 1967). Therefore, the soothing function of sucking need not be learned through experience.

Parents find many other ways to soothe infants, including **swaddling** them (Lipton et al., 1965) and rocking them (Pederson & Ter Vrugt, 1973). Speaking to infants in a soothing, low voice and picking them up also have quieting effects.

Learning occurs quickly during the soothing process. Parents learn by trial and error what types of embraces and movements are likely to soothe their infants. And infants learn quickly that crying is followed by being picked up or other forms of intervention.

When babies cry because of hunger or another recognizable form of discomfort, parents usually pick them up, do what needs to be done, and, perhaps after a play period, put them down again. If the baby starts to cry again, perhaps because he or she would rather be held than go to sleep, parents are often at a loss as to what to do. They may feel damned if they do and damned if they don't. That is, if they ignore the baby, he or she will continue to cry (and presumably suffer), at least for a while. If they pick the baby up quickly, they may worry that they are reinforcing the baby for crying. In this way, the child may become "spoiled" and find it progressively more difficult to engage in self-soothing to get to sleep.

What of it? Do babies who are picked up quickly cry more often or less often? Does picking them up reassure and soothe them, or does it simply rein-

Pacifier An artificial nipple or teething ring that soothes babies.

Swaddling Wrapping in bands of cloth that restrict movement. (See Chapter 1 for a historical perspective on swaddling.)

*This type of crying may begin abruptly when babies are sleeping peacefully, and they may sometimes sleep through it. At other times they waken and nothing can be done to soothe them. Colic tends to disappear by the third to sixth month, as a baby's digestive system matures. Although crying from colic can be severe and persistent—sometimes lasting for hours—it is not known to cause any long-term physical or psychological problems for the child. Still, inability to soothe a colicky baby is one of the great contributors to parental feelings of inadequacy.

▶ ▶ ▶ ▶

force crying? A classic study by Mary Ainsworth and her colleagues (1974) suggests that parents may not have to worry about whether they are attempting to soothe their babies too quickly. The Ainsworth group visited the homes of newborn babies every three weeks for the first year. Babies who were picked up and soothed quickly cried *less*, not more, frequently than those who were picked up after more time had elapsed. At least this one study suggests that the main effect of picking up babies may be to soothe and reassure them rather than to encourage further crying (Crockenberg & Smith, 1982).

Before leaving the Ainsworth study, we must issue the caveat that we issue with all correlational studies. The researchers did not randomly assign one group of mothers to quick soothing and another group of mothers to delayed soothing. Instead, they compared the behavior of babies whose mothers *chose* to soothe quickly or to delay. It could be, for example, that the mothers who chose to soothe quickly were generally more affectionate and concerned about their babies' moods and that this in itself might account for the behavioral differences in the babies.

Fortunately, as infants mature and learn, crying tends to become replaced by less upsetting verbal requests for intervention. And among adults, soothing techniques take very different forms—a delicate wine, a sunbelt condo, and admission that one started the argument.

Summary

1. Childbirth begins with the onset of regular contractions of the uterus. The fetus may signal the mother through hormones that it is mature enough to be born. Maternal hormones (prostaglandins and oxytocin) then stimulate labor contractions.

2. There are three stages of childbirth. In the first, which lasts an average of 12 to 24 hours in a first pregnancy, the cervix becomes effaced (thinned) and dilated (opened). During the first stage, fetal monitoring may be initiated. Transition is said to occur when the head of the fetus begins to move into the birth canal.

3. The second stage begins when the fetus first appears at the opening of the birth canal (vagina) and lasts for from a few minutes to a few hours. It ends when the baby has been born.

4. Once the head of the baby is out of the mother's body, suction is used to clear mucus from the respiratory tract. When the baby is completely out, the umbilical cord is cut. The baby usually receives an antibiotic treatment for the eyes, in order to prevent infection, and an injection of vitamin K. The Apgar scale is used to assess the neonate's color, heart rate, reflex irritability, muscle tone, and respiratory effort.

5. During the third stage of childbirth, the placenta detaches from the uterine wall and passes from the mother's body.

6. Childbirth is frequently painful, and many women receive general or local anesthetics during childbirth. Anesthetics are passed through the placenta and tend to depress the activity of the neonate's nervous system. Evidence is mixed as to whether medicated childbirth has any negative long-term effects.

▶ ▶ ▶ ▶

7. Dick-Read's natural childbirth method did not rely on anesthetics. Instead, women were educated about the childbirth process, encouraged to become physically fit, and taught breathing and relaxation exercises.

8. Prepared childbirth was brought to the West by Fernand Lamaze. In the "Lamaze method," women attend classes accompanied by a coach who expects to be present at birth. Women are educated about childbirth, taught muscle relaxation, and encouraged to exercise the muscles that will be used in childbirth.

9. The Leboyer method eases the baby gently into a dimly lit, warm, hushed room; gives the baby a warm bath; and places the baby on the mother's abdomen.

10. Caesarean sections are frequently carried out when the baby is in the breech (feet downward) position, or when difficult labor is expected for another reason.

11. So-called alternate birth centers are frequently located within or next to medical centers, but the birthing rooms are decorated like cheerful bedrooms, and family and friends are allowed to be present. Home births have grown in popularity, but they place the mother and baby at a disadvantage if emergency medical procedures are required.

12. Anoxia, or oxygen deprivation, at birth may be caused by pressure against the umbilical cord and can result in neurological or intellectual impairment.

13. Babies born at 37 weeks of gestation or less are considered preterm, and babies who weigh less than 5½ pounds are considered low-birth-weight. Preterm and low-birth-weight babies are at higher risk for infant mortality and tend to lag behind in academic achievement. Preterm infants are usually given stimulation in an effort to foster development and counter passivity. Parents frequently have more negative attitudes toward preterm babies, in part because of their appearance.

14. Within days following birth, many mothers experience temporary feelings of depression that may be hormonal in nature and are termed maternity blues. Prolonged depression, called postpartum depression, may reflect some combination of fluctuating hormone levels, a history of problems, stress, a difficult temperament in the neonate, and lack of social support.

15. Many researchers have argued that eye contact, cuddling, and other mother–infant interactions during the postpartum period are essential to the bonding process. Some studies have suggested that extended early contact promotes bonding, but there are methodological flaws in these studies.

16. Breast milk appears to be preferable to cow's milk or formula for infants. It is better balanced nutritionally and carries antibodies that appear to protect babies from certain infections. Moreover, breast-fed babies show fewer allergic reactions and digestive upsets. However, most formula-fed U.S. babies thrive. Bottle-fed babies are not malnourished when their parents carefully attend to their nutritional needs.

17. Neonates possess a number of reflexes or stereotyped responses to specific patterns of stimulation. Breathing is reflexive. Some reflexes disappear as infants mature, and reflexes are taken as indexes of neurological development. In the rooting reflex, a baby turns the mouth toward a stimulus that

▶ ▶ ▶ ▶

touches the cheek or corner of the mouth. Infants reflexively suck objects placed in the mouth. The Moro reflex occurs when the infant suddenly loses support or is startled; it involves flexing the legs and reaching outward. Neonates will usually support their weight by grasping fingers or other objects placed in the palms of their hands (palmar reflex). Neonates also eliminate waste products reflexively; toilet training involves learning to inhibit these particular reflexes.

18. Neonates engage in processes of sensation and perception. They are nearsighted but generally hear well, and they can discriminate among different odors and tastes.

19. Most neonates appear capable of learning by means of classical and operant conditioning. However, they may require large numbers of repetitions as compared with older children. Social learning does not appear to begin until 2 to 4 months of age.

20. Neonates sleep about 16 hours per day, and nearly half of this sleep is rapid-eye-movement (REM) sleep. It may be that REM sleep stimulates neurological development. Neonates distribute sleep into about six cycles of waking and sleeping per day.

21. Infants cry for reasons such as hunger, anger, pain, and fatigue. Mothers quickly learn to interpret their infants' cries. Infants can be soothed in many ways, by being rocked, swaddled, spoken to, and picked up. Mothers may fear that picking up infants quickly when they cry will "spoil" them or encourage crying. However, research suggests that infants who are soothed rapidly do not cry more frequently than infants whose mothers delay in picking them up.

T R U T H ▸ O R ▸ F I C T I O N ▸ R E V I S I T E D

The fetus signals the mother when it is ready to be born. *Probably true.* There is evidence that hormones secreted by the fetus normally stimulate the mother to begin childbirth.

Soon after birth, babies are slapped on the buttocks to clear passageways for air and stimulate independent breathing. *False.* Today the babies' air passages are cleared by suction.

The way in which the umbilical cord is cut determines whether the child will have an "inny" or an "outy" as a "belly button." *False.* The stump dries up and falls off.

Local or regional anesthetics used by mothers during childbirth have no effect on the child. *False.* All anesthetics have immediate effects. The question as to their long-term effects still remains somewhat open.

Women who give birth according to the Lamaze method experience no pain during labor. *False.* Women bearing children according to this method are better prepared for childbirth. However, they frequently ask for anesthetics as childbirth progresses.

▶ ▶ ▶ ▶

Most hospitals exclude fathers from participating in the birth process. *False.* Today the great majority of U.S. hospitals invite participation by the father.

Home births are as safe as hospital births for women who have given birth before and who are in good health. *False.* Back-up equipment and medical personnel are more readily available in the hospital (or the birthing clinic) if unanticipated problems arise.

Once their physical needs have been taken care of, preterm infants should be left undisturbed as much as possible until they achieve normal birth weights. *False.* It seems that stimulation fosters their development.

It is essential for parents to have extended early contact with their newborn children if adequate bonding is to take place. *False.* Today most scholars agree that early extended contact is just one possible element of a complex and prolonged bonding process.

Breast-feeding and bottle-feeding are equally healthful for infants. *Probably not.* Although formula-fed infants usually thrive, breast-feeding more reliably provides a healthful diet and, through the presence of the mother's antibodies, also affords infants greater protection from certain illnesses.

Women cannot become pregnant while they are breast-feeding their babies. *False.* The likelihood of conception is lowered, but breast-feeding is not a reliable birth-control method.

Newborn babies who are placed face down in comfortably warm water will attempt to swim. *True.* Swimming movements are reflexive and may reflect our evolutionary history.

Newborn babies are capable of learning. *True.* They may be conditioned, but many repetitions and immediate reinforcements are required.

Newborn babies require about twice the amount of sleep that adults do. *True.* They sleep 16 hours per day on the average.

Babies who are picked up as soon as they start to cry become spoiled and cry more often than babies whose mothers wait a while to pick them up. *False.* Babies who are picked up quickly may cry less, not more, frequently than babies who are picked up after a delay.

▶ ▶ ▶ ▶

5

Physical and Motor Development

C H A P T E R ▸ O U T L I N E

▸
▸
▸
▸
▸
▸
▸

▶
▶
▶
▶
▶
▶
▶

- The head of the newborn child only doubles in length by adulthood, but the legs increase in length by about five times.
- Infants triple their birth weight by age 1.
- Boys and girls are about equal in height through age 9 or 10.
- Children who undergo the adolescent growth spurt early end up taller than children who undergo the growth spurt relatively late.
- Children are growing taller than their parents.
- One reason that babies tend to be "cute" is that their noses and mouths are proportionately smaller than they will be when they have matured.
- We are born with all the bones we'll ever have.
- The Chinese used to bind the feet of nobly born infant girls to make them smaller.
- Vitamin D and sunshine help harden the bones.
- We are born with all the nerve cells we'll ever have.
- A child's brain reaches nearly 90 percent of its adult weight by the age of 5, although the child will still triple in overall weight by adulthood.
- Some cells in your body stretch all the way down your back to your big toe.
- Some people are left-brained, others are right-brained.
- Nocturnal emissions in boys accompany "wet dreams."
- Girls are capable of becoming pregnant after they have their first menstrual periods.
- Girls who mature early have higher self-esteem than those who mature late.
- Seventy-five-year-old adults can react to a stimulus more rapidly than 9- and 11-year-old children can.
- A disproportionately high percentage of 12- and 13-year-old math whizzes are left-handed.
- Hopi babies spend the first year of life strapped to a board, yet they begin to walk at about the same time as children who are reared in other cultures.

General Principles of Growth and Development

My wife and I are keen observers of children—that is, our own—and, from our experiences, we have discovered ten basic principles of physical growth and development:

1. An infant always weighs too little or too much, even if it is by a tiny fraction of an ounce.

2. Just when you think that your child has finally begun to make regular gains in weight, she will begin to lose weight or go for several months without gaining an ounce.

3. Just when your child is starting to look as if she has a little extra meat on her bones (so that she will have something in reserve if she should become ill), your pediatrician will warn you about the lifelong hazards of early obesity.

4. No matter how early your child sits up or starts to walk, your neighbor's child did it earlier.

5. Children first roll over when one parent is watching, but then steadfastly refuse to repeat it, at least for several days, when the other parent is called in.

6. Children begin to "get into everything" *before* you get child-proof latches on the cabinets.

7. Every advance in locomotor ability provides the child with new ways in which to get hurt.

8. Children display their most exciting developmental milestones when there is no film in the camera.

9. Children become sexually mature before their parents have developed a way of discussing sexual maturity with them.

10. One must worry continuously about every aspect of a child's growth until it occurs, and after it occurs one must endlessly ruminate over whether it occurred properly.

Parents who are also developmentalists might group these principles into the topics of *cephalocaudal development*, *proximodistal development*, and *differentiation*.

Cephalocaudal Development

Pediatrician Arnold Gesell is credited with having identified the principles of cephalocaudal and proximodistal development. The word **cephalocaudal** derives from the Greek *kephale*, meaning "head" or "skull," and from the Latin *cauda*, meaning "tail." It refers to the fact that development proceeds from head to "tail," or, more accurately, from the upper part of the head to the lower parts of the body.

When we consider the central role of the brain, which is contained within the skull, the cephalocaudal sequence appears quite logical. The brain regulates essential functions, such as heart beat. Through the secretion of hor-

Cephalocaudal (SEFF-uh-low-CAW-d'l). From top to bottom. From "head" to "tail."

▶ ▶ ▶ ▶

Proximodistal *From near to far. From the central axis of the body outward to the periphery.*

Differentiation *The processes by which behaviors and physical structures become more specialized.*

Neurological *Of the nervous system.*

mones, the brain also regulates the growth and development of the body and influences basic drives, such as hunger and thirst.

In the embryo the head develops most rapidly. By eight weeks after conception the head comprises half of the entire length of the embryo. The brain develops more rapidly than the spinal cord. Arm buds form before leg buds. Neonates have a strong, well-defined sucking reflex, although their legs are spindly and their limbs move back and forth only in diffuse excitement or agitation. Infants can hold up their heads before they gain control over their arms, their torsos, and finally their legs. They can sit up before they can crawl and walk. When they first walk, they use their arms to hold on.

The lower parts of the body, because they get off to a later start, must do more growing to reach adult size. For example, the head doubles in length between birth and maturity, but the torso triples in length. The arms increase their length about four times, but the legs and feet do so by about five.

Proximodistal Development

The **proximodistal** principle reflects the fact that growth and development appear to proceed from the trunk outward—from the body's central axis toward the periphery. This principle, too, makes a good deal of sense. The brain and spinal cord follow a central axis down through the body, and it is essential that the nerves be in place before the infant can gain control over the arms and legs. Also, the life functions of the newborn baby—heart beat, respiration, digestion, and elimination of wastes—are all carried out by organ systems close to the central axis. These must be in operation or ready to operate when the child is born.

In terms of motor development, babies gain control over their trunks and their shoulders before they can control their arms, hands, and fingers. They make clumsy swipes at objects with their arms before they can grasp them.* Babies can grab large objects before picking up tiny things with their fingers. Similarly, infants gain control over their hips and upper legs before they can direct their lower legs, feet, and toes.

Babies gain control over their heads and upper bodies before they gain control over their lower bodies.

Differentiation

As children mature, their physical reactions become less global and more specific. The tendency of responses to become more specific and distinct is termed **differentiation.** If a neonate's finger is pricked or burned, he or she may withdraw the finger, but will also thrash about, cry, and show general signs of distress. Toddlers are also likely to cry and show distress, but are more likely to withdraw the finger and less likely to thrash about. An older child or adult is also likely to withdraw the finger, but less likely to wail and show general distress. The older child or adult is also more likely to intellectually evaluate the need for assistance and to decide whether to consult another person for advice or help.

The process of differentiation is spurred by **neurological** developments. As noted in Chapter 4, neonates possess a variety of reflexes, many of which are basic to their survival. Reflexes such as sucking may be relatively sophisti-

Babies can grab large objects before picking up tiny things with their fingers. This baby's control of the rattle remains questionable.

---

*Here I am talking about voluntary or intentional reaching and grasping, not the grasping reflex.

▶ ▶ ▶ ▶

cated, involving the coordination of other reflexes, such as swallowing and breathing. However, all reflexes occur automatically and are under the control of the spinal cord or midbrain (an older, more primitive part of the brain). Voluntary sucking, like other voluntary activities, also involves the sensorimotor coordination made possible by the cerebral cortex—that wrinkled, mushroom-shaped mass beneath your skull that gives your head its delightfully well-rounded appearance.

Reflexive grasping, to return to an earlier example, is controlled by the spinal cord and midbrain. It occurs automatically, in response to pressure in the hand. We do not speak of the neonate's "knowing how" to grasp. Voluntary grasping, however, involves the cerebral cortex. In voluntary grasping, the object to be grasped is "represented" in sensory (for example, visual) areas of the cortex, and the grasping motions are represented in motor areas of the cortex. Differentiated voluntary grasping differs from reflexive grasping in many ways. The motor activity more accurately fits the shape, size, and weight of the object, and voluntary grasping is begun or suspended at will. It now seems appropriate to say that the baby "knows how" to reach for and grasp objects.

We shall return to these developmental principles as the chapter becomes differentiated into various aspects of physical growth and development: changes in height and weight; the development of bones, muscles, and the nervous system; and sexual and motor development.

Growth Patterns in Height and Weight

Height and weight provide two of the most obvious dimensions of physical growth. Children generally become taller and heavier as they grow older, and children's size has a good deal to do with their self-concept and self-esteem. Young children must literally "look up" to nearly everyone else. They must stretch to reach doorknobs and countertops and to look out of windows. With the exception of furniture and toys made especially for them, the artifacts of civilization seem designed to provide them with frustration.

Tallness is a "plus" among men in our culture (Berkowitz et al., 1971), but tall women are not viewed so positively (Gillis & Avis, 1980). Tall girls of dating age frequently find that shorter boys are reluctant to approach them or to be seen with them. Occasionally tall girls walk with a slight hunch, as if trying to minimize their height.

Plumpness has been valued in many preliterate societies, and Western paintings of former centuries suggest that there was a time when (literally) well-rounded women were the ideal. But in contemporary Western culture, slenderness is valued both in males and females (Harris et al., 1982). Obesity is clearly out of fashion, and pediatricians are recommending that children stay slender to avoid obesity in adulthood. There is good reason for this. Obesity in childhood may trigger the multiplication of **fat cells** that remain in increased numbers for a lifetime. And individuals with high numbers of fat cells may feel food-deprived unless they overeat, as we shall see in Chapter 14.

Infancy

The most dramatic gains in height and weight occur during prenatal development. Within a span of nine months, children develop from a zygote

Fat cells Cells that store fat.

▶ ▶ ▶ ▶

172   5 PHYSICAL AND MOTOR DEVELOPMENT

Growth spurt *A period during which growth advances at a dramatically rapid rate.*

Peak growth *The period during which the rate of growth is at its maximum.*

about ¹⁄₁₇₅th of an inch long to a neonate about 20 inches in length. Weight increases by a factor of *billions.*

During the first year after birth, gains in height and weight are also dramatic, although not by the standards of prenatal gains. Babies usually double their birth weight in about five months and triple it by the first birthday. Their height increases by about ten inches in the first year, so that a girl whose length at birth was 20 inches is likely to be about two and a half feet tall (30 inches) at 12 months.

Infants grow another four to six inches during the second year, and gain about four to seven pounds. There is an old rule of thumb that they reach half of their adult height by the second birthday. If we take half as a "ballpark figure," this rule may not be far from the mark, but there are many exceptions. Girls, for example, mature more quickly than boys and may be more likely to reach half of their adult height a few months earlier. Also, taller-than-average infants, as a group, tend to slow down in their growth rates. Shorter-than-average infants, as a group, tend to speed up. This is not to suggest that there is no relationship between infant and adult heights, or that we all wind up in an average range. Tall infants as a group wind up taller than short infants, but in most cases not by so much as seemed likely during infancy.

Early and Middle Childhood

Following the dramatic gains in height of the first two years, boys and girls tend to gain about two to three inches in height throughout early and middle childhood. This pattern of gradual gains does not vary significantly until they reach the adolescent **growth spurt** (see Figure 5.1). Weight gains also remain fairly even at about four to six pounds per year. During the years of 6 to 12, children become proportionately thinner in appearance as they gain in height.

There are some interesting additional features to note about Figure 5.1. Boys as a group remain slightly taller and heavier than girls from infancy through the ages of 9 or 10. The growth curves then cross, and girls tend to be heavier and taller than boys until about the ages of 13 or 14, at which time boys are at the peak of their adolescent growth spurt. When the curves cross again, boys rapidly outdistance their female age-mates and eventually wind up some four to six inches taller and 25 to 30 pounds heavier.

Noticeable variations in growth patterns also occur from child to child. Some children show more rapid growth at various times. Children who are malnourished may be shorter and lighter than well-nourished children. The great majority of U.S. children have enough to eat, but in many countries throughout the world poor children tend to be significantly smaller than wealthier children.

Adolescence

The stable growth patterns in height and weight that characterize early and middle childhood come to an abrupt end with the adolescent growth spurt. Girls start to spurt in height sooner than boys, at an average age of 10¼. Boys start to spurt about a year and a half later, at an average age of 11¾ (Hamill et al., 1973). Girls and boys tend to reach their periods of **peak growth** in height

▶ ▶ ▶ ▶

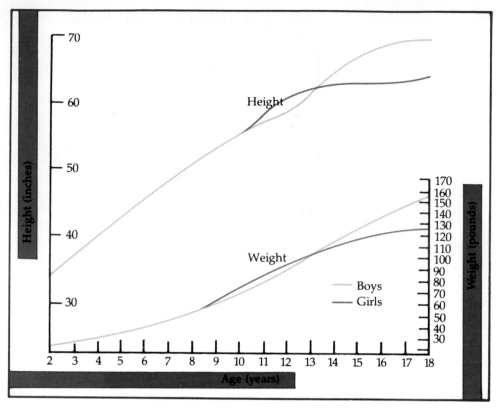

Figure 5.1 Growth Curves for Height and Weight
Gains in height and weight are most dramatic during the first two years. During the first year, height can increase by 10 inches and birth weight can triple. After the first two years, gains become more regular until the adolescent growth spurt.

at 11¾ and 13¼ respectively (see Figure 5.2). The girls' spurt in height lasts about 2¼ years, ending at 12½. The boys' spurt lasts longer—2¾ years—ending at 14½.

Adolescents begin to spurt in weight about half a year after they begin to spurt in height—girls at 10¾ and boys at 12¼. As is the case with height, the period of peak growth in weight occurs about a year and a half after the onset of the spurt, or at about 12¼ in girls and 13¾ in boys. The girls' growth spurt in weight lasts about 2½ years, ending at 13¼. The boys' spurt lasts about 2¾ years, ending at 15.

Since the spurt in weight lags behind the spurt in height, many adolescents are relatively slender as compared with their preadolescent and post-adolescent statures. However, adolescents tend to eat enormous quantities of food in order to fuel their growth spurts. Active 14- and 15-year-old boys may consume 5,000 to 6,000 calories a day without becoming obese. If they were to eat this much 20 years later, they might gain upwards of *100 pounds per year*. Little wonder that adults fighting the dismal battle of the bulge stare at adolescents in amazement as they wolf down French fries and shakes at the fast-food counter and later go out for pizza!

► ► ► ►

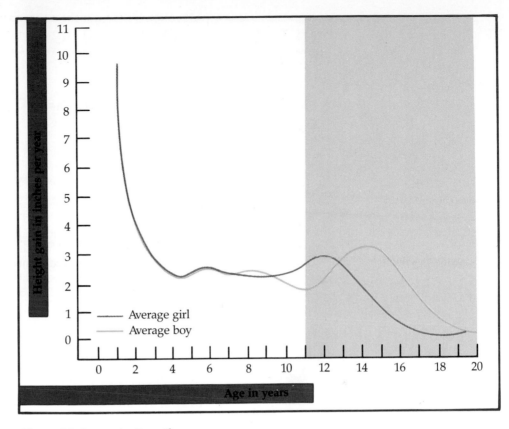

Figure 5.2 Spurts in Growth
Girls begin the adolescent growth spurt about a year and a half earlier than boys. The spurt in height precedes the spurt in weight by about half a year.

Individual Differences in Growth-Spurt Patterns   The figures given above are averages. Few of us begin or end our growth spurts right on the mark. One study found, however, that there is greater variation in the age at which the growth spurt in boys begins than when it ends (Broverman et al., 1964). For this reason, children who spurt earlier are likely to have growth spurts of longer duration. Children who spurt earlier are also likely to wind up with somewhat shorter legs and longer torsos, while children who spurt late are somewhat longer-legged. However, there are no significant differences in the total height attained at maturity (Faust, 1977).

Regardless of the age at which the growth spurt begins, there is a moderate-to-high correlation between a child's height at the onset of adolescence and at maturity (Stolz & Stolz, 1951). Are there exceptions? Of course. However, everything else being equal, a tall child has a reasonable expectation of becoming a tall adult, and vice versa.

Differences in Height and Weight: Racial, Ethnic, and Socioeconomic Factors
Differences in growth patterns and size at maturity are linked to racial, ethnic, and socioeconomic factors. Among Caucasians, for example, persons of northern European extraction, particularly Scandinavian (Norwegian, Swedish, Dan-

▶ ▶ ▶ ▶

Are We Still Growing Taller Than Our Parents?

▷
▷
▷
▷

▷ Children in the twentieth century have grown dramatically more rapidly and wound up taller than children from earlier times. Figure 5.3 shows that white American males grew more rapidly in 1960 than they did in 1880 and ended up several centimeters taller. At the age of 15, they were more than five inches taller, on the average, and 33 pounds heavier than their counterparts from the previous century (Meredith, 1963). Studies of the remains of Englishmen buried 600 to 900 years ago show that they reached an average height of about 5 feet 6 inches. Today the average

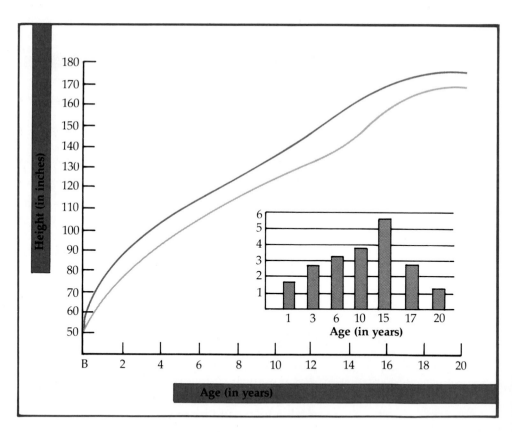

Figure 5.3 Are We Still Growing Taller Than Our Parents?
Twentieth-century children have grown more rapidly and grown taller than children in preceding centuries. However, it seems that children from affluent families are no longer growing taller than their parents. But children from the lower part of the socioeconomic spectrum are still doing so.

▶ ▶ ▶ ▶

male Englishman is three to four inches taller.

However, it turns out that American children from the upper three-quarters of the socioeconomic spectrum have now *stopped* growing taller, whereas their poorer counterparts continue to make gains in height from generation to generation. Why?

Nutrition apparently plays an important role in the rate of growth and size at maturity. U.S. government surveys have shown that children from middle- and upper-class families are taller and heavier than their age-mates from lower-class families. This in and of itself would not be very convincing. It could, for example, be argued that genetic factors provide clusters of advantages that increase the chances for financial gain as well as for greater height and weight. But remember that children from the upper three-quarters of the socio-economic spectrum are no longer growing taller. Perhaps Americans who have had nutritional and medical advantages have simply reached their full genetic potential in height. Continuing gains among families of lower socioeconomic status suggests that poorer children are still benefiting from gradual improvements in nutrition.

ish, or Finnish), tend to be slightly taller than those of southern European descent (for example, Italian or Greek). Men from some African tribes reach a height of seven feet, whereas Pygmies reach a height of about four feet. Whites and blacks (other than Pygmies) tend to be taller than Asians.

Black children in the United States tend to grow slightly more rapidly and end up slightly taller than whites (Bayley, 1965; Owen et al., 1974). These findings hold even for black children reared in poor environments with marginally adequate nutrition.

Changes in Body Proportions   Greek classical sculptors followed the rule, in rendering the human form, of the "Golden Section": The length of the head must equal one-eighth of the height of the body (including the head). The ideal of human beauty may be so, but the reality is that, among adults, the length of the head actually varies from about one-eighth to one-tenth of the entire body. Among children, the head is proportionately larger (see Figure 5.4).

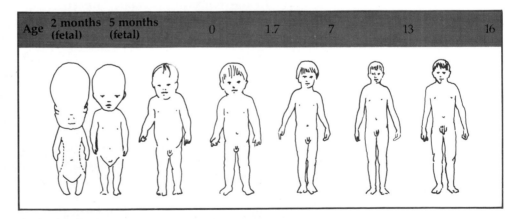

Figure 5.4 Changes in the Proportions of the Body
Development proceeds in a cephalocaudal direction. The head is proportionately larger among younger children.

► ► ► ►

Asynchrony (a-SIN-crow-knee). *Imbalance; not occurring at the same time.*

Canalization *The tendency of growth rates to return to genetically determined patterns after undergoing environmentally induced change.*

Cartilage *A tough elastic tissue that mostly turns to bone as the child matures.*

Development proceeds in a cephalocaudal manner. A few weeks after conception, an embryo is almost all head. When entering the fetal stage, the head is about half the length of the unborn child. In the neonate, it is about one-quarter of the length of the body. The head gradually diminishes in proportion to the rest of the body, even though it doubles in size by adulthood.

Among adults the arms are nearly three times the length of the head. The legs are about four times as long—nearly half the length of the body. Among newborns, the arms and legs are about equal in length. Each is only about one and a half times the length of the head. By the first birthday, the neck has begun to lengthen visibly. So have the arms and legs. The arms grow more rapidly than the legs do at first, and by the second birthday the arms are actually longer than the legs. But then the legs grow more rapidly, soon catching up with and surpassing the arms in length.

Asynchrony   Adolescents are often referred to as awkward and gawky. A major reason for this is **asynchrony**—different parts of the body grow at different rates. In an exception to the principle of proximodistal growth, the hands and feet mature before the arms and legs do. As a consequence, adolescent girls and boys may complain of big hands or feet. Temporarily, too, the nose or another facial feature may gain unwanted prominence.

Catch-up Growth

A child's growth can be slowed from its genetically predetermined course by many factors, including illness and dietary deficiency. However, once the problem is alleviated, the child's rate of growth frequently accelerates and returns to approximate its normal, deflected course. The tendency to return to one's genetically determined pattern of growth is referred to as **canalization.**

Small women with large husbands frequently give birth to smaller-than-average babies who then make greater-than-average gains in height and weight. In this way, a woman with a relatively narrow birth canal may be somehow protected from having too large a baby. But catch-up growth then spurs the baby on to the expression of his or her genetic heritage.

In the following sections, we shall see how changes in height and weight are influenced by the development of bones, muscle, the nervous system, and reproductive capacity.

Development of Bones

You may have noticed that many 6-month-old babies enjoy sucking their toes. In order to suck them, of course, they must be able to place them in their mouths. While you may have wondered about the advisability of these contortions, you may also have felt a twinge of jealousy that that your own body is no longer so supple—unless you are a ballet dancer. Babies are capable of extraordinary flexibility, because at birth much of the skeleton is composed of **cartilage** rather than hard bone. Also, most of the bones that are in place are separated by relatively large spaces.

▶ ▶ ▶ ▶

The Role of the Pituitary Gland

Bone development
hypothalamus
↓
Pituitary
↓
growth hormone

Bones first begin to develop at about the eighth week of fetal life. Their formation is governed by secretions of the **pituitary gland**—also referred to as the "master gland" because of the large number of bodily functions it regulates—and sex hormones. A major secretion of the pituitary gland is **growth hormone,** which regulates the growth of bones, muscles, and glands. An excess of growth hormone can lead to *giantism,* a condition in which people may grow two to three feet taller than their genetically predetermined heights. Children whose growth patterns are abnormally slow often catch up to their age-mates when growth hormone is administered. A recently discovered substance, growth hormone releasing factor (or hGRF), is produced by the **hypothalamus.** It causes the pituitary to produce growth hormone (Taylor, 1985).

Development of the Skull

As the baby matures, bones will be formed from cartilage, as in the wrists and ankles. In some cases, a number of small bones will join together. The head of a newborn baby is flexible so that the fetus can pass through the birth canal. When the child is born, the head may be quite distended. By and large, the skull returns to its genetically predetermined shape as the neonate matures. Then it hardens. This process is made possible by the fact that children are born with many skull bones, rather than one. These bones are separated by soft membranous areas called **fontanels.** But the fontanels fill in with bone by about the age of 2. At this age we can speak of the toddler as having a single skull bone.

The skeletal system also grows at different rates, so that skeletal growth is a major contributor to changes in body proportions. Consider the skull again. Figure 5.5 compares the skull of the neonate to that of an adult. The length of the head doubles from birth to maturity, so do not take the shown sizes literally. Do note, however, that the **cranium** and the eye sockets of the neonate are larger, proportionately speaking, than those of the adult. This means that the cranium and the eyes grow less rapidly than other parts of the head and facial features. And so the "cute, tiny" noses and mouths of babies are generally destined to become relatively larger than they appear at birth.

Some General Patterns of Skeletal Development

Although there are exceptions, as in the case of the closing of the fontanels, the skeletal system generally develops in three ways: Bones tend to increase in number and to become larger and harder.

The hands, wrists, ankles, and feet gain the greatest number of bones during childhood. The wrist and hand of the 1-year-old contain three bones, for example, but develop another 25 bones by the end of adolescence to yield the adult complement of 28.

The bones of infants are softer than those of adults, because they have more water but less mineral content. This composition, which seems adaptive, makes them more pliable and less susceptible to fracture. However, the same pliancy makes children's bones susceptible to deformation, as can occur with

Pituitary gland *The body's "master gland" located near the lower center part of the brain, which secretes growth hormone, prolactin, and many others.*

Growth hormone *A pituitary hormone that regulates growth.*

Hypothalamus *(high-poe-THAL-uh-muss). A pea-sized brain structure located above the pituitary gland that is involved in the regulation of body temperature, motivation (e.g., hunger, thirst, sex, etc.), and emotion.*

Fontanel *A soft membranous area found between the skull bones of a child (eventually filled in with bone).*

Cranium *(KRAY-knee-um). The skull—the bones forming the enclosure of the brain.*

▶ ▶ ▶ ▶

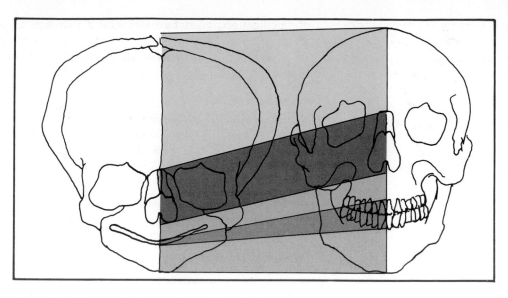

Figure 5.5 Changes in Proportions of the Skull
After birth, the cranium and eyes grow less rapidly than other parts of the head. The cranium
and eye sockets of the neonate are larger, proportionately, than those of the adult.

dietary deficiency or certain diseases. Before the twentieth century, the feet of Chinese girls born into well-to-do families were bound during late infancy and early toddlerhood. The process resulted in small feet—a sign of nobility. In various preliterate societies, the pliancy of infants' bones has been used to elongate necks, to flatten heads, and to create other deformities valued by the culture.

Calcification   Bones become denser and harden steadily through the deposit of calcium in the form of lime salts—a process called **calcification.** This process continues from birth through puberty. Vitamin D and sunshine promote the process of calcification. Lack of vitamin D and insufficient exposure to sunshine can lead to a condition called **rickets,** in which the bones remain soft and are subject to bending. Children with rickets may appear bowlegged or sway-backed.

Bones also change in shape as children mature. The long bones of the arms and legs lengthen. Some bones continue to lengthen and change shape until age 25 or so. We shall discuss the process by which the long bones stop growing in the section on sexual development.

Development of Teeth

What do baby teeth and hardwood trees have in common? They are both **deciduous**—that is, baby teeth fall out as do the leaves of oaks and maples. People have 20 "baby teeth" (also referred to as "milk teeth") and 32 permanent teeth.

Teeth begin to form late in the embryonic stage. Through the process

Calcification The process of depositing calcium (in the form of lime salts) in bones to make them harder and denser.

Rickets A skeletal disease usually caused by lack of vitamin D and sunshine that results in softening of bones.

Deciduous (dee-SID-you-us). Falling off at a certain stage of growth.

of calcification, all baby teeth and a number of permanent teeth are already developing at birth. However, with most neonates they will not yet have erupted through the gums. Babies usually get their first baby teeth at about 6 or 7 months, although there is wide variation.

Teething Parents frequently know that their babies are **teething** when they cry suddenly or persistently for no apparent reason.* Other signs of teething are drooling; sudden or persistent biting ("gumming" would be more accurate) on toys or the breast; rubbing the nose (actually the upper lip) against things; fever; and a runny nose. Teething babies may also spit up frequently—another reason that parents of formerly colicky children may at first wonder whether colic has returned.

Time, of course, brings teething pain to an end. Fortunately, there is no evidence that a difficult teething process influences the child's personality or later adjustment. Teething pain can sometimes be relieved by giving babies hard objects or cold ones to chew (some teething rings are refrigerated between usages); by rubbing over-the-counter or prescription gels on their gums; or by using pain relievers. Parents are well-advised to consult their pediatricians about any medication, whether or not it is an over-the-counter preparation.

Many parents assume that they need not be concerned about their children's permanent teeth until they come in, beginning at about the ages of 6 or 7. However, most of the permanent teeth have begun to develop about midway through the first year. So new parents have good reason to be concerned about issues such as vitamins and **fluoridation** of water. Parents may also wish to consult their pediatricians about vitamin and fluoride supplements.

Development of Muscles

Babies are not very strong, but the number of muscle fibers they will have as adults is fixed by about the fifth month of fetal life. During the last trimester, and after birth, muscle development occurs from gains in the length and thickness of muscle fibers.

Muscle development generally follows the pattern of growth in height. Gains are rather consistent through the childhood years and then accelerate at puberty, spurred on by sex hormones.

At puberty the muscle strength of boys begins to develop much more rapidly than that of girls. By the end of puberty, boys on the average are approximately twice as strong as girls in terms of the amount of weight they can lift (Faust, 1977). A larger proportion of a male's body weight is composed of his muscle mass, whereas a relatively larger part of a female's body weight is composed of fatty tissue.

Rigorous modern training methods have vastly increased the athletic capabilities of males and females. In fact, women today are breaking the records set only a few years ago by males in sports ranging from long-distance running to short-distance swimming. But these same training methods continue to give males the advantage in most events.

---

*Even colicky babies have usually shown major improvements by the time they begin to get baby teeth, and the causes of the resurgence of crying may therefore seem mysterious.

▶ ▶ ▶ ▶

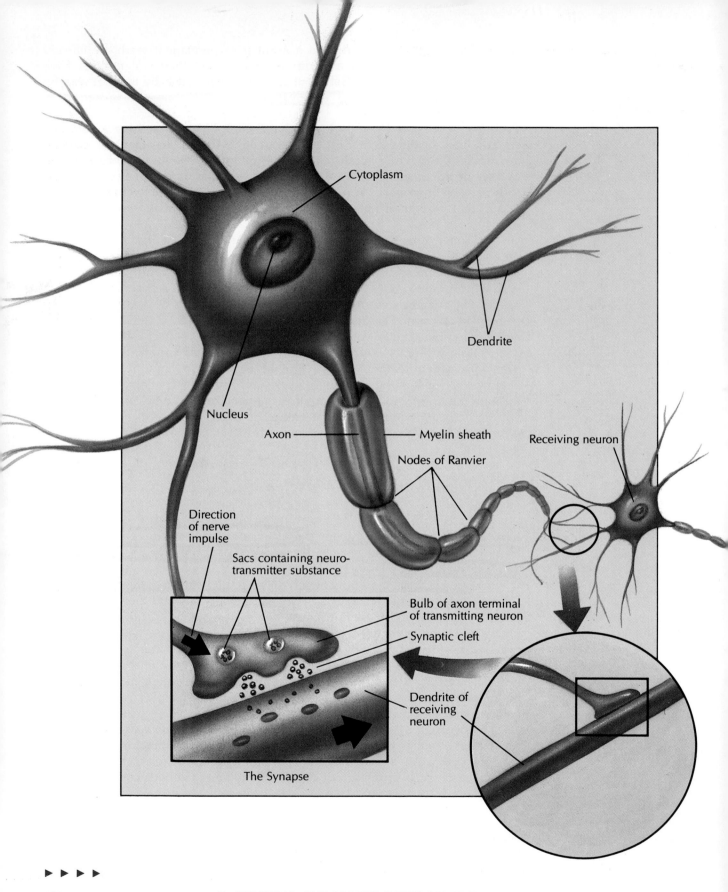

The Synapse

Development of the Nervous System

Nerves *Bundles of* axons *from many neurons.*

Neurons *Nerve cells.*

Glial cells *(GLEE-al). Cells that produce myelin and engage in "housekeeping" chores for neurons.*

Dendrite *A rootlike structure attached to the cell body of a neuron. Dendrites receive impulses from other neurons. (From the Greek* dendron, *meaning "tree.")*

Axon *A long, thin part of a neuron that transmits impulses to other neurons through small branching structures called axon terminals.*

Neurotransmitter *A chemical substance involved in the transmission of neural impulses from one neuron to another.*

Myelin sheath *(MY-uh-lin). A fatty, whitish substance that encases and insulates neurons, permitting more rapid transmission of neural impulses.*

During my own childhood there was a time when it seemed that a "nervous" system was not a good thing to have. That is, if one's system were not nervous, one would be less likely to jump at strange noises.

At some point I learned that a nervous system is not a system that is nervous, but a system of **nerves** involved in heart beat, visual-motor coordination, thought and language, and so on. The human nervous system is more complex than that of lower animals. Although elephants and whales have heavier brains, our brains comprise a larger proportion of our body weight.

Development of Neurons

The brain is but one part—although a very important part—of the nervous system. The basic units of the nervous system are **neurons.** Neurons are cells that are specialized to receive and transmit "messages" from one part of the body to another. The messages transmitted by neurons somehow account for phenomena as varied as reflexes, the perception of an itch from a mosquito bite, the visual–motor coordination of a skier, the composition of a concerto, and the solution of a math problem.

We are born with about 12 billion neurons in the brain, which is all that we shall ever have. The nervous system also contains billions of **glial cells,** which outnumber the neurons by a ratio of about ten to one (Arms & Camp, 1987). Glial cells nourish neurons, direct their growth, and remove waste products from the nervous system.

Neurons vary according to their functions and locations in the body. Some neurons in the brain are only a fraction of an inch in length, while neurons in the leg grow to be several feet long. Each neuron possesses a cell body, dendrites, and an axon (see Figure 5.6). The **dendrites** are short fibers that extend from the cell body and receive incoming messages from up to 1,000 adjoining neurons. The **axon** extends trunklike from the cell body and accounts for much of the differences in length in neurons, ranging up to several feet in length if it is carrying messages from the toes upward. Axons end in smaller, branching terminals with bulbous ends. Messages are released from axon terminals in the form of chemicals called **neurotransmitters.** These messages are then received by the dendrites of adjoining neurons, muscles, or glands.

As the child matures, the axons of neurons grow in length, and the dendrites and axon terminals proliferate, creating vast interconnected networks for the transmission of complex messages. The number of glial cells also increases as the nervous system develops and contributes to the dense appearance of the structures of the nervous system.

Myelination Many neurons are tightly wrapped with white, fatty **myelin sheaths.** Myelin actually consists of the membranes of the type of glial cell called

Figure 5.6 (opposite) The Anatomy of a Neuron
"Messages" enter neurons through dendrites, are transmitted along the axon, and then are sent through axon terminals to muscles, glands, and other neurons.

▶ ▶ ▶ ▶

the **Schwann cell.** The membranes of Schwann cells expand and wrap tightly around the axons of neurons several times. The high fat content of the Schwann cells insulates the neuron from electrically charged atoms in the fluids that encase the nervous system. In this way, leakage of the electric current being carried along the axon is minimized, and messages are conducted more efficiently. Myelin does not uniformly coat the surface of an axon. As noted in Figure 5.6, it is missing at points called **nodes of Ranvier.**

The term **myelination** refers to the process by which Schwann cells come to insulate neurons. Myelination is not complete at birth. Myelination is part of the maturation process that leads to the abilities to crawl and walk during the first year after birth. Babies are not physiologically "ready" to engage in activities involving visual–motor coordination until the coating process has reached a certain level (Kinsborne & Hiscock, 1983). In the disease **multiple sclerosis,** myelin is replaced by a hard, fibrous tissue that throws off the timing of neural transmission and in this way interferes with muscular control. If neurons that control breathing are afflicted, the child can die from suffocation.

Development of the Brain

In all the animal kingdom, you (and about 5 billion other human beings) are unique because of the capacities for learning and thought made possible by your brain. The brain of the neonate weighs a little less than a pound—nearly one-fourth of its adult weight. In keeping with the principle of cephalocaudal growth, the brain triples in weight, reaching nearly 70 percent of its adult weight by the first birthday (see Figure 5.7). And by the age of 5, the brain reaches nearly 90 percent of its adult weight, although the total weight of the 5-year-

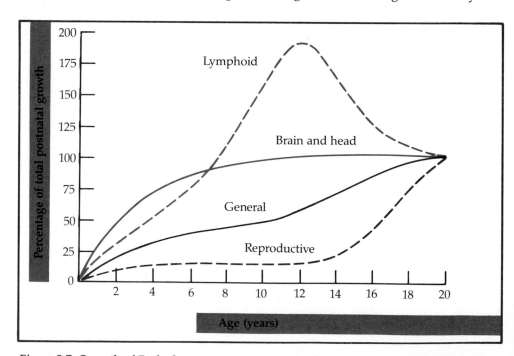

Figure 5.7 Growth of Body Systems as a Percentage of Total Postnatal Growth
The brain of the neonate weighs about one-fourth its adult weight. In keeping with the principle of cephalocaudal growth, it will have tripled in weight by the first birthday, reaching nearly 70 percent of its adult weight.

► ► ► ►

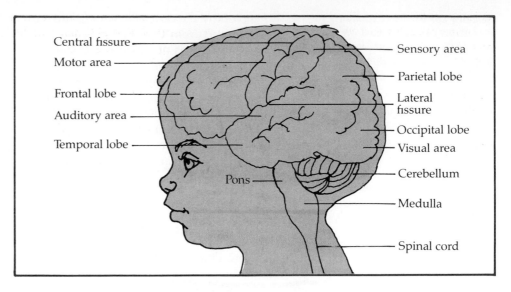

Figure 5.8 A Cutaway View of the Brain

old will triple by adulthood (Tanner, 1978). Let us look at the brain, as shown in Figure 5.8, and discuss the development of the structures within.

The Structures of the Brain   Many nerves that connect the spinal cord to higher levels of the brain pass through the **medulla oblongata.** The medulla oblongata is vital in the control of basic functions such as heart beat and respiration. The **pons,** which means "bridge" in Latin, lies forward of the medulla. Like the medulla, it is involved in respiration. The pons also transmits information concerning body movement. In Chapter 4 we saw that one theory holds that stimulation from the pons activates the parts of the brain that are involved in dreaming.

Behind the pons lies the **cerebellum,** which means "little brain" in Latin. The cerebellum helps the child maintain balance, control motor behavior, and coordinate eye movements with bodily sensations. Injury to the cerebellum may impair coordination and motor development and lessen muscle tone.

The **cerebrum** is the crowning glory of the brain. Only in human beings does the cerebrum comprise such a large proportion of the brain. The surface of the cerebrum consists of two hemispheres—left and right—that become increasingly wrinkled, or convoluted, as the child develops, coming to show ridges and valleys called fissures. This surface is the cerebral cortex. The convolutions allow a great deal of surface area to be packed into the brain.

The left and right hemispheres of the cerebral cortex are each divided into four parts, or lobes, as shown in Figure 5.8: the frontal lobe, the parietal lobe, the temporal lobe, and the occipital lobe. When light strikes the retinas of the eyes, neurons in the vision area of the occipital lobe are activated. As a result, we see. Direct electrical stimulation of the occipital lobe can also produce visual sensations. The hearing or auditory area of the cortex lies in the temporal lobe along the lateral fissure. Sounds activate the receptors for hearing in the ears, and, in turn, neurons in the auditory area of the cortex are activated. As a result, we hear.

Medulla oblongata *(meh-DULL-ah). An oblong-shaped area of the hindbrain involved in heartbeat and respiration.*

Pons *A structure of the hindbrain involved in respiration.*

Cerebellum *A part of the hindbrain involved in muscle coordination and balance.*

Cerebrum *(sir-REE-brum). The large mass of the forebrain, which consists of two hemispheres.*

▶ ▶ ▶ ▶

Just behind the central fissure in the parietal lobe lies the **sensory cortex.** Messages received from the skin senses all over the body are projected here. These are sensations as of warmth and coldness, touch, pain, and movement. Neurons in different parts of the sensory cortex are active depending on whether a baby is reaching for an object (and receiving messages from the muscles, joints, and tendons of the arm) or sucking his or her toes (and receiving messages from the lips, tongue, and toes).

The **motor cortex** lies in the frontal lobe, just across the valley of the central fissure from the sensory cortex. Neurons in the motor cortex are active when parts of the body are moved. If a surgeon were to stimulate part of your motor cortex with an electrode, you would raise your leg. Raising the leg would be sensed in the sensory cortex, and you might be perplexed as to whether you had "intended" to raise that leg or not.

The Growth Spurts of the Brain The brain makes gains in size and weight in different ways. One is in the formation of neurons, a process complete by birth. The first major growth spurt of the brain occurs during the fourth and fifth months of prenatal development, when neurons proliferate. A second growth spurt in the brain occurs between the twenty-fifth week of prenatal development and the end of the second year after birth. Whereas the first growth spurt of the brain was due to the formation of neurons, the second growth spurt is due primarily to the proliferation of dendrites and axon terminals.

Brain Development in Infancy There is a clear link between what infants can do and the myelination of areas within the brain. At birth the parts of the brain involved in heart beat and respiration, sleeping and arousal, and reflex activity are fairly well myelinated and functional.

Myelination of motor pathways allows newborn infants to show stereotyped reflexes, but otherwise their motor activity tends to be random and diffuse. Myelination of the motor area of the cortex begins at about the fourth month of prenatal development. Myelin develops rapidly along the major motor pathways from the cerebral cortex during the last month of pregnancy and continues after birth. The development of voluntary motor activity coincides with myelination as the diffuse movements of the neonate come under increasing control. The process of myelinating the motor pathways is largely complete by the age of 2 (Parmelee & Sigman, 1983).

Although newborn babies respond to touch and can see and hear quite well, the sensory, vision, and hearing areas of the cortex are less well myelinated at birth. As myelination progresses and the interconnections between the various areas of the cortex thicken, children become increasingly capable of complex and integrated sensorimotor activities.

In Chapter 3 it was noted that the neonates of women who read *The Cat in the Hat* aloud during the last few weeks of pregnancy showed a preference for this story. It turns out that myelination of the neurons involved in the sense of hearing begins at about the sixth month of pregnancy—coinciding with the period in which fetuses begin to respond to sound. In Chapter 10 we shall see that this early ability to respond to sound may predispose newborns to become attached to their natural mothers. Myelination of these pathways is developing rapidly at term and continues until about the age of 4.

Although the fetus shows some response to light during the third trimester, it is hard to imagine what use the fetus could have for vision. It turns

▶ ▶ ▶ ▶

out that the neurons involved in vision begin to myelinate only shortly before full term, but then they complete the process of myelination rapidly. Within a short five to six months, vision has become the dominant sense.

Early and Middle Childhood   Later in this chapter we shall see that we do not develop fine-motor skills until the middle of early childhood, at about the age of 4. The development of fine-motor skills coincides with the completion of the myelination of the neural pathways that link the cerebellum to the cerebral cortex. The cerebellum is involved in balance as well as coordination, and our balancing abilities also increase dramatically as myelination of these pathways nears completion.

The parts of the brain that enable the child to sustain attention and screen out distractions become increasingly myelinated between the ages of about 4 and 7 (Higgins & Turnure, 1984). As a consequence, most children are ready to focus on schoolwork at some time between these ages. Learning to read requires prolonged attention as well as perceptual abilities.

Right Brain/Left Brain?   In recent years it has become popular to speak of some people as being "right-brained" or "left-brained." I have even heard it said that some instructional methods are aimed at the right brain (presented in an emotionally laden, aesthetic way), while others are aimed at the left brain (logical and straightforward).

The notion is that the hemispheres of the brain are involved in different kinds of intellectual and emotional functions and responses. For the great majority of us, the left hemisphere is looked on as more concerned with logic and problem solving, understanding and producing language, and mathematical computation. The right hemisphere is considered more involved in decoding visual information, aesthetic and emotional responses, imagination, understanding metaphors, and creative mathematical reasoning (Levy, 1987; McKean, 1987).

Actually, these functions are not split up so precisely as has been popularly believed. The functions of the left and right hemispheres overlap to some degree, and the hemispheres also tend to respond simultaneously as we focus our attention on one thing or another. They are aided to "cooperate" by the myelination of the **corpus callosum**—a thick bundle of nerve fibers that connect the hemispheres. Myelination of the corpus callosum proceeds rapidly during early and middle childhood and is largly complete by the age of 8. By that time we apparently have greater ability to integrate logical and emotional functioning.

The process of myelination of the brain slows down beyond these early years but progresses until the age of 15 or so. As a result, we continue to show incremental improvements in our language abilities and overall intellectual functioning well into our teens. The intellectual gains that occur in later years are more the result of experience than maturation.

Plasticity of the Brain   Because of the differentiation of a number of structures in the brain, parts of the brain tend to have specialized functions. Specialization allows our behavior to be more complex. But specialization also means that injuries to certain parts of the brain can result in loss of these functions.

Fortunately, the brain also shows **plasticity.** The brain frequently can compensate for injuries to particular areas. This compensatory ability is greatest

Corpus callosum The thick bundle of nerve fibers that connects the left and right hemispheres of the brain.

Plasticity The tendency of new parts of the brain to take up the functions of other parts of the brain that have been injured.

▶ ▶ ▶ ▶

up until the ages of 8 or 9 (Williams, 1983). When we suffer damage to the areas of the brain that control language, we may lose the ability to speak or to understand language. However, other areas of the brain may assume these functions in young children who suffer such damage. As a result, they sometimes dramatically regain the ability to speak or to comprehend language (Gardner, 1982). In adulthood and adolescence, regaining such functions may be impossible.

There are at least two factors involved in the brain's plasticity. One is "sprouting," or the growth of new dendrites. New dendrites to some degree can allow for the rearrangement of neural circuits. The second is the redundancy of certain neural connections. In some cases, similar functions are found in two or more locations within the brain, although they are developed to different degrees. If one location is damaged, the other one, in time, may be able to develop greater proficiency in performing the function.

Nature and Nurture in the Development of the Brain

Development of the sensory and motor areas of the brain starts on course as a result of maturation, but Arthur Parmelee and Marian Sigman (1983) suggest that sensory stimulation and motor activity during early infancy also contribute to their development. Experience seems to "fine tune" the unfolding of the genetic code.

"Fine Tuning" the Development of the Brain Cross-species research shows how the flood of sensory stimulation that impacts upon newborns apparently spurs cortical growth. For example, young apes whose limbs were restrained did not develop normal climbing behavior once the restraints were removed.

Researchers have created rat "amusement parks" to demonstrate the effects of enriched environments on neural development. Rats have been given toys such as ladders, platforms, and boxes. They have been provided with exploratory sessions in mazes and in fields with barriers. In these studies, the "enriched" rats invariably develop heavier brains than control animals (Greenough, 1976; Rosenzweig, 1966, 1969). The weight differences in part reflect greater numbers of dendrites and axon terminals (Greenough, 1976). Enriched early experiences also appear to increase the activity of a number of neurotransmitters (Rosenzweig et al., 1972).

The environments of the young rats in some of these studies were especially enriched with sources of visual stimulation. As a result, the vision areas of their brains made the proportionately greatest gains in weight (Rosenzweig, 1966). Rats raised in darkness show shrinkage of the vision areas of their occipital lobes (Cummins et al., 1979; Rosenzweig & Bennett, 1970). People with sensory deficits (for example, blindness or deafness) similarly show **atrophy** of the parts of the brain involved in these functions. But other areas of the cortex, such as the area that projects tactile stimulation, are normal. In short, the great adaptability of the brain appears to be a double-edged sword. Adaptability allows us to develop different patterns of neural connections in order to meet the demands of our different environments (or universes of stimulation). However, lack of stimulation—especially during critical early periods of development—can apparently impair our adaptability.

Atrophy *To wither away.*

▶ ▶ ▶ ▶

Nourishment   The nourishment that the brain receives, like early experience, plays a role in its achieving the upper limits of the reaction range permitted by the child's genes. Inadequate nutrition, especially during the prenatal growth spurt of the brain, has several negative effects. These include smallness in the overall size of the brain, the formation of fewer neurons, and less myelination (Dobbing, 1976).

Inadequate nutrition in the fetus can be directly related to the nutrition received by the mother. In Chapter 3 we noted how important a proper diet was to a pregnant woman and her fetus. The placentas of mothers who do not eat adequately tend to be lighter in weight and smaller in size than the placentas of women who eat well. Smaller placentas, in turn, apparently do not carry as adequate a supply of nutrients—food and oxygen—to the fetus. Experiments with pregnant rats have shown that the pups of deprived mothers with smaller placentas have fewer brain cells (Stephan & Chow, 1969; Winick, 1970).

Sexual Development

According to the Old Testament, Adam came into being first and Eve was created from one of Adam's ribs. But according to our modern understanding of development, we shall see that it would be more accurate to say that *Adams* (that is, males) develop from *Eves* (that is, females).

In this section we focus on the processes of sexual differentiation that occur during prenatal development and at puberty. During prenatal development the genetic code and hormones spur the development of male or female gonads, ducts, and external genitals. During puberty, which signals the beginnings of adolescence, hormones once more stoke the body, spurring the additional sexual development that makes reproduction possible.

Prenatal Sexual Differentiation

At about five to six weeks after conception, when the embryo is only a quarter to a half of an inch long, primitive **gonads,** ducts, and external genitals have already been formed. However, the sex of the embryo cannot yet be distinguished (see Figures 5.9 and 5.10). By about the seventh week following conception, the genetic code (XX or XY) begins to assert itself, leading to rapid changes in the gonads, genital ducts, and external genitals.

If a Y sex chromosome is present, **androgens** cause the gonads to become more compact. The gonads develop into testes, and the structures within the testes that will manufacture sperm become organized. If such differentiation does not begin by the end of the seventh week, the embryo will probably remain female. But the forerunners of the follicles that will bear ova are not found until the fetal stage, about ten weeks after conception.

Descent of the Testes and the Ovaries   The testes and ovaries develop from slender structures high in the abdominal cavity (Figure 5.9). By about ten weeks after conception, they have descended so that they are almost even with the upper edge of the pelvis. The ovaries remain here for the remainder of the prenatal period. Later they rotate and descend farther, to their adult position in the pelvis.

Gonads *Organs that produce reproductive cells—testes and ovaries.*

Androgens *Male sex hormones.*

▶ ▶ ▶ ▶

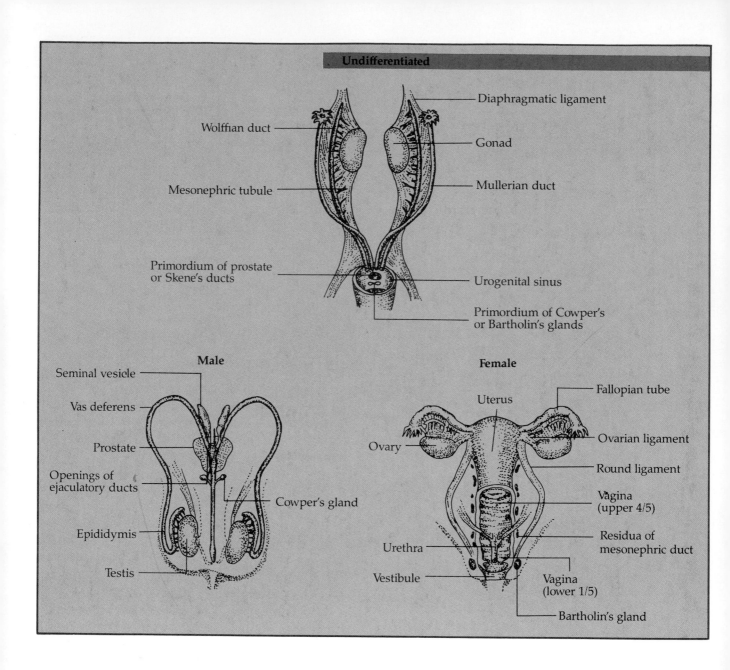

Figure 5.9 Development of the Internal Sex Organs
Five to six weeks following conception, the internal sex organs remain undifferentiated. By about the seventh week, visible differentiation begins to occur, followed by rapid changes in the gonads, genital ducts, and external genitals.

▶ ▶ ▶ ▶

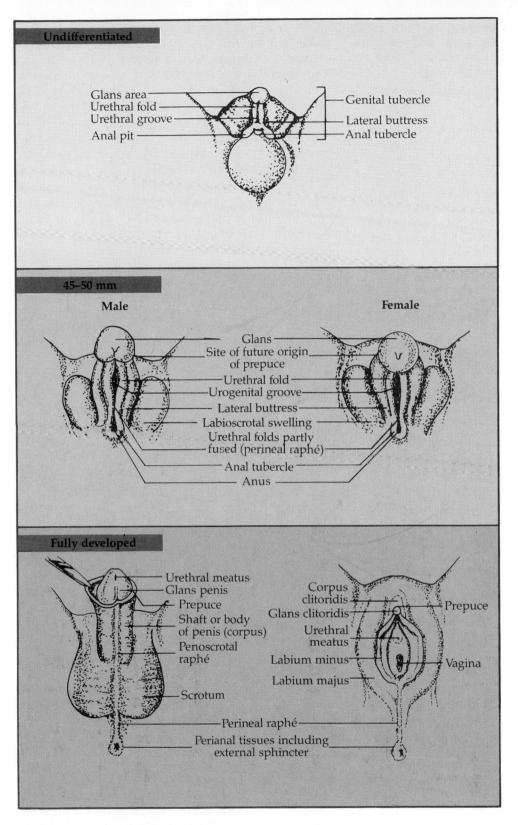

Undifferentiated

Glans area
Urethral fold
Urethral groove
Anal pit

Genital tubercle
Lateral buttress
Anal tubercle

45–50 mm

Male

Female

Glans
Site of future origin of prepuce
Urethral fold
Urogenital groove
Lateral buttress
Labioscrotal swelling
Urethral folds partly fused (perineal raphé)
Anal tubercle
Anus

Fully developed

Urethral meatus
Glans penis
Prepuce
Shaft or body of penis (corpus)
Penoscrotal raphé

Scrotum

Corpus clitoridis
Glans clitoridis
Prepuce
Urethral meatus
Labium minus
Vagina
Labium majus

Perineal raphé
Perianal tissues including external sphincter

Figure 5.10 Prenatal Development of the External Sex Organs

▶ ▶ ▶ ▶

SEXUAL DEVELOPMENT

191

About four months after conception, the testes normally descend into the scrotum through a passageway called the **inguinal canal.** After their descent, this passageway is closed. But in 1 to 2 percent of males, one or both testes remain in the abdomen, or undescended, at birth (Campbell, 1970). In most cases of undescended testes (also called **cryptochidism,** or "hidden testes"), the testes migrate to the scrotum during infancy. Still others descend by puberty. Men with undescended testes are usually treated through surgery or hormonal therapy, since they are at higher risk for cancer of the testes. Sperm production is also impaired in cryptochidism, because the testes are subjected to higher-than-optimal temperatures when they are contained within the body. Their normal hanging away in the scrotal sac serves to provide a perfect temperature for the production and maintenance of sperm.

Complications may also develop if the inguinal canal does not close properly after the descent of the testes, or reopens during later years. Intestinal loops may enter the scrotum—a condition known as **inguinal hernia,** which is corrected readily by surgery.

The Genital Ducts   Once the testes develop in the embryo, they produce the male sex hormone testosterone. Testosterone further stimulates prenatal differentiation of male sex organs. Later it will prompt the development of **secondary sex characteristics** such as the beard, the deepened voice, the growth of muscle and bone, and the sperm-producing ability of the testes.

Testosterone promotes differentiation of each **Wolffian duct** (see Figure 5.9) into ducts that will later carry and nourish sperm. In the absence of male sex hormones, the Wolffian ducts degenerate.

When male sex hormones are not present, the **Müllerian ducts** develop into fallopian tubes, the uterus, and the inner part of the vagina. Female sex hormones are not needed to induce these changes. For this reason, if a fetus with XY (male) sex chromosomal structure were prevented from producing androgens, it would develop the genital ducts of a female. In male fetuses, a substance secreted by the testes prevents the Müllerian ducts from developing into the female genital duct system.

The outer part of the female's vagina, the male's **prostate gland,** and the **urethras** of both sexes develop from parts of the urinary system.

The External Genitals   Androgens also spur the development of male external genitals (Figure 5.10). Without them, female external genitals will develop. By about four months after conception, males and females show the distinct external structures seen in Figure 5.10.

Homologous and Analogous Sex Organs   Male and female organs that develop from the same embryonic tissue are said to be **homologous.** Organs that are similar in function are called **analogous.** Table 5.1 summarizes homologous and analogous sex organs. Note that analogous organs are also homologous, but not all homologous organs are analogous.

Hormonal Errors   John Money (1966) reports the case of a pregnant Brazilian who possessed testes as well as ovarian tissue and claimed to be both father and mother of his/her unborn child. The mother was probably not also the child's father, since the hormones produced by her ovarian tissue would normally have sterilized the testes. But hormonal errors during prenatal development have led to the birth of a number of individuals with mixed genital tissue.

▶ ▶ ▶ ▶

Table 5.1 Homologous and Analogous Sex Organs in the Male and Female

EMBRYONIC TISSUE	HOMOLOGOUS ORGANS		ANALOGOUS ORGANS	
	MALE	FEMALE	MALE	FEMALE
	INTERNAL SEX ORGANS			
Gonad	Testes	Ovaries	Testes	Ovaries
Urogenital sinus	Cowper's glands	Bartholin's glands	Cowper's glands	Bartholin's glands[a]
	Prostate	Skene's glands	Prostate	Skene's glands[b]
	EXTERNAL SEX ORGANS			
Labioscrotal swelling	Scrotum	Labia majora	Scrotum	Labia majora
Genital tubercle	Penis	Clitoris[c]		
	Glans of penis	Glans of clitoris	Glans of penis	Glans of clitoris[d]
	Underside of penis	Labia minora		
	Corpora cavernosa (penile)	Corpora cavernosa (clitoral)	Corpora cavernosa (penile)	Corpora cavernosa (clitoral)[e]
	Prepuce (foreskin)	Prepuce (clitoral hood)	Prepuce (foreskin)	Prepuce (clitoral hood)[f]

[a] These glands both produce small amounts of lubricating fluid when the person is sexually aroused.
[b] Also these glands secrete fluids related to sexual activity; prostatic fluid, however, provides the bulk of seminal fluid, whereas the secretions of Skene's glands are unessential.
[c] The penis and clitoris are both sensitive to sexual stimulation, but the penis also carries urine and seminal fluid.
[d] The penile and clitoral glanses both receive and transmit sexual sensations.
[e] These bodies both swell when the person is sexually aroused.
[f] Both folds of skin protect sensitive glanses.

Hermaphrodite *(her-MAFF-row-dite). A person with both ovarian and testicular tissue.*

Pseudohermaphrodite *(SOO-doe-. . .). A person with the gonads of one sex but with external sex organs that are ambiguous or characteristic of the opposite sex.*

Testicular feminizing syndrome *A form of pseudohermaphroditism in which a genetic male is insensitive to testosterone and therefore develops female external genitals.*

Androgenital syndrome *A form of pseudohermaphroditism in which a genetic female is masculinized because of prenatal exposure to androgens.*

People with both testicular and ovarian tissue are called **hermaphrodites,** after the Greek myth of the son of Hermes and Aphrodite, whose body became united with that of a nymph while he was bathing. One type of hermaphrodite is the genetic (XX) female with male external genitals and breasts. In some cases, a vaginal opening lies below the penis. Others may have one testicle and one ovary, or structures that combine testicular and ovarian tissue. There may be one fallopian tube and an underdeveloped uterus. Some hermaphrodites menstruate. As noted in Chapter 12, regardless of the genetic sex, hermaphrodites usually assume the identity and sex role of the gender to which they are assigned.* **Pseudohermaphrodites** ("false" hermaphrodites) have testes or ovaries, but not both. Their external genitals are ambiguous or typical of the opposite sex. One form of pseudohermaphroditism is **testicular feminizing syndrome,** in which a genetic (XY) male embryo produces normal amounts of testosterone. But because of genetic defects that are only poorly understood (Mittwoch, 1973), the embryo is insensitive to testosterone. As a result, the external genitals develop as female.

In **androgenital syndrome,** another type of pseudohermaphroditism, the external sex organs of a genetic (XX) female become masculinized because

*Gender assignment in such cases typically involves labeling the child as male or female, cosmetic surgery during infancy, rearing the child as a male or female, and, possibly, continuous or intermittent hormonal therapy.

▶ ▶ ▶ ▶

the adrenal glands, located near the kidneys, produce excessive amounts of androgens during prenatal development. As noted in Chapter 12 cosmetic surgery and hormonal therapy are required if the child with androgenital syndrome is to be reared as a boy. And as noted in Chapter 2, progestin-induced hermaphroditism has occurred in a number of genetic females whose mothers threatened to miscarry and were given progestin, a chemical compound similar to androgens, to help them maintain their pregnancies. For this reason, progestin is no longer used so frequently to help women avoid miscarriages.

Pseudohermaphroditism, fortunately, is found in perhaps one infant in 1,000, and hermaphroditism is even rarer (Green & Green, 1965).

Puberty

Following their prenatal differentiation, the sex organs do not change significantly until puberty. With the advent of puberty, a clock in the brain somehow stirs the intense hormone secretion that makes people capable of reproducing within a span of just a few years. Puberty is defined as a stage of development that begins with the appearance of secondary sex characteristics and ends when the long bones make no further gains in length. The onset of adolescence coincides with the advent of puberty. Adolescence, however, ends with psychosocial markers such as the assumption of "adult responsibilities." Puberty is a biological concept, but adolescence is a psychosocial concept with biological correlates.

Puberty begins in U.S. girls between the ages of about 9 and 12 and a few years later in U.S. boys. **Menarche** (first menstruation) commonly occurs between the ages of 11 and 14, and a boy's first ejaculation at about 13 or 14. In the middle 1800s European girls first menstruated at about the age of 17, as shown in Figure 5.11. But during the past century and a half, the processes of puberty have occurred at progressively earlier ages in Western nations, probably because of improved nutrition and health care, so that by the 1960s and 1970s the average age of menarche in the United States had plummeted to between 12½ and 13 (Chumlea, 1982; Muuss, 1970; Roche, 1979). Why? One view is that body weight may trigger pubertal changes, and, as noted earlier, today's children are larger. The critical body weight for triggering menarche would be about 103 to 109 pounds (Frisch, 1972; Frisch & Revelle, 1970), but no single theory of the onset of puberty has found wide acceptance. In any event, the average age of the advent of puberty appears to have leveled off in recent years. The precipitous drop suggested in Figure 5.11 seems to have come to an end.

Pubertal changes have many psychological correlates. For one thing, they are often accompanied by striving toward increased autonomy. Pubertal changes may lead to increased conflict between adolescents and parents, and increase the emotional distance between them (Steinberg, 1987). Other changes are discussed below.

Pubertal Changes in Boys At puberty, the pituitary gland stimulates the testes to increase their output of testosterone, leading to further development of the male genitals. The first visible sign of puberty is accelerated growth of the testes, which begins at an average age of about 11½, although a range of ages of plus or minus two years is considered perfectly normal. Testicular growth further accelerates testosterone production and other pubertal changes. The penis be-

Menarche (men-NARK-ee). *The onset of menstruation.*

▶ ▶ ▶ ▶

5 PHYSICAL AND MOTOR DEVELOPMENT

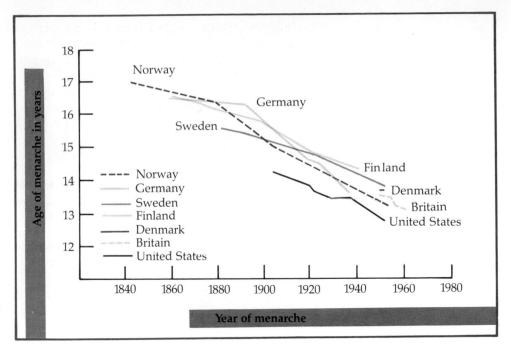

Figure 5.11 The Changing Age of Menarche
During the past century and a half, Western girls have begun to menstruate at progressively earlier ages. However, in recent years the drop shown in this figure has leveled off.

gins a spurt of accelerated growth about a year later, and still later pubic hair begins a growth spurt (see Figure 5.12).

Underarm, or **axillary**, hair appears at about age 15. Facial hair is at first a fuzz on the upper lip. An actual beard does not develop for another two to three years—only half of American boys shave (of necessity) by 17. The beard and chest hair continue to develop past the age of 20.

At 14 or 15 the voice deepens because of growth of the "voice box," or **larynx,** and the lengthening of the vocal cords. The developmental process is gradual, and adolescent boys sometimes encounter an embarrassing cracking of the voice. Because women were not allowed to sing in the opera during most of pre-nineteenth-century Europe, many boys with promising voices were **castrated** so that they could assume women's roles later on. So-called *castrati* were used in the pope's choir until early in the last century. At that time nothing was known of hormones, so it was not understood that castration prevented the appearance of secondary sex characteristics in boys by depriving them of testosterone.

Males are capable of producing erections in early infancy (and some male babies are indeed born with erections), but the phenomenon is not a frequent one until age 13 or 14. Many junior high school boys worry that they will be caught walking between classes with erections, or be asked to stand before the class. The organs that produce **semen** grow rapidly, and boys typically ejaculate seminal fluid by age 13 or 14—about one and a half years after the penis begins its growth spurt (Tanner, 1972)—although here too there is much individual variation. About a year later they begin to have **nocturnal emissions**, also called "wet dreams" because of the myth that emissions accompany erotic dreams. However, nocturnal emissions and erotic dreams need not coincide at all. Mature sperm are found in ejaculatory emissions by about the age of 15.

Axillary *Underarm.*

Larynx *(LAR-inks). The part of the throat that contains the vocal cords.*

Castrate *To remove the testes, preventing production of sperm and testosterone.*

Semen *The fluid that contains sperm.*

Nocturnal emission *Emission of seminal fluid while asleep.*

▶ ▶ ▶ ▶

SEXUAL DEVELOPMENT

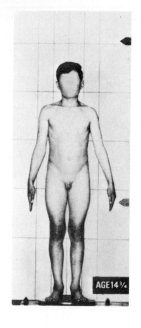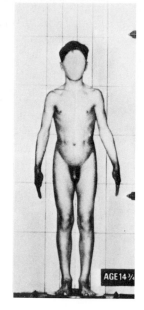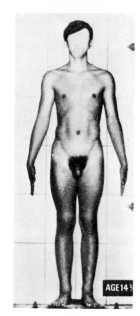

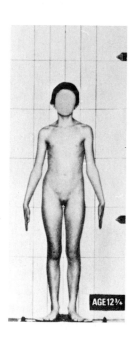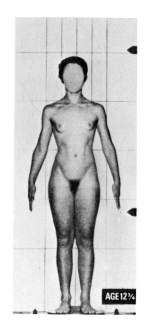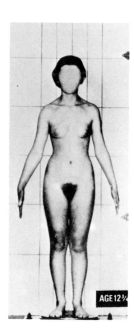

Figure 5.12 Variations in Pubertal Development
There are individual differences in the time of the onset of puberty.

Epiphyseal closure (ep-pee-FEES-ee-al). The turning to bone of the cartilage that separates the long end (epiphysis) of a bone from the main part of the bone.

▶ ▶ ▶ ▶

And so ejaculation is not adequate evidence of reproductive capacity. Ejaculatory ability in boys usually precedes the presence of mature sperm by at least a year. Girls also typically menstruate before they can reproduce.

As noted earlier, both boys and girls undergo general growth spurts during puberty. In males, the muscle mass increases in weight, and there are gains in shoulder width and chest circumference. At 20 or 21, men stop growing taller because testosterone causes **epiphyseal closure,** preventing the long bones from making further gains in length. And so puberty draws to a close.

Pustule *A skin elevation that contains pus; a pimple.*

Gynecomastia *(gone-uh-co-MAST-tee-uh). Temporary enlargement of the breasts in adolescent males.*

Mammary glands *Glands that secrete milk.*

Labia *The major and minor lips of the female's genitalia.*

Clitoris *A female sex organ that is highly sensitive to sexual stimulation, but not directly involved in reproduction.*

Acne Many 15- to 16-year-old boys are afflicted with acne due to androgen production, which also causes acne in pubescent girls. Although girls are less prone to acne than boys, we cannot say that they "suffer less" from it. In our society, a smooth complexion has a higher value for girls than boys, and girls with cases of acne that boys would consider "mild" may suffer terribly.

Severe acne is manifested by multiple pimples and blackheads on the face, chest, and back. **Pustules** reflect clogged oil-producing glands. Inappropriate treatment of acne—as in careless squeezing—can cause scarring. Since acne can cause great concern, afflicted adolescents may profit from consulting a dermatologist rather than waiting for it to clear up by itself. Dermatologists often recommend alternating several over-the-counter and prescription cleansers, and may also use ultraviolet light and antibiotics. Touted "miracle preparations" are less than miraculous, but persistence with cleansers and other facial preparations can make great inroads in controlling the problem.

Nearly four boys in five also experience temporary enlargement of the breasts, or **gynecomastia.** This condition probably stems from the small amount of female sex hormones secreted by the testes.

Pubertal Changes in Girls In girls, the pituitary gland signals the ovaries to vastly increase estrogen production at puberty. Estrogen may stimulate the growth of breast tissue ("breast buds") as early as the ages of 8 or 9, but the breasts usually begin to enlarge during the tenth year. The development of fatty tissue and ducts elevates the areas of the breasts surrounding the nipples, and causes the nipples themselves to protrude. The breasts typically reach full size in about three years, but the **mammary glands** do not mature fully until childbirth.

Estrogen also promotes the growth of the fatty and supporting tissue in the hips and buttocks, which, along with the widening of the pelvis, causes the hips to become rounded. Growth of fatty deposits and connective tissue varies considerably. For this reason, some girls develop pronounced breasts, whereas others may have relatively large hips. Our culture has long idealized the "hourglass" figure, in which rounded breasts and hips, nearly equal in circumference, are punctuated by a slender waist. Unfortunately, few girls can meet this rather arbitrary standard. In one study, over 40 percent of girls reported that they frequently felt unattractive (Offer et al., 1981). In a *Psychology Today* poll, 25 percent of women respondents expressed dissatisfaction with their breasts, 43 percent with their buttocks, and 49 percent with their hips. By comparison, only 11 percent expressed dissatisfaction with their overall facial attractiveness (Berscheid et al., 1973).

Small amounts of androgens produced by girls' adrenal glands, along with estrogen, stimulate the growth of pubic and axillary hair, beginning at about the age of 11. Excessive androgen production can darken or increase the amount of facial hair.

While estrogen causes the **labia,** vagina, and uterus to develop during puberty, androgens cause the **clitoris** to develop. The vaginal lining varies in thickness according to the amount of estrogen in the bloodstream.

Estrogen typically brakes the female growth spurt some years before testosterone brakes that of males. Girls deficient in estrogen during their late teens may grow quite tall, but most girls reach their heights because of normal genetically determined variations.

▶ ▶ ▶ ▶

Hormonal Regulation of the Menstrual Cycle   While testosterone levels remain fairly stable in boys, estrogen and progesterone levels vary markedly and regulate the menstrual cycle. Following menstruation—the sloughing off of the endometrium—estrogen levels increase, leading once more to the growth of endometrial tissue. Once girls have begun to ovulate, which usually occurs about 12 to 18 months after menarche, the surge of estrogen also causes an ovum to ripen. The ripe ovum is released by the ovary when estrogens reach peak blood levels. Then the inner lining of the uterus thickens in response to the secretion of progesterone. In this way it gains the capacity to support an embryo if fertilization should occur. If the ovum is not fertilized, estrogen and progesterone levels drop suddenly, triggering menstruation once again.

The average menstrual cycle is 28 days, but variation between girls and in the same girl is common. Girls' cycles are often irregular for a few years after menarche, but later tend to assume patterns that are reasonably regular. Menstruation follows ovulation at fairly reliable 14-day intervals, although in one large-scale survey, 87 percent of women had encountered variations of at least seven days in their menstrual cycles (Chiazze et al., 1967).

Psychological Impact of Menarche   In different times, in different places, menarche has had different meanings. The Kurtatchi, who live on an island off the green coast of New Guinea, greet menarche with elaborate ceremony (Matlin, 1987). The girl's mother announces the event to friends and relatives, who go into seclusion with the girl in her hut. There they fast and paint their bodies for several days in preparation for public ceremonies. The girl and her entourage emerge from the hut, perform a dance, and blow on a conch shell. The girl parades among male and female villagers, who rejoice enthusiastically. Then there is a feast.

In the West, menstruation has historically received a mixed response. The menstrual flow itself has generally been seen, erroneously, as polluting, and menstruating women have been stereotyped as irrational. Menarche itself has generally been perceived as the event in which a girl suddenly develops into a woman, but because of taboos and the unjustified prejudice against menstruating women, girls usually matured in ignorance of menarche.

Things are changing. In the United States today most of the negative stereotypes about menstruation are diminishing, but menstruation is still not considered an appropriate topic for "polite conversation" (Grief & Ulman, 1982). A minority of 9- to 12-year-old girls in suburban Midwest schools still clung to certain "taboos" and negative feelings: 36 percent of them believed that menstruating women should not go swimming; 16 percent believed that strenuous sports should be avoided; and 10 percent still saw menstruation as dirty or unclean (Williams, 1983). On the positive side, 64 percent of the 9- to 12-year-old girls in the Williams (1983) study agreed that "Menstruation is exciting because it means a girl is growing up" (p. 146). Also, most premenarcheal girls today hope that they will "get their periods" when their age-mates do (Peterson, 1983), just as they hope that their busts will develop at the same time.

About 90 to 95 percent of girls receive advance information about menstruation, usually from their mothers, sisters, and girlfriends (Brooks-Gunn & Ruble, 1983). Early information about menstruation appears to foster more positive feelings toward it (Golub, 1983).

Matlin (1987) notes that menarche may be a "dividing time" for females. Young girls often play football with boys or lounge around all afternoon in the home, even the bedroom, of the boy next door. Now and then fathers invite them to sit on their laps. But after menarche mothers often caution, "You're too big for that now."

Early and Late Maturers

I remember Al from my high school days. Al was short for Alfonse, but nobody dared call him that. As I entered eleventh grade, Al entered into the ninth. He was all of 14, but he was also about 6 feet 3 inches tall, with broad shoulders and arms thick with muscle. His face was cut from rock, and his beard was already dark.

Al paraded down the hallways with an entourage of male and female admirers. He literally looked down on the rest of us with a cocky grin. When there were shrieks of anticipation, you could bet that Al was coming around the corner. We all gave Al a wide birth in the boys' room. He would have to lean back when he combed his waxed hair up and back—otherwise his head would be too high for the mirror.

At that age my friends and I were very glad to be able to remind ourselves that Al was not all that bright. We were going to college; he was probably going to jail. He could whip any two or three of the older boys in the school, but he was also starting to get into trouble with the law. He had the present, but we rationalized that we had the future.

I don't know what happened to Al. I hope my friends and I were correct in our predictions. If not, there is no justice.

Al had matured early, and he had experienced the positive aspects of maturing early. It may be that his maturing early was the major accomplishment in his life, and that things went downhill from there. (Okay, okay—my wishful thinking again.) Early or late maturation can play an extremely important role in the self-esteem and adjustment of adolescent males and females, and sometimes with negative results.

Early and Late Maturation in Boys Studies are somewhat mixed in their findings about boys who mature early, but the weight of the evidence suggests that the effects of early maturation are generally positive.

Classic research by psychologists Mary Cover Jones and Paul Mussen (Jones, 1957; Mussen & Jones, 1957) on a cohort of children who participated in the Berkeley Growth Study found that early-maturing boys are more popular than their late-maturing peers and are more likely to be leaders in school. Early-maturing boys were also found to be more poised, relaxed, and good-natured. Their edge in sports and the admiration of their peers heightens their sense of self-worth. Some studies have suggested that the stereotype of the mature, tough-looking boy as dumb is just that—a stereotype. James Tanner (1982) and other researchers (e.g., Gross & Duke, 1980) report that early-maturing boys may also be somewhat ahead of their peers intellectually. However, these differences are slight and, where they exist, they tend to evaporate by adulthood (Jones, 1957).

On the negative side, early maturation may hit some boys before they are psychologically prepared to live up to the expectations of those who admire their new bodies. Coaches may expect too much of them in sports, and peers may want them to fight their battles for them. Sexual opportunities may create

▶ ▶ ▶ ▶

demands before they know how to respond to them. Some early maturers may therefore be very worried about living up to the expectations of others.

Late maturers have the advantage of avoiding this early pressure, They are not rushed into maturity. On the other hand, late-maturing boys often feel dominated by early-maturing boys. They have been found more dependent and insecure. Although they are smaller and weaker than early maturers, they may be more rebellious and more likely to get into fights—perhaps in an effort to prove themselves to be adult (Livson & Peskin, 1980; Wadsworth, 1979). But there are many individual differences. While some late maturers appear to fight their physical status and get into trouble, others adjust to their physical developmental status and find acceptance through academic achievement, music, clubs, and other nonathletic extracurricular activities. Late-maturing boys also show more flexibility and social sensitivity and a greater sense of humor than their early-maturing counterparts. Still, follow-ups of the late-maturing boys from the Berkeley Growth Study found them less likely than early maturers to take on leadership roles in business and social organizations once they were in their middle 30s (Livson & Peskin, 1980).

Cultural Differences   Michael Rutter (1980) found that the benefits of early maturation are greatest among lower-class adolescents, because physical prowess is valued more highly among these youngsters than among middle- or upper-class adolescents. Middle- and upper-class adolescents are also likely to place more value on the types of achievements—academic and so on—available to late-maturing boys.

Early and Late Maturation in Girls   The situation is somewhat reversed for girls. Whereas early maturation poses distinct advantages for boys, the picture is mixed for girls. Early-maturing girls outgrow not only their late-maturing counterparts, but also their male age-mates. With their tallness and their developing bustlines, they quickly become very conspicuous, and, unless adolescents are very sure of themselves (as Al was), they shy away from being the center of attention. Boys their own age may tease them about their breasts and their height. Older boys, who find them appealing, may attempt to pressure them into sexual activity before they are ready (Simmons et al., 1983).

In the United States today, well-developed bosoms are found attractive. However, there are stereotypes attached to large breasts. Kleinke and Staneski (1980) ran a study with college students in which they varied the breast sizes of women shown in photographs by padding and other means. The same females were rated as less intelligent, less competent, less moral, and less modest when they *appeared* to have large breasts! The large-breasted young girl clearly stands out, and teachers and her age-mates are likely to jump to unwarranted conclusions about her.

In any event, a number of studies show that the parents of early-maturing girls may increase their vigilance and restrictiveness (Hill et al., 1985; Petersen, 1985; Savin-Williams & Small, 1986). Increased restrictiveness, in turn, can lead to new child-parent conflicts.

The data in the Berkeley Growth Study showed that early-maturing girls are less poised, sociable, and expressive than their late-maturing counterparts during the latter part of middle childhood (Jones, 1958), but that they appear to adjust by the time they reach high school (Livson & Peskin, 1980). Once in high school, they do not stand out so much, and their size may earn them

▶ ▶ ▶ ▶

Pincer Grasp *The oppositional thumb is first used by babies at about 9 to 12 months, permitting them to pick up tiny objects for inspection.*

admiration rather than curiosity. At this time early-maturing girls may also take on the roles of cosmetic and sexual advisers to later-maturing age-mates. Perhaps the task of coping with the problems posed by early maturation also helps them develop coping mechanisms that they use to their advantage in later years.

One of the great things about adolescence is that it does not last forever. One of the terrible things about life is that adolescence does not last forever.

Motor Development

"When did your baby first sit up?" "When did he walk?" "Jordan reached for my nose and bit it, or gummed it—to be precise, before she was 6 months old." "I remember how scared I was the first time Allyn climbed the stairs without holding on." "She couldn't walk yet at 10 months, but she zoomed after me in her walker, giggling her head off."

These are some of the types of comments parents make about their children's motor development. Motor development provides some of the most fascinating changes in infants, in part because so much seems to happen so quickly—and so much of it during the first year.

Infancy

Motor development, like other dimensions of development, follows patterns of cephalocaudal and proximodistal development, and differentiation. As suggested by Figure 5.13, infants gain control of their heads and upper torsos before they can effectively use their arms. And they can reach for and control objects with their hands before they can control their legs.

Lifting and Holding the Torso and Head   Newborn babies can move their heads slightly to the side. This permits them to avoid suffocation if they are lying face down and their noses or mouths are obstructed by the bedding. At about 1 month babies raise their heads. By about 2 months they can also lift their chests while lying in a prone position.

When neonates are held, their heads must be supported. But by 3 to 6 months of age, babies generally manage to hold their heads quite well, so that supporting the head is no longer necessary. Unfortunately, babies who can normally support their heads cannot do so when they are lifted or moved about in a jerky manner, and a number of babies who are not handled carefully develop neck injuries.

Control of the Hands   Babies will track (follow) slowly moving objects with their eyes from shortly after birth, but generally speaking will not reach for them. They show a grasp reflex, as described in Chapter 4, but do not reliably reach for the objects that appear to interest them. Voluntary reaching and grasping require visual-motor coordination. By about 3 months of age infants will make clumsy swipes at objects, failing in efforts to grasp them, because their aim is poor or they close their hands too soon or too late.

The development of hand skills is a clear example of the process of differentiation. By about 6 months, most infants successfully grasp objects and tend to bring them to the mouth to suck or gum. However, they may not "know

▶ ▶ ▶ ▶

	0 mo.	1 mo.	2 mo.	3 mo.	4 mo.	5 mo.
	Fetal posture	Chin up	Chest up	Reach and miss	Sit with support	Sit on lap Grasp object

	6 mo.	7 mo.	8 mo.	9 mo.	10 mo.
	Sit on high chair Grasp dangling object	Sit alone	Stand with help	Stand holding furniture	Creep

	11 mo.	12 mo.	13 mo.	14 mo.	15 mo.
	Walk when led	Pull to stand by furniture	Climb stair steps	Stand alone	Walk alone

Figure 5.13 Motor Development in Infants
Motor development, like other dimensions of development, follows patterns of cephalocaudal and proximodistal development and differentiation. Infants gain control of their heads and upper torsos before they can effectively use their arms. They can reach for and control objects with their hands before they can control their legs. Although there is variation in the timing of the marker events shown in this figure, the sequence of events is largely invariant.

how'' to let go of an object and may hold onto it indefinitely, until their attention is diverted and the hand opens accidentally. Four to 6 months is a good age for giving children rattles, large plastic spoons, mobiles, and other brightly colored hanging toys that are harmless when they wind up in the mouth.

Babies first hold objects between their fingers and their palm. The oppositional thumb does not come into play until 9 to 12 months or so. Use of the thumb gives infants the ability to pick up tiny objects in what is called a **pincer grasp.** By about 11 months, infants can hold objects in each hand and inspect them in turn.

Another measure of visual-motor coordination is the ability to stack blocks. On the average, children can stack two blocks at the age of 15 months, three blocks at 18 months, and five blocks at 24 months. It is also not until about 24 months that children can copy horizontal and vertical lines.

Locomotion   **Locomotion** is movement from one place to another. Children gain the capacity to move their bodies about through a sequence of activities that includes rolling over, sitting up, crawling, creeping, walking, and running.

Pincer grasp *The use of the opposing thumb to grasp objects.*

Locomotion *Movement from one place to another.*

▶ ▶ ▶ ▶

5   PHYSICAL AND MOTOR DEVELOPMENT

There is a great deal of variation in the ages at which infants first engage in these activities, but the sequence remains generally invariant. A number of children will skip a step, however. For example, an infant may creep without ever having crawled.

Most infants can roll over, from back to stomach and stomach to back, by about 6 months. They are also capable of sitting (and holding their upper bodies, necks, and heads) for extended periods if they are supported by a person or placed in a seat with a strap or brace, such as a high chair. By about 7 months infants usually begin to sit up by themselves.

At about 8 to 9 months most infants begin to crawl, a motor activity in which they lie prone and use their arms to pull themselves along, dragging their bellies and feet behind. Creeping, a more sophisticated form of locomotion in which infants move themselves along up on their hands and knees, requires a good deal more coordination and usually appears a month or so after crawling.

There are fascinating alternatives to creeping. Some infants travel from one place to another by rolling over and over. Some lift themselves and swing their arms while in a sitting position, in effect driving along on their behinds. Still others do a "bear walk" in which they "walk" on their hands and feet, without allowing their elbows and knees to touch the floor. And some, as noted, just crawl until they are ready to stand and walk from place to place while holding on to chairs, other objects, and people.

At about 8 or 9 months, many parents give their children jumpers and walkers. Jumpers have been controversial for a number of years, with claims that they promote development of leg muscles and counterclaims that they may be harmful to the spine. At present the arguments have died down to some degree, and the most important question seems to be whether the individual child will enjoy a jumper. Some pediatricians advise against walkers for the reason that they encourage some infants to walk on their toes, rather than using the surface of the entire foot. Children as young as 5 to 6 months often find walkers a good place to sit and chew a variety of objects placed in (and tied down to!) their trays. Children of 9 to 10 months can learn to use them with astounding coordination and velocity—going forward, backward, and pivoting about, all with great glee.

Standing overlaps with crawling and creeping. Most infants can remain in a standing position if holding onto something by about 8 or 9 months. At this age they may also be able to walk a bit when supported by adults. This walking is voluntary, and does not have the stereotyped appearance of the walking reflex described in the previous chapter. About two months later they can pull themselves to a standing position by holding onto the sides of their cribs or other objects and can also stand briefly without holding on. Shortly afterward they walk about unsteadily while holding on, and by 12 to 15 months or so they walk by themselves. Walking by themselves earns them the name **toddler,** even though the term *infant* remains appropriate until they can talk.

Toddlers soon run about in a bowlegged fashion, supporting their relatively heavy heads and torsos by spreading their legs. Because they are top-heavy and inexperienced, they fall frequently. Some toddlers require a good deal of consoling when they fall. Others spring right up and run on again with barely an interruption. The ability to move about on the legs provides children with new freedom. It allows them to get about rapidly and grasp objects that were formerly out of reach. A large ball to toss and run after is about the least expensive and most enjoyable toy toddlers can be given.

Toddler *A child who walks with short, uncertain steps. Characteristic of children aged approximately 18–30 months.*

▶ ▶ ▶ ▶

MOTOR DEVELOPMENT

203

By 8 or 9 months, most children can assume a standing position so long as they have something to hold onto.

By age 8 children are showing the balance necessary to ride motorbikes.

As children mature, their muscle strength, the density of their bones, and their balance and coordination all improve. By 18 months they can climb steps, placing both feet on each step. By 2 years they run well, walk backward, climb ladders, and go down slides.

Early and Middle Childhood

Motor development continues through early and middle childhood, as noted in Tables 5.2 and 5.3. At about the age of 3 children can balance on one foot. By 3 or 4 they can walk up stairs, as adults do, by placing a foot on each step. By 4 or 5 they can skip and pedal a tricycle. Preschool children largely appear to acquire motor skills by teaching themselves and observing the behavior of other children. The opportunity to play with other children seems more important than adult instruction at this age.

School-age children are usually eager to participate in group games and athletic activities that require the movement of large muscles, such as catching and throwing balls. Children are hopping, jumping, and climbing by age 6 or so, and by 6 or 7, they are usually capable of pedaling and balancing on a bicycle. By the ages of 8 to 10, children are showing the balance, coordination, and strength that allows them to engage in gymnastics and team sports.

Reaction Time   One of the important factors in athletic performance is **reaction time,** or the amount of time required to respond to a stimulus. Reaction time is basic to the child's timing of a swing of the bat in order to meet the ball. Reaction time is basic to adjusting to a fly ball or a pass of a football. Reaction time is also involved in children's responses to cars and other (sometimes deadly) obstacles when they are riding their bicycles or running down the street.

Reaction time The amount of time required to respond to a stimulus.

A study of reaction time in people aged 7 to 75 found that it gradually improves (that is, *decreases*) from middle childhood to adulthood (Stern et al., 1980). In the Stern study, the experimental task was to press a button as soon as a light was flashed. The 7-year-olds took almost twice the amount of time

▶ ▶ ▶ ▶

5 PHYSICAL AND MOTOR DEVELOPMENT

Table 5.2 Development of Locomotion During Early and Middle Childhood

AGE	SKILLS
2 years	Takes wide stance; runs well; walks up stairs, one foot at a time; kicks a large ball; jumps 12 inches
3 years	Stands on one foot; walks up stairs alternating the feet; jumps from bottom stair; hops with two feet
4 years	Pedals a tricycle; runs smoothly; throws a ball overhand; gallops; skips on one foot
5 years	Walks a straight line; wa0lks down stairs alternating the feet; marches in rhythm; catches a bounced ball
6 years	Hops; jumps; climbs
7 years	Peddles and balances on a bicycle
8 years	Has good body balance
9 years	Engages in vigorous bodily activities, especially team sports such as baseball, football, volleyball, and basketball
10 years	Balances on one foot for 15 seconds; catches a fly ball
12 years	Displays some awkwardness as a result of asynchronous bone and muscle growth

The ages presented in the table are averages, and there are wide individual variations.
Source: Adapted from Olle Jane Z. Sahler & Elizabeth R. McAnarney, *The Child from Three to Eighteen*. (St Louis: Mosby, 1981).

Table 5.3 Development of Manipulative Skills During Early and Middle Childhood

AGE	SKILLS
2–3 years	Places simple geometric shapes in correct holes
	Easily picks up blocks
	Strings beads with a large needle
	Can turn the pages of a book
	Holds a glass in one hand
	Copies a circle accurately
	Unbuttons clothes
	Throws a ball about 10 feet
4–5 years	Uses a pencil with the correct hand grip
	Copies a square correctly
	Catches a small ball
	Walks on a balance beam
	Begins to form written letters
	Colors within lines (when desired)
6–7 years	Ties shoelaces
	Throws ball by using wrist and finger release
	Holds pencil with fingertips
	Follows simple mazes
	May be able to hit a ball with a bat
8–9 years	Spaces words when writing
	Writes and prints accurately and neatly
	Copies a diamond correctly
	Swings a hammer well
	Sews and knits
	Shows good hand–eye coordination

There are wide variations in the timing of the acquisition of the manipulative skills shown in this table.
Source: Adapted from Arnold Gesell, *The Embryology of Behavior* (Westport, CT: Greenwood, 1972).

► ► ► ►

Control over the wrists and fingers enables children to hold a pencil, play musical instruments, and, as shown in these photographs, to play with stack toys.

(.75 seconds) as the average adult (.37 seconds). Reaction time was progressively lower at the ages of 9 and 11, but the adults showed the lowest reaction times. Even the 75-year-olds outperformed the children! Baseball and volleyball may be "child's play," but, everything else being equal, adults will respond to the ball more quickly.

Fine-Motor Skills   **Fine-motor skills** develop gradually and lag behind gross-motor skills. Control over the wrists and fingers enables children to hold a pencil properly, play musical instruments, sew, and create detailed works of art. Pre-schoolers can labor endlessly in attempting to tie their shoelaces, squeeze toothpaste onto the toothbrush, and get their jackets zipped. There are terribly frustrating (as well as funny) scenes in alternating between steadfast refusal to allow a parent to intervene and requesting the parent's help. By 6 to 7 years, however, children can usually tie their shoelaces and hold their pencils as adults do (Kress, 1982). The abilities to fasten buttons, zip zippers, brush teeth, wash themselves, and coordinate a knife and fork all develop during the early school years.

Success in motor skills reflects children's physical maturity, their opportunities to learn, and their personality factors such as persistence and self-confidence. Competence in motor skills enhances children's peer acceptance and self-esteem.

Sex Differences   Throughout early and middle childhood boys and girls are not far apart in their motor skills. Girls show somewhat greater limb coordination and overall flexibility, which aids them in balancing, gymnastics, and dancing (Cratty, 1979; Tanner, 1970). Boys, on the other hand, show slightly greater overall strength, and, in particular, more forearm strength, which is valuable in swinging a bat or throwing a football. There is also some evidence

Fine-motor skills Skills involving use of the small muscles, as in the fingers.

▶ ▶ ▶ ▶

By the age of 6, children usually have the abilities to hop, jump, and, as shown in this photograph, to climb "jungle gyms."

that between the ages of 7 to 12, boys on the average can run faster, throw farther, and jump higher than girls (Espenschade, 1960)

Boys, of course, are also expected to excel in sports like football and baseball, which can spur their motivation. But throughout the middle years, girls and boys usually have the capacity to participate in the same motor activities. As suggested earlier in the chapter, however, the girl who wants to play football will usually find herself lagging significantly behind her male teammates in strength, once the group enters adolescence.

Individual differences are more impressive than sex differences throughout early and middle childhood. Some children develop motor skills earlier than others. Some are genetically predisposed toward developing better coordination or more strength than others. Motivation and practice are extremely important in children's acquisition of motor skills. Nevertheless, heredity appears to provide a reaction range (limits) on the upper boundaries of performance.

Handedness **Handedness** emerges during early and middle childhood. Ninety percent of us are right-handed, and left-handedness is found more frequently in boys than girls (McKean, 1987). Children are usually labeled right-handed or left-handed on the basis of their handwriting preferences. However, we should note that some people write with one hand but pitch a baseball with the other. In fact, some people hold a tennis racket with one hand and throw a ball with the other.

It has been generally believed that children who prefer the left hand for writing are less well-coordinated and more disposed toward reading disabilities and other academic problems than right-handed children. In fact, the word *sinister*, with its connotations of unlucky or unfavorable, derives from the Latin for the left or unpreferred side. Because of the stereotypical conception of left-handedness, left-handed children for many years were encouraged to switch to

Handedness *The tendency to prefer using the left or right hand in writing and other activities.*

► ► ► ►

writing with their right hands (Hardyck & Petrinovich, 1977). However, recent research strongly suggests that the stereotype of the left-handed child may be exaggerated.

In one recent study, Tan (1985) examined the correlations between handedness and motor competence among 4-year-old preschoolers. More than 90 percent of her sample of 512 children were right-handed, 41 were left-handed, and 23 lacked a hand preference. Tan found no differences in motor skills between right- and left-handed children, but children lacking a hand preference performed less well than the other groups. Tan concludes that left-handed children may be assumed to be less well-coordinated than right-handed children, because their motor behavior *looks* so different. She also concludes that lack of hand preference may be a sign of a developmental lag in motor skills and suggests that such children receive direct training to enhance their motor coordination.

In a recent series of studies, Camilla Benbow and Julian Stanley (1980, 1983) related handedness and other factors to scores on the math part of the Scholastic Aptitude Test (SAT) among 12- and 13-year-olds. (The SAT is designed to assess older adolescents applying for college admission.) Most of the 292 12- and 13-year-olds who scored extremely well on the math subtests were boys,* and 20 percent were left-handed. Only 10 percent of the general population is left-handed, so it appears that left-handed children are more than adequately represented among the most academically gifted.

However, the gifted 292, including the left-handed children among them, were more prone to nearsightedness and allergies than the general population. The understanding and production of language are normally controlled in the left hemisphere of the cerebral cortex, and mathematical reasoning seems associated with the right hemisphere (McKean, 1987). For most of us, male and female, the left hemisphere of the cerebral cortex is also dominant, and this dominance is associated with right-handedness. But it has been theorized that prenatal hormonal influences often cause males to experience greater development of their brains' right hemispheres at the expense of the left. In some boys, then, right-hemisphere development could account for a combination of math ability *and* left-handedness. In others, the most notable effect of right-hemisphere development might be problems in reading.

In sum, there is little or no convincing evidence that left-handed children are clumsier than right-handed children. Left-handed children may be somewhat more prone toward developing allergies (Marx, 1982). Academically speaking, left-handedness is associated with positive as well as negative academic performances. And since handedness appears to reflect the differential development of the hemispheres of the cortex, it is doubtful that struggling to write with the nondominant hand would correct any academic shortcoming that might exist in some left-handed children—any more than training right-handed children to write with their left hands would increase their math ability!

Nature and Nurture in Motor Development

As noted, there seems to be little doubt that maturation (nature) and experience (nurture) both play indispensable roles in various aspects of motor development. Certain types of voluntary motor activities do not seem possible

*We shall explore these sex differences further in Chapter 12.

▶ ▶ ▶ ▶

until the brain has matured in terms of myelination and the differentiation of the motor areas of the cortex. While it is true that the neonate shows walking and swimming reflexes, these behaviors are controlled by more primitive areas of the brain. They disappear when cortical development inhibits some of the functions of the lower areas of the brain, and, when they reappear, their quality is quite different.

Infants also need some opportunity for motor experimentation before they can engage in milestones such as sitting up and walking. But although it may take them several months to sit up and, as described earlier, more months to take their first steps, most of this time can apparently be attributed to maturation. In a classic cross-cultural study, Wayne Dennis (Dennis & Dennis, 1940) reported on the motor development of Native American Hopi children, who spend their first year strapped to a cradleboard. Although denied a full year of experience in locomotion, Hopi infants gain the capacity to walk early in their second year, at about the same time as do children reared in other cultures. A more recent cross-cultural study (Hindley et al., 1966) reported that infants in five European cities began to walk at about the same time (generally speaking, between 12 to 15 months), despite cultural differences in encouragement to walk.

On the other hand, evidence is mixed as to whether specific training can accelerate the appearance of motor skills. For example, in a classic study with identical twins, Arnold Gesell (1929) gave one twin extensive training in hand coordination, block building, and stair climbing from early infancy. The other was allowed to develop on his own. But as time passed, the untrained twin became as skilled in these activities as the other.

In a related classic study, Myrtle McGraw (1935, 1939) gave one member of a pair of identical twins training in crawling and standing. Gesell had refrained from training the other twin, but McGraw actually *prevented* the other twin from practicing these skills. McGraw's twins also eventually performed the targeted motor skills at about the same age, providing additional evidence for the central importance of the gradual unfolding of the child's genetic heritage.

More recent research does suggest that the appearance of motor skills can be accelerated by training (Zelazo et al., 1972). Yet this effect is slight, at best; guided practice in the absence of neural maturation can have only limited results. There is also no evidence that this sort of training leads to eventual superior motor skills or other advantages.

Although being strapped to a cradleboard did not permanently prevent the motor development of Hopi infants, Dennis (1960; Dennis & Najarian, 1957) reported that many institutionalized infants were significantly retarded in their motor development. In contrast to the Hopi infants, the institutionalized infants were exposed to extreme social and physical deprivation. Under conditions of social isolation and minimal nourishment, they grew apathetic, and all aspects of development suffered. But there is also a bright side to this tale of deprivation. The motor development of infants in a Lebanese orphanage accelerated dramatically in response to such minimal intervention as being propped up in their cribs and being given a few colorful toys (Dennis & Sayegh, 1965).

Nature, as noted, provides the reaction range for the expression of inherited traits. Nurture determines whether the child will develop skills in accord with the upper limits of the inherited range. There may be little purpose in trying to train children to enhance their motor skills before they are ready.

▶ ▶ ▶ ▶

However, once they are ready, teaching and practice do make a difference. One does not become an Olympic athlete without "good genes." But one also usually does not become an Olympic athlete without high-quality training. And since motor skills are important to the self-concepts of children, good teaching is all the more important.

As my wife and I, and probably every other parent, have discovered, it is a basic fact of life that new locomotor abilities also provide young children with a vastly expanded array of ways in which they can get hurt. The thing to do, of course, is to childproof one's home as well as possible and then adopt a philosophical attitude to the effect that a child will now and then get hurt and there's no point in blaming oneself too much when it happens.

If you find a way to accept this "philosophy," please get in touch—my wife and I have a good deal to learn from you.

Summary

1. Physical growth and development is characterized by cephalocaudal and proximodistal sequences and differentiation. Development proceeds from "head to tail" (cephalocaudal) and from the trunk or central axis to the extremities (proximodistal). Parts of the body and motor capacities also become increasingly distinct and specific in function (differentiation).

2. Changes in height and weight are regulated largely by growth hormone, a secretion of the pituitary gland. They are most dramatic during the first year, with infants adding about ten inches (50 percent) to their height and tripling their birth weight. Throughout early and middle childhood, boys and girls tend to gain two to three inches and four to six pounds per year.

3. The adolescent growth spurt begins in girls at about 10 years 3 months and a year and a half later in boys. During this spurt boys surpass girls in height and weight (and also greatly increase their muscle strength). Throughout most of this century children were growing taller than their parents, probably because of improved nutrition and medical care, but middle- and upper-class Americans have stopped growing taller—at least for the time being.

4. Illness and dietary deficiency can slow children from growing at their genetically predetermined rates. However, they tend to catch up once the problem is ameliorated.

5. Babies are born with soft, membranous areas in the skull called fontanels, which permit their skulls to become distended as they pass through the birth canal. The skull bones form a single hard unit by about age 2. Bones grow by increasing their numbers (as in the feet and hands), their size, and their density (through calcification).

6. "Baby teeth" and permanent teeth are formed in the jaw before they erupt through the gums. Bone development and health are promoted by calcium, vitamin D, and—in the case of teeth—fluoride.

7. Children are born with all the muscle fibers they will ever have. Muscle strength increases as fibers grow in length and weight. Because of androgens, males end up with proportionately larger muscle masses than females.

▶ ▶ ▶ ▶

8. Children also have all the neurons they will ever have at birth, although the number of glial cells in the nervous system continues to increase. The brain undergoes a prenatal growth spurt during which neurons are formed. There is also a growth spurt that begins during the last months of pregnancy and continues through infancy; the second growth spurt is due to proliferation of dendrites and axon terminals. At birth the brain has 25 percent of its adult weight, and, in an example of cephalocaudal development, it attains about 70 percent of its adult weight by the first birthday.

9. Myelination insulates the axons of neurons from electrically charged ions in the surrounding body fluids, thereby facilitating conduction of messages. There is a strong link between the progress of myelination and the development of voluntary, complex behavior patterns. Parts of the brain that are involved in basic bodily functions and reflexes are well developed at birth, while the areas that are involved in vision, hearing, and perception of the skin senses reach mature functioning afterward.

10. The functions of the left and right hemispheres of the brain are somewhat specialized, with the left side more involved in logic and language functions, and the right side more involved in aesthetic and emotional responses. However, the two sides of the brain usually respond to events simultaneously, and, once the connecting corpus callosum is myelinated, they appear to work together.

11. The brain shows plasticity in early childhood, so that injury-related losses of function can sometimes be taken up by new areas of the brain. Experience appears to "fine tune" development of the brain, so that laboratory animals raised in enriched environments show greater numbers of dendrites and axon terminals in their brains.

12. Androgens promote the prenatal and pubertal development of male genital organs and secondary sex characteristics. At six to seven weeks after conception, testes and ovaries begin to differentiate from primitive gonads. Male genital ducts develop from Wolffian ducts, and female ducts develop from Müllerian ducts. Hormonal errors can lead to the development of hermaphrodites and pseudohermaphrodites.

13. Puberty, like the adolescent growth spurt, has been arriving at younger ages. Girls in the United States today experience menarche (first menstruation) at an average of less than 13 years. Girls can usually reproduce about one and one-half years after menarche, and boys about one to one and one-half years after seminal fluid is first emitted. The menstrual cycle is regulated by hormone levels. In our society girls receive mixed messages about menarche. Negative stereotypes about menstruation to some degree remain, but menarche is generally perceived as the point at which girls become young women.

14. Research shows that early-maturing boys are usually more sociable, poised, and relaxed than their late-maturing counterparts. Their physiques tend to make them admired by boys and girls alike. Early maturation for girls may initially result in teasing and sexual pressures for which they are not prepared. But by the high school years, early maturing girls usually have the respect and admiration of their age-mates.

► ► ► ►

15. Motor development follows generally invariant sequences, although the ages at which developmental milestones occur vary widely. Some children may even skip a step or two. Babies develop the visual–motor coordination to grasp and hold objects voluntarily by about 5 to 6 months. Newborn babies can move their heads to the side, but it takes a couple of months before they can raise their heads and chests. Infants sit up alone at about 7 months, creep a couple of months later, and begin to walk without support by about 13 to 14 months.

16. In early to middle childhood, children make incremental gains in their balancing abilities and in their fine-motor skills. Boys and girls are usually not too far apart in motor development during these years, but girls tend to be somewhat more flexible, and boys tend to be slightly stronger.

17. There are stereotpyes that left-handed children are less well-coordinated and more prone to academic problems than right-handed children, but recent research does not support these stereotypes.

18. Infants who are prevented from practicing motor skills nevertheless tend to reach milestones such as sitting up and walking at normal ages, suggesting that maturation plays a powerful role in motor development. On the other hand, early training in motor skills has limited effects. Extreme social and physical deprivation can retard motor development along with other aspects of development. However, deprived children who later receive encouragement show some capacity to catch up.

T R U T H ▸ O R ▸ F I C T I O N ▸ R E V I S I T E D

The head of the newborn child only doubles in length by adulthood, but the legs increase in length by about five times. True. This is because, at birth, the head is already well-developed relative to the limbs.

Infants triple their birth weight by age 1. True. They also add about ten inches to their height.

Boys and girls are about equal in height through age 9 or 10. False. Boys, as a group, are slightly taller throughout these years.

Children who undergo the adolescent growth spurt early end up taller than children who undergo the growth spurt relatively late. False. Early and late spurters wind up with equal gains in height.

Children are growing taller than their parents. Not all of them. This is truer for poor families than for wealthy families. Better nourished children tend to grow taller than poorly nourished parents.

One reason that babies tend to be "cute" is that their noses and mouths are proportionately smaller than they will be when they have matured. True. In keeping with the principle of cephalocaudal development, the upper part of the head is proportionately larger among babies.

We are born with all the bones we'll ever have. False.

▶ ▶ ▶ ▶

The Chinese used to bind the feet of infant girls to make them smaller. *True.* Pliancy of the bones during infancy has allowed people to deform their children (in an effort to produce beauty) in culturally desired ways.

Vitamin D and sunshine help harden the bones. *True.* They promote calcification.

We are born with all the nerve cells we'll ever have. *True.* However, the nervous system grows through the proliferation of glial cells, dendrites, and axon terminals, and through the lengthening of axons.

A child's brain reaches nearly 90 percent of its adult weight by the age of 5, although the child will still triple in overall weight by adulthood. *True.* This is another example of the principle of cephalocaudal growth. The brain develops relatively early.

Some cells in your body stretch all the way down your back to your big toe. *True.* The axons of sensory and motor neurons are responsible for this great length.

Some people are left-brained, others are right-brained. *False.* It may be that some people are more logical or more emotional than others, but the two sides of the brain tend to function together.

Nocturnal emissions in boys accompany "wet dreams." *False.* Nocturnal emissions can occur when boys are dreaming about nonerotic themes, or when they are not dreaming at all.

Girls are capable of becoming pregnant after they have their first menstrual periods. *False.* Mature ova may not be produced until one to one and one-half years after menarche.

Girls who mature early have higher self-esteem than those who mature late. *Not at first.* Prior to high school, early-maturing girls may be exceptionally conspicuous and the butt of teasing.

Seventy-five-year-old adults can react to a stimulus more rapidly than 9- and 11-year-old children can. *True.* Reaction time improves steadily from middle childhood to adulthood.

A disproportionately high percentage of 12- and 13-year-old math whizzes are left-handed. *True.* This phenonmenon may be related to greater development in the right sides of their brains.

Hopi babies spend the first year of life strapped to a board, yet they begin to walk at about the same time as children who are reared in other cultures. *True.* Maturation seems to be the central factor in the development of basic motor skills. Any negative effects from sensorimotor deprivation do not appear to last in Hopi children.

► ► ► ►

6

Perceptual Development

CHAPTER ▸ OUTLINE

▶
▶
▶
▶
▶
▶
▶

T R U T H ▶ O R ▶ F I C T I O N ?

- Newborn babies are nearsighted.
- Newborn babies may look at one object with one eye and another object with the other eye.
- Newborn babies make rhythmic eye movements, scanning left and right, even in the dark.
- Four-month-old babies who have been looking at a green circle will accept its replacement by a blue circle. However, they may cry and show other signs of distress when a blue circle is replaced by a green circle.
- Two-month old babies prefer to look at human faces rather than at brightly colored objects.
- Infants need to have some experience crawling before they develop fear of heights.
- Four-month-old infants enjoy multiple mirror images of their mothers, but 6-month-old infants are frightened by them.
- When favorite toys are placed behind a screen, they no longer exist—so far as 5-month-old babies are concerned.
- Newborn babies crudely orient their heads in the direction of sounds.
- Newborn babies do not show any preference for the sounds of human speech.
- By the age of 3 months, most babies imitate musical notes sung by their mothers.
- When presented with nursing pads used by their own mothers and other mothers, babies only a few days old will turn toward the pads used by their own mothers.
- Newborn babies prefer sweet-tasting foods.
- Newborn babies do not experience pain.
- Newborn kittens prevented from seeing horizontal lines for several months will not be able to perceive horizontal lines later on.
- Boys are more likely than girls to have reading problems.
- Some children cannot learn to read, even when they are average in intelligence, come from homes where reading is encouraged, and are 6 years old or older.
- Children tend to "outgrow" early reading problems.

What a world we live in. Green hills and reddish skies; rumbling subways, clamoring cars, murmuring brooks and voices; the sweet and the sour; the acrid and the perfumed; the metallic and the fuzzy. What an ever-changing display of sights, sounds, tastes, smells, and touches. What a delight—what a horror.

The pleasures of the world, and its miseries, are known to us through sensory impressions and the organization of these impressions into personal inner maps of reality. Our eyes, our ears; the sensory receptors in our noses and our mouths; our skin senses—these are our tickets of admission to the world.

In 1890, William James, one of the founders of modern psychology, wrote that the newborn baby must sense the world "as one great booming, buzzing confusion." The neonate emerges from being literally suspended in a temperature-controlled environment to being—again, in James' words—"assailed by eyes, ears, nose, skin, and entrails at once." In this chapter we see how children sense and perceive the world. We describe the sensory capabilities of newborn children, and we see that James, for all his eloquence, probably exaggerated the disorganization of the neonate.

We follow children over the course of the years to learn how they develop their abilities to integrate disjointed sensory impressions into meaningful patterns of events. We see what sorts of things capture the attention of young babies, and we see how children become purposeful seekers of information—selecting the sensory impressions they will choose to capture, and weeding out the sensory chaff.

In so doing, we shall also see that many things that are obvious to us are not obvious to young infants. You may know that a coffee cup is the same whether you see it from above or from the side, but make no such assumptions about the baby. You may know that the toes a baby is sucking are the same toes that are within the baby's field of vision, but do not assume that the baby agrees with you. You might be distressed to see three duplicates of your mother smiling and beckoning to you, but make no such assumptions about a 3-month-old.

As we survey all these things, the obvious and the not so obvious, we shall also witness some of the most clever research methodology that has been devised. We cannot ask newborn babies and very young children to explain why they look at some things and not at others. Nor can we ask them whether they think that the mother they saw in the morning is the same mother they saw in the afternoon. But the methods that have been devised by investigators of childhood sensation and perception to answer these questions provide us with fascinating insights into the perceptual processes of even the neonate.

Development of Vision

Newborn puppies and kittens can stumble around and find their mothers' nipples, even though their eyes are shut and do not open for several days. Human babies cannot stumble around, but their eyes are open and admit light.

In nearly all cultures, light is a symbol of goodness and knowledge. We describe capable people as "bright" or "brilliant." People who aren't "in the know" are said to be "in the dark."

▶ ▶ ▶ ▶

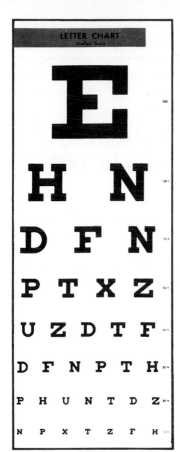

LETTER CHART
Snellen Scale

Figure 6.1 The Snellen Chart

Visual Capabilities at Birth

Unless they are blind, newborn babies respond to light. Neonates are clearly not "in the dark." Even so, their responses to light do not convince us that they are very much "in the know." Let us begin our discussion of the development of vision by examining the visual capacities the baby brings into the new world. In following sections we shall explore the development of visual processes throughout childhood.

The Pupillary Reflex   Neonates are born with the **pupillary reflex.** The pupil is the dark circular opening in the iris of the eye that permits light to enter. Even at birth, the pupil widens to admit more light in a dark environment, and narrows in bright light (Sherman et al., 1936).

Visual Acuity and Peripheral Vision   Neonates can see, but they do not possess great sharpness of vision, or **visual acuity.** Visual acuity is expressed in numbers such as 20/20 or 20/200. Think for a moment of the big E on the Snellen Chart (Figure 6.1), which you have probably seen on many eye examinations. If you were to stand 20 feet from the Snellen Chart and could see only the E, we would say that your vision is 20/200. This would mean that you can see from a distance of 20 feet what a person with normal vision can discriminate from a distance of 200 feet. In such a case you would be quite nearsighted. You would have to be unusually close to an object to discriminate its details. A person who could read the smallest line on the chart from 20 feet would have 20/15 vision and would be somewhat farsighted.

Expressed in these terms, investigators have arrived at various approximations of the visual acuity of newborn babies, with the best estimates in the neighborhood of 20/600 (Banks & Salapatek, 1981, 1983). Neonates can see best objects that are about seven to nine inches away from their eyes.

Newborn babies also see best through the centers of their eyes. They do not have the peripheral vision of older children.

Despite their nearsightedness, 22–93-hour-old infants appear to prefer the faces of their mothers to the faces of women strangers (Field et al., 1984). However, the authors concede that their methods left open the possibility that the infants were responding to odors associated with the faces rather than to the sight of the faces. In the section on development of smell, we shall see that newborns quickly come to respond positively to the odors of secretions from their mother's breasts and underarms.

Perception of Movement   Neonates can visually detect movement, and many neonates can **track** movement during the first day after birth. In fact, they appear to prefer (that is, they spend more time looking at) moving objects than at stationary objects.

In one study (Haith, 1966), 1- to 4-day-old neonates were exposed to moving or nonmoving lights while sucking on a pacifier. The frequency of their sucking decreased significantly when moving lights were presented, suggesting that this visual stimulus distracted them. In another study, a brightly colored ring was moved slowly from side to side above the heads of neonates (Greenman, 1963). Right after birth, one newborn in four followed the ring with his or her eyes. By two days (48 hours) after birth, three neonates in four did so.*

*It is still unclear, however, how well neonates can perceive color. It may be that the brightness of the ring and not the color stimulated the tracking.

▶ ▶ ▶ ▶

Pupillary reflex *The reflexive tendency of the pupils of the eyes to narrow or widen in response to the brightness of light.*

Visual acuity *Keenness or sharpness of vision.*

Track *Visually follow.*

Studying Visual Acuity in Newborn Infants: How Do You Get Babies to Tell You How Well They Can See?

▷
▷
▷
▷
▷   How do psychologists determine the visual acuity of neonates? Naturally, they can't ask babies to report how well they see, but they can determine what babies are looking at and draw conclusions from this information.

The Looking Chamber

One method of observing what a baby is looking at is by using a "looking chamber" of the sort used in research by Robert Fantz and his colleagues (see Figure 6.2). In this chamber, the baby lies on the back, with two panels above. Each panel contains a visual stimulus. From his position above, the researcher can observe the ba-

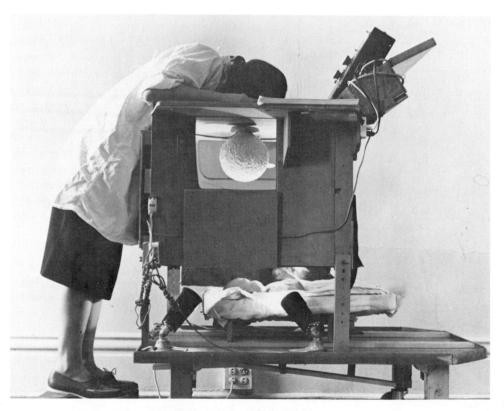

Figure 6.2 The Looking Chamber
With this chamber, the researcher can observe the baby's eye movements and record how much time is spent looking at a visual stimulus.

▶ ▶ ▶ ▶

by's eye movements and record how much time is spent looking at each panel.

A similar strategy can be carried out in the baby's natural environment. Filtered lights and a movie or TV camera can be trained on the baby's eyes. Reflections from objects in the environment can then be recorded to show what the baby is looking at.

Psychologist Daphne Maurer and her husband Charles (1976) found that newborn babies will stare at almost any nearby object for minutes—golf balls, wheels, checkerboards, bull's-eyes, circles, triangles, even lines. But babies have their preferences, as measured by the amount of time they spend *fixating on* (looking at) certain objects. For example, they will spend more time looking at black and white stripes than at gray blobs.

Stripes Are More Interesting Than Dull, Gray Blobs

The fact that infants spend more time looking at black and white stripes than gray blobs suggests one strategy for measuring visual acuity in the neonate. As black and white stripes become narrower, they eventually take on the appearance of that dull gray blob. And, as they are progressively narrowed, we can assume that babies continue to discriminate them as stripes only so long as they spend more time looking at them than at blobs.

Studies such as these suggest that newborn infants are very nearsighted. But we should remember that they, unlike adults or older children, are not motivated to "perform" in such experiments. If they were, they might show somewhat greater acuity.

In the Greenman study, neonates more successfully tracked the visual stimulus when they were cradled in the arms of the investigator. The feeding position apparently aroused the newborns, in a sense increasing their "motivation" to respond to environmental stimulation.

Visual Accommodation   **Visual accommodation** refers to the self-adjustments made by the lens of the eye in order to bring objects into focus. If you hold your finger at arm's length and bring it gradually nearer, you will feel tension in your eyes as your lenses automatically foreshorten and thicken in an effort to maintain the image in focus. When you move the finger away, the lens accommodates by lengthening and flattening, thereby keeping the finger in focus.

Neonates do not show visual accommodation. They see as through a fixed-focus camera. Objects placed somewhere between seven and nine inches away are in clearest focus for most neonates, although this range can be somewhat expanded when lighting conditions are very bright. Interestingly, this is about the distance of the face of an adult who is cradling the newborn in the arms. It has been speculated that this sensory capacity for gazing into others' eyes may promote bonds of attachment between neonates and caregivers. Visual accommodation improves dramatically within the first six weeks, and approaches adult levels by the time infants are 4 months old (Haynes et al., 1965).

Retinal Disparity and Convergence   Try bringing your finger from arm's length to the tip of your nose as you allow your eyes to "relax." As you do so, you may see two images of your finger, not one. An image of the finger is being projected onto the retina of each eye, and each image is slightly different because the finger is being seen from different angles. The difference between the projected images is referred to as **retinal disparity.** Retinal disparity serves as a **binocular cue** for the perception of depth. Note that the closer your finger

Visual accommodation The automatic adjustments made by the lenses of the eyes in order to bring objects into focus.

Retinal disparity A binocular cue for depth based on the fact that the same object creates different or disparate images on each of the retinas when it is nearby.

Binocular cue A cue for the perception of depth that requires simultaneous use of both eyes.

▶ ▶ ▶ ▶

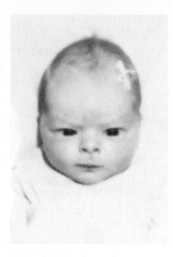

Figure 6.3 Convergence of the Eyes
Convergence is a cue for depth. The nearer objects become, the greater the tension we experience from convergence of muscles in the eyes.

Convergence *The inward movement of the eyes as they focus on an object that is drawing nearer.*

Strabismus *A disorder in which both eyes cannot focus on the same point at the same time.*

Intensity *Brightness.*

Saturation *Richness, purity.*

Hue *Color.*

Rods *Rod-shaped receptors of light that are sensitive to their intensity only. Rods permit black-and-white vision.*

Cones *Cone-shaped receptors of light that transmit sensations of color.*

▶ ▶ ▶ ▶

comes, the farther apart the "two fingers" appear. Nearby objects have greater retinal disparity.

Newborn babies do not show evidence of responding to retinal disparity as a cue for depth. Later in the chapter we shall see that there is apparently a critical period for learning to respond to retinal disparity. If medical problems prevent children from focusing simultaneously on the same object with both eyes during the critical period, they may never develop this binocular cue for depth. However, under normal conditions, babies will respond to retinal disparity as a cue for depth by 3½ to 6 months of age (Fox et al., 1980).

Now bring the finger toward your eyes again, but this time try to maintain a single image of the approaching finger. If you do so it is because your eyes turn inward, or *converge* on the finger, resulting in a "cross-eyed" look and feelings of tension in the eye muscles (see Figure 6.3).

Convergence is made possible by the coordination of the eye muscles. Neonates do not have the muscular control to converge their eyes on an object. For this reason, one eye may be staring off to the side while the other fixates on an object straight ahead. Convergence does not occur until 7 or 8 weeks of age, leading to some interesting observations. First, as noted by Wickelgren (1967), if two objects are held along a horizontal plane about nine inches away from a newborn baby's face, the baby's left eye may fixate on the object to the left, and the right eye may fixate on the object to the right.

The second observation stems from the fact that convergence gives rise to a second binocular cue for the perception of depth. As objects (such as fingers) come nearer, our eyes must converge in order to maintain a single image, resulting in greater tension in the eyes. This increased tension becomes perceived as a cue that the object is closer. However, this cue, like retinal disparity, is also absent in newborns, which may be one reason that they do not perceive depth very well. But there are many other cues that make the perception of depth possible, as we shall see later.

Strabismus Every year some 50,000 children or so are found to have **strabismus.** In this condition, the eye muscles do not work together. The child appears wall-eyed and seems to be looking at an object with one eye only. Unfortunately, note the Maurers (1976), many corrective operations are not performed early enough. They recommend that children be evaluated by a specialist if the eyes are not properly converging on an object by the age of 6 months.

Color Vision The degree to which neonates perceive color remains an open question. The research problem is that colors vary in **intensity** (that is, brightness) and **saturation** (richness) as well as in **hue.** For this reason, when babies show preference for one "color" over another, we cannot be certain that they are responding to the hue. They may also be responding to the difference in brightness or saturation. So, you say, simply change hues and keep intensity and saturation constant? A marvelous idea—but easier said than done, unfortunately.

Physiological observations also cast doubt on the capacity of neonates to perceive color. There are two types of cells in the retina of the eye that are sensitive to light: **rods** and **cones.** Rods transmit sensations of light and dark, and cones transmit sensations of color. At birth, the cones are less well-developed than rods in structure.

However, studies suggest that babies may be able to discriminate white

By the age of 4 months, babies tend to show preferences for the colors red and blue.

and colored lights at 2 months (Teller et al., 1978). By 2 to 3 months, infants can see most if not all the colors of the visible spectrum. At the age of 4 months, infants prefer the colors blue and red as measured by the amount of time fixating on them—just as college students do (Bornstein & Marks, 1982).

In one study on color preferences, babies a few months old were given either blue or green mobiles that they could move with their feet (Fagan, 1980). They kicked at the blue mobiles significantly more often than at the green ones. After three days of kicking, the mobiles were switched. Infants who had been given green mobiles were now given blue, and vice versa. Babies switched from green to blue continued to kick at them, but most of the infants who had been switched from blue to green started to cry and show other signs of distress after only a few minutes. For many subjects, in fact, the study had to be discontinued. Emotionally speaking, green seems to make infants blue.

Development of Visual Acuity and Peripheral Vision

As noted, neonates are very nearsighted. The most dramatic gains in visual acuity are made between birth and 6 months of age, with acuity reaching about 20/50 in children who will have normal vision during that time. Gains in visual acuity then taper off to more gradual increments, approximating adult levels by 1 to 5 years of age (Pirchio et al., 1978; Teller et al., 1974).

Neonates also have poor peripheral vision. Adults can perceive objects that are nearly 90 degrees off to the side (that is, directly to the left or right), although objects at these extremes are unclear. Newborn babies cannot perceive

▶ ▶ ▶ ▶

visual stimuli that are off to the side by an angle of more than 30 degrees, but their peripheral vision expands to an angle of about 45 degrees by the age of 7 weeks (Macfarlane et al., 1976). By 6 months of age, their peripheral vision is about equal to that of an adult (Cohen et al., 1979).

Typical three-year-olds can briefly focus on tiny images, such as small letters of the alphabet (Hillerich, 1983). But prior to the age of 6, which is when they are usually taught to read in school, most children's eye muscles are usually not mature enough to permit them to scan systematically a series of small letters (van Oeffelen & Vos, 1984).

Let us now consider the development of visual perception. In so doing we shall see that infants frequently prefer the strange to the familiar and will avoid going off the deep end—sometimes.

Visual Preferences: How Do You Capture a Child's Attention?

This is a big, complex world, and none of us can attend to everything at once. When we are babies, certain types of stimuli are more likely to capture our attention than others. Objects that contrast sharply with their backgrounds, bright objects, and moving objects seem to capture the gaze of the young infant in a rather mechanical fashion. At older ages we do not focus our attention so mechanically. We make finer discriminations, profit from life experience and education, and, frequently, seek out softer, more refined sources of stimulation. At older ages, in fact, we may choose not to attend to the stimuli of the outer world for extended periods of time, and to look within ourselves, "lost in meditation."

What are the things that capture the attention of babies? How do visual preferences develop?

As noted earlier, young babies attend longer to stripes than blobs, a finding that has been used in much of the research on visual acuity. Three researchers into perception among infants—Robert Fantz, Joseph Fagan, and Simon Miranda (1975)—wondered whether babies had preferences for curved lines and objects over straight ones. To investigate this question, they presented babies with curved and straight lines, bull's-eyes (concentric circles) and lines, and circles and rectangles. They found that, prior to 6 to 8 weeks, babies have no preference for straight or curved lines or for rectangles or circles. But by 8 to 12 weeks, most babies show distinct preferences for the curved lines, as measured by fixation time.

Preference for Human Faces Robert Fantz (1961) wondered whether there was something intrinsically interesting about the human face that drew the attention of babies. In order to investigate this question, he showed 2-month-old infants the six disks illustrated in Figure 6.4. One contained a caricature of human features, another newsprint, and still another a bull's-eye. The remaining three were featureless, but colored red, white, and yellow. In this study, the babies fixated significantly longer on the human face.

Subsequent studies have suggested that the 2-month-old babies in the Fantz (1961) study may not have preferred the human face so much because it was a face as because it had a complex, intriguing pattern of dots (eyes) within an outline (Caron et al., 1973). In other studies (Haaf, 1977; Haaf et al., 1983), babies have been shown facelike patterns that differed either according to the

▶ ▶ ▶ ▶

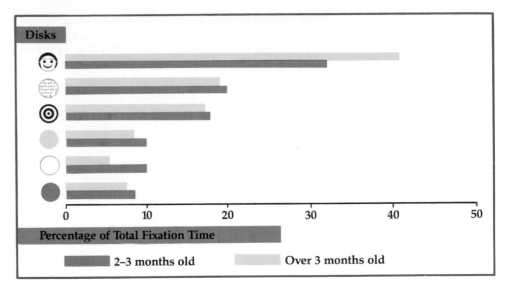

Figure 6.4 Infant Preferences for Visual Stimuli
Infants appear to prefer complex to simple visual stimuli. By the time they are 15 to 20 weeks old, they also tend to show preference for the human face.

number of visual elements or the degree to which they were organized to match the human face. Five- to 10-week-old babies pay more attention to (fixate longer on) patterns that have high numbers of elements. Their organization—that is, the degree to which they resemble the face—is less significant. But by the time infants are 15 to 20 weeks old, the organization of the patterns also becomes important, and they look longer at patterns that are most facelike.

By 3 to 6 months, babies become more sophisticated in their responses to faces. At 3 months they recognize photographs of their mothers and respond differently to various maternal facial expressions (Barrera & Maurer, 1981a, 1981b). By 6 months children prefer happy facial expressions to sad and angry ones, and they can discriminate men's faces from women's (Cohen et al., 1979). By this age they also respond differently to photographs of strangers they have seen several times, as opposed to photographs they are viewing for the first time.

Judith Langlois and her colleagues (1987) at the University of Texas ran a fascinating experiment in which 2- to 8-month-old infants preferred attractive faces to unattractive faces. About 90 percent of the children were Caucasian. The stimuli were color slides of adult Caucasian women that had been rated as attractive or unattractive by adults. The women had all posed a neutral facial expression. None wore glasses. Clothing cues were masked. The researchers suggest that "The results challenge the commonly held assumption that standards of attractiveness are learned through gradual exposure to the current cultural standard of beauty" (p. 363). This research was only recently carried out. In time other researchers may challenge the findings and their implications.

In from the Edge Newborn babies appear to direct their attention to the edges of objects. This pattern persists for the first several weeks. When they are given the opportunity to look at human faces, 1-month-old babies may briefly scan

▶ ▶ ▶ ▶

the eyes, but they tend to pay most attention to the "edges"—that is, the chin, an ear, or the hairline (Haith et al., 1977; Maurer & Salapatek, 1976). Two-month-old babies move in from the edge. They focus their attention particularly on the eyes (Hainline, 1978; Haith et al., 1977), although they also inspect other inner features, such as the mouth and nose (Maurer & Salapatek, 1976).

We do not know why the eyes take on such importance at about 2 months of age. It is tempting to look for physiological causes, since control of vision shifts from primitive areas of the brain to the visual area of the cortex at about this time. But a 2-month-old infant has also had the opportunity to learn that much about people's feelings and intentions is communicated through the eyes and the mouth.

By the age of 2 months, babies and their parents have even had ample opportunity to condition each other. Parents have had the chance to learn how to gain their babies' attention—by talking, stroking, making faces, and so on. Babies reinforce their parents for these behaviors with attention—that is, by looking into their eyes. Parents then reinforce their babies for looking into their eyes with additional gestures, smiles, laughs, high-pitched baby talk, and other responses. Thus, the baby is likely to come to direct his or her gaze at the eyes even more frequently. In such a way, social learning may also play a role.

Researchers such as Marshall Haith (1979) and Philip Salapatek (1975) explain babies' tendencies to scan from the edges of objects inward by noting that for the first several weeks of life, babies seem to be essentially concerned with *where* things are. Their attention is captured by movement and sharp contrasts in brightness and shape as are found where the edges of objects stand before their backgrounds. But by about 2 months, babies tend to focus on the *what* of things. They may locate objects by looking at their edges, but now they scan systematically within the boundaries of objects. They attend to facial features and to the difference between curved and straight lines.

Familiar versus Novel Stimulation   During the third month, the factor of novelty enters into the preferences of babies. Babies at this age can become habituated to familiar visual stimuli, and their attention can be captured by less familiar objects. In one study, Fagan (1971) found that 7-week-old infants preferred to look at familiar stimuli, as measured by fixation time, but that 10-week-olds preferred novel stimulation.

The results were similar in a well-known study with normal, scrambled, and incomplete faces (Haaf & Bell, 1967). Infants of various ages were shown four drawings. The first had all the features of a normal face in their proper places. The second was mildly scrambled, with a missing eye, an extra mouth, and some squiggles. The third drawing contained the facial outline, but only a nose within, and the fourth contained nothing but squiggles in the outline. Two-month-old babies showed no preferences, suggesting that their attention was still captured by the edges of the drawings, which were all the same. Three-month-old infants preferred the proper and scrambled faces, in that order. Thus, their attention was captured by familiarity, but second place was given to the complex and mildly novel image. One-year-olds paid most attention to the scrambled face, suggesting that they had become highly habituated to the normal face by that age.

Fagan, Fantz, and Miranda (1971) found strong evidence that the maturation of the visual system (nature) plays a more central role in the development of the child's preferences than does experience (nurture). Their subjects

▶ ▶ ▶ ▶

Discrepancy hypothesis *The view that children (and adults) prefer stimuli that are moderately different from the stimuli to which they have become accustomed.*

Habituate *To become accustomed to a repetitive stimulus.*

consisted of two groups: 11-week-old full-term babies and 11-week-old babies who had been born one month prior to full term. The full-term babies clearly preferred novel visual stimuli, while the preterm babies tended to prefer familiar stimuli—even though the preterm babies had had as much postnatal experience. However, by 15 weeks of age, the preferences of the preterm babies were indistinguishable from those of the 11-week-old full-term babies. Therefore, the amount of time since conception was the crucial factor—not visual and social experiences.

The Discrepancy Hypothesis Jerome Kagan (1971) explains babies' preference for moderately novel stimuli through the **discrepancy hypothesis.** According to this view, babies (and, perhaps, the rest of us) become **habituated** to objects they perceive over and over again. For this reason, they may play extensively with a new rattle, but spend less time with it on future occasions. At the age of 6 or 7 months, if no new rattle or toy has been received recently, they may go from rattle to rattle and toy to toy, seeming somewhat disgruntled and playing with none of them for very long. When older, they may go from familiar book to familiar book in a similar manner. It seems as though the child's sensory system has perceived everything there is to perceive about the object and must move on to other things.

The discrepancy hypothesis also maintains that babies will attend to stimuli that are *moderately* different from familiar stimuli. When new events are

Babies appear to prefer stimuli that are moderately different from familiar stimuli, according to the discrepancy hypothesis. When new events are too different, they might not capture the attention. Instead, they may evoke fear.

► ► ► ►

DEVELOPMENT OF VISION

too different, the babies have no frames of reference for understanding or interpreting them. In such cases, novel stimuli may not capture the attention. They may even evoke fear. For example, children are less likely to explore novel objects when they are in unfamiliar settings (Parry, 1972). When babies (and adults?) are insecure, they are apparently more likely to resort to the tried and true.

Depth Perception: On *Not* Going Off the Deep End

Infants are generally able to perceive depth long before they are able to crawl around, and, by the time they do crawl, they have usually developed fear of heights. This is adaptive for obvious reasons. It helps prevent them from "going off the deep end"—falling down staircases and off counters, beds, and various other artificial and natural hazards. However, as we shall see, a number of babies will go off the (apparently) deep end. In some cases this may occur by their developing crawling skills too early for their own good.

In a classic study on depth perception, Eleanor Gibson and Richard Walk (1960) placed infants of various ages on a fabric-covered runway that ran across the center of a clever device called a visual cliff (see Figure 6.5). The visual cliff consists of a sheet of plexiglas that covers material with a high-

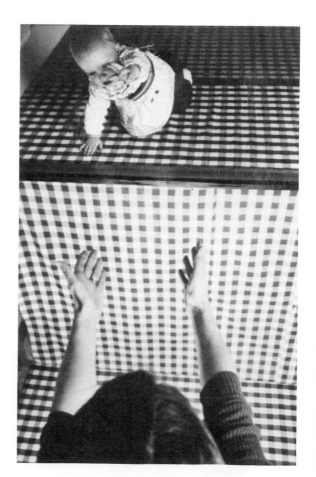

Figure 6.5 The Classic Visual Cliff Experiments
This young explorer has the good sense not to crawl out onto an apparently unsupported surface, even when Mother beckons from the other side.

▶ ▶ ▶ ▶

contrast checkerboard pattern. On one side the pattern is placed immediately beneath the plexiglas, and on the other, it is dropped about 4 feet below. Since the plexiglas alone would easily support the infant, this is a "visual" cliff rather than an actual cliff.

In this study, 81 percent of the infants who had begun to crawl refused to venture out over the seemingly unsupported surface. Babies are more likely to crawl out onto the visual cliff when their mothers show happiness or interest in them (Sorce et al., 1985). But in the Gibson and Walk study, most babies refused to crawl out over the visual cliff, even when their mothers beckoned encouragingly from the other side. When the researchers applied a (painless!) device that allowed the babies to use only one eye, the results were the same. Therefore, the babies relied on one-eyed or **monocular cues** to perceive depth. One monocular cue may have been **perspective**—the fact that objects equal in size look smaller if they are farther away. Babies are able to use relative size as a cue to the distance of objects by 5½ months of age (Yonas et al., 1982, 1985), and the pattern on the cliff side of the apparatus consisted of smaller (that is, more distant) squares.

Other studies have also shed light on babies' responses to the visual cliff. In one, Joseph Campos and his colleagues (1970) placed infants of different ages face-down on the visual cliff and monitored their heart rates. On **polygraphs** and in studies on emotional response, an accelerated heart rate is usually interpreted as a sign of anxiety or fear. A lowered heart rate is interpreted as a sign of placid interest. One-month-old infants showed no differences in heart rate, but the heart rates of 2-month-olds decreased slightly. The heart rates of 9-month-olds sped up. It appears that the 1-month-olds did not perceive the depth of the cliff, but that the older infants did—as suggested by changes in heart rate. But the 2-month-olds apparently did not experience fear on the cliff, while the older infants did.

It may be that infants need to have some experience crawling about (and, perhaps, accumulating some bumps) before they develop fear of heights. The 9-month-olds but not the 2-month-olds had had such experience. Other studies support the view that babies usually do not develop fear of heights until they can move around (Campos et al., 1978; Scarr & Salapatek, 1970).

But as noted by Gibson and Walk, not all babies who have experienced crawling around show fear of the visual cliff. A study by Richards and Rader (1981) suggests that the age at which babies begin to crawl plays a role in the development of fear of depths. In this study, babies who had begun crawling before the age of 6½ months were significantly more likely to cross the visual cliff than babies who had begun crawling at later ages. The researchers noted that the early and late crawlers seemed to have somewhat different crawling styles. The late crawlers were more likely to inspect the surface ahead of them visually as they moved about. From this observation, they suggest that early crawlers may make relatively greater use of **haptic** information than late crawlers do. For this reason, early crawlers would be less sensitive to visually perceived sources of danger.

Development of Perceptual Constancies

It may not astonish you that a 12-inch ruler is the same length whether it is two feet or six feet away. Or that a door across the room is a rectangle whether closed or ajar. Or that your home continues to exist (we hope) whether

► ► ► ►

you are in it or at school. Awareness of these three facts depends not on sensation alone, but on the development of **perceptual constancies.** Perceptual constancy is the tendency to perceive an object to be the same, even though the sensations produced by the object may differ under various conditions.

The perceptual constancies also suggest the overlaps between perceptual development and cognitive development. Perceptual constancies arise as a result of the mental representation of objects sensed in the external world. In Chapter 8 we shall see that mental representation of objects develops according to a certain sequence of changes. We shall thoroughly explore in Chapter 8 these changes and the theoretical issues that surround them. Here let us simply note that, once objects become mentally represented, they can be mentally manipulated. For example, once we have a cup in memory, we can rotate it in the mind and imagine what it might look like from different perspectives. Let us now consider a number of the perceptual constancies that are closely related to the sense of vision.

Size Constancy   Consider again the example of the ruler. When it is two feet away, its image, as focused on the retina, is a certain length. This length is the image's "retinal size." From six feet away, the 12-inch ruler is only one-third as long in terms of retinal size, but we perceive it as being the same size because of **size constancy.** Size constancy is the tendency to perceive the same objects as being of the same size even though their retinal sizes vary as a function of their distance. From six feet away, a 36-inch yardstick casts an image equal in retinal size to the 12-inch ruler at two feet, but—if recognized as a yardstick— it is perceived as longer, again because of size constancy. The development of size constancy, like the development of so many other perceptual abilities, depends on experience and maturation.

A case study highlights the role of experience in the development of size constancy. Colin Turnbull (1961) found that an African pygmy, Kenge, thought that buffalo seen across an open field were a form of insect. Kenge normally did not view large animals from great distances, because he lived in a thick tropical rain forest, and so his expectations did not mesh with the visual sensations being focused on his retinae. We may joke that large animals or people look like ants from airplanes, but we *know* that they remain large animals or people.

Research concerning the development of size constancy has yielded contradictory results. In one study, for example, Thomas Bower (1974) conditioned 2½- to 3-month-old babies to turn their heads to the left when shown a 12-inch cube from a distance of three feet. He then presented them with three experimental stimuli: (1) a 12-inch cube nine feet away, whose retinal size was smaller than that of the original cube; (2) a 36-inch cube three feet away, whose retinal size was larger than that of the original cube; and (3) a 36-inch cube nine feet away, whose retinal size was the same as that of the original cube. In this study, the infants turned their heads most frequently in response to the first experimental cube, although its retinal image was only one-third the length of that to which they had been conditioned, suggesting that they had achieved size constancy.

However, a review of the literature on development of size constancy (McKenzie et al., 1980) suggests that infants may not show solid evidence of size constancy prior to 4 months of age. The development of size constancy may at least to some degree be limited by the nearsightedness of the very young

▶ ▶ ▶ ▶

Shape constancy *The tendency to perceive objects as being the same shape, although viewing them from different angles may cause the images projected onto the retina to differ in shape.*

Object concept *Broad understanding that the existence of objects transcends the immediate sensory impressions they make.*

Object identity *Recognition that an object is the same object, regardless of its setting or superficial changes.*

infant. Poor visual acuity, that is, may place certain limits on the visual experience of babies. And perhaps because of developing visual acuity, the distance over which size constancy is perceived grows dramatically among infants. For example, at the ages of 6 to 8 months, infants show evidence of size constancy up to a distance of slightly over two feet (28 inches), but not at over three feet. Since the experimental stimuli in the Bower (1974) study were from three to nine feet distant, the results are somewhat in doubt.

Size constancy develops throughout early and middle childhood.

Shape Constancy **Shape constancy** is the tendency to perceive an object as having the same shape, even though when perceived from another angle, the shape projected onto the retina may change dramatically. When a cup or a dish is seen from above, the visual sensations are in the shape of a circle. When seen from a slight angle, the sensations are elliptical, and when seen from the side, the opening is sensed as a straight line. However, we still "perceive" the opening to be a circle, because of our familiarity with the object. In the first few months after birth, young babies see the features of their mothers, of bottles, of cribs, and of toys from all different angles, so that by the time they are 4 or 5 months old, a broad grasp of shape constancy seems to be firmly established.

Development of the Object Concept

Size constancy and shape constancy are two aspects of the constancy of objects, two reflections of the fact that objects may remain the same, even if they appear to be different because of changes in location, position, lighting conditions, and so on. These examples of object constancy are very closely related to what is termed the **object concept**—the broad recognition that objects have an existence that transcends the immediate sensory impressions that may be made by them. For this reason, objects remain the same even though they move from place to place, and they continue to exist even when they are out of sight.

Put another way, objects maintain their identities and continue to exist in and of themselves, not *because* they make a continuous impact on our sensory receptors. My car continues to exist when it is in a section of the parking lot that cannot be seen from my window (or else I had better call my insurance agent and then get someone to drive me home), and a baby's mother continues to exist even when she is in another room. My "perceiving" that my car exists, although out of view, is because of the object concept. If a baby acts as as if his or her mother no longer exists when she is out of sight, the baby does not have the object concept.

Object Identity and Object Permanence The object concept consists of two parts: *object identity* and *object permanence*. **Object identity** is recognition that an object is the same object regardless of where or when one sees it, and regardless of superficial changes in its characteristics. When I hop into my blue station wagon and turn on the ignition, I expect it to respond in certain ways because it is the same car that it was earlier.* Infants show object identity when they

*Yes, I know it's a bit more rusted and dirty, but it's still the same car (sad to say) and not *another* car.

▶ ▶ ▶ ▶

Strategies for Studying the Development of Shape Constancy

▷
▷
▷
▷

▷ People are said to show shape constancy when they perceive an object as having the same shape even though, when viewed from another angle, the shape projected onto the retina may be very different. How can we determine whether babies have developed shape constancy? Through the process of *habituation*.

Habituation

Recall that once they are a few months old, infants show a preference for novel objects. They have become habituated to familiar objects and—if we can take the liberty of describing their responses in adult terms—they are apparently "bored" by them. We also correlate certain bodily responses with interest in an object—for example, a slower heart rate (as with 2-month-old babies placed face-down on a visual cliff) and concentrated gazing. Therefore, when infants have become habituated to an object, their heart rates speed up moderately, and they no longer show concentrated gazing.

Here, then, is the research strategy. Show an infant stimulus A for a prolonged period of time. At first the heart rate will slow, and the infant will focus on the object. But as time goes on, the heart rate will again rise to prestimulated levels, and the baby's gaze will wander. Now show the infant stimulus B. If the heart rate again slows, and the gaze again becomes concentrated, we can infer that stimulus B is perceived as a novel (different) object. But if the heart rate and pattern of gazing does not change, we can infer that the baby does not perceive a difference between stimuli A and B.

Here is the 64-day-old question: *If stimuli A and B are actually the same object, but are seen from different angles, what does it mean when the baby's heart rate and pattern of gazing do not change?* We can assume that lack of change means that the baby perceives stimuli A and B to be the same—in this case, the same object. Therefore, we can conclude that the baby has developed shape constancy.

Using a strategy similar to the above, Cook and his colleagues (1978) found that 3-month-old babies who were experimentally habituated to a cube did not show different responses when they were presented with a wedge. These two shapes, when rotated, could project identical images on the retina. However, babies habituated to the cube did show different responses when later shown an L-shaped block. The cube could not be rotated to take on the characteristics of an "L." Therefore, it seems that the babies perceived the L-shaped block as novel. And so it seems that the babies had developed at least a primitive form of shape constancy—one that did not stimulate them to show a different response pattern to the wedge, even though it was a novel object.

Eleanor Gibson and her colleagues (1978) used a similar procedure and found that 5-month-old babies apparently have shape constancy for circular objects. The infants were habituated to a circular rubber disk as shown straight on. Then the disk was shown at an angle, such that its image was elliptical. The babies did not seem to regard it as a new object. However, when the disk was squeezed so that its surface was distended, the babies did respond as if it were novel. Apparently it had lost a characteristic of surface smoothness that was basic to the infants' concept of the object.

It would be not be possible to use the habituation method to try to investigate whether 1- or 2-month-old babies have shape constancy, because infants this young have not developed distinct preferences for novel objects.

▶ ▶ ▶ ▶

Object permanence Recognition that objects continue to exist even when they are not
sensed.

behave as though their mothers are the same person when seen in the living
room or the bedroom; in the morning, afternoon, or evening; in a dress or in
blue jeans; when smiling or when frowning; and when slender or 6 months
pregnant with a sibling. **Object permanence** is recognition that mother continues to exist when she is out of sight (or hearing, touch, smell, or taste).

According to Jean Piaget, various facets of the object concept develop
during infancy and correspond to the stages and substages of the child's general
cognitive development. As we shall see in Chapter 8, children's object concepts
are tied into their concepts of space and time and their general tendency to
form mental representations of sensory impressions.

Neonates show no tendency to respond to objects that are not within
their immediate sensory grasp. By 2 months, infants may show some surprise
if an object (such as a toy duck or elephant) is placed behind a screen and then
taken away, so that when the screen is lifted it is absent. However, they make
no effort to search for the missing object. But through the first six months or
so, when the screen is placed between the object and the baby, the baby behaves
as though it is no longer there (see Figure 6.6).

But wait, you say? Won't 3- or 4-month-old babies cry when mother
leaves and then stop crying when their mothers come and pick them up?
Doesn't this behavior pattern show object permanence? Don't these babies
"miss" their mothers when they are gone (that is, perceive their continued
existence in their absence) and try to get them back? Excellent question, but the
answer is "Not necessarily." Babies appear to appreciate the comforts provided
by their mothers' presence and to express displeasure when they come to an
end (as when their mothers leave the room). It so happens that the expression
of displeasure (crying, screeching, thrashing about, and so on) frequently results
in the reinstatement of pleasure (being held, fed, spoken to, and so on). Therefore, babies may learn to engage in these "protests" when their mothers leave
or are absent because of the effects of protesting—and not because they have
developed object permanence.

In any event, there are some interesting advances in the development
of the object concept by about the sixth month. For example, a baby at this age
will tend to look for an object that has been dropped, behavior that not only
suggests some form of object permanence, but also that the baby has learned
something about gravity—that is, that things move in a downward direction
when they are unsupported. By this age there is also reason to believe that the
baby perceives a mental representation (image) of an object, such as a favorite
toy, in response to sensory impressions of part of the object. This is shown by
the baby's reaching for a preferred object when it has been partially hidden by
a cloth.

By the ages of 8 to 12 months, infants will seek to retrieve objects that
have been completely hidden behind screens (Dunst et al., 1982). But experiments with Piaget's own children (Piaget, 1952) suggest that object permanence,
at least through the first nine months, is still markedly different from that of
an older child or adult. Piaget repeatedly hid a toy behind a screen, and each
time his infant removed the screen and retrieved it. Then, as the infant watched,
Piaget hid the toy behind another screen in a different place. Now the infant
was faced with two screens and no toy. The infant had observed Piaget as he
had hidden the toy behind the second screen. Still, the infant tried to recover
the toy by swiping aside the first screen! It is as though the child had learned
that a certain motor activity would reinstate the missing toy. Therefore, this

▶ ▶ ▶ ▶

Figure 6.6 Development of Object Permanence
To the infant at the top, who is 6 months old, out of sight is out of mind. Once a sheet of paper is placed between the baby and the toy elephant, the baby shows no inclination to find the elephant. From this sort of evidence, Piaget concluded that the toy is not yet mentally represented. The child below is several months older. He does mentally represent objects, as shown by his pushing through a towel to reach a toy that was screened from sight.

action pattern would be brought to bear even when the toy had most recently been seen in another location. The child's concept of the object did not, at this age, extend to recognizing that objects usually remain in the place where they have been most recently mentally represented.

In Chapter 10 we shall see that most children have developed the object concept before they develop emotional bonds to specific caregivers. Many psychologists argue that the object concept is a prerequisite for such specific attachments. For example, before you become attached to your mother, it seems logical that you should consider your mother as having an identity and as still

Strategies for Studying the Development of Object Identity and Object Permanence in Infants

▷
▷
▷
▷

▷ How can we determine whether a young baby "has" object identity? Obviously we cannot ask babies questions such as "How many Mommys do you have?" and "Is Mommy the same person as she was yesterday?" But a number of clever experiments by Thomas Bower highlight the type of methodology that can lead to suggestive results.

If One Mother Is Good, How About Three?

In one study Bower (1975) placed babies of various ages in infant seats before a window in which they could see an image of their mother that was produced with mirrors and lighting effects. After the image had been presented for a while, it was multiplied into three. Now the infants saw three mothers, not one. Prior to the age of 5 months, infants showed some signs of increased pleasure in response to the multiplied image. They probably perceived nothing strange about this example of maternal proliferation. But by about 22 to 24 weeks, infants' reactions changed markedly. Now they showed signs of anxiety and fear at the multiple image. By this age perhaps they "knew" that they had only one mother—that the mother who appeared then reappeared had a single identity. Sensory impressions of three mothers were at major variance with their expectations and caused distress.

The Case of the Disappearing Mother

In an earlier study with similar apparatus, Bower (1971) gradually dissolved the images of the babies' mothers while they were observing her in the mirror. Prior to 24 weeks or so, infants watched the dis-

solution process without signs of distress. However, 6-month-old infants showed significant levels of distress and scanned the area, apparently searching for their mothers. By 6 months, the infants apparently perceived their mothers to have object permanence, despite the waning of their sensory impressions. And so they became concerned about where their mothers had gone.

Object Permanence Makes the Eyes Go Round

Another well-known study, this one by Alastair Mundy-Castle and Jeremy Anglin (1969), presents a very different sort of experimental situation. It also shows some development of object permanence by 4 months of age. In this study the researchers placed infants in front of a screen behind which an object moved in a circular pattern. There were two portholes in the screen, to the left and right (see Figure 6.7). The infant could observe the object as it moved up through one porthole and then, after some time had elapsed, as it moved down through the second.

Prior to the age of 4 months, infants did eventually began to anticipate the appearance of the object. They showed anticipation by moving their eyes to the left or right across a horizontal plane, readying themselves to see the object when it was visible through the next porthole. Note that they clearly expected *an* object to appear in the proper place, but there is no reason to assume that they perceived the subsequent appearance to be of the *same* object. The eye movements of the 4-month-olds, however, traced the circular path of the object behind the screen. By this age they apparently continued to "per-

▶ ▶ ▶ ▶

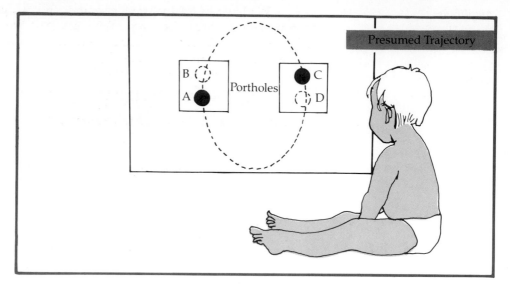

Figure 6.7 Any Porthole in an Experiment?
By the age of 4 months, infants' eyes tend to trace a circular path as they anticipate the appearance of the moving object, instead of simply looking to the left or right. Perhaps by this age they have begun to assume that the object about to appear is the same object.

ceive'' the object (that is, to assume that the object had a continuing presence, or permanence) when it was out of sight.

It is not clear why the Mundy-Castle and Anglin study suggests a more rapid development of the object concept than the Bower studies. It is always possible that such discrepancies are due to inaccuracies within the studies themselves, which is why scientists find it worthwhile to repli-

cate research. However, it is also possible that different experimental conditions elicit different aspects of a process—in this case, the development of the object concept. Remember that even 2-month-old infants seem to show some surprise when a toy that has been placed behind a screen is found missing. The object concept possesses many aspects.

existing when she is not in sight. However, we shall also see that not all psychologists agree with this view.

Now let us turn our attention to developments in the other senses, and to the development of sensory and sensorimotor coordination.

Development of Hearing

Fetuses respond to sounds months before they are born, as noted in Chapter 3. Although myelination of the auditory pathways is not complete prior to birth, fetuses' middle and inner ears normally reach their mature shapes and sizes before they are born (Aslin et al., 1983). Normal neonates can also hear remarkably well, unless their middle ears are clogged with amniotic fluid. In fact, most neonates will turn their heads toward unusual sounds, such as that of a shaking rattle, and suspend other activities while they listen (Muir & Field, 1979).

▶ ▶ ▶ ▶

Amplitude Height. The higher the amplitude of sound waves, the louder they are.

Pitch The highness or lowness of a sound, as determined by the frequency of sound waves.

We have heard that music soothes the savage breast. It also seems that continuous sounds can have a soothing effect on the agitated neonate (Brackbill, 1970). Newborn infants have the capacity to respond to sounds of different duration, **amplitude,** and **pitch.** By the third day following birth, babies can detect the difference between tones of 200 and 1,000 cycles per second, as shown by changes in bodily movements and patterns of breathing (Leventhal & Lipsitt, 1964). Newborns are more likely to be startled by high-pitched sounds than by low-pitched sounds. Speaking to infants softly, in a relatively low-pitched voice, can have a soothing effect.

It may well be that the sense of hearing plays a role in the formation of affectional bonds between neonates and their mothers that goes well beyond the soothing potential of the mothers' voices. Newborns can sense sounds that have the loudness and pitch of speech about as well as adults can (Sinnott et al., 1983). Moreover, neonates show more frequent and vigorous responses to a female human voice than to bells that are similar in duration, loudness, and pitch (Freedman, 1971). Findings with infant rhesus monkeys suggest that these primates, too, show greatest responsiveness to the vocalizations of adult females, and that this selective responsiveness is present at birth (Sackett, 1970).

More recent research with humans suggests that 3-day-old babies prefer their mothers' voices to those of other women, but do not show similar preferences for the voices of their fathers (DeCasper & Fifer, 1980; DeCasper & Prescott, 1984; Prescott & DeCasper, 1981). It may seem tempting to conclude that the human nervous system is ''prewired'' to respond positively to the voice of one's biological mother. However, neonates have already had several months of ''experience'' in utero, and, for a good part of this time, they have been capable of sensing sounds. Since they are predominantly exposed to prenatal sounds produced by their mothers, learning (nurture) may also play a role in neonatal preferences.

There is fascinating evidence that newborns are particularly responsive to the sounds and rhythms of speech, although they do not show preferences for specific languages. Condon and Sander (1974) filmed the bodily responses of 12-hour- to 2-week-old infants to human speech (English or Chinese), disconnected vowel sounds, and tapping. In a careful analysis that broke movements down according to minute fractions of a second, it was found that these babies—most of whom were under 2 days old—tended to synchronize the movements of their heads, arms (elbows and hands), and legs (including hips and toes) to the pattern of speech. They were equally adept at ''dancing'' to the sounds of English and Chinese, but showed little synchronization with the disconnected vowels or the tapping. Using the habituation method, it has also been shown that 3-day-old babies can discriminate between new sounds of speech and those that they have heard before (Brody et al., 1984).

As infants mature, the range of the pitch of the sounds they can sense gradually expands to include the adult 20 to 20,000 cycles per second. Auditory acuity also improves gradually over the first several years, although the hearing of babies can be so fine that many parents complain that their napping infants will awaken at the slightest sound.*

By the age of 1 month, infants perceive differences between sounds that

---

*Some do, especially if parents have been ''overprotective'' in attempting to keep their rooms as silent as possible. Babies who are normally exposed to a backdrop of moderate noise levels become habituated to them and are not likely to awaken unless there is a sudden, sharp noise.

are highly similar. In one study relying on the habituation method, babies of this age could activate a recording of "bah" by sucking on a nipple (Eimas et al., 1971). As time went on, habituation occurred, as shown by decreased sucking in order to hear the "bah" sound. Then the researchers switched from "bah" to "pah." If the sounds had seemed the same to the infants, their lethargic sucking patterns would have continued. But they immediately sucked harder, suggesting that they perceived the difference. Other researchers have found that within a few more weeks, babies will reliably discriminate two-syllable words such as *bada* and *baga* (Morse & Cowan, 1982).

Just as 3½-month-old babies can visually identify their parents, it appears that they can discriminate the sounds of their voices. Infants of this same age were oriented toward their parents as they reclined in baby seats. The researchers (Spelke & Owsley, 1979) played recordings of the mother's or father's voice, while the parents themselves remained inactive. The babies reliably looked at the parent whose voice was being played.

By the time infants are 3 to 5 months old, they gain the capacity to imitate sounds of various pitches. In a study by William Kessen and his colleagues (1979), babies actually "sang along" with their mothers—in a limited fashion. The mothers encouraged their babies to make sounds, and then reinforced their vocalizations by singing a musical note. Soon the babies were imitating their mothers. Musicians evaluated tape recordings of these sessions and concluded that all of the babies showed some ability to approximate the pitch of their mothers' notes, and that the babies' notes did not generally differ from the mothers' by more than a quarter tone. This capacity to match pitch seems to be inborn, and may be lost as time goes on.

Neonates can crudely orient their heads in the direction of a sound (MacFarlane, 1978). Before they are a month old, they can consistently turn their heads in the direction of a popcorn-filled bottle that is being shaken (Field et al., 1980). And the accuracy of the sound-localizing ability of the 6-month-old baby is astounding. When she is supporting herself in her crib on her hands, you may make deliberately soft sounds as you enter the room so as not to startle her. Even so, she may find you immediately and reward you with a grand smile.

A major cue for determining the location of a sound is its relative loudness in each ear. For example, if a sound is equally loud in each ear, we will profit from scanning the "midline"—straight ahead, up, down, or in back. If the sound is slightly louder in the right ear than in the left, there is a good chance you will locate it by turning your head slightly to the right. If, for all practical purposes, you sense the sound with the right ear only, you would do well to turn sharply to the right. This strategy cannot tell us whether the sound is above or below, in front or in back. Still, as a result of experience and general awareness of what is in front of us, we develop the ability to locate sounds rather quickly.

There is also evidence that babies can begin to perceive some of the typical patterns of the language spoken by their parents well before they are a year old. Kagan and his colleagues (1971) simply read four "sentences" to a number of 8-month-old baby boys. Two of the sentences were real sentences, with meaningful words—including the familiar "Daddy" and "smile"—and logical word order. The other two were nonsensical in word order and contained unfamiliar sounds. Even though the babies were too young to know what the words in the sentences symbolized, they responded more favorably to the real sentences by increasing the frequency of their **babbling.**

Babbling *The child's first vocalizations that have the sound of speech (see Chapter 7).*

▶ ▶ ▶ ▶

6 PERCEPTUAL DEVELOPMENT

By the time they are a year old, of course, auditory discrimination becomes further refined. By the first birthday many infants understand many words, and some may even have a word or two of their own. During infancy the auditory apparatus for language learning is well in place.

Development of Smell: The Nose Knows Rather Early

Neonates can definitely discriminate distinct odors, such as those of onions and anise (licorice). They show more rapid breathing patterns and increased bodily activity in response to powerful odors. They also turn away from unpleasant odors, such as ammonia and vinegar, as early as the first day after birth (Engen & Lipsitt, 1965; Rieser et al., 1976). Newborns can also become habituated to powerful odors, as shown by the tendency for the breathing and activity levels to return to normal as exposure to these odors is prolonged.

Jacob Steiner and his colleagues (Steiner, 1979; Ganchrow et al., 1983) have found that the nasal preferences of newborns are quite similar to those of older children and adults. Newborn infants spat, stuck out their tongues, wrinkled their noses, and blinked their eyes when a cotton swab saturated with the odor of rotten eggs was passed beneath their noses. However, they showed smiles and licking motions when presented with the odors of chocolate, strawberry, vanilla, butter, bananas, and honey. It would be interesting to run a longitudinal study to determine whether newborns who show relatively less response to the aromas of chocolate, butter, and honey are slenderer during later childhood and adulthood.

Research by Aidan MacFarlane (1975, 1977) of Oxford University and others suggests that the sense of smell, like hearing, may provide a vehicle for mother–infant recognition and attachment. MacFarlane suspected that neonates may be sensitive to the smell of milk, because, when held by the mother, they tend to turn toward her nipple before they have had a chance to see or touch it. In his first experiment, MacFarlane placed nursing pads above and to the sides of neonates' heads. One pad had absorbed milk from the mother, and the other was clean. Neonates less than a week old spent significantly more time turning to look at their mothers' pads than at the new pads.

In the second phase of this research, MacFarlane suspended pads with milk from the neonates' mothers and strangers to the sides of the babies' heads. For the first few days following birth, the infants showed no preference for the pads. However, by the time they were 1 week old, they spent significantly more time looking at their mothers' pads than at the strangers'. It appears that they learned to respond positively to the odor of their mothers' milk during the first few days. Afterward, a source of this odor received preferential treatment even when they were not nursing.

Jennifer Cernoch and Richard Porter (1985) of Vanderbilt University found that 15-day-old breast-fed infants also preferred their mother's axillary (underarm) odor to odors produced by other lactating women and by nonlactating women. Bottle-fed infants did not prefer their mother's axillary odor. The authors explain the difference by suggesting that breast-fed infants are more likely than bottle-fed infants to be exposed to their mother's axillary odor. That is, mothers of bottle-fed infants can remain clothed. Axillary odor along with odors from breast secretions might contribute to the early development of attachment.

▶ ▶ ▶ ▶

Development of Taste

It has been known for more than half a century that infants respond differently in their patterns of sucking to milk, water, and solutions of salt and sugar (Jensen, 1932). Recent research shows that newborn infants form facial expressions similar to those of adults in response to various kinds of fluids. In a study of 175 full-term and 20 premature neonates, the babies swallowed without showing any facial expression suggestive of a positive or negative response when distilled water was placed on their tongues (Steiner, 1979). Sweet solutions were met with smiles, licking, and eager sucking. Sour fluids frequently elicited pursing of the lips, nose-wrinkling, and eye-blinking, while bitter solutions stimulated spitting, gagging, and sticking out of the tongue.

Newborns can also discriminate between various concentrations of sweet solutions (Cowart, 1981). Crook and Lipsitt (1976) found that the heart rates of newborn infants *increase* when they are presented with sweeter solutions, suggestive of heightened arousal, but that they tend to *slow down* their rates of sucking. Some have interpreted this finding as an infant effort to savor the sweeter solution—to make the flavor last. However, with neonates it may be that this slowing down occurs for neurological reasons that are not yet clearly understood. Although we do not know why infants ingest sweet foods more slowly, this difference is useful in preventing overeating. Sweet foods tend to be high in calories, and by eating them slowly infants give their brains more time (a) to respond to bodily signals that they have eaten enough, and (b) to consequently stimulate them to stop eating. Ah, to have the wisdom of a newborn baby!

Development of Touch

Newborn babies are sensitive to touch. As noted in Chapter 4, many reflexes—including the rooting, sucking, Babinski, and palmar reflexes, to name a few—are activated by pressure against the skin. Babies can also apparently draw comfort from being held against the skin of a caretaker. However, they do not seem so sensitive to pain as they will be in the near future. Considering the squeezing that takes place during childbirth, relative insensitivity to pain may be quite adaptive.

Although they are less sensitive to pain, newborns do perceive pain. For example, babies who are circumcised show prolonged periods of fussiness accompanied by disturbances in their sleep patterns (Gunnar & Malone, 1985).

Interestingly, neonates react in different ways to having their diffuse movements restricted. When babies are born with **jaundice,** red blood cell counts must be taken repeatedly. The skin of a foot is pricked and the foot is held still while a sample of blood is drawn. Newborn babies may not respond dramatically to the pinprick itself, but they may "scream bloody murder" because their feet are being held immobile. On the other hand, babies are sometimes soothed by being swaddled, which severely curtails their movements.

The sense of touch is an extremely important avenue of learning and communication for babies. Not only do the skin senses provide information about the external world, but the sensations of skin against skin also appear to provide feelings of comfort and security that may be major factors in the for-

Taste preferences of children are nearly identical to those of adults.

Jaundice *A condition in which the skin becomes abnormally yellow because of bile pigments in the blood.*

▶ ▶ ▶ ▶

mation of bonds of attachment between infants and their caregivers, as we shall see in Chapter 10.

The lips are very sensitive to tactile sensations, and infants frequently mouth objects, not just to suck them, but also to gather information about them. Shape, texture, and hardness are just a few examples of the types of information babies gain from mouthing nipples, rattles, blocks, diapers (so keep them out of reach), and even the mesh nets of playpens.

The fact that 10-month-olds prefer novel to familiar sources of stimulation provided Sherri Soroka and her colleagues (1979) with a strategy for demonstrating that they can learn to recognize objects on the basis of tactile information. The babies in this study were allowed to play with wooden rings or crosses for a two-minute period in a dark room. Although there were individual differences, generally speaking the babies handled them and placed them in their mouths. During a second play session, still in the dark, babies were again given an object. Half again received the object with which they had already become familiar, and the other half received the new object. Babies who received the new object handled it significantly longer than babies who received the same object twice. Apparently, (1) the babies had become habituated to the object they had already handled, and (2) they were able to discern its familiarity in the dark through their sense of touch.

Development of Coordination

It seems likely that babies are neurologically "prewired" to coordinate the various senses and to coordinate sensing (as in seeing) with motor activity (as in reaching for objects).

Development of Coordination of the Senses

Newborn babies crudely orient their heads toward sounds and pleasant odors. In this way, they increase the probability that the sources of the sounds and odors will also be sensed through visual scanning. Newborn babies also show particular sensitivity to the human voice. As found by Mendelson and Haith (1976), a male voice causes them to widely open their eyes, concentrate their gaze, and scan the midline of their visual fields with small eye movements.

Further evidence that this early effort to coordinate the auditory and visual modalities is mechanical is found in the study by Jeffrey Field and his colleagues (1980) cited earlier, in which the experimenters shook a bottle filled with popcorn. They found that most of the babies who turned their heads toward the bottle during the first month no longer did so by the age of 2 months. It was as if a mechanical response had dropped out as they had matured. By the time another month had passed, however, most babies were turning toward the sound again. But now it seemed as though there was "intention" in their responses. The infants appeared to be *looking in order to see*, not just *looking and seeing*.

Development of Visual-Motor Coordination

Think of all the athletic activities that require sensorimotor coordination. In baseball, one must coordinate the swinging of a bat with the perception of

▶ ▶ ▶ ▶

a rapidly moving ball, or one must run toward and catch the ball as it flies in a high arc through the air. In tennis and golf, one must also coordinate muscular activity and hit a ball. In wrestling, one frequently coordinates one's own muscular activity on the basis of tactile sensations of the opponent's body. (There have been a number of successful blind wrestlers in the college ranks.) In weightlifting, one coordinates muscle activity with sensory impressions of the shifting weight of the barbells.

In Chapter 5 we saw that, although 2- to 3-month-old infants may make clumsy swipes at objects, they usually do not have the ability to reach for and grasp them efficiently until about 4½ to 6 months (Gibson & Walker, 1984).

Sensorimotor coordination continues to improve throughout early and middle childhood. Refer to Table 5.2 to see when most children are first capable of successfully swinging a bat or catching a ball, for example. During these years, as also noted in Chapter 5, the muscles are growing stronger, and the pathways that connect the cerebellum to the cortex are becoming increasingly myelinated. Experience also plays an indispensable role in refining many sensorimotor abilities—especially at "championship" levels, but there are also individual differences that seem inborn. Some people, for example, have better visual acuity or better depth perception than others. For reasons such as these, they will have an edge in playing the outfield or hitting a golf ball.

Theoretical Issues in Perceptual Development

Now that we have chronicled the development of perception in children, let us consider some of the theoretical issues involved in perceptual development.

First we must explain why so much of the focus in this chapter has been on the perception of development during infancy. The reason is that our sensory capabilities tend largely to mature by the end of infancy. Within months babies are sensing the world pretty much as adults do. Changes beyond infancy appear to be minor. Of course infants' interpretations of the world remain quite different from ours for many years, but interpretation of the world involves cognitive development as much as perceptual development.

And so, in later chapters we shall see that perceptual issues are labeled cognitive issues, or issues in selective attention or discrimination training. In this section, let us return to two of the controversial issues in child development raised in Chapter 1 and see how they apply to perceptual development: (1) Are children active or passive? (2) Are developmental processes basically guided by nature or nurture?

The Development of Perception and Attention: Are Children Active or Passive?

Newborn infants may have more sophisticated sensory capabilities than you expected. Still, their ways of perceiving the world are largely mechanical, or passive. The metaphor of a stimulus as *capturing* a baby's attention seems quite appropriate. Neonates seem to be generally at the mercy of external stimuli. When a bright light strikes, they attend to it. If the light moves slowly across the plane of their vision, they track it.

As time passes, broad changes occur in the perceptual processes of children, and the child's role in perception appears to become decidedly more active. Developmental psychologist Eleanor Gibson (1969) notes a number of these changes:

1. *Intentional action replaces "capture."* As infants mature and gain experience, purposeful scanning and exploration of the environment take the place of mechanical movements and passive responses to potent stimulation.

   Consider the scanning "strategies" of newborn infants. In a lighted room, newborn babies move their eyes mostly from left to right and back again. Mechanically they sweep a horizontal plane. If they "hit" an object that contrasts sharply with the background, their eye movements bounce back and forth against the edges. However, even when they awaken in a dark room, they show the stereotypical horizontal scanning pattern, with about two eye movements per second (Haith, 1980).

   The stereotypical quality of these initial scanning movements suggests that they are inborn. They provide strong evidence that the neonate is neurologically prewired to gather and seek visual information. They do not reflect what we would consider a purposeful, or intentional, effort to learn about the environment. As do so many other inborn behaviors (such as reflexes), these early scanning movements have apparent survival value. The scanning of neonates appears to provide a primitive method by which they begin to gather sensory information. However, the movements are basically mechanical and do not reflect purpose or intention on the part of the neonate.

2. *Systematic search replaces unsystematic search.* Over the first several years, infants and toddlers become more active as they develop systematic ways of exploring the environment. They come to pay progressively more attention to details of objects and people, and to make finer and finer discriminations.

3. *Attention becomes selective.* Older children become capable of selecting the information they need from the "booming" welter of confusion in the environment. For example, when older children are separated from their parents in a department store, they have the capacity to systematically scan for people of their parents' height, hair color, vocal characteristics, and so on. They are also more capable of discriminating the spot where the parent was last seen. A younger child is more likely to be confused by the welter of voices and faces and aisles, and to be unable to extract essential information from this backdrop.

4. *Irrelevent information becomes ignored.* Older children gain the capacity to screen out, or deploy their attention away from, stimuli that are irrelevent to the task at hand. This might mean shutting out the noise

▶ ▶ ▶ ▶

of cars in the street or radios in the neighborhood in order to focus on a book. It might mean eliminating "distractors" (incorrect choices) on a multiple-choice test. On another level, it may mean ignoring the hard-sell features of an advertisement to pick out useful information about a product.

Children, in short, develop from passive, mechanical reactors to—and from perceptual "victims" of—the world about them into active, purposeful seekers and organizers of sensory information. They develop from beings whose attention is diffuse and "captured" into people who make decisions as to what they will attend to. This is a process that, like so many others, appears to depend on both maturation and experience.

Let us now screen out distractions and deploy our attention to more formal consideration of the importance of maturation and experience in perceptual development.

Nativism and Empiricism in Perceptual Development: Does Perceptual Development Reflect Nature or Nurture?

The nature–nurture issue is found in perceptual development as in other dimensions of development. In the area of perception, the issue can be traced to the philosophers of the seventeenth and eighteenth centuries. René Descartes and Immanuel Kant took the **nativist** view that children are born with predispositions to perceive the world in certain ways. Kant, for example, believed that our innate makeup causes us to sense and organize the objects of the world according to certain "categories." We perceive some things and are oblivious to others because of our inborn ways of organizing the world outside.

George Berkeley and John Locke took the **empiricist** view that experience determines our ways of perceiving the world. Locke, for example, argued that mental representations reflect the impact of the world on the sense organs. There is no particular inborn way of organizing sensations of the world. The world, instead, impresses the mind with its own stamp.

Today few developmentalists subscribe to either extreme. Most would agree that nature (the nativist view) and nurture (the empiricist view) interact to give shape to perceptual development.

Evidence for the Nativist View   There is compelling evidence that our inborn sensory capacities play a crucial role in our perceptual development. For one thing, newborn babies have already come into the world with a good number of perceptual skills. They can see nearby objects quite well, and their hearing is usually fine. They are also born with "rules" that guide them to track moving objects, to systematically scan the horizon, and to prefer certain kinds of stimuli to others. Preferences for different kinds of visual stimuli appear to unfold on schedule as the first months wear on. Sensory changes, like the motor changes discussed in Chapter 5, appear to be linked to maturation of the nervous system.

Let us also not ignore the evidence that stems from simple observation of the abilities and limits of our sensory organs. Visible light, for example, is one small part of the entire array of electromagnetic energy. But our visual systems sense only that small band of electromagnetic energy that ranges in wavelength from about 400 to 700 nanometers (billionths of a meter). We per-

Nativism *The view that children are born with predispositions to perceive the world in certain ways.*

Empiricism *The view that experience determines the ways in which children perceive the world.*

▶ ▶ ▶ ▶

ceive this energy as the colors found in the rainbow—violet through red. The wavelengths of gamma rays and cosmic rays are shorter than 400 nanometers, and we cannot see them. The wavelengths of radio waves and microwaves are longer than 700 nanometers. We cannot see them either. Similarly, our auditory systems allow us to hear sounds that vary in frequency from about 20 to 20,000 cycles per second. Dogs can hear sounds that are higher in pitch, such as those emitted by "dog whistles," but we cannot.

For these reasons it seems clear that we do have certain inborn ways of responding to sensory input—certain "categories" and built-in limits—that allow us to perceive certain aspects of the world of physical reality.

Evidence for the Empiricist View   Evidence that experience plays a crucial role in perceptual development is also compelling. We could use any of hundreds of studies with children and other species to make the point, but, for the sake of convenience, let us limit our discussion to a number of experiments with kittens that appear to confirm observations of children.

Numerous studies have shown, for example, that there are critical periods in the perceptual development of children and lower animals. Failure to receive adequate sensory stimulation during these critical periods can result in permanent sensory deficits (Aslin & Banks, 1978; Banks & Salapatek, 1983). Newborn kittens raised with a patch over one eye wind up with few or no cells in the visual area of the cerebral cortex that would normally be activated by sensations of light that enter that eye. In effect, that eye becomes blind, even though sensory receptors in the eye itself may fire in response to light. On the other hand, if the eye of an adult cat is patched for the same amount of time, the animal will not lose vision in that eye. The critical period apparently will have passed. Similarly, if medical problems require that a child's eye must be patched for an extensive period of time during the first year, the child's visual acuity in that eye may be impaired.

As noted earlier in the chapter, simultaneous use of both eyes is required to perceive binocular cues for depth. In an experiment on the development of binocular vision, newborn kittens were prevented from using both eyes at the same time for several months (Blake & Hirsch, 1975). On alternate days, the left and right eyes were covered by opaque contact lenses. Following this treatment the kittens showed difficulty in depth perception. Why? It turns out that the treatment had spurred the development of two sets of cells in the visual cortex—one set activated by the left eye, the other by the right. Normally, cells in the cortex would receive impulses from both eyes. Strabismus places some children in a situation similar to that of the kittens, because the eyes of children with strabismus point in different directions. If strabismus is not corrected by about the age of 5, children will have few binocular cells in the cortex and·will not show adequate binocular depth perception. Like the experimental kittens, they will have been denied critical early experience in focusing two eyes on the same object.

In still other experiments, newborn kittens have been placed for five months in environments with only horizontal or only vertical stripes. Afterward, they cannot perceive lines running in the other direction. Once the critical period is over, the neurons in the cortex that would have been activated by the lines they never saw appear to have degenerated (Movshon & Van Sluyters, 1981). **Astigmatism** is a visual disorder in which vertical and horizontal contours cannot be simultaneously focused upon. If astigmatism is not corrected early in

Astigmatism A visual disorder caused by abnormal curvature of the lens, so that images are indistinct or distorted.

▶ ▶ ▶ ▶

childhood, the child will develop poor acuity for one of these types of contours. Children have a longer opportunity to recover from visual deprivation than kittens do. Still children are most vulnerable to deprivation during infancy, and their critical period for visual development appears to last up to eight·years (Aslin & Banks, 1978).

And so, with perceptual development, as with other dimensions of development, nature and nurture play indispensable roles. Nature continues to guide the unfolding of the child's physical systems. Nurture continues to interact with nurture in the development of these systems. In Chapter 5 we saw how sensorimotor experiences thicken the cortex of the brain. In Chapter 6 we see how sensory experiences are linked to the development of neurons in the cortex. Cortical neurons even run the risk of degenerating in the absence of appropriate experience. Inborn physical structures place limits on our abilities to respond to the world, but experience continues to help shape our most basic physical structures.

The Development of Reading Skills: An Application of Perceptual Development

Imagine a couple of monsters with purple, shaggy fur on the television screen. On the left side of the screen is the letter *c,* and the monster looking down at it makes a hard c sound ("kuh"). On the right side of the screen is the letter combination *at,* and the monster looking down at it says "at." Now the letters gradually move toward the center of the screen as the monsters continue to take turns sounding them out. Eventually they come together to form the word *cat,* and in an excited moment of recognition, the monsters say "Oh, cat!" and repeat the word a number of times. Then the monsters repeat the process for "h" and "at," "b" and "at," and so on, forming the words "hat," "bat," and many others that rhyme with them.

This is one of the ways in which the television program *Sesame Street* helps teach young children how to read, by sounding out letters and letter combinations, and showing how they are blended to form words.

The Integration of Auditory and Visual Information

Reading is a complex process that relies on skills in the integration of visual and auditory information. Accurate awareness of the sounds in the child's language is an important factor in reading readiness, as measured by reading performance in the first grade (Zifcak, 1981).

The Making of Visual Discriminations: Children Must "Mind Their P's and Q's"   Reading also requires the ability to make basic visual discriminations. In reading, for example, children must "mind their *p*'s and *q*'s." That is, in order to recognize letters, children must be able to perceive the visual differences between letters such as *b* and *d,* or *p* and *q.*

During the years of infancy and toddlerhood, neurological maturation and experience combine to allow most children to make visual discriminations between different letters with relative ease. By the time preschoolers are 5 to 5½, they have normally had enough experience with their own written languages to discriminate between its written characters better than they can be-

▶ ▶ ▶ ▶

tween the characters in foreign languages that use different alphabets (Keislar et al., 1972). That is, they are more capable of correctly noticing that an "a" is not a "b" than they are of noticing that a Greek alpha is not a Greek beta.*

How do children acquire this basic familiarity with their own written languages? More and more today, U.S. children are being exposed to TV programs such as *Sesame Street* and *The Electric Company*, but these are relatively recent educational innovations. Children are also exposed to books, street signs, names of stores and restaurants, and to writing on packages, especially at the supermarket. Some children, of course, have more books in the home than others do. It is no secret that children from affluent homes where books and other sources of stimulation are plentiful learn to read more readily than children from impoverished homes.

One study of 4-year-old readers and nonreaders found that the early readers had preferred to play with reading readiness toys such as alphabet cards and books, whereas the nonreaders had preferred toys like blocks and vehicles (Thomas, 1984). There were no consistent differences in intelligence or family background. It was not shown that the parents of the early readers made greater efforts to encourage their children to play with the reading-readiness toys. It may be that early readers are also neurologically capable of making the visual discriminations necessary for reading at earlier ages.

Methods of Teaching Reading

When they read, children integrate visual and auditory information (associate what they see with sounds), whether they are reading by the *word-recognition method* or by the *phonetic method*. If they are using the **word-recognition method,** they must be able to associate visual stimuli such as *cat* and *Robert* with the sound combinations that produce the spoken words "cat" and "Robert." This capacity is usually acquired by **rote learning,** or extensive repetition.

In the **phonetic method,** children first learn to associate written letters and letter combinations (such as *ph* or *sh*) with the sounds they are meant to indicate. Then they "sound out" words from left to right, decoding them. The phonetic method has the obvious advantage of giving children skills that they can use to decode (read) new words. However, some children learn more rapidly at early ages through the word-recognition method. The phonetic method can also slow them down when it comes to familiar words. Most children and adults, in fact, tend to read familiar words by the word-recognition method (regardless of the method of their original training), and to make some effort to "sound out" new words.

A controversy that we cannot resolve here rages over which method is superior. Some words in English can be read only by the word-recognition method—consider the numbers "one" and "two." This method is useful when it comes to words such as "Danger," "Stop," "Poison," and the child's name, for it helps provide children with a basic **sight vocabulary.** But decoding skills must be acquired at some point if children are to be able to read new words on their own.

Word-recognition method A method for learning to read in which children come to recognize words through repeated exposure to them.

Rote learning Learning by repetition.

Phonetic method (fo-NET-tick). A method for learning to read in which children decode the sounds of words based on their knowledge of the sounds of letters and letter combinations.

Sight vocabulary Words that are immediately recognized on the basis of familiarity with their overall shapes, rather than decoded.

*The study referred to was actually carried out with Roman (English), Chinese, and Hindi alphabets, but the Greek example is used to make the point in the text because it is more familiar than Chinese or Hindi.

▶ ▶ ▶ ▶

Reading Disorders

In many ways, reading is a key to unlocking the benefits our society has to offer. Good readers find endless pleasure in literature, reading and re-reading favorite poetic passages countless times. Reading makes textbook learning possible. Reading also permits us to identify subway stops, to consider the contents of food packages, to assemble children's swing sets and barbecue grills, and to learn how to use a microcomputer.

When people cannot read, obviously, important areas of experience are closed off to them. Others, particularly schooling, are made cruelly aversive. There are, of course, many reasons why a number of children do not learn how to read—or do not learn how to read well enough to ease their paths through the intellectual mazes of our culture (see Table 6.1).

One is general impairment in intellectual functioning, or mental retardation. In this instance, difficulty in learning to read is secondary to general slowness in learning. As noted in Chapter 9, many intelligence tests allow psychologists and educators to determine a child's general level of cognitive ability. However, as noted in the Diagnostic and Statistical Manual of the American Psychiatric Association (1987), there are many instances of mild mental retardation in which children's reading levels are still markedly below what could be expected of them. In these cases, the reading disorder should not simply be attributed to retardation and swept under the rug. Remedial efforts may be of use.

Cultural-familial impoverishment and inadequate schooling also contribute to low reading levels. In many cases, poor readers come from homes that do not share in the cultural abundance of information and reading materials. Because of poverty or lack of orientation toward common educational values, parents in such homes may not possess television sets, books, magazines, newspapers, or other materials that could spark an interest in reading. School systems, similarly, may not measure up to national norms in the fostering of reading skills.

Reading ability relies heavily on the integration of visual and auditory information. For this reason, impaired sensory processes of vision and hearing will also hinder the development of reading skills. Problems with vision and hearing can be determined by screening tests.

Specific Developmental Reading Disorder—Dyslexia   A specific developmental reading disorder, frequently referred to as **dyslexia,** can be puzzling, because there is every indication that the child *ought* to be able to read. Frequently the child is at least average in intelligence and from a middle-class background. His* school system is renowned for excellent reading-level scores, and his vision and hearing check out as perfectly normal. However, problems in developing reading skills persist.

Researchers have identified a number of frequently occurring characteristics of dyslexic children, and these are listed in Table 6.2. The origins of dyslexia are less well catalogued. There is controversy over whether it is primarily caused by neurological or by experiential factors (learning deficiencies).

Dyslexia (dis-LEGS-see-uh). A reading disorder characterized by problems such as letter reversals, mirror reading, slow reading, and reduced comprehension.

▶ ▶ ▶ ▶

*This is one instance in which it seems appropriate to use the male pronoun when referring to children in general. Dyslexia is at least twice as common among boys as girls.

6   PERCEPTUAL DEVELOPMENT

Table 6.1 Causes of Reading Disorders

Mental retardation
Cultural-familial deprivation
Inadequate schooling
Physical vision problems
Physical hearing problems
Developmental reading disorder (dyslexia)

Table 6.2 Characteristics of Dyslexic Children

Usually first recognized during early school years
Omissions and additions of words
Reversal or rotation of letters of the alphabet—confusing "b" with "d" and "p" with "q"
Mirror reading and writing—reading and writing words that look normal when viewed in a
    mirror, as in reading "saw" when presented with the visual stimulus *was*
Slow reading
Reduced reading comprehension
Subtle language difficulties, such as impaired sound discrimination (although overall auditory
    acuity is within normal limits)
At least some impairment in general academic functioning
May be easily distracted, fail to listen or to finish things that he or she has started
May be impulsive, call out in class, find it difficult to wait in lines
More common among twins, prematurely born children, children born to older mothers, and
    children who have sustained head injuries
More common among boys
Reading, speech, and language problems more common in family than in general population
Problem frequently continues into adolescence and adulthood

Origins of Dyslexia Hypotheses about the origins of dyslexia fall into two main camps: hypotheses about neurological factors and hypotheses about faulty learning.

One neurological hypothesis centers on the possibility of "minimal brain damage." Dyslexic boys, for example, frequently show a number of behaviors found among children with *frank*, or known, brain damage. These include a short attention span and difficulty sitting still. And so it has been speculated that children with dyslexia may also be brain damaged, even though the brain damage is so minimal that it cannot be detected by direct means.

If there is "minimal" brain damage, or another sort of neurological problem, where might the dysfunction lie? Paul Rozin (1976; Gleitman & Rozin, 1977) suggests that it might be in the "wiring" that connects the auditory system to the visual system. For this reason, visual cues, such as written letters of the alphabet, might not trigger images of the correct sounds. (That is, the child may see *b* but "hear" *d*.)

Another neurological approach is found in studies of the brains of dyslexic individuals who have died by accident. Through dissection, neurologists Albert Galaburda and Thomas Kemper have found patterns of abnormal neurological development, particularly in the left hemisphere, which is linked to language functions (Blakeslee, 1984). Neurologist Norman Geschwind suggested that such patterns of neurological development may stem from excessive

▶ ▶ ▶ ▶

prenatal exposure to the male hormone testosterone, particularly during the second trimester of pregnancy (Blakeslee, 1984).

Research by Sandra Witelson (1979) suggests that excessive prenatal exposure to male sex hormones may lead to dyslexia by causing greater-than-normal differentiation of the left hemisphere of the cerebral cortex. Witelson's research strategy was made possible by the fact that language functions are linked to structures that are usually found in the left hemisphere. But spatial abilities and emotional responses (Saxby & Bryden, 1985) are usually more localized in the right hemisphere.

One test of spatial abilities is the capacity to identify objects by the sense of touch. Handling an object allows us to construct an image of it and thereby identify it. Now consider that sensory pathways largely cross over in the brain, so that objects perceived with the right eye or right hand are more directly projected in the left hemisphere, and vice versa (see Figure 6.8). Since spatial abilities are usually more highly developed in the right hemisphere, children most often are better at identifying unseen objects with their left hands. In Witelson's research, however, dyslexic children seemed equally adept at identifying objects with either hand. Thus it may be that an unusually high development of spatial abilities in the left hemisphere somehow impairs reading ability.

Faulty-learning hypotheses focus on lack of appropriate prerequisites and the accumulation of anxiety when being taught how to read. Dyslexic children, for example, often cannot be taught to reliably discriminate between letter-pairs such as *b* and *d*, even though the pairs are presented hundreds of times, and wrong responses are consistently corrected. From this perspective, anxiety and fear become associated with trying to discriminate letters, even if children

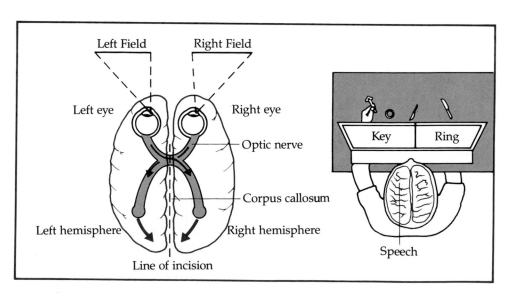

Figure 6.8 A View of the Brain from Above
Objects perceived by the right eye are more directly projected in the left hemisphere of the cortex, and vice versa. Language functions are linked to structures found in the left hemisphere, but spatial abilities and emotional responses are somewhat more localized in the right hemisphere.

▶ ▶ ▶ ▶

6 PERCEPTUAL DEVELOPMENT

do not shake and quiver as they try to read. High levels of emotion have been shown to prompt conflicting responses to simple stimuli. Therefore, the persistent effort to teach dyslexic children to discriminate among letters and simple words may backfire. The anxiety that attends repeated trials causes conflicting tendencies to say "b" and "d" in response to the visual stimulus *b* to persist. The more anxious children become about saying the right letter, the more likely it is that they will err.

Both broad explanations of dyslexia remain somewhat speculative. The faulty-learning view has great difficulty explaining the common patterns of deficiency that appear (such as letter reversal and mirror writing). Also, many dyslexic children do not appear at all anxious when they are receiving concentrated remediation.

The neurological hypotheses also have their problems. For example, the very concept of *minimal* brain damage admits that investigators may be searching for something that is impossible to detect by independent means. It is not enough to say that children behave *as though* they had a bit of brain damage. At some point we have to be able to put our finger—or a scientific instrument—on the damage and say, "Here it is." Evidence for Rozin and Witelson's views remains indirect. However, researchers are currently attempting to replicate their findings and to determine whether remedial programs based on their hypotheses are effective. Some of the research concerning Rozin's views is encouraging.

Programs for working with children with specific reading disorders focus on factors such as attempting to enhance perceptual abilities and to bring more senses to bear on the reading process. Dyslexic children, for example, not only spend hours in the reading laboratory. They also match designs with pegs; piece puzzles together; trace letters and words with their fingers before saying them or writing them; match and classify objects into categories; and, literally, hop, skip, and jump. As of today, we cannot prescribe any particular program with surety. Fortunately, however, many programs have apparently been of help with some children, and a few other children show apparently spontaneous improvements in reading ability as they mature.

In this chapter we have seen how children come into the world with sensitivity to language and with inborn "categories" that seem to guide their perceptual processes. In the next two chapters we follow the courses of language development and cognitive development. In so doing, we gather further insight into ways in which children perceive and represent the world.

Summary

1. Neonates show the pupillary reflex; that is, their eyes adjust to the brightness of their environments. Neonates are nearsighted, with their visual acuity estimated at about 20/600, and they have poor peripheral vision.

2. Many neonates can visually track moving objects on the first day after birth. Neonates do not show visual accommodation. Nor do they respond to retinal disparity and convergence as binocular cues for depth. Babies perceive color by 2 to 3 months, and prefer reds and blues by about 4 months.

▶ ▶ ▶ ▶

3. The most dramatic gains in visual acuity are made between birth and 6 months, with acuity approaching adult levels by the ages of 1 to 5. Peripheral vision approximates that of adults at 6 months.

4. Young babies prefer stripes to blobs. Two-month-old babies prefer to view faces rather than brightly colored disks, apparently because they are intrigued by complex patterns with dots (eyes). One-month-olds are visually captured by the edges of objects (such as the outlines of faces), while 2-month-olds prefer to scan within the edges (and focus, for example, on the eyes). Seven-week-old babies prefer to look at familiar stimuli, while 10-week-olds prefer novel stimuli. At 1 year, infants prefer to look at scrambled faces rather than accurately drawn faces, apparently because of their discrepancy.

5. According to the discrepancy hypothesis, infants who have reached certain ages become habituated to familiar stimuli and pay them less attention. Discrepant stimuli are novel enough to capture the attention once more, but not so different as to frighten the infant or be totally without recognizable features.

6. Babies develop some form of depth perception by about 2 months of age, as suggested by lowered heart rate and concentrated gazing when placed face down on the visual cliff. But by 7 to 9 months of age, when they have developed the capacity to crawl, most infants show fear when placed on the visual cliff, as manifested by increased heart rate. Experience with moving about apparently stimulates the development of fear of the possibility of falling.

7. Babies develop size constancy by about 4 to 6 months, and shape constancy by about the same age.

8. The object concept is the perception that objects have an existence that does not hinge upon their making sensory impressions upon us. Two aspects of the object concept are object identity and object permanence. Object identity is the perception that objects maintain their identity in between occasions on which they are sensed. Object permanence is the perception that objects continue to exist whether or not they are sensed.

9. Infants gradually develop more sophisticated forms of the object concept during the first two years. They first search for dropped objects at about 6 months and first search for objects hidden behind screens at about 9 months. During the sixth month infants show distress when they view multiple images of their mothers, suggesting that they know that mother has a single identity.

10. Fetuses respond to sound a couple of months before birth. The structures of the middle and inner ears are formed by birth, and hearing acuity at birth is normally excellent, unless the ears are blocked by amniotic fluid. Neonates crudely orient their heads in the direction of sounds and can detect differences in amplitude and pitch. Neonates prefer vocalizations by adult women to other sounds that are similar in pitch, and, within a few days, they prefer their own mothers' voices. They also synchronize their body movements to the sounds of speech.

11. Auditory acuity improves somewhat over the first months, and the range of detectable pitches expands. By 1 month babies can discriminate "pah" from "bah." By 3 to 5 months they can imitate sounds of different pitches.

▶ ▶ ▶ ▶

6 PERCEPTUAL DEVELOPMENT

12. Neonates can discriminate odors, and their preferences are similar to those of adults. By about 1 week they show preference for (turn toward) nursing pads that have been used by their own mothers, showing that they can discriminate the odor of their mothers' milk.

13. Neonates can discriminate various tastes, and show preference for sweet-tasting liquids, as manifested by harder sucking.

14. Neonates are sensitive to touch, and many of their most basic reflexes are stimulated by the sense of touch. Neonates' response to pain may be relatively low during the first few days. By 10 months they can discriminate objects through the sense of touch.

15. There is an inborn tendency for children to coordinate the auditory and visual modalities, as shown by turning their heads to look at an object they hear. Efficient visual-motor coordination does not develop until about 4½ to 6 months.

16. Many theoretical issues are involved in perceptual development. One is whether children's perceptual processes are basically active or passive. Gibson chronicles four shifts in perception and attention that take place during childhood, and it appears that perceptual processes become increasingly active: (1) Intentional action replaces capture of the senses. (2) Systematic search replaces unsystematic search. (3) Attention becomes selective. (4) Irrelevant information becomes ignored.

17. Another issue concerns nature and nurture: the extent to which perceptual development is guided by inborn tendencies to perceive the world in certain ways (the nativist view) or by experience (the empiricist view). The "rules" that guide the perceptions of newborns provide evidence for the nativist view. However, experiments with kittens that reveal a critical period for the development of cells in the visual cortex provide evidence for the empiricist view. Developmentalists today avoid both extremes in their theorizing.

18. The process of reading requires the integration of auditory and visual stimulation (spoken sounds and written letters or words) and the making of visual discriminations—for example, perceiving the difference between the written letters *b* and *d*. Most children can make appropriate discriminations by about the ages of 5 to 5½.

19. Reading is taught by the word-recognition and the phonetic methods. In the word-recognition method, children learn to say words on the basis of repeated visual presentation. In the phonetic method, children learn to decode words by sounding out their letters and letter combinations.

20. Children may have difficulty learning to read because of mental retardation, inadequate schooling, or problems in vision or hearing. Children who do not have these handicaps, but who still have serious difficulty reading, are said to have dyslexia.

21. Different theories have attempted to link dyslexia to neurological problems or to faulty learning. Possible neurological problems include "minimal" brain damage, problems in the "wiring" between the auditory and the visual systems, and *over*development of the left hemisphere of the cerebral cortex. However, the status of the research into the causes of dyslexia suggests that it would be premature to draw conclusions.

▶ ▶ ▶ ▶

Newborn babies are nearsighted. *True.* By 6 months their visual acuity will approach adult norms.

Newborn babies may look at one object with one eye and another object with the other eye. *True.* Their eyes do not necessarily yet converge on objects.

Newborn babies make rhythmic eye movements, scanning left and right, even in the dark. *True.* This innate scanning strategy provides evidence for the nativist point of view.

Four-month-old babies who have been looking at a green circle will accept its replacement by a blue circle. However, they may cry and show other signs of distress when a blue circle is replaced by a green circle. *True.* By this age, babies have distinct color preferences.

Two-month-old babies prefer to look at human faces rather than at brightly colored objects. *True.* The question is whether they prefer faces because they are faces or because faces are complex stimuli.

Infants need to have some experience crawling about before they develop fear of heights. *Apparently so.* Infants typically do not show fear of the visual cliff unless they have had such experience.

Four-month-old infants enjoy multiple mirror images of their mothers, but 6-month-old infants are frightend by them. *True.* Apparently by 6 months the object concept is developed to the point where multiple images of mother are severely discrepant with infants' expectations.

When favorite toys are placed behind a screen, they no longer exist—so far as 5-month-old babies are concerned. *True.* At this age, "out of sight" apparently means "out of existence."

Newborn babies crudely orient their heads in the direction of sounds. *True.* This inborn response promotes the coordination of the visual and auditory modalities.

Newborn babies do not show any preference for the sounds of human speech. *False.* Babies seem "prewired" to attend to speech.

By the age of 3 months, most babies imitate musical notes sung by their mothers. *True.* Infants show fine auditory discriminative ability quite early.

When presented with nursing pads used by their own mothers and other mothers, babies only a few days old will turn toward the pads used by their own mothers. *True.* The sense of smell is well developed at birth.

Newborn babies prefer sweet-tasting foods. *True.* Babies' taste preferences are very much like those of older children and adults.

Newborn babies do not experience pain. *False.* However, at first they may be relatively less sensitive to pain than older children and adults.

Newborn kittens prevented from seeing horizontal lines for several months will not be able to perceive horizontal lines later on. *True.* Such evidence with kittens supports the view that there are critical periods for the development of visual abilities.

Boys are more likely than girls to have reading problems. *True.* It may have something to do with the structure of boys' brains.

Some children cannot learn to read, even when they are average in intelligence, come from homes where reading is encouraged, and are 6 years old or older. *True.* Such children are said to have a primary reading disorder—one that is not caused by other problems.

Children tend to "outgrow" early reading problems. *False.* Serious reading problems tend to persevere.

▶ ▶ ▶ ▶

7

Language Development

C H A P T E R ▶ O U T L I N E

▶
▶
▶
▶
▶
▶
▶

T R U T H ▸ O R ▸ F I C T I O N ?

- Chimpanzees and gorillas have been taught how to use sign language.
- Crying is the child's earliest use of language.
- Children babble only the sounds of their parents' language.
- Deaf children do not babble.
- Once children acquire their first word, other words follow "fast and furiously."
- Most of children's earliest words are names for things.
- To a 2-year-old, the word combinations "Go Mommy" and "Mommy go" have the same meaning.
- Three-year-olds say "Daddy goed away" instead of "Daddy went away" because they *do* understand rules of grammar.
- Parents have to coach 4- and 5-year-olds in how to use "baby talk" with their younger siblings.
- Children learn language faster when their parents correct their errors.
- Children acquire grammar by imitating their parents.
- Children are "preprogrammed" to listen to language in such a way that they pick out rules of grammar.
- Children must understand the concepts for things before they can learn the words for things. That is, children must know what a dog is before they can learn the word *doggy*.
- People cannot learn new languages after they have reached sexual maturity.
- The Black English sentence "She the one I talking about" is produced by using systematic rules of grammar.
- Some black children can switch back and forth between Black English and standard English.
- Bilingual children encounter more academic problems than children who know only one language.
- The best way to teach English to children who speak Spanish in the home is to immerse them totally in English once they enter school.
- Deaf children reared by deaf parents show superior language development as compared to deaf children reared by parents who can hear.

Did you hear the one about the judge who pounded his gavel and yelled, "Order! Order in the court!"? "A hamburger and French fries, Your Honor," responded the defendant.

Or how about this one? "I saw a man-eating lion at the zoo." "Big deal! I saw a man eating snails at a restaurant."

Or how about, "Make me a glass of chocolate milk!"? "Poof! You're a glass of chocolate milk."

These children's jokes are based on ambiguities in the meanings of words and phrases. The joke about "order in the court" will not be found funny by most children until they are about the age of 7 and can recognize that the word *order* has more than one meaning. The jokes about the man-eating lion and the chocolate milk will not strike most children as funny until about the age of 11, when they can understand ambiguities in grammatical structure.

This chapter traces language development from the **prelinguistic** sounds children make early in the first year through the complex language they usually use during middle childhood. Vocabulary can continue to grow for a lifetime, but children normally become sophisticated producers of language before adolescence.

It may seem a bit odd, but we shall begin our exploration of language development with a recounting of efforts to teach language to apes. This brief overview will help us appreciate what is so special about the human use of language—even at very early ages.

Then we focus formally on some of the basic concepts we shall need to understand language development: phonology, morphology, syntax, and semantics. Once these fundamentals have been discussed, we shall be ready to trace language development from early crying and cooing through the production of complex, unique sentences. Next we consider theoretical views of language development. Developmentalists broadly agree that native factors in the nervous system lay the groundwork for language acquisition and that experience plays an indispensable role. But as in so many other areas of development, they differ in their relative emphases on nature and nurture. Finally, we consider examples of the varieties of development, including Black English, bilingualism, and language learning by deaf children.

On Language and Apes

When I was in high school, I was taught that we differ from other creatures that walk, swim, or fly the Earth because only we use language and tools. Then I found out that lower animals use tools too. Otters use rocks to open clam shells. Chimpanzees throw rocks as weapons and use sticks to dig out grubs for food.

In recent years, our exclusive claim to the use of language has also been challenged, for chimpanzees and gorillas have been taught to communicate by making signs with their hands or by pressing keys on an electric typewriter (Figure 7.1).

Washoe, a female chimp raised by Beatrice and Allen Gardner (1980), was the first primate who came to our notice. The Gardners and their assistants raised Washoe from the time she was a year of age. Instead of speaking to her, they employed **American Sign Language** (ASL), the language used by deaf Americans, to communicate.

Prelinguistic *Prior to the development of language.*

American Sign Language *The communication of meaning through the use of symbols that are formed by moving the hands and arms and associated gestures. The language used by deaf people.*

▶ ▶ ▶ ▶

By the age of 5, Washoe could use more than 160 signs, including signs for actions (verbs), such as *come, gimme,* and *tickle;* signs for things (nouns), such as *apples, flowers,* and *toothbrush;* and signs for more abstract concepts, such as *more.* She could also combine signs to form simple, brief sentences that were largely **telegraphic,** like those of young children. Consider these two-word sentences: *More tickle, More banana,* and *More milk*—which doesn't sound like too bad a way to spend a lazy Sunday afternoon. As time passed Washoe signed longer sentences, such as *Please sweet drink, Come gimme drink* and *Gimme toothbrush hurry.*

Washoe tended to extend the meanings of words to cover objects for which she had no words, a process called **overextension** that also characterizes children's language. During the second year, for example, children may overextend the word "doggy" to refer to many animals, including dogs, horses, and cows. At 2½ years, many children refer to objects and situations that elicit a variety of strong emotional responses as "funny" or "silly," because they cannot yet use words such as "interesting," "intriguing," and "delightful."

Some observers believe that Washoe's communications showed failings by human standards. For example, we are not certain of the degree to which Washoe and other apes have attended to grammar, as shown by word order (Terrace et al., 1980). Washoe's words were frequently strung together in assorted combinations. One day she might sign *Come gimme toothbrush,* but the next day, *Hurry toothbrush gimme.* Even the language productions of human 1-year-olds tend to have reliable word order. Children appear to share an **intuitive** grasp of grammar, but apes may not. Still, in recent years Washoe and her companions have been observed spontaneously signing to one another, and mother chimpanzees may teach their infants to use signs to communicate (Bernstein, 1987; Fouts & Fouts, 1985).

Ann and David Premack (1975) taught another female chimp, Sarah, to communicate by arranging symbols on a magnet board (see Figure 7.1). Eventually Sarah learned such simple telegraphic sentences as *Place orange dish.* Her word order was less sporadic than Washoe's. The Premacks consider their work with Sarah a demonstration of the role of operant conditioning in the learning of language. Sarah was reinforced for selecting the proper symbols to make a request and for following instructions communicated by symbols.

Still another chimp, Lana, was trained to communicate by means of a keyboard controlled by a computer (Savage-Rumbaugh & Rumbaugh, 1980). Lana learned to manipulate about 100 keys, each of which showed a different symbol. She would press various combinations of keys to communicate simple ideas (Figure 7.1), and also tended to maintain a consistent word order.

The investigative team who worked with Lana have also worked with other chimps. In a recent study, they found that two chimps could use symbols to correctly categorize novel objects as foods or tools (Savage-Rumbaugh et al., 1980). In this way, they demonstrated a relationship between cognitive development and language development in apes.

Some of the most impressive claims for teaching language to an ape have been made by Francine (Penny) Patterson (1980). Patterson taught a gorilla named Koko to use some 375 signs regularly, including signs for *friend, airplane, lollipop, belly button,* even *stethoscope.* Patterson also reports that at the ages of 5, 6, and 7, Koko earned scores on intelligence tests just below those of children of comparable ages. She characterizes Koko's use of language as almost "human," in that Koko tells lies and at times does the exact opposite of what she

▶ ▶ ▶ ▶

Figure 7.1 Apes Use Signs to Communicate
Operant conditioning was used to teach a chimpanzee named Sarah (left) to communicate by using plastic symbols. Psychologists reinforced Sarah for selecting the proper symbols, or for following commands made with symbols. Here Sarah will follow directions to place the apple in the pail and the banana in the dish. Lana (right) was taught to express simple ideas by pressing keys on a computer-controlled keyboard.

is told to do. Patterson also reports that Koko has produced some creative insults in ASL—for example, "You dirty toilet devil" and "Rotten stink." Koko, like children, has also created words (signs) of her own, such as tucking her index finger under her arm as a sign for thermometer (Patterson et al., 1987). Apes, like children, name objects. But some **linguists** argue that Koko, like other apes, shows little if any understanding of grammar.

Now that we have described the skills of a number of well-known apes, let us wrestle with the issue: Can apes really understand and produce language? To answer this question, we shall also discuss some of the major features of language.

Properties of Human Language: Semanticity, Productivity, and Displacement

According to **psycholinguist** Roger Brown (1973), three properties are used today to distinguish between human language and the communications systems of lower animals: *semanticity, productivity,* and *displacement*. **Semanticity** refers to the fact that words serve as symbols for actions, objects, relational concepts (over, in, more, and so on), and other ideas.

Many species have systems of communication. Birds warn other birds of predators. They communicate that they have taken possession of a certain tree or bush through characteristic chirps and shrieks. The "dances" shown by bees inform other bees of the approximate direction and distance of a food source or of an invading enemy. The purrs and howls of cats express content-

Linguists *Scientists who study the structure, functions, and origins of language. (From the Latin* lingua, *meaning "tongue.")*

Psycholinguist *A scientist who specializes in the study of the relationships between psychological processes and language.*

Semanticity *Meaning. The quality of language in which words are used as symbols for objects, events, or ideas.*

▶ ▶ ▶ ▶

258   7 LANGUAGE DEVELOPMENT

Productivity *The capacity to combine words into original sentences.*

Syntax *The rules in a language for placing words in proper order to form meaningful sentences. (From the Latin syntaxis, meaning "joining together.")*

Displacement *The quality of language that permits one to communicate information about objects and events in another time and place.*

ment or horror. Vervet monkeys can emit sounds that warn their kind of the distance and species of predators.

However, all these species-specific communication patterns are innate and, in contrast to human language, largely unmodifiable by experience. They also lack semanticity. That is, sounds and—in the case of bees—waggles do not symbolize specific objects, distances, and other concepts. Although apes have been taught to use signs to earn rewards, we do not know whether most of them understand that the signs are symbols.

Productivity refers to the capacity to combine words into original sentences. Our standard for originality is not rigid. An "original" sentence is *not* one that has never been spoken before. It is a sentence that is produced by the individual instead of being imitated. In order to produce original sentences, children must have a basic understanding of **syntax,** or the structure of grammar. Two-year-old children string signs (words) together in novel combinations, but questions have been raised as to whether apes combine signs into original sentences (Terrace et al., 1980). Lana, for example, appeared to learn a number of standard sentences into which she could insert new verbs and nouns, but her productivity was limited.

Terrace has concluded that apes cannot master the basics of grammar. Terrace (1987) also argues that what looks like spontaneous signing is actually signing for "a variety of concrete incentives"—that is, tricks to gain rewards. There are some exceptions, but apes generally use signs in the situations in which they have been taught to use them. What apes produce is very similar to what they have been taught to produce. After reviewing videotapes and reports of others who taught language to apes, Terrace reluctantly wrote, "The closer I looked, the more I regarded the many reported instances of language as elaborate tricks for obtaining rewards" (Terrace, 1980).

Displacement is the capacity to communicate information about events and objects in another time or place.* Language makes possible the efficient transmission of large amounts of complex knowledge from one person to another, and from one generation to another. Displacement permits parents to warn children of their own mistakes. Displacement allows children to tell their parents what they did in school. Referring to the significance of displacement, Roger Brown writes, "The important thing about language is that it makes life experiences cumulative; across generations and within one generation, among individuals. Everyone can know much more than he [or she] could possibly learn by direct experience" (1970, p. 212).

In sum, if we use Brown's criteria for defining language, some critics argue that apes fall short. However, Michael Maratsos (1983) of the University of Minnesota Institute of Child Development notes that Brown's strict criteria are relatively new on the scene. "Apes can probably learn to use signs to communicate meanings," Maratsos writes. "As this used to be the old boundary for language, it seems unfair to [now] raise the ante and say that [using signs to communicate meaning] is not really language" (1983, p. 771). But Maratsos adds that the questions as to whether apes can use word order and other aspects of grammar in the way we do remain problematic to the supporters of apes.

We have not really answered the question as to whether apes can use

---

*The word *displacement* has a very different meaning within Sigmund Freud's psychoanalytic theory of personality development, as we saw in Chapter 2.

▶ ▶ ▶ ▶

ON LANGUAGE AND APES

language. My apologies—the issue remains controversial. Nonetheless, our discussion of the language of apes has given us some insight into our own facility with language—even at very young ages.

The Basics of Language

ASL does not contain sounds, because it is intended for use by deaf people. But the components of other languages include sounds (*phonology*) and a number of other features: *morphology* (units of meaning), *syntax* (word order), and *semantics* (the meanings of words and groups of words). An understanding of these basics of language will provide a framework for following the language development of children.

Phonology

Phonology (foe-NOLL-oh-gee). *The study of the basic sounds in a language. (From the Greek* phone, *meaning "sound" or "voice.")*

Phoneme *A basic sound in a language.*

Phonology is the study of the basic sounds in a language. There are 26 letters in the English alphabet, but a greater number of basic sounds or **phonemes.** These include the *t* and *p* in *tip*, which a psycholinguist may designate as the /t/ and /p/ phonemes. The *o* in *go* and the *o* in *gone* are different phonemes. Although they are spelled with the same letter, they sound different. English phonemes are shown in Table 7.1. English speakers who learn French may be confused because /o/, as in the word *go*, has various spellings in French, including *o, au, eau,* even *eaux*.

At one time or another, you may have heard someone trying to be humorous or witty by speaking English with a mock German or Japanese accent. Why can these two languages be mocked so readily in English? One answer is

Table 7.1 Frequently Used English Phonemes

CONSONANT PHONEMES

p	(pass)	δ	(this)	n	(no)
b	(but)	s	(so)	rj	(ring)
t	(to)	z	(zero, boys)	l	(love)
d	(do)	š	(should)	w	(wish)
k	(kiss, calm)	ž	(azure)	hw	(when)
g	(go)	č	(church)	y	(yes)
f	(for)	ĵ	(Jim)	r	(run)
v	(value)	m	(more)	h	(how)
θ	(thing)				

VOWEL PHONEMES

i	(bit)	e	(bet)	ae	(map)
i	(children)	e	(above)	a	(not)
u	(put)	o	(boat)	c	(law)

From J. DeVito, *The Psychology of Speech and Language* (New York: Random House, 1970), p. 72.

▶ ▶ ▶ ▶

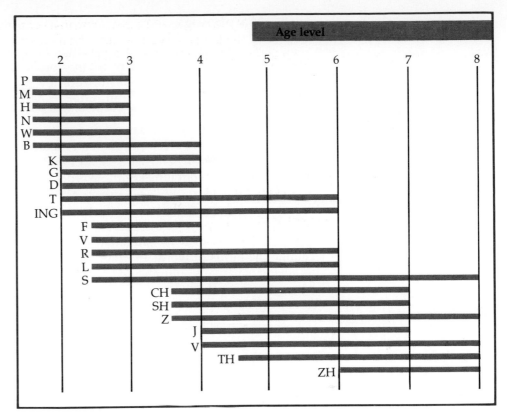

Figure 7.2 Acquisition of the Sounds of Speech
The solid bar for each sound of speech begins at the age by which 50 percent of children pronounce it properly. The bar ends at the age by which 90 percent of children are pronouncing the sound correctly. P's and b's are relatively easy to acquire. Fifty percent of children acquire the s sound before their third birthdays, but not until the age of 8 do 90 percent of children pronounce s properly.

that different languages use different phonemes. English speakers learning French, Spanish, or German must practice different-sounding "rolling r's." Japanese has no r phoneme. For this reason, many Japanese pronounce the English words *right* and *wrong* as *light* and *long*.

Phoneme Perception and Production   As noted in Chapter 6, newborn babies can discriminate the sounds of speech from other sounds as shown by different responses to speech. By the age of 1 or 2 months, babies can also discriminate among different phonemes, even the similar sounding /d/ and /t/, and /b/ and /p/ (Eimas, 1975).

Some English sounds are more difficult than others for young children to pronounce. In Figure 7.2, the left end of each solid bar shows when 50 percent of the children observed begin to pronounce the sound correctly. The right side of the bar shows the age by which 90 percent of children are pronouncing the sound correctly. As you can see, the P and M sounds are pronounced correctly by the vast majority of children by the age of 3. However, many children do not correctly pronounce S and TH sounds until the eighth year.

▶ ▶ ▶ ▶

Morphology

Morphemes are the smallest units of meaning in a language. A morpheme consists of one or more phonemes pronounced in a certain order. Some morphemes such as *dog* and *cat* function by themselves as words, but other morphemes must be combined in order to be used. The words *dogs* and *cats* each consist of two morphemes. Adding /z/ to *dog* makes the word plural. Adding /s/ to *cat* serves the same function.

An *ed* morpheme at the end of a regular verb places it in the past tense, as with *add* and *added*, and with *subtract* and *subtracted*. A *ly* morpheme at the end of an adjective often makes the word an adverb, as with *strong* and *strongly* and *weak* and *weakly*.

Inflections Morphemes such as *s* and *ed* tacked on to the ends of nouns and verbs are referred to as grammatical "markers," or **inflections.** Inflections change the forms of words in order to indicate grammatical relationships such as *number* (singular or plural) and *tense* (for example, present or past). Languages have grammatical rules for the formation of plurals, tenses, and other inflections. Children tend to grasp these rules at an early age.

Syntax

Syntax concerns the customary arrangement of words in phrases and sentences in a language. Syntax deals with the ways words are to be strung together, or ordered, into phrases and sentences. The precise rules for word order are the *grammar* of a language.

In English, statements usually follow the pattern *subject, verb,* and *object of the verb.* Note this example:

The young boy (subject) → has brought (verb) → the book (object).

The sentence would be confusing if it were written "The young boy *has* the book *brought*." But this is how the sentence would be written in German. German syntax differs from that of English. In German, a past participle ("brought") is placed at the end of the sentence, and the helping verb ("has") follows the subject. Although the syntax of German differs from the English, children reared in German-speaking homes acquire German syntax as readily as children reared in English-speaking homes acquire English syntax.

Children's early vocalizations include simple subject-verb relationships. However, by the age of 3 or 4, as children mature and gain experience, they learn to reverse this word order and to use auxilliary verbs to phrase questions. It is not until the elementary school years, however, that children spontaneously produce passive sentences, such as "The hamburger was eaten by Daddy."

Semantics

The meanings of a language are the concern of **semantics.** Semantics is defined as the study of the relationship between language and the objects or events language depicts. Words that sound (and are even spelled) alike can have different meanings, depending on their usage. Compare these sentences:

Morpheme The smallest unit of meaning in a language.

Inflections Grammatical markers that change the forms of words to indicate grammatical relationships such as number and tense.

Semantics The study of the meanings of a language—the relationships between language and objects and events.

▶ ▶ ▶ ▶

7 LANGUAGE DEVELOPMENT

"I Have My Nose Too Hard Scratched. How She Hurts."

▷
▷
▷
▷

▷ Although English and German have common origins, the syntax and many other features of the languages differ. However, children who hear these languages spoken in the home acquire either one without difficulty. But an adult who learned one language as a child may have difficulty acquiring the other.

Mark Twain, the American humorist, wrote an essay "The Awful German Language" to describe the horrors of trying to learn German syntax, or word order, as an adult. Twain presents the following translation of a passage from a German newspaper to make his point. The faint-of-heart may wish to overlook the passage. For the stouthearted, here it is:

In the daybeforeyesterdayshortly after eleveno'clock Night, the inthistownstandingtavern called "The Wagoner" was downburnt. When the fire to the onthedownburninghouseresting Stork's Nest reached, flew the parent storks away. But when the byteraging, firesurrounded Nest itself caught Fire, straightway plunged the quickreturning Motherstork into the flames and died, her wings over her young ones outspread.

All German nouns have gender or sex—male, female, or neuter (none). In English, only nouns that are actually male (like *man* or *boy* or *ram)* would be referred to by pronouns like *he* or *him.* But, as Mark Twain noted in *A Tramp Abroad* (1880), the sex of German nouns is not always assigned so logically:

A tree is male, its buds are female, its leaves are neuter; horses are sexless, dogs are males, cats are females,—Tom-cats included, of course; a person's mouth, neck, bosom, elbows, fingers, nails, feet, and body are of the male sex, and his head is male or neuter according to the word selected to signify it, and *not* according to the sex of the individual who wears it,—for in Germany all the women wear either male heads or sexless ones; a person's nose, lips, shoulders, breast, hands, and toes are of the female sex; and his hair, eyes, chin, legs, knees, heart, and conscience haven't any sex at all. The inventor of the language probably got what he knew about a conscience from hearsay.

Of course, the rules of German gender seem natural to a native-born German, even if they seem arbitrary to us.

In French all things are either male or female, including rocks and avocados. I struggled with gender in high school French for four years. French children usually know what things are "male" and which are "female" by the age of 3, even though they cannot explain why (Karmiloff-Smith, 1979). I still don't know why.

► ► ► ►

A rock sank the boat.
Don't rock the boat.

In the first sentence, *rock* is a noun and the subject of the verb *sank*. The sentence probably means that the hull of a boat was ripped open by an underwater rock, causing the boat to sink. In the second sentence, *rock* is a verb. The second sentence is probably a figure of speech in which a person is being warned not to change things—not to "upset the apple cart."

Or compare these sentences:

The chicken is ready for dinner.
The lion is ready for dinner.
The shark is ready for dinner.

The first sentence probably means that a chicken has been cooked and is ready to be eaten. The second sentence probably means that a lion is hungry, or about to devour its prey. Our interpretation of the phrase "is ready for dinner" reflects our expectations concerning chickens and lions. Whether or not we expect a shark to be eaten or to do some eating would reflect on our seafood preferences or on how recently we had seen the movie *Jaws*.

Noam Chomsky differentiates between the *surface structure* and the *deep structure* of sentences. The **surface structure** involves the superficial grammatical contruction of the sentence. The surface structure of the "ready for dinner" sentences is the same. The **deep structure** of a sentence refers to its underlying meaning. The "ready for dinner" sentences clearly differ in their deep structure. "Make me a peanut butter 'n' jelly sandwich" has an ambiguous surface structure, allowing different interpretations of its deep meaning—and the typical child's response: "Poof! You're a peanut butter 'n' jelly sandwich!" In the section on theories of language development, we shall see that Chomsky believes that children have an inborn tendency to grasp the deep structures of sentences.

To 2- and 3-year-old children, the sentence "The mouse was chased by the bear" may mean the same thing as "The bear was chased by the mouse" (Strohner & Nelson, 1974). At these young ages, children find passive sentences difficult to understand. There is a relationship between cognitive development and language development, and the syntax of this sentence is lost on the child who does not yet understand the idea that the sentence is attempting to communicate. Young children, that is, have certain expectations about the behavior of bears and mice, and they interpret what they hear according to their expectations. A slightly older child may consider the sentence in which the mouse chases the bear to be "silly," but the younger child may not "hear" it correctly.

Now that we have looked at the structure of language, we can better appreciate the "child's task" of acquiring language, which we follow in the next section.

Patterns of Language Development

Now that we have become familiar with the elements of language, let us chronicle language development. Children develop language according to an invariant sequence of steps or stages, as outlined in Table 7.2. We begin with the prelinguistic vocalizations of crying, cooing, and babbling.

▶ ▶ ▶ ▶

Table 7.2   Milestones in Language Development

APPROXIMATE AGE	VOCALIZATION AND LANGUAGE
Birth	Cries
12 weeks	Markedly less crying than at 8 weeks; when talked to and nodded at, smiles, followed by squealing-gurgling sounds usually called cooing that is vowel-like in character and pitch-modulated; sustains cooing for 15–20 seconds
16 weeks	Responds to human sounds more definitely; turns head; eyes seem to search for speaker; occasionally some chuckling sounds
20 weeks	The vowel-like cooing sounds begin to be interspersed with more consonantal sounds; acoustically, all vocalizations are very different from the sounds of the mature language of the environment
6 months	Cooing changing into babbling resembling one-syllable utterances; neither vowels nor consonants have very fixed recurrences; most common utterances sound somewhat like *ma, mu, da,* or *di*
8 months	Reduplication (or more continuous repetitions) becomes frequent; intonation patterns become distinct; utterances can signal emphasis and emotions
10 months	Vocalizations are mixed with sound-play such as gurgling or bubble-blowing; appears to wish to imitate sounds, but the imitations are never quite successful*
12 months	Identical sound sequences are replicated with higher relative frequency of occurrence and words (*mamma* or *dadda*) are emerging; definite signs of understanding some words and simple commands ("Show me your eyes")
18 months	Has a definite repertoire of words—more than 3, but fewer than 50; still much babbling but now of several syllables with intricate intonation pattern; no attempt at communicating information and no frustration for not being understood; words may include items such as *thank you* or *come here,* but there is little ability to join any of the items into spontaneous two-item phrases; understanding is progressing rapidly
24 months	Vocabulary of more than 50 items (some children seem to be able to name everything in environment); begins spontaneously to join vocabulary items into two-word phrases; all phrases seem to be own creations; definite increase in communicative behavior and interest in language
30 months	Fastest increase in vocabulary with many new additions every day; no babbling at all; utterances have communicative intent; frustrated if not understood by adults; utterances consist of at least two words; many have three or even five words; sentences and phrases have characteristic child grammar; that is, they are rarely verbatim repetitions of an adult utterance; intelligibility is not very good yet, though there is great variation among children; seem to understand everything that is said to them
3 years	Vocabulary of some 1,000 words; about 80 percent of utterances are intelligible even to strangers; grammatical complexity of utterances is roughly that of colloquial adult language, although mistakes still occur
4 years	Language is well established; deviations from the adult norm tend to be more in style than in grammar

*Here we are talking about imitating the sounds of speech. Infants of this age have already imitated the pitch of their parents' sounds quite well for a number of months, as noted in Chapter 6.

The ages in this table are approximations. Parents need not assume that their children will have language problems if they are somewhat behind. Source: Adapted from E. H. Lenneberg, *Biological Foundations of Language* (New York: Wiley, 1967), pp. 128–130.

▶ ▶ ▶ ▶

Prelinguistic Vocalizations

Parents soon learn that their babies' cries can have different meanings, indicating hunger, fatigue, gas, or other sources of distress.

Crying   Newborn children, as parents are well aware, have an unlearned but highly effective form of verbal expression: crying and more crying. Studies with the **spectrograph** show that crying is a simple form of vocalizing that is accomplished by blowing air through the vocal tract. Although crying can be prolonged and vigorous and can vary in pitch, there are no distinct, well-formed sounds. In addition to serving as a signal that help is needed, crying appears to foster cardiovascular development and increase the capacity of the lungs. These physical effects do not prove that crying is necessary for proper physical development, but parents can at least take comfort in the thought that crying serves some positive functions.

Psychologist Ann M. Frodi has found that parents and other people, including children, have similar physiological responses to infant crying—bursts of autonomic activity highlighted by increases in heart rate, blood pressure, and sweating. Crying makes them feel irritated and anxious and motivates them to run to the baby to try to relieve the distress.

In a series of experiments, Frodi (1981, 1985) compared the effects on adults of preterm babies' cries to those of full-term infants. She found that the cries of preterm babies are an octave higher. They also have different rhythm, pauses and inhalation-exhalation patterns, as well as a more aversive effect on the listener. Although such cries signal greater urgency, they can threaten the formation of parent-child bonds of attachment. Frodi notes that "If there is too much crying or the sound is too grating, you may opt to relieve your own distress by trying to get away from the cry or by becoming violent" (Sobel, 1981).

Certain cries may also be signs of infant illness. Conditions ranging from fetal malnutrition to high blood pressure in the pregnant mother can give her baby a high-pitched cry of 700 to 800 cycles per second, as compared to the normal 300 to 400 cycles per second (Sobel, 1981).

The rhythm and pitch of infants' cries can also serve as aids in diagnosing a number of neurological disorders that cannot be easily detected in other ways. Barry Lester and Sandy Zeskind (Lester & Zeskind, 1982; Zeskind, 1983) of Children's Hospital Medical Center in Boston have been working to associate features of infants' cries with specific disorders. A striking example of the link between crying and a physical disorder is the syndrome called "cri du chat," French for cry of the cat. This is a genetic disorder that produces abnormalities in the brain, atypical facial features, and a high-pitched, squealy cry. Research is underway to determine whether certain patterns of crying can predict Sudden Infant Death Syndrome (SIDS), a disorder that has so far eluded many other diagnostic approaches.

Spectrograph   An instrument that converts sounds to graphs or pictures according to their acoustic qualities.

Cooing   Prelinguistic, articulated vowel-like sounds that appear to reflect feelings of positive excitement.

▶ ▶ ▶ ▶

Cooing   Crying is just about the only sound that infants make during the first month after birth. During the second month, babies also begin **cooing.** Cooing, like crying, is unlearned. Babies use their tongues when they coo, and for this reason coos take on more articulated sounds than cries. Coos are frequently vowel-like, and may resemble repeated "oohs" and "ahs." Cooing appears associated with feelings of pleasure or positive excitement. Babies tend not to coo when they are hungry, tired, or experiencing distress in the digestive tract.

Parents soon learn that different cries and coos have different meanings and indicate different things: hunger, gas, or pleasure at being held or rocked.

Although cries and coos are innate, they can be modified by experience, a fact that provides some limited support for learning-theory views of language development. For example, cooing increases when parents respond positively to it by talking, smiling, and imitation. Early parent-child "conversations," in which parents respond to coos and then pause so that the baby can coo again, may foster early infant awareness of "turn-taking" as a way of verbally relating to other people.

Remember that true language has *semanticity;* that is, sounds (or signs, in the case of ASL) are symbols. For this reason, crying and cooing are prelinguistic events—not true language. Cries and coos do not represent objects or events. By about 8 months cooing decreases markedly. By about the fifth or sixth month, children have already begun to babble.

Babbling   **Babbling** is the first vocalizing that sounds like human speech. Babbling children utter phonemes found in several languages, including the throaty German *ch,* the clicks of certain African tribes, and rolling *r*'s (Atkinson et al., 1970; McNeill, 1970). In their babbling, babies frequently combine consonants and vowels, as in "ba," "ga," and, sometimes, the much valued "dada." "Dada" at first is purely coincidental (sorry, you Dads), despite the family's jubilation over its appearance.

Babbling, like crying and cooing, appears inborn. Children whose parents speak very different-sounding languages all seem to babble the same sounds, including many they would not have had the opportunity to hear (Oller, 1981). Deaf children at first babble as much as children who can hear, even though they cannot hear the speech of others. Babbling might produce sounds (or, in the case of deaf babies, vibrations in the throat) that children repeat because of their novelty. In this sense, babbling can be considered a form of play.

Despite the fact that it is innate, babbling is readily modified by experience. In one of the classic studies of the effects of reinforcement on babies' vocalizations, Harriet Rheingold, Jacob Gewirtz, and Helen Ross (1959) demonstrated that smiling, soft sounds, or pats on the infant's abdomen can increase the frequency of babbling. Infants also babble more when adults imitate them or simply attend to their babbling (Haugan & McIntire, 1972).

In verbal interactions between infants and adults, the adults frequently repeat the syllables produced by their babies. They are likely to say "Dadada" or "Bababa" instead of simply "Da" or "Ba." Such redundancy apparently helps infants discriminate these sounds (Goodsitt et al., 1984) from others, and further encourages them to imitate their parents.

By 8 months most infants will attend to and try to "join in" or interrupt the conversations of others (Rubin & Fisher, 1982). Their heads may turn back and forth from one speaker to another as though they were at a tennis match. Some 8-month-olds will even shout for attention.

Children seem to single out the types of phonemes used consistently in the home within a few months. By the age of 9 or 10 months these phonemes are repeated regularly. "Foreign" phonemes begin to drop out. Although there is an overall reduction in the varieties of phonemes that infants produce, their use of combinations of sounds creates a greater diversity in the overall numbers of sounds they produce. The babbling of deaf infants never begins to approximate the sounds of the parents' language, and deaf children tend to lapse into silence by the end of the first year, further suggestive of the role that experience plays in language development.

▶ ▶ ▶ ▶

Babbling   The child's first vocalizations that have the sounds of speech.

Echolalia (eck-oh-LAY-lee-uh). *Automatic repetition of sounds or words.*

Intonation *The use of pitches of varying levels to help communicate meaning.*

Receptive vocabulary *The extent of one's knowledge of the meanings of words that are communicated to one by others.*

Expressive vocabulary *The sum total of the words that one can use in the production of language.*

After infants have been babbling for a few months, parents often believe that their children are having conversations with themselves. At 10 to 12 months infants tend to repeat syllables, showing what linguists refer to as **echolalia.** [*] Parents overhear them going on and on, repeating consonant–vowel combinations ("Ah-bah-bah-bah-bah," etc.), pausing, then switching to other combinations.

Toward the end of the first year, infants are also using patterns of rising and falling **intonation** that resemble the sounds of adult speech. Given this intonational quality and the loss of many "foreign" phonemes, it may sound as if the infant is trying to speak the parents' language. In fact, parents may think that their children are "babbling *in* English," or in whatever tongue is spoken in the home.

Although babbling, like crying and cooing, is a prelinguistic event, infants usually understand much of what others are saying well before they utter their own first words. Comprehension precedes production, and infants demonstrate comprehension with their actions and gestures.

Development of Vocabulary

Vocabulary development refers to the child's learning of the meanings of words. Generally speaking, children's **receptive vocabulary** development outpaces their **expressive vocabulary** development. This means that at any given time, they can understand more words than they can use.

Now let us have a look at that exciting milestone—a child's first words.

The Child's First Words(!)   Ah, that long-awaited first word! What a thrill! What a milestone! Sad to say, many parents miss this milestone. They are not quite sure when their infants utter their first word, often because the first word is not pronounced with perfect clarity.

First words tend to be brief, consisting of one or two syllables. Each syllable is likely to consist of a consonant followed by a vowel. Parental comprehension is also impaired by the fact that both consonant and vowel may vary from usage to usage. "Ball" may be pronounced "ba," "bee," or even "pah" on separate occasions (Ferguson & Farwell, 1975).

By about 18 months, children are producing nearly two dozen words (see Figure 7.3). Many of them are quite familiar, such as *no, cookie, mama, hi,* and *eat.* Others, like *allgone* and *bye-bye,* may not be found in the dictionary, but they function clearly as words. That is, they are used consistently to symbolize the same meaning, which is the standard suggested by Scollan (1976, 1979) to determine what is a word for an infant.

Vocabulary acquisition is slow at first. According to Katherine Nelson (1973), it generally takes children three to four months to achieve a ten-word vocabulary after their first word is spoken. Children at 18 months may be able to utter only three to 50 words, but, as suggested in Table 7.3, they can understand simple commands of many more words at about 12 months.

Figure 7.3 represents a classic study in the learning of words reported by Madorah Elizabeth Smith in 1926. According to Smith, the average child

---

[*]The term *echolalia* is used in a different way by psychologists concerned with behavior disorders, as we shall see in Chapter 14.

▶ ▶ ▶ ▶

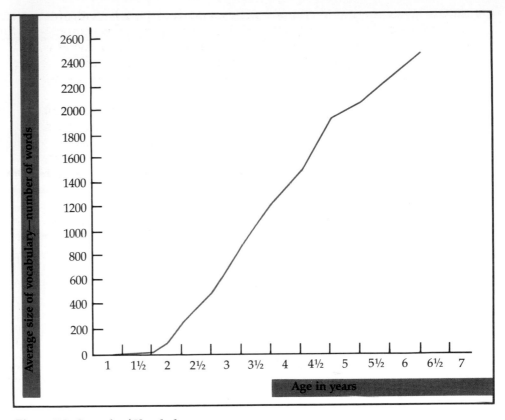

Figure 7.3 Growth of Vocabulary
The average child can speak perhaps three words by the end of the first year. Growth is slow until 18 months or so, when there is a minor "explosion." Children tend to acquire some 250 additional words by the second birthday.

(whom I have never met) has perhaps three words by the end of the first year. Within the next few months there is a very minor "explosion" to about 19 words, but then another period of slow acquisition to about 18 months. But now comes a continuous blossoming in vocabulary, with children acquiring about 250 words during the next six months (by the age of 2), and hundreds of words each year thereafter.

Nominals More than half (65 percent) of children's first words comprise what Katherine Nelson (1973) refers to as "general nominals" and "specific nominals." General nominals are like nouns in that they include the names of classes of objects (car, ball, doggy), animals (doggy, poo-cat), and people (boy). But they also include both personal and relative pronouns (she and that). Specific nominals are proper nouns, such as Daddy (used as the father's name, not the category of men to which he belongs) and Rover. As noted in Chapter 6, the attention of infants seems to be captured by movement. Nelson (1973, 1981) found that of children's first 50 words, the most common words were names for people, animals, and objects that move (Mommy, car, doggy) or that can be moved (dolly, milky, diapy); action words (bye-bye); a number of modifiers (big, hot); and expressive words (no, hi, ooh).

Nelson found a surprising diversity in the nominals used by these chil-

▶ ▶ ▶ ▶

Table 7.3 Some Uses of Children's Two-Word Utterances

TYPE OF UTTERANCE	EXAMPLE	TYPE OF KNOWLEDGE SUGGESTED BY UTTERANCE
Naming, locating	That ball. Car there. See doggy.	Objects exist and they have names.
Negating	Milk allgone. No eat. Not doggy.	Objects may become used up or leave. People may choose *not* to do things.
Demanding, expressing desire	Want Mommy. More milk. Want candy.	Objects can be reinstated; quantities can be increased.
Agent-action	Mommy go. Daddy sit. Doggy bark.	People, animals, and objects act or move.
Action-object	Hit you.	Actions can have objects.
Agent-object	Daddy car.	People do things to objects (although, in this two-word utterance, the action is not stated).
Action-location	Sit chair.	A person (unstated) is engaging in an act in a place.
Action-recipient	Give Mama.	An object (unstated) is being moved in relation to a person.
Action-instrument	Cut knife.	An instrument is being used for an act.
Attribution	Pretty Mommy. Big glass.	People or objects have traits or qualities.
Possession	Mommy cup. My shoe.	People possess objects.
Question	Where Mommy? Where milk?	People can provide information when they are prompted.

Adapted from Slobin, 1972.

dren, reflecting the objects that surrounded them and what was important to their parents. Some children, for example, may number words as exotic as "ohgi" (yogurt) and "bay" (bagel) among their first 50 or so, whereas others accumulate more traditional nominals such as duck, doggy, cookie, and diapy.

Referential and Expressive Styles in Language Development Katherine Nelson (1981) also found that some children seem to prefer a *referential* approach in their language development, whereas others take a more *expressive* approach.

Children who show the **referential language style** use language primarily to label objects in their environments. Their early vocabularies consist mainly of nominals. Children who use an **expressive language style** use language primarily as a means for engaging in social interaction. Children with an expressive style use more pronouns and many words expressive of social routines, such as "stop," "more," and "all gone." Nelson found that most children actually use a combination of the styles.

Why do some children adopt a referential style and others an expressive style? It may be that some children are naturally oriented toward the world of objects, whereas others are primarily interested in social relationships. Nelson also finds that the mother's ways of teaching her children play a role. Some mothers focus on labeling objects for their children as soon as they notice their

Referential language style
Using language primarily as a means for labeling objects.

Expressive language style
Using language primarily as a means for engaging in social interaction.

vocabularies expanding in the second year. Other mothers are more oriented toward social interactions themselves, teaching their children to say "hi," "please," and "thank you."

Nelson (1981) also found the expressive style more common among later-born children. For one thing, the older brothers and sisters of later-born children are more likely to issue commands (such as "Don't do that," and "Let me play with that now") to control their behavior than to name objects. Parents, too, have less time to label objects for later-born children. The more children in the home, the more likely parents seem to be to issue directives than teach labels.

Overextension   It seems that young children are motivated to talk about more objects than they have words for. And so they frequently extend the meaning of one word to refer to things and actions for which they do not have words (see Table 7.4). Eve Clark (1973, 1975) studied diaries of infants' language development and found that overextensions are generally based on perceived similarities in function or form between the original object or action and the new one to which the first word is being extended. She provides the example of the word "em," which one infant originally used to designate a worm, and then extended to include other small moving animals and objects, such as insects and waving grass. Another example is "mooi," which one child originally used to designate the moon. Then "mooi" became overextended to designate all round objects, including the letter O and cookies and cakes.

The diaries also provided Eve Clark (1973) with case studies that showed that overextensions gradually pull back to their proper references as the child's vocabulary and ability to classify objects develops. Consider the example of a boy who first refers to a dog as a "bow-wow." The word *bow-wow* then becomes overextended to also refer to horses, cats, sheep, and cows. These other "bow wows" are similar to dogs in many ways, of course. They all move on four legs,

Table 7.4   Some Examples of Allyn's Speech During the Third Year

(Objecting to something I say:) "No, that is not a good talk to say. I don't like that."
(Describing her younger sister:) "Jordan is very laughy today."
(On the second floor of our home:) "This is not home. This is upstairs."
(Objecting to my leaving:) "Stay here for a couple of whiles."
(After I sniff meatballs and A-B-C's:) "Did you have a great smell?"
(When I ask if I may have the book she is looking at:) "You may see it after I read it all up."
(Directing me to turn up the stereo:) "Make it a big louder, not a small louder."
"I see two policemans."
"I goed on the choo-choo."
"I gived it to Mommy."
(Requesting a nickel:) "Give me another money."
(Explaining that she and Mommy are finished singing a song:) "We singed it all up."
(Requesting an empty cup:) "Give me that. I need it to drink nothing."
(After I thank Allyn for giving me something:) "Thank you for asking me that you wanted it."
"That car is blue, just like us's."
(When I am holding Allyn but she apparently wants to feel closer:) "I want you to pick up me."
   ("What am I doing?") "Pick upping me."
(Responding to "Am I a good Daddy to you?":) "I think you're a silly Daddy to me."
(Directing me to turn on the stereo:) "Push the button and make it too loud." (A minute later:)
   "Make it more louder."
(Refusing to answer a question:) "I don't want you to ask that to me."
(Confessing what she did with several coins:) "I taked those money and put it on the shelf."

▶ ▶ ▶ ▶

have eyes, ears, and other recognizable attributes. In effect, "bow-wow" comes to mean something akin to "familiar walking and running animal." Next the boy learns to use the word "moo" to refer to cows. But "bow-wow" still remains extended to horses, cats, and sheep. Then the boy acquires the word "gee-gee" for horses.

As the boy's vocabulary develops, he acquires a word for sheep ("baa") and the words "doggy" and "horsie." So dogs and cats may now be referred to either with "bow-wow" or "doggy," and horses may be called "gee-gee" or "horsie." Eventually, each animal has one or more correct names. Cats, for example, can become "cat," "kitty," "pussycat," and other variations, but not "meow."

Children overextend well past their first words. At the age of 2½, Allyn made the following overextensions: "We taked Jordan [her younger sister] to the doctor to get her *fixed*," and "Lisa is swinging higher but I'm swinging *small* [lower]." One particular overextension, a description of the springtime, was inadvertently poetic: "The trees are sticking out their leaves." Other overextensions are found in Table 7.4.

Language and Cognitive Development   Language and cognitive development become strongly interwoven. The child gradually gains the capacity to discriminate between animals on the basis of distinct features, such as size, patterns of movement, relationships to people, and other behaviors, including the sounds they make. At the same time, the child will also be acquiring proper words that represent superordinate categories, such as "mammal" and "animal." But the correct application of these concepts may take years. Later we shall consider cognitive approaches to understanding language development.

Knowledge of the meaning of words is the single best indicator of a child's overall level of intellectual functioning, and adults can continue to add to their vocabularies for a lifetime. Note carefully, however, that many children who begin speaking relatively late can fully understand what is being said by others and show no intellectual deficits as the years go by. I have a friend whose son was still "staunchly resisting talking," as my friend put it, at 2 years 3 months. However, once he began speaking, brief sentences followed one-word utterances almost overnight, and today he is at grade level in verbal skills.

Development of Syntax: Telegraphic Speech

Although children first use one-word utterances, these utterances appear to express the meanings found in complete sentences. Harvard University psychologist Roger Brown (1973) calls brief expressions that have the meanings of sentences telegraphic speech. When we as adults write telegrams, we are allowed only a certain number of words. Therefore we use principles of syntax to cut out all the "unnecessary" words. "Home Tuesday" might stand for "I expect to be home on Tuesday." Similarly, only the "essential" words are used in children's telegraphic speech—in particular, nouns, verbs, and some modifiers.

Mean Length of Utterance   Brown (1973, 1977) has extensively studied telegraphic speech in children. He has found it useful to describe telegraphic speech in terms of children's **mean length of utterance,** or MLU. The MLU is defined as the average number of morphemes children use in their sentences. In Figure

Mean length of utterance The average number of phonemes used in an utterance.

▶ ▶ ▶ ▶

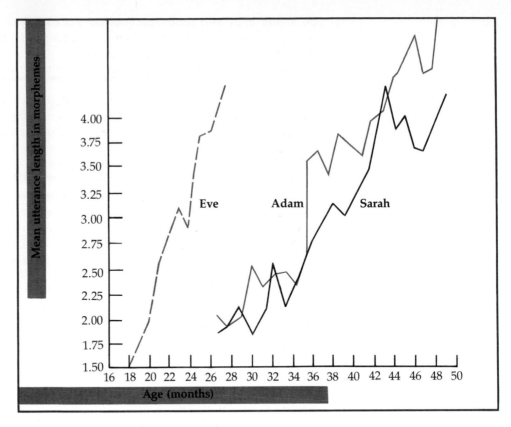

Figure 7.4 Mean Length of Utterance for Three Children
Some children begin speaking earlier than others. However, the mean length of utterance increases rapidly once speech begins.

7.4, we see the relationship between chronological age and MLU for three children tracked by Brown: Eve, Adam, and Sarah. The patterns of growth in MLU are similar for each child, showing swift upward movement, broken by intermittent and brief regressions. Figure 7.4 also shows us something about individual differences. Eve was precocious compared to Adam and Sarah, extending her MLU at much earlier ages. However, as suggested earlier, the receptive language of all three children would have exceeded their expressive language at any given time. Also, Eve's earlier extension of MLU does not guarantee that she will show more complex expressive language than Adam and Sarah at maturity.

Let us now consider the syntactic features of two types of telegraphic speech: the *holophrase* and *two-word utterances*.

Holophrases Single words that are used to express complex meanings are called **holophrases.** For example, *Mama* may be used by the child to signify meanings as varied as "There goes Mama," "Come here, Mama," and "You are Mama." Similarly, *poo-cat* can signify "There is a pussycat," "That stuffed animal looks just like my pussycat," "I want you to give me my pussycat right now!" Most children teach their parents their intended meaning quite readily. Not only do they utter the holophrase; they also gesture, use intonations, and apply reinforcements in the manner of professional learning theorists—that is,

Holophrase A single word used to express complex meanings.

▶ ▶ ▶ ▶

by acting delighted when parents do as requested, and crying when they do not.

Two-Word Sentences Toward the end of the second year, children begin to speak in simple two-word sentences.

The Pivot and Open-Class Word Controversy In the 1960s Martin Braine (1963) described the grammar of two-word sentences as consisting of a *pivot word* and an *X* or *open-class word*.

According to Braine, open-class words usually express concrete concepts that could be described in a single word. *Mommy, Daddy, car,* and *milk* are open class words. Pivot words are often small, such as *go,* and are attached to the (usually larger) open-class words. "Mommy go," "Daddy go," and "Car go" are utterances with the pivot word in the second position. In "More milk" the pivot word is in the first position. "Big," "my," "see," and "allgone" are other examples of pivot words. Pivot words would not be used by themselves, and they would stand for phrases. In "Car go," *go* stands for "is going." In "More milk," *more* stands for "I want more."

Recent observations have raised serious questions about the pivot-word and open-class-word approach to children's two-word utterances. For example, "pivot words" such as "bye-bye," "allgone," and "hi" are frequently used by themselves.

Two-word utterances also tend to be more complex than Braine suggested (Bates et al., 1982). Consider an illustration offered by Lois Bloom (1973). Bloom recorded a child's utterance "Mommy sock." According to Braine, "Mommy" would probably be the descriptive pivot word in the utterance. The utterance would mean "The sock is Mommy's," in the sense that "allgone sock" might mean "The sock is lost." But Bloom noticed that the child also said "Mommy sock" when mother was dressing the child with the *child's* sock. Therefore, "Mommy sock" could also mean "Mommy is putting my sock on my foot."

Types of Two-Word Sentences Two-word utterances, like holophrases, are examples of telegraphic speech. In the sentence "That ball," the words *is* and *a* are implied. Several types of two-word utterances are used by young children and are listed in Table 7.3. Each shows a certain level of cognitive development and grasp of the appropriate syntax to express the concepts involved.

Two-word utterances appear at about the same time in the development of languages other than English (Slobin, 1973). Morever, the types of two-word utterances that tend to be used first in English (for example, agent-action, action-object, location, and possession) also tend to be used first in languages as divergent as Luo (an African tongue), German, Russian, and Turkish (Slobin, 1971, 1983). This is one of the finer examples of the point that language develops in a series of steps that appear to be invariable. The lack of impact of wide cultural differences in the developmental sequence can be seen as supporting the view that the human tendency to develop language according to universal processes is innate.

Two-word utterances, while brief and telegraphic, still show an early understanding of syntax. The child will say "Sit chair" to tell a parent to sit in a chair, not "Chair sit." (Apes do not reliably make this distinction.) The child will say "My shoe," not "Shoe my," to show possession. "Mommy go" means

▶ ▶ ▶ ▶

On Yum-Yum, Da-Da, Wa-Wa, and Poo-Poo: Some Thoughts on "Motherese"

▷
▷
▷
▷
▷   If you spend time in the company of infants, you are likely to hear words such as "yum-yum," "da-da," "wa-wa," and "poo-poo." Sometimes they will even be uttered by the infants. But much of the time if the infants do not utter these "words," their parents will. For this reason, utterances such as these have been labeled "baby talk" or "motherese." But "motherese" is a limiting term, because fathers, siblings, and people who are not related at all, including older children, also use motherese when talking to babies (Jacobson et al., 1983; Tomasello & Mannle, 1985).

Developmentalists who have studied motherese find that it has a number of characteristics (Blewitt, 1983; Jacobson et al., 1983; Mervis & Mervis, 1982; Schachter & Strage, 1982):

1.   Motherese is spoken more slowly

Parents model certain sounds or words clearly, like "Mama" or "Dada," and encourage children to repeat them. Parents also tend to repeat the sounds that their children make, and to reinforce them heavily for any early language efforts.

► ► ► ►

than speech addressed to adults. Motherese is spoken at a higher pitch, and there are distinct pauses between ideas.

2. Sentences are brief, and adults make the effort to speak in a grammatically correct manner.

3. Sentences are simple in syntax. There is focus on nouns, verbs, and just a few modifiers.

4. The diminutive morpheme "-y" is frequently added to nouns. "Dad" becomes "Daddy," and "horse" becomes "horsey."

5. Motherese is repetitive. Adults repeat sentences several times, sometimes using minor variations, as in "Show me your nose." "Where is your nose?" "Can you touch your nose?" "Come on, touch your nose with your finger." Adults also repeat children's utterances, often rephrasing them in an effort to expand children's awareness of their expressive opportunities. If the child says, "Baby shoe," the mother may reply, "Yes, that is your shoe. Do you want me to put it on your foot? Shall Mommy put the shoe on baby's foot?"

6. Motherese includes a type of repetition called reduplication. "Yummy" becomes "yummy-yummy." "Daddy" may alternate with "Da-da."

7. Vocabulary is concrete, referring, when possible, to objects that are in the immediate environment. In general, readily recognizable labels are used. For example, stuffed lions and leopards may be referred to as "kitties" or "pussycats." Geese as well as ducks become "duckies." This purposeful overextension is intended to avoid confusing the child by adding too many new labels.

8. Objects may be overdescribed by being given compound labels. Rabbits may become "bunny-rabbits," and cats may become "kitty-cats." In this way parents may try to be sure that they are connecting with the child by using at least one label that the child will recognize.

9. Parents speak for the children, as in "Is baby tired?" "Oh, we're so tired." "Does baby want to go nappy?" "We want to take our nap now, don't we?" This parent is pretending to have a two-way conversation with the child. In this way parents seem to be trying to help their children express themselves by offering children models of sentences that they can use later on.

10. Users of motherese stay a step ahead of the child. As children's vocabularies grow and their syntax develops, adults step up their own language levels—remaining just ahead of the child, like the carrot and the horse. In this way adults seem to be encouraging the child to continue to play catch-up.

And so adults and other children use a variety of strategies to communicate with young children and to draw them out. Does it work? Does motherese foster language development?

Research in the effects of motherese is supportive of its use. The short, simple sentences used in motherese are more likely to produce a response from the child than are complex sentences (Glanzer & Dodd, 1975). Children who hear their utterances repeated and recast do seem to learn from the adults who are modeling the new expressions (Nelson, 1977). Repetition of children's vocalizations also appears to be one method of reinforcing vocalizing.

In sum, motherese may be of significant help in fostering children's language development. There is no evidence that it hurts. So the next time you're with a young child, don't be self-conscious—just go ahead and do all the "Does-baby-love-kitty-cat?-Yes!"-ing you like.

Mommy is leaving, while "Go Mommy" expresses the wish for Mommy to go away. For this reason, "Go Mommy" is not heard frequently. Moreover, when children between 18 to 30 months are asked to repeat sentences, their word order generally shows clear grasp of syntax, even when their utterances are markedly telegraphic. For example, children asked to repeat "I see the doggy" are more likely to say "See doggy" than "Doggy see." That is, they show that they are locating the dog, not that the dog is the agent of the act.

▶ ▶ ▶ ▶

7 LANGUAGE DEVELOPMENT

Development of Syntax: Toward More Complex Language

Between the ages of 2 and 3, children's sentence structure generally expands to include the words that were missing in telegraphic speech.

Articles, Conjunctions, and Possessive and Demonstrative Adjectives   It is usually during the third year that children add to their vocabulary an impressive array of articles (*a, an, the*), conjunctions (*and, but, or*), possessive and demonstrative adjectives (*your, her, that*), pronouns (*she, him, one*), and prepositions (*in, on, over, around, under,* and *through*). Their continued use of syntax to produce words and phrases is further evident in language oddities such as "your one" instead of "yours," and "his one" instead of, simply, "his."

Combinatory Rules   It is also usually between the ages of 2 and 3 that children show knowledge of rules for combining phrases and clauses into complex sentences. An early example of a complex sentence is "You goed and Mommy goed, too." A more advanced example is "What will we do when we get there?" In this example we can note the use of the interrogatory "when," the formation of the future tense through use of the auxiliary verb "will," and the correct use of the idiomatic English "to get" to a place. During the third year, *and* is the child's most frequently used conjunction (Bloom et al., 1980). Other commonly used connective words include *when, what,* and *because. But, if, that,* and *then* may also sprinkle the child's speech at this age, but not so frequently.

Overregularization   One of the more intriguing language developments is based on the fact that children acquire grammatical rules as they learn language. At very young ages they tend to apply these rules rather strictly, even in cases that call for exceptions. But first consider the formation of the past tense and of plurals in English. The general rules are to add *d* or *ed* phonemes to verbs and *s* or *z* phonemes to nouns. Thus, *walk* becomes *walked* and *look* becomes *looked. Pussycat* becomes *pussycats* and *doggy* becomes *doggies.*

But then there are irregular verbs and irregular nouns. For example, *see* becomes *saw, sit* becomes *sat,* and *go* becomes *went. Sheep* remains *sheep* (plural) and *child* becomes *children.*

At first it seems that children learn a small number of these irregular verbs by imitating their parents. As noted by Stan Kuczaj (1977, 1978), 2-year-olds tend to form them correctly—temporarily! However, then they become aware of the syntactic rules for forming the past tense and plurals in English. As a result, they tend to make charming "errors" (Bowerman, 1982). Some 3- to 5-year-olds, for example, are more likely to say "I seed it" than "I saw it," and more likely to say "Mommy sitted down" than "Mommy sat down." They are likely to talk about the "gooses" and "sheeps" they "seed" on the farm, and about all the "childs" they ran into at the playground. This tendency to regularize the irregular is termed **overregularization.**

Parents may be acutely sensitive to the fact that their children were forming the past tense of irregular verbs correctly, and that then they began to make errors. The important fact for them to remember is that overregularization *does represent an advance in the development of syntax.* Overregularization stems from accurate knowledge of grammatical rules—not from faulty language acquisition. In another year or two, *mouses* will become boringly transformed into *mice,* and Mommy will no longer have *sitted* down. So parents should enjoy

Overregularization The application of regular grammatical rules for forming inflections (e.g., past tense and plurals) to irregular verbs and nouns.

▶ ▶ ▶ ▶

This is a wug   Now there are two of them.   There are two _____ .

Figure 7.5 Wugs
Many bright, sophisticated college students have not heard of "wugs." Here are several wugs—actually, make-believe animals used in a study to learn whether preschool children can use rules of grammar to form the plurals of unfamiliar nouns.

overregularization while they can and not worry about their children's syntax.

Of course, there are also some charming mixes of the regular and the irregular as language development undergoes transitions: Consider Allyn's reference to turning down a particular aisle in the supermarket at age 2½: "Do you know what I *sawed* when you goed there? Lobsters!" Or: "I thoughted that you boughted it for me." If you think that you "have it bad," remember this: For children who are overregularizing, it is not unusual for things that are bad to become "worser," and for things that are really worser to become "worsest."

Wugs   In an experiment designed to show that preschool children are not just clever mimics in their formation of plurals, but have actually grasped rules of grammar, Berko (1958) showed children pictures of nonexistent animals, as in Figure 7.5. She first showed them a single animal and said, "This is a wug." Then she showed them a picture of two animals and said, "Now there are two of them." Then she said, "There are two _____," asking the children to finish the sentence. Ninety-one percent of the children said "wugs," correctly pluralizing the bogus word. This percentage was approximated in similar language tasks.

Pronouns and Prepositions   As language develops beyond the third year, children show increasing facility with the use of pronouns such as *it* and *she*. Their facility with prepositions such as *in, before,* or *on,* which represent physical or temporal relationships among objects and events, also develops. Cognitive development is intertwined with language development, so that during the early school years children come to understand words that describe relationships between people, such as *uncle* and *aunt*. Aunt Elizabeth is no longer simply the person designated repeatedly as Aunt Elizabeth. She is now understood to be Aunt Elizabeth *because* she is Mother's sister.

Questions   Children's first questions are telegraphic and characterized by a rising pitch (which signifies a question mark in English) at the end. "More milky?" for example, can be translated into "May I have more milk?", "Would you like more milk?", or "Is there more milk?", depending on the context.

It is usually during the third year that the *wh* questions appear. Consistent with the child's general cognitive development, certain *wh* questions (*what, who,* and *where*) appear earlier than others (*why, when, which,* and *how*) (Bloom et al., 1982). *Why* is frequently too philosophical for the 2-year-old, and *how* too involved. Two-year-olds are also likely to be now-oriented, so that *when,* too, is of less than immediate concern. By the fourth year, most children are spontaneously producing *why, when,* and *how* questions.

► ► ► ►

By the fourth year, children are asking each other and adults questions, taking turns talking, and engaging in lengthy conversations.

These *wh* words are initially tacked on to the beginnings of sentences. "Where Mommy go?" can stand for "Where is Mommy going?", "Where did Mommy go?", or "Where will Mommy go?", and its meaning must be derived from context. Later on auxiliary verbs will be added, so that the child can indicate whether the question concerns the present, past, or future. Auxiliary verbs also permit the child to say "I want you to tell me what you *are* doing" instead of "I want you to tell me what you doing"; and "What are you doing?" instead of "What you doing?"

"What are you doing?" may seem like a rather simple question to phrase. But note that it involves (a) tacking on the *wh* word ("What"), (b) reversing the normal subject–verb word order ("are you" instead of "you are"), and (c) separating the auxiliary verb ("are") from the participle "doing." All this is automatic enough to adults and older children, but they may call for some grammatical acrobatics on the part of the 2-year-old.

Passive Sentences   Passive sentences, such as "The food is eaten by the dog," are difficult for 2- and 3-year-olds to understand and are almost never produced by them. In a fascinating study of children's comprehension carried out by Katherine Nelson and a colleague (Strohner & Nelson, 1974), 2- to 5-year-olds acted out a number of sentences that were read to them with puppets and toys. Two- and 3-year-olds in the study made errors in acting out passive sentences (for example, "The car was hit by the truck") 70 percent of the time. Older children had less difficulty interpreting the meanings of passive sentences correctly. However, most children usually do not produce passive sentences spontaneously even during the early grammar-school years of 5 and 6.

Pragmatics   **Pragmatics** in language development refers to the practical aspects of communication. For example, children are showing pragmatism when they adjust their speech to fit the social situation. How many times have we heard children gushing with excitement and rudeness in their interactions with one another, and then standing still and carefully articulating "Yes, sir," when they are dressed down by an adult?

Children also show greater formality in their choice of words and syntax when they are role-playing high-status figures, such as teachers or physicians,

Pragmatics The practical aspects of communication. Adaptation of language to fit the social context.

► ► ► ►

PATTERNS OF LANGUAGE DEVELOPMENT

in their games. They also say "please" more often when making requests of high-status people (Rice, 1982, 1984).

Children also show pragmatism in their adoption of motherese when they are addressing a younger child. Four-year-olds' motherese shows brief sentences, high pitch, and precise articulation, similar to the motherese of adults (Sachs & Devin, 1976; Tomasello & Mannle, 1985).

Pragmatism provides another example of the ways in which cognitive and language development are intertwined. Preschoolers tend to be **egocentric;** that is, they show some difficulty in taking the viewpoints of other people. A 2-year-old telling another child "Gimme my book," without specifying which book, is not just assuming that the other child knows what she herself knows. She is also overestimating the clearness of her communication and how well she is understood (Beal & Flavell, 1983). Once children can perceive the world as through the eyes of others, however, they advance in their abilities to make themselves understood to others. Now the child recognizes that the other child will require a description of the book or of its location in order to carry out the request.

Developments in the "Understanding of Understanding"   Young children fail to understand much that is being said to them, but they often do not know it. It takes a bit of linguistic sophistication to be able to pinpoint what we are missing in our comprehension of speech.

Cognitive psychologist John Flavell and his colleagues (1981) demonstrated this point in a study with kindergartners and second-graders. The children were given the experimental task of making a building from blocks on the basis of the audiotaped instructions of another child. What the children did not know is that the instructions were pieced together to be purposefully ambiguous, incomplete, and self-contradictory. Still, the children dutifully went about constructing their imperfect edifices.

The second-graders were more likely than the kindergartners to pause or show confusion at the flawed passages. They were more aware that they could not comprehend what was being said to them. The kindergartners, like the older children, built flawed structures, but they took the instructions more in stride.

In Chapter 8 we shall see that children become progressively more aware of their own cognitive processes. This self-awareness is termed *metacognition,* and children who show it develop more efficient strategies for solving problems. Awareness of the possibilities created by language, and of the limitations of language, are closely related to metacognition. Such awareness offers a good example of the relationships between language and cognition.

Other Language Developments   By the fourth year, children are asking adults and each other questions, taking turns talking, and engaging in lengthy conversations. By the age of 6, their vocabularies have expanded to 10,000 words, give or take a few thousand. By 7 to 9, most children realize that words can have different meanings, and they become entertained by riddles and jokes that require semantic sophistication ("What's black and white, etc."). By the age of 8 or 9, children are able to form "tag questions," in which the question is tagged on to the end of a declarative sentence (Dennis et al., 1982). "You want more ice cream, don't you?" and "You're sick, aren't you?" are examples of tag questions. Between elementary school and high school years, vocabulary continues

► ► ► ►

Metaphor *The use of words or phrases characteristic of one situation in another situation. A figure of speech that dramatizes a description by applying imagery from another situation.*

to grow rapidly. Children also make subtle advances in articulation and in the capacity to use complex syntax.

In Chapter 8 we shall see that appreciation of **metaphors,** such as "The ship *plowed* through the water," tends to develop at about the time of puberty. Appreciation of metaphor is made possible, according to Jean Piaget, by the fact that many children are beginning to show the capacity for abstract or *formal operational* thought at about this time.

Individual Differences in Language Development

Although the sequences of development are the same from child to child, there are individual differences in the rate of language development. Moreover, there are sex and social-class differences. As we shall see in Chapter 12, girls may be slightly superior to boys in their language development. Infant girls may begin to build their vocabularies a bit faster than infant boys, and appear to articulate (pronounce words) more clearly. By adolescence, girls, as a group, are superior to boys in spelling skills, punctuation, reading comprehension, and verbal reasoning (Maccoby & Jacklin, 1974).

It appears that children from families of lower socioeconomic status have poorer vocabularies than children from middle- or upper-class families (Lesser et al., 1965). When we consider that knowledge of the meanings of words is the single strongest predictor of overall scores on tests of intellectual functioning, it is not surprising, then, that children from middle- and upper-class families, as a group, attain higher test scores.

Many of the children from poorer homes are black, and, as we shall see in Chapter 9, political as well as developmental issues are involved in trying to account for and erase these differences. But even though children from poor families may know fewer words, they seem to acquire knowledge of syntax at about the same rate as other children. Later in the chapter we shall see, however, that the syntax of Black English differs from that of general English, so that some observers have (erroneously) concluded that the syntax of Black English is inferior.

Theories of Language Development

Countless billions of children have learned the languages spoken by their parents and others around them. They have continued to pass these languages down, with minor changes, from generation to generation. In this section we discuss the insights and limitations of learning-theory, nativist, and cognitive approaches to understanding language development.

Learning-Theory Views

In previous chapters we saw that learning plays a role in motor development and perceptual development. The role of learning in language development is even more obvious. Children who are reared in English-speaking homes learn English, not Japanese or Russian.

The principles of learning that have been used to explain language development include imitation and reinforcement.

▶ ▶ ▶ ▶

The Role of Imitation From a social-learning perspective, parents serve as **models.** It seems likely that many vocabulary words, especially nouns and verbs, including irregular verbs, are learned by observing and imitating models.

Children at first tend to repeat accurately the irregular verb forms they observe—a modeling effect. But the social-learning view of learning is limited by the fact that children begin to overregularize irregular verbs once they attain an understanding of syntax.

More generally, as noted by cognitive psychologist George Rebok (1987), imitative learning does not explain why children spontaneously utter phrases and sentences that they have not heard. Parents are unlikely to say things such as "bye-bye sock" and "allgone Daddy," but children do.

Stan Kuczaj (1982) notes that children sometimes seem to steadfastly avoid imitating certain language forms that are suggested by adults, even when the adults try repeatedly to model these forms. Note the following exchange recorded by Kuczaj (1982, p. 48) between 2-year-old Ben and a (very frustrated!) adult:

> BEN: I like these candy. I like they.
> ADULT: You like them?
> BEN: Yes. I like they.
> ADULT: Say *them.*
> BEN: Them.
> ADULT: Say "I like *them.*"
> BEN: I like them.
> ADULT: Good.
> BEN: I'm good. These candy good too.
> ADULT: Are they good?
> BEN: Yes. I like they. You like they?

Ben is not resisting the model because of obstinancy. He does repeat "I like them" verbatim, when asked to do so. But when he is given the opportunity, afterward, to construct the object "them," he reverts to using the subjective form, "they." Ben is more likely at this period in his development to use his (erroneous) understanding of syntax spontaneously to produce his own language, instead of just imitating his model. His language production is active.

The Role of Reinforcement In his landmark book, *Verbal Behavior,* psychologist B. F. Skinner outlined his view of the role of reinforcement in language development: "A child acquires verbal behavior when relatively unpatterned vocalizations, selectively reinforced, assume forms which produce appropriate consequences in a given verbal community" (Skinner, 1957, p. 31).

Skinner allows that prelinguistic vocalizations such as cooing and babbling may be inborn. But parents reinforce children for babbling that approximates the form of real words, such as "da," which, in English, resembles "dog" or "daddy." Numerous experiments have shown that children, in fact, do increase their babbling when adults smile at them, stroke them, and talk back as a consequence of babbling. We have seen that as the first year progresses, children babble the sounds of their native tongues with increasing frequency. "Foreign" sounds tend to drop out. The behaviorist would explain this pattern of changing frequencies in terms of reinforcement (of the sounds of the adults' language) and **extinction** (of foreign sounds). An alternate (nonbehavioral) explanation is that children actively attend to the sounds in their linguistic environments and are intrinsically motivated to utter them.

▶ ▶ ▶ ▶

Shaping *In learning theory, the gradual building of complex behavior patterns by means of reinforcing successive approximations to the target behavior.*

From Skinner's (1957; 1983) perspective, children acquire their early vocabularies through **shaping**—that is, by adults' requiring that children's utterances be progressively closer to actual words before they are reinforced. Skinner views multiword utterances as complex stimulus–response chains that can also be taught by shaping. As children's mean length of utterance increases, parents reinforce syntactically correct word order by uttering sentences and reinforcing their imitation. As with Ben, when children make grammatical errors, parents recast their utterances correctly, and then reinforce the children for repeating them correctly.

But remember Ben's "refusal" to be shaped into correct syntax. We would be able to show that parents' selective reinforcement of their children's utterances facilitated their learning of phonetics, syntax, and semantics, if the reinforcement explanation of language development were accurate.

It does not seem that we have such evidence. For one thing, Roger Brown (1973) found that parents are more likely to reinforce their children for the accuracy or "truth value" of their utterances than for their grammatical correctness. Parents, in other words, are generally accepting of the syntax of their children's language efforts. The child who points down and says "The grass is purple" is not likely to be reinforced, despite correct syntax. But the child who shows her empty plate and blurts out "I eated it all up" is likely to be reinforced, despite overregularization of *to eat*.

Also, selective reinforcement of children's pronunciation can actually backfire. Katherine Nelson (1973) found that children whose parents reward proper pronunciation but correct poor pronunciation develop vocabulary *more slowly* than children of parents who are more tolerant of pronunciation.

Learning-theory approaches also cannot account for the invariant sequences of language development and for children's spurts in acquisition. The various types of two-word utterances emerge in a consistent sequence in diverse cultures. There are individual differences in timing, but the sequencing of types of questions, tag questions, passive versus active sentences, and so on also remains constant. It is unlikely that parents around the world teach language skills in the same sequence.

In sum, it seems that we must look to other theoretical approaches to explain the regularity of the sequences of language development. Perhaps the sequences are governed in some way by the development of biological structures, according to the unfolding of the genetic code. Perhaps the sequences are linked to the building of cognitive structures.

Nativist Views

Earlier in the chapter, we noted that many scholars question the ability of apes to grasp syntax, the grammatical structure of language. A related issue is: Why can't apes *talk?*

Apes, it happens, have structures in their throats that look similar to human vocal tracts. Scientists have also maximized environmental influences by rearing apes with human families. Still, apes have never gained the ability to produce the sounds of language. Why not? Apes must lack *something else* that allows children to vocalize.

What children probably have, and apes do not, is a *native* capacity to speak. Children probably *bring something* to the observation and processing of language that apes do not. The view that innate or inborn factors cause children

▶ ▶ ▶ ▶

to attend to and acquire language in certain ways is termed the nativist view of language development (Maratsos, 1983). Perhaps children bring certain neurological "prewiring" that involves the speech areas of the brain to language learning.

There are various nativist views on language development. Among them are the perspectives of David McNeill, Noam Chomsky, and Eric Lenneberg. McNeill's and Chomsky's views are referred to as *psycholinguistic theory.* Lenneberg's theory hypothesizes the existence of a period during which children are particularly sensitive to acquiring the structures of a language.

Psycholinguistic Theory   According to **psycholinguistic theory,** language acquisition involves an interaction between environmental influences, such as exposure to parental speech and reinforcement, and an inborn tendency to acquire language (Chomsky, 1968, 1980; Rosenthal, 1980). Evidence for an inborn tendency is found in the universality of human language abilities; in the regularity of the early production of sounds, even among deaf children; and in the invariant sequences of language development, regardless of which language the child is learning. In Urdu, Russian, and English, children tend to say their first words at about 1 year. They begin to use two-word utterances by 18 to 24 months. They usually grasp the most complex rules of grammar by 4 to 5.

The Language Acquisition Device (LAD)   David McNeill (1970) labeled this inborn tendency the **Language Acquisition Device** (LAD). He believed that the LAD is a prewiring of the human nervous system that suits it to learn grammar. On the surface, languages differ immensely. However, the LAD serves children all around the world, because languages share what Chomsky refers to as a "universal grammar"—an underlying deep structure or set of rules for turning ideas into sentences. Consider an analogy with computers: According to psycholinguistic theory, the universal grammar that resides in the LAD is the basic operating system of the computer, whereas the particular language that a child learns to use is the "software."

Transformational Grammar   Children begin to develop language with the tool of a universal grammar that sensitizes them to the deep structure of utterances. However, as language develops, children learn rules for transforming deep structure into sentences that have an appropriate surface structure. These rules involve the ways in which phonemes, morphemes, and syntax are woven together to symbolize events and yield meaning. For example, the 22-month-old child utters "Mommy sit," which has a basic meaning that might be the same in any language. In future years the child will transform this deep structure into the English surface structure: "Mommy is sitting down." Children also acquire transformational rules that allow them to produce negative forms of the same statement: at first, perhaps, "Mommy no sit," and later, "Mommy is not sitting down." Their knowledge of transformational rules for forming questions will enable them to say, "Is Mommy sitting down?" Still later, they will be able to apply transformational rules to combine negation with the tag question: "Mommy is not sitting down, is she?" Different languages have different sets of transformational rules, but a child's system for turning basic ideas into sentences is that child's **transformational grammar.**

Chomsky believes that the LAD gives children the capacity to learn the transformational rules for turning ideas (deep structure) into sentences (surface

► ► ► ►

Construct (CON-struct). A concept or theory designed to integrate strands of information. "Ego" (see Chapter 2) and "intelligence" (see Chapter 9) are examples of constructs.

Aphasia A disruption in the ability to understand or produce language.

structure). Children, from this perspective, are predisposed to attend to language and to pick out the transformational rules.

Brain Structures Involved in Language   The LAD is a **construct** hypothesized to be present in people that permits us to comprehend and produce language. The biological structures that provide the basis for the functions of the LAD might be based mostly in the left hemisphere of the cerebral cortex for right-handed people (more than 90 percent of the population), and in the right hemisphere for about half of the left-handed people. The hemisphere that controls language also receives sensory impressions more directly from the "dominant" eye and ear and controls the dominant hand. Incoming and outgoing information largely cross over in the brain, so that for right-handed people the left hemisphere is dominant.

Dennis and Victoria Molfese (1979) have found that even at birth the sounds of speech elicit greater electrical activity in the left hemisphere than the right, as indicated by brain waves. Children are more likely to report hearing the sounds of speech with the right ear as early as the age of 3, and the right ear tends to become progressively more dominant through about the age of 7 (Geffen, 1976). Interestingly, this pattern does not hold for nonspeech-related sounds. Music tends to elicit greater electrical activity in the right hemispheres of infants (Molfese et al., 1975).

Within the dominant (usually left) hemisphere of the cortex, the two areas most involved in speech are Broca's area and Wernicke's area (see Figure 7.6). The late neurologist Norman Geschwind (1979) found that even in the human fetus, the left hemisphere is usually larger than the right, a difference that can be attributed to the language areas. Damage to either area is likely to cause an **aphasia,** or disruption in the ability to understand or produce language.

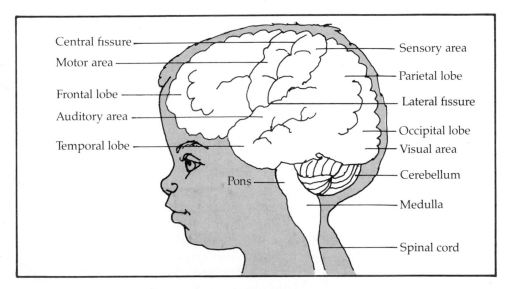

Figure 7.6 Broca's and Wernicke's Areas of the Brain
In Broca's aphasia, people speak slowly and laboriously, using simple sentences. In Wernicke's aphasia, people speak rapidly enough and with proper syntax; however, their abilities to comprehend the speech of others and to summon up the right words to express their own ideas are impaired.

▶ ▶ ▶ ▶

THEORIES OF LANGUAGE DEVELOPMENT

Broca's aphasia *A form of aphasia caused by damage to Broca's area and characterized by slow, laborious speech.*

Wernicke's aphasia *A form of aphasia caused by damage to Wernicke's area and characterized by impaired comprehension of speech and difficulty in attempting to produce the right word.*

Sensitive period *In linguistic theory, the period from about 18 months to puberty when the brain is thought to be particularly capable of learning language because of plasticity.*

Broca's area is located in the frontal lobe, near the section of the motor cortex that controls the muscles of the tongue, throat, and parts of the face that are used when speaking. When Broca's area is damaged, people speak slowly and laboriously, with simple sentences—a pattern known as **Broca's aphasia**. In more severe cases, their comprehension and use of syntax may be seriously impaired (Carlson, 1984; Schwartz et al., 1980).

Wernicke's area lies in the temporal lobe (Figure 7.6), near the auditory cortex. It appears to be involved in the integration of auditory and visual information. Broca's area and Wernicke's area are connected by nerve fibers. People with damage to Wernicke's area (that is, with **Wernicke's aphasia**) usually speak freely and with proper syntax. But their abilities to comprehend the meaning of other people's speech and to find the words to express their thoughts are impaired (Carlson, 1984; Gardner, 1978). They may even spout nonsense syllables. Wernicke's area therefore seems essential to semanticity—that is, to the relationship between words and meaning.

The Sensitive Period Eric Lenneberg (1967) and a number of other scholars propose that there is a **sensitive period** for learning language that begins at about 18 to 24 months and lasts until puberty. This "window" for language learning reflects that status of neural maturation. During the sensitive period, neural development (as in the differentiating of brain structures) provides a degree of plasticity that facilitates language learning.

Neural development also provides the basis for cognitive development. By 18 to 24 months, neural maturation permits the child to begin to entertain *preoperational thought*, as we shall see in the next chapter, and to vastly accelerate the processes of acquiring words and stringing them together to express meaning. By the time children have reached sexual maturity, brain tissue has also reached adult levels of differentiation. Language learning can occur afterward but is more laborious (Elliot, 1981).

Evidence for a sensitive period is found in recovery from brain injuries. Injuries to the dominant hemisphere can impair or destroy the ability to speak. But prior to puberty, brain-injured children frequently recover a good deal of speaking ability. Lenneberg (1967) suggests that in very young children, dominant-hemisphere damage may encourage the development of language functions in the other hemisphere. But adaptation ability wanes in adolescence.

Researchers also frequently refer to children's and adults' abilities to acquire second languages in their studies of the sensitive-period hypothesis. When families emigrate to foreign lands, for example, the sensitive-period hypothesis would predict that the younger children would acquire the language of the land with greater facility than siblings in their late teens or their parents. Evidence on this issue is mixed. Labov (1970), for example, observes that adult immigrants usually find learning the language of their new lands difficult, and tend to retain "foreign" accents. But their young children generally acquire the new language quickly and speak without an accent. In a study of English immigrants in Holland, however, Snow and Hoefnagel-Höhle (1978) found that adolescents and parents learned Dutch more readily than did preschoolers aged 3 to 5.

The Case of Genie: When a Child Past the "Sensitive Period" Attempts to Learn Language The best way to determine whether people are capable of acquiring

▶ ▶ ▶ ▶

language once they have passed puberty would be to run an experiment in which one or more children was reared in such severe isolation that they were not exposed to language until puberty. Of course, such an experiment could not be run because of ethical and legal barriers. In fact, if such a study were legal, developmentalists would be channeling their energies into changing the law, and not into such harmful research.

However, the disturbing case history of Genie, an abused California girl, provides very similar results (Curtiss, 1977). And so it offers insights into the issue of whether there is a sensitive period for language development. Genie's father locked her in a small room at the age of 20 months and kept her there until she was 13½. Her social contacts during this period were limited to her nearly blind mother, who entered the room only to feed Genie, and to beatings at the hands of her father. When Genie's situation was brought to the attention of authorities, she was past the advent of puberty but looked like a young child and weighed only about 60 pounds. She did not speak, was not toilet trained, and could barely stand.

Genie was placed in a foster home, where she was exposed to English for the first time in nearly twelve years. Of special interest is the fact that her language development followed the normal sequence of much younger children in a number of ways. But there were two major exceptions: (1) Her language acquisition was relatively rapid; and (2) she never acquired the proficiency of children reared under normal circumstances. For example, she produced single words only five months after being placed in the foster home, and most of them were nominals. Two-word utterances appeared three months later and followed the patterns shown in Table 7.3. Genie did not, however, show the overextension of younger children. She gave the name *dog* to dogs—not to cats, horses, sheep, or cows.

Five years after her liberation, Genie's language remained largely telegraphic. She still showed significant problems with syntax—failing, for example, to reverse subjects and verbs to phrase spontaneous questions. She showed confusion concerning the use of the past tense (adding *-ed* to words), and had difficulty using negative helping verbs such as *isn't* and *haven't*. Although Genie's speech showed some simple command of syntax and she produced telegraphic speech spontaneously, her abilities clearly fall below normal levels.

Genie's language development provides some support for the sensitive-period hypothesis, although it is possible that her language problems can also be attributed to her long years of malnutrition and abuse. Her efforts to acquire English after puberty were clearly laborious. Also, the results are substandard when compared even to the language of many 2- and 3-year-olds. On the other hand, it seems that she was able to acquire the meanings of many words and many rules of syntax, and to demonstrate semanticity, productivity, and displacement. So the possible loss of plasticity did not prevent her from gaining some competence in English.

In sum, there is probably some kind of neurological prewiring that permits children to grasp the basic operating rules of languages. This prewiring probably involves Broca's and Wernicke's areas of the cortex. It probably contributes to the largely invariant sequences of language development found around the world. Apes might be partially prewired to learn language. Partial prewiring could explain why apes learn to use ASL, even though their syntax and productivity remain open questions. And apes are apparently not prewired to speak, although they can produce sounds.

▶ ▶ ▶ ▶

There might also be a sensitive period for learning language that begins at about 18 to 24 months and ends with sexual maturity. But this sensitive period might only denote a period during which language learning is relatively easier. People are capable of learning language throughout adulthood.

In the next section, we consider the relationships between language and thought, or cognition.

Cognitive Views

Cognitive views of language development focus on the relationships between cognitive development and language development. Cognitive theorists tend to hold a number of assumptions. Two of the most basic are:

1. Language development is made possible by cognitive analytical abilities (Bates & MacWhinney, 1982; Maratsos, 1983).
2. Children are active agents in language learning. Children's motivation for learning syntax and vocabulary grows out of their "desire to express meanings that conceptual development makes available to them" (Maratsos, 1983).

Jean Piaget believed that cognitive development precedes language development. He argued that children must first understand concepts before they can use words that describe the concepts (1976). In Chapter 6 it was noted that object permanence emerges toward the end of the first year. Piaget believed that words that relate to the disappearance and appearance of people and objects (such as "allgone" and "bye-bye") are used only after the emergence of object permanence. Piaget's followers argue that even learning the word *dolly* is facilitated by the child's recognition that dolls continue to exist when they are not in view.

From Piaget's perspective, the meaning of a concept comes before the word that represents the concept. This perspective, as stated by Katherine Nelson and her colleagues (Nelson, 1982; Nelson et al., 1977), holds that children learn words in order to describe classes or categories that they have already created. Children can learn the word *doggy* because they have already perceived the characteristics that distinguish dogs from other things.

Does Cognitive Development Precede Language Development?   The cognitive view of language development is not monolithic. Many theorists argue that cognitive development precedes language development, but others reverse the causal relationship. The opposing point of view, as expressed by Eve Clark (1973, 1983), holds that children create cognitive classes *in order to understand things that are labeled by words.* The word can come before the meaning. When children hear the word *dog,* they strive to understand it by searching for characteristics that separate dogs from other things.

Cognitive psychologist Jerome Bruner (1964, 1983) agrees with Clark that by kindergarten age, language is permeating every aspect of the child's conceptual development. Words not only represent experience; words can transform experience. As language ability develops, children can make finer distinctions between similar concepts. Consider emotion: A 3-year-old may label herself "angry" when she has to wait for her favorite television show to come on. In later years she may substitute "frustrated" for "angry." She may also

▶ ▶ ▶ ▶

learn the words "disappointed," "disapproving," "enraged," "irked," "annoyed," and so on. In the process, her expanded vocabulary actually acquires the capacity to transform her emotional experience.

An Interactionist View Today most cognitive psychologists find something of value in each of these cognitive views (Greenberg & Kuczaj, 1982). In the early stages of language development, concepts often precede words, so that many of the infant's words describe classes that have already been developed. But later on language is not merely the handmaiden of thought; language influences thought. As Lois Bloom expresses it, "There is a developmental shift between learning to talk and talking to learn" (1975).

Similar ideas were advanced by the Russian psychologists A. R. Luria and Lev Vygotsky more than half a century ago. Vygotsky, for example, believed that during most of the first year, vocalizations and thought are separate. But usually during the second year, thought and speech—cognition and language—combine forces. "Speech begins to serve intellect and thoughts begin to be spoken" (Vygotsky, 1962, p. 43). Usually during the second year, children discover that objects have labels. Learning labels becomes more active, more self-directed. At some point, children ask what new words mean. Learning new words clearly fosters the creation of new categories and classes. An interaction develops in which classes are filled with labels for new things, and labels nourish the blossoming of new classes.

Vygotsky's concept of **inner speech** is a key feature of his position. At first, according to Vygotsky, children's "thoughts" are spoken aloud. You can overhear the 3-year-old giving herself instructions as she plays with toys. At this age her vocalizations may serve to regulate her behavior. But language gradually becomes internalized. What was spoken aloud at 4 and 5 becomes an internal dialogue by 6 or 7. This internal dialogue, or "inner speech," is the ultimate binding of language and thought. Inner speech is essential to the development of planning and self-regulation.

Putting It All Together

The ideas of a number of scholars suggest that a synthesis of the learning-theory, nativist, and cognitive views is possible (Kuczaj, 1982; Maratsos, 1983; Rebok, 1987).

First of all, learning plays an indispensable role in language development. Children's tendencies to imitate others explains, in part, why French children learn French and German children learn German. Moreover, very young children apparently imitate their parents in correctly forming the past tense of some irregular verbs. Overregularization does not occur until knowledge of rules for forming the past tense emerges.

It also seems that children do most of their language learning from their mothers. As noted earlier, mothers, other adults, even older children use "motherese" in conversing with young children. But even here the learning is not all one way. Mothers respond to cues from their children when they use motherese, and they accept the most minimal responses as signs that they are headed in the right direction (Molfese et al., 1982). But children learn even when their mothers use complex speech, suggesting that the children apply basic listening strategies that help them learn (Gleitman et al., 1984). The early use of such strategies brings us back to the nativist and the cognitive positions.

▶ ▶ ▶ ▶

The nativist view holds, first of all, that "Language learning must build on a biological base that equips the organism for understanding and producing speech" (Rebok, 1987, p. 217). Children are "preprogrammed" or neurologically "prewired" to prefer the sounds of language to nonlanguage sounds that are similar in pitch and tone. Children do attend to language—even complex sentences—in such a way that they pick out rules of grammar. By early childhood children are actively using grammatical rules to produce their own sentences; they are not just imitating models. In fact, knowledge of rules makes children resistant to imitation.

Cognitive development also appears to interact with language development. The infant's cognitive development makes early words meaningful. The word *doggy* is meaningful because the concept for "dog" exists. However, by about the age of 2 or so, most children also appear to strive to form new concepts because they hear new words. And so, there seems to come a time when cognitive development and language development stimulate each other.

While we as adults continue to struggle with complex concepts to explain language development, 1- and 2-year-olds go right on learning language all around us.

At this point, let us leave the struggle behind. Children will go on learning language, regardless of whether we understand exactly how they do it. Let us turn our attention to some varieties of linguistic experience: Black English, bilingualism, and language learning by deaf children.

Varieties of Linguistic Experience

This chapter has been written largely from the perspective of middle-class U.S. children who are exposed to standard spoken English. But some U.S. children are exposed to nonstandard English. Others are exposed to English plus a second language. Some are not exposed to the sounds of language at all, for they are deaf. Let us explore their linguistic experiences.

Black English

main difference in pronunciation

Segments of the U.S. black community speak a form of English called Black English. Since Black English has taken hold most strongly in poor black neighborhoods, members of the white (and black) communities have in many cases assumed that Black English, because it is different or nonstandard, is not good English.

Consider an example offered by Anastasiow and Hanes. They report a study in which an audiotape of standard English was played to poor black children who were asked to repeat what they had heard. The taped sentence was "I asked him if he did it, and he said he didn't do it." One 5-year-old black girl recast the sentence in Black English as follows: "I asks him if he did it, and he says he didn't did it, but I knows he did" (1976, p. 3).

As the example suggests, the major differences between Black English and standard English lie in the use of verbs. Tenses are formed differently in Black English. For example, "She-ah hit us" may be used in the place of the standard English "She will hit us." Consider the verb "to be." In Black English, "He be gone" indicates the standard "He has been gone for a long while," and

▶ ▶ ▶ ▶

7 LANGUAGE DEVELOPMENT

Dialect *The variety of a spoken language particular to a region, community, or social group. Dialects of a language tend to be understandable by speakers using another dialect without special training in that dialect, but languages are not.*

"He gone" signifies "He is gone right now" in standard English.

Some observers have felt that standard English verbs are used haphazardly in Black English, as if the bare bones of English are being adapted and downgraded. As a consequence, school systems have in some instances reacted to Black English with contempt. However, many linguists, such as William Labov (1972), have argued that Black English is just one **dialect** of English. The grammatical rules of Black English differ from those of standard English. Yet the rules of Black English are consistent, and they allow for the expression of thoughts that are as complex as those permitted by standard English. Black English, from this viewpoint, is different, but not inferior.

"To Be or Not to Be": Use of the Verb "to Be" in Black English   Let us consider a couple of examples of rules in Black English—rules involving use of the verb "to be" and negation. In standard English, "be" is part of the infinitive form of the verb used in the formation of the future tense, as in "I'll be angry tomorrow." Thus "I be angry" is incorrect. But in Black English, "be" is used to denote a continuing state of being. "I am angry" would be perfectly good standard English *and* Black English. But the Black English sentence "I be angry" means in standard English, "I have been angry for a while," and is good Black English.

Black English also *omits* the verb *to be* in some cases (Rebok, 1987), usually when standard English would use a contraction. For example, "She's the one I'm talking about" could be translated as "She the one I talking about." Omitting the verb in Black English is no more careless than contracting it in standard English. Contraction follows a rule of standard English; omission in the example follows a rule of Black English. The Black English sentence is no "simpler" than the standard one.

"Not to Be or Not to Be Nothing": Negation in Black English   Black English also differs in the use of the double negative. Consider the sentence, "I don't want no trouble," which, of course, is commendable. Middle-class white chil-

Language is an indispensable tool for the communication of the knowledge and skills that are required to forge ahead in today's high-tech society. Some black children come from homes in which Black English is spoken. Although Black English is complex and has systematic rules of grammar of its own, black children sometimes have difficulty communicating with white teachers.

dren would be corrected for this instance of double negation and encouraged to say either "I don't want any trouble" or "I want no trouble." Such double negation is not incorrect in Black English, but teachers who use standard English are likely to "jump on" black children who speak this way.

Some black children can switch readily from standard English to Black English. Their facility in doing so is a fine example of their use of the pragmatics of speech. That is, they tailor their language to their social situations. They use standard English in a conference with their teacher or in a job interview, but they use Black English "in the neighborhood."

Other children do not show facility in switching back and forth. For them, the ever-present frowns of standard-English-speaking teachers become part of their burden of poverty.

Standard English is spoken by the majority. For this reason, black children who want to succeed will usually find it to their advantage to use standard English—at least in college, on the job, and in similar social situations. However, if the teachers who instruct black children realize that Black English is just as complex and rule-governed as standard English, they will treat Black-English-speaking children with greater respect—even as they help provide black children with the "mainstream" linguistic alternative.

In the next section, we shall learn more about how showing children respect helps them acquire a "second" language in the schools.

Bilingualism

It may seem strange to U.S. citizens, but most people throughout the world speak two or more languages (Grosjean, 1982). Most countries have minority populations who speak languages in the home that differ from the national tongue. Nearly all Europeans are taught English and the languages of neighboring nations. Consider the Netherlands. Dutch is the native tongue, but all elementary school children are also taught French, German, and English, and they are expected to become fluent in each of them. For millions of U.S. children, English is a second language. Spanish, Russian, Vietnamese, or Arabic is spoken in the home and, perhaps, in the neighborhood. Many of these children do not receive training in English until they enter school.

A few decades ago, it was widely believed that children reared in **bilingual** homes were retarded in their cognitive and language development (Rebok, 1987). However, recent analysis of older studies in bilingualism shows that the families observed were also often low in socioeconomic status and level of education. Lack of education, not bilingualism per se, now appears to have caused the problems of the children. Today most linguists consider it advantageous for children to be bilingual (Diaz, 1985). For one thing, knowledge of more than one language expands children's awareness of different cultures and broadens their perspectives.

In terms of cognitive development, bilingual children learn early to distinguish between words and their meanings. Linguist Dan Slobin's English-speaking daughter was taught German in the homes of relatives beginning at the age of 2½. By 3 she was asking what things were called in the other language (Slobin, 1978). Despite fears that learning two languages at a young age can confuse children, the evidence suggests that bilingual children perform at least as well as monolingual children on intelligence tests and related tests of cognitive functioning (Segalowitz, 1981).

Bilingual Using or capable of using two languages with nearly equal or equal facility.

▶ ▶ ▶ ▶

In 1974 Congress enacted legislation requiring that non-English–speaking children be given the chance to study in their own language in order to smooth the transition into U.S. life. The official purpose is to help foreign-speaking children use their native tongue to learn English quickly, but bicultural programs that reinforce the children's primary cultural heritages have also been set up.

Bilingual Kids further ahead N ometalinguistic education

Bilingual Education   Despite the positive aspects of bilingualism, many U.S. children who speak a different language in the home have problems learning English in school. Early in the century, the educational approach to teaching English to non-English-speaking children was simple: sink or swim. Children were taught in English from the outset. It was incumbent upon them to catch on as best they could. Most children swam. Some sank.

A more formal term for the sink-or-swim method is **total immersion.** Total immersion has a checkered history. There are, of course, many successes with total immersion, but there are also more failures than the U.S. educational system is willing to tolerate. For this reason, **bilingual education** has been adopted in many school systems. In bilingual education, children are at first taught in the language spoken in the home. Their exposure to English is increased gradually. As suggested in the nearby box on "The Three R's in 70 Tongues," bilingual education also has its critics.

Iris Rotberg (1982) suggests that bilingual education has been most successful when four criteria have been met: (1) The child begins with mastery of the language spoken in the home, providing a secure linguistic base. (2) The bilingual program focuses specifically on teaching English, and does not just start teaching other subjects in English, even at a low level. (3) The child's parents understand and support the goals and methods of the program. (4) Teachers, parents, and other members of the community have mutual respect for one another and for each others' languages.

When instruction in a second language is carried out carefully, there is little evidence to suggest that it interferes with the first language (McLaughlin, 1984; Rebok, 1987). Under such circumstances, children show little confusion between the languages.

All in all, it seems that following Rotberg's principles will accomplish more than just teaching children English. The principles will also help ensure that bilingual children will be proud of the ethnic heritage they bring with them into the mainstream culture. Children may attain the language skills necessary to forge ahead in today's workplace and participate in political and social processes, while they retain a sense of ethnic identity and self-esteem.

▶ ▶ ▶ ▶

Total immersion   *A method of language instruction in which a person is placed in an environment in which only the language to be learned is used.*

Bilingual education   *A method of instruction that uses both the language the child has learned in the home and the language of the mainstream culture.*

The Three R's in 70 Tongues: Debating the Uses of Bilingual Instruction

▷
▷
▷
▷
▷   Imagine a school with 2,617 students culled from 57 different countries and cultures. In one classroom, the teacher copies the word *farming* on a blackboard—first in English, moving from left to right, then in Assyrian, moving from right to left. A murmur of Chinese rises from a history class. Soft Spanish vowels punctuate a science lesson. A model international academy? Hardly. It is Chicago's Nicholas Senn High School on the city's ethnically mixed North Side, where foreign-born students enroll in special bilingual programs that allow them to study a regular curriculum in their native languages as well as in English.

Scarcely a decade ago, such a welter of tongues would have been unspeakable in a U.S. public school. For more than a century, the great melting-pot theory decreed that foreign-speaking children be taught solely English to speed their assimilation into the mainstream. The children of 50 million immigrants were forced to master English that way. Some 22 states even outlawed teaching in foreign languages.

But in the 1960s a spectacular popularization of ethnic pride took place, and cultural heterogeneity emerged as the new ideal. Bilingual-education legislation, passed by Congress in 1974, declared that non-English-speaking children should be given the chance to study in their own language in order to smooth the transition into U.S. life. Going a step further, the act also set up a number of bicultural programs, so that children could reinforce, rather than shed, their primary cultural heritage.

The official purpose of the federal bilingual programs is to help foreign-speaking children use their native tongue to learn English rapidly, then switch to a regular school program. Yet the degree of emphasis on English differs markedly from program to program.

So-called transitional programs shoot their students into regular English-speaking classrooms as quickly as possible. Under a second technique, called the maintenance method, rapid mastery of English is still the goal. But students continue studying their own culture and language. A third approach, being tried in areas with large Hispanic enclaves, such as New York, Florida, and Southern California, is bilingual and bicultural: The programs encourage native-born U.S. citizens to achieve fluency in a foreign language even as their counterparts are learning English. In Miami's Coral Way Elementary School, which inaugurated the bicultural method to cope with the huge influx of refugees from Cuba, all students study for half a day in Spanish and for the other half in English.

Critics of the bilingual experiment contend that the movement is often more political than educational, with Spanish-surnamed children segregated in separate classes long after they can handle lessons conducted in English. "We fully recognize the benefits of cultural pluralism," says James Ward of the American Federation of Teachers. "But we must be sure that the central effort is to bring students into the mainstream of American life." Some foreign-born parents share his concern. Manuel Llera, principal of a junior high school in California's Sweetwater Union School District, near the Mexican border, has been forced by parental pressure to remove some Chicano children from the bilingual program. Parents, he says, "are afraid that their kids are going to get a second-class education and that they won't learn English."

▶ ▶ ▶ ▶

Language Learning by Deaf Children

Deaf children in many cases have been severely handicapped in their language development. Their deafness per se is not usually the main problem. Instead, the problem is that parents may not take steps early enough to teach language (usually in the form of American Sign Language [ASL]) to their deaf children. In many cases, parents do not even recognize that their children have major or complete hearing losses for several months or more. About 90 percent of deaf children are born to parents who hear, and hearing parents are unlikely to have an intuitive grasp of deaf children's language problems.

Deaf children, as noted earlier, babble "on schedule"—at the same time as children who can hear. However, instead of gradually winnowing the phonemes they utter to those of the language spoken in the home, they lapse into silence. But the process takes time and may serve only to mask their hearing problems to their parents. In some cases parents do not suspect that their children cannot hear until they have failed to produce any words by the end of the second year. When children have not completely lost their hearing, parental recognition of the problem may be further delayed. Parents of moderately deaf children may not realize that their children's language development is lagging at all. The limitations in verbal expression of moderately deaf children may first be recognized when they are given hearing tests upon entering school. (It seems wise that all parents routinely question their pediatricians about the hearing abilities of their infants.)

When hearing problems are diagnosed during the first two years, medical intervention or special education usually prevents the development of language and cognitive problems. By school age, however, children may have missed much of the theoretical "sensitive period" during which language development is thought to come most readily. By this time, early linguistic isolation from parents may have saddled deaf children with difficulties in producing speech, in comprehending and using complex syntax, and even in reading (Schlesinger & Meadow, 1972). Also, most deaf children do not read lips very well.

This is the bad news. The good news is that deaf children reared by parents who are sensitive to their problems need suffer no language deficits. For instance, deaf children reared by deaf parents usually read, write, and speak better than the deaf children of parents who can hear (Liben, 1978).

In many cases, deaf children who receive early instruction in sign language perform just as well—in ASL—as hearing children perform in spoken English. Moreover, they seem to have no trouble translating back and forth between signs and English words later on. Hilde Schlesinger and Kathryn Meadow (1972) reported the case of one precocious deaf child, Ann, who signed two words ("wrong" and "pretty") at 10 months and was using more than 100 signs by the age of 18 months. By this early age, she had also learned many letters of the manual alphabet.

It may even be that learning ASL facilitates language development in children with normal hearing. Normal children may be able to produce words as signs before they can speak them. John Bonvillian and his colleagues (1983) followed several hearing infants who were being reared by one or two deaf parents. Instead of being handicapped, the infants signed their first words at an advanced average age of 8 months. Their vocabulary growth outpaced that of children reared by two parents who could hear.

▶ ▶ ▶ ▶

Full Circle In a sense, language learning by deaf children brings us full circle. Deaf children, like the apes mentioned at the outset of the chapter, are usually taught to communicate their ideas by means of ASL. Of course, they go farther with ASL than apes do.

Duane Rumbaugh, one of the pioneers in teaching apes to use symbols to communicate, has recently found that a number of severely retarded people who had never learned to speak could be taught from two dozen to upwards of 70 symbols (Rathus, 1987). Whether or not the language development of apes truly parallels our own, our experiences with apes have taught us a great deal about helping other humans.

Summary

1. Apes have been taught to use ASL and other symbol systems to communicate. However, apes may not have the intuitive grasp of grammar shown by children.

2. As defined by Roger Brown, language has the characteristics of semanticity, productivity, and displacement. Semanticity refers to the fact that words serve as symbols. Productivity refers to the capacity to combine words into original sentences. Displacement is the ability to communicate information about other times and places.

3. There are several basic components of language: phonology, morphology, syntax, and semantics. Phonology is the study of the basic sounds (phonemes) of a language. Morphemes are the smallest units of meaning in a language. They consist of one or more phonemes pronounced in a particular order. Syntax is the system of rules (grammar) that determines how words are strung together into sentences. Semantics concerns the meanings of a language; it is the study of the relationship between language and objects or events. Sentences have a surface structure, or superficial grammatical construction, and a deep structure, or underlying meaning.

4. Prelinguistic vocalizations include crying, cooing, and babbling. Newborn children cry and begin to coo by about 2 months. Parents readily learn to interpret most of their children's cries. Preterm children, sick children, and children at risk for certain developmental disorders frequently have telltale cries—sometimes a high-pitched, extremely irritating cry.

5. Babbling emerges at about 5 to 6 months and is the first type of vocalization that has the sounds of speech. Children at first babble phonemes found in many languages, but gradually the phonemes are reduced to those spoken in the home. Deaf children babble also.

6. First words are frequently spoken toward the end of the first year. Children use single words (holophrases) at about 18 months and two-word utterances a few months later. These brief utterances express complex meanings and are therfore referred to as telegraphic speech. Most holophrases consist of nominals. Two-word utterances consist of a number of commonly used and syntactically correct combinations, for example, agent–action, agent–object, and action–object. The order of emergence of usage of two-word utterances is the same in different languages.

▶ ▶ ▶ ▶

7. Some children show a referential language style, in which they use language primarily to label objects. Others show an expressive language style, in which they use language primarily to engage in social interaction. Most children use a combination of these styles.

8. Vocabulary growth is slow at first, but by the end of the second year is advancing at the rate of several hundred words every few months. The rate of acquisition of receptive vocabulary outpaces that of expressive vocabulary.

9. Young children overextend the meanings of words so that they can be used in situations for which they do not have words.

10. Brown describes children's telegraphic utterances in terms of the mean length of utterance (MLU), or the number of phonemes that are used per utterance. Growth patterns in MLU show swift upward movement, although some children spurt earlier than others.

11. Parents (and children) use motherese when speaking to very young children. Their speech is slow, high-pitched, simple, brief, repetitive, overdescriptive, and concrete.

12. Children in the second and third years overregularize inflections such as word endings in forming the past tense of irregular verbs and in forming the plurals of irregular nouns. *Sit* may become *sitted*, and *child* may become *childs*. These "errors" are made because children *are* applying grammatical rules, not because of lack of knowledge of them.

13. As development progresses, children attain the capacities to produce articles, conjunctions, and adjectives; questions; and passive sentences. They also become more sensitive to the practical aspects of communication—the pragmatics—of language.

14. There are a number of approaches to attempting to explain language development, including learning-theory, nativist, and cognitive approaches. Learning-theory approaches emphasize the roles of imitation and reinforcement in learning. However, children do not learn grammar purely by means of imitation, and the effectiveness of reinforcement in fostering language development is spotty at best.

15. Nativist views emphasize innate factors in language development. Psycholinguistic theory hypothesizes the existence of a language acquisition device (LAD)—neural prewiring that spurs children to attend to and pick out rules of grammar. Chomsky believes that the LAD permits children to acquire rules for transforming basic meaning (the deep structure of sentences) into sentences with correct surface structure.

16. For right-handed people, language functions appear to be based on structures in the left hemisphere of the cerebral cortex: Broca's area and Wernicke's area. Observation of people whose brains have been damaged suggests that Broca's area is involved in the person's abilities to understand and use syntax (grammar), and that Wernicke's area is involved in the ability to comprehend the meanings of words and to find the right words to express thoughts.

17. Lenneberg suggests that there is a sensitive period for language acquisition that ends with sexual maturity. This view holds that the brain is not sufficiently differentiated to permit language production prior to 18 to 24

▶ ▶ ▶ ▶

months, and that the brain has become fully differentiated—and thus lost its "plasticity"—by the time of sexual maturity. Nonetheless, adults can learn new languages, even if not so readily as children.

18. The cognitive view holds that language development is made possible by cognitive analytical abilities and that children are active, self-motivated agents in language learning. However, a number of cognitive theorists, such as Lev Vygotsky, have pointed out that language learning sometimes precedes and promotes the development of cognitive structure.

19. Black English is a dialect that follows consistent rules of grammar. Two facets of Black English are the omission of the verb "to be" and double negation.

20. Bilingual children do not necessarily suffer language or academic problems when they are adequately educated. In bilingual education, children are at first instructed in the language spoken in the home.

21. Deaf children do not necessarily show language deficits when their hearing loss is detected early and they receive special education, as when they are taught sign language.

T R U T H ▸ O R ▸ F I C T I O N ▸ R E V I S I T E D

Chimpanzees and gorillas have been taught how to use sign language. *True.* They have been taught to communicate by using American Sign Language, the language of the deaf.

Crying is the child's earliest use of language. *False.* Crying, along with cooing and babbling, are *prelinguistic* vocalizations.

Children babble only the sounds of their parents' language. *False.* Children babble phonemes found in all languages.

Deaf children do not babble. *False.* Babbling appears in children who cannot hear, providing evidence that babbling emerges innately and does not represent imitation.

Once children acquire their first word, other words follow "fast and furiously." *False.* Words come slowly at first.

Most of children's earliest words are names for things. *True.* They are referred to as nominals.

To a 2-year-old, the word combinations "Go Mommy" and "Mommy go" have the same meaning. *False.* The different word orders express different meanings.

Three-year-olds say "Daddy goed away" instead of "Daddy went away" because they do understand rules of grammar. *True.* They are overregularizing because they are applying rules for forming the past tense to an irregular verb.

▶ ▶ ▶ ▶

Parents have to coach 4- and 5-year-olds in how to use "baby talk" with their younger siblings. False. Children appear to acquire the fundamentals of baby talk—otherwise known as "motherese"—on their own.

Children learn language faster when their parents correct their errors. False. One study, for example, found that correcting children's pronunciation actually slows down language development.

Children acquire grammar by imitating their parents. False. It appears that they attend to language in such a way that they pick out rules of grammar and then apply them to produce their own sentences.

Children are "preprogrammed" to listen to language in such a way that they pick out rules of grammar. True.

Children must understand the concepts for things before they can learn the words for things. That is, a child must know what a dog is before she can learn the word **doggy**. False. The perception of words can also motivate the child to develop concepts that explain them.

People cannot learn new languages once they have reached sexual maturity. False. However, there may be an early sensitive period during which language is acquired relatively more readily.

The Black-English sentence "She the one I talking about" is produced by using systematic rules of grammar. True. Black English systematically omits the verb "to be" under certain circumstances, such as in cases when contractions would be used in standard English.

Some black children can switch back and forth between Black English and standard English. True. This is a fine example of pragmatism in language usage.

Bilingual children encounter more academic problems than children who know only one language. False. Bilingualism can be advantageous for children who know both languages well.

The best way to teach English to children who speak Spanish in the home is to totally immerse them in English once they enter school. Not necessarily. The total-immersion method has produced a number of failures along with its successes.

Deaf children reared by deaf parents show superior language development as compared to deaf children reared by parents who can hear. True. Deaf parents are usually more sensitive to the potential language problems of their children, and they begin to teach their children sign language at the appropriate early age.

► ► ► ►

8

Cognitive Development

▸
▸
▸
▸
▸
▸
▸

T R U T H ▶ O R ▶ F I C T I O N ?

- Cognitive development does not occur prior to development of the ability to use language.
- Two-year-olds tend to assume that their parents are aware of everything that is happening to them, even when their parents are not present.
- Four-year-olds think that a row of five spread-out pennies contains more pennies than a row of five bunched-up pennies.
- A 4-year-old may believe that it is dark out because it is time to go to sleep.
- A 4-year-old may believe that the sky is blue because someone has painted it.
- Most 4-year-olds may not be able to correctly line up a series of ten sticks according to height.
- Adolescents tend to be rigid and unyielding in their idealism, because they are not yet capable of adult reasoning.
- Two-year-old boys show better memory for trains and puzzles, while 2-year-old girls show better memory for dolls and teddy bears.
- If you ask a 3-year-old what letter comes after N, he probably won't know the answer. But if you recite the alphabet with him and stop short at N, he is likely to say, "O, P," and so on.
- Some children have photographic memories.
- Toddlers develop emotions such as jealousy and pride only after they become self-aware.
- When asked to define themselves, adolescents are more likely to focus on their physical characteristics than on personality traits.

At the age of 2½, one of my children confused me when she insisted that I continue to play "Billy Joel" on the stereo. Put aside the question of her taste in music. My problem stemmed from the fact that when Allyn asked for Billy Joel, the name of the singer, she could be satisfied only by my playing the first song of the album, "Moving Out." When "Moving Out" had ended and the next song, "The Stranger," had begun to play, she would insist that I play "Billy Joel" again. "That *is* Billy Joel," I would protest. "No, no," she would insist, "I want *Billy Joel!*"

We would go around in circles. There were many arguments and tears until it dawned on me that "Billy Joel," for her, symbolized the song "Moving Out," not the name of the singer. Of course my insistence that the second song was also "Billy Joel" could not satisfy her! She was conceptualizing *Billy Joel* as a *property* of a particular song, not as the name of a person who could sing many songs.

From about the ages of 2 to 4, children tend to show a good deal of confusion between symbols and the objects they represent. At their level of cognitive development they do not recognize that words are arbitrary symbols for objects and events, and that people could get together and decide to use different words for things. Instead, they tend to think of words as inherent properties of objects and events.

This chapter chronicles the developing thought processes of children — that is, their cognitive development. Much of the chapter chronicles the stages of cognitive development hypothesized by Swiss psychologist Jean Piaget. Piaget looked into many cognitive-developmental issues, including the ways in which children come to understand the relationships between symbols and objects, how children go about solving problems, children's knowledge of cause and effect, and their abilities to classify objects and engage in categorical thinking.

Then we consider other views of cognitive development: the information-processing approaches that have been stimulated by our experience with that "high tech" phenomenon, the computer. Finally, we turn our attention to a fascinating aspect of cognitive development: the development of the self-concept.

Jean Piaget's Stages of Cognitive Development

Scheme *According to Piaget, an action pattern or mental structure that is involved in the acquisition or organization of knowledge.*

Assimilation *According to Piaget, the process by which new events are responded to according to existing schemes.*

Accommodation *According to Piaget, the changing of existing schemes so that new events or knowledge can be incorporated.*

▶ ▶ ▶ ▶

Cognitive development focuses on the development of children's ways of perceiving and mentally representing the world. As noted in Chapter 2, Piaget labeled children's concepts of the world **schemes.** Piaget hypothesized that children attempt to **assimilate** new events to existing schemes and, when assimilation does not allow the child to make sense of novel events, children try to **accommodate** by modifying existing schemes.

Piaget (1963) hypothesized that children's cognitive processes develop in an orderly sequence or series of stages. As is the case with motor and language development, some children may be more advanced than others at particular ages, but the developmental sequence does not normally vary. Piaget identified four major stages of cognitive development (see Table 8.1): *sensorimotor, preoperational, concrete operational,* and *formal operational.*

Table 8.1   Piaget's Stages of Cognitive Development

STAGE	APPROXIMATE AGE*	DESCRIPTION
Sensorimotor	Birth–2 years	Behavior suggests that child lacks language and does not use symbols or mental representations of objects in the environment. Simple responding to the environment (through reflexive schemes) draws to an end, and intentional behavior—such as making interesting sights last—begins. The child develops the object concept and acquires the basics of language.
Preoperational	2–7 years	The child begins to represent the world mentally, but thought is egocentric. The child does not focus on two aspects of a situation at once, and therefore lacks conservation. The child shows animism, artificialism, and immanent justice.
Concrete operational	7–12 years	The child shows conservation concepts, can adopt the viewpoint of others, can classify objects in series (for example, from shortest to longest), and shows comprehension of basic relational concepts (such as one object being larger or heavier than another).
Formal operational	12 years and above	Mature, adult thought emerges. Thinking seems characterized by deductive logic, consideration of various possibilities before acting to solve a problem (mental trial and error), abstract thought (for example, philosophical weighing of moral principles), and the formation and testing of hypotheses.

*Many researchers have found that Piaget's age estimates were often inaccurate, as we shall see throughout the chapter.

The Sensorimotor Stage

Piaget's descriptions of the cognitive development of infants during the first two years generally rely on observations of their sensory and motor activity. Although it may be difficult for us to imagine how we can develop and use cognitive processes in the absence of language, children actually do so in many ways.

One sign of the development of cognitive processes is the appearance of object permanence (see Chapter 6). The development of object permanence, in fact, has been considered the major cognitive task of the sensorimotor period. But there is much more. During the sensorimotor stage, infants progress from responding to events with reflexes, or "ready-made" schemes, to goal-oriented behavior that involves awareness of past events. During this stage, they come to form mental representations of objects and events, to hold complex pictures of past events in mind, and to solve problems by mental trial and error. Newborn infants do not distinguish themselves from the world around them, but 2-year-olds typically see themselves as one of the many objects in the environment.

▶ ▶ ▶ ▶

Piaget divided the sensorimotor stage into six substages, each of which is characterized by more complex behavior than the preceding substage. But there is also continuity from substage to substage. Each could be characterized as a variation on a theme in which earlier forms of behavior are repeated, varied, and coordinated. The approximate time periods of the substages and some characteristics of each are summarized in Table 8.2.

Ready-Made Schemes The first substage covers the first six weeks or so after birth. It is dominated by the assimilation of sources of stimulation to ready-made schemes (reflexes) such as grasping, visual tracking, crying, sucking, and crudely turning the head toward a sound. Ready-made schemes at first may show a stereotypical, inflexible quality. But even within the first few hours, neonates begin to modify reflexes as a result of experience. For example, infants may initially suck only when their mouths are touched, but within days they will root for the breast or bottle when their cheeks are stroked. Neonates will adapt (accommodate) patterns of sucking to the shape of the nipple and the rate of flow of fluid.

During the first month or so, infants apparently make no connection between stimulation perceived through different sensory modalities. They make no effort to grasp objects that they visually track. Crude turning toward sources of auditory and olfactory stimulation has a ready-made look about it that cannot be considered purposeful searching.

Table 8.2 The Six Substages of the Sensorimotor Stage, According to Piaget

	SUBSTAGE	SOME MAJOR EVENTS
1.	Ready-made schemes (0–1 month)	Assimilation of new objects to reflexive responses; babies "look and see." Ready-made schemes can be modified by experience.
2.	Primary circular reactions (1–4 months)	Repetition of actions that may have initially occurred by chance but that have satisfying or interesting results; babies "look in order to see"; babies imitate actions within their repertoires. Babies do not yet distinguish between themselves and the external world.
3.	Secondary circular reactions (4–8 months)	Repetition of learned schemes that have interesting results. There is initial awareness that schemes can influence the external world.
4.	Coordination of sensorimotor schemes (8–12 months)	Coordination of sensorimotor schemes, such as looking and grasping, to attain specific goals; imitation of actions not already in infants' repertoires.
5.	Tertiary circular reactions (12–18 months)	Purposeful adaptation of established schemes to specific situations; behavior takes on experimental quality; overt trial and error in problem solving.
6.	The transition to symbolic thought (18–24 months)	Mental trial and error in problem solving; mental detours based on cognitive maps; deferred imitation; symbolic play. Infants' cognitive advances are made possible by their mental representations and the beginnings of symbolic thought.

▶ ▶ ▶ ▶

In the substage of primary circular reactions, the infant tends to repeat unlearned actions that provide stimulation. The 3-month-old in this picture is also beginning to coordinate visual and motor sensorimotor schemes—that is, looking at the hand is becoming coordinated with holding it in the field of vision.

Primary Circular Reactions   The second substage lasts from about 1½ to 4 months of age and is characterized by the beginnings of the coordination of various sensorimotor schemes. It is labeled the stage of **primary circular reactions,** because babies tend to repeat unlearned actions that provide stimulation.

In *The Origins of Intelligence in Children,* Piaget (1936) describes his 2-month-old son, Laurent, in the process of learning to coordinate visual and motor schemes in order to maintain interesting stimulation:

> At 2 months 4 days, Laurent by chance discovers his right index finger and looks at it briefly. At 2 months 11 days, he inspects for a moment his open right hand, perceived by chance. At 2 months 17 days, he follows its spontaneous movement for a moment, then examines it several times while it searches for his nose or rubs his eye. . . .
>
> At 2 months 21 days, he holds his two fists in the air and looks at the left one, after which he slowly brings it toward his face and rubs his nose with it, then his eye. A moment later the left hand again approaches his face; he looks at it and touches his nose. He recommences and laughs five or six times in succession while moving the left hand to his face. He seems to laugh before the hand moves, but looking has no influence on its movement. He laughs beforehand but begins to smile again on seeing the hand. Then he rubs his nose. At a given moment he turns his head to the left, but looking has no effect on the direction. The next day, same reaction. At 2 months 23 days, he looks at his right hand, then at his clasped hands (at length). At 2 months 24 days, at last it may be stated that looking acts on the orientation of the hands which tend to remain in the visual field (pp. 96–97).

And so Laurent early in the third month visually tracks the behavior of his hand, but his visual observations do not seem to influence their movement. At about 2 months 21 days, Laurent can apparently exert some control over his hands, because he seems to know when a hand is about to move (and entertain him). But the link between looking at and moving the hands remains weak. A few days later, however, his looking "acts" on the hands, causing them to remain in his field of vision. Sensorimotor coordination has been achieved. An action is repeated because it stimulates the infant. Prolonged repetition and the child's laughter give this sort of assimilation the quality of play.

In terms of assimilation and accommodation, the child is attempting to assimilate the motor scheme (moving the hand) to the sensory scheme (looking at it). But the schemes do not automatically fit. Several days of apparent trial and error pass during which the infant seems to be trying to make accommodations so that they will fit.

Goal-directed behavior makes significant advances during the second substage. During the month after birth, infants visually track objects that contrast with their backgrounds, especially moving objects. But this ready-made behavior is largely automatic, so that the infant is "looking and seeing." But by the third month, as with Laurent, objects may be examined repeatedly and intensely. It seems clear that the infant is no longer simply looking and seeing, but is now "looking *in order* to see." And by the end of the third month, Laurent seems to be moving his hands *in order to look* at them.

Since Laurent (and other infants) will repeat actions that allow them to see, cognitive-developmental psychologists consider sensorimotor coordination self-reinforcing. Laurent does not seem to be looking or moving his hands because these acts allow him to satisfy a "more basic" drive such as hunger or thirst. The desire to prolong stimulation may be just as basic.

Primary circular reactions
The repetition of unlearned actions that provide stimulation.

▶ ▶ ▶ ▶

During the substage of primary circular reactions, infants appear to engage in their first voluntary imitation of facial expressions and sounds made by adults.* This imitation seems to occur most efficiently when the adult first repeats something that the infant just did. The adult's imitation seems to be assimilated to the infant's scheme, and the infant further repeats the act in order to prolong the source of stimulation.

Secondary Circular Reactions   The third substage lasts from about 4 to 8 months or so and is characterized by **secondary circular reactions,** in which learned patterns of activity are repeated because of the stimulation that they provide. In the second substage, infants prolong chance occurrences. In the third substage, they appear to search purposefully for and select actions that have interesting results.

In the third substage, infants begin to distinguish between themselves and objects in the external world. Infants may now learn to pull strings in order to make a plastic face appear, or to shake an object in order to hear it rattle. They may intentionally drop rattles and blocks so that they can then look down for them. Infants now seem to recognize that their actions are means to ends that are achieved in the external world.

Although infants in this substage track the trajectory of moving objects, they abandon their searches when the objects disappear from view. As noted in Chapter 5, the object concepts of infants are quite limited at these ages, especially the age at which the third substage begins.

Coordination of Sensorimotor Schemes   In the fourth substage, infants no longer act simply in order to prolong interesting occurrences. Now they can coordinate schemes in order to attain specific goals. Now they may lift a piece of cloth in order to reach a toy that they had seen a parent place under the cloth earlier. In this example, the sensorimotor scheme of picking up the cloth is coordinated with the sensorimotor scheme of reaching for the toy.

The above example implies that the infant has mentally represented the toy placed under the cloth. Quite so. The fourth stage is also marked by advances in the object concept. Consider another example. At the age of 5 months, one of Piaget's daughters, Lucienne, was reaching across her crib for a toy. As she did so, Piaget obscured the toy with his hand. Lucienne pushed her father's hand aside, but in doing so, she became distracted and began to play with the hand. Perhaps she had briefly maintained an image of the toy, but then this image was readily displaced by a more recent stimulus. A few months later, Lucienne did not allow her father's hand to distract her from the goal of reaching the toy. She moved the hand firmly to the side and then grabbed the toy. The mental representation of the object appears to have become more persistent. The intention of reaching the object was also maintained, and so the hand was perceived as a barrier, and not as another interesting stimulus.

Infants' development of attachment to their primary caregivers may also be related to the development of the object concept. It would appear logical that infants must have permanent mental representations of their mothers, for example, before they would show distress at being separated from their mothers. But the "proof" is not this simple. By the time a few months have passed,

Secondary circular reactions
The repetition of learned actions that provide stimulation.

▶ ▶ ▶ ▶

*In Chapter 4, it was noted that neonates engage in reflexive imitation.

infants have had ample opportunity to learn that their needs are more likely to be met when someone who looks like mother is present. This would also provide them with ample motivation to show pleasure when mother is present and to cry when she is absent, simply in response to the perceived situation at hand.

During the fourth substage, infants also gain the capacity to copy actions that are not in their own repertoires. Infants can now imitate many gestures and sounds that they had previously ignored. The imitation of a new facial gesture implies that infants have mentally represented their own faces and can tell what parts of their faces they are moving through feedback from facial muscles. For example, when a girl imitates her mother sticking out her tongue, it would appear that she has coordinated moving her own tongue with feedback from muscles in the tongue and mouth. In this way, imitation suggests a great deal about the child's emerging self-concept as well.

Tertiary Circular Reactions   In the fifth substage, which lasts from about the ages of 12 to 18 months, Piaget looks upon the behavior of infants as characteristic of budding scientists. Infants now engage in **tertiary circular reactions,** or purposeful adaptations of established schemes to specific situations. Behavior takes on a new experimental quality, and infants may now repeat actions dozens of times in order to learn how things work.

Consider Piaget's description of Laurent's behavior at 10 months 29 days:

> Laurent examines a watch chain hanging from his index finger. At first he touches it very lightly, simply "exploring" it without grasping it. He then starts it swinging a little and . . . continues this. [Instead of stopping,] he grasps the chain with his right hand and swings it with his left while trying some new combinations. In particular, he slides it along the back of his left hand and sees it fall off when it reaches the end. Then he holds the end of the chain (with his right index finger and thumb) and lets it slide slowly between the fingers of his left hand. . . . He studies it carefully at the moment when the chain falls from his left hand and repeats this ten times. Afterward, still holding the end of the chain in his right hand, he shakes it violently, which makes it describe a series of varied trajectories in the air. He then slows these movements in order to see how the chain slides along the quilt when he merely pulls it. Finally, he drops it from different heights. . . .
>
> [Laurent] repeated this kind of experiment with everything that his hand came upon: my notebook, "plugs," ribbons, etc. (1936, p. 269).

Piaget reports two examples of the use of learned or secondary circular reactions by his daughter Jacqueline. In an episode described in *The Construction of Reality in the Child* (Piaget, 1937), Jacqueline at the age of 15 months caught her skirt on a nail. Instead of pulling hard and ripping the dress, she stepped back (a tertiary circular reaction) and carefully detached her skirt (a second tertiary circular reaction).

The second episode was an experiment in which Piaget placed a stick outside of Jacqueline's playpen, which had wooden bars (Piaget, 1936). At first Jacqueline grasped the stick and tried to pull it sideways into the playpen. The stick was too long and could not fit through the bars. Over a number of days of trial and error, however, Jacqueline discovered that she could bring the stick between the bars by turning it upright. In future presentations she would immediately turn the stick upright and bring it in.

Tertiary circular reactions
The purposeful adaptation of established schemes to new situations.

▶ ▶ ▶ ▶

Jacqueline's eventual success with the stick was the result of overt trial and error. In the sixth substage, described below, the solution to problems is often more sudden, suggesting that children have manipulated the elements of the problems in their minds and engaged in mental trial and error before displaying the correct overt response.

The Transition to Symbolic Thought   The sixth substage lasts from about 18 to 24 months. It serves as a transition between sensorimotor development and the symbolic thought that characterizes the preoperational stage.

Recall Jacqueline's trials (in more ways than one) with the stick. Piaget cleverly waited until his other children, Lucienne and Laurent, were 18 months old, and then he presented them with the playpen and stick problem. By waiting until 18 months, he could attribute differences in their performance to advanced age instead of a possible "warm-up effect" from earlier tests. Rather than engage in overt trial and error, the 18-month-old children sat and studied the situation for a few moments. Then they grasped the stick, turned it upright, and brought it into the playpen with little overt effort.

Jacqueline had at first failed with the stick. She then turned it every which way, happening upon a solution almost by chance. Lucienne and Laurent solved the problem fairly rapidly, and their performance was error-free. It seems logical to conclude that the older children mentally represented the stick and the bars of the playpen and perceived that the stick would not fit through as it was. They must then have rotated the mental image of the stick, holding the image of the bars constant, until they perceived a position that would allow the stick to pass between the bars.

Children in the sixth substage also show the ability to construct and "read" cognitive maps. Piaget (1937) offers an observation of Jacqueline at 18 months. Jacqueline threw a ball under a sofa and sought to retrieve it. However, she did not bend down to look for it in the place where it disappeared. Instead, she realized that the ball's trajectory must have carried it beyond the sofa. So Jacqueline turned her back on the sofa and walked around a couple of pieces of furniture to retrieve the ball. This episode shows object permanence and a capacity to make "mental detours." Such detours can be efficiently made only when one has mentally represented the entire layout (in this case, the furniture in a room) or arena of the problem. But infants may begin to make short detours around opaque barriers to retrieve objects several months earlier (Lockman, 1984).

At about 18 months, children can also engage in **deferred imitation.** That is, they imitate people and events that may have occurred hours, days, or even weeks earlier. They may do excellent imitations of Mommy at the lawnmower or Daddy changing the baby (by using a doll), even picking up incidental mannerisms.

The presence of deferred imitation suggests that children have mentally represented complex behavior patterns and actions. Perhaps the capacity to store these types of mental images must be "in place" before children are ready to use language to talk about past events. After all, words for objects and actions would have no meanings, if they could not be linked to images that are in place.

At around 18 months children may also use imitation to symbolize or stand for a plan of action. Consider the way in which Lucienne goes about retrieving a watch chain her father has placed in a match box. It seems that symbolic imitation serves her as a way of thinking out loud:

Deferred imitation *The imitation of people and events that occurred hours, days, or weeks ago.*

▶ ▶ ▶ ▶

8   COGNITIVE DEVELOPMENT

I put the chain back into the box and reduce the opening. [Lucienne] is not aware of [how to open and close] the match box. [She] possesses two preceding schemes: turning the box over in order to empty it of its contents, and sliding her fingers into the slit to make the chain come out. [She] puts her finger inside and gropes to reach the chain, but fails. A pause follows during which Lucienne manifests a very curious reaction. . . .

She looks at the slit with great attention. Then, several times in succession, she opens and shuts her mouth, at first slightly, then wider and wider! Apparently Lucienne understands the existence of a cavity . . . and wishes to enlarge that cavity. The attempt at representation which she thus furnishes is expressed plastically. That is to say, due to inability to think out the situation in words or clear visual images, she uses a simple motor indication as "signifier" or symbol. [Lucienne then] puts her finger in the slit, and, instead of trying as before to reach the chain, she pulls so as to enlarge the opening. She succeeds and grasps the chain (Piaget, 1936, pp. 337–338).

In Chapter 10 it will be seen that children at this age may use symbolic (or "pretend") play as a way of helping resolve conflicts or meeting unsatisfied needs. For example, if an 18- to 24-month-old child is scolded by parents for throwing food, he or she may later return the scolding through play with dolls, or even imaginary figures. Children at this age may similarly act out a visit to the doctor in which they behaved courageously, or pretend that they are playing with an animal that frightens them.

Language takes on greater importance in the subsequent stages of cognitive development, when children have become highly verbal. But we shall see that children's early usages of language leave something to be desired in the realm of logic.

The Preoperational Stage

According to Piaget, the **preoperational stage** of cognitive development lasts from about the age of 2 to 6 or 7. Preoperational thought is characterized by early use of words and the manipulation of symbols to represent objects and the relationships among them. But be warned—any resemblance between the logic of children between the ages of 2 to 7 and your own very often appears purely coincidental.

The peculiar nature of young children's logic reflects the fact that they are generally not capable of performing what Piaget refers to as **operations.** Or, if they can perform some operations, the circumstances under which they can perform them are limited.

Operations are mental "acts" (or schemes) in which objects are changed or transformed and can then be returned to their original states. Mental operations are flexible and reversible.

Consider the example of planning a move in checkers or chess. A move in either game requires knowledge of the rules of the game. The child who plays the game well (as opposed to just making moves) is able to picture the results of the move—how in its new position the piece will support or be threatened by other pieces, and how other pieces might be left undefended by the move. Playing checkers or chess well requires that the child be able to picture, or focus on, different parts of the board and on relationships between pieces at the same time. By considering several moves, the child shows flexibility. By

Preoperational stage The second stage in Piaget's scheme, characterized by inflexible and irreversible mental manipulation of symbols.

Operations Flexible, reversible mental manipulations of objects—in which objects can be mentally transformed, then returned to their original states.

▶ ▶ ▶ ▶

picturing the board as it would be after a move, and then as it is, the child shows reversibility.

Having said all this, let me return to the fact that this section is about *preoperational* children—children who cannot yet engage in flexible and reversible mental operations. The preoperational stage of cognitive development is characterized by many features, including egocentrism; immature notions about causality in the physical world; confusion between symbols and the objects that they represent; ability to focus on only one dimension at a time; and confusion about the identity of people and objects.

Egocentrism　When Allyn was 2 years 7 months old, I asked her to tell me about a trip with her mother to the store. Her response was, "You tell me." I tried to explain that I could not do so, because I had not been on the trip. But when I asked her to tell me about the trip again, she repeated, "You tell me." Apparently it did not occur to her that I did not share her experiences, that I could not see the world through her eyes.

Allyn's confusion may have been a reflection of what Piaget has labeled the **egocentrism** of preoperational children. Egocentrism, in Piaget's use of the term, does not mean that preoperational children are selfish (although, of course, they may be). It means that they have not yet developed a complete understanding that other people may have different perspectives on the world. They often view the world as a stage that has been erected to meet their own needs or to amuse them.

Egocentric thought and lack of knowledge lead young children to express some interesting concepts about the nature of the universe. When asked "Why does the sun shine?" preoperational children may respond, "To keep me warm."

Causality　Preoperational children's responses to questions such as "Why does the sun shine?" may show some other facets of egocentrism. At the age of 2 or so, they may simply answer that they do not know, or change the subject. But as budding psychologists, children a year or two older may report themselves as doing things because they *want* to do them, or, perhaps, "Because Mommy wants me to." In egocentric fashion, this explanation of behavior is extended to inanimate objects. And so the sun may be thought of as shining because it wants to shine, or because someone (or something) else wants it to shine.

When the sun is conceptualized as shining to keep the child warm, its behavior is thought of as being caused by *will*—perhaps the sun's voluntary wish to bathe the child in its rays, or the child's wish to remain warm. In either case, such an answer places the child at the center of the conceptual universe. The sun itself becomes an artifact, as much an instrument as is a light bulb.

Precausal Thinking　Piaget considers this type of structuring of cause and effect **precausal.** Preoperational children believe that things happen for reasons, and not by accident. However, unless preoperational children are quite familiar with the natural causes of an event, their reasons are likely to have an egocentric, psychological flavor, and not to be based on physical causes or natural law.

Preoperational children are likely to offer mechanical explanations for familiar events (Berzonsky, 1971; Gelman, 1978), such as how food gets onto a dish ("Mommy put it there") or why a tower of blocks falls ("It's too tall"). But

▶ ▶ ▶ ▶

Studying Egocentrism among Preoperational Children

▷
▷
▷
▷
▷

The Three-Mountains Test

In his own research, Piaget used the so-called three-mountains test (see Figure 8.1) to show that egocentrism means that young children literally cannot take the viewpoints of others. In this demonstration, the child sits at a table before a model of three mountains. The mountains differ in color. One also has a house on it, and another a red cross at the summit.

Piaget then places a doll elsewhere around the table and asks the child what the doll sees. The language abilities of very young children do not permit them to provide verbal descriptions of what can be seen from where the doll is situated, so they can answer in one of two ways. They can either select a photograph taken from the proper vantage point, or they can construct another model of the mountains, as they would be seen by the doll. The results of an experiment with the three-mountains test by Monique Laurendeau and Adrien Pinard (1970) suggest that 4-year-olds frequently do not understand the problem, and that 5- and 6-year-olds usually select photos or build models that correspond to their own viewpoints.

Other Methods— Different Results

Margaret Donaldson (1978) argues, however, that the difficulty young children have with the three-mountains test may not be due to egocentrism. Instead, she attributes much of their problem to the **demand characteristics** of the three-mountains test—to the demands that this particular experimental approach make on the young child.

Donaldson believes that the three-mountains test presents a "cold-blooded" scene, devoid of people and human motives. By contrast, she has found that when children are asked to place a doll of a little boy behind tabletop screens, so that it cannot be "seen" by police dolls, 3½-year-olds succeed in doing so most of the time.

In a similar experiment by John Flavell and his colleagues Susan Shipstead and Karen Croft (1978), 16 children aged 2½ were asked to hide a Snoopy doll where it could not be seen by an adult seated elsewhere at a table. Thirteen of them successfully hid the figure behind a screen, so that it could not be seen from the vantage point of the adult. However, when asked to place the doll where they could not see it themselves, only eight of the children successfully hid the doll in terms of their own vantage points.

In another study, John Flavell (1980) instructed 2½- to 4-year-olds to close their eyes and cover them with their hands. When asked, most of the children correctly stated that the researcher could not see their eyes, but could see their arms and objects in front of them.

Demand Characteristics

It seems that young children are more capable of responding successfully when the demand characteristics of the experiments require them to hide things from others rather than to depict how abstract scenes might appear from others' points of view. But these very young children are also better able to hide things from others than to place them so that they are out of sight from themselves. Perhaps they have difficulty imagining what would have to happen so that things stand in different relation to themselves. Perhaps the concept of *not* being able to see something that they can see is too hypothetical for them.

Figure 8.1 The Three-Mountains Test
Piaget used the so-called three-mountains test to learn whether children at certain ages were egocentric or could take the viewpoints of others. Other methods for assessing egocentrism show different findings.

Demand characteristics *The demands that a specific experimental approach or task makes on a subject, as opposed to the demands that would be made by the theoretical concepts if they were tested in a different way.*

▶ ▶ ▶ ▶

Developing language skills may also play a role in tests of children's egocentrism and other aspects of cognitive development. Young children, that is, may not quite understand what is being asked of them in the three-mountains test, even though they may proceed to select the (wrong) photograph rather quickly. Let me give you an example. I was interested in knowing whether Allyn, at 2 years 9 months, thought that her mother could see her from another room. "Can Mommy see you now?" I asked. "Sure," said Allyn, "if she wants to." Allyn had interpreted my question as asking whether her mother could *have permission* to see her, not whether she had the capacity to see Allyn from behind a wall. In other words, there was an essential difference between what I wanted to find out and what the demand characteristics of my question would allow me to find out. Very young children also have difficulty differentiating among the various *wh* questions.

This is no small matter. It is important that children show the seeds of taking on the viewpoints of others earlier than Piaget suggested. One result is that they are more likely to be concerned about the feelings of others than they would otherwise be.

consider the question "Why does it get dark outside?" The preoperational child usually does not have knowledge of the Earth's rotation and is likely to answer something like "So I can go to sleep." With this response, the child is also using an effect (setting the stage for sleeping) as a cause—a type of precausal thinking that Piaget refers to as **absolute finalism.**

Preoperational children also show **animism** and **artificialism** in their attributions of causality. In animistic thinking, they attribute life and intentions to inanimate objects, such as the sun and the moon. ("Why is the moon gone during the day?" "It is afraid of the sun.") Artificialism is the belief that environmental features such as rain and thunder have been designed and constructed by people. In *Six Psychological Studies,* Piaget (1967) wrote that "mountains 'grow' because stones have been manufactured and then planted. Lakes have been hollowed out, and for a long time the child believes that cities are built [prior to] the lakes adjacent to them" (p. 28).

Concepts of the Origins of Dreams Preoperational children's conceptions of the origins of dreams show an interesting reversal of the tendency to attribute psychological causes to natural events. Dreams *are* psychological activity. Dreams are cognitive events that originate within the dreamer, and they seem to be perceived through the dreamer's sensory modalities (eyes, ears, and so on), even though the eyes are closed and the silent night casts not a sound upon the ears.

These facts were understood by 7-year-olds interviewed by Laurendeau and Pinard (1962). However, many 4-year-olds conceptualized dreams as akin to films. They attributed dreams to external sources (thought that they came from the outside), and reported (incorrectly) that their eyes were open when they dreamed.

Other examples of precausal thinking are shown in Table 8.3.

Confusion between Symbols and the Objects They Represent Children from about the ages of 2 to 4 tend to show a good deal of confusion between symbols and the objects or things that they represent. Egocentrism contributes to the assumption that their thoughts are exact reflections of external reality. They do

Absolute finalism *A type of precausal thinking in which effects are perceived as causes.*

Animism *The attribution of life and intentionality to inanimate objects.*

Artificialism *The belief that environmental features were made by people.*

► ► ► ►

8   COGNITIVE DEVELOPMENT

Table 8.3 Examples of Preoperational Thought

TYPE OF THOUGHT	SAMPLE QUESTIONS	TYPICAL ANSWERS
Absolute finalism (The effect is seen as the cause.)	Why does it get dark out?	So I can go to sleep.
	Why does the sun shine?	To keep me warm.
	Why is there snow?	For me to play in.
	Why is grass green?	Because that's my favorite color.
	What are TV sets for?	To watch my favorite shows and cartoons.
Animism (attributing life to inanimate objects)	Why do trees have leaves?	To keep them warm.
	Who do stars twinkle?	Because they're happy and cheerful.
	Why does the sun move in the sky?	To follow children and hear what they say.
	Where do boats go at night?	They sleep like we do.
Artificialism (assuming that environmental features have been fashioned by people)	What makes it rain?	Someone emptying a watering can.
	Why is the sky blue?	Somebody painted it.
	What is the wind?	A man blowing.
	What causes thunder?	A man grumbling.
	How does a baby get in Mommy's tummy?	Just make it first. (How?) You put some eyes on it, put the head on (etc.).

Source: Adapted from Cowan, 1978; Turner & Helms, 1983.

not recognize that words are arbitrary, and that people could agree to use different words to refer to things.

In *Play, Dreams and Imitation in Childhood,* Piaget (1946) asks a 4-year-old child, "Could you call this table a cup and that cup a table?" "No," the child responds. "Why not?" "Because," explains the child, "you can't drink out of a table!"

At 3 years 2 months, my daughter Jordan showed less than perfect understanding of the concept of eating—or at least of the consequences of being eaten. We were watching a television show, and she asked me why the doggy was chasing the bunny. I was a bit skittish but opted in favor of the truth: "I think the dog wants to eat the bunny." "Well," replied Jordan after mulling things over, "if the dog eats the bunny, then the bunny will eat him right back." Justice is justice.

Focus on One Dimension at a Time To gain further insight into preoperational thinking, first consider these two problems: Imagine that you pour water from a low, wide glass into a tall, thin glass, as in Figure 8.2. Now, does the tall, thin glass contain more than, less than, or the same amount of water as was in the low, wide glass? I won't keep you in suspense. If you said the same (with possible minor exceptions for spilling a drop and evaporation), you were correct.

Now that you're rolling, here's another problem. If you flatten a ball of clay into a pancake, do you wind up with more, less, or the same amount of clay? If you said the same, you are correct once more. To arrive at the correct

▶ ▶ ▶ ▶

"If It's Dark Outside, I Must Be Sleeping": Some Notes on Transductive Reasoning

▷
▷
▷
▷

▷ Arguing with a 4-year-old is one of life's less productive activities. For example, I was trying to convince one of my children that she should eat because it was dinnertime. I confess that this logic did not make perfect sense to me; nonetheless, the argument had worked in the past. But this time Allyn responded that it could *not* be dinnertime because she was *not* eating.

The view that one eats *because* it is dinnertime is an example of what Piaget refers to as **transductive reasoning.** In transductive reasoning, children jump to conclusions sideways or backwards, but not from a clear understanding of cause and effect. Older children and adults usually show *inductive reasoning* and *deductive reasoning*. In inductive reasoning, we go from the specific to the general, as in, "I get tired when I jog; therefore, exercise must be fatiguing." (A good reason for avoiding jogging.) In deductive reasoning, we go from the general to the specific, as in, "Exercise is fatiguing; therefore, if I jog I'll get tired." (Another good reason for avoiding jogging.)

In one type of transductive reasoning, children go sideways from the specific to the specific. For example, a 3-year-old may argue that she should go on her swings in the back yard *because* it is light outside. Or that she should *not* go to sleep because it is light outside. That is, separate events, daylight and going on the swings (or being awake) are thought of as having cause-and-effect relationships.

In another example of transductive reasoning, children illogically assume that if B is like A in one way, B must be like A in all ways. For example, Mommy and Daddy (who are people) are good to me; therefore, all people will be good to me. Because of this type of illogical thinking, parents must warn young children against trusting strangers.

By the way, why are there income taxes? So that I can suffer every April. This is one example of transductive logic that I think we'll all admit is quite sound.

In another type of transductive reasoning, *absolute finalism,* children reason backward, from effects to causes. Pre-operational children may answer the question "Why is there snow?" by saying "For me to play in." Being able to play in the snow is, of course, an *effect* of snow, not a cause. But this confusion of cause and effect does not trouble the typical 4-year-old.

Transductive reasoning *Illogical reasoning, as in reasoning from the specific to the specific, or as in assuming that objects that share one property share all properties.*

Conservation *The principle that properties of substances such as weight and mass remain the same (are conserved) when superficial characteristics such as their shapes or arrangement are changed.*

Center *Focus.*

▶ ▶ ▶ ▶

answers to these questions, you must understand the law of **conservation.** This law holds that properties of substances such as their weight and mass remain the same—that is, weight and mass are *conserved*—even if you change their shape or arrangement.

Conservation Conservation requires the ability to focus, or **center,** on two aspects of a situation at once, such as height and width. Conserving the weight or mass of a substance requires recognition that a change in one dimension can

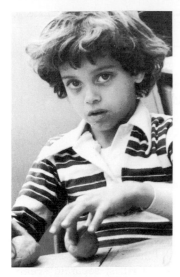

Figure 8.2 Conservation of Volume
The law of conservation holds that basic properties of substances such as weight, mass, and volume remain the same (are "conserved") even if their superficial arrangement is changed. In order to conserve the volume of water as it is poured from glass to glass, children must be able to center on two aspects of the situation at once—height and width.

Figure 8.3 Conservation of Mass
This preoperational girl has rolled two clay balls. In the top photo, she agrees that both have the same amount (mass) of clay. In the photo above, she (gleefully) flattens one clay ball. Now, when asked which piece has more clay, she replies that the flattened one does. Why? She is looking down on the clay and centering on the greater width of the flattened piece. Since she is in the preoperational stage, she does not recognize that despite the change in shape, the mass of the clay has been conserved.

compensate for a change in another. But the girl in Figure 8.3, who is in the preoperational stage, focuses only on *one dimension at a time.* When she is first presented with the two balls of clay, shown at the left, she agrees that they have the same amount of clay. Then she flattens one ball into a pancake, as shown at the right. Asked which piece now has more clay, she points to the pancake. Why? When she looks down on both pieces of clay, the pancake is wider.

The preoperational child focuses on the most apparent dimension of the situation only—in this case, perhaps, the greater width of the flattened piece of clay. She does not realize that the decrease in height compensates for the gain in width. By the way, if you ask her whether any clay has been added or taken away in the flattening process, she will readily reply no. But if you then repeat the question as to which piece has *more* clay, she will again point to the pancake.

If all this sounds rather illogical, that is because it is illogical—or, to be precise, preoperational. But if you have any doubts concerning its accuracy, borrow a brilliant 4-year-old and try the clay experiment for yourself.

After you have tried the experiment with the clay, try the following.

► ► ► ►

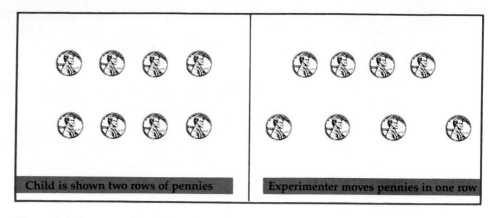

Figure 8.4 Conservation of Number
In this demonstration, we begin with two rows of pennies spread out equally (left). Then one row of pennies is spread out (right). Then we ask the child, "Which row has more pennies?" Do you think that a preoperational child will conserve the number of pennies or center on the length of the row?

Make two rows with five pennies in each, about half an inch apart. As a 3-year-old child is watching, move the pennies in the second row to about an inch apart, as in Figure 8.4. Then ask the child which row has more pennies. What do you predict the child will say?* Why?

You can also ask the 3-year-old to count the pennies in one row, tell you their number, and then do the same with the second row. Many 3-year-olds can count to five quite reliably and will state that the first row has five pennies; afterward, they will also say that the second row has five pennies. But when you again ask them which row has more pennies, they will indicate that the more spread-out row does.

Piaget states that preoperational children generally do not have the **number concept,** even though they may count quite well. The number concept requires understanding that the number of objects in an array is conserved, even if their arrangement is altered.

A study by Rochel Gelman and C. R. Gallistel (1968) suggests that many 4- and 5-year-old children are on the edge of acquiring the number concept. They can arrive at the correct number of objects in an array by counting them from one side or the other, or even by starting with an object in a location selected at random. They can add and subtract small amounts and correctly indicate whether two arrays, with objects arranged differently, are equal in number of objects. But in order to do so, they must invariably count the objects.

Identity Children gradually develop the concept of object identity. They come to recognize that people and objects retain their identities when superficial characteristics change. But in the early years of the preoperational stage, children show confusion about identity.

Number concept Awareness that the number of objects in an array remains the same even if they are rearranged.

▶ ▶ ▶ ▶

*Yes, yes! The child will say that the row that is more spread-apart has more pennies. I thought that this answer was obvious, but I include this confirmation in order to appease an editor.

A Potpourri of Experiments in Conservation

▷

▷

▷

▷

▷   A number of investigators have questioned the accuracy of Piaget's age estimates concerning children's failures (or apparent failures) to conserve quantities. Recall experiments in which Piaget and other experimenters fill two identical beakers with the same amount of water, and then pour the water from one into a beaker of another shape. Before pouring the water from one beaker into another, the experimenter typically does two things. First, he or she asks the child whether both beakers have the same amount of water. Second, the child is instructed to watch the pouring carefully. A variation on this experiment by Susan Rose and Marion Blank (1974) suggests that this approach gives the experiment demand characteristics that push the child toward the wrong answer.

Rose and Blank simply avoided questioning their young subjects as to whether the amounts in the two beakers were the same before the water was poured from one beaker to another. With this approach, 6-year-olds were significantly more likely to state that the differently shaped glasses did contain the same amount of water. The researchers suggest that the initial asking of children whether the beakers have the same amount of water can prime them to expect a change. The instruction to watch the pouring process closely can then reinforce the expectation of change. And so, Piaget and other researchers may have been systematically underestimating the age at which children can conserve quantities of water, because of the different demand characteristics of their experimental approach.

The Roles of Experience and Education

Another issue concerning the appearance of conservation has to do with the roles of experience and education. Can we accelerate children's ability to focus on more than one dimension at a time by purposefully teaching them to do so?

In one study on this question, Gilbert Botvin and Frank Murray (1975) tested first-graders for ability to conserve quantities. They then assembled the children into small discussion groups made up of two children who did show conservation and three who did not. Each group member offered reasons for his or her responses to the conservation problems, and these reasons were discussed by the group. Ultimately, all group members agreed that the answers that suggested conservation were correct.

However, the children who were initially able to conserve quantities offered explanations that differed in substance from those of the converted nonconservers. The nonconservers more often than not explained conservation by saying that the quantities retain their identity. That is, the water in the squat glass is the same water that was in the tall glass. Children who had already shown the capacity to conserve quantity were more likely to explain that the amounts were the same because the process could be reversed. That is, the water in the squat glass could be poured back into the taller glass.

We can draw a number of conclusions from the Botvin and Murray study. First, there are different ways of arriving at correct answers to many problems. Second, in many cases experience and instruction can prompt children to find more advanced solutions to specific problems. But, third, the reasoning processes (that is, the mental operations) of children may be less easy to modify. Advanced ways of thinking about the world may have to unfold largely according to the child's inner clock.

▶ ▶ ▶ ▶

The "American Question"

U.S. educators would ask Piaget to suggest ways in which children's cognitive development could be accelerated through education. Piaget would not directly answer this "American question." For one thing, Piaget was more concerned with learning *why* children made incorrect answers than he was with fostering correct answers. Also, Piaget assumed that the foundation of cognitive development was maturational, and maturation cannot be greatly accelerated by education or experience. Recall that Piaget also believed that cognitive activity was self-reinforcing. Given exposure to educational materials, children would achieve when they were ready to achieve. A message here seems to be that many of us (and our children) might be better served if we relaxed and enjoyed observing them as they develop, instead of trying to force development.

Let us for the moment put aside the issue of the ages at which certain types of thought processes occur. There are other fascinating consequences to the young child's inability to center on two dimensions at the same time. As you can see in the following extract from a study by Hartley and Hartley (1955), young children cannot conceptualize belonging to two classes at the same time:

One child, 3½ years old replied to the question, "Are you American?" with *"No, I'm a cowboy."* Another child (4 years 5 months) when asked, "Are you Catholic?" replied, *"No, I'm Richie."* A third, the same age, to, "Are you Jewish?" said, *"No, I'm only four. I'll get Jewish."* Still another faced with "Are you American?" replied, *"No, my father is American. I'm a girl."*

Piaget demonstrated young children's confusion about identity by pouring water from one glass to another and asking children whether it was still the same water. Or he bent a wire and asked whether it remained the same wire. Or he asked whether a seedling remained the same plant when it blossomed. Very young children typically responded that the water was different water, or that the wire was a different piece of wire. Not until about the age of 7 do children recognize that growing plants retain their identities as they change in size and shape.

In one study of children's concepts of identity, Rheta DeVries (1969) showed 3- to 6-year-olds a cat and then made some changes in the cat's appearance as they watched. First she showed the children the cat, and they all identified its species correctly. Then she turned the cat around, placed a dog or rabbit mask on its head, turned it back to the children, and asked again what animal it was. The 3-year-olds responded that it was a dog or rabbit, depending on the mask. The 4-year-olds generally responded with the new label also, even though they had earlier stated that the cat would retain its identity, whether or not its appearance was altered. Despite their predictions, it seems that once they were faced with the mask they could only focus on the mask (one dimension at a time), and not conserve the cat's identity. But the 5- and 6-year-olds were able to conserve the cat's identity. Five- and 6-year-olds generally responded that the cat remained a cat, regardless of its mask.

Young children may or may not think of themselves as different persons at different ages. They usually correctly label pictures of themselves at earlier ages, for example. However, this stability in identity may not reach into children's projections of their futures. Lawrence Kohlberg (1966, 1967) has found that 4-year-olds do not necessarily assume they will retain their genders once they grow up—that is, that girls will become women or boys will become men. Young children may even think it possible that they could change into animals, or that animals could change into people, as happens in some myths.

▶ ▶ ▶ ▶

Children's Concepts about Sex and Elimination

▷

▷

▷

▷

▷ I recall a trip to the pediatrician when my wife and I were struggling to find the right word to discuss our first child's bowel movements. After we fumbled about a bit, the pediatrician happily pronounced the word *poo. Poo,* it turned out, was not only a noun (as in "The child made *poo"),* but also a verb (as in, "The child *poos").* Since then we have, with a bit of self-consciousness (after all, we are both educated), used the word *poo* with all our children, and, in this way, also taught the word to them.

A typical exchange upon detecting a familiar odor emanating from the diaper:

> US: "Do you have something to tell us?"
>
> CHILD (perhaps a bit embarrassed): "Poo."

Parents are also often concerned about what they will say when their children first ask them about sexual matters, such as where babies come from. Ann Bernstein (Bernstein, 1976; Bernstein & Cowan, 1975) reversed the process by asking preoperational children where *they* thought babies came from. She found that 3- to 4-year-old children held geographic concepts concerning the issue. Children at this age tended to assume that the baby had always existed and that the issue really was *where* the baby had come from. It was apparently this type of thinking that led them to give answers such as: "You go to the baby store and buy one"; "From tummies"; "From God's place."

James Moore and Diane Kendall (1971) interviewed 3- to 5½-year-old children and found that 41 percent of the boys and 50 percent of the girls thought that babies came from their mothers' stomach—usually expressed as "tummy." Other popular answers included "the hospital," "the doctor," "the nurse," and "God." Only 7 percent of the girls and none of the boys knew that babies came from the uterus.

Bernstein and Cowan (1975) found that many 7- to 8-year-old children could refer to three aspects of the creation of babies: a social relationship between parents, something about the mechanics of sexual relations, and something about the combining of materials contributed by each parent. But little understanding of the fact that sperm and egg cells unite, and that babies develop from zygotes, was shown by children younger than 11 or 12.

Moore and Kendall also asked their subjects, "What do you call the water that comes out of your body when you use the toilet?" Only two of the 38 girls interviewed, and one of 31 boys, said "urine." The most frequently given answer was "pee pee." Other answers included "potty water," "tinkle," "wee wee," and "wet." Two children had no answer.

Children's lack of knowledge, of course, reflects both the status of their cognitive development and the presence (or lack) of accurate information. I am generally in favor of giving children accurate labels and explanations, but the term "bowel movement" does seem unwieldy for a 1-year-old.

Still, the use of the word *poo* did create a problem or two when our children were ready to hear about *Winnie the Pooh.*

▶ ▶ ▶ ▶

Adding numbers is a reversible operation. The numbers can also be subtracted. Concrete operational children recognize that certain relationships exist among numbers—that operations can be carried out according to certain rules. This understanding lends concrete operational thought flexibility and reversibility.

The Concrete Operational Stage

According to Piaget, the typical child is entering the stage of **concrete operations** by the age of 6 or 7. As noted earlier, operations are mental actions, or schemes, that are flexible and reversible.

Recall the planning of moves in the games of checkers and chess as examples of operations. Adding the numbers two and three to get five is another kind of operation. This operation is reversible, in that the child can then subtract two from five in order to get three. There is flexibility in that the child can also subtract three from five in order to get the number two. To the concrete operational child, adding and subtracting are not simply rote activities. The concrete operational child recognizes that there are certain relationships among numbers—that operations can be carried out according to certain rules. It is this understanding that lends concrete operational thought its flexibility and reversibility.

In the stage of concrete operations, which lasts until about the age of 12, children show the beginnings of the capacity for adult logic. They understand basic rules of logic that Piaget referred to as "groupings." However, their thought processes, or operations, generally involve tangible objects rather than abstract ideas. This is why we refer to their thinking as concrete.

Egocentrism Concrete operational children are less egocentric. Their abilities to take on the roles of others and view the world, and themselves, from other peoples' perspectives are greatly expanded. They recognize that people see things in different ways, because of different situations and different sets of values.

Decentration As compared with preoperational children, who can focus on only one dimension of a problem at a time, concrete operational children can engage in **decentration**. That is, they can focus simultaneously on multiple dimensions or aspects of a problem.

Decentration has implications for conservation, categorical thinking, and other intellectual undertakings.

Concrete operations The third stage in Piaget's scheme, characterized by flexible, reversible operations concerning concrete, specific objects and events.

Decentration Simultaneous focusing (centering) on more than one aspect or dimension of a problem or situation.

▶ ▶ ▶ ▶

Conservation   Concrete operational children show understanding of the laws of conservation. The girl in Figure 8.3, now a few years older, would say that the flattened ball still has the same amount of clay. If asked why, she might reply, "Because you can roll it up again like the other one"—an answer that shows reversibility.

The concrete operational girl is also aware of the principle that objects can have several properties or dimensions. Things that are tall can also be heavy or light. Things that are red can also be bright or dull, or round or square, or thick or thin. Knowledge of this principle allows her to *decenter* and avoid focusing on only the diameter of the clay pancake. By paying simultaneous attention to both the height and the width of the clay, she recognizes that the loss in height compensates for the gain in width.

Researchers such as Carol Tomlinson-Keasey and her colleagues (1979) have found that children do not develop conservation in all kinds of tasks simultaneously. For example, conservation of mass usually develops first, followed by conservation of weight and conservation of volume. Piaget referred to the sequential development of concrete operations as **horizontal décalage.** As Piaget theorized, the cognitive gains of the concrete operational stage are so tied to specific events that achievement in one area does not automatically transfer to achievement in another.

Transitivity   I have asked you some tough questions in this book, but here is a real ogre: If your parents are older than you are, and you are older than your children, are your parents older than your children? The answer, of course, is yes. (Were you concerned for a moment that it might not be?) But how did you arrive at this answer? If you said yes simply on the basis of knowing that your parents are older than your children (for example, 58 and 56 as compared to 5 and 3), your answer was not based on concrete operational thought. Concrete operational thought requires awareness of the principle of **transitivity:** If A exceeds B in some property (say age or height), and B exceeds C, then A must also exceed C.

Seriation   **Seriation** is the placing of objects in a series, or order, according to some property or trait. Seriation (for example, lining up one's family members according to age, height, or weight) is made easier when one has knowledge of transitivity, but this knowledge is not always required. Let us consider some examples with preoperational and concrete operational children.

Piaget frequently assessed children's abilities at seriation by asking them to place ten sticks in order of size, or to match dolls of different sizes to "walking sticks." Four- to 5-year-old children usually place the sticks in a random sequence, or in small groups, as in small, medium, or large. They show similar arrangements with the dolls and walking sticks.

Six- to 7-year-old children, who are in transition between the preoperational and concrete operational stages, may arrive at proper sequences. However, they usually do so by trial and error, rearranging their series a number of times. In other words, they are capable of comparing two sticks and deciding that one is longer than the other, but their overall perspective seems limited to the pair they are comparing at the time, and does not seem to encompass the entire array.

But consider the approach of 7- or 8-year-olds who are capable of concrete operations. They go about the task systematically, usually without error.

▶ ▶ ▶ ▶

Horizontal décalage (day-kah-lahzh). *The sequential unfolding of the ability to master different kinds of cognitive tasks within the same stage.*

Transitivity *The principle that if A > B in a property, and B > C, then A > C.*

Seriation *Placing objects in an order or series according to a property or trait.*

In the case of the ten sticks, they look over the array, then select either the longest or shortest and place it at the point from which they will build their series. Then they select the next longest (or shortest) and continue in this fashion until the task is complete.

Knowledge of the principle of transitivity allows concrete operational children to go about their task unerringly. They realize that if stick A is longer than stick B, and stick B is longer than stick C, then stick A is also longer than stick C. After putting stick C in place, they need not double check in hope that it will be shorter than stick A; they *know* that it will be.

Concrete operational children also have the decentration capacity to allow them to seriate in two dimensions at once. Consider a seriation task used by Piaget and his longtime colleague Bärbel Inhelder (see Figure 8.5). In this test, children are given 49 leaves and asked to classify them according to size and brightness (from small to large and from dark to light). As the grid is completed from left to right, the leaves become lighter. As it is filled in from top to bottom, the leaves become larger. Preoperational 6-year-olds can usually order the leaves according to size or brightness, but not both simultaneously. But concrete operational children of 6 or 7 can work with both dimensions at once and fill in the grid properly.

As with other dimensions of cognitive development, a number of researchers (for example, Brainerd, 1978; Bryant & Trabasso, 1971; Flavell, 1977; Trabasso, 1977) have argued that children develop seriation ability earlier than Piaget believed, and that Piaget's results reflected the demand characteristics of his experiments. This may be so, but again, the sequence of developments in seriation and transitivity seems to have been captured fairly well by Piaget.

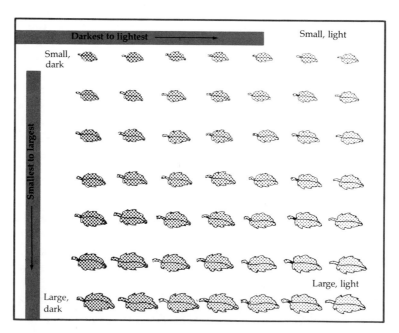

Figure 8.5 A Grid for Demonstrating the Development of Seriation
In order to properly classify 49 leaves, children must be able to center on two dimensions at once: size and brightness. They must also recognize that if quantity A exceeds quantity B and quantity B exceeds quantity C, then quantity A must also exceed quantity C. This relationship is called the principle of transitivity.

▶ ▶ ▶ ▶

8 COGNITIVE DEVELOPMENT

Classification   Another example of an operation is class inclusion, or the organizing of objects into categories. One classification operation is the grouping of three red roses and four yellow roses to make up seven roses. One can then include these seven roses in the same class with four daisies to make up 11 flowers. One can go on to include the 11 flowers with three trees to make up 14 plants. Roses, flowers, and plants are just some examples of the types of classes that we can form when we travel up the hierarchy of living things, but I think I will stop here since the point has made and I'm afraid I'll run out of classes.

Classes are determined by the characteristics shared by their members. Only closed geometric figures with four sides equal in length fit into the class of squares. But both circles and squares fit into the class of geometric figures. Yellow and red roses both fit into the class of roses, because they have in common the characteristics that make up roses. However, red roses do not fit into the class called yellow roses, because they do not share the essential sameness of color.

Researchers usually study children's classification abilities by presenting them with various objects and asking them to group the ones that go together. In one approach, Inhelder and Piaget (1959) gave children 20 geometric shapes and asked them to group the ones that went together: five blue squares, five blue circles, five red squares, and five red circles. Many 2- to 4-year-old children do not understand the task at all, while others may group them according to either color or shape (blue and red figures, or circles and squares), centering on one dimension only.

Four- to 5-year-old children frequently make two piles and then further divide one of them, so that they wind up with three piles (for example, blue figures, red circles, and red squares). Or children at this age may make four separate piles, as shown in Figure 8.6, but there may be some trial and error, and they may show difficulty focusing simultaneously on the dimensions of shape and color when interviewed. In the latter case, a typical interview would go like this:

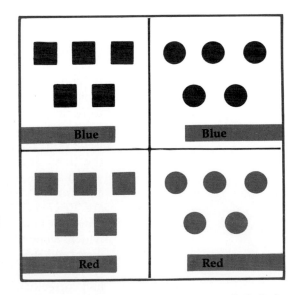

Figure 8.6 A Demonstration of Classification Ability in Children
These objects may be grouped according to shape and color. Many 2- to 4-year-old children do not know what to do when asked to put together the pieces that go together. Others at this age may group according to color or shape, centering on one dimension only.

▶ ▶ ▶ ▶

RESEARCHER: Can we put these [the two blue] piles together?
5-YEAR-OLD CHILD: Yes.
RESEARCHER: If we put them together, what are they like?
CHILD: Like squares.
RESEARCHER: Is that all?
CHILD: They're like circles, too.
RESEARCHER: Can we put them together?
CHILD: Sure.
RESEARCHER: Why?
CHILD: You tell me.
RESEARCHER: Why can we put them together?
CHILD: I don't know.

Even though the 5-year-old in this extract placed the shapes into four categories according to color and shape, she showed difficulty shifting from one shape concept to another, and from focusing on shapes to focusing on colors. Her thought processes, in other words, did not show the flexibility and reversibility that are characteristic of operational children.

Concrete operational 7- and 8-year olds will usually stop to think for a moment when asked to group the 20 figures, and then they will construct four piles rapidly and without error. When asked to explain the rationale behind their behavior, they will readily refer to the shapes and colors of the figures. Their mental structures permit decentration; they can focus simultaneously on multiple characteristics of objects.

Consider another example. Let us imagine that you place three roses and four daffodils in front of a 4-year-old, so that there are seven flowers altogether. If you ask the child whether there are more daffodils or more flowers, what will the child say? Oh, look, I'll tell you even more about the child. She knows what roses and daffodils are, and she also knows that they are both types of flowers. Now what do you think she will say?

Experiments have found that preoperational children usually think there are more daffodils than flowers (Piaget, 1952). According to the rules that govern class inclusion, if A (flowers) is composed of B_1 (roses) and B_2 (daffodils), then there is more of A than of either B_1 or B_2. But preoperational children may not be able to focus on classes (A) and subclasses (B_1 or B_2) simultaneously, and so they cannot readily compare the two.

Concrete operational children can focus on two dimensions (in this case, classes and subclasses) at the same time. Therefore, they more likely to answer the question about the daffodils and the flowers correctly. But their thought remains concrete in that they will give you the correct answer if you ask them about daffodils and flowers (or lemon drops and candy), but not if you attempt to phrase the question in terms of abstract symbols, such as A, B_1 and B_2.

As with other areas of cognitive development, researchers have taken issue with Piaget's views of the ages at which classification skills develop, and they have argued that language continues to pose hazards for the children being tested. One review of the literature on class inclusion suggested that many children cannot answer standard class-inclusion questions correctly until they are 10 years old, or even older (Winer, 1980). In an experiment reported by Margaret Donaldson (1979), 6-year-olds were shown four cow figures, three of which were black. All the cows were placed on their sides and the children were told that they were alseep. Only one child in four correctly answered the typical question "Are there more black cows or more cows?" However, nearly half correctly answered the question "Are there more black cows or more sleeping cows?" Why? The researcher suggests that it is possible that the adjective *sleeping* helped direct the children's attention to the entire group (A). However, it is also possible that the 6-year-olds conceptualized black cows and sleeping cows as two subgroups (B_1 and B_2, rather than B_1 and A), so that they were still not thinking simultaneously about a class and a subclass.

Let us now turn our attention to the cognitive developments that signify the transition from concrete operational thought to formal operational thought.

The Formal Operational Stage

Formal operations The fourth stage of Piaget's scheme, characterized by the capacity for flexible, reversible operations concerning abstract ideas and concepts, such as symbols, statements, and theories.

The stage of **formal operations** is the final one in Piaget's scheme—the stage of cognitive maturity. For many children in Western societies, formal operational thought begins at about the time of puberty—the age of 11 or 12. However, not all children enter this stage at the time of puberty, and some people never reach it.

The major tasks of the stage of formal operations involve classification, logical thought, and the ability to hypothesize. Central features are the ability to think about ideas as well as objects and to group and classify ideas—symbols, statements, entire theories. The flexibility and reversibility of operations, when applied to statements and theories, allow adolescents to follow arguments from premises to conclusions and back again.

There are several features of formal operational thought that give the adolescent a generally greater capacity to manipulate and appreciate the outer environment and the world of the imagination: hypothetical thinking, systematic problem solving, the ability to use symbols to stand for symbols, and deductive reasoning.

Hypothetical Thinking As Cowan notes, it is in formal operational thought that children—by now, adolescents—"discover the world of the hypothetical" (1978, p. 249). Adolescents can project themselves into situations that transcend their immediate experience, and, for this reason, they may become wrapped up in lengthy fantasies. Many adolescents can explore endless corridors of the mind, perceiving what would happen as one decision leads to another choice

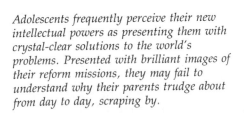

Adolescents frequently perceive their new intellectual powers as presenting them with crystal-clear solutions to the world's problems. Presented with brilliant images of their reform missions, they may fail to understand why their parents trudge about from day to day, scraping by.

▶ ▶ ▶ ▶

The Puzzle and the Pendulum

▷
▷
▷
▷
▷   If you hang a weight from a string and set it swinging back and forth, you have a pendulum. Bärbel Inhelder and Jean Piaget (1958) used a pendulum to explore ways in which children of different ages went about solving problems.

The researchers showed the children several pendulums, with different lengths of string and with different weights at their ends, as in Figure 8.7. They attached the strings to rods and sent the weights swinging. They dropped them from various heights and gave them pushes with forces of various intensities. The question they posed—the puzzle—was as follows: *What determines how fast the pendulum will swing back and forth?*

The researchers had varied four factors: the amount of weight, the length of the string, the height from which the weight was released, and the force with which the weight was pushed. The answer lies either in one of these factors, or in some combination of them. That is, the answer could involve one factor, two factors, three factors, or all factors. It could be expressed as 1, 2, 3, or 4; or 1 *and* 2, 1 and 3, 1 and 4; 2 and 3, etc.

One could try to solve this problem by deducing the answer from principles of physics, and physicists would probably prefer to use a deductive approach. However, one can also arrive at an empirical solution by trying out each possible com-

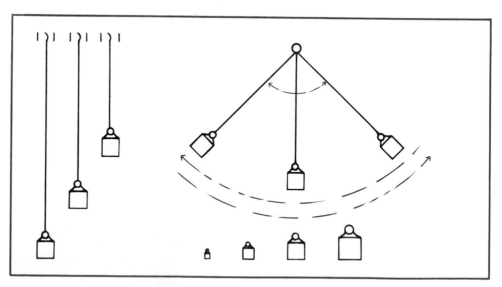

Figure 8.7 The Pendulum Problem
What determines how fast the pendulum will swing back and forth? the amount of the weight? the length of the string? the height from which the weight is released? the force with which the weight is pushed? or a combination of the above? Formal operational children attempt systematically to exclude each factor.

▶ ▶ ▶ ▶

bination of factors. Since most children (and most adults) are not physicists, they usually undertake the empirical approach.

Of the subjects tested by Inhelder and Piaget, children between the ages of 8 and 13 could not arrive at the correct answer. The fault lay largely in their approach, which was only partly systematic. They made some effort to account for the different factors, but did not control carefully for every single possibility. For example, one child compared a pendulum with a light weight and a short string to a pendulum with a heavy weight and a long string. They swung at different speeds, and so the child concluded that both factors, weight and length, were involved. After "getting the problem down" to the two factors, the child did not attempt to control for weight by switching weights while holding the length constant.

In the same study, the 14- and 15-year-olds generally set about solving the problem more systematically. First, they sat back and reflected for a while before beginning to manipulate the factors. Then, in contrast to the younger children, who hap-

hazardly varied two or more factors at a time, the older children attempted systematically to exclude each factor. They used what we call the "process of elimination" when we take multiple-choice tests. Not all of the 14- or 15-year-olds solved the problem, but the researchers concluded that, as a group, their approach was more advanced and more likely to succeed.

According to Inhelder and Piaget, the approach of the 14- and 15-year-olds was characteristic of formal operational thought. The approach of the 8- to 13-year-olds was characteristic of concrete operational thought. As with so many other aspects of Piaget's views and his experimental methods, we have to be somewhat flexible about the age estimates at which children are assumed to be capable of solving this problem. Robert Siegler and his associates (1973), for example, were able to train 10-year-olds to approach the problem in a way that allowed them to isolate the crucial factor of the length of the string. Here, too, is evidence that education and training can make a difference in the development of cognitive skills.

point, and then still another decision is made. Adolescents become aware that situations can have different outcomes. They can think ahead, systematically "trying out" various possibilities.

In a sense, it is during the stage of formal operations that people tend to emerge as theoretical scientists—even though they may think of themselves as having little or no interest in science. Adolescents may conduct daily "experiments" to determine whether their hypotheses are correct. I am not talking about experiments carried out in the laboratory with calipers or Bunsen burners. It is more common for adolescents to experiment with different tones of voice, different ways of carrying themselves, and different ways of treating others to see which sorts of behavior are most effective for them.

Endless Alternatives—Worlds without End   Adolescents, who can look ahead to multiple outcomes, may also see varieties of possibilities for themselves. Some become acutely aware that they have the capacity, to a large extent, to create or fashion themselves according to their own images of what they are capable of becoming. In terms of career decisions, the wealth of possible directions leads some adolescents to experience anxiety as to whether they will pick the one career that really "is" them, and to experience a sense of loss that they probably will have the opportunity to choose only one.

This capacity to look ahead, to fashion futures, also frequently leads to **utopian** thinking. Just as adolescents can foresee many possibilities for themselves, they can also imagine different outcomes for suffering humanity. "What

Utopian Having to do with an idealistically perfect vision of society.

▶ ▶ ▶ ▶

if'' thinking enables adolescents to fashion schemes for putting an end to hunger, disease, and international strife. Adolescents frequently adopt "young" political figures who claim to have "new ideas" with a religious fervor.

Systematic Problem Solving   The ability to form hypotheses and to test them out enables formal operational children to use more systematic ways of solving problems. Contrast the ways in which children at different ages set about solving a typical problem posed by Inhelder and Piaget (1958) in the nearby box, "The Puzzle and the Pendulum."

Sophisticated Use of Symbols   Elementary school children can understand what is meant by abstract symbols such as 1 and 2. They can also perform operations in which these numbers, and others, are manipulated—added, subtracted, and so on. But now consider X, that unknown (and, sometimes, evasive!) quantity in algebra. X may be a familiar letter of the alphabet, but its designation as a symbol for an unknown quantity is a formal abstract operation. One symbol (an X) is being made to stand for something just as abstract (the unknown). Children through the age of 11 or 12 or so usually cannot fully understand this concept, even if they can be taught the mechanics of "solving for X" in simple equations. But older, formal operational children show a sophisticated grasp of the nature of symbols that allows them to grasp intuitively what is "meant" by X. Formal operational children, or adolescents, can perform mental operations with symbols that stand for nothing in their own experience.

This also means that formal operational children may be ready for geometry. In geometry they learn "proofs" for relationships between points, lines, and perfect figures (such as circles and squares) that have no existence in the real world. Geometrical knowledge will ultimately allow them to engage in engineering and architecture—to engage, that is, in formal operations (manipulation of geometric symbols) in such a way that they derive solutions to problems with real materials and objects.

Formal operational thought is not a universal step in cognitive development. The ability to solve abstract problems, such as those found in algebra and the pendulum problem, is much more likely to be developed in "high-tech" Western societies, or in major cities, than in rural areas of less well-developed nations (Keating & Clark, 1980; Super, 1980). Moreover, reviews of the literature (Keating, 1980; Neimark, 1975) suggest that formal operational thought, as it is traditionally assessed, is found only among 40–60 percent of college first-year students. We are also more likely to use formal operational thought in the academic areas on which we focus. Some of us are formal operational in math or science, but not in the study of literature, and vice versa.

Appreciation of Metaphor   Formal operational individuals can also understand, appreciate, and sometimes produce **metaphors**. Metaphors are figures of speech in which words or phrases that ordinarily signify one thing are applied to another.

Consider the sentence "The ship plowed through the water." A plow is an instrument that furrows the soil. Portraying a ship as plowing through water suggests a comparison between the ship and the plow, and creates an image of "cutting through" and "turning up" water, as the plow does to the soil.

Metaphors play with words as symbols. Words are poetically assimi-

Metaphor *A figure of speech in which the words used to describe one thing are applied to another, increasing appreciation of both things.*

▶ ▶ ▶ ▶

lated to new schemes (as plowing is assimilated to our understanding of the movements of ships). But accommodation also occurs as the schemes are transformed in the process; the plowing metaphor transforms our image of the ship. The adaptation of words as metaphors requires the verbal fluency* and mental flexibility to associate words with situations that are perceived as having some property in common (for example, the common *movements* of the ship and plow).

We find endless examples of metaphor in literature, but consider for a moment how everyday figures of speech enhance and transform our experience: *squeezing* out a living; *aiming barbs* at someone; *glowing* in the *warmth* of someone's embrace, or *basking in the sunshine* of fame or glory; *narrowing in* on a solution; *hanging by a thread*; *jumping* to conclusions; and so on.

Deductive Reasoning Formal operational individuals can reason deductively, or draw conclusions about specific objects or people once they have been classified accurately. Consider this frequently cited **syllogism:** "All men are mortal. Socrates is a man. Therefore Socrates is mortal." Formal operational people can follow the logical process in this syllogism. First, a statement is made about a class or group of objects ("All *men* are mortal"). Second, a particular object or event (in this case, Socrates) is assigned to that class—that is, "*Socrates* is a man." Finally, it is concluded, or deduced, that what is true for the class (men) is also true for the particular object or event (Socrates)—that is, "Socrates is mortal."

As we shall see in Chapter 14, when we discuss Lawrence Kohlberg's theory of moral development, the moral judgments of many adolescents and adults are based on formal operational thought. That is, they derive their judgments about what is right and wrong in specific situations by reasoning from general moral principles. Their capacity for decentration also allows them to take a "broad view" of the situation. That is, they can focus on many aspects of a situation at once in arriving at their judgments and solving moral dilemmas.

Idealism Adolescents may be proud of their new logical abilities. A new sort of egocentrism can develop in which adolescents adamantly press for acceptance of their political and social ideas without recognition of the practical problems that are often considered by adults. Consider this example. "It is wrong to hurt people. Industry A occasionally hurts people (perhaps through pollution or economic pressures). Therefore, Industry A must be severely punished or dismantled." This thinking is not illogical. But it is idealistic, in that it does not take into account "practical" considerations. For example, there could be thousands of layoffs if the industry were precipitously dismantled. The industry may also be supplying a vital need, and other arrangements may have to be made before production can be discontinued.

Adolescents' new intellectual powers often present them with what seem to be crystal-clear solutions to the world's problems, and they may become intolerant of the relative stodginess of their parents. Their own brilliant images of how to reform the world cause them to be unsympathetic to their parents' earthbound pursuit of a livelihood and other mundane matters.

It is, of course, something of a pity that adolescents eventually become

*Verbal fluency is one of the concepts concerning the study of intelligence that we shall discuss in the next chapter.

weighed down by the ifs, ands, and buts of the real world. Taking the broader view seems gray, indeed, by comparison.

Evaluation of Piaget's Cognitive-Developmental Theory

Although Piaget's theory has led many U.S. developmentalists to recast their concepts of children, it has also met with criticism on several grounds.

Was Piaget's Timing Accurate?   Some researchers have shown that Piaget underestimated the abilities of preschoolers. In regard to their egocenticity, as we have seen, researchers who present preschool children with different task demands arrive at different impressions of how egocentric they are. We have also seen how modified task demands suggest that children are capable of conservation and other concrete operational tasks earlier than Piaget believed.

Was Piaget's Use of Concepts Too Global?   A number of investigators have found that Piaget's use of such terms as *egocentrism*, *centration*, and *conservation* may have been too global. Research has suggested that these terms encompass a variety of skills and knowledge. Consider egocentrism. One aspect of ego-centrism is literally taking the viewpoint of another, as in the three-mountains test. However, as we shall see in our discussion of social and emotional development, many children show empathy for the problems of other people prior to the age of 2.

Is Cognitive Development Really Discontinuous?   Perhaps the most potentially damaging of the criticisms leveled at Piaget is that cognitive skills such as egocentrism and conservation appear to develop more independently and continuously than Piaget thought—not in general stages. For example, Piaget described the classification abilities of 2- to 8-year-old children in three stages. These include (1) grouping items to form a design (as in combining shapes to build a house), (2) grouping according to criteria that may shift during the task (first grouping shapes by color, then by form), and (3) grouping according to stable criteria. However, Nancy Denney's (1972) research with U.S. children suggests that their classification skills may develop more continuously. Her 2- to 4-year-olds first showed inability to classify shapes of different colors and sizes according to similarity. Next, they showed partial grouping by similarity. Finally, they grouped on the basis of similarity. Moreover, 23 of the 36 4-year-olds in Denney's study were able to classify according to similarity—several years younger than Piaget's subjects.

A number of researchers, including John Flavell (1982), take(s) Denney's findings one step further. They argue that cognitive development is "*not* very stage-like" at all (Flavell, 1982, p. 17). The heart of the stage-theory approach is that changes are discontinuous. In the case of cognitive-developmental theory, children's ways of representing the world and solving problems would have to change relatively suddenly. Their responses to the world, as governed by their cognitive processes, would have to change dramatically. Flavell admits that "later cognitive acquisitions build on or are otherwise linked to earlier ones, and in their turn similarly prepare the ground for later ones" (1982, p. 18). However, the "acquisitions" process may be gradual, not discontinuous.

▶ ▶ ▶ ▶

In one example of Flavell's point, children's cognitive skills at a given age show *horizontal* inconsistencies. As noted in the discussion of horizontal décalage, conservation does not arrive all at once. Instead, children develop conservation for mass, weight, and volume at different ages. The onset of conservation may be more *continuous* than cognitive-developmental theory suggests. If this is so, the onset of conservation could be viewed in terms of the gradual accumulation of problem-solving abilities, instead of in terms of changing cognitive structures (Flavell, 1982; Scholnick, 1983).

Are the Sequences of Development Invariant?   Here we can probably offer a reasonably assured *yes*. While the notion of horizontal décalage is inconsistent with some of Piaget's ideas, it may not refute the heart of Piaget's concepts. The sequences of cognitive change—even within horizontal décalage—appear to remain invariant. I think it is fair to say that the sequences of development are more essential to Piaget's theory than their timing.

What About the Effects of Training? Back to the "American Question"   Nancy Denney (1972) suggests that her 2- to 4-year-olds may have been more advanced than Piaget's, because contemporary U.S. children profit from television and preschooling in ways that Piaget had not anticipated. Thus Denney's findings also bring us to another criticism of Piaget—the extent to which education can accelerate children's cognitive development.

As noted, Piaget's stages are not completely age-bound. He allowed that some children develop different capacities earlier than others. Piaget also acknowledged that training could foster cognitive advances—although in minor and meaningless increments. This is why Piaget paid little attention to the "American question" as to how education could be tailored to foster cognitive development. However, the achieving of a stage *several years* prior to Piaget's expectations is not a minor or meaningless discrepancy. Such a difference creates major problems for Piaget's concept of the timing of cognitive development.

In another study, Denney and her colleagues (1977) found that children could develop conservation as a result of demonstrations, instruction, and practice. Piaget had suggested that such advancements would usually be temporary, unless children were on the brink of arriving at concepts by themselves. However, a study by Dorothy Field (1981) found that 4-year-olds who were taught conservation of number retained their training several months later.

In sum, Piaget's theoretical edifice has been rocked, but it has not been dashed to rubble. Though research continues to wear away at his timing and at his views on the futility of attempting to accelerate cognitive development, his observations on the sequences of development appear to remain relatively inviolate.

The great majority of developmentalists regard Piaget as a towering figure in the study of cognitive development, but it is erroneous to view his approach as the only one. There are many others, including information-processing approaches. Information-processing approaches focus on children's memories and problem-solving abilities. However, whereas Piaget used the biological models of assimilation and accommodation as his model for cognition, information-processing theorists have turned to the computer and artificial intelligence.

▶ ▶ ▶ ▶

Information-Processing Approaches to Cognitive Development

Piaget looked upon children as budding scientists, but it could be said that **information-processing** approaches view children (and adults) as similar in some ways to computer systems. Computers receive information about problems (input), store the information permanently or in "working memory," process the information according to certain programs, and then yield answers (output). Similarly, children can be conceptualized as attaining information from the environment, storing the information, retrieving and manipulating the information as needed, and then responding to it overtly.

The central goal of the information-processing approach appears to be to learn how children store, retrieve, and manipulate information—how their "mental programs" develop. Information-processing theorists also study the development of children's strategies for processing information.

Although there may be something to be gained from thinking of children as analogous to computers, children, of course, are not computers. Children are self-aware and capable of creativity and intuition. How then, we may also ask, does self-awareness influence the development of information processing?

Developments in the Storage and Retrieval of Information

In the midst of these abstract concepts, it may be comforting to point out that psychologists use the familiar term **memory** to refer to the processes of storing and retrieving information. The development of memory permeates every aspect of the child's cognitive development, including the development of social values such as altruism, equality, and helping the group (Knight et al., 1985).

Some aspects of development that have been thought to reflect increasing capacity for the complexity and quality of thought may actually reflect an increasing capacity for memory (Gelman & Baillargeon, 1983). In Chapter 13, for example, we shall see that Jean Piaget studied children's processes of moral reasoning by telling them stories about other children. In one story, Child A breaks four cups while trying to help his mother set the dinner table. Child B breaks one cup while trying to steal a cookie from the cookie jar. Who is naughtier—Child A or Child B?

Most 5-year-olds would say that Child A is naughtier, because he broke more cups, whereas 8-year-olds would usually consider Child B naughtier, because he was doing something wrong when he broke the cup. Piaget explained this age difference in terms of 5-year-olds' tendencies to focus on the amount of damage done instead of the intentions of the wrongdoer. However many 5-year-olds say that Child A is naughtier, because it is easy to remember that he broke more cups, but they do not remember all the details of the two stories. When the stories are repeated a few times, and effort is made to make sure that children remember them well, even 5-year-olds frequently consider the intentions of the wrongdoer as well as the amount of damage done.

Now let us follow some of the more important developments in information processing during childhood.

Information processing An approach to understanding cognitive processes in which children are compared to computers, which deal with the input, storage, retrieval, manipulation, and output of information. The focus is on how children's "mental programs" develop.

Memory The processes by which we store and retrieve information.

► ► ► ►

Development of Selective Attention

The world is an ever-changing display of sights and sounds and other sources of sensory stimulation, but only some of these are remembered. Memory first requires that children pay attention to a stimulus or image, whether a new toy, a new name, or an idea. Paying attention somehow separates it from the surrounding stimuli, which the child is less likely to retain.

The attention of infants is first captured by stimuli that have salient features—for example, moving stimuli, contrasting stimuli, stimuli that resemble the face, and stimuli that are red or blue as opposed to green or yellow. But as infants develop, they begin to intentionally focus their attention. One experiment found that 2-year-old boys are more likely to attend to and remember toys like cars, puzzles, and trains, while 2-year-old girls are more likely to attend to and remember dolls, dishes, and teddy bears (Renninger & Wozniak, 1985). Even by this age, sex-role expectations may exert their influence on cognitive processes.

The ability to focus one's attention and screen out distractions advances steadily through middle childhood (Pick et al., 1975). Preoperational children engaged in problem solving tend to focus (or center) their attention on one element of the problem at a time—a major reason that they lack conservation. Concrete and formal operational children, by contrast, can attend to multiple aspects of the problem at once, permitting them to conserve number, volume, and so on.

A classic experiment by Eleanor Maccoby and John Hagen (1965) illustrates how selective attention develops during middle childhood. The researchers showed children between 6 and 12 years of age pictures of elephants, buckets, scooters, and other objects and instructed them to remember only the colors of the *backgrounds* of the pictures. They were told that the subjects themselves were immaterial. Recall of the background colors improved regularly with age, with 12-year-olds recalling about twice as many colors accurately as 6-year-olds. Then the researchers turned the tables on the children by asking them to recall the *subjects* of the pictures. Ironically, the 12-year-olds recalled *fewer* subjects correctly than the 6-year-olds, apparently because of their greater ability to focus their attention according to the original task demands.

The Structure of Memory

Psychologists divide memory functioning into three major processes or structures: *sensory memory, short-term memory,* and *long-term memory.*

Sensory Memory   When a 3-month-old infant looks at a new mobile hanging above the crib and then blinks the eyes, the visual impression of the mobile lasts for only a fraction of a second in what is called **sensory memory,** or the **sensory register.** Then the "trace" of the stimulus decays (Figure 8.8). Although research on the subject is limited (Rebok, 1987), it appears that the "life" of the stimulus trace is comparable in children of various ages and adults (Hoving et al., 1978).

Short-Term Memory   When the child focuses his or her attention on a stimulus in the sensory register, it will tend to be retained in **short-term memory** for up to 30 seconds or so after the trace of the stimulus decays. Ability to maintain

► ► ► ►

Sensory memory The structure of memory first encountered by sensory input. Information is maintained in sensory memory only for a fraction of a second.

Sensory register Another term for sensory memory.

Short-term memory The structure of memory that can hold a sensory stimulus for up to 30 seconds after the trace decays. Also called working memory.

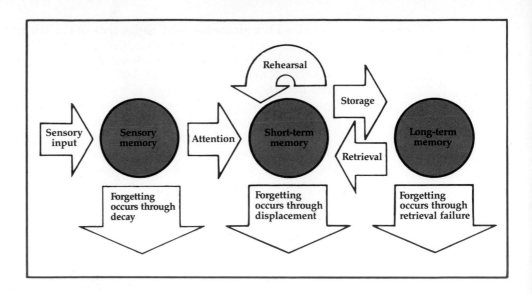

Figure 8.8 The Processing of Information
Sensory information impacts upon the sensory memory. If children attend to it, it is transferred to short-term memory. By encoding information, children are more likely to remember it and relate it to material that is already known. Information is processed more efficiently when children are aware of their cognitive processes and use strategies.

information in short-term memory depends on cognitive strategies as well as basic capacity to continue to perceive a vanished stimulus.

It is possible to focus on maintaining a visual image in the short-term memory (Fisher & Karsh, 1971), and this is all that young infants can do. But it is more common for older children to transform visual information into forms that are more easily remembered. Auditory stimuli can be maintained longer in short-term memory than can visual stimuli (Keele, 1973). For this reason, one strategy for promoting memory is to **encode** visual stimuli as sounds, or auditory stimulation. Then the sounds can be repeated out loud or mentally. That is, the sounds can be **rehearsed.**

Encoding visual material is an example of a cognitive *strategy* that enhances the ability to recall that material. Older children are more successful at recalling information, both because of improvements in the basic capacities of their short-term memories and because of their sophistication in employing strategies for enhancing memory.

Capacity of Short-Term or Working Memory The basic capacity of the short-term memory may be described in terms of the number of "bits" or chunks of information that may be kept in memory at once. To remember a new phone number, for example, one must keep seven chunks of information in short-term memory simultaneously—that is, one must rehearse them consecutively.

The average adult can keep about seven chunks of information—plus or minus two—in short-term memory at a time (Miller, 1956). As measured by the ability to recall digits, the typical 3-year-old can work on one chunk of information at a time. At the ages of 5 and 6, the typical child can recall two digits. The ability to recall series of digits improves throughout middle child-

Encode To transform sensory input into a form that is more readily processed.

Rehearse Repeat.

▶ ▶ ▶ ▶

8 COGNITIVE DEVELOPMENT

Rote *Mechanical repetition.*

Acoustic code *A code in which visual or other sensory input is transformed into sounds that are capable of being rehearsed.*

Long-term memory *The memory structure capable of relatively permanent storage.*

hood, and 15-year-olds, like adults, can keep about seven chunks of information in short-term memory at the same time (Pascual-Leone, 1970). Adolescents are typically capable of effectively rehearsing a new phone number to transfer it to long-term memory.

Pascual-Leone and Case's View Pascual-Leone and Case have advanced an information-processing view that focuses on children's capacity for memory and their use of cognitive strategies (Case, 1978; Case & Sandlos, 1980; Pascual-Leone et al., 1978; Pascual-Leone, 1980). They note, for example, that certain Piagetan tasks require several cognitive strategies instead of one, and that young children frequently fail at such tasks because they cannot hold many pieces of information in their working memories at the same time. Put another way, 3- and 4-year-old children can solve problems that have only one or two steps, whereas older children can retain information from earlier steps as they go on to subsequent steps.

How, then, do young children remember the alphabet, which is 26 chunks of information? Children learn the alphabet by **rote**—simple associative learning based on repetition. After the alphabet is repeated many, many times, *M* triggers the letter *N*, *N* triggers *O*, and so on. The typical 3-year-old who has "learned" the alphabet by rote will not be able to answer the question "What letter comes after *N?*" However, if you recite, *"H, I, J, K, L, M, N"* with the child and then pause, the child is likely to say, *"O, P!"* The 3-year-old probably will not realize that he or she can find the answer by using the cognitive strategy of reciting the alphabet, but many 5- or 6-year-olds will.

Acoustic Codes One of the simplest ways to convert visual information to an **acoustic code** is to label it. Children, therefore, are at a disadvantage for remembering stimuli until they have learned labels for them. Two-year-old children may be shown two squares and one triangle and asked to remember what they have seen. Unless they know the words *square* and *triangle* (and most 2-year-olds do not), it is unlikely that they will be able to apply and rehearse an acoustic code for this information. If, after some time has passed, they can recognize another card with two squares and a triangle as being the same, it will probably be because they have managed to maintain the trace of the original image—an unlikely event.

Long-Term Memory Think of **long-term memory** as a vast storehouse of information containing names, dates, places, what Johnny did to you in second grade, what Susan said about you when you were 12. Long-term memories may last days, years, or, for practical purposes, a lifetime.

There is no known limit to the amount of information that can be stored in long-term memory. From time to time it may seem that we have forgotten, or "lost," a long-term memory, such as the names of elementary or high school classmates. But it is more likely that we simply cannot find the proper cues to help us retrieve the information. It is "lost" in the same way as when we misplace an object, but know that it is still in the house. It remains there somewhere for the finding.

Transferring Information from Short-Term to Long-Term Memory How is information transferred from short-term to long-term memory? By and large, the more often chunks of information are rehearsed, the more likely they are

▶ ▶ ▶ ▶

Eidetic Imagery: How Do Researchers Determine Whether Children Have "Photographic Memories"?

▷
▷
▷
▷
▷ Some children have short-term memories that are capable of storing many more than seven or nine chunks of information. About 5 percent of elementary school children tested are capable of what has been called photographic memory, or eidetic imagery (Haber, 1980). Even then this ability declines with age, and is all but gone by adolescence.

How do researchers determine whether a child has eidetic imagery? In a strategy used by Haber (1969), a child first views a complex picture for 20–30 seconds. The picture is then removed and the child continues to look at a gray (neutral) background. The child is then asked detailed questions about the picture for many minutes and can answer these questions correctly only if he or she is still, in effect,

"seeing" the picture (Haber, 1969). The accuracy of children's responses suggests that a small percentage continue to perceive the picture in relatively sharp detail.

Figure 8.9 provides another example of a test of eidetic imagery. Children are asked to look at the first drawing in the series for 20–30 seconds, after which it is removed. The children then continue to observe a neutral background. Several minutes later they are shown the second drawing. When asked what they see, a few report "a face." A face would be seen only if the children had retained the first-seen image and fused it with the second-seen image, yielding the image shown in the last part of the figure. Retaining the details of the first image over several minutes is suggestive of eidetic imagery.

Figure 8.9 A Test for Eidetic Imagery
Children look at the first drawing for 20 to 30 seconds. Then it is removed. Now children look at a neutral background for several minutes. Then they are shown the second drawing. When asked what they see, children with the capacity for eidetic imagery report seeing a face. The face is perceived only by children who superimpose the second image over the first. Thus the first image would have been retained all the while that the child was staring at the neutral surface.

▶ ▶ ▶ ▶

Elaborative rehearsal *A method for increasing retention of new information by relating it to well-known information.*

Semantic code *A code based on the meaning of information.*

to be transferred to long-term memory (Rundus, 1971). Older children are more likely to rehearse than are younger children (Fabricius & Wellman, 1983). But pure rehearsal, with no attempt to make information meaningful by linking it to past learning, is no guarantee the information will be stored permanently (Craig & Watkins, 1973).

A more effective method than simple rehearsal is to purposefully relate new material to well-known information. Relating new material to well-known material is known as **elaborative rehearsal** (Postman, 1975). English teachers encourage children to use new vocabulary words in sentences to help them remember them. Each new usage is an instance of elaborative rehearsal. In this way, children are building extended **semantic codes** that will help them retrieve their meanings in the future.

Before proceeding to the next section, let me ask you which of the following words is spelled correctly: *retreival* or *retrieval*. The spellings sound alike, so an acoustic code for reconstructing the correct spelling would not be of help. But a semantic code, such as the spelling rule "*I* before *e* except after *c*," would allow you to reconstruct the correct spelling: retri*e*val. This is why children are taught rules and principles. Of course, whether or not these rules are retrieved in the appropriate situation is another question.

Organization in Long-Term Memory   As children's knowledge of concepts advances, the storehouse of their long-term memory becomes gradually organized according to categories. Preschoolers tend to organize their memories by grouping objects that share the same function (Lucariello & Nelson, 1985). "Toast" may be grouped with "peanut butter sandwich," because they are both edible. Only during the early elementary school years are toast and peanut butter likely to be joined into a single category with the term *food* applied to both.

David Bjorklund and Melanie de Marchena (1984) found that as children advanced from the first grade to the seventh grade, they became as likely to remember the names of animals that were linked categorically (e.g., dog and rabbit) as associatively (e.g., dog and cat). This finding suggests that the seventh-grade children were more likely to include dogs and rabbits (and cats) in the same category ("animals"), whereas the first graders were more likely to link dogs and cats just on the basis of their usually going together around the house.

When items are correctly organized in long-term memory, children and adults are also more likely to recall accurate information about them. For instance, do you "remember" whether whales breathe underwater? If you did not know that whales are mammals, or knew nothing about mammals, a correct answer might depend on some remote instance of rote learning. You might recall some details from a documentary on whales, for example. But if you *did* know that whales are mammals, you would be able to "remember" (or reconstruct the fact) that whales do not breathe underwater because mammals breathe air. Similarly, you might "remember" that whales, like other mammals, are warm-blooded, nurse their young, and are more intelligent than, say, sharks and tunas, which are fish.

If children have incorrectly classified whales as fish, they might search their "memories" and construct the incorrect answer that whales do breathe underwater. Correct categorization, in sum, expands children's knowledge and allows them to retrieve information more readily. As they develop, children's

► ► ► ►

knowledge becomes increasingly organized to form complex hierarchies of concepts.

But it has also been shown that when the knowledge of children in a particular area surpasses that of adults, the children show superior capacity to store and retrieve related information. For example, Micheline Chi (1978) found that chess experts were superior to novice chess players at remembering where chess pieces had been placed on the board. In this study the experts were 8-to-12-year-old children while the novices were adults. The same adults showed superiority to the 8-to-12-year olds in their memory for numbers, a task on which neither group had special knowledge. The point is that enhanced knowledge of relationships between concepts improves memory functioning, so that children can outperform adults in those areas in which they have received special training.

Developments in the Memory Tasks   The three basic memory tasks are *recognition, recall,* and *relearning.* Studying these memory tasks has led to several conclusions about the nature of forgetting.

Recognition   Recognition is the easiest type of memory task. This is why multiple-choice tests are easier than fill-in-the-blank or essay tests. We can recognize or identify photos of former classmates more easily than we can recall their names (Tulving, 1974).

Children are apparently capable of simple recognition from birth. We saw in Chapter 4 that neonates only a few days old "recognize" nursing pads with their mothers' milk, as shown by turning toward them reliably (Macfarlane, 1975). Jeffrey Fagen and his colleagues (1984) have shown that after 24-hour intervals, 3-month-olds recognize mobiles that have been linked to rewards, as shown by kicking at them.

Recall   What is the capital of Wyoming? Who wrote *Hamlet?* These are a couple of the recall tasks commonly given schoolchildren. Recall is more difficult than recognition. In a recognition task, one simply indicates whether an item has been seen before, or which of a number of items is paired with a stimulus (as in a multiple-choice test). But in a recall task, children must retrieve information, with another piece of information serving as a cue.

As children develop, their capacity for recalling information increases. Their memory improvement appears to be linked to their ability to quickly process (e.g., scan and categorize) the stimulus cues (Case, 1985; Howard & Polich, 1985). In one study, Robert Kail and Marilyn Nippold (1984) asked 8-, 12-, and 21-year-olds to name as many animals and pieces of furniture as they could during separate seven-minute intervals. The number of items increased with age both for animals and furniture. At all age groups, items were retrieved according to clusters, or classes. That is, in the animal category, a series of fish would be named, a series of birds, and so on.

Another experiment suggests how the use of categorical thinking contributes to the superior recall abilities of older children and adults. Liberty and Ornstein (1973) asked fourth graders and college students to memorize 28 words printed on cards. The children and college students were also instructed to sort the cards into groups while they were learning them. The college students organized the cards into four content categories, while the fourth graders used

▶ ▶ ▶ ▶

a greater number of less distinct categories. Not surprisingly, the recall of the college students was superior.

In another experiment on how categorizing information helps children remember, pictures of objects that fell into four categories (animals, clothes, furniture, and transporation) were placed on a table before first through sixth graders (Neimark et al., 1971). The children were allowed three minutes to arrange the pictures as they wished and to remember as many of them as they could. Children in the first and second grades made no effort to categorize the pictures and also showed poorest recall of them. A few third graders placed the pictures into categories, and this classification became more pronounced among the fourth to sixth graders. The tendency to categorize the pictures was directly related to the capacity to recall them.

Motivation apparently also contributes to recall, even among young children. For example, 2- and 3-year-olds do quite well at recalling the names of their friends and relatives, the locations of their toys, and the details of birthday parties (Bjorklund, 1985; DeLoache et al., 1985).

Relearning: Is Learning Easier the Second Time Around? Relearning is a third method of measuring retention. Do you remember having to learn all the state capitals in grade school? What were the capitals of Wyoming and Delaware? Even when we cannot recall or recognize material that had once been learned, we can relearn it more rapidly the second time, like Cheyenne for Wyoming and Dover for Delaware. Similarly, as we go through our 30s and 40s we may forget a good deal of our high school French or geometry. But we could learn what took months or years much more rapidly the second time around.

Since time is saved when we relearn things we had once known, this method of measuring retention is also known as measuring "savings."

Development of Metacognition and Metamemory

Metacognition refers to children's awareness and purposeful control of their cognitive abilities. The ability to formulate problems, awareness of the cognitive processes required to solve a problem, the activation of cognitive rules and strategies, keeping one's attention focused on the problem, and checking one's answers—all these are evidence of the emergence of metacognition.

Pascual-Leone and Case suggest that children's problem-solving abilities are largely made possible by (1) neurological developments that expand the working (short-term) memory, and (2) growing automaticity in applying cognitive strategies. The younger child may have to count three sets of two objects each one by one in order to arrive at a total of six objects. The older child, with a larger working memory, familiarity with multiplication tables, and greater perceptual experience, is likely to automatically arrive at a total of six when three groups of two are perceived. Automaticity in adding, multiplying, and so on allows older children to solve math problems with several steps. Younger children, meanwhile, become lengthily occupied with individual steps, losing sight of the whole. In Chapter 9 we shall see that automaticity in processing information is an element in Robert Sternberg's (1985) theory of intelligence.

Metamemory **Metamemory** more specifically refers to the child's awareness of the functioning of his or her memory processes. Older children not only

Metacognition Awareness of and control of one's cognitive abilities, as shown by the intentional use of cognitive strategies in solving problems.

Metamemory Knowledge of the functions and processes involved in one's storage and retrieval of information (memory), as shown by use of cognitive strategies to retain information.

▶ ▶ ▶ ▶

show superiority in information processing; they also show greater insight into how their processing of information works (Brown et al., 1983; Kail, 1984). The capacity of the short-term memory, as measured by recall of digits, improves throughout childhood. But another important reason that older children store and retrieve information more effectively than younger children is the greater sophistication of their metamemory (Liben, 1982; Stern, 1985).

For example, kindergarten children and first graders frequently announce that they have memorized educational materials before they have actually done so. Older elementary school students are more likely to assess accurately the extent of their knowledge (Flavell & Wellman, 1976).

Older children also show more knowledge of strategies that can be used to facilitate memory. For example, 2- and 3-year-olds do not use rehearsal when asked to remember a list of items. Four- and 5-year-olds will usually use rehearsal if someone else suggests that they repeat the list out loud, but not until about the ages of 6 or 7 do children use rehearsal without being instructed to do so (Flavell & Wellman, 1976; Paris et al., 1982). However, prior to the age of 7 or so, many children will not use metacognition and cognitive strategies such as rehearsal on their own (Flavell, 1985). Also, 6- and 7-year-olds frequently rehearse items aloud, while 9- and 10-year-olds will usually rehearse items "to themselves"—that is, silently.

As children develop, they also become more likely to use selective rehearsal in order to remember important information. That is, they more efficiently exclude the meaningless mass of perceptions milling about them by confining rehearsal to that which they are attempting to remember. This selectivity in rehearsal is found significantly more often among 15- and 18-year-olds than among 11-year-olds (Bray et al., 1985).

If you are trying to remember a new phone number, you would know to rehearse it several times or to write it down—before doing a series of math problems. However, 5-year-olds, asked whether it would make a difference if they jotted the number down before or after doing the math problems, do not reliably report that doing the problems first would matter. Ten-year-olds, however, are aware that new mental activities (the math problems) can interfere with old ones (trying to remember the telephone number) and usually suggest jotting the number down before attempting the math problems.

Your metamemory is advanced to the point, of course, where you recognize that it would be poor judgment to read this book while watching *Wheel of Fortune* or fantasizing about your next vacation, isn't it? Quickly, now—what are the capitals of Wyoming and Delaware?

Development of the Self-Concept

We are not born knowing that we exist. At birth, the world may be a confusing blur of sights, sounds, and inner sensations. When our hands first come into view, they may appear to do so at random, and there is little reason for us to assume that they differ in ownership from other external objects. Even when we start to learn to bring our hands into focus, there is little evidence that we *realize* that that hand "belongs" to us, and that we are somehow separate and distinct from the world outside.

▶ ▶ ▶ ▶

Self-concept One's impression
of oneself; self-awareness.

The sense of self, or the **self-concept,** appears to emerge gradually during infancy. At some point infants understand that the hand they are moving in and out of sight is "their" hand. At some point they understand that their own bodies extend only so far, and that at a certain point external objects and the bodies of others begin. As pointed out by psychologists L. Alan Sroufe (1979) and Joseph Campos and his colleagues (1983), self-awareness has a powerful impact on social and emotional development. Knowledge of the self carries the possibility of possession. The possibility of possession, of conceptualizing traits and objects as "mine," provides the basis for social conflict and emotions such as jealousy and pride. Guilt and shame also depend on the emergence of the self-concept, because in these cases the child is responding emotionally to the concept of having injured or fallen short in the eyes of another human being. Awareness of other people as separate entities allows feelings of both defiance and affection to blossom.

Toddlers may fly into rages more frequently than younger children, in part because they understand that other people frustrate them by setting limits. But they also realize that they can frustrate other people. Judy Dunn and Penny Munn (1985) found that as compared to the age of 14 months, toddlers at 18 months express anger four times as often and laugh three times as often when their mothers try to set limits. By their second birthday, the same toddlers express anger eight times as often, and laugh four times as often. Between 14 and 24 months of age, the toddlers become gradually more likely to initiate the conflict with their mothers, and react increasingly more self-assertively when their mothers attempt to remonstrate with them.

The Mirror Technique   The Dunn and Munn study assumes that the toddlers' self-awareness increased between 14 and 24 months of age. However, developmentalists have devised ingenious methods to assess the development of the self-concept among infants. One of these is the mirror technique, which relies on sensorimotor evidence.

The mirror technique involves the use of a mirror and a dot of rouge. Before the experiment begins, the researcher observes the infant for baseline data on how frequently the infant touches his or her nose. Then the mother places rouge on the infant's nose, and the infant is placed before a mirror. Not until about the age of 18 months do infants begin to touch their own noses upon looking in the mirror (Bertenthal & Fischer, 1978; Lewis & Brooks-Gunn, 1979). This is the age at which Dunn and Munn also found that children appear to have developed self-awareness.

Nose-touching suggests that children recognize themselves, and that they have a mental picture of themselves that allows them to perceive that the dot of rouge is an abnormality. At 18 to 24 months, children also spend more time looking at pictures of themselves as compared to other children, and they name themselves in the pictures.

The Hat Test   Infants will reach out to touch their images in mirrors by 6 months of age (Bertenthal & Fischer, 1978). Moreover, as shown by the "hat test," it may be that they perceive that the mirror image reflects some aspect of the world of objects at as early as 10 months.

► ► ► ►

At some point infants develop self-awareness, which has a powerful impact on social and emotional development.

In the hat test, the infant wears a vest, and a hat is affixed to a wooden rod ascending from the back of the vest. In this way the hat moves along with the child, but the child cannot see the hat without looking in a mirror. At about 10 months, children will look back at the actual hats after seeing them in the mirror, suggesting awareness that the mirror reflects objects according to certain optical rules. But at 10 months, children will not touch the rouge on their noses—and so knowledge of the rules of reflection apparently precedes but is distinct from self-awareness.

Middle Childhood and Adolescence

Psychologist Eleanor Maccoby (1980) writes that children's self-concepts or "self-definitions" initially focus on concrete external traits, such as appearance, activities, and living situations. But as children undergo the cognitive

▶ ▶ ▶ ▶

developments of middle childhood, their more abstract internal traits or personality characteristics take on a role in their self-definition. As they develop further, social relationships and group memberships also take on significance.

The Twenty Statements Test   An investigative method called the Twenty Statements Test bears out Maccoby's views and highlights the relationships between the self-concept and general cognitive development.

In this method, children are given a sheet of paper with the question "Who am I?" and 20 spaces in which to write answers. Consider the answers offered by a 9-year-old boy and by 11- and 17-year-old girls (Montemayer & Eisen, 1977, pp. 317–318):

Nine-year-old boy: My name is Bruce C. I have brown eyes. I have brown hair. I have brown eyebrows. I'm 9 years old. I LOVE! sports. I have 7 people in my family. I have great! eye site. I have lots! of friends. I live on 1923 Pinecrest Drive. I'm going on 10 in September. I'm a boy. I have a uncle that is almost 7 feet tall. My school is Pinecrest. My teacher is Mrs. V. I play hockey! I'm also the smartest boy in the class. I LOVE! food. I love fresh air. I LOVE school.

Eleven-year-old girl: My name is A. I'm a human being. I'm a girl. I'm a truthful person. I'm not pretty. I do so-so in my studies. I'm a very good cellist. I'm a very good pianist. I'm a little bit tall for my age. I like several boys. I like several girls. I'm old-fashioned. I play tennis. I am a very good musician. I try to be helpful. I'm always ready to be friends with anybody. Mostly I'm good, but I lose my temper. I'm not well liked by some girls and boys. I don't know if boys like me or not.

Seventeen-year-old girl: I am a human being. I am a girl. I am an individual. I don't know who I am. I am Pisces. I am a moody person. I am an indecisive person. I am an ambitious person. I am a big curious person. I am not an individual. I am lonely. I am an American (God help me). I am a Democrat. I am a liberal person. I am a radical. I am conservative. I am a pseudoliberal. I am an atheist. I am not a classifiable person (i.e., I don't want to be).

Only the 9-year-old lists his age and address, discusses his family, and focuses on physical traits such as eye color in his self-definition. The 9-year-old mentions his likes, which may be considered rudimentary psychological traits, but they are tied to the concrete, as would be expected of a concrete operational child.

The 9- and 11-year-olds list their names, but perhaps the 17-year-old considers her name too superficial to note. The 9- and 11-year-olds list their competencies. The 11-year-old's struggle to bolster her self-esteem—her insistence on her musical abilities despite her qualms about her attractiveness—may elicit your sympathy.

The 17-year-old shows the formal operational capacity to toy with categories such as liberal and conservative. She also appears to be struggling with the identity crises hypothesized by Erik Erikson (see Chapter 2)—particularly her political and religious identities. She would appear to be attempting to define herself in terms of the "isms" that pervade her intellectual environment. Discussing the role of the self-concept brings us full circle and shows how cognitive development is intertwined with the social, emotional, and personality development of the child.

▶ ▶ ▶ ▶

Summary

1. Cognitive development concerns the ways in which children mentally represent the world and manipulate symbols at various ages and stages of development.

2. Piaget hypothesized the existence of four stages and a number of substages of cognitive development. He saw these stages as differing in quality, but continuous in the sense that one level of cognitive development could be described as repeating and coordinating the accomplishments of lower levels.

3. The sensorimotor stage is said to last from the ages of 0–2, and is characterized by sensory and motor responses (prelinguistic behavior). The first substage (0–1½ months) is dominated by ready-made action patterns, or schemes (reflexive responses).

4. The second substage is characterized by primary circular reactions, in which infants repeat unlearned schemes to prolong stimulating occurrences.

5. In the substage of secondary circular reactions, infants repeat learned schemes to prolong stimulation and show some awareness that schemes can influence the external world.

6. The fourth stage is characterized by the coordination of sensorimotor schemes, as in coordinating looking and grasping, or as in lifting a piece of cloth to then grasp a toy below.

7. In the fifth substage, infants use tertiary circular reactions, which are purposeful adaptations of established schemes to specific situations. They also show overt trial and error in solving simple problems.

8. In the transition to symbolic thought, which occurs at about 18–24 months, infants show capacity for mental representation in using mental trial and error to solve simple problems.

9. Piaget theorized that preoperational thought characterized the ages of 2–7 years. Preoperational thought is symbolic but relatively inflexible, and leads to consequences such as egocentrism (inability to take the viewpoints of others); precausal ideas about causality (for example, transductive reasoning, animism, and artificialism); confusion between symbols and the objects that they represent; the ability to focus, or center, on only one dimension at a time when solving problems, such that preoperational children cannot conserve mass, number, and other variables; and lack of perceiving the identity of people and objects to be stable when superficial changes are made.

10. Critics of Piaget have shown that the demand characteristics of his experimental methods have led him to underestimate the cognitive abilities of many children below the age of 7. For example, some 2½-year-olds do not appear egocentric, and many 5- and 6-year-olds show conservation when presented with different experimental approaches.

11. Operations are mental acts or schemes in which objects and events can be transformed and then returned to their original forms. Operations are char-

▶ ▶ ▶ ▶

acterized by flexibility and reversibility. They allow the child to show de-centration—to focus on several aspects of a situation at once.

12. Piaget theorized that children can engage in operations concerning concrete objects and events (as opposed to abstract ideas) between about the ages of 7 and 12. As a consequence, they can take the perspective of others (egocentrism decreases); they can conserve mass, number, and other variables; they show transitivity (awareness that if A is greater than B, and B is greater than C, then A is greater than C), which allows them to engage in efficient seriation; and they show efficient class inclusion, which permits categorical thinking.

13. Piaget theorized that at about the age of 12 or so, many children enter the stage of formal operations, in which they can manipulate abstract concepts and ideas with the flexibility and reversibility they showed earlier in regard to concrete objects and events. Formal operational thought allows hypothetical thinking (thinking about the possible and the impossible, perceiving many alternatives); systematic problem solving (testing hypotheses and excluding nonessential factors); sophisticated use of symbols (as in the abilities to solve algebraic and geometric problems, and to appreciate metaphorical language); and deductive thinking (as in the syllogism).

14. Formal operational thought may evolve only in technologically advanced societies, but even in the United States, only about half of college first-year students demonstrate it.

15. Piaget's views have been criticized on three major grounds: (1) The timing of development may have been inaccurate. (2) Cognitive development may be more continuous than Piaget theorized. (3) Cognitive development may be accelerated by training to a greater extent than Piaget thought possible. However, Piaget's observations of the sequences of development appear correct.

16. Information-processing theorists view cognitive development in terms that are derived from computer technology: e.g., storing and retrieving information, and using "mental programs" to solve problems. As children develop, their attention becomes selective and they screen out distractions. Their concepts become structured into complex hierarchies.

17. Pacual-Leone and Case theorize that children become more capable of solving problems because of improvements in their short-term (working) memory, their increasingly sophisticated application of cognitive strategies, and increasing automaticity in solving elements of problems.

18. Children seem to become self-aware, as assessed by the mirror method, by about 18 months. Self-awareness lays the groundwork for the development of emotions such as pride, jealousy, and guilt, and for the display of defiance in social relationships.

19. The self-definition of older children, as measured by the Twenty Statements Test, seems to follow their overall cognitive development. Concrete operational children tend to define themselves in terms of specific acts and superficial traits. Formal operational children define themselves in terms of abstract concepts such as beliefs and motives.

▶ ▶ ▶ ▶

Cognitive development does not occur prior to development of the ability to use language. False. Many cognitive developments—for example, the attainment of mental representation and of mental trial and error—take place during the sensorimotor stage.

Two-year-olds tend to assume that their parents are aware of everything that is happening to them, even when their parents are not present. True. Two-year-olds tend to be egocentric—to assume that others perceive the world as they do.

Four-year-olds think that a row of five spread-out pennies contains more pennies than a row of five bunched-up pennies. True. This occurs because they cannot center on two dimensions at once. When they center on the greater width of the spread-out row, they cannot simultaneously center on the number of coins in each row.

A 4-year-old may believe that it is dark out because it is time to go to sleep. True. This type of precausal thinking is termed absolute finalism, in which the effect (sleeping) is perceived to be the cause.

A 4-year-old may believe that the sky is blue because someone has painted it. True. This type of precausal thinking is termed artificialism—the belief that natural objects and events take form because of someone's will or action.

Most 4-year-olds may not be able to correctly line up a series of ten sticks according to height. True. This is because they lack transitivity, or recognition that if A exceeds B and B exceeds C, then A must exceed C.

Adolescents tend to be rigid and unyielding in their idealism because they are not yet capable of adult reasoning. False. It is precisely their new adult powers of hypothetical thinking and deductive reasoning that lead them to assume that they have an inside track on truth.

Two-year-old boys show better memory for trains and puzzles, while 2-year-old girls show better memory for dolls and teddy bears. True. It may be that cultural sex-role stereotypes have contributed to the preferences—and selective attention—of children by this early age.

If you ask a 3-year-old what letter comes after N, he probably won't know the answer. But if you recite the alphabet with him and stop short at N, he is likely to say, "O, P," and so on. True. The 3-year-old may "know" the alphabet by rote, even if he or she does have an unreliable mental representation of the alphabet.

Some children have photographic memories. True. "Photographic memory" is more technically referred to as eidetic imagery, and it is found in about 5 percent of children.

▶ ▶ ▶ ▶

Toddlers develop emotions such as jealousy and pride only after they become self-aware. True. Emotions such as jealousy and pride only have meaning in terms of children's relationships with others; and children do not begin to relate to others cognitively until they realize that they are separate and distinct from others.

When asked to define themselves, adolescents are more likely to focus on their physical characteristics than on personality traits. False. Adolescents are more likely than younger children to define themselves in terms of their motives and beliefs.

▶ ▶ ▶ ▶

9

The Development of Intelligence

C H A P T E R ▸ O U T L I N E

T R U T H ▶ O R ▶ F I C T I O N ?

- Musical ability is a kind of intelligence.
- Knowing what problem to tackle is an aspect of intelligent behavior.
- Highly intelligent children are also creative.
- Creative children tend to be independent and nonconformist.
- Intelligence and "IQ" mean the same thing.
- Two children can answer exactly the same items on an intelligence test correctly, yet one can be above average in intelligence and the other can be below average in intelligence.
- Tests have been developed for measuring intelligence in neonates.
- We can predict how intelligent a person will be as an adult as early as the age of 2.
- Mentally retarded children cannot acquire the social and vocational skills required to become independent.
- Intellectually gifted children tend to be unpopular with their agemates.
- Japanese children attain higher IQ scores than U.S. children.
- Intelligence tests are actually achievement tests.
- There is no such thing as an unbiased intelligence test.
- High intelligence runs in families.
- IQ test scores of adopted children correlate more highly with the IQ scores of their adoptive parents than with those of their natural biological parents.
- Children whose mothers are more involved with them attain higher IQs.
- Head Start programs have raised children's IQs.

What form of life is so adaptive that it can survive in desert temperatures of 120° F, or Arctic climes of −40° F? What form of life can run, walk, climb, swim, live underwater for months on end, and fly to the moon and back? I won't keep you in suspense any longer. Human beings are that form of life. But our naked bodies do not allow us to be comfortable in these extremes of temperature. It is not brute strength that allows us to live underwater or travel to the moon. We attribute our success in adapting to these different conditions, and in challenging our physical limitations, to our **intelligence.**

You have heard about intelligence since you were a young child. At an early age we gain impressions of how intelligent we are as compared to other family members and schoolmates. Expressions like "That's a smart thing to do" and "What an idiot!" are heard each day. We think of some people as "having more" intelligence than others. We associate intelligence with academic success, advancement on the job, and appropriate social behavior. Psychologists use intelligence as a **trait** in an effort to explain why people do (or fail to do) things that are adaptive and inventive.

Despite our sense of familiarity with the concept of intelligence, intelligence cannot be seen, touched, or measured physically. For this reason, intelligence is subject to various interpretations. Theories about intelligence are some of the most controversial issues in psychology today.

In this chapter we follow the development of intelligence throughout childhood and adolescence. In order to do so, we also discuss different ways of looking at intelligence and discuss the relationship between intelligence and creativity. We shall see how intelligence is measured and discuss individual and group differences in intelligence. In the section on "the testing controversy," we shall see that few developmental issues stir as much debate as differences in intelligence. Finally we shall return to the issue of nature versus nurture when we examine the determinants of intelligence: heredity and the environment.

Intelligence *A complex and controversial concept, defined by David Wechsler as the "capacity . . . to understand the world [and] resourcefulness to cope with its challenges."* (*From the Latin* inter, *meaning "among," and* legere, *meaning "to choose." Intelligence implies the capacity to make adaptive choices.*)

Trait *A distinguishing quality or characteristic that is presumed to account for consistency in behavior.*

Achievement *That which is attained by one's efforts and presumed to be made possible by one's abilities.*

▶ ▶ ▶ ▶

Theories of Intelligence

Psychologists generally distinguish between **achievement** and intelligence. Achievement is what a child has learned, the knowledge and skills that have been gained by experience. Achievement involves specific content areas like English, history, and math. Educators and psychologists use achievement tests to measure what children have learned in academic areas. We would not be surprised to find that a student who has taken Spanish, but not French, does very well on a Spanish achievement test, but poorly on a French achievement test. The strong relationship between achievement and experience seems obvious.

The meaning of intelligence is more difficult to pin down (Green, 1981). Most developmentalists would agree that intelligence somehow provides the cognitive basis for academic achievement. Intelligence is usually perceived as a measure of a child's underlying *competence* or *learning ability*, whereas achievement reflects a child's current *performance*. But developmentalists disagree as to what is meant by a child's underlying competence or learning ability, and how it develops.

9 THE DEVELOPMENT OF INTELLIGENCE

In this section we consider the two major theoretical approaches to understanding the meaning of intelligence: factor and cognitive theories. Then we explore the relationships between intelligence and a related concept—creativity.

Factor Theories

Factor A condition or quality that brings about a result—in this case, "intelligent" behavior. A cluster of related items, such as those found on an intelligence test.

Many investigators have viewed intelligence as consisting of one or more major mental abilities, or **factors.** Alfred Binet, for example, the Frenchman who developed intelligence testing methods at the turn of the century, believed that intelligence consists of several related factors. Other investigators have argued that intelligence consists of one, two, or hundreds of factors.

g Spearman's symbol for general intelligence—a general factor that he believed underlay more specific abilities.

G and s factors   In 1904 British psychologist Charles Spearman suggested that the various behaviors we consider intelligent have a common, underlying factor. He labeled this factor **g,** for "general intelligence." He felt that *g* represented broad reasoning and problem-solving abilities. He supported this view by noting that people who excel in one area generally show the capacity to excel in others. But he also noted that even the most capable people seemed more capable in some areas—perhaps music or business or poetry—than in others. For this reason, he also suggested that **s,** or specific capacities, accounted for a number of individual abilities.

s Spearman's symbol for specific or s factors *that he believed accounted for individual abilities.*

Factor analysis A statistical technique that allows researchers to determine the relationships among large number of items, such as those found on intelligence tests.

In order to test his views, Spearman developed a statistical method called **factor analysis.** Factor analysis allows researchers to determine the relationships among large numbers of items, such as those found on intelligence tests. Items that cluster together are labeled factors. In his research on relationships between tests of verbal, mathematical, and spatial reasoning, Spearman repeatedly found evidence supporting the existence of *s* factors. The evidence for *g* was more limited.

Primary mental abilities According to Thurstone, the basic abilities that compose intelligence.

Primary Mental Abilities   American psychologist Louis Thurstone (1938) used Spearman's factor-analytic method with various tests of individual abilities and also found only limited evidence for the existence of *g*. Thurstone concluded that Spearman had oversimplified the concept of intelligence. Thurstone's data suggested the presence of nine specific factors, which he labeled **primary mental abilities** (see Table 9.1). Thurstone suggested that we might have high word

Table 9.1   Louis Thurstone's Primary Mental Abilities

ABILITY	BRIEF DESCRIPTION
Visual and spatial abilities	Visualizing forms and spatial relationships
Perceptual speed	Grasping perceptual details rapidly, perceiving similarities and differences between stimuli
Numerical ability	Computing numbers
Verbal meaning	Knowing the meanings of words
Memory	Recalling information (words, sentences, etc.)
Word fluency	Thinking of words quickly (rhyming, doing crossword puzzles, etc.)
Deductive reasoning	Deriving examples from general rules
Inductive reasoning	Deriving general rules from examples

▶ ▶ ▶ ▶

fluency, enabling us rapidly to develop lists of words that rhyme, yet not be efficient at solving math problems (Thurstone & Thurstone, 1963). A version of Thurstone's Primary Mental Abilities Test (the PMA) remains in use today. It consists of five factors: numerical ability, word fluency, verbal meaning, reasoning ability, and spatial ability.

This view seems to make sense. Most of us know children who are "good at" math but "poor in" English, and vice versa. Nonetheless, some link seems to connect different mental abilities, even if it is not so strong as the links among the items that define specific factors. The data still show that the person with excellent reasoning ability is likely to have a larger-than-average vocabulary and better-than-average numerical ability. There are few, if any, people who exceed 99 percent of the population in one mental ability, yet are exceeded by 80 or 90 percent of the population in others.

Structure-of-intellect model
Guilford's three-dimensional model of intelligence, which focuses on the operations, contents, and products of intellectual functioning.

The Structure-of-Intellect Model   The **structure-of-intellect model** proposed by psychologist J. P. Guilford (1959) greatly expands the numbers of factors found in intellectual functioning. Guilford used a combination of factor analysis and logical reasoning to arrive at 120 factors in intellectual functioning. Each of the 120 factors consists of three elements, as shown in Figure 9.1.

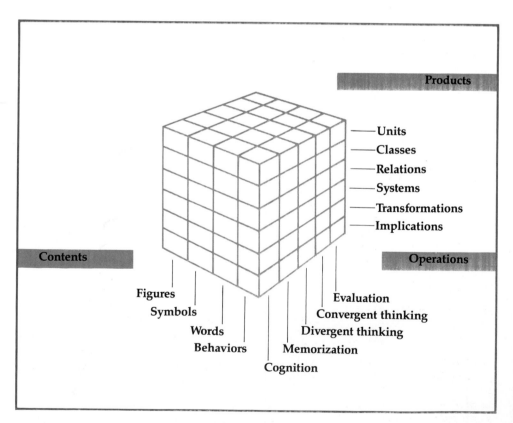

Figure 9.1 Guilford's Structure of Intellect Model
With this model, Guilford hypothesizes the existence of 120 factors in intelligence.

▶ ▶ ▶ ▶

1. Operations—the kinds of cognitive processing that are involved.
2. Contents—the type of information that is processed.
3. Products—the forms that the information takes.

Guilford and his associates have developed test items to measure performance in many of the 120 factors. Consider the following examples:

1. Name as many objects as you can that are both white and edible.
2. Give as many sentences as you can that would fit into the form: W _____ c _____ s _____ d _____. Example: "Workers can seldom deviate."

The operation in each example is **divergent thinking**—the ability to generate many novel associations to a stimulus. The content of each example consists of words. However, the products differ. The products in the first example consist of single objects, or *units.* The products in example 2 consist of organized sequences of words, or *systems.*

In more recent writings, Guilford (1982) has expanded his model to 150 factors. The problem with this approach seems to be that the greater the number of factors generated, the more overlap there is among them. As pointed out by Rebok (1987), developmentalists are more concerned with how intellectual functioning changes with age than with a potentially endless expansion of the numbers of factors.

The Theory of Fluid and Crystallized Intelligence   The theory of *crystallized intelligence* and *fluid intelligence* was proposed by Raymond Cattell (1963, 1971). This model is also based on factor analysis, but it focuses on only two factors and on their development over the life span.

Crystallized intelligence includes primary abilities such as reasoning ability, verbal comprehension, and concept formation. Crystallized intelligence depends on education and cultural influences, and it increases steadily over most of the life span. It is measured by means such as vocabulary tests ("What does *camel* mean?") and tests of general information ("How far is it from New York to Los Angeles?").

Fluid intelligence includes primary abilities, such as inductive reasoning, associative memory, and the ability to visualize the rotation of objects in space. It is best described as the processes that make incidental or casual learning possible (Horn, 1982). Fluid intelligence, in contrast to crystallized intelligence, is considered largely independent of school learning and **acculturation.** The development of fluid intelligence is thought to be based largely on the unfolding of neurological and physiological patterns and structures. The child's learning of the concept of **conservation,** as discussed in Chapter 8, is an example of the effects of fluid intelligence. Few school systems purposefully teach Piaget's concepts.* Children tend to arrive at such concepts on their own—on the basis of their fluid intelligence.

---

*Recall that Piaget himself did not see a purpose to directly instructing children in concepts such as conservation.

Divergent thinking *A thought process that attempts to generate multiple solutions to problems. Free and fluent associations to the elements of a problem.*

Crystallized intelligence *Cattell and Horn's view of those intellectual functions that depend on education and cultural influences.*

Fluid intelligence *Cattell and Horn's view of those intellectual functions that are based on the unfolding of neurological structures and account for incidental learning.*

Acculturation *The process by which children adapt to the patterns or customs of a culture.*

Conservation *Piaget's term for recognition that basic qualities of objects (such as their number) remain the same when superficial characteristics (such as their arrangement) are altered. See Chapter 8.*

▶ ▶ ▶ ▶

Because of their theoretical origins, crystallized and fluid intelligence are believed to have different developmental courses, as shown in Figure 9.2. Crystallized intelligence (C) increases most rapidly during infancy, because of the young child's wealth of new experiences (nearly everything is new to a baby!). The rate of increase remains rapid during early and middle childhood, largely due to formal education. Then it tapers off but continues to make slow gains, by and large, for a lifetime, as educational experiences (E) also accumulate. Fluid intelligence (F) is also rapid at first, as neural structures (M) mature. However, underlying neural capacities begin to decline even prior to adolescence (M). The effects of their decline are compounded by accumulated injuries (I) to the nervous system. As a consequence, fluid intelligence (F) also declines past childhood. When we combine the contributions of crystallized and fluid intelligence, we arrive at overall ability (G). G declines after adolescence because of losses in fluid intelligence, not crystallized intelligence. Research has been more supportive of the gains in crystallized and fluid intelligence that occur during childhood than the theorized losses of the adult years (Horn & Cattell, 1967; Schaie, 1979).

Multiple Intelligences Psychologist Howard Gardner (1983) uses the following anecdote to introduce his model of multiple intelligences. Two Martians land on Earth and are curious about the functioning of the mind. One wanders into a U.S. university and consults an educational psychologist. The psychologist explains the concept of intelligence and how it is measured by IQ tests. What are the questions? asks the Martian. A sampling: What does "belfry" mean?

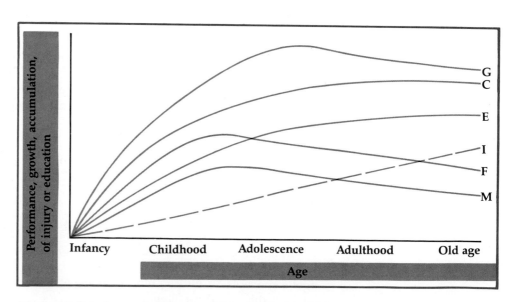

Figure 9.2 Developmental Courses of Crystallized and Fluid Intelligence
According to Cattell and Horn, fluid intelligence (F) declines beginning in adolescence, suffering from an accumulation of neurological injuries. Crystallized intelligence (C) reflects educational experiences and can advance for a lifetime. Overall general intellectual functioning (G) reflects the courses of crystallized and fluid intelligence.

▶ ▶ ▶ ▶

9 THE DEVELOPMENT OF INTELLIGENCE

Psychologist Howard Gardner argues that there are many intelligences, not just one, including bodily talents as expressed through dancing or gymnastics. Each "intelligence" is an inborn talent that must be developed through educational experiences, if it is to be expressed, and peaks at a certain age.

What do a chair and a table have in common? How much is 8 times 3? Who wrote *The Iliad?*

The second Martian wanders the planet. He sees Indian yogis, tennis players, computer programmers, concert violinists, Balinese dancers in grass skirts, presidents, peasants, and Melanesian sailors. The second Martian concludes that there are many kinds of minds, many kinds of "intelligences."

To Gardner, intelligence—or intelligences—reflect much more than logical and problem-solving abilities. Gardner labels several different kinds of intelligence. Two are familiar: verbal ability and logical-mathematical reasoning. The others are spatial intelligence, bodily–kinesthetic intelligence (as shown by dancers and gymnasts), musical intelligence, interpersonal intelligence (as shown by empathy and ability to relate to others), and personal knowledge (self-insight). Occasionally individuals show great "intelligence" in one area—as the young Mozart with the piano, or the illiterate island boy who can intuitively navigate his small boat to hundreds of islands by observing the changing patterns of the stars—without notable abilities in others.

Gardner's critics argue that he has included what other people would label specific "talents" as kinds of intelligence (Scarr, 1985). Perhaps we do not, as a culture, sufficiently reward dancers, musicians, and persons with interpersonal skills. But this does not mean that these talents address the same issues dealt with by the concept of intelligence.

Cognitive Theories

Cognitive theorists tend to view intelligence in terms of information processing. They focus on how information "flows" through us and is modified by us as we adapt to and act to change our environments. Two cognitive theories have been proposed by Arthur Jensen and Robert Sternberg.

▶ ▶ ▶ ▶

Level I and Level II Intelligence   Arthur Jensen's concern has been to explain social-class differences in intelligence. He does so by hypothesizing the existence of two different levels of intelligence: Level I and Level II.

Level I intelligence involves associative abilities. They are measured by tasks involving rote learning and memorization. One example would be memorizing a song. Another would be repeating a series of numbers that has been read aloud, such as 7-4-9-6-2-5. Still another would be associating letters and sounds, as in learning the alphabet. Level I skills are not strongly linked to school performance, as measured by academic grades (Rebok, 1987).

Level II intelligence involves conceptual abilities. It includes verbal ability, logical reasoning, and problem-solving skills. All of these are related to cognitive learning and development. They are measured by items such as ones that require conceptual thinking ("How are good and bad alike?"), mathematical reasoning ("If two candy bars cost 25 cents, how many candy bars can you buy for one dollar?"), and general comprehension ("Why should pregnant women check with their doctors about the drugs they use?"). Level II skills are more strongly correlated with academic grades than are Level I skills.

Jensen argues that all social classes possess adequate degrees of Level I intelligence. However, he asserts, and this has aroused great controversy, that the middle and upper classes possess more Level II intelligence, and that this difference accounts for their superior academic grades and performance in professional positions. Jensen (1969, 1980, 1985) further believes that our potentials at each level are basically inherited and are therefore largely unmodifiable by experience. We shall explore these ideas further in the section on the determinants of intelligence.

A Triarchic Model of Intelligence   Robert Sternberg (1985) has constructed a **triarchic**, or three-level, model of intelligence. The three levels are *contextual*, *experiential*, and *componential*. Individual differences are found at each level.

The Contextual Level   The **contextual level** concerns the environmental setting. It is assumed that intelligent behavior permits people to adapt to the demands of their environments. For example, keeping a job by changing one's behavior to meet the requirements of one's employer is adaptive. But if the employer is making unreasonable or immoral demands, reshaping one's environment (by changing one's employer's attitudes) or selecting an alternate environment (finding a more suitable job) are also adaptive.

Adaptive behaviors in one setting may be maladaptive in another. For instance, assertive social interaction is often helpful in the U.S. workplace, but in Japan deference and avoidance of eye contact are valued more highly. It is "intelligent" of U.S. and Japanese citizens to modify their interpersonal behavior when they visit or are transferred to one another's workplaces.

The Experiential Level   On the **experiential level**, intelligent behavior is defined by the abilities to cope with novel situations and to process information automatically. The ability to relate novel situations to familiar situations quickly (that is, to perceive their similarities and differences) fosters adaptation. Moreover, as a result of experience, we come to solve problems more rapidly. Coping with novelty and automaticity interact to enhance one another. For example, the child who gathers experience in reading processes familiar words more or less automatically and also fosters skills that allow decoding of new words. In sum, it is "intelligent" to profit from experience.

Triarchic   *Governed by three. Descriptive of Sternberg's view that intellectual functioning occurs on three levels: contextual, experiential, and componential.*

Contextual level   *Those aspects of intelligent behavior that permit people to adapt to their environment.*

Experiential level   *Those aspects of intelligence that permit people to cope with novel situations and process information automatically.*

▶ ▶ ▶ ▶

Componental level *The level of intelligence that consists of metacomponents, performance components, and knowledge-acquisition components.*

Metacomponents *Components of intelligence that are based on self-awareness of our intellectual processes.*

Performance components *The mental operations used in processing information.*

Knowledge-acquisition components *Components used in gaining knowledge, such as encoding and relating new knowledge to existing knowledge.*

Creativity *The ability to generate novel solutions to problems. A trait characterized by flexibility, ingenuity, and originality.*

The Componential Level   The **componential level** of intelligence consists of three processes: *metacomponents*, *performance components*, and *knowledge acquisition components*.

Metacomponents concern our awareness of our own intellectual processes. Metacomponents are involved in deciding what problem to solve, selecting appropriate strategies and formulas, monitoring the solution, and changing performance in the light of knowledge of results.

Performance components are the mental operations or skills used in solving problems or processing information. Performance components include encoding information, combining and comparing pieces of information, and generating a solution. Consider Sternberg's (1979) analogy problem:

Washington is to *one* as *Lincoln* is to (a) *five*, (b) *ten*, (c) *fifteen*, (d) *fifty*.

In order to solve the analogy, we must first correctly *encode* the elements— Washington, one, and Lincoln—by identifying them and comparing them to relevant concepts in long-term memory. We must first encode Washington and Lincoln as the names of presidents,* and then try to combine Washington and *one* in a meaningful manner. Perhaps two possibilities come to mind. Washington was the first president, and Washington's picture is on the one dollar bill. We can then generate two possible solutions and try them out. First, what number president was Lincoln? Second, on what bill is Lincoln's picture found? (Do you need to consult a history book or peek into your wallet at this point?)

Knowledge-acquisition components are used in gaining new knowledge. These include encoding information (e.g., Roger Smith as the founder of Rhode Island or as the president of General Motors), combining pieces of information, and comparing new information with what is already known.

Sternberg's model is quite complex, but it does a promising job of capturing what most investigators mean by intellectual functioning. David Wechsler, the originator of a series of widely used intelligence tests, described intelligence in terms that are much simpler but, I think, consistent with Sternberg's view. Intelligence, wrote Wechsler, is the "capacity of an individual to understand the world [and the] resourcefulness to cope with its challenges" (1975, p. 139). Intelligence, to Wechsler, involved accurate representation of the world (which Sternberg discusses as encoding, comparing new information to old information, and so on) and effective problem solving (adapting to one's environment, profiting from experience, selecting the appropriate formulas and strategies, and so forth).

Intelligence and Creativity

What is creativity? What is the relationship between intelligence and creativity?

Creativity is an enigmatic concept. Creativity is difficult to characterize (Feldman, 1980), although we usually have little difficulty recognizing the products of creativity (Amabile, 1982). When I was an undergraduate, a favorite professor remarked that there is nothing new under the sun, only novel com-

---

*There are other possibilities. Both are the names of memorials and cities, for example.

▶ ▶ ▶ ▶

binations of existing elements. To him, the core of creativity was the ability to generate many novel combinations of these elements.

My professor's view was similar to that held by many developmentalists. Mednick (1962), for example, argues that creativity is the ability to make unusual, sometimes remote, associations to the elements of problems, so that new solutions may be generated. According to Amabile (1983), an essential aspect of a creative response is the apparent leap from the elements of the problem to the novel solution. That is, using a standard solution is not particularly creative, even if it is difficult and complex.

Creativity and Divergent Thinking   Creativity demands divergent thinking rather than convergent thinking (Guilford & Hoepfner, 1971). In **convergent thinking** one tries to narrow his or her thought processes to find the single best solution to a specific problem. In divergent thinking one associates more freely and fluently to all aspects of a problem. One allows "leads" to run a nearly limitless course to determine whether they will eventually combine in a useful manner.

Factors in Creativity   What factors contribute to creativity? Guilford (1959) noted that creative people show the cognitive characteristics of flexibility, fluency in generating words and ideas, and originality. Getzels and Jackson (1962) found that creative schoolchildren express rather than inhibit their feelings and are playful and independent. Conger and Peterson (1984) concur that creative people tend to be independent and nonconformist. However, independence and nonconformist behavior are not in and of themselves signs of creativity.

Unfortunately, creative children are often at odds with their teachers because of their independence. Faced with the task of managing large classes, teachers often prefer quiet, submissive, "good" children. In Chapter 11 we shall see that a recent innovation in education, referred to as "open education," is designed to foster creativity and independence.

As Conger and Peterson (1984) note, independence and nonconformity have been discouraged more frequently in girls than in boys. Why? These traits are inconsistent with the traditional passive and compliant feminine social role. Creative behavior requires freedom from social constraints (Amabile, 1983). Because of the women's movement, the numbers of women in the sciences and creative arts are growing rapidly today. In the past the creativity of many girls may have been nipped in the bud.

Intelligence and creativity sometimes, but not always, go hand in hand. Persons low in intelligence are also generally low in creativity, but high intelligence does not guarantee creativity (Crockenburg, 1972). In most cases creativity is found only among people who are above average in intelligence, but the correlation between intelligence and creativity breaks down for highly intelligent people. It also sometimes happens, as noted by Howard Gardner (1983), that people of only moderate intelligence excel in some aspects of creativity, especially in fields like music and art.

Convergent thinking A *thought process that attempts to narrow in on the single best solution to a problem.*

▶ ▶ ▶ ▶

A Canadian study found that highly intelligent ("gifted") boys and girls aged 9 to 11 were, as a group, more creative than less intelligent children (Kershner & Ledger, 1985). Still, not all of the gifted children were more creative than their less intelligent peers. The girls in this study, by the way, were significantly more creative than their male agemates, especially on verbal tasks!

9 THE DEVELOPMENT OF INTELLIGENCE

Tests that measure intelligence—as defined traditionally—are not useful in measuring creativity. Intelligence-test questions require convergent thinking, not creative thinking, to focus in on the single right answer. On intelligence tests, ingenious responses that differ from the designated answers are marked wrong. Tests of creativity, by contrast, are oriented toward determining how flexible and fluent one's thinking can be. Such tests include items like suggesting improvements or unusual uses for a familiar toy or object, naming things that belong in the same class, producing words similar in meaning, and writing different endings for a story.

Here is an item from a test of creativity used to measure ability to freely associate to words (Getzels & Jackson, 1962): "Write as many meanings as you can for each of the following words: (a) duck; (b) sack; (c) pitch; (d) fair." Those who write several meanings for each word, rather than only one, are rated as potentially more creative.

The Remote Associates Test measures creativity in terms of ability to find words related to stimulus words (Matlin, 1983). A set of three words is provided, such as "rough," "resistance," and "beer," and the test-taker tries to associate to another word that will be related to the three. "Draft" is an answer to the example, because of the phrases "rough draft," "draft resistance," and "draft beer." Can you find a word related to each of the following sets of three? The answers follow.

1. charming	student	valiant
2. food	catcher	hot
3. hearted	feet	bitter
4. dark	shot	sun
5. Canadian	golf	sandwich
6. tug	gravy	show
7. attorney	self	spending
8. arm	coal	peach
9. type	ghost	story

Answers to Remote Associates Test: prince, dog, cold, glasses, club, boat, defense, pit, writer. Source: Matlin (1983).

Measurement of Intelligence

Although there are disagreements about the nature of intelligence, but thousands of intelligence tests are administered by psychologists and educators every day.

The Stanford-Binet Intelligence Scale (SBIS) and the Wechsler scales for preschool children, school-age children, and adults are the most widely used and well-respected intelligence tests. The SBIS and Wechsler scales yield scores called **intelligence quotients,** or **IQs.** Each of them has been carefully developed and revised over the years. Each of them has been used to make vital decisions about the academic careers of children. In many cases, children whose test scores fall below or above certain cut-off scores are placed in special classes for the retarded or the gifted.

It must be noted just as emphatically that each test has been accused of discriminating against racial minorities such as black and Hispanic children,

Intelligence quotient (1) Originally, a ratio obtained by dividing a child's score (or "mental age") on an intelligence test by his or her chronological age. (2) Generally, a score on an intelligence test.

IQ Intelligence quotient.

► ► ► ►

the foreign-born, and the children of the socially and economically disadvantaged.

In this section we first explore some basic characteristics of intelligence tests. We see that intelligence tests must be reliable, valid, and adequately standardized. Then we examine the major tests in use today.

Characteristics of Intelligence Tests

Correlation coefficient A number that indicates the direction (positive or negative) and strength of the relationship between two variables.

Reliability In psychological tests and measurements, consistency of scores.

Test–retest reliability A method for determining the reliability of a test by comparing (correlating) test-takers' scores from separate occasions.

Aptitude An ability or talent to succeed in an area in which one has not yet been trained.

Validity In psychological testing, the degree to which a test measures or predicts what it is supposed to measure or predict.

Since important decisions are made on the basis of intelligence tests, they must be *reliable, valid,* and properly *standardized.* Psychologists use statistical techniques, especially the *correlation coefficient,* to study the reliability and validity of tests.

A **correlation coefficient** is a number that indicates how strongly two or more things, like height and weight, or age and weight, are related. Correlation coefficients vary from −1.00 (a perfect negative correlation) to +1.00 (a perfect positive correlation). In order for a test to be considered reliable, correlations between a group's test results on separate occasions should be positive and high—about +.90 (see Table 9.2).

Reliability The **reliability** of a measure is its consistency. A measure of height would not be reliable if a person appeared taller or shorter every time a measurement was taken. A reliable measure of intelligence, like a good tape measure, must yield similar results on different testing occasions.

There are different ways of showing a test's reliability, all of which rely on the correlation coefficient. One of the most commonly used is **test–retest reliability,** which is shown by comparing scores of tests taken on different occasions. The measurement of test–retest reliability may be confused in tests of intelligence and **aptitude** by the fact that people often improve their scores from one occasion to the next because of familiarity with the test items and the testing procedure.

Validity The **validity** of a test is the degree to which it measures what it is supposed to measure. In order to determine whether a test is valid, we see whether it actually predicts an outside standard or external criterion. A proper

Table 9.2   Interpretations of Some Correlation Coefficients

CORRELATION COEFFICIENT	INTERPRETATION
+1.00	Perfect positive correlation, as between temperature Fahrenheit and Centigrade
+0.90	High positive correlation, adequate for test reliability
+0.60 to +0.70	Moderate positive correlation, usually considered adequate for test validity
+0.30	Weak positive correlation, unacceptable for test reliability or validity
0.00	No correlation between variables (no association indicated)
−0.30	Weak negative correlation
−0.60 to −0.70	Moderate negative correlation
−0.90	High negative correlation
−1.00	A perfect negative correlation

▶ ▶ ▶ ▶

9   THE DEVELOPMENT OF INTELLIGENCE

standard or criterion for determining the validity of a test of musical aptitude is the ability to learn to play a musical instrument. Tests of musical aptitude, therefore, should correlate highly with ability to learn to play a musical instrument. It may be that musical ability correlates to some degree with drawing ability and general intelligence. Still, a test of musical aptitude should show a stronger correlation with ability to learn to play an instrument than with either of the others.

In order to determine the validity of an intelligence test, first we ask what more intelligent people can do that less intelligent people cannot do. Then we find out whether the intelligence test predicts that type of behavior, or criterion.

Most psychologists assume that intelligence is one of the factors responsible for academic success. For this reason, intelligence test scores have frequently been correlated with school grades, which serve as one external standard or criterion, to see whether the scores are valid. Other indexes of academic success include scores on achievement tests and teacher ratings of cognitive ability. Intelligence tests generally correlate from about +0.60 to +0.70 with school grades (Lavin, 1965; McCall, 1975; McClelland, 1973). Since we would also expect people who are more intelligent to be placed in white-collar and professional jobs, there should also be a positive correlation between intelligence-test scores attained during childhood and the status of one's occupation as an adult. In one longitudinal study, intelligence-test scores attained after the age of 7 were indeed shown to correlate moderately positively with occupational status (McCall, 1977).

As noted in Table 9.2, a correlation of about +0.60 to +0.70 is generally considered adequate for purposes of assessing test validity. However, such a correlation does not approach a perfect positive relationship. This suggests that factors *other* than performance on intelligence tests contribute to academic and occupational success. Motivation to do well and one's general level of personal adjustment are two of them (Anastasi, 1983; Hrncir et al., 1985; Scarr, 1981).

Standardization   In order to judge how well children perform on an intelligence test, we must be able to compare their scores to those of other children. Children's abilities to answer items correctly on these tests develop with age. That is, in the normal course of things, children answer more items correctly at age 9 than they did at age 6, and still more items correctly at, say, the age of 12. And so, when we are interpreting children's scores, we must compare them to the scores of children from the same age group. However, the capacity to answer more questions correctly usually stabilizes during late adolescence. For this reason, when we evaluate adult scores, it is less important to compare scores to those of people of the same age.

Test developers establish **norms** for intelligence tests by administering them to groups of children of various age groups. Since an effort is made to **standardize** tests according to the performance of a representative sample of children, U.S. reference groups generally reflect the performances of the numerically predominant groups of U.S. children, who are middle class and white.

Because the language of middle-class white children in the United States is English, the history of intelligence testing is checkered with instances of labeling non-English-speaking people as retarded *because of their inability to respond correctly to tests administered in English.* But we should also note that most middle-class white children share certain types of interests and learning op-

Norms *Scores typical of a certain group.*

Standardization *The process of determining how children of different ages perform on a psychological test. This process provides data that permit psychologists and educators to interpret test scores as deviations from a norm.*

▶ ▶ ▶ ▶

What Happens to Brilliant Children? Some Notes on the Terman "Studies of Genius"

▷
▷
▷
▷
▷ How valid are intelligence tests? Can they identify exceptionally bright children? What happens to children whose intelligence test scores suggest that they are headed for success?

The classic longitudinal study described by Stanford University psychologist Lewis Terman (1959) in his "Studies of Genius" provides insight into the validity of intelligence-test results and also into the contribution that personality factors make to success. In 1921 Terman began to track the progress of some 1,500 California schoolchildren who had attained IQ scores of 135 or above. The average score was 150, which places these children in a very superior group. As adults the group was extremely successful in terms of level of education (nearly 10 percent had earned doctoral degrees), socioeconomic status, creativity (the group had published over 90 books and many more shorter pieces), and personal adjustment (the incidence of suicide and mental illness was below the national average).

However, not all group members were so successful. A number of the gifted children did not go on to excel in their careers. The central factor that differentiated the successful from the unsuccessful was not IQ—their scores differed by only six points (Oden, 1968). There were, in fact, a number of more powerful predictors of success: achievement motivation (the desire to get ahead), personal adjustment, and the *sex* of the person.

The influences of achievement motivation and adjustment seem obvious enough. If children have no particular desire to get ahead, or if they are disorganized and distracted by personal problems, their accomplishments are bound to suffer. But what about sex? We must keep in mind that the Terman studies began in the 1920s, when it was generally agreed that a woman's place was in the home. And so many women who today might have climbed the corporate ladder, or distinguished themselves in literature or the arts, became homemakers.

portunities that may not be available or of interest to all American children. For this reason, a number of critics have argued that different norms—and, perhaps, different tests—should be developed for children from different ethnic and racial backgrounds.

Now that we have examined some of the issues concerning the measurement of intelligence, let us have a look at some of the intelligence tests in use today, including the SBIS and the Wechsler scales.

The Stanford-Binet Intelligence Scale

The SBIS originated through the work of Frenchmen Alfred Binet and Theophile Simon early in this century. The French public-school system sought an instrument that could identify children who were unlikely to profit from the

► ► ► ►

regular classroom setting, so that they could receive special attention. Since 1905, when the Binet-Simon scale came into use, it has undergone revision and refinement.

As noted earlier, Binet believed that intelligence involved a number of factors, including reasoning, comprehension, and judgment. Despite his view that many factors were involved in intellectual functioning, Binet constructed his test to yield a single overall score, so that it could be more easily used by the school system.

Binet also assumed that intelligence increased with age. Therefore, older children should get more items right than younger children. And so, he included a series of age-graded questions, as in Table 9.3, and he arranged them in their order of difficulty, from easier to harder. Items were ordered so that they were answered correctly by about 60 percent of the children at their given age level. It was also required that they be answered correctly by significantly fewer children who were one year younger, and by a significantly greater number of children who were one year older.

Mental age *The accumulated months of credit that a person earns on the Stanford-Binet Intelligence Scale. Abbreviated MA.*

Mental Age   The Binet-Simon scale yielded a score called a **mental age,** or MA. The MA shows the intellectual level at which a child is functioning. A child with an MA of 6 is functioning, intellectually, like the average child aged 6.

In taking the test, children earned "months" of credit for each correct answer. Their MA was determined by adding the years and months of credit they attained.

Table 9.3   Some Test Items from the Stanford-Binet Intelligence Scale

LEVEL (YEARS)	ITEM
2 years	1. Children show knowledge of basic vocabulary words by identifying parts of a doll such as the mouth, ears, and hair.
	2. Children show counting and spatial skills along with visual-motor coordination by building a tower of four blocks to match a model.
4 years	1. Children show word fluency and categorical thinking by filling in the missing words when they are asked: "Brother is a boy; sister is a _____?" "In daytime it is light; at night it is _____?"
	2. Children show comprehension by answering correctly when they are asked questions such as: "Why do we have books?" "Why do we have houses?"
9 years	1. Children can point out verbal absurdities, as in this question: "In an old graveyard in Spain they have discovered a small skull which they believe to be that of Christopher Columbus when he was about ten years old. What is foolish about that?"
	2. Children show fluency with words, as shown by answering the questions: "Tell me a number that rhymes with tree." "Tell me the name of a color that rhymes with head."
Adult	1. Adults show knowledge of the meaning of words and conceptual thinking by correctly explaining the differences between "poverty and misery," "laziness and idleness," and "character and reputation."
	2. Adults show spatial skills by correctly answering the question: "What direction would you have to face so that your right hand would be to the north?"

Source: L. M. Terman & M. A. Merrill, *Stanford-Binet Intelligence Scales: 1973 Norms Edition* (Boston: Houghton Mifflin, 1973).

Louis Terman adapted the Binet-Simon scale for use with American children. The first version of the *Stanford*-Binet Intelligence Scale (SBIS)* was published in 1916. The SBIS included more items than the original test and was used with children aged 2 to 16. The SBIS also yielded an intelligence quotient, or IQ, rather than an MA, and American educators developed interest in learning the IQs of their pupils. The SBIS today may be used with children from the age of 2 onward up to adults. Items at the 2-year-level include placing blocks correctly in a three-hole form board; stating what we do with common objects; naming parts of the body; and repeating a series of two numbers. At older age levels, children are asked to define advanced vocabulary words and are asked questions that require more complex verbal reasoning, as in explaining how objects are alike or different.

IQ   The IQ reflects the relationship between a child's mental age and actual or **chronological age,** or CA. Use of this ratio reflects the fact that the same MA score can have vastly different implications for children of different ages. That is, an MA of 8 is an above-average score for a 6-year-old, but an MA of 8 is below average for a 10-year-old. The German psychologist Wilhelm Stern suggested use of the intelligence quotient to handle this problem in 1912.

The IQ is computed by the formula IQ = (Mental Age/Chronological Age) × 100, or

$$IQ = \frac{MA}{CA} \times 100$$

Using this formula, you can readily see that a child with an MA of 6 and a CA of 6 would have an IQ of 100. Children who can handle intellectual problems as well as older children will have IQs above 100. For instance, an 8-year-old who does as well on the SBIS as the average 10-year-old will attain an IQ of 125. Children who do not answer as many items correctly as other children of their age will attain MAs that are lower than their CAs. Consequently, their IQ scores will be below 100.

Since adults do not make gains in problem-solving ability from year to year in the same dramatic way children do, the above formula is not used in arriving at their IQ scores. For adults, IQ scores are derived from comparing their performances with those of other adults.

The Wechsler Scales

David Wechsler developed a series of scales for use with school-age children (Wechsler Intelligence Scale for Children), younger children (Wechsler Preschool and Primary Scale of Intelligence), and adults (Wechsler Adult Intelligence Scale). These tests are abbreviated WISC, WPPSI, and WAIS. They have been revised in recent years, so that the current versions are referred to as the WISC-R, and so on.

The Wechsler scales group test questions into a number of separate subtests (such as those shown in Table 9.4). Each subtest measures a different type of intellectual task. For this reason, the test shows how well a person does

Chronological age A person's age. Abbreviated CA.

▶ ▶ ▶ ▶

*The test is so named because Terman carried out his work at Stanford University.

Table 9.4 Subtests from the Wechsler Intelligence Scale for Children (WISC-R)

VERBAL SUBTESTS	PERFORMANCE SUBTESTS
1. *Information:* "What is the capital of the United States?" "Who was Shakespeare?"	1. *Picture Completion:* Pointing to the missing part of a picture.
2. *Comprehension:* "Why do we have zip codes?" "What does 'A stitch in time saves 9' mean?"	2. *Picture Arrangement:* Arranging cartoon pictures so that they tell a meaningful story.
3. *Arithmetic:* "If 3 candy bars cost 25 cents, how much will 18 candy bars cost?"	3. *Block Design:* Using multicolored blocks to copy pictures of geometric designs.
4. *Similarities:* "How are peanut butter and jelly alike?" "How are good and bad alike?"	4. *Object Assembly:* Putting pieces of a puzzle together so that they form a meaningful object.
5. *Vocabulary:* "What does 'canal' mean?"	5. *Coding:* Rapid scanning for and drawing of symbols that are associated with numbers.
6. *Digit Span:* Repeating series of numbers presented orally by the examiner, forward and backward.	6. *Mazes:* Using a pencil to trace the correct route from a starting point to home.

Items for verbal subtests 1–5 are similar but not identical to items on the WISC. Consider the verbal similarities subtest (#4) for a moment. What are a couple of correct answers to the first question? Did you come up with (1) Both are found on a sandwich, and (2) Both are types of food? Do you think that one of these answers suggests a higher level of intellectual functioning than the other? Why? Note that in the performance coding subtest (#5) children are shown a series of symbols that are associated with numbers. Below are found lines of numbers with empty boxes for drawing in the correct symbol. In this time-limited subtest, the sooner the child memorizes (learns by repeated association) the correct symbol for each number, the sooner he or she can stop scanning for symbols and concentrate on rapid drawing instead.

on one type of task (such as defining words) as compared with another (such as using blocks to construct geometric designs). In this way, the Wechsler scales help reveal children's relative strengths and weaknesses, as well as provide measures of overall intellectual functioning.

Verbal and Performance Subtests   As you can see in Table 9.4, Wechsler described some of his scales as measuring *verbal* tasks, and others as assessing *performance* tasks. In general, verbal subtests require knowledge of verbal concepts, while performance subtests (see Figure 9.3) require familiarity with spatial-relations concepts. But the two groupings are not actually so easily distinguished. For example, the ability to name the object being pieced together in subtest 11, a sign of word fluency and general knowledge as well as of spatial relations ability, helps the person construct it rapidly. In any event, Wechsler's scales permit the computation of verbal and performance IQs. It is not unusual for nontechnically oriented college students to attain higher verbal than performance IQs.

The Deviation IQ   Wechsler also introduced the concept of the **deviation IQ.** Instead of using mental and chronological ages to compute an IQ, Wechsler examined the distribution of the number of correct answers attained by subjects of different ages. He assigned IQ scores on the basis of how much a person's number of correct answers deviated from the average number of correct answers

Deviation IQ *A score on an intelligence test that is derived by determining how far it deviates from the norm.*

▶ ▶ ▶ ▶

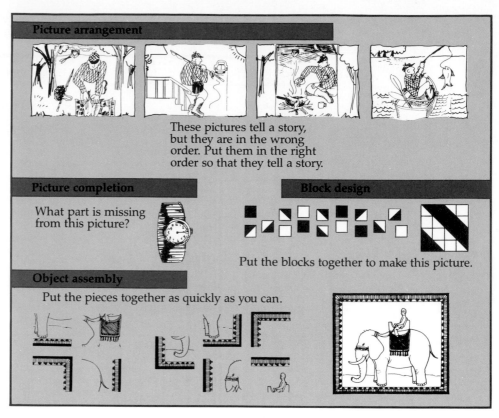

Figure 9.3 *Items Resembling Those Found in the Wechsler Intelligence Scale for Children—Revised Version*

A number of Wechsler performance subtests, such as the block design subtest, tap spatial relations abilities.

► ► ► ►

9   THE DEVELOPMENT OF INTELLIGENCE

Table 9.5 Variations in IQ Scores

RANGE OF SCORES	PERCENTAGE OF POPULATION	BRIEF DESCRIPTION OF INTELLECTUAL FUNCTIONING*
130 and above	2	Very superior
120–129	7	Superior
110–119	16	Bright normal
100–109	25	High average
90–99	25	Low average
80–89	16	Dull normal
70–79	7	Borderline deficient
Below 70	2	Intellectually deficient

*According to David Wechsler.

attained by people of the same age. The average test result at any age level is defined as an IQ score of 100. Wechsler then distributed IQ scores, so that the middle 50 percent of them would fall within the broad average range from 90 to 110. Deviation IQs are used in much the same way as the original ratio (MA/CA) IQs, even though they differ in principle (Sternberg & Powell, 1983).

As you can see in Figure 9.4, most children's IQ scores cluster around the average. Only 5 percent of the population have IQ scores of above 130 or below 70. Table 9.5 indicates the labels that Wechsler assigned to various IQ scores and the approximate percentages of the population who attain IQ scores at those levels.

Group Tests

The SBIS and Wechsler scales are administered to one child at a time. This one-to-one ratio is optimal. It allows the examiner to facilitate performance (within the limits of the standardized directions) and to observe the child closely. In such a setup, examiners do more than mechanically score answers and compute IQs. They can be alert to factors that impair performance, such as language difficulties, illness, or a noisy or poorly lit room. But large institutions with few trained examiners, like the public schools, have also wished to estimate the intellectual functioning of their charges. They require tests that can be administered simultaneously to large groups of schoolchildren.

Group tests for children, first developed during World War I, were administered to 4 million children by 1921, a couple of years after the war had ended (Cronbach, 1975). At first these tests were heralded as remarkable instruments, because they eased the huge responsibilities of school administrators. But as the years passed they came under increasing attack, because many administrators relied on them to track children. They did not seek other sources of information about the children's abilities and achievements (Reschly, 1981).

Intellectual Development Throughout Childhood

We have considered theories of intelligence and the ways in which intelligence is measured. Now let us consider the development of intelligence.

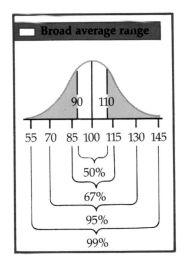

Figure 9.4 Approximate Distribution of IQ Scores David Wechsler defined the deviation IQ in such a way that 50 percent of scores fall within the broad average range of 90–110. This bell-shaped curve is referred to as a normal curve by psychologists and educators. It describes the distribution of many traits, including height.

We shall see that intelligence, as measured during infancy, does not necessarily overlap with intelligence at later ages. We shall also see that there are problems in attempting to predict intelligence during later childhood and adulthood from scores attained at very young ages.

Intelligence in Infancy

Intelligence in infants, of course, is measured differently from intelligence in older children and adults. Siegler and Richards (1982) asked introductory psychology students at Carnegie Mellon University to list the five traits that they felt best characterized intelligence at four age levels: 6 months, 2 years, 10 years, and adulthood. The students also ranked the characteristics according to their importance. As shown in Table 9.6, intelligent behaviors in infants did not at all overlap with intelligent behaviors at 10 years or, of course, adulthood. As age increased, motor and perceptual skills were mentioned less frequently. Reasoning, learning, and problem-solving abilities were mentioned more frequently.

Infants cannot, of course, be assessed by asking them to explain the meanings of words, the similarity between concepts, or the rationales for social rules. One of the most important tests of intellectual development among infants contains very different kinds of items. It is the Bayley Scales of Infant Development, constructed by psychologist Nancy Bayley.

The Bayley Scales   The Bayley test consists of 163 mental-scale items and 81 motor-scale items. Table 9.7 contains sample items from the mental and motor scales and shows the ages at which 50 percent of the infants taking the test passed the items.

The Mental Scale assesses verbal communication, perceptual skills, learning and memory, and problem-solving skills. The Motor Scale assesses gross motor skills, as in standing, walking, and climbing, and fine motor skills, as shown by ability to manipulate the hands and fingers. A behavior record is also kept. It is based on examiner observation of the child during the test. The

Table 9.6   Traits Most Frequently Mentioned as Characteristic of Intelligence at Different Age Levels

6-MONTH-OLDS	2-YEAR-OLDS	10-YEAR-OLDS	ADULTS
Recognition of people and objects	Verbal ability	Verbal ability	Reasoning
Motor coordination	Learning ability	Learning ability; Problem solving; Reasoning (all three tied)	Verbal ability
Alertness	Awareness of people and environment		Problem solving
Awareness of environment	Motor coordination		Learning ability
Verbalization	Curiosity	Creativity	Creativity

Source: R. S. Siegler & D. D. Richards (1982). In R. J. Sternberg (Ed.), *Handbook of Human Intelligence* (New York: Cambridge University Press).

Table 9.7   Items From the Bayley Scales of Infant Development

AGE	MENTAL-SCALE ITEMS	MOTOR-SCALE ITEMS
Newborn	Baby quiets when picked up.	Baby makes a postural adjustment when examiner puts her to his shoulder.
2 months	When examiner presents two objects above infant in crib, she glances back and forth from one to the other.	Baby holds her head steady when being carried about in vertical position.
5 months	Baby is observed to transfer object from one hand to the other during play.	When seated at a feeding-type table and presented with a sugar pill out of reach, baby attempts to pick it up.
8 months	When object in plain view of baby (on table) is covered by a tissue, baby removes tissue to recover toy.	Baby raises herself to a sitting position.
12 months	Baby imitates words when examiner says them.	When asked by the examiner, baby stands up from a position lying on her back on the floor.
16 months	Baby builds a tower with three small cubes after demonstration by examiner.	Baby stands on her left foot alone.

Ages given correspond to level at which 50 percent of infants pass item.
Source: N. Bayley, *Bayley Scales of Infant Development* (New York: The Psychological Corporation, 1969).

behavior record assesses attention span, goal directedness, persistence, and aspects of social and emotional development.

Scales Based on Piaget's Theory of Cognitive Development   Ina Uzgiris and J. McVicker Hunt (1975) have developed infant scales that assess cognitive development according to the theoretical concepts of Piaget. They measure sequential steps in sensorimotor development. Items focus, for example, on visual tracking of a stimulus, the development of object permanence, capacity to bring about desired environmental events, gestural and vocal imitation, the construction of operational causality, and the construction of object relations in space.

Purposes and Problems in Testing Infants   As you can imagine, it is no easy matter to test an infant. The items must be administered on a one-to-one basis by a patient tester, and it can be difficult to judge whether the infant is showing the targeted response. Why, then, do we test infants?

One reason is to screen babies for handicaps. A highly trained tester may be able to detect early signs of sensory or neurological problems. In addition to the Bayley Scales, a number of promising new tests have been developed to screen infants for such difficulties, including the Brazelton Neonatal Behavioral Assessment Scale (see Chapter 4) and the Denver Developmental Screening Test (Brooks-Gunn & Weinraub, 1983).

A second use of infant scales is to make developmental predictions. Here the scales do not fare so well.

► ► ► ►

The Instability of IQ Scores Attained at Early Ages For all the information that the Brazelton, Bayley, and Uzgiris and Hunt scales provide, they do not predict school grades or later IQ scores very well (Kopp & McCall, 1982; McCall, 1981; Rubin & Balow, 1979). Time-honored studies such as that by Anderson (1939) have found little or no relationship at all between "intelligence" as measured at the ages of 3 and 12 months and again at the age of 5 years. Nancy Bayley's (1943) own research showed no relationship between scores on her scale and SBIS scores at the ages of 6 and 7.

The fact of the matter is that IQ scores do not become very stable until preadolescence. A classic study (Honzik et al., 1948) found that IQ scores at the age of 2 correlate only .37 with scores at age 10 and .31 with scores at age 18. IQ scores taken at the age of 4 correlated .66 with scores at the age of 10, but only .42 with scores at the age of 18. Between the ages of 6 and 16, the IQ scores of 58 percent of the children studied changed by 15 or more points. The IQ scores of 35 percent of the children changed by 20 or more points.

A more recent study of 140 children by Robert McCall and his associates (1973), using data from the Fels Longitudinal Study, found that IQ scores fluctuated an average of 28.5 IQ points between the ages of 2½ and 17. About one child in six or seven showed an IQ shift of *40 points* upward or downward. Figure 9.5 shows five patterns of IQ change. Only Group 1 showed stability over the years. The four other groups showed both dramatic gains and dramatic declines. Group 4, like Group 1, wound up at age 17 close to where they had started at 2½. However, their scores shot up dramatically throughout early and most of middle childhood, only to decline just as dramatically after the age of 10.

Why do infant tests fail to predict IQ scores among preschoolers and school-aged children? First of all, cognitive functioning seems to change so quickly during infancy that measurement may be impossible (Birren et al., 1981; Ulvund, 1984). Second, the sensorimotor test items used during infancy may not be strongly related to the verbal and symbolic items used at later ages (Fagan & Singer, 1983; Rebok, 1987). Third, there is little consistency among so-called intelligent behaviors during infancy (Lewis, 1983).

Use of Visual Recognition Memory: A Recent Effort to Enhance Predictability
In a continuing effort to find aspects of intelligence that might remain consistent from infancy through later childhood, a number of researchers have recently focused on **visual recognition memory.** This procedure is based on habituation, as are so many of the methods for assessing perceptual development (see Chapter 6).

Let us consider two longitudinal studies of this type. In one, Joseph Fagan and Susan McGrath (1981) showed 7-month-old babies pictures of two identical faces. After 40 seconds the pictures were replaced with one picture of a new face and a second picture of the familiar face. The amount of time the infants spent looking at each of the second set of faces was recorded. Some infants spent significantly more time looking at the new face than the older face, suggesting that they had better memory for visual stimulation. The children were given standard IQ tests at the age of 7 years. It was found that the children with greater visual recognition memory later attained higher IQ scores. In the other study, Susan Rose and Ina Wallace (1985) obtained similar results with preterm children assessed at 6 months and again at 6 years.

Joseph Fagan (1984) reviewed 15 studies of the relationship between

▶ ▶ ▶ ▶

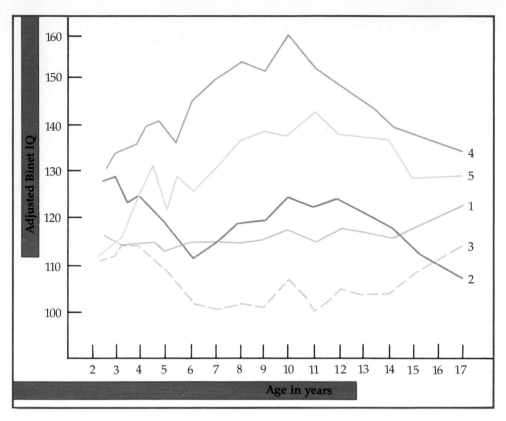

Figure 9.5 Five Patterns of Change in IQ Scores for Children in the Fels Longitudinal Study
In the Fels Longitudinal Study, IQ scores remained stable between the ages of 2½ and 17 for only one of five groups—group number 1.

infant preference for novel stimulation and later IQ scores. Correlations between the earlier and later measures ranged from + .33 to + .66, with an average correlation of + .45. These weak to moderate correlations do not permit solid prediction, but they seem stronger than the correlations attained using more traditional assessment techniques. Perhaps infants' tendencies to scan stimuli and retain images will yield more precise measures in future years.

In sum, infant scales and assessment techniques may provide useful data as screening devices, as research instruments, or simply for describing the things that infants do and do not do. However, their predictive power as intelligence tests has so far been disappointing.

Intelligence in Childhood and Adolescence

The most rapid advances in intellectual functioning occur during childhood. Within a few years, children gain the abilities to symbolize experiences and manipulate symbols to solve increasingly complex problems. Their vocabularies leap, and their sentences become more complex. Their thought processes become increasingly logical and abstract, and they gain the capacity to focus on two or more aspects of a problem at once.

There seem to be at least two major spurts in intellectual growth. The first occurs at about the age of 6. As noted by Rebok (1987), this spurt coincides with entry into a school system and also with the shift from preoperational to concrete operational thought. In using the concepts of Cattell and Horn, the school experience may begin to help "crystallize" intellectual functioning at this time. The second spurt occurs at about age 10 or 11, and possible influences are harder to pin down. Rebok suggests that this spurt may reflect general physical and psychological changes linked to approaching puberty, or, perhaps, the shift from concrete to formal operational thought.

Although there are spurts, once they reach middle childhood, children appear to undergo relatively more stable patterns of gains in intellectual functioning. As a result, intelligence tests gain greater predictive power at about this time. Returning to the study by Honzik and associates (1948), we find that intelligence test scores taken at the age of 9 correlated +.90 with scores at the age of 10 and +.76 with scores at the age of 18.

Despite the increased predictive power during middle childhood found by the Honzik group, the McCall group's 1973 study continued to find wide individual differences. As shown in Figure 9.5, two groups of children (1 and 3) made reasonably consistent gains in intelligence-test scores between the ages of 10 and 17, whereas three groups showed declines. Group 4, who had shown the most intellectual "promise" at age 10 went on to show the most precipitous decline, although they still wound up in the highest 2–3 percent of the population.

Although intelligence test scores change throughout childhood, some children show reasonably consistent patterns of below- or above-average performance. In the following section we discuss children who show consistent patterns of extreme scores—low and high.

Differences in Intelligence

The average IQ score in the United States is very close to 100, and about 50 percent of U.S. children attain IQ scores in the broad average range from 90 to 110. Nearly 95 percent attain scores between 70 and 130. But what of the other 5 percent? Children who attain IQ scores below 70 are generally labeled as intellectually deficient or mentally retarded. Children who attain scores of 130 or above are usually labeled as gifted. Both of these labels—these extreme individual differences—lead to certain expectations of children. Both can place heavy burdens on children and their parents.

There are also social-class, racial, and ethnic differences in IQ. Individual differences may tax our school systems and create the need for educational innovation, but racial and cultural differences have stimulated social and political strife. In this section we consider mental retardation; gifted children; and social-class, racial, and cultural differences in IQ.

Mental Retardation

Mental retardation is typically assessed through a combination of children's IQ scores and observations of the adaptiveness of their behavior. A number of scales have been developed to assess adaptive behavior. Items from the Vineland Adaptive Behavior Scales (Sparrow et al., 1984) are shown in Table

Mainstreamed *Placed in educational settings (e.g., schools and classrooms) for normal children.*

9.8. Later in the chapter we shall see that early in this century many immigrants were labeled "feebleminded" on the basis of intelligence tests. It was little matter to some of the examiners that the immigrants spoke Russian or Italian; the tests were given in English. However, if the adaptive behavior of these immigrants had also been assessed, the label *feebleminded* could hardly have been applied.

Table 9.9 summarizes descriptions of a number of levels of retardation. Most of the children (about 80 percent) who are retarded are mildly retarded. Mildly retarded children, as the term implies, are most capable of adjusting to the demands of educational institutions and, eventually, to society at large. The mildly retarded are also most likely to be **mainstreamed** in regular classrooms, as opposed to being placed in special-needs classes, as we shall see in Chapter 11. Mainstreaming is intended to provide mildly retarded children with the best possible education and to encourage socialization with children at all intellectual levels. Unfortunately, some mildly retarded children are overwhelmed by regular classrooms, and they are avoided by their classmates.

Children with Down syndrome are most likely to fall within the moderately retarded range. As suggested in Table 9.9, moderately retarded children can learn to speak; to dress, feed, and clean themselves; and, eventually, to engage in useful work under supportive conditions, as in the sheltered workshop. However, they usually do not acquire skills in reading and arithmetic. Severely and profoundly retarded children may not acquire speech and self-help skills, and remain highly dependent on others for survival throughout their lives.

Causes of Retardation   As noted in earlier chapters, some of the causes of retardation are biological (see Table 9.10). Retardation, for example, can stem from chromosomal abnormalities, such as Down syndrome; genetic disorders, such as phenylketonuria (PKU); and brain damage. Brain damage may have many origins, including accidents during childhood and problems during pregnancy. For example, maternal alcohol abuse, malnutrition, or diseases during pregnancy can lead to retardation in the unborn child.

Table 9.8   Items from the Vineland Adaptive Behavior Scales

AGE LEVEL	ITEM
2 years	Says at least 50 recognizable words.
	Removes front-opening coat, sweater, or shirt without assistance.
5 years	Tells popular story, fairy tale, lengthy joke, or plot of television program.
	Ties shoelaces into a bow without assistance.
8 years	Keeps secrets or confidences for more than one day.
	Orders own meal in restaurant.
11 years	Uses the telephone for all kinds of calls, without assistance.
	Watches television or listens to radio for information about a particular area of interest.
16 years	Looks after own health.
	Responds to hints or indirect cues in conversation.

Adapted from S. S. Sparrow, D. A. Ballo, & D. V. Cicchetti, *Vineland Adaptive Behavior Scales* (Circle Pines, MN: American Guidance Service, 1984).

▶ ▶ ▶ ▶

Table 9.9 Levels of Retardation, Typical Ranges of IQ Scores, and Types of Adaptive Behaviors Shown

APPROXIMATE IQ SCORE RANGE	PRESCHOOL AGE 0–5 MATURATION AND DEVELOPMENT	SCHOOL AGE 6–21 TRAINING AND EDUCATION	ADULT 21 AND OVER SOCIAL AND VOCATIONAL ADEQUACY
Mild 50–70	Often not noticed as retarded by casual observer, but is slower to walk, feed self, and talk than most children.	Can acquire practical skills and useful reading and arithmetic to a 3rd to 6th grade level with special education. Can be guided toward social conformity.	Can usually achieve social and vocational skills adequate to self-maintenance; may need occasional guidance and support when under unusual social or economic stress.
Moderate 35–49	Noticeable delays in motor development, especially in speech; responds to training in various self-help activities.	Can learn simple communication, elementary health and safety habits, and simple manual skills; does not progress in functional reading or arithmetic.	Can perform simple tasks under sheltered conditions; participates in simple recreation; travels alone in familiar places; usually incapable of self-maintenance.
Severe 20–34	Marked delay in motor development; little or no communication skill; may respond to training in elementary self-help—e.g., self-feeding.	Usually walks, barring specific disability; has some understanding of speech and some response; can profit from systematic habit training.	Can conform to daily routines and repetitive activities; needs continuing direction and supervision in protective environment.
Profound Below 20	Gross retardation; minimal capacity for functioning in sensorimotor areas; needs nursing care.	Obvious delays in all areas of development; shows basic emotional responses; may respond to skillful training in use of legs, hands, and jaws; needs close supervision.	May walk, may need nursing care, may have primitive speech; will usually benefit from regular physical activity; incapable of self-maintenance.

Adapted from L. E. Bourne, Jr., & B. R. Ekstrand, *Psychology: Its Principles and Meanings,* 4th ed. (New York: Holt, Rinehart and Winston, 1982), p. 209.

Table 9.10 Organic Diseases Associated with Mental Retardation

WHEN DISEASE DEVELOPS	TYPES OF DISEASE		
	GENETIC	INFECTIOUS	TRAUMATIC
In utero*	Down syndrome Klinefelter's syndrome Phenylketonuria Tay-Sachs disease Niemann-Pick disease Maple syrup urine disease** Hurler's syndrome Lesch-Nyhan syndrome	Rubella Syphilis Toxoplasmosis Encephalitis	Rh factor Cretinism Malnutrition Poisoning (lead, carbon monoxide, X-ray) Drugs (especially alcohol)
At or following birth		Encephalitis Meningitis	All the above (except Rh factor) *plus* Anoxia Premature birth Head injury

Based on discussion in G. C. Davison & J. M. Neale, *Abnormal Psychology,* 4th ed. (New York: Wiley, 1986), pp. 407–413.

*Conditions in which the head size is grossly distorted are not listed, because various factors may have impaired development. Examples are microcephaly, or small head in which the development of the brain has been arrested; macrocephaly, large head with abnormal growth of supportive tissues; and hydrocephaly, large head with excessive cerebrospinal fluid.

**So-called because of the characteristic odor of the infant's urine.

▶ ▶ ▶ ▶

There is also **cultural-familial retardation,** in which the child is biologically normal, but does not develop age-appropriate behaviors at the normal pace, because of social isolation of one kind or another. For example, the later-born children of impoverished families may have little opportunity to interact with adults or to play with stimulating toys. As a result, they may not develop sophisticated language skills or the motivation to acquire the kinds of knowledge that are valued in a technologically oriented society.

Naturally, we wish to encourage all children to develop to the maximum of their capacities—including retarded children. As a rule of thumb, we should keep in mind that IQs are nothing but scores on tests. They are not perfectly reliable, meaning that they can and do change somewhat from testing to testing. Thus it is more important to focus on children's current levels of achievement in the academic and self-help skills that we wish to impart, so that we can try to build these skills gradually and coherently, step by step.

In the case of children with cultural-familial retardation, there is every reason to believe that they can change dramatically when we intervene by providing enriched learning experiences, especially at early ages. Later in the chapter we shall see how Head Start programs, for example, have enabled children at cultural-familial risk to function at above-average levels.

Gifted Children

Giftedness involves more than intelligence. According to former U.S. Commissioner of Education Sidney P. Marland (1972), the category of gifted children should include children who have "outstanding abilities and are capable of high performance" in overall intelligence; a specific academic area, such as language arts or mathematics; creativity; leadership; the visual or performing arts; or bodily talents, such as gymnastics and dancing.

This view of giftedness exceeds the realm of intellectual ability alone and is consistent with Gardner's (1983) view, mentioned earlier, that there are six intelligences, not one, each of which is based in a different area of the brain. Two of these involve language ability and logic, which are familiar components of intelligence functions. But Gardner also refers to bodily talents, musical ability, spatial-relations skills, and an empathic ability—a sensitivity to one's own feelings and those of others. According to this view, one could compose magnificent symphonies or make advances in mathematical theory while remaining average in, say, language skills.

Much of our knowledge of the progress of children who are gifted in overall intellectual functioning stems from Terman's longitudinal studies of genius. And it is encouraging. As discussed earlier in the chapter, his sample went on to engage in an extraordinary number of achievements. Moreover, they tended to be well-adjusted. Other studies are also positive, showing, for example (Gallagher, 1975), that gifted children tend to be independent and popular with their peers.

Marland (1972) suggested that there is a need to identify gifted children at an early age and provide them with enriched experiences, so that they can develop their exceptional talents. I agree. But I'll venture a couple of steps further. As we shall see later in this chapter, it is also essential to provide disadvantaged children with the richest possible educational experiences from an early age. But if we enrich only the gifted and the disadvantaged, we run the risk of creating a new class of relatively deprived students—the middle 95

▶ ▶ ▶ ▶

percent of the school population. I would like to see us invest enough in education to enrich every child.

Social-Class, Racial, and Ethnic Differences

Retardation and giftedness are examples of the differences found *within* every racial and cultural group. However, there is also a body of research suggestive of differences *between* social, racial, and ethnic groups.

For example, lower-class U.S. children attain IQ scores some 10–15 points lower than those of middle- and upper-class children. Black children tend to attain IQ scores that are some 15–20 points lower than their **Caucasian** agemates (Hall & Kaye, 1980; Loehlin et al., 1975). In his analysis of the data from 11 major studies of black–white differences, Arthur Jensen (1985) concluded that the racial differences reflected different rates in processing information (Jensen's "Level II" functioning), rather than differences in specific knowledge, training, or skills ("Level I" functioning). Hispanic American and Native American children as groups also score significantly below the Caucasian norms. For the first 18 months, white, black, middle- and lower-class infants all tend to score about the same on infant scales of intelligence. Differences in IQ become apparent when children enter school, and they appear to increase throughout childhood.

Several studies on IQ have confused the factors of social class and race, because disproportionate numbers of blacks, Hispanic Americans, and Native Americans are found among the lower socioeconomic classes. But when we limit our observations to particular racial groups, we still find an effect for social class. That is, middle-class Caucasians outscore lower-class Caucasians. Middle-class blacks, Hispanic Americans, and Native Americans also all outscore lower-class members of their own racial groups.

Research has also discovered differences between Asians and Caucasians. Asian Americans, for example, frequently outscore Caucasian Americans on the math test of the Scholastic Aptitude Tests. Students in China (Taiwan) and Japan also outscore Americans on standardized achievement tests in math and science (Stevenson et al., 1986). More than a decade ago, reports were published by British psychologist Richard Lynn (1977, 1982) that the Japanese (residing in Japan) attain higher IQ scores than Caucasian Britishers or Americans. The mean Japanese IQ was 111, which just exceeds the top of the high average range in the United States.

The findings concerning Asian and U.S. children have not gone undisputed. Harold Stevenson and his colleagues (1985) gave ten cognitive tasks along with reading and math achievement tests to children from Minneapolis, Minnesota; Taiwan; and Sendai, in Japan. They selected 240 children in each of the first five school grades. Although the Asian children attained higher achievement scores than the U.S. children, their performance on the cognitive tasks was comparable.

Groups of Asian students achieve more than Caucasian Americans, but the difference in achievement may not reflect overall differences in cognitive or intellectual ability. It may be, instead, that the superior achievements of Asian children reflect different values in the home, school, or culture at large. Lynn (1982) suggested that environmental factors such as intensive educational practices have motivated Japanese children to achieve more than their American and European peers. Still, a number of scientists, such as Alan Anderson (1982),

Caucasian *Descriptive of people whose ancestors came from Europe, North Africa, and the Middle East to North India. Usually referred to as "white people," although skin color actually varies from pale reddish white to olive brown.*

▶ ▶ ▶ ▶

an editor of *Nature,* believe that the higher IQ scores of Asians may reflect genetic factors. Anderson attributes the Japanese scores, in part, to intermarriage among previously isolated groups that occurred when rural Japanese migrated to urban centers at midcentury. Intermarriage was also accompanied by increases in height and longevity. Better nutrition and prenatal care no doubt also played a role in these improvements, however. In the following sections of the chapter we shall see how difficult it can be to tease out the effects of heredity and the environment.

The differences in IQ scores between black children and Caucasian children in the United States have stimulated yet hotter disputes and have been studied with greater intensity. We shall discuss these differences in the broader contexts of the IQ testing controversy and the determinants of intelligence.

The Testing Controversy

I was almost one of the testing casualties. At 15 I earned an IQ test score of 82, three points above the track of the special education class. Based on this score, my counselor suggested that I take up bricklaying because I was "good with my hands." My low IQ, however, did not allow me to see that as desirable.

This testimony, offered by black psychologist Robert L. Williams (1974, p. 32), echoes the sentiments of many psychologists. A recent survey of psychologists and educational specialists by Mark Synderman and Stanley Rothman (1987) found that the majority believed that intelligence tests are somewhat biased against blacks and members of the lower classes. Respondents also believed that elementary and secondary schools rely on them too strongly in making educational placements.

In this section let us first gain a historical perspective on the testing controversy. Then let us examine some contemporary pressing issues.

Some Notes on the Historical Misuse of Intelligence Tests

During the 1920s intelligence tests were misused to prevent the immigration of many Europeans and others into the United States (Kamin, 1982; Kleinmuntz, 1982). Test pioneer H. H. Goddard (1917) assessed 178 newly arrived immigrants at Ellis Island and claimed that "83 percent of the Jews, 80 percent of the Hungarians, 79 percent of the Italians, and 87 percent of the Russians were 'feeble-minded' " (Kleinmuntz, 1982, p. 333). Apparently it was of little concern to Goddard that these immigrants by and large did not understand English—the language in which the tests were administered.

Such blatant misuse of intelligence tests has led psychologists like Leon Kamin to complain, "Since its introduction to America the intelligence test has been used more or less consciously as an instrument of oppression against the underprivileged—the poor, the foreign born, and racial minorities" (in Crawford, 1979, p. 664). Despite these historical notes and criticisms, group tests are administered to as many as 10 million children a year in the United States. Some states, however, like California, and some cities have outlawed their use as the sole standard for placing children in special classrooms (Bersoff, 1981). Let us explore further some of the controversy concerning the use of both individual

▶ ▶ ▶ ▶

A number of critics of intelligence tests argue that the tests are geared for middle-class white children who tend to share interests and learning opportunities not available to all children. These critics have further argued that different norms, or different tests, should be developed for children from different racial and ethnic backgrounds.

and group intelligence tests. The important issues are whether intelligence tests are still misused and misunderstood.

The Modern-Day Testing Controversy: The Quest for Culture-Free Intelligence Tests

Cultural bias *A factor hypothesized to be present in intelligence tests that provides an advantage for test-takers from certain cultural or ethnic backgrounds, but does not reflect true intelligence.*

Culture-free *Describing a test in which cultural biases have been removed. On such a test, test-takers from different cultural backgrounds would have an equal opportunity to earn scores that reflect their true abilities.*

Intelligence tests, as pointed out by critics such as Robert Williams, all measure traits that are required in modern, high-technology societies (Anastasi, 1983; Pearlman et al., 1980; Schmidt et al., 1981). The vocabulary and arithmetic subtests on the Wechsler scales, for example, clearly reflect achievement in language skills and computational ability. It is generally assumed that the broad types of achievement measured by these tests reflect intelligence. Yet we cannot rule out the possibility that they also strongly reflect cultural familiarity with the concepts required to respond correctly to test questions. In particular, the tests seem to reflect middle-class white culture in the United States (Garcia, 1981).

If scoring well on intelligence tests requires a certain type of cultural experience, the tests are said to have a **cultural bias.** Children reared to speak Black English in black neighborhoods could be at a disadvantage, not because of differences in intelligence, but because of cultural differences. For this reason, psychologists like Raymond B. Cattell (1949) and Florence Goodenough (1954) have tried to construct **culture-free** intelligence tests.

▶ ▶ ▶ ▶

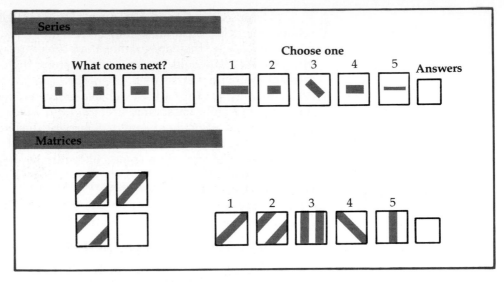

Figure 9.7 A Drawing of a Person by a 7-Year-Old
Some psychologists use children's drawings of persons as culture-fair indexes of their intelligence.

Some culture-free tests do not rely on expressive language at all. Cattell's Culture-Fair Intelligence Test evaluates reasoning ability through the child's comprehension of the rules that govern a progression of geometric designs, as shown in Figure 9.6. Goodenough's Draw-A-Person test is based on the premise that children from all cultural backgrounds have had the opportunity to observe people and note the relationships between the parts and the whole. Her instructions simply require children to draw a picture of a man or woman, as shown in Figure 9.7.

Unfortunately, culture-free tests have not lived up to their promise. First, middle-class white children still outperform blacks on them. Middle-class white children, for example, are more likely to have basic familiarity with materials such as blocks and pencils and paper. They are more likely than disadvantaged children to have arranged blocks into various designs (practice relevant to the Cattell test) and more likely to have sketched animals, people, and inanimate objects (practice relevant to the Goodenough test). Second, culture-free tests do not appear to be as valid as other intelligence tests. They do not predict academic success as well, and scholastic aptitude remains the central concern of educators.

There may really be no such thing as a culture-fair or culture-free intelligence test. Motivation to do well, for example, could be considered a cultural factor. Because of socioeconomic differences, black children in the United States often do not have the same motivation as whites to do well on tests. Highly motivated children attain higher scores on intelligence tests than do less well-motivated children (Zigler & Butterfield, 1968). And, as noted above, even basic familiarity with test-relevant materials such as pencils and paper is a cultural factor.

▶ ▶ ▶ ▶

Some of the controversy over using intelligence tests in the public schools might be diffused if they were viewed as broad achievement tests—which, of course, they are—rather than direct measures of intelligence (Humphreys, 1981). It would be clearly understood that they measure a child's performance in certain areas on a given day. The focus might be on using follow-up techniques, perhaps more extensive individual testing or interviews, to more fully outline a child's academic strengths and weaknesses, including factors like motivation and adjustment, and to determine the best strategies to help enhance the child's academic performance. Then testing would promote equal opportunity instead of excluding some children from privileges (Gordon & Terrell, 1981). It is irresponsible to make major decisions about children's lives on the basis of an isolated test score attained in an impersonal group-testing situation.

The Determinants of Intelligence: Where Do IQ Scores Come From?

In 1969 Arthur Jensen published an article called "How Much Can We Boost IQ and Scholastic Achievement?" in the *Harvard Educational Review.* Filled with statistics and technical jargon, the article gained national visibility because of Jensen's assertion that 80 percent of the variability in IQ scores is inherited. This may sound like nothing much to get excited about, yet Jensen became the focus of campus demonstrations and was sometimes booed loudly in class.

Why?

As noted earlier, blacks score below Caucasians on intelligence tests. Jensen had asserted that this difference was largely genetically determined. If so, the difference could never be decreased.

Protests from the black community were echoed by many Caucasians, including prominent psychologists and other scientists. In the political climate of the late 1960s and 1970s, "Jensen-*ism*" became equated with racism and fascism. Consider this condemnation by behavior geneticist Jerry Hirsch: "It perhaps is impossible to exaggerate the importance of the Jensen disgrace. . . . It has permeated both science and the universities and hoodwinked large segments of government and society" (1975, p. 3). Crawford (1979) suggested that Jensen's views met with opposition because they are incompatible with the basic U.S. belief that U.S. children can grow up to be whatever they want to be, even President.

What do developmentalists know about the **determinants** of intelligence? What are the roles of heredity and the environment?

Genetic Influences on Intelligence

Let us describe famous experiments with laboratory animals in order to point up some of the difficulties and shortcomings of research on genetic influences on *human* intelligence. Then we shall examine correlational research with human subjects.

Selective Breeding of Rats for Maze-Learning Ability Maze-learning ability in rats is measured by the numbers of errors (literally, the number of times they

Determinants *Factors that define or set limits.*

▶ ▶ ▶ ▶

Strategies for Studying Genetic and Environmental Influences on IQ

▷

▷

▷

▷

▷   Consider the problems in attempting to decide whether a child's performance on an intelligence test is mainly influenced by nature or nurture—that is, by genetic or environmental factors. If a superior child has superior parents, do we attribute the superiority to heredity or to the environment provided by these parents? Similarly, if a dull child lives in an impoverished home, do we attribute the dullness to the genetic potential transmitted by the parents or to the lack of intellectual stimulation in the environment?

No research strategy for attempting to ferret out genetic and environmental determinants of IQ is flawless. Still, a number of ingenious approaches have been devised. The total weight of the evidence provided through these approaches may be instructive.

Strategies for Studying Genetic Influences

The following strategies have been devised for research into genetic factors:

• Selective breeding of rats for maze-learning ability. If we can breed generations of rats who are "bright" and "dull" in their ability to learn maze routes, it may be that there is also a genetic factor in human intellectual functioning. Drawbacks? At least two: (1) Maze-learning in rats is not the equivalent of intelligent behavior in humans, and (2) there are general problems in applying findings with rats and other lower animals to humans.

• Kinship studies: Correlating the IQ scores of twins, other siblings, and parents and children who have lived together and apart. Strong positive correlations between the IQ scores of closely related children who have been reared apart could be taken as evidence of genetic influences. Psychologists and educational specialists appear to be most impressed by studies of monozygotic (identical) twins who have been reared apart (Snyderman & Rothman, 1987).

• Adoptee studies: Correlating the IQ scores of adopted children with those of their biological and adoptive parents. If the IQ scores of adoptees correlate more highly with those of their biological than their adoptive parents, we have another argument for genetic influences.

Strategies for Studying Environmental Influences

There are also several approaches to studying environmental influences on IQ:

• Discovering situational factors that affect IQ scores. If children's motivation to do well, their familiarity with testing materials, their nourishment, and their comfort in the testing situation can be shown to affect IQ scores, environmental influences play a role.

• Exploring children's abilities to rebound from early deprivation. If children who have spent some of their early lives in impoverished circumstances can make dramatic gains in IQ when stimulated later on, it would appear that IQ is subject to environmental influences.

• Exploring the effects of positive early environments. If good parent–child relations, early language stimulation, and Head Start programs are linked to gains in IQ, we have more evidence for the role of environmental influences.

In our review of the literature, we shall see that there seems to be evidence for both genetic and environmental influences on IQ. Moreover, many of the same studies—in particular, the kinship and adoptee studies—appear to provide evidence for *both* genetic and environmental influences.

▶ ▶ ▶ ▶

run down "blind alleys") the animals make in running through mazes over several trials in order to attain food goals. Maze-learning ability, of course, is limited in scope; it relies on spatial relationships and sensorimotor coordination. No verbal skills are required. But maze-learning ability still requires some capacity to profit from experience in order to meet the requirements of one's situation, and so this research is instructive.

In such studies (Rosenzweig, 1969; Tryon, 1940), a group of rats is tested for maze-learning ability. Rats making the fewest mistakes are labeled B_1, signifying the first generation of "maze-bright" rats. "Maze-dull" rats are labeled D_1. The total distribution of errors, or blind-alley entrances, made by the first (parent) generation is shown in Figure 9.8. These errors were made over a series of 19 runs in the Tryon study.

Maze-bright rats from the first generation were interbred with other maze-bright rats. Maze-dull rats were similarly interbred. The second graph in Figure 9.8 shows how the offspring (B_2) of the maze-bright parents compared

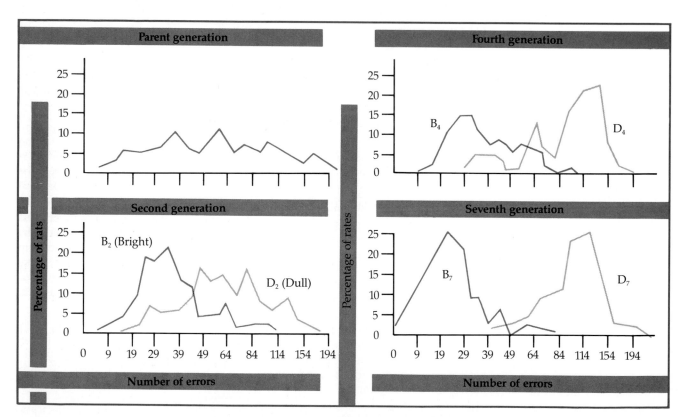

Figure 9.8 Selective Breeding for Maze-Learning Ability in Rats
In the Tryon study, the offspring of maze-bright rats were inbred for six generations. So were the offspring of maze-dull rats. As the generations progressed, there was less and less overlap in maze-learning ability between the maze-bright and maze-dull rats, although environmental influences were held as constant as possible for all offspring. Research also shows that an enriched early environment narrows the performance gap between offspring of maze-bright and maze-dull rats.

▶ ▶ ▶ ▶

9 THE DEVELOPMENT OF INTELLIGENCE

with the offspring (D₂) of the maze-dull parents in numbers of errors (blind-alley entrances). The offspring of the maze-bright rats, as a group, clearly made fewer errors than the offspring of the maze-dull, although there was considerable overlap between groups. The brightest offspring of the maze-bright were then interbred as were the dullest of the maze-dull for six consecutive generations. Fortunately for the researchers, rat generations are measured in months, not decades. Throughout their development, the environments of the rats were kept as constant as possible. Dull rat pups were often given to bright mothers for rearing, and vice versa. For this reason, a critic could not argue that the maze-learning ability of bright offspring could be attributed to an enriched environment provided by a bright mother.

After six generations there was little overlap in maze-learning performance between maze-bright and maze-dull rats. The (spatial relations) superiority of the maze-bright rats did not generalize to all types of learning tasks, and we cannot emphasize too strongly that maze-learning ability in rats is not comparable to the complex groupings of behavior that define human intelligence. However, the experimental technique provides a model that is worth noting, because we cannot replicate it with human subjects.

For ethical, legal, and practical reasons we cannot specify which people will breed together. Nor can we completely control childhood environments. These facts are fortunate from the standpoints of personal freedom and the dignity of the individual, but they also prevent experiments in selective breeding of people for the characteristic (or characteristics) of intelligence. Thus, the research on genetic influences on human intelligence must employ different strategies. Two of them involve studies of the relationships between intelligence and degree of kinship, as in the monozygotic–dizygotic (MZ–DZ) twin study, and studies of the intelligence of adopted children.

Intelligence and Family Relationship   As explained, it would be unethical and impractical to run experiments in which we selectively breed people on the basis of IQ scores or other factors. Still, we can examine the IQ scores of closely and distantly related people who have been reared together or apart. If heredity is involved in human intelligence, closely related people ought to have more similar IQs than distantly related or unrelated people, even when they are reared separately.

Figure 9.9 shows the results of 52 studies of IQ and heredity in human beings, as summarized by the journal *Science*. The lines show the range of correlations of IQ scores for pairs of people, and the mark along each line shows the average correlation for the pairs.

Figure 9.9 shows that the IQ scores of MZ twins are more alike than the scores for any other pairs, even when the twins have been reared apart. The average correlation is about +.90. Correlations between the IQ scores of DZ twins, siblings, and parents and children are generally comparable, as is their degree of genetic relationship. The correlations tend to vary from the upper +.40s to the upper +.50s. Correlations between the IQ scores of children and their natural parents are higher than those between children and adoptive parents.

There is no relationship between the IQ scores of unrelated people who are reared separately. This is as it should be since such pairs share neither heredity nor environment. But there is an average correlation in the +.30s for siblings separated at an early age and reared apart. And there is an average

▶ ▶ ▶ ▶

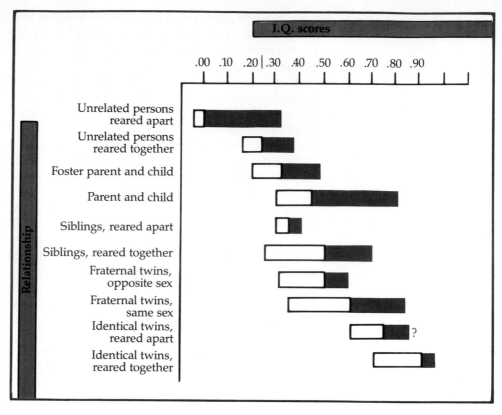

Figure 9.9 Summary of Findings of Studies on Kinship and IQ
The bars show the range of correlations for pairs of individuals in each group. The beginning of the color segment of each bar marks the average correlation for the group of studies. A question mark accompanies the data on "identical twins, reared apart" because it was recently revealed that British psychologist Cyril Burt, whose research contributed to these figures, had falsified much of his data. Nevertheless, more recent research on identical twins separated at an early age is consistent with the data shown in the figure.

correlation in the +.70s for identical twins who were separated at an early age and reared apart.

It must be pointed out that some of the data summarized in the *Science* review is suspect. Some of it was reported by the late British psychologist Sir Cyril Burt. In a scandal of the 1970s, it was discovered that Burt had falsified the names of coresearchers and fudged data to support the view that heredity is the major determinant of intelligence in humans. However, more recent studies of kinship and intelligence are still consistent with the data in Figure 9.9. For instance, a study of 500 pairs of MZ and DZ twins in Louisville, Kentucky (Wilson, 1983), found that the correlations in intelligence between MZ twins were in the range suggested for MZ twins in Figure 9.9. The correlations in intelligence between DZ twin pairs was also the same as that between other siblings.

▶ ▶ ▶ ▶

9 THE DEVELOPMENT OF INTELLIGENCE

All in all, these studies appear to provide evidence for a role for heredity in IQ scores. Note, however, that genetic pairs (like MZ twins) reared together show higher correlations between IQ scores than similar genetic pairs (like other MZ twins) who were reared apart. This finding holds for MZ twins, siblings, and unrelated people. *For this reason, the same group of studies suggests that the environment may play a role in the attaining of IQ scores.*

Studies of the Intelligence of Adoptees A third strategy for exploring genetic influences on intelligence is to compare the correlations between adopted children and their biological and adoptive parents. When children are separated from their biological parents at early ages, one can argue that strong relationships between their IQ scores and those of their natural parents may reflect genetic influences. Strong relationships between their IQs and those of their adoptive parents might reflect environmental influences.

Several recent studies with 1- and 2-year-old children in Colorado (Baker et al., 1983), children in Texas (Horn, 1983), and Minnesota children (Scarr & Weinberg, 1983) all find that there is a stronger relationship between the IQ scores of adopted children and their biological parents than there is with their adoptive parents. The Scarr and Weinberg report concerns black children reared by white adoptive parents, and we shall return to its findings in the section on environmental influences on intelligence.

And so, there may be a genetic influence on intelligence. However, as we shall see, there is also probably an environmental influence.

Environmental Influences on Intelligence

One approach in studies on environmental influences on intelligence focuses on the situational factors that determine IQ scores. Remember that an IQ is, after all, a score on a test. And so, in some cases, we need look no further than the testing situation to explain some of the discrepancy between the IQ scores of middle-class children and those of children from economically disadvantaged backgrounds. In one study, the experimenters (Zigler et al., 1982) simply made children as comfortable as possible during the test. Rather than being cold and "impartial," the examiner was warm and friendly. When care was taken to see that the children understood the directions, the children's test anxiety appears to have been markedly reduced. The children's IQ scores were six points higher than those for a control group treated in a more indifferent manner, and disadvantaged children made relatively greater gains from the procedure. *By doing nothing more than make testing conditions more optimal for all children, we may narrow the IQ gap between white and black children.*

Social behavior and intellectual functioning are both adversely influenced by early deprivation. For example, undernourished South African children have scored some 20 IQ points lower than children with adequate diets (Stock & Smythe, 1963).

The Skeels and Dye Study A classic experiment with children in an orphanage provided dramatic evidence of the ability of children to recover from deprivation (Skeels & Dye, 1939). A group of retarded 19-month-old children considered unlikely candidates for adoption was placed in the care of mildly retarded older

▶ ▶ ▶ ▶

girls who lived in an institution. The older girls spent a great deal of time playing with the children, talking to them, and generally nurturing them. When the children were able to walk, they were given stimulating toys and an enriched nursery school experience. Children who remained in the orphanage (controls) continued to receive relatively little social stimulation.

Four years after being placed with the surrogate mothers, the "retarded" children showed an average gain of 32 IQ points on standardized tests. Children remaining in the orphanage showed an average *decrease* of 21 points. Many years later, Skeels (1966) reported that most children placed with surrogate mothers had graduated from high school. About one-third had attended college.

Back to the Maze-Bright–Maze-Dull Rats   Interestingly, studies of rats selectively bred for maze-learning ability have also provided evidence for the importance of experience.

Cooper and Zubek (1958) provided young rats descended from maze-bright and maze-dull parents with different early environments. Some rats from each group were reared in a dull, featureless environment. Others were reared in rat amusement parks with ramps, ladders, wheels, and toys. Rats reared in the impoverished environment did poorly on maze-learning tasks in adulthood, regardless of their parentage. But rats reared in the "amusement park" later learned mazes relatively rapidly. An enriched early environment narrowed the gap between the performances of rats with maze-dull and maze-bright parents.

The Effects of the Early Environment on Children   Developmentalist Lois Hoffman (1985) believes that researchers have not paid enough attention to the impacts of the home environment and of styles of parenting on IQ.

Bettye Caldwell has developed a measure for evaluating children's home environments labeled, appropriately enough, *HOME*—an acronym for Home Observation for the Measurement of the Environment. With this method, researchers directly observe parent–child interaction in the home. The HOME inventory contains six subscales, as shown in Table 9.11.

HOME inventory items turn out to be better predictors of children's later IQ scores than social class or infant IQ scores (Bradley & Caldwell, 1976; Elardo et al., 1975; Elardo et al., 1977; Gottfried, 1984). In their 1975 study, Elardo, Bradley, and Caldwell observed children from poor and working-class families at 6 and 24 months, and again at 3 and 4 years. The HOME inventory was used at the early ages, and standard IQ tests were given at 3 and 4. The children of mothers who were emotionally and verbally responsive, who provided appropriate play materials, who were involved with their children, and who provided a variety of daily experiences during the early years attained higher IQ scores later on. The extent of home organization and safety has also been linked to higher IQs at later ages, and to higher achievement-test scores during the first grade (Bradley & Caldwell, 1984).

Dozens of other studies support the view that the early environment of the child is linked to IQ scores and academic achievement. For example, Ronald McGowan and Dale Johnson (1984) found that good parent–child relationships and maternal encouragement of independence were both positively linked to Mexican-American children's IQ scores by the age of 3. A number of studies

▶ ▶ ▶ ▶

Table 9.11 Scales of the HOME Inventory

SCALES	SAMPLE ITEM
Emotional and verbal responsiveness of mother	Mother spontaneously vocalizes to child during visit. Mother responds to child's vocalizations with vocal or verbal response.
Avoidance of restriction and punishment	Mother does not shout at child. Mother does not interfere with child's actions or restrict child's movements more than three times during visit.
Organization of the physical environment	Child's play environment seems to be safe and free from hazards.
Provision of appropriate play materials	Child has a push or a pull toy. Child has one or more toys or pieces of equipment that promote muscle activity. Family provides appropriate learning equipment.
Maternal involvement with child	Mother structures child's play periods. Mother tends to keep child within visual range and looks at the child frequently.
Opportunities for variety in daily stimulation	Child gets out of the house at least four times weekly. Mother reads stories to child at least three times weekly.

have also found that high levels of maternal restrictiveness and punishment at 24 months are linked to *lower* IQ scores later on (Bee et al., 1982; Yeates et al., 1983).

Head Start and Learning-to-Learn Programs   Head Start and Learning-to-Learn programs are government-funded efforts to provide preschoolers with enriched early environments in order to increase their readiness for elementary school. Head Start programs were instituted in the 1960s to enhance the cognitive development and academic skills of poor children. Children in these programs are exposed to letters and words, numbers, books, exercises in drawing, pegs and pegboards, puzzles, toy animals, and dolls, along with other materials and activities that middle-class children can usually take for granted.

Some Head Start programs emphasize the acquisition of concrete academic skills. They focus on learning the meanings of words, the alphabet, and numbers. Some programs follow a Piagetan model. They focus on teaching "operations," as in playing checkers and practicing conservation tasks. Still others provide role models and discussions of the future to build self-confidence and the desire to succeed. Learning-to-Learn programs are similar to Head Start programs, but they also focus on small-group instruction, the child's use of language, and the fostering of parental involvement.

Studies of Head Start and Learning-to-Learn programs provide further evidence that environmental enrichment can significantly enhance the learning ability of children (Darlington et al., 1980; Sprigle & Schaefer, 1985; Zigler & Berman, 1983). In a New York City study, for example, adolescent boys who had participated in Head Start attained average SBIS IQ scores of 99. Boys similar in background, but without preschooling, earned an average SBIS score of 93 (Palmer, 1976). In another study, 20 black children were provided with enriched day care from the age of 6 weeks (Heber et al., 1972). By the age of 5,

Preschoolers placed in government-funded Head Start programs have been shown to make dramatic gains in IQ.

their IQ scores averaged about 125, as compared with an average of 95 for children from similar backgrounds who did not receive day care. Children whose IQ scores were initially lowest made the greatest gains in these programs (Zigler & Valentine, 1979). In addition to positively influencing IQ scores, Head Start programs have also led to gains in knowledge of letters, numbers, vocabulary, and scores on achievement tests.

There was initial concern that the gains of the preschoolers tended to evaporate during the elementary school years. By the end of the second or third grade, it often seemed that the performance of children in these programs dropped back to the equivalent of those who had not had early enrichment experiences. However, more recent evaluations of the programs suggest more promising outcomes and attribute the early results to faulty methodology, such as the lack of carefully matched control groups.

When researchers did carefully compare the intellectual competence of graduates of Head Start programs to that of children who were carefully matched for IQ scores, racial and cultural factors, and other variables, the children from Head Start did appear to make significant and lasting gains (Lazar & Darlington, 1982). About ten years later, the Head Start children were less likely to have been left back or placed in classes for slow learners. They scored significantly higher on achievement tests in math and reading. Head Start children were more likely to graduate from high school and to undertake postgraduate training or education.

One of the tragic contributors to the perpetuation of the cycle of poverty is the incidence of pregnancy among unwed teenage girls. Pregnancy in these cases usually means that formal education comes to an end, so that the children born to unwed teenagers are destined to be reared by poorly educated mothers. Although girls from Head Start programs became pregnant as frequently as matched controls, at least they were more likely to return to school after giving birth.

And Back to the Studies of Adopted Children As noted earlier, the Minnesota adoption studies reported by Scarr and Weinberg suggest a genetic influence on intelligence. But the same studies (Scarr & Weinberg, 1976, 1977) also suggest a role for environmental influences. Black children who were adopted during the first year by white parents who were above average in income and education showed IQ scores some 15 to 25 points higher than those attained by black children reared by their natural parents (Scarr & Weinberg, 1976). Still, the adoptees' average IQ scores, about 109, remained somewhat below those of their adoptive parents' natural children—115 (Scarr & Weinberg, 1977). Even so, the adoptive early environment closed much of the IQ gap.

On Race and Intelligence: A Concluding Note

Many developmentalists believe that heredity and environment interact to influence intelligence (Plomin & DeFries, 1980). Forty-five percent of Snyderman and Rothman's (1987) sample of 1,020 psychologists and educational specialists believe that the black–white IQ difference is a "product of both genetic and environmental variation, compared to only 15 percent who feel the

▶ ▶ ▶ ▶

difference is entirely due to environmental variation. Twenty-four percent of experts do not believe there are sufficient data to support any reasonable opinion, [and] eight experts (1 percent) indicate a belief in an entirely genetic determination" (p. 141). Experts usually see genetic influences as providing the reaction range for the complex pattern of verbal and reasoning abilities and problem-solving skills that we interpret to be signs of intelligence. An impoverished environment may prevent some children from living up to their potential. An enriched environment may encourage others to realize their potential, minimizing possible differences in heredity.

Although studies in race and IQ appear to suggest that heredity plays a role in the differences in IQ scores, let us retain a note of caution. Some psychologists, such as Brian Mackenzie (1984), point out that it is wrong to assume that genetic factors play a role just because environmental explanations have not yet been shown to tell the whole story. Mackenzie refers to such falling back on genetic explanations as the "hereditarian fallacy." Mackenzie believes that we have not yet discounted every possible environmental hypothesis. Nor is he convinced that we have yet arrived at the best research designs. For example, it seems to me that bright children of bright mothers have spent a gestation period being nurtured by the bright mothers—even if they are separated at birth. Have we done everything we can to control for the possible effects of nine months of prenatal nurture?

Perhaps we need not be concerned with "how much" of a person's IQ is due to heredity and how much is due to environment. Psychology has traditionally supported the dignity of the individual. Therefore, it might be more appropriate for us to try to identify children *of all races* whose environments seem to place them at high risk for failure to develop their potential, and then do what we can to enrich these environments.

Summary

1. Achievement is what a person has learned. Intelligence is presumed to be the learning ability that underlies achievement. Intelligence has been defined by Wechsler as the capacity "to understand the world [and the] resourcefulness to cope with its challenges."

2. There are two broad theoretical approaches to understanding intelligence: factor theories and cognitive theories. Spearman believed that a common factor, *g*, underlay all intelligent behavior, while specific *s* factors accounted for specific abilities and talents. Thurstone suggested that there are nine primary mental abilities, including word fluency and numerical ability.

3. Guilford's structure-of-intellect model proposes 120 factors, each of which involves the operations, contents, and products of intellectual functioning. Cattell and Horn suggest two factors: fluid and crystallized intelligence. Crystallized intelligence depends on education and increases over the life

▶ ▶ ▶ ▶

span. Fluid intelligence consists of the processes that make incidental learning possible, and it is thought to begin to decline by adolescence. Gardner's theory of multiple intelligences proposes that such special talents as musical and bodily-kinesthetic abilities are factors of intelligence.

4. Jensen's cognitive theory proposes Level I and Level II intelligence. Level I intelligence involves associative learning abilities. Level II intelligence involves conceptual abilities. Jensen controversially attributes social-class differences in intelligence to differences in Level II cognitive functioning.

5. Sternberg's triarchic theory of intelligence proposes contextual, experiential, and componential levels of intelligence. The contextual level involves adaptation to one's environments. The experiential level involves the abilities to cope with novel situations and to process information rapidly. The componential level consists of metacomponents, performance components (mental operations used in solving problems), and knowledge-acquisition components.

6. Creativity is the ability to generate novel solutions to problems. Creative children show divergent thinking ability by associating freely to the elements of a problem. There is a correlation between intelligence and creativity, but above average intelligence is not a guarantee of creativity. Creative children tend to show independence and nonconformity.

7. Intelligence tests yield scores called intelligence quotients, or *IQs*. A good intelligence test is reliable (consistent) and valid (it measures what it is supposed to measure). It also has adequate norms as a result of the standardization process. The correlation coefficient is frequently used in the determination of reliability and validity. The validity of intelligence tests is usually assessed by correlating test scores with school performance (grades), achievement-test scores, and teacher ratings of cognitive ability.

8. The Terman "studies of genius" found that children with IQs of 135 and above went on, as a group, to excel in their careers. However, the need for achievement and personal adjustment also played major roles in their success.

9. Individual intelligence tests are more costly than group tests, but they have the advantage of allowing the examiner to develop hypotheses as to *why* a particular child performs as he or she does on a test.

10. The major individual intelligence tests are the Stanford-Binet Intelligence Scale (SBIS) and the Wechsler scales. The SBIS, originated in France by Alfred Binet, gives children "months" of credit for correct answers, which are summed up as the child's mental age. The SBIS score is a ratio IQ, which, following Stern's suggestion, was at one time derived by dividing children's mental age scores by their chronological ages (MA/CA), then multiplying by 100.

11. The Wechsler scales use deviation IQs, which are derived by comparing a person's performance to those of age-mates. Wechsler tests contain verbal and performance subtests.

▶ ▶ ▶ ▶

12. Intelligence in infancy is measured by sensorimotor types of items that do not predict later IQ scores very well. The Bayley infant scales include mental items, motor items, and a behavior record.

13. The IQ scores of young children are unstable. Not until the ages of about 6 or 7 do IQ scores begin to show moderate-to-high correlations with those attained at the ages of 10 to 18. Tests of visual-recognition memory hold better promise as predictors of later IQ, but for now the correlations between early visual-recognition memory and later IQ are weak to moderate.

14. About 5 percent of children have IQ scores below 70 and above 130. Children with scores below 70 and various problems in adaptation are usually considered mentally retarded. Retardation can have a number of biological causes, but also often reflects cultural-familial factors.

15. Gifted children are identified not only on the basis of high IQ scores, but also by exceptional talents, as in music, leadership, or other areas.

16. Upper- and middle-class children outperform lower-class children on intelligence tests. Japanese and Chinese children outperform U.S. children. In the United States, Caucasian children outperform their black, Hispanic-American, and Native-American peers.

17. Many critics assert that intelligence tests are culturally biased in favor of middle-class children. As a consequence, efforts have been made to develop culture-fair or culture-free tests. However, the main external criterion used to determine the validity of intelligence tests is academic performance, and culture-free tests are weaker predictors of this criterion than are traditional tests.

18. Many clever research designs have been used to obtain evidence concerning the determinants of intelligence. Evidence concerning genetic influences tends to focus on (a) selective breeding of lower animals, (b) kinship studies, and (c) studies of adoptees. We find, for example, that the IQ scores of adopted children correlate more highly with those of their natural parents than with those of their adoptive parents.

19. Evidence concerning environmental influences tends to focus on (a) effects of the environment on lower animals; (b) effects of the early environment, including the home environment, parenting styles, and Head Start programs; (c) kinship studies, emphasizing the differences in IQ between close relatives when reared together or apart; and (d) studies of adoptees. We find, for example, that enrichment of the child's early environment appears to narrow the IQ gap between lower- and middle-class children. We also find that the IQs of children who are reared together correlate more highly than those of children, related just as closely, who are reared apart.

20. Many developmentalists believe that genetic and environmental factors interact to determine intelligence. However, we must retain caution because of what Mackenzie labels the "hereditarian fallacy." That is, it may be that we have not yet ruled out every environmental hypothesis for differences in IQ.

▶ ▶ ▶ ▶

Musical ability is a kind of intelligence. *True,* according to Gardner. However, most psychologists view musical ability as a special talent, not as a factor in intelligence.

Knowing what problem to tackle is an aspect of intelligent behavior. *True.* Sternberg refers to this aspect of intelligence as a metacomponent of intelligence.

Highly intelligent children are also creative. *False.* Intelligence is only moderately related to creativity.

Creative children tend to be independent and nonconformist. *True.* However, nonconformity is not necessarily a sign of creativity.

Intelligence and "IQ" mean the same thing. *False.* Intelligence is a hypothetical trait. An IQ is a score on a test.

Two children can answer exactly the same items on an intelligence test correctly, yet one can be above average in intelligence and the other can be below average in intelligence. *True.* Intelligence develops with age. Therefore, the younger of the children would be considered more intelligent.

Tests have been developed for measuring intelligence in neonates. *True.* However, the types of sensorimotor functions used to screen neonates at risk for various problems do not adequately predict IQ scores attained at later ages.

We can predict how intelligent a person will be as an adult as early as the age of 2. *False.* We can determine whether certain problems in intellectual functioning are evident at that early age. However, the correlations between "intelligence" at age 2 and IQ scores attained at later ages are weak to moderate.

Mentally retarded children cannot acquire the social and vocational skills required to become independent. *False.* Mildly retarded individuals can do quite well on their own, although they may profit from occasional advice.

Intellectually gifted children tend to be unpopular with their age-mates. *False.* Gifted children tend to be popular.

Japanese children attain higher IQ scores than U.S. children. *True.* The question concerns the relative roles of nature and nurture as contributers to IQ scores.

Intelligence tests are actually achievement tests. *True.* However, they are very broad achievement tests.

There is no such thing as an unbiased intelligence test. *True,* in the sense that school adjustment and motivation to do well influence IQ. These factors are more often found among middle-class white children in the United States than among ethnic minorities or lower-class children.

High intelligence runs in families. *Not necessarily.* The evidence shows that high *IQs* run in families. IQ, as noted, is not the same thing as intelligence.

► ► ► ►

IQ test scores of adopted children correlate more highly with the IQ scores of their adoptive parents than with those of their natural biological parents. **False**. Such evidence is suggestive of a role for heredity in the development of intelligence.

Children whose mothers are more involved with them attain higher IQs. **True**. A number of home environment factors appear to influence the development of intelligence.

Head Start programs have raised children's IQs. **True**. Many kinds of early-childhood programs appear to enhance intellectual development.

▶ ▶ ▶ ▶

10

Social and Emotional Development

▶
▶
▶
▶
▶
▶
▶

T R U T H ▸ O R ▸ F I C T I O N ?

- All children develop fear of strangers at some point during the second six months of infancy.
- Children are less likely to be securely attached to abusive or neglectful parents.
- An infant's willingness to leave the mother in order to explore the environment is a sign of secure attachment.
- You can predict how strongly babies are attached to their fathers if you know how many diapers per week the father changes.
- Children must become attached to their parents before a critical period elapses, or else bonds of attachment will not form properly.
- Children become attached to their mothers earlier than they become attached to their fathers.
- Blind babies do not smile.
- Children placed in day care become less attached to their mothers than children who are cared for in the home.
- Children placed in full-time day care are more aggressive than children who are cared for in the home.
- Child abusers have frequently been the victims of child abuse themselves.
- Children who are highly indulged by their mothers during the first year of life become dependent.
- Imaginary friends are a sign that children are lonely or poorly adjusted.
- At the age of 2 or 3, children are frequently afraid of imaginary creatures.
- Adopted children are less likely to experience disturbance if they are transferred to their permanent adoptive homes within three months after birth.

If this chapter had been written by the poet John Donne, it might have begun, "No children are islands unto themselves." Not only do children issue from other people, but they come into this world crying, thrashing about, and squirming—fully dependent on others for their survival and well-being.

This chapter is about some of the consequences of that absolute dependency. It is about the social relationships between children and caregivers, and the development of the bonds of affection or attachment that usually—but not always—bind them so strongly. It is about the behaviors of children that prompt social and emotional responses from adults. It is about the behaviors of adults that prompt social and emotional responses from children. It is about being together and being apart, and the powerful emotional consequences of each.

On another level, this chapter is about the development of the emotions of love and fear. At their most extreme, these feelings can seem to make the world go round or make it stop. Let us now consider the issue of attachment, its development, and the factors that contribute to it. Then we shall consider other issues in social and emotional development: the development of independence, play, emotions, and the effects of social deprivation.

Attachment

At the age of 2, one of my daughters behaved in a way that cast doubt on whether this book would be completed. When I locked myself into my study, she positioned herself outside the door and called, "Daddy, oh Daddy." Next came, "Pencer, oh Pencer." At other times she would bang on the door or cry outside. When I would give in (several times each day) and open the door, she would run in and say, "I want you to pick up me" and hold out her arms or climb into my lap. Then she would say, "I want to play." I would beg, "I was in the middle of something. Just give me a second to finish it." Then, when I would look back briefly at the screen of my word processor, she would try to turn my face to hers or turn the computer off. Or if I were trying to jot down some notes from a journal, she would try to yank them from my hands and toss them across the room.

I am a psychologist. Solutions, therefore, came easily. For example, I could write outside my home. But this solution had the drawback of placing distance between myself and my family. Another solution was to let my daughter cry and ignore her. If I refused to reinforce crying, crying would become extinguished. There were only two problems with this solution. First, I was incapable of ignoring her crying, even though in the long run it would be "for her own good." Second, I didn't *want* to extinguish her efforts to get to me. **Attachment,** you see, is a two-way street.

Attachment is a slippery concept. Parents and children rarely say, "I am attached to you." Parents, other caregivers, and children think and speak of experiencing love for one other, not attachment.

According to Mary Ainsworth, one of the foremost researchers in the area of attachment, "Attachment may be defined as an affectional tie that one person or animal forms between himself and another specific one—a tie that binds them together in space and endures over time" (1973). Attachment appears to descend from the Greek concept of **storge,** the form of love that binds

Attachment *According to Ainsworth, the "affectional tie that one person or animal forms between himself and another . . . that binds them together in space and endures over time."*

Storge *(STORE-gay). The ancient Greek concept of love that is most similar to the contemporary concept of* attachment.

▶ ▶ ▶ ▶

parents and children. Romantic love differs from attachment in that it involves feelings of passion as well as affection and devotion. Attachment is essential to the very survival of the infant (Bowlby, 1980).

Developmentalists, when they can, prefer to discuss concepts in terms of observable behaviors. Observable behaviors are public events that are subject to scientific investigation and measurement. The behaviors that define attachment include (1) attempting to maintain contact or nearness, and (2) showing "separation anxiety." Fear of strangers was once listed as a criterion for attachment. However, many children never develop fear of strangers, yet are securely attached to their parents.

Infants try to maintain contact with caregivers to whom they are attached. They engage in eye contact, pull and tug at them, ask to be picked up, and may even jump in front of them in such a way that they will be "run over" by them if they are not picked up!

When they cannot maintain contact, infants show behaviors suggestive of **separation anxiety.** These behaviors vary according to their behavioral capacities, their ability to delay gratification, their knowledge of "what works," their temperaments, and factors such as whether they are tired or hungry. They may thrash about, fuss, cry or screech, whine, or throw things. Parents who are seeking a few minutes to attend to their own legitimate needs sometimes see these behaviors as manipulative. In a sense, they are. That is, children learn that they achieve desired ends. But what is wrong with "manipulating" a loved one to end one's distress?

By about 6 to 8 months, many babies develop fear of strangers. Whereas they previously delighted in—or calmly accepted—the effusive compliments of strangers in the supermarket, now they let out a sudden howl or burst into tears. My wife and I knew that our children had developed fear of strangers when every trip to the supermarket required us to repeat, "Don't take it personally," or "She's that way with everyone new."

Measuring Attachment

Developmentalists measure attachment via interviews and questionnaires that are filled out by parents and other caregivers, and by direct behavioral observation. Interviews and questionnaires are easy to use, but respondents may recall events inaccurately or distort answers for reasons discussed in Chapter 1. Behavioral observations are more reliable. Today much research involves videotaping parent–child interactions.

In an illustrative study, Harriet Rheingold and Carol Eckerman (1970) observed the attachment behaviors of infants who were capable of crawling and creeping. The infants were placed in a laboratory room with their mothers. From their vantage points on the floor, they could see an adjoining room and also see their mothers at the far end of their own room. With one group of infants, a brightly colored toy was placed in the adjoining room. With another group, the adjoining room was left empty. When the toy was not present, infants were significantly more likely to move toward their mothers than into the adjoining room. But when the toy was used, the infants as a group were more likely to crawl toward it. Even so, there were individual differences. Some infants approached the toy. Others crawled toward their mothers. Later in this section we shall see that there is reason to believe that willingness to move away from the mothers to explore the environment is a sign of secure attachment.

▶ ▶ ▶ ▶

The Strange Situation Method

▷
▷
▷
▷
▷   The Strange Situation method developed by Mary Ainsworth provides a uniform format for the study of attachment, and is widely used in research on social and emotional development. In this method, an infant is exposed to a series of separations and reunions with a caregiver (usually the mother) and a "stranger" who is a confederate of the researchers. Children are led through eight episodes (Ainsworth & Bell, 1970):

1. The mother carries the infant into the laboratory room. They are accompanied by an observer who then leaves.
2. The mother puts the infant down and then sits quietly in a chair. She does not interact with the infant unless the infant seeks her attention. This episode lasts three minutes.
3. A stranger enters the room and sits quietly for one minute. The stranger then converses with the mother for one minute. The stranger then gradually approaches the infant with a toy. After a third minute has passed, the mother leaves the room.
4. The stranger's behavior in this episode varies according to the infant's reactions. If the infant is involved in active play, the stranger observes unobtrusively. If the infant is passive, the stranger tries to interest him or her in the toy. If the infant shows distress (as by crying), the stranger tries to comfort him or her. The episode comes to an end if the infant cannot be comforted. Otherwise, it lasts three minutes.
5. The mother returns, pausing in the doorway, so that the infant has an opportunity to respond to her spontaneously. The stranger leaves unobtrusively. After the infant has again begun to play, the mother briefly says "bye-bye" and also departs. The duration of this episode is open-ended.
6. The infant is left alone for three minutes unless he or she shows such distress that the episode is cut short.
7. The stranger re-enters the room and behaves as described in the fourth episode for three minutes. This episode may also be cut short if the infant is distressed.
8. The mother returns and the stranger leaves.

In an illustrative study with the Strange Situation test, Mary Ainsworth and Sylvia Bell (1970) observed the attachment behaviors of 56 infants who were about 12 months old. The researchers recorded contact-maintaining behaviors and proximity- (nearness) and contact-seeking behaviors. These behaviors were relatively weak during episode 2, when the mother and baby were alone. Proximity- and contact-seeking behaviors increased only slightly during episode 3's entry and involvement of the stranger, probably because the mother was still present. However, both types of attachment behaviors showed marked increases during episodes 5 and 8. These were mother–baby reunions following the infants' spending of time alone with the stranger. In fact, the attachment behaviors were strongest during episode 8: The babies clung to their mothers strongly. Apparently the first interaction with the stranger did not reduce the babies' desires to be with their mothers during the second. At least in this study, repetition of separation seems to have sensitized the babies to separation rather than to have decreased separation anxiety.

► ► ► ►

Types of Attachment

By using the Strange Situation method, Ainsworth and her colleagues (1978) have identified various patterns of attachment. Broadly speaking, babies are either **securely attached** or insecurely attached. The two major subtypes of insecure attachment are **avoidant attachment** and **resistant attachment.** There are subdivisions within each type.

Ainsworth and other investigators have found that about 70 percent of middle-class U.S. babies are securely attached. In the Strange Situation test, babies who are securely attached show the common features of mildly protesting mother's departure, seeking interaction upon reunion, and being readily comforted by her.

Approximately 15 percent of babies show avoidant attachment. These babies are least distressed by their mothers' departure. They play without fuss when alone and ignore their mothers upon reunion. Resistant babies comprise another 10 percent of the samples. Resistant babies are the most emotional. They show severe signs of distress when their mothers leave and show ambivalence upon reunion by alternately clinging to and pushing their mothers away.

Attachment is one measure of the quality of the care that children have received during infancy (Bretherton & Waters, 1985; Sroufe, 1985). Securely attached babies cry generally less frequently than insecurely attached babies. They are more likely to show affection toward their mothers, cooperate with them, and to use their mothers as a base for exploration. Securely attached preschoolers are more likely than insecure peers to be emotionally warm, socially mature, and popular among their peers (LaFreniere & Sroufe, 1985). Securely attached children aged 2 to 7 have been found to be happier and more enthusiastic and socially active; to show more leadership qualities and greater academic persistence; and to be better able to occupy themselves when alone than insecurely attached age-mates (Brody & Axelrad, 1978; Matas et al., 1978; Lieberman, 1977; Sroufe, 1983). At age 5 children who were securely attached in infancy are rated by teachers as curious, self-reliant, and effective in seeking and using help in problem solving (Frodi et al., 1985).

Victoria Seitz (1985) followed impoverished children whose mothers had received extensive medical and social services during pregnancy and for 30 months following childbirth. The children were superior to controls whose mothers had not received these services in their social and academic adjustment. Seitz suggests that the services had improved the mothers' caregiving skills, promoting secure attachment and, consequently, better adjustment.

The mothers of securely attached babies are more likely to be cooperative, reliable, and predictable in their caregiving. They respond more sensitively to their babies' smiles, cries, and other social behaviors (Egeland & Farber, 1984; Sroufe, 1985). They hold their babies lovingly and show affection freely (Ainsworth et al., 1974).

Insecure attachment is found more frequently among babies who have been neglected or abused (Egeland & Sroufe, 1981). It is found more often among babies whose mothers are slow to meet their needs or who meet them in a cold manner. The mothers of avoidant babies respond less quickly to their signals. Mothers of avoidant babies tend to be rigid and prone to anger. They tend not to hold their babies tenderly, and they show them less affection.

Secure attachment *A type of attachment characterized by mild distress at leavetakings, seeking of nearness to an attachment figure, and being readily soothed by the figure.*

Avoidant attachment *A type of insecure attachment characterized by apparent indifference to the leavetakings of, and reunions with, an attachment figure.*

Resistant attachment *A type of insecure attachment characterized by severe distress at the leavetakings of, and ambivalent behavior at reunions with, attachment figures.*

► ► ► ►

The mothers of resistant babies tend to fit in somewhere between the mothers of the other types. For example, they hold their babies more closely than do mothers of avoidant babies, but they are more awkward.

It is tempting to seek the causes of insecure attachment in the mother's behavior, but we must be cautious in doing so. Babies also differ in their temperaments. Caregivers respond to babies' behavior just as the babies respond to caregivers' behavior. The processes of attachment may be bidirectional. Fathers and other caregivers are also involved in the attachment process. Further, we are just beginning to learn how other processes, such as our basic sensory capabilities, may influence bonds of attachment.

Stability of Attachment The literature has been mixed concerning the stability of attachment. Some research has shown that individual patterns of attachment tend to persist (Waters, 1978) and to influence other areas of behavior. For example, children who are insecurely attached during the first year relate relatively poorly to peers during the second year (Waters et al., 1979). They are less adept at problem solving and using tools (Matas et al., 1978).

Other research shows a significant incidence of change in classification patterns (Campos et al., 1983). Egeland and Sroufe (1981) followed a number of infants who were severely neglected and others who received high-quality care from 12 to 18 months. Attachment patterns remained stable (secure) for infants receiving fine care. However, many neglected infants changed from insecurely to securely attached over the six-month period, sometimes because of a relationship with a supportive family member, sometimes because home life grew less tense. Other studies show that children can become less securely attached to caregivers when the quality of home life deteriorates (Thompson et al., 1982; Vaughn et al., 1979).

Even when children are adopted as late as the age of 4, they can become securely attached to their adoptive parents (Tizard et al., 1976). Young children show resilience in their social and emotional development. Early insecurities apparently can be overcome.

Stages of Attachment

John Bowlby (1980) is credited with first outlining phases in the development of attachment between infants and caregivers. His views have since been refined by Mary Ainsworth.

A couple of classic cross-cultural studies have provided insight into the stages of attachment. In one, Ainsworth (1967) traveled to Uganda, Africa, and observed 29 infants who ranged in age from 2 to 14 months. She followed them over a nine-month period and tracked attachment behaviors including maintaining contact with the mother, smiling at her, protesting when separated, and using her as a base for exploring the environment.

At first the Ugandan infants showed **indiscriminate attachment.** That is, they clearly preferred being held or being with someone to being alone. However, they showed no particular preferences for the mother or another familiar caregiver. Specific attachment to the mother began to develop at about 4 months and grew intense by about 7 months. Fear of strangers developed one or two months afterward—if it developed at all.

The other study was carried out by Rudolf Schaffer and Peggy Emerson (1964a). Schaffer and Emerson followed 60 Scottish infants from 5 to 23 weeks

Indiscriminate attachment
The showing of attachment behaviors toward any person.

▶ ▶ ▶ ▶

Initial-preattachment phase
The first phase in the forming of bonds of attachment, lasting from birth to about 3 months and characterized by indiscriminate attachment.

Attachment-in-the-making phase *The second phase in the development of attachment, occurring at 3 or 4 months and characterized by preference for familiar figures.*

Clear-cut-attachment phase
The third phase in the development of attachment, occurring at 6 or 7 months and characterized by intensified dependence on the primary caregiver.

of age for 18 months. They interviewed their mothers about the infants' responses to separation and directly observed the infants' responses to the approach of a stranger—in this case, the interviewer. During the first six months or so after birth, the Scottish infants also showed indiscriminate attachment, as suggested by Figure 10.1. Then indiscriminate attachment waned. Specific attachments to the mother and other familiar caregivers intensified and remained at high levels through the age of 18 months. Fear of strangers occurred on the average at 8 months, a month or so after the intensity of specific attachments began to mushroom. Thus, in both studies, fear of strangers followed the development of specific attachments by a number of weeks.

From studies such as these, Mary Ainsworth (1978) identified three stages of attachment:

1. The **initial-preattachment phase,** which lasts from birth to about 3 months, and is characterized by indiscriminate attachment.

2. The **attachment-in-the-making phase,** which occurs at about 3 or 4 months, and is characterized by the selection of familiar figures over strangers.

3. The **clear-cut-attachment phase,** which occurs at about 6 or 7 months, and is characterized by intensified dependence upon the primary caregiver—usually the mother.

Bowlby has hypothesized a fourth phase occurring between the second and third and characterized by fear of strangers. But, as noted earlier, not all children show fear of strangers. Therefore, this "phase" is currently omitted.

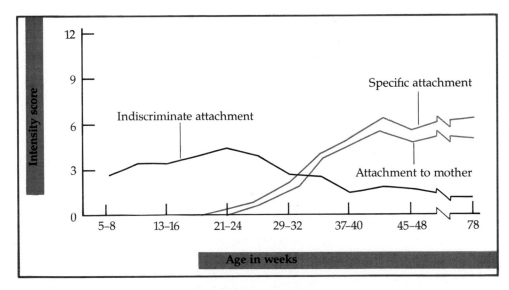

Figure 10.1 The Development of Attachment
During the first six months, infants tend to show indiscriminate attachment. Indiscriminate attachment then wanes while specific attachments grow intense and remain at high levels. If it occurs at all, fear of strangers develops a month or so after the intensity of specific attachments begins to blossom.

▶ ▶ ▶ ▶

ATTACHMENT

401

Let us also note that there are individual differences in patterns of attachment. The sequence outlined is far from universal. It did not even hold for all infants in the two cross-cultural studies we have described.

In the Ainsworth study, for example, a minority of infants who were insecurely attached to their mothers did not develop specific attachments at all. In the Schaffer and Emerson study, despite Bowlby's observations, about 25 percent of the infants developed fear of strangers *before* they developed specific attachments to their mothers. And so the development of specific attachments may not be a prerequisite for fear of strangers, even when this fear occurs.

Theoretical Views of Attachment

Evidence appears to suggest that attachment, like so many other behavior patterns, seems to develop as a result of the interaction between nature and nurture.

Consider the research on the sensory capabilities of newborn babies. As noted in Chapter 6, neonates are sensitive to the odor of breast secretions. Within a few days, they prefer nursing pads that have been used by their own mothers to those of strange women. Neonates are also sensitive to speech and will synchronize their body movements to the sounds of speech. They discriminate their mothers' voices from those of strangers, and they prefer their mothers' voices. Inborn sensitivities and early learning experiences apparently dispose neonates toward recognizing and becoming attached to their mothers.

Another source of evidence stems from research into the temperaments of infants. Schaffer and Emerson (1964b), for example, suggest that there may be innate differences in babies' responses to cuddling. Some babies are readily soothed by being cuddled and seem to fold comfortably into their caregivers' arms. Others seem to find contact less comforting or even discomforting. They avoid or resist efforts to hold them. Parents who want to cuddle their babies may be upset when the babies shun contact, and, as a result, the overall quality of parent–infant attachment may suffer.

Babies also differ in their tendencies to cry and fuss because of illness or various developmental disorders such as colic. Colicky babies, for example—through no fault of their own—may cry unconsolably for hours on end. Even the most understanding parents respond to incessant crying with distress. Occasional irritation or annoyance are also not uncommon. Although intervention might soothe their babies, parents of babies who cry frequently do not intervene as quickly as parents of babies who cry less often (Dunn, 1977). Parents of fussy babies may wait in part because they have the idea that there is little that they can do. In any event, the crying may create some distance between parent and infant.

Another view of attachment is primarily cognitive. It focuses on the apparently logical contention that an infant must have developed some form of object permanence before specific attachment becomes possible. In other words, if caregivers are to be missed when absent, perhaps the infant must perceive that they continue to exist. As noted earlier, however, infants tend to develop specific attachments at about 6 to 7 months. As noted in Chapter 6, rudimentary object permanence concerning physical objects develops somewhat earlier. In general, awareness of the permanence of people does not usually develop before permanence of physical objects (Jackson et al., 1978). However, caregivers play

▶ ▶ ▶ ▶

such central roles in infants' lives that babies may devote special attention to them and learn of their permanence relatively early.

I am confident that research findings will eventually spur the development of powerful theories of attachment that center on infant perception and cognition. The current theoretical explanations of how innate tendencies (nature) and experience (nurture) interact to produce attachment all seem limited in scope.

A Behavioral View of Attachment: Mothers as Reinforcers   Early in the century, behaviorists argued that "attachment behaviors" were learned through laws of conditioning. Infants would come to associate their mothers with gratification and learn to approach their mothers in order to meet their needs. From this perspective, a child's mother becomes a conditioned reinforcer. Because of repeated association with primary reinforcers, the mother herself acquires reinforcing properties.

The feelings of gratification that are associated with meeting specific needs generalize into feelings of security when mother is present. Behaviorists would suggest that this is why children like to have their mothers present when they are exposed to novel and threatening situations, such as meeting new people, exploring a new store, or going to nursery school for the first few times.

The Harlows' View of Attachment: Mother as a Source of Contact Comfort
University of Wisconsin psychologist Harry F. Harlow noted that infant rhesus monkeys reared without mothers or companions appeared to become attached to pieces of cloth in their cages. They maintained contact with them and showed distress when separated from them. All in all, they clung to them like security blankets. Harlow (1959) conducted an ingenious series of experiments to find out why.

In one study, Harlow placed rhesus monkey infants in cages with two surrogate mothers, as shown in Figure 10.2. One "mother" was made from wire mesh, from which a baby bottle extended. The other surrogate mother was made of soft, cuddly terry cloth. Infant monkeys, as you can see from the graph in Figure 10.2, spent most of their time clinging to the cloth mother.

A behaviorist might have expected that the wire-mesh mother would have acquired the properties of a conditioned reinforcer because it was associated with feeding. However, the rhesus infants clearly preferred the softer mothers, even though they did not gratify the infants' physiological need for food.

Harlow concluded that monkeys—and perhaps babies—have a need for **contact comfort** that is as basic as the need for food. He also argued that gratification of the need for contact comfort, rather than hunger, is the reason that infant monkeys (and babies) cling to their mothers. Put another way, it might be that the path to a baby's heart lies through its skin, not its stomach.

Harlow and Zimmerman (1959) found that a terry-cloth "mother" could also serve as a comforting base from which a rhesus infant could explore the environment. Toys like oversized wooden insects and stuffed bears were placed in cages with infant monkeys and their surrogate mothers (see Figure 10.3). When the monkeys were alone or had only wire mothers as companions, they cowered in fear so long as the "insect monster" or "bear monster" was present. But when the terry-cloth mothers were present, the infants clung to them for a while and then explored the intruding "monster."

Contact comfort (1) The pleasure derived from physical contact with another. (2) A hypothesized need or drive for physical contact with another.

▶ ▶ ▶ ▶

ATTACHMENT

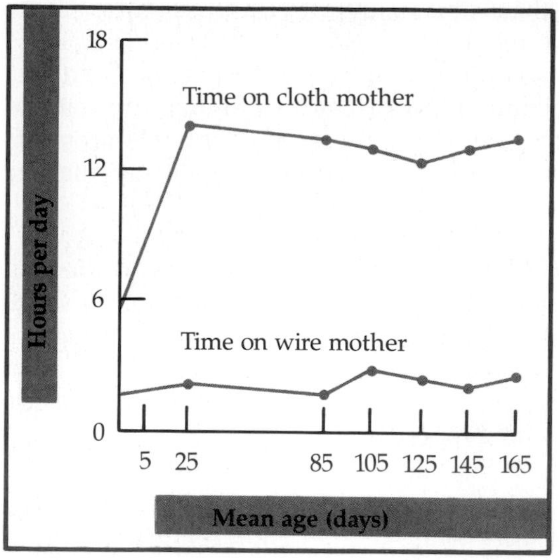
18
12
6
0
Time on cloth mother
Time on wire mother
Hours per day
5 25 85 105 125 145 165
Mean age (days)

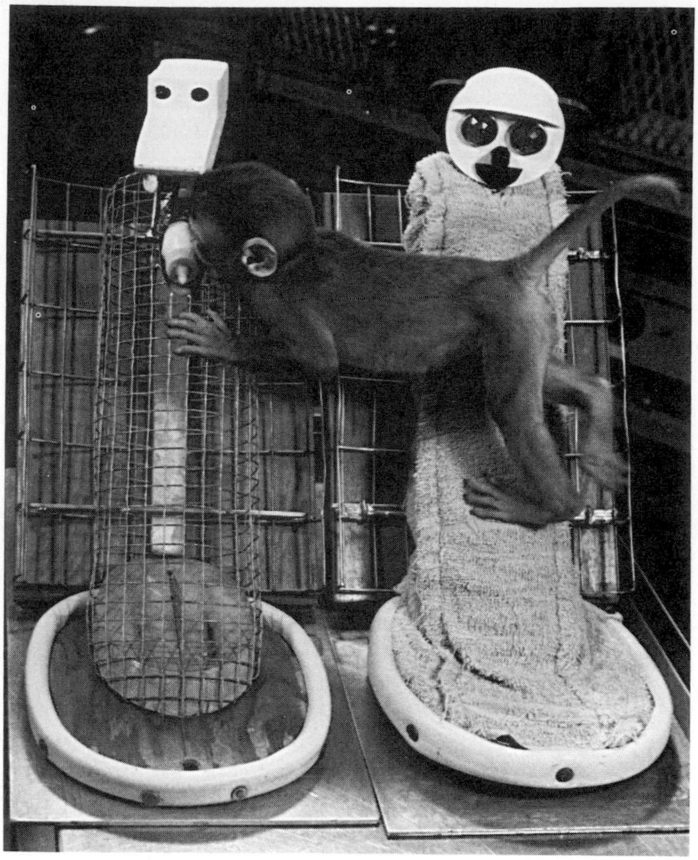

Figure 10.2 **Attachment in Infant Monkeys**

Although this infant rhesus monkey is fed by the wire "mother," it becomes attached to the terry-cloth "mother," as measured by the amount of time spent on each mother. The monkey knows where to find a meal, but contact comfort is apparently a more powerful determinant of attachment than feeding in infant monkeys—and in infant humans?

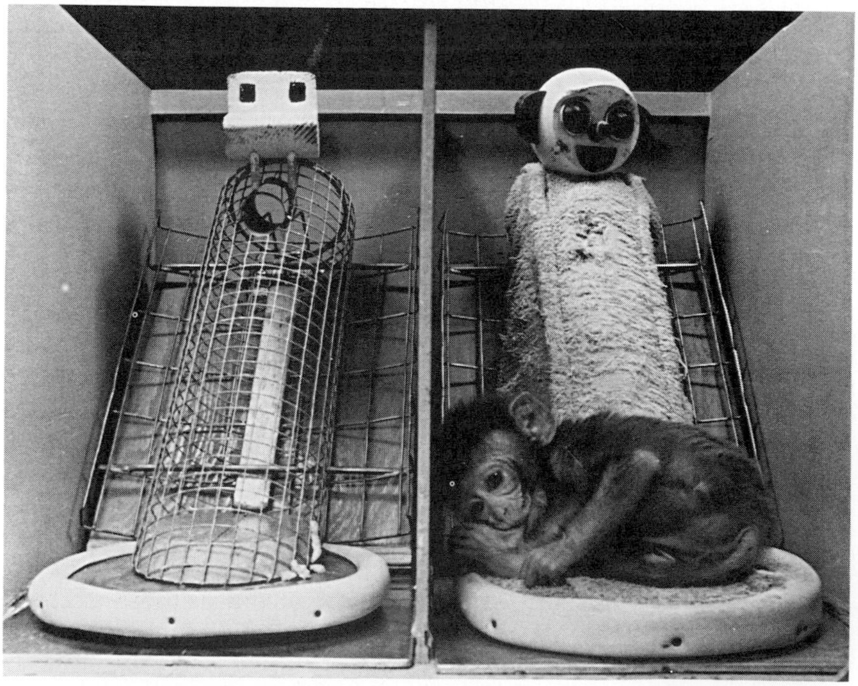

►►►►

Figure 10.3 Security
Willingness to explore the environment is a sign of secure attachment. With its terry-cloth surrogate mother nearby, this infant rhesus monkey apparently feels secure enough to explore the "bear monster" placed in its cage. But infants with only wire surrogate mothers, or with no mothers, remain cowering in a corner when the bear or other "monsters" are introduced.

Ethologist *A scientist who studies the behavior patterns that are characteristic of various species.*

Fixed action pattern *An instinct. A stereotyped form of behavior that is characteristic of a species and is triggered by a releasing stimulus. Abbreviated FAP.*

Releasing stimulus *A stimulus that elicits a FAP.*

Critical period *A period of development during which a releasing stimulus can elicit a FAP.*

Imprinting *The process by which some animals exhibit the FAP of attachment in response to a releasing stimulus. Such FAPs are difficult to modify and occur during a critical period.*

Imprinting: An Ethological View of Attachment **Ethologists** have argued that for many animals attachment is an innate **fixed action pattern** (FAP). The FAP of attachment, like others, is theorized to occur in the presence of a species-specific **releasing stimulus.** An example of a FAP and a releasing stimulus is the robin's mechanical aggressive response to anything that visually approximates the breast of another robin.

The FAP of attachment is also theorized to occur during a **critical period** of life. If it does not, it might never occur. During this period, young animals are capable of forming an instinctive attachment to their mothers or parents if the releasing stimuli are present.

Water fowl become attached during the critical period to the first moving object they encounter. The unwritten rule seems to be, "If it moves, it must be mother." It is as if the image of the moving object becomes "imprinted" upon the young animal. The process of forming an attachment in this manner is called **imprinting.**

Ethologist Konrad Lorenz (1962, 1981) became well known when pictures of his "family" of goslings were made public (see Figure 10.4). How did Lorenz acquire his "following"? He was present when the the goslings hatched, and he allowed them to follow him. The critical period for geese and ducks seems bounded at the younger end by the age at which they first engage in locomotion and, at the older end, by the age at which they develop fear of strangers.

▶ ▶ ▶ ▶

ATTACHMENT

Figure 10.4 Imprinting
Quite a following? Konrad Lorenz may not look much like Mother to you, but these goslings became attached to him because he was the first moving object that they perceived and followed. The process of imprinting occurs during a so-called critical period in the development of many species.

The extent of the goslings' attachment was shown in various ways. They followed "Mommy" persistently, ran to Lorenz when frightened, honked with distress at his departure, and tried to overcome barriers placed between them (Sluckin, 1970). If you substitute crying for honking, it all sounds rather human.

But it is unlikely that children undergo imprinting. As shown by the 4-year-old adoptees who formed strong attachments to their adoptive parents (Tizard et al., 1976), there is apparently no critical period for the development of attachment in humans. However, Marshall Klaus and John Kennell suggested that there might be a weaker "maternal-sensitive" period, governed by hormones, for becoming attached to a newborn. But even the evidence for this watered-down "sensitive" period is in disarray, as noted in Chapter 4.

In sum, attachment in humans appears to be a complex process that continues for months, or years. Certainly it includes learning in the broad sense of the term—as opposed to a limited, mechanistic-behaviorist sense. Attachment involves infant perceptual and cognitive processes, and the type of attachment that develops is related to the quality of the caregiver–infant relationship. The caregiving itself, and infant responsiveness, such as infant smiling, appear to spur the development of attachment—at least in parents who want their children. In our discussion of child abuse, sad to say, we shall see that the development of parental attachment is far from inevitable.

Let us now turn our attention to a number of specific issues concerning attachment: father–child attachment; the influences of day care and group child-rearing on attachment; and that distressing example of failed attachment—child abuse.

Fathers and Attachment

Did you know that you can predict how well attached babies are to their fathers if you know how many diapers the fathers change each week? Gail Ross and her colleagues (1975) found that the more diapers the father changed, the stronger the attachment. No, there is no magical connection between diapers and love. Rather, the number of diapers the father changes roughly reflects his involvement in child-rearing.

Until recently, fathers had been largely left out of the theory and research concerning attachment. There are a number of reasons for this. One is the traditional "division of labor" in our society. The father has traditionally been the breadwinner and the mother the primary caregiver to the children. Mothers have been given the responsible roles of feeder, changer, and comforter of children. Fathers have more or less been expected to play with, enjoy, and perhaps discipline them (Feldman et al., 1984).

A second reason has been the pervasiveness of psychoanalytic theory. Laypeople may not be acquainted with the details of Freud's views. Still, many are familiar with the general concept that the child's early emotional development involves strong sexual feelings, and that these feelings somehow get attached to the mother.*

Involvement of Fathers How involved is the average father with his children? A review of the literature by Michael Lamb (1979) found that father–child interactions differ in quality and quantity from mother–child interactions. To begin

*See Chapter 2 for a critique of Freud's views.

▶ ▶ ▶ ▶

Smile, 'Cause When You're Smiling, Your Caregivers Smile with You

▷
▷
▷
▷
▷ "Smile," goes the song, "'Cause when you're smiling, the whole world smiles with you." When babies and their caregivers smile at one another, it seems that they not only express their mutual pleasure but also tighten their bonds of attachment (Kaye & Fogel, 1980). More than 100 years ago, Charles Darwin (1872) theorized that smiling was an innate response in babies that helped ensure survival by eliciting pleasure in their caregivers.

The notion that smiling is an innate response is consistent with ethological theory. It is also consistent with evidence that concordance in the time of onset of social smiling is greater for MZ twins than for DZ twins (Plomin & DeFries, 1985).

According to John Bowlby (1969), smiling is one of many attachment behaviors that are elicited by specific stimuli. Newborn infants tend to smile reflexively when their cheeks are stroked, or in re- sponse to certain kinds of internal stimu- lation. But toward the end of the first month a smile may also be triggered by a high-pitched voice of the sort that par- ents—particularly mothers—are likely to use in motherese (Wolff, 1963). By 6 weeks or so, it appears that the human face also begins to elicit smiling (Ahren, 1954). The crucial human features that trigger smiling appear to be the eyes and a smiling mouth. At around ten weeks, the eyes alone will elicit smiles in babies, but at 5 or 6 months, most of the facial features are required.

But by the time a baby has become a few months old, it is no longer possible to differentiate between inborn and inten- tional smiling. A 5- or 6-month-old baby has had months of experience in mutual gazing and smiling with caregivers. De- spite the origins of smiling, infants and caregivers can clearly condition each other to smile by smiling in response to smiling

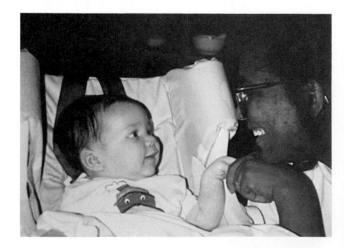

Smiling in babies is elicited by human facial features and seems to be an important ingredient in the formation of parent-infant bonds of attachment.

► ► ► ►

(Brackbill, 1958; Gewirtz & Boyd, 1977; Sroufe & Waters, 1976).

A second interesting source of evidence that smiling is innate is found in the fact that blind babies also smile in response to the human voice and in response to being touched (Freedman, 1974). Blind babies, of course, cannot perceive the smiles of caregivers, and their smiling cannot be explained in terms of learning by imitation. Even if caregivers reinforce their smiling by cuddling and gushy vocalizing, the initial smile must occur spontaneously.

Like other attachment behaviors, smiling is at first directed indiscriminately toward other people (Emde et al., 1976). But as the baby develops specific attachments, smiling becomes directed only at a select few. It is as if the baby is saying, "I only have eyes for you." And being the recipient of their infants' smiles makes parents feel proud and very, very special.

with, most fathers spend fewer than ten hours a week caring for or playing with their infants. Fathers are more likely to play with their children than to feed or clean them. Fathers more often than mothers poke their babies, toss them into the air, and mimic their behavior (Trevarthen, 1974; Parke & O'leary, 1976). Mothers are more likely to play games like pat-a-cake and peek-a-boo (Lamb, 1976a). Fathers are also less likely than mothers to use motherese and try to hold "conversations" (verbal give-and-takes) with their infants *unless* they are in the primary caregiving role. When they are the primary caregivers, their vocal and other behaviors are more like women's (Field, 1978).

Attachment to Fathers   How strongly, then, do infants become attached to their fathers? The answer seems to depend on the situation. In a laboratory setting in which their play is disrupted by a stranger, 10- to 16-month-old infants are more likely to cope by seeking contact with their mothers than their fathers (Cohen & Campos, 1974). But when they are observed at their natural activities in the home and other familiar settings, they seek proximity and contact with their fathers about as often as with their mothers (Lamb, 1977, 1981). In at least one study carried out in the home, as a matter of fact, male infants showed preference for their fathers, whereas female infants showed no preference (Lamb, 1976b).

Moreover, it appears that babies develop attachments for both parents at about the same time (Parke, 1981). This is interesting for two reasons. First, it flies in the face of Freudian theory, which argues that babies become more attached to their mothers—providers of "oral gratification"—during the first year. Second, most mothers provide a markedly greater amount of caregiving than fathers do during the first few months.

Infants who are securely attached to only one parent are also as likely to be attached to the father as the mother (Main & Weston, 1981). By and large, the quality of the time spent with the father and not the number of hours seems to determine father–child attachment (Easterbrooks & Goldberg, 1984).

The Effects of Day Care

More than half of today's U.S. mothers spend the day on the job. This figure includes 41 percent of mothers of children less than 1 year old (Klein, 1985). The ideals of the women's movement and financial pressures are likely to increase this number. When parents of young children both spend the day

▶ ▶ ▶ ▶

Center day care *Day care in a communal public or private center.*

on the job, the children must be taken care of by others, although many older "latchkey" children take care of themselves after school until their parents come home.* Many years ago, when U.S. residents were less mobile and there was more of an extended family life, young children were frequently farmed out to relatives. Today, however, their care is more often entrusted to others in one of several forms of day care.

Types of Day Care There are three major types of day care: center day care, family day care, and in-home day care (Belsky et al., 1981). In **center day care,** children receive care at a center that may be private, but is frequently affiliated with a university, church, housing project, or community agency. Family day care is provided by parents who take the children of others into their homes. In a number of states, people who offer family day care require licenses. In-home care (baby-sitting) takes place in the child's home.

Between 7 and 8 million U.S. preschool children are now placed in day-care centers, and parents express many concerns about what happens to them there. In one survey, 59 percent of working mothers reported that worrying about the care their children received increased their stress level (Trost, 1987). Fifty-six percent of parents reported difficulty arranging quality day care; 54 percent complained that the costs of day care were excessive; 51 percent had problems with the location and hours of their day-care centers; and 25 percent of working mothers considered quitting their jobs because of these problems (Trost, 1987). What types of experiences do children actually encounter in day-care centers? What are the effects of day care on parent–child bonds of attachment? On children's social development? What factors contribute to a positive day-care experience?

What Are Day-Care Centers Like? Infants' experiences in day-care centers vary. Some infants are placed in centers for a few hours a week, and others for the entire day, five days a week. Some day-care centers have an adult caregiver for every three children, and others place as many as twelve children in the care of one adult. The purposes and personnel of day-care centers also vary. Some are intended to provide early cognitive stimulation to prepare children for entry into elementary school. Others focus on custodial care and entertainment. Some have college-educated personnel. Others have caregivers who function on the basis of life experience or specific training. Standards for the licensing of day-care centers vary from locale to locale. Parents therefore need to take pains to determine the adequacy of the centers they are considering for their children.

Most parents want day-care centers to provide more than the basics of food, warmth, and security. They want these centers to stimulate their children intellectually, to provide a variety of toys and games, and to provide successful peer interactions and experience in relating to adults other than family members.

How Do Day-Care Centers Influence Bonds of Attachment? Many parents wonder whether day care will affect their children's attachment to them. After all, the child will be spending many hours away at a "vulnerable" age. During these time periods, their needs will be met by outsiders. Parents also have mixed

---

*Recent studies of latchkey children at least 9 years of age have found no significant problems on several measures of psychological and social functioning (Galambos & Garbino, 1983; Rodman et al., 1985).

▶ ▶ ▶ ▶

feelings about day care. If they had the time and money, most parents would prefer to care for their children personally. And so parents often feel some guilt about "sending away" their children. They may fear that they will be punished with loss of love for their "wrongdoing."

Whether these concerns are rational or not, studies of the effects of day care are encouraging. In their review of the literature, Jay Belsky and Laurence Steinberg (1978) concluded that day care has *not* been shown to interfere with mother–child bonds of attachments. As in other studies of attachment, infants' behavior depends on the research setting. When in the Strange Situation, infants prefer their mothers to their daytime caregivers (Cummings, 1980). But at their familiar day-care centers, infants appear as willing to spend time with center personnel as with their mothers.

In their large-scale, frequently cited study of day care, Jerome Kagan and his colleagues (1978, 1980) followed children placed in day care and a matched group cared for in the home from 3½ months to 29 months. Both groups preferred to maintain proximity and contact with their mothers in the laboratory setting. However, the day-care children also became attached to their caregivers and preferred them to adult strangers.

A study by Christine Anderson and her colleagues (1981) suggests that children's attachment to their caregivers depends on the quality of their interaction with them. Children from 19–42 months of age were observed in "high-quality" and "low-quality" day-care programs. Programs considered high in quality were rich in toys, games, and other equipment. They also had programs to foster social and cognitive development. Caregivers were assigned 12 children in both high- and low-quality centers.

In this study, the level of involvement of the caregiver was the key to the development of attachment. The general "quality" of the center was irrelevant. Children whose caregivers were highly involved with them made a greater attempt to maintain proximity and contact with them. Children were also more likely to use highly involved caregivers as a base for exploration.

The Kagan group suggests that initial enrollment in day care is less stressful for infants prior to the age of 7 months or after the age of 15 to 18 months. In this way, the infants are exposed to day-care personnel either before they may develop fear of strangers and separation anxiety, or after these fears are on the wane.

How Do Day-Care Centers Influence Social Development? Day-care centers provide an opportunity for social experiences outside the home. This fact both delights and concerns many parents. Parents generally want their children to acquire the social skills to relate to outsiders, but they may also prefer to be the caregivers (and protectors) who oversee their children's early social interactions.

Day care seems to have positive and negative influences on children's social development. First, the positive. Infants with day-care experience are more peer-oriented and play at higher developmental levels. Day-care children are also more likely to share their toys (Belsky & Steinberg, 1978, 1979). Adolescent boys who had been placed in day care before the age of 5 were rated high in sociability and were liked by their peers (Moore, 1975). And so day care may stimulate interest in peers and help in the formation of social skills.

Now, the negative. A number of studies have compared 3- and 4-year-olds who had been in full-time day care for several years with age-mates recently placed in day-care centers. The experienced children were more impulsive, more

▶ ▶ ▶ ▶

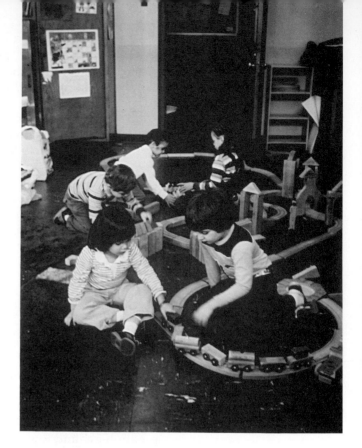

Between seven and eight million U.S. preschoolers are now placed in day-care centers. What are the effects of day care on social development and on parent-child bonds of attachment?

aggressive toward peers and adults, and more egocentric (Caldwell et al., 1970; Lay & Meyer, 1973; Schwartz et al., 1973, 1974). They were also less cooperative and showed less tolerance for frustration.

The negative characteristics found among children with extensive day-care experience seem to suggest a common theme: Day care can promote interest in peers and the development of social skills, but children frequently do not receive the individual attention or resources they would like. Placed in a competitive situation, they become somewhat more aggressive in attempting to meet their needs. Nor do they become habituated to partial attention from caregivers. Their lower tolerance for frustration suggests, instead, that intermittent attention only further sensitizes them to frustration.

There is another possibility. The studies of children in full-time day care or home care involved children whose parents had already *chosen* whether or not to use day care. It could be that pre-existing personality differences in the children played a role in influencing parents to place them, or not to place them, in day care. Perhaps parents with more impulsive but less cooperative children were more highly motivated to send their children out for care. I do not find this argument convincing, but the studies on day care have been correlational and not experimental. Infants have not been assigned at random to day care or home care. And so one must consider the possibility that group differences pre-existed and were not the result of day care.

Even if day care usually fosters impulsiveness and aggressiveness, these outcomes are not inevitable. Fewer children per caregiver and more toys would reduce competition. Unfortunately, caregivers, on the average, are assigned nearly four infants aged under 18 months or nearly six toddlers aged 18 to 24

▶ ▶ ▶ ▶

months. In many cases, they have many more. Two major obstructions stand in the way of having one caregiver for every three children, however: money and the scarceness of qualified personnel.

Selecting a Day-Care Center   Selecting a day-care center can be an overwhelming task. Standards for day-care centers vary from locale to locale, so licensing is no guarantee of adequate care. To become sophisticated consumers of day care, parents can weigh factors such as the following when making a choice:

1. Is the center licensed? By what agency? What standards must be met to acquire a license?

2. What is the ratio of children to caregivers? Everything else being equal, it would appear logical that caregivers can do a better job when there are fewer children in their charge. Jerome Kagan and his colleagues (1978) recommend that caregivers not have more than three infants or toddlers assigned to their care. But it may also be of use to look beyond numbers. Quality is frequently more important than quantity.

3. What are the qualifications of the centers' caregivers? How well aware are they of children's needs and patterns of development? Day-care workers are typically paid poorly. Financial frustrations lead many of the best-qualified workers to seek work in other fields (Saddler, 1987). According to the findings of the National Day Care Study (Ruopp et al., 1979), children fare better when their caregivers have specific training in child development. Years of day-care experience and formal degrees are less important. If the administrators of a day-care center are reluctant to discuss the training and experience of their caregivers, consider another center.

4. How safe is the environment? Do toys and swings seem to be in good condition? Are dangerous objects out of reach? Would strangers have a difficult time breaking in? Have children been injured in this center? Administrators should report previous injuries without hesitation.

5. What is served at mealtime? Is it nutritious, appetizing? Will *your child* eat it? Some babies are placed in day care at 6 months or younger, and parents will need to know what formulas are used.

6. Which caregivers will be responsible for your child? What are their backgrounds? How do they seem to relate to children?

7. With what children will your child interact and play?

8. What toys, games, books, and other educational objects are provided?

9. What facilities are present for promoting the motor development of your child? How well-supervised are children when they use new objects such as swings and tricycles?

10. Are the hours offered by the center convenient for your schedule?

11. Is the location of the center convenient?

12. Do you like the overall environment and "feel" of the center?

▶ ▶ ▶ ▶

Kibbutz (key-BOOTS). An Israeli farming community in which children are reared in group settings.

Metapelet A child-rearing professional in a kibbutz.

Perhaps no day-care center will score perfectly on each item. But some items are more important than others. Going through the list item by item may at least help focus your concerns.

Now let us consider the effects of a group child-rearing method that could be considered an extended day-care type of program—the kibbutz.

The Effects of Rearing Children in Groups

About 100,000 Israelis live in collective farm settlements known as **kibbutzim.** In the kibbutz, children are reared in group settings from shortly after birth through adolescence (Bronfenbrenner, 1973). Children spend their first year in a nursery, then advance to a toddler's house. The same group of children remains together from infancy, and their attachment to one another grows very strong.

Parents visit and play with their children frequently. Their major role appears to be to provide their children with emotional gratification (Beit-Hallahmi & Rabin, 1977). The children's primary care and training, however, is entrusted to a child-rearing specialist called a **metapelet.** Because parents are not involved in training chores, this arrangement reduces early parent–child conflict.

Despite the reduced parent–child contact, kibbutz life does not seem to impair parent–child bonds of attachment (Maccoby & Feldman, 1972). In fact, parent–child relations seem more cordial. But babies appear to become equally attached to their metapelet (Fox, 1977). This outcome would be unacceptable to parents who want their children to be primarily attached to them. As noted by Rabkin and Rabkin (1974), kibbutz life "shields the child from overprotective or domineering parents who might block his efforts to become independent."

It has been suggested that kibbutz life encourages children to be more generous and cooperative (Shapira & Madsen, 1974). One study found that first- and fifth-grade kibbutz children are more likely to distribute rewards evenly between themselves and a partner than are their city counterparts (Nisan, 1984). But another found kibbutz-reared children to be less cooperative with adult strangers than were Israeli children who were reared in the city (Levy-Shiff, 1984).

In contrast to U.S. children placed in full-time day care, kibbutz children do not seem to be more impulsive and aggressive than children reared in the home. A number of differences between U.S. day care and the kibbutz may account for this finding. First, kibbutz children sleep in the kibbutz as well as spend their days there. Second, the metapelet perceives herself as the primary caregiver and is probably more devoted to the children than are workers in U.S. day-care centers. Third, take an ecological perspective. Cultural differences between Israel and the United States are also likely to foster differences in the development of personality and social behavior.

Child Abuse: When Attachment Fails

There's no place like home—for violence, that is. Consider the following statistics from a national survey of 1,146 parents by Richard Gelles and Murray Strauss (1979):

▶ ▶ ▶ ▶

- 71 percent of parents have slapped or spanked their children.
- 46.4 percent of parents have pushed, grabbed, or shoved their children.
- 20 percent have hit their children with an object.
- 9.6 percent have thrown something at their children.
- 7.7 percent have kicked or bitten their children, or hit them with their fists.
- 4.2 percent have beaten up their children.
- 2.8 percent have threatened their children with a knife or gun.
- 2.9 percent have actually used a knife or a gun on their children.

We are concerned about the company our children keep. We teach them to look both ways when they cross the street. We know that the world at large is a violent place, and so we caution our children to avoid dark streets and alleyways. But at least 625,000 children in the United States are neglected or abused every year . . . at home (National Center on Child Abuse and Neglect, 1982). And this figure is rising (Brown, 1983).

Neglect is more common than abuse. Some children are poorly fed, poorly clothed in winter, ignored, and allowed to fend for themselves in unsafe environments. Although blatant abuse is more horrifying, more injuries, illnesses, and deaths result from neglect (Cantwell, 1980; Wolock & Horowitz, 1984).

Causes of Child Abuse   A number of factors contribute to the probability that parents will abuse their children. They include situational stress, a history of child abuse in at least one of the parent's families of origin, acceptance of violence as a way of coping with stress, failure to become attached to the children, and rigid attitudes about child-rearing (Belsky, 1984; Milner et al., 1984; Rosenblum & Paully, 1984).

There are many sources of stress, including such "life changes" as parental conflict, divorce or separation, the loss of a job, moving, and the birth of a new family member (Rathus & Nevid, 1986). Parents who are exposed to more life changes are more likely to abuse their children (Justice & Justice, 1976). Unemployment seems to be a particularly predisposing life change. Child abuse increases during periods of rising unemployment (National Center on Child Abuse and Neglect, 1982; Steinberg et al., 1981).

Stress is created by crying infants themselves (Green et al., 1987; Murray, 1985). Infants who are already in pain of some kind, and relatively difficult to soothe, may ironically be more likely to be abused (Frodi, 1981, 1985). Why? Parents tend to become frustrated and irritated when their babies show prolonged signs of distress. Some frustrated parents may even "take it personally"—that is, draw the irrational conclusion that their children are crying because they do not love them (Steele & Pollock, 1974). Similarly, abusive mothers are more likely than nonabusive mothers to assume that their children's misbehavior is intentional, even when it is not (Bauer & Twentyman, 1985). Within our culture, intentional misconduct is seen as more deserving of punishment than incidental misconduct.

Sad to say, abused children show an alarming incidence of personal and social problems and abnormal behavior patterns. Maltreatment can disturb basic patterns of attachment. Abused children are less likely than nonabused agemates to venture out to explore the world (Aber & Allen, 1987). Abused children are more likely to be depressed and aggressive than nonabused children, even at preschool ages (Hoffman-Plotkin & Twentyman, 1984; Kazdin et al., 1985).

▶ ▶ ▶ ▶

Nonabused toddlers are likely to show concern or sadness when their peers are distressed. Abused toddlers often respond to age-mates' distress with fear, anger, or physical attacks (Main & George, 1985). One study notes some similarities between child abusers and the behavior of Harry Harlow's "motherless-mother" rhesus monkeys. Spinetta and Rigler (1972) argue that the child abusers they investigated encountered social and maternal deprivation at a young age and did not feel secure or loved themselves.

Child abuse is somewhat more likely to run in families. But it must be emphasized that *the majority of children who are abused as adults do* not *abuse their own children.* According to psychologist Mindy Rosenberg, there is no evidence that women who were abused as children are more likely than other women to abuse their own children (Fisher, 1984). These facts are extremely important, because many victims of child abuse as adults are (unjustifiedly) concerned that they are destined to abuse their own children.

Why do *some* victims of child abuse become abusive themselves? One possibility is that their parents serve as violent role models. If children grow up observing their parents using violence as a means to cope with stress and feelings of anger, they are less likely to learn to diffuse anger through techniques such as humor, verbal expression of feelings, reasoning, or even "counting to ten."

Exposure to violence in their own homes may also lead some children to accept family violence as a norm. They may see little or nothing wrong in it. Certainly, there are any number of "justifications" they can find for violence—if they are seeking them. One is the age-old adage, "Spare the rod, spoil the child." Another is the belief that they are hurting their children "for their own good"—to discourage behavior that is likely to get them into trouble. Along these lines, let me note that I have seen cases in which mothers have claimed to have beaten their children in order to "protect them" from their fathers. They have claimed that their husbands, who were much stronger, were about to beat the children. By jumping in and doing it themselves, they spared their children an even rougher beating.

Still another "justification" of child abuse is the sometimes cloudy distinction between the occasional swat on the rear end and spanking or other types of repeated hitting. Child abusers may argue that all parents hit their children (which is not true) and claim not to understand why outsiders are making "such a fuss" about their private family behavior. Child abusers who come from families in which they were subjected to abuse are also more likely to have the (incorrect) perspective that "everyone does it."

What of the role of failure of attachment in abuse? In Chapter 4 we noted that parents of preterm children have more difficulty becoming attached to them. One reason is that the early parent–infant relationship is interrupted by hospital procedures. Although only one child in twelve is preterm, about one in four abused children is preterm (Klein & Stern, 1971). Preterm children are about three times as likely as their full-term counterparts to be abused. With prematurity, of course, we are not only dealing with possible failures in attachment. Preterm children are also more likely to develop illnesses and other problems. As a consequence, they may cry more frequently and generally make more demands on their parents.

What to Do Dealing with child abuse is a frustrating issue in itself. Social

▶ ▶ ▶ ▶

agencies and courts can find it as difficult to distinguish between "normal"* hitting or spanking and abuse as many abusers do. Because of the U.S. belief that parents have the right to rear their children as they wish, police and courts have also historically tried to avoid involvement in "domestic quarrels" and "family disputes."

However, the alarming incidence of child abuse has spawned new efforts at detection and prevention. Many states require helping professionals such as psychologists and physicians to report any suspicion of child abuse. Many states legally require *anyone* who suspects child abuse to report it to authorities.

Many locales also have Child Abuse Hotlines. Their phone numbers are available from the telephone information service. Private citizens who suspect child abuse may call these numbers for advice. Parents who are having difficulty controlling aggressive impulses toward their children are encouraged to use them. Some hotlines are serviced by groups such as Parents Anonymous, who have had similar difficulties and may help callers diffuse feelings of anger in less harmful ways.

Other potentially helpful measures include increased publicizing of the dimensions of the child-abuse problem. To be sure, news and entertainment media have made efforts to do so, but the campaigns may be too infrequent. The public may also need more education about where an occasional swat on the behind ends and child abuse begins. Perhaps the format for such education could be something like, "If you are doing such and such, make no mistake about it—you are abusing your child."

Finally, as with the crime of wife-beating, child abuse must be conceptualized and dealt with as a crime of violence. Whether or not child abusers happen to be victims of abuse themselves, child abusers are criminals and their children must be protected from them.

Dependence and Independence

At 2 years 6 months, Allyn said, "I'm not listening to you" when her mother asked her to do something. The remark "came out of the blue" and was met with stunned silence. My wife's facial expression must have communicated that here indeed was a behavior worthy of note, because Allyn persisted in repeating it for several days in every imaginable situation. Now, years later, Allyn still gets across this message, but in more sophisticated ways. Usually she simply does not "listen" to us, without verbal accompaniment.

Toward the end of the second year, and during the third year, children become increasingly aware that their goals and wills can differ from their parents'. At about this time children tend to push toward autonomy and may meet nearly every request or remark with a "No."

---

*I place this word in quotes because of my own horror at child abuse, and my refusal to consider any hitting of children to be normal.

▶ ▶ ▶ ▶

Executive dependence *Dependence on others to execute actions that meet one's physical needs.*

Executive independence *Ability to execute actions that meet one's own physical needs.*

Affectional dependence *Dependence on others to meet one's emotional, affectional needs.*

For the first couple of years, infants show what David Ausubel (1958) has labeled **executive dependence.** That is, infants depend on their parents to execute actions that will meet their needs. Sometimes they show "independence" in the expression of their executive dependence. For example, children may push and prod parents to the place where they want them to execute an action such as reaching for a cookie.

Young children can also have temper tantrums because they want to do things for themselves. Doing things for oneself is a sign of **executive independence.** Two- and 3-year-olds may cry, throw things, hit and screech, and whine when parents try to help them do things that they think that they can do—even when they can't. As a rule of thumb, it seems to be helpful to allow children to try to do the things they think they can do, so long as the results will not be injurious or overly messy. When children try things by themselves, and then see that they need help, they may ask for it and a tantrum will have been averted. When it is dangerous to let children do things for themselves, consistency and a brief explanation ("Do you see all these cars? If you don't hold my hand you could get hurt!") will often spur cooperation and stave off tears.

Affectional dependence is the need to have the affection and approval of other people. Jerome Kagan and Howard Moss (1962) dipped into the pool of subjects followed by the Fels Institute since the 1920s and found that highly dependent preschoolers tended to retain this trait until early adolescence. From the age of 12 or so boys tended to surge toward independence, perhaps because dependence is considered a negative trait for boys and they encounter increasing pressure to change during adolescence. Boys might also be more motivated than girls to hide feelings of dependence. Highly dependent girls tended to remain dependent as adults. They stayed close to home and took jobs that are traditional for women.

At a young age, dependence can be seen as a function of the distance that infants are willing to maintain from their primary caregivers (Rheingold & Eckerman, 1970). Two-year-olds are more willing to place distance between themselves and their caregivers than are 1-year-olds. Three-year-olds are yet more willing, and so on.

Generally speaking, children who cling to their caregivers are also more dependent than children who do not. Children who are securely attached are more likely to use their caregivers as a base for exploring the environment (Clarke-Stewart & Hevey, 1981). They are more likely to venture away from them and experiment with the skills that will lead to executive independence. Making children feel loved does not appear to keep them dependent. Promoting feelings of security seems to prompt the development of independence.

Play: Is Play Just "Child's Play"?

At around her second birthday, "Loveliness" entered Allyn's life. Loveliness was a boy or man (we think). He wore black overalls, a black shirt, black socks, and black shoes—as described by Allyn. He told Allyn to do lots of things—move things from here to there, get food for him, and so on. At times we overheard Allyn talking in her room. Looking back on it, perhaps we should

▶ ▶ ▶ ▶

Cross-Cultural Studies of the Development of Independence

▷
▷
▷
▷

▷ Cross-cultural studies provide some interesting insights into the development of independence. Among the !Kung people of Namibia, babies are kept in close contact with their mothers during the first year (Konner, 1972, 1977). Babies are fed on demand. It might be more accurate to report that they are fed *prior* to demand:

> The mother, with the infant against her skin, or in her arms, can literally feel his state changes. She makes every effort to anticipate hunger. Waking up, moving, gurgling, the pucker face, the slightest fret, a change in the rate of breathing—any of these may result in nursing (Konner, 1972).

!Kung infants are also frequently carried in slings across their mothers' hips that allow them to nurse at will—literally, all day long. The !Kung seem to follow the "commandment": The infant shall not go hungry, not even for five seconds. In every way, !Kung mothers try to respond at once to their babies, cries and whims. By Western standards, !Kung babies are incredibly indulged or spoiled.

However, overindulgence does not appear to make !Kung babies overly dependent on their mothers. By the time they are capable of walking, they do. They do not cling to their mothers. In comparison to Western children of the same age, !Kung children spend less time with their mothers and more time with their peers (Konner, 1977).

Also compare Urie Bronfenbrenner's (1973) observations of child-rearing in the United States and Russia. Russian babies as a group are more likely than U.S. babies to be cuddled, kissed, hugged, and held tightly. Russian mothers are not quite so solicitous as their !Kung counterparts, but they are highly protective as compared to U.S. mothers. Russian children are taught to take care of themselves at younger ages than U.S. children. By 18 months they are usually learning to dress themselves and are largely toilet-trained. But Russian mothers tend to hover over their children, limiting their movements for fear that they will get hurt and, perhaps, interfering with the development of their sense of autonomy. In nursery schools, Russian children are assigned communal chores, such as caring for animals and shoveling snow. They are encouraged to be altruistic, self-disciplined, and obedient. They are guided into group activities and given toys that can be made to work only when they cooperate with one another.

Russian children's taking care of themselves at very early ages may reflect obedience and conformity more than independence. Independence seems to be fostered when parents respect and encourage the developing autonomy of their children.

have respected her privacy more, but we would go into her room and ask her whom she was talking to. The answer "Loveliness" came willingly enough.

Loveliness was Allyn's first and—so far as we know—only imaginary friend. Fifteen to 30 percent of children have such friends. It does not mean that they are lonely. Nor, although it involves fantasy, does it mean that children are having difficulty maintaining contact with reality. However, it usually

▶ ▶ ▶ ▶

As children develop, play becomes more socially oriented and cooperative.

occurs between the ages of 3 and 10, not at 2, and it is most common among only and first-born children (Manosevitz et al., 1973).

Imaginary friends are one example of "pretend" or dramatic play. In this section we explore the nature of play and of the contributions of play to social and emotional development.

Patterns of play become more peer-oriented as children develop. Infants first show positive interest in one another at about 6 months. If they are placed on the floor facing one another, they will smile, occasionally imitate each other, and often touch one another. Social interaction increases over the next few months, but during the first year, contacts between infants tend to be brief and loose (Eckerman & Whatley, 1977; Hartup, 1983; Vandell et al., 1980). By about the age of 3 or so, children begin to become involved in each other's activities. Toddlers are more willing to separate from their mothers to play with attractive toys in the presence of peers (Gunnar et al., 1984), suggestive that the presence of peers helps provide them with a sense of security.

From the age of about 3 through middle childhood, children tend to prefer the company of peers of the same sex (Roopnarine, 1984). This preference is at least in part related to preference for toys that are stereotyped as appropriate for their own gender (Eisenberg et al., 1984). That is, children who prefer transportation toys to dolls may prefer to associate with children who share their preference.* I watched with amusement as Allyn, at 5, persistently encouraged 4-year-old Eric to join her in play with dolls. It took Eric a while to

---

*In Chapter 12 we shall also consider the hypothesis that same-sex companions contribute to children's sense of gender stability.

▶ ▶ ▶ ▶

become involved, and his parents—especially his father—seemed to be made uncomfortable by Allyn's insistence. But they did not know quite what to do. Part of their problem, they later admitted, was that they were too intellectually sophisticated to object to their son's playing with dolls. Still, their own sex-role training had apparently left its emotional impact.

Parten's Types of Play

In classic research on children's play, Mildred Parten (1932) observed the development of five types of play among 2- to 5-year-old nursery school children.

First is **solitary play,** in which children play with toys by themselves, independently of the children around them. Solitary players do not appear influenced by children around them. They make no effort to approach them.

Second is **onlooker play,** in which children observe other children who are at play. Onlookers frequently talk to the children they are observing and may make suggestions, but they do not overtly join in. Solitary play and onlooker play are both considered types of **nonsocial play**—that is, play in which children do not interact. Onlooker play occurs most often at the age of 2.

Third is **parallel play,** in which children play with toys similar to those of surrounding children. However, they treat the toys as they choose, and do not directly interact with other children.

Fourth is **associative play,** in which children interact and share toys. However, they do not seem to share group goals. Although they interact, individuals still treat toys as they choose. The association with the other children appears to be more important than the nature of the activity. They seem to enjoy each other's company.

Fifth is **cooperative play,** in which children interact to achieve common group goals. The play of each child is subordinated to the purposes of the group. One or two group members direct the activities of others. There is also a division of labor, with different children taking different roles. Children may pretend to be members of a family, "cowboys and Indians," animals, space monsters, and all sorts of creatures. Their imitation and instruction increases their capacity to empathize with others, and they receive ongoing feedback as to the social effectiveness of their behavior.

Parallel play, associative play, and cooperative play are types of **social play.** In each case children are influenced by other children as they are playing. Parten found that associative and cooperative play become common at age 5. Recent research continues to show that they are found among older and more experienced preschoolers (Harper & Huie, 1985).

But there are exceptions. Five-year-olds who engage in solitary play from time to time may be showing independence and the capacity to concentrate on individual tasks—not social immaturity (Roper & Hinde, 1978). Nonsocial play can involve educational activities that foster cognitive development. In fact, many 5-year-olds spend a good deal of time in parallel constructive play. For instance, they may work on puzzles or build with blocks near other children. Parallel constructive players are frequently perceived by teachers to be socially skillful and are popular with their peers (Rubin, 1982). Some toddlers are also more capable of social play than one might expect from their years alone. Two-year-olds with older siblings or a great deal of group experience may engage in advanced forms of social play.

▶ ▶ ▶ ▶

Solitary play *Play that is independent from that of nearby children, and in which no effort is made to approach other children.*

Onlooker play *Play during which children observe other children at play, but do not enter into their play themselves.*

Nonsocial play *Forms of play (solitary play and onlooker play) in which play is not influenced by the play of nearby children.*

Parallel play *Play in which children use the same toys as nearby children, but approach their toys in their own ways. No effort is made to modify the play of others.*

Associative play *Play with other children in which toys are shared and the company is enjoyed; however, there is no common goal or division of labor.*

Cooperative play *Organized play in which children cooperate to meet common goals. There is a division of labor, and children take on specific roles as group members.*

Social play *Play in which children interact with and are influenced by the play of others (parallel play, in which children use the same toys; associative play; and cooperative play).*

Social play appears to help preschoolers acquire interpersonal skills that will serve them later on. Toddlers who have had more social interaction with their age-mates approach other children more frequently and accept invitations to play with greater social skill (Mueller & Brenner, 1977).

Dramatic or "Pretend" Play

Children's "let's pretend" type of play may seem immature to busy adults meeting the realistic demands of the business world, but "pretend" or **dramatic play** requires cognitive sophistication. During the first year, play is largely sensorimotor. It involves repetitious assimilation of familiar and novel objects to sensorimotor schemes. Children mouth, shake, stack, and toss familiar and novel objects.

According to Piaget (1962), pretend play usually occurs some time during the second year, when the child is symbolizing objects. At 19 months Allyn picked up a pine cone and looked it over. Her older sister Jill said, "That's a pine cone," but Allyn heard "comb" and began to comb her hair with it. "No," said Jill, "It's a *cone*, not a *comb*." Allyn shifted gears and started pretending to lick it, like an ice-cream cone.

Pretend play increases over the next three to four years. Then it gradually wanes in favor of playing games with rules—checkers, Monopoly, athletic games, and so on. Piaget argues that the ability to engage in pretend or dramatic play is based on the use and recollection of symbols—that is, on mental representations of things that children have encountered or heard about.

Cooperative play is often dramatic, with children taking various roles. Pairs of children may pretend to be husband and wife, parent and child, or parents. Catherine Garvey found that most dramatic cooperative play, among 2- to 5-year-olds, centers around such standard domestic themes. But children may also enact characters from film and television ("I'll be Kermit and you be Miss Piggy!"), or varieties of monsters that they reshape as they play along. Cooperative fantasies become more complex beween the ages of 2 and 6 (Rubin et al., 1983).

Much theorizing has been done about dramatic play. It has been suggested that dramatic play also fosters social and emotional development. For example, dramatic play allows children to experiment with different social roles and obtain feedback from peers. Enacting the roles of other people may help them develop empathy. Finding solutions to fantastic problems may transfer to helping children find ways to solve problems in the real world. On an emotional level, it has been suggested that dramatic play allows children to express their fears and their fantasies.

We do not yet have a full understanding of the origins and functions of play. Of course, one of the wonderful things about play is that it need not serve any function at all.

Now let us consider emotional development. After all, social development and play would not be any "fun" without emotional response.

Dramatic play Play in which children enact social roles as made possible by the attainment of symbolic thought. Also referred to as pretend play, *signifying, for example, the element of fantasy in which children may pretend that toys and objects are something else.*

▶ ▶ ▶ ▶

Emotional Development

Emotions color our lives. We are green with envy, red with anger, blue with sorrow. The poets paint a thoughtful mood as a brown study. Positive emotions such as love can fill our days with pleasure. Negative emotions such as fear, depression, and anger can fill us with dread and make each day a chore.

An **emotion** is a state of feeling that has physiological, situational, and cognitive components (Rathus, 1987). Physiologically, when emotions are strong, our hearts may beat more rapidly and our muscles may tense. Situationally, we may feel fear in the presence of a threat and joy or relief in the presence of a loved one. Cognitively, fear is accompanied by the idea that we are in danger. Depression is accompanied by the idea that we have suffered a loss and, perhaps, there is little that we can do.

Theories of the Development of Emotions

There are a number of theories concerning the development of emotions. Basically they break down into two camps. The first, proposed originally by Katherine Bridges (1932), holds that we are born with a single emotion and that other emotions become differentiated as time passes. The second, proposed by Carroll Izard, holds that all emotions are present and adequately differentiated at birth. However, they are not shown all at once. Instead, they emerge in response to the child's developing needs and maturational sequences.

Bridges' and Sroufe's Theory   On the basis of her observations of babies, Bridges proposed that newborns experience one emotion—diffuse excitement. By 3 months, two other emotions have differentiated from this general state of excitement—a negative emotion, distress, and a positive emotion, delight. By 6 months, fear, disgust, and anger will have developed from distress. By 12 months elation and affection will have differentiated from delight. Jealousy develops from distress, and joy develops from delight—both during the second year.

Alan Sroufe (1979) has advanced Bridges' theory, focusing on the ways in which cognitive development may provide the basis for emotional development. Jealousy, for example, could not become differentiated without some understanding of object permanence (the continuing existence of people and objects) and possession. Anger usually results from situations in which our intentions are thwarted. For example, 7-month-old infants show anger when a biscuit is almost placed in their mouths and then removed (Stenberg et al., 1983). It may be that the development of intentionality and of rudimentary causality (the ability to perceive other people as the causes of frustration) precede the differentiation of anger.

Sroufe also links development of fear of strangers to the perceptual-cognitive capacity to discriminate the faces of familiar people from those of unfamiliar people. As noted in Chapter 6, infants usually show distress at the mother's departure after they have developed a rudimentary form of object permanence.

Izard's Theory   Carroll Izard (1978, 1979, 1982) proposes that infants are born with discrete emotional states. However, the timing of their appearance is linked to the child's cognitive development and social experiences. For example, in one study, Izard and his colleagues (1983) claim that 2-month-old babies receiving inoculations showed distress, whereas older infants showed anger.

Izard's view may sound very similar to Sroufe's. After all, both are suggesting that there is an orderly unfolding of emotions such that they become

▶ ▶ ▶ ▶

more specific as time passes. However, in keeping with Izard's view, researchers have found that a number of different emotions appear to be shown by infants at ages earlier than those suggested by Bridges and Sroufe. In one study of the emotions shown by babies during the first three months, 99 percent of the mothers interviewed reported that their babies showed the emotion of interest. Ninety-five percent of mothers reported joy; 84 percent, anger; 74 percent, surprise; and 58 percent, fear (Johnson et al., 1982). These figures are based on mothers' reports, and it is possible that the infants were actually showing more diffuse emotions (Murphy, 1983). Perhaps the mothers were "reading" specific emotions "into" the babies based on their own knowledge of appropriate (adult) emotional reactions to the infants' situations. This is a problem that extends to Izard's interpretations of infants' facial expressions.

Izard (1979) claims to have found many discrete emotions at the age of 1 month by using his Maximally Discriminative Facial Movement Scoring System. Figure 10.5 shows some infant facial expressions that Izard believes are associated with the basic emotions of anger–rage, disgust, enjoyment–joy, fear–terror, interest–excitement, and sadness–dejection. However, Joseph Campos and his colleagues (1983) suggest that this type of research is fraught with problems. First, these facial expressions seem to be fleeting in young infants, if they are drawn accurately at all. Second, we cannot know the exact relationship between a facial expression and an infant's inner feelings, which, of course, are ultimately private events. In other words, even if the drawings accurately represent young infants' facial expressions, we cannot be certain that they express the specific emotions they would suggest in the cases of older children and adults.

In sum, researchers seem agreed that a handful of emotions are shown by infants during the first few months. They agree that other emotions develop in an orderly manner. They agree that emotional development is linked to cognitive development and social experience. They do not agree as to exactly when specific emotions are first shown, or on whether discrete emotions are present at birth.

Enough disagreement. Let us discuss an emotion that we'll all agree is very little fun: fear.

Children's Fears

Children, like adults, have their fears. It seems that about 90 percent of children aged 2 to 14 report at least one fear (MacFarlane et al., 1954). In one study, 40 percent of the children between the ages of 6 to 12 had at least seven fears (Lapouse, 1966). As is the case with adults, many children's fears are rational, but some are not so rational. There are also individual differences. Some children fear objects and animals that other children find appealing or simply manage to accept without great anxiety. Some fears such as fear of snakes are unimportant because they have little impact on our lives. But other

▶ ▶ ▶ ▶

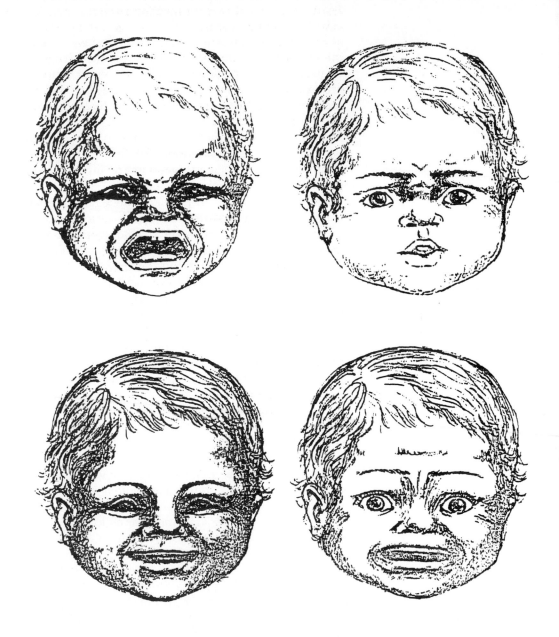

Figure 10.5 Illustrations from Carroll Izard's Maximally Discriminative Facial Movement Scoring System
What emotion do you think is being experienced by each of these infants?

▶ ▶ ▶ ▶

fears can be debilitating because they concern everyday situations and objects. Fears of dogs and cats, of meeting new children, and of talking in front of the class are some of them.

Many fears are rational and adaptive. Fear of strange places and unfamiliar people can protect us from unknown dangers. Reasonable concern about dogs and insects may help us avoid a nip now and then. However, when fears are excessive in relation to the amount of actual danger and prevent us from meeting the demands of our everyday lives, they are labeled **phobias.**

Fear of Strangers Many but not all children develop fear of strangers. By 4 or 5 months, infants show more smiling in response to their mothers than to strangers. But they may spend more time looking at strangers, presumably because of their novelty (Emde et al., 1976). At this age infants may compare the faces of strangers and their mothers, looking back and forth. At about 5 to 7 months, many infants show the beginnings of fear. Their gazes take on a sober, concerned appearance. And at about 7 to 9 months they begin to show frank distress by crying, whimpering, gazing fearfully, and arching their backs.

Securely attached children frequently use their mothers as a base for exploration. Children who have developed fear of strangers similarly show less distress in response to strangers when their mothers are present. Babies are less likely to show fear of strangers when they are sitting on their mothers' laps than when they are placed in infant seats a few feet away (Morgan & Ricciuti, 1969). Alan Sroufe and his colleagues (1974) also found that children are less likely to show fear of strangers when they in familiar surroundings, such as their homes, rather than in the laboratory.

In terms of proximity, the fear response is the mirror image of attachment. Children attempt to remain near people to whom they are attached. However, the closer they are to strangers, the greater their signs of distress (Lewis & Brooks, 1974). They are most distressed when the strangers touch them. For this reason, if you find yourself in a situation in which you are trying to comfort an infant who does not know you, it may be more effective to talk in a friendly and soothing manner *from a distance.* Reconsider rushing in and picking the child up.

When you see an unfamiliar child, also note that the way in which you behave can make a difference. Ross and Goldman (1977) found that adults who were active and friendly, who gestured, smiled, and offered toys were responded to more positively by 1-year-olds than strangers who were quiet and passive. Demeanor makes a difference.

Some strangers are also more equal than others. A parent once told me that infants can "recognize their own." That is, that they can discriminate between children and adults. Perhaps so. In studies of 7- to 24-month-old infants, Jeanne Brooks and Michael Lewis (Brooks & Lewis, 1976; Lewis & Brooks, 1974) found that the infants responded slightly positively to unfamiliar 4-year-old girls, but negatively to strange adults. In the 1976 study, Brooks and Lewis also found that infants showed negative responses to unfamiliar midgets as well as to unfamiliar full-size adults. Therefore, the critical factor in discriminating adults from children apparently is not size. It may have something to do with signs of maturity, such as facial features and proportions.

Developmental Patterns Young children are most likely to have fears that revolve around imaginary creatures and personal safety (Barnett, 1969). The

► ► ► ►

fantasies of young children frequently involve both stories they are told or read and TV and film images. Frightening images of imaginary creatures can persevere. Many young children are reluctant to have the lights put out at night because of fear that these creatures may harm them in the dark. In a sense, fears of imaginary creatures also involve personal safety.

But there are also real objects and situations that cause many children to fear for their personal safety: lightning; thunder and other loud noises; the dark; high places; sharp objects and being cut; blood; people who are unfamiliar, deformed, or who act strangely; stinging and crawling insects; other animals; and on and on. Some of these objects are also frightening because of their aversiveness, even when they are not direct threats. Children may not expect to be hurt by thunder or worms, but they may still view them as awful.

As children develop from middle childhood toward adolescence, they become less fearful of imaginary creatures and threats to personal safety. They grow more fearful of threats in school and social relationships (Barnett, 1969; Kendall & Williams, 1981). As children approach their teens, they become more fearful about whether they will be accepted by peers, about whether they will fit into the crowd. Fears of social scrutiny include fear of talking in front of the class, of making errors on tests, and of earning the disapproval of the teacher.

Helping Children Cope with Fears

A number of methods have been developed to help children cope with irrational, debilitating fears. Professionals who work with children today are most likely to use such behavior-modification methods as *desensitization, participant modeling,* and *operant conditioning* (Johnson & Melamed, 1979). Each of them is based on the principles of learning discussed in Chapter 2.

Desensitization **Desensitization** is based on principles of classical conditioning. The desensitization techniques used today are quite similar to the method used by Harold and Mary Cover Jones in the 1920s (see the nearby box, "Chocolate Chip Cookie Therapy?"). In desensitization, children are exposed gradually to the sources of their fears while they are engaging in behavior that is incompatible with feelings of fear. Fear includes bodily responses such as rapid heart rate and respiration rate. So by doing things that reduce the heart and respiration rates, children are doing something that is incompatible with fear.

A favorite desensitization technique with adults involves the progressive relaxation of muscle groups throughout the body. This technique has also been used with older children, but other techniques may be more effective with younger children, such as giving the child a treat (as the Joneses did), playing with a game or favorite toy, or asking the child to talk about a favorite book or TV hero (Johnson & Melamed, 1979).

In desensitization, the parent or helping professional brings the child gradually into closer contact with the feared object or situation, while the child remains relaxed. An excellent way to bring a child into gradual contact with a large mature dog, for instance, is to give the child a puppy. Children will frequently do things in the company of their parents that they would be afraid to do alone. Therefore, it may be helpful to desensitize a child to a new situation, such as a day-care center, by initially attending with the child. Then the parent can depart progressively earlier.

Desensitization A process in which one loses irrational fear of anxiety-evoking objects by gradually approaching them in fantasy or in real life.

▶ ▶ ▶ ▶

Chocolate Chip Cookie Therapy?

▷
▷
▷
▷
▷   Afraid of heights? Perhaps you should try munching away on nachos or double-fudge ice cream while you climb the stairs.

John Watson and Rosalie Rayner (1920) taught Little Albert to fear a rat by clanging steel bars behind his head while he played with the animal. Sad to say, they never taught him to unlearn his fear.

But just a few years later, University of California professors Harold Jones and Mary Cover Jones (Jones, 1924; Jones & Jones, 1928) tried a reversal of the Watson and Rayner technique. They reasoned that if fears could be *conditioned* by painful circumstances, then perhaps fears could be *counterconditioned* by pleasant experiences.

The Joneses tested their hypothesis on a 2-year-old boy named Peter. Peter feared rabbits intensely. He cried and whined in their presence and tried to escape. The Joneses decided that Peter would "confront" his fear—that is, approach the rabbit—but not all at once. In their search for a starting point, they noted that Peter could tolerate a rabbit that was being kept safely across the room. It also helped if Peter were engaging in some of his favorite activities at the time, like munching merrily away on candy and cookies. Peter, to be sure, cast a wary eye in the rabbit's direction, but he continued to eat.

Gradually the animal was brought closer. The Joneses suspected that if they brought the rabbit too close too quickly, the cookies left on Peter's plate, and those already eaten, might have decorated the walls. But gradually the animal could be brought nearer without upsetting the boy. Eventually Peter could eat and touch the rabbit at the same time.

The Joneses theorized that the pleasure of eating was incompatible with feelings of fear. Therefore, by bringing the rabbit gradually closer while Peter was eating, the boy had managed to countercondition progressively larger amounts of fear at each step along the way.

No, I don't know how much weight and how many cavities Peter acquired while overcoming his fear of rabbits.

Participant Modeling   **Participant modeling** is based on principles of observational learning. In participant modeling, children first observe models (ideally children similar in age) engage in the behavior that evokes fear. Then they imitate the behavior of the models. Models may be live or filmed or videotaped.

Observing the models is thought to have a number of positive effects. First, it shows children how to act in the situations, or interact with the objects, that evoke fear. Second, it communicates the idea that the object or situation is not so dreadful. Third, observing others engage in feared activities without negative results *may* extinguish some of the observer's own fear. Fourth, it may help motivate children to try to engage in the observed activities themselves.

In an often-cited experiment on participant modeling, Albert Bandura and his colleagues (1969) found that participant modeling is as effective as desensitization for people who are afraid of snakes. It also works more rapidly

Participant modeling A process in which one loses irrational fear of anxiety-evoking objects by first observing models interact with them and then imitating the models.

▶ ▶ ▶ ▶

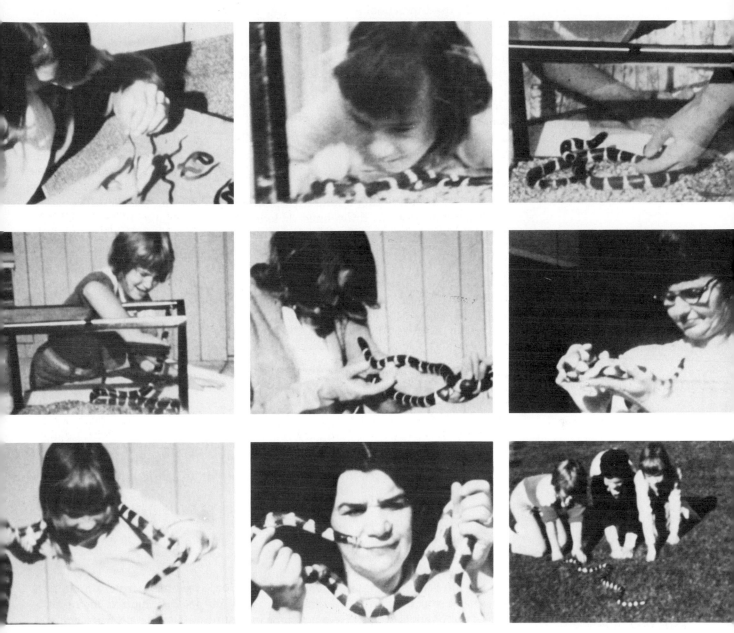

Figure 10.6 Participant Modeling
Participant modeling helps children overcome fears through principles of observational learning.
In this method, children first observe, then imitate, people who are not afraid to handle aversive
stimuli. Parents also often try to convince children that something tastes good by eating it in
front of them and saying "Mmm!"

than desensitization. Figure 10.6 shows a number of children and adults in the Bandura study who observed and then imitated the behavior of models who were unafraid of snakes.

Philip Kendall and Carolyn Williams (1981) note that videotaped models could be used in school systems and on TV programs to "immunize" children against commonly occurring fears, such as trips to the dentist, routine medical examinations, and entering school. Some programs, such as *Sesame Street*, portray children coping with the potentially stressful experiences of handling animals, making new friends, and going to a new school, among others.

Operant Techniques Operant techniques are based on principles of operant conditioning. In operant conditioning, children are guided into desirable behaviors, then reinforced for engaging in them. Reinforcement increases the frequency of desired behavior. Behavior modification in the classroom is an example of the use of operant techniques. In this method good (desired) behavior is reinforced, and misbehavior is ignored.

Parents and other adults use operant techniques all the time. They may teach children how to draw lines or letters of the alphabet by guiding their hands and saying "Good!" when the desired result is obtained. When children fear touching a dog, parents frequently take their hands and guide them physically in petting the animals. Then they say something reinforcing such as, "Look at that big boy/girl petting that doggy!" or "Isn't the puppy nice and soft and warm?" Parents also physically guide their children in the use of tricycles or slides when they show fear. Then parents say "You did it!" when the children make some show of handling the apparatus.

The Effects of Social Deprivation

The importance of meeting children's material needs is self-evident. However, the development of their social skills and emotional responses is also important. Children reared in orphanages and other institutions where they have not suffered materially, but have received little social stimulation, show retarded social and intellectual development (Spitz & Wolff, 1946; Provence & Lipton, 1962).

Experiments with Animals

Studies of children reared under deprived circumstances are limited in that they are correlational. In other words, family factors that led to the children's deprivation or to their placement in institutions may also have contributed to their developmental problems. Ethical considerations prevent us from conducting experiments in which we randomly assign children to social deprivation. However, experiments of this kind have been undertaken with dogs and rhesus monkeys. Their results are consistent with those of the correlational studies of children.

▶ ▶ ▶ ▶

Experiments with Dogs Melzack and Thompson (1956) separated a number of Scotch terriers from their mothers as soon as they were weaned. From that time on, the dogs were reared in pens isolated from other dogs and people. They had no opportunity to interact with people, even when their food and water trays were filled or their wastes were removed. Control animals lived in group pens in the laboratory or were reared as pets with human families.

As compared to the controls, the isolated dogs at the ages of 7 to 10 months showed deficits in their social and emotional responses. When placed with a control dog in a room with one food bowl, the control animal pushed aside the experimental animal on almost every trial. When exposed to unfamiliar objects such as a balloon being filled with air or a human skull, control animals ran away. About a year later the control animals growled and barked and snapped at strange objects, frequently in a playful manner. When exposed to the unfamiliar objects as pups, the experimental animals whined and showed other signs of distress and agitation. However, they made no systematic effort to move away from them. A year later, they were more likely than the control animals to become agitated and run away from the objects.

Experiments with Rhesus Monkeys As noted earlier, Harry Harlow and his colleagues conducted a number of studies of rhesus monkeys who were "reared by" wire-mesh and terry-cloth surrogate mothers. In later studies rhesus monkeys were reared even without even this questionable "social" support. Their food and water were provided, and their wastes removed, by mechanical means. The lighting in their cages was diffuse. The infant monkeys were even insulated from sounds other than their own.

Harlow (1965; Harlow & Harlow, 1970) found that rhesus infants reared in this most solitary confinement later avoided contact with other monkeys. They did not engage in the characteristic playful chasing and romping. Instead, they cowered in their presence and failed to respond to others. Nor did they make any effort to fend off attacks by other monkeys. Rather, they withdrew into themselves, as evidenced by a stereotypical huddling posture and rocking. If they did any biting in response to attack, they bit themselves. In short, they showed arousal and agitation in response to aggression, but this emotional response was not channeled into effective social behavior.

As adults, socially deprived rhesus males showed little interest in approaching sexually receptive females. Socially deprived rhesus females seemed equally unimpressed with any show of attention by adult males, even when they were in **estrus.** If "motherless mothers" later had children of their own, they tended to ignore or abuse them (Ruppenthal et al., 1976). In some cases they bit, chewed, or crushed their offspring. In no instances were there signs of attachment.

There seems to be a link between the amount of time an infant rhesus monkey has been deprived and its capacity to recover from deprivation. Monkeys reared without social stimulation for the first three months tend to adjust rapidly when placed in a community cage. But if they have been isolated for six months or more, they tend to sit clutching themselves and rocking back and forth in corners. When monkeys have been reared in isolation for twelve months, they

Estrus The periodic sexual excitement of many female mammals, during which they are receptive to advances by males.

▶ ▶ ▶ ▶

Figure 10.7 Monkey "Therapists"
In the top photo, a 3- to 4-month-old rhesus monkey "therapist" tries to soothe a monkey who was reared in social isolation. The deprived monkey remains withdrawn. She clutches herself into a ball and rocks back and forth. The bottom photo was taken several weeks afterward and shows that deprived monkeys given young "therapists" can learn to play and to adjust to community life. Socially withdrawn preschoolers have similarly profited from exposure to younger peers.

► ► ► ►

. . . are very seriously affected. Even primitive and simple play activity is almost nonexistent. With these isolated animals, no social play is observed and aggressive behavior is never demonstrated. Their behavior is a pitiful combination of apathy and terror as they crouch at the sides of the room, meekly accepting the attacks of the more healthy control monkeys (Harlow & Harlow, 1970, p. 95).

Efforts have been made to learn whether the damage done by social deprivation can be overcome. When monkeys deprived for six months or more are placed with older monkeys, they tend to remain socially withdrawn and apathetic (Erwin et al., 1974). But Suomi and Harlow (1972) found that deprived monkeys placed with younger, 3- to 4-month-old females for a couple of hours a day show greater likelihood of recovery (Figure 10.7). They may ignore the younger monkeys at first, even abuse them. But when the younger monkeys persist in their efforts to initiate social interaction with their deprived elders, many of the deprived monkeys begin to play with the youngsters after a few weeks. Many of them eventually expand their social contacts to rhesus monkeys of various ages and both sexes.

Perhaps of greater interest is the finding that socially withdrawn 4- and 5-year-old children make gains in their social and emotional development when they are provided with younger playmates (Furman et al., 1979).

Studies with Children

As noted, there are no experiments in which children have been subjected to conditions such as those in the studies with dogs and monkeys. But investigators of child development such as John Bowlby and René Spitz have reported that institutionalized children whose material needs are met nevertheless encounter problems in their physical, intellectual, social, and emotional development. Spitz (1965) noted that many institutionalized children appear to develop a syndrome characterized by withdrawal and depression. They show progressively less interest in their worlds and become progressively inactive. Some of them die.

Consider a report of life in one institution (Provence & Lipton, 1962). Infants were maintained in separate cubicles for most of their first year, in order to ward off infectious diseases. Adults tended to them only to feed and change them. As a rule, baby bottles were propped up in the infants' cribs. Attendants rarely responded to the babies' cries. The infants were rarely played with or spoken to.

By the age of 4 months, the infants in this institution showed little interest in adults. They rarely tried to gain their attention, even when in distress. A few months later, some of them sat withdrawn in their cribs and rocked back and forth, almost like Harlow's monkeys. Language deficiencies were striking. As the first year progressed, little babbling was heard within the infants' cubicles. None was speaking even one word at 12 months.

How Do We Explain the Deficits of Socially Deprived Children? Why do children whose material needs are met show such dramatic deficiencies? Is it because they do not receive the love and affection of a mother or of a stable surrogate mother? Or is it that they do not receive adequate sensory or social stimulation?

▶ ▶ ▶ ▶

The answer may in part depend on the age of the child. Studies by Leon Yarrow and his colleagues (1971; Yarrow & Goodwin, 1973) suggest that deficiencies in sensory stimulation and in social interaction may cause more problems than lack of love in infants who are too young to have developed specific attachments. However, once infants have developed specific attachments, separation from their primary caregivers can lead to major problems.

In the first study, the development of 53 adopted children was followed over a ten-year period (Yarrow et al., 1971). The researchers compared the development of three subgroups: (1) children who were transferred to their permanent adoptive homes almost immediately after birth; (2) children who were given temporary foster mothers and then transferred to permanent adoptive homes before they were 6 months old; and (3) children who were transferred from temporary foster mothers to their permanent adoptive homes after they were 6 months old. At the age of 10, children in the first two groups showed no differences in social and emotional development. However, children in the third group showed significantly less ability to relate to other people. Perhaps their deficits are to be traced to being separated from their initial foster mothers, after they had become attached to them.

In the second study, Yarrow and Goodwin (1973) followed the development of 70 adopted children who were separated from temporary foster parents between birth and the age of 16 months. The authors found strong correlations between the age at which the children were separated and feeding and sleeping problems, decreased social responsiveness, and extremes in attachment behaviors (see Figure 10.8). Disturbed attachment behaviors included

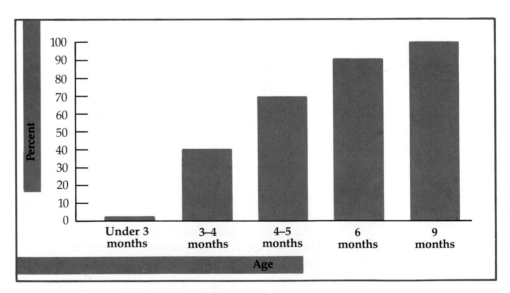

Figure 10.8 The Development of Adopted Children Separated from Temporary Foster Parents
The older the child at time of separation, the more likely it was that behavioral disturbances would occur.

▶ ▶ ▶ ▶

10 SOCIAL AND EMOTIONAL DEVELOPMENT

excessive clinging to the new mother and violent rejection of her. None of the children who were separated from the initial foster mothers prior to the age of 3 months showed moderate or severe disturbances. *All* of the children who were separated at 9 months or older did show such disturbances. From 40 to 90 percent of the children separated between the ages of 3 and 9 months showed moderate to severe disturbances. The incidence of problems increased as the age advanced.

The Yarrow studies suggest that babies in institutions may require general sensory and social stimulation more than they need a specific relationship with a primary caregiver, at least up to the age of 3 months or so. After the age of 3 months, some disturbance is likely, if there is instability in the caregiving staff. By the ages of 6 to 9 months, disturbance seems to be guaranteed, if there is instability in the position of primary caregiver. Fortunately, there is also evidence that children show some capacity to recover from early social deprivation.

The Capacity to Recover from Social Deprivation   Studies with animals and children do show that early social deprivation is linked to developmental deficits. However, other studies suggest that infants also have powerful capacities to recover from deprivation.

Kagan and Klein (1973) report that many children may be able to recover fully from 13 or 14 months of deprivation. The natives in an isolated Guatemalan village believe that fresh air and sunshine will make children ill. Children are thus kept in windowless huts until they can walk. They are also played with infrequently. During their isolation, the children behave apathetically, and they are physically and socially retarded when they start to walk. However, by the age of 3 they are as well coordinated as other children. By the age of 10 they show no social or intellectual deficits when compared with U.S. children of the same age (Kagan, 1972).

The Skeels and Dye (1939) study of retarded orphanage children, referred to in Chapter 9, also provides dramatic evidence of the ability of children to recover from social deprivation. In this study a group of 19-month-old children was placed in the care of older institutionalized girls who spent a great deal of time playing with, talking to, and generally nurturing them. This placement occurred many months past the age at which specific attachments develop. However, four years after being placed with the girls, the "retarded" children made dramatic gains in intelligence-test scores, whereas children remaining in the orphanage showed declines in IQ scores.

The children placed in the care of the older girls also appeared to be generally well adjusted. By the time Skeels reported on their progress in 1966, most were married and were rearing children of their own. Their children showed no intellectual or social deficits. Sad to say, many of the children who had been left in the orphanage were still in some type of institutional setting. Few of them had "caught up" in their social and emotional development. Few were functioning as independent adults.

The good news is that many children who have been exposed to early social deprivation can catch up in their social and emotional development and lead normal adult lives. The bad news seems to be that society has not yet allocated the resources to give all children the opportunity to do so.

▶ ▶ ▶ ▶

Summary

1. Attachment is the affectional tie that persons form between themselves and specific others "that binds them together in space and endures over time." Attachment in young children is measured by their efforts to maintain contact or proximity with caregivers and their display of separation anxiety.

2. Mary Ainsworth has developed the Strange Situation method to measure attachment in infants. In this method, infants are observed during a series of separations from parents, reunions, and exposures to strangers.

3. Ainsworth notes patterns of secure and insecure attachment. Securely attached infants seek interaction with caregivers after they have been separated from them and do not resist being held. Insecurely attached infants include avoidant and resistant infants. In avoidant attachment, infants show little interest in caregivers' efforts to interact with them and hold them. Children with resistant attachments show mixed feelings, frequently violently resisting caregivers' efforts to hold or cuddle them.

4. Securely attached infants are more likely than others to interact affectionately with their primary caregivers and to use them as a base for exploration. They are also less likely to cry. Securely attached infants are later happier, more socially active, and more self-reliant in school. Individual patterns of attachment can change as family conditions and interpersonal relationships change.

5. A common pattern of three phases of attachment has been identified: From birth to 3 months infants show indiscriminate attachment. At about 3 or 4 months they select familiar figures over strangers. At 6 or 7 months attachment becomes more clear cut, as characterized by intensified dependence on the primary caregiver.

6. There are many theoretical views of attachment. The neonate's sensitivities to the odor of the mother's milk and the sound of the mother's voice may promote attachment. Some babies, referred to as "cuddlers," may be more temperamentally predisposed to forming attachments than others. Cognitive theorists note that children must have some form of object permanence before developing specific attachments. Behaviorists view mothers as conditioned reinforcers who acquire their reinforcement value mainly by meeting the baby's basic need for food. The Harlows suggest that contact comfort is a more basic motive for attachment. Ethologists suggest that attachment is a fixed action pattern that can be triggered by a releasing stimulus during a critical period. Infant smiling is an innate response to various forms of social interaction and appears to promote attachment.

7. Babies become attached to fathers at about the same time they become attached to mothers, although they generally spend less time with their fathers and their mothers are more likely to be the ones who meet their routine needs. Babies seem to prefer to be with their mothers under stressful conditions, but not necessarily for play.

8. Day care has not been shown to impair mother–child bonds of attachment. Children in full-time day care are more peer-oriented than children cared for in the home, but they are also more aggressive and impulsive.

▶ ▶ ▶ ▶

9. Children reared in the kibbutz become attached to their metapelets as well as their parents, and their relationships with their parents are generally cordial.

10. Many factors appear to contribute to child abuse: situational stress, a history of abuse in the abusers' families of origin, acceptance of violence as normal, and failure to develop a strong attachment to one's children.

11. Children start to push strongly for independence by the end of the second year. Executive dependence is reliance on others to meet instrumental needs. Affectional dependence is reliance on others for affection, acceptance, and approval. Overindulgence does not necessarily make children more dependent.

12. Play contributes to social and emotional development. Parten's classic study chronicled the transitions from nonsocial to social play. She noted several types of play, including solitary, onlooker, parallel, associative, and cooperative play.

13. The onset of dramatic or pretend play coincides with symbolic thought. Dramatic play includes imaginary friends and cooperative play in which children take on and enact various social roles. Dramatic play permits children to practice social roles, develop empathy for others, and express fears and fantasies.

14. Theories of emotional development fall into two camps: (a) Bridges and Sroufe propose that diffuse excitement is present at birth and differentiates according to the child's cognitive development and social interactions. (b) Izard and others propose that several discrete emotions are present at birth, even if they are not all shown at once.

15. Most children have at least some fears. Young children most often have fears of imaginary creatures and concerns about personal safety, whereas older children develop social- and school-related fears.

16. Experiments with animals and studies with humans show that severe social and emotional deficits may develop when children's material needs are met but they are socially deprived. Socially deprived rhesus monkeys avoid other monkeys, fail to fend off aggression, show ineffectual sexual responses, and neglect or abuse their offspring. The longer monkeys are deprived, the harder it is for them to overcome deficits, but even monkeys deprived for six months frequently overcome deficits when exposed to the persistent social stimulation of younger monkeys. Exposure to younger children has also fostered the social development of socially withdrawn preschoolers.

17. Socially deprived children are frequently withdrawn and apathetic. It appears that babies need sensory stimulation and social interaction, and that after the age of 3 months or so it becomes relatively more important that there be stability in the role of primary caregiver. Children can also frequently recover from early social deprivation. Evidence is derived from examples such as the recovery of Guatemalan children who are isolated for the first 13 to 14 months, and the progress of the orphans in the Skeels and Dye study once they were placed with older girls.

▶ ▶ ▶ ▶

All children develop fear of strangers at some point during the second six months of infancy. False. Many children never develop fear of strangers.

Children are less likely to be securely attached to abusive or neglectful parents. True. Children more often show signs of *in*-secure attachment to abusive and neglectful parents.

An infant's willingness to leave the mother in order to explore the environment is a sign of secure attachment. True.

You can predict how strongly babies are attached to their fathers if you know how many diapers per week the father changes. True. The "diaper index" provides a rough measure of a father's involvement with his children.

Children must become attached to their parents before a critical period elapses, or else bonds of attachment will not form properly. False. This view is consistent with ethological theory, but is not borne out by evidence.

Children become attached to their mothers earlier than they become attached to their fathers. False. Despite the Freudian view of the special early importance of the mother, children appear to become attached to both parents at about the same time.

Blind babies do not smile. False; they do. Smiling appears to be an inborn behavior pattern that emerges at a certain age.

Children placed in day care become less attached to their mothers than children who are cared for in the home. False. The quality of the mother–child relationship seems to be a more central factor than the number of hours spent together.

Children placed in full-time day care are more aggressive than children who are cared for in the home. True. Perhaps relatively less individual attention, or greater exposure to peers, encourages them to become more aggressive in meeting their needs.

Child abusers have frequently been the victims of child abuse themselves. True. Many child abusers have been exposed to violent role models.

Children who are highly indulged by their mothers during the first year of life become dependent. False. It appears that the promotion of feelings of security during the first year can actually help foster independent behavior later on.

Imaginary friends are a sign that children are lonely or poorly adjusted. False. Imaginary friends are a perfectly normal type of dramatic or "pretend" play.

At the age of 2 or 3, children are frequently afraid of imaginary creatures. True. They are also frequently concerned about their personal safety.

Adopted children are less likely to experience disturbance if they are transferred to their permanent adoptive homes within three months after birth. True. At this early age they will not yet have developed specific attachments.

▶ ▶ ▶ ▶

11

Socialization Influences

CHAPTER ▶ OUTLINE

- Truth or Fiction?
- Family Influences
  Dimensions of Child Rearing   Ways in Which Parents Enforce Restrictions
  Baumrind's Typology of Patterns of Child Rearing   Fostering Achievement
  Motivation
  The Influence of Siblings   The Effects of Family Size   The Effects of Birth Order
  The Effects of Single-Parent Families   The Children of Divorce
- Peer Influences
  Development of Friendships   Conformist Tendencies   Peer Acceptance   Peers as
  Socialization Influences
- School Influences
  The Effects of the School Environment   The Effects of Open versus Traditional
  Approaches to Education   Teachers   Mainstreaming
- Summary
- Truth or Fiction Revisited

T R U T H ▸ O R ▸ F I C T I O N ?

- Trying to "reason" with children is the least effective way of fostering self-control.
- Children with strict parents are more likely than children with permissive parents to have high self-esteem.
- Parents who make high demands on their children to achieve are most likely to foster achievement motivation.
- Children from large families do not perform as well in school as children from small families.
- First-born children tend to show higher achievement motivation than later-born children.
- Later-born children tend to be more sociable than first-born children.
- Divorce is harder on young children than on adolescents.
- About 90 percent of children of divorced parents live with their mothers.
- Regular visits with their natural mothers are associated with poorer relationships between stepdaughters and their stepmothers.
- The majority of divorced fathers do not keep up with their child-support payments.
- The daughters of working women are more achievement oriented and set themselves higher career goals than the daughters of nonworking women.
- Physically attractive children are more popular with their peers.
- Children willingly accept friends from different races and social classes.
- Aggressive children tend to be looked up to by their peers.
- Children who are allowed to make many of their own decisions in the classroom tend to goof off and achieve less.
- Teachers should avoid praising some children for their accomplishments.
- Teachers who have high expectations of students frequently elicit greater achievements from them.

I must confess that my wife and I were not ready for **sibling rivalry**. With a bit of luck we managed to have two of our girls almost exactly two years apart. We spent months preparing Allyn for the appearance of the baby who turned out to be her sister, Jordan. We described all the things they would be able to do together as Jordan developed. We encouraged Allyn to touch her mother's abdomen, so that she could feel Jordan's movements in the later months of pregnancy.

For the first few weeks after Jordan was born, Allyn seemed interested and affectionate enough. She would observe us closely as we fed and changed Jordan. She also showed tolerance when we had to interrupt playing with her to pick up a waking or crying Jordan. But after a couple of months had passed, Allyn began to complain and cry when we attended to Jordan. When we brought Jordan into the room, she would say "No!" or "I don't want to see her!" or "Put her down!" Later, when Jordan was grasping objects and toys, Allyn would yell "No, Jordan!" and grab them away from her. Still later, when Jordan was creeping to get toys, Allyn would run in front of her and grab them away. Sometimes she would say, "That's mine!" Now and then she would try to hit Jordan.

Two-year-olds are not terribly consistent. Allyn would also hug and kiss Jordan and give her things from time to time. But when Allyn was hungry, or tired, or cranky for other reasons, we would hear that "No, Jordan!" and have to rescue Jordan again. The word "rescue" sounds dramatic, but I think that it is accurate.

Of course, we did not stand idly by while all this took place. We did not step in *only* to replace a toy that Allyn had taken away, or only to prevent Allyn from hurting Jordan. We also tried persistently to reward Allyn for affectionate behavior and to discourage harmful behavior. I went so far as to read the literature on child development. As a result, we explained repeatedly to her *why* she should be nicer to Jordan. We made our exhortations on both an emotional and intellectual plane. Although we praised Allyn for sharing her toys with Jordan and for showering her with affection, it was not possible to follow the behavior-modification approach outlined in Chapter 2: We could not afford to ignore Allyn's bad behavior and simply focus on reinforcing her good behavior. If we had ignored her bad behavior, it is not certain that there would have been much good behavior to reinforce—or that Jordan would still be with us.

I suppose that we stumbled through most of the ways in which families socialize children—teaching, prodding, encouraging, rewarding, and setting firm limits. Socialization becomes a daily way of relating to children, of guiding them physically and verbally, of rewarding and punishing them so that they will increasingly conform their behavior to what their families consider right, decent, and proper. Through socialization, families attempt to influence their children to meet most or all of the goals listed in Table 11.1.

The family is not the only socialization influence on the child. Peers, schools, religious institutions, clubs, and, when necessary, social-welfare and criminal-justice agencies, also play a role. In this chapter we focus on three major socialization influences: family, peers, and schools.

▶ ▶ ▶ ▶

Table 11.1 Behavior Patterns That Parents and Other Socialization
Influences Attempt to Foster in Children

Eating foods that are nourishing and healthful
Regulating cycles of sleeping and wakefulness to conform to family norms
Inhibiting reflexes that cause the elimination of waste products
Keeping out of danger
Dressing themselves
Washing and brushing themselves
Keeping some sort of order to their toys or rooms
Protecting the property of the family and others from damage
Decreasing egocentrism and developing concern for the feelings of others
Developing a sense of right and wrong
Adopting cultural and familial goals and values
Conforming to cultural and subcultural (e.g., neighborhood) ways of dressing, talking, and
   relating to others
Participating in family life
Developing relationships with peers and adults who will help perpetuate these goals and values
Acquiring skills and knowledge in school and in other important social institutions
Establishing long-range personal goals that are consistent with parental values and social reality

Family Influences

Young children usually spend most of their time within the family. Even when both parents work and children have babysitters or attend preschool programs, parents usually attempt to choose caregivers whose behavior will be compatible with their own values and goals.

According to Robert Sears, Eleanor Maccoby, and Harry Levin (1957) in their classic study of *Patterns of Child Rearing*, most parents have reasonably similar socialization goals. They want their children to develop a sense of responsibility and to conform to family routines. And they try to prevent children from damaging property. But parents have different temperaments, values, and socialization experiences of their own. And so they also have different approaches to socializing their children.

In this section we first explore parental approaches to socialization. Then we examine the influences of family size, birth order, and siblings, and the effects of change in the family structure. We dwell particularly on the effects of working mothers, divorce, and single-parent families on socialization.

Dimensions of Child Rearing

Investigators of parental approaches to child rearing have found it useful to classify them according to two broad dimensions: warmth–coldness, and restrictiveness–permissiveness. As suggested by Figure 11.1, warm parents can also be restrictive or permissive. So can cold parents.

Warmth–Coldness Whether or not parents respond to their children with warmth, love, and affection usually reflects their feelings toward their children,

▶ ▶ ▶ ▶

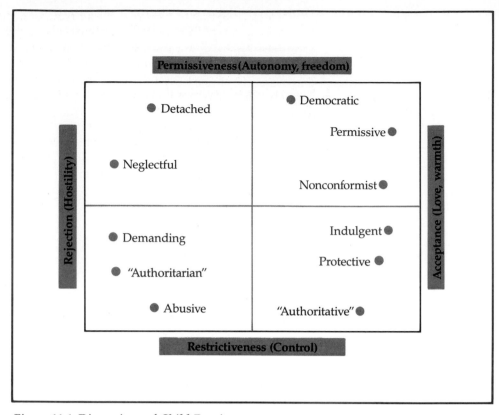

Figure 11.1 Dimensions of Child Rearing
The child-rearing dimensions of warmth–coldness and restrictiveness–permissiveness are
independent. That is, warm parents can be either restrictive or permissive. The same is true
of cold parents.

not a philosophy of child rearing. Warm parents are affectionate toward their children. They tend to hug and kiss them, and to smile at them frequently. Warm parents generally behave in ways that communicate their happiness at having children and their enjoyment in being with them (Sears et al., 1957).

Cold parents may not enjoy being with their children and may have few feelings of affection for them. They are likely to complain about their children's behavior, saying that they are naughty or have "minds of their own." Warm parents may also say that their children have "minds of their own," but they are frequently proud of and entertained by their children's stubborn behavior. Even when they are irked by it, they usually focus on attempting to change it, instead of rejecting the children outright.

It requires no stretch of the imagination to conclude that warmth is superior to coldness in rearing children. Children of parents who are accepting and warm show fewer behavior problems (Martin, 1975). They are also more likely to develop goals and values similar to their parents' than are children of cold, rejecting parents (Martin, 1975). Maternal affection, when combined with intellectually stimulating mothering, also appears to contribute to competence (Pettit & Bates, 1984), a subject we shall elaborate upon below.

▶ ▶ ▶ ▶

Restrictiveness–Permissiveness Parents must generally decide how restrictive they will be toward many of their children's behavior patterns. Consider just a brief list: diet, making excessive noise (screaming, screeching, demanding attention) when other children are sleeping or people are trying to converse, playing with dangerous objects or in dangerous areas, damaging property, keeping their rooms and other areas neat, aggression, nudity, and masturbation.

Parents who are highly restrictive tend to impose many rules and to watch their children closely (Sears et al., 1957). Parents who are restictive about one thing also tend to be restrictive about others. But some parents may focus on proprieties—cleanliness, manners (for example, saying "please" and keeping elbows off the table), and sexual behavior—while others are more concerned about grades in school. Restrictive parents generally do not allow their children to run nude or to masturbate.

Permissive parents impose few if any rules and supervise their children less closely. As a group, they are less concerned about cleanliness. They allow their children to do what is "natural"—to make noise, treat the objects in their playspaces carelessly (although they may also extensively "child-proof" their homes to prevent their children from getting hurt and to protect the furniture), and to experiment or play with their own bodies. They may also allow their children to show a good deal of aggression, intervening only when another child appears to be in serious danger—if then.

Parents may be permissive for different reasons. Some parents believe that children need the freedom to express their natural urges, if they are to become self-directed and psychologically healthy. Others may be disinterested in their children and uninvolved.

Ways in Which Parents Enforce Restrictions

Regardless of their general approaches to child rearing, most if not all parents are restrictive now and then, even if only when they are teaching their children not to run into the street or to touch the stove. However, parents use different techniques in restricting their children's behavior. In this section we describe the methods of *induction*, *power-assertion*, and *loss of love*.

Inductive Techniques **Inductive** methods attempt to provide children with knowledge that will enable them to generate desirable behavior patterns in similar situations. The major inductive technique is "reasoning," or explaining why one sort of behavior is good and another is not. Parents who rely on induction may bend over backwards in trying to avoid being arbitrary. They may also make the effort to praise their children for desirable behavior.

"Reasoning" with a 1- or 2-year-old can be primitive. "Don't do that—it hurts!" qualifies as reasoning when children are very young. After all, "It hurts!" is an explanation, if brief. "If you don't get to sleep, you'll be very tired tomorrow" also qualifies as reasoning. So does "No more peanuts—you'll get a tummy ache" (not to mention a diaper filled with pieces of peanuts).

One- and 2-year-olds may not understand all words, or may not perceive the words and ideas quite as their parents intend them. Parents are also often frustrated by young children's brief attention spans and by their interrupting explanations with tears or other distracters. Fortunately, children's abil-

most effective in fostering self-control + empathy

Inductive *Characteristic of disciplinary methods that attempt to foster an understanding of the principles behind parental demands—for example, "reasoning" with children.*

▶ ▶ ▶ ▶

Inductive methods for enforcing restrictions attempt to teach children the principles that they should use in guiding their own behavior. This mother is using the inductive technique of reasoning.

ity to understand parental explanations such as "No! If you do that you'll get hurt!" blossoms along with their abilities to run around and do those potentially harmful things.

Power-Assertive Methods Other parents use power or coercion. They tend to believe in physical rewards and punishments. They may give their children presents or special desserts when they are good and spank them when they are not. They often justify physical punishments through aphorisms such as "Spare the rod, and spoil the child." Power-assertive parents also tend to yell at their children, rather than reason with them.

A study of abusive mothers found that they used more power-assertive techniques than controls (Oldershaw et al., 1986). They issued more commands, were less flexible, were more intrusive, and more inconsistent in their use of parenting techniques than nonabusive mothers. In turn, their children were more noncompliant than the children of control mothers.

Power-assertive parents sometimes argue that their approach is necessary precisely because their children are noncompliant. In many cases it is unclear which came first—power-assertion methods or children's noncompliance. However, power-assertion and noncompliance can clearly escalate into a (literally) vicious cycle. But it should also be noted that power-assertive parents are not invariably abusive. Many of them carefully limit the extent of their punishments.

Loss of Love Still other parents attempt to control their children by threatening them with loss of love. They tend to isolate or ignore their children when they

▶ ▶ ▶ ▶

misbehave. At other times they express great disappointment. Since most children have strong needs for approval and for physical contact with their parents, loss of love can be more threatening than physical punishment.

The literature is not consistent on the effects of these different approaches toward enforcing social demands. It seems that few parents use the same approach all the time (I wish I could say that I had been more consistent over the years!). In many families, parents may be split as to which approach to use. Also, imagine the difficulties of creating experimental treatments in which parents consistently use only one form of enforcement. Imagine the difficulties of recruiting parents to respond to children in ways that are inconsistent with their own philosophies. Because of these problems, research concerning these approaches tends to be correlational and not experimental.

Still, as noted in Chapter 13, there is some evidence that the inductive approach can foster compliance and encourage the development of empathy and self-control. Physical rewards and punishments can modify behavior *in the situations in which they are applied*, but it is questionable that they foster empathy. The evidence concerning the effects of the threat of loss of love largely consists of clinical case studies, and their outcomes are not all that consistent. However, it may be that using loss of love, more than the other approaches, fosters feelings of anxiety and self-uncertainty.

Baumrind's Typology of Patterns of Child Rearing

Diana Baumrind undertook research to determine the socialization patterns of children who show **instrumental competence.** Instrumentally competent children are generally energetic and friendly. They are capable of manipulating their environments to achieve desired effects. Compared to other children, they tend to show self-reliance and independence, high levels of activity, maturity in the formation of goals and achievement orientation, cooperativeness and assertiveness in social relationships, and exploratory behavior. In her search for the pattern that might lead to instrumental competence, Baumrind (1973, 1978; Lamb & Baumrind, 1978) studied four areas of parental behavior: the extent of efforts to influence the behavior of the child; demands for the child to achieve high levels of intellectual, emotional, and social skills; communications ability; and parental warmth and involvement.

One "side effect" of Baumrind's research is very welcome: the creation of a **typology** of restrictive parents. We now have standards that allow us to discriminate among parents who might otherwise be lumped together. Baumrind has found evidence for at least two types of restrictive parents: *authoritative* and *authoritarian.*

Instrumental competence The capacity to manipulate the environment to achieve desired ends.

Typology (type-POLL-oh-gee). The study of types.

Authoritative A child-rearing style in which parents are restrictive and demanding, yet communicative and warm.

Authoritative Parents   The parents of the most instrumentally competent children were rated as high in all four areas of behavior (see Table 11.2). They made strong efforts to control their children (that is, were highly restrictive) and they made strong maturity demands. However, their restrictiveness and demands were accompanied by their ability to reason with their children and by strong support and feelings of love. The parents of the most competent children expected a lot. But they also explained why, and they supported their children. Baumrind labeled these parents **authoritative** to suggest that they knew very clearly what they wanted, but that they were also loving and respectful of their children's points of view.

▶ ▶ ▶ ▶

Table 11.2 Baumrind's Patterns of Parenting

PARENTAL STYLE	PARENTAL BEHAVIOR PATTERNS			
	RESTRICTIVENESS	DEMANDS FOR MATURE BEHAVIOR	COMMUNICATIONS ABILITY	WARMTH AND SUPPORT
Authoritarian	High (Physical punishments)	Moderate	Low	Low
Authoritative	High (Reasoning)	High	High	High
Permissive	Low (Lax)	Low	Low	High
Nonconformist	Low (Purposeful)	Moderate	Moderate	High
Harmonious	?	High	High	High

According to Baumrind, the children of authoritative parents show the greatest instrumental competence, while the children of permissive parents are the least mature.

Authoritarian Parents   **Authoritarian** parents, by contrast, tend to look upon obedience as a virtue to be pursued for its own sake. Authoritarian parents believe in strict guidelines for determining what is right and wrong. They demand that their children accept these guidelines without question. Like authoritative parents, they are controlling. Unlike authoritative parents, their enforcement methods rely on coercion. Moreover, authoritarian parents communicate poorly with their children. They do not respect their children's points of view, and they are cold and rejecting.

In Baumrind's research, the children of authoritarian parents also developed some degree of independence, although other researchers have found them to be less competent socially and academically than children of authoritative parents (Maccoby & Martin, 1983). Children of authoritarian parents also tend to be conflicted and irritable. They are less friendly and spontaneous in their social interactions (Maccoby & Martin, 1983). Perhaps they have learned to be cautious in relating to others.

Permissive versus Nonconformist Parents   Baumrind found two types of parents who were permissive as opposed to restrictive. She labeled one type "permissive" and the other "nonconformist." **Permissive** parents, as their label suggests, were rated low in their attempts to control their children and in their demands for mature behavior. Their brand of permissiveness also tended to cluster with high nurturance (warmth and support) but poor communication ability. The children, in short, were loved and accepted. However, they and their parents did not understand each other very well, and they did pretty much as they wished.

The **nonconformist** parents were also permissive in many ways. But the parents Baumrind labeled "permissive" tended to be disorganized and easygoing. Nonconformist parents, by contrast, were intellectually committed to allowing their children the freedom to develop their own abilities and points of view. Nonconformist parents actually had very high expectations for their children, which they communicated to them. Permissive parents, by contrast, were less involved.

It is not surprising, then, that the children of permissive and nonconformist parents show major differences. By and large, the children of permissive parents seem the least responsible and mature. They are frequently impulsive, moody, and aggressive. As infants they frequently show insecure patterns of attachment (Egeland & Sroufe, 1981). In adolescence, lack of parental monitoring is often linked to delinquency and poor academic performance (Loeb et al., 1980; Martin, 1981; Patterson, 1982; Pulkkinen, 1982).

The *sons* of nonconformist parents show a good deal of independence and a high achievement orientation, according to Baumrind. The daughters of nonconformist parents, however, are similar to those of authoritarian and permissive parents: They have little ambition and are somewhat withdrawn and dependent. I am at a loss to account for this sex difference. Perhaps nonconformist parents somehow impart an activist orientation to their sons, but not to their daughters.

Harmonious Parents   A fifth group of parents was characterized by Baumrind as harmonious. Harmonious parents were high in their demands for mature behavior, their communication ability, and their warmth and support. However, since their children lived up to their expectations and little family friction was generated, there was no basis for rating their restrictiveness.

Baumrind's research does not prove that certain child-rearing patterns *cause* the outcomes described. Children, as we saw in Chapter 2, also come into the world with predispositions toward developing their own personality traits. It could be that authoritativeness and instrumental competence tend to go together for genetic reasons. On the other hand, Baumrind's research suggests that we can make an effort to avoid some of the pitfalls of being authoritarian or overly permissive.

Patterns of Child Rearing and Self-Esteem   Frequently cited research by Stanley Coopersmith (1967) suggests that authoritative parenting may contribute to children's self-esteem. Coopersmith followed a sample of boys throughout the middle childhood years and found that boys with high self-esteem tended to come from homes with parents who were strict and involved, but not harsh or cruel. Parents of boys with low self-esteem were generally permissive, but harsh when exerting discipline.

High demands apparently can lead to competency. Competencies, in turn, contribute to self-esteem, whether they lie in intellectual tasks (Flippo & Lewinsohn, 1971) or in physical skills, such as swimming (Koocher, 1971).

High self-esteem in children is also related to their closeness to their parents, especially as found in father–son and mother–daughter relationships (Dickstein & Posner, 1978; Elrod & Crase, 1980). Close relationships with friends also enhance self-esteem (Mannarino, 1978). When others find children worthy of forming close relationships, apparently the children perceive themselves as worthy.

Self-esteem, once established, seems to endure. Coopersmith found that children's self-esteem remained stable after a three-year interval. Most children will encounter failure, but high self-esteem may contribute to a continuing belief that they can master adversity. Low self-esteem may become a self-fulfilling prophecy: Children with low self-esteem may not carve out much to boast about in life.

▶ ▶ ▶ ▶

We shall explore these issues further in the discussion of achievement motivation.

Fostering Achievement Motivation

Parents foster a desire to achieve beginning at an early age, although the behaviors that qualify as achievement vary as the child develops. Showing the "self-sufficiency" to play by oneself in a playpen for 15 minutes is an "achievement" for a 10-month-old. Putting toys away, not interrupting, avoiding damaging the parents' furniture, using paints and glue in crafts projects, and cleaning up qualify as achievements for a 3-year-old. By the time children are 5 or 6, achievement may take a decidedly more academic turn, with the focus on basic reading and numerical skills. But in each case, children are showing some responsibility or independence. They are acquiring the skills that will eventually allow them to function independently.

There is a saying that "success breeds success." It seems clear that early achievements create the expectancy of success. Positive expectancies, in turn, enhance motivation to perform (Bandura, 1986). So do parental demands. In a study of factors that contribute to achievement in math (Parsons et al., 1982), parents' expectations for success were more predictive than children's past performance or children's expectations. Parental expectations have a way of becoming parental demands, and parental demands for mature behavior and achievement are found throughout the literature on the development of achievement motivation (Baumrind, 1973; Hoffman, 1972; Spence & Helmreich, 1978).

High Demands   In one study of factors that contribute to children's success, Marian Winterbottom (1958) compared mothers of sons with high achievement motivation to mothers of sons with low achievement motivation. The mothers

Parents of children with high achievement motivation tend to make demands and impose restrictions, but are also warmly encouraging.

▶ ▶ ▶ ▶

of the achievers made relatively more demands and imposed more restrictions on their sons during the early school years. Even during the preschool years, the mothers of the highly motivated boys demanded that they keep their rooms and possessions neat. They required that they make their own decisions concerning clothes, that they select friends, compete as needed, and undertake difficult tasks and persist at them. But these mothers did more than make demands and impose restrictions. They also praised their sons profusely for their accomplishments.

A Key Role for Parental Warmth   There is also a key role for parental warmth in fostering achievement motivation. Bernard Rosen and Roy D'Andrade (1959) found that mothers of highly achieving sons show them a good deal of affection and respond to success with praise and warmth. Robert Sears (1970) found parental warmth linked with achievement in mathematics and reading in 12-year-olds.

There have been some sex differences in the literature. Girls, for example, have usually not been expected to do as well in math as boys (Parsons et al., 1982). The reviews by Hoffmann (1972) and Spence and Helmreich (1978) found that boys who are high achievers tend to have internalized parental demands for achievement. Successful girls, on the other hand, frequently continued to achieve to earn the approval of parents and other people important to them. In Chapter 12 we shall further discuss sex differences and look into their origins.

The Influences of Siblings

Of U.S. families with children, more than 80 percent have at least two. Therefore, siblings as well as parents have the opportunity to influence most children. In fact, the larger the family, the less chance there is for parents to interact extensively with each child. In many cases, older children, especially girls, assume some of the child-rearing chores.

Siblings serve many functions, including physical caregiving, providing emotional support and nurturance, offering advice and direction, providing role models, providing social interaction that helps develop social skills, and making demands and imposing restrictions (Lamb, 1982). Siblings spend a good deal of time relating to each other and imitating one another (Dunn & Kendrick, 1982a, 1982b). By and large, younger siblings are more likely to imitate older siblings (Abramovitch et al., 1982, 1986) and are more likely to accept their direction (Brody et al., 1985; Stoneman et al., 1984).

However, older siblings may also imitate younger siblings, especially when parents remark "how cute" the baby is being in front of the older child. When 2 years 5 months, my daughter Allyn would pretend that she could not talk every once in a while, just like her 5-month-old sister Jordan. She imitated babbling, but not very well, and tended to produce many "blahs" and "blub-blubs." Two months later, when Jordan was creeping, Allyn would also get down on all fours to scamper across the room from time to time.

In many cultures, older girls are expected to care for younger siblings. In the United States, younger siblings frequently turn to older sisters when the mother is unavailable. In response, the older sister acts as a mother surrogate

▶ ▶ ▶ ▶

more often than not (Bryant & Crockenberg, 1980; Cicirelli, 1976, 1982). Boys do not usually play this nurturing role and tend to be perceived as bossy by younger siblings (Sutton-Smith & Rosenberg, 1968). However, this social dominance can also have a positive side: Older brothers may come to the aid of siblings when they get into scrapes with outsiders or cannot handle problems in the home.

The Effects of Family Size

At the outset of the chapter, I confessed my distress at the sibling rivalry that Allyn showed when Jordan required attention. The research suggests that there is cause for sibling rivalry, and that my experience may have been pretty much the norm. When new babies come into the home, mothers usually pay relatively more attention to them (Bryant & Crockenberg, 1980). Mothers spend much less time playing games with their toddlers and looking at things together (Kendrick & Dunn, 1980). When their hands are full with their newborns, mothers also have to verbally warn their toddlers "No!" or "Stop that!" more often to prevent them from engaging in destructive acts.

As families grow larger, the problems among parents, children, and siblings become magnified. Major changes occur in the ways parents relate to their children. Children are frequently assigned chores (Bossard & Boll, 1960). Parents cannot pay each child as much attention. Perhaps for this reason, disciplinary methods become less inductive and more power-assertive (Nuttall & Nuttall, 1971). Children in large families are not supervised as closely and become less dependent on their parents at earlier ages. However, their "independence" does not also spell achievement motivation. As a group, children from larger families do not perform as well in school.

There are also social-class differences. The children of large lower-class families seem to do most poorly. Children in such families are more likely to be unplanned, and family resources do not permit adequate supervision. But when large families are affluent, parents can hire child-care assistants and domestic helpers and provide adequate physical facilities. As a result, they feel less harassed. They can maintain high-quality interaction with their children, even if they cannot afford them the individual attention they once received.

But the effects of large families are not all negative. Young children typically have a variety of role models whom they can imitate and with whom they can identify. They are unlikely to be lonely. Older siblings can also serve as teachers of academic subjects. Older sisters, especially, are likely to help their younger siblings learn the basics of the "three R's" and to generally measure up in school (Cicirelli, 1982).

But despite the availability of multiple "teachers," research shows that the larger the family, the lower the achievements and the IQ scores of the children (Belmont & Marolla, 1973). Consider Figure 11.2. It represents the IQ scores of some 400,000 men in Holland (Zajonc, 1975). As the number of children within the family increases from two to nine, the IQ scores of children in a given position (e.g., first-born, second-born, and so on) decline. Note, too, that IQ scores tend to be lower for later-born children—which brings us to our discussion of the effects of birth order.

▶ ▶ ▶ ▶

The Effects of Birth Order

Figure 11.2 suggests a negative correlation between birth order and IQ. With few exceptions, the IQ scores of later-born children (whose birth order is higher) are lower than those of earlier-born children. In large families there is some tendency for the scores of the next-to-last children to show a minor jump. Still, the overall trend is remarkably consistent—down, down, down.

Many differences in personality and achievement have been observed among first-borns as compared with later-born children. On the positive side (from the standpoint of a highly achievement-oriented adult!), first-borns and only children show higher achievement motivation; a greater sense of responsibility, as manifested by more cooperativeness and helpfulness and less aggressiveness; and a greater orientation toward relating to adults. On the negative side, first-borns and only children show greater anxiety and are less self-reliant. Later-born children are more likely to harbor feelings of inadequacy and to engage in reckless acts. (As adults, first-borns and only children are more likely to avoid occupations or leisure activities that can result in physical harm [Nisbett, 1968].) But, later-born children are more likely to acquire social skills, to be tolerant of the shortcomings of others, and to be friendly. These traits earn them higher popularity ratings by peers (Miller & Maruyama, 1976).

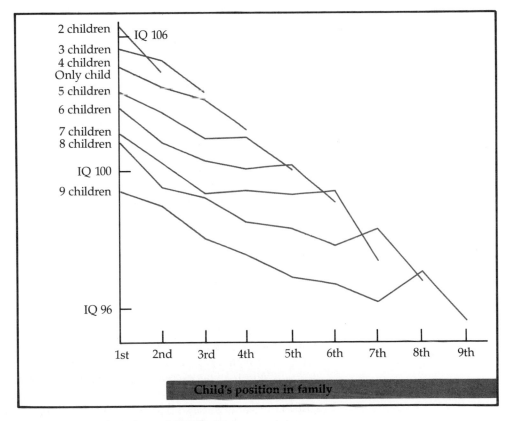

Figure 11.2 Birth Order and Intelligence
By and large, the higher the birth order, the lower the score on intelligence tests.

Differences in personality and achievement among first- and later-borns are linked to contrasting styles in parenting (Dunn & Kendrick, 1982a, 1982b; Dunn et al., 1986). First-borns start life with experience as only children. For a year or more, they receive the singular attention of both parents. They are held more, spoken to more, stimulated more. All in all, they spend more time with their parents than later-borns do (Thoman et al., 1972). Even after other children come along, parents still tend to relate to the first child more than to later-borns. Parents continue to make demands and to orient their speech toward levels that are appropriate for the first-born (Bossard & Boll, 1956). Parents have greater expectations for first-born children. They impose tougher restrictions on them and make greater demands of them. The are also more highly involved in their activities (Hilton, 1967; Rothbart, 1971).

By and large, parents are more relaxed with later-borns (Lasko, 1954). Why? There are a number of reasons. For one, they have probably gained some self-confidence in child rearing. They see that the first-born is "turning out all right" (which, most often, is accurate enough). Second, parents may interpret the first child's success as a sign of their own competence and may therefore assume that later-borns will also turn out all right. Third, some parents accept the fact that they cannot give later-borns the attention they gave the first-born. They "make the best of it."

Later-born children frequently learn that they must act aggressively in order to earn the attention of their parents and older siblings. They also tend to accept that they do not come first. As a result, their self-concepts tend to be lower than those of first-borns or of only children. They learn that they must consider the needs of their brothers and sisters. They are more tolerant of waiting in line at home and elsewhere. The social skills they acquire from dealing with and accommodating to the desires of their older siblings seem to translate into their greater popularity with peers.

And so later-borns tend to acquire skills that will make for happy moments with their peers. But first-borns and only children, with their relatively greater orientations toward achievement and adults, usually go on to higher educational and occupational status.

A word of comfort may be of use to parents or future parents who have or are considering having large families. The data we have summarized concerns group trends. There are exceptions. Furthermore, parents who have been warned about potential problems of larger families may be able to find ways of supplying all of their children with the human resources they need. Also, many parents place more value on sociability traits than on achievement—the traits that seem to be found more often among later-born children.

The Effects of Single-Parent Families

When I was a college student, I heard that the typical U.S. family consisted of a mother, a father, and about 2.4 children. It occurred to me that the third child might make things somewhat confusing for census takers, but then I left the thought alone. Today, however, the typical family is more difficult to describe, largely because nearly half (40–50 percent) of all U.S. children will spend at least part of their childhoods in single-parent families. In the great majority of cases, these single-parent families result from divorce.

▶ ▶ ▶ ▶

The Children of Divorce

Divorce requires many adjustments for children as well as for parents. Change itself is stressful, and divorce involves a multitude of changes.

Divorce turns the children's world topsy turvy. The simple things that had been taken for granted are no longer simple: Eating meals and going on trips with both parents, curling up with either parent to read a book or watch television, kissing both parents at bedtime come to an end. Divorced parents must support two households, not one. And so, children of divorce most often suffer downward movement in socioeconomic status. If the downward movement is not severe, it may require minor adjustments and loss of but a few privileges. But more than half of the children younger than 18 who live in father-absent homes must scrape by below the poverty level (Weinraub & Wolf, 1983). In severe cases, the downward trend can mean moving from a house into a cramped apartment, or from a more desirable to a less desirable neighborhood. With moving may come the switching of schools, and children may have to begin to relate to other children who share unfamiliar backgrounds and values. Divorce in families where the mother had stayed in the home may suddenly require her to rejoin the work force and place her children in day care. Such women typically suffer the stresses of task overload, as well as the other problems divorce entails (Hetherington et al., 1982).

One of the major conflicts between parents is differences in child-rearing practices. Children of parents who get a divorce have frequently heard them arguing about how they should be reared. Adolescents may understand that the differences reside in the parents. Young children, however, may focus on their own conflicts with their parents and blame themselves for the family upheaval. Younger children also tend to be more fearful than adolescents of the unknown. Adolescents have had more of an opportunity to learn that they can exert some control over what happens to them (Kurdek et al., 1981; Wallerstein & Kelly, 1974, 1975).

About 90 percent of the children of divorce live with their mothers (Salkind, 1983). Fathers usually see their children frequently during the first months after the divorce, but visitation often drops precipitously later on (Clingempeel & Repucci, 1982). Also, about two-thirds of fathers do not keep up with their child-support payments, exacerbating the family's downward trend in socioeconomic status.

Given all this outer and inner turmoil, it is not surprising that children of divorce show a number of behavior problems. In a longitudinal study run by E. Mavis Hetherington and her colleagues (1975, 1982, 1983), the adjustment of children who were 4 years old at the time of the divorce was assessed at intervals of two months and one and two years. On the basis of behavioral observations at home and school, personality tests, and interviews, it was found that both boys and girls showed disturbances that increased over the course of the first year. However, by the time two years had passed, much of the disturbance had decreased.

There were some sex differences. Boys showed greater behavioral disturbances than girls, as manifested by conduct disorders in school and increased anxiety and dependence. Boys and girls regained much of their equilibrium after two years, and the girls by and large could not be distinguished from girls from intact families.

Researchers attribute children's problems not only to the divorce, but also to a decline in the quality of child rearing that frequently follows. The

▶ ▶ ▶ ▶

Effects of Father-Absence on Girls: The Hetherington Study

▷
▷
▷
▷
▷ A study by E. Mavis Hetherington (1972) shows how many teenage daughters of divorced parents respond to their fathers' absence. Hetherington's samples consisted of 24 girls whose parents had been divorced, 24 girls whose fathers had died, and 24 girls whose families were intact. She compared the girls on a battery of personality tests, interviews, and behavioral observations at a recreation center and during the interviews. The behavioral observations included such measures of "body language" as how close the girl chose to sit to the interviewer, whether she was turned toward or away from the interviewer, and whether her legs were open or crossed.

Both groups of father-absent girls showed higher anxiety levels than the girls from intact homes, but there were few other differences on the personality tests. Both groups of father-absent girls reported feelings of insecurity around male peers and adults. They also reported relatively low levels of self-esteem as compared with girls from intact homes. However, despite their insecurity, the girls whose parents had been divorced reported higher levels of heterosexual activity than did the other two groups. Girls whose mothers had been widowed reported the least heterosexual contact. Behavioral observations showed that girls whose parents had been divorced spent more time in areas of the recreation center that were populated by males (see Figure 11.3). Their "body language" during interviews by male questioners was also more open and inviting. They sat closer to the male interviewers (see Table 11.3). They leaned forward, and their posture was more open and inviting. The daughters of the widows tended to stay away from males at the recreation center. They also tended to distance themselves from a male interviewer with a bolt-upright posture.

Table 11.3   Chairs Selected by Girls Interviewed by Men in the Hetherington Study

POSITION OF CHAIR SELECTED	NUMBER OF GIRLS WHO SELECTED CHAIR		
	DAUGHTERS OF DIVORCED MOTHERS	DAUGHTERS OF WIDOWED MOTHERS	DAUGHTERS FROM INTACT HOMES
Closest to interviewer	8	0	1
Across from interviewer	3	2	8
Farthest from interviewer	1	10	3

Data adapted from Hetherington, 1972, p. 317, Table 3.

▶ ▶ ▶ ▶

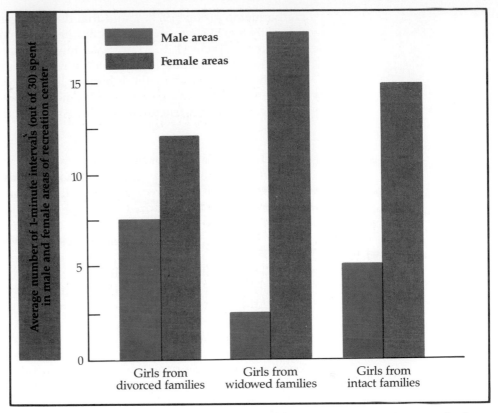

Figure 11.3 Behavior of Daughters of Divorced, Widowed, and Married Women in the Hetherington Study
As a group, daughters of divorced women tended to spend the most time in male areas of the recreation center.

Father-absence apparently contributed to feelings of insecurity around males and to low self-esteem among the daughters of divorced and widowed women. However, the two groups reacted very differently. The divorced group showed increased heterosexual interest and involvement, while the widowed group distanced themselves from males. Perhaps the divorced group felt rejected by their fathers' departures and were attempting to prove to themselves that they could arouse and hold the interest of males. The mothers who had been divorced reported the most conflict with their daughters. Daughters of divorced women were most likely to be punished for sexual activity.

In sum, father-absence alone was not responsible for the results of the Hetherington study. Group differences among the adolescent girls were linked to the reasons for father-absence. When fathers appear voluntarily to leave daughters, the girls' self-esteem as well as their security can plummet. The girls may attempt to reconstruct their self-concepts by demonstrating that they can indeed arouse the interest of men.

organization of family life tends to deteriorate after divorce (Hetherington et al., 1975). The family is more likely to eat their meals "pick-up style," as opposed to sitting down together. Children are less likely to get to school on time or to get to sleep at a regular hour. It is also more difficult for single mothers to set limits and enforce restrictions on sons' behavior (Santrock et al., 1982). The

▶ ▶ ▶ ▶

Hetherington group (1977) found that divorced parents, on the whole, are significantly less likely to show the authoritative behaviors that foster instrumental competence (Table 11.2). They make fewer demands for mature behavior, decline in communication ability, and show less nurturance and warmth. Moreover, their disciplinary methods become inconsistent. Not only do their children believe that they can "get away with more," they also come to conceptualize their worlds as unstructured places. As a consequence, their anxiety levels increase.

The Effects of Father-Absence   Since most children of divorce live with their mothers, and the fathers tend not to visit regularly, many of these children grow up, to a large degree, without fathers. The effects of father-absence are usually felt more by boys than girls, especially when the father is absent during the first five years or so of a boy's life (Hetherington & Deur, 1972; Huston, 1983). There are individual differences, but boys with absent fathers show fewer sex-typed "masculine" interests, greater dependence, and a "feminine" pattern of intellectual skills—for example, greater verbal skills than math ability.

The nearby box on the Hetherington study reports some additional findings on the effects of father-absence on teenage girls.

When Fathers Have Custody   In about 10 percent of divorces, fathers have custody of their children. As we shall see in Chapter 12, men are not usually socialized to develop parenting skills. As a result, having the sole responsibility for parenting can be overwhelming, at least at first. However, as a group, divorced fathers tend to report the same types of parenting problems encountered by divorced mothers. They also tend to be about as successful (Mendes, 1976; Orthener et al., 1976).

One of the most common problems for fathers who have custody is coordinating their work schedules with their children's schedules. Their problem is akin to that of divorced women who must remain in, or return to, the work force. Day-care centers, nursery schools, scout troops, music and dance lessons, and other organized activities ease these problems somewhat for fathers as they do for mothers. Single fathers also show few problems with chores such as shopping, cooking, cleaning, and getting children to doctors' appointments.

Consider the feelings of pride and competence that emerged in one father who was awarded custody of his two daughters:

> It was during the first year with my daughters that I realized how important a part of my life my children were. It took me almost six months to figure out I wanted them, not the carefree life of a bachelor. The whole "male mystique" about my not caring enough or not wanting to be with my children was balderdash. Yes, it was terrifying to think of raising them alone, because as men we're not raised to think we can do it. But I found delight and joy in being a single parent. Not that it wasn't difficult and horrible in all sorts of mechanical ways. But I actually liked all that dumb stuff—wiping noses, just being there for my daughters. And they were there for me. Having them helped keep me together after the marriage broke up (Molinoff, 1977, p. 16).

Studies of 6- to 11-year-olds suggest that boys do somewhat better when their fathers have custody of them, but that girls do somewhat better with their mothers (Santrock & Warshak, 1979). However, traits such as authoritativeness and warmth seem to be more important than the custodian's gender in promoting children's adjustment. It also comes down to an individual issue: Which parent truly wants the children and has the emotional resources to cope with their needs?

Regardless of which parent has custody, children's adjustment to divorce is facilitated when parents maintain their commitment to the children and set aside their own disputes long enough to agree on child-rearing practices (Hetherington, 1979; Moreland & Schwebel, 1981; Wallerstein & Kelly, 1980). It is helpful for divorced parents to encourage each other to continue to play roles in their children's lives and to avoid saying negative things about each other in front of the children.

Stepparent Families   Seventy to 75 percent of divorced people get remarried, usually within five years. Thirty-five percent of the children born in the 1980s can expect to spend some part of their lives in a stepfamily. And so, the effects of stepparenting are also an important issue in U.S. family life.

Most investigators have found that living in stepfamilies as opposed to nuclear families has little psychological impact (Ganong & Coleman, 1984). In fact, stepfathers may now and then attenuate the effects of father-absence for boys by providing male role models and companionship.

It also appears that stepmothers can have positive effects, particularly for stepdaughters. In a study of the effects of different kinds of stepfamilies on 9- to 12-year-olds, positive stepmother–stepchild relationships were associated with lower aggression in boys and girls and with high self-esteem in girls (Clingempeel & Segal, 1986). Frequent visits with the nonresident natural mother appeared to impair stepmother–stepdaughter relations, apparently by maintaining stepdaughter resistance to forming a relationship with the stepmother. On the other hand, stepmother–stepdaughter relationships generally improved over time.

Should Conflicted Parents Stay Together for the Sake of the Children?   It is good for divorced parents to cooperate in rearing their children. Is it also better for the children for parents to remain together despite their conflicts? It depends on how the parents behave in front of the children. Children as young as 2 show distress and increased aggression in response to angry adult conflict (Cummings et al., 1985). When parents argue persistently in front of the children, the children tend to develop behavior problems akin to those of children whose parents have been divorced (Emory, 1982). When parents cannot get along, divorce followed by cooperative child rearing may be the best alternative. As E. Mavis Hetherington notes, "Divorce is often a positive solution to destructive family functioning" (1979, p. 857). Given that most children begin to adjust reasonably well by a couple of years afterward, the assumption that divorce will be followed by perpetual "gloom-and-doom" may be unwarranted.

Peer Influences

Families are the most powerful socialization influences on children during the first few years. But as children develop, their activities and interests become directed progressively further away from home. Peers take on an increasing importance. By the time children reach adolescence, they tend to spend more time with peers than in the company of their parents, even if they spend

▶ ▶ ▶ ▶

Working Mothers and Their Children: Must Women Who Want What's Best for Their Children Remain in the Home?

▷
▷
▷
▷

▷ What are the effects of maternal employment on children? Must mother be available for round-the-clock love and attention? Not necessarily.

Developmentalists have found no consistent evidence that maternal employment is harmful (Easterbrooks & Goldberg, 1985; Hoffman, 1985). Children of working women do not differ from those of full-time housewives in terms of anxiety, incidence of antisocial behavior, dependence, or complaints of stress-related disorders such as headaches and upset stomachs. In fact, the children of working women see their mothers as more competent and hold fewer stereotypical sex-role attitudes (Gold & Andres, 1978a, 1978b, 1978c). Children of working women are more helpful with the housework. The daughters of working women are also more achievement ori-ented and set themselves higher career goals than the daughters of nonworking women.

More recent research suggests one negative finding about the children of mothers who work: The IQ scores and academic achievements of their sons are somewhat lower than those of full-time homemakers (Gold & Andres, 1978a, 1978b, 1978c). This group difference is rather small, but may reflect other findings to the effect that working women as compared to nonworking women pay somewhat less attention to their sons relative to their daughters (Stuckey et al., 1982). However, this does not mean that the sons of working women are neglected by them—only that working mothers are more egalitarian in their distribution of affection.

The children of working women tend to see their mothers as more competent and hold fewer sex role stereotypes.

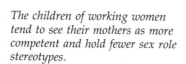

When Dad Stays Home

In some cases, the stereotypical sex roles are reversed and the father stays at home (serves as "househusband") while the mother takes the morning trek to the factory or the office. Children in these families also show fewer stereotypical sex-role attitudes but greater instrumental competence, as measured by IQ scores and the belief that they can exert control over what happens to them in life (Radin, 1982; Russell, 1982). But we cannot necessarily attribute these findings to the father's remaining in the home. It may be that the same egalitarian or nonconformist attitudes that led to the parental decision to reverse roles also caused the group differences in the children.

All in all, working women spend about half as much time caring for their infant children as housewives do, but their children develop normal attachments to them (Moore & Hofferth, 1979). The quality of the time that parents and their children spend together, along with the making of adequate child-care arrangements, outweighs the number of hours (Bralove, 1981; Easterbrooks & Goldberg, 1985). When mothers choose to work and find their work fulfilling, they are happier with their lives (Rathus & Nevid, 1986). They and their husbands are more egalitarian in their distribution of chores in the home as well as in the breadwinning role. Perhaps the working mothers' feelings of instrumental competence and high self-esteem transfer into more authoritative relationships with their children.

more hours per day in their homes (Hartup, 1970; Medrich et al., 1982).

Let us explore the ways in which friendship develops. Then we shall see how peers socialize one another.

Development of Friendships

Among young children, friendships are based on geographical closeness or **propinquity.** Friendships are relatively superficial—quickly formed, quickly broken. What matters are shared activities and who has the swing set or sandbox. Five- to 7-year-olds usually report that their friends are the children they do things with, the children with whom they have "fun" (Berndt & Perry, 1986; Damon, 1977). There is little reference to friends' traits.

Between the ages of 8 and 11, children show increased recognition of the importance of friends meeting each others' needs and possessing desirable traits (Damon, 1977). Children at these ages are more likely to say that friends are nice to one another and share interests as well as things. Not until 12 or so does the capacity to share intimate feelings and events enter children's concepts of friendship (Damon, 1977). By the early teens, children usually report that their friends give them emotional support when they are feeling bad. They can tell their friends "everything" without worrying that their friends will spread stories around town (Berndt & Perry, 1986). Girls report intimacy to be a more important factor in friendship than boys do. Girls also describe their friendships as more intimate (Berndt, 1982).

Since friends usually come from the same neighborhood, they tend to be similar in race, social class, and values. Even when children are entering kindergarten, they prefer befriending children of the same race (Finkelstein & Haskins, 1983; Singleton & Asher, 1979).

Children's numbers of friends increase throughout the school years (Riesman & Shorr, 1978). Schoolchildren are involved in more joint activities than are preschoolers. However, adolescents share their confidences with only

Propinquity Nearness.

▶ ▶ ▶ ▶

Clique (click). *A small group of friends who share activities and confidences.*

Crowd *A loosely organized number of children who share interests and activities.*

a small number of friends—that is, their **clique.** Other friends belong to the larger **crowd.** The crowd is a loosely organized group who tend to flock together because of shared interests and activities. An adolescent can belong to a number of crowds. One crowd may consist of schoolmates and another of church friends. Similarly, adolescents may belong to different cliques. One may include two best friends from school. Another may include best friends from church. Still another may include one or more members of the opposite sex. Cliques may also consist of dating couples who share similar life aspirations, such as going on to college and joining the professional ranks.

Conformist Tendencies

Not only does the amount of time spent with peers increase as children develop. The influence of peers also grows more powerful. Studies show that conformity to peer pressures increases dramatically for both sexes from about the ages of 7 to 14. It then declines gradually throughout the remainder of adolescence (Constanzo & Shaw, 1966; Gottman, 1985; Hartup, 1970).

Peer pressures are frequently at variance with parents' wishes. Involvement in conduct disorders in the school, in sexual activities, and in drugs is more likely to reflect the influences of peers than the values expressed in the home. Thomas Berndt (1979) found that 8-year-olds were more susceptible to parents' demands than peer pressures. The increase in conformity to peer pressures between the ages of 8 and 14 was accompanied by a decline in conformity to parental demands. At the age of 14, children who were subject to antisocial peer pressures felt somewhat more compelled to accede to them than to their parents' wishes. By the time adolescents reached the ages of 16 and 17, peer pressure was on the wane, and they were becoming more likely to conform to conventional adult standards.

Peer relationships take on different meanings as children develop. Five-to 7-year-olds report that friends are children with whom it is fun to be with. Children of 8 to 11 report that friends are nice to one another and share interests. Sharing confidences becomes important by about the age of 11.

▶ ▶ ▶ ▶

Peer Acceptance

Acceptance or rejection by peers is of major importance, because problems with peers are a harbinger of later social and emotional maladjustment (Cowen et al., 1973; Achenbach & Edelbrock, 1981). Peer acceptance seems to begin with secure attachment to parents. Infants who are securely attached at the age of 1 later show greater social skills as preschoolers. They approach peers less hesitantly, are more empathic, and more likely to take on leadership (Lieberman, 1977; Walters et al., 1979).

Popular children tend to share culturally valued traits (Asher et al., 1977). On a physical level, popular children tend to be attractive and relatively mature for their age, although physical attractiveness seems to be more important for girls than boys (Langlois, 1985; Vaughn & Langlois, 1983). Socially speaking, popular children are friendly and outgoing (Coie & Kupersmidt, 1983) and possess conversational skills (Bierman & Furman, 1984). Popular children also have instrumental competencies. They tend either to do well in school or to excel in valued activities such as sports. In addition to being friendly, popular children also tend to be lavish in their dispensing of praise and approval (Masters & Furman, 1981). Children who are rejected by their peers are more likely to show aggressive behavior and to disrupt group activities by bickering or deviant behavior (Asher & Hymel, 1981; Dodge, 1983).

As noted earlier, later-born children are more likely to be popular than first-borns, because they generally develop superior skills in relating to peers (but not to adults). This trend holds despite the facts that school achievement is a factor in popularity and first-borns tend to earn higher grades than later-borns. Although pressure to conform to group norms and standards can be powerful, indeed, most children who are rejected do not shape up their behavior. Instead, they tend to remain alone, on the fringes of the group. In some cases they join deviant subcultures whose values and goals differ from the mainstream. This is unfortunate, because training in social skills seems to have the capacity to increase children's popularity with peers (Bierman, 1986).

Peers as Socialization Influences

Peer relationships, then, are a major part of growing up. Peers exert powerful socialization influences and pressures to conform. As involved and authoritative as they may be, parents can only provide their children with experience in relating to adults. Children also profit from experience in relating to peers. Peers, like adults, have various needs and interests, various competencies and social skills. Not only do they belong to a different generation from parents; they also differ as individuals. For all these reasons, peer experiences broaden children.

Peers guide children and afford practice in sharing and cooperation, in relating to leaders, and in coping with aggressive impulses, including their own. Peers, like parents, help children learn what types of impulses—affectionate, aggressive, and so on—they can safely express, and with whom. Adolescents who are at odds with their parents about issues such as independence and sexuality can turn to peers as sounding boards. With peers they can compare feelings and experiences they would not bring up in the home. When children share troubling ideas and experiences with peers, they often learn that their friends have similar concerns. They realize that they are normal and not alone.

▶ ▶ ▶ ▶

In Chapters 12 and 13 we shall learn more about how peers foster the socialization process. In Chapter 12 we shall see that peers provide powerful rewards and punishments that encourage children to conform to sex-role stereotypes. In Chapter 13 we shall see how different types of experiences with peers can foster aggressive behavior in some children (or in some situations) and promote friendly, cooperative behavior in others.

As children develop, the school and school activities also come to play an increasingly important role in socialization.

School Influences

When I was doing my graduate work in psychology, a couple of my professors candidly admitted that their goals were to socialize their students into behaving as they did. Through extensive modeling and reinforcement, they hoped to show their students how to formulate scientific questions and seek the answers. They would know that they were successful if their students went on to do the things that they did—teaching, research, writing, and consulting with agencies and institutions concerning the welfare of children.

Teachers and school administrators explicitly or implicitly share some of these goals. They aim to have students adopt some of their behavior patterns, and they use extensive modeling and rewards and punishments in teaching them to do so. Of course, they cannot (and most would not want to) create carbon copies of themselves. The U.S. democratic ideal puts the individual first, and the stamping out of identical people smacks of authoritarianism. Also, children bring different bents, abilities, and talents into the school. They might not be able to fully pattern their behavior after others' even if they wanted to. Too, the goals of school personnel are often inconsistent, as in the clashing U.S. ideals of fostering cooperativeness and competitiveness. So children are likely to receive mixed messages concerning the degree to which these traits ought to be developed. Finally, despite the fact that most children attend schools for five to six hours a day 180 or so days a year, schools are just one of a number of socialization influences. Family, peers, and religious and other institutions provide different influences.

Nevertheless, it can be argued that the schools in the United States have been extremely successful in one particular form of socialization—"Americanization." With the exception of a few million Native Americans, the United States is a nation of immigrants—people who have come from various backgrounds with various purposes, languages, skills, and values. U.S. schools, more so than other institutions, have had the responsibility for Americanizing immigrant children. The schools have taught children a common tongue, acquainted them with U.S. ideals and values, and imparted the knowledge and skills required to assist children to prosper in our competitive society.

Schools, like parents, set limits on behavior; make demands for mature behavior; attempt to communicate; and are oriented toward nurturing positive physical, social, and cognitive development. The schools, like parents, have a direct influence on children's achievement motivation and career aspirations (Rutter, 1983; Walberg & Rasher, 1977). Like the family and religious institutions, schools also influence moral development (Hess & Holloway, 1984; Minuchin & Shapiro, 1983).

▶ ▶ ▶ ▶

Let us consider a number of factors that affect the processes of socialization in the schools, including the physical school environment, the educational approach (traditional or "open"), teachers, and mainstreaming.

The Effects of the School Environment

When parents consider moving to a new community, they often visit the schools in order to gain an impression of what it would mean for their children to attend them. From the outside, we are impressed by schools' sizes, their newness (or oldness), and the way buildings and grounds are maintained. Research, however, finds no consistent advantages or disadvantages associated with the size of a school (Barker & Gump, 1964). Nor does the age of a school seem to matter, so long as it is safe. Physical features that do seem to matter include class or group size, seating arrangements, student density, and the availability of equipment.

Class Size   Smaller classes or instruction groups permit students to receive more individual attention and to express their ideas more often (Minuchin & Shapiro, 1983). In an early study of kindergarten classes (Dawe, 1934), fewer children participated in the discussion as class size increased. Children's contributions were briefer. The total amount of give-and-take declined. Larger groups encourage lecturing, even when the teacher would like to have discussions. These findings have been replicated at the college level (Tuana, 1969).

Group sizes were experimentally manipulated in an English study with preschoolers (Smith & Connolly, 1980). As a general rule, the larger the group, the more likely children were to engage in impulsive rough-and-tumble activities. The smaller the group, the more likely children were to engage in activities that involved the imagination and fantasy. Smaller classes are particularly useful in teaching the "three R's" to elementary school students at risk for academic failure (Rutter, 1983).

Seating Arrangements   The student's location in the class as well as group size influences participation. In studies with first-, sixth-, and eleventh-graders, students who sat toward the front and center of the classroom were more likely to participate in discussions (Adams & Biddle, 1970). Students who choose to sit in the back of the room may be separating themselves psychologically (as well as physically) from the teacher and the school setting (Levinger & Gunner, 1967).

There are implications for socialization and the fostering of achievement. When possible, circular or other arrangements that bring more students "front and center" are preferable to the traditional rectangular seating grid. When rectangular arrangements must be maintained, it may be preferable *not* to allow students to choose their seats. Students who are most alienated from the schools will probably seize the opportunity to further distance themselves. It may also be useful to rotate seating arrangements, to bring all students front-and-center from time to time. By walking around the room as they teach, teachers may also encourage students who "take a back seat."

Student Density and Distance   Group size and seating arrangements are not the only physical factors that affect children's participation. Their density—that

► ► ► ►

is, the degree to which children are packed in or spread out—also has an influence.

In the English study by Smith and Connolly (1980), packing preschoolers into spaces in which they had 15 or fewer square feet each tended to increase aggressive behavior and dampen cooperative play. In a U.S. study, uncrowded preschoolers paid more attention than crowded children to stories and to teacher demonstrations (Krantz & Risley, 1977).

Crowding is not inevitably damaging. Cross-cultural studies suggest that some children are more comfortable under crowded conditions than others. Young black children, for example, seem normally to interact at closer distances than young Caucasians. But black adolescents seem to prefer *more* distance from one another than Caucasians do (Aiello & Thompson, 1980). Children who are reared in more crowded environments are more likely to engage in cooperative rather than aggressive activities in crowded classrooms (Fagot, 1977).

There are also age differences. Boys and girls seem to prefer more distance from one another as their grade levels advance from the first through seventh grades. Spatial requirements then level off. Girls at each grade level are comfortable in interacting more closely than boys (Aiello & Aiello, 1974).

Personality factors also have an impact. People who have low self-esteem or an **external locus of control,** or who are anxious or violent, seem to require greater distance from others (Fisher et al., 1984). Packing children with these traits into small rooms may impair their socialization and their academic progress.

Availability of Equipment   It is no secret to parents that children compete for playthings. The availability of toys and other kinds of equipment also has an influence on the social behavior of children in playgroups and classes. In the English study, groups that had duplicates of playthings behaved less aggressively than children in scantily supplied groups (Smith & Connolly, 1980). Children in less well-supplied groups were more likely to share what little they had, but they were also more likely to cry and compete for toys.

An abundance of supplies in the lower elementary school grades may help keep children occupied and lower the incidence of aggressive behavior. I keep finding ways to spend other people's money.

The Effects of Open versus Traditional Approaches to Education

In the traditional approach to education, the teacher's role has been that of an authoritarian leader. The teacher has been the autocratic leader who sets classroom policies, dictates activities, sorts children into groups, and directs group members in the completion of assigned tasks. This does not mean that the authoritarian teacher is hostile or unfriendly. Rather, there is a clear understanding of who is the leader, and student–teacher relationships are characterized by specific formal standards.

There is no question that the traditional approach, over the years, has fostered achievement and the acquisition of skills required for success in a technologically oriented society. But today teachers often try to be more democratic in their relations with students. In support of newer approaches, research shows that a more "open" kind of classroom organization and structure also fosters achievement. An open classroom may also be superior in the fostering of other

Laissez-faire (lezz-zay fair). *Noninterfering. (A French phrase meaning "allowing to do.")*

attributes. Let us first describe a classic experiment in leadership styles carried out by Kurt Lewin and his colleagues (1939). Then we shall compare some of the results of traditional and "open education."

The Lewin Study Kurt Lewin and his colleagues trained adults to lead small groups of 10-year-old boys in the completion of experimental tasks. Some leaders were trained to behave in an authoritarian manner, as described in the traditional approach to teaching. Others were trained to act in a democratic manner. Democratic leaders outlined general goals and suggested ways of completing tasks, but allowed the groups to choose their own methods. They allowed group members to split up the work and work with whomever they wished. They offered praise, as appropriate. In general, they tried to act as regular group members, although they did not do too much of the work. Still other adults were trained as **laissez-faire** leaders. Laissez-faire leaders indicated the nature of the tasks and supplied materials. However, they did not formulate policies, assign tasks, or suggest ways of completing them. They served as resources but did not participate unless asked.

In this experiment, the leadership styles led to very different results. Boys in authoritarian groups could not work efficiently unless the leader was present. They tended to be passive or rebellious in their relations with the leader. They were also frequently aggressive toward one another. Boys in the laissez-faire groups were disorganized, inefficient, and impulsive. Frequently, they stopped working altogether. Boys in the democratic group were most efficient, even when the leader was not present. They showed more cooperation and were happiest with their leader.

Thomas Good and Jere Brophy (1980) argue that the behavior of the "democratic" leader in the Lewin experiment was similar to that of the authoritative parents described by Diana Baumrind. Democratic (and authoritative) leaders (and parents) assume their responsibilities and speak as mature and experienced adults. They maintain the ultimate authority. However, instead of acting dictatorially, they explain the rationales behind their policies (communicate effectively), seek input from children, and encourage children to make

Traditional education (left) focuses more on academic skills and achievement, while open education (right) is relatively more concerned with fostering curiosity and self-confidence. Studies find little difference in academic achievement between the two approaches, but show that children in open education are more creative, independent, curious, and cooperative.

▶ ▶ ▶ ▶

SCHOOL INFLUENCES

their own decisions and act independently when they can. They also use warm encouragement and are generous in their praise (when it is due).

Laissez-faire leaders, on the other hand, have results similar to those of permissive parents. The children under their leadership have relatively little motivation to complete tasks and act impulsively.

Open Education Open education, in many ways, seeks to approximate the democratic (or authoritative) leadership style in the classroom. Open education is a broad term that refers to a variety of educational methods that encourage children to be active explorers rather than passive recipients of subject matter. In open education, children are given the opportunity to express their "individual bents," as suggested by Rousseau (see Chapter 1). They make many of their own decisions about what tasks they will complete and what they will study. Children do not merely take concrete direction from an autocratic leader. Instead, they interact informally with teachers and other students. Children in open classes usually do not sit in regimented rectangular patterns, but rather in a circle or in small groups. Also, in small groups or individually, they examine an abundance of learning materials that are scattered about the room. In many open-education programs, students from different grade levels are mixed together and grades are deemphasized. The goals of fostering lasting curiosity and self-confidence are viewed as more important than specific intellectual achievements, especially in the early grades.

I would like to be able to say that we have been able to carefully evaluate the effects of open education as compared to traditional education. In fact, this is not quite the case. As you may have gathered, open-education programs may include teachers in both democratic (authoritative) and laissez-faire roles (plus a few unwilling authoritarians), and we have not systematically sorted out the effects of each approach. "Traditional" education is also not monolithic. It includes many teachers who attempt to be as democratic as possible within the limits of their settings. Such teachers encourage students to make choices, and they attempt to communicate the rationales behind school policies and procedures.

Open education may also have very different effects in, say, a second-grade class that teaches many academic areas and a tenth-grade plane-geometry class. Again, we have not fully sorted out the effects of each approach at all grade levels and in all subjects. Another problem is that parents often choose whether their children will attend open or traditional schools. It is likely that parents who choose a nontraditional school may also be nontraditional in child-rearing practices. Thus children are as likely to reflect home influences as school influences.

Even so, the information we have about the effectiveness of open education is encouraging (Minuchin & Shapiro, 1983). In a review of numerous studies, Horwitz (1979) reported that nearly half (46 percent) found no significant differences in academic achievement. The number of studies reporting that either open (14 percent) or traditional (12 percent) schools resulted in superior achievement were about equal. But in terms of personality traits and prosocial behavior, the open schools yielded consistently superior results. For example, children in open schools were more creative, more independent, less conformist, more curious, and more cooperative. Although about half of the studies reported no significant differences in self-concept and locus of control, there were greater trends for students in open schools to show a positive self-concept and **internal locus of control.**

Internal locus of control A *personality trait in which the person perceives the power to attain reinforcements as being within the self.*

▶ ▶ ▶ ▶

Other researchers have found largely consistent results. They agree, for example, that children in low-structured learning situations do not learn more (Featherstone, 1971). Also, children in more open classes tend to be more co-operative and to engage in more frequent imaginative play (Smith & Connolly, 1980; Thomas & Berk, 1981). However, from time to time, they are also more aggressive (Huston-Stein et al., 1977). Children in open classes also tend to show higher activity levels, to express their feelings more frequently, and to like their teachers better.

I would think that we can tentatively conclude that an open-education approach does *not* impair academic achievement, at least in the elementary school. Children seem to prefer open education and are freer to express their feelings and their curiosities. On the other hand, it may be that open education, when too permissive, encourages aggressive behavior. A final evaluation must be postponed until some of the research problems I mentioned have been dealt with.

Teachers

The influence of the schools is mainly due to teachers. Teachers, like parents, set limits, make demands, communicate values, and foster development. Teacher–student relationships are more limited than parent–child relationships, but teachers still have the opportunity to serve as powerful role models and dispersers of reinforcement. After all, children spend several hours each weekday in the presence of teachers.

The Teacher as a Role Model Children are most likely to imitate the behavior of people who appear similar to themselves and who have efficient control of reinforcements. Teachers usually wish their students to adopt the behavior patterns that they (the teachers) value and model. In this context, it is interesting to note that, since most elementary school teachers are women, young boys may consider the school a sort of preserve for women and resist acquiring the skills they model. Girls may feel much more comfortable in the elementary school setting. Girls may thus make more of an effort to adopt the values and skills expressed and demonstrated by the teacher (Stein & Bailey, 1973).

Consider an experiment in the imitation of a teacher role model. The researchers (Portuges & Feshbach, 1971) created two films of a woman teaching a geography lesson. The geographical subject matter was identical. In one film the woman used a positive approach, profusely praising students for correct answers. In the other film, the woman was generally negative. She focused on criticizing incorrect answers. The models also used distinctive gestures unrelated to their teaching style, such as clasping their hands. The 8- to 10-year-old viewers were then asked to teach a geography lesson to dolls. In this way the researchers could observe if the children's approaches imitated those of the film models, and, if so, which model they imitated.

Some children used approaches of their own, but many of them imitated the film models not only in their teaching styles, but also in their incidental gestures. Their imitative behavior seemed to be of the broad sort that social-learning theorists view as a sign of an effort to identify with a model. The model with the warm, encouraging teaching style was imitated significantly more often than the negative model. However, girls imitated the filmed model more frequently than boys did, and middle-class children imitated her more often than

▶ ▶ ▶ ▶

lower-class children did. Middle-class girls, in other words, were most likely to identify with the model. Lower-class boys were least likely to do so. Again, it seems that children are more likely to imitate adults whom they perceive as similar to themselves.

We can draw a rather clear inference from studies such as these. Many lower-class children from minority ethnic backgrounds already do not possess an achievement orientation and self-confidence when they enter the school system. Once in school, they are unlikely to identify with middle-class teachers. Lower-class boys are even more unlikely to identify with middle-class women. Offering lower-class children teacher-models who have come from a similar background and mastered the skills of our technologically oriented society might be more likely to foster imitation and identification.

The Teacher as a Dispenser of Reinforcement   It will come as no surprise that students usually respond positively to praise and negatively to criticism. However, there are so many exceptions to this rule of thumb that teachers will normally profit from carefully studying their students as individuals (Brophy & Evertson, 1976; Good & Grouws, 1975). For example, some students are embarrassed by public praise. Others may identify with a subgroup of classmates who are not achievement oriented and who find teacher praise punitive. In cases such as these, teachers might be wise to offer brief praise in private rather than profuse compliments before the class. Now and then it might be wise to refrain from praise altogether and to find indirect ways of letting students know that they have excelled.

According to Jere Brophy (1981) and Thomas Good (Good & Brophy, 1980), effective praise follows guidelines such as these:

1. It is sincere, as shown by spontaneity or other indications of credibility. When teachers try to praise children to control their behavior or to make them feel good about themselves, the praise is frequently perceived as insincere (Parsons et al., 1982).

2. Its form and intensity are appropriate to the specific accomplishment. The teacher does not gush over a trivial achievement.

3. It is adapted to the needs and preferences of the individual student. For example, students who would be embarrassed by public attention are spoken to privately.

4. It is specific in describing what the student did that resulted in the praise. Specificity is a sign of credibility. It also provides the student with information that allows him or her to further develop praise-worthy behavior. Unfortunately, in one study fewer than 10 percent of the praise statements delivered by first-grade teachers specified the praiseworthy behavior (Anderson et al., 1979).

5. It explains how the student's current achievement is an advance over earlier achievements.

6. It encourages the student to view himself or herself as capable of earning future rewards from society at large. For example, the student is told that the amount of effort put into a project would also win praise within the corporate structure.

▶ ▶ ▶ ▶

Pygmalion effect *The process by which one's belief in the abilities of another person elicits competent performance from that person.*

The Importance of Teacher Expectations   There is a saying that "You find what you're looking for." In Greek mythology, the amorous sculptor Pygmalion breathed life into a beautiful statue he had carved. Similarly, in the musical *My Fair Lady*, which is a reworking of the Pygmalion legend, Henry Higgins fashions a great lady from the lower-class Eliza Doolittle.

Teachers also try to "bring out" positive traits that they believe dwell within their students. An experiment by Robert Rosenthal and Lenore Jacobson suggests the impact that teacher expectations can have. As reported in their *Pygmalion in the Classroom*, Rosenthal and Jacobson (1968) first gave students a battery of psychological tests. Then they informed teachers that a handful, although average in performance to date, were "late bloomers." The tests clearly suggested that they were about to blossom forth intellectually in the current school year.

Now the fact is that the tests had indicated nothing in particular about the "chosen" children. These children had been selected at random. The purpose of the experiment was to determine whether modifying teacher expectations could enhance student performance. As it happened, the identified children made signicant gains in intelligence test scores. But as reported by Jere Brophy and Thomas Good (1974) in a review of 60 such studies, results overall have been mixed. Some studies have shown the **Pygmalion effect.** Others have not. A more recent review of 18 such experiments found that the Pygmalion effect was most pronounced when the procedure for informing teachers of the potential in the target students had greatest credibility (Raudenbush, 1984). An appropriate conclusion would be that teacher expectations *often, but not always,* influence students' achievement motivation, self-esteem, expectancies for success, and actual achievement (Brophy, 1983; Minuchin & Shapiro, 1983).

What are teacher expectations normally like? Note the following (Braun, 1976):

1. Teachers expect that physically attractive children will be more intelligent, more achievement-oriented, and show more social skills than less attractive children. More attractive people also tend to be rated as more socially skillful. Somehow we elicit more socially competent behavior from attractive people, even if we do not know exactly how (Goldman & Lewis, 1977; Snyder et al., 1977).

2. Middle-class students are expected to receive higher grades than lower-class students. In one experiment, subjects watched videotapes of a child taking a test (Darley & Gross, 1983). One group, informed that she came from an upper-class background, rated her performance as superior. Another group watched the same tape but was informed that the girl was of lower-class origin. They rated her performance as below grade level.

3. Teachers tend to be influenced more strongly by negative information about a child (such as a low IQ score) than by neutral or positive information. A child whose schoolwork is consistently excellent over the years may be labeled an "overachiever" on the basis of an average IQ score on a single intelligence test.

4. Women teachers are more likely to perceive girls than boys to be ideal students. Why? In early grades, girls are usually more inter-

▶ ▶ ▶ ▶

SCHOOL INFLUENCES

471

ested in sedentary educational activities such as reading and artwork than boys are. Boys may be too active to focus on them with equal persistence. Thus an initial positive response from teachers may give girls self-confidence in the academic setting. A negative response may cause many boys to begin to see themselves as academic foul-ups.

By and large, teachers behave generally more positively toward students of whom they have high expectations (Cooper, 1979). They smile at them more frequently, praise them more often, supervise them more closely, and press them harder to find answers. Moreover, when they do poorly, teachers are likely to encourage them to work harder. Teachers communicate the expectancy that they have the ability to succeed—all they require is the effort and the appropriate prerequisites. But teachers are not likely to press students for whom they have low expectations. It would be cruel, they might think, to press them to achieve when they must fall short.

Teachers can go a long way toward reducing some of the detrimental effects of low expectations by doing some of the following:

1. Allowing young boys, who are frequently more active than young girls, more time to adjust to the school situation before making judgments of their academic ability.
2. Attempting to avoid prejudgments of the abilities of individual students on the basis of their physical appearance or their ethnic backgrounds, names, or social class.
3. Trying to make reasonably high demands of all students, and not singling out a few.
4. Being certain that students are praised on the basis of what they accomplish, not on the basis on what the teacher sees as their potential.
5. Avoiding going to an administrative office to compare students' scores on IQ tests.
6. Evaluating students on the basis of their performance in class, and not on the basis of the academic average brought into the class.

The educational system accomplishes very little, if several years of schooling do nothing more than bear out the predictions made for children on the basis of early test scores or failures. A superior educational system will break down these predictions by making reasonable demands of all children and praising them for their achievements, rather than judging them on irrelevant traits.

Exceptional children *Children whose emotional, intellectual, or physical traits differ significantly from those of the great majority of children.*

Mainstreaming

Special programs have been created for multitudes of **exceptional children** to meet their special needs and to protect them from the tough competition

▶ ▶ ▶ ▶

in regular classrooms. However, placing exceptional children in separate classes can also stigmatize them and segregate them from other children. Except for gifted children, special-needs classes also negatively influence teacher expectations. Neither the teacher nor the students themselves come to expect very much. This negative expectation becomes a **self-fulfilling prophecy,** and the exceptional students' achievements also suffer.

Mainstreaming is intended to counter the negative effects of special-needs classes. In mainstreaming, exceptional children are placed in regular classrooms. Children who have been mainstreamed include the emotionally disturbed; the gifted and the mildly mentally retarded; and children with physical disabilities such as blindness, deafness, or paralysis.

The mainstreaming of exceptional children seems consistent with democratic ideals and the desire to provide every child with an equal opportunity to learn. Mainstreaming also permits exceptional and other children to socialize and interact on a number of levels.

The goals of mainstreaming include inspiring handicapped students to greater achievements; providing handicapped students with better educational opportunities; and fostering normal social interactions between handicapped and nonhandicapped students, so that the handicapped will have a better chance of fitting into society as adults.

While the goals of mainstreaming are laudable, observations of the results are less promising. There is some suggestion that mildly retarded children may achieve more when they are mainstreamed (Robinson & Robinson, 1976). But a review of a number of studies suggests that many handicapped children do not fare well in regular classrooms (Linton & Juul, 1980). Rather than inspiring them to greater achievements, regular classrooms can also be overwhelming for many handicapped students and cause them to withdraw from their classmates.

Nor is it clear that placement in regular classrooms spurs socializing with handicapped students. Nonhandicapped students generally choose not to socialize with handicapped students in these classes (Ipsa, 1981; Karnes & Lee, 1979). Ironically, handicapped students sometimes become further isolated and stigmatized.

We need to learn more about what types of teacher training and what types of preparation for the nonhandicapped students will ease the way of the handicapped child in the regular classroom. We also need to find out what sort of supplementary educational experiences are needed to round out the educational and social experiences of mainstreamed children. Until we have this information, the results of mainstreaming may remain mixed.

▶ ▶ ▶ ▶

Summary

1. Families and other institutions socialize children to develop a sense of responsibilty, to conform to routines, and to avoid damaging property.

2. Many investigators classify families' approaches to socialization according to the independent dimensions of warmth–coldness (or acceptance–rejection) and restrictiveness–permissiveness.

3. Parents usually attempt to enforce restrictions by inductive, power-assertive, or loss-of-love techniques. Inductive techniques aim to teach children principles that they can use to guide their own behavior. Reasoning is an inductive technique. Power-assertive parents tend to rely on physical rewards and punishments. Parents who use loss of love to encourage compliance tend to isolate or ignore their children when they misbehave. Inductive techniques are most likely to foster empathy and self-control.

4. In her search for the origins of instrumental competence, Diana Baumrind discovered a typology of child-rearing approaches. Authoritative parents are most likely to have competent children. Authoritative parents are high in restrictiveness, demands for mature behavior, communication ability, and warmth. Authoritarian parents view obedience as a virtue for its own sake. Authoritarian parents are low in communication ability and warmth. Their children develop moderate competence, but also tend to be irritable and cautious in social interactions. Permissive parents are low in restrictiveness, maturity demands, and communication ability, but high in warmth and support. Their children tend to be least mature and most impulsive.

5. Parents who foster achievement motivation expect their children to succeed. They demand mature behavior, display warmth and encouragement, and praise accomplishments.

6. Siblings provide caregiving, nurturance, advice, role models, and social interaction for children. Mothers generally pay newborns more attention than older children, which can foster sibling rivalry. As families grow, children are more likely to be assigned specific chores in the home, and parents are more likely to become power-assertive in their discipline. Children from large families do not perform as well in school as children from small families.

7. First-born children tend to attain the highest IQ scores, the highest grades, and to be most responsible. However, they are also usually the most anxious children. Later-born children tend to acquire superior social skills and to be more popular with peers. Later-borns are also more likely to engage in dangerous activities or sports.

8. Children of divorced parents generally experience turmoil, uncertain futures, and downward movement in socioeconomic status. Young children suffer more than older children, and boys more than girls. But most children appear to adjust in about two years. The more disorganized the family after a divorce, the more the children suffer. Parents who remain committed to cooperating in child rearing after a divorce minimize the effects of divorce on their children.

▶ ▶ ▶ ▶

9. Most children of divorce live with their mothers. Boys whose fathers are absent during the first few years of life frequently show less stereotypical masculine behavior and greater dependence. Teenage daughters who reside with their mothers frequently show increased heterosexual interest and activity.

10. Peers become progressively more important as children develop. Older children spend more time with peers, and the tendency to conform to peer pressures increases dramatically from about the ages of 8 to 14. Attractive, sociable children are most likely to be popular with peers. Aggressive children tend to be rejected.

11. In addition to imparting knowledge and skills, schools socialize children to adopt U.S. ways and values. Children participate more when class size is smaller. Children who sit in the front and center of classrooms participate more than those who sit to the sides or back of the room. Children may be uncomfortable and respond aggressively when they are packed in too closely.

12. In open education, children are allowed to actively explore a rich learning environment, rather than coerced to engage in specific learning activities. Teachers in open classrooms tend to behave more democratically, to explain restrictions, elicit student input, and warmly encourage learning activities. There are major gaps in the evidence comparing the effectiveness of open and traditional approaches to education. However, both approaches may spur similar achievements, and children in open classrooms have more positive attitudes toward school and display more curiosity and creativity.

13. Teachers serve as role models and dispensers of reinforcement. Teacher praise is most effective when it is sincere, specific, and adapted to the individual needs of students. Students seem most likely to imitate (identify with) warm, positive teachers. When teachers have high expectations of certain students, they frequently elicit greater achievements from them. Teachers smile at these students more often, praise them, push them harder, and attribute their shortcomings to lack of effort rather than lack of ability.

14. Mainstreaming is intended to inspire handicapped students to greater achievements, provide them with the best educational opportunities, and encourage social interactions with nonhandicapped students. Unfortunately, some handicapped students feel overwhelmed in regular classrooms and also tend to be avoided by nonhandicapped students.

▶ ▶ ▶ ▶

Trying to "reason" with children is the least effective way of fostering self-control. False. So-called inductive methods are most likely to foster empathy and self-control.

Children with strict parents are more likely than children with permissive parents to have high self-esteem. True. Strictness appears to help foster behavioral competencies, and behavioral competencies contribute to self-esteem.

Parents who make high demands of their children to achieve are most likely to foster achievement motivation. True—especially when high demands are associated with parental warmth and encouragement.

Children from large families do not perform as well in school as children from small families. True. However, when large families have the resources to provide each child with individual attention, the children achieve more.

First-born children tend to show higher achievement motivation than later-born children. True. They are also generally more responsible, but more anxious.

Later-born children tend to be more sociable than first-born children. True. It seems that they acquire social skills that make them relatively more popular with their peers.

Divorce is harder on young children than on adolescents. True. Young children are more likely to blame themselves for the divorce and are generally more fearful about the future.

About 90 percent of children of divorced parents live with their mothers. True.

Regular visits with their natural mothers are associated with poorer relationships between stepdaughters and their stepmothers. True. Good stepmother–stepdaughter relationships promote higher self-esteem in stepdaughters.

The majority of divorced fathers do not keep up with their child-support payments. True. About two-thirds do not.

The daughters of working women are more achievement oriented and set themselves higher career goals than the daughters of nonworking women. True. The marriages and general home atmosphere of working women are also more egalitarian.

Physically attractive children are more popular with their peers. True.

Children willingly accept friends from different races and social classes. False. Schoolchildren usually select friends from their own ethnic backgrounds and social class.

Aggressive children tend to be looked up to by their peers. False. Aggressive children tend to be rejected by their peers.

▶ ▶ ▶ ▶

Children who are allowed to make many of their own decisions in the classroom tend to goof off and achieve less. False. When the student–teacher relationship is more democratic, many students achieve more. They also show more curiosity and like school better.

Teachers should avoid praising some children for their accomplishments. True—at least in public. Some children are embarrassed when teachers praise them in front of the class.

Teachers who have high expectations of students frequently elicit greater achievements from them. True. The so-called Pygmalion effect has worked many times, especially when teachers strongly believe that certain children harbor great potential.

▶ ▶ ▶ ▶

12

Development of Sex Roles and Sex Differences

C H A P T E R ▸ O U T L I N E

▶
▶
▶
▶
▶
▶
▶

- At the age of 2½, boys and girls typically think their own sex is superior.
- Three-year-olds report that women are more likely to cry than men.
- Girls are superior to boys in verbal abilities.
- Fathers are more likely than mothers to help children with their math homework.
- Girls are more likely than boys to have math anxiety.
- Girls are more likely to play with "boys' toys" than boys are to play with "girls' toys."
- Girls do not like to play with guns.
- Caring for children is apparently a sex-typed activity, while caring for pets is not.
- Girls like going to school, but boys do not.
- Boys are more aggressive than girls.
- Boys are more likely than girls to curse.
- By the time they enter school, boys and girls tend to sit and carry themselves differently.
- Women who compete with men in the business world are suffering from penis-envy they experienced as little girls.
- Fathers are more likely than mothers to treat their sons and daughters equally.
- Boys reared in father-absent homes are more dependent than boys reared in intact homes.
- Men are more often portrayed as authorities on television commercials, while women are more likely to be cast as flustered product users.
- A 2½-year-old may know that he is a boy, but still think that he can grow up to be a mommy.
- Five- and 6-year-olds tend to distort their memories so that they "recall" boys playing with trains and sawing wood—even when these activities were actually carried out by girls.
- Adolescent girls who show a number of "masculine" traits have higher self-esteem than girls who thoroughly adopt the traditional feminine sex role.

Two children were treated at Johns Hopkins University Hospital for the same problem. But the treatments and the outcomes were vastly different. Each child was genetically female, and each had the internal sex organs of a female. But because of excessive in-utero exposure to male sex hormones, each had developed external sex organs that resembled a male's (Money & Ehrhardt, 1972).

The problem was identified in one child (let's call her Nora) early. The masculinized sex organs were surgically removed when she was 2. Like many girls, Nora was tomboyish during childhood, but she was feminine in appearance and had a female **gender identity.** She dated boys, and her fantasies centered around marriage to a man. *(Poor Girl)*

The other child (let's call him Edward) was at first mistaken for a genetic male with stunted external sex organs. The error was discovered at the age of 3½. But by then Edward had a firm male gender identity. Surgery further masculinized the appearance of his sex organs. At puberty, hormone therapy fostered the development of bodily hair, male musculature, and other male secondary sex characteristics.

As an adolescent, Edward joined a gang of semidelinquents. He was accepted as one of the boys. In contrast to Nora, Edward was sexually attracted to women.

Nora and Edward both had **androgenital syndrome.** In this hormonal disorder, prenatal exposure to androgens masculinizes the sex organs of genetic females. In the case of Nora, the child was assigned to the female gender and reared as a girl. The other child, Edward, was labeled male and reared as a boy. Each child acquired the gender identity of the assigned sex.

The problems encountered by Nora and Edward are rare. Still, they raise questions about what it means to be a boy or girl in our society. Let us explore this issue further by discussing masculine and feminine sex-role stereotypes and their development. Then we shall describe research on cognitive and personality sex differences and explore their development.

Finally, we shall examine the concept of psychological androgyny. *Physical* androgyny—the possession of the sex organs of both sexes—poses many problems and is corrected medically at an early age. But *psychological* androgyny may be desirable, because it places a wider range of traits and adjustment strategies at the disposal of the individual.

Gender identity *One's concept of being male or female. (The first stage in the cognitive-developmental theory of the assumption of sex roles.)*

Androgenital syndrome *A disorder in which genetic females become masculinized as a result of prenatal exposure to male hormones.*

Stereotype *A fixed, conventional idea about a group.*

Sex roles *Complex clusters of ways in which males and females are expected to behave.*

▶ ▶ ▶ ▶

Development of Sex Roles and Stereotypes

"Why Can't a Woman Be More Like a Man?" You may recall this song title from the musical *My Fair Lady.* In the song, Henry Higgins laments that women are emotional and fickle, whereas men are logical and dependable. The emotional female is a **stereotype.** The logical male is also a stereotype. Stereotypes shape our expectations so that we assume that unknown members of the designated group share the stereotype.

Cultural stereotypes of males and females involve clusters of traits that we call **sex roles.** Laypeople tend to see the traditional feminine sex-role stereotype as dependent, gentle, helpful, kind, mild, patient, and submissive (Cartwright et al., 1983). The typical masculine stereotype is perceived as tough, protective, and gentlemanly (Myers & Gonda, 1982). Females are more often viewed as warm and emotional, while males are more frequently seen as independent and competitive. Men are more frequently expected to be the financial providers for their families. Women are more often expected to care for the kids and cook the meals (Deaux & Lewis, 1983).

Research by Deanna Kuhn and her colleagues (1978) shows that children have acquired cognitive awareness of sex-role stereotypes by the ages of 2½ to 3½. When asked to describe the differences between boys and girls, or women and men, 2½-year-old children answered concretely in terms of the things boys and girls *do* and like or dislike. Boys and girls generally agreed that boys played with transportation toys (cars, firetrucks, and so on), built things with blocks and other materials, enjoyed helping their fathers, and tended to hit others (act aggressively). Boys and girls also agreed that girls played with dolls and helped their mothers cook and clean. They perceived girls as never hitting, as talking a lot, and as frequently asking for help.

There was some "chauvinism." Children of each sex perceived their own in a somewhat better light. Boys perceived other boys, for example, as hard workers and go-getters, but viewed girls as whiny slowpokes who were less effective at getting things done. Girls perceived other girls as nicer-looking than boys, more affectionate (kissing), and nonaggressive (an attribute they viewed as positive). They saw boys as mean and liking to hit. Ironically, girls also viewed boys as "weak," even though they were more aggressive. Among adults, the male sex-role stereotype is usually viewed as more positive both by men and women.

By the age of 3, most children are also aware of stereotypical differences in the ways that males and females dress, and the types of occupations that are considered appropriate for them (Ruble & Ruble, 1980).

Williams, Bennett, and Best (1975) studied sex-role stereotypes among kindergartners to fourth-graders by asking them to point to a picture of either a woman or a man as they read a series of statements, such as "One of these people is a bully. This person is always pushing people around and getting into fights. Which person gets into fights?" (p. 636). Ninety-four percent of the youngest group—the kindergartners—pointed to the man. Men were viewed by kindergartners as strong, loud, coarse, independent, and adventurous. The kindergartners chose male pictures about as often as female pictures for statements that described female stereotypes, such as gentleness, emotionality, and soft-heartedness. That is, the feminine sex-role stereotype was not so well-developed as the masculine among the kindergartners.

Sex-role stereotypes of fourth- and fifth-graders in the United States, England, and Ireland are more clearly differentiated (Best et al., 1977; Williams et al., 1975). Fourth- and fifth-graders speak about the sexes in terms of psychological traits, not only concrete activities and preferences. The 9- and 10-year-olds in these studies, girls as well as boys, perceived females, not males, as weak. Men were viewed as dominant, strong, ambitious, aggressive, and coarse. Women were perceived as more sophisticated, soft-hearted, affectionate, and sentimental.

Reis and Wright (1982) found that children become increasingly traditional in their stereotyping between 3 and 5. Even 3-year-olds viewed "cruel" as a masculine trait, while "cries a lot" was seen as feminine. The children in this study were retested after six months, and the stereotypes had become stronger for each age level.

▶ ▶ ▶ ▶

Stereotyping seems to peak at about the fourth or fifth grade and then declines slightly over the next couple of years (Meyer, 1980; Ullian, 1981). During adolescence children apparently become somewhat more flexible in their perceptions of males and females (Emmerich & Shepard, 1982). They retain the broad stereotypes but also perceive similarities between the sexes and recognize that there are individual differences.

There are apparently some social-class and racial differences in sex-role stereotyping. Middle-class children are more likely than lower-class children to show flexibility in their sex-role concepts (Romer & Cherry, 1980). Middle-class children see the sexes as sharing many traits. Black children consider men and women equally emotionally expressive, whereas Italian-American and Jewish children see women as significantly more expressive than men.

FOCUS ▸ ON ▸ RESEARCH

Sugar and Spice and . . . Just What Are Little Girls (and Boys) Made Of?

▷
▷
▷
▷
▷   No doubt you have heard the doggerel that little girls are "sugar and spice and everything nice," while little boys are "snaps and snails and puppy-dogs' tails." Perhaps we are too sophisticated to interpret these descriptions literally. Nevertheless, in one influential study of sex roles, Inge Broverman and her colleagues (1972) found that college students had very clear ideas about what constituted proper behavior for males and females.

The researchers first had undergraduate psychology students list the traits and behaviors that they thought differentiated the sexes. A list of 122 traits, each of which was mentioned at least twice, was generated. Each trait was made into a bipolar scale, such as:

Not at all aggressive ..... Very aggressive

Another group of students indicated which pole of the scale was more descriptive of the "average" man or woman. Only traits that achieved a 75 percent agreement rate were retained. Many of the 41 traits that met this standard are shown in Table 12.1.

Further analysis broke the list down into two broad factors. One centered around competency in the realm of objects, including the business world ("instrumentality"). The second involved emotional warmth and expression of feelings (the "warmth–expressiveness cluster"). Other samples then rated the items as more desirable for men or women. In general, masculine traits in the instrumentality cluster were rated as more desirable for men, while feminine traits in this cluster were rated as more desirable for women. Respondents felt that it was desirable for women to be less rational than men, less aggressive, less competitive, and less dominant, but more emotional and dependent. The ideal woman was also seen as neater, gentler, more empathetic, and more emotionally expressive than a man.

▶ ▶ ▶ ▶

Table 12.1 Stereotypical Sex-Role Traits as Found in the Broverman Study

INSTRUMENTALITY CLUSTER (Masculine Pole Perceived as More Desirable)

FEMININE	MASCULINE
Not at all aggressive	Very aggressive
Not at all independent	Very independent
Very emotional	Not at all emotional
Does not hide emotions at all	Almost always hides emotions
Very subjective	Very objective
Very easily influenced	Not at all easily influenced
Very submissive	Very dominant
Dislikes math and science very much	Likes math and science very much
Very excitable in a minor crisis	Not at all excitable in a minor crisis
Very passive	Very active
Not at all competitive	Very competitive
Very illogical	Very logical
Very home-oriented	Very worldly
Not at all skilled in business	Very skilled in business
Very sneaky	Very direct
Feelings easily hurt	Feelings not easily hurt
Not at all adventurous	Very adventurous
Has difficulty making decisions	Can make decisions easily
Cries very easily	Never cries
Almost never acts as a leader	Almost always acts as a leader
Not at all self-confident	Very self-confident
Very uncomfortable about being aggressive	Not at all uncomfortable about being aggressive
Not at all ambitious	Very ambitious
Unable to separate feelings from ideas	Easily able to separate feelings from ideas
Very dependent	Not at all dependent
Very conceited about appearance	Never conceited about appearance
Thinks women are always superior to men	Thinks men are always superior to women
Does not talk freely about sex, with men	Talks freely about sex with men

WARMTH–EXPRESSIVENESS CLUSTER (Feminine Pole Perceived as More Desirable)

FEMININE	MASCULINE
Doesn't use harsh language at all	Uses very harsh language
Very talkative	Not at all talkative
Very tactful	Very blunt
Very gentle	Very rough
Very aware of feelings of others	Not at all aware of feelings of others
Very religious	Not at all religious
Very interested in own appearance	Not at all interested in own appearance
Very neat in habits	Very sloppy in habits
Very quiet	Very loud
Very strong need for security	Very little need for security
Enjoys art and literature	Does not enjoy art and literature at all
Easily expresses tender feelings	Does not easily express tender feelings at all

Based on responses from 74 college men and 80 college women.
Adapted from I. K. Broverman, et al., Sex-role stereotypes: A current appraisal. *Journal of Social Issues, 28*(2) (1972), 63.

► ► ► ►

Sexism

Children, like adults, are guilty of, and must cope with, **sexism.** Sexists usually assume that negative traits will eventually impair the performance of boys and girls in certain types of jobs or social situations. In Chapter 1 we noted how sexism has historically worked to the disadvantage of girls. Boys have historically been afforded more educational opportunities. Until recently, sexism excluded girls from many sports and from certain college or preprofessional preparatory programs. Women have been excluded from many occupations, with medicine and law serving as visible examples.

Sexism may lead us to interpret the same behavior in different ways when shown by girls or by boys. We may see the boy as "self-assertive," but the girl as "pushy." We may see an undecided boy as "flexible," but view an undecided girl as "fickle" and "indecisive."

Sexism can also rear its ugly head when a boy chooses to behave in ways that are stereotyped as feminine. A "sensitive" girl is simply sensitive, but a sensitive boy may be seen as a "sissy." A girl may seem "polite," whereas a boy, showing the same social behavior, may be labeled "passive" or "weak." Let us examine some studies of the power of sexism.

In one, 3- and 5-year-olds viewed a videotape of an infant who was labeled "Lisa" for some observers and "Bobby" for others (Haugh et al., 1980). Even among these preschoolers, the name induced inference of different traits. "Lisa" usually came in second-best. "Lisa" was perceived as smaller, weaker, slower, and softer than "Bobby," although the children were watching the same tape.

School Days, School Days—Dear Old Sexist School Days? Although girls were systematically excluded from formal education for centuries, today we might least expect to find sexism among teachers. Teachers, after all, are generally well educated. They are also trained to be fair-minded and sensitive to the needs of their young charges in today's changing society.

However, we may not have heard the last of sexism in our schools. Field researchers enlisted by Myra and David Sadker (1985) observed students in fourth-, sixth-, and eighth-grade classes in four states and in the District of Columbia. Teachers and students were white and black, urban, suburban, and rural. In almost all cases, findings were depressingly similar.

Boys generally dominated classroom communication, whether the subject was math (a traditionally "masculine" area) or language arts (a traditionally "feminine" area). Boys, in fact, were eight times more likely than girls to call out answers without raising their hands. So far, it could be said, we have evidence of a sex difference, but not of sexism. However, teachers were less than impartial in responding to boys and girls when they called out. Teachers, male and female, were significantly more likely to accept calling out from boys. Girls were significantly more likely to, as the song goes, receive "teachers' dirty looks"—or to be reminded that they should raise their hands and wait to be called upon. Boys, it appears, are expected to be impetuous, but girls are reprimanded for "unladylike behavior."

Despite boys' dominance of classroom communication, teachers still think of girls as more talkative than boys. In a clever experiment, the Sadkers (1985) showed teachers and administrators films of classroom discussions. Afterward they asked who were doing more talking, boys or girls. Most teachers

▶ ▶ ▶ ▶

reported that the girls were more talkative, even though, in the film, the boys spent three times as much time talking.

The Sadkers also report other instances of sexism in the classroom:

- Teachers praise preschool boys more often than girls and are more likely to give them detailed instructions.
- Girls are less likely to take courses in math and science, even when their aptitude in these areas equals or excels that of boys.
- Girls begin school with greater skills in basic computation and reading, but have lower SAT scores in quantitative and verbal subtests by the time they are graduated from high school. Perhaps the educational system does more to encourage boys to develop academic skills.

The irony is that our educational system has been responsible for the lifting of many generations of the downtrodden into the mainstream of U.S. life. Sad to say, the system appears to be doing more for boys than for girls—even in the 1980s.

Occupational Stereotypes and Career Choices

Children not only divide the world according to sex-role personality stereotypes. They also divide the workplace into "women's jobs" and "men's jobs."

In order to assess 2- and 3-year-olds' stereotypes about the workplace, Gettys and Cann (1981) showed them male and female dolls and asked them to point to the one that held a particular job. Even by this age, 78 percent of the children thought that the male doll was the construction worker. By contrast, only 23 percent pointed to the male doll as a teacher.

Children's stereotyping of occupations according to gender seems to grow more rigid up through about the fourth grade. It is also at about the fourth grade that boys and girls are most likely to restrict their socializing to members of their own sex (Matlin, 1987). Fifth- and sixth-graders seem to ease up somewhat in their assumptions (Cann & Haight, 1983; O'Keefe & Hyde, 1983; Tremaine et al., 1982).

Sex Differences in Occupational Stereotypes By and large, boys seem to be more restricted in their occupational stereotypes. Shepard and Hess (1975) gave children a list of jobs and asked respondents to indicate whether each should be performed by a man or a woman, or whether it could be performed by either. Except for kindergartners, the youngest age group, girls were more likely than boys to choose "either."

Boys are also more rigid in their own career aspirations. Lavine (1982) asked 7- to 11-year-olds what they wanted to do as adults. She coded responses according to census information that indicated the proportion of men in each position. The jobs mentioned by boys were occupied by men 89 percent of the time. The jobs chosen by girls were occupied by men 41 percent of the time. Boys chose male-sex-typed positions significantly more often than girls did. However, if we view the average "neutral" position as being occupied by men 50 percent of the time, girls' responses were more neutral. Girls, that is, were willing to accept nonstereotyped positions more often.

A recent study by Linda Dunlap and Joseph Canale (1987) of Marist

▶ ▶ ▶ ▶

College appears to clarify some of the developmental trends in choosing non-traditional careers. Dunlap and Canale assessed career aspirations among second-, fifth-, eighth-, and twelfth-graders in upstate New York. As in the Lavine (1982) study, boys chose masculine-typed jobs more often than girls did. But boys' "rigidity" peaked at the fifth grade, then declined. Seventy-eight percent of second-grade boys chose masculine-typed jobs, as compared to 100 percent of fifth-graders, 92 percent of eighth-graders, and 69 percent of twelfth-graders. The pattern for girls also showed ascent followed by decline. Only 20 percent of second-grade girls chose masculine-typed careers, as compared to 41 percent of fifth-grade girls, 59 percent of eighth-grade girls, and 39 percent of twelfth-grade girls. This developmental trend may reflect increasing awareness of non-traditional career opportunities among girls through eighth grade. At some point during high school, aspirations may become tempered by real-world opportunities and accumulating years of socialization as well as by changes in actual preferences. The same study found that the girls' parents wanted them to enter traditional feminine-typed jobs in an overwhelming majority of cases. As a consequence, a number of girls may begin to focus on more traditional occupations as they approach entry into the work force or selection of a college major.

Dunlap and Canale also found that the prestige of the mother's job influenced children's job choices—particularly at the fifth-grade level. The children of mothers with highly prestigious jobs were more likely to choose highly prestigious jobs for themselves. As more women attain highly prestigious jobs, perhaps their daughters will become more likely to aspire to them as well.

Evidence is mixed as to whether adolescent girls select careers that are as prestigious as those chosen by boys. Dunlap and Canale (1987) found that their sample of upstate New York boys generally aspire to higher-prestige jobs than girls did. This difference was most pronounced during the eighth grade. But in a study of 1,234 Illinois ninth- and twelfth-graders, Farmer (1983) found that girls chose more prestigious careers than boys.

All in all, Farmer found that the career aspirations of today's male and female adolescents more similar than different, although the girls remained more commit to homemaking than the boys. Sad to say, this double commitment on the part of girls all too often reflects the realities awaiting them in adulthood. Even when they become the vice presidents or presidents of their companies, wives remain more likely than husbands to do the laundry, plan meals and shop for food, shop for the children's clothing, and stay home with their children when they are ill (Rogan, 1984).

Sex Differences: Vive la Différence or Vive la Similarité?

If the sexes were not clearly anatomically different, this book might have been about the development of regional differences in Chinese cooking. But there are serious questions about behavioral, cognitive, and personality differences between boys and girls, especially in the light of the controversy over sex-role stereotypes. Let us now examine what is known of these differences.

▶ ▶ ▶ ▶

Differences in Infancy

Boys are somewhat longer and heavier than girls at birth, but here the physical "superiority" seems to end. Girls are slightly ahead in bone development. Boys also reach the early milestones in locomotion—sitting, crawling, and walking—later than girls do (Hutt, 1978).

Infant boys and girls show few differences in perceptual development. Shepard & Peterson (1973) reviewed the literature and found gender comparisons in 145 ways of measuring vision, hearing, and other sensory functions in infants. There were no differences in 123 of the measures. The remainder were split in showing advantages for boys or girls.

The literature is mixed as to whether boys are more active during infancy. While some studies have shown boys to be more active on some measures, others find no substantial differences (Jacklin & Maccoby, 1983; Rothbart, 1983). Rothbart (1983) similarly found no significant sex differences in crying or in the ease with which babies could be soothed over the first six months.

Infant girls may be somewhat more sociable than boys. Brooks-Gunn and Matthews (1979) reported that girls were more likely than boys to look at, smile at, and talk to their mothers throughout infancy. Infant girls may also be somewhat more responsive when their mothers speak to them (Gunnar & Donahue, 1980). Newborn girls apparently cry more than infant boys in response to the crying of other infants (Eisenberg & Lennon, 1983). However, crying at this age is reflexive. It is doubtful that we can relate neonatal crying to differences in empathy that characterize the sex-role stereotype later on.

All in all, sex differences during infancy are small and rather inconsistent (Matlin, 1987).

Differences in Cognitive Abilities

It was once believed that males were more intelligent than females, because of their greater knowledge of world affairs and their skill in science and industry. We now recognize that greater male knowledge and skill reflected not differences in intelligence, but the systematic exclusion of females from world affairs, science, and industry. Whereas there are no overall differences in cognitive abilities between the sexes, Eleanor Maccoby and Carol Nagy Jacklin (1974) found persistent suggestions that females are somewhat superior to males in verbal ability. Males, on the other hand, seem somewhat superior in visual-spatial and math abilities (Table 12.2).

Verbal Abilities Girls seem to acquire language somewhat faster than boys. Some investigators have found that girls make more prelinguistic vocalizations and utter their first word about half a month sooner—at 11.4 as compared to 12 months (Harris, 1977). Girls acquire additional words more rapidly, and their pronunciation is clearer, making them easier to understand (Nelson, 1973; Schachter et al., 1978).

Between the ages of 5 and 11 girls show greater word fluency. They can name letters, colors, and objects more rapidly than their male age-mates

▶ ▶ ▶ ▶

Table 12.2   Vive la Différence? Just How Different Are Boys and Girls?

DIFFERENCES BORNE OUT BY SOME RESEARCH STUDIES	DIFFERENCES ABOUT WHICH THERE IS GREAT DOUBT	ASSUMED DIFFERENCES THAT RESEARCH HAS SHOWN TO BE FALSE
Boys tend to be more aggressive than girls. Girls have greater verbal ability than boys. Boys have greater visual-spatial ability than girls. Boys have greater ability in math than girls.	Girls are more timid and anxious than boys. Boys are more active than girls. Boys are more competitive than girls. Boys are more dominant than girls. Girls are more sociable than boys.	Boys are more logical and analytical than girls. Girls are more suggestible than boys. Boys have higher self-esteem than girls. Girls lack achievement motivation.

It has been commonly assumed that there are great cognitive and personality differences between males and females, and that these differences represent heredity or the natural order of things. But psychological research has found that certain assumed differences do not exist, and that others are smaller than expected. Those differences that remain, such as greater verbal ability in females and greater math ability in males, may reflect cultural expectations and not heredity.
Source: Based on data from Maccoby & Jacklin, 1974.

(Denckla & Rudel, 1974). Larger sex differences in verbal abilities are found at about the age of 11, and differences continue to increase throughout the high school years (Maccoby & Jacklin, 1974). Female high school students excel in spelling, punctuation, reading comprehension, solving verbal analogies (such as "Washington : one :: Lincoln : ?), and solving anagrams (scrambled words).

As noted in Chapter 6, far more U.S. boys than girls have reading problems, such as dyslexia or simply reading below grade level. Girls appear to attend more carefully to the details that allow discrimination among letters (Smith, 1985). Cultural factors may play a role in sex differences in reading, since these differences disappear or are reversed in other cultures (Matlin, 1987). Reading is stereotyped as a feminine activity in the United States and Canada, and girls surpass boys in reading skills in these countries. Boys score higher than girls on most tests of reading in Nigeria and England, where boys have traditionally been expected to outperform girls in academic pursuits, including reading.

Spatial Abilities   Beginning in adolescence, boys usually outperform girls on tests of spatial abilty. These tests assess skills such as mentally rotating figures in space and finding figures embedded within larger designs (Maccoby & Jacklin, 1974; Petersen, 1980).

The sex difference in spatial ability may be related to the number of math courses taken. Children are likely to practice spatial skills in geometry and related courses, and boys take more math courses in high school than girls (Meece et al., 1982). One study found no sex differences in spatial ability when the number of math courses taken was considered (Fennema & Sherman, 1977).

Just as reading is considered feminine in our culture, spatial and math activities are stereotyped as masculine. "Boys'" toys provide more practice with spatial skills than "girls'" toys. Moreover, children who spend more time playing with so-called boys' toys perform better on spatial tasks than children who

In the United States, girls tend to have fewer reading problems than boys.

▶ ▶ ▶ ▶

spend more time playing with so-called girls' toys (Fagot & Littman, 1976). Adolescent boys are also more likely than adolescent girls to engage in spatially oriented leisure-time activities (Newcombe et al., 1983), which may provide further "practice" in spatial skills.

Mathematics Abilities   Maccoby and Jacklin (1974) found that boys and girls show similar math ability until late childhood. Boys begin to outperform girls at about the age of 12, and consistent sex differences appear at about 15 (Meece et al., 1982).

Consider sex differences on the mathematics test of the Scholastic Aptitude Test (SAT). The mean score is 500. Twice as many boys as girls attain scores over 500 (Benbow & Stanley, 1980). *Thirteen* times as many boys as girls attain scores over 700 (Benbow & Stanley, 1983).

Boys, as noted, are more likely to take math courses in high school than girls. There are many more reasons that boys are likely to feel more "at home" with math:

1. Fathers are more likely than mothers to help children with math homework (Meece et al., 1982; Raymond & Benbow, 1986).

2. Advanced math courses are more likely to be taught by men (Fox, 1982).

3. Teachers often show higher expectations for boys in math courses (Meece et al., 1982).

4. Teachers of math courses spend more time instructing and interacting with boys than girls (Meece et al., 1982).

Given these typical experiences with math, we should not be surprised that:

1. By junior high, boys view themselves as more competent in math than girls do, even when they receive identical grades (Meece et al., 1982).

2. By high school, students perceive math as part of the male domain (Fox, 1980).

3. By junior high, boys are more likely than girls to perceive math as useful (Meece et al., 1982).

4. Boys are more likely to have positive feelings about math. Girls are more likely to have math anxiety (Tobias & Weissbrod, 1980).

5. It becomes increasingly difficult to convince high school and college women to take math courses, even when they show superior math ability (Eccles, 1985; Fox et al., 1985; Paulsen & Johnson, 1983).

Julia Sherman (1981, 1982, 1983) found several factors related to girls' decisions to take math courses in high school. First, traits stereotyped as "masculine" were associated with mathematics and apparently dissuaded some girls from exploring it. These traits included ambition, independence, self-confidence, and spatial ability. Girls choosing to take math were less likely to view math as a male domain, and they had had positive early experiences with math.

► ► ► ►

A Cautionary Note In sum, it does appear that within our culture girls show greater verbal abilities than boys, whereas boys show greater spatial and math abilities than girls. However, three factors should caution us not to attach too much importance to these sex differences. First, in most cases they are small (Deaux, 1984; Hyde, 1981). For example, one study of 440,000 high school students found that boys did outperform girls on math tests (Fox et al., 1979). *But the average girl missed only 0.6 of an item more than the average boy.*

Second, these sex differences are *group* differences. Variation in these skills is larger *within,* than between, the sexes. Despite group differences, millions of males exceed the ''average'' female in writing and spelling skills. Millions of females outdistance the ''average'' male in math and spatial abilities. Males have produced their Shakespeares and females their Madame Curies.

Third, the small differences that appear to exist may largely reflect cultural expectations and environmental influences (Tobias, 1982). We have noted that reading ability is stereotyped as feminine in our culture, whereas spatial and math abilities are stereotyped as masculine. Female introductory psychology students given just three hours of training in various visual-spatial skills, such as rotating geometric figures, showed no performance deficit in these skills when compared to men (Stericker & LeVesconte, 1982). As noted in Chapter 9, so-called ability or aptitude tests actually measure achievement at a certain point in time.

Differences in Play and School Activities

Boys and girls develop stereotypical preferences for toys and activities early. Even within their first year, boys are more explorative and independent. Girls are relatively more quiet, dependent, and restrained (Goldberg & Lewis, 1969). By 18 to 36 months, girls are more likely to play with soft toys and dolls and to dance. Eighteen- to 36-month-old boys are more likely to play with hard objects; blocks; and toy cars, trucks, and airplanes (Fagot, 1974).

Although preferences for sex-typed toys are well developed by the ages of 15 to 36 months, girls are more likely to stray from the stereotypes. Girls select ''boys' toys'' such as cars and trucks more frequently than boys choose ''girls' toys'' such as dolls (O'Brien et al., 1983). These cross-role activities seem consistent with what we know of sexism. ''Masculine'' activities and traits carry greater prestige in U.S. culture. Therefore, a boy's playing with ''girls' toys'' might be seen as his taking on an inferior role. A girl's playing with ''boys' toys'' might be interpreted as an understandable grasping for power or esteem.

Sex-typed preferences extend to school activities and team sports. A survey of children aged 7 to 11 found that boys liked or loved rough-and-tumble sports such as football and boxing (Zill, 1985). Boys also liked playing with guns and making and fixing things. Boys did not like dancing, sewing, or playing with dolls. Girls were less enthusiatic than boys about team sports, although they generally liked them. Girls liked cooking, caring for children, sewing, dancing, and playing with dolls. Girls also had slightly positive feelings about making and fixing things, but they did not enjoy these activities as much as boys did. Girls did not like boxing or playing with guns. Boys and girls both liked a number of other activities: watching television, going to parties, caring for pets, going to school, going to church, and reading. (It is interesting that boys reported liking reading, since other studies show that reading is stereotyped as a feminine activity in our culture.) Caring for pets apparently is not sex-typed. Caring for children is.

▶ ▶ ▶ ▶

Girls Enjoying a Game of Baseball
Although preferences for sex-typed toys
and games are well established by the age
of 3, girls are more likely to stray from the
stereotypes, as in this photograph of girls
playing the masculine-typed game baseball.

Differences in Aggressiveness

In almost all cultures, with a couple of fascinating exceptions (Ford & Beach, 1951; Mead, 1935), it is the males who march off to war and who battle for glory and shaving-cream-commercial contracts. Most psychological studies of aggression have found that males behave more aggressively than females, whether the subjects are under 6 years of age (Maccoby & Jacklin, 1980; White, 1983) or older.

Boys' reputations for aggressiveness and disobedience may earn them harsh treatment from adults whether they deserve it or not. Boys are more likely than girls to be punished by parents and teachers (Maccoby & Jacklin, 1974; Mulhern & Passman, 1981). Adults apparently expect boys to be less obedient and more aggressive. I wonder how many boys have learned to behave aggressively because someone has expected the worst from them.

Ann Frodi and her colleagues (1977) reviewed 72 studies concerning sex differences in aggression. Their findings show that females are more likely to act aggressively (or to report acting aggressively) under some circumstances than others.

1. Males are more likely than females to report physical aggression in their behavior, intentions, and dreams. (Matlin [1987] notes that self-reports are notoriously vulnerable to distortion in the culturally expected direction.)

2. Males and females are about equally likely to approve of violence.

3. Males and females both appreciate hostile humor.

4. Females are more likely to feel anxious or guilty about behaving aggressively. These feelings tend to inhibit aggression.

▶ ▶ ▶ ▶

Studies find that boys tend to be more aggressive than girls. The question is why.

5. Females behave as aggressively as males when they have the means to do so and believe that their behavior is justified. For example, women act as aggressively as men in experiments in which they are given the physical capacity to do so and believe that they should act aggressively.

6. Females are more likely to empathize with the victim—to put themselves in the victim's place.

7. Sex differences in aggression decrease when the victim is anonymous. Anonymity may prevent females from empathizing with their victims.

Differences in Communication Styles: "He's Just a Chatterbox"

Despite the stereotype of women as gossips and "chatterboxes," research in communication styles suggests that males in many situations spend more time talking than women. Males are also more likely to introduce new topics and to interrupt (Brooks, 1982; Deaux, 1985; Hall, 1984). During early childhood, girls frequently do more talking than boys (Haas, 1979), which may reflect their greater verbal ability. However, boys dominate discussion by the time they enter the classroom (Sadker & Sadker, 1985). Moreover, as girls grow up, they appear to learn to let boys do the talking. Girls take a back seat to boys in mixed-sex groups (Haas, 1979; Hall, 1984).

Yet females do seem more willing to reveal their feelings and personal experiences (Cozby, 1973). Females are less likely than males to curse—with the exception of women who are bucking sex-role stereotypes. As noted in Table 12.1, use of harsh language is considered a masculine trait.

In one fascinating study on the communication styles attributed to males

▶ ▶ ▶ ▶

and females, Edelsky (1976) asked children and adults to indicate whether the following sentences and others had been spoken by men or women:

1. Damn it, the TV set broke!
2. Won't you please close the door?
3. Get me that pencil.
4. Oh dear, I lost my keys!
5. That's an adorable story.
6. You're damn right.

First-graders more often than not attributed sentences like 1, 3, and 6 to men, and sentences like 2, 4, and 5 to women. Six-year-olds, that is, already perceived that curses and orders were more likely to be uttered by males. Polite requests, expressions such as "oh dear," and words like "adorable" were perceived as more likely to be uttered by women. These differences became more pronounced among older children and adults. Other studies show that elementary-school boys are more likely to use slang and curse words than their female classmates (Jay, 1980).

Let us now consider sex differences in two aspects of nonverbal communication—personal space and body posture.

Personal space *A psychological boundary that permits one to maintain a comfortable distance from others.*

Differences in Personal Space: "Are *You* Sitting Next to *Me?*" How do you react when a stranger sits at your table in the library or the cafeteria—when someone "invades" your **personal space?**

Girls and women appear to require less personal space than boys and men do. They tend to stand and sit closer to one another than men do, as noted both in naturalistic observation of window shoppers and visitors to art exhibits (Fisher et al., 1984), and in experiments (Sussman & Rosenfeld, 1982). Preschoolers of both sexes approach women more closely than they approach men (Eberts & Lepper, 1975). Girls also prefer to have friends sit next to them, whereas boys prefer friends to sit across from them (Sommer, 1969; Fisher & Byrne, 1975).

Differences in seating preferences and personal-space requirements might reflect greater male competitiveness. Males might perceive close encounters as confrontations in which they face potential adversaries. Thus, they need to keep an eye on them from a safe distance.

Body Posture Just as they seem to require more personal space, males occupy more space with their bodies. They sit or stand with their legs apart, and their hands tend to reach out. Females are more likely to sit or stand with their legs together and with their hands folded in front of them or at their sides (Davis & Weitz, 1981; Hall, 1984).

There are also a number of sex-typed mannerisms found among girls and boys as young as age 4 (Rekers et al., 1977). Girls, for example, are more likely than boys to show fluttering arms, bent elbows, and limp wrists.

And so, there appear to be a number of differences between boys and girls. Some of them are first shown during infancy. Others emerge during middle childhood or adolescence. These include minor differences in cognitive functioning, and differences in play, school activities, aggressiveness, and communication styles. In the next section we consider the development of these differences.

▶ ▶ ▶ ▶

On Becoming a Man or a Woman: Theoretical Views on the Development of Sex Differences in Behavior

Like mother, like daughter; like father, like son—at least often, if not always. Why is it that little boys (often) grow up to behave according to the cultural stereotypes of what it means to be male? That little girls (often) grow up to behave like female stereotypes? Let us have a look at biological and psychological factors that appear to contribute to the development of sex differences.

Biological Influences

Biological views on sex differences tend to focus on two issues: brain organization and sex hormones.

Brain Organization   A number of studies suggest that we can speak of "left-brain" versus "right-brain" functions. As noted in Chapter 7, language skills seem to depend more on left-brain functioning, while right-brain functioning may be more involved in spatial relations and aesthetic and emotional responses. The brain hemishperes may be even more specialized in males than in females (Bryden, 1982).

Evidence for this view derives from adults who receive brain injuries. Men with damage to the left hemisphere are more likely to show verbal deficits than women with similar damage (McGlone, 1980). Men with damage to the right hemisphere are more likely to show spatial-relations deficits than similarly injured women.

Sex differences in brain organization might in part explain why women exceed men in verbal skills that require some spatial organization, such as reading, spelling, and crisp articulation of speech. But men might be superior at more specialized spatial-relations tasks, such as interpreting road maps and visualizing objects in space.

But let us retain a note of caution. Brain research is in its infancy, and, as noted earlier, the differences *within* the sexes remain greater than the differences *between* the sexes.

Sex Hormones in Utero   Sex hormones are responsible for the in-utero differentiation of sex organs. At the beginning of the chapter, it was noted that the sex organs of genetic females who are exposed to excess androgens in utero may become masculinized. Sex hormones in utero might not only influence the development of male or female sex organs, but also "masculinize" or "feminize" the brain by creating predispositions that are consistent with some sex-role stereotypes (Diamond, 1977; Money, 1977, 1987).

Diamond takes an extreme view. She suggests that in-utero brain masculinization can cause tomboyishness and assertiveness—even preferences for trousers over skirts and for playing with "boys' toys." Money agrees that predispositions may be created in utero, but argues that social learning plays a stronger role in the development of gender identity, personality traits, and

▶ ▶ ▶ ▶

preferences. Money claims that social learning is powerful enough to counteract many prenatal predispositions.

There is very little experimental research on prenatal hormonal influences in children. Ethical considerations prevent us from experimentally manipulating prenatal levels of sex hormones in people. But now and then sex hormones are manipulated for other reasons, and we can observe the results. Many women, for example, have taken androgens to help maintain their pregnancies. Consequently, Anke Ehrhardt and Susan Baker (1975) were able to study the effects of prenatal androgens on 17 children aged 4 to 26.

As compared to sisters who had not been exposed to androgens in utero, androgenized girls were more active during play and more likely to perceive themselves to be tomboys. They were less vain about their appearance than their unaffected sisters. They did not enjoy caring for babies or show much interest in playing with dolls or eventually marrying. The boys whose mothers had received male hormones engaged more often in outdoor sports and rough-and-tumble play than their brothers.

There are some methodological problems in the Ehrhardt and Baker report. First is the selection factor. The mothers were not assigned at random to androgens, but were a group with a history of miscarriages. This history might somehow have been responsible for the behaviors shown by their children. Second, the sample was small, rendering the evidence almost anecdotal. Third, the prenatal androgen levels required that the children receive the steroid cortisone for the rest of their lives. Cortisone has a number of side effects, among them an increased level of activity. Thus, play styles among the children could have reflected the cortisone therapy as well as prenatal androgen levels.

Sex Hormones at Puberty Sex hormones also spur sexual maturation during adolescence, and there are some interesting suggestions that sexual maturation is linked to development of cognitive skills. As noted in Chapter 5, girls usually reach sexual maturation earlier than boys. Researchers have found that late maturers, whether boys or girls, show the "masculine pattern" of exceeding early maturers on math and spatial-relations tasks (Sanders & Soares, 1986; Sanders et al., 1982; Waber et al., 1985). Early-maturing boys exceed late-maturing boys in verbal skills, and also show the "feminine pattern" of higher verbal than math and spatial-relations skills (Newcombe & Bandura, 1983). And so, early maturation would seem to favor development of verbal skills, whereas late maturation might favor development of math and spatial-relations skills. Since girls usually mature earlier than boys, time of maturation might influence the development of so-called masculine and feminine patterns of cognitive skills. How? Possibly by contributing further to the "masculinization" or "femininization" of the brain.

Let us now consider psychological views of the development of sex differences.

Psychoanalytic Theory

Sigmund Freud explained the acquisition of sex roles in terms of the concept of identification. In psychoanalytic theory, identification is the process of incorporating within ourselves the behaviors and what we perceive as the

▶ ▶ ▶ ▶

Do Girls Suffer from Penis Envy?

▷
▷
▷
▷

▷ Psychoanalytic theory in many ways has been a liberating force, allowing people to admit the importance of sexuality in their lives. But it has also been claimed that Freud's views are repressive toward women. The penis-envy hypothesis has stigmatized women who compete with men in the business world as failing to have resolved the Electra complex.

Freud believed that little girls were envious of boys' penises. Why, they would feel, should boys have something that they do not? As a consequence of this jealousy, girls would come to resent their mothers for bringing them into the world so ''ill-equipped,'' as Freud (1964) wrote in *New Introductory Lectures on Psychoanalysis*. They would then develop the wish to marry their fathers as a substitute for not having penises of their own.

Through a series of developmental transformations, Freud went on, the wish to marry the father would evolve into the desire to marry another man and bear children. A baby, especially a male child, would symbolize something growing from the genital region and bring some psychological satisfaction. Freud declared that the ideally adjusted woman would accept her husband's authority, thereby symbolizing

surrender of the wish to have a penis of her own.

Freud warned that retaining the wish to have a penis would lead to maladjustment. Persistent jealousy would cause women to develop masculine traits. They might even become competitive and self-assertive, or at worst, homosexual.

These assumptions have been attacked strongly by women and by modern-day psychoanalysts. Karen Horney (1967), a neo-Freudian, contended that little girls do not feel inferior to little boys, and that the penis-envy hypothesis is not supported by the evidence of actual observations of children. Horney wrote that Freud's view reflected a Western cultural prejudice that women are inferior to men— and not sound psychological theory.

Psychologist Phyllis Chesler (1972) argues that there has been a historic prejudice against self-assertive, competent women. Many people want women to remain passive and submissive, emotional, and dependent on men. In Freud's day these prejudices were more extreme. Psychoanalytic theory, in its original form, reflected the belief that motherhood and family life were the only proper avenues of fulfillment for women.

thoughts and feelings of other people. Freud believed that gender identity is rather flexible until the resolution of the Oedipus and Electra complexes at about the age of 5 or 6. Freud argued that the assumption of sex-appropriate sex roles requires that boys identify with their fathers and surrender the wish to possess their mothers. Girls would have to identify with their mothers and surrender the wish to have a penis. But, as noted earlier, children display stereotypical sex-role behaviors long before the arrival of the hypothetical conflicts of the phallic stage.

Let us consider the ways in which social-learning and cognitive theories account for children's early preferences for toys and activities.

► ► ► ►

Social-Learning Theory

Social-learning theorists explain the acquisition of sex roles and sex differences in terms such as observational learning, identification,* and socialization.

Much knowledge of what is "masculine" or "feminine" occurs by observational learning, as suggested by an experiment conducted by David Perry and Kay Bussey (1979). In this study, children learned how behaviors are sextyped by observing the *relative frequencies* with which men and women performed them. While 8- and 9-year-old boys and girls observed them, the adult role models in this experiment expressed arbitrary preferences for one of each of 16 pairs of items—pairs such as oranges and apples, and toy cows and toy horses. Then the children were asked to show their own preferences. Boys selected an average of 14 of 16 items that agreed with the "preferences" of the men. Girls selected an average of only three of 16 items that agreed with the choices of the men.

In a related experiment, Perry and Bussey (1979) found that children tended to imitate a same-sex adult role model *only when they believed that the model's behavior* was in accord with traditional sex-role stereotypes. Even before the age of 10, the children were unwilling to be "misled" by models with nontraditional behavior.

Much knowledge of what is considered masculine and feminine in our culture is obtained by observational learning. Children tend to imitate the behavior of adult role models of the same sex when they believe that the adult's behavior is in accord with traditional sex-role stereotypes.

*But the social-learning concept of identification differs from the psychoanalytic concept, as noted in this section.

▶ ▶ ▶ ▶

What's Sweet for Jack Is Often Sour for Jill

▷
▷
▷
▷

▷ Many parents may believe that they treat their children reasonably equally, regardless of whether they are boys or girls. But a number of observational studies and experiments suggest that boys are more equal than girls, especially when they try to engage in vigorous physical activity or to explore their environments.

In several observational studies, Beverly Fagot (e.g., 1974, 1978, 1982) found that boys and girls are treated quite differently, even when they show the same behavior. Mothers are more likely, for example, to encourage their young daughters to follow them around the house, while boys of the same age are pushed to be independent. Boys are told to run errands outside the home at earlier ages than girls (Saegert & Hart, 1976). Both parents are more likely to reinforce sons for exploring the environment and manipulating objects. Girls are more likely to be criticized for the same behavior, or warned about the prospects of getting hurt.

In a fascinating experiment, Hannah Frisch (1977) found that parents treated 14-month-old boys and girls significantly differently. The gender of the infants was visually concealed and the parents were told at random that they were boys or girls. Parents who believed that the infants were boys were more likely to encourage them to play with blocks and tricycles. Parents who believed that the children were girls spent more time talking to them and were more likely to encourage them to play with dolls and baby bottles.

Caroline Smith and Barbara Lloyd (1978) found that Frisch's results could be replicated with infants as young as 6 months. Mothers who were told that the infant was a girl were more likely to cuddle "her." Mothers who were told that the infant was a boy were more likely to encourage motor activities such as crawling and playing with toys, including a hammer.

In general, boys are given athletic equipment, cars, and guns from early ages, and are encouraged to compete aggressively. Boys are handled more frequently than girls. Girls are spoken to more often. There may be biological predispositions for boys to act more aggressively and for girls to show greater verbal skills. However, early socialization also fosters stereotypical sex-role development.

Social-learning theorists view identification as a broad, continuous learning process in which children are influenced by rewards and punishments to imitate adults of the same sex—particularly the parent of the same sex (Bronfenbrenner, 1960; Kagan, 1964; Storms, 1979). In identification as opposed to imitation, children not only imitate a certain behavior pattern. They also try to become broadly like the model.

Socialization also plays a role. Parents and other adults—even other children—inform children as to how they are expected to behave. They reward children for behavior they consider sex-appropriate. They punish (or fail to reinforce) behavior they consider inappropriate. Girls, for example, are given dolls while they still sleep in cribs. They are encouraged to rehearse care-taking behaviors in preparation for traditional feminine adult roles.

► ► ► ►

The Role of Parents   Parents are usually delighted when their children begin to refer to themselves as boys or girls. Through approval and affection, they reward children for establishing a gender identity consistent with their anatomic sex. And, as noted in the nearby box, "What's Sweet for Jack Is Often Sour for Jill," they encourage children to engage in behavior consistent with sex-role stereotypes.

Mothers generally have the major responsibility for the day-to-day nurturance of children (Belsky et al., 1984; Feldman et al., 1984). Mothers tend to provide the "emotional glue" that keeps the family integrated (Johnson, 1983; Orlofsky, 1983). Fathers are more oriented toward playing with their children and communicating norms for sex-typed behaviors (Lamb, 1981; Power, 1985). Do not misunderstand. Mothers share fathers' cultural expectations concerning "sex-appropriate" behavior patterns. It's just that they usually do not make as sharp a distinction in expressing their attitudes to their sons and daughters (McHale & Huston, 1984).

Mothers tend to have warm, expressive relationships with both their sons and their daughters. Mothers tend to provide encouragement and support, while fathers are more action-oriented. Fathers tend to encourage instrumental behavior in their sons and warm, expressive behavior in their daughters. Fathers encourage sons to be active and dominant. Girls are encouraged to comfort others and show affection (Block, 1979). Fathers toss their sons into the air and use hearty expressions with them such as "How're yuh doin', Tiger?" and "Hey you, get your keester over here" (Jacklin et al., 1984; Power & Parke, 1982). By contrast, fathers are likely to cuddle their daughters gently. I went out of my way to toss my young daughters up into the air, and the relatives yelled at me for being too rough. Of course, I modified my behavior. I learned to toss them up into the air when we were alone—not in front of the relatives.

In one study, sex differences in fathers' play with sons and daughters were noted at the age of 12 months (Snow, Jacklin, & Maccoby, 1983). Fathers more often prohibited sons from touching or playing with delicate or potentially harmful objects. They held their daughters and gave them dolls more often. However, it was not clear whether the fathers or infants initiated much of the sex-typed behavior. Boys, for example, attempted to touch objects that were prohibited more often than girls did, and girls more often elected to play with dolls and vacuum cleaners. Regardless of the exact nature of reciprocal father–child influences, sex-typed interaction with the father was established by this early age.

Effects of Father Absence   Research has also shown that boys from father-absent families show a weaker preference for the traditional masculine sex role, are more dependent, and perform less well in school than boys reared in two-parent homes. A study of 2½-year-old nursery-school children by Rachel Levy-Shiff (1982) found that boys from father-absent homes were also less well adjusted socially and more likely to encounter problems in relating to peers than boys from intact homes.

But boys from father-absent homes with older brothers are relatively more "masculine" and less dependent. They also earn higher grades in school (Santrock, 1970; Sutton-Smith et al., 1968; Wohlford et al., 1971). Boys with older sisters are more likely than boys with older brothers or no siblings to show a number of feminine-typed behaviors (Sutton-Smith & Rosenberg, 1970). Girls with older brothers are also more likely to show masculine-typed behaviors than girls with older sisters or no siblings.

▶ ▶ ▶ ▶

Evidence is more mixed on girls from father-absent homes. In the Hetherington (1972) study described in Chapter 1, the adolescent daughters of divorced women were more assertive in the company of men than the daughters of married women. Daughters of widows were, by contrast, shy and uncomfortable. Hetherington (1979) suggests that the daughters of divorced women may perceive establishing a relationship with a man as essential to happiness. The daughters of widows may have idolized their fathers and felt that other men could not compare. Although girls from each group showed some interpersonal problems with men, it does not appear that they failed to develop "sex-appropriate" behavior patterns.

The Levy-Shiff (1982) study found that girls from father-absent homes were more independent and assertive than girls from intact homes. However, there was no indication that greater independence and assertiveness was linked to social problems. While independence and assertiveness may be stereotyped as masculine, they are valuable traits for both sexes in the academic and vocational worlds.

The Role of Peers Children are also motivated to engage in "sex-appropriate" behaviors in order to earn the approval, and avoid the disapproval, of their peers. In one study, the researchers (Serbin et al., 1979) observed children in a playroom under three conditions: alone, with a peer of the same sex, or with an opposite-sex peer. Many toys were available in the room. When peers of either sex were present, the children were significantly more likely to restrict their play to toys that were consistent with the stereotypes for their sex. Boys, that is, were more likely to choose toy soldiers or transportation toys when in the presence of a peer than when alone. Girls, similarly, were more likely to play with dolls, tea sets, and housekeeping toys when they were in the company of age-mates. Several children tended to look back over their shoulders at the peer when they picked up a toy that did not fit their stereotypes. Then they selected another toy, even when the peer seemed disinterested in their behavior.

Research by Michael Lamb and his colleagues (Lamb & Roopnarine, 1979; Lamb et al., 1980) suggests that children have good reason to select "sex-appropriate" toys in the presence of their peers. Three-year-old children, for example, frequently stop playing with boys who play with dolls or tea sets, or with girls who play with toy guns, firetrucks, and hammers. Most 5-year-olds are openly critical. They criticize the choices of the other children and sometimes go so far as to prevent them from playing with the "wrong" toys. But they need not go to such extremes. Children tend to drop cross-gender behaviors very quickly when others disapprove.

The Role of Schools Schools also spur the socialization process. Girls are usually expected to outperform boys in English and language arts, while boys are expected to excel in math and science. Stereotypical socialization messages are even found in nursery schools. In one school that proclaimed a commitment to breaking down traditional sex-role stereotypes, girls were still complimented on their clothing more frequently than boys were, particularly when they wore dresses (Joffee, 1971). In high school, girls are more likely to be assigned courses in homemaking, secretarial work, and dancing. Boys are more frequently guided into shop courses and preprofessional studies (Naffziger & Naffziger, 1974).

One study highlights the power of teacher praise in sex-typing (Serbin

▶ ▶ ▶ ▶

et al., 1977). Over a two-week baseline period, the researchers recorded the frequency with which children engaged in cooperative play activities that were usually preferred by children of the opposite sex. During the next two weeks, teachers praised children for engaging in cross-gender play, and the frequency of such play increased significantly. However, when the teachers discontinued their reinforcement, cross-gender play fell back to baseline levels.

The Social Learning of Sex Differences in Aggressive Behavior Concerning the greater aggressiveness of boys, Maccoby and Jacklin note that:

> Aggression in general is less acceptable for girls, and is more actively discouraged in them, by either direct punishment, withdrawal of affection, or simply cognitive training that "that isn't the way girls act." Girls then build up greater anxieties about aggression, and greater inhibitions against displaying it (1974, p. 234).

As noted earlier, girls frequently learn to respond to social provocations by feeling anxious about the possibility of acting aggressively, whereas boys are generally encouraged to retaliate (Frodi et al., 1977). Parents usually squelch aggression in their daughters (Sears et al., 1957). Boys are likely to be permitted to express some aggression toward their parents. Many boys are encouraged to fight with peers, when necessary, in order to defend themselves and their property.

Several experiments also highlight the importance of social-learning factors in female aggressiveness. Studies by Albert Bandura and his colleagues (1963) found that boys are more likely than girls to imitate film-mediated aggressive models, because the social milieu more often frowns upon aggressiveness in girls. Other investigators find that the development of aggressive behavior in females is influenced by situational variables, such as the nature of the provocation and the possibility that someone will disapprove of them (Taylor & Epstein, 1967; Richardson et al., 1979).

In the Taylor and Epstein study, aggressive behavior was measured by the strength of the electric shock selected for delivery to another person. Subjects used a fearsome looking console (Figure 12.1) to take turns shocking other participants in the study when they failed to respond quickly enough to a stimulus. Subjects could select the strength of the shock themselves. When men

Figure 12.1 The "Aggression Machine"
Psychologists frequently use consoles like the one pictured here in studies on aggression. In the Taylor and Epstein study, the intensity of aggression was defined as the amount of shock selected by the subject.

▶ ▶ ▶ ▶

set low or moderate shock levels for women subjects, the women generally chose somewhat lower shock levels for the men when their turn came. In this way, they adhered to the feminine stereotype of nonaggressiveness. But when the men violated the **sex norm** of treating women favorably by setting high levels of shock for them, the women retaliated by setting shock levels that were equally high. Apparently the women decided that what was sauce for the gander was sauce for the goose. If men could violate sex norms and treat women aggressively, women, too, could violate sex norms and respond just as aggressively.

The development of aggressive behavior in girls is also influenced by the responses of those who monitor their behavior and reward or punish them. In the Richardson study, college women competed with men in responding quickly to a stimulus over four blocks of trials, with six trials in each block. They could not see their opponents. The loser of each trial received an electric shock whose intensity was set by the opponent. Women competed under one of three experimental conditions: "public," "private," or with a "supportive other." In the public condition, another woman observed her silently. In the private condition, there was no observer. In the supportive-other condition, another woman urged her to retaliate strongly when her opponent selected high shock levels. As shown in Figure 12.2, women in the private and supportive-other conditions selected increasingly higher levels of shock in retaliation. Presumably, the women in the study assumed that an observer—though silent—would frown on aggressive behavior. This assumption is likely to reflect their own early socialization experiences. Women who were unobserved or

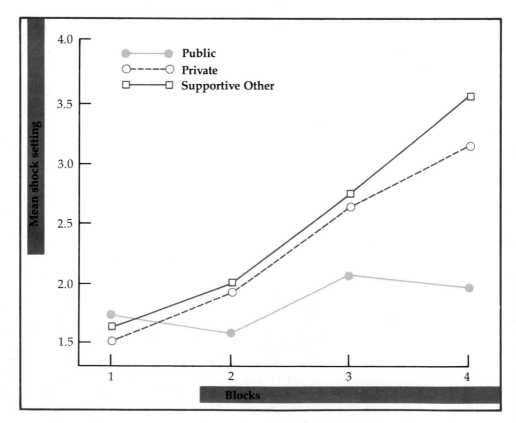

Figure 12.2 Mean Shock Settings Selected by Women in Retaliation Against Male Opponents
Women in the Richardson study chose higher shock levels for their opponents when they were alone or when another person (a supportive "other") urged them on.

▶ ▶ ▶ ▶

Noneducational Television Can Be Educational, Indeed, *or,* "I'm Popeye, the Sailor Woman"?

▷
▷
▷
▷
▷ What do Popeye, the Pink Panther, and Bugs Bunny have in common—aside from fat bank accounts? They're all *male*. In a study of children's television shows, Sternglanz and Serbin (1974) found that several shows have all-male casts and that among shows with "coed" heroes, males outnumber females two to one.

Children who watch television are learning more than how to rescue Olive Oyl and trap roadrunners. Female television characters are portrayed as less active than males and more likely to follow directions of others (especially males). Females' activities have less impact than those of males. Male characters are more likely to conceive and carry out plans, be aggressive, and just have fun (Zuckerman & Zuckerman, 1985). Children who spend more hours watching television are more likely to show stereotyped concepts of masculine and feminine behavior (Leary et al., 1982).

Commercials have also supported sex-role stereotypes. In their study of 199 television commercials, McArthur and Resko (1975) found that 70 percent of the male characters were portrayed as authorities on their products, as compared with 14 percent of females. Male figures were significantly more likely to back claims with scientific and other evidence. Men were more often shown as capable problem-solvers, while women more frequently acted ignorant, passive, and flustered. The woman's place was still in the home—only 13 percent of male product users were shown using home products, as compared to one-third of the females.

There is also disconcerting experimental evidence that television portrayals of sex-role stereotypes affect viewers. Young children shown cartoons in which characters adhere to traditional sex-role stereo-types are more likely than children shown nontraditional behavior to describe men and women according to these stereotypes (Davidson et al., 1979). But the Davidson study also showed signs of hope. Five- and 6-year-olds who observed girls in nontraditional roles, such as building a clubhouse, held stereotyped attitudes less strongly afterward.

There is also some evidence that the impact of TV on children's stereotypes can be minimized by rearing children with nontraditional sex-role attitudes. List, Collins, and Westby (1983) classified members of a sample of third-graders as either high, medium, or low stereotyped on the basis of their preferences for "masculine" or "feminine" activities. The children were then broken down into groups and either shown a film of a woman in a traditional role (wife and mother) or in a nontraditional role (physician and army officer). Children who were highly stereotyped later remembered less about the film in which the woman played the doctor and officer. However, children low in sex-role stereotyping recalled more about both films.

Another encouraging note is found in shows like "Freestyle," a TV series designed to counteract children's sex-role and racial stereotypes. "Freestyle" shows children of both sexes and a variety of ethnic backgrounds engaging in nontraditional behavior patterns. In one result, 9- to 12-year-old watchers showed increased acceptance of boys in nurturant roles and girls who were making and fixing things (Johnston & Ettema, 1982).

Television has a powerful potential to hurt, but an equally powerful potential to help. Perhaps awareness of the potential of the medium will encourage producers to eliminate sexism from a greater percentage of shows.   ▶ ▶ ▶ ▶

urged on by a supportive-other apparently felt free to violate the sex norm of nonaggressiveness when their situations called for aggressive responses.

If the Richardson experiment were replicated with boys, is it possible that boys in a room with a silent observer would also be highly aggressive? After all, their early socialization experiences might lead them to expect that an observer would disapprove of them for *failing* to respond aggressively to a provocation. Why not run such an experiment and tell me about the results?

Social-learning theory has done an admirable job of outlining the situational factors that influence children's preferences for "sex-appropriate" toys and behavior patterns. Criticisms of social-learning theory do not challenge the results of experiments such as those reported in this section. Instead, they focus on theoretical issues, such as *How do reinforcers influence children?* Do reinforcers mechanically increase the frequency of behavior, as some learning theorists would suggest? Or do reinforcers provide children with information that they use in making decisions, as cognitive theorists might suggest?

Let us now consider two cognitive-theory approaches to sex-typing: cognitive-developmental theory and gender schema theory.

Cognitive-Developmental Theory

Lawrence Kohlberg (1966) proposed a cognitive-developmental view of the development of sex roles and sex differences. Consistent with other aspects of cognitive-developmental theory, children are viewed as active participants in the development of sex roles and sex differences. These developments are seen as occurring in stages—discontinuously. They are also seen as entwined with the child's general cognitive development.

Certainly rewards and punishments influence children's choice of toys and activities. But we must come to grips with the issue as to *why* rewards and punishments influence behavior. From the cognitive perspective, rewards do not strengthen stimulus–response connections mechanically. Instead, rewards provide children with information as to when they are behaving in ways that other people desire. For this reason, even at the ages of 21 to 25 months, girls respond more positively to rewards from other girls. Boys at this age respond more positively to rewards from other boys (Fagot, 1985a). Rewards, that is, are most effective when they have been processed in terms of the gender of the "rewarder"; their effects are not mechanical.

And so there is a role for rewards and punishments in cognitive-developmental theory: They provide information. But Kohlberg views the essential aspects of sex-typing in terms of the emergence of three concepts: *gender identity*, *gender stability*, and *gender constancy*.

The first step in sex-typing is attaining gender identity. Gender identity is one's knowledge that he or she is male or female. Gender identity appears to originate in sexual assignment, or the process by which other people label the child a boy or girl. Sexual assignment is a response to the child's anatomic sex that usually occurs at birth. Gender identity is so important to parents that they usually want to know "Is it a boy or a girl?" before they begin to count fingers and toes.

Most children acquire a firm gender identity by the age of 36 months (Marcus & Corsini, 1978; McConaghy, 1979; Money, 1977). Spencer Thompson

▶ ▶ ▶ ▶

Gender stability The concept that one's gender is a permanent feature.

Gender constancy The concept that one's gender remains the same, despite superficial changes in appearance or behavior.

(1975) assessed gender identity in young children in a number of ways. In one, he simply asked them whether they were boys or girls. In another, he asked them to put pictures of themselves in with the group to which they belonged. In the second method, the children were given two groups of pictures—one group of males, the other of females. At 24 months most children could verbally state whether they were boys or girls. However, they did not show similar reliability in sorting their own pictures, suggesting that their concept of gender identity was limited. By 30 months, 75 percent of the children sorted their pictures properly according to gender. By 3 years, virtually all children showed gender identity according to both measures. By the age of 3, most children have also acquired the capacity to discriminate anatomic sex differences (Ruble & Ruble, 1980).

At around the age of 4 or 5, most children develop the concept of **gender stability.** They recognize that people retain their genders for a lifetime. Girls no longer believe that they will grow up to be daddies, and boys no longer think they can become mommies. According to cognitive-developmental theory, the emergence of gender stability contributes to the organization of sex-typed behavior (Siegal & Robinson, 1987).

By the age of 7 or 8, most children develop the more sophisticated concept of **gender constancy.** Children with gender constancy recognize that gender does not change, even if people modify their dress or their behavior patterns. Gender, that is, remains constant despite rearrangement of superficial appearances. A woman who crops her hair short remains a woman. A man who cries remains a man. We could relabel gender constancy as "conservation of gender," highlighting the theoretical debt to Jean Piaget.

Many 4-year-olds have the notion that boys could be girls if they chose to be, or if they wore their hair longer, or if they wore dresses. Note the following excerpt from a conversation recorded by Kohlberg (1966, p. 95). Jimmy is 4. Johnny is older:

> JOHNNY: I'm going to be an airplane builder when I grow up.
> JIMMY: When I grow up, I'll be a Mommy.
> JOHNNY: No, you can't be a Mommy. You have to be a daddy.
> JIMMY: No, I'm going to be a Mommy.
> JOHNNY: No, you're not a girl, you can't be a Mommy.
> JIMMY: Yes, I can.

Marcus and Overton (1978) found that the development of gender constancy was related to the general development of conservation, as described in Chapter 8. In a sample of 5- to 8-year-old children, the development of physical conservation concepts usually preceded gender constancy. For this reason, it seems that conservation concepts may lay the cognitive groundwork for gender constancy. More intelligent children also developed gender constancy earlier, further suggestive of the cognitive nature of the task.

Interestingly, Ullian (1981) found that 6-year-old children who have developed gender stability but not gender constancy tend to adhere rather rigidly to "sex-appropriate" behavior patterns. It is as if they think that behaving in inappropriate ways could actually change their genders! By the age of 8, children are more willing to engage in behavior patterns associated with the opposite sex. Perhaps they have become secure in the knowledge that they will remain as they were.

▶ ▶ ▶ ▶

In a similar vein, Smetana and Letourneau (1984) found that girls with gender stability more often chose girl playmates than did girls who had developed gender identity only. The researchers theorize that female companionship helps confirm their female self-concepts prior to the certainty of gender constancy. Once they have attained gender constancy, girls know that playing with boys will not alter their gender. For this reason, they become less rigid in use of gender as a factor in choice of playmates.

A number of studies have found that the concepts of gender identity, gender stability, and gender constancy do emerge in the order predicted by Kohlberg (Slaby & Frey, 1975). The order of emergence is confirmed in cross-cultural studies in the United States, Samoa, Nepal, Belize, and Kenya (Munroe et al., 1984).

According to cognitive-developmental theory, once children have established concepts of gender stability and constancy, they will be motivated to behave in ways that are consistent with their genders. Once girls understand that they will remain female, they will show a preference for "feminine" activities. As shown by Perry and Bussey (1979), children do appear to actively seek information as to which behavior patterns are "masculine" and which are "feminine." They are then significantly more likely to imitate the "sex-appropriate" patterns.

However, there are problems with the ages at which sex-typed play emerges. Numerous studies have shown that many children prefer sex-typed toys such as cars and dolls at the age of 2 (Huston, 1983). At this age, children are likely to have a sense of gender identity, but gender stability and gender constancy remain some years away (Fagot, 1985b). Therefore, gender identity alone seems to provide a child with sufficient motivation to assume sex-typed behavior patterns.

Cornell University psychologist Sandra Bem (1983) notes that Kohlberg's theory also does not explain why children focus on gender as a crucial factor in classifying people and behavior patterns. Another cognitive view, gender schema theory, attempts to address these shortcomings.

Gender Schema Theory: An Information-Processing View

Gender schema theory holds that children use gender as one way of organizing their perceptions of the world (Bem, 1981, 1985; Martin & Halverson, 1981). According to this view, gender has a great deal of prominence, even to young children. As a consequence, children mentally group people of the same gender together.

Gender schema theory borrows elements from social-learning theory and from cognitive-developmental theory. As in social-learning theory, sex-typing is viewed as largely learned from experience. Children learn what behavior patterns are considered appropriate for males and females by observing others. On the other hand, children's active cognitive processing of information also contributes to their sex-typing.

Consider the example of strength and weakness. Children learn that strength is linked to the male sex-role stereotype, and weakness to the female's. But they also learn that some traits, such as strong-weak, are more relevant to one gender than the other. The strong-weak dimension is more relevant for boys than girls. Bill will learn that the strength he displays in weight training

Gender schema theory The view that one's knowledge of the gender schema in one's society (the distribution of behavior patterns that are considered appropriate for men and women) guides one's assumption of sex-typed preferences and behavior patterns.

▶ ▶ ▶ ▶

or wrestling makes a difference in the way others perceive him. But most girls do not find that this trait is so important in the eyes of others, unless they are competing in gymnastics, tennis, swimming, or other sports. Even so, boys are expected to compete in these sports, and girls are not. Jane is likely to find that her gentleness and neatness are more important in the eyes of others than her strength.

And so children learn to judge themselves according to the traits that are considered relevant to their genders. Their self-concepts become blended with the gender schema of their culture. The gender schema provides standards for comparison. Children whose self-concepts are consistent with their society's gender schema are likely to have higher self-esteem than children whose self-concepts are not.

From the viewpoint of gender schema theory, gender identity would be sufficient to prompt "sex-appropriate" behavior. As soon as children understand the labels *boy* and *girl*, they have a basis for blending their self-concepts with the gender schema of their society. Children with gender identity will actively seek information concerning the gender schema. Their self-esteem will soon become wrapped up in the ways in which they measure up to the gender schema.

A number of recent studies support the view that children process information according to the gender schema (Cann & Newbern, 1984; List et al., 1983). As noted in Chapter 8, for example, boys show better memory for "masculine" toys and objects, while girls show better memory for "feminine" objects and toys (Bradbard & Endsley, 1984).

A recent study by Carol Martin and Charles Halverson (1983) sheds further light on the issue. Five- and 6-year-old boys and girls were shown pictures of actors engaged in "sex-consistent" or "sex-inconsistent" activities. The sex-consistent pictures showed boys in activities such as playing with trains or sawing wood and girls in activities such as cooking and cleaning. Sex-inconsistent pictures showed actors of the opposite sex engaged in these sex-typed activities. Each child was shown a randomized collection of pictures that included only one picture of each activity.

One week later, the children were asked who had engaged in a pictured activity, a male or a female. Boys and girls both replied incorrectly significantly more often when the picture they had seen showed sex-inconsistent activity. As in the Bradbard and Endsley (1984) study, the processing of information had been distorted to conform to the gender schema.

In sum, brain organization and sex hormones may contribute to sex-typed behavior patterns. They may play minor roles in mathematics skills and aggressive behavior patterns. However, there is also evidence that suggests that the effects of social learning may be strong enough to counteract most prenatal biological influences. Social-learning theory does an excellent job of outlining the environmental factors that influence children to assume "sex-appropriate" behavior patterns. However, it may pay insufficient attention to children's active role in acquiring sex-role information and to the role of developing concepts of masculinity and femininity. Cognitive-developmental theory views children as active seekers of information, but may overestimate the roles of gender stability and gender constancy in sex-typing. Gender schema theory integrates the strengths of social-learning theory and cognitive-developmental theory. It also highlights the ways in which children process information, so as to blend their self-concepts with the gender schema of their culture, once they attain gender identity.

▶ ▶ ▶ ▶

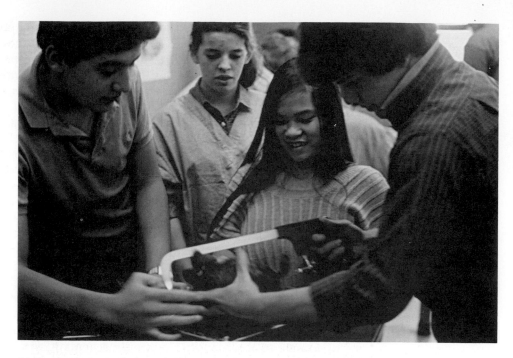

Studies have shown that psychologically androgynous girls feel more comfortable engaging in stereotyped masculine activities such as sawing wood than do feminine-typed girls.

Psychological Androgyny

We usually think of masculinity and femininity as opposite poles of one continuum (Storms, 1979). The more masculine a person is, the less feminine he or she must be, and vice versa. For this reason, a boy who shows the "feminine" traits of nurturance, tenderness, and emotionality might be considered less masculine than other boys. This is also why girls who compete with boys in sports are seen not only as more masculine than other girls, but also as less feminine.

But in recent years many behavioral scientists have argued that masculinity and femininity are independent personality dimensions. That is, a person who scores high on a measure of "masculine" traits, regardless of gender, need not necessarily score low on "feminine" traits. In terms of the clusters of traits observed by the Brovermans (1972), a person who shows *instrumentality* can also show *warmth–expressiveness* (see Table 12.1). People showing both clusters are said to possess **psychological androgyny.** People high in instrumentality *only* are typed as masculine. People high in warmth–expressiveness *only* are typed as feminine. People low in both instrumentality and warmth-expressiveness are "undifferentiated."

It has been suggested that it is worthwhile to promote psychological androgyny in children because they will then possess both the instrumentality and warmth–expressiveness that are valued in our culture (Babladelis, 1979). Research also suggests that androgynous children and adults are relatively well adjusted because they can summon a wider range of traits to meet the challenges

Psychological androgyny
Possession of instrumental and warmth–expressiveness traits.

▶ ▶ ▶ ▶

of their worlds. For example, androgynous college students are more likely than feminine, masculine, and undifferentiated students to show a combination of "high identity" and "high intimacy" (Schiedel & Marcia, 1985). That is, they are more likely to show a firm sense of who they are and what they stand for (identity) along with the capacity to form intimate, sharing relationships.

Androgynous people of both sexes show "masculine" independence under group pressures to conform and "feminine" nurturance in interactions with a kitten or a baby (Bem, 1975; Bem, Martyna, & Watson, 1976). They feel more comfortable performing a wider range of activities, including (the "masculine") nailing of boards and (the "feminine") winding of yarn (Bem & Lenney, 1976; Helmreich et al., 1979). In adolescence, they report greater interest in pursuing nontraditional occupational roles (Motowidlo, 1982). They are more likely to try to help others in need. Androgynous women rate stressful life events as less undesirable than do feminine women (Shaw, 1982). Androgynous people show greater maturity in moral judgments, greater ability to bounce back from failure (Baucom & Danker-Brown, 1979), and greater self-esteem (Flaherty & Dusek, 1980; Spence et al., 1975).

In early adolescence it appears that "masculinity" or androgyny are associated with popularity and higher self-esteem in both boys and girls (Lamke, 1982b). Given the prevalence of sexism, it is not surprising that boys fare better among their peers when they show masculine-typed traits. It is of greater interest that girls also fare better when they show some masculine-typed, instrumental traits. Apparently these traits do not compromise their "femininity"— providing more evidence that so-called masculinity and femininity are independent clusters of traits.

Other research suggests that it may be worthwhile to encourage warmth–expressiveness traits in boys, because they contribute to eventual marital happiness. Antill (1983) found that not only was husbands' happiness positively related to their wives' femininity, but also that wives' happiness was positively related to their husbands' femininity. Wives of androgynous husbands were far happier than women whose husbands adhered to a rigid masculine sex role. Women, like men, appreciate spouses who are sympathetic, warm, and tender, and who love children.

On the other hand, feminists have criticized the view that psychological androgyny is a worthwhile goal. The problem, from the feminist perspective, is that psychological androgyny is defined as the possession of both masculine and feminine personality traits. However, this very definition relies upon the presumed rigidity of masculine and feminine sex-role stereotypes. Feminists would prefer to see the dissolution of these stereotypes (Lott, 1981, 1985).

In any event, studies show that about 25 to 35 percent of high school and college students are androgynous (Bem, 1974; Lamke, 1982a). It will be interesting to see whether heightened public awareness of sexism will cause these numbers to grow in future years.

Summary

1. A stereotype is a fixed, conventional idea about a group, and a sex role is a cluster of stereotypes attributed to one of the sexes. In our society, the masculine sex-role stereotype includes aggressiveness, independence,

► ► ► ►

logic, and competence in the business world or the realm of objects ("instrumentality"). The feminine sex-role stereotype includes nurturance, passivity, and dependence ("warmth–expressiveness" traits).

2. Children by the age of about 2½ have developed basic concrete stereotypes of the things that boys and girls do or do not do, and like or dislike. Children's stereotypes are most rigid at about the ages of 9 and 10. Adolescents are less rigid in their stereotypes.

3. Sexism has made it difficult for girls to express stereotypical masculine traits (such as competitiveness) and for boys to express feminine traits (and to consider vocations such as nursing or secretarial work). Three- to 5-year-olds view girls as smaller, slower, and weaker than boys. Teachers assume that girls talk more than boys, although they do not. Teachers praise boys more often than girls, and are more likely to tolerate calling out from boys.

4. Children show stereotypical ideas as to whether certain jobs are for men or women by the ages of 2 and 3. Girls are more likely than boys to aspire to jobs considered appropriate for the opposite sex. Preference for male sex-typed jobs seems to peak for boys and girls prior to adolescence. Evidence is mixed as to whether boys or girls aspire to higher-prestige jobs.

5. Sex differences during infancy are small and inconsistent. Male neonates are larger and heavier than girls, but girls are slightly ahead in bone and locomotor development. Infant girls may be more sociable than male infants.

6. Girls generally excel in verbal abilities, while boys excel in math and spatial-relations abilities. Girls talk somewhat earlier than boys, and expand their vocabularies faster. Their pronunciation is clearer, and boys develop more reading problems. Math is more likely to be considered a male domain, while reading is viewed as a female domain in our society. It is difficult to convince even highly capable girls to take math courses in high school. However, cognitive sex differences are generally small, and abilities within genders vary more greatly than abilities between the genders.

7. Preferences for sex-typed toys develop by 15 to 36 months. Boys prefer transportation toys, and girls prefer dolls and soft toys. During middle childhood, boys like rough-and-tumble sports; girls do not. Girls like dancing and sewing; boys do not. Boys like making and fixing things more than girls do. Both sexes like caring for pets, school, and reading.

8. Boys are more aggressive than girls under most circumstances. Aggressiveness in girls may be inhibited by lesser physical strength, by anxiety (caused by aggression's inconsistency with the feminine sex-role stereotype), and by empathy with the victim.

9. In group settings, men talk and interrupt more often than women do. Boys are more likely to make demands and curse. Girls require less personal space than boys do, and they prefer to sit next to companions, while boys prefer to sit across from them. Boys' postures take up more space than girls'. Girls are more likely to show fluttering arms, bent elbows, and limp wrists.

10. Biological influences may partly explain a number of sex differences. Greater brain lateralization in boys might be associated with differences in

► ► ► ►

cognitive abilities. Prenatal influences of male sex hormones may increase activity level and masculine sex-typed preferences. But many researchers believe that social learning outweighs possible biological influences on cognitive functioning and personality.

11. According to psychoanalytic theory, sex-typing stems from resolution of the conflicts of the phallic stage. However, children assume sex roles at much earlier ages than the theory would suggest.

12. Social-learning theory explains sex-typing in terms of observational learning, identification, and socialization. Observational learning may largely account for children's knowledge of "gender-appropriate" preferences and behavior patterns. Children generally identify with adults of the same sex and attempt to broadly imitate their behavior, but only when they perceive it as gender-appropriate. Children are also guided into stereotypical sex-role behaviors by early socialization messages and reinforcement.

13. Parents treat infant boys and girls differently. They encourage physical activity in boys, and they speak to and cuddle girls more often. Fathers are more likely than mothers to treat sons and daughters differently. Boys reared in father-absent homes show weaker preference for the traditional masculine sex role, unless older brothers serve as masculine role models. Peers selectively reinforce sex-typed behavior patterns. Teacher praise can be powerful enough to encourage participation in play activities usually preferred by the opposite sex.

14. Experiments show that female college students behave as aggressively as males when they are highly provoked and when they believe that the social milieu (the people around them) will tolerate aggressive behavior from them. Over the years, television has generally reinforced traditional sex-role stereotypes by portraying males as active and authoritative, while women have been shown as dependent and flustered.

15. Cognitive-developmental theory views sex-typing in terms of the emergence of gender identity, gender stability, and gender constancy. Gender identity is one's sense of being male or being female, and develops by about 18–36 months of age. Gender stability, or recognition that people retain their gender for a lifetime, develops by ages 4 or 5. Gender constancy is the equivalent of conservation of gender, or the concept that gender is a stable attribute. Gender constancy develops soon after gender stability and involves recognition that people retain their genders, even if they change their dress, their appearance, and their behaviors.

16. Within cognitive developmental theory, it is thought that the development of gender stability fosters the organization of sex-typed behavior. However, children usually show sex-typed preferences and behavior patterns upon the emergence of gender identity.

17. Gender schema theory includes elements from social-learning theory and cognitive-developmental theory. Gender schema theory proposes that children use the gender schema of their society to organize their perceptions, and that children attempt to blend their self-concepts with the gender schema.

18. Evidence in support of gender schema theory shows that children process information according to the gender schema. Children better "remember"

▶ ▶ ▶ ▶

objects considered appropriate to their genders. Children also distort their memories to make them more consistent with the gender schema.

19. Children who show "masculine" instrumentality and "feminine" warmth–expressiveness are labeled psychologically androgynous. Psychologically androgynous children may be better adjusted than stereotypically masculine boys and feminine girls, because they can summon a wider range of traits and skills to meet the challenges of their situations.

T R U T H ▸ O R ▸ F I C T I O N ▸ R E V I S I T E D

At the age of 2½, boys and girls typically think that their own sex is superior. True. Chauvinism begins early.

Three-year-olds report that women are more likely to cry than men. True. Knowledge of stereotypical sex roles is forming rapidly by this age.

Girls are superior to boys in verbal abilities. True. Girls speak somewhat earlier than boys, have crisper pronunciation, and encounter fewer reading problems.

Fathers are more likely than mothers to help children with their math homework. True. Math is generally seen as part of the male domain in our culture.

Girls are more likely than boys to have math anxiety. True. It is difficult to convince even highly capable girls to take advanced math courses.

Girls are more likely to play with "boys' toys" than boys are to play with "girls' toys." True. Sexism leads boys to view girls' activities as inferior.

Girls do not like to play with guns. True. Nor, generally speaking, do they like boxing and other rough-and-tumble activities.

Caring for children is apparently a sex-typed activity, while caring for pets is not. It may well be so, because boys and girls both like caring for pets a great deal, but girls show a distinct preference for caring for children.

Girls like going to school, but boys do not. False. Boys and girls both generally like school.

Boys are more aggressive than girls. True.

Boys are more likely than girls to curse. True. Boys are also more likely to issue commands, while girls are more likely to make polite requests.

By the time they enter school, boys and girls tend to sit and carry themselves differently. True. Boys' postures generally take up more space.

Women who compete with men in the business world are suffering from penis-envy they experienced as little girls. False. This psychoanalytic notion is based on ignorance and prejudice.

Fathers are more likely than mothers to treat their sons and daughters equally. True. Mothers are likely to be expressive with sons and daughters, while fathers are likely to encourage instrumentality in sons.

▶ ▶ ▶ ▶

Boys reared in father-absent homes are more dependent than boys reared in intact homes. True. Boys reared in father-absent homes show weaker adherence to the masculine sex-role stereotype.

Men are more often portrayed as authorities on television commercials, while women are more likely to be cast as flustered product users. True. Children also seem to be influenced by what they watch on television.

A 2½-year-old may know that he is a boy, but still think that he can grow up to be a mommy. True. Children do not recognize that they will retain their genders until the concept of gender stability emerges at about the ages of 4 or 5.

Five- and 6-year-olds tend to distort their memories so that they "recall" boys playing with trains and sawing wood—even when these activities were actually carried out by girls. True. Evidence such as this shows that children process information according to the gender schema of their cultures.

Adolescent girls who show a number of "masculine" traits have higher self-esteem than girls who thoroughly adopt the traditional feminine sex role. True. The presence of instrumental traits apparently boosts the self-concept without compromising warmth–expressiveness traits.

▶ ▶ ▶ ▶

13

Moral Development

C H A P T E R ▶ O U T L I N E

T R U T H ▶ O R ▶ F I C T I O N ?

- Five and 6-year-old children do not have clear ideas of what is right and wrong.
- Five-year-old children generally think that people who accidentally harm others ought not to be punished.
- People who have arrived at the highest level of moral development follow their own ethical principles and may disobey the laws of the land.
- Girls lag behind boys in their moral development.
- Children who express the belief that cheating in school is wrong are unlikely to cheat.
- More intelligent children are less likely to cheat on school examinations.
- Children become more cooperative as they grow older.
- Children can be taught to make donations to charity by exposing them to generous adult models.
- Aggressive boys are likely to be aggressive as men.
- Aggressive girls are not likely to be aggressive as women.
- Human beings have inherited a killer instinct.
- Children who are physically punished are more likely to be aggressive.
- Most children mechanically imitate the aggressive behavior they observe on television and in films.

On guard. This chapter begins with a quiz. Answer each of the following questions with a yes or a no, and be ready to explain why you answered it as you did:

1. Is it okay to eat candy before supper?
2. Is it okay to bother a parent who is really busy?
3. Is it okay to brush your teeth before going to bed?
4. Is it okay to use someone else's bike without asking permission?
5. Is it okay to share your toys when a friend comes to your house?

Just in case you are in doubt, here are the correct answers: no (drat), no, yes, no (prissy?), yes. These are similar to the questions asked of 49-month-old children by Johnson, McGillicuddy, and Delisi in a 1983 study on moral development published in the journal *Child Development*. In brief, the researchers found that children's knowledge of rules and conventions increases when adults provide feedback as to whether children's verbal responses are consistent with social expectations.

Knowledge of social rules and conventions is one aspect of moral development. A child's moral development is a complex issue, with cognitive, behavioral, and affective aspects. On a cognitive level, moral development concerns whether children can deduce judgments of right and wrong from social principles. In the *Child Development* study cited above, conventional judgments of right and wrong were fostered and reinforced by the selective attention and explanations of adults. In this chapter we examine the contributions of Jean Piaget and Lawrence Kohlberg to our understanding of the cognitive aspects of moral development. In this chapter we also discuss cheating, altruism, and aggression.

Cognitive-Developmental Theories of Moral Development

Jean Piaget and Lawrence Kohlberg argue that moral reasoning undergoes a universal and invariant cognitive-developmental pattern. The moral considerations that children weigh at a given age are likely to reflect the values of the social and cultural settings in which they are being reared. However, moral reasoning is also theorized to reflect the orderly unfolding of cognitive processes. In turn, the unfolding of cognitive processes is thought to be at least partly based on the maturation of the nervous system. Patterns of moral reasoning are related to the child's overall cognitive development.

Let us describe and evaluate the contributions of each of these theorists.

Jean Piaget's Theory

In a sense, child morality throws light on adult morality. If we want to form men and women, nothing will fit us so well for the task as to study the laws that govern their formation.

—*Jean Piaget (1932, p. 9)*

▶ ▶ ▶ ▶

Moral realism *According to Piaget, the stage during which children judge acts as moral when they conform to authority or to the rules of the game. Morality at this stage is perceived as embedded in the structure of the universe.*

Objective morality *The perception of morality as objective, that is, as existing outside the cognitive functioning of people. Characteristic of Piaget's stage of moral realism.*

Objective responsibility *Judging the wrongness of an act in terms of the amount of damage done.*

For years Piaget observed children playing games like marbles and making judgments of the seriousness of the wrongdoing of characters in stories. On the basis of these observations, he concluded that children's moral judgments develop in two major overlapping stages: the stages of moral realism and autonomous morality (1932).

The Stage of Moral Realism

The earlier stage is usually referred to as the stage of **moral realism** or of **objective morality.** During this stage, which emerges at about the age of 5, children consider behavior to be correct when it conforms to authority, or to the rules of the game. Prior to this stage, marble players use idiosyncratic or shifting rules. They may not use rules at all.

At 5 or so, children perceive rules as somehow embedded in the structure of the universe. Rules, to them, reflect ultimate reality. Hence, the term *moral realism.* Rules and right and wrong are seen as unchanging and absolute. They are not seen as deriving from people in order to meet group needs.

When asked why something should be done in a certain way, the 5-year-old may answer "Because," or "Because that's the way to do it," or "Because my Mommy says so." Rules exist because they exist. Right is right, and wrong is wrong. Why? Because that's the way it is.

Why is it this way? Realism may reflect the egocentrism of the preoperational child, who frequently assumes that thoughts and mental representations are exact equivalents of external reality.

Objective Responsibility Egocentric moral reasoning yields interesting views of the social world. One is **objective responsibility.** That is, the wrongness of

How "bad" would this girl be if she dropped something on the floor and it broke? Would your answer differ if the girl were (a) trying to help her mother or (b) sneaking a treat against her mother's wishes? Children in the stage of objective morality tend to focus on the amount of damage done in making their judgments. Children in the stage of autonomous morality tend to be subjective, however; they also consider the motives of the wrongdoer.

▶ ▶ ▶ ▶

The Stories of the Cups

▷
▷
▷
▷

▷ Jean Piaget frequently studied the development of children's reasoning about moral issues by telling them stories and then asking them questions about the stories. In order to study the processes by which children arrived at moral judgments, he told them the following stories about John and Henry:

Story A. A little boy who is called John is in his room. He is called to dinner. He goes into the dining room. But behind the door there was a chair, and on the chair there was a tray with 15 cups on it. John couldn't have known that there was all this behind the door. He goes in, the door knocks against the tray, bang go the 15 cups and they all get broken.

Story B. Once there was a little boy whose name was Henry. One day when his mother was out he tried to get some jam out of the cupboard. He climbed up onto a chair and stretched out his arm. But the jam was too high up and he couldn't reach it and have any. But while he was trying to get it he knocked over a cup. The cup fell down and broke (Piaget, 1932, p. 122).

Consider the responses of a typical 6-year-old to these stories:

"Have you understood these stories? Let's hear you tell them."
"A little child was called in to dinner. There were 15 plates on a tray. He didn't know. He opens the door and he breaks the 15 plates."
"That's very good. And now the second story?"
"There was a child. And then this child wanted to go and get some jam. He gets onto a chair, his arm catches onto a cup, and it gets broken."
"Are those children both naughty, or is one not so naughty as the other?"
"Both just as naughty."
"Would you punish them the same?"
"No. The one who broke 15 plates."
"And would you punish the other one more, or less?"
"The first broke lots of things, the other one fewer."
"How would you punish them?"
"The one who broke the 15 cups, two slaps. The other one, one slap" (Piaget, 1932, p. 125).

Piaget notes that 7 was the average age for objective responsibility. Children below the age of 6 could not be questioned because of the intellectual difficulties of making the comparison.

Now, consider some responses to the stories of the cups by children who are showing autonomous morality:

[A precocious 7-year-old:]
"Which is naughtiest?"
"The second, the one who wanted to take the jam-pot, because he wanted to take something without asking."
"Did he (actually get the jam)?"
"No."
"Was he naughtiest all the same?"
"Yes."
"And the first (child)?"
"It wasn't his fault. He didn't do it on purpose."

▶ ▶ ▶ ▶

[A 9-year-old:]

"What did the first (child) do?"

"He broke 15 cups as he was opening a door."

"And the second one?"

"He broke one cup as he was taking some jam."

"Which of these . . . things was naughtiest, do you think?"

"The one where he tried to take hold of a cup was because the other boy didn't see (the cups behind the door). He (Henry) saw what he was doing."

"How many did (Henry) break?"

"One cup."

"And the other one?"

"Fifteen."

"Then which one would you punish most?"

"The one (Henry) who broke one cup."

"Why?"

"He did it on purpose. If he hadn't taken the jam, it wouldn't have happened" (Piaget, 1932, pp. 129–130).

Immanent justice *The view that retribution for wrongdoing is a direct consequence of the wrongdoing. Immanent justice reflects the belief that morality is embedded within the structure of the universe.*

Autonomous *Self-governed.*

Subjective *Existing within the mind of the person. According to Piaget, subjective responsibility is the judgment of the wrongness of an act in terms of the intentions of the wrongdoer.*

an act is judged in terms of the amount of damage done, rather than in terms of the intentions of the wrongdoer. Children in the stage of moral realism are tough jurors indeed. They do not "let off" the well-meaning transgressor, or the person who harms by accident. As an illustration, consider Piaget's stories of the broken cups in the nearby box.

Immanent Justice Another consequence of viewing rules as embedded in the fabric of the world is **immanent justice,** or automatic retribution. Punishment is perceived as structurally connected to wrongdoing. Therefore, punishment is inevitable. Five- or 6-year old children who lie or steal usually believe that they will be found out or at least punished for their acts. If they become ill or trip and scrape their knees, they may assume that this outcome represents punishment for a recent transgression.

Consider the correspondence between moral realism and preoperational thought. As noted in Chapter 8, preoperational children tend to be egocentric and to focus on one dimension at a time (in this case, the pertinent social rule or convention) in solving problems. Egocentrism and focusing on one dimension (e.g., the amount of harm done) at a time are also characteristic of moral realism.

The Stage of Autonomous Morality

Piaget found that when children reach the ages of 9 to 11, their moral judgments tend to become more **autonomous,** or self-governed. The tendency to interpret social rules strictly declines. Children come to view these rules as arbitrary agreements that can be changed. Children no longer automatically view obedience to authority figures as right. They realize that circumstances can require breaking the rules.

Children who show autonomous morality are capable of flexible operational thought. They show decentration in their ability to focus simultaneously on multiple dimensions. And so, they consider not only social rules, but also the motives of the wrongdoer and the demands of the situation.

Subjective Morality Children in this stage also show a greater capacity to take the point of view of others, to empathize with them. Decentration and increased

▶ ▶ ▶ ▶

empathy work together to prompt **subjective** moral judgments. Now the intentions of the wrongdoer may be considered more important than the amount of damage done. Still, children usually see severely harmful trangressions as deserving of punishment, despite the intentions of the wrongdoer.

As jurors, children now become capable of considering mitigating circumstances. Accidents are less likely to be considered crimes.

Piaget assumed that autonomous morality usually developed as a result of cooperative peer relationships. But he also believed that parents helped foster autonomous morality when they attempted to establish more egalitarian relationships with their children and explained the rationales for social rules.

Evaluation of Piaget's Theory of Moral Development

Many researchers agree that children's moral development proceeds from a stage of moral realism to one of autonomous morality (e.g., Hogan & Emler, 1978; Karniol, 1980; Lickona, 1976; Shultz, 1980). A number have found that very young children do make moral judgments on the basis of the consequences of an act, rather than on the intentions of the wrongdoer (Brandt & Strattner-Gregory, 1980).

Still, there are many problems with Piaget's views. One, as noted by James Rest (1983) and Judith Smetana (1985), is that many more issues than the amount of damage done and the intentions of the transgressor influence children's moral judgments. These include the ultimate outcomes of the acts, whether the object of wrongdoing was an object or a person, whether the effects of the act were physical or psychological, and so on. Smetana (1985) also notes that children, like adults, have a tendency to infer people's personality traits from their behavior. Very serious wrongdoings can encourage children to assume that the actor will commit other transgressions, even though children may focus more on motives when harmful acts are less severe.

Another pattern of criticism parallels the problems with Piaget that were noted in Chapter 8. It centers mainly on Piaget's age estimates and on the demand characteristics of his research methods. A number of studies suggest, for example, that most children show autonomous morality prior to the age of 9. Piaget's experimental stories, such as the stories of the cups, require that children remember the intentions of two people and the outcomes of two acts. Young children cannot process all this information simultaneously. But when the situations are described one at a time, or when intentions are more clearly outlined, many 5- and 6-year-olds consider the intentions of the wrongdoer in passing their moral judgments (Chandler et al., 1973; Constanzo et al., 1973; Feldman et al., 1976; Nelson, 1980; Surber, 1977).

One recent study of children aged 5, 8, 9, and 11 asked subjects to judge the wrongness of lies. All age groups considered both the amount of damage done by the lie and the intentions of the liar (Peterson et al., 1983). Lies that did no harm were judged less serious than harmful lies, but selfishly motivated lies were judged as worse than unintended lies and lies that were intended to please the listener. However, the 11-year-olds explained the wrongness of lying in terms of violation of trust and fairness in relationships. Younger children referred to the likelihood of being caught and punished. So in this study there were clear cognitive developments. Younger children judged social behavior in terms of rewards and punishments, and older children relied on abstract ethical principles that govern social relationships. But these developmental changes

▶ ▶ ▶ ▶

were not reflected in a clear transition from objective to subjective moral judgments.

In Chapter 8 we saw that children appear capable of taking the point of view of others at younger ages than Piaget believed—also, perhaps, because of flaws in his methodology. Later in this chapter we shall see that children are also apparently capable of showing empathy for others earlier than Piaget believed.

Another criticism of Piaget focuses on the presumed universality of development from moral realism to autonomous morality. For example, in our culture belief in immanent justice generally declines between ages 5 and 10 and is all but absent among fifth-graders (Suls & Kalle, 1979). However, this decline is not universal. Havighurst and Neugarten (1955) found that belief in immanent justice increased with age, rather than decreased, in 6 of 10 tribes of Native Americans. Still, in a culture in which it is recognized that social rules are conventions and not absolutes, and that wrongdoers are not always punished, belief in immanent justice is likely to decrease as children advance in cognitive development.

Lawrence Kohlberg's Theory

Psychologist Lawrence Kohlberg (1981, 1985) advanced the cognitive-developmental theory of moral development by elaborating the kinds of information children use as well as the complexities of moral reasoning. Before we consider Kohlberg's views, read the following tale used by Kohlberg (1969) in much of his research, and answer the questions below.

In Europe a woman was near death from a special kind of cancer. There was one drug that the doctors thought might save her. It was a form of radium that a druggist in the same town had recently discovered. The drug was expensive to make, but the druggist was charging 10 times what the drug cost him to make. He paid $200 for the radium and charged $2,000 for a small dose of the drug. The sick woman's husband, Heinz, went to everyone he knew to borrow the money, but he could only get together about $1,000 which was half of what it cost. He told the druggist that his wife was dying and asked him to sell it cheaper or let him pay later. But the druggist said: "No, I discovered the drug and I'm going to make money from it." So Heinz got desperate and broke into the man's store to steal the drug for his wife.

What do you think? Should Heinz have tried to steal the drug? Was he right or wrong? Heinz's story is an example of a moral dilemma in which a legal or social rule (in this case, laws against stealing) is pitted against a strong human need (Heinz's desire to save his wife). According to Kohlberg's theory, children and adults arrive at yes or no answers for different reasons. These reasons can be classified according to the level of moral development that they reflect.

Children (and adults) are faced with many moral dilemmas. Consider two issues concerning cheating that children frequently face in school. When children fear failing a test, they may be tempted to cheat. Different children may decide not to cheat for very different reasons. One child may simply fear getting caught. A second child may decide that it is more important to live up to his or her moral principles than to get the highest possible grade. In each

▶ ▶ ▶ ▶

Preconventional level *According to Kohlberg, a period during which moral judgments are based largely on expectations of rewards or punishments.*

case the child's decision is not to cheat. However, the cognitive processes behind each decision reflect different levels of reasoning.

Other children may observe a classmate cheating and decide to inform the teacher—again, for different reasons. A child with a grudge against the cheater may tell the teacher, so that the cheater will be punished. A second child may tell the teacher to prevent the cheater from getting a high grade and making other students' grades—including the informant's—look bad by comparison. A third may tell the teacher, because he or she believes that reporting cheating is the normal thing to do. A fourth may hate the idea of "squealing," but may still inform on the cheater, because of concern that the social system could break down if cheating is tolerated by peers.

As a stage theorist, Kohlberg argues that the developmental stages of moral reasoning follow an invariant sequence. Different children may progress at different rates, and not all children (or adults) reach the highest stage. However, children must experience stage 1 before they enter stage 2, and so on.

Let us return to Heinz and see how responses to the questions we have posed can reflect different levels and stages of moral development.

The Preconventional Level

In the **preconventional level,** children base their moral judgments on the consequences of their behavior. For instance, stage 1 is oriented toward obedience and punishment. Good behavior is seen as that which involves obedience and allows one to evade punishment. According to stage 1 reasoning, Heinz could be urged to steal the drug so that he *will not be blamed* for allowing his wife to die. But he could also be urged not to steal the drug so that he will not be sent to jail. (See Tables 13.1 and 13.2.)

In stage 2, good behavior is that which will allow people to satisfy their

Table 13.1 Lawrence Kohlberg's Levels and Stages of Moral Development

LEVEL AND STAGE	WHAT IS RIGHT	REASONS FOR DOING RIGHT	SOCIAL PERSPECTIVE OF STAGE
LEVEL I— PRECONVENTIONAL Stage 1—Heteronomous morality	To avoid breaking rules backed by punishment, obedience for its own sake, and avoiding physical damage to persons and property.	Avoidance of punishment, and the superior power of authorities.	*Egocentric point of view.* Doesn't consider the interests of others or recognize that they differ from the actor's; doesn't relate two points of view. Actions are considered physically rather than in terms of psychological interests of others. Confusion of authority's perspective with one's own.
Stage 2—Individualism, instrumental purpose, and exchange	Following rules only when it is in someone's immediate interest; acting to meet one's own interests and needs and letting others do the same. Right is also what's fair, what's an equal exchange, a deal, an agreement.	To serve one's own needs or interests in a world where you have to recognize that other people have their interests, too.	*Concrete individualistic perspective.* Aware that everybody has his own interest to pursue and these conflict, so that right is relative (in the concrete individualistic sense).

▶ ▶ ▶ ▶

Table 13.1 Cont.

LEVEL AND STAGE	WHAT IS RIGHT	REASONS FOR DOING RIGHT	SOCIAL PERSPECTIVE OF STAGE
LEVEL II— CONVENTIONAL Stage 3—Mutual interpersonal expectations, relationships, and interpersonal conformity	Living up to what is expected by people close to you or what people generally expect of people in your role as son, brother, friend, etc. "Being good" is important and means having good motives, showing concern about others. It also means keeping mutual relationships, such as trust, loyalty, respect, and gratitude.	The need to be a good person in your own eyes and those of others. Your caring for others. Belief in the Golden Rule. Desire to maintain rules and authority that support stereotypical good behavior.	*Perspective of the individual in relationships with other individuals.* Aware of shared feelings, agreements, and expectations that take primacy over individual interests. Relates points of view through the concrete Golden Rule, putting yourself in the other guy's shoes. Does not yet consider generalized system perspective.
Stage 4—Social system and conscience	Fulfilling the actual duties to which you have agreed. Laws are to be upheld except in extreme cases where they conflict with other fixed social duties. Right is also contributing to society, the group, or institution.	To keep the institution going as a whole, to avoid the breakdown in the system "if everyone did it," or the imperative of conscience to meet one's defined obligations.	*Differentiates societal point of view from interpersonal agreement or motives.* Takes the point of view of the system that defines roles and rules. Considers individual relations in terms of place in the system.
LEVEL III— POSTCONVENTIONAL, or PRINCIPLED Stage 5—Social contract or utility and individual rights	Being aware that people hold a variety of values and opinions, that most values and rules are relative to your group. These relative rules should usually be upheld, however, in the interest of impartiality and because they are the social contract. Some nonrelative values and rights like *life* and *liberty*, however, must be upheld in any society and regardless of majority opinion.	A sense of obligation to law because of one's social contract to make and abide by laws for the welfare of all and for the protection of all people's rights. A feeling of contractual commitment, freely entered upon, to family, friendship, trust, and work obligations. Concern that laws and duties be based on rational calculation of overall utility, "the greatest good for the greatest number."	*Prior-to-society perspective.* Perspective of a rational individual aware of values and rights prior to social attachments and contracts. Integrates perspectives by formal mechanisms of agreement, contract, objective impartiality, and due process. Considers moral and legal points of view; recognizes that they sometimes conflict and finds it difficult to integrate them.
Stage 6—Universal ethical principles	Following self-chosen ethical principles. Particular laws or social agreements are usually valid because they rest on such principles. When laws violate these principles, one acts in accordance with the principles, which are universal: the equality of human rights and respect for the dignity of human beings as individual persons.	The belief as a rational person in the validity of universal moral principles, and a sense of personal commitment to them.	*Perspective of a moral point of view* from which social arrangements derive. Perspective is that of any rational individual recognizing the nature of morality or the fact that persons are ends in themselves and must be treated as such.

Source: Adapted from L. Kohlberg, Moral stages and moralization. In T. Lickona (ed.), *Moral Development and Behavior* (New York: Holt, Rinehart and Winston, 1976), pp. 34–35.

▶ ▶ ▶ ▶

Table 13.2 Stage Levels of Illustrative Responses to the Story of Heinz Stealing the Drug for His Wife

Stage 1: "It isn't really bad to take it—he did ask to pay for it first. He wouldn't do any other damage or take anything else, and the drug he'd take is only worth $200; he's not really taking a $2,000 drug."

Stage 2: "Heinz isn't really doing any harm to the druggist, and he can always pay him back. If he doesn't want to lose his wife, he should take the drug because it's the only thing that will work."

Stage 3: "Stealing is bad, but this is a bad situation. Heinz isn't doing wrong in trying to save his wife; he has no choice but to take the drug. He is only doing something that is natural for a good husband to do. You can't blame him for doing something out of love for his wife. You'd blame him if he didn't love his wife enough to save her."

Stage 4: "The druggist is leading a wrong kind of life if he just lets somebody die like that, so it's Heinz's duty to save her. But Heinz just can't go around breaking laws and let it go at that— he must pay the druggist back and he must take his punishment for stealing."

Stage 5: "Before you say stealing is wrong, you've got to really think about this whole situation. Of course, the laws are quite clear about breaking into a store. And, even worse, Heinz would know that there are no legal grounds for his actions. Yet, I can see why it would be reasonable for anybody in this situation to steal the drug."

Stage 6: "Where the choice must be made between disobeying a law and saving a human life, the higher principle of preserving life makes it morally right—not just understandable—to steal the drug."

Source: Adapted from J. R. Rest, The hierarchical nature of moral judgment: The study of patterns of comprehension and preference with moral stages. *Journal of Personality, 41* (1974), 92–93.

own needs and, perhaps, the needs of others. A stage 2 reason for stealing the drug is that Heinz's wife needs it and that Heinz would probably not be given too severe a sentence for the act. A stage 2 reason for not stealing the drug would be that Heinz's wife might die even if he does so. Thus, he might wind up in jail needlessly.

In a study of U.S. children aged 7 through 16, Kohlberg (1963) found that stage 1 and 2 types of moral judgments were offered most frequently by 7- and 10-year-olds. There was a steep falling off of stage 1 and 2 judgments after age 10.

The Conventional Level

In the **conventional level** of moral reasoning, right and wrong are judged by conformity to conventional (family, church, societal) standards of right and wrong. According to the stage 3 "good-boy orientation," it is good to meet the needs and expectations of others. During this stage moral behavior is seen as what is "normal." Moral behavior is what the majority does, or what proper people do. From the stage 3 perspective, Heinz should steal the drug, because that is what a "good husband" would do. It is "natural" or "normal" to try to help one's wife. Or, Heinz should *not* steal the drug because "good people do not steal." Stage 3 judgments also focus on the role of sympathy— on the importance of doing what will make someone else feel good or better.

In stage 4, moral judgments are based on rules that maintain the social order. Showing respect for authority and doing one's duty are valued highly.

Conventional level According to Kohlberg, a period during which moral judgments largely reflect social conventions. A "law and order" approach to morality.

▶ ▶ ▶ ▶

From this perspective, one could argue that Heinz must steal the drug, because it would be his responsibility if he let his wife die. And, of course, he would pay the druggist when he could. Or one could argue that Heinz should not steal the drug, because he would always feel guilty for breaking the law. He might also be contributing to the breakdown of the social order. Many people do not develop beyond the conventional level.

Kohlberg (1963) found that stage 3 and 4 types of judgments are all but absent among 7-year-olds. However, they are reported by about 20 percent of 10-year-olds, and higher percentages of 13- and 16-year-olds. Stage 3 and 4 moral judgments are the types of judgments made most frequently by 13- and 16-year-olds.

A review of the research found that higher percentages of juvenile delinquents engaged in stage 2 moral reasoning than did their nondelinquent counterparts (Blasi, 1980). The comparison groups, who did not engage in delinquent behavior, were more likely to show moral reasoning that was typical of stages 3 and 4. Stage 2 reasoning (viewing what is right and wrong in terms of satisfying personal needs) is also characteristic of offenders who engage in robbery and other "instrumental" crimes (Thornton & Reid, 1982).

The Postconventional Level

Postconventional level *According to Kohlberg, a period during which moral judgments are derived from moral principles and people look to themselves to set moral standards.*

Reciprocity *The principle that actions have mutual effects and that we are dependent on one another to treat each other morally.*

In the **postconventional level**, moral reasoning is based on the person's own moral standards. In each instance, moral judgments are derived from personal values, not from conventional standards or authority figures. In stage 5's contractual, legalistic orientation, it is recognized that laws stem from agreed-upon procedures and that many rights have great value and should not be violated. But it is also recognized that there are circumstances in which existing laws cannot bind the individual's behavior. A stage 5 reason for stealing the drug might be that it is the right thing to do, even though it is illegal; Heinz would lose his self-respect if he allowed his wife to die. Conversely, it could be argued that if everyone "in need" broke the law, the legal system and the social contract would be destroyed.

In stage 6's principled orientation, people choose their own ethical principles—such as justice, **reciprocity,** and respect for individuality. Behavior derived from these principles is considered right. If a law is seen as unjust, or as contradicting the rights of the individual, it is wrong to obey it.

Postconventional people look to themselves as the highest moral authority. This point has created confusion. To some critics it suggests that it is right for people to break the law or ignore social conventions whenever convenient. But Kohlberg means that postconventional people feel obligated to do what they believe is right, even if following their beliefs leads to social disapproval and personal sacrifice.

Consider examples from recent history in which many have faced large-scale moral dilemmas that required personal sacrifice. During the 1960s many U.S. citizens broke local laws in their civil-rights demonstrations. In most cases these local laws were later overturned by the Supreme Court as discriminatory. During the 1960s and 1970s many young men who believed that U.S. military involvement in Vietnam was wrong were faced with a dilemma when they were drafted into the armed forces. If they allowed themselves to be inducted, they would be supporting what they saw as an immoral cause. But by refusing induction, they were breaking the law. In the 1980s other U.S. citizens have

▶ ▶ ▶ ▶

Juvenile delinquents tend to show lower stages of moral reasoning than do nondelinquents.

broken the law in their efforts to prevent the construction of plants for generating nuclear energy. However, they have also believed that it would be wrong for them to stand idly by while the country—from their perspective—was building machines that could lead to its own destruction. For these citizens, belief in their cause compelled them to break laws, even though they risked losing their families, careers, social status, and freedom.

Of course, it can be argued, and correctly, that not all of the demonstrators and law-breakers in the civil rights, anti-Vietnam, and antinuclear crusades have acted from such a principled perspective. Certainly some demonstrators broke the law in order to avoid the disapproval of their own peer groups. A few college students have admitted to going on demonstrations as a way of finding dates. And a few young men, of course, refused induction into the armed forces to avoid exposure to the dangers of Vietnam, despite claims to higher moral concerns. Nevertheless, many did break the law because of their interpretation of moral principles and were operating at Kohlberg's stage 6. College students at the postconventional level were more likely than peers at the conventional level of morality to participate in the campus demonstrations and civil disobedience of the 1960s (Haan et al., 1968).

Return to the case of Heinz. It could also be argued from stage 6's perspective that the principle of preserving life takes precedence over laws prohibiting stealing. Therefore, it is morally necessary for Heinz to steal the drug, even if he must go to jail. Note that it could also be asserted, from the principled orientation, that, if Heinz finds the social contract or the law to be the highest principle, he must then remain within the law, despite the consequences.

Stage 5 and 6 moral judgments were all but absent among the 7- and 10-year-olds in Kohlberg's (1963) sample of U.S. children. They increased in

▶ ▶ ▶ ▶

frequency during the early and middle teens. By age 16, stage 5 reasoning was shown by about 20 percent and stage 6 reasoning by about 5 percent of adolescents. However, stage 3 and 4 judgments were made more frequently at all ages, 7 through 16, studied by Kohlberg and other investigators (Colby et al., 1983; Rest, 1983). (See Figure 13.1.)

Sex Differences in Moral Development

One of the more controversial notions in the history of child development is that males show higher levels of moral development than females. From his psychoanalytic perspective, Freud assumed that males would have stronger "superegos" than females, because of the wrenching Oedipus complex and the male's consequent identification with authority figures and social codes. But Freud's views on the Oedipus complex were speculative, and his views on women reflected the ignorance and prejudice of his times.

However, in more recent years, a number of cognitively oriented researchers have claimed to find gender differences in moral development in the United States in terms of responses to Heinz's dilemma. Some studies have found that boys reason at higher levels of moral development than girls. Carol Gilligan (1977, 1982) argues that this sex difference reflects different patterns of socialization for boys and girls.

Gilligan makes her point through two examples of responses to Heinz's dilemma. Eleven-year-old Jake views the dilemma as a math problem. He sets up an equation showing that life has greater value than property. Heinz is thus obligated to steal the drug. Eleven-year-old Amy equivocates. She notes that stealing the drug and letting Heinz's wife die would both be wrong. Amy searches for alternatives, such as getting a loan, stating that it would profit Heinz's wife little if he went to jail and were no longer around to help her.

According to Gilligan, Amy is showing a pattern of reasoning that is as sophisticated as Jake's. Still, Amy would be rated as showing a lower level of moral development. Gilligan asserts that Amy, like other girls, has been socialized into focusing on the needs of others and foregoing simplistic judgments

Carol Gilligan

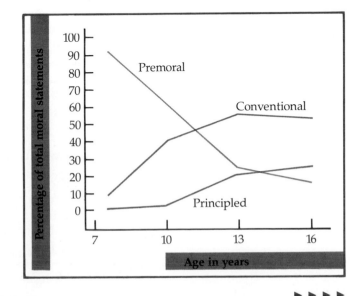

Figure 13.1 Age and Type of Moral Judgment
The incidence of preconventional (premoral) reasoning declines from greater than 90 percent of moral statements at age 7 to about 20 percent of moral statements at age 16. Conventional moral statements increase with age between 7 and 13, but then level off to account for 50–60 percent of moral statements between 13 and 16. Postconventional (principled) moral statements are all but absent at ages 7 and 10, but account for about 20–25 percent of moral statements at ages 13 and 16.

▶ ▶ ▶ ▶

of right and wrong. As a consequence, Amy is more likely to appear to show "stage 3 reasoning," which focuses in part on emphaty for others (Gilligan, 1977). Jake, by contrast, has been socialized into making judgments based "purely" on logic. To him, clear-cut conclusions are to be derived from a set of premises. Amy was aware of the logical considerations that struck Jake, of course. However, she processed them as one source of information—not as the single acceptable source. It is ironic that Amy's empathy, a trait that has "defined the 'goodness' of women," marks Amy "as deficient in moral development" (Gilligan, 1982, p. 18). Prior to his death in 1987, Kohlberg (1985) had begun efforts to correct the sexism of his scoring system.

There are individual differences. Some girls do focus essentially on abstract moral principles, and some boys do focus on the needs of others. But by and large, the cultural die of the logical boy and the empathic girl has been cast. This is unfortunate to Gilligan; she argues that ideal solutions to moral and other problems would reflect both the needs of others and abstract principles.

However, it should also be noted that some studies do not find that girls reason at lower levels than boys, even though the girls remain more likely to express sympathy for victims during the studies (e.g., Gibbs et al., 1984).

In his review of the literature on sex differences in moral reasoning, Lawrence Walker (1984) concluded that the apparent sex differences found in *some* studies could actually be attributed to differences in educational and occupational achievement—at least among older subjects. That is, subjects who showed the highest levels of moral reasoning had had more education and occupational experience at higher levels. Diana Baumrind (1986) counters that sex differences remain, even when we consider educational and occupational status. However, like Gilligan, she argues that we have yet to fully understand the specific nature of these differences.

Cultural Influences on Moral Development

Cultural background appears to influence moral reasoning. Kohlberg found postconventional thinking among a minority of U.S. adolescents, but it was all but absent among adolescents in villages in Mexico, Taiwan, Turkey (Kohlberg, 1969), and the Bahamas (White et al., 1978). Postconventional reasoning seems more likely to be found in industrialized, affluent nations. Within the United States, postconventional thinking is more likely to be voiced by persons of higher socioeconomic status. Longitudinal evidence shows that higher education also tends to foster higher levels of moral reasoning (Rest & Thoma, 1985).

Situational Influences on Moral Development

People who are capable of a certain level of moral reasoning do not always use it (Hoffman, 1980; Weiss, 1982). Situational factors apparently play an important role in whether moral judgments will be based on conventional or postconventional principles. A study by Tapp and Levine (1972), for example, suggests that it is easier to talk about higher levels of moral development in theoretical discussions than it is to apply them to one's own life. The investigators asked children and adolescents two questions: (1) "Why *should* people

▶ ▶ ▶ ▶

follow rules?" and (2) "Why do *you* follow rules?" Answers to the first question were more advanced. For example, children were more likely to say that people should follow rules to maintain the social order than they were to offer this reason for their own behavior. In their own lives, they admitted that their own behavior was more likely to be governed by expectations of reward or punishment.

An experiment also suggests the power of situational influences. In a study by Sobesky (1983), high school and college students who were told that it was certain that Heinz would go to prison for stealing the drug were significantly less likely to use principled thinking and suggest that Heinz should help his wife. Once the consequences were made so clear and certain, many of these students seemed compelled by the situation into making stage 1 moral judgments that were controlled by fear of punishment. Other students, who were told that the drug would definitely save Heinz's wife, were significantly more likely to suggest that Heinz steal the drug and to justify their decision with principled reasoning.

Moral Behavior and Moral Reasoning: Is There a Relationship?

Is there a relationship between moral cognitive development and moral behavior? Are children whose moral development is more mature less likely to commit immoral acts? Is there a correspondence between children's behavior and their moral judgments? The answer seems to be *often, but not always.*

Preadolescents whose moral reasoning is at stage 2 appear to engage in cheating and other conduct problems in the classroom more frequently than age-mates whose moral reasoning is at higher stages (Bear & Richards, 1981; Krebs, 1967). Older children at the postconventional level of morality also seem less likely to cheat in school situations than age-mates at lower levels of morality (Grim et al., 1968; Lehrer, 1967). But there are exceptions, especially among younger children. Aronfreed (1976) notes the example of a 7-year-old girl who acted violently toward her younger brother. Despite her behavior, she stated clearly that she should not have tried to hurt her brother, because it was wrong. Among young children behavior is frequently impulsive and not tempered by cognitive mediation—even when children become capable of careful deliberation (Burton, 1984).

Still, many studies have found relationships between stage of moral development and moral behavior. Experiments have also been conducted in the hope of advancing moral reasoning as a way of decreasing immoral behavior. At present I think it is fair to say that it has been shown that group discussion of moral dilemmas can elevate delinquents' level of moral reasoning (e.g., Gibbs et al., 1984). However, it has not yet been demonstrated that delinquents, as a consequence, discontinue immoral or illegal behavior.

Evaluation of Kohlberg's Theory

There is evidence that the moral judgments of children develop toward higher stages in sequence (Snarey et al., 1985), even though most children do not reach postconventional thought. Postconventional thought, when it is found, first occurs during adolescence.

▶ ▶ ▶ ▶

Why doesn't postconventional moral reasoning appear until age 13 or so? A number of studies (Tomlinson-Keasey & Keasey, 1974; Kuhn et al., 1977) suggest that formal operational thinking is a precedent. That is, postconventional reasoning appears to require the capacities to understand abstract moral principles and to empathize with the attitudes and emotional responses of other people. However, the appearance of formal operational thought does not guarantee that postconventional moral judgments will follow.

Consistent with Kohlberg's theory, children do not appear to skip stages as they progress (Kohlberg & Kramer, 1969; Kuhn, 1976; White et al., 1978). When children are exposed to adult models who engage in a lower type of moral reasoning, they can be induced to express the patterns of judgment characteristic of the earlier stage (Bandura & McDonald, 1963). But children exposed to examples of moral reasoning above and below that of their own stage generally prefer the higher level of reasoning (Rest, 1976, 1983). Thus the thrust of moral development is from lower to higher stages, even if children can be sidetracked by social influences.

One longitudinal study did find that one's level of moral reasoning can "slip backward" in response to changed circumstances. James Rest and Steven Thoma (1985) observed young adults who went on to college after high school. They showed increasingly higher levels of moral development over the course of the next six years. However, high school graduates who did not attend college showed increases in moral development over the next two years, and then their development tended to fall back to levels similar to those at time of graduation. Rest and Thoma suggest a number of explanations for the advances of the college students, including socialization into the (more principled) values likely to be held by college students, the learning of moral philosophies, and general intellectual stimulation. The educational thrust of high school may have fueled the development of non-college-attending graduates for another two years or so. But then perhaps they were socialized into groups with more of a "law-and-order" orientation. Or else perhaps decreased intellectual stimulation killed the incentive to examine moral issues.

Kohlberg believed that the stages of moral development were universal, following the unfolding of innate sequences. However, he seems to have underestimated the influence of cultural or educational institutions. It has been found that the use of inductive disciplinary methods, including discussions of the feelings of others, advances moral reasoning (Hoffman, 1984; Parke, 1977). Mothers seem to be particularly influential in fostering advanced moral reasoning because they, more so than fathers, look for children's motives and discuss the feelings of victims (Hoffman, 1982). (Are there any who still view women's moral development as inferior to men's?)

There is also cross-cultural evidence concerning the importance of the macrosystem. The fact that postconventional thinking is all but absent in nonindustrialized societies—and infrequent even in the United States—suggests that postconventional reasoning may be more reflective of the philosophical ideals of Kohlberg, and of those who share his views, than it is of a natural stage of cognitive development. Stage 6 reasoning, for example, is based on the acceptance of "universal" ethical principles. The principles of justice, equality, integrity, and the sanctity of human life may have a high appeal to you. But you were reared in a culture that idealizes them. They are not universally revered. Thus, they are more reflective of Western cultural influences than of the cognitive development of the child. In recognition of these problems, Kohlberg (1985) all but dropped stage 6 reasoning from his theory in recent years.

▶ ▶ ▶ ▶

Let us now turn our attention to the topic of cheating in school and elsewhere. We shall see that children's moral evaluation of cheating is only one of many factors that influence cheating—and perhaps not a major factor.

Cheating

Few things seem obvious in life. But perhaps one of them is that children who believe that cheating is wrong are unlikely to cheat, right? Wrong. One of the fascinating findings of Hugh Hartshorne and Mark May's (1928) classic research into children's "character" was that children who cheated in school often expressed as much disapproval of cheating as children who did not.

Studies suggest that most children cheat at least some of the time—in elementary school, in high school, and in college. Cheating, like so many other forms of behavior, is influenced by the behavior of those around us. Three- to 5-year-olds are less likely to "cheat" by playing with forbidden toys when they believe that their peers have decided not to play with them (Parke, 1974). Nonaffiliated college students are less likely to cheat on exams than are groups of fraternity brothers or sorority sisters (Hetherington & Feldman, 1964). Group living may encourage cheating by modeling effects.

In this section we examine a number of issues surrounding cheating, including the consistency of cheating behavior from one situation to another, and the personal factors that contribute to cheating.

Consistency in Cheating

In one of the most ambitious studies of child development, Hartshorne and May (1928) observed some 11,000 children who had the opportunity to lie, cheat, or steal in a variety of situations—at school, at home, at parties, during athletic contests, alone, or with peers. The researchers reported that cheating tended to be situation-specific. Children, that is, might cheat in one situation, but not in another. One could not very well predict whether children would cheat in situation B from their behavior in situation A. Many children were also

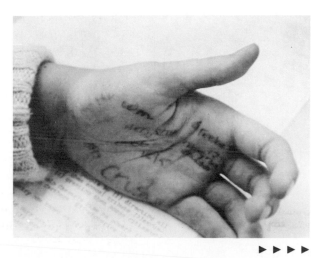

Cheating, like other forms of behavior, is influenced by the behavior of those around us.

▶ ▶ ▶ ▶

more likely to avoid cheating because of fear of detection or fear of peer disapproval than because of their own moral values.

Roger Burton (1963, 1984) reanalyzed Hartshorne and May's data with more sophisticated statistical techniques and reported that children appear to have predispositions to cheat or not to cheat in similar situations. The child who cheats at one game is likely to cheat at a second game, but not necessarily to cheat in school or lie to a parent. The child who cheats in math is likely to cheat in science, but not necessarily at baseball.

Ironically, children who cheat are more likely than noncheaters to express feelings of guilt and to state that they must make amends. Burton (1976) explains this discrepancy by suggesting that cheaters who proclaim high standards are not being sincere. Rather, they may have learned to "talk a good moral game" in order to assuage angered parents and thus avoid punishment.

Personal Characteristics and Cheating

Children who have a high need for achievement are more likely to cheat when they believe that their classmates are outperforming them on a test (Shelton & Hill, 1969). Cheating allows them to avoid the disapproval of others and to maintain self-esteem.

The dynamics of cheating among late high school and college males also suggest that cheating increases with personal need—in this case, with pressure to succeed (Hetherington & Feldman, 1964; Feldman & Feldman, 1967). In a study run during the Great Depression, students who were working their way through college—and thus under greater financial pressure—were more likely to cheat than students who were not working (Parr, 1936).

The social psychology literature suggests that, when we engage in behavior we consider immoral, we often see ourselves as being forced into it by circumstances. However, we usually attribute dishonest behavior in others to personal choice (Rathus, 1987). These observations hold true for cheating. College students tend to attribute their cheating to cutthroat competition and the unacceptable impact that poor grades would have on their job possibilities or on chances for admission to graduate school (Smith et al., 1972). Given the prevalence of cheating, children and college students are also likely to have the perception that "everyone is doing it." This perception establishes a group norm which makes cheating acceptable. It also encourages individuals to think that they might be handicapping themselves if they do not cheat.

There is an about equal incidence of cheating among boys and girls, even though teachers consider girls more trustworthy (Burton, 1976). Girls, however, are more likely to cheat when the teacher is a female. Boys are more likely to cheat when the teacher is a male. Perhaps children are more concerned about disappointing an adult of the opposite sex.

Numerous studies report that brighter students are less likely to cheat (Hartshorne & May, 1928; Hetherington & Feldman, 1964; Johnson & Gormley, 1972). Perhaps more intelligent children are less likely to *need* to cheat in order to earn high grades. Therefore, the risks of cheating outweigh the potential benefits for them. But it may also be that more intelligent children accept occasional failures as part of their overall success. In any event, Hartshorne and May (1928) found that bright students were as likely as less intelligent students to cheat in nonacademic situations, where their intelligence would do them

▶ ▶ ▶ ▶

little good. Thus, when the need of the bright student increases, he or she also becomes more likely to cheat.

Let us now turn our attention to a more positive aspect of moral development—the development of altruism.

Altruism

Altruism may be defined as unselfish concern for the welfare of others. Altruistic behavior includes cooperating with others, coming to the aid of others in distress, and sharing with others who are in need. Most of us verbally extol the virtues of cooperating with and helping others, but U.S. society—especially middle-class culture—has also been criticized for promoting competitiveness and a "dog-eat-dog" attitude.

Patterns of Helping

Children respond emotionally from a very early age when other people are in distress (Eisenberg, 1982; Hoffman, 1983). During the first year of infancy, children frequently begin to cry when they hear other children crying. Nurses on maternity wards note that one neonate's loud cries may stimulate other neonates to cry. However, this early agitated response may be largely reflexive. Crying, like other strong stimuli, can be aversive, and infants generally react to aversive stimulation by crying. Even so, this early unlearned behavior pattern might contribute to the development of **empathy.**

Developmentalists broadly agree that children show empathy during the second year, especially during the second half of the second year (Radke-Yarrow et al., 1983). Empathy apparently promotes prosocial behavior (Chap-

Children tend to show the ability to share another person's feelings during the second year. Most children try to help others who are in distress.

▶ ▶ ▶ ▶

man et al., 1987; Iannotti, 1985). During the second year many children approach other children and adults who are in distress, and they begin to attempt to help them. They may try to hug or hold a crying child. They may suggest using a Band-Aid, or they may tell the other child or adult not to cry. Jerome Kagan (1984) takes the view that the development of empathy during the second half of the second year is largely maturational—it reflects changes in the nervous system. In fact, Kagan argues that conscience and morality are natural consequences of children's increasing awareness of how their behavior affects others, and how the behavior of others affects them. To Kagan, the question is not how children acquire a "conscience." It is how some children *lose* their consciences as they grow older.

During the third year, many children apply what they can from their own limited experiences and observations. They may tell a mother to feed or change a crying infant. They may suggest calling the doctor. They may ask the distressed child or adult to tell them what is wrong—where it hurts, or where the "boo-boo" is.

By the time they are 45 to 65 months old, children have apparently acquired very different ways of conceptualizing their relationships with adults and with other children. When they explain *why* they comply with the requests of adults, they are likely to say that the adult is an authority figure or may punish them (Eisenberg et al., 1985). However, when they explain why they comply with the requests of their peers, they are significantly more likely to refer to feelings of liking and friendship, or to the other children's needs.

Another aspect of helping is sharing. Let us examine the factors that promote childhood generosity.

The Development of Sharing Behavior

At 18 months, Allyn's behavior suggested she was well aware that other people appreciated sharing. She would offer her older sister Jill food and toys.

Four-year-olds are sensitive to the needs of other children.

Maternal Influences on Helping Behavior

▷
▷
▷
▷

▷ It appears that the mother's behavior is a powerful determinant of whether her children will come to the aid of others. In a study of helping behavior in 18-month-olds, Yarrow and Waxler (1978) trained mothers to record distressful incidents and their children's responses. The reliability of the mothers' records was assessed by researchers, who observed them in the home for several hours every three weeks.

There was great variability in the frequency of helping responses, even at this early age. Some children attempted to help most of the time when they hurt someone or saw someone in distress. Other children offered aid infrequently, and some not at all.

The mother's reactions to distress and to their children's harmdoing were powerful influences on the frequency of helping behavior. Some mothers simply explained cause-and-effect relationships. That is, they described how their behavior harmed others. They might say, "Jessie is crying because you took her bunny rabbit," or "Randy is bleeding because you scratched him." Other mothers explained cause and effect and also used strong emotional injunctions. For example, "If you don't let Jessie play with her toys, I'm not going to let you go near her!" or "You must never scratch your brother!" Still other mothers used physical punishment (as in hitting or spanking), physical restraint (preventing the child from doing harm by holding him or her back or moving away), or unexplained injunctions such as "Don't do that!"

Children of mothers who explained cause-and-effect relationships were more likely to help the victim when they caused the distress. Children of mothers who explained cause and effect and also used emotional injunctions were most likely to help others regardless of who or what had caused the distress. Children whose mothers used physical punishment or restraint, or who had unexplained prohibitions, were least likely to try to come to the aid of others.

In general, then, altruistic behavior is more likely to be fostered when parents explain how harmful behavior damages others and when they encourage their children to imagine being "in the shoes" of others (Hoffman, 1981; Radke-Yarrow et al., 1983). Moreover, strong emotional messages about causing distress in others appear to heighten children's motivation to undo the distress.

▶ ▶ ▶ ▶

Sharing is influenced by rewards and punishments. Children respond more positively to peers who share than to peers who are self-centered.

Then, when Jill reached for them, Allyn yanked them away with a grunt and an explosive laugh. Jill caught on quickly. After a few repetitions she said, "No, I don't want it" when offered a toy. But Allyn insisted. Eventually Jill gave in and reached once more. Yank—laugh. When I wondered aloud how Allyn had learned this game, Jill noted acidly that my appreciative laughter seemed to be reinforcing Allyn quite nicely. Duly chastized, I left the room, but I confess that I still enjoyed the repeated grunts and laughs from inside.

About a year later, Allyn refused to share her toys with Jordan. I recall sitting with them on many occasions and saying things like, "Either let Jordan play with the pink bear or the caterpillar with sneakers. You can't play with both of them while she has nothing." When you are a parent, it seems that you find yourself talking about things like caterpillars with sneakers.

Sneakers aside, it could be argued that "sharing" behaviors begin during the first year of life, when infants try to bring interesting objects to the attention of others by excitedly pointing at them. Eighteen-month-old children frequently show and offer their toys to parents and strangers (Rheingold et al., 1976). Many of them even allow the adults to hold onto them for a while.

Although it is not possible to identify the exact origins of sharing behavior, the literature is replete with studies that show how the frequency of sharing behaviors can be increased.

Fostering Sharing Behavior through Reinforcement and Modeling

Sharing is influenced by rewards and punishments. Observations of nursery school children show that the peers of children who are cooperative, friendly, and generous respond more positively to them than they do to children whose behavior is self-centered (Hartup, 1983).

In one experiment, 4-year-olds became more likely to share their marbles with unknown peers when their generosity was rewarded with bubble gum (Fischer, 1963). Explaining to young children that they have more than others does little to prompt sharing behavior. Threatening them with punishment unless they share their bounty works wonders as a method of fostering generosity (Hartmann et al., 1974, 1976). However, it is unclear whether such isolated instances of positive or negative consequences shape patterns of sharing that endure over the years.

Some children at early ages are made responsible for housekeeping, caring for younger siblings, and other chores. They are taught helping skills, and their performances are selectively reinforced by other children and adults. Whiting and Whiting (1975) reported that children given such tasks are more likely to help and share with others than children who are not.

There is evidence that children can acquire sharing behavior by observing models who help and share. For example, children who watch *Mister Rogers' Neighborhood*, a children's program that heavily models cooperative behavior, have shown increased social interaction, sharing behavior, cooperation, and use of positive reinforcement (as opposed to punishment) in shaping the behavior of other children (Coates et al., 1976; Freidrich & Stein, 1975). (See Figure 13.2.)

In one experiment in sharing, 29- to 36-month-old toddlers were more likely to share toys with toddler playmates who first shared toys with them (Levitt et al., 1985). That is, the children reciprocated. In another experiment,

▶ ▶ ▶ ▶

Figure 13.2 A Classic Experiment in the Imitation of Aggressive Models
Children will imitate the behavior of adult models in certain situations, as shown in these pictures from a classic study by Albert Bandura and his colleagues (1963). In the top row, an adult model strikes a clown doll. The next two rows show a boy and a girl imitating the adult.

fourth- and fifth-grade children bowled for certificates that could be exchanged for toys at a local store. After the game, the children passed a box labeled "Trenton Orphan's Fund" with a picture of poorly dressed children on the front. Some of the children observed an adult model place some of his certificates in the box. Others did not. The children were then left by the box and observed surreptitiously. Nearly half (47.5 percent) of the boys and girls who had observed the generous model made contributions. None were made by children who were not exposed to adult sharing.

Altruistic values in parents seem to predict altruistic behavior in children (Hoffman, 1973), but parents' behavior in some ways speaks louder than their words. In studies similar to the above, third- and fourth-graders won money in experimental games. They were then exposed either to a charitable adult model (who donated a portion of his winnings to the March of Dimes) or a model who kept his winnings. In addition, some children heard the charitable model argue in favor of generosity (e.g., "It's good to donate to poor children"). Others heard the selfish model justify stinginess (e.g., "Why should we give

▶ ▶ ▶ ▶

any of our money to other people?"). Children were then left alone by the contribution boxes. It turned out that charitable behavior in the model fostered charitable behavior in the children, regardless of what the model preached. Preaching charity was ineffective when the model behaved selfishly.

Role Taking and Altruistic Behavior   As noted earlier in the chapter, Piaget believed that moral development in children was associated with their capacity to empathize with, or to take the roles of, others. Simply being aware that another person is in distress usually does not prompt helping behavior. The generous child is more likely to be able to feel the distress of the other person. Moreover, teaching young children what it is like to be in the victim's shoes increases altruistic behavior (Iannotti, 1978; Staub, 1971).

Consider an experiment in which Caucasian third-graders were taught to empathize with the victims of prejudice (Weiner & Wright, 1973). The children were randomly assigned to "Green" or "Orange" groups and given colored armbands for identification. First, the Greens were labeled inferior and denied social privileges. After a few days, the Greens lost self-esteem and earned poorer grades. They cried often and lost the desire to attend school. Then the pattern was reversed and the Oranges received this treatment. Children in a second class did not receive the Green–Orange treatment and served as controls.

Following the experiment, children from both classes were asked whether they wanted to go on a picnic with black children from another school. Ninety-six percent of the Green–Orange children, as compared with 62 percent of the controls, expressed an interest in attending the picnic. Taking the role of the victim of prejudice apparently enabled the Green–Orange children to empathize with blacks. They became more willing to share their experiences with them.

Middle-Class Culture and Cooperation   Finally, let us note an irony of middle-class U.S. life. The value of the community and the qualities of helpfulness, charity, and cooperation are deeply embedded in our cultural tradition. Thus, as they become more knowledgeable about their cultural heritage and egocentrism declines, children should become more cooperative. Older children, from a cognitive perspective, are more capable of taking the role of, or empathizing with, others. For this reason also, we might predict that children's behavior would become more generous and cooperative as they grew older.

Not necessarily. In one study of developmental patterns in cooperative behavior, M. C. Madsen (1971) gave pairs of children a task with marbles in which success required cooperation. He found that 4- and 5-year-old children were more successful at the task than the 7- to 10-year-olds. Why?

Madsen and his colleagues suggest that despite many of our expressed values, U.S. culture is not cooperative, but highly competitive. The corporate world, the political structure, the military, even the academic world promote the most competitive individuals to the highest positions and grant them the greatest rewards. For most U.S. residents, grades become important in grammar school. Often children must try out for clubs, teams, and societies. Later on adolescents compete in making themselves as attractive as they can. Children quickly learn of the benefits of winning and the tragedies of losing. And so, despite preaching the value of cooperation, we often practice the value of com-

▶ ▶ ▶ ▶

petition. As children develop, they become more influenced by our actual values (as expressed through our daily behavior) than by our professed values.

There is cross-cultural evidence as well. Children reared in less competitive cultures seem to work together more effectively. This is true of Mexican children (Kagan & Madsen, 1971, 1972), children reared in the Israeli kibbutz (Shapira & Madsen, 1974), and Native American Blackfoot children (Miller, 1973). Moreover, Blackfoot children educated in predominantly Caucasian schools become more competitive than counterparts attending all-Native-American schools.

At an extreme, competition can provoke aggressive behavior. We now consider a number of the questions concerning the development of aggressive behavior.

Aggression

Children, like adults, are complex beings. Not only can they be loving and altruistic. They can also be aggressive.

Developmental Patterns

Aggression, like other behaviors, seems to follow certain developmental patterns. For one thing, the aggression of preschoolers is frequently instrumental or possession-oriented (Parke & Slaby, 1983). That is, young children tend to use aggression in order to obtain the toys and things they want, such as a favored seat at the dinner table or in the family car. They may even push each other around to be the "leader" going up or down the stairs—which, of course, can be quite dangerous.

By 6 or 7, aggression becomes hostile and person-oriented. Children taunt and criticize each other and call each other names as well as attack physically. Person-oriented aggression appears to emerge because of cognitive development (Ferguson & Rule, 1980). At 6 or 7 children are more capable of processing information about the motives and intentions of other people. As a result, they are less likely to stand by idly when another child intends to hurt or ridicule them.

Other evidence for a role for information processing is found in that aggressive boys are more likely than nonaggressive boys to incorrectly interpret the behavior of other children as potentially harmful (Dodge, 1985). Of course, once children establish a repuation for being aggressive, other children may respond to them more aggressively. For this reason, aggressive children may not be all wrong in perceiving the social world as a more dangerous place.

Aggressive behavior appears to be remarkably stable (Olweus, 1982). A longitudinal study of more than 600 children found that aggressive 8-year-olds tended to remain more aggressive than their peers 22 years later, at age 30 (Eron, 1987; Huesmann & Eron, 1986). The aggressive children were more likely to have criminal convictions as adults, to abuse their spouses, and to drive while drunk.

A study by Huesmann and his colleagues (1984) found stability in aggressive behavior for both sexes. Aggressive girls were significantly more likely

▶ ▶ ▶ ▶

Dominance *Control or authority over others.*

Territory *According to ethology, an area whose possession provides privileges in feeding and mating.*

than nonaggressive peers to have criminal convictions as adults. However, the boys in this study were much more likely than the girls to show aggression. As noted in Chapter 12, boys are much more likely than girls to retaliate when they are attacked (Darvill & Cheyne, 1981). At all ages, even among preschoolers, boys are more likely than girls to start fights.

Theoretical Perspectives

For thousands of years, philosophers, clergy, scientists, and the neighborhood bartender have attempted to explain the origins of human aggression. In this section we review a number of theoretical perspectives on the development of aggressive behavior.

An Ethological Perspective From an ethological perspective, aggression is instinctive. Many animals, from birds to wolves, will instinctively engage in aggressive behavior to establish **dominance** and to defend **territories.** A territory provides feeding and mating privileges. Since stronger or more wily animals are more likely to successfully establish and defend territories, aggressive behavior also contributes to survival of the fittest. We know that these behavior patterns are instinctive in many species as a result of research in which their young have been reared in isolation but shown the behavior patterns at the appropriate ages.

Aggressive behavior in many animals is triggered by releasing stimuli. A male robin attacks when shown the red breast of another robin. The male stickleback fish attacks when shown the red belly of another male stickleback—or an oval piece of wood that has been painted red.

Aggression seems to be at least partially controlled by the structure in the brain called the hypothalamus. When certain parts of the hypothalamus are electrically stimulated, cats and rats will kill (Smith et al., 1970). Cats show stereotyped patterns of stalking, pouncing upon, and killing their prey. Rats show the stereotyped response of biting through the neck of a mouse and severing its spinal cord.

In higher animals, the hypothalamus may also be involved in aggressive behavior, but in a less mechanical manner. Electrical stimulation of an area of the hypothalamus of a male monkey may induce aggression toward less dominant males, but not toward females. Nor will a weak monkey attack a dominant male when so stimulated. Rather, it will cringe as though it were being attacked itself. The hypothalamus may therefore somehow signal a "tense situation" in primates, but not directly induce aggressive behavior. The monkey's processing of information about its situation is also an important determinant of its reaction.

This finding is promising for children. There is little reason to think that children respond automatically with aggression in any situation—even if the "right" or "wrong" buttons are being pressed. We shall pursue this concept when we discuss ways in which we can decrease the probability that children will act aggressively after being exposed to media violence.

Psychoanalytic Perspectives Sigmund Freud saw hostile impulses as instinctive and inevitable. He believed that children were basically antisocial—that is, they put their own ids first. Concern for others arose only to avoid condemnation. At first children sought to avoid the condemnation of others. After

▶ ▶ ▶ ▶

cultural values had been internalized, children also sought to avoid self-condemnation.

Freud noted that every child would encounter frustration now and then, even in infancy. He theorized that children would naturally wish to vent their frustrations toward their parents through aggression. But because children also loved their parents, they might delude themselves that they did not harbor hostile impulses toward them. These impulses might then become redirected— either toward others or inward toward themselves.

Fortunately, there is no evidence that children are basically antisocial, even though it is obvious that it takes time for them to develop awareness that other people are separate beings with needs of their own. Freud's views remain speculative. It is worth noting that many modern-day psychoanalysts have revised his pessimistic views of human nature.

Social-Learning Perspectives on the Development of Aggression Social-learning explanations of aggression tend to focus on the roles of conditioning and observational learning.

Children, like adults, are most likely to be aggressive when they are frustrated. Frustration occurs when a barrier exists between us and something we want. In the case of children, what they want might be the attention of a parent, a particular toy, or, perhaps, a good place in the school lunch line. The barrier to achieving such goals is usually another child.

Reinforcement Aggressive behavior is reinforced in some children, especially the relatively strong and well-coordinated, by removal of sources of frustration. Aggression might allow the aggressor to play with a favored toy, to get time on the swing or in the sandbox, or to grab someone else's milk money. Some children who behave aggressively might also enjoy the discomfort that is displayed by the victim.

As noted in Chapter 11, children who have the social skills to engage in alternatives to aggression such as negotiation and compromise are more popular with their peers. But despite the fact that aggressive children are less popular, field observations at nursery schools and day-care centers show that aggression is nevertheless often reinforced by peers. When children push, shove, and hit in order to grab toys or to break into a line, other children most of the time let them have their way (Patterson, 1982). Therefore, the aggressor is likely to continue to use aggressive means.

Victims show a wide range of responses. Some victims passively accede to the aggressor. Some cry. Some complain to the teacher or supervisor. Others try to get their property back. And some victims retaliate with aggressive behavior of their own. Counteraggression often discourages the attacker and might therefore be reinforced in the victim. The victim might then turn to offensive aggression when he or she is frustrated.

Modeling Effects In such dramas, former victims may acquire aggressive responses from observing the behavior of the attacker. Children learn not only from the effects of their own behavior, but also from observing the behavior of others (Bandura, 1973). In fact, children are more likely to imitate what their parents do than to heed what they say. If adults say they disapprove of aggression, but smash furniture or slap each other when frustrated, children are likely to develop the notion that this is the way to handle frustration.

▶ ▶ ▶ ▶

Does TV Violence Contribute to Aggressive Behavior in Children?

▷

▷

▷

▷

▷ Can we expect children to act civilized when they are bombarded with violence on TV shows and in films?

In 1977, a Florida adolescent killed an elderly woman. The defense claimed that he was not guilty by reason of insanity. Why? He had become "addicted" to TV violence and could no longer differentiate between fantasy and reality. (He was found guilty.) In 1974 a 9-year-old California girl was raped with a bottle by four girls who admitted they had been given the idea by a TV movie. The victim's family sued the network and the station that had screened the film. But the courts chose not to award damages to avoid setting a precedent that might interfere with the right to free expression.

It cannot be argued that TV violence directly caused these crimes. After all, with a few unfortunate exceptions, the millions who watch television do *not* imitate antisocial behavior. But TV violence poses a risk factor.

Television is one of the major sources of observational learning in our culture. By the age of 3 or 4, U.S. children average four hours a day of viewing (Pearl et al., 1982; Singer & Singer, 1981). Children spend more hours at the TV set than in school (Singer, 1983). This early devotion to television gives the medium the potential to benefit children in the development of knowledge and cognitive skills (Dorr, 1985; Liebert & Sprafkin, 1982; Wright & Huston, 1983). But as of today, TV does not appear to have lived up to this potential.

Most psychologists agree that TV violence *contributes* to aggression (NIMH, 1982; Rubinstein, 1983). How? At least four types of influence have been outlined:

Watching violence on television may contribute to aggressive behavior in children by raising their levels of arousal, disinhibiting aggressive impulses, teaching aggressive skills, and desensitizing children to violence.

▶ ▶ ▶ ▶

1. *Increased arousal.* TV violence increases the level of arousal of viewers. We are more likely to engage in dominant forms of behavior, including aggressive behavior, when we have high levels of arousal. Osborn and Endsley (1971) used galvanic skin response (GSR) as their measure of arousal and found that violent shows led to significantly higher levels of arousal among 4- and 5-year-olds than did nonviolent shows.

2. *Disinhibition.* TV violence may disinhibit the expression of aggressive impulses that would otherwise have been controlled.

3. *Observational learning.* TV violence teaches viewers aggressive skills.

4. *Habituation.* Children become habituated to many stimuli that impact upon them repeatedly. Media violence apparently has the effect of decreasing viewers' emotional response to subsequent violence (Geen, 1981; Thomas et al., 1977). Boys who watch television many hours a day show less emotional response to violent boxing films, as measured by GSR, than do boys who watch television less frequently (Cline et al., 1973). The researchers in this study did not control the number of hours the boys watched television. It might be that boys who chose to watch less frequently were also more upset by portrayals of violence than chronic viewers. Still, U.S. children have the opportunity to watch hundreds or thousands of violent assaults on television each year. It may be that they learn to perceive violence as commonplace. If so, their own attitudes toward violence could become less condemnatory, and they might place less value on self-restraint.

There seems to be a circular relationship between viewing TV violence and aggressive behavior (Eron, 1982; Fenigstein, 1979). TV violence contributes to aggressive behavior, and aggressive children are more likely to watch violent television. Aggressive children are less popular than nonaggressive children, and Eron theorizes that aggressive children watch more television because their peer relationships are less fulfilling. The high incidence of TV violence also confirms their own aggressiveness (1982, p. 210).

TV violence is one factor among many that contribute to aggressive behavior. Parental rejection and physical punishment also contribute to aggression (Eron, 1982). Harsh home life might further confirm the child's view of the world as violent, and encourage further reliance on television for companionship.

But for parents of children who will watch TV violence, there is encouraging news. Children given the following information about TV violence are rated by peers as less aggressive (Huesmann et al., 1983):

1. TV violence does *not* represent the behavior of most people.

2. The apparently aggressive behaviors are not real. They reflect camera tricks and special effects.

3. Most people use other-than-violent behavior to resolve their conflicts.

Aggressive skills alone do not cause children to act aggressively. Apparently they must also believe that aggression is appropriate for them in a given set of circumstances.

Children who are physically punished are more likely to behave aggressively themselves (Eron & Huesmann, 1984; Patterson, 1982). Physically aggressive parents serve as models for aggression and increase their children's anger. Also remember the lessons of the ecological perspective: There may be reciprocal parent-child influences. Some children, that is, may elicit more aggressive behavior from parents. Regardless of initial causes, once aggressive patterns of interaction become established, the cycles can be truly vicious.

Peer Influences Peers also serve as aggressive models. In their review of re-

▶ ▶ ▶ ▶

Disinhibit *To stimulate a response that has been suppressed (inhibited) by showing a model engaging in that response without aversive consequences.*

search concerning the acquisition of aggressive behavior, Parke and Slaby (1983) found three ways in which peers instigate and maintain aggressive behavior patterns: First, peers can serve as aggressive models, particularly if they are rewarded for aggression. Second, children may belong to a peer group—such as a gang—that reinforces aggressive behavior. Third, children may belong to a peer group in which aggressive behavior is the norm. In such a group, children can come to think of aggression as a normal element of daily life.

Media Influences   A classic study by Bandura, Ross, and Ross (1963) suggests the power of the media. One group of preschool children observed a film of an adult model hitting and kicking an inflated Bobo doll, while a control group saw an aggression-free film. The model was neither rewarded nor punished for mistreating the doll. The experimental and control children were then left alone in a room with the same doll, as hidden observers recorded their behavior. The children who had observed the aggressive model showed significantly more aggressive behavior toward the doll themselves (see Figure 13.3). Many children went so far as to imitate bizarre attack behaviors devised for the model in this experiment—behaviors that they would not have thought up themselves.

The children exposed to the aggressive model also showed aggressive behavior patterns that had not been modeled. Observing the model, therefore, not only led to imitation of modeled behavior patterns; it also apparently **disinhibited** previously learned aggressive responses. The results were similar whether children observed human or cartoon models on film.

What of the effects of Big Bird, Cookie Monster, Kermit, David and Maria, and the rest of the gang at *Sesame Street?* Research shows that even an award-winning children's show such as *Sesame Street* can contribute to violent behavior. Coates and Pusser (1975), for example, found that children who had rarely used punishments such as hitting and criticism increased these negative social interactions after viewing the show.

Does this finding seem odd? After all, *Sesame Street* is designed for educational purposes and is largely nonviolent. However, a comparative content analysis of *Mister Rogers' Neighborhood* and *Sesame Street* showed that characters on the first show used positive reinforcement about 20 times as often as they used punishment. But on *Sesame Street*, positive reinforcement was only used about three and a half times as frequently as punishment.

I am not suggesting that *Sesame Street* is harmful. Everything is relative, to coin a phrase. *Sesame Street* clearly enhances cognitive skills in preschoolers of various backgrounds (Ball & Bogatz, 1970). And, if children were not watching *Sesame Street*, they would probably be watching other shows, which average about 25 violent incidents per hour. Although *Sesame Street* characters show criticism and disapproval, violent incidents are relatively mild, and few and far between. The effects of TV violence are discussed further in the nearby box.

Summary

1. Moral development has cognitive, behavioral, and affective aspects. Cognitive-developmental theorists focus on the orderly unfolding of sequences in moral reasoning.

2. According to Jean Piaget, the egocentrism of preoperational children encourages moral realism. That is, young children believe that social rules are absolutes. In evaluating situations, preoperational children also tend to focus on only one dimension at a time. Their judgments of a transgressor, for example, do not take into account the intentions of the transgressor, but only the amount of damage done. Young children also believe in immanent justice—that punishment automatically follows trangressions.

3. According to Piaget, more advanced moral judgments are based on operational thinking, and children first show autonomous morality at about the ages of 9 to 11. (Other researchers find autonomous morality at younger ages.) Operational children are more flexible in their thinking. They understand that social rules are conventions constructed by people to meet social needs. Increased capacity for empathy and decentration (ability to focus on more than one dimension simultaneously) encourage older children to weigh the intentions of transgressors, as well as the amount of damage done.

4. Lawrence Kohlberg's cognitive theory hypothesizes three levels of moral development—preconventional, conventional, and postconventional—and two stages within each level. Preconventional morality is found among young children and generally characterized by the expectation of punishments or rewards. Conventional morality is largely based on the needs to attain the approval of others and to maintain the social order. Postconventional morality is found among a minority of individuals. It is characterized by the derivation of moral judgments from one's own moral principles. At this level the behavior that people label moral may conflict with conventional rules or laws.

5. Girls frequently show "lower" levels of moral reasoning than boys. This is because boys tend to adhere to logical deduction of judgments from moral principles. Girls tend more to empathize with all participants in disputes and to seek compromise solutions. However, girls' reasoning is as complex as boys'.

6. While the sequence of Kohlberg's stages is largely invariant, stage 6 reasoning has been shown not to be universal. Stage 6 reasoning may reflect Kohlberg's own philosophical views and not a logical developmental pattern. Moral development may also be more subject to educational and cultural influences than Kohlberg would have allowed.

7. Cheating in school and other activities is widespread in our culture. Belief that cheating is wrong does not generally deter children from cheating. Fear of getting caught or of earning the disapproval of peers may deter cheating. Cheating tends to be situation-specific: Children who cheat on academic tests do not necessarily cheat at athletic contests, and vice versa. More intelligent children are less likely to cheat on examinations—apparently because they have less need to cheat.

▶ ▶ ▶ ▶

8. Children can begin to show concern for others who are in distress as early as the first year. Most children show concern for others by the end of the second year. Children are most likely to develop empathy when parents respond emotionally to their harmful behavior and also explain the cause-and-effect relationships between their behavior and the distress of others.

9. Children are more likely to share their toys and other possessions with less fortunate children when they are rewarded for doing so, or when they fear punishment for not doing so. Modeling also promotes generosity. Children exposed to adult models who contribute to charity are more likely than other children to make contributions. Children seem more influenced by what adult models do than what they say. Children tend to imitate generous or selfish behavior they observe, but are less likely to act in accord with what the models profess to be their values.

10. Despite our professing to value cooperation, middle-class U.S. society promotes competitive behavior. As children develop, one might expect that they would become more capable of role taking and empathy with others, and that such empathy ought to promote cooperation. However, 5- and 6-year-olds are more likely to cooperate with other children than are 10-year-olds, apparently because 10-year-olds have been more socialized into competing.

11. Aggressive behavior among preschoolers tends to be instrumental. That is, it is aimed toward attainment of objects and privileges. By 6 or 7, aggressive behavior also becomes person-oriented and hostile, frequently in anticipation of the attacks of others. Hostile boys are biased toward assuming that others intend to attack them, even when this is not the case.

12. Aggressiveness tends to remain stable from middle childhood to adulthood. Boys are more aggressive than girls. They initiate fights more often and are more likely to retaliate against social provocateurs by fighting.

13. From an ethological perspective, aggressive behavior is instinctive in humans. However, there is no evidence that people have inherited aggressive tendencies.

14. From a psychoanalytic perspective, aggressive impulses are inevitable outcomes of daily frustrations.

15. From a social-learning perspective, children tend to acquire aggressive responses through principles of operant conditioning and observational learning. Violence on TV shows and in other media may promote aggressive behavior in children by increasing their levels of arousal, disinhibiting aggressive responses, promoting observational learning, and habituating viewers to violence. Parents can help mitigate the effects of media violence by explaining to children that real people usually do not resolve their conflicts violently.

▶ ▶ ▶ ▶

Five- and 6-year-old children do not have clear ideas of what is right and wrong. False. Five- and 6-year-olds have strong opinions about the morality of many types of behavior. They also tend to believe that right and wrong are absolutes.

Five-year-old children generally think that people who accidentally harm others ought not to be punished. False. Most 5-year-olds hand out punishments according to the amount of damage done by a wrongdoer.

People who have arrived at the highest level of moral development follow their own ethical principles and may disobey the laws of the land. True, according to Lawrence Kohlberg's theory of moral development. Kohlberg's views have caused a good deal of controversy, and are also frequently misunderstood.

Girls lag behind boys in their moral development. False. Girls score "below" boys, according to Kohlberg's levels of reasoning, because girls tend to be more empathic than boys. However, this does not mean that girls' reasoning processes are inferior to boys'.

Children who express the belief that cheating in school is wrong are unlikely to cheat. False. Many children express the belief that cheating is wrong, but cheat when they encounter academic and parental pressure.

More intelligent children are less likely to cheat on school examinations. True. Perhaps more intelligent children have less of a need to cheat.

Children become more cooperative as they grow older. Not in U.S. culture. Apparently because of cultural influences, middle-class U.S. children grow more competitive and less cooperative.

Children can be taught to make donations to charity by exposing them to generous adult models. True. Children are more likely to do as the models do than to listen to what the models preach.

Aggressive boys are likely to be aggressive as men. True. They are more likely to be convicted of crimes, abuse their spouses, and drive when drunk.

Aggressive girls are not likely to be aggressive as women. False. Stability in aggressive behavior holds for females as well as males.

Human beings have inherited a killer instinct. False. There is no evidence that instinctive aggressive responses can be elicited in primates.

Children who are physically punished are more likely to be aggressive. True. Their punishers model aggression and give the children the idea that it is appropriate to respond to stress by aggressive means.

Most children mechanically imitate the aggressive behavior they observe on television and in films. False. Many children may acquire aggressive skills and become somewhat habituated to violence from watching television. However, most children do not imitate the aggressive acts they observe.

▶ ▶ ▶ ▶

14

Behavior Disorders of Childhood and Adolescence

▶
▶
▶
▶
▶
▶
▶

- Most children outgrow "baby fat."
- Children who watch a great deal of television are more likely to be obese than children who do not.
- Anoretic girls eat a great deal, but have trouble keeping weight on.
- Some college women control their weight by going on cycles of binge eating followed by vomiting.
- The average U.S. college woman believes she is overweight.
- Sleepwalkers become violently agitated if they are awakened during an episode.
- There is no way of predicting which babies will be struck by sudden infant death syndrome.
- It is normal for children who have gained bladder control to continue to have "accidents" at night for a year or more.
- Boys are more likely than girls to wet their beds.
- Autistic children are highly intelligent.
- Many hyperactive children have been calmed down by stimulants.
- Schizophrenic children are likely to become schizophrenic adults.
- Children who show conduct disorders at 8 to 10 are more likely to get divorces as adults than children who do not.
- The drug most frequently abused by children is marijuana.
- Curiosity is the single most common reason that children give for trying drugs.
- Headaches and nausea can be signs of anxiety in children.
- Poor appetite is usually a sign of depression in children.

Behavior disorders of childhood can become the entire focus of parents' lives. Consider the case of Peter:

> Peter nursed eagerly, sat and walked at the expected ages. Yet some of his behavior made us vaguely uneasy. He never put anything in his mouth. Not his fingers nor his toys—nothing. . . .
>
> More troubling was the fact that Peter didn't look at us, or smile, and wouldn't play the games that seemed as much a part of babyhood as diapers. He rarely laughed, and when he did, it was at things that didn't seem funny to us. He didn't cuddle, but sat upright in my lap, even when I rocked him. But children differ and we were content to let Peter be himself. We thought it hilarious when my brother, visiting us when Peter was 8 months old, observed that "That kid has no social instincts, whatsoever." Although Peter was a first child, he was not isolated. I frequently put him in his playpen in front of the house, where the schoolchildren stopped to play with him as they passed. He ignored them, too.
>
> It was Kitty, a personality kid, born two years later, whose responsiveness emphasized the degree of Peter's difference. When I went into her room for the late feeding, her little head bobbed up and she greeted me with a smile that reached from her head to her toes. And the realization of that difference chilled me more than the wintry bedroom.
>
> Peter's babbling had not turned into speech by the time he was 3. His play was solitary and repetitious. He tore paper into long thin strips, bushel baskets of it every day. He spun the lids from my canning jars and became upset if we tried to divert him. Only rarely could I catch his eye, and then saw his focus change from me to the reflection in my glasses. . . .
>
> His adventures into our suburban neighborhood had been unhappy. He had disregarded the universal rule that sand is to be kept in sandboxes, and the children themselves had punished him. He walked around a sad and solitary figure, always carrying a toy airplane, a toy he never played with. At that time, I had not heard the word that was to dominate our lives, to hover over every conversation, to sit through every meal beside us. That word was autism (Eberhardy, 1967).

Autism is one of the most severe behavior disorders of childhood. Autistic children, like Peter, seem utterly alone in the world, despite parental efforts to bridge the gap that separates them.

Behavior disorders of childhood refer to patterns of abnormal behavior among children. In considering what is normal and abnormal, we must consider what is to be expected given the child's age, sex, family and cultural background, and the various developmental transformations that are taking place (Garber, 1984; Sroufe & Rutter, 1984). By and large, behavior patterns may be considered disordered when they meet one or more of the following criteria (Rathus, 1987):

1. They occur infrequently.
2. They are socially unacceptable.
3. They involve faulty perception, or faulty interpretation of reality.
4. They cause the child distress.

Autism *Self-absorption or fantasy as a way of avoiding social contact and escaping reality.*

Behavior disorders *Behavior problems characterized by one or more of the following: low frequency; social unacceptability; faulty perception or interpretation of reality; personal distress; self-defeating behavior; or dangerous behavior.*

▶ ▶ ▶ ▶

5. They are self-defeating.

6. They are dangerous to the child or to others.

Peter's behavior was disordered in that very few children show autism. His perceptions of the world were also very different from his age-mates'.

Other children engage in self-defeating behavior patterns, such as overeating or refusal to eat. Some children show socially unacceptable behavior patterns, as in conduct disorders and substance abuse. But keep in mind that what is socially acceptable at one age, such as not having bladder control at 12 months, may be socially unacceptable at another—not having bladder control at 48 months. Other behavior disorders, such as anxiety disorders and depression, are mainly characterized by the distress of the child. Most of the problems discussed in this chapter meet several of the criteria that define behavior disorders.

In this chapter we explore eating disorders, elimination disorders, sleep disorders, **pervasive developmental disorders,** attention-deficit hyperactivity disorder, conduct disorders, substance abuse, anxiety disorders, and depression. The behavior disorders of childhood have a particular poignancy. Many of them occur at early ages and stand in the way of children's fulfilling their developmental potentials.

In the section on sleep disorders we shall discuss sudden infant death syndrome (SIDS) which, strictly speaking, is a medical disorder and not a behavior disorder. However, SIDS does appear to be a disorder of sleep. Too, it is such a worrisome disorder that I chose to err by including it rather than by omitting it.

Eating Disorders

All of us need food in order to survive, but food means more than survival to many children and adults. Food is a symbol of family togetherness and caring. We associate food with the nurturance of the parent–child relationship and with visits "home" once we are adults. Friends and relatives offer food when we enter their homes. Saying no may be interpreted as a personal rejection.

Eating can also have its traumatic aspects. Parents may become quite concerned about the eating habits of their children. During pregnancy, many women worry about whether they will be able to produce enough milk to sustain their babies. A baby's refusal to breast-feed can seem not only like a rejection of the mother but can also lead to uncomfortable engorgement of the breasts with milk. During the third year, children often go on what seems like prolonged "hunger strikes." They eat little of anything, and certainly very little of the nutritious foods their parents want them to eat. Parents may therefore become obsessed with whether their children have had enough protein, vitamins, and minerals, such as calcium.

It is quite normal for children to be fussy eaters when they are very young. Even the partial hunger strikes of the 2-year-old occur often enough. But the eating habits of some children are extreme enough to impair their physical well-being and their social relationships. Such patterns include childhood obesity, anorexia nervosa, and bulimia nervosa.

► ► ► ►

Obesity tends to run in families and can be a way of life in many homes. Numbers of fat cells and psychological factors contribute to overeating.

Childhood Obesity

Obesity is a disorder characterized by the excessive accumulation of fat. Definitions of obesity vary, with some authorities defining it as a body weight in excess of 20 percent of the norm. Others require a weight of 40 percent or more of the norm. Judith Rodin (1977) notes that if we use the 40 percent criterion, 2 to 15 percent of American children are obese. Broadly speaking, 10 percent of children are heavy enough to profit from taking off some pounds (Grinker, 1981; Lamb, 1984).

Obese children, despite the stereotype, are usually far from jolly. Preschool children show negative attitudes toward overweight people (Fritz & Wetherbee, 1982). During middle childhood, heavy children are often the butt of their peers' jokes (Grinker, 1981). They usually perform poorly in athletic activities, which is a source of much prestige for other children. As they approach adolescence, they become even less popular, because they are less likely to be found attractive by the opposite sex. It is no surprise, then, that obese children tend to like their bodies less than children of normal weight. Moreover, overweight boys aged 11.5–14.4 and overweight girls aged 14.5–17.4 have lower general self-esteem than do peers of normal weight (Mendelson & White, 1985).

Parents (and children) frequently assume that heavy children will "outgrow" their "baby fat"—especially once they hit the growth spurt of adolescence. Not so. *Most overweight children become overweight adults* (Abraham et al., 1971; Lamb, 1984; Maloney & Klykylo, 1983). By contrast, only about 40 percent of normal-weight boys and 20 percent of normal-weight girls become obese adults.

Causes of Obesity   There is little doubt that obesity runs in families. For example, children with one obese parent have a 40 percent chance of becoming

Obesity   An eating disorder characterized by excessive accumulation of fat.

▶ ▶ ▶ ▶

Adipose tissue Fat.

obese themselves. Children with two obese parents have an 80 percent chance (Winick, 1974). But this does not necessarily mean that obesity is inherited. Rather, as noted by Hilde Bruch (1975), overeating is a "normal" way of life in many homes.

Obesity has also been related to the amount of fat cells or **adipose tissue** we have, and we may have some tendency to inherit different numbers of fat cells. Hunger seems to be related to the amount of fat stored in these cells. As time passes after a meal, the blood-sugar level drops. Fat is then drawn from fat cells to provide further nourishment, causing them to shrivel. At some point, the brain is signaled of the fat deficiency in these cells, and the hunger drive is triggered.

Children with more fat cells than other children will feel food-deprived sooner, even if equal in weight. This is presumably because more signals are being sent to the brain. The number of fat cells may be influenced by childhood dietary habits as well as heredity (Brownell, 1982; Grinker, 1981; Sjøstrøm, 1980). Obese children may develop more adipose tissue. As a result, childhood obesity may cause the adult dieter to feel persistent hunger, even after leveling off at a new desired weight. However, in his review of the literature, Alex Roche (1981) did not find a compelling connection between childhood dietary habits, formation of fat cells, and adult obesity.

Even if fat cells play a role in triggering the hunger drive, they cannot compel obese children to eat more. Moreover, obese people seem to be less sensitive than normal-weight individuals to *internal* sensations of hunger. The overweight are more sensitive than others to *external* sources of stimulation, such as the aroma of food, the sight of others eating, even the clock. That is, obese children are more likely than others to feel hungry just because it's lunchtime or dinnertime. This high sensitivity to external sources of stimulation has also been found among rats in whom a part of the hypothalamus has been destroyed. For this reason, it has been suggested that some obese children are suffering from a faulty hypothalamus. However, this view remains speculative.

A more strongly substantiated hypothesis concerns the role of TV watching in obesity. A large-scale longitudinal study showed that children in middle childhood who watched television for 25 or more hours per week were more likely to become obese as adolescents (Dietz & Gortmaker, 1985). The influence of TV watching is at least threefold: First, children tend to consume snacks while watching. Second, watching television is sedentary. We burn fewer calories sitting than engaging in strenuous physical activity. Third, television bombards children with commercials for fattening foods, such as candy and potato chips.

Bruch (1975) noted that many children overeat for "developmental" and "reactive" reasons. Developmental obesity stems from family conflict, especially when parents try to fulfill their own needs through their children. In such cases, children may be overfed and overprotected. Reactive obesity may occur in response to severe stresses, as due to bickering in the home, parental divorce, or the birth of a sibling. The idea here is that food takes the place of love. The child ingests large quantities of food to try to fill emotional emptiness. There is evidence that dieting efforts are impeded by negative emotional states such as depression (Baucom & Aiken, 1981).

Physical problems are also now and then implicated in childhood obesity (Lowrey, 1978). However, these problems are rare. Parents who attribute their children's weight problems to physical problems are probably deluding themselves.

▶ ▶ ▶ ▶

A Weight-Loss Manual for Children (and Their Parents)

▷
▷
▷
▷
▷ Health and fitness have nearly reached fad proportions. Today's parents not only want to be slimmer themselves. They are also more aware of the health benefits their children gain by avoiding obesity. However, losing weight is one of the most difficult problems in self-control—for all of us, children and adults alike.

Diet pills have side-effects and children cannot go on using them forever. Moreover, pills do nothing to teach children how to change their eating habits. Long-term, insight-oriented psychotherapy has also not been shown to be of much use. However, behavioral methods show promise of helping children lose weight (e.g., Cohen et al., 1980; Epstein et al., 1984; Foreyt & Goodrick, 1981; Israel et al., 1984). These methods include (1) improving nutritional knowledge, (2) reducing calories, (3) exercise, and (4) behavior modification. The behavioral methods involve tracking the child's weight and calorie intake, keeping the child away from temptations, setting a good example, and the systematic use of praise and other rewards (Epstein et al., 1985; Foster et al., 1985; Israel et al., 1985). Here are a number of suggestions gleaned from the literature:

Teach children about their nutritional needs—calories, protein, vitamins, minerals, fiber, food groups, and so on. Indicate which foods may be eaten in nearly unlimited quantities (e.g., green vegetables), and which foods should be eaten only sparingly (cakes, cookies, soft drinks sweetened with sugar, etc.).

Do not insist that the entire family sit down at the same time for a large meal. Allow your child to eat only when hungry. This will break down the tyranny of the clock—the expectation that he or she must be hungry because it's noontime or 6:00 P.M.

Substitute low-calorie foods for high-calorie foods. There's no way around it: Calories translate into pounds.

Don't push your child to "finish the plate." Children should be allowed to stop eating when they are no longer hungry. There is no moral or nutritional value to stuffing.

Prepare low-calorie snacks for your child to eat throughout the day. In this way, children do not become extremely deprived and feel desperate for food. Desperation can prompt binging.

Do not cook, eat, or display fattening foods when the child is at home. The sight and aroma of tantalizing foods can be more than children can bear.

Involve the child in more activities. When children are kept busy, they are less likely to think about food.

Do not take your child food-shopping, or, if you do, try to avoid the market aisles with ice cream, cake, and candy. If fattening food is left at the supermarket, it does not wind up in the child's stomach.

Prewarn relatives and friends not to offer fattening treats when you visit. Be insistent—stand up to the grandparent who's only trying to put a little more "meat" on your child's already well-fleshed-out bones.

Don't allow snacking in front of the TV set, while playing, reading, or engaging in any other activity. Allowing children to snack while watching TV makes eating a mindless habit.

Praise children profusely when they take off a pound or so. Use sincere compliments. Weigh the child frequently and point out exactly how much weight is being lost. (But try to be aware of what constitutes

▶ ▶ ▶ ▶

normal weight gains at certain ages, so that you give children credit for maintaining the same weight or making only small gains during spurts.)

Remind the child how much more popular he or she will be, how he or she will look at the pool next summer. Yes, children have body images, and they are important to them. Try to phrase your reminders like this: "You're doing well! You're going to fit into a nice swimsuit next summer! Everyone will think you look wonderful!"

Tie some physical rewards to weight loss. Praise and approval may be more important than physical rewards, but there's also nothing wrong with going on a special trip or to a special movie.

Involve the child in calorie-burning exercise. Check with the pediatrician about possible risks, but try to involve the child in activities such as swimming or prolonged bicycle riding. Exercise will burn calories, increase the child's feelings of competence and self-esteem, improve cardiovascular condition, and, possibly, promote lifetime exercise habits.

Don't assume it's a catastrophe if the child slips and goes on a binge. Don't rant and rave. Don't get overly upset. Talk over what triggered the binge with the child so that similar problems may be averted in the future. Remind the child (and yourself) that tomorrow is another day and another start.

If you and your children are overweight, lose weight together. Follow-up studies show that it is more effective for overweight children and their parents to diet and exercise together, than for the children to go it alone (Epstein et al., 1987).

Anorexia Nervosa

There is a saying that you can never be too rich or too thin. Excess money may be pleasant enough, but one certainly can be too thin, as in the case of anorexia nervosa.

Anorexia nervosa is a life-threatening eating disorder characterized by intense fear of being overweight, severe weight loss, and refusal to eat enough to reach or maintain a healthful body weight.

By and large, anorexia is a disorder that afflicts girls and young women. Nearly one in 200 school-aged girls has trouble gaining or maintaining weight (Crisp et al., 1976). Anoretic females outnumber anoretic males by estimates of about 9:1 to 20:1. The onset of anorexia is most often between the ages of 12 and 18, although girls have become anoretic in prepuberty and women as late as 30.

Anoretic girls may drop 25 percent or more of their body weight in a year. Dramatic weight loss is accompanied by **amenorrhea** and general health declines. About 5 percent of anoretic girls die from the disorder (Hsu, 1980).

In the typical pattern, girls notice some weight gain after menarche and decide that it must come off. However, dieting, and, often, exercise, continue at a fever pitch. They go on long after girls reach normal body weights, even after family and others have told them that they are losing too much. Anoretic girls almost always adamantly deny that they are wasting away. They may point to their fierce exercise regimens as proof. It seems as though their body images are distorted. While others perceive them as "skin and bones," they frequently sit before the mirror and see themselves as getting where they want to be. Or they focus on nonexistent "remaining" pockets of fat.

Although anoretic girls eat very little, they may feel quite hungry. Many anoretics become obsessed with food and are constantly "around it." They may engross themselves in cookbooks, take on the family shopping chores, and prepare elaborate dinners for others.

Anorexia nervosa (an-or-EGG-see-uh). *An eating disorder characterized by irrational fear of weight gain and severe weight loss.*

Amenorrhea (ay-men-or-REE-uh). *Lack of menstruation.*

▶ ▶ ▶ ▶

Bulimia Nervosa

Anorexia is often associated with cycles of binge eating and purging called **bulimia nervosa.** In bulimia, the person has recurrent cycles of binging and dramatic purging as by self-induced vomiting, fasting, or excessive use of laxatives or diuretics (American Psychiatric Association, 1987). Bulimia is more common than anorexia. Bulimia has become epidemic on college campuses, where nearly 5 percent of women have a history of the disorder (American Psychiatric Association, 1987). About half of college women admit to at least an occasional cycle of binging and purging (Herzog, 1982a, 1982b).

Theoretical Views   Anorexia, like obesity, may reflect problems in the hypothalamus (Bemis, 1978). But there is no hard evidence for this point of view. Most theories focus on possible psychological origins (Yager, 1982).

The frequent link between anorexia and menarche has led some theorists to suggest that anorexia may represent an effort by the girl to remain prepubescent. Anorexia allows the girl to avoid growing up, separating from the family, and assuming adult responsibilities. Weight loss also prevents rounding of the breasts and hips, suggestive that anoretic girls are conflicted about their sexuality and the possibility of pregnancy.

Some view anorexia as a "weight phobia" (Crisp, 1967). Irrational fear of gaining weight might reflect cultural idealization of the slender female. Women college students generally see themselves as significantly heavier than the figure that is most attractive to males, and heavier, still, than the "ideal" female figure (Fallon & Rozin, 1985). College men actually prefer women to be heavier than women expect—about halfway between the girth of the average woman and what the woman thinks is most attractive.

Self-starvation also has a brutal effect on parents and might be used as a weapon when family relationships become disturbed (Bemis, 1978).

Treatment   Anorexia is difficult to treat. Individual psychotherapy usually fails. The patient is frequently placed in a hospital setting, given drugs to heighten hunger and inhibit vomiting, and denied privileges unless she gains weight (Hsu, 1980). **Family therapy,** which focuses on problems in family interaction rather than the disorders of one member, may also be of some use. In one encouraging report (Rosman et al., 1976), more than 80 percent of the girls whose families were seen in therapy had retained weight gains in follow-ups ranging from a few months to a few years.

A follow-up of 63 anoretics two years after completing treatment found that they had resumed menstruating, had most often returned to school or work, and had made additional weight gains. However, most continued to believe they were overweight, even though they averaged 8 percent below their ideal weight (Nussbaum et al., 1985). This persistent perceptual distortion suggests that we must remain cautious concerning the long-term outlook, even for anoretics who have "successfully" completed therapy.

Sleep Disorders

A number of disorders disturb the sleep of children. In this section we shall discuss sleep terrors and nightmares, sleepwalking, and sudden infant death syndrome (SIDS).

▶ ▶ ▶ ▶

The Girl in the Gilded Cage

▷
▷
▷
▷
▷ "I'm only a bird in a gilded cage," goes the song. In her book *The Gilded Cage*, Hilde Bruch (1978) compares anoretic girls to exotic birds who spend their time, doll-like, within the protected golden cages of their homes.

Consider Bruch's description of Alma:

> When she came for consultation, she looked like a walking skeleton, scantily dressed in shorts and a halter, with her legs sticking out like broomsticks, every rib showing, and her shoulder blades standing up like little wings. Most striking was the face—hollow like that of a shriveled-up old woman with a wasting disease, sunken eyes, a sharply pointed nose on which the juncture between bone and cartilage was visible. When she spoke or smiled—and she was quite cheerful—one could see every movement of the muscles around her mouth and eyes, like an animated anatomical representation of the skull. Alma insisted that she looked fine and that there was nothing wrong with her being so skinny.
>
> At 15 Alma had been healthy and well-developed, had menstruated at age 12, was five feet six inches tall, and weighed 125 pounds. At that time her mother urged her to change to a school with higher academic standing, a change she resisted. Her father suggested that she should watch her weight, an idea that she took up with great eagerness, and she began a rigid diet. She lost rapidly and her menses ceased. That she could be thin gave her a sense of pride, power, and accomplishment. Alma also began a frantic exercise program, would swim by the mile, play tennis for hours, or do calisthenics to the point of exhaustion. Whatever low point her weight reached, Alma feared that she might become "too fat" if she regained as little as an ounce. There were many efforts to make her gain weight, which she would lose immediately, and she had been below 70 pounds most of the time. There was also a marked change in her character and behavior. Formerly sweet, obedient, and considerate, she became more and more demanding, obstinate, irritable, and arrogant. There was constant arguing, not only about what she should eat but about all other activities as well (pp. 1–2).

Sleep Terrors and Nightmares

Sleep terrors are much more severe than the anxiety dreams we refer to as "nightmares." For one thing, sleep terrors usually occur during deep (stages 3 and 4) sleep. Nightmares take place during rapid-eye-movement (REM) sleep, when about 80 percent of normal dreams occur. Sleep terrors tend to occur early during the night, nightmares in the morning hours (Hartmann, 1981).

Sleep terrors usually begin between the ages of 4 and 12 (American Psychiatric Association, 1987). Children who encounter sleep terrors might sit

Sleep terrors Frightening dreamlike experiences that occur during the deepest stage of NREM sleep. Nightmares, by contrast, occur during REM sleep.

▶ ▶ ▶ ▶

Insomnia *Sleeping problems—difficulty falling asleep, difficulty remaining asleep during the night, or waking early.*

Ruminative *Given to endless turning things over in the mind. (From the Latin* ruminare, *meaning "to chew [the cud].")*

Somnambulism *Sleepwalking. (From the Latin* somnus, *meaning "sleep," and* ambulare, *meaning "to walk.")*

up suddenly with a surge in heart and respiration rates, talk incoherently, and thrash about wildly. They sometimes scream piercingly.

Children are not completely awake during sleep terrors and may fall back into more restful sleep as suddenly as they awoke. It can be difficult to awaken them during sleep terrors. Once awakened, children may be disoriented and difficult to soothe. Children often remember their nightmares quite well. Memories of sleep terrors are less vivid and usually cannot be recalled at all.

The heart and respiration rates of children who are having nightmares show less arousal. Children are easier to awaken during nightmares, and tend to recall them more vividly.

Children who have frequent nightmares or sleep terrors may come to fear going to sleep. They may show distress at bedtime, refuse to get into their pajamas, and insist that the lights be kept on during the night. As a result, they can also develop **insomnia.**

Fortunately, the incidence of sleep terrors wanes dramatically as children develop and spend progressively less time in deep sleep. They are all but absent among adults.

Children most likely to suffer frequent nightmares are those who are anxious and **ruminative** (Anthony, 1959). Children are also more likely to encounter nightmares when they are undergoing situational stress, such as moving to a new neighborhood, attending school for the first time, or adjusting to a divorce. Children with frequent nightmares need their parents' understanding and affection. Yelling at them to stop their "immature" refusal to have the lights out and return to sleep will not alleviate their anxieties.

Sleepwalking

Sleepwalking, or **somnambulism,** is much more common among children than adults. As do sleep terrors, sleepwalking also tends to occur during deep (stages 3 and 4) sleep (American Psychiatric Association, 1987). Onset is usually between the ages of 6 and 12.

During medieval times it was believed that sleepwalking was a sign of possession by evil spirits. Psychoanalytic theory suggests that sleepwalking allows people the chance to express feelings and impulses that they would inhibit while awake. But children who sleepwalk have not been shown to have any more trouble controlling impulses than other children do. Moreover, what children *do* when they sleepwalk is usually too boring to suggest exotic motivation. They may rearrange toys, go to the bathroom, go to the refrigerator and have a glass of milk, or get dressed and take a walk in the garden. Then they return to their rooms and go back to bed. In the morning they seem to have no recall of the episode, which is consistent with sleep terrors, which also occur during deep sleep. Sleepwalking episodes may be very brief. Most tend to last no longer than half an hour.

There are some myths about sleepwalking—namely that sleepwalkers' eyes are closed, that they will avoid harm, and that they will become violently agitated if they are awakened during an episode. All of these are false. Sleepwalkers' eyes are usually open, although they may respond to onlooking parents as furniture to be walked around, and not as people. Children may incur injury when sleepwalking, just as they may when awake. And, finally, children

▶ ▶ ▶ ▶

may be difficult to rouse when they are sleepwalking, as during sleep terrors. But if they are awakened, they are more likely to show confusion and disorientation (again, as during sleep terrors) than violence.

Today, sleepwalking among children is assumed to reflect immaturity of the nervous system and not the "acting out" of dreams or of psychological conflicts. As in the case of sleep terrors, the incidence of sleepwalking drops dramatically as children develop. When sleep terrors or sleepwalking are persistent, it may be wise to discuss them with the pediatrician.

Sudden Infant Death Syndrome (SIDS)

In the United States annually **SIDS,** or crib death, kills 6,000 to 7,000 infants during their first year. This represents about one child in 500. In the typical case of SIDS, the baby goes to sleep, apparently in perfect health, and is found dead the next morning (Levine, 1983). There is no sign that the baby struggled or was in pain (DeFrain et al., 1982). New parents frequently live in dread of SIDS and check their babies regularly through the night to see if they are breathing. It is not abnormal, by the way, for babies to occasionally suspend breathing for a moment. The intermittent suspension of respiration is termed **apnea,** and the build-up of carbon dioxide usually spurs a return to breathing. Babies who succumb to crib death may have more eposides of apnea than normal (Steinschneider, 1975).

Although it is known that SIDS does not result from suffocation, from choking on undigested food, or from drowning on regurtigated food or a propped-up baby bottle, its causes remain largely obscure. Still, there are a number of **risk factors** associated with the disorder, and parents whose situations seem to fit the stereotypical picture may wish to take special heed:

1. SIDS most often strikes between the ages of 2 to 4 months. Its likelihood drops off dramatically after 6 months.

2. SIDS occurs at more than chance frequency during the winter months.

3. SIDS is more likely to strike male infants.

4. SIDS frequently follows a minor respiratory problem such as a cold or a viral infection.

5. SIDS is more common among later-born than first-born children.

6. SIDS is more common among preterm babies.

7. SIDS is more common among babies with lower-than-average Apgar scores (Lipsitt et al., 1979).

8. SIDS is more common among babies whose mothers smoked during pregnancy (Rhead, 1977).

9. SIDS is more common among infants of mothers who received inadequate or marginal prenatal care and nutrition.

10. SIDS is more common among blacks, poor families, and the babies of teenagers (Lipsitt, 1982).

▶ ▶ ▶ ▶

Although we do not know the exact causes of SIDS, recurring factors allow us to speculate. For example, the fact that babies "grow out of" the age of risk suggests that maturational factors, even if unknown, are linked to SIDS. A major possibility, for example, is that prenatal factors interact to deprive the fetus of oxygen or to delay maturation of areas of the nervous system involved in respiration. The damaged or immature areas of the nervous system could lie in the brain stem or the central nervous system. Both of these areas are intimately involved in respiration.

No remedy for SIDS is in the offing. However, parents whose babies are at risk may be somewhat cheered by the fact that monitoring systems have been developed to alert them to episodes of apnea and to give them time to intervene—as by artificial respiration. In essence, a monitor is placed in the baby's crib, and an alarm is triggered if the baby stops breathing. The alarm alone triggers breathing in some babies. These monitors are now standard equipment for dealing with sick children at high risk in the hospital setting. They may be purchased for home use as well.

Elimination Disorders

The elimination of waste products occurs reflexively in neonates. As children develop, their task is to learn to *inhibit* the reflexes that govern urination and bowel movements. The process by which parents teach their children to inhibit these reflexes is referred to as toilet training. The inhibition of eliminatory reflexes makes polite conversation possible.

In *Patterns of Child Rearing,* Robert Sears and his colleagues (1957) reported that U.S. children were toilet trained at an average age of 18 months. However, nighttime bladder "accidents" remained frequent until about 24 months. More recent studies tend to report more advanced ages. Today most U.S. children are reasonably well toilet trained between the ages of 2 and 3. They continue to have accidents at night for about another year.

In toilet training, as in so many other areas of physical growth and development, maturation plays a crucial role. During the first year, only an exceptional child can be toilet trained, even when parents devote a great deal of time and energy to the task. If parents do not begin toilet training until the third year, the process usually runs relatively rapidly and smoothly.

Parents are motivated to toilet train their children not only because of the "mess" of changing diapers. Parents often experience pressure from grandparents, other relatives, and friends who point out that so-and-so's children were all toilet trained before the age of— (You fill it in. Choose a number that will make most of us feel like inadequate parents). Parents in turn may pressure their children to become toilet trained. And so, toilet training can become a major arena for parent–child conflict.

Children who do not become toilet trained within reasonable time frames are said to have either *enuresis, encopresis,* or both.

Enuresis (en-you-REE-sis). Failure to control the bladder (urination) once the normal age for control has been reached.

▶ ▶ ▶ ▶

Enuresis

Enuresis is the failure to control the bladder (urination) once the "normal" age for achieving control of the bladder has been reached. Conceptions

Bed-wetting *Failure to control the bladder during the night.*

as to the normal age vary. The American Psychiatric Association (1987) is reasonably lenient on the issue and places the cut-off age at 5 years. The frequency of "accidents" is also an issue. The American Psychiatric Association does not consider that children are displaying enuresis unless they have accidents at least twice a month for 5- and 6-year-olds, or once a month for children who are older. Here the association is not quite as lenient. Perhaps as many as 8 percent of schoolchildren wet their beds once a month or more (LaPouse & Monk, 1959).

A nighttime accident is referred to as **bed-wetting.** Nighttime control is more difficult to achieve than daytime control. At night children must first wake up when their bladders are full. Only then can they go to the bathroom.

Bed-wetting is about twice as common among boys as girls. In the United States, where parents usually feel that early bladder control is important, only 10 to 15 percent of children wet their beds at the ages of 3 and 4 (Baller, 1975). Bruno Bettelheim (1969) found that in the Israeli kibbutz, where there is less concern about toilet training, as many as 40 percent of the children still wet their beds at the age of 9.

Causes of Enuresis   Enuresis can have organic causes, such as infections of the urinary tract or kidney problems. Numerous psychological explanations of enuresis have also been advanced.

Psychoanalytic theory suggests that enuresis is a way of expressing hostility toward parents (because of their harshness in toilet training) or a form of symbolic masturbation. These views are largely unsubstantiated. Learning theorists point out that enuresis is most common among children whose parents attempted to train them early. Early failures might have conditioned anxiety to attempts to control the bladder. Conditioned anxiety, then, prompts rather than inhibits urination.

Situational stresses seem to play a role. Children are more likely to wet their beds when they are entering school for the first time, when a sibling is born, or when they are ill. There may also be a genetic component, in that the concordance rate for enuresis is higher among MZ twins than among DZ twins (American Psychiatric Association, 1987).

It has also been noted that bed-wetting, the most common form of enuresis, tends to occur during the deepest stage of sleep. This is also the stage when sleep terrors and sleepwalking take place. For this reason, bed-wetting could be considered a sleep disorder. Like sleepwalking, bed-wetting could reflect immaturity of certain parts of the nervous system. Just as children "outgrow" night terrors and sleepwalking, they also tend to outgrow bed-wetting. In most cases bed-wetting resolves itself by adolescence, and usually by the age of 8.

Treatment   When parents (and children) feel that they cannot wait for bed-wetting to resolve itself, they may turn to behavioral methods that condition the child to awaken when their bladders are full. One reasonably reliable method for conditioning is Mowrer's bell-and-pad method (Doleys, 1977), described in Chapter 2.

Often all that is needed is reassurance that neither parents nor children are necessarily "to blame" for bed-wetting, and that most children will outgrow it.

▶ ▶ ▶ ▶

Encopresis

Soiling, or **encopresis,** is lack of control over the bowels. Soiling, like enuresis, is more common among boys. However, the overall incidence of soiling is lower than that of enuresis. About 1 to 2 percent of children at the ages of 7 and 8 have problems controlling their bowels. Encopresis is all but absent by the middle teens (Schaefer, 1979), except among the severely and profoundly retarded.

Soiling, in contrast to enuresis, is more likely to occur during the day. Thus it can be acutely embarrassing to the child. Classmates may avoid or poke fun at the soiler. Since bowel movements have a powerful odor, teachers may find it difficult to "tough it out" and function as though nothing of importance has occurred. Parents, too, eventually become aggravated by persistent soiling and may heighten their demands for self-control, using powerful punishments for failure. As a result of all this, the child may begin to hide soiled underwear (Ross, 1981). He may isolate himself from schoolmates, pretending to be sick in the morning to stay at home. His anxiety level increases. And since anxiety prompts bowel movements, control can become increasingly elusive.

Causes of Encopresis   With few exceptions, encopresis stems from psychological factors rather than physical causes. Frequently, soiling seems to follow harsh punishment of one or two accidents, especially in children who are already anxious or under stress. It is as if the harshness of the punishment focuses the child's attention on soiling. The child then begins to ruminate about soiling, so that it becomes a major concern of his young life.

Treatment: Toilet Training in a Day?   Operant conditioning methods are usually helpful in dealing with soiling. They use reward (by praise and other means) of incidents of self-control, which parents would normally take for granted. They use mild punishments for continued soiling, such as a gentle reminder to pay more attention to bowel sensations and having the child clean his own underwear.

Richard Foxx and Nathan Azrin (1973) trained children ranging in age from 20 to 36 months to control their bladders and bowels through only one day of intense operant conditioning. They shaped self-control by reinforcing the children for engaging in each of the steps involved in using the potty— approaching the potty, taking down their pants, sitting, eliminating, wiping themselves, and so on. Reinforcers included praise, embraces, and special treats. Following treatment, the children had an average of one accident a week, as compared with a pretreatment average of six a day.

While these principles and treatment methods are simple enough, parents of children who soil frequently do not understand this approach or may resist it. In these cases it may be necessary for therapists to work on family interactions as well as potty-training.

Pervasive Developmental Disorders

Pervasive developmental disorders used to be classified as *psychoses* by the American Psychiatric Association. **Psychoses** in adults are major disorders in which they have difficulty meeting the demands of everyday life and may

Encopresis *Failure to control the bowels once the normal age for bowel control has been reached. Also called* soiling.

Psychosis *(sigh-CO-sis). A severe behavior disorder characterized by inability to meet the demands of everyday life and faulty perception of reality. Plural:* psychoses.

▶ ▶ ▶ ▶

Infantile autism *A pervasive developmental disorder marked by aloneness, communication problems, preservation of sameness, and ritualistic behavior.*

Mutism *Inability or refusal to speak.*

Echolalia *Immediate and persistent repetition of the words of others.*

lose contact with reality. Psychotic adults also usually lack insight that anything is wrong. Young children would not be expected to understand that there is something amiss in their psychological functioning, even under most normal circumstances. However, their failure to develop normal patterns of social interaction and their sometimes bizarre behavior leave little doubt in the minds of others that something, indeed, is very wrong.

The use of the term *pervasive developmental disorders* represents recent recognition that these problems differ from adult psychoses. They are referred to as *pervasive*, because they affect many areas of development: cognitive, social, and emotional (American Psychiatric Association, 1987; Prior, 1984; Waterhouse & Fein, 1984). In this section we examine two related pervasive developmental disorders: *infantile autism* and *childhood schizophrenia*. Both are more prevalent among boys.

Infantile Autism

Infantile autism strikes 4 to 5 children in 10,000 before the age of 30 months, and is three to four times more common among boys than girls (American Psychiatric Association, 1987). Perhaps the most poignant feature of infantile autism is the child's utter aloneness, as seen with Peter at the outset of the chapter. Other symptoms of infantile autism include communication problems, preservation of sameness, and ritualistic or stereotypical behavior (see Table 14.1).

Parents of autistic children frequent report that they were "good babies." This usually means that they made few demands. However, as autistic children develop, they tend to shun affectionate contacts such as hugging, cuddling, and kissing (Schopler & Mesibov, 1984).

Their speech development lags. There is a dearth of babbling and communicative gesturing during the first year. They may show **mutism, echolalia,** and pronoun reversal, referring to themselves as "you" or "he."

Autistic children become bound by ritual, in their demands of others and in their own behavior. For example, the teacher of a 5-year-old autistic girl would greet her each morning with "Good morning, Lily, I am very, very glad to see you" (Diamond et al., 1963). Lily would not respond, but if the teacher

Table 14.1   Symptoms of Infantile Autism

Onset by 30 months of age

Extreme aloneness: Autistic children shun human contact, resist cuddling, treat other people as though they were furniture, do not notice distress in others, and play with objects but not peers

Communication problems: These include infrequent, meaningless babbling during first year; mutism; echolalia; and pronoun reversal

Absence of imaginative play and activity

Preservation of sameness: Autistic children become very upset if toys are out of place, if breakfast differs from day to day, or if others vary their greetings

Ritualistic behavior: There are repetitive motor acts such as rocking back and forth, spinning, hand-flicking, and finger twiddling.

There may be persistent staring at moving inanimate objects

▶ ▶ ▶ ▶

omitted one of the "verys," Lily would scream. The self-concepts of autistic children do not become well differentiated (Ferrari & Matthews, 1983). About 30 percent of them aged 3 to 12 fail to recognize their mirror images (Spiker & Ricks, 1984), although such recognition is almost universal among normal 2-year-olds (see Chapter 8). Despite their odd behavior, autistic children are frequently exceptionally attractive. Despite low scores on intelligence tests, they appear to have an "intelligent look" about them.

Causes of Autism Psychoanalytic and learning-theory approaches have argued that children become autistic in response to rejection by, or lack of adequate reinforcement from, their parents. From this perspective, autistic behavior patterns shut out the cold outside world.

Neurological-cognitive views of autism are coming into vogue. They suggest that autism involves organizations in the central nervous system that regulate the processing of information (Greenspan & Porges, 1984). For one thing, the onset is extremely early, and parents of autistic children appear to have been as loving and supportive as other parents. Second, there is a rather specific pattern of cognitive dysfunctioning in autistic children (Hoffmann & Prior, 1982). It is unlikely that infants from around the world would adopt similar bizarre behaviors in response to rejection. Third, autistic behaviors resemble behavior patterns that sometimes follow brain diseases such as encephalitis and congenital syphilis.

It should also be noted that many autistic children have abnormal brain wave patterns or seizures (Lotter, 1974). Others have been found to have brain damage (DeMyer et al., 1973) or cognitive behavior patterns suggestive of brain damage (Hoffmann & Prior, 1983).

Also consider twin studies. In one twin study four of eleven identical twins of autistic children showed the disorder, as compared with none of ten fraternal twins of autistic children (Folstein & Rutter, 1978). And another four of the identical twins shared one or more autistic symptoms, such as delayed speech or tendencies toward pronoun reversal.

Having said this, it must be admitted that we have not yet discovered the exact neurological-cognitive basis of autism. Therefore, we should remain open to shifts of thinking on the subject in the future.

The most poignant feature of autism is the child's utter aloneness.

▶ ▶ ▶ ▶

Treatment and Outcome The effectiveness of treatment for infantile autism is far from encouraging. Behavioral methods for attacking autistic behavior patterns have met with some success. For example, operant conditioning methods have encouraged autistic children to play with other children (Romanczyk et al., 1975), to pay attention to a therapist (Lovaas, 1977), and to stop self-mutilative behavior. UCLA psychologist O. Ivar Lovaas (1987) has recently reported the results of a long-term experiment with autistic children who received 40 hours of one-to-one behavior modification per week for at least two years. Nine of 19 children (47 percent) in the program made significant intellectual and educational gains, permitting them to succeed in first grade. The results are somewhat confounded by the fact that a number of autistic children were not accepted into the program because of extremely low levels of functioning. Still, the study offers more encouragement than we usually find.

There are also reports now and then (e.g., Clark & Witherspoon, 1984; Geller et al., 1982) that drugs are showing some promise with autistic children. Other approaches have included educational mainstreaming, involvement of families in treatment, and residential programs (Anderson et al., 1986; Harris, 1986; Romanczyk, 1986). Over the years only a small minority of autistic children have developed into adults who live independently and hold jobs (DeMyer et al., 1981; Kernberg, 1979; Lotter, 1978; Rutter, 1983).

We may have to gain a clearer picture of the causes of autism before we can devise more effective treatments.

Childhood Schizophrenia

Childhood schizophrenia is marked by a significant decline in contact with reality and social adjustment. Its onset occurs after 30 months. It was once assumed that childhood schizophrenia was an earlier version of the adult disorder. However, childhood schizophrenics do not usually become adult schizophrenics, even if their adult functioning remains impaired.

In childhood, as among adults, schizophrenia is marked by social withdrawal, confusion and disorientation, problems in speech, bizarre motor activities, **loose associations, hallucinations,** and **delusions.** But not all children with the disorder display all these symptoms. Schizophrenic children often report bizarre imaginary events, which suggests that their perceptions of the world are severely distorted.

There are some important differences between infantile autism and childhood schizophrenia. To me the most visible one concerns patterns of attachment. Autistic children generally show indifference to their parents and other people. However, they may become attached to inanimate objects, as shown by the distress they display when separated from them. Schizophrenic children, on the other hand, seem insecurely attached to their parents. They may cling to them obsessively and scream at minor separations.

Childhood schizophrenia, more clearly than autism, seems to follow a family pattern suggestive of genetic factors (Kallman & Roth, 1956). As with adult schizophrenics, current research into the neurological bases for childhood schizophrenia is now focusing on the levels of neurotransmitters such as **serotonin** and **dopamine.** Drugs that lower the amount of dopamine available to the brain have been found reasonably effective in the treatment of childhood schizophrenia (Kernberg, 1979).

Childhood schizophrenia *A pervasive developmental disorder marked by significant declines in contact with reality and in social adjustment that begin after the age of 30 months.*

Loose associations *A symptom of a thought disorder marked by difficulty sticking to one topic or producing coherent speech.*

Hallucinations *(hal-loose-sin-NAY-shuns). Perceptions in the absence of sensation—as in "seeing" or "hearing things." (From the Latin* hallucinari, *meaning "to wander mentally.")*

Delusions *Firmly held beliefs that are inconsistent with reality.*

Serotonin *A neurotransmitter implicated in behavior disorders such as schizophrenia and depression.*

Dopamine *A neurotransmitter implicated in schizophrenia.*

▶ ▶ ▶ ▶

Attention-Deficit Hyperactivity Disorder

Many parents feel that their children do not pay enough attention to them—that they tend to run around as the whim strikes and to do things in their own way. Some inattention, especially at early ages, is to be expected. But in **attention-deficit hyperactivity disorder** (ADHD), as diagnosed by the American Psychiatric Association (1987), the child shows "developmentally inappropriate" lack of attention, impulsivity, and **hyperactivity**.

The onset of ADHD occurs by age 7 (American Psychiatric Association, 1987). The behavior pattern must have persisted for at least six months for the diagnosis to apply. Such children's activity and restlessness impair their ability to function in school. They simply cannot sit still.

Sad to say, ADHD is *not* rare. It is diagnosed in about 3 percent of children and is the most common cause of childhood referrals to mental-health clinics (Trites & Caprade, 1983). It is about six to nine times more common in boys than in girls (American Psychiatric Association, 1987). Inattention appears to be the core problem (McGee et al., 1985). Associated problems include stubbornness, bullying, temper tantrums, and lack of response to punishment (Hechtman & Weiss, 1983). A more complete list of problems is shown in Table 14.2.

The *degree* of hyperactive behavior is crucial, since many normal children are labeled overactive and fidgety from time to time. In fact, if "talking too much" were the sole criterion for ADHD, the label would have applied to me.

Table 14.2   Symptoms of Attention-Deficit Hyperactivity Disorder (ADHD)

Lack of attention	Frequently fails to finish projects
	Does not seem to pay attention
	Is readily distracted
	Cannot sustain concentration on schoolwork or related tasks
	Does not sustain interest in play activities
Impulsivity	Frequently acts without thinking
	Shifts from activity to activity
	Cannot organize tasks or work
	Requires constant supervision
	Often "calls out" in class
	Does not wait his turn in line, games, etc.
Hyperactivity	Constantly runs around or climbs on things
	Cannot sit still; fidgets constantly
	Does not remain in his seat in class
	Shows excessive motor activity when asleep
	Is constantly on the go, running like a "motor"

Children who are diagnosed as showing ADHD display many of the behaviors listed in this table. Their academic functioning and sometimes their social functioning suffer as a result.
Source: Adapted from American Psychiatric Association, *Diagnostic and Statistical Manual of the Mental Disorders,* Third edition–Revised (Washington, DC: American Psychiatric Press, Inc., 1987), pp. 50–53.

▶ ▶ ▶ ▶

Causes of Hyperactivity   In the case of ADHD, most theorists focus on possible physical causes. For one thing, ADHD tends to run in families (Gross & Wilson, 1974; Morrison & Stewart, 1973). The mothers of children who become hyperactive have often had difficult pregnancies. In infancy, the children are more prone to neurological disorders such as seizures and encephalitis. Recordings of brain waves frequently show abnormalities as well.

All in all, ADHD children display behavior patterns similar to some caused by brain damage. However, brain damage cannot usually be demonstrated with ADHD children. For this reason, some investigators have suggested that ADHD children are "minimally" brain-damaged, or "minimally neurologically impaired." These labels, of course, do not add much to efforts to locate and remedy possible damage.

One other physical hypothesis should be mentioned. Pediatrician Ben Feingold created a stir with his 1975 book, *Why Your Child Is Hyperactive*. He argued that the chemical additives in processed food were largely responsible for hyperactivity. However, experimental studies of the "Feingold diet," which was purported to remove such additives from children's food, have not been encouraging.

Hyperactive children are continually on the go, as if their "motors" are constantly running. Hyperactivity as an abnormal syndrome is not to be confused with the normal high activity levels of children.

▶ ▶ ▶ ▶

ATTENTION-DEFICIT HYPERACTIVITY DISORDER

567

Treatment and Outcome The most widespread treatment for ADHD is medical—the use of **stimulants** such as Ritalin and Dexedrine. It may seem ironic that stimulants would be used with children who are already overly active. The rationale is that the activity of the hyperactive child stems from inability of the cerebral cortex to inhibit more primitive areas of the brain. The drugs, in theory, act to stimulate the cortex and facilitate cortical control of primitive areas.

Stimulants have been shown to reduce disruptive, annoying, and aggressive behaviors among hyperactive children (e.g., Abikoff & Gittelman, 1985; Whalen et al., 1987). However, their use is controversial. Some critics argue that stimulants suppress gains in height and weight, do not contribute to academic gains, and lose effectiveness over time (Friman & Christopherson, 1983). Supporters of stimulant treatment counter that the suppression of growth appears to be related to the dosage and the specific drug chosen (Mattes & Gittelman, 1983; Rapport, 1984). Recent studies suggest that stimulants may increase self-control (Barkley et al., 1984), prolong the attention span, and decrease fidgeting in school (O'Leary, 1980). They may also lead to academic gains of 10 to 24 percent (Kavale, 1982). Finally, there seem to be few, if any, scientifically rigorous studies on the outcomes of long-term treatment with stimulants (Pelham, 1983; Rapport, 1984).

Operant conditioning methods have also been used with some success, both in decreasing hyperactivity and in increasing the amount of time spent on academic work (O'Leary et al., 1976). It may be that a combination of behavior therapy and stimulants will prove to be the most effective approach to treating ADHD children (Hinshaw et al., 1984; Pelham et al., 1980).

In any event, ADHD most often declines by adolescence. Even so, problems in attention and learning may persist. By the time they are young adults, most formerly hyperactive children attain jobs and are satisfied with their lives (Weiss et al., 1979). A few remain impulsive. Some become antisocial.

Conduct Disorders

Children who show **conduct disorders** persistently break rules or violate the rights of others. Conduct disorders are much more prevalent among boys than girls (Herbert, 1978). Their onset is typically just prior to puberty or during puberty. In order to receive this label, children must have engaged in the troublesome behavior pattern for at least six months (American Psychiatric Association, 1987).

Children with conduct disorders are often involved in sexual activity prior to puberty, smoking, drinking, and the abuse of various other substances. They typically have a low tolerance for frustration and may have temper flare-ups. They are biased in their processing of social information: They assume that others intend them ill when they do not (Dodge & Frame, 1982; Jurkovic, 1980). They usually blame other people for the scrapes they get into. They believe that they are misperceived and treated unfairly. Their academic accomplishments are usually below grade level, and their intelligence is usually at least average.

Conduct disorders show a good deal of stability. One longitudinal study showed that children who show conduct disorders in kindergarten through third grade have more contacts with police through adolescence (Spivack et al., 1986). Longitudinal data from the Berkeley Guidance study show that children

▶ ▶ ▶ ▶

who had temper tantrums at 8 to 10 were more likely to have erratic work lives and get divorced as adults (Caspi et al., 1987).

Origins of Conduct Disorders   There may be a genetic component in conduct disorders, because they are more likely to be found among the biological parents than the adoptive parents of adopted children (Mednick, 1985). But the presence of sociopathic models in the family, inconsistent discipline, and family stress can also contribute to antisocial behavior (Bond & McMahon, 1984; Griest et al., 1980; Margolin, 1981; Olweus, 1980; Rutter & Garmezy, 1983). Conduct disorders in children also sometimes appear to be direct reflections of marital problems (Emery, 1982; Christensen et al., 1983).

Treatment of Conduct Disorders   The treatment of conduct disorders is challenging and less than satisfactory. Psychotherapy has not been reliably shown to help. Imprisonment may temporarily protect society from young offenders. But prison too often serves as a school for acquiring "advanced" deviant skills that are practiced upon release. It may be that placing children with conduct disorders in programs or settings with concrete rules and clear rewards for obeying them offers the greatest promise (Barkley et al., 1976; Henggeler et al., 1986; Phillips et al., 1976; Stumphauzer, 1981). Such programs may use operant conditioning. Some of them use a **token economy.**

In one approach, architect Harold Cohen (Cohen & Filipczak, 1971) and his colleagues provided a special training program for delinquents in Washington, DC. The children enrolled in courses such as remedial math, history, and electronics, and they were permitted to earn money for their achievements. Extra cash flowed for A's. As a group, the children acquired study skills that they consequently put to good use in the public schools. The most significant finding is that they got into fewer scrapes with the law during the two years following the program.

Other approaches include teaching aggressive children various methods for coping with feelings of anger that will not violate the rights of others. In one promising method, "problem-solving therapy," aggressive boys learned to reconceptualize the social confrontations that had previously provoked them to violence as problems to be solved (Lochman et al., 1984). They then generated nonviolent solutions to these social "problems" and tried out the most promising ones. As a consequence, they showed significant decreases in aggressive and disruptive behavior in the classroom, and less aggression in the home.

Sometimes the child's parents must be integrated into treatment (Baumrind, 1983). Scott Henggeler and his colleagues (Brunk et al., 1987; Henggeler, 1982; Henggeler & Cohen, 1984; Henggeler et al., 1986) have innovated an even broader "family-ecological" approach based on Bronfenbrenner's (1979) ecological theory. Henggeler, like Bronfenbrenner, sees the child as embedded within several systems. He focuses on the reciprocal relationships between the juvenile offender and the systems with which he interacts. The techniques employed are not unique. Rather, the family-ecological approach attempts to identify as many of the determinants of conduct disorders as possible, and to change the child's interactions with as many systems as needed.

Again, we are reminded that children are not islands unto themselves. They influence and are influenced by others. Reciprocal influences need to be studied more carefully if we are to make the most effective interventions.

▶ ▶ ▶ ▶

Substance Abuse

We live in a drug-oriented society. We use drugs not only to cope with medical problems, but also with daily tensions, run-of-the-mill depression, even boredom. Drugs are used properly when they are required to maintain or restore health, but we use drugs for many other reasons. Many prepubertal children and adolescents use drugs for the same reasons that adults do. But they also use drugs because their friends do or because their parents tell them not to. They use drugs to experience pleasure, to deaden pain, and to earn prestige among their peers.

Patterns of Substance Abuse among Adolescents Following a dropoff in popularity during the 1960s, alcohol has reasserted its dominance among the drugs used on college campuses and in the high schools. More than 90 percent of U.S. high school students have tried alcohol, and 70 percent report using it within the past 30 days (Brooke & Whiteman, 1983; Johnston et al., 1982). The incidence of marijuana use appears to have peaked in the late 1970s. Still, nearly 60 percent of high school students have tried marijuana. Just under 30 percent have used it in the last 30 days.

Perhaps 20 to 30 percent of college students and 16 percent of high school students have tried the stimulant cocaine. But only about 5 percent have used it recently, perhaps because the drug has been so expensive. However, its street price has been dropping. Even the potent cocaine derivative "crack" can be afforded by many adolescents, at least occasionally. It is possible that this stimulant, which had once been the toy of the well-to-do, will find more regular use among lower-income adolescents.

Nearly 30 percent of high school students have tried stimulants. About 15 percent have tried **sedatives, hallucinogenics,** and tranquilizers. Only a small minority of these percentages use the drugs regularly. Still fewer adolescents—only 1 to 2 percent—have tried heroin. Very few use heroin regularly.

Most adolescents who use drugs do not do so regularly. However, some fall prey to patterns of usage that are labeled *substance abuse* and *substance dependence* by the American Psychiatric Association (1987).

Substance Abuse and Dependence There are many ways to define substance abuse. From a legal standpoint, the use of drugs by minors or the use of proscribed substances may be defined as abuse. The American Psychiatric Association (1987) uses the diagnosis **substance abuse** for continued use of the substance despite the fact that usage impairs one's social, academic, or physical well-being. Children and adolescents who are repeatedly **intoxicated** in the classroom, or who miss classes or cut school because they are "high" or sleeping off the effects of drugs, fit the pattern. Sad to say, there are some students who smoke marijuana or gulp an alcoholic beverage between classes and stay high for the day.

Substance dependence is more severe than substance abuse. It is characterized by factors such as the following: a pattern of increasing usage, difficulty in limiting usage, devotion of a great deal of time and energy to procuring the substance, problems at school or work because of intoxication or withdrawal, the changing of daily activities so that they revolve around the substance and peers who use the substance, and increased tolerance of the substance. Substance dependence usually implies **physiological dependence.**

Sedatives *Drugs that soothe or quiet restlessness or agitation. (From the Latin* sedare, *meaning "to settle.")*

Hallucinogenics *Drugs that give rise to hallucinations.*

Substance abuse *A persistent pattern of use of a substance such that one is frequently intoxicated and well-being is impaired.*

Intoxicated *Drunk.*

Substance dependence *A pattern of usage in which one orients one's life toward getting and using the substance despite harmful effects. Usually accompanied by physiological dependence.*

Physiological dependence *Biological dependence on a substance, as evidenced by tolerance or an abstinence syndrome.*

Perhaps 20 to 30 percent of college students and about 16 percent of high school students have tried cocaine. The street price of this drug has been dropping, and for this reason its use among lower-income adolescents may increase.

Physiological dependence is made evident either by *tolerance* or by the presence of an *abstinence syndrome* upon a sudden decline in usage. **Tolerance** is the body's habituation to a drug. Tolerance results from regular usage and requires that progressively higher doses be used to achieve similar effects. An **abstinence syndrome** consists of a characteristic cluster of symptoms that are experienced when the level of usage is suddenly curtailed. For example, the abstinence syndrome for alcohol includes anxiety, **tremors,** restlessness, weakness, rapid pulse, and high blood pressure.

Children who abuse substances may become psychologically dependent on them and be anxious about what would happen to them if they had to go without them. The physical symptoms of anxiety (shakiness, rapid pulse, and so on) are similar to the abstinence syndromes for many substances, and so substance abusers may think that they are physiologically dependent when they are not.

Causes of Abuse   The most frequently cited reason for trying drugs is curiosity (Jalali et al., 1981). However, children and adolescents also use drugs for other reasons:

Modeling   Children whose parents use drugs such as alcohol, tobacco, tranquilizers, and stimulants are more likely to turn to drugs themselves (Brook et al., 1980; Kandel, 1980). Modeling increases children's awareness of drugs and shows them when to use them—for example, when they are anxious and depressed.

In preadolescence and adolescence, children are also exposed to peers who use drugs. When peers seem similar to themselves and are admired for maturity and coping skills, they are most likely to be imitated.

Conformity   In Chapter 11 it was noted that children are highly vulnerable to peer pressure from about 8 to 14. Parents may consider the ages of 10 to 14 as their children's most vulnerable years. If children of this age group are closely involved with a group that uses proscribed substances, they may experience enormous pressure to do so themselves.

Tolerance *Habituation to a drug with the result that increasingly higher doses of the drug are needed to achieve similar effects.*

Abstinence syndrome *A characteristic cluster of symptoms that results from sudden decrease in the level of usage of a substance.*

Tremors *Shaking or shivering.*

▶ ▶ ▶ ▶

Abuse is not an inner-city problem. Every U.S. city and suburban area has its crowds or subcultures that abuse drugs. Children become involved with them even in the wealthiest suburbs. The pattern of child rearing that is associated with inducing instrumental competence may help children cope with peer pressures to become involved in drugs (Konopka, 1976)—that is, high parental involvement, the setting of strict limits, demands for mature behavior, inductive enforcement techniques, democratic discussion of values and goals, and warmth and encouragement. This view remains largely to be tested.

Rebellion   Some children are in rebellion and abuse drugs in part because they savor the misery it causes their parents—or would cause their parents if they knew about it.

Authoritarian parents may be most likely to have rebellious children. The children of permissive parents may be drawn to substance abuse because of their immaturity and impulsivity more so than because of rebelliousness.

Self-Handicapping   Many adolescents use alcohol as a self-handicapping strategy. In one experiment, students were given cognitive tasks and allowed to drink as much as they wished during their completion (Tucker et al., 1981). Some students had access to study materials and, as a result, they expected to succeed on the tasks. Others did not have access to these materials. Students who could use the study aids drank significantly less than students who could not. The researchers suggest that subjects who were more likely to fail turned to alcohol as a self-handicapping strategy. That is, if they did fail, they could attribute failure to the alcohol, rather than to their own abilities. In this way they could maintain their self-esteem.

The Effects of the Substances   I have said little, until now, about the possible lures of the effects of the substances themselves. After they try a drug, adolescents are most likely to try it again if it makes them feel good (Mizner et al., 1970). For example, most adolescents drink alcohol in order to "get high," not to prove that they are adults (Carman et al., 1983). But there are other reasons that adolescents seek the effects of drugs. Adolescents who are anxious about their prospects for developing vocational and advanced educational skills, or who have difficulties socializing, may be drawn to the calming effects of alcohol, marijuana (in certain doses), tranquilizers, and sedatives. Adolescents with low self-confidence and self-esteem may be drawn to the ego-bolstering effects of drugs such as **amphetamines** and cocaine. A number of adolescents have attempted to escape the poverty, anguish, and tedium of life in the inner city through heroin and similar drugs (Hollister, 1983).

Physiological Dependence   More children and adolescents try drugs than use them regularly. Those who choose to use them regularly may be more in need of, or sensitive to, their effects. Because of tolerance, regular use of many drugs diminishes the effects for which they were first used. And so, many adolescents who begin to use substances such as alcohol for the pleasure of it wind up using them to escape the withdrawal symptoms of the abstinence syndrome.

Amphetamines (am-FET-uh-means). *Stimulants derived from* alpha-*methyl-beta-*phenyl-ethyl-*amine, a colorless liquid consisting of carbon, hydrogen, and nitrogen.*

Possible Genetic Factors   We have discussed psychological reasons for special sensitivity to the effects of certain drugs, but genetic factors may also be in-

▶ ▶ ▶ ▶

Can You Make Your Children Immune to Alcohol Abuse?

▷
▷
▷
▷
▷ Prevention has become a buzz word. No longer are we as willing to sit back and deal with the consequences of illness or problem behavior when they strike as we once were. Now the focus has shifted to ways in which we can change our daily lives to avert medical and behavioral problems.

Drug abuse is one such problem, and alcohol is the most widely abused drug by children and adolescents. Various prevention projects have sprung into being for use with elementary school children as well as for adolescents and adults. Unfortunately, the results of these programs are mixed (Marlatt, 1985; Miller & Nirenberg, 1984). Sometimes they help. Other times they backfire, with drinking rates among children increasing after they have been exposed to program materials.

Perhaps there is no single way to be absolutely sure that your children will not develop alcohol problems, but Barclay Martin (1981) compiled a number of cultural and family factors that are associated with a low incidence of abuse in nations where alcohol is used freely, such as the United States. Obviously, there are no guarantees, but it seems reasonable to become aware of these factors and to weigh their potential for your family:

1. Expose children to alcohol early in life, within a strong family or religious group. Whatever the beverage, it is served in diluted and small quantities, with consequent low blood alcohol levels.

2. Use beverages that contain relatively large amounts of nonalcoholic components (wines and beers), which also give low blood alcohol levels.

3. Use beverages that are considered mainly as food and are usually consumed with meals, again with consequent low blood alcohol levels.

4. Present an example of moderate drinking.

5. Attach no moral importance to drinking. Speak of it neither as a virtue nor a vice.

6. Do not view drinking as proof of adulthood or virility.

7. Make abstinence socially acceptable. Teach children that it is no more rude or ungracious to decline a drink than to decline a piece of cake.

8. Express the view that excessive drinking or intoxication is not socially acceptable. Show that excessive drinking is not to be considered stylish, comic, or tolerable (Martin, 1981, p. 472).

volved. There is growing evidence that we can have a genetic predisposition toward physiological dependence on certain substances (Vaillant, 1982). For example, rats have been selectively bred to show preference for alcohol over other beverages (Sigovia-Riquelma et al., 1971). Moreover, children of alcoholics who are reared by adoptive parents are more likely to develop alcohol-related problems than are the natural children of the adoptive parents (Cadoret et al., 1980; Goodwin, 1979).

Prenatal Factors The prenatal environment may also play a role. Julien (1978) reports that even small amounts of alcohol drunk by mothers during certain stages of pregnancy can predispose the child to excessive drinking later on.

▶ ▶ ▶ ▶

Anxiety Disorders

Children encounter many fears and anxieties that are considered normal, because they are widespread and appear to reflect natural cognitive-developmental processes. During the second half of the first year, it is normal for children to develop separation anxiety and fear of strangers. Other childhood anxieties concern supernatural and imaginary creatures, being left alone or in the dark, noise, attack by animals, pain and bodily injury. During the first six years, fears of noises, strange objects and people, and pain decline. Fears of ridicule, animals, the dark, and real sources of danger increase. By sixth grade fears of imaginary creatures and animals have waned, and concerns over physical danger have increased (Bauer, 1976).

We discuss two anxiety disorders listed by the American Psychiatric Association (1987) that may occur in childhood or adolescence: *avoidant disorder* and *overanxious disorder*.

Avoidant Disorder

While some fear of strangers is to be expected in children, children diagnosed as having an **avoidant disorder** show persistent and excessive avoidance of contact with strangers. They show normal needs for affection and acceptance and have warm relationships with their families. However, their avoidance of people outside the family is sufficient to interfere with the development of peer relationships. For example, they usually avoid playgrounds and neighborhood children. Their discomfort at being around other children in the classroom can have a detrimental effect on their academic progress.

Avoidant disorders develop after normal fear of strangers has disappeared, at the age of 2½ or afterward. They may be complicated by feelings of isolation and depression, since children with the problem usually fail to form social bonds that extend beyond the immediate family. In some cases, avoidant children have simply not had experience in relating to other children, but they relate relatively freely to adults (Scarlett, 1980).

Avoidant disorder has not been studied very extensively, in part because it is difficult to tell where run-of-the-mill shyness ends and an avoidant disorder begins. In any event, shy, withdrawn children have been helped by behavior-therapy methods that rely on operant conditioning and observational learning. For example, they have been "drawn out" when day-caregivers and teachers reinforce efforts at socializing and ignore withdrawn behavior (Hart et al., 1968). They have also been encouraged to try to relate to peers by being shown films of withdrawn children gradually increasing the extent of their social interactions with peers (O'Connor, 1969).

Overanxious Disorder

Avoidant disorder Persistent avoidance of strangers and peers such that social functioning is impaired.

Overanxious Excessively anxious. Highly sensitive to social criticism.

Overanxious children appear generally worried and fretful. Instead of overreacting to one or two specific objects or events, their concerns extend to future events, such as tests and visits to the doctor; to past events, such as whether they said the right thing to a friend or answered a test item properly; and their overall competence, in school, sports, and social relationships (see Table 14.3).

Table 14.3   Signs of Anxiety in Children

Unrealistic concern about the future—tests, deadlines, doctors' visits, etc.
Rumination about past performances—adequacy in sports, social interactions, tests, etc.
Excessive concern about competence in school, sports, with peers, etc.
Strong need for reassurance
Physical complaints that are frequently associated with anxiety—a "lump in the throat," loose
   bowels, headaches, nausea, shortness of breath, dizziness, insomnia, "butterflies in the
   stomach"
Excessive self-consciousness; ready embarrassment
Tension—motor restlessness, nervous habits such as pulling hair or biting nails
Nightmares

Adapted from American Psychiatric Association (1987), pp. 64–65.

Overanxious children frequently saddle themselves with self-doubts and perfectionism. They also may show "nervous habits" such as biting their nails or pulling their hair.

Causes and Treatment   Overanxious children are displaying a general pattern of anxious behavior, and not a reaction to specific events or stimuli. For this reason, the causes are difficult to pin down. Still there are a number of theoretical views. According to psychoanalytic theory, generalized anxiety reflects difficulty in repressing primitive urges, particularly sexual and aggressive impulses. Learning theorists might suggest that pervasive anxiety indicates anxiety about broad themes, such as general fear of rejection. Perhaps fears about competence and rejection have become generalized to most areas of achievement and social interaction. As suggested in Chapter 11, there is also some evidence that the children of parents who discipline their children by threatening loss of love are more anxious than children of parents who discipline through inductive methods. The anxieties of these children might reflect deep-seated fears that unless they act perfectly they will be unworthy of love.

There is also probably a genetic component to anxiety disorders. Anxiety disorders run in families (Turner et al., 1987), and there is a higher concordance rate for anxiety disorders and anxiety-related traits among identical twins than fraternal twins (Floderus-Myrhed et al., 1980; Matheny, 1983; Scarr & Kidd, 1983; Torgersen, 1983).

Whatever the sources of pervasive anxieties, there are many approaches to dealing with them. Among adults, the most prevalent treatment is tranquilizing drugs. This treatment is problematic, because people rapidly build tolerance for tranquilizers. Drugs also provide no guidance in helping them cope with the sources of their anxieties. Psychological treatments focus on various aspects of anxiety listed in Table 14.3. In one behavior-therapy approach, for example, people are taught how to relax their bodies without resorting to drugs. In this way, they learn to reduce symptoms such as muscle-tension headaches and "butterflies" in the stomach. In a cognitive approach, people are helped to get more in touch with, and to challenge, their irrational expectations and perfectionistic self-demands. So-called "habit-reversal" techniques, largely pioneered by psychologist Nathan Azrin, have also helped people gain control of nervous habits such as nail-biting and hair-pulling. These psychological approaches have also been found to have some utility with children (Kendall & Williams, 1981).

► ► ► ►

Anxiety is often found to be associated with another emotional problem in children—depression (Wolfe et al., 1987).

Depression

Because of its prevalence, depression has been referred to as the "common cold" of the behavior disorders. Depressed adults may feel sad, blue, "down in the dumps." They may complain of poor appetite, insomnia, lack of energy and inactivity, loss of self-esteem, difficulty concentrating, loss of interest in other people and activities they usually enjoy, pessimism, crying, feelings of hopelessness and helplessness, and thoughts of suicide. Depressed people also tend to be dependent in their social relationships and self-critical.

There is not much of a continuity between childhood schizophrenia and adult schizophrenia, but the opposite is true of depression. Depressed children frequently have depressive episodes as adults (Cantwell, 1982).

Many of the symptoms of depression found in adults are found in children (Asarnow & Carlson, 1985). For example, in middle childhood depressed children report feelings of sadness, shame, and hostility directed toward others and the self (Blumberg & Izard, 1985). But many depressed children do not report, and are not aware of, feelings of sadness. Part of the problem is cognitive-developmental. Children do not usually recognize depression in themselves until the age of 7 or so. The capacity for concrete operations apparently contributes to children's abilities to perceive internal feeling states (Glasberg & Aboud, 1982).

When children cannot report their feelings, depression is inferred from behavior. Depressed children in middle childhood, like depressed adults, engage in less social activity and are less emotionally expressive (less given to smiling and frowning) than nondepressed peers (Kazdin et al., 1985). But in some cases childhood depression is "masked" by apparently unrelated behaviors. Now and then conduct disorders, physical complaints, academic problems, even hyperactivity might stem from depression. Among adolescents, sexual and aggressive **acting out** has been linked to depression (Achenbach & Edelbrock, 1981; Carlson, 1980).

Depression in adults is often accompanied by poor appetite. Children at various ages might show relatively poor appetites, and so we need to be aware of developmental norms before we draw conclusions about children's behavior.

Despite these problems, a number of scales for measuring childhood depression have been developed (e.g., by Asarnow & Carlson [1985], by Kovacs & Beck [1977], and by Lefkowitz & Tesiny [1980]). The self-rating scale reported by Joan Asarnow and Gabrielle Carlson (1985) includes items such as "I feel like running away," "I have horrible dreams," "I feel very lonely," and "My mind wanders and I cannot concentrate." In the method developed by Monroe Lefkowitz and Edward Tesiny, children are asked to identify peers who are described by items such as "Who says they can't do things?" and "Who often looks sad?" Scores on this test tend to be reliable and to be inversely related to children's popularity, self-esteem, and school achievement (Tesiny & Lefkowitz, 1982). Depression thus appears to impair not only children's states of happiness, but also their peer relationships and their academic progress.

We still do not have a very clear idea of how many children are depressed, although estimates run as high as one-third of all children.

Acting out *Expressing primitive impulses and ideas that are usually inhibited.*

▶ ▶ ▶ ▶

Depression has complex psychological and, in some cases, biological origins. However, adults can help depressed children by involving them in enjoyable activities, encouraging the development of competencies, offering praise when appropriate, and pointing out when children are being too hard on themselves.

Origins of Depression   The origins of depression are complex and varied, and there are psychological and biological approaches to understanding them. Psychoanalysts, for example, have suggested that depressed children (and adults) have typically been severely threatened with parental loss of love for their shortcomings. They tend to repress rather than express feelings of anger. The net result is that they turn their anger inward upon themselves—experiencing it as misery and self-hatred.

Some social-learning theorists focus on relationships between competencies (knowledge and skills) and feelings of self-esteem in explaining depression. Children who gain academic, social, and other competencies also usually have high feelings of self-esteem. Perceived low levels of competence are linked to helplessness, low self-esteem, and depression in children and adolescents (McCranie & Bass, 1984; Weisz et al., 1987). Children who have not developed competencies because of lack of training opportunities, inconsistent parental reinforcement, and so on, may also develop feelings of helplessness and hopelessness. Some children do have competencies, but excessive parental expectations might prevent them from crediting themselves for them. For this reason, overly anxious, perfectionistic children are also frequently depressed. They cannot meet their own high standards.

Our perceived reasons for our shortcomings—our **attributional styles**— can also contribute to feelings of helplessness and hopelessness. Consider the case of two children who do poorly on a math test. John thinks, "I'm a jerk! I'm just no good in math! I'll never learn." Jim thinks, "That test was tougher than I thought it would be. I'll have to work harder next time." John is perceiving the problem as global (he's "a jerk") and stable (he'll "never learn"). Jim perceives the problem as specific (related to the type of math test the teacher makes up) and unstable (he can change the results by working harder). Depressed children tend to explain negative events in terms of internal, stable, and global causes (Blumberg & Izard, 1985). As a result, they, like John, are more likely than Jim to be depressed.

Attributional style   The way in which one interprets failures or shortcomings—for example, whether one is predisposed toward placing blame on oneself or on external factors.

▶ ▶ ▶ ▶

Norepinephrine *A neurotrans-mitter implicated in depression.*

Parents have a major influence on their children's attributional styles. When parents who disapprove of their children's behavior tell them that they're "bad" or "dumb," children are likely to conclude that they cannot change their behavior for the better and to feel helpless and depressed—or rebellious, when the underlying feelings are "masked." Children whose parents tell them that they love them but who demand *specific behavioral changes* are more likely to have children with high self-esteem, and a non-self-defeating attributional style.

There is also evidence for genetic factors in depression. Children of depressed parents are at greater risk for depression and other disorders (Beardslee et al., 1983). On a neurological level, there is evidence that persistent depression is associated with low utilization of the neurotransmitters serotonin and **norepinephrine.** Especially when children show severe, unrelenting feelings of depression, it might be that neurological factors are involved. Antidepressant drugs have shown some usefulness with children, and they are thought to act by increasing utilization of these neurotransmitters (Petti & Connors, 1983).

Parents and teachers can also do a good deal to alleviate more common feelings of depression among children. They can involve children in enjoyable activities, encouraging the step-by-step development of instrumental competencies; offer praise when appropriate; and point out when children are being too hard on themselves.

A Look Back

It happens that the last topic in this book is depression, but I do not want to end on a depressing note. Let us remember that the majority of children do *not* encounter the behavior disorders discussed in this chapter. There are also two other encouraging notes:

First, many children are apparently invulnerable to the behavioral problems that beset their troubled parents and their distressed siblings (Goleman, 1987). These children have been exposed to horrendous environmental conditions, ranging from extremes of poverty to parental neglect and abuse; yet they are resilient. Despite hardship, they become self-confident and thrive.

No single cluster of characteristics sets resilient children apart from their vulnerable peers. Still, as noted by Ellen Farber and Byron Egeland (1987), a number of traits appear to protect them almost from birth. For example, at birth they tend to be attentive and alert. At the age of 1 they tend to be securely attached to their mothers, although their mothers may become abusive or incompetent as time goes on. At 2 years they are independent, easygoing, and persistent. They continue to work at building tall towers of blocks, whereas their peers quit after a tumble or two. Later in childhood they show a knack for enlisting the aid of adults outside the family who provide them with encouragement, support, and role models.

Second, as noted by Arthur Parmelee, Jr. (1986), past president of the Society for Research in Child Development, childhood problems can have positive outcomes in other ways. Problems provide opportunities for children to increase their self-knowledge and can promote the development of empathy for the plights of others. Disordered children in the family can also foster the development of empathy and caring behavior in siblings.

▶ ▶ ▶ ▶

Childhood can be the most enjoyable and exciting time of life. If you don't think so, I leave you with a question: At what other time of life can we pull out the tape measure and actually look forward to the changes we will find?

Summary

1. Behavior disorders of childhood and adolescence refer to patterns of behavior that may (1) be infrequent, (2) be socially unacceptable, (3) involve faulty perception, (4) cause personal distress, (5) be self-defeating, or (6) be dangerous.

2. Obese children are likely to become obese adults. The causes of obesity have been linked to the child's number of fat cells, which reflect both heredity and early eating habits. However, some investigators dispute the fat-cell hypothesis. Some children overeat because overeating is the normal family pattern. Others overeat because of family conflict or other sources of stress.

3. Anorexia nervosa is characterized by dramatic weight loss and intense fear of being overweight. Anoretic females have a distorted body image, viewing themselves as overweight when others perceive them to be dangerously thin. Anorexia is most often found in adolescent girls and may reflect concerns about assuming the roles of adult women.

4. In bulimia nervosa, there are cycles of binging and purging.

5. Sleep terrors are more severe than nightmares and occur during deep (non-REM) sleep. Most nightmares occur during REM sleep. Children may awaken screaming with sleep terrors, with accelerated heart and respiration rates.

6. Sleepwalking also occurs during deep sleep. Despite myths to the contrary, sleepwalkers walk with their eyes open, may hurt themselves, and are not violent when awakened, although they may be disoriented and confused.

7. In sudden infant death syndrome (SIDS), apparently healthy children go to sleep and fail to awaken in the morning. The causes of SIDS are unknown, but may reflect immaturity of the parts of the nervous system involved in breathing. A number of risk factors for SIDS have been identified. For example, SIDS is more common among male babies who are later-born and have shown respiratory problems.

8. Enuresis is failure to control the bladder after the normal age for gaining control. Enuresis is more common among boys. Most children "outgrow" enuresis. Treatments such as the bell-and-pad method are available.

9. Encopresis, or lack of bowel control, is also more common among boys. Encopresis is frequently a source of humiliation for the boy and his family. Enuresis and encopresis are most common among children whose parents attempt to toilet train them early and use harsh training techniques.

10. Pervasive developmental disorders are severe and affect many areas of psychological development—cognitive, social, and emotional. Infantile autism has its onset by 30 months and is characterized by extreme aloneness, communication problems, preservation of sameness, and ritualistic behavior.

▶ ▶ ▶ ▶

11. Childhood schizophrenia occurs after 30 months and is characterized by social withdrawal, confusion, bizzare behavior, loose associations, and, sometimes, hallucinations and delusions. Neurological and cognitive factors appear to play a role in both types of pervasive developmental disorders.

12. Attention-deficit hyperactivity disorder (ADHD) is most often found in boys and is characterized by lack of attention, impulsivity, and hyperactivity. Hyperactivity is characterized by running around, fidgeting, not remaining seated, and having excessive motor activity while asleep. Hyperactivity is thought to reflect neurological problems and has been treated by stimulants (which facilitate cortical control over primitive areas of the brain) and behavior therapy.

13. Children with conduct disorders are in frequent conflict with society. Physical aggression, stealing, drug abuse, and sexual behavior are common among children with conduct disorders.

14. Substance abuse is more frequent among adolescents than younger children. Adolescents are most likely to abuse alcohol and marijuana. Substance abuse is a pattern of usage that is characterized by impaired functioning and problems with self-control. Substance dependence is more severe and is characterized by tolerance or an abstinence syndrome (a pattern of withdrawal symptoms). Children and adolescents try and use drugs because of curiosity, modeling, peer pressure, self-handicapping, and the effects of the drugs themselves. Genetic factors may predispose some youngsters toward abusing certain drugs.

15. A number of anxiety disorders affect children. Children with an avoidant disorder show persistent and excessive avoidance of contact with strangers. Overanxious children seem generally worried and fretful. They tend to worry about their performance and competence, need excessive reassurance, and frequently develop anxiety-related physical symptoms.

16. Childhood depression is characterized by feelings of sadness and hopelessness, low self-esteem, social withdrawal, and inactivity. However, some "symptoms" are said to be able to "mask" depression. These include conduct disorders and hyperactivity. Depression may stem from lack of competence, a self-defeating attributional style, and, possibly, neurological factors.

T R U T H ▸ O R ▸ F I C T I O N ▸ R E V I S I T E D

Most children outgrow "baby fat." False. Obese children run a high risk of becoming obese adults.

Children who watch a great deal of television are more likely to be obese than children who do not. True. Watching television is a sedentary activity. Children also tend to snack while they watch.

Anoretic girls eat a great deal, but have trouble keeping weight on. False. They eat dangerously little, apparently because of excessive fear of putting on weight.

▶ /▶ ▶ ▶

Some college women control their weight by going on cycles of binge eating followed by vomiting. True.

The average U.S. college woman believes she is overweight. True. Unrealistic slenderness is valued as the ideal in U.S. society.

Sleepwalkers become violently agitated if they are awakened during an episode. False. They may be disoriented and confused, but violence is very rare.

There is no way of predicting who will be struck by sudden infant death syndrome. False. The exact causes of the disorder are unknown, but several risk factors have been identified.

It is normal for children who have gained bladder control to continue to have "accidents" at night for a year or more. True.

Boys are more likely than girls to wet their beds. True. Boys are also more likely to soil.

Autistic children are highly intelligent. False. However, they frequently have an "intelligent look" about them.

Many hyperactive children have been calmed down by stimulants. True. The stimulants apparently help the cortex inhibit the activity of more primitive areas of the nervous system.

Schizophrenic children are likely to become schizophrenic adults. False. There is little continuity between childhood and adult schizophrenia.

Children who show conduct disorders at 8 to 10 are more likely to get divorces as adults than children who do not. True. There is continuity between misconduct as a child and a violent, irresponsible life style as an adult.

The drug most frequently abused by children is marijuana. False. It is alcohol.

Curiosity is the single most common reason that children give for trying drugs. True.

Headaches and nausea can be signs of anxiety in children. True. They can have the same meaning for adults.

Poor appetite is usually a sign of depression in children. Not necessarily. Poor appetite is a sign of depression in adults, but children may "normally" show disinterest in food at certain times during the developmental process. One must be aware of developmental norms before attributing behavior patterns to problems.

▶ ▶ ▶ ▶

G L O S S A R Y

Absolute finalism In cognitive-developmental theory, a type of precausal thinking in which effects are perceived as causes.

Abstinence syndrome A characteristic cluster of symptoms that results from sudden decrease in the level of usage of a substance.

Accommodation According to cognitive-developmental theory, the modification of existing schemes in order to allow the incorporation of new events or knowledge. See *Assimilation.*

Acculturation The process by which children adapt to the patterns or customs of the cultures in which they are reared.

Achievement That which is attained by one's efforts and presumed to be made possible by one's abilities. See *Aptitude, Intelligence.*

Acoustic code A code in which visual or other forms of sensory input are transformed into sounds that can be rehearsed in order to facilitate long-term storage.

Acquired immune deficiency syndrome A fatal, sexually transmitted disease that is caused by a virus and cripples the body's immune system, rendering the victim vulnerable to "opportunistic" diseases. Abbreviated *AIDS.*

Acting out Expressing primitive impulses that are normally inhibited.

Active As a developmental concept, influencing or acting upon the environment.

ADD See *Attention deficit disorder.*

Adipose tissue Fat.

Adolescence The stage of development bounded by the advent of puberty at the lower end and the capacity to assume adult responsibilities at the upper end.

Adrenalin A hormone that generally arouses the body, increasing the heart and respiration rates. Also called *epinephrine.*

Affect The expressed emotions.

Affectional dependence Dependence on others to meet one's emotional, affectional needs.

Age of viability The age at which a fetus can sustain independent life.

AIDS See *Acquired immune deficiency syndrome.*

Allele A member of a pair of genes.

Alphafetoprotein assay A blood test that assesses maternal blood level of alphafetoprotein, a substance that is linked with neural-tube defects in the fetus.

Altruism Unselfish concern for the welfare of others that is usually characterized by helping behavior.

Amenorrhea Lack of menstruation.

American Sign Language The communication of meaning through forming symbols by means of movements and gestures, primarily of the hands and arms. Abbreviated *ASL.*

Amniocentesis A procedure for drawing and examining fetal cells sloughed off into amniotic fluid in order to determine the presence of various disorders in the fetus.

Amniotic fluid Fluid within the amniotic sac that suspends and protects the fetus.

Amniotic sac The sac containing the fetus.

Amphetamine A kind of stimulant drug.

Amplitude Height. The higher the amplitude of sound waves, the louder they are.

Anal-expulsive In psychoanalytic theory, descriptive of traits and behavior patterns characterized by unregulated self-expression, such as messiness.

Analogous organs Male and female organs that are similar in function, such as the testes and the ovaries.

Anal-retentive In psychoanalytic theory, descriptive of traits and behavior patterns characterized by expression of self-control, or "holding in."

▶ ▶ ▶ ▶

Anal stage The second stage of psychosexual development in psychoanalytic theory, during which gratification is hypothesized to be attained primarily by means of anal activities, such as the elimination or holding in of wastes.

Androgenital syndrome A form of pseudohermaphroditism in which a genetic female is masculinized because of prenatal exposure to androgens.

Androgens Male sex hormones.

Anesthetics Agents that produce partial or total loss of the sense of pain. See *General anesthesia, Local anesthesia.*

Animism In cognitive-developmental theory, the attribution of life and intentionality as a way of explaining the behavior of inanimate objects. Characteristic of preoperational thought.

Anorexia nervosa An eating disorder most prevalent among adolescent females and characterized by irrational fear of obesity, distorted body image, and severe weight loss.

Anoxia Oxygen deprivation.

Antisocial personality The American Psychiatric Association (1980) diagnosis given a person who is in frequent conflict with society but is undeterred by punishment and experiences little or no feelings of guilt and anxiety. Also referred to as *sociopathy.*

Aphasia A disruption in the ability to understand or produce language.

Apnea Temporary suspension of breathing.

Aptitude An ability or talent to succeed in an area in which one has not yet received training.

Artificial insemination Use of instruments to inject sperm into the uterus in order to fertilize an ovum.

Artificialism In cognitive-developmental theory, the belief that natural environmental features were made by people. A type of preoperational thought.

ASL See *American Sign Language.*

Assertive behavior Behavior that is characterized by requesting one's rights and expressing one's feelings but not by aggression (attack, threats, or insults).

Assimilation According to cognitive-developmental theory, the incorporation of new events or knowledge into existing schemes. See *Accommodation.*

Associative play Play with other children in which toys are shared and the company is enjoyed. However, there is no common goal or division of labor.

Astigmatism A visual disorder caused by abnormal curvature of the lens, so that images are indistinct or distorted.

Asynchronous growth Imbalanced growth, such as that which occurs during the early part of adolescence and causes many adolescents to appear "gawky."

Atrophy Wither away.

Attachment According to Ainsworth, the "affectional tie that one person or animal forms between himself and another . . . that binds them together in space and endures over time."

Attachment-in-the-making phase The second phase in the development of attachment, which occurs at 3 or 4 months of age and is characterized by preference for familiar figures.

Attention deficit disorder A behavior disorder characterized by lack of attention and impulsiveness, and frequently associated with hyperactivity. Abbreviated *ADD* (or *ADD-H,* when associated with hyperactivity).

Attributional style The way in which one is disposed toward interpreting failures or shortcomings, as in tending to place blame on oneself or on external factors.

Authoritarian style A child-rearing style in which parents demand obedience for its own sake from their children.

Authoritative style A child-rearing style in which parents are restrictive and demanding but also communicative and warm.

Autism Self-absorption or fantasy as a means of avoiding contact with others. See *Infantile autism.*

Autonomous morality The second stage in Piaget's congitive-developmental theory of moral development. In this stage, children base moral judgments on concepts such as reciprocity and the intentions of the wrongdoer as well as on the amount of damage done.

Autonomy Self-direction; independence.

Autosome Either member of a pair of chromosomes (with the exception of sex chromosomes).

Autostimulation theory The view that REM sleep in infants fosters the development of the brain by stimulating neural activity.

Avoidance learning A kind of learning in which organisms learn to engage in responses that avert aversive (painful) stimulation.

Avoidant attachment A type of insecure attachment characterized by apparent indifference to the leave-takings of, and reunions with, an attachment figure.

Avoidant disorder A behavior disorder characterized by persistent avoidance of strangers and peers such that social functioning is impaired.

Axillary Of the underarm, as in axillary hair or axillary odor.

Axon A long, slender part of a neuron that transmits impulses or messages to other neurons through small branching stuctures called axon terminals.

Babbling The child's first vocalizations that have the sound of speech.

Babinski reflex A reflex in which infants fan their toes in response to stroking the undersides of their feet.

▶ ▶ ▶ ▶

Babkin reflex A reflex that occurs when infants lie on their backs. In this position, infants will open their mouths and attempt to lift their heads in response to pressure against the palms of their hands.

Baby biography A meticulous account of the development of a baby, attending to the sequences and timing of changes.

Bed-wetting Failure to control the bladder during the night, resulting in urination while in bed.

Behavior disorders Behavior problems characterized by one or more of the following: low frequency; social unacceptability; faulty perception or interpretation of reality; personal distress; self-defeating behavior; dangerous behavior.

Behaviorism The school of psychology founded by John B. Watson that focuses on observable behavior and investigates relationships between stimuli and responses.

Behavior modification The systematic application of principles of learning to the reversal or amelioration of behavior problems.

Bilingual Using or capable of using two languages with equal or nearly equal facility.

Bilingual education A method of instruction which uses both the language that the child has learned in the home and the language of the mainstream culture.

Binocular cue for depth A cue for the perception of depth that involves the simultaneous use of both eyes. See *Monocular cue.*

Blastocyst A stage within the germinal stage of prenatal development, when the embryo has the form of a sphere of cells surrounding a cavity of fluid.

Bonding The process of forming bonds of attachment between children and parents.

Braxton-Hicks contractions The first contractions of childbirth, which are usually painless.

Breech position A problematic feet-downward position for childbirth in which the fetus's backside first enters the birth canal.

Broca's aphasia A type of aphasia caused by damage to Broca's area of the cerebral cortex and characterized by slow, laborious speech.

Bulimia An eating disorder most prevalent among women and characterized by cycles of binge eating and vomiting as a means of controlling weight gains.

CA See *Chronological age.*

Caesarean section A method of childbirth in which the fetus is delivered through a surgical incision in the abdomen.

Calcification The process by which bones become harder and denser as a result of the depositing of calcium in the form of lime salts.

Canalization The tendency of growth rates to return to genetically determined patterns after they have undergone environmentally induced changes.

Carrier A person who carries and transmits genetic (or other) abnormalities, but who does not show them himself or herself.

Cartilage A tough, elastic tissue that mostly turns to bone as the child matures, as in the case of cartilage found in the skull of the neonate.

Case study A carefully drawn biography of the life of an individual or of the lives of a small group of individuals that seeks to discover influences on behavior and development.

Castration Removal of the testes, which prevents production of sperm and the hormone testosterone.

Caucasian Descriptive of people whose ancestors came from Europe, North Africa, and the Middle East to North India. Usually referred to as "white people."

Center A term used in cognitive-developmental theory, meaning "to focus" one's attention. See *Decentration.*

Center day care Day care in a communal public or private setting.

Cephalocaudal development One of the principles of development, according to which development proceeds from the upper part (head) of the child to the lower extremities.

Cerebellum A structure of the hindbrain that consists of two hemispheres and is involved in muscle coordination and balance.

Cerebral cortex The wrinkled surface area of the brain, which makes possible the functions of thought and language.

Cerebrum The large mass of the forebrain, which consists of two hemispheres.

Cesarean section An alternate spelling for *Caesarean section.*

Child A person undergoing the period of development from infancy through puberty.

Childhood schizophrenia A pervasive developmental disoder characterized by significant declines in reality testng and social adjustment and by onset after the age of 30 months.

Chorionic villi sampling A method for the prenatal detection of genetic abnormalities that samples tissue from the membrane that envelops the amniotic sac and fetus.

Chromosome A rodlike structure composed of genes that is found within the nuclei of cells.

Chronological age A child's age in years and months, which was historically compared to his or her mental age score on the Stanford-Binet Intelligence Scale in order to derive an IQ score. Abbreviated *CA.*

Classical conditioning A simple form of learning in which a previously neutral stimulus comes to elicit the response usually brought forth by a second stimulus by being paired repeatedly with the second stimulus.

▶ ▶ ▶ ▶

Clear-cut-attachment phase The third phase in the development of attachment, which occurs at 6 or 7 months and is characterized by intensified dependence on the primary caregiver.

Clique A small group of friends who share activities and confidences.

Clitoris A female sex organ that is highly sensitive to sexual stimulation but not directly involved in reproduction.

Cognitive Concerning mental activities and functions, such as thought, language, intelligence, dreams, and fantasies.

Cognitive-developmental theory A stage theory of development that views the child as active and holds that children's abilities to represent the world mentally and to solve problems unfold as a result of the interaction between the maturation of neurological structures and experience.

Cohort effect Similarities in behavior and development among a group of peers that stem from the fact that they are of approximately the same age. (A confounding effect in *Cross-sectional research*.)

Colic A digestive disorder in young infants which results in painful gas, irritability, and crying. Colic usually comes to an end at about 6 months as the digestive system matures.

Componential level In triarchic theory, the level of intelligence that consists of metacomponents, performance components, and knowledge acquisition components.

Conception The process by which a sperm cell joins with an ovum to begin a new life.

Concordance Agreement.

Concrete operations The third stage in Piaget's cognitive-developmental theory, characterized by flexible, reversible operations concerning concrete (as opposed to abstract) objects and events.

Conditioned response A learned response to a previously neutral (conditioned) stimulus. Abbreviated *CR*.

Conditioned stimulus A previously neutral stimulus that elicits a (conditioned) response, because it has been paired repeatedly with another stimulus that already brought forth that response. Abbreviated *CS*.

Conditioning A simple form of learning in which stimuli and responses are associated. See *Classical conditioning* and *Operant conditioning*.

Conduct disorders Disorders marked by persistent breaking of the rules and violations of the rights of others.

Cones Cone-shaped receptors for light that transmit sensations of color.

Congenital Present at birth. Usually used as descriptive of children's disorders that can be attributed to conditions in the prenatal environment.

Conscious Self-aware.

Conservation In cognitive-developmental theory, a type of operational thought in which it is recognized that basic properties of substances such as mass and weight remain the same (are conserved), even though superficial characteristics such as their shapes or arrangement are changed. For example, in conservation of mass it is recognized that the mass of a ball of clay is conserved, even when the ball of clay is flattened.

Construct (CON-struct). A concept or theory designed to integrate strands of information. "Intelligence" and "language acquisition device" are examples of constructs.

Contact comfort (1) The pleasure derived from physical contact with another. (2) According to Harlow, a need or drive for physical contact with another that provides a basis for the formation of bonds of attachment.

Contextual level In triarchic theory, those aspects of intelligent behavior that permit people to adjust to their environments or to seek or create new environments.

Continuous reinforcement Reinforcement of every correct response. See *Intermittent reinforcement*.

Control subjects Participants in an experiment who do not receive the experimental treatment, but for whom all other conditions are comparable to those of experimental subjects. See *Experimental subjects*.

Conventional level According to Kohlberg, a period during which moral judgments largely reflect social rules and conventions. A "law-and-order" approach to morality.

Convergence In visual perception, a binocular cue for depth that occurs because the eyes move inward as they focus on an object that is drawing nearer.

Convergent thinking A thought process that attempts to narrow in on the single best solution to a problem. See *Divergent thinking*.

Cooing Prelinguistic, articulated vowel-like sounds that appear to express feelings of positive excitement among young infants.

Cooperative play Organized play in which children cooperate to meet common goals. There is division of labor, and children take on specific goals as group members.

Corpus callosum The thick bundle of nerve fibers that connects the left and right hemispheres of the brain.

Correlated Associated; linked.

Correlation coefficient A number derived by statistical techniques that indicates the direction (positive or negative) and the strength of the relationship between two variables.

CR See *Conditioned response*.

Cranium The skull—the bones forming the enclosure of the brain.

Creativity The ability to generate novel solutions to problems. A trait

▶ ▶ ▶ ▶

characterized by flexibility, ingenuity, and originality.

Crib death   See *Sudden infant death syndrome.*

Critical period   (1) A period of time during which a developing organism is particularly sensitive to certain sources of stimulation. For example, there are critical periods during which the embryo is especially vulnerable to certain teratogens. (2) In ethological theory, a period of development during which a releasing stimulus can elicit a fixed action pattern. For example, there is a critical period following hatching when ducklings and goslings form attachments by following a moving stimulus. See *Sensitive period.*

Cross-cultural   With or of another culture.

Cross-sectional research   A method of investigating developmental processes in which measures are taken of children of different age groups. It may be assumed that these measures reflect changes that might occur in the same children as they develop. See *Longitudinal research.*

Cross-sequential research   A method of investigating development that combines the longitudinal and cross-sectional methods. Individuals of different age groups are followed for abbreviated periods of time in an effort to discover longitudinal trends but to avoid some of the confounding that is introduced by cohort effects.

Cross-species   With or of another species.

Crowd   A loosely organized group of children who share interests and activities.

Cryptochidism   The disorder defined by undescended testes.

Crystallized intelligence   Cattel and Horn's view of those intellectual functions which depend on education and cultural influences and which may thus show growth over a lifetime. See *Fluid intelligence.*

CS   See *Conditioned stimulus.*

C-section   See *Caesarean section.*

Cultural bias   A factor hypothesized to be present in intelligence tests that provides an advantage for test-takers from certain cultural or ethnic backgrounds but does not reflect true intelligence.

Cultural-familial retardation   Substandard intellectual performance that is presumed to stem from lack of opportunity to acquire knowledge and strategies for solving problems considered important within a cultural setting.

Culture-free   Descriptive of a test in which cultural biases have been removed. On such a test, test-takers from different cultural backgrounds would have an equal opportunity to earn scores that reflect their true abilities.

Debriefing   Receiving information about a just-completed research procedure in an effort to mitigate possible harmful effects of that procedure.

Decentration   In cognitive-developmental theory, simultaneous focusing (centering) on more than one aspect or dimension of a problem, such that flexible, reversible thought is possible. See *Center.*

Deciduous   Falling off or out at a certain stage of growth, as in the case of ''baby teeth.''

Deep structure   The underlying meaning of a sentence, e.g., as determined by the context of the sentence as well as word order. See *Surface structure.*

Defense mechanism   In psychoanalytic theory, an unconscious function of the ego that protects the ego from anxiety-evoking ideas by distorting them or ejecting them from consciousness.

Deferred imitation   The imitation of people and events that have occurred in the past (perhaps hours or days past). Deferred imitation suggests that the behavior patterns being imitated have been mentally represented.

Delusions   Firmly held beliefs that are inconsistent with reality. Symptoms of a thought disorder.

Demand characteristics   the demands made on a subject by a specific experimental approach or task. The implication is that the theoretical inferences drawn from the study might have been different if tasks with different demand characteristics had been used.

Demographic variables   Variables concerning vital statistics, such as place of birth and ethnic background.

Dendrite   A rootlike part of a neuron which receives impulses or messages from other neurons.

Deoxyribonucleic acid   Genetic material found in the nuclei of cells that takes the form of a double helix composed of phosphates, sugars, and bases. Abbreviated *DNA.*

Dependent variable   A measure of an assumed effect of an independent variable. See *Independent variable.*

DES   See *Diethylstilbestrol.*

Desensitization   A process in which one loses irrational fear of anxiety-evoking objects by gradually approaching them in fantasy or in real life.

Determinants   Factors that define or set limits, such as the determinants of intelligence.

Development   The processes by which organisms unfold features and traits, grow, and become more complex and specialized in structure and function.

Deviation IQ   A score on an intelligence test derived from comparing an individual's performance to norms for his or her peers. See *Ratio IQ.*

Dialect   The variety of a spoken language particular to a region, community, or social group. Dialects tend to be understandable to persons who speak another dialect of

▶ ▶ ▶ ▶

the language without special training, whereas other languages are not.

Diethylstilbestrol A powerful estrogen that was prescribed for women threatening miscarriage, but which has been linked to cancer in the reproductive organs of their children. Abbreviated *DES*.

Differentiation The processes by which physical structures and behavior patterns become more specialized as they develop.

Dilate Make wider or larger.

Discrepancy hypothesis The view that children (and adults) prefer stimuli that are moderately different from stimuli to which they have bcome habituated, or accustomed.

Discrete Separate and distinct; made up of distinct parts.

Disinhibition In social-learning theory, stimulation of a response that has been suppressed by showing a model engaging in that response without aversive consequences.

Displacement (1) In language development, the quality of language which permits one to communicate information about objects and events in another time and place. (2) In psychoanalytic theory, a defense mechanism in which ideas or impulses are transferred from threatening or unsuitable objects onto less threatening objects.

Divergent thinking A thought process that attempts to generate multiple solutions to problems. Free and fluent associations to the elements of a problem. See *Convergent thinking*.

Dizygotic twins Twins that derive from two zygotes and are thus related as other siblings. Fraternal twins. Abbreviated *DZ twins*. See *Monozygotic twins*.

DNA See *Deoxyribonucleic acid*.

Dominance Control or authority over others.

Dominant trait A trait that is expressed. See *Recessive trait*.

Dopamine A neurotransmitter that is implicated in schizophrenia.

Down syndrome A chromosomal abnormality characterized by mental retardation and caused by an extra chromosome in the twenty-first pair.

Dramatic play Play in which children enact social roles as made possible by the attainment of symbolic thought. Also referred to as *pretend play*, signifying an element of fantasy in which children may pretend that objects and toys are other than what they are.

Dyslexia A reading disorder characterized by problems such as letter reversals, mirror reading, slow reading, and reduced comprehension.

DZ twins See *Dizygotic twins*.

Echolalia Automatic repetition of sounds or words.

Ecological theory Urie Bronfenbrenner's approach to understanding child development, which focuses on the reciprocal influences among children and the settings which comprise their environment.

Ecology A field of biology that investigates the relationships between living organisms and their environments.

Ectoderm The outermost cell layer of the newly formed embryo, from which the skin and nervous system develop.

Edema Swelling.

EEG See *Electroencephalograph*.

Efface Rub out or wipe out; become thin.

Ego According to psychoanalytic theory, the psychic structure which develops following the id. The ego is characterized by self-awareness, planning, and delay of gratification.

Egocentrism Assumption that others view the world as one does oneself; inability to take the vantage point of others. In cognitive-developmental theory, hypothesized to be characteristic of preoperational thought.

Ego identity According to Erik Erikson, one's sense of who one is and what one stands for.

Elaborative rehearsal A strategy for increasing retention of new information by relating it to well-known information.

Electra complex A conflict of the phallic stage of psychosexual development in psychoanalytic theory, in which the girl longs for her father and resents her mother.

Electroencephalograph An instrument that measures electrical activity of the brain. Abbreviated *EEG*.

Elicit Bring forth; evoke.

Embryonic disk The platelike inner part of the blastocyst which differentiates into the ectoderm, mesoderm, and endoderm of the embryo.

Embryonic stage The stage of prenatal development that lasts from implantation through the eighth week, and which is characterized by the differentiation of the major organ systems.

Embryonic transfer The transfer of a 5-day-old embryo from the uterus of the woman who conceived it to the uterus of another woman, where it will become implanted and develop to term.

Emotion A feeling state that has physiological, situational, and cognitive components.

Empathy The ability to share another person's feelings or emotions.

Empirical Based on observation and experimentation.

Empiricism The view that experience determines the ways in which children perceive the world. Contrast with *Nativism*.

Enactive mode Bruner's term for the cognitive style in which representation is by means of action.

Encoding The transformation of sensory input into a form that is more readily processed.

▶ ▶ ▶ ▶

Encopresis Failure to control the bowels once the normal age for bowel control has been reached. Also called *soiling*.

Endoderm The inner layer of the newly formed embryo, from which the lungs and digestive system develop.

Endometriosis A condition caused by inflammation of endometrial tissue that is sloughed off into the abdominal cavity rather than out of the body during menstruation and characterized by abdominal pain and, sometimes, infertility.

Endometrium The inner lining of the uterus which is normally sloughed off during menstruation.

Enuresis Lack of bladder control at an age by which control is usually attained.

Epinephrine See *Adrenalin*.

Epiphyseal closure The process by which the cartilage that separates the long end (epiphysis) of a bone from the main part of the bone turns to bone, thus preventing further gains in length.

Episiotomy A surgical incision in the perineum that widens the birth canal, preventing random tearing during childbirth.

Equilibration In cognitive-developmental theory, the creation of a balance between assimilation and accommodation, thereby facilitating acquisition of knowledge.

Erogenous zone An area of the body that is sensitive to sexual sensations.

Eros In psychoanalytic theory, the basic instinct to preserve and perpetuate life.

Estrus The periodic sexual excitement of many female mammals, during which they are receptive to advances by males.

Ethical Moral; of a system of morals.

Ethologist A scientist who studies the behavior patterns characteristic of various species.

Exceptional children Children whose emotional, intellectual, or physical traits differ significantly from those of the great majority of children.

Executive dependence Dependence on others to execute actions that meet one's physical needs.

Executive independence Ability to execute actions that meet one's own physical needs.

Exosystem In ecological theory, community institutions and settings that indirectly influence the child, such as the school board and the parents' workplaces.

Experiential level In triarchic theory, those aspects of intelligence that permit people to become increasingly efficient in coping with novel situations and processing information.

Experiment A method of scientific investigation that seeks to discover cause-and-effect relationships by introducing independent variables and observing their effects on dependent variables.

Experimental subjects (1) Subjects receiving a treatment in an experiment. (2) More generally, participants in an experiment. See *Control subjects*.

Expressive language style The child's use of language primarily as a means for engaging in social interaction. See *Referential language style*.

Expressive vocabulary The sum total of words that one can use in the production of language. See *Receptive vocabulary*.

External locus of control A personality trait in which the person perceives the power to grant reinforcements as being largely outside the self. See *Internal locus of control*.

Extinction (1) In classical conditioning, repeated presentation of the CS in the absence of the US, leading to inhibition of the CR in response to the CS. (2) In operant conditioning, repeated performance of a learned response in the absence of reinforcement, leading to inhibition of that response.

Extraversion A personality trait characterized by sociability and impulsiveness. See *Introversion*.

Factor A condition or quality that brings about a result. A cluster of related items, such as those found on an intelligence or personality test.

Factor analysis A statistical technique that allows researchers to determine the relationships among large numbers of items, such as those found on intelligence or personality tests.

Fallopian tube A strawlike tube in the woman's abdomen that conducts ova from an ovary to the uterus.

Family therapy A form of therapy in which the family unit is treated and family members are taught to relate to one another more productively.

FAP See *Fixed action pattern*.

FAS See *Fetal alcohol syndrome*. (In future years, *FAS* may also stand for "Fetal AIDS Syndrome.")

Fat cells Cells that store adipose tissue, or fat.

Fetal alcohol syndrome A cluster of symptoms, including mental retardation and characteristic facial features, found among babies of women who drink alcohol during pregnancy. Abbreviated *FAS*.

Fetal monitoring The use of instruments to track the heart rate and oxygen levels of the fetus during childbirth.

Fetal stage The stage of development that lasts from the beginning of the ninth week of pregnancy through birth and is characterized by gains in size and weight and the maturation of organ systems that were given their basic form during the embryonic stage.

▶ ▶ ▶ ▶

Fetoscopy Surgical insertion of a narrow tube into the uterus in order to examine the fetus.

Fetus The unborn child from the beginning of the ninth week of pregnancy through birth.

Field study A method of scientific observation in which subjects are carefully observed in their natural environments.

Fine-motor skills Skills involving use of the small muscles, such as those in the fingers.

Fixation In psychoanalytic theory, arrested psychosexual development. Attachment to objects characteristic of a certain stage, when one's development should have progressed such that one is attached to objects characteristic of a more advanced stage.

Fixed action pattern An instinct. A stereotyped form of behavior that is characteristic of a species and triggered by a releasing stimulus. Abbreviated *FAP*.

Fluid intelligence Cattell and Horn's term for those intellectual functions which are based primarily on the unfolding of neurological structures, account for incidental learning, and tend to peak at about adolescence. See *Crystallized intelligence*.

Fluoridation The process of adding fluorides (fluorine compounds) to drinking water in order to decrease the incidence of cavities in the teeth.

Fontanel A soft membraneous area found between the skull bones of an infant and eventually filled in with bone.

Forceps A curved instrument that fits around the head of the baby and permits it to be pulled through the birth canal as a way of facilitating childbirth.

Formal operations The fourth stage in Piaget's cognitive-developmental theory, characterized by the capacity for flexible, reversible operations concerning abstract ideas and con-cepts, such as symbols, statements, and theories.

g Spearman's term for general intelligence—a general factor that he believed underlies more specific abilities. See *s*.

Galvanic skin response A measure of anxiety based on the amount of electricity conducted by the sweat in the palm of the hand. Abbreviated *GSR*.

Gender constancy The third stage in the cognitive-developmental theory of the assumption of sex roles: the concept that one's gender remains the same despite superficial changes in appearance or behavior.

Gender identity One's concept of being male or female. The first stage in the cognitive-developmental theory of the assumption of sex roles.

Gender schema The distribution of behavior patterns that are considered appropriate for males and females within a cultural setting.

Gender schema theory A cognitive theory of sex typing which holds that one's gender identity and knowledge of the gender schema in one's society stimulates and guides one's assumption of sex-typed preferences and behavior patterns.

Gender stability The second stage in the cognitive-developmental theory of the assumption of sex roles: the concept that one's gender is a permanent feature.

Gene The basic unit of heredity. Genes are composed of deoxyribonucleic acid (DNA). See *Chromosome*.

General anesthesia The process of eliminating pain by putting people to sleep, such as during childbirth. See *Local anesthesia*.

Genetic counseling Advice concerning the probabilities that a couple's children will show genetic abnormalities.

Genital stage The fifth and final stage of psychosexual development in psychoanalytic theory, characterized by the preferred expression of libidinal energy by means of sexual intercourse with an adult of the opposite sex.

Genotype The genetic form or constitution of an organism as determined by heredity. See *Phenotype*.

Gentle childbirth See *Leboyer method*.

German measles See *Rubella*.

Germ cells Ova and sperm. The cells from which organisms develop.

Germinal stage The period of development between conception and the implantation of the embryo in the uterine wall. Also called *Period of the ovum*.

Gestation period The period of carrying young from conception to birth.

Glial cells Cells that perform "housekeeping" chores for neurons and also form myelin to insulate the axons of neurons from bodily fluids and thereby facilitate the conduction of "messages."

Gonads Organs—testes and ovaries—that produce reproductive cells.

Grasping reflex See *Palmar reflex*.

Growth The processes by which organisms increase (and eventually decrease) in size, weight, power, and other traits as development progresses.

Growth hormone A hormone secreted by the pituitary gland that regulates growth.

Growth spurt A period during which growth advances at a dramatically rapid rate as compared to other periods.

GSR See *Galvanic skin response*.

Gynecomastia Temporary enlargement of the breasts in adolescent males.

Habituation Adaptation to repetitious stimuli, such that response is discontinued.

Hallucinations Perceptions in the absence of sensation, such as "seeing" or "hearing things." Frequently a symptom of a thought disorder or of substance abuse.

► ► ► ►

Hallucinogenics   Drugs that give rise to hallucinations.

Handedness   The tendency to prefer the left or right hand in writing and in other manual tasks.

Haptic   Of the sense of touch; tactile.

Head Start   A type of program intended for disadvantaged preschoolers which provided training in the intellectual and social skills that are considered essential to success in kindergarten and primary grades.

Hemophilia   A genetic disorder in which the blood does not clot properly.

Heredity   The transmission of traits and characteristics from parent to child by means of genes.

Hermaphrodite   A person born with both ovarian and testicular tissue.

Heterozygous   Having two different alleles for a trait, as in showing brown eyes although one also has recessive blue alleles in the nuclei of one's cells. See *Homozygous*.

Hindbrain   The back part of the brain, containing the medulla, pons, and cerebellum.

Holophrase   A single word used by a child to express complex meanings. An example of *Telegraphic speech*.

Homologous organs   Male and female organs that are similar in structure, such as the head of the penis and the head of the clitoris.

Homozygous   Having two identical alleles for a trait, as in showing brown eyes and *not* having recessive blue alleles in the nuclei of one's cells. See *Heterozygous*.

Horizontal décalage   The sequential unfolding of the ability to master different kinds of cognitive tasks within the same stage. For example, children do not master all kinds of conservation tasks simultaneously, but rather, master them in an orderly sequence.

Hue   Color.

Huntington's chorea   A fatal genetic neurological disorder whose onset is in middle age.

Hyaluronidase   An enzyme that promotes the penetration of sperm through the wall of the ovum.

Hyperactivity   A behavior disorder of childhood characterized by excessive restlessness, low tolerance for frustration, and short attention span. Not to be confused with misbehavior or with normal high activity levels that occur during childhood. Technically termed *Attention Deficit Disorder with Hyperactivity (ADD-H)*.

Hypothalamus   A pea-sized structure which is located above the pituitary gland in the brain and is involved in the regulation of body temperature, motivation (e.g., hunger, thirst, sex), and emotion.

Hypothesis   An assumption about behavior that is tested by empirical research.

Iconic mode   Bruner's term for the cognitive style in which representation is by means of visual mental images.

Id   In psychoanalytic theory, the psychic structure that is theorized to be present at birth, unconscious, and representative of physiological drives.

Identification   A process in which one person becomes like another through broad imitation and assumption of the second person's personality traits. In psychoanalytic theory, identification is viewed as defensive and partly unconscious. In social-learning theory, the focus is on the role of observational learning.

Identity crisis   According to Erik Erikson, a period of inner conflict during which one examines one's values and makes decisions about life roles.

Immanent justice   The view that retribution for wrongdoing is a direct consequence of wrongdoing, reflective of the belief that morality is embedded within the structure of the universe.

Imprinting   The process by which some animals exhibit the fixed action pattern (FAP) of attachment in response to a releasing stimulus. This FAP occurs during a critical period and is difficult to modify.

Incubator   A heated, protective container for premature babies.

Independent variable   In a scientific study, a condition that is manipulated (changed) so that its effect may be observed. See *Dependent variable*.

Indiscriminate attachment   The showing of attachment behaviors toward any person.

Inductive disciplinary method   A method for restricting behavior, such as reasoning, that attempts to foster understanding of the principles underlying parental demands.

Infancy   Babyhood. The period of very early childhood, characterized by lack of speech. The first two years after birth.

Infanticide   The practice of killing babies.

Infantile autism   A pervasive developmental disorder of childhood characterized by extreme aloneness, communication problems, preservation of sameness, and ritualistic behavior.

Inflection   A grammatical marker that changes the form of words to indicate grammatical relationships such as number (singular or plural) and tense (e.g., past or present).

Information-processing theory   The view in which cognitive processes are compared to the functions of computers. The theory deals with the input, storage, retrieval, manipulation, and output of information, and the focus is on the development of children's strategies for solving problems—their "mental programs."

► ► ► ►

Inguinal canal A fetal canal that allows the testes to descend into the scrotum.

Inguinal hernia The disorder in which intestinal loops enter the scrotum through the inguinal canal.

Initial-preattachment phase The first phase in the forming of bonds of attachment, which lasts from birth to about 3 months of age and is characterized by indiscriminate attachment.

Inner speech Vygotsky's concept of the ultimate binding of language and thought. Inner speech originates in vocalizations that regulate the child's behavior and become internalized by 6 or 7.

Insomnia One or more of a number of sleep problems, including difficulty falling asleep, difficulty remaining asleep, and waking early.

Instinct An inborn tendency to behave in a way that is characteristic of one's species.

Instrumental competence The capacity to manipulate the environment to achieve desired ends.

Intelligence A complex and controversial concept defined by David Wechsler as the ''capacity . . . to understand the word [and the] resourcefulness to cope with its challenges.'' Intelligence implies learning ability and the capacity to make the right choice in a given academic or social situation.

Intelligence quotient A score on an intelligence test. Abbreviated *IQ*. See *Ratio IQ* and *Deviation IQ*.

Intensity The strength of a stimulus, as the brightness of a light.

Intermittent reinforcement Reinforcement of some but not all correct responses, accomplished by varying the number of correct responses required or the amount of time that must elapse following a correct response before reinforcement is made available. Contrast with *Continuous reinforcement*.

Internal locus of control A personality trait in which the person perceives the power to attain reinforcements as being largely within the self. See *External locus of control*.

Intonation In language, the use of pitches of varying levels to help communicate meaning.

Intoxication Drunkenness.

Intuition Direct knowledge or learning without conscious use of reason.

In vitro fertilization Fertilization of an ovum in a laboratory dish.

IQ See *Intelligence quotient*.

Jaundice A condition in which the skin becomes abnormally yellowed because of bile pigments in the blood.

Kibbutz An Israeli farming community in which children are reared in group settings.

Klinefelter's syndrome A chromosomal disorder found among males that is caused by an extra X sex chromosome and characterized by infertility and mild mental retardation.

Knowledge acquisition components In triarchic theory, those aspects of intelligence that are applied in gaining knowledge, such as encoding and relating new knowledge to existing knowledge.

Labia The major and minor lips of the female's genitalia.

LAD See *Language acquisition device*.

Laissez-faire A French phrase translated as ''noninterfering.''

Lamaze method A childbirth method in which women learn about childbirth, learn to relax and to breathe in patterns that conserve energy and lessen pain, and have a coach (usually the father) present at childbirth. Also termed *Prepared childbirth*.

Language acquisition device In the psycholinguistic theory of language development, neural ''prewiring'' that facilitates the child's learning of grammar. Abbreviated *LAD*.

Lanugo Fine, downy hair that covers much of the body of the neonate, especially preterm babies.

Larynx The part of the throat that contains the vocal cords.

Latency stage The fourth stage of psychosexual development in psychoanalytic theory, characterized by repression of sexual impulses.

Latent Hidden.

Leboyer method A childbirth method that focuses on gently easing the neonate into the world. Also termed *Gentle childbirth*.

Level of arousal The body's general level of activation or readiness for action.

Libido In psychoanalytic theory, the energy of eros; the sexual instinct.

Life crisis According to Erik Erikson, an internal conflict that characterizes each stage of psychosexual development. Generally positive resolution of life crises sets the stage for generally positive resolution of subsequent life crises.

Linguist A scientist who specializes in the structure, functions, and origins of language.

Local anesthesia The process of reducing pain in a specific area of the body, as during childbirth. See *General anesthesia*.

Locomotion Movement from one place to another.

Longitudinal research A method of investigating developmental processes in which repeated measures are taken of the same children at various times throughout their development. See *Cross-sectional research*.

Long-term memory The structure of memory capable of relatively permanent storage of information.

Loose associations A symptom of a thought disorder in which the individual has difficulty sticking to one topic or producing coherent speech.

Luteinizing hormone A hormone produced by the pituitary gland that causes ovulation.

▶ ▶ ▶ ▶

MA See *Mental age.*

Macrosystem In ecological theory, the basic institutions and ideologies that influence the child, such as U.S. ideals of freedom of expression and equality under the law.

Mainstreaming The practice of placing exceptional children in educational settings with nonexceptional children.

Mammary glands Glands that secrete milk.

Maternity blues A condition characterized by crying, sadness, anxiety and tension, irritability, and anger that afflicts half or more of women for a couple of days or so following childbirth. Not so severe as *Postpartum depression.*

Maturation The unfolding of genetically determined traits, structures, and functions.

Maturational theory Arnold Gesell's view which holds that development is self-regulated by the unfolding of natural plans (that is, heredity) and processes.

Mean length of utterance The average number of phonemes used in an utterance. A rough measure of the sophistication of the child's use of language.

Medulla oblongata An oblong-shaped structure of the hindbrain that is involved in heartbeat and respiration.

Meiosis The type of cell division in which germ cells are formed. Each pair of chromosomes in the parent cell splits apart, so that one member of each pair moves to each new cell. As a result, each new cell has 23 chromosomes. See *Mitosis.*

Memory The processes by which we store and retrieve information.

Menarche The onset of menstruation.

Mental age The accumulated "months" of credit that a child earns on the Stanford-Binet Intelligence Scale. Abbreviated *MA.*

Mesoderm The central layer of the embryo, from which the bones and muscles develop.

Mesosystem In ecological theory, the interlocking settings that influence the child, such as the interaction of the school and the larger community, when children are taken on field trips.

Metacognition Awareness and control of one's cognitive abilities as shown by the intentional use of cognitive strategies in solving problems.

Metacomponents In triarchic theory, components of intellectual functioning that are facilitated by self-awareness of intellectual processes.

Metamemory Knowledge of the functions and processes involved in one's storage and retrieval of information (memory) as shown by intentional use of cognitive strategies to retain information.

Metapelet A child-rearing professional in a kibbutz.

Metaphor A figure of speech that amplifies meaning and dramatizes description by adopting imagery from another situation.

Microsystem In ecological theory, the immediate settings with which the child interacts, such as the home, the school, and the maternity ward.

Midwife A woman (nonphysician) who is especially trained to help other women in childbirth.

Mitosis The form of cell division in which each chromosome splits lengthwise to double in number. Half of each chromosome then moves to each new cell, where it combines with chemicals in the cell fluid to retake its original form. See *Meiosis.*

Model In social-learning theory, a person who engages in behavior that is observed and imitated by another person.

Modifier genes Genes that alter the action of the phenotypical expression of other genes.

Monocular cue for depth A cue for depth that can be perceived by one eye. See *Binocular cue.*

Monozygotic twins Twins that derive from a single zygote which has divided into two separate zygotes and that thus carry the same genetic code. Identical twins. Abbreviated *MZ twins.* See *Dizygotic twins.*

Moral realism According to Piaget, the stage during which children judge acts as moral when they conform to authority or to the rules of the game. Morality in this stage is perceived as embedded in the structure of the universe from which the corollary of immanent justice is derived.

Moro reflex A reflex in which infants arch their backs and draw up their legs in response to a sudden change in position.

Morpheme The smallest unit of meaning in a language.

Motility Self-propulsion. A measure of the viability of sperm cells.

Motor cortex The section of the cerebral cortex that lies in the frontal lobe, just across the central fissure from the sensory cortex. Neural impulses in the motor cortex are linked to muscular responses throughout the body.

Motor development The development of the capacity for movement, particularly as made possible by maturation of the nervous system and muscles.

Müllerian ducts Embryonic structures that develop into fallopian tubes, uterus, and inner vagina in the female. See *Wolffian duct.*

Multifactorial problems Problems that stem from the interaction of heredity with environmental factors.

Multiple sclerosis A disease in which myelin is replaced by hard, fibrous tissue that impairs the conduction of neural impulses.

▶ ▶ ▶ ▶

Muscular dystrophy   A chronic disease characterized by progressive wasting away of the muscles.

Mutation   A sudden variation in an inheritable characteristic, as by an accident that affects the composition of genes.

Mutism   Inability or refusal to speak.

Myelination   The process by which axons of neurons are sheathed in myelin.

Myelin sheath   A fatty whitish substance formed by glial cells that encases and insulates the axons of neurons, permitting more rapid conduction of neural impulses.

MZ twins   See *Monozygotic twins*.

Nativism   The view that children have inborn predispositions to perceive the world in certain ways. See *Empiricism*.

Natural childbirth   Dick-Read's method of childbirth in which women use no anesthesia but are given other strategies for coping with discomfort and are educated about childbirth.

Naturalistic-observation method   A method of scientific observation in which subjects are carefully observed in their natural settings. Also referred to as the *field study*.

Nature   The processes within an organism that guide the organism to unfold structures and traits according to its genetic code. See *Nurture*.

Negative reinforcer   A reinforcer that, when removed, increases the frequency of a response. Pain and fear usually but not always function as negative reinforcers. Note that a negative reinforcer increases the frequency of a response, whereas punishment suppresses a response. See *Positive reinforcer*.

Neonate   A newborn child.

Nerve   A bundle of axons from many neurons.

Neural tube   A hollowed-out area in the blastocyst from which the nervous system will develop.

Neurological   Of the nervous system.

Neuron   A nerve cell.

Neuroticism   A personality trait characterized by anxiety and emotional instability.

Neurotransmitters   Chemical substances that transmit impulses (carry "messages") from one neuron to another.

Night terrors   Frightening dreamlike experiences that occur during the deepest stages of NREM sleep. Nightmares, by contrast, are dreams that occur during REM sleep. Also called *Sleep terrors*.

Nocturnal emission   Emission of seminal fluid in one's sleep.

Node of Ranvier   A noninsulated segment of an axon of a neuron that is elsewhere sheathed in myelin.

Nonconformist style   A child-rearing style in which parents are permissive because of an intellectual commitment to encouraging children to develop their own abilities and values.

Non-rapid-eye-movement sleep   Periods of sleep during which we are unlikely to dream. Abbreviated *NREM sleep*. See *Rapid-eye-movement sleep*.

Nonsocial play   Forms of play (such as solitary and onlooker play) in which play is not influenced by the play of nearby children.

Noradrenalin   See *Norepinephrine*.

Norepinephrine   A neurotransmitter that is implicated in depression. Also called *noradrenalin*.

Norms   Group averages or standards that indicate how children at a certain age level behave or are expected to behave.

NREM sleep   See *Non-rapid-eye-movement sleep*.

Number concept   In cognitive-developmental theory, recognition that the number of objects in an array remains the same, even if their arrangement is changed.

Nurture   The processes external to an organism that provide nourishment as it develops according to its genetic code or that cause it to swerve from its genetically programmed course. Environmental factors that influence development. See *Nature*.

Obesity   An eating disorder characterized by excessive accumulation of fat.

Object concept   Broad recognition that the existence of objects transcends the immediate sensory impressions made by them.

Object identity   Recognition that an object is the same object regardless of its setting or of superficial changes.

Objective morality   The perception of morality as objective, or as existing outside the cognitive functioning of people. A characteristic of Piaget's stage of moral realism.

Objective responsibility   Judging the wrongfulness of an act in terms of the amount of damage done instead of the intentions of the wrongdoer. See *Subjective responsibility*.

Object permanence   Recognition that objects continue to exist even when they are not sensed.

Observational learning   In social-learning theory, the acquisition of expectations and skills by observing others. As opposed to operant conditioning, in observational learning, skills can be acquired without being emitted and reinforced.

Oedipus complex   A conflict of the phallic stage of psychosexual development in psychoanalytic theory, in which the boy wishes to possess his mother sexually and perceives his father as a rival in love.

Onlooker play   Play during which children observe other children at play but do not enter into their play themselves.

Ontogeny recapitulates phylogeny   The nineteenth-century view that the development of the individual retraces the evolution of the species.

▶ ▶ ▶ ▶

Open education A relatively unstructured approach to education in which children are encouraged to explore actively a rich learning environment.

Operant conditioning A simple form of learning in which an organism learns to engage in behavior because it is reinforced. See *Classical conditioning*.

Operations In cognitive-developmental theory, flexible and reversible mental manipulations of objects such that objects can be mentally transformed and then returned to their original states. Planning a number of different moves in checkers or chess is an example.

Oral stage The first stage of psychosexual development in psychoanalytic theory, during which gratification is hypothesized to be attained primarily by means of oral activities, such as sucking and biting.

Orienting reflex An unlearned, stereotyped response in which an organism pays attention to a stimulus.

Ovary A female reproductive organ located in the abdomen that produces female reproductive cells, or ova.

Overanxious Excessively anxious. Highly sensitive to social criticism.

Overextension A normal aspect of language development in which words are used in situations in which their meanings become extended, or inappropriate, as in an infant's extension of the label "doggy" to several types of four-legged animals.

Overregularization A normal aspect of language development in which the child applies regular grammatical rules for forming inflections (e.g., past tense and plurals) to irregular verbs and nouns.

Overt behavior Observable behavior.

Ovulation The release of an ovum from an ovary.

Ovum A female reproductive cell. Plural: ova.

Oxytocin A pituitary gland that stimulates labor contractions.

Pacifier An artificial nipple or teething ring that is used to soothe babies.

Palmar reflex A reflex in which infants grasp objects that create pressure in the palms of the hands. Also termed *Grasping reflex*.

Parallel play Play in which children use the same toys as nearby children but approach their toys in their own ways. No effort is made to modify the play of others.

Participant modeling A process in which one loses irrational fear of anxiety-evoking objects by observing models interact with them and then imitating the models.

Passive As a developmental concept, influenced or acted upon by environmental stimuli as opposed to acting upon the environment. See *Active*.

Patriarchy A social system which is dominated by the father or the eldest male.

Peak growth A period of growth during which the growth rate is at a maximum.

Peer A child of the same age. More generally, a person of similar background and social standing.

Pelvic inflammatory disease Any of a number of diseases that infect the abdominal region, impairing fertility. Abbreviated *PID*.

Penis-envy In psychoanalytic theory, jealousy of the male sex organ attributed to girls in the phallic stage.

Perception The process by which sensations are organized into mental representations of the world.

Perceptual constancy The tendency to perceive objects as the same although sensations produced by them differ as, for example, they shift in position or the lighting changes.

Performance components In triarchic theory, those aspects of intelligence that are identified by the adequacy of the mental operations used in processing information.

Perineum The area between the female's genital region and the anus. See *Episiotomy*.

Period of the ovum See *Germinal stage*.

Permissive style A child-rearing style in which parents are neither controlling nor restrictive.

Personal space A psychological boundary that permits one to maintain a comfortable distance from others.

Perspective The perception of depth on the basis of the apparent distance and relative positions of objects. That is, objects that are smaller tend to be perceived as more distant.

Pervasive developmental disorders Severe behavior disorders that impair the child's cognitive, social, and emotional development.

Phallic stage The third stage of psychosexual development in psychoanalytic theory, characterized by a shift of libido to the phallic region and the Oedipus complex.

Phenotype The actual form or constitution of an organism as determined by the interaction of heredity and environmental factors. See *Genotype*.

Phenylketonuria A genetic abnormality in which a child cannot metabolize phenylalanine, which consequently builds up in the form of an acid and causes mental retardation. Abbreviated *PKU*.

Phobia An intense, excessive fear.

Phoneme A basic sound in a language.

Phonetic method A method for learning to read in which children decode the sounds of words based on their knowledge of the sounds of letters and combinations of letters.

Phonology The study of the basic sounds in a language.

▶ ▶ ▶ ▶

Physiological dependence Biological addiction to a substance, as evidenced by tolerance or an abstinence syndrome.

PID See *Pelvic inflammatory disease.*

Pincer grasp The use of the opposing thumb in grasping objects.

Pitch The highness or lowness of a sound, as determined by the frequency of sound waves.

Pituitary gland The body's "master gland" which is located in the lower central part of the brain and secretes many hormones essential to development, such as oxytocin, prolactin, and growth hormone.

PKU See *Phenylketonuria.*

Placenta An organ connected to the fetus by the umbilical cord. The placenta serves as a relay station between mother and fetus, allowing the exchange of nutrients and wastes.

Placing reflex A reflex in which infants lift their legs in response to pressure on the top of the foot.

Plantar reflex A reflex in which infants curl their toes downward in response to pressure against the balls of the feet.

Plasticity of the brain The tendency of new parts of the brain to take up the functions of injured parts of the brain.

Polygenic Descriptive of traits that result from many genes.

Polygraph An instrument that suggests emotional response by measurement of heart rate, blood pressure, and other biological variables.

Pons A bridgelike structure of the hindbrain that is involved in respiration.

Positive reinforcer A reinforcer that, when applied, increases the frequency of a response. Food and attention usually but not always function as positive reinforcers. See *Negative reinforcer.*

Postconventional level According to Kohlberg, a period during which moral judgments are derived from moral principles and people look to themselves to set moral standards.

Postpartum depression Severe, prolonged depression that afflicts 10–15 percent of women after childbirth, and is characterized by sadness, apathy, feelings of worthlessness, difficulty concentrating, and physical symptoms. More severe than *Maternity blues.*

Postpartum period The period that immediately follows childbirth.

Pragmatics The practical aspects of communication, such as adaptation of language to fit the social context.

Precausal thinking In cognitive-developmental theory, a type of thought characterized by an explanation of natural cause-and-effect relationships in terms of will and other preoperational concepts.

Preconscious In psychoanalytic theory, descriptive of mental content that is not in awareness but can be readily brought into awareness by the focusing of attention.

Preconventional level According to Kohlberg, a period during which moral judgments are based largely on expectations of rewards or punishments.

Prelinguistic vocalizations Vocalizations such as crying, cooing, and babbling that occur prior to the use of language.

Premature Born before the baby is mature enough to sustain independent life with relative ease.

Prenatal development Development prior to birth. See *Germinal stage, Embryonic stage,* and *Fetal stage.*

Preoperational stage The second stage in Piaget's cognitive-developmental theory, characterized by inflexible and irreversible mental manipulation of symbols.

Prepared childbirth See *Lamaze method.*

Pretend play See *Dramatic play.*

Preterm Born prior to full term (37 weeks of gestation).

Primary circular reactions In cognitive-developmental theory, a substage in the sensorimotor period during which the infant repeats unlearned actions that provide stimulation.

Primary mental abilities According to Thurstone, the basic factors such as reasoning and numerical abilities that compose intelligence.

Primary reinforcer An unlearned reinforcer, such as food, warmth, or pain. See *Secondary reinforcer.*

Primates An order of mammals, including humans, apes, and monkeys.

Productivity The characteristic of language defined as the capacity to combine words into original sentences.

Progestin A hormone that is used to maintain pregnancy but that has been linked with masculinization of the fetus.

Programmed learning A learning method in which complex tasks are broken down into simple steps. The proper performance of each step is reinforced, whereas incorrect responses are not reinforced.

Propinquity Nearness, closeness. A factor in the formation of friendships.

Prostaglandins Hormones that stimulate uterine contractions.

Prostate gland The gland that secretes the bulk of seminal fluid.

Proximodistal development One of the principles of development, according to which development proceeds from the inner part (or axis) of the child's body outward.

Pseudohermaphrodite A person with the gonads of one sex whose external sex organs are ambiguous or characteristic of the opposite sex.

▶ ▶ ▶ ▶

Psychic structure In psychoanalytic theory, a hypothesized mental structure (e.g., ego) used to explain aspects of behavior.

Psychoanalytic theory The school of psychology founded by Sigmund Freud that emphasizes the importance of unconscious, primitive motives and conflicts as determinants of behavior and personality development.

Psychodynamic Descriptive of Freud's view that psychological forces move throughout the personality and determine behavior.

Psycholinguist A scientist who specializes in the the relationships between psychological processes and language.

Psycholinguistic theory The view that language acquisition involves an interaction between environmental influences and an inborn tendency to learn language. The emphasis is on the inborn tendency.

Psychological androgyny Possession of both instrumental and warmth-expressiveness traits.

Psychological trait An aspect of personality that is inferred from behavior and assumed to account for behavioral consistency.

Psychosexual development In Freud's psychoanalytic theory, the process by which different erogenous zones express libidinal energy during five stages of development.

Psychosis A severe behavior disorder characterized by faulty perception of reality and inability to meet the demands of everyday life.

Psychosocial development Erik Erikson's eight-stage theory of development which, in contrast to Freud's theory of development, downplays the importance of sexual impulses and focuses on social relationships and the conscious assumption of various life roles.

Puberty The biological stage of development characterized by changes that lead to reproductive capacity.

Puberty signals the beginning of adolescence.

Punishment An aversive or unpleasant stimulus that suppresses the behavior it follows. Contrast with *Negative reinforcement*.

Pupillary reflex The reflexive tendency of the pupils of the eyes to narrow or widen in response to the intensity of light.

Rapid-eye-movement sleep A period of sleep during which the eyes move back and forth rapidly beneath closed lids, suggestive of dreaming. Abbreviated *REM sleep*.

Ratio IQ A score on an intelligence test derived by comparing a child's mental age to his or her chronological age. See *Deviation IQ*.

Rationalization A defense mechanism in psychoanalytic theory, in which the individual finds self-deceptive justifications for unacceptable ideas or behavior patterns.

Reaction range The variability in the expression of inherited traits as a function of environmental influences.

Reaction time The amount of time required to respond to a stimulus.

Receptive vocabulary The extent of one's knowledge of the meaning of words that are communicated to one by others. See *Expressive vocabulary*.

Recessive trait A trait (such as blue eyes) that is not expressed when the gene or genes involved have been paired with dominant genes (such as those determining brown eye color). But recessive traits are transmitted to future generations and expressed if they are paired with other recessive genes. See *Dominant trait*.

Reciprocal Done, felt, or given in return. Referring to a mutual exchange in which each side influences the other.

Reciprocity The principle that actions have mutual effects and that people are dependent upon one another to treat each other morally.

Referential language style The child's use of language primarily as a means for labeling objects. See *Expressive language style*.

Reflex An inborn, stereotyped response to an environmental stimulus.

Regression A defense mechanism in psychoanalytic theory, in which the individual, under stress, shows behavior patterns characteristic of earlier stages of development.

Rehearsal In information processing, the mental repetition of information in order to facilitate long-term storage.

Reinforcement Any stimulus or change in the environment that follows a behavior pattern and has the effect of increasing the frequency of that behavior pattern.

Releasing stimulus A stimulus that elicits a fixed action pattern.

Reliability In tests and measurements, consistency of scores.

REM sleep See *Rapid-eye-movement sleep*.

Repression The major defense mechanism in psychoanalytic theory, which is hypothesized to protect the ego from anxiety by ejecting anxiety-evoking ideas from awareness.

Resistant attachment A type of insecure attachment characterized by severe distress at the leavetakings of, and ambivalent behavior at reunions with, attachment figures.

Respiratory distress syndrome A cluster of breathing problems, including weak and irregular breathing, to which preterm babies are especially prone.

Retinal disparity A binocular cue for depth that occurs because the same object creates different (disparate) images on the retina of each eye when it is nearby.

Retinoblastoma A type of blindness caused by a dominant gene.

▶ ▶ ▶ ▶

Retrolintal fibroplasia A type of blindness caused by excessive oxygen, as may be found in an incubator.

Reward A pleasant stimulus that increases the frequency of the behavior it follows. Contrast with *Reinforcement*.

Rh incompatibility A condition in which antibodies produced by a pregnant women are transmitted to the fetus and may cause brain damage or death to the fetus.

Rickets A disease that is caused by deficiencies of vitamin D and sunshine and characterized by softening of the bones.

Risk factors Variables such as ethnicity and social class that do not directly cause problems but are associated with them.

Rods Rod-shaped receptors for light that are sensitive to the intensity of light only. Rods permit black-and-white vision.

Role diffusion According to Erik Erikson, inconsistency in behavior and susceptibility to charismatic leaders that stems from the lack of ego identity.

Role model A person who enacts a social role that is observed and imitated by another person.

Rooming-in The practice of having a newborn baby remain in the hospital room with the mother instead of residing in the nursery.

Rooting reflex A reflex in which infants turn their mouths and heads in the direction of a tactile stimulus that strokes the cheek or the corner of the mouth.

Rote learning Learning by repetition.

Rubella A viral infection that can cause mental retardation and heart disease in the embryo. Also called *German measles*.

Rumination (1) In biology, repeated rejection of the contents of the stomach through the mouth; vomiting.

(2) In psychology, turning things over in the mind repeatedly.

s Spearman's term for specific factors that he believed account for individual mental abilities. See *g*.

Saturation In visual perception, the richness or purity of a color.

Scheme According to cognitive-developmental theory, an action pattern or mental structure that is involved in the acquisition and organization of knowledge.

Schwann cell A kind of glial cell that extends its membrane and wraps it tightly around the axon of a neuron, in this way creating a myelin sheath.

Secondary circular reactions In cognitive-developmental theory, a substage in the sensorimotor period during which the infant repeats learned actions that provide stimulation.

Secondary reinforcer A reinforcer, such as money or social approval, whose effectiveness is based on association with established reinforcers. See *Primary reinforcer*.

Secondary sex characteristics Sex-linked characteristics other than differences in reproductive organs, such as the depth of voice and distribution of bodily hair.

Secure attachment A type of attachment characterized by mild distress at leavetakings, seeking of nearness to the attachment figure, and being readily soothed by the figure.

Sedatives Drugs that soothe or quiet restlessness or agitation.

Self-fulfilling prophecy An event that occurs because of one's belief that it will occur.

Semantic code In information processing, a code based on the meaning of information.

Semanticity Meaning. The quality of language in which words are used as symbols for objects, events, and ideas.

Semantics The study of the meanings of a language—the relationships between objects, events, and language.

Semen The fluid that contains sperm.

Sensation A process involving the stimulation of sensory receptors and the transmission of sensory information to the spinal cord and brain.

Sensitive period In language development, the period from about 18 months of age to puberty, when the child is thought to be especially capable of learning language because of plasticity of the brain. A sensitive period is less dramatic in its effects than a ''critical'' period: If a behavior pattern is not acquired during a so-called critical period, it is unlikely to be acquired at all.

Sensorimotor stage The first stage in Piaget's cognitive-developmental theory, characterized by lack of language and by attainment of the object concept.

Sensory cortex The section of the cerebral cortex that lies in the parietal lobe just behind the central fissure and where tactile sensory information is projected.

Sensory memory The structure of memory first encountered by sensory input. Sensory memory is maintained for only a fraction of a second.

Sensory register Another term for *Sensory memory*.

Separation anxiety Fear of being separated from a target of attachment—usually a primary caregiver.

Separation anxiety disorder An American Psychiatric Association (1980) diagnosis given an extreme form of otherwise normal separation anxiety that is characterized by persistent refusal to attend school. The goal is to remain with the parent or in the home.

Seriation Placement of objects in order or in a series according to an increasing or decreasing property or trait.

▶ ▶ ▶ ▶

Serotonin A neurotransmitter that is implicated in behavior disorders such as schizophrenia and depression.

Sex chromosome A chromosome in the shape of a Y (male) or an X (female) that determines the sex of the child.

Sexism The prejudgment that a person, on the basis of gender, will possess negative traits or perform inadequately.

Sex-linked genetic abnormalities Abnormalities that stem from genes that are found on the X sex chromosome. They are thus more likely to be shown by male offspring (who do not have an opposing gene from a second X sex chromosome) than by female offspring.

Sex norm An expectation about what sort of social behavior is appropriate in social interactions between males and females.

Sex role A complex cluster of behavior patterns that are considered stereotypical of males or females within a culture.

Shape constancy The tendency to perceive an object as being the same shape, although when viewed from a different position, the shape projected onto the retina differs.

Shaping An operant-conditioning procedure for teaching complex behavior patterns in which the components of the pattern are reinforced separately, before they are combined into a complete performance.

Short-term memory The structure of memory that can hold a sensory stimulus for up to 30 seconds after the trace decays. Also called *Working memory.*

Sibling rivalry Rivalry or jealousy among brothers and sisters.

Sickle cell anemia A genetic disorder, for which blacks are at greatest risk, that decreases the blood's capacity to carry oxygen.

SIDS See *Sudden infant death syndrome.*

Sight vocabulary Words that are recognized on the basis of familiarity with their overall shapes, rather than decoded.

Significant others Erik Erikson's term for people who have a major impact on one's development, including parents, peers, and lovers.

Size constancy The tendency to perceive objects as being the same size although the sizes of their retinal images differ as a function of distance.

Sleep terrors Frightening, dreamlike experiences that occur during NREM (stages 3 and 4) sleep.

Small-for-dates Descriptive of newborn babies who are unusually small given the amount of time that has passed since conception.

Socialization A process by which children are guided into socially acceptable behavior patterns by means of guidance, rewards and punishments, and exposure to role models.

Social-learning theory A contemporary theory of learning that views children as active and asserts that most human learning takes place by means of observation.

Social play Play in which children interact with, and are influenced by, the play of others. Examples include associative play, cooperative play, and parallel play in which children use the same toys.

Sociopath See *Antisocial personality.*

Soiling See *Encopresis.*

Somnambulism Sleepwalking.

Solitary play Play which is independent from that of nearby children. No effort is made to approach other children.

Sonogram A procedure in which ultrasound waves are used in order to create a "picture" of an embryo or fetus.

Spectrograph An instrument that converts sounds to graphs or pictures in order to facilitate the study of their acoustic qualities.

Spermatid A cell with 23 chromosomes that results from meiosis of spermatocytes and develops into a sperm cell.

Spermatocyte A cell with 46 chromosomes from which sperm cells are formed.

Spontaneous abortion Unpremeditated, accidental abortion.

Stage A distinct period of life that differs markedly in quality from other periods. Stages are hypothesized to be discontinuous and to follow one another in an invariant sequence.

Stage theory A theory of development in which discrete stages are hypothesized.

Standardization The process of determining how various groups (such as age groups) perform on a test in order to establish norms. Norms permit interpretation of individual test scores.

Stepping reflex A reflex in which infants take steps when they are held under the arms and leaned forward, such that their feet press against the ground.

Stereotype A fixed, conventional idea about a group.

Stillbirth The birth of a dead fetus.

Stimulants Drugs that increase the activity of the nervous system.

Stimulus A change in the environment that leads to a change in behavior.

Storge The ancient Greek concept of love that is similar to the contemporary concept of attachment.

Strabismus A disorder in which both eyes cannot focus on the same point at the same time.

Structure-of-intellect model Guilford's three-dimensional model of intelligence, which focuses on the operations, contents, and products of intellectual functioning.

Stupor A condition in which responsiveness is dulled or slowed down.

► ► ► ►

Subjective responsibility According to Piaget, the judgment of the wrongfulness of an act in terms of the intentions of the wrongdoer.

Substance abuse A persistent pattern of use of a substance characterized by frequent intoxication and impairment of physical, social, or emotional well-being.

Substance dependence A persistent pattern of use of a substance that is accompanied by physiological addiction.

Successive approximations An operant-conditioning procedure for teaching behavior in which responses generally similar to the target behavior are reinforced at first, but then only behaviors progressively more like the target behavior are reinforced.

Sudden infant death syndrome The death, while asleep, of apparently healthy babies who stop breathing for unknown medical reasons. Abbreviated *SIDS*.

Superego In psychoanalytic theory, the last psychic structure to develop. The superego functions as a conscience: It sets forth high standards for behavior and floods the ego with feelings of guilt and shame when immoral behavior is carried out or contemplated.

Supermale A male with XYY sex chromosomal structure.

Surface structure The superficial construction of a sentence, for example, as determined by word order. See *Deep structure*.

Surrogate mother A woman who is artificially inseminated and carries to term a child who is then given to another woman, typically the spouse of the man who donated the sperm used in insemination. (Social critics note that the adoptive mother is actually the substitute or surrogate mother, whereas the woman who conceives and carries the child to term is the real biological mother.)

Swaddling The practice of wrapping babies in long, narrow bands of cloth, usually in an effort to foster proper physical development or to soothe.

Syllogism A type of reasoning in which two statements or premises are set forth and a logical conclusion is drawn from them.

Symbolic mode Bruner's term for the cognitive style in which representation is by means of language.

Syntax The rules in a language for placing words into an order that will form meaningful sentences.

Syphilis A sexually transmitted disease.

Tabula rasa A Latin phrase meaning "blank slate," referring to the view that children are born without innate cultural, ethical, or vocational preferences, and that such preferences are shaped by the environment.

Tay-Sachs disease A fatal genetic neurological disorder for which Jews of Eastern European origin are at greatest risk.

Teething The often painful process of cutting teeth through gums.

Telegraphic speech Speech in which only the essential words are used, such as in children's one- and two-word utterances.

Teratogen An agent that gives rise to abnormalities in the embryo or fetus.

Term A set period of time, such as the normal duration of the gestation period.

Territory In ethological theory, an area whose possession provides privileges in feeding and mating.

Tertiary circular reactions In cognitive-developmental theory, a substage of the sensorimotor period in which the infant purposefully adapts established schemes to new situations.

Testicular feminizing syndrome A form of pseudohermaphroditism in which a genetic male is insensitive to testosterone while undergoing prenatal development and thus develops female external genitals.

Testosterone A male sex hormone produced by the testes.

Test-retest reliability A method for determining the reliability of a test in which persons' scores from separate testing occasions are correlated.

Thalidomide A sedative used in the 1960s that has been linked to birth defects, especially deformed or absent limbs.

Theory A formulation of relationships underlying observed events. Theories involve assumptions and logically derived explanations and predictions.

Time out A behavior-modification procedure for discouraging misbehavior: A child who misbehaves is temporarily placed in a drab, restrictive environment in which reinforcement is unavailable.

Toddler A child who walks with short, uncertain steps. "Toddlerhood" lasts from about 18 to 30 months of age.

Token economy A behavior-modification technique in which persons receive tokens for desirable behavior that can later be exchanged for desired objects and privileges.

Tolerance Habituation to a drug such that increasingly higher doses are needed to achieve similar effects.

Total immersion A method of language instruction in which a person is placed in an environment in which only the language to be learned is used.

Toxemia A life-threatening disease that can afflict pregnant women and which is characterized by high blood pressure.

Trait A distinguishing characteristic of an organism. See *Psychological trait*.

Tranquilizer An agent that reduces feelings of anxiety and tension.

▶ ▶ ▶ ▶

Transductive reasoning A type of preoperational thought in which the child reasons from the specific to the specific, or assumes that objects that share one property share all properties.

Transformational grammar The child's system for turning basic ideas into sentences. The child uses transformational grammar to generate the surface structure of sentences from their deep structure.

Transition In childbirth, the initial movement of the head of the fetus into the birth canal.

Transitivity Recognition that if A > B in a property, and B > C, then A > C.

Transverse position A problematic position for childbirth in which the fetus lies crosswise across the opening to the birth canal.

Treatment In an experiment, a condition received by subjects so that its effects may be observed.

Tremors Shaking or shivering.

Triarchic theory Robert Sternberg's cognitive theory which views intellectual functioning as occurring on three levels: contextual, experiential, and componential.

Trophoblast The outer part of the blastocyst, from which the amniotic sac, placenta, and umbilical cord develop.

Turner's syndrome A chromosomal disorder found among females that is caused by having one X sex chromosome and characterized by infertility.

Ultrasound Sound waves too high in pitch to be sensed by the human ear. See *Sonogram*.

Umbilical cord A tube that connects the fetus to the placenta.

Unconditioned response An unlearned, stereotyped response to a stimulus. Abbreviated *UR*.

Unconditioned stimulus A stimulus that elicits an unlearned, stereotyped response from an organism. Abbreviated *US*.

Unconscious In psychoanalytic theory, descriptive of mental content that is not available to awareness under ordinary means, such as focusing of attention.

UR See *Unconditioned response*.

Urethra The duct through which urine is excreted.

US See *Unconditioned stimulus*.

Uterus The hollow organ within females in which the embryo becomes implanted and develops to term.

Vacuum extraction tube An instrument that uses suction to pull the baby through the birth canal as a way of facilitating childbirth.

Validity In tests and measurements, the degree to which a test measures what it is supposed to measure.

Variable In research, a quantity that can vary from subject to subject or from occasion to occasion, such as height, weight, intelligence, and attention span.

Vernix An oily, white substance that coats the skin of the neonate, especially in preterm babies.

Visual accommodation The automatic adjustments made by the lenses of the eyes in order to bring objects into focus.

Visual acuity Keenness or sharpness of vision.

Visual recognition memory Ability to discriminate previously seen objects from novel objects. An experimental measure of infant intelligence.

Visual tracking Following a moving object with one's eyes. The term usually applies to tracking in infants.

Wernicke's aphasia A type of aphasia caused by damage to Wernicke's area of the cerebral cortex and characterized by impaired comprehension of speech and difficulty in attempting to produce the right word.

Wet nurse A lactating woman hired to suckle and, usually, to rear another woman's child.

Withdrawal reflex A reflex in which infants draw back or recoil from a painful stimulus.

Wolffian duct An embryonic structure that develops into the duct system that will carry and nourish sperm in the mature male. See *Müllerian ducts*.

Womb simulator An artificial environment used primarily with preterm babies that mimics some of the features of the womb, particularly temperature, sounds, and rocking motions.

Word-recognition method A method for learning to read in which children come to recognize words through repeated exposure to them.

Working memory See *Short-term memory*.

Zona pellucida A gelatinous layer surrounding an ovum.

Zygote A fertilized ovum.

R E F E R E N C E S

Abel, E. L. (1980). Fetal alcohol syndrome: Behavioral teratology. *Psychological Bulletin, 87*, 29–50.

Aber, J. L., & Allen, J. P. (1987). Effects of maltreatment on young children's socioemotional development: An attachment theory perspective. *Developmental Psychology, 23*, 406–414.

Abikoff, H., & Gittelman, R. (1985). The normalizing effects of methylphenidate on the classroom behavior of ADDH children. *Journal of Abnormal Child Psychology, 13*, 33–44.

Abraham, S., Collins, G., & Nordsieck, M. (1971). Relationship of childhood weight status to morbidity in adults. *Public Health Reports, 86*, 273–284.

Abramovitch, R., Corter, C., Pepler, D. J., & Stanhope, L. (1986). Sibling and peer interaction: A final followup and a comparison. *Child Development, 57*, 217–229.

Abramovitch, R., Peplar, D. J., & Corter, C. (1982). Patterns of sibling interaction among preschool-age children. In M. E. Lamb & B. Sutton-Smith (Eds.), *Sibling relationships*. Hillsdale, NJ: Erlbaum.

Abrams, K. I., & Bennet, J. W. (1981). Changing etiological perspectives in Down's syndrome: Implications for early intervention. *Journal of the Division for Early Childhood, 2*, 109–112.

Abravanel, E., & Gingold, H. (1985). Learning via observation during the second year of life. *Developmental Psychology, 21*, 614–623.

Abravanel, E., & Sigafoos, A. D. (1984). Exploring the presence of imitation during early infancy. *Child Development, 55*, 381–392.

Achenbach, T. M., & Edelbrock, C. S. (1981). Behavioral problems and competencies reported by parents of normal and disturbed children aged 4 through 16. *Monographs of the Society for Research in Child Development, 46* (Whole No. 188).

Adams, R. S., & Biddle, B. J. (1970). *Realities of teaching*. New York: Holt, Rinehart and Winston.

Adamson, L. B., & Bakeman, R. (1985). Affect and attention: Infants observed with mothers and peers. *Child Development, 56*, 582–593.

Ahrens, R. (1954). Beitrage zur Entwicklung des Physiognomie und Mimikerkennens. *Zeitschrift fur Experimentelle und Angewandte Psychologie, 2*, 599–633.

Aiello, J. R., & Aiello, T. D. (1974). Development of personal space: Proxemic behavior of children six to sixteen. *Human Ecology, 2*, 177–189

Aiello, J. R., & Thompson, D. E. (1980). Personal space, crowding, and spatial behavior in a cultural context. In I. Altman, J. F. Wohlwill, & A. Rapoport (Eds.), *Human behavior and environment*, Vol. 4. New York: Plenum Press.

Ainsworth, M. D. S. (1963). The development of infant–mother interaction among the Ganda. In D. M. Foss (Ed.), *Determinants of infant behavior*, Vol. 2. New York: Wiley.

Ainsworth, M. D. S. (1967). *Infancy in Uganda: Infant care and the growth of love*. Baltimore: Johns Hopkins University Press.

Ainsworth, M. D. S. (1979). Infant–mother attachment. *American Psychologist, 34*, 932–937.

Ainsworth, M. D. S., & Bell, S. M. (1970). Attachment, exploration, and separation: Illustrated by the behavior of one-year-olds in a strange situation. *Child Development, 41*, 49–67.

Ainsworth, M. D. S., Bell, S. M., & Stayton, D. J. (1974). Infant-mother attachment and social development: Socialization as a product of reciprocal responsiveness to signals. In M. P. M. Richards (Ed.), *The integration of the child into a social world*. London: Cambridge University Press.

Ainsworth, M. D. S., Blehar, M. C., Waters, E., & Wall, S. (1978). *Patterns of attachment: A psychological study of the strange situation*. Hillsdale, NJ: Erlbaum.

Alemi, B., Hamosh, M., Scanlon, J. W., Salzman-Mann, C., & Hamosh, P. (1981). Fat digestion in very low-birth-weight infants: Effects of addition of human milk to low-birth-weight formula. *Pediatrics, 68,* 484–489.

Allport, G. W. (1937). *Personality: A psychological interpretation.* New York: Holt, Rinehart and Winston.

Allport, G. W. (1961). *Pattern and growth in personality.* New York: Holt, Rinehart and Winston.

Almy, M., Monighan, P., Scales, B., & Van Hoorn, J. (1983). Recent research on playing: The perspective of the teacher. In L. Katz (Ed.), *Current topics in early childhood education,* Vol. 5. Norwood, NJ: Ablex.

Amabile, T. M. (1982). Social psychology of creativity: A consensual assessment technique. *Journal of Personality and Social Psychology, 43,* 997–1013.

Amabile, T. M. (1983). The social psychology of creativity: A componential conceptualization. *Journal of Personality and Social Psychology, 45,* 357–376.

American Psychiatric Association (1987). *Diagnostic and statistical manual of the mental disorders,* Third edition-Revised. Washington, DC: American Psychiatric Press, Inc.

Anastasi, A. (1983). Evolving trait concepts. *American Psychologist, 38,* 175–184.

Anastasiow, N. J., & Hanes, M. L. (1976). *Language patterns of children in poverty.* Springfield, IL: Charles C Thomas.

Anderson, A. (1982). The great Japanese IQ increase. *Nature, 297,* 180–181.

Anderson, C. W., Nagle, R. J., Roberts, W. A., & Smith, J. W. (1981). Attachment to substitute caregivers as a function of center quality and caregiver involvement. *Child Development, 52,* 53–61.

Anderson, L. D. (1939). The predictive value of infant tests in relation to intelligence. *Child Development, 10,* 202–212.

Anderson, S. R., Christian, W. P., & Luce, S. C. (1986). Transitional residential programming for autistic individuals. *The Behavior Therapist, 9,* 205–211.

Antill, J. K. (1983). Sex role complementarity versus similarity in married couples. *Journal of Personality and Social Psychology, 45,* 145–155.

Apgar, V. (1953). A proposal for a new method of evaluation in the newborn infant. *Anesthesia and Analgesia, 52,* 260–267.

Ardrey, R. (1961). *African genesis.* New York: Dell Books.

Aries, P. (1962). *Centuries of childhood.* New York: Knopf.

Arms, K., & Camp, P. S. (1987). *Biology,* 3d ed. Philadephia: Saunders College Publishing.

Aronfreed, J. (1968). *Conduct and conscience: The socialization of internalized control over behavior.* New York: Academic Press.

Aronfreed, J. (1976). Moral development from the standpoint of a general psychological theory. In T. Lickona (Ed.), *Moral development and behavior.* New York: Holt, Rinehart and Winston.

Asarnow, J. R., & Carlson, G. A. (1985). Depression self-rating scale: Utility with child psychiatric inpatients. *Journal of Consulting and Clinical Psychology, 53,* 491–499

Asher, S., & Hymel, S. (1981). Children's social competence in peer relations: Sociometric and behavioral assessment. In J. D. Wine & M. D. Smys (Eds.), *Social competence.* New York: Guilford.

Aslin, R. N., & Banks, M. S. (1978). Early visual experience in humans: Evidence for a critical period in the development of binocular vision. In S. Schneider, H. Liebowitz, H. Pick, & H. Stevenson (Eds.), *Psychology: From basic research to practice.* New York: Plenum Press.

Aslin, R. N., Pisoni, D. B., & Jusczyk, P. W. (1983). Auditory development and speech perception in infancy. In P. H. Mussen (Ed.), *Handbook of child psychology,* 4th ed. New York: Wiley.

Atkinson, K., MacWhinney, B., & Stoel, C. (1970). An experiment on recognition of babbling. In *Papers and reports on child language development.* Stanford, CA: Stanford University Press.

Austin, C. R., & Short, R. V. (1972). *Reproduction in mammals.* London: Cambridge University Press.

Ausubel, D. P. (1958). *Theory and problems of child development.* New York: Grune & Stratton.

Auvenshire, & Enriquez. (1985). *Maternity nursing.* Monterey, CA: Wadsworth.

Babladelis, G. (1979). Accentuate the positive. *Contemporary Psychology, 24,* 3–4.

Baker, L. A., DeFries, J. C., & Fulker, D. W. (1983). Longitudinal stability of cognitive ability in the Colorado adoption project. *Child Development, 54,* 290–297.

Bakwin, H. (1970, August 29). Sleepwalking in twins. *Lancet,* pp. 446–447.

Bakwin, H. (1971a). Car-sickness in twins. *Developmental Medicine and Child Neurology, 13,* 310–312.

Bakwin, H. (1971b). Constipation in twins. *American Journal of Diseases of Children, 121,* 179–181.

Bakwin, H. (1971c). Enuresis in twins. *American Journal of Diseases of Children, 121,* 222–225.

Bakwin, H. (1971d). Nail-biting in twins. *Developmental Medicine and Child Neurology, 13,* 304–307.

Ball, S., & Bogatz, G. A. (1970). *The first year of Sesame Street: An evaluation.* Princeton, NJ: Educational Testing Service.

Baller, W. R. (1975). *Bed-wetting: Origin and treatment.* Elmsford, NY: Pergamon Press.

► ► ► ►

Bandura, A. (1973). *Aggression: A social learning analysis*. Englewood Cliffs, NJ: Prentice-Hall.

Bandura, A. (1977). *Social learning theory*. Englewood Cliffs, NJ: Prentice-Hall.

Bandura, A. (1981). Self-referrant thought: A developmental analysis of self-efficacy. In J. H. Flavell & L. Ross (Eds.), *Social cognitive development: Frontiers and possible futures*. Cambridge: Cambridge University Press.

Bandura, A. (1982). Self-efficacy mechanism in human agency. *American Psychologist, 37*, 122–147.

Bandura, A. (1986). *Social foundations of thought and action: A social-cognitive theory*. Englewood Cliffs, NJ: Prentice-Hall.

Bandura, A., Blanchard, E. B., & Ritter, B. (1969). The relative efficacy of desensitization and modeling approaches for inducing behavioral, affective, and cognitive changes. *Journal of Personality and Social Psychology, 13*, 173–199.

Bandura, A., & McDonald, F. J. (1963). Influence of social reinforcement and the behavior of models in shaping children's moral judgments. *Journal of Abnormal and Social Psychology, 67*, 274–281.

Bandura, A., Reese, L., & Adams, N. E. (1982). Microanalysis of action and fear arousal as a function of differential levels of perceived self-efficacy. *Journal of Personality and Social Psychology, 43*, 5–21.

Bandura, A., & Rosenthal, T.L. (1966). Vicarious classical conditioning as a function of arousal level. *Journal of Personality and Social Psychology, 3*, 54–62.

Bandura, A., Ross, D., & Ross, S. A. (1963a). A comparative test of the status envy, and the secondary reinforcement theories of identificatory learning. *Journal of Abnormal and Social Psychology, 67*, 527–534.

Bandura, A., Ross, S. A., & Ross, D. (1963b). Imitation of film-mediated aggressive models. *Journal of Abnormal and Social Psychology, 66*, 3–11.

Banks, M. S. (1982). The development of spatial and temporal contrast sensitivity. *Current Eye Research, 2*, 191–198.

Banks, M. S., & Salapatek, P. (1981). Infant pattern vision: A new approach based on the contrast selectivity function. *Journal of Experimental Child Psychology, 31*, 1–45.

Banks, M. S., & Salapatek, P. (1983). Infant visual perception. In M. M. Haith & J. Campos (Eds.), *Handbook of child psychology*, Vol. 2. New York: Wiley.

Barker, R. G., & Gump, P. V. (1964). *Big school, small school*. Stanford, CA: Stanford University Press.

Barkley, R. A., Hasting, J. E., Tousel, R. E., & Tousel, S. E. (1976). Evaluation of a token system for juvenile delinquents in a residential setting. *Journal of Behavior Therapy and Experimental Psychiatry, 7*, 227–230.

Barkley, R. A., Karlsson, J., Strzelecki, E., & Murphy, J. V. (1984). Effects of age and Ritalin dosage on the mother–child interactions of hyperactive children. *Journal of Consulting and Clinical Psychology, 52*, 750–758.

Barnard, K. E., & Bee, H. L. (1983). The impact of temporally patterned stimulation on the development of preterm infants. *Child Development, 54*, 1156–1167.

Barnes, A., Colton, T., Gunderson, J., Noller, K., Tilley, B., Strama, T., Townsend, D., Hatab, P., & O'Brien, P. (1980). Fertility and outcome of pregnancy in women exposed in utero to diethylstilbestrol. *The New England Journal of Medicine, 302*, 609–613.

Barr, H. M., Streissguth, A. P., Martin, D. C., & Herman, C. S. (1984). Infant size at 8 months of age: Relationship to maternal use of alcohol, nicotine, and caffeine during pregnancy. *Pediatrics, 74*, 336–341.

Barrera, M. E., & Maurer, D. (1981a). The perception of facial expressions by the three-month-old child. *Child Development, 52*, 203–206.

Barrera, M. E., & Maurer, D. (1981b). Discrimination of strangers by the three-month-old child. *Child Development, 52*, 558–563.

Baruch, G., Barnett, R., & Rivers, C. (1983). *Lifeprints*. New York: McGraw-Hill.

Bates, E., Bretherton, I., Beeghly-Smith, M., & McNew, S. (1982). Social bases of language development: A reassessment. In H. W. Reese & L. P. Lipsitt (Eds.), *Advances in child development and behavior*, Vol. 16. New York: Academic Press.

Bates, E., & MacWhinney, B. (1982). A functionalist approach to grammatical development. In L. Gleitman & H. E. Wanner (Eds.), *Language acquisition: The state of the art*. Cambridge: Cambridge University Press.

Bates, J. E., & Bayles, K. (1984). Objective and subjective components in mothers' perceptions of their children from age 6 months to 3 years. *Merrill Palmer Quarterly, 30*, 111–130.

Baucom, D. H., & Aiken, P. A. (1981). Effect of depressed mood on eating among obese and nonobese dieting and nondieting persons. *Journal of Personality and Social Psychology, 41*, 577–585.

Baucom, D. H., & Danker-Brown, P. (1979). Influence of sex roles on the development of learned helplessness. *Journal of Consulting and Clinical Psychology, 47*, 928–936.

Bauer, D. H. (1976). An exploratory study of developmental changes in children's fears. *Journal of Child Psychology and Psychiatry, 17*, 69–74.

Bauer, W. D., & Twentyman, C. T. (1985). Abusing, neglectful, and comparison mothers' responses to child-related and non-child-related stressors. *Journal of Consulting and Clinical Psychology, 53*, 335–343.

Baumrind, D. (1967). Child care practices anteceding three patterns of preschool behavior. *Genetic Psychology Monographs, 75*, 43–88.

▶ ▶ ▶ ▶

Baumrind, D. (1968). Authoritarian vs. authoritative parental control. *Adolescence, 3,* 255–272.

Baumrind, D. (1972). Socialization and instrumental competence in young children. In W. W. Hartup (Ed.), *The young child: Reviews of research,* Vol. 12. Washington, DC: National Association for the Education of Young Children.

Baumrind, D. (1973). The development of instrumental competence through socialization. In A. D. Pick (Ed.), *Minnesota symposia on child psychology,* Vol. 7. Minneapolis: University of Minnesota Press.

Baumrind, D. (1983). Rejoinder to Lewis's reinterpretation of parental firm control effects: Are authoritative families really harmonious? *Psychological Bulletin, 94,* 132–142.

Baumrind, D. (1986). Sex differences in moral reasoning: Response to Walker's (1984) conclusion that there are none. *Child Development, 57,* 511–521.

Bayley, N. (1943). Mental growth during the first three years. In R. G. Barker, J. S. Kounin, & H. F. Wright (Eds.), *Child behavior and development.* New York: McGraw-Hill.

Bayley, N. (1965). Comparisons of mental and motor test scores for ages 1–15 months by sex, birth order, race, geographical location, and education of parents. *Child Development, 36,* 379–411.

Bazar, J. (1980, January). Catching up with the ape language debate. APA *Monitor,* 4–5, 47.

Beal, C. R., & Flavell, J. H. (1983). Young speakers' evaluation of their listeners' comprehensions in a referential communication task. *Child Development, 54,* 148–153.

Beal, C. R., & Flavell, J. H. (1984). Development of the ability to distinguish communicative intention and literal message meaning. *Child Development, 55,* 920–928.

Bear, G. G., & Richards, H. C. (1981). Moral reasoning and conduct problems in the classroom. *Journal of Educational Psychology, 73,* 644–670.

Beardslee, W. R., Bemporad, J., Keller, M. B., & Klerman, G. L. (1983). Children of parents with major affective disorder: A review. *American Journal of Psychiatry, 140,* 825–832.

Beckman, L. J., & Houser, B. B. (1982). The consequences of childlessness on the social-psychological well-being of older women. *Journal of Gerontology, 37,* 243–250.

Beckwith, L., & Parmelee, A. H., Jr. (1986). EEG patterns of preterm infants, home environment, and later IQ. *Child Development, 57,* 777–789.

Bee, H. L., et al. (1982). Prediction of IQ and language skill from perinatal status, child performance, family characteristics, and mother–infant interaction. *Child Development, 53,* 1134–1156.

Behrman, R. E., & Rosen, T. S. (1976). HEW Publication No. 05 76–128, 12–1–12–116.

Behrman, R. E., & Vaughn, V. C., III. (1983). *Pediatrics.* Philadelphia: W. B. Saunders Co.

Beit-Hallahmi, B., & Rabin, A. I. (1977). The kibbutz as a social experiment and a child-rearing laboratory. *American Psychologist, 32,* 532–544.

Belmont, L., & Marolla, F. A. (1973). Birth order, family size, and intelligence. *Science, 182,* 1096–1101.

Belsky, J. (1980). Child maltreatment: An ecological integration. *American Psychologist, 35,* 320–335.

Belsky, J. (1981). Early human experience: A family perspective. *Developmental Psychology, 17,* 3–23.

Belsky, J. (1984). The determinants of parenting: A process model. *Child Development, 55,* 83–96.

Belsky, J., Gilstrap, B., & Rovine, M. (1984). The Pennsylvania infant and family development project, I: Stability and change in mother–infant and father–infant interaction in a family setting at one, three, and nine months. *Child Development, 55,* 692–705.

Belsky, J., & Most, R. K. (1981). From exploration to play: A cross-sectional study of infant free play behavior. *Developmental Psychology, 17,* 630–639.

Belsky, J., & Steinberg, L. D. (1978). The effects of day care: A critical review. *Child Development, 49,* 929–949.

Belsky, J., & Steinberg, L. D. (1979, July–August). What does research teach us about day care? A follow-up report. *Children Today,* pp. 21–26.

Belsky, J., Steinberg, L. D., & Walker, A. (1982). The ecology of day care. In M. E. Lamb (Ed.), *Nontraditional families: Parenting and child development.* Hillsdale, NJ: Erlbaum.

Bem, S. L. (1974). The measurement of psychological androgyny. *Journal of Consulting and Clinical Psychology, 42,* 151–162.

Bem, S. L. (1975). Sex role adaptability: One consequence of psychological androgyny. *Journal of Personality and Social Psychology, 31,* 634–643.

Bem, S. L. (1981). Gender schema theory: A cognitive account of sex typing. *Psychological Review, 88,* 354–364.

Bem, S. L. (1983). Gender schema theory and its implications for child development: Raising gender-aschematic children in a gender-schematic society. *Signs: Journal of Women in Culture and Society, 8,* 598–616.

Bem, S. L. (1985). Androgyny and gender schema theory: A conceptual and empirical integration. In T. B. Sonderegger (Ed.), *Nebraska symposium on motivation, 1984: Psychology and gender.* Lincoln: University of Nebraska Press.

Bem, S. L., & Lenney, E. (1976). Sex typing and the avoidance of cross-sexed behaviors. *Journal of Personality and Social Psychology, 33,* 48–54.

Bem, S. L., Martyna, W., & Watson, C. (1976). Sex typing and androgyny: Further explorations of the expressive domain. *Journal of Personality and social psychology, 34,* 1016–1023.

▶ ▶ ▶ ▶

Bemis, K. M. (1978). Current approaches to the etiology and treatment of anorexia nervosa. *Psychological Bulletin, 85,* 593–617.

Benbow, C. P., & Stanley, J. C. (1980). Sex differences in mathematical ability: Fact or artifact? *Science, 210,* 1262–1264.

Benbow, C. P., & Stanley, J. C. (1983). Sex differences in mathematical reasoning: More facts. *Science, 222,* 1029–1031.

Benedek, E., & Vaughn, R. (1982). Voluntary childlessness. In M. Kirkpatrick (Ed.), *Women's sexual experience.* New York: Plenum Press.

Berezin, N. (1980). *The gentle birth book: A practical guide to Leboyer family-centered delivery.* New York: Pocket Books.

Berko, J. (1958). The child's learning of English morphology. *Word, 14,* 150–177.

Berkowitz, W. R., Nebel, J. C., & Reitman, J. W. (1971). Height and interpersonal attraction: The 1960 mayoral election in New York City. Paper presented to the meeting of the American Psychological Association, Washington, D.C.

Berman, P. W., & Goodman, V. (1984). Age and sex differences in children's responses to babies: Effects of adults' caretaking requests and instructions. *Child Development, 55,* 1071–1077.

Bernard, J., & Sontag, L. W. (1947). Fetal reactivity to sound. *Journal of Genetic Psychology, 70,* 205–210.

Berndt, T. J. (1979). Developmental changes in conformity to peers and parents. *Developmental Psychology, 15,* 608–616.

Berndt, T. J. (1982). The features and effects of friendships in early adolescence. *Child Development, 53,* 1447–1460.

Berndt, T. J., & Perry, T. B. (1986). Children's perceptions of friendships as supportive relationships. *Developmental Psychology, 1986,* 640–648.

Bernstein, A. C. (1976, August). How children learn about sex and birth. *Psychology Today,* p. 31.

Bernstein, A. C., & Cowan, P. A. (1975). Children's concepts of how people get babies. *Child Development, 46,* 77–92.

Bernstein, E. (1987). Response to Terrace. *American Psychologist, 42,* 272–273.

Berscheid, E., Walster, E., & Bohrnstedt, G. (1973, June). Body image, the happy American body: A survey report. *Psychology Today,* pp. 119–123, 126–131.

Bersoff, D. N. (1981). Testing and the law. *American Psychologist, 36,* 1159–1166.

Bertenthal, B. I., & Fischer, K. W. (1978). Development of self-recognition in the infant. *Developmental Psychology, 14,* 44–50.

Berzins, J. I., Welling, M. A., & Wetter, R. E. (1977). The PRF ANDRO scale: User's manual. Unpublished manuscript, University of Kentucky.

Best, D. L., Williams, J. E., Cloud, J. M., Davis, S. W., Robertson, L. S., Edwards, J. R., Giles, H., & Fowles, J. (1977). Development of sex-trait stereotypes among young children in the United States, England, and Ireland. *Child Development, 48,* 1375–1384.

Bettelheim, B. (1969). *Children of the dream.* London: Collier-Macmillan.

Betz, N. E., & Hackett, G. (1981). The relationships of career-related self-efficacy expectations to perceived career options in college women and men. *Journal of Counseling Psychology, 28,* 399–410.

Bierman, K. L. (1986). Process of change during social skills training with preadolescents and its relation to treatment outcome. *Child Development, 57,* 230–240.

Bierman, K. L., & Furman, W. (1984). The effects of social skills training and peer involvement on the social adjustment of preadolescents. *Child Development, 55,* 151–162.

Binet, A. (1909). *Les idées modernes sur les enfants.* Paris: Schleicher.

Bing, E. D. (1983). *Dear Elizabeth Bing: We've had our baby.* New York: Pocket Books.

Birch, L. L., Marlin, D. W., & Rotter, J. (1984). Eating as the "means" activity in a contingency: Effects on young children's food preference. *Child Development, 55,* 431–439.

Birren, J. E., Kinney, D. K., Schaie, K. W., & Woodruff, D. S. (1981). *Developmental psychology: A life-span approach.* Boston: Houghton Mifflin.

Bjorklund, D. F. (1985). The role of conceptual knowledge in the development of organization in children's memory. In C. J. Brainerd & M. Pressley (Eds.), *Basic processes in memory development.* New York: Springer-Verlag.

Bjorklund, D. F., & de Marchena, M. R. (1984). Developmental shifts in the basis of organization in memory: The role of associative versus categorical relatedness in children's free recall. *Child Development, 55,* 952–962.

Blake, R., & Hirsch, H. V. B. (1975). Deficits in binocular depth perception in cats after alternating monocular deprivation. *Science, 190,* 1114–1116.

Blakeslee, S. (1984, November 11). The learning disabled: Brain studies shed light on disorders. *The New York Times,* Education, Fall Survey, p. 45.

Blank, M. (1974). Cognitive functions of language in the preschool years. *Developmental Psychology, 10,* 229–245.

Blasi, A. (1980). Bridging moral cognition and moral action: A critical review of the literature. *Psychological Bulletin, 88,* 1–45.

Blewitt, P. (1983). *Dog* versus *collie:* Vocabulary in speech to young children. *Developmental Psychology, 19,* 602–609.

Block, J. H. (1979). Personality development in males and females: The

▶ ▶ ▶ ▶

influence of differential socialization. Master lecture presented at the meeting of the American Psychological Association, New York.

Block, J. H. (1983). Differential premises arising from differential socialization of the sexes: Some conjectures. *Child Development, 54,* 1335–1354.

Bloom, L. (1973). *One word at a time.* The Hague: Mouton.

Bloom, L. (1975). Language development. In F. D. Horowitz (Ed.), *Review of child development research,* Vol. 4. Chicago: University of Chicago Press.

Bloom, L., Lahey, L., Hood, L., Lifter, K., & Fiess, K. (1980). Complex sentences: Acquisition of syntactic connectives and the semantic relations they encode. *Journal of Child Language, 7,* 235–261.

Bloom, L., Merkin, S., & Wootten, J. (1982). *Wh*-questions: Linguistic factors that contribute to the sequence of acquisition. *Child Development, 53,* 1084–1092.

Blumberg, S. H., & Izard, C. E. (1985). Affective and cognitive characteristics of depression in 10- and 11-year-old children. *Journal of Personality and Social Psychology, 49,* 194–202.

Boismier, J. D. (1977). Visual stimulation and wake–sleep behavior in human neonates. *Developmental Psychology, 10,* 219–227.

Bond, C. R., & McMahon, R. J. (1984). Relationships between marital distress and child behavior problems, maternal personal adjustment, maternal personality, and maternal parenting behavior. *Journal of Abnormal Psychology, 93,* 348–351.

Bonica, J. (1972). *Principles and practices of obstetric analgesia and anesthesia,* Vols. 1 & 2. Philadelphia: F. A. Davis.

Bonvillian, J. D., Orlansky, M. D., & Novack, L. L. (1983). Developmental milestones: Sign language acquisition and motor development. *Child Development, 54,* 1435–1445.

Bornstein, M. H., Kessen, W., & Weiskopf, S. (1976). The categories of hue in infancy. *Science, 191,* 201–202.

Bornstein, M. H., & Marks, L. E. (1982, January). Color revisionism. *Psychology Today,* pp. 64–73.

Borstelmann, L. J. (1983). Children before psychology: Ideas about children from antiquity to the late 1800s. In W. Kessen (Ed.), *Handbook of child psychology.* New York: Wiley.

Bossard, J. H. S., & Boll, E. (1956). *The large family system.* Philadelphia: University of Pennsylvania Press.

Bossard, J. H. S., & Boll, E. (1960). *The sociology of child development.* New York: Harper & Row.

Botvin, G. J., & Murray, F. B. (1975). The efficacy of peer modeling and social conflict in the acquisition of conservation. *Child Development, 46,* 796–799.

Bourne, L. E., Ekstrand, B. R., & Dominowski, R. L. (1971). *The psychology of thinking.* Englewood Cliffs, NJ: Prentice-Hall.

Bower, T. G. R. (1971, October). The object in the world of the infant. *Scientific American, 225,* 30–38.

Bower, T. G. R. (1974). *Development in infancy.* San Francisco: W. H. Freeman.

Bower, T. G. R. (1975). Infant perception of the third dimension and object concept development. In L. B. Cohen & P. Salapatek (Eds.), *Infant perception: From sensation to cognition,* Vol. 2. New York: Academic Press.

Bower, T. G. R. (1977). *The perceptual world of the child.* Cambridge, MA: Harvard University Press.

Bowerman, M. F. (1982). Starting to talk worse: Clues to language acquisition from children's late speech errors. In S. Strauss (Ed.), *U-shaped behavioral growth.* New York: Academic Press.

Brackbill, Y. (1958). Extinction of the smiling response in infants as a function of reinforcement schedule. *Child Development, 29,* 115–124.

Brackbill, Y. (1970). Continuous stimulation and arousal level in infants: Additive effects. Paper presented to the American Psychological Association.

Brackbill, Y. (1976). Long-term effects of obstetrical anesthesia on infant autonomic function. *Developmental Psychobiology, 9,* 353–358.

Brackbill, Y. (1979). Obstetrical medication and infant behavior. In J. D. Osofsky (Ed.), *Handbook of infant development.* New York: Wiley-Interscience.

Bradley, R. H., & Caldwell, B. M. (1976). The relation of infants' home environments to mental test performance at fifty-four months: A follow-up study. *Child Development, 47,* 1172–1174.

Bradley, R. H., & Caldwell, B. M. (1984). The relation of infants' home environments to achievement test performance in first grade: A follow-up study. *Child Development, 55,* 803–809.

Braine, M. D. S. (1963). The ontogeny of English phrase structure: The first phase. *Language, 39,* 1–13.

Brainerd, C. J. (1978). *Piaget's theory of intelligence.* Englewood Cliffs, NJ: Prentice-Hall.

Bram, S. (1984). Voluntarily childless women: Traditional or nontraditional? *Sex Roles, 10,* 195–206.

Brandt, M. M., & Strattner-Gregory, M. J. (1980). Effect of highlighting intention on intentionality and restitutive justice. *Developmental Psychology, 16,* 147–148.

Braun, C. (1976). Teacher expectations: Sociopsychological dynamics. *Review of Educational Research, 46* (2), 185–213.

Bravlove, M. (1981, December 7). Keeping work world out of family life is growing problem for two-job couples. *The Wall Street Journal.*

Bray, N. W., Hersh, R. E., & Turner, L. A. (1985). Selective remembering during adolescence. *Developmental Psychology, 21,* 290–294

► ► ► ►

Brazelton, T. B. (1970). Effects of prenatal drugs on the behavior of the neonate. *American Journal of Psychiatry, 37,* 180–189.

Brazelton, T. B. (1973). *Neonatal behavioral assessment scale.* London: Heinemann.

Bretherton, I., & Waters, E. (1985). Growing points of attachment theory and research. *Monographs of the Society for Research in Child Development, 50* (1, 2, Serial No. 209).

Bridges, K. (1932). Emotional development in early infancy. *Child Development, 3,* 324–341.

Brigham, T. A., Hopper, C., Hill, B., de Armas, A., & Newsom, P. (1985). A self-management program for disruptive adolescents in the school: A clinical replication analysis. *Behavior Therapy, 16,* 99–115.

Brody, G. H., Stoneman, Z., MacKinnon, C. E., & MacKinnon, R. (1985). Role relationships and behavior between preschool-aged and school-aged sibling pairs. *Developmental Psychology, 21,* 124–129.

Brody, L. R., Zelazo, P. R., & Chaika, H. (1984). Habituation-dishabituation to speech in the neonate. *Developmental Psychology, 20,* 114–119.

Brody, S., & Axelrad, S. (1978). *Mothers, fathers, and children.* New York: International Universities Press.

Broman, S. H., Nichols, P. L., & Kennedy, N. A. (1975). *Preschool IQ: Prenatal and early developmental correlates.* Hillsdale, NJ: Erlbaum.

Bronfenbrenner, U. (1960). Freudian theories of identification and their derivatives. *Child Development, 31,* 15–40.

Bronfenbrenner, U. (1970). *Two worlds of childhood: U.S. and U.S.S.R.* New York: Russell Sage Foundation.

Bronfenbrenner, U. (1973). The dream of the kibbutz. In *Readings in human development.* Guilford, CT: Dushkin.

Bronfenbrenner, U. (1977). Toward an experimental ecology of human development. *American Psychologist, 32,* 513–531.

Bronfenbrenner, U. (1979). *The ecology of human development: Experiments by nature and design.* Cambridge, MA: Harvard University Press.

Bronfenbrenner, U. (1986). Ecology of the family as a context for human development: Research perspectives. *Developmental Psychology, 22,* 723–742.

Bronfenbrenner, U., & Crouter, A. C. (1983). The evolution of environmental models in developmental research. In P. H. Mussen (Ed.), *Handbook of child psychology: Vol. 1. History, theory, and methods.* New York: Wiley.

Brook, J. S., Lukoff, J. F., & Whiteman, M. (1980). Initiation into adolescent marijuana use. *Journal of Genetic Psychology, 137,* 133–142.

Brook, J. S., & Whiteman, M. (1983). Stages of drug use in adolescence: Personality, peer and family correlates. *Developmental Psychology, 19,* 269–277.

Brooks, J., & Lewis, M. (1976). Infants' responses to strangers: Midget, adult, and child. *Child Development, 47,* 323–332.

Brooks, V. R. (1982). Sex differences in student dominance behavior in female and male professors' classrooms. *Sex Roles, 8,* 683–690.

Brooks-Gunn, J., & Lewis, M. (1984). Maternal responsivity in interactions with handicapped infants. *Child Development, 55,* 782–793.

Brooks-Gunn, J., & Matthews, W. S. (1979). *He and she: How children develop their sex-role identity.* Englewood Cliffs, NJ: Spectrum.

Brooks-Gunn, J., & Ruble, D. N. (1983). The experience of menarche from a developmental perspective. In J. Brooks-Gunn & A. C. Petersen (Eds.), *Girls at puberty.* New York: Plenum Press.

Brooks-Gunn, J., & Weinraub, M. (1983). Origins of infant intelligence testing. In M. Lewis (Ed.), *Origins of intelligence: Infancy and early childhood,* 2d ed. New York: Plenum Press.

Brophy, J. E. (1983). Research on the self-fulfilling prophecy and teacher expectations. *Journal of Educational Psychology, 75,* 631–661.

Brophy, J. E., & Good, T. L. (1974). *Teacher-student relationships: Causes and consequences.* New York: Holt, Rinehart and Winston.

Broverman, I. K., Vogel, S. R., Broverman, D. M., Clarkson, F. E., & Rosenkrantz, P. S. (1972). Sex-role stereotypes: A current appraisal. *Journal of Social Issues, 28,* 59–78.

Brown, A. L., Bransford, J. D., Ferrara, R. A., & Campione, J. C. (1983). Learning, remembering, and understanding. In J. H. Flavell & E. M. Markman (Eds.), *Handbook of child psychology: Vol. 3. Cognitive development.* New York: Wiley.

Brown, L. (1983). Status of child protective services in the United States: An analysis of issues and practice. In J. E. Leavitt (Ed.), *Child abuse and neglect: Research and innovation.* The Hague: Martinus Nijhoff.

Brown, N. A., Goulding, E. H., & Fabros, S. (1979). Ethanol embryotoxicity: Direct effects on mammalian embryos in vitro. *Science, 206,* 573–575.

Brown, R. (1970). The first sentences of child and chimpanzee. In R. Brown (Ed.), *Psycholinguistics.* New York: Free Press.

Brown, R. (1973a). Development of the first language in the human species. *American Psychologist, 28,* 97–106.

Brown, R. (1973b). *A first language: The early stages.* Cambridge, MA: Harvard University Press.

Brown, R. (1977). Introduction. In C. A. Snow & C. Ferguson (Eds.), *Talking to children.* New York: Cambridge University Press.

Brownell, K. D. (1982). Obesity: Understanding and treating a serious, prevalent, and refractory disorder. *Journal of Consulting and Clinical Psychology, 50,* 820–840.

▶ ▶ ▶ ▶

Bruch, H. (1957). *The importance of overweight*. New York: Norton.

Bruch, H. (1978). *The golden cage: The enigma of anorexia nervosa*. Cambridge, MA: Harvard University Press.

Bruden, M. P. (1982). *Laterality*. New York: Academic Press.

Bruner, J. S. (1964). The course of cognitive growth. *American Psychologist, 19,* 1–15.

Bruner, J. S. (1983). *Child's talk: Learning to use language*. New York: Norton.

Bruner, J.S., Goodnow, J.J., & Austin, G.A. (1956). *A study of thinking*. New York: Wiley.

Bruner, J. S., & Kenney, J. (1966) On multiple ordering. In J. S. Bruner, R. R. Olver, & P. M. Greenfield (Eds.), *Studies in cognitive growth*. New York: Wiley.

Brunk, M., Henggeler, S. W., & Whelan, J. P. (1987). Comparison of multisystemic therapy and parent training in the brief treatment of child abuse and neglect. *Journal of Consulting and Clinical Psychology, 55,* 171–178.

Bry, B. H. (1983). Predicting drug abuse: Review and reformulation. *International Journal of the Addictions, 18,* 223–233.

Bryant, B. J. (1982). Sibling relationships in middle childhood. In M. E. Lamb & B. Sutton-Smith (Eds.), *Sibling relationships*. Hillsdale, NJ: Erlbaum.

Bryant, B. J., & Crockenberg, S. (1980). Correlates and dimensions of prosocial behavior. *Child Development, 51,* 529–544.

Bryant, P. (1982). Piaget's questions. *British Journal of Psychology, 73,* 157–163.

Bryant, P., & Trabasso, T. (1971). Transitive inferences and memory in young children. *Nature, 232,* 456–458.

Bullock, M. (1985). Animism in childhood thinking: A new look at an old question. *Developmental Psychology, 21,* 217–225.

Burton, R. V. (1963). Generality of honesty reconsidered. *Psychological Review, 70,* 481–499.

Burton, R. V. (1976). Honesty and dishonesty. In T. Lickona (Ed.), *Moral development and behavior*. New York: Holt, Rinehart and Winston.

Burton, R. V. (1984). A paradox in theories and research in moral development. In W. M. Kurtines & J. L. Gewirtz (Eds.), *Morality, moral behavior and moral development*. New York: Wiley.

Bushnell, E. W., & Maratsos, M. P. (1984). *Spooning* and *basketing*: Children's dealing with accidental gaps in the lexicon. *Child Development, 5,* 893–902.

Bustillo, M., Buster, J. E., Cohen, S. W., Hamilton, F., Thorneycroft, I. H., Simon, J. A., Rodi, I. A., Boyers, S., Marshall, J. R., Louw, J. A., Seed, R., & Seed, R. (1984). Delivery of a healthy infant following nonsurgical ovum transfer. *Journal of the American Medical Association, 251,* 889.

Butler, N. R., & Goldstein, H. (1973). Smoking in pregnancy and subsequent child development. *British Medical Journal, 4,* 573–575.

Cadoret, R. J. (1978). Psychopathology in adopted-away offspring of biologic parents with antisocial behavior. *Archives of General Psychiatry, 36,* 176–184.

Cadoret, R. J., Cain, C. A., & Grove, W. M. (1980). Development of alcoholism in adoptees raised apart from alcoholic biologic relatives. *Archives of General Psychiatry, 37,* 561–563.

Cairns, R. B. (1983). The emergence of developmental psychology. In P. H. Mussen (Ed.), *Handbook of child psychology: Vol. 1. History, theory, and methods*. New York: Wiley.

Caldwell, B. M. (1964). The effects of infant care. In M. L. Hoffman & L. W. Hoffman (Eds.), *Review of child development research*, Vol. 1. New York: Russell Sage.

Caldwell, B. M., & Bradley, R. H. (1984). *Home observation for the measurement of the environment*. New York: Dorsey Press.

Caldwell, B. M., Wright, C. M., Honig, A. S., & Tannenbaum, J. (1970). Infant day care and attachment. *American Journal of Orthopsychiatry, 40,* 397–412.

Callaghan, J. W. (1981). A comparison of Anglo, Hopi and Navajo mothers and infants. In T. M. Field, A. M. Sostel, P. Vietze, & P. H. Leiderman (Eds.), *Culture and early interactions*. Hillsdale, NJ: Erlbaum.

Campbell, F. L., Townes, B. D., & Beach, L. R. (1982). Motivational bases of childbearing decisions. In G. L. Fox (Ed.), *The childbearing decision*. Beverly Hills, CA: Sage.

Campbell, M. (1970). Anomalies of the genital tract. In M. Campbell & J. Harrison (Eds.), *Urology*, Vol. 2. Philadelphia: W. B. Saunders.

Campos, J. J. (1976). Heart rate: A sensitive tool for the study of emotional development. In L. Lipsitt (Ed.), *Developmental psychobiology: The significance of infancy*. Hillsdale, NJ: Erlbaum.

Campos, J., Barrett, K., Lamb, M., Goldsmith, H., & Stenberg, C. (1983). Socioemotional development. In. M. M. Harth & J. J. Campos (Eds.), *Handbook of child psychology: Vol. 2. Infancy and developmental psychobiology*. New York: Wiley.

Campos, J. J., Hiatt, S., Ramsay, D., Henderson, C., & Svejda, M. (1978). The emergence of fear on the visual cliff. In M. Lewis & L. Rosenblum (Eds.), *The origins of affect*. New York: Plenum Press.

Campos, J. J., Langer, A., & Krowitz, A. (1970). Cardiac responses on the visual cliff in prelocomotor human infants. *Science, 170,* 196–197.

Campos, J. J., & Stenberg, C. (1981). Perception, appraisal, and emotion: The onset of social referencing. In M. E. Lamb & L. R. Sherrod (Eds.), *Infant social cognition: Empirical and*

▶ ▶ ▶ ▶

theoretical considerations. Hillsdale, NJ: Erlbaum.

Cann, A., & Haight, J. M. (1983). Children's perceptions of relative competence in sex-typed occupations. *Sex Roles, 9,* 767–773.

Cann, A., & Newbern, S. R. (1984). Sex stereotype effects in children's picture recognition. *Child Development, 55,* 1085–1090.

Cantor, P. (1983). Depression and suicide in children. In C. E. Walker & M. C. Roberts (Eds.), *Handbook of clinical child psychology.* New York: Wiley.

Cantwell, D. P. (1975). *The hyperactive child: Diagnosis, management, current research.* New York: Spectrum Books.

Cantwell, D. P. (1980). A clinician's guide to the use of stimulant medication for the psychiatric disorders of children. *Developmental and Behavioral Pediatrics, 1,* 133–140.

Cantwell, D. P. (1982). Childhood depression: A review of current research. In B. B. Lahey & A. E. Kazdin (Eds.), *Advances in clinical child psychology.* New York: Plenum Press.

Cantwell, H. B. (1980). Child neglect. In C. H. Kempe & R. E. Helfer (Eds.), *The battered child,* 3d ed. Chicago: University of Chicago Press.

Caputo, D. V., & Mandell, W. (1970). Consequences of low birth weight. *Developmental Psychology, 3,* 363–383.

Carlson, B. E. (1984). The father's contribution to child care: Effects on children's perceptions of parental roles. *American Journal of Orthopsychiatry, 54,* 123–136.

Carlson, G. A. (1980). Unmasking masked depression in children and adolescents. *American Journal of Psychiatry, 137,* 445–449.

Carlson, N. R. (1987). *Psychology: The science of behavior,* 2d ed. Boston: Allyn & Bacon.

Carman, R. B., Fitzgerald, J., & Holmgren, C. (1983). Drinking motivations and alcohol consumption among adolescent females. *Journal of Psychology, 114,* 79–82.

Caron, A. J., & Caron, R. F. (1981). Processing of relational information as an index of infant risk. In S. L. Friedman & M. Sigman (Eds.), *Preterm birth and psychological development.* New York: Academic Press.

Caron, A. J., & Caron, R. F. (1982). Cognitive development in infancy. In T. M. Field, A. Huston, H. C. Quay, L. Troll, & G. E. Finley (Eds.), *Review of human development.* New York: Wiley.

Caron, A. J., Caron, R. F., Caldwell, R. C., & Weiss, S. J. (1973). Infant perception of the structural properties of the face. *Developmental Psychology, 9,* 385–399.

Carpenter, C. J., & Huston-Stein, A. (1980). The relation of children's activity preference to sex-typed behaviors. *Child Development, 51,* 862–872.

Carroll, J. L., & Rest, J. R. (1982). Moral development. In B. Wolman (Ed.), *Handbook of developmental psychology.* Englewood Cliffs, NJ: Prentice-Hall.

Carter, D. B., & McCloskey, L. A. (1983). Peers and maintenance of sex-typed behavior: The development of children's conceptions of cross-gender behavior in their peers. *Social Cognition, 2,* 294–314.

Carter, D. B., & Patterson, C. J. (1982). Sex roles as social conventions: The development of children's conceptions of sex-role stereotypes. *Developmental Psychology, 18,* 812–824.

Carter, D., & Welch, D. (1981). Parenting styles and children's behavior. *Family Relations, 30,* 191–195.

Carter-Saltzman, L. (1980). Biological and sociocultural effects on handedness: Comparison between biological and adoptive families. *Science, 209,* 1263–1265.

Case, R. (1984). The process of stage transition: A neo-Piagetan view. In R. Sternberg (Ed.), *Mechanisms of cognitive development.* New York: Freeman.

Case, R. (1985). *Intellectual development: Birth to adulthood.* New York: Academic Press.

Casper, R. C., Eckert, E. O., Halmi, K. A., Goldberg, S. C., & Davis, J. M. (1980). Bulimia: Its incidence and clinical importance in patients with anorexia nervosa. *Archives of General Psychiatry, 37,* 1030–1035.

Caspi, A., Elder, G. H., Jr., & Bem, D. J. (1987). Moving against the world: Life-course patterns of explosive children. *Developmental Psychology, 23,* 308–313.

Cassill, K. (1982) *Twins reared apart.* New York: Atheneum.

Cattell, R. B. (1949). *The culture-free intelligence test.* Champaign, IL: Institute for Personality and Ability Testing.

Cernoch, J., & Porter, R. (1985). Recognition of maternal axillary odors by infants. *Child Development, 56,* 1593–1598.

Chaiklin, H. (1979). The treadmill of lead. *American Journal of Orthopsychiatry, 49,* 571–573.

Chandler, M. J., Greenspan, S., & Barenboim. (1973). Judgments of intentionality in response to videotaped and verbally presented moral dilemmas: The medium is the message. *Child Development, 44,* 315–320.

Chapman, M., Zahn-Waxler, C., Cooperman, G., & Iannotti, R. (1987). Empathy and responsibility in the motivation of children's helping. *Developmental Psychology, 23,* 140–145.

Charbonneau, C., Robert, M., Bourassa, G., & Glady-Bissonnette, S. (1976). Observational learning of quantity conservation and Piagetan generalization tasks. *Developmental Psychology, 12,* 211–217.

Chasnoff, I. J., Burns, W. J., Schnoll, S. H., & Burns, K. A. (1985). Cocaine use in pregnancy. *The New*

▶ ▶ ▶ ▶

England Journal of Medicine, 313, 666–669.

Chesler, P. (1972). *Women and madness.* New York: Doubleday.

Chesno, F. A., & Kilmann, P. R. (1975). Effects of stimulation intensity on sociopathic avoidance learning. *Journal of Abnormal Psychology, 84,* 144–151.

Chess, S. (1983). Mothers are always the problem—Or are they? *Pediatrics, 71,* 974–976.

Chess, S., & Thomas, A. (1982). Infant bonding: Mystique and reality. *American Journal of Orthopsychiatry, 52,* 213–222.

Chi, M. T. H. (1976). Short-term memory limitations in children: Capacity or processing deficits? *Memory and Cognition, 4,* 559–572.

Chi, M. T. H. (1978). Knowledge structures and memory development. In R. S. Siegler (Ed.), *Children's thinking: What develops?* Hillsdale, NJ: Erlbaum.

Chi, M. T. H., & Koeske, R. D. (1983). Network representations of a child's dinosaur knowledge. *Developmental Psychology, 19,* 29–39.

Chilman, C. S. (1982). Adolescent childbearing in the United States: Apparent causes and consequences. In T. M. Field, A. Huston, H. C. Quay, L. Troll, & G. E. Finley (Eds.), *Review of human development.* New York: Wiley.

Chomsky, C. S. (1969). *The acquisition of syntax in children from five to ten.* Cambridge, MA: Massachusetts Institute of Technology Press.

Chomsky, N. (1965). *Aspects of the theory of syntax.* Cambridge, MA: Massachusetts Institute of Technology Press.

Chomsky, N. (1968). *Language and mind.* New York: Harcourt, Brace & World.

Chomsky, N. (1980). *Rules and representations.* New York: Columbia University Press.

Christensen, A., Phillips, P., Glasgow, R. E., & Johnson, S. M. (1983). Parental characteristics and interactional dysfunction in families with child behavior problems: A preliminary investigation. *Journal of Abnormal Child Psychology, 11,* 153–166.

Chumlea, W. C. (1982). Physical growth in adolescence. In B. B. Wolman (Ed.), *Handbook of developmental psychology.* Englewood Cliffs, NJ: Prentice-Hall.

Cicchetti, D., & Pogge-Hesse, P. (1981). The relation between emotion and cognition in infant development. In M. E. Lamb & L. R. Sherrod (Eds.), *Infant social cognition: Empirical and theoretical considerations.* Hillsdale, NJ: Erlbaum.

Cicirelli, V. G. (1975). Effects of mother and older sibling on the problem-solving behavior of the younger child. *Developmental Psychology, 11,* 749–756.

Cicirelli, V. G. (1976). Siblings help siblings. In V. L. Allen (Ed.), *Children as tutors.* New York: Academic Press.

Cicirelli, V. G. (1982). Sibling influence throughout the life-span. In M. E. Lamb & B. Sutton-Smith (Eds.), *Sibling relationships.* Hillsdale, NJ: Erlbaum.

Clark, E. V. (1973). What's in a word? On the child's acquisition of semantics in his first language. In E. Moore (Ed.), *Cognitive development and the acquisition of language.* New York: Academic Press.

Clark, E. V. (1975). Knowledge, context, and strategy in the acquisition of meaning. In D. P. Date (Ed.), *Georgetown University roundtable on language and linguistics.* Washington, DC: Georgetown University Press.

Clark, E. V. (1977). Strategies and the mapping problem in first language acquisition. In J. Macnamara (Ed.), *Language learning and thought.* New York: Academic Press.

Clark, E. V. (1979). Building a vocabulary: Words for objects, actions, and relations. In P. Fletcher & M. Gorman (Eds.), *Language acquisition.* Cambridge: Cambridge University Press.

Clark, E. V. (1982). The young word maker: A case study of innovation in the child's lexicon. In E. Wanner & L. R. Gleitman (Eds.), *Language acquisition: The state of the art.* Cambridge: Cambridge University Press.

Clark, E. V. (1983). Meanings and concepts. In J. H. Flavell & E. M. Markman (Eds.), *Handbook of child psychology,* Vol. 3. New York: Wiley.

Clark, E. V., Gelman, S., & Lane, N. (1985). Compound nouns and category structure in young children. *Child Development, 56,* 84–94.

Clark, H. H., & Clark, E. V. (1977). *Psychology and language: An introduction to psycholinguistics.* New York: Harcourt Brace Jovanovich.

Clark, M., & Witherspoon D. (1984, May 28). Using drugs to fight autism. *Newsweek,* pp. 90–91.

Clarke, A. E., & Ruble, D. N. (1978). Young adolescents' beliefs concerning menstruation. *Child Development, 49,* 231–234.

Clarke, A. M., & Clarke, A. D. B. (Eds.) (1976). *Early experience: Myth and evidence.* New York: Free Press.

Clarke-Stewart, K. A. (1982). *Day care.* Cambridge, MA: Harvard University Press.

Clarke-Stewart, K. A. (1984). Day care: A new context for research and development. In M. Perlmutter (Ed.), Parent–child interactions and parent–child relations in child development. *The Minnesota symposium on child psychology,* Vol. 17. Hillsdale, NJ: Erlbaum.

Clarke-Stewart, K. A., & Fein, G. G. (1983). Early childhood programs. In P. H. Mussen (Ed.), *Handbook of child psychology: Vol. 2. Infancy and developmental psychobiology.* New York: Wiley.

▶ ▶ ▶ ▶

Clarke-Stewart, K. A., & Hevey, C. M. (1981). Longitudinal relations in repeated observations of mother-care interaction from one to two and one-half years. *Developmental Psychology, 17,* 127–145.

Clausen, J. A. (1975). The social meaning of differential physical and sexual maturation. In S. E. Dragastin & G. H. Elder (Eds.), *Adolescence in the life cycle: Psychological change and social context.* New York: Wiley.

Cleckley, H. (1964). *The mask of sanity.* St. Louis: Mosby.

Clifton, R. K. (1974). Heartrate conditioning in the newborn infant. *Journal of Experimental Child Psychology, 18,* 9–21.

Clifton, R. K., Morrongiello, B. A., Kulig, J. W., & Dowd, J. M. (1981). Newborns' orientation toward sound: Possible implications for cortical development. *Child Development, 52,* 833–838.

Clifton, R. K., Siqueland, E. R., & Lipsitt, L. P. (1972). Conditioned head turning in human newborns as a function of conditioned response requirements and states of wakefulness. *Journal of Experimental Child Psychology, 13,* 43–57.

Cline, V. B., Croft, R. G., & Courrier, S. (1973). Desensitization of children to television violence. *Journal of Personality and Social Psychology, 27,* 360–365.

Clingempeel, W. G., & Repucci, N. D. (1982). Joint custody after divorce: Major issues and goals for research. *Psychological Bulletin, 91,* 102–127.

Clingempeel, W. G., & Segal, S. (1986). Stepparent–stepchild relationships and the psychological adjustment of children in stepmother and stepfather families. *Child Development, 57,* 474–484.

Coates, B., & Pusser, H. E. (1975). Positive reinforcement and punishment in "Sesame Street" and "Mister Rogers' Neighborhood." *Journal of Broadcasting, 19,* 143–151.

Coates, B., Pusser, H. E., & Goodman, I. (1976). The influence of "Sesame Street" and "Mister Rogers' Neighborhood" on children's social behavior in the preschool. *Child Development, 47,* 138–144.

Cohen, E. A., Gelfand, D. M., Dodd, D. K., Jensen, J., & Turner, C. (1980). Self-control practices associated with weight-loss maintenance in children and adolescents. *Behavior Therapy, 11,* 26–37.

Cohen, H. L., & Filipczak, J. (1971). *A new learning environment.* San Francisco: Jossey-Bass.

Cohen, L. B., DeLoache, J. S., & Strauss, M. S. (1979). Infant visual perception. In J. D. Osofsky (Ed.), *Handbook of infant development.* New York: Wiley-Interscience.

Cohen, L. J., & Campos, J. J. (1974). Father, mother, and stranger as elicitors of attachment behavior in infancy. *Developmental Psychology, 10,* 146–154.

Cohn, J. F., & Tronick, E. Z. (1983). Three-month-old infants' reaction to simulated maternal depression. *Child Development, 54,* 185–193.

Coie, J. D., & Kupersmidt, J. B. (1983). A behavioral analysis of emerging social status in boys' groups. *Child Development, 54,* 1400–1416.

Colby, A., Kohlberg, L., Gibbs, J., & Lieberman, M. (1983). A longitudinal study of moral judgment. *Monographs of the Society for Research in Child Development, 48* (Serial No. 200).

Cole, N. S. (1981). Bias in testing. *American Psychologist, 36,* 1067–1077.

Colletti, L. F. (1979). Relationship between pregnancy and birth complications and the later development of learning disabilities. *Journal of Learning Disabilities, 12,* 659–663.

Condiotte, M. M., & Lichtenstein, E. (1981). Self-efficacy and relapse in smoking cessation programs. *Journal of Consulting and Clinical Psychology, 49,* 648–658.

Condon, W. S., & Sander, L. W. (1974a). Neonate movement is synchronized with adult speech. *Science, 183,* 99–101.

Condon, W. S., & Sander, L. W. (1974b). Synchrony demonstrated between movements of the neonate and adult speech. *Child Development, 45,* 456–462.

Conger, J. J., & Petersen, A. (1984). *Adolescence and youth: Psychological development in a changing world,* 3d ed. New York: Harper & Row.

Conway, E., & Brackbill, Y. (1970). Delivery medication and infant outcome: An empirical study. *Monographs of the Society for Research in Child Development, 35* (4), 24–34.

Cook, A. S., West, J. S., & Hamner, T. J. (1982). Changes in attitude toward parenting among college women: 1972 and 1979 samples. *Family Relations, 31,* 109–113.

Cook, M., Field, J., & Griffiths, K. (1978). The perception of solid form in early infancy. *Child Development, 49,* 866–869.

Coons, S., & Guilleminault, C. (1982). Development of sleep-wake patterns and non-rapid-eye-movement sleep stages during the first six months of life in normal infants. *Pediatrics, 69,* 793–798.

Cooper, H. M. (1979a). Pygmalion grows up: A model for teacher expectation communication and performance influence. *Review of Educational Research, 49,* 389–410.

Cooper, H. M. (1979b). Statistically combining independent studies: A meta-analysis of sex differences in conformity research. *Journal of Personality and Social Psychology, 37,* 131–146.

Cooper, R., & Zubek, J. (1965). Effects of enriched and restricted early environments on the learning ability of bright and dull rats. *Canadian Journal of Psychology, 12,* 159–164.

Coopersmith, S. (1967). *The antecedents of self-esteem.* San Francisco: W. H. Freeman.

▶ ▶ ▶ ▶

Costanzo, P. R., Coie, J. D., Grument, J. F., & Farnill, D. (1973). A reexamination of the effects of intent and consequence of children's moral judgments. *Child Development, 44,* 154–161.

Costanzo, P. R., & Shaw, M. E. (1966). Conformity as a function of age level. *Child Development, 37,* 967–975.

Cowan, C. A., Langer, J., Heavenrich, J., & Nathanson, M. (1969). Social learning and Piaget's cognitive theory of moral development. *Journal of Personality and Social Psychology, 11,* 261–274.

Cowan, P. A. (1978). *Piaget with feeling.* New York: Holt, Rinehart and Winston.

Cowart, B. J. (1981). Development of taste perception in humans: Sensitivity and preference throughout the life span. *Psychological Bulletin, 90,* 43–93.

Cozby, P. C. (1973). Self-disclosure: A literature review. *Psychological Bulletin, 79,* 73–91.

Craighead, W. E., Kazdin, A. E., & Mahoney, M. J. (1981). *Behavior modification: Principles, issues, and applications,* 2d ed. Boston: Houghton Mifflin.

Craik, F. I. M., & Watkins, M. J. (1973). The role of rehearsal in short-term memory. *Journal of Verbal Learning and Verbal Behavior, 12,* 599–607.

Cratty, B. (1979). *Perceptual and motor development in infants and children,* 2d ed. Englewood Cliffs, NJ: Prentice-Hall.

Crawford, C. (1979). George Washington, Abraham Lincoln, and Arthur Jensen: Are they compatible? *American Psychologist, 34,* 664–672.

Crisp, A. H. (1967). The possible significance of some behavioural correlates of weight and carbohydrate intake. *Journal of Psychosomatic Research, 11,* 117–131.

Crnic, K. A., Ragozin, A. S., Greenberg, M. T., Robinson, M. N., & Basham, R. B. (1983). Social interaction and developmental competence of preterm and full-term infants during the first year of life. *Child Development, 54,* 1199–1210.

Crockenberg, S. B. (1972). Creativity tests: A boon or boondoggle for children? *Review of Educational Research, 42,* 27–45.

Crockenberg, S. B. (1981). Infant irritability, mother responsiveness, and social support influences on the security of the mother-infant attachment. *Child Development, 52,* 857–865.

Crockenberg, S. B., & Smith, P. (1982). Antecedents of mother-infant interaction and infant irritability in the first three months of life. *Infant Behavior and Development, 5,* 105–119.

Cronbach, L. J. (1975). Five decades of public controversy over mental testing. *American Psychologist, 30,* 1–14.

Crook, C. K., & Lipsitt, L. P. (1976). Neonatal nutritive sucking: Effects of taste stimulation upon sucking rhythm and heart rate. *Child Development, 47,* 518–522.

Cruise, M. O. (1973). A longitudinal study of the growth of low birth weight infants: 1. Velocity and distance growth, birth to 3 years. *Pediatrics, 51,* 620–628.

Cummings, E. M. (1980). Caregiver stability and day care. *Developmental Psychology, 16,* 31–37.

Cummings, E. M., Iannotti, R. J., & Zahn-Waxler, C. (1985). Influence of conflict between adults on the emotions and aggression of young children. *Developmental Psychology, 21,* 495–507.

Cummins, R. A., Livesey, P. J., Evans, J. G. M., & Walsh, R. N. (1979). Mechanism of brain growth by environmental stimulation. *Science, 205,* 522.

Curtiss, S. (1977). *Genie: A psycholinguistic study of a modern-day "wild child."* New York: Academic Press.

Cutrona, C. E. (1983). Causal attributions and perinatal depression. *Journal of Abnormal Psychology, 92,* 161–172.

Cutrona, C. E., & Troutman, B. R. (1986). Social support, infant temperament, and parenting self-efficacy: A mediational model of postpartum depression. *Child Development, 57,* 1507–1518.

Dale, P. (1976). *Language development: Structure and function.* Hinsdale, IL: Dryden Press.

Damon, W. (1977). *The social world of the child.* San Francisco: Jossey-Bass.

Daniels, D., & Plomin, R. (1985). Origins of individual differences in infant shyness. *Developmental Psychology, 21,* 118–121.

Daniels, P., & Weingarten, K. (1982). *Sooner or later: The timing of parenthood in adult lives.* New York: Norton.

Darley, J. M., & Gross, P. H. (1983). A hypothesis-confirming bias in labeling effects. *Journal of Personality and Social Psychology, 44,* 20–33.

Darlington, R. B., Royce, J. M., Snipper, A. S., Murray, H. W., & Lazar, I. (1980). Preschool programs and later school competence of children from low-income families. *Science, 208,* 202–204.

Darvill, D., & Cheyne, J. A. (1981). Sequential analysis of response to aggression: Age and sex effects. Paper presented to the biennial meeting of the Society for Research in Child Development, Boston.

Darwin, C. A. (1972). *The expression of the emotions in man and animals.* London: J. Murray.

Davies, J. M., Latto, I. P., Jones, J. G., Veale, A., & Wardrop, C. A. (1979). Effects of stopping smoking for 48 hours on oxygen availability from the blood: A study of pregnant women. *British Medical Journal, 2,* 355–356.

Davis, E. (1983). *A guide to midwifery: Heart and hands.* New York: Bantam Books.

Davis, M., & Weitz, S. (1981). Sex differences in body movements and positions. In C. Mayo & N. M. Henley (Eds.), *Gender and nonverbal behavior.* New York: Springer-Verlag.

▶ ▶ ▶ ▶

REFERENCES

Dawe, H. C. (1934). The influence of size of kindergarten group upon performance. *Child Development, 5,* 295–303.

Deaux, K. (1984). From individual differences to social categories: Analysis of a decade's research on gender. *American Psychologist, 39,* 105–116.

Deaux, K. (1985). Sex and gender. *Annual Review of Psychology, 36,* 49–81.

Deaux, K., & Lewis, L. L. (1983). Assessment of gender stereotypes: Methodology and components. *Psychological Documents, 13* 25 (Ms. No. 2583).

DeCasper, A. J., & Fifer, W. P. (1980). Of human bonding: Newborns prefer their mothers' voices. *Science, 208,* 1174–1176.

DeCasper, A. J., & Prescott, P. A. (1984). Human newborns' perception of male voices: Preference, discrimination, and reinforcing value. *Developmental Psychobiology, 17,* 481–491.

De Frain, J., Taylor, J., & Ernst, L. (1982). *Coping with sudden infant death.* Lexington, MA: Lexington Books.

DeFries, J. C., Plomin, R., & LaBuda, M. C. (1987). Genetic stability of cognitive development from childhood to adulthood. *Developmental Psychology, 23,* 4–12.

DeLoache, J. S., Cassidy, D. J., & Brown, A. L. (1985). Precursors of mnemonic strategies in very young children's memory. *Child Development, 56,* 125–137.

DeMyer, M. K., Barton, S., DeMyer, W. E., Norton, J. A., Allen, J., & Steele, R. (1973). Prognosis in autism: A follow-up study. *Journal of Autism and Childhood Schizophrenia, 3,* 199–246.

DeMyer, M. K., Hingtgen, J. N., & Jackson, R. K. (1981). Infantile autism reviewed: A decade of research. *Schizophrenia Bulletin, 7,* 388–451.

Denckla, M. B., & Rudel, R. (1974). Rapid "automatized" naming of pictured objects, colors, letters, and numbers by normal children. *Cortex, 10,* 186–202.

Denney, N. W. (1972). Free classification in preschool children. *Child Development, 43,* 1161–1170.

Denney, N. W., Zeytinoglu, S., & Selzer, C. S. (1977) Conservation training in four-year-old children. *Journal of Experimental Child Psychology, 24,* 129–146.

Dennis, M., Sugar, J., & Whitaker, H. A. (1982). The acquisition of tag questions. *Child Development, 53,* 1254–1257.

Dennis, W. (1940). Does culture appreciably affect patterns of infant behavior? *Journal of Social Psychology, 12,* 305–317.

Dennis, W. (1960). Causes of retardation among institutional children: Iran. *Journal of Genetic Psychology, 96,* 47–59.

Dennis, W., & Dennis, M. G. (1940). The effect of cradling practices upon the onset of walking in Hopi children. *Journal of Genetic Psychology, 56,* 77–86.

Dennis, W., & Najarian, P. (1957). Infant development under environmental handicap. *Psychological Monographs, 71,* 436.

Dennis, W., & Sayegh, Y. (1965). The effect of supplementary experiences upon the behavioral development of infants in institutions. *Child Development, 36,* 81–90.

Desmond, M. M., & Wilson, G. S. (1975). Neonatal abstinence syndrome: Recognition and diagnosis. *Addictive Diseases: An International Journal, 2,* 113–121.

DeVries, R. (1969). Constancy of generic identity in the years three to six. *Monographs of the Society for Research in Child Development, 34* (Serial No. 127).

Diamond, M. (1977). Human sexual development: Biological foundations for social development. In F. A. Beach (Ed.), *Human sexuality in four perspectives.* Baltimore: Johns Hopkins University Press.

Diamond, M. (1978, September). Aging and cell loss: Calling for an honest count. *Psychology Today,* p. 126.

Diamond, M. (1984, November). A love affair with the brain. *Psychology Today,* pp. 62–73.

Diamond, S., Baldwin, R., & Diamond, R. (1963). *Inhibition and choice.* New York: Harper & Row.

Diaz, R. M. (1985). Bilingual cognitive development: Addressing three gaps in current research. *Child Development, 56,* 1376–1388.

Dick-Read, G. (1944). *Childbirth without fear: The principles and practices of natural childbirth.* New York: Harper & Bros.

Dickstein, E., & Posner, J. M. (1978). Self-esteem and relationship with parents. *The Journal of Genetic Psychology, 133,* 273–276.

Dietz, W. H., Jr., & Gortmaker, S. L. (1985). Do we fatten our children at the television set? Obesity and television viewing in children and adolescents. *Pediatrics, 75,* 807–812.

Dobbing, J. (1976). Vulnerable periods of brain development. In D. E. Roberts (Ed.), *The biology of human fetal growth.* New York: Halsted Press.

Dodge, K. A. (1983). Behavioral antecedents of peer social status. *Child Development, 54,* 1386–1399.

Dodge, K. A. (1985). A social information processing model of social competence in children. In M. Perlmutter (Ed.), *Minnesota symposium on child psychology.* Hillsdale, NJ: Erlbaum.

Dodge, K. A., & Frame, C. L. (1982). Social cognitive biases and deficits in aggressive boys. *Child Development, 53,* 620–635.

Doherty, W. J., & Jacobson, N. S. (1982). Marriage and family. In B. B. Wolman (Ed.), *Handbook of developmental psychology.* Englewood Cliffs, NJ: Prentice-Hall.

▶ ▶ ▶ ▶

Doleys, D. M. (1977). Behavioral treatments for nocturnal enuresis in children: A review of the recent literature. *Psychological Bulletin, 8*, 30–54.

Dollard, J., Doob, L. W., Miller, N. E., Mowrer, O. H., & Sears, R. R. (1939). *Frustration and aggression.* New Haven, CT: Yale University Press.

Donaldson, M. (1979). *Children's minds.* New York: Norton.

Dooker, M. (1980, July/August). Lamaze method of childbirth. *Nursing Research*, pp. 220–224.

Dorr, A. (1985). Contexts for experience with emotion with special attention to television. In M. Lewis & C. Saarni (Eds.), *The socialization of emotion.* New York: Plenum Press.

Dunlap, L., & Canale, J. (1987). Factors influencing the career aspirations of primary and secondary grade students. Paper presented at the annual meeting of the Eastern Psychological Association, Arlington, VA.

Dunn, H. G., McBurney, A. K., Ingram, S., & Hunter, C. M. (1977). Maternal cigarette smoking during pregnancy and the child's subsequent development: II. Neurological and intellectual maturation to the age of 6½ years. *Canadian Journal of Public Health, 68*, 43–50.

Dunn, J. (1977). *Distress and comfort.* Cambridge, MA: Harvard University Press.

Dunn, J., & Kendrick, C. (1980). The arrival of a sibling: Changes in patterns of interaction between mother and firstborn child. *Journal of Child Psychology and Psychiatry, 21*, 119–132.

Dunn, J., & Kendrick, C. (1982a) Interaction between young siblings: Association with the interaction between mother and firstborn. *Developmental Psychology, 17*, 336–343.

Dunn, J., & Kendrick, C. (1982b). Siblings and their mothers: Developing relationships within the family. In M. E. Lamb & B. Sutton-Smith (Eds.), *Sibling relationships.* Hillsdale, NJ: Erlbaum.

Dunn, J., & Munn, P. (1985). Becoming a family member: Family conflict and the development of social understanding in the second year. *Child Development, 56*, 480–492.

Dunn, J., Plomin, R., & Daniels, D. (1986). Consistency and change in mothers' behavior toward young siblings. *Child Development, 57*, 348–356.

Dunst, C. J., Brooks, P. H., & Doxsey, P. A. (1982). Characteristics of hiding places and the transition to stage IV performance in object permanence tasks. *Developmental Psychology, 18*, 671–681.

Easterbrooks, M. A., & Goldberg, W. A. (1984). Toddler development in the family: Impact of father involvement and parenting characteristics. *Child Development, 55*, 740–752.

Easterbrooks, M. A., & Goldberg, W. A. (1985). Effects of early maternal employment on toddlers, mothers, and fathers. *Developmental Psychology, 21*, 774–783.

Eberhardy, F. (1967). The view from "the couch." *Journal of Child Psychology and Psychiatry, 8*, 257–263.

Eberts, E. H., & Lepper, M. R. (1975). Individual consistency in the proxemic behavior of preschool children. *Journal of Personality and Social Psychology, 32*, 841–849.

Eccles, J. S. (1985). Sex differences in achievement patterns. In T. Sonderegger (Ed.), *Nebraska symposium on motivation.* Lincoln: University of Nebraska Press.

Eccles, J. S., & Hoffman, L. W. (1984). Sex roles, socialization, and occupational behavior. In H. W. Stevenson & A. E. Siegel (Eds.), *Research in child development and social policy*, Vol. 1. Chicago: University of Chicago Press.

Edelsky, C. (1976). Subjective reactions to sex-linked language. *Journal of Social Psychology, 99*, 97–104.

Egeland, B., & Farber, E. A. (1984). Infant-mother attachment: Factors related to its development and changes over time. *Child Development, 55*, 753–771.

Egeland, B., & Sroufe, L. A. (1981a). Attachment and early maltreatment. *Child Development, 52*, 44–52.

Egeland, B., & Sroufe, L. A. (1981b). Developmental sequelae of maltreatment in infancy. *New Directions for Child Development, 11*, 77–92.

Ehrhardt, A. A., & Baker, S. W. (1975). Hormonal aberrations and their implications for the understanding of normal sex differentiation. In P. H. Mussen, J. J. Conger, & J. Kagan (Eds.), *Basic and contemporary issues in developmental psychology.* New York: Harper & Row.

Eiger, M. S., & Olds, S. W. (1986). *The complete book of breast-feeding*, 2d ed. New York: Bantam Books.

Eimas, P. D. (1975). Developmental studies of speech perception. In L. B. Cohen & P. Salapatek (Eds.), *Infant perception.* New York: Academic Press.

Eimas, P. D., Sigueland, E. R., Jusczyk, P., & Vigorito, J. (1971). Speech perception in infants. *Science, 171*, 303–306.

Eisenberg, L. (1980). Adolescent suicide: On taking arms in a sea of troubles. *Pediatrics, 66*, 315–320.

Eisenberg, N. (1982). *The development of prosocial behavior.* New York: Academic Press.

Eisenberg, N., & Lennon, R. (1983). Sex differences in empathy and related capacities. *Psychological Bulletin, 94*, 100–131.

Eisenberg, N., Lennon, R., & Roth, K. (1983). Prosocial development: A longitudinal study. *Developmental Psychology, 19*, 846–855.

Eisenberg, N., Lundy, T., Shell, R., & Roth, K. (1985). Children's justifications for their adult and peer-directed compliant (prosocial and nonprosocial) behaviors. *Developmental Psychology, 21*, 325–331.

▶ ▶ ▶ ▶

Eisenberg, N., Tryon, K., & Cameron, E. (1984). The relation of preschoolers' peer interaction to their sex-typed toy choices. *Child Development, 55,* 1044–1050.

Elardo, R., Bradley, R. H., & Caldwell, B. M. (1975). The relation of infants' home environments to mental test performance from six to thirty-six months: A longitudinal analysis. *Child Development, 46,* 71–76.

Elardo, R., Bradley, R. H., & Caldwell, B. M. (1977). A longitudinal study of the relation of infants' home environments to language development at age three. *Child Development, 48,* 595–603.

Elias, S., & Annas, G. (1986). Social policy considerations in noncoital reproduction. *Journal of the American Medical Society, 255,* 62–68.

Elliot, A. J. (1981). *Child language.* Cambridge, MA: Cambridge University Press.

Elrod, M. M., & Crase, S. J. (1980). Sex differences in self esteem and parental behavior. *Psychological Reports, 46,* 719–727.

Emde, R. N., Gaensbauer, T. J., & Harmon, R. J. (1976). *Emotional expression in infancy: A biobehavioral study.* New York: International Universities Press.

Emde, R. N., Harmon, R. J., Metcalf, D., Koenig, K. L., & Wagonfeld, S. (1971). Stress and neonatal sleep. *Psychosomatic Medicine, 33,* 491–497.

Emery, R. E. (1982). Interpersonal conflict and the children of discord and divorce. *Psychological Bulletin, 92,* 310–330.

Emmerich, W., & Shepard, K. (1982). Development of sex-differentiated preferences during later childhood and adolescence. *Child Development, 18,* 406–417.

Endsley, R. C., & Bradbard, M. (1976). The wise guide to quality day care. Unpublished manuscript, University of Georgia.

Endsley, R. C., Hutcherson, M. A., Garner, A. P., & Martin, M. J. (1979). Interrelationships among selected maternal behaviors, authoritarianism, and preschool children's verbal and non-verbal curiosity. *Child Development, 50,* 331–339.

Engen, T., & Lipsitt, L. P. (1965). Decrement and recovery of responses to olfactory stimuli in the human neonate. *Journal of Comparative and Physiological Psychology, 59,* 312–316.

English, H. B. (1929). Three cases of the "conditioned fear response." *Journal of Abnormal and Social Psychology, 34,* 221–225.

Epstein, L. H., Wing, R. R., Koeske, R., Andrasik, F., & Ossip, D. J. (1981). Child and parent weight loss in family-based behavior modification programs. *Journal of Consulting and Clinical Psychology, 49,* 674–685.

Epstein, L. H., Wing, R. R., Koeske, R., & Valoski, A. (1987). Long-term effects of family-based treatment of childhood obesity. *Journal of Consulting and Clinical Psychology, 55,* 91–95.

Epstein, L. H., Wing, R. R., Woodall, K., Penner, B. C., Kress, M. J., & Koeske, R. (1985). Effects of family-based behavioral treatment on obese 5-to-8-year-old children. *Behavior Therapy, 16,* 205–212

Epstein, L. H., Woodall, K., Goreczny, A. J., Wing, R. R., & Robertson, R. J. (1984). The modification of activity patterns and energy expenditure in obese young girls. *Behavior Therapy, 15,* 101–108.

Erikson, E. H. (1963). *Childhood and society.* New York: Norton.

Erikson, E. H. (1975). *Life history and the historical moment.* New York: Norton.

Erikson, E. H. (1983). Cited in Hall, E. (1983, June). A conversation with Erik Erikson. *Psychology Today,* pp. 22–30.

Eron, L. D. (1982). Parent-child interaction, television violence, and aggression of children. *American Psychologist, 37,* 197–211.

Eron, L. D. (1987). The development of aggressive behavior from the perspective of a developing behaviorism. *American Psychologist, 42,* 435–442.

Eron, L. D., & Huesmann, L. R. (1984). The control of aggressive behavior by changes in attitudes, values and the conditions of learning. In R. J. Blanchard & C. Blanchard (Eds.), *Advances in the study of aggression,* Vol. 2. New York: Academic Press.

Erwin, J., Maple, T., Mitchell, G., & Willott, J. (1974). Follow-up study of isolation-reared rhesus monkeys paired with preadolescent cospecifics in late infancy: Cross-sex pairings. *Developmental Psychology, 6,* 808–814.

Espenschade, A. (1960). Motor development. In W. R. Johnson (Ed.), *Science and medicine of exercise and sports.* New York: Harper & Row.

Evans, H. J. (1981). Abnormalities and cigarette smoking. *Lancet, 1,* 627–634.

Ewy, D., & Ewy, R. (1976). *Preparation for childbirth.* New York: New American Library.

Fabricius, W. V., & Wellman, H. M. (1983). Children's understanding of retrieval cue utilization. *Developmental Psychology, 19,* 15–21.

Fagan, J. F., III. (1971). Infants' recognition memory for a series of visual stimuli. *Journal of Experimental Child Psychology, 11,* 244–250.

Fagan, J. F., III. (1984). The intelligent infant: Theoretical implications. *Intelligence, 8,* 1–9.

Fagan, J. F., III, Fantz, R. L., & Miranda, S. B. (1971). Infants' attention to novel stimuli as a function of postnatal and conceptual age. Paper presented to the Society for Research in Child Development, Minneapolis.

Fagan, J. F., III, & McGrath, S. (1981). Infant recognition memory and later intelligence. *Intelligence, 5,* 121–130.

▶ ▶ ▶ ▶

Fagan, J. F., III, & Singer, L. T. (1983). Infant recognition memory as a measure of intelligence. In L. P. Lipsitt (Ed.), *Advances in infancy research*, Vol. 2. Norwood, NJ: Ablex.

Fagen, J. W. (1980). Stimulus preference, reinforcer effectiveness, and relational responding in infants. *Child Development, 51,* 372–378.

Fagen, J. W., Morrongiello, B. A., Rovee-Collier, C., & Gekoski, M. J. (1984). Expectancies and memory retrieval in three-month-old infants. *Child Development, 55,* 936–943.

Fagot, B. I. (1974). Sex differences in toddlers' behavior and parental reaction. *Developmental Psychology, 10,* 554–558.

Fagot, B. I. (1977). Consequences of moderate cross-gender behavior in preschool children. *Child Development, 48,* 902–907.

Fagot, B. I. (1978). The influence of sex of child on parental reactions to toddler children. *Child Development, 49,* 459–465.

Fagot, B. I. (1981). Male and female teachers: Do they treat boys and girls differently? *Sex Roles, 7,* 263–272.

Fagot, B. I. (1982). Adults as socializing agents. In T. M. Field (Ed.), *Review of human development.* New York: Wiley.

Fagot, B. I. (1985a). Beyond the reinforcement principle: Another step toward understanding sex role development. *Developmental Psychology, 21,* 1097–1104.

Fagot, B. I. (1985b). Changes in thinking about early sex role development. *Developmental Review, 5,* 83–98.

Fagot, B. I., Hagan, R., Leinbach, M., & Kronsberg, S. (1985). *Child Development, 56,* 1499–1505.

Fagot, B. I., & Littman, I. (1976). Relation of preschool sex-typing to intellectual performance in elementary school. *Psychological Reports, 39,* 699–704.

Fallon, A. E., & Rozin, P. (1985). Sex differences in perceptions of desirable body shape. *Journal of Abnormal Psychology, 94,* 102–105.

Fallon, A. E., Rozin, P., & Pliner, P. (1984). The child's conception of food: The development of food rejections with special reference to disgust and contamination sensitivity. *Child Development, 55,* 566–575.

Fantz, R. L. (1961). The origin of form perception. *Scientific American, 204,* 66–72.

Fantz, R. L., Fagan, J. F., III, & Miranda, S. B. (1975). Early visual selectivity. In L. B. Cohen & P. Salapatek (Eds.), *Infant perception: From sensation to cognition,* Vol. 1. New York: Academic Press.

Farber, E., & Egeland, B. (1987). *The invulnerable child.* New York: Guilford Press.

Farmer, H. S. (1983). Career and homemaking plans for high school youth. *Journal of Counseling Psychology, 30,* 40–45.

Faust, M. S. (1977). Somatic development of adolescent girls. *Monographs of the Society for Research in Child Development, 42* (Whole #169).

Faux, M. (1984). *Childless by choice.* Garden City, NY: Doubleday/Anchor Press.

Featherstone, J. (1971, September 11). Open schools—the British and U.S. *The New Republic,* pp. 20–25.

Feingold, B. F. (1975). Hyperkinesis and learning disabilities linked to artificial food flavors and colors. *American Journal of Nursing, 75,* 797–803

Feldman, N. S., Klosson, E. C., Parsons, J. E., Rholes, W. S., & Ruble, D. N. (1976). Order of information presentation and children's moral judgments. *Child Development, 47,* 556–559.

Feldman, S. E., & Feldman, M. T. (1967). Transition of sex differences in cheating. *Psychological Reports, 20,* 957–958.

Feldman, S. S., Nash, S. C., & Aschenbrenner, B. G. (1983). Antecedents of fathering. *Child Development, 54,* 1628–1636.

Fenigstein, A. (1979). Does aggression cause a preference for viewing media violence? *Journal of Personality and Social Psychology, 37,* 2307–2317.

Fennema, E., & Sherman, J. (1977). Sex-related differences in mathematics achievement, spatial visualization and affective factors. *American Educational Research Journal, 14,* 51–71.

Ferguson, C. A., & Farwell, C. (1975). Words and sounds in early language acquisition: English consonants in the first 50 words. *Language, 51,* 419–439.

Ferguson, T. J., & Rule, B. G. (1980). Effects of inferential sex, outcome severity and basis of responsibility on children's evaluations of aggressive acts. *Developmental Psychology, 16,* 141–146.

Ferrari, M., & Matthews, W. S. (1983). Self-recognition deficits in autism: Syndrome-specific or general developmental delay? *Journal of Autism and Developmental Disorders, 13,* 317–325.

Fetterly, K., & Graubard, M. S. (1984). Racial and educational factors associated with breast-feeding—United States, 1969 and 1980. *Morbidity and Mortality Weekly Report, 33*(11), 153–154. U.S. Centers for Disease Control.

Field, D. (1981). Can preschool children really learn to conserve? *Child Development, 52,* 326–334.

Field, J., Muir, D., Pilon, R., Sinclair, M., & Dodwell, P. (1980). Infants' orientation to lateral sounds from birth to three months. *Child development, 51,* 295–298.

Field, T. M. (1978). Interaction behaviors of primary versus secondary caretaker fathers. *Developmental Psychology, 14,* 183–184.

Field, T. M. (1980). Interactions of high risk infants: Quantitative and quali-

▶ ▶ ▶ ▶

tative differences. In D. B. Sawin, R. C. Hawkins, L. P. Walker, & J. H. Penticuff (Eds.), *Exceptional infant: Vol. 4. Psychosocial risks in infant environmental transactions.* New York: Brunner/Mazel.

Field, T. M., Cohen, D., Garcia, R., & Greenberg, R. (1984). Mother-stranger face discrimination by the newborn. *Infant Behavior and Development, 7,* 19–25.

Field, T. M., Dempsey, J. R., & Shuman, H. H. (1981). Developmental follow-up of preterm and post-term infants. In S. L. Friedman & M. Sigman (Eds.), *Preterm birth and psychological handicap.* New York: Academic Press.

Field, T. M., Gewirtz, J. L., Cohen, D., Garcia, R., Greenberg, R., & Collins, K. (1984). Leave-takings and reunions of infants, toddlers, preschoolers, and their parents. *Child Development, 55,* 628–635.

Field, T. M., Widmayer, S. M., Stringer, S., & Ignatoff, E. (1980). Teenage, lower-class, black mothers and their preterm infants: An intervention and developmental follow-up. *Child Development, 51,* 426–436.

Filsinger, E. E., & Fabes, R. A. (1985). Odor communication, pheromones, and human families. *Journal of Marriage and the Family, 47,* 349–360.

Finkelstein, N. W., & Haskins, R. (1983). Kindergarten children prefer same-color peers. *Child Development, 54,* 502–508.

Fischer, W. F. (1963). Sharing in preschool children as a function of amount and type of reinforcement. *Genetic Psychology Monographs, 68,* 215–245.

Fisher, D. F., & Karsh, R. (1971). Modality effects and storage in sequential short-term memory. *Journal of Experimental Psychology, 87,* 410–414.

Fisher, J. D., Bell, P. A., & Baum, A. (1984). *Environmental psychology,* 2d ed. New York: Holt, Rinehart and Winston.

Fisher, J. D., & Byrne, D. (1975). Too close for comfort: Sex differences in response to invasions of personal space. *Journal of Personality and Social Psychology, 32,* 15–21.

Fisher, K. (1984). Family violence cycle questioned. *APA Monitor, 15* (12), 30.

Fitzgerald, H. E., & Brackbill, Y. (1976). Classical conditioning in infancy: Development and constraints. *Psychological Bulletin, 83,* 353–376.

Flaherty, J. F., & Dusek, J. B. (1980). An investigation of the relationship between psychological androgyny and components of the self-concept. *Journal of Personality and Social Psychology, 38,* 984–992.

Flavell, J. H. (1980, Fall). A tribute to Piaget. *Society for Research in Child Development Newsletter.*

Flavell, J. H. (1982). Structures, stages, and sequences in cognitive development. In W. A. Collins (Ed.), *The Concept of Development: The Minnesota Symposia on Child Psychology,* Vol. 15. Hillsdale, NJ: Erlbaum.

Flavell, J. H. (1985). *Cognitive development.* Englewood Cliffs, NJ: Prentice-Hall.

Flavell, J. H., Shipstead, S. G., & Croft, K. (1978). Young children's knowledge about visual perception: Hiding objects from others. *Child Development, 49,* 1208–1211.

Flavell, J. H., Speer, J. R., Green, F. L., & August, D. L. (1981). The development of comprehension monitoring and knowledge about communication. *Monographs of the Society for Research in Child Development, 46* (5, Serial No. 192).

Flavell, J. H., & Wellman, H. M. (1976). Metamemory. In R. V. Kail & J. W. Hagen (Eds.), *Perspectives on the development of memory and cognition.* Hillsdale, NJ: Erlbaum.

Flippo, J. R., & Lewinsohn, P. M. (1971). Effects of failure on the self-esteem of depressed and nonde-pressed subjects. *Journal of Consulting and Clinical Psychology, 36,* 151.

Floderus-Myrhed, B., Pederson, N., & Rasmuson, I. (1980). Assessment of heritability for personality based on a short form of the Eysenck Personality Inventory: A study of 12,898 twin pairs. *Behavior Genetics, 10,* 153–162.

Fogelman, K. (1980). Smoking in pregnancy and subsequent development of the child. *Child Care, Health, and Development, 6,* 233–251.

Folstein, S., & Rutter, M. (1978). A twin study of individuals with infantile autism. In M. Rutter & E. Schopler (Eds.), *Autism: A reappraisal of concepts and treatment.* New York: Plenum Press.

Ford, C. S., & Beach, F. A. (1951). *Patterns of sexual behavior.* New York: Harper & Row.

Foreyt, J. P., & Goodrick, G. K. (1981). Childhood obesity. In E. J. Mash & L. G. Terdal (Eds.), *Behavioral assessment of childhood disorders.* New York: Guilford.

Forman, M. R., Graubard, B. I., Hoffman, H. J., Beren, R., Harley, E. E., & Bennett, P. (1984). The Pima infant feeding study: Breast feeding and gastroenteritis in the first year of life. *American Journal of Epidemiology, 119,* 335–349.

Foster, G. D., Wadden, T. A., & Brownell, K. D. (1985). Peer-led program for the treatment and prevention of obesity in the schools. *Journal of Consulting and Clinical Psychology, 53,* 538–540.

Fouts, R. S., & Fouts, D. H. (1985). *Friends of Washoe, 4* (4), 3–8.

Fox, L. H. (1980). Conclusions: What do we know and where should we go? In L. H. Fox, L. Brody, & D. Tobin (Eds.), *Women and the mathematical mystique.* Baltimore: Johns Hopkins University Press.

Fox, L. H. (1982). Sex differences among the mathematically gifted. Paper presented at the annual meeting of the American Association for

▶ ▶ ▶ ▶

the Advancement of Science, Washington, DC.

Fox, L. H., Brody, L., & Tobin, D. (1985). The impact of early intervention programs upon course-taking and attitudes in high school. In S. F. Chipman, L. R. Brush, & D. M. Wilson (Eds.), *Women and mathematics: Balancing the equation.* London: Erlbaum.

Fox, L. H., Tobin, D., & Brody, L. (1979). Sex-role socialization and achievement in mathematics. In M. A. Wittig & A. C. Petersen (Eds.), *Sex-related differences in cognitive functioning.* New York: Academic Press.

Fox, N. (1977). Attachment of kibbutz infants to mother and metapelet. *Child Development, 48,* 1228–1239.

Fox, R., Aslin, R. N., Shea, S. L., & Dumais, S. T. (1980). Stereopsis in human infants. *Science, 207,* 323–324.

Foxx, R. M., & Azrin, N. H. (1973). *Toilet training the retarded: A rapid program for day and night time independent toileting.* Champaign, IL: Research Press.

Francoeur, R. T. (1985). Reproductive technologies: New alternatives and new ethics. *SIECUS Report, 14,* 1–5.

Franklin, D. (1984). Rubella threatens unborn in vaccine gap. *Science News, 125,* 186.

Freedman, D. (1965). An ethological approach to the genetic study of human behavior. In S. G. Vandenberg (Ed.), *Methods and goals in human behavior genetics.* New York: Academic Press.

Freedman, D. (1971). Behavioral assessment in infancy. In G. B. A. Stoelinga & J. J. van der Werff Ten Bosch (Eds.), *Normal and abnormal development of brain and behavior.* Leiden: Leiden University Press.

Freedman, D. (1974). *Human infancy: An evolutionary perspective.* Hillsdale, NJ: Erlbaum.

Freud, S. (1909). Analysis of a phobia in a five-year-old boy. In *Collected papers,* Vol. 3, translated by A. & J. Strachey. New York: Basic Books, 1959.

Freud, S. (1927). A religious experience. In *Standard edition of the complete psychological works of Sigmund Freud,* Vol. 21. London: Hogarth, 1964.

Freud, S. (1933). New introductory lectures. In *Standard edition of the complete psychological works of Sigmund Freud,* Vol. 22. London: Hogarth, 1964.

Fried, P. A., Watkinson, B., & Willan, A. (1984). Marijuana use during pregnancy and decreased length of gestation. *American Journal of Obstetrics and Gynecology, 150,* 23–27.

Friedrich, L. K., & Stein, A. H. (1975). Prosocial television and young children: The effects of verbal labeling and role playing on learning and behavior. *Child Development, 46,* 27–38.

Friman, P. C., & Christopherson, E. R. (1983). Behavior therapy and hyperactivity: A brief review of therapy for a big problem. *The Behavior Therapist, 6,* 175–176.

Frisch, H. L. (1977). Sex stereotypes in adult-infant play. *Child Development, 48,* 1671–1675.

Frisch, R. E. (1972). Weight at menarche: Similarity for well-nourished and undernourished girls at differing ages, and evidence for historical constancy. *Pediatrics, 50,* 445–450.

Frisch, R. E., & Revelle, R. (1970). Height and weight at menarche and a hypothesis of critical body weights and adolescent events. *Science, 169,* 397–399.

Fritz, J., & Wetherbee, S. (1982). Preschoolers' beliefs regarding the obese individual. *Canadian Home Economics Journal, 33,* 193–196.

Frodi, A. M. (1981). Contribution of infant characteristics to child abuse. *American Journal of Mental Deficiency, 85,* 341–349.

Frodi, A. M. (1985). When empathy fails: Infant crying and child abuse. In B. M. Lester & C. F. Z. Boukydis (Eds.), *Infant crying.* New York: Plenum Press.

Frodi, A. M., Bridges, L., & Grolnick, W. (1985). Correlates of master-related behavior: A short-term longitudinal study of infants in their second year. *Child Development, 56,* 1291–1298.

Frodi, A. M., Macauley, J., & Thome, P. R. (1977). Are women always less aggressive than men? A review of the experimental literature. *Psychological Bulletin, 84,* 634–660.

Furman, W., Rahe, D., & Hartup, W. W. (1979). Social rehabilitation of low-interactive preschool children by peer intervention. *Child Development, 50,* 915–922.

Galambos, N. L., & Garbarino, J. (1983, July–August). Identifying the missing links in the study of latchkey children. *Children Today,* pp. 2–4, 40–41.

Gallagher, J. J. (1975). *Teaching the gifted child.* Boston: Allyn & Bacon.

Ganchrow, J. R., Steiner, J. E., & Daher, M. (1983). Neonatal facial expressions in response to different qualities and intensities of gustatory stimuli. *Infant Behavior and Development, 6,* 189–200.

Gansberg, J. M, & Mostel., A. P. (1984). *The second nine months.* New York: Tribeca.

Garber, J. (1984). Classification of childhood psychopathology: A developmental perspective. *Child Development, 55,* 30–48.

Garcia, J. (1981). The logic and limits of mental aptitude testing. *American Psychologist, 36,* 1172–1180.

Gardner, B. T., & Gardner, R. A. (1980). Two comparative psychologists look at language acquisition. In K. E. Nelson (Ed.), *Children's language,* Vol. 2. New York: Gardner Press.

Gardner, H. (1978, March). The loss of language. *Human Nature, 1,* 76–84.

Gardner, H. (1982). *Art, mind, and brain: A cognitive approach to creativity.* New York: Basic Books.

▶ ▶ ▶ ▶

Gardner, H. (1983). *Frames of mind: The theory of multiple intelligences.* New York: Basic Books.

Garvey, C. (1977). *Play.* Cambridge, MA: Harvard University Press.

Gath, A. (1985). Down's syndrome in the first nine years. In A. R. Nicol (Ed.), *Longitudinal studies in child psychology and psychiatry.* New York: Wiley.

Geen, R. G. (1981). Behavioral and physiological reactions to observed violence: Effects of prior exposure to aggressive stimuli. *Journal of Personality and Social Psychology, 40,* 868–875.

Geffen, G. (1976). Development of hemispheric specialization for speech perception. *Cortex, 12,* 337–346.

Geller, E., Ritvo, E. R., Freeman, B. J., & Yuwiler, A. (1982). Preliminary observations on the effect of fenfluramine on blood serotonin and symptoms in three autistic boys. *New England Journal of Medicine, 307,* 3.

Gelles, R. J., & Strauss, M. A. (1979). Violence in the American family. *Journal of Social Issues, 35,* 15–38.

Gelman, R. (1978). Cognitive development. *Annual Review of Psychology, 29,* 297–332.

Gelman, R., & Baillargeon, R. (1983). A review of some Piagetan concepts. In J. Flavell & E. Markman (Eds.), *Handbook of child psychology.* New York: Wiley.

Gelman, R., & Gallistel, C. R. (1978). *The child's understanding of number.* Cambridge, MA: Harvard University Press.

Gerson, M. (1980). The lure of motherhood. *Psychology of Women Quarterly, 5,* 207–218.

Gerson, M. (1984). Feminism and the wish for a child. *Sex Roles, 11,* 389–399.

Gerson, M., Alpert, J. L., & Richardson, M. S. (1984). Mothering: The view from psychological research. *Signs, 9,* 434–453.

Geschwind, N. (1979, September). Specialization of the human brain. *Scientific American, 241,* 180–201.

Gesell, A. (1928). *Infancy and human growth.* New York: Macmillan.

Gesell, A. (1929). Maturation and infant behavior patterns. *Psychological Review, 36,* 307–319.

Gettys, L. D., & Cann, A. (1981). Children's perceptions of occupational sex stereotypes. *Sex Roles, 7,* 301–308.

Getzels, J. W., & Jackson, P. W. (1962). *Creativity and intelligence: Explorations with gifted students.* New York: Wiley.

Gewirtz, J. L., & Boyd, E. F. (1977). Does maternal responding imply reduced infant crying? A critique of the 1972 Bell and Ainsworth report. *Child Development, 48,* 1200–1207.

Gibbs, J. C., Arnold, K. D., Ahlborn, H. H., & Cheesman, F. L. (1984). Facilitation of sociomoral reasoning in delinquents. *Journal of Consulting and Clinical Psychology, 52,* 37–45.

Gibbs, J. C., Arnold, K. D., & Burkhart, J. E. (1984). Sex differences in the expression of moral development. *Child Development, 55,* 1040–1043.

Gibson, E. J. (1969). *Principles of perceptual learning and development.* New York: Appleton-Century-Crofts.

Gibson, E. J., Owsley, C. J., & Johnston, J. (1978). Perception of invariants by five-month-old infants: Differentiation of two types of motion. *Developmental Psychology, 14,* 407–415.

Gibson, E. J., & Walk, R. D. (1960, April). The visual cliff. *Scientific American, 202,* 64–71.

Gibson, E. J., & Walker, A. S. (1984). Development of knowledge of visual-tactual affordances of substance. *Child Development, 55,* 453–460.

Gilligan, C. (1982). *In a different voice.* Cambridge, MA: Harvard University Press.

Gillis, J. S., & Avis, W. E. (1980). The male-taller norm in mate selection. *Personality and Social Psychology Bulletin, 6,* 396–401.

Glanzer, P. D., & Dodd, D. H. (1975). Developmental changes in the language spoken to children. Paper presented to the biennial meeting of the Society for Research in Child Development, Denver.

Glasberg, R., & Aboud, F. (1982). Keeping one's distance from sadness: Children's self-reports of emotional experience. *Developmental Psychology, 18,* 287–293.

Glass, R. H., & Ericsson, R. (1982). *Getting pregnant in the 1980s.* Berkeley: University of California Press.

Gleicher, N. (1984). Caesarean section rates in the United States. *Journal of the American Medical Association, 252,* 3273–3276.

Gleitman, L. R., Newport, E. L., & Gleitman, H. (1984). The current status of the motherese hypothesis. *Journal of Child Language, 11,* 43–79.

Gleitman, L. R., & Rozin, P. (1977). The structure and acquisition of reading. In A. S. Reber & D. L. Scarborough (Eds.), *Toward a psychology of reading.* Hillsdale, NJ: Erlbaum.

Goddard, H. H. (1917). Mental tests and the immigrant. *The Journal of Delinquency, 2,* 243–277.

Golbus, M., Loughman, W., Epstein, C., Halbasch, G., Stephens, J., & Hall, B. (1979). Prenatal genetic diagnosis in 3,000 amniocenteses. *The New England Journal of Medicine, 300,* 157–163.

Gold, D., & Andres, D. (1978a). Comparisons of adolescent children with employed and nonemployed mothers. *Merrill-Palmer Quarterly, 24* (4), 243–254.

Gold, D., & Andres, D. (1978b). Developmental comparisons between ten-year-old children with employed and nonemployed mothers. *Child Development, 49,* 75–84.

► ► ► ►

Gold, D., & Andres, D. (1978c). Relations between maternal employment and development of nursery school children. *Canadian Journal of Behavioral Science, 10,* 116–129.

Goldberg, S. (1983). Parent-infant bonding: Another look. *Child Development, 54,* 1355–1382.

Goldberg, S., & Lewis, M. (1969). Play behavior in the year-old infant: Early sex differences. *Child Development, 40,* 21–31.

Goldman, W., & Lewis, P. (1977). Beautiful is good: Evidence that the physically attractive are more socially skillful. *Journal of Experimental Social Psychology, 13,* 125–130.

Goldsmith, H. H. (1983). Genetic influences on personality from infancy to adulthood. *Child Development, 54,* 331–355.

Goldsmith, H. H., & Campos, J. J. (1986). Fundamental issues in the study of early temperament: The Denver twin temperament study. In M. Lamb & A. Brown (Eds.), *Advances in developmental psychology.* Hillsdale, NJ: Erlbaum.

Goldstein, K. M., Caputo, D. V., & Taub, H. V. (1976). The effects of perinatal complications on development at one year of age. *Child Development, 47,* 613–621.

Goleman, D. (1987). Thriving despite hardship: Key childhood traits identified. *The New York Times,* October 13, pp. C1, C11.

Golub, S. (1983). Menarche: The beginning of menstrual life. In S. Golub (Ed.), *Lifting the curse of menstruation.* New York: Haworth.

Good, T. L., & Brophy, J. E. (1980). *Educational psychology: A realistic approach,* 2d ed. New York: Holt, Rinehart and Winston.

Goodenough, F. L. (1926). *Measurement of intelligence by drawings.* New York: Harcourt.

Goodsitt, J. V., Morse, P. A., Ver Hoeve, J. N., & Cowan, N. (1984). Infant speech recognition in multisyllabic contexts. *Child Development, 55,* 903–910.

Goodwin, D. W. (1979). Alcoholism and heredity: A review and hypothesis. *Archives of General Psychiatry, 36,* 57–61.

Gordon, E. W., & Terrell, M. D. (1981). The changed social context of testing. *American Psychologist, 36,* 1167–1171.

Gottfried, A. W. (1984). Home environment and early cognitive development: Integration, meta-analyses, and conclusions. In A. W. Gottfried (Ed.), *Home environment and early cognitive development.* San Francisco: Academic Press.

Gottman, J. M. (1985). The world of coordinated play: Same- and cross-sex friendship in young children. In J. M. Gottman & J. G. Parker (Eds.), *The conversations of friends.* New York: Cambridge University Press.

Graziano, A. M., DeGiovanni, I. S., & Garcia, K. A. (1979). Behavioral treatment of children's fears: A review. *Psychological Bulletin, 86,* 804–830.

Green, B. F. (1981). A primer of testing. *American Psychologist, 36,* 1001–1011.

Green, D. S., & Green, B. (1965, March). Double sex. *Sexology,* pp. 561–563.

Green, J. A., Jones, L. E., & Gustafson, G. E. (1987). Perception of cries by parents and nonparents: Relation to cry acoustics. *Developmental Psychology, 23,* 370–382.

Greenberg, E. R., Barnes, A. B., Resseguie, L., Barrett, J. A., Burnside, S., Lanza, L. L., Neff, R. K., Stevens, M., Young, R. H., & Colton, T. (1984). Breast cancer in mothers given diethylstilbestrol in pregnancy. *New England Journal of Medicine, 311,* 1393–1398.

Greenberg, J., & Kuczaj, S. A., II. (1982). Towards a theory of substantive word-meaning acquisition. In S. A. Kuczaj, II (Ed.), *Language development, Vol. 1: Syntax and semantics.* Hillsdale, NJ: Erlbaum.

Greenman, G. W. (1963). Visual behavior of newborn infants. In A. J. Solnit & S. A. Provence (Eds.), *Modern perspectives in child development.* New York: Hallmark.

Greenough, W. T. (1976). Enduring brain effects of differential experience and training. In M. R. Rosenzweig & E. L. Bennett (Eds.), *Neural mechanisms of learning and memory.* Cambridge: MA: MIT Press.

Greenspan, S. I., & Porges, S. W. (1984). Psychopathology in infancy and early childhood: Clinical perspectives on the organization of sensory and affective-thematic experience. *Child Development, 55,* 49–70.

Grief, E. B., & Ulman, K. J. (1982). The psychological impact of menarche on early adolescent females: A review of the literature. *Child Development, 53,* 1413–1430.

Griest, D., Forehand, R., Wells, K., & McMahon, R. J. (1980). An examination of differences between nonclinic and behavior problem clinic-referred children and their mothers. *Journal of Abnormal Psychology, 89,* 497–500.

Grim, P., Kohlberg, L., & White, S. (1968). Some relationships between conscience and attentional processes. *Journal of Personality and Social Psychology, 8,* 239–253.

Grinker, J. A. (1981). Behavioral and metabolic factors in childhood obesity. In M. Lewis & L. A. Rosenblum (Eds.), *The uncommon child.* New York: Plenum Press.

Grosjean, F. (1982). *Life with two languages: An introduction to bilingualism.* Cambridge, MA: Harvard University Press.

Gross, M. B., & Wilson, W. C. (1974). *Minimal brain dysfunction.* New York: Brunner/Mazel.

Gross, R. T., & Duke, P. (1980). The effect of early versus late physical maturation on adolescent behavior. In I. Litt (Ed.), *Symposium on adolescent medicine. The Pediatric Clinics of North America, 27,* 71–78.

► ► ► ►

Guilford, J. P. (1959a). Three faces of intellect. *American Psychologist, 14,* 469–479.

Guilford, J. P. (1959b). Traits of creativity. In H. H. Anderson (Ed.), *Creativity and its cultivation.* New York: Harper & Row.

Guilford, J. P. (1980) Fluid and crystallized intelligence: Two fanciful concepts. *Psychological Bulletin, 88,* 408–412.

Guilford, J. P. (1982). Cognitive psychology's ambiguities: Some suggested remedies. *Psychological Review, 89,* 48–59.

Guilford, J. P., & Hoepfner, R. (1971). *The analysis of intelligence.* New York: McGraw-Hill.

Gunderson, V. M., Grant, K. S., Burbacher, T. M., Fagan, J. F., & Mottet, N. K. (1986). The effect of low-level prenatal methylmercury exposure on visual recognition memory in infant crab-eating macaques. *Child Development, 57,* 1076–1083.

Gunnar, M. R., & Donahue, M. (1980). Sex differences in social responsiveness between six months and twelve months. *Child Development, 51,* 262–265.

Gunnar, M. R., & Malone, S. (1985). Coping with aversive stimulation in the neonatal period: A longitudinal and comparative study of normal and disturbed youths. *Child Development, 56,* 824–834.

Gunnar, M. R., Senior, K., & Hartup, W. W. (1984). Peer presence and the exploratory behavior of eighteen- and thirty-month-old children. *Child Development, 55,* 1103–1109.

Gupta, C., Yaffe, S. J., & Shapiro, B. H. (1982) Prenatal exposure to phenobarbital permanently decreases testosterone and causes reproductive dysfunction. *Science, 216,* 640–642.

Haaf, R. A. (1977). Visual response to complex facelike patterns by 15- and 20-week-old infants. *Developmental Psychology, 13,* 77–78.

Haaf, R. A., & Bell, R. Q. (1967). A facial dimension in visual discrimination by human infants. *Child Development, 38,* 893–899.

Haaf, R. A., Smith, P. H., & Smitley, S. (1983). Infant response to facelike patterns under fixed trial and infant-control procedures. *Child Development, 54,* 172–177.

Haan, N., Smith, M. B., & Block, J. (1968). Moral reasoning of young adults: Political-social behavior, family background, and personality correlates. *Journal of Personality and Social Psychology, 10,* 183–201.

Haas, A. (1979). Male and female spoken language differences: Stereotypes and evidence. *Psychological Bulletin, 86,* 616–626.

Haber, R. N. (1969). Eidetic images. *Scientific American, 220,* 36–55.

Haber, R. N. (1980, November). Eidetic images are not just imaginary. *Psychology Today,* pp. 72–82.

Haber, R. N., & Hershenson, M. (1980). *The psychology of visual peception.* New York: Holt, Rinehart and Winston.

Hack, M. (1983). The sensorimotor development of the preterm infant. In A. A. Fanaroff, R. J. Martin, & J. R. Merkatz (Eds.), *Behrman's neonatal-perinatal medicine.* St. Louis: Mosby.

Hahn, S. R., & Paige, K. E. (1980). American birth practices: A critical review. In J. E. Parsons (Ed.), *The psychology of sex differences.* New York: McGraw-Hill.

Hainline, L. (1978). Developmental changes in visual scanning of face and nonface patterns by infants. *Journal of Experimental Child Psychology, 25,* 90–115.

Hains, A. A., & Ryan, E. B. (1983). The development of social cognitive processes among juvenile delinquents and nondelinquent peers. *Child Development, 54,* 1536–1544.

Haith, M. M. (1966). The response of the human newborn to visual movement. *Journal of Experimental Child Psychology, 3,* 235–243.

Haith, M. M. (1979). Visual cognition in early infancy. In R. B. Kearsly & I. E. Sigel (Eds.), *Infants at risk: Assessment of cognitive functioning.* Hillsdale, NJ: Erlbaum.

Haith, M. M., Bergman, T., & Moore, M. J. (1977). Eye contact and face scanning in early infancy. *Science, 198,* 853–855.

Hall, E. (1983, June). A conversation with Erik Erikson. *Psychology Today,* pp. 22–30.

Hall, J. A. (1984). *Nonverbal sex differences: Communication accuracy and expressive style.* Baltimore: Johns Hopkins University Press.

Hall, V. C., & Kaye, D. B. (1980). Early patterns of cognitive development. *Monographs of the Society for Research in Child Development, 45* (2), Serial No. 184.

Hamill, P. V., Johnston, F. E., & Lemeshow, S. (1973). Height and weight of children: Socio-economic status: United States. Rockville, MD: Publication No. HRA 74–1608 of the DHEW.

Hanson, J. W., Streissguth, A. P., & Smith, D. W. (1978). The effects of moderate alcohol consumption during pregnancy on growth and morphogenesis. *The Journal of Pedatrics, 92,* 457–460.

Hardy-Brown, K., & Plomin, R. (1985). Infant communicative development: Evidence from adoptive and biological families for genetic and environmental influences on rate differences. *Developmental Psychology, 21,* 378–385.

Hardyck, C., & Petrinovich, L. F. (1977). Left-handedness. *Psychological Bulletin, 84,* 385–404.

Hare, R. D. (1980). *Personality and individual differences.* New York: Pergamon Press.

Hare-Mustin, R. T., & Broderick, P. C. (1979). The myth of motherhood: A study of attitudes toward motherhood. *Psychology of Women Quarterly, 4,* 114–128.

▶ ▶ ▶ ▶

Harlap, S. (1979). Gender of infants conceived on different days of the menstrual cycle. *New England Journal of Medicine, 300,* 1445–1448.

Harlap, S., & Shiono, P. H. (1980). Alcohol, smoking, and incidence of spontaneous abortions in the first and second trimester. *Lancet, 2,* 173–176.

Harlow, H. F. (1959). Love in infant monkeys. *Scientific American, 200,* 68–86.

Harlow, H. F. (1965). Sexual behavior in the rhesus monkey. In F. A. Beach (Ed.), *Sex and behavior.* New York: Wiley.

Harlow, H. F., & Harlow, M. K. (1966). Learning to love. *American Scientist, 54,* 244–272.

Harlow, H. F., & Zimmermann, R. R. (1959). Affectional responses in the infant monkey. *Science, 130,* 421–432.

Harper, L. V., & Huie, K. S. (1985). The effects of prior group experience, age, and familiarity on the quality and organization of preschoolers' social relationships. *Child Development, 56,* 704–717.

Harris, L. J. (1977). Sex differences in the growth and use of language. In E. Donelson & J. Gullahorn (Eds.), *Women: A psychological perspective.* New York: Wiley.

Harris, M. B., Harris, R. J., & Bochner, S. (1982). Fat, four-eyed, and female: Stereotypes of obesity, glasses, and gender. *Journal of Applied Social Psychology, 12,* 503–516.

Harris, S. L. (1986). Families of children with autism: Issues for the behavior therapist. *The Behavior Therapist, 9,* 175–177.

Hart, B. M., Reynolds, N. J., Baer, D. M., Brawley, E. R., & Harris, F. R. (1968). Effect of contingent and noncontingent social reinforcement on the cooperative play of a preschool child. *Journal of Applied Behavior Analysis, 1,* 73–76.

Harter, S. (1983). Developmental perspectives on the self-system. In P. H. Mussen (Ed.), *Handbook of Child Psychology,* Vol. 4. New York: Wiley.

Hartmann, D. P., Gelfand, D. M., Smith, C. L., Paul, S. C., Cromer, C. C., & Lebenta, D. V. (1974, April). Help or else: The effects of avoidance training procedures on children's altruistic behavior. Paper presented to the meeting of the Western Psychological Association, San Francisco.

Hartshorne, H., & May, M. A. (1928). *Studies in the nature of character,* Vol. 1: *Studies in deceit.* New York: Macmillan.

Hartup, W. W. (1970). Peer interaction and social organization. In P. H. Mussen (Ed.), *Carmichael's manual of child psychology,* Vol. 2. New York: Wiley.

Hartup, W. W. (1983). The peer system. In P. H. Mussen & E. M. Hetherington (Eds.), *Handbook of child psychology, Vol 4: Socialization, personality, and social development,* 4th ed. New York: Wiley.

Haugen, G. M., & McIntire, R. W. (1972). Comparisons of vocal imitation, tactile stimulation, and food as reinforcers for infant vocalizations. *Developmental Psychology, 6,* 201–209.

Haugh, S. S., Hoffman, C. D., & Cowan, G. (1980). The eye of the very young beholder: Sex typing of infants by young children. *Child Development, 51,* 598–600.

Havighurst, R. J., & Neugarten, B. L. (1955). *American Indian and white children.* Chicago: University of Chicago Press.

Haynes, H., White, B. L., & Held, R. (1965). Visual accommodation in human infants. *Science, 148,* 528–530.

Heber, R., Garber, H., Harrington, S., & Hoffman, C. (1972, December). Rehabilitation of families at risk for mental retardation. Progress report, Research and Training Center, University of Wisconsin.

Hechtman, L., & Weiss, G. (1983). Long-term outcome of hyperactive children. *American Journal of Orthopsychiatry, 53,* 522–541.

Hedrick, T. E., & Chance, J. E. (1977). Sex differences in assertive achievement patterns. *Sex Roles, 3,* 129–139.

Helmreich, R. L., Spence, J. T., & Holahan, C. K. (1979). Psychological androgyny and sex-role flexibility: A test of two hypotheses. *Journal of Personality and Social Psychology, 37,* 1631–1644.

Henggeler, S. W. (Ed.) (1982). *Delinquency and adolescent psychopathology: A family-ecological systems approach.* Littleton, MA: Wright-PSG.

Henggeler, S. W., & Cohen, R. (1984). The role of cognitive development in the family-ecological systems approach to childhood psychopathology. In B. Gholson & T. L. Rosenthal (Eds.), *Applications of cognitive developmental theory.* New York: Academic Press.

Henggeler, S. W., Rodick, J. D., Borduin, C. M., Hanson, C. L., Watson, S. M., & Urey, J. R. (1986). Multisystemic treatment of juvenile offenders: Effects on adolescent behavior and family interaction. *Developmental Psychology, 22,* 132–141.

Henn, F. A., Bardwell, R., & Jenkins, R. L. (1980). Juvenile delinquents revisited: Adult criminal activity. *American Journal of Psychiatry, 37,* 1160–1163.

Henneborn, W. J., & Cogan, R. (1975). The effect of husband participation on reported pain and probability of medication during labor and birth. *Journal of Psychosomatic Research, 19,* 215–222.

Hennigan, K. M., DelRosario, M. L., Heath, L., Cook, T. D., Wharton, J. D., & Calder, B. J. (1982). Impact

▶ ▶ ▶ ▶

of the introduction of television on crime in the United States. *Journal of Personality and Social Psychology, 42,* 461–477.

Herbert, M. (1978). *Conduct disorders of childhood and adolescence.* New York: Wiley.

Herrnstein, R. IQ. (1971, September). *Atlantic Monthly,* pp. 43–64.

Herzog, D. B. (1982a). Bulimia in the adolescent. *American Journal of Diseases of Children, 136,* 985–989.

Herzog, D. B. (1982b). Bulimia: The secretive syndrome. *Psychosomatics, 23,* 481–487.

Hess, R. D., & Holloway, S. D. (1984). Family and school as educational institutions. In R. D. Parke (Ed.), *Review of child development research,* Vol. 7. Chicago: University of Chicago Press.

Hetherington, E. M. (1967). The effects of familial variables on sex typing, on parent-child similarity, and on imitation in children. In J. P. Hill (Ed.), *Minnesota symposia on child psychology,* Vol. 1. Minneapolis: University of Minnesota Press.

Hetherington, E. M. (1972). Effects of father absence on personality development in adolescent daughters. *Developmental Psychology, 7,* 313–326.

Hetherington, E. M. (1979a). Divorce: A child's perspective. *American Psychologist, 34,* 851–858.

Hetherington, E. M. (1979b). Play and social interaction in children following divorce. *Journal of Social Issues, 34* (4), 111–117.

Hetherington, E. M., Camara, K. A., & Featherman, D. L. (1983). Achievement and intellectual functioning of children from one-parent households. In J. Spence (Ed.), *Achievement and achievement motives.* San Francisco: Freeman.

Hetherington, E. M., Cox, M., & Cox, R. (1975). Beyond father absence: Conceptualization of effects of divorce. Paper presented at the meeting of the Society for Research in Child Development, Denver.

Hetherington, E. M., Cox, M., & Cox, R. (1977). The aftermath of divorce. In J. H. Stevens, Jr., & M. Matthews (Eds.), *Mother-child, father-child relations.* Washington, DC: National Association for the Education of Young Children.

Hetherington, E. M., Cox, M., & Cox, R. (1982). Effects of divorce on parents and children. In M. E. Lamb (Ed.), *Nontraditional families: Parenting and child development.* Hillsdale, NJ: Erlbaum.

Hetherington, E. M., & Duer, J. (1972). The effects of father absence on child development. In W. W. Hartup (Ed.), *The young child: Review of research,* Vol. 2. Washington, DC: National Association for the Education of Young Children.

Hetherington, M. S., & Feldman, S. E. (1964). College cheating as a function of subject and situational variables. *Journal of Educational Psychology, 55,* 212–218.

Hiatt, S., Campos, J. J., & Emde, R. (1979). Facial patterning and infant emotional expression. *Child Development, 50,* 1021–1035.

Higgins, A. T., & Turnure, J. E. (1984). Distractibility and concentration of attention in children's development. *Child Development, 55,* 1799–1810.

Hill, J., Holmbeck, G., Marlow, L., Green, T., & Lynch, M. (1985). Menarcheal status and parent-child relations in families of seventh-grade girls. *Journal of Youth and Adolescence, 14,* 301–316.

Hillerich, R. L. (1983). *The principal's guide to improving reading instruction.* Boston: Allyn & Bacon.

Hilton, I. (1967). Differences in the behavior of mothers toward first- and later-born children. *Journal of Personality and Social Psychology, 7,* 282–290.

Hindley, C. B., Filliozat, A. M., Klackenberg, G., Nicolet-Neister, D., &

Sand, E. A. (1966). Differences in age of walking for five European longitudinal samples. *Human Biology, 38,* 364–379.

Hinshaw, S. P., Henker, B., & Whalen, C. K. (1984). Cognitive-behavioral and pharmacologic interventions for hyperactive boys: Comparative and combined effects. *Journal of Consulting and Clinical Psychology, 52,* 739–749.

Hirsch, J. (1975). Jensenism: The bankruptcy of "science" without scholarship. *Educational Theory, 25,* 3–28.

Hittleman, J. N., O'Donohue, N., Zilkha, S., & Parekh, A. (1980). Mother-infant assessment of the LeBoyer "nonviolent" method of childbirth. Paper presented to the meeting of the American Psychological Association, Montreal.

Hobson, J. A., & McCarley, R. W. (1977). The brain as a dream state generator: An activation-synthesis hypothesis of the dream process. *American Journal of Psychiatry, 134,* 1335–1348.

Hoffman, L. W. (1972). Early childhood experiences and women's achievement motives. *Journal of Social Issues, 28,* 129–155.

Hoffman, L. W. (1985a). The changing genetics/socialization balance. *Journal of Social Issues, 41,* 127–148.

Hoffman, L. W. (1985b, August). Work, family, and the child. Master lecture presented at the annual meeting of the American Psychological Association, Los Angeles.

Hoffman, L. W., & Manis, J. D. (1978). Influences of children on marital interaction and parental satisfaction and dissatisfaction. In R. M. Lerner & G. B. Spanier (Eds.), *Child influences on marital and family interaction.* New York: Academic Press.

Hoffman, M. L. (1973, August). Altruistic behavior and the parent-child relationship. Report #36, Developmental Program, Department of Psychology, University of Michigan.

▶ ▶ ▶ ▶

Hoffman, M. L. (1980). Moral development in adolescence. In J. Adelson (Ed.), *Handbook of adolescent psychology*. New York: Wiley.

Hoffman, M. L. (1981a). Is altruism part of human nature? *Journal of Personality and Social Psychology, 40,* 121–137.

Hoffman, M. L. (1981b). Development of the motive to help others. In J. P. Rushton & R. M. Sorrentino (Eds.), *Altruism and helping*. Hillsdale, NJ: Erlbaum.

Hoffman, M. L. (1982). The role of the father in internal moralization. In M. E. Lamb (Ed.), *The role of the father in child development*. New York: Wiley.

Hoffman, M. L. (1983). Affective and cognitive processes in moral internalization. In E. T. Higgins, D. N. Ruble, & W. W. Hartup (Eds.), *Social cognition and social development*. Cambridge: Cambridge University Press.

Hoffman, M. L. (1984). Empathy, its limitations, and its role in a comprehensive moral theory. In W. M. Kurtines & J. L. Gewirtz (Eds.), *Morality, moral behavior and moral development*. New York: Wiley.

Hoffmann, W., & Prior, M. (1982). Neuropsychological dimensions of autism in children: A test of the hemispheric dysfunction hypothesis. *Journal of Clinical Neuropsychology, 4,* 27–42.

Hoffmann, W., & Prior, M. (1983). Processing deficits relating to frontal-lobe problems in autistic children. Unpublished data cited in Prior (1984).

Hoffman-Plotkin, D., & Twentyman, C. T. (1984). A multimodal assessment of behavioral and cognitive deficits in abused and neglected preschoolers. *Child Development, 55,* 794–802.

Hoffnung, M. (1984). Motherhood: Contemporary conflict for women. In J. Freeman (Ed.), *Women: A feminist perspective,* 3d ed. Palo Alto, CA: Mayfield.

Hogan, R., & Emler, N. P. (1978). Moral development. In M. E. Lamb (Ed.), *Social and personality development*. New York: Holt, Rinehart and Winston.

Hollenbeck et al. (1984). Labor and delivery medication influences on parent-infant interaction in the first post-partum month. *Infant Behavior and Development, 7,* 201–209.

Hollestedt, C., Dahlgren, L., & Rydbert, U. (1983). Outcome of pregnancy in women treated at an alcohol clinic. *Acta Psychiatr. Scand., 67,* 236–248.

Hollister, L. E. (1983). Drug abuse in the United States: The past decade. *Drug and Alcohol Dependence, 11,* 49–53.

Holmes, D. L., Nagy, J., Slaymaker, F., Sosnowski, R. J., Prinz, S., & Pasternak, J. (1982). Early influences of prematurity, illness, and prolonged hospitalization on infant behavior. *Developmental Psychology, 18,* 744–750.

Honzik, M. P., Macfarlane, J. W., & Allen, L. (1948). The stability of mental test performance between two and eighteen years. *Journal of Experimental Education, 17,* 309–324.

Hook, E. (1981). Rates of chromosome abnormalities at different maternal ages. *Obstetrics and Gynecology,* 282–284.

Hooker, K., Nesselroade, D. W., Nesselroade, J. R., & Lerner, R. M. (1987). The structure of intraindividual temperament in the context of mother-child dyads: P-technique factor analyses of short-term change. *Developmental Psychology, 23,* 332–346.

Hopkins, J., Marcus, M., & Campbell, S. B. (1984). Postpartum depression: A critical review. *Psychological Bulletin, 95,* 498–515.

Horn, J. L. (1982). The aging of human abilities. In B. B. Wolman (Ed.), *Handbook of developmental psychology*. Englewood Cliffs, NJ: Prentice-Hall.

Horn, J. L., & Cattell, R. B. (1967). Age differences in fluid and crystallized intelligence. *Acta Psychologia, 26,* 107–129.

Horn, J. M. (1983). The Texas adoption project: Adopted children and their intellectual resemblance to biological and adoptive parents. *Child Development, 54,* 268–275.

Horney, K. (1967). *Feminine psychology*. New York: Norton.

Horton, D. L., & Turnage, T. W. (1976). *Human learning*. Englewood Cliffs, NJ: Prentice-Hall.

Horton, M., & Markman, E. M. (1980). Developmental differences in the acquisition of basic and superordinate categories. *Child Development, 51,* 708–719.

Horwitz, R. A. (1979). Psychological effects of the "open classroom." *Review of Educational Research, 49,* 71–86.

Householder, J., Hatcher, R., Burns, W., & Chasnoff, I. (1982). Infants born to narcotic-addicted mothers. *Psychological Bulletin, 92,* 453–468.

Houser, B. B., Beckman, S. L., & Beckman, L. J. (1984). The relative rewards and costs of childlessness for older women. *Psychology of Women Quarterly, 8,* 395–398.

Hoving, K. L., Spencer, T., Robb, K., & Schulte, D. (1978). Developmental changes in visual information processing. In P. A. Ornstein (Ed.), *Memory development in children*. Hillsdale, NJ: Erlbaum.

Howard, L., & Polich, J. (1985). P300 latency and memory span development. *Developmental Psychology, 21,* 283–289.

Hrncir, E. J., Speller, G. M., & West, M. (1985). What are we testing? *Developmental Psychology, 21,* 226–232.

Hsu, L. K. G. (1980). Outcome of anorexia nervosa: A review of the literature. *Archives of General Psychiatry, 37,* 1041–1046.

Huesmann, L. R., & Eron, L. D. (1986). *Television and the aggressive child: A*

▶ ▶ ▶ ▶

cross-national comparison. Hillsdale, NJ: Erlbaum.

Huesmann, L. R., Eron, L. D., Klein, R., Brice, P., & Fischer, P. (1983). Mitigating the imitation of aggressive behaviors by changing children's attitudes about media violence. *Journal of Personality and Social Psychology, 44*, 899–910.

Huesmann, L. R., Lagerspetz, K., & Eron, L. D. (1984). Intervening variables in the TV violence-aggression relation: Evidence from two countries. *Developmental Psychology, 20*, 746–755.

Humphreys, L. G. (1981). The primary mental ability. In M. P. Friedman, J. P. Das, & N. O'Connor (Eds.), *Intelligence and learning*. New York: Plenum Press.

Huston, A. C. (1983). Sex typing. In P. H. Mussen (Ed.), *Handbook of child psychology, Vol. 4: Socialization, personality, and social development*, 4th ed. New York: Wiley.

Huston-Stein, A., Friedrich-Cofer, L., & Susman, E. J. (1977). The relation of classroom structure to social behavior, imaginative play, and self-regulation of economically disadvantaged children. *Child Development, 48*, 908–916.

Hutt, C. (1978). Biological bases of psychological sex differences. *American Journal of Diseases of Children, 132*, 170–177.

Huxley, A. (1932). *Brave new world*. New York: Harper.

Hyde, J. S. (1981). How large are cognitive gender differences? *American Psychologist, 36*, 892–901.

Iannotti, R. J. (1978). Effect of role taking experiences on role taking, empathy, altruism and aggression. *Developmental Psychology, 14*, 119–124.

Iannotti, R. J. (1985). Naturalistic and structured assessments of prosocial behavior in preschool children: The influence of empathy and perspective taking. *Developmental Psychology, 21*, 46–55.

Inhelder, B., & Piaget, J. (1955). *The growth of logical thinking from childhood to adolescence*. New York: Basic Books, 1958.

Inhelder, B., & Piaget, J. (1959). *The early growth of logic in the child: Classification and seriation*. New York: Harper & Row, 1964.

Ipsa, J. (1981). Social interactions among teachers, handicapped children, and nonhandicapped children in a mainstreamed preschool. *Journal of Applied Developmental Psychology, 1*, 231–250.

Israel, A. C., & Stolmaker, L. (1980). Behavioral treatment of obesity in children and adolescents. In M. Hersen, R. M. Eisler, & P. M. Miller (Eds.), *Progress in Behavior Modification*, Vol. 10. New York: Academic Press.

Israel, A. C., Stolmaker, L., & Andrian, C. A. G. (1985). The effects of training parents in general child management skills on a behavioral weight loss program for children. *Behavior Therapy, 16*, 169–180.

Israel, A. C., Stolmaker, L., Sharp, J. P., Silverman, W. K., & Simon, L. G. (1984). An evaluation of two methods of parental involvement in treating obese children. *Behavior Therapy, 15*, 266–272.

Jacklin, C. N., DiPietro, J. A., & Maccoby, E. E. (1984). Sex-typing behavior and sex-typing pressure in child-parent interaction. *Sex Roles, 13*, 413–425.

Jacklin, C. N., & Maccoby, E. E. (1983). Issues of gender differentiation. In M. D. Levine, W. B. Carey, A. C. Crocker, & R. T. Gross (Eds.), *Developmental-behavioral pediatrics*. Philadelphia: W. B. Saunders.

Jackson, E., Campos, J. J., & Fischer, K. W. (1978). The question of décalage between object permanence and person permanence. *Developmental Psychology, 14*, 1–10.

Jacobson, J. L., Boersma, D. C., Fields, R. B., & Olson, K. L. (1983). Paralinguistic features of adult speech to infants and small children. *Child Development, 54*, 436–442.

Jacobson, S. W. (1979). Matching behavior in the young infant. *Child Development, 50*, 425–430.

Jalali, B., Jalali, M., Crocetti, G., & Turner, F. (1981). Adolescents and drug use: Toward a more comprehensive approach. *American Journal of Orthopsychiatry, 3*, 120–130.

Jelliffe, D. B., & Jelliffe, E. F. P. (1983). Recent scientific knowledge concerning breastfeeding. *Rev. Epidem. et Sante. Publ., 31*, 367–373.

Jensen, A. R. (1969). How much can we boost IQ and scholastic achievement? *Harvard Educational Review, 39*, 1–123.

Jensen, A. R. (1980). *Bias in mental testing*. New York: Free Press.

Jensen, A. R. (1982). Level I/Level II: Factors or categories? *Journal of Educational Psychology, 74*, 868–873.

Jensen, A. R. (1985). The nature of the black-white difference on various psychometric tests: Spearman's hypothesis. *The Behavioral and Brain Sciences, 8* (2), 193–219.

Jensen, K. (1932). Differential reactions to taste and temperature stimuli in newborn infants. *Genetic Psychology Monographs, 12*, 363–479.

Jensen, & Bobak. (1985). *Maternity and gynecologic care*. St. Louis: Mosby.

Jersild, A. T., & Holmes, F. B. (1935). *Children's fears*. New York: Teachers College Press.

Jiao, S., Ji, G., & Jing, Q. (1986). Comparative study of behavioral qualities of only children and sibling children. *Child Development, 57*, 357–361.

Joffee, C. (1971). Sex role socialization and the nursery school: As the twig is bent. *Journal of Marriage and the Family, 33*, 467–475.

Johnson, C. D., & Gormley, J. (1972). Academic cheating: The contribution of sex, personality and situational variables. *Developmental Psychology, 6*, 320–325.

▶ ▶ ▶ ▶

Johnson, J. E., & McGillicuddy-Delisi, A. (1983). Family environment factors and children's knowledge of rules and conventions. *Child Development, 54*, 218–226.

Johnson, S. B., & Melamed, B. G. (1979). The assessment and treatment of children's fears. In B. Lahey & A. E. Kazdin (Eds.), *Advances in clinical child psychology*, Vol. 2. New York: Plenum Press.

Johnson, W., Emde, R. N., Pannabecker, B., Stenberg, C., & Davis, M. (1982). Maternal perception of infant emotion from birth to 18 months. *Infant Behavior and Development, 5*, 313–322.

Johnston, J., & Ettema, J. S. (1982). *Positive images: Breaking stereotypes with children's television.* Beverly Hills, CA: Sage.

Johnston, L. D., Bachman, J. G., & O'Malley, P. M. (1982). *Student drug use, attitudes, and beliefs: 1975–1982.* U.S. Department of Health and Human Services Publication No. ADM 82-1260. Washington, DC: National Institute on Drug Abuse.

Jones, H. E., & Jones, M. C. (1928). Fear. *Childhood Education, 5*, 136–143.

Jones, K. L. (1975). The fetal alcohol syndrome. In R. D. Harbison (Ed.), *Perinatal addiction.* New York: Halsted Press.

Jones, M. C. (1924). Elimination of children's fears. *Journal of Experimental Psychology, 7*, 381–390.

Jones, M. C. (1957). The late careers of boys who were early- or late-maturing. *Child Development, 28*, 115–128.

Jones, M. C. (1958). The study of socialization patterns at the high school level. *Journal of Genetic Psychology, 93*, 87–111.

Jones, M. C., & Mussen, P. H. (1958). Self-conceptions, motivations, and interpersonal attitudes of early- and late-maturing girls. *Child Development, 29*, 491–501.

Joos, S. K., Pollitt, E., Mueller, W. H., & Albright, D. L. (1983). The Bacon Chow study: Maternal nutritional supplementation and infant behavioral development. *Child Development, 54*, 669–676.

Jost, H., & Sontag, L. (1944). The genetic factor in autonomic nervous system function. *Psychosomatic Medicine, 6*, 308–310.

Julien, R. M. (1978). *A primer of drug action.* San Francisco: Freeman.

Jurkovic, G. J. (1980). The juvenile delinquent as a moral philosopher: A structural-developmental perspective. *Psychological Bulletin, 88*, 709–727.

Justice, B., & Justice, R. (1976). *The abusing family.* New York: Human Sciences Press.

Kagan, J. (1964). Acquisition and significance of sex-typing and sex-role identity. In M. L. Hoffman & L. W. Hoffman (Eds.), *Review of child development research*, Vol. 1. New York: Russell Sage Foundation.

Kagan, J. (1971). *Change and continuity in infancy.* New York: Wiley.

Kagan, J. (1972). The plasticity of early intellectual development. Paper presented to the meeting of the Association for the Advancement of Science, Washington, DC.

Kagan, J. (1984). *The nature of the child.* New York: Basic Books.

Kagan, J., Kearsley, R. B., & Zelazo, P. R. (1978). *Infancy: Its place in development.* Cambridge, MA: Harvard University Press.

Kagan, J., & Klein, R. E. (1973). Cross-cultural perspectives on early development. *American Psychologist, 28*, 947–961.

Kagan, J., & Moss, H. A. (1962). *Birth to maturity: A study in psychological development.* New York: Wiley.

Kagan, S., & Madsen, M. C. (1971). Cooperation and competition of Mexican, Mexican-American, and Anglo-American children of two ages under four instructional sets. *Developmental Psychology, 5*, 32–39.

Kagan, S., & Madsen, M. C. (1972). Experimental analyses of cooperation and competition of Anglo-American and Mexican children. *Developmental Psychology, 6*, 49–59.

Kail, R. (1984). *The development of memory in children*, 2d ed. New York: W. H. Freeman.

Kail, R., & Nippold, M. A. (1984). Unconstrained retrieval from semantic memory. *Child Development, 55*, 944–951.

Kallman, F. J., & Roth, B. (1956). Genetic aspects of preadolescent schizophrenia. *American Journal of Psychiatry, 112*, 599–606.

Kamin, L. J. (1982). Mental testing and immigration. *American Psychologist, 37*, 97–98.

Kandel, D. B. (1980). Drug and drinking behavior among youth. *Annual Review of Sociology, 6*, 235–285.

Kaplan, R. M., & Singer, R. D. (1976). Television violence and viewer aggression: A reexamination of the evidence. *Journal of Social Issues, 32*, 35–70.

Karmiloff-Smith, A. (1979). *A functional approach to child language.* Cambridge: Cambridge University Press.

Karnes, M. B., & Lee, R. C. (1979). Mainstreaming in the preschool. In L. G. Katz (Ed.), *Current topics in early childhood education*, Vol. 2. Norwood, NJ: Ablex.

Karniol, R. (1980). A conceptual analysis of immanent justice responses in children. *Child Development, 51*, 118–130.

Karp, L. (1980). The arguable propriety of preconceptual sex determination. *American Journal of Medical Genetics, 6*, 185–187.

Katchadourian, H. A. (1985). *Fundamentals of human sexuality.* New York: Holt, Rinehart and Winston.

Kavale, K. (1982). The efficacy of stimulant drug treatment for hyperactivity: A meta-analysis. *Journal of Learning Disabilities, 15*, 280–289.

▶ ▶ ▶ ▶

Kazdin, A. E., Esveldt-Dawson, K., Sherick, R. B., & Colbus, D. (1985). Assessment of overt behavior and childhood depression among psychiatrically disturbed children. *Journal of Consulting and Clinical Psychology, 53,* 201–210.

Kazdin, A. E., Moser, J., Colbus, D., & Bell, R. (1985). Depressive symptoms among physically abused and psychiatrically disturbed children. *Journal of Abnormal Psychology, 94,* 298–307.

Keating, D. P. (1980). Thinking processes in adolescence. In J. Adelson (Ed.), *Handbook of adolescent psychology.* New York: Wiley-Interscience, pp. 211–246.

Keating, D. P., & Clark, L. V. (1980). Development of physical and social reasoning in adolescents. *Developmental Psychology, 16,* 23–30.

Keele, S. W. (1973). *Attention and human performance.* Santa Monica, CA: Goodyear.

Keislar, E. R., Hsieh, B., & Bhasin, C. (1972). An intercultural study: Discrimination and informal experience. *Reading Teacher, 12,* 1–10.

Keller, W. D., Hildebrandt, K. A., & Richards, M. (1981). Effects of extended father-infant contact during the newborn period. Paper presented to the biennial meeting of the Society for Research in Child Development, Boston.

Kendall, P. C., & Fischler, G. L. (1984). Behavioral and adjustment correlates of problem solving: Validational analysis of interpersonal problem-solving measures. *Child Development, 55,* 879–892.

Kendall, P. C., & Williams, C. L. (1981). Behavioral and cognitive behavioral approaches to outpatient treatment with children. In W. E. Craighead, A. E. Kazdin, & M. J. Mahoney, *Behavior modification: Principles, issues, and applications,* 2d ed. Boston: Houghton Mifflin.

Kendrick, C., & Dunn, J. (1980). Caring for a second baby: Effects on inter-action between mother and first-born. *Developmental Psychology, 16,* 303–311.

Kennedy, W. A. (1965). School phobia: Rapid treatment of fifty cases. *Journal of Abnormal Psychology, 70,* 285–289.

Kennell, J. H., Jerauld, R., Wolfe, H., Chesler, D., Kreger, N. C., McAlpine, W., Steffa, M., & Klaus, M. H. (1974). Maternal behavior one year after early and extended post-partum contact. *Developmental Medicine and Child Neurology, 16,* 172–179.

Kennell, J. H., & Klaus, M. H. (1984). Mother-infant bonding: Weighing the evidence. *Developmental Review, 4,* 275–282.

Kernberg, P. F. (1979). Childhood schizophrenia and autism: A selective review. In L. Bellak (Ed.), *Disorders of the schizophrenic syndrome.* New York: Basic Books.

Kershner, J. R., & Ledger, G. (1985). Effect of sex, intelligence, and style of thinking on creativity: A comparison of gifted and average IQ children. *Journal of Personality and Social Psychology, 48,* 1033–1040.

Kessen, W. (1965). *The child.* New York: Wiley.

Kessen, W., Haith, M. M., & Salapatek, P. (1970). Human infancy: A bibliography and guide. In P. H. Mussen (Ed.), *Carmichaels's manual of child psychology,* Vol. 1, 3d ed. New York: Wiley.

Kessen, W., Leutzendoff, A. M., & Stoutsenberger, K. (1967). Age, food deprivation, non-nutritive sucking and movement in the human newborn. *Journal of Comparative and Physiological Psychology, 63,* 82–86.

Kessen, W., Levine, J., & Wendich, K. A. (1979). The imitation of pitch in infants. *Infant Behavior and Development, 2,* 93–100.

Kessner, D. M. (1973). *Infant death: An analysis by maternal risk and health care.* Washington, DC: National Academy of Sciences.

Keuthen, N. (1980). Subjective probability estimation and somatic structures in phobic individuals. Unpublished manuscript, State University of New York at Stony Brook.

Kinsborne, M., & Hiscock, M. (1983). The normal and deviant development of functional lateralization of the brain. In P. H. Mussen (Ed.), *Handbook of Child Psychology,* Vol. 2. New York: Wiley.

Klaus, M. H., & Kennell, J. H. (1978). Parent-to-infant attachment. In J. H. Stevens, Jr., & M. Mathews (Eds.), *Mother/child, father/child relationships.* Washington, D.C.: National Association for the Education of Young Children.

Klein, M., & Stern, L. (1971). Low birth weight and the battered child syndrome. *American Journal of Diseases of Childhood, 122,* 15–18.

Klein, R. P. (1985). Caregiving arrangements by employed women with children under 1 year of age. *Developmental Psychology, 21,* 403–406.

Kleinke, C. L., & Staneski, R. A. (1980). First impressions of female bust size. *Journal of Social Psychology, 100,* 123–134.

Kleinmuntz, B. (1982). *Personality and psychological assessment.* New York: St. Martin's Press.

Knaub, P. K., Eversoll, D. B., & Voss, J. H. (1983). Is parenthood a desirable adult role? An assessment of attitudes held by contemporary adult women. *Sex Roles, 9,* 355–362.

Knight, G. P., Dubro, A. F., & Chao, C. (1985). Information processing and the development of cooperative, competitive, and individualistic social values. *Developmental Psychology, 21,* 37–45.

Kogan, B. A. (1973). *Human sexual expression.* New York: Harcourt Brace Jovanovich.

Kohlberg, L. (1963). Moral development and identification. In H. W. Stevenson (Ed.), *Child psychology:*

62nd yearbook of the National Society for the Study of Education. Chicago: University of Chicago Press.

Kohlberg, L. (1966). A cognitive-developmental analysis of children's sex-role concepts and attitudes. In E. E. Maccoby (Ed.), *The development of sex differences.* Stanford, CA: Stanford University Press, pp. 82–173.

Kohlberg, L. (1969). Stage and sequence: The cognitive-developmental approach to socialization. In D. A. Goslin (Ed.), *Handbook of socialization theory and research.* Chicago: Rand McNally, pp. 347–480.

Kohlberg, L. (1976). Moral stages and moralization: The cognitive-developmental approach. In T. Lickona (Ed.), *Moral development and behavior: Theory, research, and social issues.* New York: Holt, Rinehart and Winston.

Kohlberg, L. (1981). *The meaning and measurement of moral development.* Worcester, MA: Clark University Press.

Kohlberg, L. (1985). *The psychology of moral development.* San Francisco: Harper & Row.

Kohlberg, L., & Kramer, R. B. (1969). Continuities and discontinuities in childhood and adult moral development. *Human Development, 12,* 93–120.

Kolata, G. B. (1985). Down syndrome–Alzheimer's linked. *Science, 230,* 1152–1153.

Konner, M. J. (1972). Aspects of the developmental ethology of a foraging people. In N. Burton Jones (Ed.), *Ethological studies of child behavior.* London: Cambridge University Press.

Konner, M. J. (1977). Infancy among the Kalahari San. In P. H. Leiderman, S. R. Tulkin, & A. Rosenfeld (Eds.), *Culture and infancy: Variations in the human experience.* New York: Academic Press.

Koocher, G. P. (1971). Swimming, competence, and personality change. *Journal of Personality and Social Psychology, 18,* 275–278.

Koop, C. E. (1987). Cited in Koop urges AIDS test before getting pregnant. *New York Times,* March 25, 1987, p. B4.

Kopp, C. B., & McCall, R. B. (1982). Predicting later mental performance for normal, at-risk, and handicapped infants. In P. B. Baltes & O. G. Brim, Jr. (Eds.), *Lifespan development and behavior,* Vol. 4. New York: Academic Press.

Korner, A. F., Kraemer, H. C., Hoffner, E., & Cosper, L. M. (1975). Effects of waterbed flotation on premature infants: A pilot study. *Pediatrics, 56,* 361–367.

Korsch, B. M. (1983). More on parent-infant bonding. *Journal of Pediatrics, 103,* 249–250.

Kovacs, M., & Beck, A. T. (1977). An empirical-clinical approach toward a definition of childhood depression. In J. G. Schulterbrandt & A. Raskin (Eds.), *Depression in childhood: Diagnosis, treatment, and conceptual models.* New York: Raven Press.

Krantz, P. J., & Risley, T. R. (1977). Behavioral ecology in the classroom. In K. D. O'Leary & S. G. O'Leary (Eds.), *Classroom management.* New York: Pergamon Press.

Krebs, R. L. (1968). *Some relationships between moral judgment, attention, and resistance to temptation.* Unpublished doctoral dissertation, University of Chicago.

Kress, G. (1982). *Learning to write.* Boston: Routledge and Kegan Paul.

Kuczaj, S. A., II (1982). On the nature of syntactic development. In S. A. Kuczaj, II (Ed.), *Language development: Vol. 1. Syntax and semantics.* Hillsdale, NJ: Erlbaum.

Kuhn, D. (1976). Short-term longitudinal evidence for the sequentiality of Kohlberg's early stages of moral development. *Developmental Psychology, 12,* 162–166.

Kuhn, D., Kohlberg, L., Langer, J., & Haan, N. (1977). The development of formal operations in logical and moral judgment. *Genetic Psychology Monographs.*

Kuhn, D., Nash, S. C., & Brucken, L. (1978). Sex-role concepts of two- and three-year-olds. *Child Development, 49,* 445–451.

Kurdek, A., Blisk, D., & Siesky, A. E. (1981). Correlates of children's long-term adjustment to their parents' divorce. *Developmental Psychology, 17,* 565–579.

Labov, W. (1970). The logic of nonstandard English. In F. Williams (Ed.), *Language and poverty: Perspectives on a theme.* Chicago: Markham.

Labov, W. (1972). The study of language in its social context. In W. Labov (Ed.), *Sociolinguistic patterns.* Philadelphia: University of Pennsylvania Press.

Lacey, J., & Lacey, I. (1958). The relationship of resting autonomic activity to motor impulsivity. *Research Publication of the Association for Research on Nervous and Mental Diseases, 36,* 144–209.

LaFreniere, P. J., & Sroufe, L. A. (1985). Profiles of peer competence in the preschool: Interrelations between measures, influence of social ecology, and relation to attachment history. *Developmental Psychology, 21,* 56–69.

Lahey, B. B., & Drabman, R. S. (1981). Behavior modification in the classroom. In W. E. Craighead, A. E. Kazdin, & M. J. Mahoney (Eds.), *Behavior modification: Principles, issues, and applications,* 2d ed. Boston: Houghton Mifflin.

Lakin, M. (1957). Personality factors in mothers of excessively crying (colicky) infants. *Monographs of the Society for Research in Child Development, 22* (Whole No. 64).

Lamaze, F. (1981). *Painless childbirth.* New York: Simon & Schuster.

Lamb, D. R. (1984). *Physiology of exercise: Response and adaptation,* 2d ed. New York: Macmillan.

▶ ▶ ▶ ▶

Lamb, M. E. (1976a). Effects of stress and cohort on mother- and father-interaction. *Developmental Psychology, 12,* 435–443.

Lamb, M. E. (1976b). Interactions between eight-month-old children and their fathers and mothers. In M. E. Lamb (Ed.), *The role of the father in child development.* New York: Wiley.

Lamb, M. E. (1977). Father-infant and mother-infant interaction in the first year of life. *Child Development, 48,* 167–181.

Lamb, M. E. (1979). Paternal influences and the father's role. *American Psychologist, 34,* 938–943.

Lamb, M. E. (1981). The development of father-infant relationships. In M. E. Lamb (Ed.), *The role of the father in child development.* New York: Wiley.

Lamb, M. E. (1982a). Sibling relationships across the lifespan. In M. E. Lamb & B. Sutton-Smith (Eds.), *Sibling relationships.* Hillsdale, NJ: Erlbaum.

Lamb, M. E. (1982b). Early contact and maternal-infant bonding: One decade later. *Pediatrics, 70,* 763–768.

Lamb, M. E., & Baumrind, D. (1978). Socialization and personality development in the preschool years. In M. E. Lamb (Ed.), *Social and personality development.* New York: Holt, Rinehart and Winston.

Lamb, M. E., Easterbrooks, M. A., & Holden, G. W. (1980). Reinforcement and punishment among preschoolers: Characteristics, effects, and correlates. *Child Development, 51,* 1230–1236.

Lamb, M. E., Frodi, A., Hwang, C. P., & Frodi, M. (1982). Varying degrees of paternal involvement in infant care: Correlates and effects. In M. E. Lamb (Ed.), *Nontraditional families.* Hillsdale, NJ: Erlbaum.

Lamb, M. E., Hwang, C. P., Frodi, A., & Frodi, M. (1982). Security of mother and father infant attachment and its relation to sociability with strangers in traditional and nontraditional Swedish families. *Infant Behavior and Development, 5,* 355–368.

Lamb, M. E., & Roopnarine, J. L. (1979). Peer influences on sex-role development in preschoolers. *Child Development, 50,* 1219–1222.

Lamke, L. K. (1982a). Adjustment and sex-role orientation. *Journal of Youth and Adolescence, 11,* 247–259.

Lamke, L. K. (1982b). The impact of sex-role orientation on self-esteem in early adolescence. *Child Development, 53,* 1530–1535.

Lancioni, G. E. (1980). Infant operant conditioning and its implications for early intervention. *Psychological Bulletin, 88,* 516–534.

Landesman-Dwyer, S., & Emanuel, I. (1979). Smoking during pregnancy. *Teratology, 19,* 119–126.

Lang, P. J., & Melamed, B. B. (1969). Case report: Avoidance conditioning therapy of an infant with chronic ruminative vomiting. *Journal of Abnormal Psychology, 74,* 1–8.

Langlois, J. H. (1985). From the eye of the beholder to behavioral reality: The development of social behaviors and social relations as a function of physical attractiveness. In C. P. Herman (Ed.), *Physical appearance, stigma, and social behavior.* Hillsdale, NJ: Erlbaum.

Langlois, J. H., Roggman, L. A., Casey, R. J., Ritter, J. M., Rieser-Danner, L. A., & Jenkins, V. Y. (1987). Infant preferences for attractive faces: Rudiments of a stereotype? *Developmental Psychology, 1987,* 363–369.

LaPouse, R. (1966). The epidemiology of behavior disorders in children. *American Journal of Diseases of Children, 111,* 594–599.

LaPouse, R., & Monk, M. (1959). Fears and worries in a representative sample of children. *American Journal of Orthopsychiatry, 29,* 803–818.

Larsen, J. (1984, March 19). Cited in Sad news for the happy hour. *Newsweek,* p. 67.

Larsen, S. A., & Homer, D. R. (1978). Relation of breast versus bottle feeding to hospitalization for gastroenteritis in a middle-class U.S. population. *The Journal of Pediatrics, 92,* 417–418.

Lasko, J. K. (1954). Parent behavior towards first and second children. *Genetic Psychology Monographs, 49,* 5–39.

Laurendeau, M., & Pinard, A. (1962). *Causal thinking in the child: A genetic and experimental approach.* New York: International Universities Press.

Lavin, D. E. (1965). *The prediction of academic performance: A theoretical analysis and review of research.* New York: Russell Sage Foundation.

Lavine, L. O. (1982). Parental power as a potential influence on girls' career choice. *Child Development, 53,* 658–663.

LaVoie, J. C. (1973). Punishment and adolescent self-control. *Developmental Psychology, 8,* 16–24.

Lay, M., & Meyer, W. (1973). Teacher/child behaviors in an open environment day care program. Syracuse: Syracuse University Children's Center.

Lazar, I., & Darlington, R. (1982). Lasting effects of early education: A report from the Consortium of Longitudinal Studies. *Monographs of the Society for Research in Child Development, 47* (2–3), Serial No. 195.

Leary, M. A., Greer, D., & Huston, A. C. (1982, April). The relation between TV viewing and gender roles. Paper presented at the meeting of the Southwestern Society for Research in Human Development, Galveston, TX.

LeBoyer, F. (1975). *Birth without violence.* New York: Knopf.

Lefkowitz, M. M., & Tesiny, E. P. (1980). Assessment of childhood depression. *Journal of Consulting and Clinical Psychology, 48,* 43–50.

Lehrer, L. (1967). Sex differences in moral behavior and attitudes. Un-

▶ ▶ ▶ ▶

published doctoral dissertation, University of Chicago.

Lehtovaara, A., Saarinen, P., & Jarvinen, J. (1965). *Psychological studies of twins: 1. GSR reactions.* Helsinki, University of Helsinki Press.

Leifer, A. D., Leiderman, P. H., Barnett, C. R., & Williams, J. A. (1972). Effects of mother-infant separation on maternal behavior. *Child Development, 43,* 1203–1218.

Leifer, M. (1980). *Psychological effects of motherhood: A study of first pregnancy.* New York: Praeger.

Lenneberg, E. H. (1967). *Biological foundations of language.* New York: Wiley.

Lepper, M. R. (1981). Intrinsic and extrinsic motivation in children: Detrimental effects of superfluous social controls. In W. A. Collins (Ed.), *Minnesota symposia on child psychology,* Vol. 14. Hillsdale, NJ: Erlbaum.

Lepper, M. R., Greene, D., & Nisbett, R. E. (1973). Undermining children's intrinsic interest with extrinsic rewards. *Journal of Personality and Social Psychology, 28,* 129–137.

Lesser, G. S., Fifer, G., & Clark, D. H. (1965). Mental abilities of children from different social class and cultural groups. *Monographs of the Society for Research in Child Development, 30* (Whole No. 102).

Lester, B. M. (1978). The organization of crying in the neonate. *Journal of Pediatric Psychology, 3,* 122–130.

Lester, B. M., Als, H., & Brazelton, T. B. (1982). Regional obstetric anesthesia and newborn behavior: A reanalysis toward synergistic effects. *Child Development, 53,* 687–692.

Lester, B. M., & Zeskind, P. S. (1982). A biobehavioral perspective on crying in early infancy. In H. Fitzgerald, B. M. Lester, & M. W. Yogman (Eds.), *Theory and Research in Behavioral Pediatrics,* Vol. 1. New York: Plenum Press.

Leventhal, A. S., & Lipsitt, L. P. (1964). Adaptation, pitch discrimination, and sound localization in the neonate. *Child Development, 35,* 759–767.

Levine, S. (1983). A psychobiological approach to the ontogeny of coping. In N. Garmezy & M. Rutter (Eds.), *Stress and coping in early childhood.* New York: McGraw-Hill.

Levine, S. (1987, March 18). Personal communication.

Levinger, G., & Gunner, J. (1967). The interpersonal grid: Felt and tape techniques for the measurements of social relationships. *Psychonomic Science, 8,* 113–174.

Levitt, M. J., Weber, R. A., Clark, M. C., & McDonnell, P. (1985). Reciprocity of exchange in toddler sharing behavior. *Developmental Psychology, 21,* 122–123.

Levy, J. (1987). Right brain, left brain: Fact and fiction. In M. G. Walraven & H. E. Fitzgerald (Eds.), *Psychology 87/88.* Guilford, CT: Dushkin.

Levy-Shiff, R. (1982). The effects of father absence on young children in mother-headed families. *Child Development, 53,* 81–86.

Levy-Shiff, R. (1983). Adaptation and competence in early childhood: Communally raised kibbutz children versus family raised children in the city. *Child Development, 54,* 1606–1614.

Lewin, K., Lippitt, R., & White, R. K. (1939). Patterns of aggressive behavior in experimentally created "social climates." *Journal of Social Psychology, 10,* 271–299.

Lewis, M. (1969). A developmental study of information processing within the first three years of life: Response decrement to a redundant signal. *Monographs of the Society for Research in Child Development, 34,* (Whole No. 133).

Lewis, M. (1983). On the nature of intelligence: Science or bias? In M. Lewis (Ed.), *Origins of intelligence: Infancy and early childhood,* 2d ed. New York: Plenum Press.

Lewis, M., & Brooks, J. (1974). Self, other, and fear: Infants' reactions to people. In M. Lewis & L. Rosenblum (Eds.), *The origins of fear.* New York: Wiley.

Lewis, M., & Brooks-Gunn, J. (1979). *Social cognition and the acquisition of self.* New York: Plenum Press.

Lewis, M., Feiring, C., McGuffog, C., & Jaskir, J. (1984). Predicting psychopathology in six-year-olds from early social relations. *Child Development, 55,* 123–136.

Liben, L. S. (1978). The development of deaf children: An overview of issues. In L. S. Liben (Ed.), *Deaf children: Developmental perspectives.* New York: Academic Press.

Liben, L. S. (1982). The developmental study of children's memory. In T. M. Field, A. Huston, H. C. Quay, L. Troll, & G. E. Finley (Eds.), *Review of human development.* New York: Wiley.

Liberty, C., & Ornstein, P. A. (1973). Age differences in organization and recall: The effects of training in categorization. *Journal of Experimental Child Psychology, 15,* 169–186.

Lickona, T. (1976). Research on Piaget's theory of moral development. In T. Lickona (Ed.), *Moral development and behavior.* New York: Holt, Rinehart and Winston.

Lieberman, A. F. (1977). Preschoolers' competence with a peer: Relations with attachment and peer experience. *Child Development, 48,* 1277–1287.

Liebert, R. M., & Sprafkin, J. N. (1982). *The early window.* Elmsford, NY: Pergamon Press.

Linn, S., Reznick, J. S., Kagan, J., & Hans, S. (1982). Salience of visual patterns in the human infant. *Developmental Psychology, 18,* 651–657.

Linn, S., Schoenbaum, S., Monson, R., Rosner, B., Stubblefield, R., & Ryan, K. (1982). Coffee and pregnancy. *New England Journal of Medicine, 306,* 141–145.

▶ ▶ ▶ ▶

Linton, T. E., & Juul, K. D. (1980). Mainstreaming: Time for reassessment. *Educational Leadership, 37,* 433-437.

Lipsitt, L. P. (1982). Perinatal indicators of psychophysiological precursors of crib death. In J. Belsky (Ed.), *In the beginning.* New York: Columbia University Press.

Lipsitt, L. P., Sturner, W. Q., & Burke, P. (1979). Perinatal indicators and subsequent crib death. *Infant Behavior and Development, 2,* 325–328.

Lipton, E. L., Steinschneider, A., & Richmond, J. B. (1965). Swaddling, a child care practice: Historical, cultural and experimental. *Pediatrics, 35,* 521–567.

List, J. A., Collins, W. A., & Westby, S. D. (1983). Comprehension and inferences from traditional and nontraditional sex-role portrayals on television. *Child Development, 54,* 1579–1587.

Livson, N., & Peskin, H. (1980). Perspectives on adolescence from longitudinal research. In J. Adelson (Ed.), *Handbook of adolescent psychology.* New York: Wiley.

Lochman, J. E., Burch, P. R., Curry, J. F., & Lampron, L. B. (1984). Treatment and generalization effects of cognitive-behavioral and goal-setting interventions with aggressive boys. *Journal of Consulting and Clinical Psychology, 52,* 915–916.

Lockman, J. L. (1984). The development of detour ability during infancy. *Child Development, 55,* 482–491.

Loeb, R. B., Horst, L., & Horton, P. J. (1980). Family interaction patterns associated with self-esteem in preadolescent girls and boys. *Merrill-Palmer Quarterly, 26,* 203–217.

Loehlin, J. C., Lindzey, G., & Spuhler, J. N. (1975). *Race differences in intelligence.* San Francisco: Freeman.

Loehlin, J. C., Willerman, L., & Horn, J. M. (1982). Personality resemblances between unwed mothers and their adopted-away offspring. *Journal of Personality and Social Psychology, 42,* 1089–1099.

Lorenz, K. (1962). *King Solomon's ring.* London: Methuen.

Lorenz, K. (1981). *The foundations of ethology.* New York: Springer-Verlag.

Lott, B. (1981). A feminist critique of androgyny: Toward the elimination of gender attributions for learned behavior. In C. Mayo & N. M. Henley (Eds.), *Gender and nonverbal behavior.* New York: Springer.

Lott, B. (1985). The potential enrichment of social/personality psychology through feminist research and vice versa. *American Psychologist, 40,* 155–164.

Lotter, V. (1974). Factors related to outcome in autistic children. *Journal of Autism and Childhood Schizophrenia, 4,* 263–277.

Lotter, V. (1978). Follow-up studies. In M. Rutter & E. Schopler (Eds.), *Autism: A reappraisal of concepts and treatment.* New York: Plenum Press.

Lovaas, O. I. (1977). *The autistic child: Language development through behavior modification.* New York: Irvington.

Lovaas, O. I. (1987). Behavioral treatment and normal educational and intellectual functioning in young autistic children. *Journal of Consulting and Clinical Psychology, 55,* 3–9.

Lowrey, G. H. (1978). *Growth and development of children,* 7th ed. Chicago: Year Book Medical Publishers.

Lucariello, J., & Nelson, K. (1985). Slot-filler categories as memory organizers for young children. *Developmental Psychology, 21,* 272–282.

Lutjen, P., Trounson, A., Leeton, J., Findlay, J., Wood, C., & Renou, P. (1984). The establishment and maintenance of pregnancy using in vitro fertilization and embryo donation in a patient with primary ovarian failure. *Nature, 307,* 174–175.

Lykken, D. T. (1957). A study of anxiety in the sociopathic personality. *Journal of Abnormal and Social Psychology, 55,* 6–10.

Lykken, D. T. (1982). Fearlessness: Its carefree charm and deadly risks. *Psychology Today, 16* (9), 20–28.

Lynn, R. (1977). The intelligence of the Japanese. *Bulletin of the British Psychological Society, 30,* 69–72.

Lynn, R. (1982). IQ in Japan and the United States shows a growing disparity. *Nature, 297,* 222–223.

Maccoby, E. E. (1980). *Social development: Psychological growth and the parent-child relationship.* New York: Harcourt Brace Jovanovich.

Maccoby, E. E., & Jacklin, C. N. (1974). *The psychology of sex differences.* Stanford, CA: Stanford University Press.

Maccoby, E. E., & Jacklin, C. N. (1980). Sex differences in aggression: A rejoinder and reprise. *Child Development, 51,* 964–980.

Maccoby, E. E., & Martin, J. A. (1983). Socialization in the context of the family: Parent-child interaction. In P. H. Mussen (Ed.), *Handbook of child psychology: Vol. 4. Socialization, personality, and social development.* New York: Wiley.

Macfarlane, A. (1977). *The psychology of childbirth.* Cambridge, MA: Harvard University Press.

Macfarlane, A. (1978, February). What a baby knows. *Human Nature.*

Macfarlane, A., Harris, P., & Barnes, I. (1976). Central and peripheral vision in early infancy. *Journal of Experimental Child Psychology, 21,* 532–538.

Macfarlane, J. A. (1975). Olfaction in the development of social preferences in the human neonate. In M. A. Hofer (Ed.), *Parent-infant interaction.* Amsterdam: Elsevier.

Macfarlane, J. W., Allen, L., & Honzik, M. P. (1954). *A developmental study of the behavior problems of normal children between 21 months and 14 years.* Berkeley, University of California Press.

Mackenzie, B. (1984). Explaining race differences in IQ: The logic, the methodology, and the evidence. *American Psychologist, 39,* 1214–1233.

▶ ▶ ▶ ▶

Madsen, C. H., Becker, W. C., & Thomas, D. R. (1968). Rules, praise, and ignoring: Elements of elementary classroom control. *Journal of Applied Behavior Analysis, 1,* 139–150.

Mahoney, M. J. (1974). *Cognition and behavior modification.* Cambridge, MA: Ballinger.

Main, M., & George, C. (1985). Responses of abused and disadvantaged toddlers to distress in agemates: A study in the day care setting. *Developmental Psychology, 21,* 407–412.

Main, M., & Weston, D. R. (1981). The quality of the toddler's relationship to mother and to father: Related to conflict behavior and the readiness to establish new relationships. *Child Development, 52,* 932–940.

Malatesta, G. Z., Grigoryev, P., Lamb, C., Albin, M., & Culver, C. (1986). Emotion socialization and expressive development in preterm and full-term infants. *Child Development, 57,* 316–330.

Malatesta, G. Z., & Haviland, J. (1982). Learning display rules: The socialization of emotional expression in infancy. *Child Development, 53,* 991–1003.

Malatesta, G. Z., & Haviland, J. (1985). Signals, symbols, and socialization. In M. Lewis & C. Saarni (Eds.), *The socialization of emotions.* New York: Plenum Press.

Maloney, M. J., & Klykylo, W. M. (1983). An overview of anorexia nervosa, bulimia, and obesity in children and adolescents. *Journal of the American Academy of Child Psychiatry, 22,* 99–107.

Mankiewicz, F., & Swerdlow, J. (1977). *Remote control.* New York: Quadrangle.

Mannarino, A. (1978). Friendship patterns and self-concept development in preadolescent males. *Journal of Genetic Psychology, 133,* 105–110.

Manning, M. M., & Wright, T. L. (1983). Self-efficacy expectancies, outcome expectancies, and the persistence of pain control in childbirth. *Journal of Personality and Social Psychology, 45,* 421–431.

Manosevitz, M., Prentice, N. M., & Wilson, F. (1973). Individual and family correlates of imaginary companions in preschool children. *Developmental Psychology, 8,* 72–79.

Manstead, A. S. R., Proffitt, C., & Smart, J. L. (1983). Predicting and understanding mothers' infant-feeding intentions and behavior: Testing the theory of reasoned action. *Journal of Personality and Social Psychology, 44,* 657–671.

Marano, H. (1979). Breast-feeding. New evidence: It's far more than nutrition. *Medical World News, 20,* 62–78.

Maratsos, M. (1983). Some current issues in the study of the acquisition of grammar. In J. H. Flavell & E. M. Markman (Eds.), *Handbook of child psychology: Vol. 3. Cognitive development.* New York: Wiley.

Marcia, J. E. (1980). Identity in adolescence. In J. Adelson (Ed.), *Handbook of adolescent psychology.* New York: Wiley.

Marcus, D. E., & Overton, W. F. (1978). The development of cognitive gender-constancy and sex role preference. *Child Development, 49,* 434–444.

Marcus, T. L., & Corsini, D. A. (1978). Parental expectations of preschool children as related to child gender and socioeconomic status. *Child Development, 49,* 243–246.

Margolin, G. (1981). The reciprocal relationship between marital and child problems. In J. P. Vincent (Ed.), *Advances in family intervention, assessment and theory: An annual compilation of research.* Greenwich, CT: JAI Press.

Marks, G., Miller, N., & Maruyama, G. (1981). Effect of targets' physical attractiveness on assumption of similarity. *Journal of Personality and Social Psychology, 41,* 198–206.

Marland, S. P. (1972). *Education of the gifted and talented.* Washington, DC: U.S. Office of Education.

Marlatt, G. A. (1985) Review of *Prevention of alcohol abuse. The Behavior Therapist, 8,* 80–81.

Marlatt, G. A., & Gordon, J. R. (1980). Determinants of relapse: Implications for the maintenance of behavior change. In P. O. Davidson & S. M. Davidson (Eds.), *Behavioral medicine: Changing health lifestyles.* New York: Brunner/Mazel.

Martin, B. (1975). Parent-child relations. In F. D. Horowitz, E. M. Hetherington, S. Scarr-Salapatek, & G. M. Siegel (Eds.), *Review of child development research,* Vol. 4. Chicago: University of Chicago Press.

Martin, B. (1981). *Abnormal psychology,* 2d ed. New York: Holt, Rinehart and Winston.

Martin, C. L., & Halverson, C. F., Jr. (1981). A schematic processing model of sex typing and stereotyping in children. *Child Development, 52,* 1119–1134.

Martin, C. L., & Halverson, C. F., Jr. (1983). The effect of sex-typing schemas on young children's memory. *Child Development, 54,* 563–574.

Martinez, G. A., & Krieger, F. W. (1985). The 1984 milk-feeding patterns in the United States. *Pediatrics, 76,* 1004–1008.

Marx, J. L. (1982). Autoimmunity in left-handers. *Science, 217,* 141–144.

Masters, J. C., & Furman, W. (1981). Popularity, individual friendship selection, and specific peer interaction among children. *Developmental Psychology, 17,* 344–350.

Masters, W. H., Johnson, V. E., & Kolodny, R. C. (1985). *Human sexuality,* 2nd ed. Boston: Little, Brown.

Matas, L., Arend, R., & Sroufe, L. A. (1978). Continuity of adaptation in the second year: The relation between quality of attachment and later competence. *Child Development, 49,* 547–556.

▶ ▶ ▶ ▶

Matheny, A. P., Jr. (1983). A longitudinal twin study of stability of components from Bayley's Infant Behavior Record. *Child Development, 54,* 356–360.

Matheny, A. P., Jr., Wilson, R. S., & Thoben, A. S. (1987). Home and mother: Relations with infant temperament. *Developmental Psychology, 23,* 323–331.

Matlin, M. W. (1987). *The psychology of women.* New York: Holt, Rinehart and Winston.

Mattes, J. A., & Gittelman, R. (1983). Growth of hyperactive children on maintenance regimen of methylphenidate. *Archives of General Psychiatry, 40,* 317–321.

Maurer, D. M., & Maurer, C. E. (1976, October). Newborn babies see better than you think. *Psychology Today,* pp. 85–88.

Maurer, D. M., & Salapatek, P. (1976). Developmental changes in the scanning of faces by infants. *Child Development, 47,* 523–527.

May, K. A., & Perrin, S. P. (1985). Prelude: Pregnancy and birth. In S. M. H. Hanson & F. W. Bozett (Eds.), *Dimensions of fatherhood.* Beverly Hills: Sage Publications.

McArthur, L. Z., & Resko, B. G. (1975). The portrayal of men and women in American film commercials. *Journal of Social Psychology, 97,* 209–220.

McAuliffe, K., & McAuliffe, S. (1983, November 6). Keeping up with the genetic revolution. *New York Times Magazine,* pp. 40–44, 92–97.

McCall, R. B. (1975). *Intelligence and heredity.* Homewood, IL: Learning Systems Company.

McCall, R. B. (1977). Children's IQ as predictors of adult educational and occupational status. *Science, 297,* 482–483.

McCall, R. B. (1981). Early predictors of later IQ: The search continues. *Intelligence, 5,* 141–148.

McCall, R. B., Applebaum, M. I., & Hogarty, P. S. (1973). Developmental changes in mental performance. *Monographs of the Society for Research in Child Development, 38* (Whole No. 150).

McCall, R. B., Parke, R. D., & Kavanaugh, R. (1977). Imitation of live and televised models in children 1–3 years of age. *Monographs of the Society for Research in Child Development, 42* (Whole No. 173).

McClelland, D. C. (1973). Testing for competence rather than for intelligence. *American Psychologist, 28,* 1–14.

McConaghy, M. J. (1979). Gender permanence and the genital basis of gender: Stages in the development of constancy of gender identity. *Child Development, 50,* 1223–1226.

McCord, W., & McCord, J. (1964). *The psychopath: An essay on the criminal mind.* New York: Van Nostrand Reinhold.

McCranie, E. W., & Bass, J. D. (1984). Childhood family antecedents of dependency and self-criticism: Implications for depression. *Journal of Abnormal Psychology, 93,* 3–8.

McFalls, J. A. (1983). Where have all the children gone? The future of reproduction in the United States. In O. Pocs (Ed.), *Human Sexuality, 83/84.* Guilford, CT: Dushkin.

McGee, R., Williams, S., & Silva, P. A. (1985). Factor structure and correlates of ratings of inattention, hyperactivity, and antisocial behavior in a large sample of 9-year-old children from the general population. *Journal of Consulting and Clinical Psychology, 53,* 480–490.

McGlone, J. (1980). Sex differences in human brain asymmetry: A critical survey. *Behavioral and Brain Sciences, 3,* 215–263.

McGowan, R. J., & Johnson, D. L. (1984). The mother-child relationship and other antecedents of childhood intelligence: A causal analysis. *Child Development, 55,* 810–820.

McGraw, M. B. (1935). *Growth: A study of Johnny and Jimmy.* New York: Appleton-Century-Crofts.

McGraw, M. B. (1939). Later development of children specially trained during infancy: Johnny and Jimmy at school age. *Child Development, 10,* 1–19.

McHale, S., & Huston, T. (1984). Men and women as parents: Sex role orientations, employment, and parental roles with infants. *Child Development, 55,* 1349–1361.

McKean, K. (1987). Intelligence: New ways to measure the wisdom of man. In M. G. Walraven & H. E. Fitzgerald (Eds.), *Psychology 87/88.* Guilford, CT: Dushkin.

McKenzie, B. E., Tootell, H. E., & Day, R. H. (1980). Development of visual size constancy during the first year of human infancy. *Developmental Psychology, 16,* 163–174.

McLaughlin, B. (1984). *Second language acquisition in childhood: Vol. 1. Preschool children,* 2d ed. Hillsdale, NJ: Erlbaum.

McNeill, D. (1970). The development of language. In P. H. Mussen (Ed.), *Carmichael's manual of child psychology,* Vol. 1, 3d ed. New York: Wiley.

Mednick, S. A. (1962). The associative basis of the creative process. *Psychological Review, 69,* 220–232.

Mednick, S. A. (1985, March). Crime in the family tree. *Psychology Today,* pp. 58–61.

Medrich, E. A., Rosen, J., Rubin, V., & Buckley, S. (1982). *The serious business of growing up: A study of children's lives outside of school.* Berkeley: University of California Press.

Meece, J. L., Parsons, J. E., Kaczala, C. M., Goff, S. B., & Futterman, R. (1982). Sex differences in math achievement: Toward a model of academic choice. *Psychological Bulletin, 91,* 324–348.

Meehan, A. M. (1984). A meta-analysis of sex differences in formal operational thought. *Child Development, 55,* 1110–1124.

Meichenbaum, D. (1977). *Cognitive behavior modification: An integrative approach.* New York: Plenum.

▶ ▶ ▶ ▶

Meltzoff, A. N., & Moore, M. K. (1983). Newborn infants imitate facial gestures. *Child Development, 54,* 702–709.

Mendelson, B. K., & White, D. R. (1985). Development of self-body-esteem in overweight youngsters. *Developmental Psychology, 21,* 90–96.

Mendelson, M. J., & Haith, M. M. (1976). The relation between audition and vision in the human newborn. *Monographs of the Society for Research in Child Development, 41* (Whole No. 167).

Mendes, H. A. (1976). Single fathers. *Family Coordinator, 25,* 439–444.

Meredith, H. V. (1963). Change in the stature and body weight of North American boys during the last 80 years. In L. P. Lipsitt & C. C. Spiker (Eds.), *Advances in child development and behavior,* Vol. 1. New York: Academic Press.

Meredith, H. V. (1975). Relation between tobacco smoking of pregnant women and body size of their progeny: A compilation and synthesis of published studies. *Human Biology, 47,* 451–472.

Mervis, C. B., & Mervis, C. A. (1982). Leopards are kitty-cats: Object labeling by mothers for their thirteen-month-olds. *Child Development, 53,* 267–273.

Meyer, B. (1980). The development of girls' sex-role attitudes. *Child Development, 51,* 508–514.

Michie, S. (1985). Development of absolute and relative concepts of number in preschool children. *Developmental Psychology, 21,* 247–252.

Millar, W. S., & Watson, J. S. (1979). The effect of delayed feedback on infant learning reexamined. *Child Development, 50,* 747–751.

Miller, A. G. (1973). Integration and acculturation of cooperative behavior among Blackfoot Indian and non-Indian Canadian children. *Journal of Cross-Cultural Psychology, 4,* 374–380.

Miller, C. A. (1985). Infant mortality in the United States. *Scientific American, 235,* 31–37.

Miller, G. A. (1956). The magical number seven, plus or minus two: Some limits on our capacity to process information. *Psychological Review, 63,* 81–97.

Miller, M. L., Chiles, J. A., & Barnes, V. E. (1982). Suicide attempters within a delinquent population. *Journal of Consulting and Clinical Psychology, 50,* 490–498.

Miller, N., & Maruyama, G. (1976). Ordinal position and peer popularity. *Journal of Personality and Social Psychology, 33,* 123–131.

Miller, N. E., & Dollard, J. (1941). *Social learning and imitation.* New Haven, CT: Yale University Press.

Miller, P. M., & Nirenberg, T. D. (1984). *Prevention of alcohol abuse.* New York: Plenum Press.

Miller, S. M. (1980). Why having control reduces stress: If I can stop the roller coaster I don't want to get off. In J. Garber & M. E. P. Seligman (Eds.), *Human helplessness: Theory and research.* New York: Academic Press.

Milner, J. S., Gold, R. G., Ayoub, C., & Jacewitz, M. M. (1984). Predictive validity of the child abuse potential inventory. *Journal of Consulting and Clinical Psychology, 52,* 879–884.

Minnett, A. M., Vandell, D. L., & Santrock, J. W. (1983). The effects of sibling status on sibling interaction: Influences of birth order, age, spacing, sex of child and sex of sibling. *Child Development, 54,* 1064–1072.

Minuchin, P. P., & Shapiro, E. K. (1983). The school as a context for social development. In P. H. Mussen (Ed.), *Handbook of child psychology: Vol. 4. Socialization, personality, and social development.* New York: Wiley.

Mischel, W. (1986). *Introduction to personality,* 4th ed. New York: Holt, Rinehart and Winston.

Mittler, P. (1971). *The study of twins.* Baltimore: Penguin Books.

Mittwoch, U. (1973). *Genetics of sex differentiation.* New York: Academic Press.

Mizner, G. L., Barter, J. T., & Werme, P. H. (1970). Patterns of drug use among college students: A preliminary report. *American Journal of Psychiatry, 127,* 15–24.

Modahl, C., & Newton, N. (1979). Mood state differences between breast and bottle-feeding mothers. In L. Carenza & L. Zichella (Eds.), *Emotion and reproduction.* New York: Academic Press.

Molfese, D. L., Freeman, R. B., Jr., & Palermo, D. S. (1975). The ontogeny of brain lateralization for speech and nonspeech stimuli. *Brain and Language, 2,* 356–368.

Molfese, D. L., & Molfese, V. J. (1979). Hemisphere and stimulus differences as reflected in the cortical responses of newborn infants to speech stimuli. *Developmental Psychology, 15,* 505–511.

Molfese, D. L., Molfese, V. J., & Carrell, P. L. (1982). Early language development. In B. B. Wolman (Ed.), *Handbook of developmental psychology.* Englewood Cliffs, NJ: Prentice-Hall.

Molinoff, D. (1977, May 22). Life with father. *New York Times Magazine,* pp. 12–17.

Money, J. (1966, August). The strange case of the pregnant hermaphrodite. *Sexology,* pp. 7–9.

Money, J. (1968). *Sex errors of the body.* Baltimore: Johns Hopkins University Press.

Money, J. (1974). Prenatal hormones and postnatal socialization in gender identity differentiation. In J. K. Cole & R. Bienstbier (Eds.), *Nebraska Symposium on Motivation.* Lincoln: University of Nebraska Press.

Money, J. (1977). Human hermaphroditism. In F. A. Beach (Ed.), *Human sexuality in four perspectives.* Baltimore: Johns Hopkins University Press.

▶ ▶ ▶ ▶

Money, J., & Ehrhardt, A. A. (1972). *Man and woman, boy and girl: The differentiation and dimorphism of gender identity from conception to maturity.* Baltimore: Johns Hopkins University Press.

Montemayor, R., & Eisen, M. (1977). The development of self-conceptions from childhood to adolescence. *Developmental Psychology, 13,* 314–319.

Montrose, M. (1978, May). New options in childbirth, Part 1: Family-centered maternity care. *American Baby,* pp. 52–54, 58ff.

Moore, J. E., & Kendall, D. G. (1971). Children's concepts of reproduction. *Journal of Sex Research, 7,* 42–61.

Moore, T. (1975). Exclusive early mothering and its alternatives: The outcome to adolescence. *Scandinavian Journal of Psychology, 16,* 255–272.

Moro, E. (1918). Das erste trimenon. *Münchener Medizinische Wochenschrift, 65,* 1147–1150.

Morrison, E. S., Starks, K., Hyndman, C., & Ronzio, N. (1980). *Growing up sexual.* New York: Van Nostrand.

Morrison, J. R., & Stewart, M. A. (1973). The psychiatric status of the legal families of adopted hyperactive children. *Archives of General Psychiatry, 28,* 888–891.

Morse, P. A., & Cowan, N. (1982). Infant auditory and speech perception. In T. M. Field, A. Houston, H. C. Quay, L. Troll, & G. E. Finley (Eds.), *Review of human development.* New York: Wiley.

Motowidlo, S. T. (1982). Sex role orientation and behavior in a work setting. *Journal of Personality and Social Psychology, 42,* 935–945.

Movshon, J. A., & Van Sluyters, R. C. (1981). Visual neural development. *Annual Review of Psychology, 32,* 477–522.

Mueller, E., & Brenner, J. (1977). The origins of social skills and interaction among playgroup toddlers. *Child Development, 48,* 854–861.

Muir, D., & Field, J. (1979). Newborn infants orient to sounds. *Child Development, 50,* 431–436

Mulhern, R. H., & Passman, R. H. (1981). Parental discipline as affected by the sex of the parent, sex of the child, and the child's apparent responsiveness to discipline. *Developmental Psychology, 17,* 604–613.

Mundy-Castle, A. C., & Anglin, J. (1969). The development of looking in infancy. Paper presented to the Society for Research in Child Development, Santa Monica.

Munroe, R. H., Shimmin, H. S., & Munroe, R. L. (1984). Gender role understanding and sex role preference in four cultures. *Developmental Psychology, 20,* 673–682.

Murphy, L. B. (1983). Issues in the development of emotion in infancy. In R. Plutchik & H. Kellerman (Eds.), *Emotion: Theory, research, and experimentation.* New York: Academic Press.

Murray, A. D. (1985). Aversiveness is in the mind of the beholder. In B. M. Lester & C. F. Z. Boukydis (Eds.), *Infant crying.* New York: Plenum Press.

Murray, A. D., Dolby, R. M., Nation, R. L., & Thomas, D. B. (1981). Effects of epidural anesthesia on newborns and their mothers. *Child Development, 52,* 71–82.

Mussen, P. H., & Jones, M. C. (1957). Self-conceptions, motivations, and interpersonal attitudes of late- and early-maturing boys. *Child Development, 28,* 243–256.

Muuss, R. E. (1970). Adolescent development and the secular trend. *Adolescence, 5,* 267–284.

Myers, A. M., & Gonda, G. (1982). Utility of the masculinity-femininity construct: Comparison of traditional and androgyny approaches. *Journal of Personality and Social Psychology, 43,* 514–523.

Myers, B. J. (1984). Mother–infant bonding: The status of this critical period hypothesis. *Developmental Review, 4,* 283–288.

Naeye, R. L. (1978). Relationship of cigarette smoking to congenital anomalies and perinatal death. *American Journal of Pathology, 90,* 269–293.

Naeye, R. L., & Peters, E. C. (1984). Mental development of children whose mothers smoked during pregnancy. *Obstetrics and Gynecology, 64,* 601.

Naffziger, C. C., & Naffziger, K. (1974). Development of sex role stereotypes. *Family Coordinator, 23,* 251–258.

Nagelman, D. B., Hale, S. L., & Ware, S. L. (1983). Prevalence of eating disorders in college women. Paper presented to the annual meeting of the American Psychological Association, Anaheim, CA.

National Center on Child Abuse and Neglect Report (1982, January–February). *Children Today,* pp. 27–28.

Neimark, E. D. (1975). Intellectual development during adolescence. In F. D. Horowitz (Ed.), *Review of child development research,* Vol 4. Chicago: University of Chicago Press.

Neimark, E. D., Slotnik, N., & Ulrich, T. (1971). Development of memorization strategies, *Developmental Psychology, 5,* 427–432.

Nelson, K. (1973). Structure and strategy in learning to talk. *Monographs for the Society for Research in Child Development, 38* (Whole No. 149).

Nelson, K. (1977). Facilitating children's syntax acquisition. *Developmental Psychology, 13,* 101–107.

Nelson, K. (1981). Individual differences in language development: Implications for development of language. *Developmental Psychology, 17,* 170–187.

Nelson, K. (1982). The syntagmatics and paradigmatics of conceptual development. In S. A. Kuczaj, II (Ed.), *Language development, Vol. 2: Lan-*

▶ ▶ ▶ ▶

guage, thought, and culture. Hillsdale, NJ: Erlbaum.

Nelson, K., Rescorla, L., Gruendel, J., & Benedict, H. (1977). Early lexicons: What do they mean? Paper presented to the biennial meeting of the Society for Research in Child Development, New Orleans.

Nelson, N., Enkin, M., Saigal, S., Bennett, K., Milner, R., & Sackett, D. (1980). A randomized clinical trial of the Leboyer approach to childbirth. The New England Journal of Medicine, 302, 655–660.

Nelson, S. A. (1980). Factors influencing young children's use of motives and outcomes as moral criteria. Child Development, 51, 823–829.

Newcombe, N., & Bandura, M. M. (1983). The effect of age at puberty on spatial ability in girls: A question of mechanism. Developmental Psychology, 19, 215–224.

Newcombe, N., Bandura, M. M., & Taylor, D. G. (1983). Sex differences in spatial ability and spatial activity. Sex Roles, 9, 377–386.

Newman, H. H., Freeman, F. H., & Holzinger, K. J. (1937). Twins: A study of heredity and environment. Chicago: University of Chicago Press.

Newton, N. (1971). Psychologic differences between breast and bottle feeding. American Journal of Clinical Nutrition, 24, 993–1004.

Newton, N. (1972a). Battle between breast and bottle. Psychology Today, 6, 68–70, 88–89.

Newton, N. (1972b). Childbearing in broad perspective. In Boston Children's Medical Center (Ed.), Pregnancy, birth, and the newborn baby. New York: Delacorte.

Newton, N. (1979). Key psychological issues in human lactation. In L. R. Waletzky (Ed.), Symposium on human lactation. Rockville, MD: DHEW Publication No. HSA 79–5107.

Nicholls, J. G., Patashnick, M., & Mettetal, G. (1986). Conceptions of ability and intelligence. Child Development, 57, 636–645.

Nichols, P. L. (1977). Minimal brain dysfunction: Associations with perinatal complications. Paper presented to the meeting of the Society for Research in Child Development, New Orleans.

Nieberg, P., Marks, J. S., McLaren, N. M., & Remongton, P. L. (1985). The fetal tobacco syndrome. Journal of the American Medical Association, 253, 2998–2999.

NIMH (1982). See Pearl, Bouthilet, & Lazar (1982).

Nisan, M. (1984). Distributive justice and social norms. Child Development, 55, 1020–1029.

Nisbett, R. E. (1968). Birth order and participation in dangerous sports. Journal of Personality and Social Psychology, 8, 351–353.

Notman, M. T., & Nadelson, C. C. (1982). Changing views of the relationship between femininity and reproduction. In C. C. Nadelson & M. T. Notman (Eds.), The woman patient, Vol. 2. New York: Plenum Press.

Nussbaum, M., Shenker, I. R., Baird, D., & Saravay, S. (1985). Follow-up investigation in patients with anorexia nervosa. The Journal of Pediatrics, 106, 835–840.

Nuttall, E., & Nuttall, R. (1971). The effects of size of family on parent-child relationships. Proceedings of the American Psychological Association, 6, 267–268

O'Brien, M., Huston, A. C., & Risley, T. (1983). Sex-typed play of toddlers in a day care center. Journal of Applied Developmental Psychology, 4, 1–9.

O'Connor, R.D. (1969). Modification of social withdrawal through symbolic modeling. Journal of Applied Behavior Analysis, 2, 15–22.

Oden, M. H. (1968). The fulfillment of promise: 40-year follow-up of the Terman gifted group. Genetic Psychology Monographs, 77, 3–93.

Offer, D., Ostrov, E., & Howard, K. I. (1981). The adolescent: A psychological self-portrait. New York: Basic Books.

Ogra, P. L., & Greene, H. L. (1982). Human milk and breast feeding: An update on the state of the art. Pediatric Research, 16, 266–271.

O'Hara, M. W., Neunaber, D. J., & Zekoski, E. M. (1984). Prospective study of postpartum depression: Prevalence, course, and predictive factors. Journal of Abnormal Psychology, 93, 158–171.

O'Keefe, E. S. C., & Hyde, J. S. (1983). The development of occupational sex-role stereotypes: The effects of gender stability and age. Sex Roles, 9, 481–492.

Oldershaw, L., Walters, G. C., & Hall, D. K. (1986). Control strategies and noncompliance in abusive mother-child dyads: An observational study. Child Development, 57, 722–732.

O'Leary, K. D. (1980). Pills or skills for hyperactive children? Journal of Applied Behavior Analysis, 13, 191–204.

O'Leary, K. D., Pelham, W. E., Rosenbaum, A., & Price, G. H. (1976). Behavioral treatment of hyperkinetic children: An experimental evaluation of its usefulness. Clinical Pediatrics, 15, 510–515.

Oller, D. K. (1981). Infant vocalizations: Exploration and reflectivity. In R. E. Stark (Ed.), Language behavior in infancy and early childhood. New York: Elsevier.

Olweus, D. (1980). Familial and temperamental determinants of aggressive behavior in adolescent boys: A causal analysis. Developmental Psychology, 16, 644–660.

Olweus, D. (1982). Development of stable aggressive reaction patterns in males. In R. J. Blanchard & C. Blanchard (Eds.), Advances in the study of aggression, Vol. 1. New York: Academic Press.

Orenberg, C. L. (1981). DES: The complete story. New York: St. Martin's Press.

▶ ▶ ▶ ▶

Orthener, D. K., Brown, T., & Ferguson, D. (1976). Single-parent fatherhood: An emerging family life style. *Family Coordinator, 25,* 429–437.

Osborn, D. K., & Endsley, R. C. (1971). Emotional reactions of young children to TV violence. *Child Development, 42,* 321–331.

Palmer, F. H. (1976). *The effects of minimal early intervention on subsequent IQ scores and reading achievement.* Report to the Education Commission of the States, contract 13–76–06846, State University of New York at Stony Brook.

Papoušek, H. (1967). Conditioning during early postnatal development. In Y. Brackbill & G. G. Thompson (Eds.), *Behavior in infancy and early childhood.* New York: Free Press.

Paris, S. G., Newman, R. S., & McVey, K. A. (1982). Learning the functional significance of mnemonic actions: A microgenetic study of strategy acquisition. *Journal of Experimental Child Psychology, 34,* 490–509.

Parke, R. D. (1974). Rules, roles, and resistance to deviation in children: Explorations in punishment, discipline, and self-control. In A. Pick (Ed.), *Minnesota symposia on child psychology,* Vol. 8. Minneapolis: University of Minnesota Press.

Parke, R. D. (1977). Punishment in children: Effects, side effects, and alternate strategies. In H. L. Hom & P. A. Robinson (Eds.), *Psychological processes in early education.* New York: Academic Press.

Parke, R. D., & Collmer, C. W. (1975). Child abuse: An interdisciplinary analysis. In E. M. Hetherington, J. W. Hagen, R. Kron, & A. H. Stein (Eds.), *Review of child development research,* Vol. 5. Chicago: University of Chicago Press.

Parke, R. D., & O'Leary, S. E. (1976). Father-mother-infant interaction in the newborn period: Some findings, some observations, and some unresolved issues. In K. Riegel & J. Meachem (Eds.), *The developing individual in a changing world, Vol. 2: Social and environmental issues.* The Hague: Mouton.

Parke, R. D., & Slaby, R. G. (1983). The development of aggression. In P. H. Mussen (Ed.), *Handbook of child psychology: Vol. 4. Socialization, personality and social development.* New York: Wiley.

Parke, R. D., & Tinsley, B. R. (1981). The father's role in infancy: Determinants of involvement in caregiving and play. In M. E. Lamb (Ed.), *The role of the father in child development.* New York: Wiley.

Parmelee, A. H., Jr. (1986). Children's illnesses: Their beneficial effects on behavioral development. *Child Development, 57,* 1–10.

Parmelee, A. H., Jr., & Sigman, M. D. (1983). Perinatal brain development and behavior. In P. H. Mussen (Ed.), *Handbook of child psychology: Vol. 2. Infancy and developmental psychobiology.* New York: Wiley.

Parr, F. W. (1936). The problem of student honesty. *Journal of Higher Education, 7,* 318–326.

Parry, M. H. (1972). Infants' responses to novelty in familiar and unfamiliar settings. *Child Development, 43,* 233–237.

Parsons, J. E., Adler, T. F., & Kaczala, C. M. (1982). Socialization of achievement attitudes and beliefs: Parental influences. *Child Development, 53,* 310–321.

Parten, M. B. (1932). Social participation among preschool children. *Journal of Abnormal and Social Psychology, 27,* 243–269.

Pascual-Leone, J. (1970). Mathematical model for the transition rule in Piaget's developmental stages. *Acta Psychologica, 63,* 301–345.

Pascual-Leone, J. (1980). Constructive problems for constructive theories: The current relevance of Piaget's work and a critique of information-processing simulation psychology. In R. H. Kluwe & H. Spada (Eds.), *Developmental models of thinking.* New York: Academic Press.

Pascual-Leone, J., Goodman, D., Ammon, P., & Subelman, I. (1978). Piagetan theory and neo-Piagetan analysis as psychological guides in education. In J. M. Gallagher & J. A. Easley (Eds.), *Knowledge and development,* Vol. 2. New York: Plenum Press.

Passman, R. H., & Blackwelder, D. E. (1981). Rewarding and punishing by mothers: The influence of progressive changes in the quality of their sons' apparent behavior. *Developmental Psychology, 17,* 614–619.

Pastor, D. L. (1981). The quality of mother-infant attachment in its relationship to toddlers' initial sociability with peers. *Developmental Psychology, 17,* 326–335.

Patterson, F. G. (1978). Conversations with a gorilla. *National Geographic, 154,* 438–465.

Patterson, F. G. (1980). Innovative uses of language by a gorilla: A case study. In K. E. Nelson (Ed.), *Children's language, Vol. 2.* New York: Gardner Press.

Patterson, F. G., Patterson, C. H., & Brentari, D. K. (1987). Language in child, chimp, and gorilla. *American Psychologist, 42,* 270–272.

Patterson, G. R. (1982). *Coercive family processes.* Eugene, OR: Castilia Press.

Paulsen, K., & Johnson, M. (1983). Sex-role attitudes and mathematical ability in 4th, 8th, and 11th grade students from a high socioeconomic area. *Developmental Psychology, 19,* 210–214.

Pavlov, I. (1927). *Conditioned reflexes.* London: Oxford University Press.

Pearl, D., Bouthilet, L., & Lazar, J. (Eds.) (1982). *Television and behavior: Ten years of scientific progress and implications for the eighties,* Vols. 1 & 2. Washington, DC: U.S. Government Printing Office.

► ► ► ►

Pearlman, K., Schmidt, F. L., & Hunter, J. E. (1980). Test of a new model of validity generalization: Results for job proficiency and training criteria in clerical operations. *Journal of Applied Psychology, 65,* 373–406.

Pederson, D. R., & Ter Vrugt, D. (1973). The influence of amplitude and frequency of vestibular stimulation on the activity of two-month-old infants. *Child Development, 44,* 122–128.

Pelham, W. E. (1983). The effects of psychostimulants on academic achievement in hyperactive and learning-disabled children. *Thalamus, 3,* 1–49.

Pelham, W. E., Schnedler, R. W., Bologna, N. C., & Contreras, J. A. (1980). Behavioral and stimulant treatment of hyperactive children: A therapy study with methylphenidate probes in a within-subject design. *Journal of Applied Behavior Analysis, 13,* 221–236.

Perry, D. G., & Bussey, K. (1979). The social learning theory of sex differences: Imitation is alive and well. *Journal of Personality and Social Psychology, 37,* 1699–1712.

Petersen, A. C. (1980). Biopsychosocial processes in the development of sex-related differences. In J. E. Parsons (Ed.), *The psychobiology of sex differences and sex roles.* Washington, DC: Hemisphere.

Petersen, A. C. (1983). Menarche: Meaning of measures and measuring meaning. In S. Golub (Ed.), *Menarche.* Lexington, MA: Lexington Books.

Petersen, A. C. (1985). Pubertal development as a cause of disturbance: Myths, realities, and unanswered questions. *Genetic Psychology Monographs, 111,* 207–231.

Peterson, C. C., Peterson, J. L., & Seeto, D. (1983). Developmental changes in ideas about lying. *Child Development, 54,* 1529–1535.

Peterson, L., & Gelfand, D. M. (1984). Causal attributions of helping as a function of age and incentives. *Child Development, 55,* 504–511.

Petri, E. (1934). Studies on the onset of menarche. *Journal of Morphological Anthropology, 33,* 43–48.

Petti, T. A., & Connors, C. K. (1983). Changes in behavioral ratings of depressed children treated with imipramine. *Journal of the American Academy of Child Psychiatry, 22,* 355–360.

Pettit, G. S., & Bates, J. E. (1984). Continuity in individual differences in the mother-infant relationship from six to thirteen months. *Child Development, 55,* 729–739.

Phillips, E. L., Wolf, M. M., Fixsen, D. L., & Bailey, J. S. (1976). The achievement place model: A community-based, family-style, behavior modification program for predelinquents. In E. Ribes-Inesta & A. Bandura (Eds.), *Analysis of delinquency and aggression.* Hillsdale, NJ: Erlbaum.

Piaget, J. (1924). *The child's conception of the world.* New Jersey: Littlefield, Adams, 1964.

Piaget, J. (1927). *The child's conception of physical causality.* New Jersey: Littlefield, Adams, 1960.

Piaget, J. (1932). *The moral judgment of the child.* London: Kegan Paul.

Piaget, J. (1936). *The origins of intelligence in children.* New York: Norton, 1963.

Piaget, J. (1937). *The construction of reality in the child.* New York: Ballantine, 1971.

Piaget, J. (1946). *Play, dreams and imitation in childhood.* New York: Norton, 1962.

Piaget, J. (1964). In D. Elkind (Ed.), *Six psychological studies.* New York: Random House, 1967.

Piaget, J. (1968). *On the development of memory and identity.* Worcester, MA: Clark University Press.

Piaget, J. (1976). *The grasp of consciousness: Action and concept in the young child.* Cambridge, MA: Harvard University Press.

Pick, A. D., Frankel, D. G., & Hess, V. (1975). Children's attention: The development of selectivity. In E. M. Hetherington (Ed.), *Review of child development research,* Vol. V. Chicago: University of Chicago Press.

Pirchio, M., Spinelli, D., Fiorentini, A., & Maffei, L. (1978). Infant contrast sensitivity evaluated by evoked potentials. *Brain Research, 141,* 179–184.

Plomin, R. (1982). Quoted in Pines, M. (1982, June 19). Behavior and heredity: Links for specific traits are growing stronger. *New York Times,* pp. C1–C2.

Plomin, R., & DeFries, J. C. (1980). Genetics and intelligence: Recent data. *Intelligence, 4,* 15–24.

Plomin, R., & DeFries, J. C. (1985). *Origins of individual differences in infancy.* New York: Academic Press.

Porter, F. L., Miller, R. H., & Marshall, R. E. (1986). Neonatal pain cries: Effect of circumcision on acoustic features and perceived urgency. *Child Development, 57,* 790–802.

Postman, L. (1975). Verbal learning and memory. *Annual Review of Psychology, 26,* 291–335.

Power, T. G. (1985). Mother- and father-infant play: A developmental analysis. *Child Development, 56,* 1514–1524.

Power, T. G., & Parke, R. D. (1982). Play as a context for early learning: Lab and home analyses. In L. M. Laosa & I. E. Sigel (Eds.), *The family as a learning environment.* New York: Plenum Press.

Powledge, T. M. (1981). Unnatural selection. In H. B. Holmes, B. B. Hoskins, and M. Gross (Eds.), *The custom-made child? Women-centered perspectives.* Clifton, NJ: Humana Press.

Prechtl, H. F. R. (1965). Problems of behavioral studies in the newborn infant. In D. S. Lehrman, R. A. Hinde, & E. Shaw (Eds.), *Advances in the study of behavior,* Vol. 1. New York: Academic Press.

▶ ▶ ▶ ▶

Premack, A. J., & Premack, D. (1975). Teaching language to an ape. In R. C. Atkinson (Ed.), *Psychology in progress*. San Francisco: W. H. Freeman.

Prescott, P., & DeCasper, A. J. (1981). Do newborns prefer their fathers' voices? Apparently not. Paper presented to the meeting of the Society for Research in Child Development, Boston.

Prior, M. (1984). Developing concepts of childhood autism: The influence of experimental cognitive research. *Journal of Consulting and Clinical Psychology, 52,* 4–16.

Provence, S., & Lipton, R. C. (1962). *Infants in institutions.* New York: International Universities Press.

Pulkkinen, L. (1982). Self-control and continuity from childhood to adolescence. In P. B. Baltes & O. G. Brim (Eds.), *Life-span development and behavior,* Vol. 4. New York: Academic Press.

Purtillo, D. F., & Sullivan, J. L. (1979). Immunological basis for superior survival of females. *American Journal of Diseases of Children, 133,* 1251–1253.

Rabkin, L. Y., & Rabkin, K. (1974). Children of the kibbutz. *Readings in psychology today,* 3d ed. Del Mar, CA: CRM Books.

Radin, N. (1982). Primary caregiving and role-sharing fathers. In M. E. Lamb (Ed.), *Nontraditional families: Parenting and child development.* Hillsdale, NJ: Erlbaum.

Radke-Yarrow, M. E., Cummings, M., Kuczynski, L., & Chapman, M. (1985). Patterns of attachment of 2- and 3-year-olds in normal families and families with parental depression. *Child Development, 56,* 884–893.

Radke-Yarrow, M. E., Zahn-Waxler, C., & Chapman, M. (1983). Children's prosocial dispositions and behavior. In P. H. Mussen (Ed.), *Handbook of child psychology, Vol. 4:*

Socialization, personality, and social development, 4th ed. New York: Wiley.

Rapport, M. D. (1984). Hyperactivity and stimulant treatment: *Abusus non tollit usum. The Behavior Therapist, 7,* 133–134.

Rassin, D. K., Richardson, J., Baranowski, T., Nader, P. R., Guenther, N., Bee, D. E., & Brown, J. P. (1984). Incidence of breast-feeding in a low socioeconomic group of mothers in the United States: Ethnic patterns. *Pediatrics, 73,* 132–137.

Rathus, S. A. (1983). *Human sexuality.* New York: Holt, Rinehart and Winston.

Rathus, S. A. (1987). *Psychology,* 3d ed. New York: Holt, Rinehart and Winston.

Rathus, S. A., & Nevid, J. S. (1986). *Adjustment and growth: The challenges of life,* 3d ed. New York: Holt, Rinehart and Winston.

Raudenbusch, S. W. (1984). Magnitude of teacher expectancy effects on pupil IQ as a function of credibility of expectancy induction: A synthesis from 18 experiments. *Journal of Experimental Psychology, 76,* 85–97.

Raymond, C. L., & Benbow, C. P. (1986). Gender differences in mathematics: A function of parental support and student sex typing? *Developmental Psychology, 22,* 808–819.

Rebok, G. W. (1987). *Life-span cognitive development.* New York: Holt, Rinehart and Winston.

Reis, H. T., & Wright, S. (1982). Knowledge of sex-role stereotypes in children aged 3 to 5. *Sex Roles, 8,* 1049–1056.

Rekers, G. A., Amaro-Plotkin, H. D., & Low, B. P. (1977). Sex-typed mannerisms in normal boys and girls as a function of sex and age. *Child Development, 48,* 275–278.

Renninger, K. A., & Wozniak, R. H. (1985). Effect of interest on attentional shift, recognition, and recall in young children. *Developmental Psychology, 21,* 624–632.

Reschly, D. J. (1981). Psychological testing in educational classification and placement. *American Psychologist, 36,* 1094–1102.

Rest, J. R. (1983). Morality. In P. H. Mussen (Ed.), *Handbook of child psychology: Vol. 3. Cognitive Development.* New York: Wiley.

Rest, J. R., & Thoma, S. J. (1985). Relation of moral judgment development to formal education. *Developmental Psychology, 21,* 709–714.

Rhead, W. J. (1977). Smoking and SIDS. *Pediatrics, 59,* 791–792.

Rheingold, H. L., & Eckerman, C. O. (1970). The infant separates himself from his mother. *Science, 168,* 78–83.

Rheingold, H. L., Gewirtz, J. L., & Ross, H. W. (1959). Social conditioning of vocalizations in the infant. *Journal of Comparative and Physiological Psychology, 52,* 68–73.

Rheingold, H. L., Hay, D. F., & West, M. J. (1976). Sharing in the second year of life. *Child Development, 47,* 1148–1158.

Rholes, W. S., & Ruble, D. N. (1984). Children's understanding of dispositional characteristics of others. *Child Development, 55,* 550–560.

Rice, M. L. (1982). Child language: What children know and how. In T. M. Field, A. Huston, H. C. Quay, L. Troll, & G. E. Finley (Eds.), *Review of human development.* New York: Wiley.

Rice, M. L. (1984). Cognitive aspects of communicative development. In R. L. Schiefelbusch & J. Pickar (Eds.), *The acquisition of communicative competence.* Baltimore: University Park Press.

Richards, J. E., & Rader, N. (1981). Crawling-onset age predicts visual cliff avoidance in infants. *Journal of Experimental Psychology: Human Perception and Performance, 7,* 382–387.

Richards, T. W., & Nelson, V. L. (1938). Studies in mental development: 2. Analyses of abilities tested at six months by the Gesell sched-

▶ ▶ ▶ ▶

ule. *Journal of Genetic Psychology, 52,* 327–331.

Richardson, D. C., Bernstein, S., & Taylor, S. P. (1979). The effect of situational contingencies on female retaliative behavior. *Journal of Personality and Social Psychology, 37,* 2044–2048.

Richardson, S. (1972). Ecology of malnutrition: Nonnutritional factors influencing intellectual and behavioral development. In Pan American Health Organization Scientific Publication No. 251, *Nutrition, the nervous system and behavior.*

Rieser, J., Yonas, A., & Wikner, K. (1976). Radial localization of odors by human newborns. *Child Development, 47,* 856–859.

Ritvo, E. R., Freeman, B. J., Mason-Brothers, A., Mo, A., & Ritvo, A. M. (1985). Concordance for the syndrome of autism in 40 pairs of afflicted twins. *American Journal of Psychiatry, 142,* 74–77.

Robinson, N., & Robinson, H. B. (1976). *The mentally retarded child.* New York: McGraw-Hill.

Roche, A. F. (1979). Secular trends in stature, weight, and maturation. In A. F. Roche (Ed.), *Secular trends in human growth, maturation, and development. Monographs of the Society for Research in Child Development, 44* (Whole No. 179).

Roche, A. F. (1981). The adipocyte-number hypothesis. *Child Development, 52,* 31–43.

Rodhölm, M. (1981). Effects of father-infant postpartum contact on their interaction three months after birth. *Early Human Development, 5,* 79–86.

Rodin, J. (1977). Research on eating behavior and obesity: Where does it fit in personality and social psychology? *Personality and Social Psychology Bulletin, 3,* 335–355.

Rodman, H., Pratto, D. J., & Nelson, R. S. (1985). Child care arrangements and children's functioning: A comparison of self-care and adult-care children. *Developmental Psychology, 21,* 413–418.

Roe, K. V., Drivas, A., Karagellis, A., & Roe, A. (1985). Sex differences in vocal interaction with mother and stranger in Greek infants: Some cognitive implications. *Developmental Psychology, 21,* 372–377.

Roffwarg, H. P., Muzio, J. N., & Dement, W. C. (1966). Ontogenetic development of the human sleep-dream cycle. *Science, 152,* 604–619.

Rogan, H. (1984, October 30). Executive women find it difficult to balance demands of job, home. *Wall Street Journal,* pp. 33, 55.

Rogers, M. F. (1985). AIDS in children: A review of the clinical, epidemiological and public health aspects. *Pediatric Infectious Disease, 4,* 230–236.

Romanczyk, R. G. (1986). Some thoughts on future trends in the education of individuals with autism. *The Behavior Thrapist, 8,* 162–164.

Romanczyk, R. G., Diament, C., Goren, E. R., Trunell, G., & Harris, S. L. (1975). Increasing isolate and social play in severely disturbed children: Intervention and postintervention effectiveness. *Journal of Autism and Childhood Schizophrenia, 5,* 730–739.

Romer, N., & Cherry, D. (1980). Ethnic and social class differences in children's sex-role concepts. *Sex Roles, 6,* 245–263.

Roopnarine, J. L. (1984). Sex-typed socialization in mixed-age preschool classrooms. *Child Development, 55,* 1078–1084.

Roper, R., & Hinde, R. A. (1978). Social behavior in a play group: Consistency and complexity. *Child Development, 49,* 570–579.

Rorvik, D., & Shettles, L. B. (1970). *Your baby's sex: Now you can choose.* New York: Dodd, Mead.

Rosch, E. H. (1978). Principles of categorization. In E. H. Rosch & B. B. Lloyd (Eds.), *Cognition and categorization.* Hillsdale, NJ: Erlbaum.

Rosch, E. H., Mervis, C. B., Gray, W. P., Johnson, D. M., & Braehm, P. (1976). Basic objects in natural categories. *Cognitive Psychology, 8,* 382–439.

Rose, S. A. (1983). Differential rates of visual information processing in full-term and preterm infants. *Child Development, 54,* 1189–1198.

Rose, S. A., & Blank, M. (1974). The potency of context in children's cognition: An illustration through conservation. *Child Development, 45,* 499–502.

Rose, S. A., & Wallace, I. (1985). Visual recognition memory: A predictor of later cognitive functioning in preterms. *Child Development, 56,* 843–852.

Rosen, B. C., & D'Andrade, R. (1959). The psychological origins of achievement motivation. *Sociometry, 22,* 185–218.

Rosenberg, M. S. (1987). New directions for research on the psychological maltreatment of children. *American Psychologist, 42,* 166–171.

Rosenberg, M. S., & Repucci, N. D. (1985). Primary prevention of child abuse. *Journal of Consulting and Clinical Psychology, 53,* 576–585.

Rosenblum, L. A., & Paully, G. S. (1984). The effects of varying environmental demands on maternal and infant behavior. *Child Development, 55,* 305–314.

Rosenthal, D. M. (1970). *Genetic theory and abnormal behavior.* New York: McGraw-Hill.

Rosenthal, D. M. (1980). The modularity and maturation of cognitive capacities. *Behavior and Brain Science, 3,* 32–34.

Rosenthal, R., & Jacobson, L. (1968). *Pygmalion in the classroom.* New York: Holt, Rinehart and Winston.

Rosenzweig, M. R. (1966). Environmental complexity, cerebral change, and behavior. *American Psychologist, 21,* 321–332.

Rosenzweig, M. R. (1969). Effects of heredity and environment on brain chemistry, brain anatomy, and learning ability in the rat. In

▶ ▶ ▶ ▶

M. Manosovitz et al. (Eds.), *Behavioral genetics.* New York: Appleton.

Rosenzweig, M. R., & Bennett, E. L. (1970). Effects of differential environments on brain weights and enzyme activities in gerbils, rats, and mice. *Developmental Psychobiology, 2,* 87–95.

Rosenzweig, M. R., Bennett, E. L., & Diamond, M. C. (1972, February). Brain changes in response to experience. *Scientific American, 226,* 22–29.

Rosett, H. L., & Sander, L. W. (1979). Effects of maternal drinking on neonatal morphology and state regulation. In J. D. Osofsky (Ed.), *Handbook of infant development.* New York: Wiley-Interscience.

Rosman, B. L., Minuchin, S., & Liebman, R. (1976). Input and outcome of family therapy of anorexia nervosa. In J. L. Claghorn (Ed.), *Successful psychotherapy.* New York: Brunner/Mazel.

Ross, A. O. (1981). *Psychological disorders of childhood: A behavioral approach to theory, research, and practice,* 2d ed. New York: McGraw-Hill.

Ross, G. (1985). Use of Bayley scales to characterize abilities of premature infants. *Child Development, 56,* 835–842.

Ross, G., Kagan, J., Zelazo, P., & Kotelchuck, M. (1975). Separation protest in infants in home and laboratory. *Developmental Psychology, 11,* 256–257.

Ross, H. S., & Goldman, B. D. (1977). Infants' sociability toward strangers. *Child Development, 48,* 638–642.

Rotberg, I. C. (1982). Some legal and research considerations in establishing federal policy in bilingual education. *Harvard Educational Review, 52,* 149–168.

Rothbart, M. K. (1971). Birth order and mother-child interaction in an achievement situation. *Journal of Personality and Social Psychology, 17,* 113–120.

Rothbart, M. K. (1983). Longitudinal observation of infant temperament. Unpublished manuscript, Department of Psychology, University of Oregon, Eugene.

Rotter, J. B. (1972). Beliefs, social attitudes, and behavior: A social learning analysis. In J. B. Rotter, J. E. Chance, & E. J. Phares (Eds.), *Applications of a social learning theory of personality.* New York: Holt, Rinehart and Winston.

Rovet, J., & Netley, C. (1983). The triple X chromosome syndrome in childhood: Recent empirical findings. *Child Development, 54,* 831–845.

Rozin, P. (1976). The evolution of intelligence and access to the cognitive unconscious. In J. M. Sprague & A. N. Epstein (Eds.), *Progress in Psychobiology and Physiological Psychology,* Vol. 6. New York: Academic Press.

Rubin, K. H. (1982). Nonsocial play in preschoolers: Necessary evil? *Child Development, 53,* 651–657.

Rubin, K. H., Fein, G. G., & Vandenberg, B. (1983). Play. In P. H. Mussen (Ed.), *Handbook of child psychology: Vol. 4. Socialization, personality, and social development.* New York: Wiley.

Rubin, R. R., & Balow, B. (1979). Measures of infant development and socioeconomic status as predictors of later intelligence and school achievement. *Developmental Psychology, 15,* 225–227.

Rubin, R. R., & Fisher, J. J. (1982). *Ages 3 and 4: Your preschooler.* New York: Macmillan.

Rubin, Z. (1980). *Children's friendships.* Cambridge, MA: Harvard University Press.

Rubinstein, E. A. (1983). Television and behavior: Research conclusions of the 1982 NIMH report and their policy implications. *American Psychologist, 38,* 820–825.

Ruble, D. N., & Ruble, T. L. (1982). Sex stereotypes. In A. G. Miller (Ed.), *In the eye of the beholder: Contemporary issues in stereotyping.* New York: Praeger.

Rundus, D. (1971). Analysis of rehearsal processes in free recall. *Journal of Experimental Psychology, 89,* 63–77.

Ruopp, R. (1979). *Children at the center: Final report of the national day care study.* Cambridge, MA: Abt Associates.

Rush, D., Stein, Z., & Susser, M. (1980). *Diet in pregnancy: A randomized controlled trial of nutritional supplements.* New York: Liss.

Russell, G. (1982). Shared-caregiving families: An Australian study. In M. E. Lamb (Ed.), *Nontraditional families: Parenting and child development.* Hillsdale, NJ: Erlbaum.

Rutter, M. (1980). *Changing youth in a changing society: Patterns of adolescent development and disorder.* Cambridge, MA: Harvard University Press.

Rutter, M. (1981). *Maternal deprivation reassessed,* 2d ed. Middlesex, England: Penguin Books.

Rutter, M. (1983a). Cognitive deficits in the pathogenesis of autism. *Journal of Child Psychology and Psychiatry, 24,* 513–531.

Rutter, M. (1983b). School effects on pupil progress: Research findings and policy implications. *Child Development, 54,* 1–29.

Rutter, M., & Garmezy, N. (1983). Developmental psychopathology. In P. H. Mussen (Ed.), *Handbook of child psychology: Vol. 4. Socialization, personality and social development.* New York: Wiley.

Sachs, B. P., McCarthy, B. J., Rubin, G., Burton, A., Terry, J., & Tyler, C. W. (1983). Caesarean section. *Journal of the American Medical Association, 250,* 2157–2159.

Sachs, J., & Devin, J. (1976). Young children's use of age-appropriate speech styles in social interaction and role playing. *Journal of Child Language, 3,* 82–98.

Sackett, G. P. (1966). Monkeys reared in isolation with pictures as visual input: Evidence for an innate releasing mechanism. *Science, 154,* 1468–1473.

► ► ► ►

Sackett, G. P. (1970). Innate mechanisms, rearing conditions and a theory of early experience effects. In M. R. Jones (Ed.), *Miami symposium on the prediction of behavior: Early experience.* Coral Gables: University of Miami Press.

Saddler, J. (1987, February 12). Low pay, high turnover plague day-care industry. *Wall Street Journal,* p. 27.

Sadker, M., & Sadker, D. (1985, March). Sexism in the schoolroom of the '80s. *Psychology Today,* pp. 54–57.

Sadowitz, P. D., & Oski, F. A. (1983). Iron status and infant feeding practices in an urban ambulatory center. *Pediatrics, 72,* 33–36.

Saegert, S., & Hart, R. (1976). The development of sex differences in the environmental competence of children. In P. Burnett (Ed.), *Women in society.* Chicago: Maaroufa Press.

Salapatek, P. (1975). Pattern perception in early infancy. In L. B. Cohen & P. Salapatek (Eds.), *Infant perception: From senstion to cognition,* Vol. 1. New York: Academic Press.

Salkind, N. J. (1983). The father-child post divorce relationship and child support. In J. Cassely (Ed.), *The parental child-support obligation.* Lexington, MA: Lexington Books.

Sameroff, A. J. (1968). The components of sucking in the human newborn. *Journal of Experimental Child Psychology, 6,* 607–623.

Sameroff, A. J. (1971). Can conditioned responses be established in the newborn infant? *Developmental Psychology, 5,* 1–12.

Sameroff, A. J., & Chandler, J. J. (1975). Reproductive risk and the continuum of caretaking casualty. In F. D. Horowitz (Ed.), *Review of child development research,* Vol. 4. Chicago: University of Chicago Press.

Sameroff, A. J., & Seifer, R. (1983). Familial risk and child competence. *Child Development, 54,* 1254–1268.

Sanders, B., & Soares, M. P. (1986). Sexual maturation and spatial ability in college students. *Developmental Psychology, 22,* 199–203.

Sanders, B., Soares, M. P., & S'Aquila, J. M. (1982). The sex difference on one test of spatial visualization: A nontrivial difference. *Child Development, 53,* 1106–1110.

Santrock, J. W. (1970). Paternal absence, sex typing, and identification. *Developmental Psychology, 2,* 264–272.

Santrock, J. W., & Warshak, R. A. (1979). Father custody and social development in boys and girls. *Journal of Social Issues, 35* (4), 112–125.

Santrock, J. W., Warshak, R. A., Lindbergh, C., & Meadows, L. (1982). Children's and parents' observed social behavior in stepfather families. *Child Development, 53,* 472–480.

Savage-Rumbaugh, E. S., & Rumbaugh, D. M. (1980). Language analogue project I, phase II: Theory and tactics. In K. E. Nelson (Ed.), *Children's language,* Vol. 2. New York: Gardner Press.

Savage-Rumbaugh, E. S., Rumbaugh, D. M., & Boysen, S. (1980). Do apes use language? *American Scientist, 68,* 49–61.

Savage-Rumbaugh, E. S., Rumbaugh, D. M., Smith, S. T., & Lawson, J. (1980). Reference: The linguistic essential. *Science, 210,* 922–924.

Savin-Williams, R., & Small, S. (1986). The timing of puberty and its relationship to adolescent and parent perceptions of family interaction. *Developmental Psychology, 22,* 322–347.

Saxby, L., & Bryden, M. P. (1985). Left visual-field advantage in children for processing visual emotional stimuli. *Developmental Psychology, 21,* 253–261.

Scanlon, J. W., Brown, W. V., Jr., Weiss, J. B., & Alper, M. H. (1974). Neurobehavioral responses of newborn infants after maternal epidural anesthesia. *Anesthesiology, 40,* 121–128.

Scarlett, W. A. (1980). Social isolation from agemates among nursery school children. *Journal of Child Psychology and Psychiatry, 21,* 231–240.

Scarr, S. (1981a). Testing *for* children: Assessment and the many determinants of intellectual competence. *American Psychologist, 36,* 1159–1166.

Scarr, S. (1981b). *Race, social class, and individual differences in IQ.* Hillsdale, NJ: Erlbaum.

Scarr, S. (1985a). An author's frame of mind. (Review of *Frames of mind,* by H. Gardner). *New Ideas in Psychology, 3,* 95–100.

Scarr, S. (1985b). Constructing psychology: Making facts and fables for our times. *American Psychologist, 40,* 499–512.

Scarr, S., & Kidd, K. K. (1983). Developmental behavior genetics. In M. Haith & J. J. Campos (Eds.), *Handbook of child psychology.* New York: Wiley.

Scarr, S., & Salapatek, P. (1970). Patterns of fear development during infancy. *Merrill-Palmer Quarterly, 16,* 53–90.

Scarr, S., Webber, P. L., Weinberg, R. A., & Wittig, M. A. (1981). Personality resemblance among adolescents and their parents in biologically related and adoptive families. *Journal of Personality and Social Psychology, 41,* 885–898.

Scarr, S., & Weinberg, R. A. (1976). IQ test performance of black children adopted by white families. *American Psychologist, 31,* 726–739.

Scarr, S., & Weinberg, R. A. (1977). Intellectual similarities within families of both adopted and biological children. *Intelligence, 1,* 170–191.

Scarr, S., & Weinberg, R. A. (1983). The Minnesota adoption studies: Genetic differences and malleability. *Child Development, 54,* 260–267.

Scarr-Salapatek, S., & Williams, M. (1972). The effects of early stimulation on low-birthweight infants. *Child Development, 43,* 509–519.

▶ ▶ ▶ ▶

Schachter, F. F., Shore, E., Hodapp, R., Chalfin, S., & Bundy, C. (1978). Do girls talk earlier? Mean length of utterance in toddlers. *Developmental Psychology, 14*, 388–392.

Schachter, F. F., & Strage, A. A. (1982). Adults' talk and children's language development. In S. G. Moore & C. R. Cooper (Eds.), *The young child: Reviews of research*, Vol. 3. Washington, DC: National Association for the Education of Young Children.

Schaefer, C. E. (1979). *Childhood encopresis and enuresis*. New York: Van Nostrand.

Schaefer, M., Hatcher, R. P., & Barglow, P. D. (1980). Prematurity and infant stimulation: A review of research. *Child Psychiatry and Human Development, 10*, 199–212.

Schaffer, H. R. (Ed.) (1971). *The origins of human social relations*. New York: Academic Press.

Schaffer, H. R., & Emerson, P. E. (1964a). The development of social attachments in infancy. *Monographs of the Society for Research in Child Development, 29* (Whole No. 94).

Schaffer, H. R., & Emerson, P. E. (1964b). Patterns of response to physical contact in early human development, *Journal of Child Psychology and Psychiatry, 5*, 1–13.

Schaie, K. W. (1979). The primary mental abilities in adulthood: An exploration in the development of psychometric intelligence. In P. B. Baltes & O. G. Brim, Jr. (Eds.), *Lifespan development and behavior*, Vol 2. New York: Academic Press.

Scheinfeld, A. (1973). *Twins and supertwins*. Baltimore: Penguin Books.

Scher, J., & Dix, C. (1983). *Will my baby be normal? Everything you need to know about pregnancy*. New York: Dial Press.

Schiedel, D. G., & Marcia, J. E. (1985). Ego identity, intimacy, sex role orientation, and gender. *Developmental Psychology, 21*, 149–160.

Schlesinger, H. S., & Meadow, K. P. (1972). *Sound and sign*. Berkeley, University of California Press.

Schmidt, F. L., Hunter, J. E., & Pearlman, K. (1981). Task differences as moderators of aptitude test validity in selection: A red herring. *Journal of Applied Psychology, 66*, 161–185.

Schmitt, M. H. (1970, July). Superiority of breast-feeding: Fact or fancy? *American Journal of Nursing,* pp. 1488–1493.

Scholnick, E. K. (1983). Why are new trends in conceptual representation a challenge to Piaget's theory? In E. K. Scholnick (Ed.), *New trends in conceptual representation: Challenges to Piaget's theory*. Hillsdale, NJ: Erlbaum.

Schopler, E., & Mesibov, G. B. (Eds.) (1984). *The effects of autism of the family*. New York: Plenum Press.

Schroeder, M. L., Schroeder, K. G., & Hare, R. D. (1983). Generalizability of a checklist for assessment of psychopathy. *Journal of Consulting and Clinical Psychology, 51*, 511–516.

Schuckit, M. A. (1986). Alcoholism and affective disorders: Genetic and clinical implications. *American Journal of Psychiatry, 143*, 140–147.

Schuckit, M. A. (1987). Biological vulnerability to alcoholism. *Journal of Consulting and Clinical Psychology, 55*, 301–309.

Schwartz, A., Campos, J. J., & Baisel, E. (1973). The visual cliff: Cardiac and behavioral correlates on the deep and shallow sides at five and nine months of age. *Journal of Experimental Child Psychology, 15*, 85–99.

Schwartz, D., & Mayaux, F. (1982). Female fecundity as a function of age. *New England Journal of Medicine, 306*, 404–406.

Schwartz, J. C., Strickland, R. G., & Krolick, G. (1974). Infant day care: Behavioral effects at preschool age. *Developmental Psychology, 10*, 502–506.

Schwartz, M. F., Saffran, E. M., & Marin, O. S. M. (1980). The word order problem in agrammatism. I: Comprehension. *Brain and Language, 10*, 249–262.

Scollan, R. (1976). *Conversations with a one-year-old*. Honolulu: University of Hawaii Press.

Scollan, R. (1979). A real early stage: An unzipped condensation of a dissertation on child language. In E. Ochs & B. B. Schieffelin (Eds.), *Developmental pragmatics*. New York: Academic Press.

Scott, W. J., & Morgan, C. S. (1983). An analysis of factors affecting traditional family expectations and perceptions of ideal fertility. *Sex Roles, 9*, 901–914.

Sears, R. R. (1970). Relation of early socialization experiences to self-concepts and gender role in middle adulthood. *Child Development, 41*, 267–290.

Sears, R. R., Maccoby, E. E., & Levin, H. (1957). *Patterns of child rearing*. New York: Harper & Row.

Segalowitz, N. S. (1981). Issues in the cross-cultural study of bilingual development. In H. C. Triandis & A. Heron (Eds.), *Handbook of cross-cultural psychology: Vol. 4. Developmental psychology*. Boston: Allyn & Bacon.

Seitz, V., Rosenbaum, L. K., & Apfel, N. H. (1985). Effects of family support intervention: A ten-year follow-up. *Child Development, 56*, 376–391.

Self, P. A., & Horowitz, F. D. (1980). The behavioral assessment of the neonate: An overview. In J. D. Osofsky (Ed.), *The handbook of infant development*. New York: Wiley-Interscience.

Serbin, L. A., Conner, J. M., Burchardt, C. J., & Citron, C. C. (1979). Effects of peer presence on sex-typing of children's play behavior. *Journal of Experimental Child Psychology, 27*, 303–309.

Serbin, L. A., Tonick, I. J., & Sternglanz, S. H. (1977). Shaping cooperative cross-sex play. *Child Development, 48*, 924–929.

Serrill, M. S. (1987, February 16.) In the grip of the scourge. *Newsweek,* pp. 58–59.

▶ ▶ ▶ ▶

Shapira, A., & Madsen, M. C. (1970). Cooperation and competitive behavior of urban Afro-American, Anglo-American, Mexican-American, and Mexican village children. *Developmental Psychology, 3*, 16–20.

Shapira, A., & Madsen, M. C. (1974). Between and within group cooperation and competitive behavior among kibbutz and nonkibbutz children. *Developmental Psychology, 10*, 140–145.

Shaw, J. S. (1982). Psychological androgyny and stressful life events. *Journal of Personality and Social Psychology, 43*, 145–153.

Shaywitz, S., Cohen, D., & Shaywitz, B. (1980). Behavior and learning difficulties in children of normal intelligence born to alcoholic mothers. *The Journal of Pediatrics, 96*, 978–982.

Shelton, J., & Hill, J. P. (1969). Effects on cheating of achievement anxiety and knowledge of peer performance. *Developmental Psychology, 1*, 449–455

Shepard, W., & Hess, D. T. (1975). Attitudes in four age groups toward sex role division in adult occupations and activities. *Journal of Vocational Behavior, 6*, 27–39.

Shepard, W., & Peterson, J. (1973). Are there sex differences in infancy? *JSAS: Catalog of Selected Documents in Psychology, 3* (Ms. No. 474).

Sheppard, J. J., & Mysak, E. D. (1984). Ontogeny of infantile oral reflexes and emerging chewing. *Child Development, 55*, 831–843.

Sherman, J. A. (1981). Girls' and boys' enrollment in theoretical math courses: A longitudinal study. *Psychology of Women Quarterly, 5*, 681–689.

Sherman, J. A. (1982). Mathematics and critical filter: A look at some residues. *Psychology of Women Quarterly, 6*, 428–444.

Sherman, J. A. (1983). Factors predicting girls' and boys' enrollment in college preparatory mathematics. *Psychology of Women Quarterly, 7*, 272–281.

Sherman, M., Sherman, J. C., & Flory, C. D. (1936). Infant behavior. *Comparative Psychology Monographs, 12* (4).

Shettles, L. B. (1972, June). Predetermining children's sex. *Medical Aspects of Human Sexuality*, p. 172.

Short, R. V. (1984). Breast feeding. *Scientific American, 250* (4), 35–41.

Shultz, T. (1980). Development of the concept of intention. In W. A. Collins (Ed.), *Minnesota symposia on child psychology*, Vol. 13. Hillsdale, NJ: Erlbaum.

Siegal, M., & Robinson, J. (1987). Order effects in children's gender-constancy responses. *Developmental Psychology, 23*, 283–286.

Siegler, R. S., Liebert, D. E., & Liebert, R. M. (1973). Inhelder and Piaget's pendulum problem: Teaching preadolescents to act as scientists. *Developmental Psychology, 9*, 97–101.

Siegler, R. S., & Richards, D. (1982). The development of intelligence. In R. Sternberg (Ed.), *Handbook of human intelligence*. New York: Cambridge University Press.

Sigman, M., Cohen, S., Beckwith, L., & Parmelee, A. H., Jr. (1981). Social and familial influences on the development of preterm infants. *Journal of Pediatric Psychology, 6*, 1–13.

Signorella, M. L., & Liben, L. S. (1984). Recall and reconstruction of gender-related pictures: Effects of attitude, task difficulty, and age. *Child Development, 55*, 393–405.

Signorielli, N., Gross, L., & Morgan, M. (1982). Violence in television programs: Ten years later. In D. Pearl, L. Bouthilet, & J. Lazar (Eds.), *Television and behavior: Ten years of scientific progress and implications for the eighties*, Vol. 2. Washington, DC: U.S. Government Printing Office.

Simcock, B. Sons and daughters—a sex preselection study. *Medical Journal of Australia, 142*, 541–542.

Simmons, R. G., Blyth, D. A., & McKinney, K. L. (1983). The social and psychological effects of puberty on white females. In J. Brooks-Gunn & A. C. Petersen (Eds.), *Girls at puberty: Biological and psychosocial aspects*. New York: Plenum Press.

Singer, D. G. (1983). A time to reexamine the role of television in our lives. *American Psychologist, 38*, 815–825.

Singer, J. L., & Singer, D. G. (1981). *Television, imagination and aggression: A study of preschoolers*. Hillsdale, NJ: Erlbaum.

Singer, J. L., & Singer, D. G. (1983). Psychologists look at television: Cognitive, developmental, personality, and social policy implications. *American Psychologist, 38*, 826–834.

Singleton, L. C., & Asher, S. R. (1979). Racial integration and children's peer preferences: An investigation of developmental and cohort differences. *Child Development, 50*, 936–941.

Sinnott, J. M., Pisoni, D. B., & Aslin, R. N. (1983). A comparison of pure auditory thresholds in human infants and adults. *Infant Behavior and Development, 6*, 3–18.

Siqueland, E., & Delucia, C. A. (1969). Visual reinforcement of non-nutritive sucking in human infants. *Science, 165*, 1144–1146.

Sjøstrøm, L. (1980). Fat cells and body weight. In A. J. Stunkard (Ed.), *Obesity*. Philadelphia: W. B. Saunders.

Skeels, H. M. (1966). Adult status of children with contrasting early life experiences: A follow-up study. *Monographs of the Society for Research in Child Development, 31* (3), 1–65.

Skeels, H. M., & Dye, H. B. (1939). A study of the effects of differential stimulation on mentally retarded children. *Proceedings of the American Association for Mental Deficiency, 44*, 114–136.

Skinner, B. F. (1957). *Verbal behavior*. New York: Appleton.

► ► ► ►

Skinner, B. F. (1979). *The shaping of a behaviorist.* New York: Knopf.

Skinner, B. F. (1983). *A matter of consequences.* New York: Knopf.

Slaby, R. G., & Frey, K. S. (1975). Development of gender constancy and selective attention to same-sex models. *Child Development, 46,* 849–856.

Slater, E., & Shields, J. (1969). Genetic aspects of anxiety. In M. H. Luder (Ed.), *Studies of anxiety.* Ashford, England: Headley Brothers.

Slobin, D. I. (1971). *Psycholinguistics.* Glenview, IL: Scott, Foresman.

Slobin, D. I. (1972, July). Children and language: They learn the same way all around the world. *Psychology Today,* pp. 71–74ff.

Slobin, D. I. (1973). Cognitive prerequisites for the development of grammar. In C. A. Ferguson & D. I. Slobin (Eds.), *Studies of child development.* New York: Holt, Rinehart and Winston.

Slobin, D. I. (1978). A case study of early language awareness. In A. Sinclair, R. J. Jarvella, & W. J. M. Levelt (Eds.), *The child's conception of language.* Berlin: Springer-Verlag.

Slobin, D. I. (1983). Crosslinguistic evidence for basic child grammar. Paper presented to the biennial meeting of the Society for Research in Child Development, Detroit.

Sluckin, W. (1970). *Early learning in man and animal.* London: G. Allen.

Smetana, J. G. (1985). Children's impressions of moral and conventional transgressors. *Developmental Psychology, 21,* 715–724.

Smetana, J. G., Kelly, M., & Twentyman, C. T. (1984). Abused, neglected, and nonmaltreated children's conceptions of moral and social-conventional transgressions. *Child Develoment, 55,* 277–287.

Smetana, J. G., & Letourneau, K. J. (1984). Development of gender constancy and children's sex-typed free play behavior. *Developmental Psychology, 20,* 691–696.

Smith, C. P., Ryan, E. R., & Diggins, D. R. (1972). Moral decision making: Cheating on examinations. *Journal of Personality, 40,* 640–660.

Smith, D., King, M., & Hoebel, B. G. (1970). Lateral hypothalamic control of killing: Evidence for a cholinoreceptive mechanism. *Science, 167,* 900–901.

Smith, M. O. (1985). Examining reading problems as a means to uncovering sex differences in cognition. In T. Schlechter & M. Toglia (Eds.), *New directions in cognitive science.* Norwood, NJ: Ablex.

Smith, P. K., & Connolly, K. J. (1980). *The ecology of preschool behavior.* Cambridge: Cambridge University Press.

Smye, M. D., & Wine, J. D. (1980). A comparison of female and male adolescents' social behaviors and cognitions: A challenge to the assertiveness literature. *Sex Roles, 6,* 213–230.

Snarey, J. R., Reimer, J., & Kohlberg, L. (1985). Development of social-moral reasoning among kibbutz adolescents: A longitudinal cross-cultural study. *Developmental Psychology, 21,* 3–17.

Snow, C. E., & Hoefnagel-Hohle, M. (1978). The critical period for language acquisition: Evidence from second language learning. *Child Development, 49,* 1114–1128.

Snow, M. E., Jacklin, C. N., & Maccoby, E. E. (1983). Sex-of-child differences in father-child interaction at one year of age. *Child Development, 54,* 227–232.

Snyder, M., Tanke, E. D., & Berscheid, E. (1977). Social perception and interpersonal behavior: On the self-fulfilling nature of social stereotypes. *Journal of Personality and Social Psychology, 35,* 656–666.

Snyderman, M., & Rothman, S. (1987). Survey of expert opinion on intelligence and aptitude testing. *American Psychologist, 42,* 137–144.

Sobesky, W. E. (1983). The effects of situational factors on moral judgments. *Child Development, 54,* 575–584.

Sokol, R. J. (1984, March 19). Cited in "Sad news for the happy hour." *Newsweek,* p. 67.

Sommer, R. (1969). *Personal space.* Englewood Cliffs, NJ: Prentice-Hall.

Sontag, L. W. (1944). Differences in modifiability of fetal behavior and psychology. *Psychosomatic Medicine, 6,* 151–154.

Sontag, L. W. (1966). Implications of fetal behavior and environment for adult personality. *Annals of the New York Academy of Science, 134,* 782–786.

Sontag, L. W., & Richards, T. W. (1938). Studies in fetal behavior: Fetal heart rate as a behavioral indicator. *Child Development Monographs, 3,* No. 4.

Sorce, J. F., Emde, R. N., Campos, J. J., & Klinnert, M. D. (1985). Maternal emotional signaling: Its effect on the visual cliff behavior of 1-year-olds. *Developmental Psychology, 21,* 195–200.

Soroka, S. M., Corter, C. M., & Abramovitch, R. (1979). Infants' tactile discrimination of novel and familiar stimuli. *Child Development, 50,* 1251–1253.

Sparrow, S. S., Ballo, D. A., & Cicchetti, D. V. (1984). *Vineland Adaptive Behavior Scales.* Circle Pines, MN: American Guidance Service.

Spearman, C. (1904). "General intelligence" objectively determined and measured. *American Journal of Psychology, 15,* 201–293.

Spelke, E. S., & Owsley, C. (1979). Intermodal exploration and knowledge in infancy. *Infant Behavior and Development, 2,* 13–27.

Spence, J. T., & Helmreich, R. L. (1978). *Masculinity and femininity.* Austin: University of Texas Press.

Spence, J. T., Helmreich, R., & Stapp, J. (1975). Ratings of self and peers

▶ ▶ ▶ ▶

on sex-role attributes and their relation to self-esteem and concepts of masculinity and femininity. *Journal of Personality and Social Psychology, 32*, 29–39.

Spezzano, C. (1981). Prenatal psychology: Pregnant with questions. *Psychology Today, 15* (5), 49–57.

Spiker, D., & Ricks, M. (1984). Visual self-recognition in autistic children: Developmental relationships. *Child Development, 55*, 214–225.

Spinetta, J., & Rigler, D. (1972). The child-abusing parent: A psychological review. *Psychological Bulletin, 77*, 296–304.

Spitz, R. A. (1964). Hospitalism: A follow-up report. In D. Fenschel et al. (Eds.), *Psychoanalytic studies of the child*, Vol. 2. New York: International Universities Press.

Spitz, R. A. (1965). *The first year of life: A psychoanalytic study of normal and deviant object relations*. New York: International Universities Press.

Spitz, R. A., & Wolff, K. M. (1946). Anaclitic depression: An inquiry into the genesis of psychiatric conditions in early childhood: II. In A. Freud et al. (Eds.), *The psychoanalytic study of the child*, Vol. 2. New York: International Universities Press.

Spivack, G., Marcus, J., & Swift, M. (1986). Early classroom behaviors and later misconduct. *Developmental Psychology, 22*, 124–131.

Sprigle, J. E., & Schaefer, L. (1985). Longitudinal evaluation of the effects of two compensatory preschool programs on fourth- through sixth-grade students. *Developmental Psychology, 21*, 702–708.

Sroufe, L. A. (1979). Socioemotional development. In J. Osofsky (Ed.), *Handbook of infant development*. New York: Wiley.

Sroufe, L. A. (1983). Individual patterns of adaptation from infancy to preschool. In M. Perlmutter (Ed.), *Minnesota symposium on child psychology*, Vol. 16. Hillsdale, NJ: Erlbaum.

Sroufe, L. A. (1985). Attachment classification from the perspective of infant-caregiver relationships and infant temperament. *Child Development, 56*, 1–14.

Sroufe, L. A., Fox, N. E., & Pancake, V. R. (1983). Attachment and dependency in developmental perspective. *Child Development, 54*, 1615–1627.

Sroufe, L. A., & Rutter, M. (1984). The domain of developmental psychopathology. *Child Development, 55*, 17–29.

Sroufe, L. A., & Waters, E. (1976). The ontogenesis of smiling and laughter: A perspective on the organization of development in infancy. *Psychological Review, 83*, 173–179.

Sroufe, L. A., & Waters, E. (1977). Attachment as an organizational construct. *Child Development, 48*, 1184–1199.

Sroufe, L. A., Waters, E., & Matas, L. (1974). Contextual determinants of infant affectional response. In M. Lewis & L. Rosenblum (Eds.), *The origins of fear*. New York: Wiley.

Stamps, L. E., & Porges, S. W. (1975). Heartrate conditioning in newborn infants: Relationships among conditionability, heartrate variability and sex. *Developmental Psychology, 11*, 424–431.

Starfield, B. (1972). Enuresis: Its pathogenesis and management. *Clinical Pediatrics, 11*, 343–350.

Steele, B. F., & Pollock, C. B. (1974). A psychiatric study of parents who abuse infants and small children. In R. E. Helfer & C. H. Kempe (Eds.), *The battered child*, 2d ed. Chicago: University of Chicago Press.

Stein, A. H., & Bailey, M. M. (1973). The socialization of achievement orientation in females. *Psychological Bulletin, 80*, 345–366.

Stein, G. (1982). The maternity blues. In I. F. Brockington & R. Kumar (Eds.), *Motherhood and mental illness*. London: Academic Press.

Stein, Z., Susser, M., Saenger, G., & Morolla, F. (1975). *Famine and human development: The Dutch hunger-winter of 1944–1945*. New York: Oxford University Press.

Steinberg, L. (1987). Impact of puberty on family relations: Effects of pubertal status and pubertal timing. *Developmental Psychology, 23*, 451–460.

Steinberg, L., Catalano, R., & Dooley, D. (1981). Economic antecedents of child abuse and neglect. Paper presented to the meeting of the Society for Research in Child Development, Boston.

Steiner, J. E. (1979). Facial expressions in response to taste and smell discrimination. In H. W. Reese & L. P. Lipsitt (Eds.), *Advances in child development and behavior*, Vol. 13. New York: Academic Press.

Steinmetz, J. L., Lewinsohn, P. M., & Antonuccio, D. O. (1983). Prediction of individual outcome in a group intervention for depression. *Journal of Consulting and Clinical Psychology, 51*, 331–337.

Steinschneider, A. (1975). Implications of the sudden infant death syndrome for the study of sleep in infancy. In A. D. Pick (Ed.), *Minnesota symposia on child psychology*, Vol. 9. Minneapolis: University of Minnesota Press.

Stenberg, C. R., Campos, J. J., & Emde, R. N. (1983). The facial expression of anger in 7-month-old infants. *Child Development 54*, 178–184.

Stenchever, M. A., Williamson, R. A., Leonard, J., Karp, L. E., Ley, B., Shy, K., & Smith, D. (1981). Possible relationship between in utero diethylstilbestrol exposure and male fertility. *American Journal of Obstetrics and Gynecology, 140*, 186–193.

Stephan, C. W., & Langlois, J. H. (1984). Baby beautiful: Adult attributions of infant competence as a function of adult attractiveness. *Child Development, 55*, 576–585.

▶ ▶ ▶ ▶

Stephan, J. K., & Chow, B. F. (1969). The fetus and placenta in maternal dietary restriction. *Federation Proceedings, 28,* 915.

Stericker, A., & LeVesconte, S. (1982). Effect of brief training on sex-related differences in visual-spatial skill. *Journal of Personality and Social Psychology, 43,* 1018–1029.

Stern, J. A., Oster, P. J., & Newport, K. (1980). Reaction time measures, hemispheric specialization, and age. In L. W. Poon (Ed.), *Aging in the eighties: Psychological issues.* Washington, DC: American Psychological Association.

Stern, L. (1985). *The structures and strategies of human memory.* Homewood, IL: Dorsey Press.

Stern, M., & Hildebrandt, K. A. (1986). Prematurity stereotyping: Effects on mother-infant interaction. *Child Development, 57,* 308–315.

Sternberg, R. J. (1979). Stalking the IQ quark. *Psychology Today, 13* (9), 42–54.

Sternberg, R. J. (1985). *Beyond IQ: A triarchic theory of human intelligence.* New York: Cambridge University Press.

Sternberg, R. J., & Powell, J. S. (1983). The development of intelligence. In J. H. Flavell & E. M. Markman (Eds.), *Handbook of child psychology: Vol. 3. Cognitive development.* New York: Wiley.

Sternglanz, S. H., & Serbin, L. A. (1974). Sex role stereotyping in children's television programs. *Developmental Psychology, 10,* 710–715.

Stevenson, H. W., Lee, S. Y., & Stigler, J. W. (1986). Mathematics achievement of Chinese, Japanese, and American children. *Science, 231,* 693–699.

Stevenson, H. W., Stigler, J. W., Shin-Ying, L., Lucker, G. W., Kitamura, S., & Hsu, C. (1985). Cognitive performance and academic achievement of Japanese, Chinese, and American children. *Child Development, 56,* 718–734.

Stock, M. B., & Smythe, P. M. (1963). Does undernutrition during infancy inhibit brain growth and subsequent intellectual development? *Archives of Disorders in Childhood, 38,* 546–552.

Stolkowski, J., & Choukroun, J. (1981). Preconception selection of sex in man. *Israeli Journal of Medical Sciences, 17,* 1061–1067.

Stolz, H. R., & Stolz, L. H. (1951). *Somatic development of adolescent boys: A study of the growth of boys during the second decade of life.* New York: Macmillan.

Stoneman, Z., Brody, G. H., & MacKinnon, C. (1984). Naturalistic observations of children's activities while playing with their siblings and friends. *Child Development, 55,* 617–627.

Storms, M. D. (1980). Theories of sexual orientation. *Journal of Personality and Social Psychology, 38,* 783–792.

Streissguth, A. P., Barr, H. M., & Martin, D. C. (1983). Maternal alcohol use and neonatal habituation assessed with the Brazelton scale. *Child Development, 54,* 1109–1118.

Streissguth, A. P., Landesman-Dwyer, S., Martin, J. C., & Smith, D. W. (1980). Teratogenic effects of alcohol in humans and laboratory animals. *Science, 209,* 353–361.

Streissguth, A. P., Martin, D. C., Barr, H. M., Sandman, B. M., Kirchner, G. L., & Darby, B. L. (1984). Interuterine alcohol and nicotine exposure: Attention and reaction time in 4-year-old children. *Developmental Psychology, 20,* 533–541.

Strohner, H., & Nelson, K. E. (1974). The young child's development of sentence comprehension: Influence of event probability, nonverbal context, syntactic form, and strategies. *Child Development, 45,* 567–576.

Stuckey, M. F., McGhee, P. E., & Bell, N. J. (1982). Parent-child interaction: The influence of maternal employment. *Developmental Psychology, 18,* 635–644.

Stumphauzer, J. S. (1981). Behavior modification with delinquents and criminals. In W. E. Craighead, A. E. Kazdin, & M. J. Mahoney (Eds.), *Behavior modification: Principles, issues, and applications,* 2d ed. Boston: Houghton Mifflin.

Suls, J., & Kalle, R. J. (1979). Children's moral judgments as a function of intention, damage, and an actor's physical harm. *Developmental Psychology, 15,* 93–94.

Sunday, S., & Lewin, M. (1985). Integrating nuclear issues into the psychology curriculum. Paper presented at the annual meeting of the Eastern Psychological Association.

Suomi, S. J., & Harlow, H. (1972). Social rehabilitation of isolate-reared monkeys. *Developmental Psychology, 6,* 487–496.

Suomi, S. J., Harlow, H. F., & McKinney, W. T. (1972). Monkey psychiatrists. *American Journal of Psychiatry, 128,* 927–932.

Super, C. M. (1980). Cognitive development: Looking across at growing up. In C. M. Super & S. Harkness (Eds.), *New directions for child development, No. 8. Anthropological perspectives on child development.* San Francisco: Jossey-Bass.

Surber, C. F. (1977). Developmental processes in social inference: Averaging of intentions and consequences in moral judgment. *Developmental Psychology, 13,* 654–665.

Sussman, N. M., & Rosenfeld, H. M. (1982). Influence of culture, language, and sex on conversational distance. *Journal of Personality and Social Psychology, 42,* 66–74.

Sutton-Smith, B., & Rosenberg, B. G. (1970). *The sibling.* New York: Holt, Rinehart and Winston.

Sutton-Smith, B., Rosenberg, B. G., & Landy, F. (1968). The interaction of father absence and sibling presence on cognitive abilities. *Child Development, 39,* 1213–1221.

Svejda, M. J., Campos, J. J., & Emde, R. N. (1980). Mother-infant "bond-

▶ ▶ ▶ ▶

ing": Failure to generalize. *Child Development, 51,* 775–779.

Tan, L. (1985). Laterality and motor skills in four-year-olds. *Child Development, 56,* 119–124.

Tanner, J. M. (1970). Physical growth. In P. H. Mussen (Ed.), *Carmichael's manual of child psychology,* 3d ed., Vol. 1. New York: Wiley.

Tanner, J. M. (1972). Sequence, tempo, and individual variation in growth and development of boys and girls aged twelve to sixteen. In J. Kagan & R. Coles (Eds.), *Twelve to sixteen: Early adolescence.* New York: Norton.

Tanner, J. M. (1978). *Fetus into man: Physical growth from conception to maturity.* Cambridge, MA: Harvard University Press.

Tanner, J. M. (1982). *Growth at adolescence,* 2d ed. Oxford: Scientific Publications.

Tapp, J. L., & Levine, F. J. (1972). Compliance from kindergarten to college: A speculative research note. *Journal of Adolescence and Youth, 1,* 233–249.

Taylor, S. P., & Epstein, S. (1967). Aggression as a function of the interaction of the sex of the aggressor and the sex of the victim. *Journal of Personality, 35,* 474–486.

Taylor, W. N. (1985). Super athletes made to order. *Psychology Today, 19* (5), 62–66.

Teller, D. Y., Morse, R., Borton, R., & Regal, D. (1974). Visual acuity for vertical and diagonal gratings in human infants. *Vision Research, 14,* 1433–1439.

Teller, D. Y., Peeples, D. R., & Sekel, M. (1978). Discrimination of chromatic from white light in two-month-old human infants. *Vision Research, 18,* 41–48.

Terkel, J., & Rosenblatt, J. S. (1972). Humoral factors underlying maternal behavior at parturition: Cross transfusion between freely moving rats. *Journal of Comparative and Physiological Psychology, 80,* 365–371.

Terman, L. M. (Ed.) (1959). *Genetic studies of genius,* Vol. 5. Stanford, CA: Stanford University Press.

Terman, L. M., & Oden, M. (1959). The gifted group at mid-life. In L. M. Terman (Ed.), *Genetic studies of genius,* Vol. 5. Stanford, CA: Stanford University Press.

Terrace, H. S. (1980). *Nim: A chimpanzee who learned sign language.* New York: Knopf.

Terrace, H. S. (1987). Reply to Bernstein and Kent. *American Psychologist, 42,* 273.

Terrace, H. S., Petitto, L. A., Sanders, R. J., & Bever, T. G. (1980). On the grammatical capacity of apes. In K. E. Nelson (Ed.), *Children's language,* Vol. 2. New York: Gardner Press.

Tesiny, E. P., & Lefkowitz, M. M. (1982). Childhood depression: A 6-month follow-up study. *Journal of Consulting and Clinical Psychology, 50,* 778–780.

Thoman, E. B., Liederman, P. H., & Olson, J. P. (1972). Neonate-mother interaction during breast feeding. *Developmental Psychology, 6,* 110–118.

Thomas, A., & Chess, S. (1977). *Temperament and development.* New York: Brunner/Mazel.

Thomas, A., & Chess, S. (1980). *The dynamics of psychological development.* New York: Brunner/Mazel.

Thomas, B. (1984). Early toy preferences of four-year-old readers and nonreaders. *Child Development, 55,* 424–430.

Thomas, M. H., Horton, R. W., Lippincott, E. C., & Drabman, R. S. (1977). Desensitization to portrayals of real-life aggression as a function of exposure to television violence. *Journal of Personality and Social Psychology, 35,* 450–458.

Thomas, N. G., & Berk, L. E. (1981). Effects of school environments on the development of young children's creativity. *Child Development, 52,* 1153–1162.

Thompson, R. A., Lamb, M. E., & Estes, D. (1982). Stability of infant-mother attachment and its relationship to changing life circumstances in an unselected middle-class sample. *Child Development, 53,* 144–148.

Thompson, S. K. (1975). Gender labels and early sex role development. *Child Development, 46,* 339–347.

Thomson, M. E., & Kramer, M. S. (1984). Methodologic standards for controlled clinical trials of early contact and maternal-infant behavior. *Pediatrics, 73,* 294–300.

Thornton, D., & Reid, R. L. (1982). Moral reasoning and type of criminal offense. *British Journal of Social Psychology, 21,* 231–238.

Thurstone, L. L. (1938). Primary mental abilities. *Psychometric Monographs, 1.*

Thurstone, L. L., & Thurstone, T. G. (1963). *SRA primary abilities.* Chicago: Science Research Associates.

Tisak, M. S., & Turiel, E. (1984). Children's conceptions of moral and prudential rules. *Child Development, 55,* 1030–1039.

Tizard, B., Philips, J., & Plewis, I. (1976). Play in preschool centres. *Journal of Child Psychology and Psychiatry, 17,* 265–274.

Tobias, S. (1982, January). Sexist equations. *Psychology Today,* pp. 14–17.

Tobias, S., & Weissbrod, C. (1980). Anxiety and mathematics: An update. *Harvard Educational Review, 50,* 63–70.

Tomasello, M., & Mannle, S. (1985). Pragmatics of sibling speech to one-year-olds. *Child Development, 56,* 911–917.

Tomlinson-Keasey, C., Eisert, D. C., Kahle, L. R., Hardy-Brown, K., & Keasey, B. (1979). The structure of concrete operational thought. *Child Development, 50,* 1153–1163.

Tomlinson-Keasey, C., & Keasey, C. B. (1974). The mediating role of cognitive development in moral judgment. *Child Development, 45,* 291–298.

▶ ▶ ▶ ▶

Torgersen, S. (1983). Genetic factors in anxiety disorders. *Archives of General Psychiatry, 40,* 1085–1089.

Trabasso, T. (1977). The role of memory as a system in making transitive inferences. In R. V. Kail, Jr., & J. W. Hagen (Eds.), *Perspectives on the development of memory and cognition.* Hillsdale, NJ: Erlbaum.

Tremaine, L. S., Schau, C. G., & Busch, J. W. (1982). Children's occupational sex typing. *Sex Roles, 8,* 691–710.

Trevarthen, C. (1974, May 2). Conversations with a 2-month-old. *New Scientist,* pp. 230–235.

Trites, R. L., & Caprade, K. (1983). Evidence for an independent syndrome of hyperactivity. *Journal of Child Psychology and Psychiatry, 24,* 573–586.

Trost, C. (1987, February 12). Childcare center at Virginia firm boosts worker morale and loyalty. *Wall Street Journal,* p. 27.

Tryon, R. C. (1940). Genetic differences in maze learning in rats. *Yearbook of the National Society for Studies in Education, 39,* 111–119.

Tuana, S. (1969). Study cited in R. Sommer (1969). *Personal space.* Englewood Cliffs, NJ: Prentice-Hall, 1969.

Tucker, J. A., Vichinich, R. E., & Sobell, M. B. (1981). Alcohol consumption as a self-handicapping strategy. *Journal of Abnormal Psychology, 90,* 220–230.

Turkington, C. (1984, November). Hormones in rats found to control sex behavior. *APA Monitor,* pp. 40–41.

Turnbull, C. M. (1961). Notes and discussions: Some observations regarding the experiences of the Bambute pygmies. *American Journal of Psychology, 7,* 304–308.

Turner, S. M., Beidel, D. C., & Costello, A. (1987). Psychopathology in the offspring of anxiety disorders patients. *Journal of Consulting and Clinical Psychology, 55,* 229–235.

Ullian, D. Z. (1976). The development of conceptions of masculinity and femininity. In B. Lloyd & J. Archer (Eds.), *Exploring sex differences.* New York: Academic Press.

Ullian, D. Z. (1981). The child's construction of gender: Anatomy as destiny. In E. K. Shapiro & E. Weber (Eds.), *Cognitive and affective growth.* Hillsdale, NJ: Erlbaum.

Ulvund, S. E. (1984). Predictive validity of assessments of early cognitive competence in light of some current issues in developmental psychology. *Human Development, 27,* 76–83.

Ungerer, J. A., & Sigman, M. (1983). Developmental lags in preterm infants from one to three years. *Child Development, 54,* 1217–1228.

Uzgiris, I. C., & Hunt, J. McV. (1975). *Toward ordinal scales of psychological development in infancy.* Champaign: University of Illinois Press.

Vaillant, G. E. (1982). *The natural history of alcoholism.* Cambridge, MA: Harvard University Press.

Vandell, D. L., Wilson, K. S., & Buchanan, N. R. (1980). Peer interaction in the first year of life: An examination of its structure, content, and sensitivity to toys. *Child Development, 51,* 481–488.

Van Oeffelen, M. P., & Vos, P. G. (1984). The young child's processing of dot patterns: A chronometric and eye movement analysis. *International Journal of Behavioral Development, 7,* 53–56.

Vaughn, B. E., Egeland, B., & Sroufe, L. A. (1979). Individual differences in infant-mother attachment at 12 and 18 months: Stability and change in families under stress. *Child Development, 50,* 971–975.

Vaughn, B. E., Kopp, C. B., & Krakow, J. B. (1984). The emergence and consolidation of self-control from eighteen to thirty months of age: Normative trends and individual differences. *Child Development, 55,* 990–1004.

Vaughn, B. E., & Langlois, J. H. (1983). Physical attractiveness as a correlate of peer status and social competence in preschool children. *Developmental Psychology, 19,* 561–567.

Venn, J. R., & Short, J. G. (1973). Vicarious classical conditioning of emotional responses in nursery school children. *Journal of Personality and Social Psychology, 28,* 249–255.

Verne, G. B. (1977). The effects of four-hour delay of punishment under two conditions of verbal instructions. *Child Development, 48,* 621–624.

Vygotsky, L. S. (1962). *Thought and language.* Cambridge, MA: Massachusetts Institute of Technology Press.

Waber, D. P., Mann, M. B., Merola, J., & Moylan, P. M. (1985). Physical maturation rate and cognitive performance in early adolescence: A longitudinal examination. *Developmental Psychology, 21,* 666–681.

Wadsworth, M. E. J. (1979). *Roots of delinquency: Infancy, adolescence, and crime.* Oxford: Martin Robinson.

Waldholz, M. (1985, July 22). Breakthroughs in prenatal testing give hope to high-risk couples. *Wall Street Journal,* p. 21.

Wales, E., & Brewer, B. (1976). Graffiti in the 1970s. *Journal of Social Psychology, 99,* 115–123.

Walker, E., & Emory, E. (1983). Infants at risk for psychopathology: Offspring of schizophrenic parents. *Child Development, 54,* 1269–1285.

Walker, L. J. (1984). Sex differences in the development of moral reasoning: A critical review. *Child Development, 55,* 677–691.

Wallerstein, J. S., & Kelly, J. B. (1974). The effects of parental divorce: The adolescent experience. In A. Koupernik (Ed.), *The child in his family: Children at psychiatric risk,* Vol. 3. New York: Wiley.

Wallerstein, J. S., & Kelly, J. B. (1975). The effects of parental divorce: Experience of the preschool child. *Journal of the American Academy of Child Psychiatry, 14,* 600–616.

▶ ▶ ▶ ▶

Wallerstein, J. S., & Kelly, J. B. (1982). *Surviving the breakup: How children and parents cope with divorce.* New York: Basic Books.

Wallis, C. (1984, August 27). Can science pick a child's sex? Doctors challenge new methods of granting an ancient wish. *Time,* p. 59.

Waterhouse, L., & Fein, D. (1984). Developmental trends in cognitive skills for children diagnosed as autistic and schizophrenic. *Child Development, 55,* 236–248.

Waters, E. (1978). The reliability and stability of individual differences in infant-mother attachment. *Child Development, 49,* 483–494.

Waters, E., Wippmann, J., & Sroufe, L. A. (1979). Attachment, positive affect, and competence in the peer group. *Child Development, 50,* 821–829.

Watson, J. B. (1924). *Behaviorism.* New York: Norton.

Watson, J. B., & Rayner, R. (1920). Conditioned emotional reactions. *Journal of Experimental Psychology, 3,* 1–14.

Watson, J. D., & Crick, F. H. C. (1958). Molecular structure of nucleic acids: A structure for deoxyribose nucleic acid. *Nature, 171,* 737–738.

Wechsler, D. (1975). Intelligence defined and undefined: A relativistic appraisal. *American Psychologist, 30,* 135–139.

Wehren, A., & DeLisi, R. (1983). The development of gender understanding: Judgments and explanations. *Child Development, 54,* 1568–1578.

Weinberg, R. S., Yukelson, S., & Jackson, A. (1980). Effect of public and private efficacy expectations on competitive performance. *Journal of Sport Psychology, 2,* 340–349.

Weiner, M. J., & Wright, F. E. (1971). Effects of undergoing arbitrary discrimination upon subsequent attitudes toward a minority group. *Journal of Applied Social Psychology, 3,* 94–102.

Weinraub, M., & Wolf, B. M. (1983). Effects of stress and social supports on mother-child interactions in single- and two-parent families. *Child Development, 54,* 1297–1311.

Weiss, G., Hechtman, L., Perlman, T., Hopkins, J., & Wener, A. (1979). Hyperactives as young adults. *Archives of General Psychiatry, 36,* 675–681.

Weiss, R. J. (1982). Understanding moral thought: Effects on moral reasoning and decision-making. *Developmental Psychology, 18,* 852–861.

Weisz, J. R., Weiss, B., Wasserman, A. A., & Rintoul, B. (1987). Control-related beliefs and depression among clinic-referred children and adolescents. *Journal of Abnormal Psychology, 96,* 58–63.

Westoff, C. R., & Rindfuss, R. R. (1974). Sex preselection in the United States: Some implications. *Science, 184,* 633–636.

Whalen, C. K., Henker, B., Swanson, J. M., Granger, D., Kliewer, W., & Spencer, J. (1987). Natural social behavior in hyperactive children: Dose effects of methylphenidate. *Journal of Consulting and Clinical Psychology, 55,* 187–193.

White, C. B., Bushnell, N., & Regnemer, J. L. (1978). Moral development in Bahamian school children: A three-year examination of Kohlberg's stages of moral development. *Developmental Psychology, 14,* 58–65.

White, J. W. (1983). Sex and gender issues in aggression research. In R. G. Geen & E. I. Donnerstein (Eds.), *Aggression: Theoretical and empirical reviews,* Vol. 2. New York: Academic Press.

White, R. W. (1959). Motivation reconsidered: The concept of competence. *Psychological Review, 66,* 297–333.

Whiting, B. B., & Whiting, J. W. M. (1975). *Children of six cultures: A psycho-cultural analysis.* Cambridge, MA: Harvard University Press.

Wickelgren, L. W. (1967). Convergence in the human newborn. *Journal of Experimental Child Psychology, 5,* 74–85.

Wideman, M. V., & Singer, J. F. (1984). The role of psychological mechanisms in preparation for childbirth. *American Psychologist, 34,* 1357–1371.

Williams, H. (1983). *Perceptual and motor development.* Englewood Cliffs, NJ: Prentice-Hall.

Williams, J. E., Bennett, S. M., & Best, D. L. (1975). Awareness and expression of sex stereotypes in young children. *Developmental Psychology, 11,* 635–642.

Williams, L. R. (1983). Beliefs and attitudes of young girls regarding menstruation. In S. Golub (Ed.), *Menarche.* Lexington, MA: Lexington Books.

Williams, R. L. (1974, May). Scientific racism and IQ: The silent mugging of the black community. *Psychology Today.*

Wilson, G. T. (1982). Psychotherapy process and procedure: The behavioral mandate. *Behavior Therapy, 13,* 291–312.

Wilson, R. S. (1983). The Louisville twin study: Developmental synchronies in behavior. *Child Development, 54,* 298–316.

Winer, G. A. (1980). Class-inclusion reasoning in children: A review of the empirical literature. *Child Development, 51,* 309–328.

Winick, M. (1970). Cellular growth in intrauterine malnutrition. *Pediatric Clinics of North America, 17,* 69–77.

Winick, M. (1975). *Childhood obesity.* New York: Wiley.

Winick, M. (1981, January). Food and the fetus. *Natural History,* pp. 16–81.

Winick, M., & Noble, A. (1966). Cellular response in rats during malnutrition at various ages. *Journal of Nutrition, 89,* 300–306.

Winterbottom, M. (1958). The relation of need for achievement to learning experiences in independence and mastery. In J. Atkinson (Ed.), *Motives in fantasy, action, and society.* Princeton, NJ: Van Nostrand.

▶ ▶ ▶ ▶

Witelson, S. F. (1979). Developmental dyslexia: Research methods and inferences. *Science, 203,* 201–203.

Witkin, H. A., Mednick, S. A., Schulsinger, F., Bakkestrom, E., Christiansen, K. O., Goodenough, D. R., Hirschhorn, K., Lundsteen, C., Owen, D. R., Philip, J., Rubin, D. B., & Stocking, M. (1976). Criminality in XYY and XXY men. *Science, 193,* 547–555.

Wohlford, P., Santrock, J. W., Berger, S., & Liberman, D. (1971). Older brothers' influence on sex-typed, aggressive, and dependent behavior in father-absent children. *Developmental Psychology, 4,* 124–134.

Wolfe, D. A., Katell, A., & Drabman, R. S. (1982). Parents' and preschool children's choices of disciplinary child-rearing methods. *Journal of Applied Developmental Psychology, 3,* 167–176.

Wolfe, V. V., Finch, A. J., Jr., Saylor, C. F., Blount, R. L., Pallmeyer, T. P., & Carek, D. J. (1987). Negative affectivity in children: A multitrait-multimethod investigation. *Journal of Consulting and Clinical Psychology, 55,* 245–250.

Wolff, P. H. (1963). Observations on the early development of smiling. In B. M. Foss (Ed.), *Determinants of infant behavior,* Vol. 2. London: Methuen.

Wolock, I., & Horowitz, B. (1984). Child maltreatment as a social problem: The neglect of neglect. *American Journal of Orthopsychiatry, 54,* 530–543.

Wolpe, J., & Rachman, S. (1960). Psychoanalytic "evidence": A critique based on Freud's case of Little Hans. *Journal of Nervous and Mental Disease, 131,* 135–147.

Wright, J. C., & Huston, A. C. (1983). A matter of form: Potentials of television for young viewers. *American Psychologist, 38,* 835–843.

Wright, J. T., Waterson, E. J., Barrison, I. G., Toplis, P. J., Lewis, I. G., Gordon, M. G., MacRae, K. D., Morris, N. F., & Murray Lyon, I. M. (1983, March 26). Alcohol consumption, pregnancy, and low birthweight. *The Lancet,* pp. 663–665.

Yager, J. (1982). Family issues in the pathogenesis of anorexia nervosa. *Psychosomatic Medicine, 44,* 43–60.

Yarrow, L. J., & Goodwin, M. S. (1973). The immediate impact of separation: Reactions of infants to a change in mother figures. In L. J. Stone, H. T. Smith, & L. B. Murphy (Eds.), *The competent infant: Research and commentary.* New York: Basic Books.

Yarrow, L. J., Goodwin, M. S., Manheimer, H., & Milowe, I. D. (1971, March). Infant experiences and cognitive and personality development at ten years. Paper presented to the meeting of the American Orthopsychiatric Association, Washington, DC.

Yarrow, M. R., Scott, P. M., & Waxler, C. Z. (1973). Learning concern for others. *Developmental Psychology, 8,* 240–260.

Yeates, K. O., MacPhee, D., Campbell, F. A., & Ramey, C. T. (1983). Maternal IQ and home environment as determinants of early childhood intellectual competence: A developmental analysis. *Developmental Psychology, 19,* 731–739.

Yogev, S., & Vierra, A. (1983). The state of motherhood among professional women. *Sex Roles, 9,* 391–397.

Yonas, A., Granrud, C. E., & Pettersen, L. (1985). Infants' sensitivity to relative size as information for distance. *Developmental Psychology, 21,* 161–167.

Yonas, A., Pettersen, L., & Granrud, C. E. (1982). Infants' sensitivity to familiar size as information for distance. *Child Development, 53,* 1285–1290.

Zahn-Waxler, C., Cummings, E. M., & Cooperman, G. (1984). Emotional development in childhood. *Annals of Child Development, 1,* 45–106.

Zahn-Waxler, C., Friedman, S. L., & Cummings, E. M. (1983). Children's emotions and behaviors in response to infants' cries. *Child Development, 54,* 1522–1528.

Zajonc, R. B. (1975). Birth order and intelligence: Dumber by the dozen. *Psychology Today, 8,* 37–43.

Zajonc, R. B. (1976). Family configuration and intelligence. *Science, 192,* 227–236.

Zajonc, R. B., & Markus, G. B. (1975). Birth order and intellectual development. *Psychological Review, 82,* 74–88.

Zelazo, N. A., Zelazo, P. R., & Kolb, S. (1972). Walking in the newborn. *Science, 176,* 314–315.

Zeskind, R. S. (1983). Production and spectral anaylsis of neonatal crying and its relations to other biobehavioral systems in the infant at risk. In T. M. Field & A. Sostek (Eds.), *Infants born at risk: Physiological, perceptual and cognitive processes.* New York: Grune & Stratton.

Zifcak, M. (1981). Phonological awareness and reading acquisition. *Contemporary Educational Psychology, 106,* 117–126.

Zigler, E., Abelson, W. D., Trickett, P. K., & Seitz, V. (1982). Is an intervention program necessary in order to improve economically disadvantaged children's IQ scores? *Child Development, 53,* 340–348.

Zigler, E., & Berman, W. (1983). Discerning the future of early childhood intervention. *American Psychologist, 38,* 894–906.

Zigler, E., & Butterfield, E. C. (1968). Motivational aspects of change in IQ test performance of culturally deprived nursery school children. *Child Development, 39,* 1–14.

Zigler, E., & Valentine, J. (Eds.) (1979). *Project Head Start: A legacy of the war on poverty.* New York: Free Press.

Zill, N. (1985). *Happy, healthy, and insecure: A portrait of middle childhood in the United States.* New York: Cambridge University Press.

Zuckerman, D. M., & Zuckerman, B. S. (1985). Television's impact on children. *Pediatrics, 75,* 233–240.

▶ ▶ ▶ ▶

Photo Credits

Chapter 1: *page 7,* Beryl Goldberg; *page 15,* Arvind Garg; *page 21,* Roe DiBona—copyright © 1987 *Psychology Today* Magazine; *page 22,* John Running.

Chapter 2: *pages 43, 48,* National Library of Medicine; *page 49,* Harvard University Archives; *page 54,* The Ferdinand Hamburger, Jr., Archives of The Johns Hopkins University; *page 55,* The Bettmann Archive; *page 67,* Black Star; *page 73* (left), Cornell University, (right) University of Virginia.

Chapter 3: *page 84,* Peter Arnold, Inc.; *page 95,* March of Dimes; *page 97,* copyright © 1987 *Psychology Today* Magazine; *page 100,* Photo Researchers; *page 101,* Dr. L. B. Shettles; *pages 106, 109, 111, 112,* Science Source / Photo Researchers; *page 123,* American Cancer Society.

Chapter 4: *page 136,* Pat Hansen; *page 140* (top), Hazel Hankin, (bottom), Biomedical Communications / Peter Arnold, Inc; *page 142,* Suzanne Arms / Jeroboam; *page 146,* Roe DiBona—copyright © 1987 *Psychology Today* Magazine; *page 152,* Bernard Wolff / UNICEF; *page 155,* Prof. Dr. Heinz P. R. Prechtl, University Hospital, Groningen, The Netherlands.

Chapter 5: *page 171* (top), Four by Five, (bottom), Bob Delucia; *page 196,* J. M. Tanner M.D., The Institute of Child Health, University of London; *page 201,* Four by Five; *page 204* (top), J. Russell Boersma, (middle), John Eastcott / Yva Momatiuk / The Image Works; *pages 206, 207,* Four by Five.

Chapter 6: *page 218,* David Linton, courtesy of Ann Linton, Stowe, Vermont; *page 220,* Dr. L. B. Shettles; *page 221,* Katherine Abbe; *page 225,* Ewing Galloway; *page 226,* Enrico Ferorelli / Dot; *page 232,* Zimbel / Monkmeyer Press; *page 238,* Julia Price.

Chapter 7: *page 258* (left), © 1972 Scientific American, Inc. (right), Jean-Pierre Laffont / Sygma; *page 266,* Suzanne Szasz; *page 275,* Mimi Cotter; *page 279,* Michael Weisbrot; *page 291,* Bill Price / Photo Researchers; *page 293,* Sybil Shelton / Monkmeyer Press.

Chapter 8: *page 305,* Ed Lettau / Photo Researchers; *page 320,* Lew Merrim / Monkmeyer Press; *page 325,* Fernandez / Black Star; *page 342,* Susan Szasz.

Chapter 9: *page 355,* Samuel Teicher; *page 366,* Nancy Hays / Monkmeyer Press; *page 378,* John Coletti / Stock, Boston; *page 379,* Drawing by Sara Katz; *page 387,* Ellis Herwig / Stock Boston.

Chapter 10: *pages 404, 405,* Harlow Primate Laboratory, University of Wisconsin; *page 406,* Nina Leen / *Life* Magazine—Time Inc.; *page 407,* Charlyce Jones Owen; *page 412,* Jerry Howard / Positive Images; *page 420,* Alan Carey / The Image Bank; *pages 424, 425,* from C. E. Izard, *Maximally Discriminative Facial Movement Scoring System* (1979); *pages 432, 433,* Harlow Primate Laboratory, University of Wisconsin.

Chapter 11: *page 446,* Richard Frieman / Photo Researchers; *page 450,* Elizabeth Crews; *page 460,* Francene Keery; *page 462,* Stock, Boston; *page 464,* Donald Dietz / Stock, Boston:

▶ ▶ ▶ ▶

INDEXES

Name Index

Ainsworth, M., 15, 164, 396, 398
Allport, G., 41
Amabile, T.M., 358
Anastasiow, F., 290
Anderson, A., 376–377
Anderson, C., 411
Anderson, L.D., 370
Anglin, J., 233–234
Antill, J.K., 509
Apgar, V., 137
Aristotle, 7–8, 104
Aronfreed, J., 529
Asarnow, J., 576
Ausubel, D., 418
Azrin, N., 562, 575

Baker, S., 495
Bandura, A., 65, 428–429, 501, 544
Barnard, K., 147
Baumrind, D., 23, 447–449, 467, 528
Bayley, N., 368, 370
Bee, H., 147
Bell, S., 398
Belsky, J., 411
Bem, S., 506
Benbow, C., 208
Bennett, W., 481
Benstein, A., 319
Berkeley, G., 242
Berko, J., 278
Berndt, T., 462
Bettelheim, B., 561
Binet, A., 11, 13, 351, 362–365
Bjorklund, D., 337
Blank, M., 317
Bloom, L., 274, 289
Bonvillian, J., 296
Botvin, G., 317
Boverman, I., 482, 508
Bower, T., 228–229, 233–234
Bowlby, J., 400–402, 407, 433

Bradbard, M., 507
Bradley, R.H., 386
Braine, M., 274
Brainerd, C.J., 322
Brazelton, T.B., 157
Bridges, K., 423–424
Broderick, P.C., 83
Bronfenbrenner, U., 18, 72–75, 419, 569
Brooks, J., 426
Brooks-Gunn, J., 487
Brophy, J., 467, 470–471
Brown, L., 103
Brown, R., 258–259, 283
Bruch, H., 553, 557
Bruner, J., 288
Burt, C., 384
Burton, R., 532
Bussey, K., 497, 506

Caldwell, B.M., 386
Campos, J., 227, 341, 424
Canale, J., 485
Cann, A., 485
Carlson, G., 576
Case, R., 335, 339
Cattell, R.B., 353, 371, 378–379
Cernoch, J., 237
Chesler, P., 496
Chess, S., 42, 72
Chi, M., 338
Chomsky, N., 264, 284
Clark, E., 271, 288
Cohen, H., 569
Collins, W.A., 515
Condon, W.S., 235
Conger, J.J., 358
Connolly, K.J., 466
Cook, M., 230
Cooper, R., 386
Coopersmith, S., 449

Cowan, P.A., 319, 325
Crawford, C., 380
Crick, F., 87
Croft, K., 311
Crook, K.C., 238

D'Andrade, R., 451
Daniels, D., 42
Darwin, C., 11–13, 407
Davidson, H., 515
DeCasper, A.J., 111
DeFries, J.C., 15
Delisi, A., 516
De Marchena, M., 337
Dement, W.C., 161–162
Denney, N., 330–331
Dennis, W., 209
Descartes, R., 242
DeVries, R., 318
Diamond, M., 494
Dick-Read, G., 139
Donaldson, M., 311, 324
Dunlap, L., 485
Dunn, J., 341
Dye, H.B., 435

Eckerman, C., 397
Edelsky, C., 493
Egeland, B., 400
Ehrhardt, A., 495
Elardo, R., 387
Emerson, P., 400–402
Endsley, R.C., 507, 543
Epstein, S., 501
Ericsson, R., 105
Erikson, E., 40, 44, 48–53, 75–76, 343
Evans, H.J., 124

Fagan, J.F., 220, 224
Fagen, J.W., 338, 370–371
Fagot, B., 498

▶ ▶ ▶ ▶

▶ ▶ ▶ ▶

▶ ▶ ▶ ▶

Wechsler, D., 357, 364–367
Weinberg, R.A., 385, 388
Westby, S.D., 515
White, R.W., 58
Whiting, B.B., 536
Whiting, J.W.M., 536
Wickelgreen, L.W., 220

Williams, C., 430
Williams, L.R., 198
Williams, R.L., 377–378
Winterbottom, M., 450
Witelson, S., 248–249
Wright, S., 481

Yarrow, L., 434–435
Yarrow, M.R., 535

Zeskind, S., 266
Zimmermann, R.R., 403
Zubek, J., 386

► ► ► ►

Subject Index

Page numbers in **boldface** indicate running glossary terms.

▶ ▶ ▶ ▶

► ► ► ►

▶ ▶ ▶ ▶

► ► ► ►

▶ ▶ ▶ ▶

▶ ▶ ▶ ▶

Insomnia, **558**
Instincts, **13**
Institutionalized children
   motor development retarded in,
      209
   social deprivation effects in, 430,
      433–435
Instrumental competence, **447–449**,
   456, 461, 463, 572
Intelligence, 15, 339
   conduct disorders and, 568
   creativity and, 357–359
   determinants of, 356, 380–389
   environmental influences on, 381,
      385–388
   genetic influences on, 380–385,
      388–389
   in infancy, 368–371
   maturation and, 41–42
   in middle childhood and adoles-
      cence, 371
   range of differences in, 371–377
   reading readiness and, 245
   social class, racial, and ethnic dif-
      ferences in, 356, 372, 376–377
   theories of, **350–357**
   See also Cognitive development; In-
      telligence tests; IQ (intelligence
      quotient)
Intelligence tests, 13, 246
   bilingualism and, 292
   characteristics of, 360–366
   culture-free, quest for, 378–379
   group, 367
   historical misuse of, 377–378
   kinds of, 359–367
   See also IQ (intelligence quotient)
Intensity of colors, **220**
Intentional action, 239–242
Intermittent reinforcement, **61–62**
Internal locus of control, **468**
Intonation, **268**
Intoxication, **570**
Intrinsic reinforcers, 58
Intuitive knowledge, **257**
In vitro fertilization, **103**
IQ (intelligence quotient), **22, 359,**
   364
   birth order and, 453
   family size and, 452
   maternal smoking and, 124
   working mothers and, 460–461
   See also Intellience

Jaundice, **238**

Jews, 94, 485
Jumpers, 203

Kibbutzim, **414**
Kinship studies, 381
Klinefelter's syndrome, **93**, 374
Knowledge-acquisition components,
   357

Labia, **197**
Laissez-faire leaders, **267–268**
Lamaze method, 134, **140–141**
Language
   apes in experiments with, 256–260
   basics of, 260–264
   biological and environmental influ-
      ences on, 16
   brain damage and, 188
   brain structures involved in,
      285–286
   cognitive development and, 280,
      303, 309, 312
   crying and, 162
   in deaf children, 295–296
   first words, 268–270, 284
   hearing and, 236–237
   individual differences in levels of,
      281
   motherese, 275–276, 289, 407
   overextension, 271–272
   patterns of development of,
      264–281, 283
   properties of, 162, 258–260
   referential and expressive styles in,
      270–271
   sensitive period for, 286–288, 295
   syntax, 262–263, 274, 277–281
   theories of development of,
      281–290
   two-word sentences, 272, 274, 276
   varieties of experience with,
      290–296
Language Acquisition Device (LAD),
   284–285
Lanugo, **145**, 153
Larynx, **195**
Latchkey children, **410**
Latency stage, **47**
Latent skills, **64**
Leadership styles, 467–468
Learning theories, 76
   of anxiety, 575
   of autism, 564
   of language development, 267,
      281–283

Learning-to-Learn programs, 387–388
Leboyer method, 141–142
Libido, **45**
Life crisis, **50**, 52
Lightening, 132
Linguists, **258**
Local anesthetic, **138**
Locomotion, **202–203**
Longitudinal research, **28–30**
Long-term memory, **335**, 337–338
Loose association, **565**
Loss of love, threats of, 446–447, 575

Macrosystem, **74**, 530
Mainstreaming, **373**, **472–473**, 565
Mammary glands, **197**
Marijuana, 570
   prenatal development and, 119–120
Masturbation, Freudian view of,
   48–49, 561
Maternal age, 95, 125–126, 247
Maternal depression, 148–149
Maternal diet, 114–115, 189, 559
Maternal diseases and disorders,
   115–118, 373
Maternal stress, 124–125
Maternity blues, **148–149**
Math skills, 495, 507
   intelligence and, 351–352
   sex differences in, 23, 489–490
   stereotyped as masculine, 488,
      500
Maturation, **16**, 67
   cognitive-developmental theory of,
      67
   toilet training and, 560
Maturational theory, 13, 75
   evaluation of, 42
   focus of, **40–41**
   psychological traits and, 41–42
Maximally Discriminative Facial
      Movement
   Scoring System, 424
Medicated childbirth, 138–139
Medulla oblongata, **185**
Meiosis, **86–88**, 101
Memory
   development of, **332**
   metacognition, 339–340
   metamemory, 339–340
   structure of, 333–339
Menarche, **194–195**
   anorexia and, 556
   psychological impact of, 198–199

▶ ▶ ▶ ▶

▶ ▶ ▶ ▶

► ► ► ►

► ► ► ►

Rooting, **53**
Rooting reflex, **154**–155, 238
Rote learning, **245**
Rubella (German measles), 110, 115–**116**, 120
Ruminative children, 63, 66, **558**
Running, 203–205

Saturation of colors, **220**
Schemes, **69**–70, **302**, 304, 309
Scholastic Aptitude Test (SAT), 208, 459
School activities, sex differences in, 490
Schools, 11, 367
    AIDS and, 118
    behavior modification used in, 63–64
    bilingual education and, 293–294
    cheating in, 532–533
    mainstreaming and, 373, 472–473, 565
    participant modeling in, 463
    physical environment in, 465–466
    punishment effects in, 60
    reinforcers in, 58
    sex-role stereotypes and, 484–485, 500 501
    socialization process and, 464–473, 500–501
    and views of children as active or passive beings, 17–18
    See also Education; Teachers
Schwann cell, **184**
Scientific method, 18–19
Seating arrangements, 465
Secondary circular reactions, 304, **306**
Secondary reinforcer, **58**
Secondary sex characteristics, **192**
Secure attachment, **399**–400, 418
Sedatives, **570**
Selective attention, 240–241, 333
Self-concept
    birth order and, 454
    cognitive development and, 340–343
    in infancy and early childhood, **340**–342
    in middle childhood and adolescence, 342–343
Self-esteem
    child rearing patterns and, 449
    depression and, 577–578
    in overweight children, 552
    substance abuse and, 572

working mothers and, 461
Self-fulfilling prophecy, **473**
Self-handicapping, 572
Semantic codes, **337**
Semanticity, **258**, 267, 287
Semantics, **262**–264
Semen, **195**
Sensation, in neonates, **157**–158
Sensitive period for language development, 286–288, 295
Sensorimotor stage, 71
    age and characteristics of, 303
    substages of, 303–309
Sensory cortex, **186**
Sensory memory, **333**
Separation anxiety, **397**
Seriation, **321**–322
Serotonin, **565**, 578
Sex, children's concepts about, 319
Sex differences
    in achievement motivation, 451
    in adjustment to nursery school, 20
    in aggressiveness, 491–492, 501–504, 540
    in bed-wetting incidence, 561
    biological theories of, 494–495
    in cognitive abilities, 487–490
    cognitive-developmental theory of, 504–506
    in communication styles, 492–493
    gender schema theory of, 506–507
    in hyperactivity incidence, 566
    in impact of father absence, 22–23, 499–500
    in infancy, 487
    in language development, 281
    in moral development, 527–528
    in motor skills, 206–207
    in occupational stereotypes, 485–486
    in play and school activities, 490
    psychoanalytic theories of, 495–496
    in response to divorce of parents, 455
    social-learning theory of, 497–504
    See also Boys; Girls
Sex differentiation, prenatal, 109
Sex hormones
    at puberty, 495
    sex-typed behavior patterns and, 507
    in utero, 494–495
Sexism, 509
    impact of, **484**

in schools, 484–485, 500–501, 532
sex-selection technology and, 104–105
Sex-linked chromosomal abnormalities, 92–93
Sex-linked genetic abnormalities, **94**
Sex norm, **502**
Sex roles, 15, 39, **480**
    cognitive development and, 5–6
    Freud's view of, 49
    modeling of, 66
    nature-nurture question and, **16**
    psychological androgeny and, 508–509
    See also Sex differences; Sex-role stereotypes
Sex-role stereotypes
    in adolescents, 483
    in children, 460–462, 480–481, 496
    cognitive development and, 333
    creativity and, 358
    development of, 480–486
    occupation and, 485–486
    sexism and, 484–485
    social class and racial differences in, 483
    television and, 503
    traits associated with, 480–483
    working mothers and, 460–462
Sex-selection technology, 104–105
Sexual development, 189–194
S factor, **351**
Shape constancy, **229**–230
Shaping, **62**, **283**
Sharing behavior, 534, 536–538
Short-term memory, **333**–337
    metacognition and, 339
Shyness, 86, 574
Sibling rivalry, **442**, 452
Siblings, socialization process and, 451–454
Sickle-cell anemia, 92, 97
    characteristics and cause of, **94**–05
Sight vocabulary, 245
Significant others, **50**
Sitting up, 203–205, 209
Size constancy, **228**–229
Skeletal development, 179–180
Skipping, 204
Skull development, 179
Sleep disorders, 556–560
Sleep patterns, in newborns, 160–162
Sleep terrors, **557**–559, 561
Sleepwalking, 558–559, 561
Small for dates, **145**

▶ ▶ ▶ ▶

▶ ▶ ▶ ▶

Transition, **134**
Transition to symbolic thought, 304,
308–309
Transitivity, **321**
Transverse position, **142**
Treatment, **24**
Tremors, **571**
Triarchic model of intelligence,
356–357
Trophoblast, **106**
Turner's syndrome, 93
Twins
identical and fraternal, 88–90
incidence of, 89
Twin studies, 24, 41–42, 564
Two-word sentences, 272, 274, 276,
283–284
Typology, **447**

Ultrasound, **97**
Umbilical cord, **110**, 112, 141, 154
Unconditioned response (UR), **56**
Unconditioned stimulus (US), **55**–56
Unconscious mind, **44**
Urethra, **192**
Utopian thinking, **328**

Vacuum extraction tube, **134**
Validity, **360**–351
Variables, **22**
Verbal abilities
intelligence and, 351–352
sex differences in, 23, 487–488, 495,
500
Vernix, **145**, 153
Vision
depth perception and, 226–227
in infancy and early childhood,
221–234
myelination and, 186–187
nature-nurture issue and, 242–244
in newborns, 158, 216–221
perceptual constancies and,
227–234
peripheral, 217, 221–222
reading skills and, 244–247
Visual accomodation, **219**
Visual acuity, **217**–219, 221–222, 240
Visual-motor coordination
development of, 239–240
hand control and, 201–202
myelination and, 184
Visual recognition memory, **370**–371
Vitamin K, 136
Vitamins, 120–121

Vocabulary development, 268–276
Voluntary actions, **154**–155

Walkers, 203
Walking, 203–205, 209
Walking reflex, 203, 209
Warm parents, 443–444, 451
Wechsler scales, 359, 367, 378
Weight
growth patterns in, 172–178
racial, ethnic, and socioeconomic
factors in, 175, 177
Weight-loss methods, 554–555
Wernicke's aphasia, **286**
Wernicke's area, 285–287
Wet dreams, 195
Wet nurses, 7
Withdrawal reflex, **157**
Wolffian duct, **192**
Womb simulator, **147**
Women's movement, 358, 409, 509
Word-recognition method, **245**
Working mothers, 409–410
children of, 460–461
divorce and, 455
World Health Organization, 152

Zona pellucida, **101**–102

▶ ▶ ▶ ▶

Developing Today

▶ ▶ ▶ ▶